Cassell's Illustrated History Of The Russo-turkish War

Edmund Ollier

Part 1 PRESENTATION PLATE. [To be Completed in 24 Parts.] Price 7d.

NEW EDITION.

269

Osman Pasha.

General Todleben.

CASSELL'S

Illustrated History

OF THE

RUSSO-TURKISH WAR.

Czar Alexander II.

By EDMUND OLLIER.

CASSELL & COMPANY, Limited:

London, Paris, New York & Melbourne.

Magazines that should find a place in every Home.

The Spectator, **Dec. 20, 1884, says:—"So much trouble is taken with these periodicals, so much ability is at the disposal of their conductors, that it is difficult to bestow the praise which is really deserved without seeming extravagant."**

The Quiver *for* ***February****, price* **6d.**, *contains—*

Church Work in South London. By the LORD BISHOP OF ROCHESTER.—**Some of the King's Servants.**—**Some Singular Steeples.**—**Restful Talks in the Rush of Life.**—By Rev. W. M. STATHAM.—**Boodle's Doctor.** Short Story.—**Scripture Lessons for School and Home.** THE CHILDREN OF THE BIBLE.—**A Word about the Amalekites.** By Very Rev. Dean MARTYN HART, M.A.—**Sunday Thoughts in Venice.** By Rev. J. STOUGHTON, D.D.—**The Growth of the New Testament.** By Ven. Archdeacon GORE, M.A.—**"O Lord of all Creation."** Original Hymn Tune.—**"One more for the Lifeboat Crew."**—**A Child's Legacy.** Short Story.—**Popular American Preachers.** NEW YORK. By Rev. LL. D. BEVAN, D.D.—**The Marks of the Lord Jesus.** By Rev. HORATIUS BONAR, D.D.—**Short Arrows.**—**"The Quiver" Bible Class.**—*Serial Stories:* (1) **Mollie's Maidens.** (2) **A Poor Man's Wife.**—&c. &c.

"'THE QUIVER' is the best of all the magazines devoted to Sunday reading."—*Saturday Review.*

Cassell's Family Magazine *for* ***February****, price* **7d.**, *contains—*

What to do in the County Court. By a BARRISTER.—**Life at an American College.**—**Our Model Reading Club.**—**Grandmamma's Valentine.**—**Remunerative Employments for Gentlewomen.**—**The Garden in February.**—**The Island Suburb of Foochow.**—**Two Modern American Fables.**—**Our Autograph Books.**—**On Making Home Beautiful.**—**The Humours of the Sun.**—**A New Order of Odd Fellows.** THE MAN WHO TAKES THINGS EASY.—**How to Treat Emotional Nervousness.** By a FAMILY DOCTOR.—**Prize Story.** A LOST OPPORTUNITY.—**Dress for Exercise.** By OUR PARIS CORRESPONDENT.—**New Music.** DAME FORTUNE.—**The Gatherer.**—**"Words for Music" Competition Award.**—*Serial Stories:* (1) **A Diamond in the Rough.** (2) **Sweet Christabel.**—&c. &c.

"In 'CASSELL'S FAMILY MAGAZINE' we find articles to suit all members of the household, with a strong infusion of the useful and instructive."—*The Times.*

Little Folks *for* ***February****, price* **6d.**, *contains—*

Russell Escott's Victory. A School Story.—**Some Notable Pictures and their Story.** "The Last Supper," by LEONARDO DA VINCI.—**Third Mate of the "Polly-Anne."** A Tale of the Greenland Seas.—**A Strange Railway Journey.** A Fairy Story. By JULIA GODDARD.—**The "Children of the Rock."**—**A New Kind of Patchwork.**—**Pussy's Letter to Nan.**—**A Game of Romps.**—**A Chat about Robins.**—**Jack's Ride to Town.**—**Legends and Stories of Famous Rivers.** THE RHINE.—**How Bertie was Rescued.**—**In Valentine Land.** A February Story.—**The Children's Own Garden in February.**—**Singing through the Storm.** Illustrated by GIACOMELLI.—**Music.** DOLLY'S LULLABY.—**The Editor's Pocket-Book.**—*Serial Stories:* (1) **Not Found Out.** (2) **King Charles's Page.**—&c. &c. With Illustrations on nearly every page.

"'LITTLE FOLKS' begins charmingly for the new year. It more than ever merits the distinction of being *the best of all the juvenile publications* brought out in this country."—*Daily Chronicle.*

The Magazine of Art *for* ***February****, price* **1s.**, *contains—*

"The Wonder Story." Painted by ARTHUR HACKER. *Frontispiece.*—**The Royal Institute.** With Three Illustrations.—**The "Madonna Ansidei."** By CLAUDE PHILLIPS. With Two Engravings.—**"A Tuscan May-day."** Picture in Colour. By A. MARY F. ROBINSON and W. J. HENNESSY.—**The Romance of Art: Temple and Tomb.** By LINDA VILLARI.—**Artists' Homes: Mr. Frank Holl's, in Fitzjohn's Avenue.** By HELEN ZIMMERN. With Five Illustrations.—**Nicolas Poussin.** By RICHARD HEATH. With Two Illustrations.—**Early Sculptured Stones in England.** By Rev. G. F. BROWNE. With Nine Examples.—**"Alva's Last Ride through Amsterdam."** From the Picture by CHARLES ROCHUSSEN.—**The Artist in Corsica.** By E. T. COMPTON. With Six Illustrations.—**Portraiture in France.** By R. A. M. STEVENSON. With Six Illustrations.—**Mr. Ruskin on English Art.** By the EDITOR.—&c.

"Contains better literature than any of the other Art periodicals."—*Pall Mall Gazette.*

"Its exquisite beauty should carry it into every home."—*Standard.*

CASSELL & COMPANY, LIMITED, *Ludgate Hill, London.*

"TREASURE ISLAND, written for boys, has fascinated a Prime Minister and become a Classic."

FOURTH EDITION, *now ready*, **5s.** *post free.*

Treasure Island, A Story of Pirates and the Spanish Main, by R. L. STEVENSON.

"Mr. Stevenson's 'Treasure Island' does not contain a dull page, no, nor a dull line either."—*Spectator.*

"A book for boys which will be delightful to all grown men who have the sentiment of treasure-hunting."—*Saturday Review.*

CASSELL & COMPANY, LIMITED, *Ludgate Hill, London.*

NOW READY, *price* **2s. 6d.**

The Sea Fathers. A Series of Lives of Great Navigators of Former Times. By CLEMENTS MARKHAM, C.B., F.R.S., Secretary of the Royal Geographical Society. Crown 8vo, 256 pages.

"We commend the 'Sea Fathers' to those who want a healthy book full of absorbing interest to place in a boy's hands."—*Naval and Military Gazette.*

CASSELL & COMPANY, LIMITED, *Ludgate Hill, London.*

Weekly, 1d.; Monthly, 6d.

CASSELL'S Saturday Journal.

Some Recent Reviews.

The Times says—

"'CASSELL'S SATURDAY JOURNAL' professes itself a magazine of useful and entertaining reading for the homes of the people, and assuredly the people get value for their money. It is full of instruction, entertainment, and sensation."

The Spectator says—

"We found ourselves spending more time over 'CASSELL'S SATURDAY JOURNAL' than the numerous claims of the season could well allow. Its funny stories and sayings, its fiction, its miscellaneous articles (containing, by the way, not a few promising first efforts by prize-winners), will furnish entertainment for many hours of amusement to happy people who have leisure."

The Court Circular says—

"We do not wonder, then, at the extraordinary popularity it has attained, for it fulfils a real want in many a household."

The Queen says—

"'CASSELL'S SATURDAY JOURNAL' is so well conducted and so cheap that its circulation ought to be promoted by the friends of the less favoured classes as an antidote to the trash which is so very easy to get and so mischievous."

CASSELL & COMPANY, LIMITED, *London; and all Booksellers.*

MEETING OF THE CONFERENCE AT CONSTANTINOPLE.

CASSELL'S

ILLUSTRATED HISTORY

OF THE

RUSSO-TURKISH WAR

BY

EDMUND OLLIER,

AUTHOR OF "CASSELL'S ILLUSTRATED HISTORY OF THE UNITED STATES," ETC. ETC.

VOL. I.

FROM THE COMMENCEMENT OF THE WAR TO THE FALL OF PLEVNA.

INCLUDING

An Historical Sketch of the Russian and Turkish Empires.

CASSELL & COMPANY, LIMITED:

LONDON, PARIS, NEW YORK & MELBOURNE.

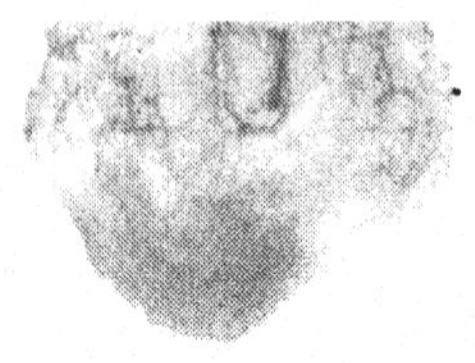

BODLEIAN
7 MAR 87
OXFORD

CONTENTS.

CHAPTER XVI.

CHAPTER XVII.

CHAPTER XVIII.

CHAPTER XIX.

CHAPTER XX.

CHAPTER XXI.

CHAPTER XXII.

CHAPTER XXIII.

CHAPTER XXIV.

CHAPTER XXV.

CHAPTER XXVI.

CHAPTER XXVII.

CHAPTER XXVIII.

CHAPTER XXIX.

CHAPTER XXX.

CHAPTER XXXI.

CHAPTER XLII.

CHAPTER XLIII.

CHAPTER XLIV.

CHAPTER XLV.

CHAPTER XLVI.

LIST OF ILLUSTRATIONS.

CHAPTER I.

The Herzegovina, and its Relations to Turkey—The Insurrection of 1875—Active Propaganda—Excesses of the Turkish Troops—Progress of the Rebellion—Action of the Powers—Disastrous Condition of the Ottoman Empire—Pecuniary Embarrassment, and Partial Suspension of Interest on the Foreign Loan—Effect on Europe—Purchase by the English Government of Shares in the Suez Canal—The Andrassy Note—Its Acceptance in England and in Turkey—Fighting in the Herzegovina—Fruitless Attempt at Pacification—Extravagant Demands of the Insurgents—Increased Financial Difficulties at Constantinople—Salonica and its Associations—Outbreak of Religious Fanaticism—The Berlin Memorandum, expressing the Views of Russia, Austria, and Germany—Its insolent Pretensions, and covert Threat of War—The Memorandum supported by Italy and France—Refusal of the British Government to abet the Design—Policy of the Three Northern Empires.

Far away from Constantinople, in the north-western parts of European Turkey, is a province, mainly occupied by Christians of the Greek Church, which did not come under the sway of the Ottoman Porte until a comparatively recent period. This region, now known as the Herzegovina, was originally a part of Croatia, but was united with Bosnia in 1326. Bosnia was at that time tributary to the Hungarian monarchs, but in 1389 fell beneath the dominion of the Turks. Herzegovina, however, maintained its independence until 1699, when it was ceded to Turkey by the Treaty of Carlowitz, which also secured Hungary to Austria. It is a somewhat narrow territory, lying on the eastern shores of the Adriatic, with Montenegro to the south; and is now once more considered, for purposes of government, a part of Bosnia, though it still retains something of a distinct individuality. The Herzegovinians have never been well affected towards their Mohammedan masters, and some insurrections have occurred in recent times. Of these, the most formidable was that which broke out on the 1st of July, 1875, and from which, by a gradual sequence of events, the War between Russia and Turkey derived its origin. The revolt seems to have been due to Montenegrin promptings. Early in the preceding winter, about a hundred and sixty-four inhabitants of the district of Nevesinje left their homes, and went into the country of the Black Mountain. After remaining there some months, they petitioned the Porte to be allowed to return, and, with a little hesitation, their prayer was granted. That they brought disaffection back with them, is certain. Appearing in open revolt shortly afterwards, they refused to pay their taxes, or to admit the representatives of Turkish authority. Some Mohammedans were murdered, with circumstances of savage cruelty; and the flame of insurrection spread.* Fuel for supporting it was certainly not absent. The people had actual grievances, of which the most was made. The harvest of 1874 had been a failure; but the tax-farmers had exacted the utmost they could by any possibility wring from the impoverished people. It has been stated that, as a rule, the peasant did not gain more than a third of the crop which he sowed and reaped; and the hardship was now aggravated by prevalent distress. In some cases, where payment was refused, the defaulters were beaten and imprisoned, while those who complained were threatened with arrest. Such were the facts which the refugees from Nevesinje unfolded to the Montenegrins. The object of their visit was doubtless to solicit help. They returned with a revolutionary programme.

The oppression of the people was due not so much to the Turkish Government itself as to the rapacity of the tax-farmers, who, by a vicious system, are permitted to get as much out of the peasantry as they can. When the disturbances broke forth, the Mutessarif or Governor of Mostar invited the malcontents to that town, that they might state their grievances, at the same time assuring them that they would be redressed; but they refused to go, and shortly afterwards cut to pieces a man who had been to Mostar about some other business.† There was probably a fear that they would be seized and punished, if once they placed themselves in the power of the Mutessarif; there was also, it can hardly be questioned, a desire to foment and extend the outbreak, for ulterior purposes. By a free exercise of intimidation, the insurgents compelled many who would gladly have abstained from the revolt to swell its forces. The peaceably inclined were threatened with death if they did not join the malcontents. Their houses were destroyed, and their prospects made dependent on active co-operation with the revolution. In this way the movement was kept alive, and the excesses committed by some of the Turkish troops added bitterness to the feud. Persons not engaged in the disturbances are said to have been murdered, because of their presumed sympathies with the disaffected. The Christians were insulted, and religious antagonism was aroused at a moment when the elements of disorder were already sufficiently numerous and sufficiently violent to need no increase. Yet the quarrel might have been composed, but for the determination of political intriguers not to let it rest. It happened at that time that the Emperor of Austria was making a tour in Dalmatia, a province which immediately adjoins the Herzegovina. The leaders of the rebellion believed that he had formed a design of purchasing Bosnia from the Sultan, and they may perhaps have thought that the prosecution of a vigorous insurrection would incline Abdul-Aziz to get rid of so disloyal and troublesome a province. Some of them even went the length of sending petitions to the Kaiser, requesting him to redress their wrongs. Dervish Pasha, the Governor of Bosnia, was of course greatly incensed at this attempt to open negotiations with a foreign Power, and the bad understanding between the Turks and Herzegovinians became more extreme than ever. Several actions took place, with varying fortunes and no very definite results. The insurrection did not make extensive progress; but on the other hand it was not extinguished. The Government troops were too few in number to act with decision, and the insurgents were too feebly supported to carry out their purposes. That they had the sympathy and encouragement of the Montenegrins is admitted on all hands; but those warlike barbarians were withheld from active interference by the commands of the Czar, who doubted whether the right time had come for quarrelling with Turkey. Prince Milan, of Servia, refused to follow his warlike Ministry into a policy of aggression; Austria hesitated as to diplomatic intervention; and Germany had no motive for forcing her action in any way. Thus it was that for a long while matters

* Consul Holmes: official letters from Bosna-Seraï, July 2nd and 9th, 1875.

† *Ibid*, July 2nd.

remained in suspense, though the country continued to be torn by frequent conflicts between the troops and the insurgents.

While refraining from actual intervention, the European Powers were necessarily interested spectators of a contest which threatened to re-open the terrible Eastern Question, with all its certain evils and uncertain risks. On the 22nd of August, 1875, they recommended the Porte to send a commission to the Herzegovina for the redress of grievances; were insecure. Some amount of exaggeration may have entered into these statements; but it is probable that they were true in a considerable degree, and they constituted a severe indictment against Turkish rule. The Ministers of the Porte conceived that something might yet be done by a policy of conciliation. On the 2nd of October an Iradé, and on the 12th of December a Firman, granting concessions to all Christian subjects, were issued by the Sultan. The act is said to have been prompted by

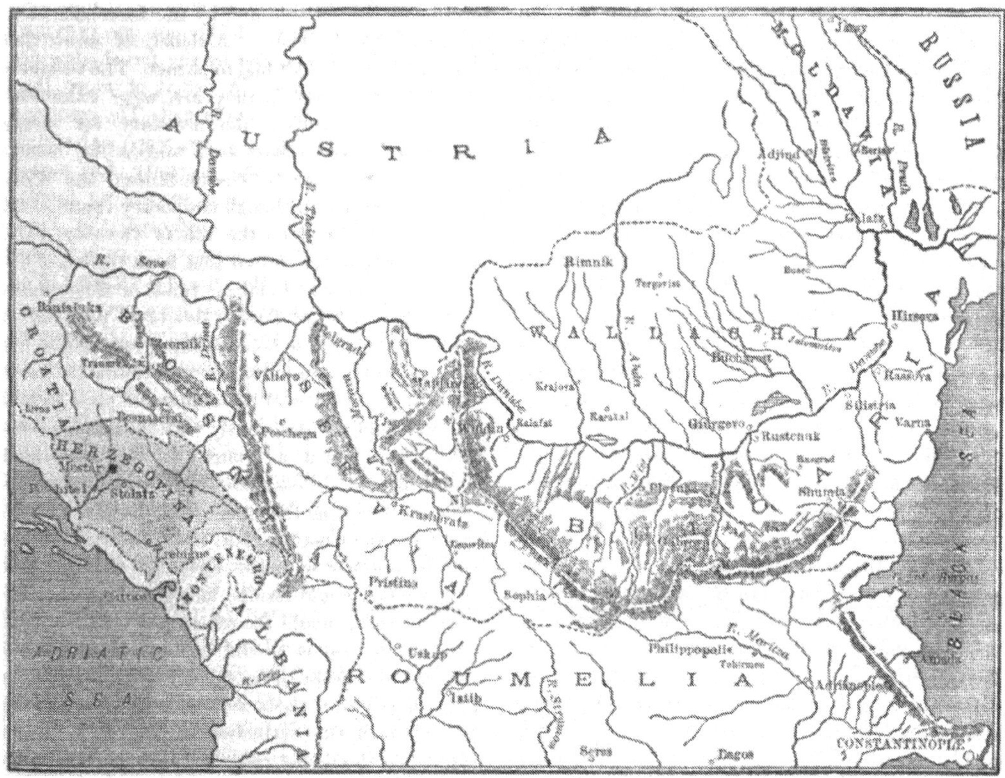

MAP OF THE HERZEGOVINA AND NEIGHBOURING COUNTRIES.

and some remonstrances to the Ottoman Government were made by the representatives of England and Russia in the course of the autumn. The insurgents themselves, on the 12th of September, formulated their complaints in a document which described their sufferings for the sake of religion, demanded complete freedom, and declared that they would never again be subject to the Turks. The so-called tithe, they alleged, had been advanced twelve and a half per cent. The taxes had been collected with great unfairness. Christians had been made to undergo forced labour on the public roads. The horses of the people had been used for the army. The Aghas were tyrannical; the law-courts were corrupt; and property, life, and honour General Ignatieff, the Russian Ambassador at Constantinople. By these edicts, equality was in most respects established between the Christians and Mohammedans, and a liberal redress of grievances was promised. The Courts of Justice, from the highest to the lowest, were re-organised, and it was declared that the Judges of the chief tribunals should be chosen from persons having the capacity and integrity to merit general confidence, and should not be dismissed without lawful cause. The members of other judicial and administrative bodies were to be elected by the subjects of the Porte without distinction, and suits between Mussulmans and non-Mussulmans were to be referred to civil tribunals. It was further provided that taxation should be lightened and equalized; that a fourth part of the tithe should be permanently taken off; that the tithe should no longer be collected by the arbitrary procedure of the tax-farmers; that the collectors should be chosen by the population without distinction of creed; that forced labour should be abolished; and that the Minister of Commerce should confer with competent persons upon the measures necessary for a more thorough development of agriculture, manufactures, and trade. Powers previously granted to the heads of the Eastern Church and other ecclesiastical authorities, for managing the affairs of their communities, and for the free profession of their religious belief, were confirmed, and a solemn undertaking was given that every official rank and all public functions should thenceforth be accessible to non-Mussulman subjects. The tax for exemption from military service was to be paid only by Christians between the ages of twenty and forty years, and was to be reduced. Permission was granted to all non-Mussulman subjects to acquire property in land and houses, and their testamentary dispositions were to be respected. Finally, the people were to be at liberty to address the Porte whenever they might have legitimate occasion of complaint.

In themselves, these reforms were admirable. The only fear was lest, as on previous occasions, they should be imperfectly carried out. On the other hand, the sanguine were not without some ground for hoping that the Sultan would see the necessity, even for his own sake, of entering sincerely and earnestly on the path of reform. The position of the Empire was becoming every day more serious and alarming. Famine was desolating Asia Minor. A large part of the European population was openly or secretly disaffected. Russia was awaiting her opportunity for dismembering the Ottoman dominions as soon as the internal processes of disintegration had sufficiently advanced. Nations which had once been friendly were beginning to look cold; and, to add to the misfortunes of the time, a state of more than usual pecuniary embarrassment had set in. Turkey had often before been involved in money troubles, owing to profligate expenditure and disregard of political economy. After the Peace of Adrianople, in 1829, Mahmud II. was so impoverished by a long series of wars and internal commotions that he soon found himself unable to provide the whole of the indemnity which Russia had exacted, and was compelled to solicit the remittance of nearly a third. But until 1854 —the period of the Crimean war—Turkey had no national debt. Since then, her obligations have increased beyond the ability of the State to pay the entire interest on what has been borrowed. The Turkish debt, which was only £3,000,000 sterling when it commenced, had in twenty years augmented with such fearful rapidity that in 1874 it amounted to £180,000,000. In June, 1875, the Imperial expenditure stood at £26,299,178, while the estimated receipts did not go beyond £21,711,764. Such was the financial condition in which the Turkish Ministers found themselves while confronted by an obstinate rebellion in one province, by discontent in others, and by the foreshadowings of foreign complications. A deficit of more than four millions and a half had to be met. The resources of the Empire, great as they are, were exhausted, and at the same time the necessity for money became more urgent with each succeeding month. Under these desperate circumstances, the Porte resolved on a partial though temporary repudiation. A decree was issued on the 6th of October, 1875, by which it was announced that for a period of five years the interest and sinking funds of the internal and external debts of Turkey should be paid half in cash, and half in new bonds bearing interest at five per cent. per annum; that the interest on the bonds delivered in payment of the moiety not paid in cash should be paid simultaneously with the other moiety paid in specie; that, as security for the payment of the half payable in cash, and of the interest on the bonds representing the other half, the revenue derived from the Customs, salt, and tobacco, would be pledged, together with the Egyptian tribute; that the sheep-tax would also be mortgaged as an additional security, should the others prove inadequate; and that, in case it should be impossible for the Treasury to redeem the new bonds at the expiration of the five years, their reimbursement would be deferred until the extinction of the first foreign loan which should be redeemed through the operation of its sinking fund, and the guarantees applicable to the loan so paid off would secure the ultimate payment of the bonds representing the half not paid in cash.

Europe was both astonished and angered at the publication of this decree. The financial world was thrown into a state of feverish excitement, and politicians began to speculate on the approaching collapse of the Ottoman Empire. All who had lent money on the faith of Turkish solvency felt that they were being robbed for the support of a system of misgovernment, the errors of which they had not until then discovered. Vehement and unmeasured was the outcry against the offending State, and it cannot be doubted that the fiery denunciation of Turkey in the following year was in some degree heightened by the exasperated feelings of unlucky investors. The Turkish Government, however, pursued its way with true Oriental imperturbability. On the 7th of October—the day following that on which the decree of partial repudiation was issued —a circular note remitted taxes, and promised economical and commercial reforms; and on the 20th of the same month another note represented the object of the Government to be the stopping of onerous loans, and the development of the Imperial resources.

Even before the outbreak of the Herzegovinian revolt, the state of Turkey had engaged the attention of the English House of Commons, where, on the 18th of June, Mr. Yorke brought forward a motion for papers bearing on the subject. The motion was negatived, but it led to an interesting debate. Mr. Yorke contended that the Ottoman Empire was in a state of rapid decay; that the promises of the Porte had been broken, and that corruption and misgovernment were paramount. Quoting from an account of the Sultan's personal expenses given by Mr. (now Sir T.) Brassey, who had visited Constantinople in 1874, he said: —"The authorised civil list is about £1,200,000, and, by means of various more or less arbitrary grants, it is actually little short of £2,000,000 a year. All along the shores of the Bosphorus, vast palaces and elaborate kiosks occur in succession, at a distance of little more than a mile apart. Some of these buildings are furnished in the most costly style. The daily dinner of the Sultan—he always dines alone—consists of ninety-four dishes; and ten other meals are prepared, in case it should be his fancy to partake of them. He has eight hundred horses, and seven hundred wives, attended and guarded by three hundred and fifty eunuchs. For this enormous household, forty thousand oxen are yearly slaughtered, and the purveyors are required to furnish daily two hundred sheep, a hundred lambs or goats, ten calves, two hundred hens, two hundred pairs of pullets, a hundred pairs of pigeons, and fifty green geese." When Abdul-Aziz ascended the throne, in 1861, it was believed that he was a man of simple and domestic tastes, disinclined to the polygamous habits of his fellow-religionists, and desirous of reducing the extravagant expenditure of his brother, Abdul-Medjid. But these hopes were speedily disappointed, and Turkey became every year more deeply plunged in debt. In the opinion of Mr. Yorke, England was entitled, under the ninth clause of the Treaty of Paris (1856), to interfere by friendly remonstrances with the Turkish Government; and these remonstrances, he submitted, should at once be made.

The Government, however, was of a different opinion. The Premier (Mr. Disraeli) abstained from speaking; but Mr. Bourke, the Under-Secretary for Foreign Affairs, boldly asserted that we had no direct concern with the internal condition of Turkey. That condition, he believed, had improved of late years, and, although all the promises of internal reform had not been fulfilled, the fault lay rather with subordinates than with leading Turkish statesmen. The Treaty of Paris, as interpreted by this speaker, gave England no right to interfere in the administration of the Ottoman Empire; and the same resolve to adopt a policy of non-intervention was followed by the Government of Mr. Disraeli on a much more trying occasion. When the act of partial repudiation became known in England, a deputation of Turkish bondholders waited on the Foreign Secretary, and urged on him to devise some measures for enforcing full payment of the interest on the loans. But Lord Derby denied that there was any obligation on the part of the Government to take up the case of the bondholders. He questioned the existence of a guarantee by Great Britain, though some rather imprudent language by Lord Palmerston and Lord John Russell might have encouraged that impression. Other official utterances in the course of the year showed that Ministers were watchful, but that they believed, or at any rate affected to believe, that Europe would be saved from war by the moderation of the Powers. The purchase by the Government, in November, of the Khedive's shares in the Suez Canal—now the main approach to India—looked like a determination to be prepared for any eventuality that might result from a war between Russia and Turkey, by acquiring a preponderating influence in the management of that great water-highway.

At the close of 1875, the insurrection in Herzegovina was still unsuppressed; indeed, it had by that time acquired proportions more formidable than it originally presented. A general opening of the Eastern Question was feared by many, and perhaps hoped by some; and the Emperors of Russia, Germany, and Austria began to enter into a mutual understanding. The result was a circular note to the Western Powers, in which Count Andrassy, the Austrian Chancellor, gave expression to the combined views of what are sometimes called the three Northern Courts. The date of this note was December 30th, 1875, and the document went at some length into the great questions affecting the stability of the Turkish Empire. Count Andrassy recommended the adoption of those reforms which the Sultan had already promised in his Firman of the 12th of December, and he added that the execution of the necessary measures should be placed under the care of a special commission, half the members of which should be Mussulmans, and half Christians. The State, he held, should sell portions of its waste lands to the peasantry on easy terms; and, as the people would not trust the bare word of the Porte, the Powers must obtain from the Sultan a solemn confirmation of his Imperial promises, and a formal acceptance of the demands to be presented by the European Governments. Glancing at the future, the Count remarked that the indefinite promises recently made by the Porte would only exalt without contenting the hopes of the insurgents. All the rebellious populations, he averred, believed that the spring would bring them reinforcements from Bulgaria, Crete, and other places. The Governments of Servia and Montenegro, which already had great difficulty in holding aloof from the movement, would then be unable to resist the current; and the existing force of public opinion in those countries was preparing them to take a speedy part in the struggle.

ALI PASHA, GOVERNOR-GENERAL OF THE HERZEGOVINA.

When this collective note of the three Empires (for such it was) came before the English Government, Lord Derby intimated that he and his colleagues would give a general sanction to Count Andrassy's proposals. The Porte had previously requested the London Cabinet to communicate those proposals to itself, if they were not altogether objectionable; and the note was presented at Constantinople (though not officially) on the 31st of January, 1876. The Sultan accepted all the demands, save the one defining the purposes to which the direct and indirect taxes of the insurrectionary provinces should be applied; yet even in this respect he promised that a certain sum should be set apart out of the Imperial revenue for the local wants of Bosnia and Herzegovina. The reply of the Porte was given in a circular to the Powers, bearing date February 13th; but by that time the Andrassy Note had ceased to be regarded as having any practical value in connection with the great problem of the day. Nothing, indeed, could be more unsatisfactory than that document. It was either mischievous or futile, and could hardly, under any circumstances, have been productive of good results. Mainly inspired by Russia, it was so conceived as to promote her designs by facilitating the downfall of the Ottoman Power. "The proposals of Count Andrassy," very pertinently remarked Lord Derby in a communication to Sir Henry Elliot, our

MURDER OF THE FRENCH AND GERMAN CONSULS AT SALONICA.

Ambassador at Constantinople, "amount to little more than a request that the Porte will execute the Hatti-Scheriff of Guilhané of 1839, the Hatti-Humayoun of 1856, and the Iradé and Firman of October 2nd and December 12th, 1875; in short, that the measures for the improvement of the condition of the non-Mussulman and rural populations generally throughout the Empire, which have been publicly proclaimed, should be brought into practical application."* So far, the suggestions were idle; for, if the Porte had neglected hitherto to carry out its own reforms, though urged to do so by the European Powers, a mere renewal of the requests would not be likely to result in better fortune. But something more than a renewal of requests was contemplated. The note contained suggestions pointing to intervention in the affairs of Turkey. The commission for superintending the execution of the promised reforms was, indeed, to be elected by the people; but it is easy to see how it would have worked. Such a commission, supposing it to have been formed, would in all probability have fallen under the influence of Russia, and would at any rate have destroyed the independence of the Porte, by introducing an element which would have been simply a foreign element in disguise. The destruction of that independence is what Russia has been endeavouring to effect for many years; and it would clearly have answered her purposes much better than a war, the issues of which are always uncertain, while the cost is inevitable and onerous. In exact proportion to the weakening of the Sultan's authority is the gain to the Czar's ultimate designs; for the Christian provinces are too feeble to stand alone, and will gravitate towards St. Petersburg if released from Constantinople.

While these matters were being discussed, the struggle in Herzegovina was proceeding with increased bitterness. Several actions were fought in the early part of 1876, and one of the leaders of the insurrection was killed. Secretly aided, it is well known, by Montenegro and Servia, the rebels maintained the contest with great spirit, and occasionally gained successes over the Ottoman troops. Ali Pasha, the Governor-General of Herzegovina, offered them an amnesty on the 24th of March; but they refused to accept it. On the 30th of the same month, however, an armistice of ten days was arranged, to enable General Rodich, an envoy from the Austrian Government, to open negotiations with the malcontents; but this well-meant attempt at pacification came to nothing, owing to the extravagant demands of the Herzegovinians, which Count Andrassy thought quite inadmissible, though Prince Gortschakoff, the head of the Russian Ministry, considered them worthy of discussion. It was required by the insurgents that a third part of the land should become the property of the Christians; that the Turkish troops should be concentrated in the garrison towns; that the Porte should rebuild the houses and churches destroyed by the Mohammedans; that the peasantry should be supplied, at the cost of the Government, with food and agricultural implements for at least a year; that they should be exempt from taxes for three years; that they should be allowed to retain their weapons until the Mussulmans were disarmed; and that the money for compensating the Christians should be paid to a European Commission. Even had Austria agreed with Russia in supporting these terms, it is certain that the Government of the Sultan would not have accepted them. Only a Power in the utmost extremity would have consented to such demands; and the Herzegovinians were in no position to enforce their wishes. On the whole, the Turks prevailed in the open field against their ill-disciplined foes; yet the rebellion flourished among the mountains, and the army was unable to crush it out.

The financial difficulties of the Porte continued to increase with the development of its other troubles. The consolidated debt of the Empire had now reached the alarming total of about £200,000,000, the interest on which amounted to £14,000,000 a year; and besides this there was a floating debt, the proportions of which are not exactly stated, but which certainly counted for several millions more. A part of the debt had, as we have seen, been repudiated for a time; but what the Government then contracted to pay had been honestly met, and the Grand Vizier, Mahmud Pasha, had placed at the disposal of the creditors the revenue arising from the indirect taxes, the tribute due to the Porte by the Khedive or Viceroy of Egypt, and a portion of the income derived from the sheep-tax. Fresh complications, however, arose in the course of 1876, and it was found a hard matter to provide a sum of £120,000, needed to pay the coupons of the loan of 1858. The money was at length obtained from the financial companies of Galata; but this was only a temporary assistance. It was not long before the bondholders of the loans of 1854, 1855, and 1871, began to protest against the Egyptian tribute being diverted to the payment of creditors under any other loan. In respect of the three loans to which allusion has been made, there had been an express stipulation that the tribute should be paid into the Banks of

* Despatch of January 25th, 1876.

England and France, for the benefit of the shareholders of those two countries. No such stipulation existed in the case of the other loans, which had been contracted for on specially advantageous terms. The latter formed by far the larger part of the Turkish debt; and when Mahmud Pasha found that for payment of the interest on that portion he could not depend on the Egyptian tribute, he was almost reduced to despair. Towards the end of March, he felt compelled to defer payment of the dividend (amounting to about £1,200,000) of the public debt due in April. The postponement was to be until July, and the bondholders were promised interest at the rate of six per cent. It was evident that such a device merely put off the evil day for a little while, and accumulated greater embarrassment for the near future. Something of more permanent effect was necessary, and the Porte accordingly summoned to its counsels a number of eminent financiers from several European capitals. Various proposals were made, all of a more or less unsatisfactory character, as sacrificing to some extent the claims of the bondholders; but nothing was settled, and the several schemes were still under consideration when troubles of a more serious nature arose at a distance from the metropolis.

The outbreak of religious fanaticism which took place at Salonica, early in May, is involved in a good deal of obscurity, and it is not easy to speak with entire confidence of its origin and development. Salonica is a town in Macedonia, situated at the head of the Gulf of Salonica, and containing a large Christian population. It is the Thessalonica of earlier days, of which we read in ancient history and in the Acts of the Apostles. Under the Roman Empire it was a place of great importance, the metropolis of the Illyrian provinces, and a seat of commerce both with the east and with the west. It has still a flourishing trade, and many foreign consuls reside there. Very interesting remains of Greek and Roman architecture are scattered about its streets and public places; but the genius of Mohammedanism is predominant over all, and the severe Monotheism of the Arabian Prophet is preached in temples that were once Pagan, and in fanes that formerly echoed with the Christian rites. The city has a bad reputation for massacre. Near the end of the fourth century, the commander of the garrison and his principal officers were murdered by the people for having imprisoned a favourite rider in the circus, who had committed some profligate offence. The crime was great, but the punishment was out of all proportion. Possibly without intending more than a just retribution, the Emperor Theodosius I. let loose on the citizens a body of barbarian soldiers, by whom, in an indiscriminate carnage of three hours' duration, seven thousand persons (according to some accounts, fifteen thousand) were slaughtered in cold blood.

The catastrophe of May, 1876, was a small matter in comparison with this tragedy; yet it was sufficiently lamentable. On the 5th of that month, a Bulgarian girl who had been converted to the Mohammedan faith arrived by train at Salonica, for the purpose of authenticating her change of religion before the proper authority. The news soon spread abroad, and it was asserted by many of the Christians that the person was an unwilling convert. A number of Greeks determined that she should be rescued from what they regarded as an evil fate, and, on the way from the station to the Governor's house, the girl was torn from her escort, and carried off, first to the residence of the American vice-consul, and afterwards to a place of concealment in the Greek quarter. It is easy to understand the fierce excitement which such an act would produce among the Mussulman population of the town. Let us imagine a parallel case, and suppose a convert from Judaism to Christianity forcibly abducted by a mob of Israelites in the streets of some Christian city where religious feeling is a powerful and ruling sentiment; or let us suppose a similar act committed by Protestants against Romanists, or by Romanists against Protestants. In all such instances a sanguinary outbreak would be inevitable, unless the civil power were sufficiently strong to suppress any movement at the very commencement. The civil power at Salonica was not strong enough, or perhaps not watchful enough, to prevent mischief. On the day following the outrage, five thousand Mussulmans went to the official residence of the Governor, and demanded the restoration of the girl, declaring that her forcible seizure was a public affront, as indeed it was. Quieting assurances were given, and the authorities succeeded after a while in dispersing the crowd, the members of which, however, shortly afterwards re-assembled in an adjacent mosque, for the purpose of insisting on their demands. While they were still there, the German and French consuls very imprudently proceeded to the edifice, which they entered in the midst of the excited mob. It was believed that the girl was in the house of the German consul; and, after some fierce altercation, the representatives of Germany and France were barbarously murdered. The girl herself soon appeared upon the scene; but the tragedy was by that time fully consummated. A great crime had been committed, and the difficulties of the Turkish Empire were incalculably increased by the acts of two bodies of fanatics, indifferent to all considerations but the indulgence of their unreasoning passions.

The utmost indignation at this terrible event was expressed, not only in France and Germany, but all over Europe. For a moment it appeared doubtful whether it would not lead to an immediate foreign intervention. French and German squadrons were sent to Salonica; large bodies of troops were landed, under whose protection the funerals of the murdered men took place with great solemnity and pomp; and a demand for reparation, and for the punishment of the offenders, was made. Some of the chief persons concerned in the murder were executed on the 16th of May; others were imprisoned; and it is said that £40,000 were afterwards paid to the families of the victims. The immediate danger was thus averted; but it was so evident that the Ottoman Empire was in the throes of revolution, and that the Continental Powers might take advantage of this state to intervene for the promotion of their own views, that the British fleet was sent to Besika Bay, near the entrance to the Dardanelles, for the protection of English residents in Constantinople, and for keeping a watchful eye on the interests of this country in the East. The naval force was afterwards augmented, and Mr. Disraeli, in a debate occurring on the 30th of July, said that it was not sent to uphold the Turkish Empire, but to protect the British Empire. Its duty was in truth to be prepared for all eventualities, and that duty might be interpreted in many ways.

Almost immediately after the Salonica outrage, the three Northern Powers renewed their insidious and mischievous attempt at interference in the internal affairs of Turkey. The murder of the consuls took place on the 6th of May: on the 11th of that month, Prince Gortschakoff and Count Andrassy met Prince Bismarck at Berlin, in order that they might confer on the existing state of the Ottoman Empire. It was not enough that the Porte had voluntarily decreed all the most essential reforms, even before the concoction of the Andrassy Note—reforms which it was impossible to carry out on the instant, whilst a portion of the country was distracted by a civil war. It was not enough that, with only one exception, of no primary importance, the Sultan had accepted the propositions contained in the celebrated circular of the Austrian Chancellor, and that there was as yet no reason for charging him with breach of faith. The real object was to humiliate Turkey in the eyes of the world—to discover pretexts for intervention, so that the Ottoman dominion might be ruined, and the Ottoman territory divided amongst the three military and Divine Right monarchies. This object engaged the attention of the Russian, Austrian, and German statesmen at their interviews on the 11th and 12th of May; and the result was the composition of a circular known as the Berlin Memorandum, the date of which is May 13th. The document, thus compiled by an act of conspiracy against a friendly Power, started with the extraordinary argument that the Sultan, by accepting the reforms specified in the Andrassy Note, had given the Powers a moral right to insist that he should keep his word. It need scarcely be pointed out that this monstrous assumption placed Turkey in the position of a vassal State, and that the very placability of the Sultan was used as an instrument against him. The Christians, it was insultingly added, could not trust to the promises of the Turks—an argument

BULGARIAN GIRL.

which defeated itself, for in that case there was no remedy for the evil, short of the complete separation of the Christian provinces from the rule of the Porte, which, however much it may have been really contemplated by the three Empires, was of course not among the avowed objects of the note. It had become necessary, continued the document, "to establish certain guarantees, of a nature to ensure beyond doubt the loyal and full application of the measures agreed upon between the Powers and the Porte." An armistice of two months was to be insisted on by the united voice of the Great Powers; the Porte and its insurrectionary subjects were to open negotiations for peace, and the points to be taken as the bases of discussion were almost identical with those which the insurgents themselves had advanced a few weeks before, and which Count Andrassy had then considered inadmissible. The proposal with respect to a mixed commission, contained in the Andrassy Note of December 30th, was repeated, and it was added that the consuls or delegates of the Powers should preside over the application of the reforms in general, and of particular measures arising out of them. In this last provision, that which had been distantly and craftily approached in the earlier note was boldly assumed as a declared principle. The government of the Christian provinces of Turkey was to be handed over to a committee of the European Powers, in which it is obvious that Russia hoped to find an instrument for the promotion of her own designs. It may well be doubted whether so insolent a demand was ever before made upon any Power untouched by defeat, capable of asserting its independence, and under not the slightest obligation, of any sort whatever, to those who put forward the pretension. Diplomacy is often dishonest. It was here audacious and impertinent.

What made the terms of the three Emperors more nakedly brutal was the scarcely disguised threat of war with which the Memorandum concluded. "If," said the authors of that document, "the armistice should expire without the objects of the Powers being attained, the three Imperial Courts are of opinion that it will become necessary to reinforce diplomatic action by the sanction of an understanding with a view to those efficacious measures which would appear to be demanded, in the interests of the general peace, to arrest the mischief, and prevent its further development." The language of diplomatic intercourse is usually diffuse and involved, and the art of evading a distinct expression of intentions was certainly carried to perfection in this remarkable sentence. Yet there cannot be a question as to the meaning so carefully wrapped up. Turkey was to yield her sovereignty, or to be desolated by a remorseless invasion. The subtle phrases covered without concealing the mortal design. A dagger is not less a dagger because it is muffled in the assassin's cloak.

Austria acted throughout this business as the servant of Russia. The ignominy of her position was pitiable. She had been the mouthpiece of the Czar in the production of the Andrassy Note. She now consented, as regarded the Herzegovina, to endorse the very terms which Count Andrassy himself had but recently set aside. Her own proper interests were in no respect concerned in the humiliation and ruin of Turkey; but that community of ideas which generally binds together the three Northern Courts, and which has so often proved disastrous to the best interests of Europe, determined the policy of Austria at this juncture, and determined it in favour of the designs of Russia. The particular motives which influenced the German Emperor and his astute Chancellor, Prince Bismarck, are not so easy to discover. Germany is too strong to need the countenance of any other Power; and her position towards Turkey is not such as to create even imaginary interests out of any condition into which the Ottoman Empire may lapse. But, in the event of a European war arising from the contemplated attack on Turkey, the German monarch doubtless hoped to snatch something out of the chaos.* Italy afterwards accepted the Memorandum because, as a young Power anxiously looking for support and for favourable opportunities of action, she perceived an advantage in ranging herself with great military Empires like those of the North. France also gave her sanction to the demands of St. Petersburg, Vienna, and Berlin; but France was no longer a first-rate Power, and could not afford to quarrel with the league of despots. Ever since the disastrous war of 1870–71, and the equally disastrous revolution which expelled the

* Sir H. Drummond Wolff, M.P., speaking at Bournemouth on the 28th of September, 1877, said:—"It had been stated to him through a private source that what the Turkish Government really feared was, not only the arms of Russia, but a European combination which would postively mean the destruction and partition of the Turkish Empire. Their idea was that Germany sought to humiliate France, and would therefore assist Russia to work her own will in Eastern Europe. Austria was to be offered the dominion of Bosnia and Herzegovina, Italy was to take Nice and Savoy, while England was to have Egypt and Candia. Russia did not so much desire to possess Constantinople as to be left alone without molestation to deal with Turkey in the manner she desired. No doubt, Russia would be satisfied with this arrangement, provided the free passage of the Dardanelles was thrown open to her. Even if this were done, Turkey would merely submit to the domination of Russia until she was strong enough to oppose it."

Napoleonic dynasty for a Republic of imbecility and intrigue, France had been of little weight in the counsels of Europe. She therefore joined the others, and, together with Italy, assumed the perilous honours of the situation. Fortunately, which her enemies asked her to accept by a voluntary act. In that event, the Powers must have gone to war; and, as the interests of some differ widely from those of others, the allies would speedily have been at issue among themselves. The Government

A GROUP OF ARMED MONTENEGRINS.

however, England disapproved of such a course, and by so doing broke up the conspiracy. It is most improbable that Turkey would have accepted such demands—demands striking at the very root of her existence as a sovereign State—even had they been presented by the six Great Powers in concert. No nation abdicates, except on dire necessity. Turkey would have tried the worst, which could hardly in any case have exceeded the humiliation of Mr. Disraeli showed a provident forethought in declining such responsibilities; but it is to be regretted that the refusal was not placed on the direct ground that this country had neither the right to interfere in the internal affairs of Turkey, nor any interest in destroying Turkish rule. Instead of this, it was based mainly on the disinclination of the Government to adopt a plan in the preparation of which it had not been consulted, and which it did not believe would succeed.* No doubt it would have been exceedingly undignified of England to accept a foregone conclusion, with respect to which her opinion had not been previously asked; but there were considerations even more important than that.

which freedom is more native, every attempt at progress, every struggle of the popular mind, every hope arising in the popular heart. The three witches of Shakespeare's fancy, brewing their fell enchantments in the cave of Acheron, are the fittest analogues of the three Divine Right monarchies

THE EMPEROR OF RUSSIA. THE EMPEROR OF GERMANY. THE EMPEROR OF AUSTRIA.

For many generations, the three Northern Courts, whether in their single or their united action, have been the menace and the affliction of Europe. Representing little beyond organized brute force and military dictatorship, they have suppressed or rendered difficult every aspiration of lands to which have their capitals at St. Petersburg, Berlin, and Vienna. The eighteenth century felt the weight of their mailed hands. The nineteenth century is not yet safe from their oppressions. Murdered Poland accuses them. France, thwarted of the fruits of her great revolution, brings against them the impeachment of a grievous wrong. Italy, long divided and enslaved, bears witness to the fatal

* Lord Derby to Lord Odo Russell (British Minister at Berlin), May 19th, 1876.

league. Hungary cherishes the memory of her rights defeated, of her patriots murdered, of her years of anguish and denial. The public life of England itself, in the time of our fathers, was debauched by the principles of the Holy Alliance. At this day, European liberty exists but on sufferance, where it exists at all, from the Baltic to the Danube, and from the Rhine to the Ural Mountains. Yet even this was not sufficient, and more was to be sought. The Berlin Memorandum was a masked attempt to spread the principles and the power of the three military Empires, but especially of Russia, to the vicinity of the Mediterranean and the gates of Asia.

CHAPTER II.

English Opinion on the Eastern Question in May, 1876—Bulgaria and its People—Dissensions between the Bulgarians and the Greeks in respect of the National Church—The Jurisdiction of the Patriarch of Constantinople repudiated by the Bulgarians—Various Religious Bodies in Bulgaria—Liberal Policy of the Porte—The Bulgarians and the Russians—Intrigues of Russia in European Turkey—Attempts to revolutionise Bulgaria—Greek Agents and their Disappointments—Condition of Bulgaria in 1875-6—Russian Designs in the East of Europe—Secret Societies in Russia for the Propagation of Revolutionary Doctrines—The Sclavonic Race, and its Position in European Turkey—Ambition of the Czars to reign at Constantinople—The National Sentiment and the Sentiment of Race—The Sclavonic Committee and its Branches—Objects of the Propaganda, and Methods by which it is worked—Opinions of the *Moscow Gazette*—Insurrectionary Movements in Turkey prompted by Pan-Sclavism—The Bulgarian Rising of 1876—The Revolt stimulated and sustained by Revolutionary Agents—Premature Commencement of the Insurrection—Massacre of Mussulmans, with Circumstances of great Cruelty—Employment of Volunteers by the Turks—General Description of the Disturbed Province—Philippopolis and its Characteristics.

When the leading Ministers of the three military Empires met at Berlin for the concoction of their famous Memorandum, opinion in England was not strongly agitated with regard to Eastern affairs in any sense whatever. On the one hand was to be found a general and perhaps rather vague impression, derived from the political teachings of Lord Palmerston, that the integrity of the Turkish Empire was necessary to the defence of our Indian realms. On the other hand, a natural and creditable sympathy with races which had unquestionably been misgoverned, and which were then struggling for independence, induced many persons to wish well to the insurgent populations of South-eastern Europe. But neither opinion was very vehemently expressed. The feeling of friendliness towards Turkey, and the belief in her regeneration, development, and progress, which at one time was almost universal, had undoubtedly suffered some decay, and the principles of Mr. Cobden and Mr. Bright were accepted by many more persons than would have acknowledged them twenty years earlier. Yet it cannot be said that dislike or distrust of Turkey was general amongst the English people in May, 1876. It was known that that country was in a very disturbed state; it was seen that her finances were desperately involved; and those who had lent money to the Sultan's Government, and doubted whether they should get either their principal or their interest, were in a mood of sullen discontent, which very little would suffice to inflame. Nevertheless, England was somewhat indifferent to the progress of Eastern affairs, while trusting that the ambition of Russia would not violently reopen a question which carried in its bosom so much lurking mischief.

An extraordinary series of events, however, soon riveted the attention of the whole world, and made the state of Turkey the most important topic of the day. The Memorandum so carefully elaborated at Berlin was never presented at Constantinople, owing to that series of events; and all the manifold interests contained in what is called the Eastern Question were handed over to the domain of prejudice and passion. A few days before the meeting of the three Chancellors at Berlin, an insurrection broke out in a part of Turkey commonly, but perhaps incorrectly, designated Bulgaria, the leaders of which hoped to co-operate (though distantly) with the rebels in Herzegovina, and, by increasing the embarrassments of the Porte, to promote the designs of Pan-Sclavism. Bulgaria is a province of European Turkey, situated north of Roumelia (which contains the Imperial capital), south of Wallachia and Moldavia, east of Servia, and west of the Black Sea. It comprises the greater part of ancient Mœsia, which was peopled by a race of Sclavonic origin. Various Gothic tribes afterwards colonised the land; but in the seventh century Upper Mœsia was given by the Greek Emperor Heraclius to the Serbs and other Sclavonic peoples, so that the main element is analogous with that which enters so largely into the composition of the Russian nationality. The Bulgarians themselves were Finns, of the Ugrian stock, from the banks of the Volga. They entered Lower Mœsia about the middle of the sixth century, but in the course of a few generations blended with the native population. Their name became in time the name of the country and the people, and the Bulgarians soon acquired a distinct position in the East of Europe, which they have not yet renounced. In truth, their race and language extend far south of the geographical limits now assigned to Bulgaria, and form important elements in the provinces of Thrace and Macedonia, which come under the general denomination of Roumelia; and it was in those more southern regions that the insurrection broke out. The population of Bulgaria, so called, is computed at about 3,000,000, but, taking the whole of European Turkey, the people altogether count for many more. For some centuries, their kings were willing vassals of the Greek Emperors, whose protection they were glad to receive; but in 1185 they declared their entire independence, observing that the Greek Empire needed protection more than Bulgaria. The country, however, has never been long free from the domination of some stronger Power. That sovereignty which was at one time exercised by the Roman Emperors, and afterwards by those of Constantinople, was seized during the Middle Ages by the Hungarian monarchs, though Bulgaria had still its petty kings, who were allowed to rule, on paying fealty to their superior. But the Turks were by this time acquiring a position in Europe, and the Bulgarians were unable to resist their onslaught when it came. The conquest of the country by the Ottomans took place in 1392, and ever since then the independence of Bulgaria has been a dream. The general character of the land is fertile, except where it is traversed by the great mountain chain called the Balkans,—the Hæmus of the ancients. In the plains and valleys, the ground is well cultivated. Agriculture flourishes more in Bulgaria than in any other part of Turkey, and the comfort and prosperity of the people, for many years previous to the recent outbreak, seem to prove that the oppression of the Christians by the Mohammedan Pashas, which Russia has always alleged as one of her chief causes of complaint against the Turkish Government, was at least considerably exaggerated. A semi-Oriental character is visible in the province itself, in the towns, and in the people; indeed, many of the inhabitants, even among the actual Bulgarians, are Moslems by religion. These are, no doubt, greatly out-numbered by the Christians, who are reckoned at about two-thirds of the whole; but the existence of this element must be taken into the account in any estimate of the political or social state of the country.

When it is said that the majority of the Bulgarians are Christians, it should be recollected that their Christianity is divided against itself into distinct bodies. At the period of the Turkish conquest, the people mostly belonged to the Greek Church; yet by the Greeks themselves they were regarded as heterodox, since they repudiated the jurisdiction of the Patriarch of Constantinople. It was not until 1767 that the Bulgarian Church was placed under the authority of that Pontiff. This act was followed by the dismissal of the native Bishops and clergy, by the occupation of their sees and parishes by Greeks, by the seizure of their monasteries and schools, together with the revenues attached to those institutions, and by the disuse of the Bulgarian language in all educational establishments. The subjection of the Bulgarians to the Greeks in matters of Church government was brought about by an agreement between the Hellenes and the Turks; and the consequence is that the one Christian race dislikes the other as much as both detest the Mohammedans. In some quarters, even the Russians are distrusted. The subjects of the Czar, while patronising the Bulgarians for their own purposes, are disposed to treat them with contempt, as inferior members of the Sclavic family. That the Turks were not the chief oppressors of these usually quiet people, is proved by the fact that some years ago they appealed to the Porte for protection against the persecutions of the Greek ecclesiastics. The appeal was ineffectual, and between the years 1840 and 1845 some wealthy merchants of Philippopolis and other districts organised a national opposition to their tyrants, and insisted on a revival of their own tongue. Despite the bitter antagonism of the Greeks, the Bulgarians at length carried their point, and schools distinct from those of the Hellenes were opened in 1850 in some of the district towns. Education then rapidly advanced, and the Bulgarians made great progress in intelligence and material prosperity.*

Religious dissent from the domination of the Greek Pontiff continued to increase, and steps were taken to found an independent Bulgarian Church. About 1860, the people of Philippopolis renounced their allegiance to the Patriarch of Constantinople, appropriated the ecclesiastical domains, tenements,

* "Turkey in Europe," by Lieut.-Colonel James Baker, M.A., 1877, chap. ii.

and revenues of the diocese, and devoted a portion of the funds to educational purposes. This example was speedily followed, and the Bulgarians once more enjoyed their own Church government. Whatever opposition they experienced came from the Greeks: the Sultan and his Ministers threw no difficulties in their way, and seem, indeed, to have been favourably disposed towards them. Whether they would have met with as much leniency from the Russians, the most rigid and orthodox members of the Greek Church, is more than doubtful. A Bulgarian colony which settled, several years ago, in a part of Bessarabia, then belonging to Russia, was denied the use of its own language until after the annexation of the territory to Roumania by the Treaty of Paris, in 1856.* Another Bulgarian colony, which was recently granted lands on the Russian Steppe, found a state of things so uncongenial in many respects that its members talked of returning to their old homes.† In this instance, the causes of discontent had reference chiefly to the disappointment of the people's hopes as colonists; but the Russian has never treated the Bulgarian with much generosity. The latter has always been regarded either as the tool or as the poor relation of the former.

Religion is a powerful sentiment with all Bulgarians—the most powerful of any by which they are actuated. They dislike the Turk because he is a Mohammedan; they dislike the Greek because in their opinion he is worldly-minded and intriguing. Yet they have sometimes been glad to avail themselves of Turkish protection against the violence of their own religious factions, when it has been only the Moslem scimetar that has prevented one sect from flying at the throats of another. The Bulgarian Christians may formerly have been nearly all of one Church; but that is not so now. American Foreign Missions have introduced Protestantism into the country, and of late years there have been several Roman Catholics. It was even stated, in January, 1861, that the Bulgarian people had gone over as a body to the Western Church; but this was a great exaggeration. Still, a certain number of converts were made, and the Romanists are now sufficiently strong to be a disturbing element in the State. They are a good deal persecuted by the Eastern Christians, and are inclined to favour the Ottoman Power, which protects them against the fanaticism of their fellow-Christians of a different ritual. The Porte has in truth acted with great impartiality, for the last twenty years or so, towards the several denominations of Bulgarians. Protestants and Romanists have been allowed a fair amount of freedom, and those of the Eastern Church have been suffered to emancipate themselves from Greek tyranny. The Imperial Firman of February, 1870, by which the Bulgarian Church was released from the Patriarchate, and established as an independent religious body, was received by the great majority of the people with the utmost joy and gratitude. In a general letter from the Bulgarian Synod sitting at Constantinople on the 3rd of March, 1870, and from the Bulgarian University at the Ottoman capital, addressed to the Bulgarian provinces on the issue of this Firman, we read:—"After so many evils, after so much unjust suffering, after ten years of laborious efforts, we see to-day the desire of our fathers—the toils and patience of the nation, and of us all, rewarded and crowned under the righteous judgment and impartiality of the Imperial Government. The decision of our 'question,' which has drawn out our efforts and attracted our attention for so many years, is the plain proof of the good will and love which the Imperial Government cherishes towards the Bulgarians. It is a bright evidence that it wishes to have us under its immediate protection and care; it is a demonstration that it raises even us Bulgarians to the rank of its true subjects." In revenge for these transactions, the Greek Patriarch excommunicated all Bulgarians who acknowledged the independence of the national Church.

Although the feeling entertained by many Bulgarians towards the Porte became extremely friendly in consequence of the Firman of 1870, others omitted no opportunity of conspiring against the Ottoman Power. Russia, owing to affinity of race and of religion, has always had a strong attraction for a certain proportion of the people. It is true that, as we have seen, the Russians treat their humble congeners with great superciliousness. Several young Bulgarians are every year educated in schools established by the Russian Government at Odessa and Nicolaieff, and in these schools every effort is made to discourage a distinctive Bulgarian sentiment, and to merge the nationality of the province in that of the huge Northern Power. Yet numerous Bulgarians are so besotted with the love of Russia as to abet the designs of the Czar in every way they can; and the young men who have been trained in Russian seminaries return to their own land as the agents of Muscovite intrigue. That an active propaganda has been carried on in Turkey by the Emperors of Russia for years, is quite incapable of any but the most audacious denial; and it is easy to understand how great an

* Colonel Baker's "Turkey in Europe."

† "Russia," by D. Mackenzie Wallace, M.A., 1877, vol. ii., chap. xxiv.

obstacle this must have presented to the effectual application of the reforms which have from time to time been promised. At the Peace of Bucharest, in 1812, when one of the numerous wars between Russia and Turkey was brought to a close, and it was agreed that the Pruth should be the dividing line between the two Empires, Russia acquired a right of protectorate, as regarded the Greek Church, in certain parts of Turkey; and from that time forward the influence of St. Petersburg over a large number of Turkish subjects was facilitated and assured. The partial independence of Greece was to some extent brought about by the secret action, as afterwards by the avowed support, of Russia; though of course we must not forget the natural and legitimate aspirations of a great historic race, or the grinding tyranny of the Pashas.

Since then, the Russians have made several attempts to revolutionise Bulgaria, one of the most noticeable of which took place in 1867, at the period of the Cretan insurrection. At that time, a horde of Greeks of the worst character was sent among the Bulgarians, with instructions to slaughter the people far and wide. except on condition of their joining in a movement against the Turkish Government. It was hoped in this way to create such a state of anarchy as would afford a plausible excuse for foreign intervention; but the Bulgarians themselves were so disgusted by the ferocity of these brigands (who took their orders from a secret committee sitting at Bucharest, in Wallachia, and of course in communication with Russia) that they hunted them down without remorse, and delivered them over to the Ottoman authorities. In opposition to the revolutionary propaganda, the Christians were to the full as earnest as the Mohammedans. The late Lord Strangford has preserved, in one of his writings on the subject, a remarkable address by a Greek agent, named Costaki, to the Bucharest Committee by which he had been employed. This man was taken prisoner, and, while lying under sentence of death, wrote to his principals that they had deceived him, for that he had found the Bulgarian peasantry fiercely hostile to the movement, whereas he had been led to suppose that they were eager to rise against the Sultan. "We are shot down on the plains," he said, "and starved in the mountains, and have nothing for it but to surrender ourselves to law. Is that the way you pretend to regenerate a people, and to work for the good of the Bulgarian race? Is that your holy work, in the name of civilisation and progress? My worldly goods are destroyed, my house is desolate, my life I am about to lay down in the flower of my age. May God smite you, and all those who act with you—smite you with a chastisement even more terrible than that which your victims are doomed to suffer!" The man was shot shortly after he was taken prisoner, and the letter was found on his person.

While these events were happening, Midhat Pasha, afterwards Grand Vizier for a few weeks, was Governor of Bulgaria. Midhat is a man of great energy, and of very liberal ideas. Under his rule, Bulgaria flourished, and enjoyed a degree of prosperity which seemed likely to increase. He made roads, suppressed brigandage, and otherwise added to the well-being of the country; and, although these improvements were allowed to languish after his removal, the province was tranquil and happy when the Herzegovinian revolt broke out, in 1875. If there were any hardships from which the people suffered, they were not so serious as to produce a wide-spread feeling of disloyalty. Some of the Bulgarians were. undoubtedly, influenced by a sentimental affection for Russia, which the young students from Odessa and Nicolaieff did their utmost to foster; but there was no more desire for insurrection then than had existed in 1867. The Bulgarian was at ease in all his surroundings; he was well fed, well clothed, possessed even of superfluities, and at liberty, by the wise concessions of the Sultan, to manage his religious affairs according to his own wishes. A correspondent of the *Daily News*—a journal bitterly opposed to Turkey and all things Turkish—bore remarkable testimony, during the war of 1877, to the enviable condition of Bulgaria before its desolation by contending armies, and to the systematic misrepresentations by which the Russian soldiers had been deceived. Several officers of high rank, and more than one in the personal suite of the Emperor, declared to him that they had laboured under a profound misconception as to the state of the Bulgarian Christians. "They had believed them," said the correspondent, "oppressed, impoverished, impeded in the exercise of their religion, sure not for an hour of their lives, of the honour of their women, of their property. It was in this belief that they thrilled with enthusiasm for a veritable war of liberation. And, they continue, how do we actually find the Bulgarians? They live in the most perfect comfort; the Russian peasant cannot compare with them in comfort, competence, or prosperity. Personally, I may add that I should be glad if the English peasantry were at all near them in these attributes. Their grain-crops stretch far and wide. Every village has its teeming herd of cattle, brood-mares with foals, goats, and sheep. The houses are palaces compared with the subterranean hovels of the Roumanian peasants. Last year's straw is yet in their stack-yards. Milk may be bought in every house. In the villages, for one mosque there are half a dozen Christian churches. No man experiences anywhere a difficulty in getting silver for a napoleon."* The deception practised on the Russian army must in the main have been due to Russian statesmen and political agents.

Lord Palmerston remarked in the House of Commons, on the 25th of March, 1854, that, from the time of Peter the Great, Russia had persistently laboured to effect the subjugation of Turkey. This is a fixed idea on the part, not only of the Emperors and the bureaucratic classes, but of a large number among the Russians themselves. The Pan-Sclavic sentiment—the conviction that the whole of the enormous Sclavonian race must in time be united under the rule of Holy Russia—has taken possession of the popular mind, and is professed with all the fervour of a religious creed. Secret societies exist for its support and dissemination, and in some of these it is combined with revolutionary and socialistic principles which make it still more formidable. The Russian monarchs, with all their despotic power, dare not resist it, even if so inclined, for it could always re-inforce itself by the most disturbing influences. No country in the world is more thoroughly penetrated with anarchical ideas than that which still rests in delusive quiet beneath the sceptre of the Czars. The Nihilists—a body of reformers, so called because they propose to destroy every established institution, and begin society afresh on the most extreme communistical theories—are preparing the way for convulsions that will probably equal the worst of which Paris has at any time been the theatre. One of the founders of the celebrated International Association, a few years ago—a Russian named Michael Bakounine, who died in Switzerland on the 1st of July, 1876—declared himself opposed to every species of creed, to all accepted ideas of virtue, to all forms of law, and all descriptions of personal property. An Imperial rescript, addressed in 1875 to the Russian nobility, called attention to the prevalence of these ideas, and declared that the entire Empire was "sapped by socialism." Count Pahlen, the Minister of Justice, at the same time issued an official proclamation, stating that, in spite of all attempts at repression, "the most criminal propaganda, threatening alike religion, morality, and property," had struck deep roots into the Russian population. Even persons in official station had secretly adopted the same dangerous creed. The Minister of Public Instruction also bore testimony to the same effect, in a circular to the heads of Universities and schools, in which he alleged that communistical ideas were being widely disseminated among the students and pupils of the various academies throughout the Empire. A number of incendiary fires, attributed to the Nihilists, occurred in various parts of Russia in the course of 1875, and several arrests were made, in the vain hope of crushing out the evil.

MIDHAT PASHA.

It must be borne in mind that most of these ultra-revolutionists are devoted to the belief that all the scattered members of the Sclavonic family must be united with Russia. They accordingly add immensely to the force of the Pan-Sclavist idea, and it is only by yielding to them in this respect that the Emperor can stave off dangers which threaten his dynasty, and menace the whole fabric of society in that part of the world. The Sclaves of European Turkey amount to between eleven and twelve millions, as well as can be ascertained in countries where statistical information cannot be had with exactness. The total number of Sclaves in Europe altogether (including not only Russia, but Austria, Poland, and some parts of Germany) is supposed to be upwards of ninety millions. To bring the whole of this immense family under one rule, is the object of Pan-Sclavism. As a large part of the popula-

* *Daily News*, Aug. 9th, 1877.

tion of Turkey in Europe is Sclavonian, it is a favourite dream of Russians to obtain possession of Servia, Bosnia, the Herzegovina, Montenegro, and Bulgaria; but a design of this nature must always be approached cautiously, and under cover of a pretended sympathy with the oppressed and suffering. Another motive, besides affinity of race, influences the policy of Russia in this respect. If the northern provinces of European Turkey can be subjugated, or established as nominally independent States under the tutelage and protection of St. Petersburg, a very important step will have been taken towards the acquisition of Constantinople; and the possession of that city by Russia, in addition to her other dominions, will give her the command of the East, together with a preponderating influence in the Mediterranean, and over a large part of Europe. To absorb the outlying members of the Sclavonian race is therefore one part of the Russian policy; to establish the seat of government on the Bosphorus, and thus be in a position unequalled by any other country in the world, is the other part. It is true that the Suez Canal has opened a new route to Eastern Asia; but the command of the Mediterranean, which would fall to the lot of any aggressive Power holding Constantinople, is an object that Russia will never willingly relinquish. The Czars have long believed that they are destined to inherit the old dominions of the Byzantine Emperors, to which they seem almost to consider that they have a prescriptive right; though how such a right is to be shown, it would be difficult to say. But with Russia at Constantinople, an Empire would be created, far larger and more formidable than any which has ever before been ruled from that ancient and historic city. This it is which creates in so many quarters so much jealousy of the designs of Russia; this it is also which makes Russia so resolved to win the prize, either by force or cunning. She is now land-locked to the south, being unable to quit the Black Sea, which is a mere interior lake. In the case supposed, her naval power would be felt throughout the world, and might in time surpass all others.

BULGARIAN AGRICULTURAL LABOURERS.

The appeal to the sentiment of race, by which

Russia hopes to effect her purpose, is one extremely well adapted to mislead several minds by a fallacious appearance of generosity, but is at the same time a motive peculiarly liable to abuse. It seems often to be confounded with the sentiment of nationality, from which, however, it is in truth perfectly distinct. Where a clearly-defined nation, with a common history, a common language, and a common centre of national life, has been conquered, despoiled, and divided, a legitimate occasion exists for the most eager aspirations after a revival of the murdered country in all its plenitude and all its glory. Such, until recently, was the case with Italy; such is still the case with Poland. In quarrels like these, conspiracy appears respectable; revolt is noble; success, when it comes, is a vindication of natural justice; and no nation that lives honestly has any reason to fear or to regret the progress of events in that direction. But the sentiment of race is little better than a pretext for ambition, conquest, and robbery. Races separate into nations, and there is no divinely-appointed head to all the subdivisions. Between the Russian and the Serb, or the Russian and the Bulgarian, nothing but a remote ethnological affinity can be said to exist. The Servians, the Bosnians, the Bulgarians, may be Sclaves, but they were never Russians. They do not speak the Russian tongue; they were never at any time ruled from Moscow or St. Petersburg; their traditions are distinct; it may be doubted whether, if left to themselves, they would desire incorporation with the great Northern Empire, though a friendly alliance would of course be natural. Yet Russia has so contrived that all these populations have been half won over to her sway. She has made the most of the Pan-Sclavic idea, and has bent it to the purposes of self-aggrandisement.

One of the chief associations for the diffusion of this idea is the Sclavonic Committee, a body divided into three sections, the principal of which sits at Moscow, the second at St. Petersburg, and the third at Kief. A writer favourable to Russia denies that the Committee is a secret or revolutionary society, but acknowledges that nearly all its members are more or less influenced by Sclavophil sentiments, that some are probably actuated by political or semi-political motives, and that, whether intentionally or unintentionally, they have fostered among the Bulgarians and other branches of the Sclave race those feelings of discontent, mingled with political aspirations, which had in the first instance been engendered by tyranny and misrule.* The Committee is authorised by Government, and holds its meetings in public; and its members have for several years been subscribing funds for the education of the Southern Sclaves, and for the maintenance of the "Orthodox" churches in Austria and Turkey. But the same authority admits that these ladies and gentlemen (for the association includes both) have —whether with or without any such design— inspired many Sclaves in both Empires with the belief that they would find in Russia a protector in the hour of danger. It is therefore obvious, even on the most friendly showing, that the Sclavonic Committee of Russia had much to do with fomenting disloyalty and the desire of rebellion in Bulgaria and other parts of European Turkey. The general design has still more influential patrons. Sir Henry Elliot, writing from Constantinople to Lord Derby on the 14th of February, 1876, said that at Ragusa, in Austrian Dalmatia, the Russian consulate was the open resort of the insurgent chiefs concerned in the Bosnian and Herzegovinian movements; that their correspondence was sent to the consul, who was a party to all their projects; and that so little attempt at concealment was made, that, on the occasion of one of the chiefs being killed in action, the Russian flag at the consulate was hoisted at half-mast, and the representative of Russia joined in the funeral procession. This gentleman's conduct was afterwards brought to the notice of Prince Gortschakoff; but the latter merely replied that he could not rebuke his subordinate for kindness of heart. It is well known that the same ends are promoted by societies of a secret nature, whose designs are more extreme than those of the Sclavonic Committee, whose agents are more subtle, and whose operations are probably attended by greater success, as they are conducted with a bolder hand and a more thorough unscrupulousness.

The flame is still further supported by an influence which in Russia is extremely powerful. The priest omits no opportunity of representing to his flock the oppressed and miserable condition of their fellow-Christians in Turkey, or of urging on them the sacred duty of aiding the sufferers by every means in their power, even to the extent of sacrificing their lives for the triumph of the one true faith. Under these powerful appeals, subscriptions have never been wanting for the various organisations which professed to be mainly concerned in the education of Bulgarian children, or the adornment of South Sclavonian churches, but which were in reality engaged in preparing the way for revolutionary movements. Thus, three impulses combine in urging the Russian people towards one

* Mr. Mackenzie Wallace's "Russia," vol. ii., pp. 450–51.

end: Governmental policy, revolutionary fervour, and religious faith. The complicity of the higher classes in this movement, during several years, rests on evidence the most certain. Not to go farther back, a very remarkable paper appeared in the *Moscow Gazette* of February 17th, 1867. The journal in question is not official, but expresses the views of influential persons, and is therefore an important witness in all such questions. "The new era," said the *Gazette*, glancing, doubtless, at the Cretan insurrection which had broken out a few months before, "has at length begun, and for us Russians it has a peculiar call. This era is our own; it calls to life a new world hitherto waiting in obscurity the hour of destiny—the Greco-Sclavonian world. After ages of resignation and servitude, this world approaches at last the hour of renovation. The present generation will witness great changes, great events, and great formations. Already in the Balkan peninsula, and beneath the rotten covering of Ottoman tyranny, three groups of strong and energetic nationalities are awakening — the Hellenic, the Sclavonian, the Roumanian. Closely united to each other by a common faith and by historical traditions, these three groups are equally united to Russia by all the ties of religious and national life. When once these three national groups are reconstructed, Russia will stand forth in a new light. She will no longer be alone in the world: instead of a sombre Asiatic Power, she will become a moral force indispensable to Europe. She must assume towards the Sclavonian races the attitude which France has assumed to the Latin races, and Prussia to the German races; and she must employ all her forces to realise it."

BULGARIAN BISHOP OF THE GREEK CHURCH.

In the spring of 1868, a great Sclavonic Congress was held at Moscow, where representatives of the race assembled from all parts of Europe. They were received with much honour by the Imperial family and the official world, and in turn called upon the Czar to plant the Russian standard on the Dardanelles and the church of St. Sophia. At that very time, Bulgarian committees were sitting in the capital of Wallachia, and in other Danubian towns, for the purpose of exciting disturbances in Bulgaria, and arms were actually being supplied to the people direct from Russia.* The Cretan revolt of 1867—8 was undoubtedly fostered by the Northern Power. Great toleration in religion had been allowed by Turkey for several years; and it is doubtful whether the grievances which really existed would have provoked an outbreak without some foreign stimulus. The systematic interference of Russia in the East was well known to Austria, and correctly appreciated by that Power, at the period of the rising in Crete. Count Beust was at that time Chancellor of the Austrian Empire; and on the 22nd of January, 1867, he addressed to the Internuncio at Constantinople a despatch, in which he remarked that the Governments of Europe must be desirous to maintain the general peace; that all, with one exception, must be interested in finding a pacific solution for the Eastern Question, without disturbing their mutual good relations; but that Russia might be supposed to take a different view, and to be bent on pursuing another object than the common interest, by turning to her own purposes the multifarious relations she had established in South-eastern Europe. "The experience of the last ten years," added Count Beust, "shows that her exertions are incessant to keep up the agitation of those countries." The experience of the *next* ten years proved that Austria herself,

* *Edinburgh Review* for January, 1877, in an article containing the above passage from the *Moscow Gazette*, as quoted by M. Klacko, in his "Deux Chanceliers."

under the guidance of another Minister, was persuaded to become an accomplice in that fatal policy.

Such were the steps which led up to the Bulgarian rising. A movement of a seditious character had taken place in 1873, and again in 1875; but both were easily suppressed. The exciting causes, however, remained, and a fresh outbreak was planned for the 1st of May, 1876. It is believed that the Bulgarians generally had no desire to join in such an enterprise; but a certain number were persuaded by Russian and Roumanian agitators to raise the standard of revolt. Mr. Walter Baring, of the British Legation at Constantinople, writing to his chief in the early part of August, 1876, said there could not be the slightest doubt that the Russian consul at Philippopolis had had a leading share in creating the troubles.* The foreign emissaries told the unfortunate people that the insurrection would be assisted from abroad, not only with weapons and munitions of war, but with reinforcements. Chests of gold, it was said, would be sent from Russia to repay them for the probable loss of their homes, flocks, and herds. The religious motive was powerfully excited, and the heads of the Bulgarian Church, forgetful that their independence from Greek dictation had been secured to them by the Porte, encouraged whatever feeling of disaffection already existed. The most active and uncompromising of the Pan-Sclavist Committees was established at Bucharest, which, being on the northern side of the Danube, in the newly-formed State of Roumania, was at once excellently situated for operating on Bulgaria and the adjacent provinces, and conveniently removed from the observation and power of the Turkish Government. The members of this Committee are believed to have been revolutionists of the most extravagant description; but they had probably no objection to employing the religious fanaticism of the Bulgarian peasantry as a means towards the promotion of their own designs, while the Russian Government was equally willing to use the Nihilists as agents in preparing the desired catastrophe. The revolutionary chiefs met in council, during the first week of April, at a Bulgarian village, where the details of the plot were finally arranged. It was decided that the Mussulmans were to be massacred; that, as far as possible, the railways were to be destroyed, together with the rolling stock; that Adrianople should be fired in one hundred, and Philippopolis in sixty, places; that a large number of villages should be plundered and burned; that certain important positions should be occupied; that Tatar-Bazardjik should be attacked with three thousand men, and the Government stores seized; that the rising should be general and simultaneous; and that such Bulgarians as refused to join the insurrection should be forced into it by violence and terrorism. Direct promises were held out that the Russians would speedily arrive to their assistance; and in the meanwhile the people were to help the cause as much as they could by acts of assassination. The document setting forth this insurrectionary programme consisted of thirty-six articles, and one of these gave the number of fighting men who were at the disposal of the revolutionists. Another contained statistics of the houses, the inhabitants, and the estimated value of property, in every village of Bulgaria.*

The movement broke out prematurely on the 1st of May. This was owing to the design having been communicated to the Turkish authorities at Bazardjik by one of the conspirators, named Tetko, who, never having liked the scheme, determined to betray his comrades. A knowledge of the plot, according to the information of this man, had been spread over the whole province. The emissaries had been at work for three months, and their projects were by that time fully organised. They had chosen as their revolutionary centres the villages among the Balkans inhabited exclusively by Bulgarians, some of which villages were in the Philippopolis district, while others were in the vicinity of Bazardjik; and they had introduced into the country, from Russia, Roumania, and Servia, large stores of arms and ammunition. The Governor of Bulgaria, believing the statements of Tetko (which were doubtless true in the main, though they may have been heightened by fear or interest), sent Achmet Agha to Otloukeui, and Nedjib Agha to Avrat-Alan. Both these officers were police magistrates, and they were accompanied by some rural constabulary. On the 1st of May, Nedjib Agha, observing some signs of disturbance, arrested two of the rioters, and threw them into jail. The leaders of the conspiracy, believing that their plans had been discovered, at once prepared for action. They demanded the immediate release of the two imprisoned men, and, on this being refused, broke out into open rebellion, and rushed upon the small force commanded by Nedjib Agha. The zaptiehs, or rural policemen, were unarmed, and speedily fell victims to the sudden fury of the attack. Nedjib Agha, however, escaped with a few

* Telegraphic Despatch of Sir Henry Elliot to the Earl of Derby, August 11th, 1876.—Blue Book on Turkey, No. 1 (1877).

* These particulars are derived from Turkish official documents, and must therefore be received subject to some abatement; but they were substantially adopted by Mr. Baring in his official inquiry on behalf of the British Government, and are supported by probability and by independent evidence.

wounds, and conveyed information of the rising to the Government authorities, by whom the troops quartered at Philippopolis were ordered to proceed to Avrat-Alan and the adjoining districts. Before the arrival of these soldiers, several Mussulmans (according to the official report) had been massacred, with circumstances of prolonged and atrocious cruelty. The massacres and the cruelty were afterwards denied by the Bulgarians, and by various writers in this country, but apparently for no better reason than that everything is to be believed against a Turk, and nothing against his adversary. The statements, however, were in some degree credited by Mr. Baring in his report on the rising and its consequences; and they are indirectly confirmed by the shocking barbarities committed during the ensuing war by the Bulgarian peasants and their Russian allies—barbarities too clearly proved by the testimony of English newspaper correspondents to admit of any doubt. The Bulgarians are a quiet, pastoral, inoffensive people, as long as nothing occurs to rouse their passions; but let their religious fanaticism be excited, or their fears be quickened, and they are capable of as much ferocity as more warlike races.

The fact of there having been any rising at all was repudiated by the Bulgarians with the utmost energy of protest. Two delegates from Bulgaria to England—Messrs. D. Zancof and Marco D. Balabanow—published in London, during the autumn of 1876, a narrative of events which proceeded on the assumption that the Turkish reformers, for reasons not clearly made out, determined, without any provocation whatever, to exterminate the Christians. The motives imputed were—fear lest Servia should make war on the Porte, and be assisted by the Bulgarians; and the mere rage and fury of religious fanaticism. But, as the event afterwards abundantly proved, Turkey had no occasion to dread the arms of Servia: and the modern Turk is not fanatical, unless his fanaticism is kindled by opposition or the sense of danger. Of late years, indeed, he has been singularly tolerant. Sir George Campbell, a gentleman well known in connection with the Indian civil service, and a witness not at all favourable to Turkish rule, has declared, as the result of his own observations, that the toleration of the Ottoman Government towards Christians and Jews has even been "excessive."* That the Mohammedans, without any exciting cause, should have suddenly fallen on the Christians, and committed a series of wanton atrocities, at a time when the Empire was already sufficiently embarrassed, is an assertion too wildly improbable for any but the most reckless partisan to believe.

After raising the standard of rebellion, the insurgents concentrated their forces at six different centres, where they erected redoubts and barricades to resist the progress of the Turkish troops until the arrival of succours from beyond the frontier. Possessing very little military force in those parts, the Government authorities were compelled to meet the revolt by arming the adult Mussulman population at the threatened centres of Philippopolis and Bazardjik, and thus creating an improvised militia as the only means of suppressing the sedition. This show of energy over-awed the insurgents in the neighbourhood of the large towns; but the small villages were attacked with all the greater vehemence, as it was believed that the Turks were in no position to follow the rapidly-moving bodies of agitators. After some days, during which (if we may believe the statement put forth by the Turkish Commissioners who subsequently conducted an inquiry) there seemed every probability of the danger spreading, the Grand Vizier ordered the employment of more volunteers, who, uniting with the regular troops as the latter slowly arrived, began to act vigorously against the rebels. In a little while the flame of insurrection was extinguished; but, in the process of stamping it out, a series of atrocities was committed by the exasperated Moslems, which justly moved the horror and indignation of the civilised world, and which undoubtedly exceeded beyond all measure any amount of provocation that may have been received.

Before proceeding to relate those atrocities, it may be advisable to glance at the country in which they took place. The scene of the rising, and of the dreadful acts by which it was avenged, is on the southern slopes of the Balkans, which there strike out into innumerable ranges of rocky heights and narrow valleys. According to the boundaries usually assigned to Bulgaria, the country is not in that province at all, but, as we have said, in Roumelia; yet the people in the main are Bulgarians, and the land is therefore identified with the race, and generally called after their name. No more picturesque scenery exists in any part of Europe than is to be found in this region of mountains and forests. Much of the territory remains in all its primitive wildness, as it may have appeared to Greek colonists or explorers when it bore the name of Thrace, and was peopled with savage barbarians who worshipped Mars as their chief deity. The narrow glens are overshadowed and rendered melancholy by the natural ramparts of

* A Handy Book of the Eastern Question. By Sir George Campbell, M.P., 1876.

BULGARIAN PRIEST PREACHING INSURRECTION.

vast precipices; but in many spots cultivation is carried on with the assiduity of a simple and industrious race. Far up the mountain sides, the smoke of humble dwellings tells of small villages isolated from their fellows by sterile roads, by tracts of forest, or by walls of rock. Here and there, valleys of exquisite beauty—green, fresh, and sparkling with the fluent silver of the water-courses—spread themselves out beneath the austere eminences of the Balkan spurs. In their recesses lie a number of small towns, some of which are associated with the ancient world, while others are scarcely known beyond the limits of the province. Among the principal of these, having regard to the districts most disturbed, are Tatar-Bazardjik, Philippopolis, and Eski-Zaghra. Philippopolis is a very old city, in which the distant past seems absolutely ineradicable. A recent traveller found amongst the current coin of the people a piece of money of the reign of Philip of Macedon!* Yet at the present day the prevailing element is Oriental.

PHILIPPOPOLIS.

Even in those quarters which are Bulgarian or Greek, the houses have a character that is partly Turkish. The East of Europe has in many ways received the stamp of Asia, and even the disappearance of the Osmanlis could not for many generations obliterate that stamp, or change the habits to which a long association has given rise.

* Under the Balkans: Notes of a Visit to the District of Philippopolis in 1876. By Robert Jasper More. 1877.

CHAPTER III.

Influence of the Russian Ambassador over Sultan Abdul-Aziz—Irregular Forces of the Turkish Empire—The Bashi-Bazouks—The Circassians and their History—Violent Suppression of the Bulgarian Rising—Commission of great Atrocities by the Turks—Narrative by the Constantinople Correspondent of the *Daily News*—The Subject discussed in the British Parliament—Statements by Mr. Disraeli and Lord Derby—Unjust Imputations against the Prime Minister and Sir Henry Elliot—Reasons why the Government was not better informed—Turkish Official Reports—Inquiry by the Special Commissioner of the *Daily News* (Mr. J. A. MacGahan)—Horrible Condition of Batak—Reports of Mr. Schuyler, the American Consul-General for Turkey—Mission of Mr. Baring, Secretary to the British Legation at Constantinople—Principal Features of that Gentleman's Report—Contradictions between his Assertions and those of Mr. Schuyler—Programme of the Insurgents—Testimony of two Christian Commissioners—Reasons for doubting some of the worst Narratives—Maltreatment of Prisoners—Rewards bestowed on the Chief Wrong-doers—Anarchical Condition of Bulgaria after the Suppression of the Revolt—Trial of the Persons implicated—Alleged Renewal of the Outrages in the Autumn of 1876—Probability that the Statements were exaggerated.

When the disturbances broke out in Herzegovina, and afterwards in what is sometimes called Bulgaria, Turkey was ruled by a weak, incapable, and debauched sovereign, who had suffered himself to fall under the influence of a plausible diplomatist, sent there, strange to say, by the very country which all Turkish Sultans have the most reason to dread. Russia was at that time represented at Constantinople by General Ignatieff, a soldier of gay, facile, and agreeable manners, who pleased even the grave and leisurely Turks by his brightness and apparent good-fellowship, and who inspired the half-imbecile Abdul-Aziz with a profound idea of his wisdom. General Ignatieff has been described as the Mephistopheles of the late Sultan. It was said that he encouraged him in his vices, and supported, if he did not prompt, the most unpopular acts of his reign in recent times. The contraction of fresh loans, and their partial repudiation, have been attributed to him; and it was openly averred in many quarters that his object was to lure the Empire and its ruler to destruction. These imputations may be chiefly due to popular hatred and prejudice; but it is certain that the Russian Ambassador was earnestly desirous of promoting the designs of his Government. A wiser monarch than Abdul-Aziz would have distrusted such a person, and declined his advice, as likely to be dictated by a sinister motive. But the Sultan was surrounded by dangers, feeble in character, and disposed to accept any counsel which promised fairly. Confronted by a rebellion, he listened to the recommendations of Ignatieff as to the best way of suppressing it.

The General represented the movement as one of the very slightest importance. It could easily be suppressed by a mere handful of men. Why send regular troops upon so paltry a service? The desultory militia of the province — the Bashi-Bazouks and Circassians—would soon make an end of the business. The Sultan, unfortunately, adopted this suggestion, and the troops principally employed in suppressing the revolt were men of whom every excess was to be anticipated, and who in the event did not belie their reputation. The Bashi-Bazouks are little better than a tribe of brigands, imperfectly disciplined, loosely commanded, thievish in their habits, and ferocious in their passions. Literally construed, the word means light-headed, or foolish; and certainly these irregular troops seem to be of little worth. They were employed by us in the Crimea, but proved insubordinate, ruffianly, and valueless. The idle, profligate, and reckless of many different races swell the ranks of this body of fighting men; and the Turks themselves dislike them as much as the Christians. Of the Circassians more is to be said, though they have the faults of a barbarian race in ample measure. Their story is one of great suffering and oppression, and it should be borne in mind when we are considering their misdeeds.

The Circassians are aliens in Turkey. They are colonists introduced from the northern declivities of the Caucasus, to save them from the tyranny of Russia. Their country was formally ceded to that Power by the Porte (which had in truth only slight jurisdiction over it) by the Treaty of Adrianople, in 1829; but the mountaineers hated their Christian masters, and resisted them with indomitable spirit for many years. Schamyl, their leader, attracted the admiration of all men by his heroism, and in the popular esteem he ranked with Abd-el-Kader, Kossuth, and Garibaldi. So deadly was the struggle, so difficult the conduct of a war amongst rocky passes and on the slopes of beetling precipices, that Russia every year lost many thousands of her best troops in the desperate endeavour to subdue a race of warriors trained to freedom and to arms, and hating the domination of Christians as at once an injury and an affront. It was a contest in which no quarter was given on either side; but the ferocity of the Russians was worthy of Genghiz Khan or Tamerlane. They slaughtered men, women, and children, in cold blood; they drove 300,000 of the people from their lands; they employed against them every agency by which they might be reduced to despair. The officers who ordered or sanctioned these atrocities were neither punished nor removed from command; and it cannot be doubted that they carried out, perhaps with an occasional excess of zeal, the general instructions they had received from St. Petersburg. The misery of the Circassians was so intolerable that in April, 1864, they appealed to Queen Victoria to mediate between them and their oppressors; but the request was not granted. Schamyl had been captured in 1859, and the struggle for independence had become hopeless. Twenty thousand Circassians emigrated to Constantinople in 1860, and many more followed in June, 1864, after the capture of the last mountain stronghold, and the close of the war. Towards the support of these exiles, the Turkish Government, at a period when it was much embarrassed, devoted a sum of £200,000. They were settled in various localities, but soon proved to be very troublesome subjects. While maintaining their gallant struggle with Russia, they were regarded by English newspaper writers with great admiration; but in truth their chief virtues are courage, patriotism, and hospitality. Dishonest and turbulent, they are constantly involved in some sanguinary feud, and they have more than once defied and resisted the Turkish Government. They sell their daughters to the harems of rich Pashas, and insist on keeping their hereditary slaves, though it is against the law of their adopted country. No more fanatical Mohammedans than the Circassians are anywhere to be found; but this does not seem to have established between them and the Turks any great bond of union, and the settlers from the Caucasus are a danger to the land where they have pitched their tents.

Sir Henry Elliot, the British Ambassador at Constantinople in 1876, remonstrated with the Turkish Government more than once on the danger of employing irregular troops in the suppression of the disturbances among the Christians. But his advice was not taken, and, in the closing days of his reign, Abdul-Aziz directed a horde of Bashi-Bazouks and Circassians, but chiefly the former, against the rebellious Bulgarians. The Beys of Philippopolis and Adrianople had previously sent numerous telegrams to the Porte for regular troops; but these were refused—whether owing solely to the influence of General Ignatieff, or partly to that, and partly to the fact that troops were not then readily available, may be an open question. Left entirely to their own resources, the Beys armed the Mohammedan population, and sent them, together with a few regulars, into the Bulgarian villages. The resistance they encountered was not energetic. In several places, the insurgents surrendered their arms on the first demand. At other points, there was a despairing attempt to maintain the insurrection by fighting; but the pacific Bulgarians could make but a poor stand against the onslaught of the more warlike Moslems, and the Russian or Roumanian instigators were too few in number to alter the conditions of the struggle. Had the contest ended here, no blame could have been cast on the Turkish Government. But, unhappily, the madness of fanaticism had been aroused, and it was not without some exciting causes of a genuine character. The Mohammedans knew that villages inhabited by their fellow-believers had been burned; that several persons had been cruelly massacred; and that a Christian conspiracy, fomented from abroad, threatened the very existence of the Empire. They probably believed the danger to be greater than it was; and in a transport of rage and fear they swept down on the Christian communities, and repaid their wrongs a hundredfold in acts of merciless revenge. Non-combatants suffered equally with combatants; neither age nor infancy was any protection against brutal murder; small towns and flourishing hamlets were reduced to ashes; and in many instances women and children were subjected to abominable outrage before being despatched or turned adrift upon the world. The regular troops, for the most part, behaved with proper discipline and self-restraint, though the rule was not without some marked exceptions, such as are to be found in every army in periods of excitement. But the Bashi-Bazouks and Circassians worked their will upon the wretched people with unmitigated ferocity; and the country over which they passed was turned, in several localities, to a desert and a charnel-house.

These dreadful events took place in the first half of May. It was not until the 23rd of June that the English public knew anything about them. On that day, the *Daily News* published a letter from its regular correspondent at Constantinople (dated June 16th), in which it was written:—"Dark rumours have been whispered about Constantinople, during the last month, of horrible atrocities committed in Bulgaria. The local newspapers have given mysterious hints about correspondence from the interior which they have been obliged to suppress. I have hitherto refrained from mentioning these rumours, or from stating what I have heard; but they are now gradually assuming definiteness and consistency, and cruelties are being revealed which place those committed in Herzegovina and Bosnia altogether in the background." It was added that the atrocities complained of were not the work of soldiers, but of Bashi-Bazouks. "Turkish soldiers," said the correspondent, "are always a rough, undisciplined lot; but they had to deal with men who were not very much better, and who were in rebellion." It was too soon then to state, with any exactness, the number of persons killed; but an intelligent Turk who had just arrived in Constantinople estimated it at 18,000, while Bulgarians spoke of 30,000, and of the destruction of upwards of a hundred villages. That it was impossible in the first instance to set down the numbers with precision is not at all surprising. Wild rumours were flying about, and the most conscientious chronicler could not at the moment detect the degree of exaggeration which belonged to each. But it is much to be regretted that the *Daily News* and its correspondent should, in support of a foregone conclusion, and in pursuance of a policy which could have no other effect than to encourage the aggressive ambition of Russia, have clung to those exaggerations as if they contained the very essence of truth. On the 30th of June, the Constantinople correspondent wrote that not one of the rumours published in his former letter had, as far as he was aware, been disproved, while some had been established. In the same letter, he mentioned the report of a consular agent, in which the number of killed, amongst the non-combatants only, but including men, women, and children, was fixed at 12,000. This was the lowest estimate; but reports were quoted which spoke of 20,000 and 25,000. On the 11th of July, the correspondent asserted that the destroyed towns and villages amounted to nearly ninety. He re-affirmed all that he had said in his first letter, and stated deliberately that the evidence which had since come to hand showed that he had under-estimated, rather than over-estimated, the outrages committed on the Bulgarians by the Bashi-Bazouks and Circassians. A special correspondent sent by the same paper to Constantinople telegraphed on the 21st of July that all the evidence obtainable on the subject was in favour of the other writer's statements, which no one, even amongst the upholders of Turkey, ventured to contradict or doubt. The accuracy of his first details was once more maintained by the regular correspondent on the 18th of July; and on the 21st of the same month he repeated that his original allegations were under-estimates, and, without any expression of dissent, quoted an assertion by a correspondent of the Paris *Figaro*, to the effect that a hundred and twenty villages had been burned, and upwards of 40,000 persons killed.* It thus appears that the estimates had a tendency to swell with time, and that the correspondent was nevertheless still nervously anxious on the score of under-statement. He did not, indeed, commit himself to any one number; but the general impression evidently sought to be produced was that the numbers were to be reckoned by tens of thousands. In certain quarters, mention was made of as many as 60,000 persons having been slaughtered without justification, and scarcely a day passed without the publication of frightful tales of outrage, some of which afterwards proved to be baseless. The most extravagant view of the facts was pertinaciously maintained by the *Daily News* in its leading columns, and the English public were given to understand, not merely that a terrible crime had been committed, but that the proportions of that crime were much greater than there was any probable ground for supposing, or than afterwards turned out to be the truth.

ABDUL-AZIZ.

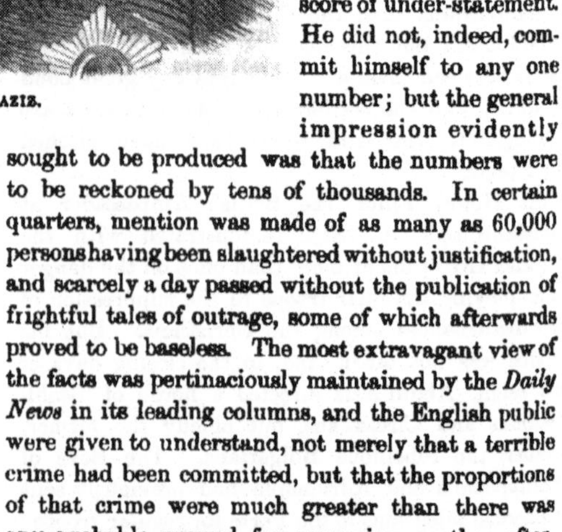

* *Daily News*, July 8th, 19th, 24th, 25th, and 29th, 1876.

The original statement, published on the 23rd of June, not unreasonably attracted much attention. The subject was brought before Parliament on the 26th of the same month, when Mr. W. E. Forster asked the Premier whether he could give the House any information as to the alleged misdeeds of the Turkish irregulars. Mr. Disraeli replied that the Government was in possession of no information which justified the statements to which reference had been made. "The persons," he said, "who are called Bashi-Bazouks and Circassians, are persons who have settled in the country, and have a stake in it. I have not the slightest doubt myself that the war, if you can call it a war, between the invaders and the Bashi-Bazouks and Circassians, was carried on with great ferocity. One can easily understand, in the circumstances under which these outrages occurred, and with such populations, that that might happen. I am told that no quarter was given, and no doubt scenes took place which we must all entirely deplore. But in the month of May the attention of Sir Henry Elliot was called to this state of things from some information which reached him, and he immediately communicated with the Porte, who at once ordered some regular troops to repair to Bulgaria, and steps to be taken by which the action of the Bashi-Bazouks and Circassians might be arrested. Very shortly after, the disturbances in Bulgaria seem to have ceased." The description of the Bashi-Bazouks and Circassians in this reply is applicable only to the latter; but in other respects the statement seems unexceptionable. Mr. Disraeli, however, went on to repeat that the information which the Government had at various times received did not justify the statements made in the journal mentioned by Mr. Forster. This called down much wrath on the head of the Prime Minister; and it was afterwards, on several occasions, most disingenuously alleged that the right honourable gentleman had at first, and as long as he could, denied the commission of any atrocities by Circassians or Bashi-Bazouks; though the brief observations of Mr. Disraeli contained a distinct assertion that the struggle had in all probability been carried on with great ferocity, that no quarter had been given, and that deplorable scenes had occurred.

The Duke of Argyll made some remarks on the subject, on the same evening, in the House of Lords, and, like Mr. Forster in the Lower House, asked whether any official information was forthcoming. Lord Derby replied that the reports he had received did not bear out in any degree the statements which the noble Duke had quoted from the *Daily News*, and, in the absence of any such official confirmation, he thought the House should be slow to believe those statements. They had heard of acts of cruelty committed on both sides, but on nothing like the scale spoken of by the correspondent. "I have a lively recollection," said Lord Derby, "of the extraordinary and sensational circumstances which reached us day by day, and week by week, nine years ago, during the insurrection in Crete. I ventured then to express some doubts as to their accuracy; and I make bold to say that nine-tenths of those reports turned out to be untrue." The Foreign Secretary appears to have adopted a more confident tone than the Prime Minister; and it is certain that if others over-estimated he under-estimated the proportions of the crime that had been committed. On the 10th of July, Mr. W. E. Forster referred to statements that a large number of Bulgarian girls had been sold publicly as slaves, and that several Bulgarians were then undergoing torture in prison. Mr. Disraeli's response to the right honourable gentleman's question, as to whether the Government would lay on the table any papers or despatches on the subject, provoked much comment at the time, and exposed the head of the Ministry to some very severe criticisms, the justice of which was less apparent than the bitterness. He stated that communications had been made between our Ambassador at Constantinople and the consuls at the seats of disturbance, and that all the information the Government had received would be laid before Parliament. In the meanwhile, he expressed a hope, for the sake of human nature itself, that, on the receipt of fuller information, it would be found that the original statements were "scarcely warranted." Yet Mr. Disraeli again affirmed his belief in the commission of many abominable deeds. "That there have been proceedings of an atrocious character in Bulgaria," he remarked, "I never for a moment doubted. Wars of insurrection are always atrocious. These are wars not carried on by regular troops—in this case not even by irregular troops—but by a sort of *posse comitatus* of an armed population. . . . . I cannot doubt that atrocities have been committed in Bulgaria; but that girls were sold into slavery, or that more than 10,000 persons have been imprisoned, I doubt. In fact, I doubt whether there is prison accommodation for so many, or that torture has been practised on a great scale among an Oriental people, who seldom, I believe, resort to torture, but generally terminate their connection with culprits in a more expeditious manner. These are circumstances which lead me to hope that in time we may be better informed. I have no doubt there may be much to deplore in what has been done, and we may even become convinced that scenes have occurred which must bring to every one feelings of the deepest regret. Still, I cannot but cherish a hope that some of the heart-rending statements we have heard have the most heartless levity. It would certainly have been better to use expressions which not even partisanship could misinterpret; but it is evident that the words were really dictated by a feeling of

GROUP OF BASHI-BAZOUKS.

not that foundation which some honourable gentlemen believe they possess."

Two rather ill-chosen expressions in this brief address were fastened on by critics of the Government with a sort of fierce avidity. The phrases "prison accommodation," and "terminate their connection with culprits in a more expeditious manner," were held up to odium as exhibitions of indignant sarcasm at the hasty cruelty with which semi-civilised Powers deal with political prisoners. The whole of Mr. Disraeli's observations turned on the assumption that the Turkish authorities were guilty of serious enormities; yet, because he did not at once admit that everything stated in the newspapers was strictly correct (and subsequent inquiries showed how well-founded was his doubt),

THE BURNING AND SACK OF BATAK.

the Premier was for several months assailed by unjust imputations, as if he had found a subject for merriment in the agony of Bulgarian peasants. Sir Henry Elliot seems also to have been inconsiderately blamed for not having discovered the atrocities sooner, although it is clear that before the newspapers said anything on the subject—indeed, as early as May—he had remonstrated with the Porte on the use of irregular troops, and that this was in consequence of what he had heard concerning their misconduct. The Government was in constant communication with its Ambassador, and on the morning of that same 10th of July Lord Derby had telegraphed to Sir Henry to communicate what he knew with the least possible delay. On the 17th of July, Mr. Disraeli made some elaborate explanations to the House, from which it was evident that the English Ambassador had spoken strongly to the Grand Vizier on the atrocities that had been committed at the scene of the disturbances before the *Daily News* called attention to the subject, though he was undoubtedly ignorant of the full extent of the evil. That Ministers were not better informed as to the details of the atrocities, and were therefore ignorant of their exact proportions, is attributable to the fact that, although we had consuls at Belgrade, Ragusa, Cettinje, Scutari, and Galatz, we had none at any of the towns in the districts immediately affected. Russia, Austria, France, and Greece, were duly represented at Philippopolis; but, from motives of false economy, enforced by the House of Commons, Great Britain had no consul nearer than Adrianople, and this gentleman was in so shattered a state of health as to be quite unfit for service. Sir Henry Elliot, therefore, had no means of knowing with precision what was going on under the shadow of the Balkans, and the Government was consequently not so well instructed as it should have been. The Ambassador might, indeed, on hearing rumours of the atrocities in May, have sent an *attaché* to make inquiries; but, considering the state of affairs at that time, and the many demands on his attention, the omission, though regrettable, does not seem open to serious blame.

The statements of the *Daily News* were now supported by those of the *Times*. Other journals suggested doubts as to their accuracy, except in a minor degree, and the Turkish Government declared that they were exaggerations of a most extreme order. It was alleged that the Bulgarians set fire to their own villages, as well as to those of the Mussulmans. Five hundred and thirty Mohammedans, according to an official report, had been killed by the Christians; the number of Bulgarians slain by the Turkish troops in their measures of repression was not more than 1,836. On the restoration of order, and the return to their homes of those insurgents who were not detained as prisoners, the Mussulmans restored to the Christians the property of the latter which they had saved from the burning villages. Such was the defence of the Ottoman Porte. It is right that it should be considered and borne in mind; but it was naturally received with scepticism at the time, and is not likely at any period to be regarded with much faith. A singular statement, however, in the report of the Extraordinary Tribunal instituted at Philippopolis for the trial of offenders, seems to derive some colour of probability from collateral testimony of an independent character. According to the report, some Bulgarians, who had contemplated a massacre of Mussulmans in the village of Ostona, afterwards took refuge in the same place, where, with their children, they were provided with food and other necessaries for five days, after which they were delivered over to the commander of the troops. The collateral evidence which renders this less improbable is the statement of an influential Bulgarian to the English Ambassador at Constantinople, to the effect that many fatherless children had been received both into Turkish and Greek families.* Some of these were afterwards restored to their relatives.

Being challenged as to the accuracy of its statements, the *Daily News* resolved on sending a Special Commissioner into the disturbed districts, with instructions to make a searching investigation. The person selected for this duty was Mr. J. A. MacGahan, an American gentleman, who was accompanied by Mr. Eugene Schuyler, the American Consul-General for Turkey. The inquiry was entirely independent both of the British Embassy at Constantinople and of the Turkish Government. Many of the peasantry were examined; and, besides these, foreign consuls, Greek residents, Germans in the employ of the Turkish Government, Turks themselves, and Americans occupied in the work of education in Bulgaria, tendered a large body of evidence incriminatory of the Ottoman troops. Mr. MacGahan reached Philippopolis, the centre of the disturbed districts, on the 25th of July, and his first letter to the *Daily News* bears date the 28th. His communications were published during the month of August, and added greatly to the excitement already existing in England. The Special Correspondent found everywhere the signs of horrible cruelty; heard in all directions the most appalling narratives of murder, rape, indescribable

* Sir Henry Elliot to Lord Derby, July 6th, 1876.

outrage, and incendiarism. The condition of Batak, a village among the mountains, was frightful beyond conception. It was one vast open grave, filled with decaying bodies of men, women, children, and infants; and amongst the tottering ruins of burned houses wandered, or idly sat, a few of the survivors, moaning in hopeless agony of mind over the desolation that had been wrought. Similar scenes were witnessed in other places; and before all the revelations had been published, Mr. Bourke, Under-Secretary of State for Foreign Affairs, said, speaking in the House of Commons on the 11th of August:—"I feel bound to admit frankly that the Government really had no idea of the events which have occurred in Bulgaria until attention was called to them in the House; and I gladly take this opportunity of saying that the Government and the country are very much indebted to the newspaper correspondents through whom those events have become known." Mr. Bourke was a little too ingenuous in these admissions; for it is clear from the original statements of Mr. Disraeli, on the 26th of June, that neither the Government nor Sir Henry Elliot was at that date entirely ignorant of what had occurred. Their information, however, was vague and unsatisfactory; and newspaper enterprise, as not unfrequently happens, effected more than official zeal.

The reports of Mr. Schuyler to the Hon. Horace Maynard, the United States Minister at Constantinople, were to the same general purport as the letters of Mr. MacGahan to the *Daily News*, though they were of course written in a more restrained and less emotional style. The American Consul-General said he had been "unable to find that the Bulgarians committed any outrages or atrocities, or any acts which deserve that name." He alleged that the massacre at Batak was perpetrated without any resistance having been offered by the people; that the village in fact surrendered without firing a shot, after a promise of safety given by Achmet Agha, who had command of the Bashi-Bazouks. As soon as the people had rendered up such arms as they possessed, Achmet ordered the destruction of the hamlet and the indiscriminate slaughter of the inhabitants, with the exception of about a hundred girls, who were reserved for the vilest purposes. Not a house was left standing; the saw-mills on the river were burned; and, of the 8,000 inhabitants, not 2,000 were known to survive. The letters of Mr. MacGahan and the reports of Mr. Schuyler were valuable contributions towards a knowledge of this dismal series of transactions; but they were too obviously written with a strong bias against the Turks to be entirely satisfactory guides, taken by themselves. What those gentlemen saw with their own eyes they doubtless reported with accuracy, though the highly pictorial style of Mr. MacGahan stood a little in the way of the reader's calm appreciation of facts. But they appear to have credited every hideous story told them by exasperated peasants and hysterical women; and it is certain that at such a period of anger and excitement many circumstances would be invented, and many others imagined. Being ignorant of Turkish, they had to depend on Bulgarian interpreters in communicating with the Ottomans, and were therefore at the mercy of any amount of misrepresentation which might be considered patriotic. Some less prejudiced testimony was needed, and it was furnished by an official representative of Great Britain.

When the statements of the *Daily News* and *Times* acquired gravity by repetition, Mr. Walter Baring, one of the Secretaries of the British Legation at Constantinople, was ordered to proceed into the devastated localities, and report to his chief. His investigations were made at the same time that the two American gentlemen were conducting theirs; but they were carried on in a more judicial spirit, and resulted in a report which bore greater marks of impartiality. That report is dated "Therapia, September 1st, 1876." In transmitting it to the Earl of Derby, Sir Henry Elliot observed that it established only too clearly that cruelties had been perpetrated on a scale fully sufficient to justify the indignation they had called forth, although the number of victims was shown to have been vastly exaggerated, and particular incidents were proved to be untrue, or very much over-coloured. Mr. Baring had the advantage of understanding Turkish, which most of the Bulgarians can speak, and he emphatically testified to the courtesy manifested towards him by the Turkish authorities and people wherever he went, and to the fact that not once did the authorities endeavour to place obstacles in his way, or try to prevent his visiting particular localities, or holding perfectly free communication with the natives. His inquiries confirmed the Turkish statements that there had been a veritable rising of the Bulgarians, prompted by the revolutionary Committee sitting at Bucharest—a fact which even Mr. Schuyler admits. It also came out very plainly that the insurgents had in the first instance committed some barbarous crimes. "The place," wrote Mr. Baring, "where the Bulgarians showed the greatest ferocity was at Avrat-Alan, for here they massacred seventy Mussulmans in cold blood; viz., the Mudir and his secretary, three zaptiehs, sixty-four gipsies, and one Turkish girl." On the whole, about two hundred Mussulmans (including women and children) appear to have been deliberately murdered; but some stories of torture and outrage committed on persons of that faith by Christians could not be brought to proof, though they were not necessarily false on that account. Mr. MacGahan himself acknowledged that the killing of the gipsies (whose number he stated at forty) was "really inexcusable;" but he hastened to add that these gipsies were secretly arming themselves, and were "suspected, but only suspected," of an intention to join the Bashi-Bazouks. The bias of this inquirer's mind may be judged by observing the very different tone with which he speaks of Christian and of Turkish offences.

Mr. Schuyler, in summing up the evidence with respect to insurrectionary acts committed by the Bulgarians, said:—"No Turkish women or children were killed in cold blood. No Mussulman women were violated. No Mussulmans were tortured. No purely Turkish village was attacked or burned. No Mussulman house was pillaged. No mosque was desecrated or destroyed." Some of these statements are contradicted by Mr. Baring, to say nothing of the Turkish official reports, which, however questionable in certain respects, may not have been without a measure of truthfulness. Mr. Baring believed that twelve Turkish women and children had been murdered—certainly a very small number as compared with the number on the other side, but one which would in all likelihood have been augmented, had not the movement been so speedily suppressed. "It has been denied," wrote the English Secretary of Legation, "that a single Mussulman village was burned, or a single mosque destroyed, when with my own eyes I have seen the ruins of both." That some of the Christian villages were fired by the insurgents themselves, or by the foreign instigators of the revolt, seems highly probable. The programme of the conspiracy, which was laid before the Extraordinary Tribunal at Philippopolis, expressly directed that all villages whose existence should interfere with the insurrection were to be absolutely destroyed. A copy of this programme was enclosed by Sir Henry Elliot to the Foreign Office, and Mr. Baring believed in its authenticity. Moreover, two Christian Commissioners, sent by the Porte to inquire into the atrocities committed by the Turkish irregular troops, gave testimony to similar effect. These Commissioners were Blacque Bey and Yovantcho Effendi—the latter not merely a Christian, but a Bulgarian. They expressed themselves satisfied that deeds of great atrocity had been committed by their fellow-religionists at the beginning of the insurrection, and that they had formed part of a deliberate scheme for rendering the movement more likely to succeed. It was hoped and desired that these acts would provoke extreme retaliations, which would in their turn excite the Bulgarians to rise as one man against their Turkish rulers. The Christian inhabitants of a village near Tirnova related to Blacque Bey, who afterwards repeated the story to an English vice-consul, that at the beginning of the revolt the insurgents seized a wealthy Turk of the locality, universally beloved for his justice and benevolence, buried him up to his waist in the earth, and then stoned him to death.* Such, at any rate, are the statements of Christians with respect to their own community.

Yet, after all due weight has been given to the provocation received, and to the danger which really threatened the Turks, the fact still remains that a frightful series of atrocities was committed by the Ottoman troops. Mr. Baring did severe justice to both sides alike, and refused to let his judgment be warped by prejudice or passion, in whatsoever direction they might lean. He denied or doubted the truth of some appalling stories which had found their way into the English newspapers, to the effect that cartloads of human heads had been paraded about the streets of different towns; that women and children had been publicly sold in the streets of Philippopolis and Tatar-Bazardjik; that horrible tortures had been practised on the prisoners; that forty young girls had been ravished, and then burned alive in a barn; that at least 25,000 perfectly innocent persons had been massacred; and that a large number of villages, differently estimated at from sixty to a hundred, had been destroyed. The question whether the prisoners had been subjected to torture he admitted to be very difficult of decision; but, while he believed that the captives had been treated with great harshness and brutality, he questioned the fact of their having been tortured. The brutality, however, was often so extreme as to amount to torture, though not coming specifically under that designation. While being conveyed to Philippopolis from the places where they were captured, many of the prisoners were savagely ill-used. "This," wrote Mr. Baring, "was especially the case with four hundred men who were marched, heavily chained, from Bazardjik to Philippopolis, and who, on their entry into the latter place, were mercilessly beaten by their escort, and pelted and insulted by the Mussulman mob. Again, eighty prisoners were sent from Philippopolis to Sofia; five of them died on the road. Immediately after the suppression of the insurrection, when the feeling

* Acting Vice-Consul Calvert to Sir Henry Elliot, Aug. 29th, 1876.—Blue Book on Turkey, No. 1 (1877).

against the Bulgarians was strongest, the zaptiehs even beat the prisoners while escorting them from the prison to the place of trial. When the great mass of prisoners came in from the surrounding country, there is no doubt that the overcrowding in the prisons at Philippopolis was terrific. Two hundred and sixty-five men were confined for four days in a bath, in which there was not the smallest attempt at drainage, the stench becoming so fearful that the guards could not even sit in the ante-room, but had to stay in the street." Owing to fear of a pestilence, the prisoners were afterwards removed to a khan.

Mr. Baring substantially confirmed the terrific account of the condition of Batak given by Mr. MacGahan in the *Daily News;* and with respect to many other villages he related a fearful tale of murder, devastation, outrage, and foul atrocity. As regarded the total number of Christians killed in those awful days, the English Commissioner mentioned that during his journey he heard it stated by a Bulgarian gentleman at 200,000, but that to the best of his belief it was in reality about 12,000—in itself, a sufficiently appalling calculation. Mr. Layard, who succeeded Sir Henry Elliot at Constantinople, has since declared his opinion that even this was greatly in excess of the truth. He believes that the whole number did not exceed 3,500.* But in any case the tragedy was on an immense scale, and was attended by circumstances of loathsome horror, which for several weeks weighed like a nightmare on the whole of civilized Europe. The Sultan and his Ministers, moreover, identified themselves with these iniquities by the course they afterwards pursued. It is very probable they never intended the commission of such acts; it is possible they were ignorant, until some time after, of their having occurred; but it is certain that they recompensed the chief perpetrators. Achmet Agha, who ordered the atrocious slaughter of men, women, and children at Batak, after he had sworn to hold them harmless on their surrendering, was adorned with the Order of the Medjidié. Nedjib Effendi, who suffered his men to pillage and burn Yenikeui after all resistance was at an end, was likewise decorated. Shefket Pasha received a high place at the palace. "The Porte," said Mr. Baring, "has given a powerful handle to its enemies and detractors by the way it has treated those who took an active part in the suppression of the insurrection. Those who have committed atrocities have been rewarded; while those who have endeavoured to protect the Christians from the fury of the Bashi-Bazouks and others have been passed over with contempt." But this impartial chronicler added, not without reason, that those agitators who, to serve the selfish ambition of States whose only object was territorial aggrandisement, had incited ignorant peasants to revolt, and had thus desolated thousands of homes, should not be allowed to escape without their share of public execration. The blame of arming the Bashi-Bazouks and other irregulars rested, according to Mr. Baring, on Aziz Pasha, who issued the fatal order; but the Grand Vizier, Mahmud Pasha, was in his opinion none the less plainly convicted of culpable negligence in not having sent regular troops the moment they were asked for.

The remonstrances of the European Powers subsequently induced the Porte to punish some of the persons concerned in the atrocities. On the 8th of June, 1877, Achmet Agha, Metto Bektash, and Achmet Chaoush, the three persons chiefly implicated in the Batak massacre, were sent as prisoners from Philippopolis to Constantinople; but their ultimate fate is not exactly known. Promises were made that taxes should be remitted in the devastated villages, and that various sums of money should be paid to the priests of those villages, in compensation for the injury that had been inflicted; but these promises have been very remissly carried out. Mr. Baring mentioned in his report that the Government officials were endeavouring to extort taxes out of the people whose villages had been destroyed. He also accused the authorities of resorting to forced labour in a way that, under the circumstances, was both unjust and injudicious. Before the disturbances, the people of Bellova had four hundred oxen; after it, they possessed but sixty. Yet five yoke were taken for working at the reconstruction of the blockhouse destroyed by the insurgents. A Government order arrived for eighty oxen to transport stores. Only half that number was forthcoming, and the soldiers on their arrival beat the people. In many instances, the clothes of the unfortunate peasants were stolen; food was deficient, and the prospects of the winter were alarming. In the province of Slimnia, however, the Mutessarif did something towards helping the inhabitants to rebuild their houses. Another act of generosity on the part of a Mussulman should not be omitted. When the troops of Shefket Pasha—an officer of the regular army—were pillaging Yamboli, Hafiz Effendi took as many Christian families into his house as he could, and, going to Shefket, insisted that the plundering should be stopped. But for the most part the feeling between Christian and Moslem was bitter in the extreme, and it was deepened by the state of

* Blue Book on Turkey, No. 26, published shortly after the close of the Parliamentary session of 1877.

anarchy which succeeded the abortive rising and its cruel suppression. The Christians, according to Mr. Baring, were afraid to go about the country, and the peasants dared not even work in the fields at any distance from their villages. Wandering bands of Circassians, armed to the teeth, struck terror into the miserable Bulgarians, and to resist their extortions was a matter of no slight peril.

The punishment of the persons engaged in the rising was of various degrees of severity. The official list of prisoners tried, condemned, or released by the Special Tribunal of Philippopolis up to the 5th of August, at which time Mr. Baring was making his inquiries, stated that sixty had been condemned to hard labour; that two had been sentenced to death, but not executed; that twenty-five had suffered the extreme penalty; that 1,400 had been released; that a hundred and fifty had been sent to Adrianople or elsewhere, on account of the non-competence of the tribunal; that twenty-five had died natural deaths, and that two hundred and ninety-four remained in prison. This gave a total of 1,956. Mr. Baring believed that 1,200 people were imprisoned at Adrianople, that eleven had been hanged for being concerned in the late revolt, and that seven had suffered for implication in a rising at Eski-Zaghra in October, 1875. These persons were tried before tribunals composed of Turkish, Bulgarian, Greek, Armenian, and Jewish members, sitting at Philippopolis, Adrianople, and Tirnova. The prisoners were primarily examined before the Tribunal of First Instance, where their depositions were taken, and then before the Special Commission. Some of these men confessed their guilt; but it is said that their self-criminatory admissions were wrung from them by torture. Of this, however, there has never been anything like satisfactory proof. Mr. Baring was in court when four men were tried, all of whom had made confessions, while not one denied the truth of what he had previously stated, or alleged that it had been extorted from him by unfair means. There is considerable force in the argument of Mr. Baring, that, if these men had been intimidated or tortured, they would, at the last moment, when feeling the rope about their necks, have taken advantage of the presence of Europeans to declare their innocence.

A CIRCASSIAN.

It has been asserted by the Bulgarians and their friends that the atrocities of May were resumed in August, September, and October. Messrs. Zancof and Balabanow, to whose pamphlet reference has already been made, published a long list of outrages committed in several small towns and villages. The Bashi-Bazouks and Circassians, it was stated, insulted and plundered the people, and repeatedly struck them with cudgels. In the villages, they unreservedly entered the Bulgarian houses, and compelled the owners to lodge and feed them free of charge. From Pirot to Widdin, forty-eight villages had been burned between August and

October. Churches were ransacked, and the ecclesiastical vessels and crosses carried away. All who dared complain to the authorities were thrown into prison. Murder, torture, and outrage, according to this account, were of daily occurrence, and the superior authorities did nothing to prevent, check, or punish the criminals. That the country altogether was in a terribly disturbed state, is certain; and it is but too probable that the Circassians and Bashi-Bazouks indulged their fanaticism and their love of plunder by isolated acts of cruelty and rapine. But it is doubtful whether any crimes on a scale of great magnitude were committed after the attention of Europe had been directed to the shocking events occurring in the spring. The testimony of irritated Bulgarians was in itself far from conclusive; and in this instance it was not supported by evidence of equal value with that which had to a considerable extent confirmed the earlier charges.

SIR HENRY ELLIOT.

CHAPTER IV.

Political Discontent at Constantinople—Demands of the Softas—Ministerial Changes—Mehemet Ruchdi made Grand Vizier—Influence of Midhat Pasha over his Colleagues in the Cabinet—Determination of the Ministers to Depose Sultan Abdul-Aziz—Measures by which the Deposition was effected—Proclamation of Murad V.—Imperial Hatt, foreshadowing Reforms—Suicide of the deposed Sultan—Assassination of Turkish Ministers by Hassan, a disgraced Circassian Officer—Designs of Servia—Secret Understanding between the Servian Prince and the Russian Emperor—Geographical Character of Servia, and previous History of the Country—Struggles of the Principality to obtain Freedom from Ottoman Rule—Progress of the Servians since their Partial Independence—Prince Milan and his Policy—Declaration of War by Servia against Turkey—War also Declared by Montenegro—Historical Sketch of the Montenegrins—Servia under the Government of Milosch Obrenowitsch—Unjustifiable Character of the Servian Attack on Turkey—Evil Influence of Russia—Progressive Steps by which a War of Fanaticism had been created.

AFFAIRS at Constantinople were hastening to a crisis when the chief Ministers of Russia, Austria, and Germany were consulting at Berlin on the proper method of dealing with the Christian provinces, and when the Turkish irregulars were cruelly avenging an abortive insurrection in the Balkans. A strong feeling of political discontent had for some time been growing up at the seat of Government. It was held by many that the Sultan and his Ministers had been too subservient to foreign influence; that the Christians had received too many privileges; and that Russia was acquiring a dangerous ascendency over the mind of the sovereign. General Ignatieff was believed to be persuading the weak-minded Abdul-Aziz to accept an arrangement similar to that which was effected by the Treaty of Unkiar-Skelessi, on the 8th of July, 1833, by which Russia undertook to place her naval and military forces at the disposal of Sultan Mahmud II. A corps of troops, it is alleged, was ready to sail for the Bosphorus, and the demand for their intervention, as a means of saving the Sultan from the insurrections which Russia had herself contrived, was either signed, or about to be signed, when a remarkable movement among a certain section of the citizens put a stop to the intrigue.* The most patriotic, or at least the most national, class in Turkey is that of the Softas, or legal students at the universities. To these young men, everything foreign is an abomination. In religion they are fanatically Mohammedan; and they are, for the most part, deeply persuaded that only by reviving the old Turkish spirit of predominance can the ancient glories of the Empire be restored. In all this there is a great deal of narrow-mindedness and prejudice; but in some respects the Softas are men of liberal and enlightened views. They demand for Turkey an honest and a capable Government; they require the purification of abuses; and they complain, not without reason, of the State being made a field of contention for rival ambitions. Foreign patronage and foreign intrigue have for many years been the two great afflictions of Turkey. The Softas perceived that fact very clearly; and they placed in the front rank of reforms the liberation of the country from secret and self-interested counsels.

Some riots of an alarming character occurred at Constantinople on the 12th of May, when the Softas raised the cry of "Turkey for the Turks!" and demanded Ministerial changes. The consequence was that Mahmud Pasha, the Grand Vizier, was replaced by Mehemet Ruchdi, who urged on the Sultan the expediency of adopting certain reforms in the administration, chiefly based on a scheme put forward by Midhat Pasha, who had been a member of Mahmud's Cabinet up to the previous December. Mehemet proposed that the civil list should be curtailed, that the arbitrary power of the sovereign should be subjected to some limits, and that the Sultan, abjuring the treacherous influence of Russia, should enter into friendly relations with the old and trusty ally of Turkey,—England. Abdul-Aziz, in what might almost be described as the blindness of fate, haughtily refused to entertain any such projects; but the new Grand Vizier and his colleagues determined that the country should not be ruined because of the obstinacy of one man. Midhat Pasha was now once more a member of the Administration, though not holding any portfolio; and his influence was supreme. It was given on behalf of bold and even revolutionary measures. The Sultan resisted reform: nothing, therefore, remained but to effect his deposition.

A Council of Ministers was held towards the latter end of May, at which Mehemet Ruchdi Pasha, Hussein Avni Pasha (the Minister of War), and Midhat Pasha, were present. At this meeting, the removal of the Sultan from the head of the State was finally resolved on, and it was arranged

* *Edinburgh Review*, October, 1876.—The writer of the article says he has great reason to believe the statements to be true.

that the change should be accomplished at half-past twelve o'clock, noon, on Tuesday, the 30th of May. The deposition of a Sultan was no new fact in Ottoman history. Such a catastrophe had taken place several times before, and, in days when the Janizaries were supreme, the event was often accompanied by murder. Although recognised, by virtue of his office, as Commander of the Faithful, the Sovereign of Turkey is not surrounded personally by that superstitious veneration which former ages attached to the idea of an anointed Christian King. He cannot set himself up above the law, as the law is expounded in the Koran. He cannot disregard the public good, and plead some mysterious Divine Right as his warrant. That is to say, he cannot theoretically do these things; though of course a strong-willed Sultan, popular with the army, and surrounded by able Ministers devoted to his person, may act pretty nearly as he likes. But Abdul-Aziz was weakness itself; he had done nothing to secure the affection of his soldiers; and his own Ministers turned against him. He had sufficient adherents, however, to obtain a knowledge of the plot before it could be brought to pass. At ten p.m. on the night of the 29th of May, Hafiz Pasha, the first chamberlain of the Sultan, received information of what was intended for the following day, and at once communicated the project to his sovereign. The Sultan thereupon summoned Hussein Avni to the palace at Dolmabatcheh; but the War Minister refused to appear, alleging that he was ill. Another message was sent to the same Pasha, commanding his immediate attendance, and informing him that the conspiracy was discovered; but Hussein Avni refused to stir. He was, in fact, holding a council with the other two Ministers at the Seraskierate, or War Office, to which were admitted several dignitaries, both of the State and of the Church. As it was considered advisable to proceed with a regard to forms and precedents, and not by mere violence, the opinion of the Sheikh-ul-Islam, the head of the hierarchy of Ulemas, or expounders of the Sacred Law, was solicited and received. According to this high authority, the Sultan could be legally dethroned, and it was added that his proper successor was Mehemet Murad Effendi, nephew of the reigning Sultan, and eldest son of Abdul-Medjid, who died in 1861. This arrangement was approved by the Council without a dissentient voice, and the conspirators at once proceeded to put their design in execution.

Preparations had already been commenced. Redif Pasha, President of the Council of War, had, in obedience to instructions from Hussein Avni, surrounded the Dolmabatcheh Palace with troops on the land side, and with steam-launches on the Bosphorus. Ahmed Kaisserli, Minister of Marine, had gone on board the ironclad, *Messoudieh*, which had been recently purchased by the Government, and then lay at anchor in front of the palace. But a difficulty presented itself at the very outset. The Prince, who was usually called by his second name, Murad, was detained by the Sultan as a sort of hostage, and it was not easy to get at him. It was believed by the Council that his acceptance of the Imperial dignity was certain; yet when an invitation was conveyed to him, begging that he would receive the investiture, he declined—probably from motives of prudence. Hussein Avni, perceiving that the refusal was not genuine, went to the palace, accompanied by two squadrons of horse, and, by help of some of the servants, contrived to get the Prince away, and to take him in a private carriage to the Seraskierate, where he was proclaimed as Sultan Murad V., in the presence of Abdul Muhtaleb, the Grand Scherif of Mecca, and of five or six hundred persons, including both Mohammedans and Christians, who had assembled outside.* As daybreak of the 30th came stealing along the waters of the Bosphorus, a hundred and one discharges of artillery announced the commencement of the new reign—a reign destined to be short indeed, yet full of troubles. The Imperial standard was hoisted on the tower of the Seraskierate, and on the old Genoese tower at Galata, one of the suburbs of the great city. Telegrams were sent off to the Governors of the several provinces, and, by the same agency, the Ottoman Ambassadors abroad were informed of the change that had been effected.

The dawn was wild and stormy, with a heavy downfall of rain. Abdul-Aziz, knowing what was going on, and probably fearing lest his life should be taken, retired into the harem for safety. In the early hours of the morning, Redif Pasha

* The four previous Murads are generally known to history by the name of Amurath. They reigned in the fourteenth, fifteenth, sixteenth, and seventeenth centuries of the Christian era. These were the sovereigns to whom Shakespeare alluded in the Second Part of "Henry IV." (Act V., sc. 2):—

"Not Amurath an Amurath succeeds,
But Harry Harry."

The poet seems to have been under the impression that the fourth Amurath immediately succeeded to the third, who died a little before the date of the play. Each of the Amuraths was in fact divided from his predecessor of the same name by several years—in one instance, by more than a century. It has been suggested that "Amurath" is not a proper name at all, but a Hellenised form of the Oriental word "Emir," signifying a sovereign or ruler. Shakespeare, however, and other writers of his time, undoubtedly used it as a proper name.

entered the palace, accompanied by several officers of rank, and by a detachment of troops, and desired to see the Sultan. A few of the eunuchs tried to cry out and resist, but were at once gagged and bound; and Abdul-Aziz, apprehending the nounced Redif Pasha as a liar, but was sternly bidden to look out at the windows. The dull light, struggling through clouds and rain, showed the forces of the Revolution arrayed by land and water in support of the new order; and resistance was

DEMONSTRATION OF SOFTAS.

worst, refused to grant the request for an interview. Word was then sent to him that, if he did not appear, the women's quarters would be entered—an extreme step in any Mohammedan community. Thus coerced, the deposed sovereign presented himself, accompanied by his mother, with her hair dishevelled, and was informed that his reign had ceased, and that he must immediately quit the palace. Transported with rage, Abdul-Aziz denounced Redif Pasha as a liar, but was sternly bidden to look out at the windows.

evidently hopeless. He was told that if he valued his life he must set out without delay. Instantaneously changing his mood, the ex-Sultan permitted himself to be escorted by water to Top Capou, where he was assigned a temporary residence in the Old Palace near the Seraglio Point. On entering the caïque, he cursed his nephew, and exclaimed, "Had I known what kind of plant that Murad was, I should have watered him with poison."

He now professed his readiness to accept the reforms which he had refused a few days before; but it was too late. His sun had set; the night was coming fast upon him in madness and in horror.

Murad V. was in the thirty-sixth year of his age when called to the throne. He was a Prince in feeble health, weak of mind, unacquainted with the affairs of the world, and enervated by that confinement to the seraglio which is usual with the younger members of the Turkish Royal family. It is obvious that he was little else than an instrument in the hands of the reforming party. The Imperial Hatt, or Message, by which he announced his accession, was of course the production of his Ministers. It was read with great solemnity on the 1st of June before a large number of persons, and commenced with the statement that his Majesty had been called to reign by the grace of God and the will of all. The latter clause of this sentence has a singularly democratic sound; but, though possibly true, it was of course quite unwarrantable, since the people had never been consulted on the subject. The Sultan charged his Ministers—which was in fact another way of saying that his Ministers charged *him*—to reform the administration of justice, and to remove those internal and external causes of discontent which had led to disturbance in certain provinces. It would be the duty of the Ministers to devise a government which should best guarantee the liberties of all; and they were to rivet more and more closely the ties of friendship which bound the Empire to foreign Powers. The decree recommended that an equilibrium of the budget should be effected, that public education should be immediately improved, and that the Council of State and other departments of the Government should be reorganised. As a proof of his own personal desire to aid the country in its troubles, the Sultan proposed to strike off £300,000 sterling from the Civil List, thus reducing it to £720,000 a year; also to renounce the income accruing from the Crown Mines, and from other Crown property, which would thenceforth be devoted to the benefit of the State. These announcements were received with much satisfaction, and it was believed that Turkey had entered on a new era of retrenchment and reform. It was not considered how great were the obstacles to any thorough amendment of abuses which had grown inveterate with time.

The fate of the deposed Sultan excited considerable uneasiness in most European countries, where the tendency of Turkish revolutions to end in murderous violence was remembered with misgiving. No longer back than the year 1808, Mustapha IV. was killed by his brother Mahmud II., after having a few months before strangled Selim III., who had been removed from power by the Janizaries in 1807. It did not create much surprise, therefore, when the announcement went forth that Abdul-Aziz had been found dead on the morning of June 4th. The first impression was that he had been assassinated; but, though the suspicion cannot be said to have been entirely removed by subsequent details, it appears not improbable that the act was one of suicide. On the day after his deposition, he wrote to his nephew, congratulating him on his promotion, assuring him of his best wishes, and asking as a favour to be removed from the Old Seraglio, and conveyed to one of the pavilions of the palace of Cheragan, which he had built for himself. The request was granted, and the ex-Sultan and his family were carried in boats across the Golden Horn—the port of Constantinople, dividing the city from its European suburbs—to the place indicated. They arrived there on the evening of May 31st; but on the following day Abdul-Aziz, according to the accounts put forth, exhibited signs of insanity. He was restless and moody; took scarcely any food; and menaced with a revolver the sentries posted at his door. His attendants removed all weapons from his reach; but on the morning of Sunday, June 4th, he was found lying half across the sofa in his apartment, with his feet on the floor in a great pool of blood. Nineteen physicians, of different nationalities (including Dr. Dickson, of the British Embassy), were at once called in, and all agreed that the direction and nature of the wounds were such as to make it apparent that the deceased had died by his own hand. The weapon employed seems to have been a pair of scissors, with which the unhappy man had opened the arteries of his arms. It may, perhaps, never be known with certainty whether the death of Abdul-Aziz was voluntary or not; but there is at least a strong presumption in favour of the affirmative hypothesis.

Any danger that might have threatened the power of the new Sultan in consequence of the prolonged existence of his predecessor was thus at an end; but the State was still at the mercy of unforeseen perils. An extraordinary set of events took place in the middle of June—events which created a feeling of dismay at Constantinople, and again attracted the astonished attention of Europe. On the 15th of the month, the members of the Cabinet were holding a meeting in the Palace of Midhat Pasha, when a disgraced Circassian officer, named Hassan, entered the room, and fired at the War Minister, Hussein Avni. Struck with fear and horror, the other Ministers, with the exception of Raschid Pasha, the Foreign Minister, and Ahmed Kaïsserli, the Minister of Marine, rushed through one of the doors into an inner apartment. Raschid appeared spell-bound or petrified; but Ahmed flung himself upon the assassin, and endeavoured to pinion his arms. Hassan, however, got his right hand free, and with a long Circassian knife stabbed the Minister of Marine in several places, compelling him to release his hold, and take to flight. Hussein Avni, though badly wounded by the pistol-shot, was not dead, and he now endeavoured to crawl fired through the door, but without hitting any one; flung down the furniture in a wild access of rage; set fire to the curtains, and broke the chandelier, so that the apartment remained dimly lighted by a single taper. After awhile, two of the Ministers—Ahmed Agha and Chukri Bey—ventured back into the room, but were instantaneously shot dead by the assassin. When at length the police and soldiery from the nearest post reached the spot, they found the floor deluged with blood, and Hassan still in a state of mad excitement. One of the police officers

ABDUL-AZIZ ON HIS WAY TO TOP CAPOU.

towards the door of entrance. Seeing this, Hassan rushed after him, and hacked at his person with the knife until he had ceased to breathe. Raschid Pasha had in the meanwhile never stirred from his place, and it is supposed that he actually died of fright. But Hassan determined to put it out of his power to give any alarm. "Do you stop here to arrest me?" he exclaimed; and shot him through the head. He next proceeded to the door of the inner apartment, which was now fastened on the other side, and, shaking it, called out, "Grand Vizier, open the door! No harm is intended to you." Mehemet Ruchdi, who was an old man, replied, in tones of great terror, "My son, not now; you are too much excited to listen to reason." Hassan then was killed, and six of the constables and soldiers were wounded before the murderer could be secured. In the struggle, he was himself seriously injured, and in this state was taken to the Seraskierate, where on the following day he was tried and sentenced to death. He would not allow the surgeons to bind up his wounds, and was much exhausted by loss of blood when, on the 17th, he was hanged in an open space in front of the War Office.* This singular combination of crimes does not seem to have been prompted by political motives, but simply by private malice; though it has been attributed to revenge for the deposition of Abdul-Aziz. Never-

* Constantinople Correspondent of the *Times*; and other authorities.

RECEPTION OF THE SULTAN MURAD.

theless, coming at such a time, it added to the general belief that the dissolution of the Turkish power in Europe could not be long deferred.

This conviction was very strongly entertained by the Prince of Servia, and it appeared to him that the time was propitious for throwing off his allegiance to the Porte, and adding to his dominions. Early in 1876, Prince Milan had begun to think of war with his suzerain, under pretence of sympathising with the insurgents in Bosnia and the Herzegovina. He was preparing for hostilities, and the attention of Sir Henry Elliot was drawn to the subject. That diplomatist reported to his Government, on the 8th of February, a declaration of the Prince that if the Herzegovina were annexed to Montenegro (as the rebels were said to desire) he would at once declare war. He would equally do so "if an Austrian force were to occupy any portion of Bosnia for the purpose of ensuring an equitable treatment of the people; and he would resist the grant to them of an autonomy, or the appointment of a Christian Governor." The motive avowed before the world, that Servia was acting on grounds of humanity and chivalrous regard for oppressed races, was therefore nothing better than a hypocritical mask. Prince Milan frankly told the British Ambassador that he cared nothing about the equitable treatment of the people, or their freedom: what he wanted, and meant to have, was more territory. As the spring advanced, Russia professed great anxiety that the proposals of the insurgents should not be rejected, that peace should be restored, and that the existing concert of the European Powers should be maintained. But all this while she was encouraging the Servian Government to plot against Turkey; and towards the end of May the Czar permitted General Tchernaieff to enter the service of Prince Milan: an act which every one saw could have but one meaning—a speedy declaration of war on the part of Servia, and an underhand support of that principality by the great Northern Empire.

Servia is perhaps the most distinct nationality in European Turkey. It has a history not unworthy to be so called—an inheritance from the past, and a prospect of future distinction, if greed, subserviency, and bad faith do not ruin all. The country is situated on the right or southern bank of the Danube, which, together with the Save, separates it from the Austro-Hungarian Empire; and it has for its other neighbours Roumania, Bulgaria, Bosnia, and Albania. Its territorial dimensions are but slight, being not more than a hundred and forty-five miles in length from east to west, and a hundred and fifty in breadth from north to south. The land is almost entirely mountainous, and a great deal of the soil is covered with ancient forests. The population, therefore, is very insignificant, and a million and a half would more than number them all. Views of the most striking picturesqueness meet the traveller at every turn, in the woody valleys and on the rugged mountain slopes; and over all is that charm of simplicity which belongs to a pastoral people and the ways of untamed nature. The Servians are physically a very fine race—tall, well-formed, and handsome, with light hair and blue eyes. They are Sclaves with scarcely any intermixture, and their language is one of the most polished dialects of the Sclavonian tongue. In the Middle Ages they formed a rather powerful State, which often defied the strength of the Greek Emperors, and even encroached on their dominions. The Servian Czardom, as it was called, had its seat in what is now designated Old Servia—at the present day, a part of Albania, and therefore not included in the realm of Prince Milan. In that small territory, cut off from its old companionship, two modern travellers have discovered the fountain-head of Servian popular song—a whole literature of wild and passionate poetry, dealing with the triumphs and the sufferings of the race. The valleys of Old Servia, now but little explored, abound in evidences of past greatness; in old cities, still maintaining a certain stately air, in ancient churches of Byzantine architecture, and in frescoes of early Italian art.* After the Turks had established themselves in Europe, some of their Sultans married with the Royal house of Servia; but the jealousy of the rival races and the rival religions could not be subdued. The Servians underwent a terrific defeat at the hands of the Moslems in 1389; and from that time their prosperity declined. But the country was not over-run by the Turks until 1459; and even then, Belgrade, the capital, held out, with the assistance of the Hungarians, until 1522. A portion of Servia was conquered by Austria in 1717, but regained by the Turks in 1739. The most remarkable period of its modern history was in the early part of the present century, when a peasant named George Petrowitsch—otherwise Kara or Black George—headed an insurrection against the Janizaries, and in a few years completely conquered them. In this movement he was aided by the Turkish Sultan, who desired to curb the insolence of his prætorian troops. Thus, in 1807, Servia became a sort of military republic, under the presidency of Kara George, and to some extent recognised by the Porte. The

* Travels in the Sclavonic Provinces of Turkey in Europe. By Miss Mackenzie and Miss Irby.

peasant-hero did not get on well with his colleagues, and endeavoured to divert their discontent by incursions into neighbouring provinces; but, after a career of some success, the star of his fortunes waned. He had now provoked the opposition of the Turkish Government, and Servia had to fight for her existence. The Ottoman troops re-conquered the country in 1813, and Kara George fled into Austria, and afterwards into Bessarabia, then recently become a Muscovite possession. The insurrection in Servia was renewed by Milosch Obrenowitsch, originally a swineherd, but a man of courage and ability; and, after a prolonged struggle, varied by occasional agreements with the Ottomans, the Turks, in 1830, recognised the quasi-independence of the country, and the commencement of a hereditary dynasty in the person of Milosch—a chief of very indifferent political character, who sometimes sided with the Russians, and sometimes with the Turks, as he believed his interests to lie.

A Constitution had been framed for Servia by Kara George in the days of his power. That daring revolutionist re-entered Servia in 1816, but encountered an unexpected enemy in Milosch, who, either from rivalry, or to save his own life by propitiating the Turks, or, as his admirers say, to rescue the country from the danger of a rising at an unpropitious moment, put him to death as he slept in a hut. Nevertheless, the Constitution remained, though with some modifications. The criminal code was based mainly on that of France, and the clergy were made amenable to the same courts as the laity. But the political institutions of the country were either worth little in themselves, or were so frequently set aside by the personal will of the Prince as to be wholly ineffective in guarding the rights of the subject. The Servians soon found that they had far less liberty under the rule of their own countryman than under that of the Turks, who had in fact let them do pretty nearly what they liked as long as they paid their taxes. Milosch was an avaricious man, and, being suspected of misappropriating the public funds, came into collision with the Senate, which in 1839 ordered an examination into the national accounts. As a consequence, he was compelled to resign, and retire into Wallachia. He was succeeded, after a period of change and disturbance, by Alexander Kara Georgewitsch, son of Black George, who ruled from 1842 to 1858, when, being regarded as a tool in the hands of Austria, he was deposed by a popular movement, which is thought to have been instigated by Russia. Servia had had nearly thirty years of recognised freedom from Turkish interference, though the sovereignty of the Porte was still maintained. Yet the progress of the country had been anything but satisfactory, and the people, in their want of faith in the younger generation, turned their eyes once more to Milosch Obrenowitsch. Milosch was now an old man, but his mind was vigorous, and he had often said that he *would* not die except as Prince of Servia. He was restored to power on the 23rd of December, 1858, but expired in less than two years after. His son, Prince Michael, who quietly took up the reins of government, had travelled through the greater part of Europe, and was a man of education and culture. He at once enlisted the affections of the people by declaring that thenceforward the law should be supreme in Servia; but it was not long ere he encroached very considerably on the popular powers. The movement for freeing the country entirely from Imperial rule was encouraged by Prince Michael. Ottoman supremacy was represented in a certain number of fortresses, including that of Belgrade, where Turkish garrisons were posted. To obtain the withdrawal of these garrisons, whose presence sometimes led to sanguinary collisions, was one of the chief objects of the patriotic party. A demand for their removal was made by the Servian Government in October, 1866, and was supported by the Government of the late Lord Derby, in which his son, the present Lord Derby, then Lord Stanley, held the seals of the Foreign Office. The garrison towns were evacuated in March, 1867, and on the 30th of the same month Prince Michael thanked the Sultan in person at Constantinople. The policy of the English Government in supporting the requirements of the Servian Government in the matter of the fortresses is open to serious question, if it be really an object of importance to resist the advance of Russia in South-eastern Europe. It must have been evident to any observer that the Servians would not be propitiated towards Turkey by the really liberal concession that had been made; that their inclinations towards Russia would be equally great, and that their opportunities of intrigue would be indefinitely magnified by the removal of every restraint. So it proved. The independence of Servia was now nearly complete. With the exception of a merely formal acknowledgment of the Porte's supremacy, and a yearly payment of £20,000 to the Imperial exchequer, she stood on the same footing as any other country which has its own rulers and its own laws. But in effect the principality has been simply an out-lying portion of the Russian Empire, and its sovereign is a willing tool in the hands of the Czar for the ruin of European Turkey.

The reign of Prince Michael extended over but

few years. He was assassinated on the 10th of June, 1868, and it was very generally believed at the time that the murder had been brought about by the Kara Georgewitsch family—a suspicion which seems never to have been clearly justified by facts. Michael was succeeded by his nephew, Prince Milan, who was then scarcely fourteen years of age, but who attained his majority in August, 1872. The government in the meanwhile was carried on by a regency, and in 1869 a Constitution was proclaimed, declaring the hereditary right to be in the Obrenowitsch family. Prince Milan was in Paris when called to the throne, and may be supposed to have imbibed some Western ideas during his residence in France. But his sympathies are wholly Russian, and although, at the beginning of the Herzegovinian insurrection, he was compelled, as a matter of prudence, to restrain the impatience of his people, his heart was with the movement, and he was ready at any time to aid the designs of Russia. A new Ministry, hostile to Turkey, was formed in the early autumn of 1875, but was forced in a few weeks to give place to a more pacific Cabinet. The feeling of opposition to Turkey, however, was only held in check, and in June, 1876, began once more to make itself clearly manifest.

The storm had been gathering for some time, and at length, on the 22nd of June, Prince Milan addressed to the Grand Vizier a letter, which plainly foreshadowed a declaration of war. On the 1st of July he formally announced, in an address to the Servian people, that he intended to join his arms to those of Bosnia and Herzegovina, to secure the liberation of the Sclavonic Christians from their state of oppression. "Our movement," he said, "is purely national. It excludes every element of social revolution and religious fanaticism. We do not carry with us revolution, fire, and destruction, but right, order, and security. Spare those of foreign nationality; extend to them that moral friendship which distinguishes the Servian; respect the borders of the neighbouring Monarchy [that of Austria], and give the Imperial and Royal Government no cause for discontent. That Government has acquired a claim to our respect by taking thousands of Bosniaks and Herzegovinians under its protection, giving them shelter and food. Brothers, full of confidence in your patriotism and your warrior qualities, I shall march with you and at your head. With us are our brave Montenegrin brothers, led by their chivalrous chief, my brother, Prince Nicholas. With us are those valiant heroes, the Herzegovinians, and those martyrs, the Bosniaks. Our brave brothers, the Bulgarians, are waiting for us; and we may expect that the glorious Hellenes, the descendants of Themistocles and Botzaris, will not long remain away from the field of battle. Forward, then, noble heroes! Let us march in the name of Almighty God, the protector of all the rights of nations; let us march in the name of right, liberty, and civilisation." The Parisian training of Prince Milan had clearly not been without some effect. Nothing could be more French in style than this manifesto. Its melodramatic attitudinising would have done credit to the most experienced revolutionist of the Latin Quarter, allowing for a few phrases which the revolutionist would object to, as being too monarchical and pious.

The declaration of war by Servia was immediately followed by Montenegro, the Prince of which State signified his intention on the 2nd of July. The native designation of this wild territory is Czerna Gora, which, like the Italian name commonly used in Europe, signifies the Black Mountain. No title could give a better idea of the general aspect of the country, which is that of a great mountain range, darkened by the shadows of immense forests. Montenegro is a very small State, with Herzegovina to the north-west, Albania to the south-east, and Bosnia to the north. As a matter of fact, it is independent of any foreign Power; but, while it is nominally under the protection of Austria, it is generally regarded as a sort of rebellious fief of Turkey. The people are a fierce and warlike race, numbering about 120,000; courageous in the highest degree, but savagely barbarian in their animosities, and fanatical in their attachment to the Greek Church. Like the other nationalities in that part of Europe, they are of Sclavonic race, and their hatred of the Turks is nothing short of a devouring passion. The country was conquered by the Sultan Solyman II. in 1526, but never quietly submitted to Ottoman rule. It rebelled early in the eighteenth century, when the Montenegrins established an hereditary hierarchical government in the family of Petrowitsch Njegosch. In the early years of the present century, they had a desperate struggle with the French, to whom, by the Treaty of Presburg, in 1805, some territory in the vicinity of their mountains had been granted. But for many years past their arms have been entirely directed against the Turks, into whose dominions they have made incursions out of number, doing as much damage as they could effect, cutting off the heads of their slain enemies, and then escaping into the rocky fastnesses of their own land. Up to 1851, the Montenegrin sovereigns had been priests as well as temporal rulers; but in that year Prince Danieli, on succeeding to power, declined to assume the ecclesiastical function. In the following year he made war on Turkey, and the Porte retorted by blockading all the coast approaches to the country, and by sending an army of 20,000 men under Omar Pasha, who stormed the village of Grahovo, and occupied all accessible positions. The mediation of Austria procured the withdrawal of the Turks at the close of February, 1853; but another war, less successful for the Ottomans, occurred in 1858. Prince Danieli, who ruled tyrannically, was assassinated in August, 1860, and the present ruler, Prince Nikita (or Nicholas), succeeded him. In 1861, war with Turkey again broke out, and Omar Pasha once more invaded the province. He had with him an army of 32,000 men, and, after suffering some reverses, succeeded in forcing the mountaineers to accept a peace, of which one of the conditions was that the supremacy of Turkey should be recognised. This was in September, 1862; but the spirit of the Montenegrins was not broken. Their sympathy with the Herzegovinians in 1875 very nearly precipitated a collision with the Porte, and in 1876 the collision came. As the whole adult male population of Montenegro are soldiers (the very priests being as ready to fight as to administer the offices of religion), the alliance of that State with Servia was an important accession of strength.

In the frequent wars between the Montenegrins and the Turks, during a period of many years, the former seem always to have been the aggressors; and it is difficult to find that they acted from any other motives than fanatical hatred and love of rapine. But their conduct was not so bad as the conduct of Servia in her declaration of war against Turkey in 1876. The injustice of that proceeding has hardly ever been surpassed. Servia had no ground of complaint against the Porte. For nearly half a century she had received nothing but favours at the hands of the Ottoman Government. Every demand had been granted, until Servia stood in the position of an independent country, for all practical purposes of self-government and freedom. Yet, at the bidding of Russia, and to promote the designs of that Power, she turned against her suzerain in the days of his misfortune, without the smallest provocation, without the ability even to allege one wrongful act committed by the Porte against herself. We have seen, by the admissions of Prince Milan, that the plea of sympathy with kindred races suffering oppression was a falsehood. Nor could the Bulgarian atrocities have had much to do with the event, for the war was planned and put in training some months before the atrocities took place. Desire of augmented territory was one motive; a still greater, was subserviency to Russia. Muscovite influence, exercised solely with a view to its own ends, has always been the curse of Servia, and of the other Christian provinces in South-eastern Europe. Kara George, the most high-minded of modern Servians—the truest and most patriotic of the race for the last hundred years—refused to ally himself with Russia, which he said would be simply throwing off one tyrant to submit to a greater. His words were abundantly justified by facts.

During the war of independence, Russia trifled with the Servians in the most heartless manner; encouraging the insurrection as long as she was at war with Turkey, in order to keep a certain number of the Ottoman troops employed, and coolly throwing the unhappy principality over at the peace in 1812. Nevertheless, a large number of the people have always felt that servility towards Russia which is commonly exhibited by the weak towards the strong. Milosch Obrenowitsch was the chief upholder of this policy, and he received the support of the Czar when, in the course of a few years, it again became the interest of that potentate to stir up disaffection in the dominions of the Sultan. The very genius of Czarism seems to have entered into the nature of Milosch. He was a thorough despot, and his bigotry was equal to his tyranny. No Mussulmans, with the exception of the soldiers in the garrison towns, were to be permitted to reside in the country, though it was agreed that a certain time should be allowed for the emigration of those who were already there. In other respects, the rule of Milosch was stern and illiberal; so much so that in 1829-30 the Porte itself took up the cause of the people, and by two Hatti-scheriffs made provision for the rights and liberties of the commonalty. It was stipulated that, although the Servians were to pay to their Prince the sum required for his maintenance and expenses, the impost "must not be an intolerable burden on the poor." Moreover, the Representative Council was not to be dismissed unless it had been guilty of some grave offence towards the Porte, or towards the laws and constitution of the country. Milosch, however, defied the people, and attempted to rule by his own personal will, like a veritable Czar. In 1838, the Servians appealed to the Porte to protect them against their own ruler, and received a fresh charter of their liberties, and a Constitution of a very popular character. But Milosch refused to execute this Constitution, and next year was expelled, for reasons already stated. The short reigns which followed—those of his two sons, one of whom died, while the other was dethroned for peculation like his father's—were periods of anarchy, during which Russia supported the despotic party, and Turkey the cause of the people. While Kara George's son, Alexander, was in power, Servia enjoyed a time of reasonable liberty; but it was also a time of disturbance, for Russia, after opposing the succession of the Prince to the utmost of her power, endeavoured to embroil the Servians with the Turks, though without success. The prosperity of the country made great progress, and the Turks were regarded rather as the friends than as the enemies of the people. At the commencement of the Crimean war, the Emperor Nicholas tried to induce Servia to attack the Porte; but the Government of the principality replied in a memorandum which must here be quoted for its emphatic language:—

HASSAN BEY.

HUSSEIN AVNI PASHA.

RASCHID PASHA.

"The whole nation is perfectly convinced that the most precious interests impose upon it the maintenance of tranquillity and order, and the avoidance of anything which could involve it in war, and turn Servia into a battle-field. Filled with a deep gratitude to the Suzerain Court for the privileges which have been so graciously confirmed to them, and for the attitude which they have been allowed to hold during this war, the Government and people of Servia are too much alive to their own interests, and too much attached to the happiness of their country, to hesitate a moment as to the line of conduct to be followed: their consciousness of their own situation will preserve them, better than any threats whatever, from all false and injurious measures. In other respects, since the war has broken out, has not Servia sufficiently shown that she both knows, and will remain faithful to, her duties and obligations? Notwithstanding all that may have been said, she has never ceased following a line of conduct, retiring, it is true, but loyal, and conformable to her engagements.

SERVIAN TROOPS LEAVING BELGRADE.

Neither will she henceforward deviate from this line of conduct. The Sublime Porte may be perfectly sure of this."

After the return of Milosch, the Russian intrigues against Turkey acquired additional force. The English Consul-General at Belgrade, Mr. Longworth, reported to his Government that Christian brigands were introduced into Servia, with orders to assume Mussulman names, and assail the Christians, so as to create a general disturbance. During the reign of Prince Michael, the Turks in Servia were treated with murderous violence, under the pretence that they were arming—a charge for which there seems to have been no foundation. At length, the Mohammedans, being repeatedly struck, gave back blow for blow, and a good deal of bloodshed ensued. The Turkish quarter of Belgrade was attacked in 1862, and Mr. Longworth saw a cart-load of slaughtered Turkish women in that part of the town. Ultimately, the Turkish garrison bombarded the city, for which act the Pasha was dismissed, though the provocation had certainly been great. Shortly afterwards, Russia secretly supplied the Servians with arms and ammunition; and when the Porte concentrated troops on the Servian frontier, an outcry was raised by several of the Continental Powers.* Such were among the causes of the recent war. Had it not been for the evil and selfish influence of the Northern Empire, Servia might at the present moment be a prosperous and happy State. That she is not so, is the fitting punishment of a tortuous, dishonest, and mistaken policy.†

* Colonel Baker's Turkey in Europe, chap. 13.

† The superior toleration of the Mussulmans, as compared with some denominations of Christians, is curiously illustrated by an historical anecdote. When Hunniades, Voivode of Transylvania, was besieging Varna, in 1444, he was asked by George Brankowitsch, of the Greek Church, what he would do if victory declared in his favour. He answered that he would compel all the people to become Romanists. Brankowitsch then went to Sultan Mahomet II., and put the same question to him. The Sultan replied that he would build a church near every mosque, and allow the people to bow in the mosques or cross themselves in the churches, according as they desired. The Servians therefore thought it better to submit to the Turks. (Colonel Baker's work on Turkey, chap. 13.) Of course it must not be forgotten that Mohammedans have often been intolerant enough; but their tendency for several years has been towards a liberal treatment of opponents, when not irritated by fanatical opposition.

CHAPTER V.

Beginning of the Servian War—Insincerity of the Pretences by which the War was preceded—Interchange of Notes with Turkey —Servia and the South Sclavonic Nationalities—Numbers and Composition of the Servian Army—The Servian Troops pass the Fortified Position of the Turks at Nisch—Defeat of the Army on several Occasions—Servia entered by the Turks —Serious Reverse of the Servians before Alexinatz—Russian Volunteers in the Servian Forces—Cowardice of the Servians —Proposals for an Armistice—Suspension of Hostilities agreed to—Montenegrin Successes—Prince Milan proclaimed King of Servia by the Army—The Dignity not accepted—Suggestions by Lord Derby for bringing the War to a Close—Renewal of Hostilities—Crushing Defeats of the Servians and their Russian Auxiliaries—Fall of Alexinatz and Occupation of Deligrad—Another Revolution at Constantinople—Murad V. succeeded by Abdul-Hamid II.—The Autumn Agitation in England on the Subject of the Bulgarian Atrocities—Outbreak of Religious Fanaticism—Excitement of Public Opinion—Views of Mr. Gladstone on the Eastern Question—Retrospect in Regard to the Conduct of Russia on the Question of Black Sea Neutralization—Subserviency of Mr. Gladstone to the Policy of Russia—Pamphlet by that Statesman on "Bulgarian Horrors"—Exaggerated Statements, False Arguments, and Dangerous Conclusions—Mr. Carlyle on Russia and Turkey—Lord Beaconsfield's Speech at Aylesbury—Influence of the Secret Societies—Vacillation of Lord Derby—His Despatch to Sir Henry Elliot, reproving the Sultan and his Government for their Conduct in connection with the Bulgarian Massacres—Questionable Policy of that Despatch—Development of English Opinion during the Autumn of 1876—Vigorous Attacks on Russia—The Turning of the Tide.

SERVIA took a venturous step in defying the power of her suzerain; but she counted on the assistance of the Czar, and knew that in any case Europe would not permit her to be entirely crushed. Her preparations were deliberately, and even openly, made. The representatives of Russia, Austria, and France counselled moderation; but, however sincere this counsel on the part of the two last-named Powers, it could have been nothing but a diplomatic pretence, for the sake of deceiving Europe, on the part of the first. Russia, while verbally advising Servia not to make war on the Porte, had been helping on the movement for some time, and it began in earnest as the spring ripened into summer. The march of the Servian troops and militia towards the frontier commenced in June, a month before the declaration of war. The Belgrade Town Council, in a proclamation to their fellow-citizens about the same time, requested ample and immediate contributions towards the new National Loan, which, they said, was raised "to free all men of Servian descent from foreign yoke, and to restore the ancient Empire of the United Servians, which flourished centuries ago." A Vienna paper asserted that the Servian armaments were practically complete for war. The Ministry of War had at its disposal 200,000 breech-loading rifles and 100,000 good muzzle-loaders, twenty-five batteries of artillery, of twelve guns each, and ample stores of ammunition. Extensive preparations were made for provisioning the army in the field. Steam machinery was sent to the frontier for baking bread sufficient to turn out 250,000 rations a day. Even the field-telegraph department was fully organised, while the country was still nominally at peace. Mills for grinding corn were put up along the entire frontier. Schools were closed, in order to be used as hospitals; and public buildings were converted for the time into magazines, arsenals, and provision-stores.

Well might the Porte, in view of these extraordinary facts, require some explanation of the Servian Government. The reply of that Government, despatched in the early part of June, was a model of duplicity. Prince Milan, speaking through his Ministers, alleged that Servia was merely completing her military organization on the principle of the universal obligation to military service. "The idea of waging war, or of threatening the integrity of Turkey," continued the reply, "could not possibly be entertained, inasmuch as the preservation of that integrity is really the basis of Servia's highest interests. A temporary occupation of the frontier is imposed upon Servia by the extraordinary circumstances existing in the frontier provinces, and especially by the violations of Servian territory which have occurred, though, of course, against the wishes of the local Turkish authorities. The Servian Government has at heart the settlement of certain difficulties which have arisen, and for that purpose it will send a special plenipotentiary to Constantinople." Immediately afterwards, Prince Milan despatched an envoy to the Imperial capital, to present an autograph letter acknowledging his allegiance to the new Sultan. But the Turkish Government was not so readily satisfied. On the 10th of June, three notes from Constantinople were received at Belgrade. In the first of these, Turkey demanded the immediate payment of certain arrears of the Servian tribute, then over-due. In the second, she required that the Servian troops should be at once withdrawn from the frontier. In the third, she signified that the accession of Murad V. must be solemnly proclaimed at Belgrade, with a salute of a hundred and twenty-one rounds. Nevertheless, the Servian armaments continued, and the troops were not withdrawn from the frontier. On the contrary, fresh militia detachments were sent south from the interior counties of the principality, and everything spoke of imminent hostilities. Montenegro was equally defiant and threatening in her attitude. The official organ of the Montenegrin Government contained an article, in its impression of the 1st of June, which clearly revealed what was contemplated. It announced the determination of the insurgents in the rebellious Turkish provinces to fall upon the Turks in conjunction with the whole Servian race, and to accept no armistice. The revolt of Bosnia and the Herzegovina was at that time proceeding with redoubled fury, and in a little while the rising in Bulgaria again broke out, excited by foreign agents from Russia, Servia, Roumania, and elsewhere. Then came the letter of Prince Milan to the Grand Vizier, and then the declaration of war.

The Servian Prince wore the mask of plausible pretences as long as he could; but it can have deceived no one. To Turkey, and to all the European Powers, it must have been obvious that he hoped to profit by the existing disturbances, and to extend the bounds of his small dominion. Servia aims at being the leader of the South Sclavonic races, and at re-establishing the old Servian Czardom which the Turks destroyed in the fifteenth century. That monarchy, in the days of its strength, spread from the Danube to the Adriatic, and included Bosnia, Herzegovina, Montenegro, a part of Albania, and some other lands. But this was not for long. It cannot be said that at the present day the Servian nationality includes any one of those provinces, though the same race peoples all. There has never, in fact, been any great nationality in that part of Europe. If such is to be created, Servia has perhaps the best historic claim to form its nucleus. But the claim is by no means strong. South-eastern Europe was peopled, in the decline of the Roman power, by certain Sclavonic tribes, who seem to have had the tribal much more than the national instincts. For a time, the military genius of some of the Servian Kings held several of these in a kind of union; but no great nation was created, and it has never been shown that the South Sclavonians are willing to merge their distinct provincialities in a large Servian monarchy, as the divided members of the Italian family were willing to accept the lead of Piedmont, that a free Italy might be created, with Rome for its capital. Before Prince Milan can hope to be a Victor Emmanuel, he must fashion a Servia such as never yet existed.

At the head of the Servian armies, as regarded the practical duties of command, was General Tchernaieff, a Russian officer of distinction, who had recently edited a Pan-Sclavist journal, and who, on arriving at Belgrade, is said to have presented the Servian Government with £50,000, as a donation from the Sclavonic societies in Russia. The nominal chief was Prince Milan himself, then barely twenty-two years of age. The head-quarters were at Alexinatz, near the southern frontier, and therefore not far from Nisch, in Bulgaria, where the Turks were posted. Nisch (or Nissa, as it is sometimes called) is an important place from a military point of view, being the key to the communications between Thrace, Bulgaria, and Servia. It is strongly fortified, and provided with cannon of large calibre. The Servians, however, rashly resolved to pass this fortress, and leave it in their rear. Their army numbered from 45,000 to 50,000 men; but only a very small proportion—less than 4,000—were trained soldiers. By some writers the Servians have been described as a martial people, who could upon occasion bring into the field an army of 150,000 foot and 10,000 horse. In 1876, however, they did nothing of the kind, and, with but few exceptions, the character of their soldiers was as indifferent as their numbers were inadequate. Yet with these insufficient resources they determined, under the leadership of Tchernaieff, to cross the Morava, and strike boldly into the enemy's country.

The invading force was divided into two columns, which, escaping the observation of the Turks, passed over the mountains on both sides of Nisch, and descended into the valleys beyond—one corps arriving at Akpalanka, to the left, the other reaching Miramor, to the right. In their entrenched camp at Nisch, the Turks had 35,000 men; and to leave such a force in the rear was an act of daring which nothing but success could justify. The commander of the Turkish position was considered blamable for letting the enemy pass him; and Abdul Kerim Pasha was sent from Constantinople to retrieve his error. The Servians were rapidly pursued, defeated in two or three actions, and compelled to retreat precipitately towards their own land. On the 31st of July, the Turks forced their way, though not without a severe struggle, into Servia, which they entered by Gramada and Randevola; and on the 5th of August the Servians were driven from their positions at Kujazevatz, and obliged to retire still farther into the country. The Ottoman troops now held such favourable positions that the prospect of a serious reverse to their enemy appeared imminent. A column under Hassan Pasha occupied the defile of Vraternitza and the village of Galjan on the 6th of August, and the Servians fell back along the whole line of the Timok valley. Prince Milan returned to Belgrade, and on the 18th of the same month held a Cabinet Council, at which, notwithstanding the unhopeful aspect of affairs, it was determined to prosecute the war to the utmost. The Turks, however, continued to advance; the Servians sustained fresh defeats; and a few days later the invading hosts appeared before Alexinatz, the chief position of the ill-advised provokers of the war.

Matters now looked alarming, and Prince Milan considered it high time to seek the mediation of the Powers. On the 24th of August, he summoned the foreign consuls to the palace, and signified to them his willingness to accept intervention for the purpose of bringing about a cessation of hostilities. Before this could be accomplished, the Turks had added very materially to their successes, and in the 1st of September the aggressors were most disastrously beaten before the walls of Alexinatz, and compelled to fly in disorder towards Deligrad. The Servians did not show much fighting capacity in this unfortunate and unnecessary war; but the conduct of their artillerymen in the struggle before Alexinatz is said to have been excellent. They had by this time been reinforced by large numbers of Russian volunteers; and these men, being well-trained soldiers, did a good deal towards introducing better discipline into the disorderly ranks of their allies. Russia was in truth making war on Turkey while pretending to be at peace. No more flagrant breach of neutrality was ever committed. Soldiers, and officers to command them, were sent by Russia, with scarcely an attempt at concealment, to take part in the Servian war; and the campaign was in this way prolonged far beyond the date at which it must otherwise have collapsed. The number of Russians was at first rather small; but when it became evident that the Servians were greatly overmatched by the Turks, a constant supply of Russian soldiers flowed into the little principality. The Government of Prince Milan was of course very glad of their assistance; but the Servian troops grew jealous after awhile, and began to look on them more in the light of invaders than of friends. On the other hand, the Russians regarded the Servians with no little contempt. As a rule, the latter were cowardly and worthless soldiers, and it was only with great difficulty that they could be made to face the Turks at all. Such was the testimony of the Special Correspondent of the *Daily News;* such also is the evidence of a young English gentleman who took service with these half-hearted patriots, and who has related that, although driven into action at the point of the sword, it was found impossible to keep them under fire for any length of time, and that they would run away, discharging their guns in all directions, and leaving the officers to their fate.*

PRINCE MILAN.

On the very day that the Servians were so seriously defeated before Alexinatz, the British Government proposed that an armistice of a month's duration should be concluded between the belligerents. To this the Porte objected, but at the same time expressed a willingness to offer peace, on condition that Prince Milan should do homage to the Sultan at Constantinople, that four of the Servian fortresses should be garrisoned by Turkish troops, that the number of the Servian forces should be limited to 10,000 men, with two batteries of artillery, that all recent fortresses should be demolished, that Servia should pay either an indemnity or a larger tribute, and that the Turkish Government should be permitted to construct and work a railway through the principality. The Powers, however, declared these demands to be inadmissible; but on the 16th of September, previous to this intimation, the Porte agreed to a suspension of hostilities until the 25th. While the Servians were being steadily pressed back from their advanced positions, the more warlike Montenegrins were achieving some marked successes. Prince

* Two Months with Tchernaieff in Servia. By Philip H. B. Salusbury. 1877.

Nikita defeated the Turks under Mukhtar Pasha at the latter end of July, and again in the early days of August; but these exploits did little towards neutralising the misfortunes that had been sustained by Servia. The cause, on the whole, was gravely, if not hopelessly, damaged; yet at this very time Prince Milan, listening to the unwise advice of General Tchernaieff, took a step which could only have been reasonably taken at a period of triumph, but which under the circumstances made his position all the worse. He suffered himself, on September 16th, to be proclaimed King of Servia and Bosnia at Deligrad. He was at Belgrade when this happened; but there can be no doubt that he knew beforehand what was about to be done. A son and heir had been born to him on the 14th of August, and it was perhaps desired in this way to signalise the event. Tchernaieff, in telegraphing to the Prince an account of the ceremony, said that the movement was so strong it was impossible to prevent it. Officers and privates alike, he declared, had expressed their determination to fight to the last drop of their blood for the independence of the country and the glory of his Majesty. The enthusiasm had been indescribable. Priests, and deputations from all parts of the army, arrived at head-quarters, and General Protich, speaking in the name of the Servian nation, dedicated their lives and property to the Fatherland and the King. To this address, General Tchernaieff replied:—"The voice of the people is the voice of God; and nothing remains for me but to cry with you, 'Long live the King of Servia, Milan Obrenowitsch, the Queen, and the Servian Prince!'" At a subsequent church-service, more than fifty priests officiated. Milan was again proclaimed King of Servia, and, after an address by the Chief Priest, and the singing of a *Te Deum*, the whole army swore allegiance to the King, to the Queen, and to the infant Prince. Doubtless the scene was impressive, but the act was imprudent; and Prince Milan, finding that his new dignity was generally disapproved by the Powers, consented to waive the honour.

The English Government was very desirous of bringing this petty war to an end, lest it should reopen the dreaded Eastern Question; and on the 21st of September Lord Derby proposed a new basis of discussion, which was to the effect that the *status quo*, speaking roughly, should be maintained in Servia and Montenegro, and that administrative reforms, for the purpose of establishing local self-government, without any question of the creation of tributary States, should be established in Bosnia and Herzegovina, with guarantees of a similar kind against maladministration in Bulgaria. These terms were adopted by the other Powers. Turkey offered to prolong the suspension of hostilities until the 2nd of October; but Prince Milan, obeying the fatal influence of St. Petersburg, foolishly declined to accept any other arrangement than a formal armistice. The war was accordingly resumed after the 25th of September, and the Servians made still more desperate efforts to wring success from the stubborn and disciplined hosts of the Ottoman. Fresh battalions from Russia poured into the country, until the total number amounted to many thousands; and under their tuition and example the Servians began to acquire greater steadiness in the field. Severe fighting before Alexinatz took place on the 26th, 27th, 28th, and 29th of September. On the two latter of those days, the combined Servians, Montenegrins, and Russians furiously attacked the Turks, but were repulsed with great slaughter. For a time, in the action of the 28th, the fortune of the day seemed to incline towards the assailants, who flanked the Turks on both sides, so that only their rear was open. Had Tchernaieff been supported by strong reinforcements, he might perhaps have achieved a victory; but these were wanting, and in the end the Servians were compelled to retreat. The losses on both sides were very heavy, and it is said that sixty Russian officers were left dead upon the field. Every day, indeed, made it more clear that the struggle was unequal, notwithstanding the irregular assistance of Russia, and the advantage to the Servians of their strongly fortified positions amongst the woody defiles of steep and rugged hills. The Turks showed much the greater fighting capacity, and success after success rewarded their valour. After a sanguinary struggle of several days' duration, they carried the position of Djunis on the 23rd of October, and the Servians retreated before them in different directions. On the 31st, Alexinatz was captured, and Deligrad was occupied on the 1st of November. The road to Belgrade was now completely open, and Servia lay at the mercy of her angered suzerain.

Before these events had reached their crisis, Constantinople was the scene of another revolution. Murad V. was originally a person of weak character and indifferent health. He was entirely destitute of the ability to command; and the terrible events immediately succeeding his accession to the throne, combined with the responsibilities of office, completely shattered his nervous system. It has been said that he was addicted to drink, and that his intemperate habits increased so fearfully after his assumption of power as to bring on two attacks of *delirium tremens* within a short period. However

SERVIANS ATTACKING THE TURKISH ENTRENCHED CAMP AT BABINA-GLAVA.

this may have been, he was undoubtedly reduced to the most pitiable imbecility. His position seems to have stupefied him, and he would sit for days in a state of moody silence, crushed by the weight of sovereignty and the horrors of the time. The death of his uncle especially afflicted his spirits, as he believed it would be regarded as his own act. The dread of assassination possessed him, and his fits of speechless despair were at times varied by violent paroxysms, during which the palace echoed with his cries. At length, his inability to attend to any matters of business became so total that the choice of a successor was inevitable. After a reign of three months, he was deposed on the 31st of August, and succeeded by his brother, Abdul-Hamid, the second Sultan of that name—a man of four-and-thirty, vigorous in health, and reputed to be well-inclined towards the Christians.

The progress of the Servian war was accompanied, in England, by an extraordinary outburst of indignation against Turkey, on account of the Bulgarian massacres. A feeling of mingled pity and anger had been growing up in many sections of the British population ever since the publication by the *Daily News*, on the 23rd of June, of the first letter from its Constantinople correspondent on the subject of the alleged misdeeds. That feeling was immensely increased by the reports of the Special Commissioner of the same journal, published in August, and by statements which appeared in other newspapers. The official report by Mr. Walter Baring, issued in the latter half of September, did nothing to allay the excitement, although its effect was certainly to reduce the magnitude of the earlier revelations, and to consign some of the horrors to the limbo of exploded fictions. The popular emotions had been deeply stirred, and for several weeks scarcely anything was talked about, or written about, save the diabolical wickedness of Turkey, and the wrongs of the Eastern Christians. It was altogether forgotten, or flatly denied, that it was the Eastern Christians themselves who began the hellish work, and that the Turks only repeated and magnified the villany they had been taught. A wild tempest of unreflecting wrath swept over the land, and any one who ventured to suggest greater moderation stood a very fair chance of being set down as a species of Bashi-Bazouk, or at least

PROCLAIMING PRINCE MILAN KING OF SERVIA AND BOSNIA.

as a hard-hearted and selfish wretch. Meetings were held in every part of Great Britain, to denounce Turkey to the detestation of the whole civilised world. Many of these gatherings were spontaneous and genuine; but others were undoubtedly got up by political bodies for party ends. As Mr. Disraeli (who about the middle of August was promoted to the Upper House as Earl of Beaconsfield) had expressed a prudent disbelief in the entire accuracy of the first reports, a question which had really nothing to do with party was argued out on party grounds; and the milk of human kindness (setting Turks aside), which flowed undiluted in some quarters, was in others a good deal acidulated, and therefore curdled, by the vinegar of political hate.

No agent was more active in giving an extreme character to the agitation than the journal which first called attention to the subject. Day after day, that journal published, in its leading columns and in its correspondence, the most bitter diatribes against the Turks—the most passionate incentives to a war of hatred and fanaticism. These provocations fell on ears well fitted to receive them. In every community there are thousands of men, and tens of thousands of women, who mistake their animosities, their jealousies, and their fears, for religious convictions, and act accordingly in the blindness of their mood. England has fewer such than most other countries, because of the breadth and variety of her culture, and the activity of her freedom; but the race is not unknown even here, and the sudden strength with which the passion of religious bigotry glared forth in the autumn of 1876 was truly startling. This journal—which had probably been actuated by no other motive than a feeling of humanity, and a cherished craze in the region of foreign politics—was soon followed by papers more extreme, and less guarded by the checks of intellect. The religious world was awakened, and fancied the appointed time had come for the overthrow of Islam. The High Church raged at Mohammedan Turkey, because the gaudy sentimentalism of Eastern Christianity has an attraction for High Church minds. The Low Church joined in chorus, because the coming destruction of a religion professed by a hundred millions of devout believers was thought to be foreshadowed in the Book of Revelation. A veritable crusade was preached by men who should have known better than to turn an honest sentiment of indignation at abominable crimes into a means of advancing their own factious ends.

The "atrocity" meetings were attended, in most instances, by enthusiastic crowds, and resolutions condemning the Government, and pointing to armed interference between the Porte and its Christian subjects, were carried with acclamation. If any one dared to say a word for the Turk, or to hint that there were considerations of policy which ought not to be entirely put out of view, he was generally silenced. Nothing could be more excellent than the feeling of humanity which prompted a large number of the speakers; nothing could be more lamentable than the want of judgment, of thought, and of knowledge, which characterized most, and which drowned every reasonable utterance in the shrieks of hysteria. Even the better part of this emotion degenerated after awhile, as every ill-regulated and unbalanced sentiment is sure to do. What was pity in the beginning, became morbid appetite in the end. People gloated over the horrors of massacre and licence, and several of the newspapers continued to publish disgusting and frightful narratives after the necessity for exposure had passed away. The intention was obvious. It was hoped to lash the people of England into a new crusade, or at any rate to prevent the Government taking steps against Russia, whatever the designs of that Power might be. Assuredly, Russia was well served on the English press during that eventful time, and in the great struggle that followed. In certain quarters, everything was interpreted in her favour, with a vehemence of advocacy, a subtlety of rhetoric, an ingenuity of misapplication, that afforded matter for sorrowful wonder. The opposite side, however, was very ably supported by other journals; noticeably by the *Daily Telegraph* and the *Pall Mall Gazette*.

The anti-Turkish party soon found a powerful ally in Mr. Gladstone. That remarkable man and somewhat eccentric politician had preserved throughout the session a guarded tone with respect to events in the East. He had refrained from any serious opposition to the policy of Government, and had even, on the 31st of July, defended the Crimean war, which he said was very properly undertaken to resist external interference, and to give Turkey an opportunity of reforming her administration, as it then seemed probable she would do. He also defended it on the ground that whereas, up to 1853, Russia by herself had at all times the privilege of interfering in the affairs of Turkey, under pretence of defending the Eastern Christians, the Peace of 1856 transferred that responsibility—not formally, but as a matter of moral right—to the guaranteeing Powers generally. But Mr. Gladstone's support of the Crimean war, at the time it was going on, was of a listless and feeble character, and he retired from the Palmerston Cabinet (though on a side issue) while the struggle was yet proceeding. The disposition of his mind to take a Russian view of Continental politics was strongly exhibited in the latter part of 1870, during the progress of the war between France and Germany. The memorable transaction by which the neutralization of the Black Sea was abolished, and the results of the Crimean war were modified, deserves some consideration in this place, as it cannot be doubted that it had much to do with the subsequent course of Russia.

The Treaty of Paris, at the conclusion of the Crimean war in 1856, contained a provision by which the waters and ports of the Black Sea, while left open to the mercantile marine of all nations, were formally and perpetually interdicted to ships of war of any nation whatever, with the exception of a few small Russian and Turkish vessels, the number and nature of which were determined by a Special Convention concluded between the two Powers on the 30th of March, the same day that the Treaty of Peace was signed. This is what is meant by the neutralization of the Euxine. Russia and Turkey also engaged neither to construct nor maintain any naval or military arsenal on the coast; and the effect of these provisions was not merely to restrain the ambition of Russia, but to remove or prevent many fertile occasions of disagreement between the two rival Powers. It is not easy to see in what respect such an arrangement could have injured any legitimate interest, or how either Turkey or Russia could have objected to its continuance, unless the one entertained a secret design of attacking the other at the first convenient opportunity. In point of fact, Turkey made no objection, but Russia did. On the 20th of October, 1870, Prince Gortschakoff addressed to Baron Brunnow, the Russian Ambassador at the Court of St. James's, a despatch affirming that the Treaty of 1856 had been broken in various ways to the detriment of Russia, and that consequently his Imperial master had resolved to re-establish the balance founded in the East by that agreement. The despatch was communicated to the British Government on the 9th of November, and was followed soon afterwards by a circular to the European Powers, dated October 31st, in which it was asserted that the stipulations with reference to the Euxine had not been fairly carried out, and that, "in reality, while Russia disarmed in the Black Sea, and, by a declaration contained in the minutes of the Conference, likewise loyally deprived herself of the possibility of taking measures for an effectual maritime defence in the adjoining seas and ports, Turkey preserved her privilege of having an unlimited number of men-of-war in the Archipelago and Straits, while France and England were also at liberty to assemble their squadrons in the Mediterranean." Complaint was further made that under the treaty in question the war-flag of all nations was formally and perpetually prohibited an entry into the Black Sea, while at the same time the so-called Straits Treaty closed the Straits only in time of peace to men-of-war. Accordingly, the Emperor Alexander gave notice that he could no longer hold himself bound by those stipulations of the Treaty of March 30th, 1856, which restricted the exercise of his sovereign rights in the Black Sea; that he would no longer regard as valid the special and additional convention appended to the said treaty, which fixed the number and size of the men-of-war which the two Powers bordering on the Black Sea should keep in that sea; and that his Imperial Majesty restored to the Sultan the full exercise of his sovereign rights in this respect, reclaiming the like privilege for himself.

TCHERNAIEFF.

At the time this notification was made, Mr. Gladstone was Prime Minister, and Lord Granville Foreign Secretary. The Russian sympathies of the former found an admirable opportunity for their gratification, and it was resolved that the opportunity should not be allowed to slip. Russia had chosen her time extremely well. France was torn with revolution, and prostrate beneath the heel of foreign invasion. Germany was deeply indebted to Russia for taking so friendly a view of the existing war. Austria was not at all likely to trouble herself in the matter; and in fact England stood alone. It was hardly to be expected that the British Government should, without allies, enter into a war with Russia in defence of the neutralization of the Black Sea; but Mr. Gladstone showed an alacrity in meeting the views of that Power, which revealed the satisfaction he felt in undoing some portion of the work that had been accomplished by the war of 1854-6. Lord Granville did indeed protest against the right assumed by Russia of setting aside, at her own will and pleasure, a treaty by which she was bound in common with other Powers. But a willingness to consider the alleged grievances, together with the other co-signatories of the treaty, was intimated by the Government; and when Mr. (now Lord) Odo Russell represented to Count Bismarck that, if Russia persisted in her course, we should be compelled, with or without allies, to go to war, Mr. Gladstone said in Parliament that such a statement was going too far. Russia having expressed her readiness to consult the co-signatories of the Treaty of 1856, if that could be effected (though in saying so she repeated her determination to repudiate, under any circumstances, the clauses to which she objected), the representatives of the Powers, following a suggestion made by Prussia, met in London on the 17th of January, 1871, and on the 13th of March signed a new treaty, by which the neutralization of the Black Sea was abrogated. By the second article of this treaty, it was provided that "the principle of the closing of the Straits and of the Bosphorus is maintained, with power to his Imperial Majesty the Sultan to open the said Straits in time of peace to the vessels of war of friendly and allied Powers, in case the Sublime Porte should judge it necessary in order to secure the execution of the stipulations of the Treaty of Paris." The tenth article of that treaty confined the right of the Porte with respect to opening the Straits to times of war; so that the clause in the later treaty was some compensation for the abandonment of the neutralization of the Black Sea, since it permitted the Sultan to call in foreign vessels, even if only threatened with Russian interference. Before the assembling of the Conference, the Russian Chancellor withdrew his claim to the maintenance of a foregone conclusion as the basis of the discussion, and admitted that the plenipotentiaries might record any opinion they pleased on the question of principle; and at the first meeting of the Conference a protocol was agreed to, recording it to be an essential element in the law of nations that no Power can liberate itself from the engagements of a treaty without the consent of the other contracting parties. Yet, on the whole, Russia gained by the alteration in the earlier treaty which she had succeeded in effecting. To disturb the settlement of 1856 in *any* way was a valuable triumph; and to obtain an European sanction to her possession of ships of war in the vicinity of Constantinople was a matter even more important. A new naval harbour in the Black Sea had been commenced by the Russian Government, in 1863, at the town of Poti, situated at the mouth of the river Rion, not many miles from the Turkish frontier; and a Steamboat Company was formed at Odessa, all the ships belonging to which were at the disposal of the Government, and so constructed that they could easily be plated with armour, and armed with twelve guns each. For these devices there was no longer any necessity. By the treaty of 1871, Russia might maintain in the Black Sea any armament she pleased.

Such being the known policy of Mr. Gladstone in connection with Russia and Turkey, it ought not to have been a surprise to any one, despite the moderation of his tone during the Parliamentary session of 1876, that he should have come forward in the autumn of that year as a bitter opponent of the latter Power. Early in September he published a pamphlet bearing the suggestive title of "Bulgarian Horrors and the Question of the East." Its object was to show that the Turks were utterly effete as a governing race; that they were impotent yet proud, feeble yet ferocious; that they had made no progress even during the twenty years of peace which foreign arms had secured to them as a consequence of the Crimean war; that the Bulgarian horrors were without provocation, excuse, or mitigation; that the Government of Mr. Disraeli had trifled with the question in a spirit of cynical levity; and that the right thing then to be done was to insist that Turkey should grant to its Christian subjects a species of independent Government (similar to that of Servia and Roumania), at the same time retaining its titular sovereignty. Towards the close of his pamphlet, Mr. Gladstone wrote:—

"An old servant of the Crown and State, I entreat my countrymen, upon whom, far more than perhaps any other people of Europe, it depends, to require, and to insist, that our Government, which has been working in one direction, shall work in the other, and shall apply all its vigour to concur with the other States of Europe in obtaining the extinction of the Turkish executive power in Bulgaria. [In another page he spoke also of Bosnia and the Herzegovina.] Let the Turks now carry away their abuses in the only possible manner, namely, by carrying off themselves. Their Zaptiehs and their Mudirs, their Bimbashis and their Yuzbashis, their Kaimakams and their Pashas, one and all, bag and baggage, shall, I hope, clear out from the province they have desolated and profaned. This thorough riddance, this most blessed deliverance, is the only reparation we can make to the memory of those heaps on heaps of dead; to the violated purity alike of matron, of maiden, and of child; to the civilization which has been affronted and shamed; to the laws of God, or, if you like, of Allah; to the moral sense of mankind at large. There is not a criminal in an European gaol, there is not a cannibal in the South Sea Islands, whose indignation would not rise and overboil at the recital of that which has been done, which has too late been examined, but which remains unavenged; which has left behind all the foul and all the fierce passions that produced it, and which may again spring up in another murderous harvest, from the soil soaked and reeking with blood, and in the air tainted with every imaginable deed of crime and shame. That such things should be done once, is a damning disgrace to the portion of our race which did them; that a door should be left open for their ever-so-barely-possible repetition would spread that shame over the whole. . . . We may ransack the annals of the world, but I know not what research can furnish us with so portentous an example of the fiendish misuse of the powers established by God 'for the punishment of evil-doers, and for the encouragement of them that do well.' No Government ever has so sinned; none has so proved itself incorrigible in sin, or, which is the same, so impotent for reformation."

It is not surprising that Mr. Gladstone's pamphlet produced an immense effect. The high position and authority of its author, the eloquence of the writing, and the skilful manner in which a natural feeling of indignation was turned to the service of a political idea, were certain to be attended by important results. The pamphlet had an enormous sale; its most striking passages were reproduced in every newspaper; and its arguments and exhortations added incalculably to the agitation of the autumn months. Yet its exaggeration of tone was glaring; its partisanship flagrant; its lack of prudence remarkable in a man so long accustomed to the responsibilities of office and the complexity of public affairs. It entirely suppressed the important fact that the animosities of the Christians and the Mohammedans had been fostered and fomented by Russia. It denied the provocations by which the massacres had been provoked. It suggested that those massacres were only an intensification of the ordinary characteristics of Turkish rule in Bulgaria; whereas it is certain that the grievances of the Bulgarians, though real, were not extreme. It clung with feverish and morbid eagerness to the original reports of the Bulgarian massacres, though there was reason even then to believe that they had been overstated. It took no account of the actual position of the European provinces of Turkey, which have been under their present rulers for between four and five centuries, and where there is a large Mohammedan population native to the soil. It disregarded with serene indifference the patent fact that the Christian populations of Turkey are not sufficiently strong to stand by themselves, and that if established in a position of independence, under the nominal suzerainty of the Porte, they would very soon become, in effect, as we see in the cases of Servia and Roumania, mere adjuncts of the Czardom. Lastly, it outraged one of the most obvious truths of foreign politics, but one which a certain section of politicians is too apt to forget or deny—namely, that neither England nor any other Power has the smallest treaty right to interfere in the internal affairs of Turkey, or to dictate to her in what manner she shall govern her own subjects. Such a right was in fact expressly disavowed by the Ninth Article of the Treaty of Paris. Mr. Gladstone admitted this in his speech of July 31st; but, adopting some expressions by Lord Palmerston, he talked of a "moral right," which in the region of statesmanship means nothing more than a fanciful claim which no one is bound to acknowledge. England, France, and Sardinia (now Italy), defended Turkey, at the period of the Crimean war, out of no abstract principles of love and generosity, but to serve their own purposes, and could not on that account assert a right of coercion where the question was simply one between a Sovereign Power and its subjects. As those nations were not responsible for the sins of Turkish misgovernment, so also were they under no obligation to apply the remedy; nor had they the right, supposing they possessed the desire.

Mr. Gladstone's hyperbole about the criminals in gaol and the cannibals in the South Sea Islands boiling over with virtuous indignation at the recital of Turkish misdeeds may be passed over as a mere figure of rhetoric, though the use of such absurdly exaggerated language is no bad measure of the intemperate and hectic spirit in which the writer approached his subject. But the "bag-and-baggage" policy must be taken as deliberate. That policy meant nothing else than the removal of many thousands of Mohammedans from their homes and the homes of their ancestors, or their oppression by religious foes, of whose tender mercies, both to Moslems and Jews, we have had abundant evidence in Roumania and Servia. As Mr. Gladstone included under the designation of Bulgaria the scenes of the recent tragedies, which were in fact in Roumelia, he practically removed from the dominion of the Sultan, and practically placed under the dominion of the Czar, a tract of country approaching to within a short distance of Constantinople. By such an arrangement the Balkans would have been lost to Turkey as a military defence, and the approach of Russia to the Imperial capital would have been enormously facilitated. For this, "Bulgarian horrors" were pleaded as the justification. Nothing was said about the horrors of Russian rule in Poland, in Circassia, and in many other places, though they would equally justify an interference in the internal affairs of the Northern Empire. In those Muscovite possessions, not only have atrocious massacres taken place as the punishment of revolt, but a degree of misgovernment has existed—systematic, persistent, cold-blooded, and relentless—which in European Turkey has not been nearly equalled for many years. All this, however, was to be kept out of view, and in the last resort to be denied, with miserable equivocations, with disingenuous suppressions, with frantic and despairing struggles to hide the truths which nothing could hide. The preachers of the new crusade were insincere in their virtue. They hated the Turk, not because he was a sinner, but because he was a Mohammedan.

SERVIAN SOLDIERS.

Another one-sided utterance on the subject of Russia and Turkey appeared during this epoch of tumultuous views. On the 24th of November. Mr. Carlyle addressed to a friend a letter on the topic of the day, which soon got into print. It was certainly not remarkable that a writer who admires Frederick the Great, who was enamoured of negro slavery, who found in the Jamaica atrocities of 1865 occasions for deep thankfulness, and who delighted in Bismarck's policy of blood and iron, should discover that the Russians "have dominions in this quarter of the globe, and England, apparently, was to take Egypt, for the sake of the Suez Canal. To bring about a proper concord among the three Great Powers (France, of course, being of no account), we were to seek the advice of

MR. GLADSTONE AT BLACKHEATH.

done signal service to God and man in drilling into order and peace" (by proceedings similar to the Bulgarian massacres) "anarchic populations all over their side of the world." But perhaps few were prepared to find Mr. Carlyle going even farther than Mr. Gladstone himself. This, however, was the case. England and the other Powers were to tell the Turk, peremptorily, that he was to turn his face to the eastward, and to quit Europe altogether. Russia and Austria were to divide his

Prince Bismarck, "a magnanimous, noble, and deep-seeing man," with "no national aims or interests in the matter!" But, added Mr. Carlyle, "the only clear advice I have to give is, as I have stated, that the unspeakable Turk should be immediately struck out of the question, and the country left to honest European guidance; delaying which can be profitable or agreeable only to gamblers on the Stock Exchange, but distressing and unprofitable to all other men." Such were the opinions of Mr. Carlyle on the Eastern Question. They would not be worth a moment's consideration, were it not for the name and position of their author.

Although Parliament was now prorogued, various Ministerial utterances were heard from time to time. On the 20th of September, the Prime Minister delivered a speech at an agricultural dinner at Aylesbury, in which he admitted that the policy of the Government was unpopular, but gave reasons why, in his opinion, it was entitled to the support of the country. He severely condemned the Servians for attacking their suzerain, in defiance of every principle of international law, of public morality, and of honour; but he attributed their conduct to the action of the secret societies of Europe, which had declared war on Turkey. "In the attempt to conduct the government of this world," he remarked, "there are new elements to be considered, which our predecessors had not to deal with. We have now to deal not merely with Emperors, with Princes, and with Ministers. There are the secret societies—an element which we must take into account, and which at the last moment may baffle all our arrangements; societies which have regular agents everywhere, which countenance assassination, and which, if necessary, could produce a massacre." These statements were much ridiculed by the opponents of the Government; but they contained a good deal of truth. The International Association was believed, as far back as 1870, to consist of 800,000 members; and by writers favourable to that body it was said to claim a total, in Europe and America, of from five to seven millions. Admitting that this may be an over-statement, it is yet certain that the numbers are very large; and, as the subordinate branches are directed from a common centre, the power wielded is immense. The Paris Commune of 1871 was contrived, matured, and ordered to be carried into effect, by this secret league of revolutionists; and the Pan-Sclavist Societies of Russia and Roumania obey the same impulse. Lord Beaconsfield was therefore right in saying that a new power had arisen, with which it was particularly difficult to deal.

Indications of the Ministerial policy were also given, during September, by Lord Derby, the Secretary for Foreign Affairs. They were chiefly remarkable as showing that the popular agitation was beginning to have an effect on the Government, and that a disposition to make some approach towards Mr. Gladstone's views was growing up within the Cabinet itself. Replying to certain deputations on the 11th of the month, Lord Derby averred—much to the astonishment of most political observers—that neither he nor any of his colleagues had ever shown any hostility in principle to a further extension of constitutional changes within the borders of the Ottoman Empire, similar to those which had already been carried out in Roumania, in Servia, and in a less degree in Crete. But he still hesitated to make such a demand, in view of the difficulties attending its accomplishment, and he warned his auditors against any attempt to "blot out the Turks from the map of Europe"—an attempt which would assuredly bring on a fierce religious war, in the course of which deeds of blood would be committed, infinitely greater than those which were at that time agitating the minds of Englishmen. This was evidently an endeavour to take the ground from under the feet of Mr. Gladstone, whose pamphlet was then a few days old. It was a suggestion that after all the question might be settled by granting autonomy to Bulgaria and the other Christian provinces. It was in short the first sign of yielding—the first indication of that policy of ambiguous, insincere, and contradictory speech which cast so much discredit on the Government, and had so large a share in bringing on the war. With characteristic hesitation, Lord Derby receded somewhat from this position in an answer, delivered on the 27th of September, to a deputation headed by the Lord Mayor, which conveyed to him a series of resolutions passed at a meeting at the Guildhall. But at the same time he mentioned that a despatch had been sent to Sir Henry Elliot, charging him to repeat to the Sultan the facts concerning the Bulgarians established by Mr. Baring's report, to denounce by name the chief authors of the outrages, and to make the Sultan realise his obligations in the matter. This despatch bore date September 21st, and is perhaps the most imperious address ever submitted to an independent Power. The Porte was reminded that neither the Government of Great Britain, nor any of the signatory Powers of the Treaty of Paris, could show indifference to the sufferings of the Bulgarian peasantry under the recent outbreak of vindictive cruelty; and the despatch then went on:—

"Your Excellency will, in the name of the Queen and her Majesty's Government, call for reparation and justice, and urge that the rebuilding of the houses and churches should be begun at once, and necessary assistance given for the restoration of the woollen and other industries, as well as provision made for the relief of those who have been reduced to poverty; and, above all, you will point out that it is a matter of absolute necessity that the eighty women [said to have been taken away from Batak] should be found, and restored to their families. Your Excellency will likewise urge that striking examples should be made on the spot of those who have connived at, or taken part in, the atrocities. The persons who have been decorated or promoted, under a false impression of their conduct, should be tried and degraded, where this has not been done already, and every effort made to restore public confidence. With this view, it would seem advisable, as a provisional measure, and without prejudice to such future arrangements as may be made in concert with the Powers, that the disturbed districts should be at once placed under an able and energetic Commissioner, specially appointed for the purpose, who, if not himself a Christian, should have Christian counsellors, in whom trust could be reposed by the Christian population."

That this reproof was thoroughly merited by the wretches who had committed the massacres, and by the Government which made itself a partner in iniquity by rewarding the chief perpetrators, will not be questioned by any one. But on political grounds it may well be doubted whether the Foreign Secretary's despatch was either justifiable or prudent. Lord Derby addressed the Turkish Sultan as if he were a Viceroy of the British Crown, though he had no more right to lecture him on his misdeeds (or rather the misdeeds of his predecessors) than he had to lecture Russia on the numerous cruelties of her rule. In principle, everything was conceded to that Power by the English despatch of September 21st. What Russia had been labouring to establish was a right of interference between the Porte and its subjects. This had been strenuously opposed by the Government of Lord Beaconsfield, and very reasonably so: firstly, because the principle is one of the most dangerous that can be admitted, with reference to any State whatever; secondly, because, in the particular case in question, it would have aided the ulterior purposes of Russia. Yet here was the whole point given up. If Turkey was to receive orders from London, there was no reason why she should not receive them from St. Petersburg. If her rulers were to be reproved by Lord Derby, it is hard to say why they should not be cashiered by Prince Gortschakoff. The ill-considered agitation of the autumn had borne its fruit in vacillation and false principle; and that was soon to bear its bitter consequences in a sanguinary and disastrous war. Russia had won the first move on the chess-board.

The popular agitation continued throughout several weeks. Mr. Gladstone wrote letters and articles on the subject, and addressed public meetings; noticeably, a great gathering at Blackheath, on the 9th of September, when the speaker urged co-operation with Russia in the policy of giving a qualified autonomy to the northern provinces of European Turkey. The Duke of Argyll, Mr. Bright, Mr. Lowe, and other leading Liberals, energetically seconded the exertions of Mr. Gladstone; but Lord Hartington and Mr. Forster, who both made tours in the East, spoke with greater reserve and deliberation, and actual dissent from the bag-and-baggage policy was expressed by Lord Fitzwilliam, the Duke of Somerset, and several Liberals belonging to a different section of the party from that which followed Mr. Gladstone. In the course of October, a reaction set in, which deepened with the advancing autumn; and it was now sought to turn the tables on the anti-Turks by blazoning forth the crimes committed by Russia in various parts of the world, and proving how little right she had to speak in the name of humanity. Just at this time, Mr. Eugene Schuyler, the American Consul-General for Turkey, and the author of the well-known report on the Bulgarian atrocities, published a work relating his personal observations in Russian Turkistan and other parts of Central Asia recently subjected to the Czar, from which it appeared that deeds of excessive cruelty had been committed in those countries by the deliberate order of Russian Generals, who, so far from being punished, had actually been rewarded for their doings. The *Pall Mall Gazette* dwelt with great emphasis on these details, and Mr. Gladstone replied in an article contributed to the November number of the *Contemporary Review*. The controversy between these two authorities was conducted with great bitterness, each accusing the other of dishonest suppressions; but the main result was that, although there may have been error on one or two points, the conduct of the Russians in Central Asia was shown to have been grossly inhuman. Of course, Russian crimes were no excuse for Turkish crimes; but when an influential party advocated a policy the effect of which (whether intended or not) was to increase the influence of Russia over a large and important region, it was not amiss to inquire if the best interests of the world would be any gainers by the change.

CHAPTER VI.

Commencement of a New Phase in the Events—Russia coming more unreservedly on the Scene—Proposals by the Czar for a Joint Military Occupation of Bosnia and Bulgaria—Lord Derby on the Settlement of Affairs—Views of Austria—Protest by England against the Presence of Russian Volunteers in Servia—Excited State of Popular Feeling in Russia and Turkey—English Plan of Reform rejected by the Porte, which propounds its own Scheme—Formal Demand by Russia on Turkey for an Armistice of a Month or Six Weeks—Suggestion by Turkey of an Armistice of Six Months—Discussion on the Subject—The Russian Ultimatum—Acceptance of the Shorter Armistice—Ideas of the English Government—Pacific Assurances of the Russian Emperor—Bad Faith of the Northern Power—Proposals by Lord Derby for a Conference—Speech of Lord Beaconsfield at Guildhall—Speech of the Emperor Alexander at Moscow—Despatch of Prince Gortschakoff on the Treaty of 1856—Objects and Methods of Proceeding of the Turkish Government—Anti-Turkish Opinions of Lord Derby—Lord Beaconsfield and the *Golos*—Departure of Lord Salisbury from London to attend the Conference at Constantinople—His Instructions—Suggestions for Turkish Reform, and for the obtaining of Guarantees—The "National Conference" at St. James's Hall.

WITH the collapse of the Servian war commences the second stage of the events which we are now relating. Russia doubtless hoped to secure her ends, first by exciting revolts in Bosnia, Herzegovina, and Bulgaria, and afterwards by putting forward Servia to fight the battle, with ample auxiliaries supplied from her own army. Had these means prevailed, the Northern Power would have effected its objects without being compelled to appear openly on the scene, and would thus have avoided the necessity of giving explanations to other Powers, and the danger of complications that might be embarrassing. In the case supposed, a number of independent States would have been formed out of the Sultan's European dominions, with every probability of their speedily becoming mere satrapies of the Russian Empire; and, although every one would have known that the work was Russia's own doing, there would have been a plausible pretence for saying that the change had been brought about by the spontaneous movements of populations long enslaved, but now resolved to be free. The energy and good generalship of the Turks put an end to these hopes, and it was imperative for the chief agent to come forward more unreservedly. On the 26th of September, just as Servia was renewing the war, with but little chance of success, Count Schouvaloff communicated to Lord Derby certain proposals from the Russian Government, to the effect that, in the event of the terms of peace being refused by the Porte, Bosnia should be occupied by an Austrian and Bulgaria by a Russian force, while the united fleets of the Powers should enter the Bosphorus. At the same time, however, Russia stated her willingness to abandon the proposed occupation, if the naval demonstration were considered sufficient by her Majesty's Government. This looked very like a suggestion for dividing the property of "the sick man," though it was not clear what share England was to have in the booty. The idea was first promulgated by the Emperor of Russia in a letter to the Emperor of Austria, written during the month of September, from Livadia, on the southern coast of the Crimea, where he was then staying. The Czar here remarked that in his opinion the misrule of Turkey should be put an end to by force; and the joint occupation of the principalities was how it was to be brought about. Of course the plan met with no countenance from the British Government, nor does it seem to have been favourably regarded by Austria.

Matters being thus complicated, and Russia showing signs of impatience by submitting to the Powers that the war should be arrested by immediately "imposing" a short truce on both parties, so as to afford the mediating Governments time to consider the means of effecting a definite arrangement, Lord Derby and his colleagues decided to give their support to the idea of an armistice of not less than a month, in the event of Turkey rejecting the suggested terms for concluding a peace. At the termination of the truce, it was proposed that a Conference should immediately follow. Sir Henry Elliot was instructed on the 5th of October to express these views to the Porte, and to state that, in case of a refusal, he was to leave Constantinople, "as it would then be evident that all further exertions on the part of her Majesty's Government to save the Porte from ruin would have become useless." * This was another step in the new policy which Lord Derby—whether by his own inclination, or by the influence of his colleagues—had recently inaugurated. Turkey was to do as she was told, or to be coerced. She was to accept the plan submitted to her, under a direct threat of the consequences if she refused. Nothing was more likely to encourage

* Despatch from Lord Derby to Lord Augustus Loftus, the British Ambassador at St. Petersburg, Oct. 30th, 1876: a communication containing a summary of the whole transactions up to that date.

Russia, which, taking the tone now assumed by the English Government in conjunction with the autumnal meetings, the writings of Mr. Gladstone, and the utterances of important organs of opinion, must have supposed that England was desirous of seeing the Turks expelled from Europe, and would even be pleased to find the Czar undertaking that task.

To the proposals of the British Government, Austria raised some objections. She was not very well inclined to the project of a Conference, though prepared to accept it, if so managed as to ensure the desired results. Russia, moreover, was disposed to stipulate for the exclusion of Turkish representatives from at least the first portion of the deliberations of the Conference—a step which, as Lord Derby reasonably remarked, seemed to make it undesirable that Constantinople should be the place of meeting, but to which, nevertheless, he ultimately assented. In the meanwhile, Russian volunteers kept pouring into Servia by way of Roumania, thus compromising the neutrality of that State, which its ruler, Prince Charles, professed a desire to maintain. Lord Derby brought the subject under the notice of Count Schouvaloff at the beginning of October, when he remarked that "the presence of Russian officers and soldiers in the Servian army had assumed proportions little short of national assistance." It was pointed out that the help thus openly given to Servia must excite irritation and suspicion in the minds of the Turkish Ministers, and disincline the Servians to listen to reasonable terms, in the hope that by these irregular means they might accomplish their desires. The Porte itself, on October 12th, referred to the subject in a note to the representatives of the mediating Powers at Constantinople. It was certainly a very serious grievance, and a grave impeachment of the good faith of Russia, as the Imperial Government could at once have stopped the influx, had it chosen, instead of permitting and even encouraging it. That the feeling in the country itself, however, was general and sincere, cannot be questioned. "In the large towns of Russia," wrote the *Daily News* on the 14th of September, "the war in Turkey [Servia] is the one thing of which everybody is talking from morning to night. The poorest subscribe with all their heart to the funds being raised in aid of Servia, while those who have but little money take small amounts of the Servian loan. Boxes for contributions in aid of the war are introduced in all societies, and noble ladies thrust them into the windows of carriages in the streets. The volunteers are blessed by the priests, and applauded by the people, as they depart for the south, to make their way to the army of General Tchernaieff." The enthusiasm became even greater after the renewal of the war by Servia in the final days of September; and the remonstrances of the British Government fell on unheeding ears.

But the feeling of fanatical devotion to national interests, or what were supposed to be such, was quite as strong in Turkey as in Russia. The pride of race and the pride of religion were powerfully excited among the subjects of Abdul-Hamid, and the Government had to take account of these emotions. The Mohammedans were so inflamed by the fear of foreign dictation that the walls of Constantinople were posted in the early autumn with placards threatening death to any Ministers who should flinch from asserting the dignity and independence of Islam. It was also felt by many that the submission of the Porte to the advice of Europe would lead to a general massacre of the Christians. Possibly these fears were exaggerated; but the Turkish Ministers were doubtless right in not accepting the plans of reform put forward by Lord Derby in September, and adopted by the Continental Powers, and of which the principal feature was the creation of a species of municipal autonomy in Bosnia, Herzegovina, and Bulgaria. The Porte not unnaturally felt that to issue a protocol promising reforms in the insurgent provinces at the bidding of foreign Governments would greatly impair its authority in all parts of the Empire; and this feeling was plainly expressed to the British representative at Constantinople. But, on the 2nd of October, the Turkish Government, while rejecting the idea of autonomy in any shape as impracticable, promised a series of reforms even greater than what had been required. Much had already been granted by the Firman of December, 1875, and, if those concessions had not been carried out, the fault may fairly be ascribed to the state of civil war that had existed ever since. It was now proposed to create a National Council, composed of members of both religions, to free the Christians from all remaining disabilities, and to extend the new political system to the whole Empire. The official promulgation of these reforms took place on the 12th of October, when it was announced that they would consist of the establishment of a Senate and of a Representative Assembly, to vote the budget and taxes, a revision of the system of taxation, the reorganization of the provincial administrations, the full execution of the law of the vilayets (administrative divisions of the first class), a large extension of the right of election, and other measures of an ameliorative character, including those which had been promised for Bosnia and the Herzegovina. Such was the answer which the Porte made to the demand of the Powers that it should reform its administration. It would not accept the schemes sought to be imposed on it by the will of foreign Governments; but it would introduce, of its own free choice, a system much more comprehensive, and of a nature never before attempted in the Ottoman dominions.

The question of the armistice, however, had still to be settled. Early in October, when it was obvious that matters were not going well for the Servians, the St. Petersburg Cabinet made a formal demand on Turkey for an armistice of a month or six weeks. To the Turkish Government it appeared that so short a truce would be injurious to the interests of the Empire, since, should it fail to lead to peace, it would expose Turkey to the risk of having to resume hostilities in the winter. A longer period would enable the Sultan's Ministers to calm the excited feelings of the Moslem population, and to carry out those reforms which it was hoped would render peace more permanent and certain. This, however, did not suit the objects which Russia had in view, and which would have been admirably served by a brief armistice, giving time for the concentration of reinforcements in Servia, and compelling Turkey to renew the struggle under climatic conditions the most unfavourable to her troops. In the note to the mediating Powers delivered on October 12th, the Turkish Ministry declared their willingness to conclude a regular armistice, but considered that it should extend to six months, from October 1st to March 31st. Lord Derby immediately urged on the several Powers concerned the importance of inducing Servia to accept these terms; but the Russian Ambassador at London expressed his doubt whether so long an armistice would be sanctioned by his Imperial master. This proved to be the case. Prince Gortschakoff telegraphed from Livadia that Russia could not ask Servia to accept the proposed truce, because the principality could not keep its army on a war-footing for so many months without putting too severe a strain on its resources. The armistice should therefore, in the opinion of Russia, be for a period not exceeding six weeks at the utmost. Italy, which throughout these transactions exhibited a strong Muscovite leaning, took the same view as Russia. The English Foreign Secretary then made an appeal to Prince Bismarck to use the influence of Germany to procure the acceptance of some compromise, in order that a serious war might be averted. But on the 19th of October the German Chancellor replied that, although an armistice of six months appeared unobjectionable in itself, he could not put pressure on any other Power to induce acceptance. Germany and Russia perfectly well understood one another, and were not likely to be found at issue. France and Austria supported the Turkish proposal, and Lord Derby informed the Russian Ambassador that her Majesty's Ministers were not prepared to withdraw their acceptance of that proposal, or to make any new suggestion. The Government of the Sultan, however, ultimately informed that of Russia that Turkey would agree to an armistice of six weeks, on condition that, if the negotiations were not concluded by that time, the truce should be renewed for a similar term, and again for two months, if the second period passed without result. It is evident that Turkey was animated by a very conciliatory spirit, and that her concessions only stopped short of a renunciation of her sovereign rights as an independent State. Her qualified acceptance of the six weeks' armistice should have been sufficient to satisfy the requirements of Russia, and would doubtless have been so considered had that Power really desired peace. But Turkey was to be humiliated, if she could not be despoiled. On the 31st of October—the same day that Alexinatz fell before the victorious Ottomans, and that the Servian war was nearly brought to a close—General Ignatieff, who had recently returned to Constantinople after a period of absence, handed in to the Porte an ultimatum calling on Turkey to agree to the shorter armistice, pure and simple, within forty-eight hours. In case of a refusal, he was at once to leave the country. The successes of the Turkish troops, enabled the Government to grant what was demanded, and the crisis was delayed for a while.

In an interview with Count Schouvaloff during the progress of the negotiations, Lord Derby warned his Excellency that, however strong might be the feeling of national indignation against the Turks for their cruelty towards the Bulgarians, it would be superseded by a very different sentiment if it were once believed that Constantinople was threatened. The rejection by Russia of the Turkish proposal would be understood as indicating a fixed purpose of going to war; and the Foreign Minister consequently entreated the Ambassador of Russia to omit no effort to make his Government understand the light in which such a resolution would be viewed by the English people.* These representations appeared so serious to the Czar that on the 2nd of November he considered it advisable to assure Lord Augustus Loftus, in the course of an interview at Livadia, that he was not acting with any covert intention. According to the telegraphic report of

* Despatch to Lord Augustus Loftus, Oct. 30th, 1876.

DESCENT OF MOUNT JAVALAR.

the British Ambassador, "he pledged his sacred word of honour, in the most earnest and most solemn manner, that he had no intention of acquiring Constantinople, and that, if necessity should oblige him to occupy a portion of Bulgaria, it would only be provisionally, and until the peace and safety of the Christian population were secured." He denounced as "absurd" the notion that Russia intended to conquer India, and declared that there was no question of erecting Servia and Roumania into kingdoms. It would be, he said, a folly to do so, and he had only allowed his officers (after they had left the Imperial service) to go to Servia in the hope that the popular agitation might in that way be quieted. But he also remarked that he "could not understand, when both countries had a common object—namely, the maintenance of peace, and the amelioration of the condition of the Christians—and when he had given every proof that he had no desire for conquest or aggrandisement, why there should not be a perfect understanding between England and Russia; an understanding based on a policy of peace, which would be equally beneficial to their mutual interests, and to those of Europe at large." Finally, he requested the Ambassador to do his utmost to dispel the cloud of suspicion and distrust of Russia which had gathered in England. These assurances were very well as far as they went; but it is obvious that they did not amount to much. They proved nothing more than that the Russian Emperor wished to keep on good terms with England, and that, like every other monarch, he was earnestly desirous of repudiating any design which might be viewed with disfavour by a great Power. But it is the unfortunate habit of diplomatic intercourse to use language in a certain mobile and flexible way, and to be always ready with an unanticipated explanation when events appear to falsify the spoken word. In January, 1873, Russia most positively stated that she would not annex Khiva; yet Khiva was virtually annexed on the 24th of August in the same year, and it was then maintained that the Imperial promises had not been violated, because the town of Khiva, as distinct from the country so called, had not been occupied by Russian troops, and the Khan had not been actually deposed, but had only signed a treaty making himself the humble vassal of the Czar, and ceding the whole of the right bank of the Amou Darya, and the adjacent lands, which had previously been considered as belonging to Khiva. The words of a despotic sovereign must always be construed with reference to what he is likely to regard as his interest, to the known tendencies of his nation, and to the general teachings of history. The Emperor Alexander may not have been consciously insincere in his speech to Lord Augustus Loftus; yet all the while he was acting in a way which, if successful, would have the effect of bringing the Russian power, practically, to the vicinity of Constantinople.

On the 3rd of November, Lord Derby telegraphed to Lord Augustus Loftus that he and his colleagues had received the assurances of the Russian Emperor with the greatest satisfaction; and on the following day the Foreign Minister signified to Sir Henry Elliot the intention of the British Government to renew its suggestion that a Conference should meet at Constantinople. At this date, affairs wore a somewhat pacific aspect, though attentive observers could not fail to perceive the many possibilities, and even probabilities, of mischief which lurked beneath the surface. A rather unfortunate speech by Lord Beaconsfield at Guildhall, on the 9th of November, when the leading members of the Government were present at the Lord Mayor's banquet, gave a different turn to men's thoughts, though it is doubtful whether it had any important influence on the course of events. The popular agitation of August and September had declined; it had even been followed by a reaction; and in the latter half of October there were signs that the English people were beginning to think that Russian ambition was a matter which concerned them more than Turkish misgovernment. Those who had always dissented from the outcry against Turkey, and who had looked with suspicion on the proceedings of the Northern Power, declared that the nation was recovering its sanity; and it was now boldly proclaimed that England was as little inclined to witness the advance of Russia in the East as in the days of Lord Palmerston and the Crimean war. The original agitation and the subsequent reaction brought out a curious fact in the composition of the English Government. It could hardly be doubted that there were two parties in the Cabinet—not to the extent of a division, but to the extent of mutual embarrassment. The Prime Minister, at one end of the scale, represented a Turkish view of the questions in dispute. The Marquis of Salisbury, Secretary of State for India, at the other end of the scale, represented the Russian view. Lord Derby occupied a middle position, inclining sometimes to one extremity and sometimes to the other, according to the stress of public opinion and the turn of events. Matters had altered a good deal since, on the 20th of September, Lord Beaconsfield had confessed at Aylesbury that the Ministerial policy was unpopular. He felt now that people were in a better mood to listen to his utterances, and in his speech at the civic banquet he took high ground. After declaring that his first object had been peace, and his second the amelioration of the suffering nationalities, he glanced at the possibility of war, and at the power of England to meet such a condition. "We have nothing to gain by war," he said. "We are essentially a non-aggressive Power. There are no cities and no provinces that we desire to appropriate. We have built up an empire of which we are proud, and our proudest boast is this—that that empire subsists as much upon sympathy as upon force. But, if the struggle comes, it should also be recollected that there is no country so prepared for war as England, because there is no country whose resources are so great. In a righteous cause—and I trust that England will never embark in war except in a righteous cause, a cause that concerns her liberty, her independence, or her empire—England is not a country that will have to inquire whether she can enter into a second or a third campaign. In a righteous cause, England will commence a fight that will not end until right is done." These expressions were received with loud and prolonged cheering; but on the eve of a Conference, the object of which was to discover some pacific solution of existing difficulties, the speech was certainly injudicious. What made it doubly objectionable was the fact that the Prime Minister was already in possession of the telegraphic despatch from Lord Augustus Loftus giving a report of the Czar's pacific assurances, of which, however, the English public had at that time no knowledge. Those assurances, as we have observed, were of but little value; yet they should have had some effect in determining the language of the Premier.

The very next day, the Russian Emperor made a similar demonstration of warlike enthusiasm, in a speech delivered to a body of representatives of the nobles and communal council of Moscow, in St. George's Hall of that city. "It is already known to you," said his Majesty, "that Turkey has yielded to my demands for the immediate conclusion of an armistice, in order to put an end to useless slaughter in Servia and Montenegro. In this unequal struggle, the Montenegrins have, as on all previous occasions, shown themselves to be real heroes. Unfortunately, the same thing cannot be said of the Servians, notwithstanding the presence of our volunteers in the Servian ranks, many of whom have shed their blood for the Sclavonian cause. I know that all Russia most warmly sympathises with me in the sufferings of our brethren and co-religionists. The true interests of Russia, however, are dearer to me than all, and I should wish to the uttermost to spare Russian blood from being shed. This is the reason why I have striven, and shall still strive, to obtain a real improvement in the position of the Christians in the East by peaceful means. In a few days negotiations will commence in Constantinople between the representatives of the Great Powers, to settle the conditions of peace. My most ardent wish is that we may arrive at a general agreement. Should this, however, not be achieved, and should I see that we cannot obtain such guarantees as are necessary for carrying out what we have a right to demand of the Porte, I am firmly determined to act independently, and I am convinced that in this case the whole of Russia will respond to my summons, should I consider it necessary, and should the honour of Russia require it. I am also convinced that Moscow, as heretofore, will lead the van by its example. May God help us to carry out our sacred mission!" The Municipal Council replied to this speech in an address of the most effusive and flowery description. "Thanks to thee, O Czar!" exclaimed the representatives of the holy city. "O most pacific of Czars, of the most pacific of nations! thanks to thee for thy wisdom in waiting, and in predetermining the hour when thy Czarish patience will be exhausted, and the moment for the independent action of Russia shall have come." It was at first supposed in England that the Emperor had received a telegraphic report of Lord Beaconsfield's speech on the previous evening, and that his own martial strain had been provoked by that of the English Premier; but it subsequently appeared that his Majesty knew nothing of the Guildhall banquet when he spoke,* so that his tone of defiance had not the excuse which was suggested by some English journalists.

Apparently thinking that he had gone too far for prudence, and possibly desiring at once to put the English Premier in the wrong, and to show the world how peaceful were his own wishes, the Czar made, through his representative in London, a formal request that the explanations given to Lord Augustus Loftus at Livadia should be published. They were accordingly printed in the *London Gazette* of the same evening—the 21st of November. In a despatch to the British Ambassador, issued at the same time, Lord Derby drily observed that the publication of the Livadia statements might be opportune, as the last few days had brought intelligence of the mobilisation of a considerable Russian force, and of the emission of a new loan for 100,000,000 roubles. Russia was in truth

* Lord Augustus Loftus to the Earl of Derby, December 5th, 1876.

steadily advancing on the road to war, though a few diplomatic pretences were still kept up. On the 19th of November, Prince Gortschakoff wrote to Count Schouvaloff to the effect that European action in Turkey had been condemned had no right to interfere. It is worthy of remark that when Russia signified her intention to be no longer bound by the stipulations securing the neutralization of the Black Sea, Prince Gortschakoff specifically declared that "his Imperial Majesty

A CIRCASSIAN OUTPOST.

to powerlessness by the stipulations of 1856, and that for twenty years the Porte had pursued, with the assurance of complete impunity, a system alike ruinous to the Empire and to its Christian subjects, disastrous to the general peace, and revolting to the sentiments of humanity and the conscience of Christian Europe. He might have stated his meaning more succinctly by saying that for twenty years Russia had been restrained from interfering with the internal affairs of Turkey, with which she fully adhered to his consent to the general principles of the treaty of 1856, which had fixed the position of Turkey in the European system."* The Emperor even expressed his willingness to renew the other stipulations of that treaty; and he did in fact renew them by the treaty signed in London on the 13th of March, 1871. To many at that time it was apparent that the objection to the

* Circular of Prince Gortschakoff to the European Powers, October 31st, 1870.

Black Sea clauses was only the first step towards a more sweeping conclusion. In less than six years, the whole treaty was denounced as an injury and a clog.

"If," said the Russian Chancellor, in his despatch of November 19th, 1876, "the Great Powers wish to accomplish a real work, and not expose themselves to the periodical and aggravated return of this dangerous crisis, it is impossible that that they should persevere in the system which permits the germs of it to exist and develop with the inflexible logic of facts. It is necessary to escape from this vicious circle, and to recognise that the independence and integrity of Turkey must be subordinated to the guarantees demanded by humanity, the sentiments of Christian Europe, and the general peace. The Porte has been the first to infringe the engagement which she contracted by the treaty of 1856 with regard to her Christian subjects. It is the right and duty of Europe to dictate to her the conditions on which alone it can on its part consent to the maintenance of the political *status quo* created by that treaty; and since the Porte is incapable of fulfilling them, it is the right and duty of Europe to substitute itself for her, to the extent necessary to ensure their execution." Russia, it was added, was more directly and seriously interested in the matter than any other Power; but she regarded it none the less as one of general interest, and her own views were free from any concealed intention. This despatch was important, since it contained a clear exposition of those principles which governed the subsequent Conference, and proved the causes of its failure.

In his reiterated endeavours to relieve the English people of their fears, Prince Gortschakoff argued that the best arrangement for Russian interests was to leave the keys of the Black Sea in hands feeble enough not to close that commercial outlet against Russia, or to menace her security. Turkish dominion answered this purpose; but the Turks had abused their dominion by rendering it intolerable to the Christians, and English policy had contributed to the abuse. It need scarcely be remarked that the commercial objects would be attained by the possession of Constantinople as the southern capital of the Russian Empire, and that such a climax would place that Empire in the most magnificent position for aggressive purposes that it is possible to conceive. The advance towards the city of the Eastern Cæsars on the part of Russia has been going on for many years, and the demand for Bulgarian autonomy was only another step in the great march. At the same time, it is not difficult of belief that Russia would be very well content to leave the final step for a later generation. If she could have got the consent of England to the creation of a number of quasi-independent States north and south of the Balkans, she could easily have afforded to let the remainder of the drama work itself out by a natural process. No one really supposes that a Bosnian or a Bulgarian principality would be any obstacle to the fulfilment of Russian designs when the proper moment should be held to have arrived.

Lord Beaconsfield announced in the course of his Guildhall speech that Lord Salisbury would proceed to Constantinople as the Plenipotentiary of England at the approaching Conference. The Indian Secretary was a very unfortunate choice for such a mission. He is a man of great ability, largely acquainted with Oriental politics; but at this time his bias towards Russia was well known. Lord Salisbury is as a Tory of Tories, and his sympathy with the politics of St. Petersburg was then a natural consequence. On this occasion he received the cordial support of that section of the Liberal party which, to the confusion and stultification of all Liberal principles, has for some years past been exalting the character and aims of Russia. He of course received his instructions from Lord Derby, the Foreign Secretary; but a good deal was left to his discretion, and Lord Derby himself, with all his oscillations, had strong leanings towards an anti-Turkish policy. On the 19th of October, 1864, while he was still Lord Stanley, the present Earl delivered a speech to his constituents, in which he dwelt on the advisability of creating fresh political organisations in place of the decaying Ottoman Empire. He believed the breaking up of the Turkish dominion to be only a question of time, and probably not a very long time. The Turks had played their part in history; they had had their day, and that day was over; and the speaker confessed he did not understand, unless it were from the influence of diplomatic traditions, why the statesmen of the old school (it must be borne in mind that Lord Palmerston was then living) were so determined to stand by Turkey, whether right or wrong. "I think," he went on to say, "we are making for ourselves enemies of races which will very soon become, in Eastern countries, dominant races. I think we are keeping back countries by whose improvement we, as the great traders of the world, should be the chief gainers, and that we are doing this for no earthly advantage, present or prospective. I admit that England has an interest, and a very strong one, in the neutrality of Egypt, and some interest also, though to a less extent, in Constantinople not falling into the hands of a great European Power; but, these two points set aside, I can conceive no injury arising to Great

RETURNING HOME.

Britain from any transfer of power which might affect the Turkish Empire." A Minister holding such views as these was a very ill-omened occupant of the Foreign Office at a time when Russia was renewing her former attempts in the East. Lord Derby, in the autumn of 1876, often spoke and acted in a contrary sense; but he could not be relied on for a day. Whenever the Russian party in the Cabinet gained the ascendant, he was a willing ally; when the other section was predominant, he went with that also; but his personal inclination was probably as it had been in 1864,—and that was to favour a "transfer of power" such as Russia desired to accomplish in the region of the Balkans.

The Premier himself was apparently unwavering

in his desire to maintain the Turkish Empire as part of a political system the destruction of which would entail great danger to the interests of England. He was viewed with so much disfavour in Russia that, in the course of the autumn, a well-known journal, called the *Golos*, twice attacked him with great bitterness on personal grounds, alleging that he had amassed a colossal fortune by speculating in Eastern securities, and that his policy had been directed by a desire to advance his private ends. He had entered, it was said, into partnership with the firm of Erlanger, and had realised enormous sums by the depreciation of silver, the purchase of the Suez Canal shares, and the Servian war. The Russian Government inserted in the *Journal de St. Petersbourg* a formal expression of regret for these diatribes; but the author was not called to account, and it is probable that he had the support of a large number of his countrymen. Had Lord Beaconsfield been omnipotent in the Cabinet, he would perhaps have adopted a firmer and more consistent tone. But he was old, weary, and out of health, and younger men seized much of the influence which some years earlier would have been exercised by himself. Hence the Russianising tendencies which from time to time became apparent.

PORT SAID, THE NORTHERN ENTRANCE TO THE SUEZ CANAL.

The principle of a Conference having been accepted by Turkey (though, considering its implied interference with her domestic affairs, a refusal would not have been surprising), Lord Salisbury left

London for Constantinople on the 20th of November. The communication from the Foreign Office setting forth his instructions was dated the same day. Lord Derby here stated that her Majesty's Government submitted, as the bases for the deliberations of the Conference, the following propositions:—1. The independence and territorial integrity of the Ottoman Empire. 2. A declaration that the Powers would not seek for any territorial advantage, any exclusive influence, or any concession with regard to the commerce of their subjects, which those of every other nation might not equally obtain. 3. The basis of pacification proposed to the Porte near the end of September.* It was furthermore desired that the reforms already agreed to by the Porte, in the note addressed to the representatives of the Powers on the 13th of February, 1876 (those, that is, which were promulgated in the Firman of December 12th, 1875), should be included in the administrative arrangements for Bosnia and the Herzegovina, and, so far as they might be applicable, for Bulgaria. These bases had met with general acceptance by the other Powers, and were therefore to be considered as regulating the deliberations of the Conference, and marking the limits within which its discussions should be confined. With respect to Montenegro, a suggestion was offered that it would be politic on the part of the Porte, and of general benefit to the populations concerned, if some territorial concession were made to that principality, which would have the effect of bringing under the rule of Prince Nikita certain adjacent lands, which, in the opinion of her Majesty's Government, were only a source of weakness to Turkey. These concessions would include the port of Spitza, on the Adriatic, which the Montenegrins had long coveted, and which Mr. Consul Holmes believed might very properly be granted them.

After referring to the objections entertained by the Porte to the introduction of any form of administrative autonomy into the provinces, and to the interference of the Powers in matters of internal government, which it would regard as an infringement of the Turkish rights of sovereignty and the independence of the Empire, Lord Derby observed:—"The immediate necessity of the situation is to restore tranquillity to the disturbed provinces. The course of events has made it obvious that this can now only be done by concert with the Powers, and it is in vain for the Porte to expect that the Powers will be satisfied with the mere general assurances which have already been so often given, and have proved to be so imperfectly executed. If the Conference should decide upon a scheme of administration for these particular provinces which may be applicable and advantageous to other provinces, it will be open to the Porte to extend it to them. No doubt the Conference will give due weight to the reforms already promulgated, which will properly form an important element for consideration; but pacification cannot be attained by proclamations, and the Powers have a right to demand, in the interest of the peace of Europe, that they shall examine for themselves the measures required for the reform of the administration of the disturbed provinces, and that adequate security shall be provided for carrying those measures into operation." Anticipating that the Porte would probably again put forward the objections to which allusion had already been made, Lord Salisbury was instructed to state positively that they could not be entertained.

The Foreign Secretary next proceeded to point out the main defects in the administration of European Turkey, and to indicate with some detail the most advisable reforms. He then touched upon a matter of the most important nature—one which nothing but a mistaken view of the whole question would ever have suffered to appear, and which in fact carried within itself the final ruin of the Conference, and the immediate cause of war. Besides giving the Christian populations some control over their own local affairs, the bases of the Conference, according to Lord Derby (who seems, however, to have adopted a latitude of interpretation of the most amazing kind), provided that there should be other "guarantees" against the exercise of arbitrary authority in Bosnia and Herzegovina, and also against maladministration in Bulgaria. In the bases as laid down by himself at the beginning of the despatch, the guarantees appear to be nothing more than the forms of local self-government which it was proposed to establish. It now appeared, however, that there were to be guarantees quite independent of those, and having an "external" character. The vilayets, it was suggested, might be placed under Valis, whose nomination by the Porte should, as a temporary arrangement, be subject to the approval of the Ambassadors of the Guaranteeing Powers, or a majority of them. Moreover, the Vali was to be irremovable, even on conviction of crime, corruption, or incapacity, except with the concurrence of the Ambassadors, or a majority of them; and the Mutessarifs and Judges, though selected by the Porte, were to be subject temporarily to the veto of the same body. Her Majesty's Government would not indeed countenance the introduction into the Conference of any proposal for bringing foreign armies into Turkish territory, in violation of the engagements by which the

* See *ante*, p. 53.

Guaranteeing Powers were bound; but the Porte was distinctly given to understand that if, by obstinacy or apathy, it opposed the efforts which were then being made to place the Ottoman Empire on a more secure basis, the responsibility for the consequences which might ensue would rest solely with the Sultan and his advisers. Turkey was to abdicate her sovereignty in favour of a Commonwealth of Ambassadors, representing the most antagonistic views, or she was to be abandoned to her fate.

Lord Derby had in fact resolved to carry out to their legitimate and disastrous conclusion the principles which he had laid down in a despatch to Sir Henry Elliot on the 5th of September, which he then admitted to be indefensible in the abstract, but which he said had been forced on the Government by the atrocity meetings. He there wrote:—"The accounts of outrages and excesses, committed by the Turkish troops upon the unhappy and for the most part unresisting population, have raised a universal feeling of indignation in all classes of English society; and to such a pitch has this risen that, in the extreme case of Russia declaring war against Turkey, her Majesty's Government would find it practically impossible to interfere in defence of the Ottoman Empire. Such an event, by which the sympathies of the nation would be brought into direct opposition to its treaty engagements, would place England in a most unsatisfactory and even humiliating position; yet it is impossible to say that, if the present conflict continues, the contingency may not arise." Never before, surely, did an English Minister threaten to break the most solemn treaty engagements, and to place his country in what he himself described as an unsatisfactory and humiliating position, because he was told to do so by the irresponsible orators of the platform.

While the question of peace or war was pending, the anti-Turkish party in England was doing its utmost to revive the autumn agitation. The managers of that party were stung by repeated assertions that the fever of two months back had worn itself out; that the people in the main were ashamed of their excitement, and had awakened to a conviction that the question was not one to be determined by mere emotion, but must be settled on grounds of policy and reason. To disprove these statements, a great demonstration at St. James's Hall was arranged for the early part of December, and took place on the 8th of that month. There were in fact two meetings—one in the afternoon, and one in the evening. The chair on the earlier occasion was taken by the Duke of Westminster; on the latter, by Lord Shaftesbury. The chief speakers were the two chairmen, Sir George Campbell, Mr. Anthony Trollope, Sir Thomas Fowell Buxton, the Bishop of Oxford, Mr. Evelyn Ashley, Professor Bryce, Sir Henry Havelock, Canon Liddon (who carried his partisanship to the irrational length of demanding that the whole Mohammedan population of European Turkey should be disarmed, and that England should send 100,000 men into the dominions of the Porte), Mr. Trevelyan, Mr. Freeman (who desired that the interests of England should perish, rather than that we should speak one word on behalf of Turkey), Professor Fawcett, and Mr. Gladstone. A great deal of eloquence was expended on these two occasions; but it was for the most part of a wild and hysterical order. The Duke of Westminster suggested that the fleets and armies of England should be sent to Constantinople, not to oppose Russia, but to coerce Turkey; and the Bishop of Oxford supported the same view. One temperate and reasonable utterance varied this Babel of furious and bitter passions. It was that of Sir George Campbell, an Anglo-Indian administrator, who had recently visited Turkey, and who admitted that while the Turkish Government was as execrably bad as it was possible for any Government to be, the Turkish people were themselves not nearly so black as they had been painted. Oppressed as the Christians no doubt were, Sir George said he was in a position to assert, that although the Turkish Government was not so efficient, or not so severe in some senses, and although it did not exercise so stringent a police system, as some of the despotic Governments of Europe, yet more personal freedom had been enjoyed by the Christians than was the case under that system of serfage to which many of the peoples of Europe had been subjected. He believed, in fact, that they had considerably prospered and considerably advanced, and that they were in a very much better position than his auditors were inclined to suppose. The meeting was paraded as a "National Conference;" but such a title was a misnomer, if not an imposition. The demonstration was not national, and it was in no respect a conference. It made no approach towards representing the varied opinions of the English people, and instead of "conferring" it declaimed.

CHAPTER VII.

Journey of Lord Salisbury to Constantinople—His Visits to Paris, Berlin, Vienna, and Rome—Opinions of the French, German, Austrian, and Italian Governments on the Conference and its Objects—Position of Germany with respect to the Eastern Question—The Alliance of the Three Emperors—Ambiguous Utterances of Prince Bismarck—Article in the *Agence Russe* on the approaching Conference—Proposal for a Belgian Occupation of Bulgaria—Article in the *Novaya Vremia*—Question as to whether the Christians of Turkey were placed by the Treaty of 1856 under a European Protectorate—Mr. Gladstone's Speech on the Subject in the House of Commons—Fallacy pervading the View usually accepted—Lord Salisbury and General Ignatieff—First Meeting of the Preliminary Conference at Constantinople (Dec. 11th)—Demands on Turkey formulated by the Powers—Austrian and Greek Objections to them—Encouragement given to the South Sclavonic Element—Hesitating Attitude of the English Government—Earnest Warnings of Sir Henry Elliot—Evident Determination of the Turks to resist Dictation to the last Extremity—Russia and Turkey both arming—Appointment of Midhat Pasha as Grand Vizier—First Meeting of the Plenary Conference (Dec. 23rd)—Proclamation of the Turkish Constitution—Its chief Provisions—Probabilities of the Future—The Plenipotentiaries attending the Conference—Proceedings in the Earlier Stages of the Discussion—The Sultan and the English Plenipotentiary.

LORD SALISBURY pursued his way to Constantinople by a devious route. It was considered advisable that he should ascertain the views of the chief European Governments, not parties to the quarrel, before attending the council-chamber in the Turkish capital. He accordingly paid visits in the first instance to Paris, Berlin, Vienna, and Rome, at all of which cities he held discussions with the leading Ministers. Any inclination to follow an anti-Russian policy which may have been entertained by a section of the English Cabinet received signal discomfiture in the course of these interviews—a discomfiture which could not have been otherwise than highly gratifying to the English Plenipotentiary. At Paris, on the 21st of November, the Duc Decazes told him that France was not prepared to place herself in opposition to Russia on the Eastern Question. At Berlin, where he arrived on the 22nd, he had prolonged conversations with Prince Bismarck, the Foreign Minister, the Crown Prince, and the Emperor himself; and from all these distinguished personages he received the assurance that Germany would be neutral in any war that might ensue, and that, although Prussia was a consenting party to the Treaty of Paris, by which the independence and the territorial integrity of the Ottoman Empire were recognised and guaranteed, Germany would not interfere on behalf of Turkey, should hostilities break out. Prince Bismarck even confessed his sympathy with the Czar, and the German Emperor was necessarily well-inclined towards his nephew, not only by reason of the ties of relationship, but also on account of the assistance which Russian neutrality had rendered to Prussia in the great struggle with France. Proceeding to Vienna, on the 24th of November, Lord Salisbury exchanged views with Count Andrassy, the Austrian Chancellor, and with M. Tisza, the Prime Minister of the Hungarian Kingdom. Both these statesmen exhibited some degree of willingness to support Turkey in certain eventualities; but their tone was very undecided, and it was doubtful whether any serious opposition to Russia would come from that quarter. Count Andrassy was strongly opposed to the formation by the Conference of any new tributary States, and also to the idea of a Russian occupation, which he hoped England would not sanction. He agreed with the English Minister on the necessity of obtaining guarantees for the effectual execution of those reforms which had already been granted; but the disarming of the Mussulmáns was admitted by both statesmen to be a matter too difficult to be carried into effect.

On arriving at Rome, which he reached on the 29th, the Marquis found that Italy had as little disposition as the other Powers to interpose between Turkey and any action on the part of the Czar. By Signor Melegari, the Minister of Foreign Affairs, the principles of Italian policy were declared to be —the maintenance of the territorial integrity of Turkey; liberal measures of reform for the insurgent provinces, under an international guarantee or engagement, which would give the Powers the right of seeing to their application; neutrality in the event of war, but diplomatic opposition to military occupation of the provinces by any foreign Power whatever. None of the Continental Governments took so decided a stand on what may be called a coercive policy as that of Italy. In his interview with Lord Salisbury, Signor Melegari urged with much emphasis that the action of the Powers ought not to be derived from or limited by the Treaty of Paris, but that their functions were rather those of mediators, deriving their title simply from the events of the war, and the acceptance of the Conference by the Porte. They ought, he considered, to be unrestricted, in their search for a solution of the questions to be submitted to the Conference, by any obligations imposed by that treaty; and he was not prepared to admit that the Porte would be at liberty to reject any decision to which the Conference might come.* Well satisfied with this exposition of principles, Lord Salisbury left Rome for Brindisi on the 1st of December. He had quitted London on the 20th of November; he arrived at Constantinople on the 5th of the following month.

The position of Germany was one of the most important elements in the whole question, considered with reference to the probabilities of the future. Had Russia been opposed by the Emperor William, she would have refrained from placing herself in such a position as to render a contest unavoidable, except in the unlikely event of Turkey doing whatever she was told. With the support of Germany, Russia might safely proceed, unless England should again come to the rescue, as in 1854. Of this there was no immediate probability. The autumn agitation, and the evident retrogression of the Government from the ground first assumed, left little to apprehend on that score. The pro-Russian party in the Cabinet had got the upper hand, and Lord Salisbury talked of guarantees, and almost of coercion, as glibly as Prince Gortschakoff himself. It was necessary, however, to be assured of Germany. The Czar and his advisers doubtless knew from the very first that the Emperor William would be their friend. There can be no question that the matter had been fully discussed at those meetings of the despotic sovereigns which take place from time to time, and at which the fate of Europe is settled with the secrecy of conspirators and the morals of brigands. But the Russian people knew little or nothing as to what Prince Bismarck and his master would do, until about the period of Lord Salisbury's journey. Some sentences in the speech of the German Emperor at the opening of the Parliament, on the 30th of October, had encouraged the Muscovites to take a hopeful view of German policy; but they had no certain information until the observations of Bismarck to the British Plenipotentiary were made public. Thenceforward, the devotion of the Russian press to Germany was unbounded. It was ostentatiously proclaimed that the alliance of the three Empires was secure (though in truth the designs of Austria were still rather doubtful), and that the rest of Europe had nothing to do but to obey. The motives of Germany have been differently interpreted. By some it has been thought that she desired to lure Russia into an exhausting conflict, in order that, when completely ruined, she might herself stand forward as the one great arbiter of the destinies of Europe. But the more probable explanation is that she anticipated the outbreak of a general war, and hoped to share material results with the Czar.

Russia, then, was satisfied with the policy of the German Government; yet Prince Bismarck still thought it advisable to keep up some degree of mystification. At a Parliamentary dinner given at Berlin on the 1st of December, at which the President, Vice-President, and all the leading members of the Reichstag were present, the German Chancellor delivered a speech, in which, referring to the Eastern Question, he dwelt so strongly on the absolute neutrality which would be observed by the Emperor, and insisted so much on the importance he attached to the preservation of good relations with Austria, that people began to ask themselves whether, after all, Germany was not acting on behalf of Turkey. He even went so far as to declare that war was being urged on by the Russian press and the Pan-Sclavist committees. Speaking for himself, he said that he had never advised the occupation of Bulgaria; and he added that, should peace be impossible, Germany would seek to localise the war, and that the moment for her interference would be when Austria, whose existence was of the highest importance to Germany and Europe, should be endangered in her vital interests. All this looked rather unfriendly towards Russia; but in truth it meant very little. It was exceedingly improbable that the Czar would seek to obtain the Sclavonic provinces of Austria, unless forced into a position of hostility by Austria herself; and that was the only contingency which Prince Bismarck contemplated as likely to draw Germany into the field. A speech in the Reichstag, on the 5th of December, gave more guarded expression to the Chancellor's views; besides which, it was obvious to all that, in so important a matter of foreign policy, the personal wishes of the Emperor would count for even more than the calculations of the Prince.

As the period of the Conference drew near, the tone of the Russian Government grew more moderate—probably because it began to be evident that the Powers were agreed on some of the most essential points of the political programme, and that this partial unity might be endangered by a too eager insistance on matters likely to create dissension. In the early days of December, the *Agence Russe*, of St. Petersburg, contained an article which, being clearly of official inspiration, was considered by Lord Augustus Loftus of sufficient importance to be brought before the notice of his Government. The journalist commenced by referring to a previous

* The Marquis of Salisbury to the Earl of Derby: Rome, Nov. 30th, 1876.—Blue Book on Turkey, No. 2 (1877).

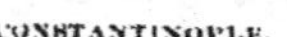

CONSTANTINOPLE.

declaration that Russia, while considering an occupation of Turkish territory the most efficacious and practical of guarantees, had no wish to impose her own view on the other Powers, nor to suggest that the desired end could only be obtained in the way indicated. Consequently, Russia would willingly adhere to any other means, equally efficacious, which might be proposed. The article then proceeded to say that, after the assurances given by the Emperor, no advantage could be derived from, but rather a heavy charge imposed on Russia by, a periodical occupation of the Christian provinces of the Balkans. As for military glory, Russia did not require it. The English and Russian Governments, the writer remarked, were agreed both on the urgency of reforms, and the necessity of some guarantee for their execution. The only point of divergence between them was the *modus agendi;* and the article then sought to prove that, although the Treaty of 1856 required the maintenance of the Ottoman Empire in its integrity, the welfare of the Christian population was by the same instrument placed under the protectorate of the guaranteeing Powers.* Lord Augustus Loftus believed that this article gave a very correct idea of the views of the Imperial Government, and of the course which

LORD BEACONSFIELD.
(*From a Photograph by Messrs. W. & D. Downey.*)

* Lord Augustus Loftus to the Earl of Derby, December 6th, 1876.

the Emperor's representatives would take in the approaching Conference. It appeared to him intended to prepare the public mind for a renunciation of the idea of occupying Bulgaria—an idea which had for some time been entertained and discussed. The plan was shortly afterwards revived in a different form. It was then suggested by the Russian Government that Bulgaria should be temporarily occupied by Belgian troops; but the proposal came to nothing, and it is difficult to believe that it can ever have been seriously intended. At the close of the year, we find the St. Petersburg journal, *Novaya Vremia*, returning to the original idea of a Russian occupation. "If Turkish obstinacy has to be broken," said that paper, "there can be no doubt that such a task cannot be performed by a neutral Power, but only by one which has an interest in the matter; that, so far as Bulgaria is concerned, Russia alone possesses sufficient strength to secure the lives and properties of the population, sufficient good will to help an unhappy people which cries out for brotherly assistance, and sufficient knowledge and capacity to give the Bulgarians a solid political organization. The occupation can, and must, be effected by Russia only, and that not at some future time, but now."

A phrase in the article from the *Agence Russe* expressed very tersely the position taken up by the Russian Government, and by the English advocates of a Muscovite policy. The Christian population of Turkey, it was remarked, was placed by the Treaty of 1856 under the protectorate of the Guaranteeing Powers. Mr. Gladstone, reviewing the whole question in the House of Commons on the 31st of July, 1876, maintained that the arrangement of twenty years earlier had thrown on those Powers the responsibility of upholding the rights of the Christians, and enforcing on the Porte a proper recognition of their claims. Up to that date, the right honourable gentleman observed, Russia was the sole champion of Christianity in Turkey, and she had the power of fixing her own construction on the privileges granted to the Christian subjects of the Porte, and of threatening the Sultan with war if he did not do exactly what was desired at St. Petersburg. But by the peace of 1856 the treaty rights of Russia to interfere in Turkey were destroyed. For a generation before the Crimean war, the Christians of Turkey had a protector in Russia; but the war abolished the functions of that protector, and it was not to be supposed, argued Mr. Gladstone, that Lord Palmerston and the other statesmen of that day intended to leave the Eastern Christians in a worse condition than before. The treaty therefore substituted for the dangerous prerogative of Russia, which had been used by the Emperor Nicholas as a means of destroying the peace of Europe, a collective guarantee of the European Powers. Consequently, in the opinion of the speaker, a moral responsibility rested on those Powers, who were bound to see that the Christians were treated by the Porte with justice and humanity. The whole argument, however, rested on an assumption totally at variance with the terms of the Treaty of 1856. There was no collective guarantee in that treaty with reference to the Christian population of Turkey. The principalities of Wallachia and Moldavia, and the principality of Servia, were placed, as regarded their quasi-independence, under such a guarantee; but the Christians of Turkey proper were left to the operation of the Hatti-Sherif, a copy of which was communicated to the Powers assembled in Conference, and acknowledged by them with an express admission that it did not confer any right to interfere in the domestic affairs of the Ottoman Empire. So clear and absolute is this provision that Mr. Gladstone himself, after talking in the speech in question about the "collective guarantee," and "the concerted and general action of the European Powers," was obliged to confess that nothing more than a moral right of interference had been obtained. The plain fact is, that, whether wisely or not, the amelioration of the lot of the Christians did not enter into the designs of the Powers, either in making war or in concluding peace. The great objects of the struggle were to restrain the ambition of Russia, and to uphold Turkey as a necessary part of the European system; and those were the ideas which dominated the Treaty of Paris of March 30th, 1856. The Powers said they were pleased to find that the Sultan had issued a Firman recording his generous intentions towards his Christian subjects; but that was all.* Nor did the Treaty of 1871 make any alteration in this respect, but, on the contrary, re-enacted everything contained in the earlier document, with the excep-

* It may be as well to append in this place the exact words of the Treaty of 1856:—"Art. IX.—His Imperial Majesty the Sultan, having, in his constant solicitude for the welfare of his subjects, issued a Firman which, while ameliorating their condition without distinction of religion or of race, records his generous intentions towards the Christian population of his empire, and wishing to give a further proof of his sentiments in that respect, has resolved to communicate to the Contracting Parties the said Firman, emanating spontaneously from his sovereign will. The Contracting Powers recognise the high value of this communication. It is clearly understood that it cannot, in any case, give to the said Powers the right to interfere, either collectively or separately, in the relations of his Majesty the Sultan with his subjects, nor in the internal administration of his empire."

tion of the Black Sea clauses, and those having reference to the Straits of the Dardanelles and the Bosphorus, and the condition of the Danube, which were either abrogated or amended. Yet so frequently and boldly was the contrary asserted in the autumn of 1876, that in time members of the Government itself, and even Lord Beaconsfield, were found admitting that the Powers generally, and England in particular, had duties and responsibilities towards the Christians. These duties and responsibilities were to be carried out by means of the Conference, and to be enforced by guarantees. In the then heated state of the public mind, it was in vain to suggest that since the exclusion of foreign interference the condition of the Christians had greatly improved, and that it would probably have improved still more but for the constant provocations to insurrection which had been sedulously maintained by Russian agents. The party of Mr. Gladstone had triumphed, and Ministers were either frightened, or secretly in league with the agitators of St. James's Hall. Divided among themselves, they endeavoured to please both parties, and of course pleased neither. Such were the radical errors out of which the Conference was born. That it should be a failure was almost inevitable from the first.

Lord Salisbury, as we have said, represented the pro-Russian party in the Cabinet, and immediately on arriving at Constantinople he became exceedingly friendly with General Ignatieff. It was the policy of the Russian Ambassador to please the English Plenipotentiary, and to encourage his Muscovite leanings by a few concessions. The project of a Russian occupation of Bulgaria was therefore all but abandoned, and Lord Salisbury seems thenceforward to have been very much at the disposal of General Ignatieff. The first meeting of the preliminary Conference, from which the representatives of Turkey were excluded, took place on the 11th of December at the Russian Embassy; the final meeting, as regarded this initiatory stage, was on the 17th. After discussion, it was agreed that Bulgaria (including under that designation the scenes of the recent outrages, which were really in Roumelia) should be divided into two vilayets, each to be ruled by a Christian Vali, or Governor-General, who might be a foreigner or an Ottoman subject. Provision was made for the local government of the province so created, and for securing to the Powers a veto over the appointments of the Porte. The relief measures of the Andrassy Note were to be adopted; the regular army, as a rule, was to be concentrated in the fortresses and great towns; and a Christian militia, with officers of all creeds, was to be appointed by the Vali. The persons concerned in the atrocities of May were to be punished; and an amnesty was to be granted to the insurgents. Similar, though not identical, arrangements were to be made for Bosnia and Herzegovina; the terms of peace, as regarded Servia and Montenegro, were in both cases to include a small cession of territory by the Turks; and the reforms were to be carried out under the direction of an International Commission, appointed for a year, with the assistance of a foreign military force. Lastly, the representatives of the Six Powers proposed to adhere to the general principles laid down, and, in the event of the Turks refusing compliance, to quit Constantinople in a body.

It will be seen that the plans thus adopted were extremely coercive. They were mainly inspired by General Ignatieff, and were doubtless conceived with a desire to break down the sovereignty of Turkey, and, though by slow degrees, to make way for the influence of Russia. When Ignatieff's original proposals, as informally stated by him in conversation, were brought before the notice of Count Andrassy, that statesman expressed to Sir Andrew Buchanan, the British Ambassador at Vienna, his great dissatisfaction with them, though he afterwards gave a qualified support to the plan as settled by the Conference. He considered that the adoption of Ignatieff's programme would be the first step towards the decomposition of Turkey, and he characterised the plan as directed against the future independence and development of the Greek population, and as being merely designed to promote Pan-Sclavist and Russian interests.* The Greeks themselves held the same view. The Hellenic community at Philippopolis protested against any part of the country south of the Balkans being included in the proposed scheme of autonomy, and the Government of the Kingdom of Greece took up the subject with much animation. The Armenian Patriarch was also opposed to the scheme. It was in truth a Russian project pure and simple, and the eagerness with which General Ignatieff pressed it on the acceptance of the other Powers shows how implicitly Russia reckoned on the South Sclavonic populations, when possessed of autonomy, advancing her ulterior views. For some years after the creation of the Greek Kingdom, that small and feeble State was used as the chief agent towards the same end, and answered the purpose extremely well. But Greece had recently exhibited more independence, and was obviously coming into the field as a rival to the Northern Power for the possession of Constantinople and the southern provinces, whenever

* Sir Andrew Buchanan to the Earl of Derby, December 11th, 1876.

the final collapse of the Ottoman Empire should occur. The Sclavonic element was therefore to be brought forward, even to the injury of the Hellenic; and the next stepping-stones to the capital—two having been already secured in Servia and Roumania—were to be Bosnia and Bulgaria.

The hesitating attitude of the English Government was made apparent in a despatch from the Earl of Derby to the Marquis of Salisbury, dated December 22nd, 1876. "I have the honour to inform your Excellency," said the Foreign Secretary, "that her Majesty's Government have decided that England will not assent to, or assist in, coercive measures, military or naval, against the Porte. The Porte must, on the other hand, be made to understand, as it has from the first been informed, that it can expect no assistance from England in the event of war." Should the Government of the Sultan persistently refuse to make the required concessions, and the Conference result in failure, the Marquis was at once to leave, and Sir Henry Elliot was to depart for England, there to report on the situation, leaving a secretary in charge of the Embassy. In the first of these intimations we see the policy of Lord Beaconsfield; in the second, that of an influential section of the Cabinet, which inclined to views highly favoured at St. Petersburg. The two clauses had no reasonable connection with one another. If the sin of the Porte in rejecting the conditions of the Powers was so great as to merit desertion, it was surely great enough to merit a more positive sentence; at any rate, the punishment that was certain to ensue should not have been left solely to the discretion of others. Such an announcement, if it failed to intimidate the Sultan, could have no other effect than to invite the aggression of the Czar. It was proclaiming that Turkey, in the case supposed, would deserve chastisement, and at the same time making over the sword to the very hands most likely to use it to our detriment.

The Government of Lord Beaconsfield had in fact entered on a most dangerous path; but there was one clear head at Constantinople which saw the truth, and gave expression to it. Sir Henry Elliot wrote to Lord Derby on the 10th of December, pointing out in very earnest language the inevitable effect of driving the Turks to despair and defiance, and showing that the force of any protest which the Government might wish to make against coercive measures adopted by Russia would be diminished by the fact of the rejected proposals having been approved by England herself. "I perceive in the English newspapers," said the Ambassador, in sentences that have an important bearing on the subsequent course of events, "the prevalence of a conviction that, provided the Marquis of Salisbury and General Ignatieff can come to an understanding upon the measures to be expected from the Porte, no further difficulty need be apprehended, as the acquiescence of the Imperial Government will be a matter of course. This I believe to be an entire delusion. The united action of Great Britain and Russia must have immense weight with the Porte; but the influence of her Majesty's Government as a friendly adviser is not what it was a short time ago. The declaration of important personages that the Turks must be driven out of Europe causes a feeling of distrust against anything we may recommend in concert with Russia. Convinced that Russia intends to attack it, the whole nation has resolved to offer the best resistance in its power, and that resistance will certainly be stubborn, though probably futile; but the Turks say that there would be less discredit in being driven by force from their territories than in being cajoled out of them. The Christian populations are as unanimously opposed to the threatened Russian aggression as the Turks, for they know it to be undertaken in the interest of a particular nationality which they dread, and at the same time despise." The writer added that, although the Marquis of Salisbury would report to his Lordship everything connected with the proceedings of the Conference, he thought it his duty to keep her Majesty's Government informed of the temper of the nation, which it was necessary to take into account if a successful issue was to be hoped for, and a knowledge of which, observed the Ambassador, with a significant glance at his colleague who had instantaneously become so cordial with General Ignatieff, could not well be obtained in a few days. Sir Henry believed from what he had learned that the Turkish Ministers would be found disposed to grant most of the desired concessions—those, that was to say, which came fairly within the limits of the bases upon which the Conference was accepted by them; but if measures were proposed which they would regard as contrary to the engagement that both the territorial integrity and the independence of the Porte should be respected, their resistance, according to this competent observer, whose forecastings were speedily realised as regarded the immediate contingency, would be very great, and probably insuperable.

In the meanwhile, both sides were busily arming. A large proportion of the Russian troops was mobilised; Prince Nicholas (brother of the Emperor) left St. Petersburg, about the close of November, to take command of the Army of the South; and the new loan, which did not prove very successful, was made for the present to furnish the necessary funds. Turkey also began to put herself in readiness for the contest which it was but too probable would break out in the ensuing spring, if not earlier; and thus the Conference which was to establish peace commenced with every indication of approaching war. As if to make more clearly manifest the determination of the Sultan to resist dictation, yet at the same time to follow the path of reform with energy and thoroughness, the post of Grand Vizier was now taken from Mehemet Ruchdi Pasha, and conferred on Midhat Pasha, a man of highly liberal views, and an administrator of great ability, yet a decided enemy to Russian intrigues. Midhat was opposed to granting special institutions to the Sclave provinces; but he had always advocated the equality of Mussulmans and Christians, and he wished for a constitutional control over the power of the Grand Vizier, as well as that of the Sultan. Perceiving the evils of excessive centralisation, he was in favour of giving the provincial populations much control over their local affairs, and was generally regarded as the hope of the Mussulman reformers and of the Christians.* Nevertheless, his strongly national feelings were a warrant that he would not obey foreign influence to any extent inconsistent with the dignity of the Empire. This was made perfectly clear to Lord Salisbury at an interview which he had with the new Grand Vizier on the 21st of December, when the appointment of an International Commission was firmly protested against, and it was intimated that any form of guarantee except the promise of the Sultan would be opposed. The first meeting of the plenary Conference took place on the 23rd; but, as the Turkish Plenipotentiaries had not yet received their instructions, the proceedings were purely formal. The occasion, however, was signalised by a remarkable event, which seems to have been dramatically timed to produce the greatest possible effect under existing circumstances.

Soon after the Plenipotentiaries had taken their places, salvoes of artillery were heard, and the chief representative of Turkey, Safvet Pasha, Minister for Foreign Affairs, informed the assembled statesmen that this was to proclaim the new Constitution which the Sultan had just conferred on the Empire. A copy of the document, in French, was at once transmitted by Sir Henry Elliot to Lord Derby. It revealed a truly noble scheme for the government of the Empire, though of course the very important questions remained, whether it would be honestly carried out, and whether the Ottoman race and its subject nationalities were capable of receiving and applying the political ideas of Western Europe. The Constitution started with the assertion that the Ottoman Empire, including its existing territories and possessions, and its semi-dependent provinces, formed an indivisible whole, from which no portion could be detached under any pretext whatever. The Sultan was to be a Constitutional Sovereign, irresponsible and inviolate. The liberty of his subjects was to be guaranteed by the laws. Islamism was, as formerly, to be the State religion; but all other faiths professed in the Empire were to be freely exercised, and to be protected in their privileges, on condition that public order and morality were not disturbed. The press, within strictly defined limits, was to be free, and education was to be carried out under State supervision. All subjects of the Sultan, whether Mussulman or Christian, were to be equal in the eye of the law, and alike eligible for public offices. Taxes were to be equally distributed, property was to be guaranteed, and the domicile was declared inviolable, except in cases legally prescribed. Torture and inquisition under any form were absolutely forbidden. The proceedings of the law-courts were to be public; prisoners might be defended by all lawful means; and the judges were to be irremovable. As in England, the Ministers were to be responsible to Parliament, and, on the Chamber of Deputies demanding their impeachment, they might be tried by the High Court of Justice. If they should be defeated in Parliament on any important question, the Sultan would change them, or appeal to the country. Public officials were not to be dismissed without legal and sufficient cause; yet they were not to shelter themselves under the orders of a superior, if they committed acts contrary to law. With respect to the Legislative Body, it was decreed that this should consist of a House of Lords, or Senate, and a Chamber of Deputies. For every fifty thousand inhabitants there was to be one deputy; the votes to be taken by ballot; general elections to recur every four years. The persons of the deputies were declared inviolate, except under certain conditions; provision was made for the government of the provinces by administrative councils; and the Constitution was not at any time to be changed without the sanction of both Chambers and the concurrence of the Sultan.

The chief features of this Constitution were admirable. They embodied the best elements of English and French constitutional law, and offered the most complete guarantees for the future progress of the Empire, provided only the Sultan was sincere in his

* Sir Henry Elliot to Lord Derby, December 19th, 1876.

reforming zeal, and the nation equal to the great destiny held out to it. But these, no doubt, were very serious provisos. Previous Sultans had introduced many other excellent reforms; but, although they had not been so completely violated as was frequently declared by political enemies, the acts were always imperfectly carried out, and Europe had been taught mistrust by numerous instances of bad faith. With respect to the capability of the Turks and their fellow-subjects to adopt a constitutional system, very little could be predicted. The experiment is one of a novel character, and there were but few precedents, as regards an Oriental people, to help the judgment to a satisfactory conclusion. The natural, or at least the acquired and hereditary, tendency of the Asiatic mind is towards despotism. Turks are Asiatics, overflowing into Europe, yet retaining their eastern characteristics but slightly impaired. So far, the conditions were against the problem; the past was a heavy drag upon the future. The diversity of races, the haughtiness of long predominance, the memory of old wrongs, the clash of rival religions, the mutual hatred of opposing fanaticisms—these also were rocks ahead in the track of the best-devised Parliamentary system. Yet the prospect was not altogether hopeless. The Turks, apart from official corruption, have many virtues. They are brave, strong, temperate, and in some respects high-minded; simple-living, grave, and self-reliant; humane, when not excited to frenzy (at which periods, no doubt, the old Tartar blood flames out in uncontrollable excesses); very capable of toleration, if not insulted or endangered on the score of their own faith; and possessed of a certain tranquil dignity, not at all ill-adapted to the forms of constitutional government. We are too apt to judge the whole Turkish people by the Pashas and office-holders whom we principally know, and who are often deeply stained by the worst vices of Oriental despotism. The humbler Ottoman is neither "unspeakable," according to Mr. Carlyle, nor "anti-human," as Mr. Gladstone would have us believe.* He is a man, with the virtues and the

PROCLAMATION OF THE CONSTITUTION AT CONSTANTINOPLE.

* The expression occurs in Mr. Gladstone's pamphlet, "Lessons in Massacre," and for a long time enjoyed considerable popularity in certain quarters. As a matter of immediate grammatical construction, it is applied to the Turkish Government; but it is evident from the context that the whole Turkish people are included.

faults of a conquering race. If his religion is narrow and restrictive, it is also deep and sincere; intense in its subjection of the individual to the will of the Divine Being, and open to many tender susceptibilities in the region of charity and mutual helpfulness. All this might do but little towards enabling the Turk to conquer the difficulties of the new future that was set before him; but it permitted some degree of hope. And it must not be forgotten that the Constitution, if successful, will in time cure, as nothing else can cure, the manifold evils from which Turkey has been suffering for centuries, and which Russia has made the pretext for continual interference. Misgovernment cannot long co-exist with the forms of Parliamentary life, supposing the system to be honestly worked. The objection to such institutions in the case of Turkey, that they will be merely an instrument in the hands of a Mohammedan majority, applies with equal force to every Empire where there is a dominant race, and a religion of the majority differing from that of the smaller number. It is the argument of the Irish against the Imperial Parliament of which they constitute a part. But it is the peculiar excellence of popular governments that in time they work themselves free of their own injustice and their own errors. We have seen this already in the West: let us hope, so long as hope is not impossible, that coming generations may see it in the East as well.

When the full Conference assembled, it consisted of eleven gentlemen, all of whom were persons of distinction in the councils of Europe. Germany, Italy, and Russia were represented by only one delegate each; England, France, Austria, and Turkey had each two representatives. The meetings took place at the Admiralty Palace, Constantinople, on the left bank of the inner Golden Horn, close to the Arsenal. The representatives of Turkey were Safvet and Edhem Pashas, the first of whom was Foreign Minister of the Porte, and formerly Ambassador at Paris during the reign of Napoleon III. Edhem Pasha also was high in the service of the Sultan, and had had personal experience of the nations of Western Europe. The French delegates were the Comte François de Bourgoing, the resident Ambassador at Constantinople, and the Comte de Chaudordy, who, during the siege of Paris, was the representative of the French Foreign Office in the Delegate Government established first at Tours, and afterwards at Bordeaux, and had therefore much to do in conducting the difficult negotiations of that time.

PRINCE GORTSCHAKOFF. GENERAL IGNATIEFF.

Germany was represented by Baron Werther, Ambassador to the Porte—a diplomatist of whom it was ominously recorded that he was Ambassador at Copenhagen before the Danish war, at Vienna previous to the brief struggle between Austria and Prussia, and at Paris before the outbreak of hostilities with Germany. Count Corti was the representative of Italy. The views of the Austro-Hungarian Monarchy were expounded by Count Zichy, a Hungarian nobleman, and Baron Calice, the Austrian diplomatic agent and consul-general in Roumania. Russia had an effective champion in General Ignatieff; and the dignity of England was sustained by the Marquis of Salisbury, her Special Plenipotentiary, and Sir Henry Elliot, the British Ambassador in Turkey. The Conference being held at Constantinople, Safvet Pasha, the senior Turkish delegate, acted as President.

At the first sitting of the plenary Conference, on the 23rd of December, the European representatives laid before those of Turkey the proposals for the better government of Bulgaria, Bosnia, and the Herzegovina, which had been settled at the preliminary meetings. The Turkish Plenipotentiaries read a long paper on the subject of the civil war in the provinces, against some portions of which, referring in laudatory terms to the conduct of the Turkish authorities in Bulgaria, Lord Salisbury thought it right to protest. The second meeting of the Conference, thus fully constituted, took place on the 28th of December, when the Servian and Montenegrin armistice was prolonged for two months, with the concurrence of General Ignatieff. The proposals of the Six Powers were then considered in a discussion which lasted four hours. The Turkish Ministers took everything *ad referendum*, but in the meanwhile raised objections to all the proposals. It cannot be doubted that their dislike of the suggested reforms was greatly increased by the affront to Turkey involved in the fact of the scheme having been first elaborated at a series of meetings from which, though held in her own capital, and dealing with the affairs of her own Empire, she was herself excluded. On the 30th of December the delegates met again, and the representatives of the Porte then stated that they had counter-proposals to present, which were not at the moment ready for production. General Ignatieff urged them to give a definite answer to the terms submitted by the Powers, and read a telegram from Prince Gortschakoff, stating that he had accepted an irreducible minimum of concessions. The Turkish counter-project was communicated to the Ministers of the Six Powers after the sitting had broken up. It consisted of an elaborate plan for the local government of the provincial communes by councils elected by the people, for the reform of various abuses, and for the suppression of tithes, and of the system of farming the taxes. The details were considered at a meeting of the Plenipotentiaries of the Six Powers on the 31st of December; but the suggestions met with no favour.

An agreement was evidently most improbable. The Sultan was as little inclined to yield as Midhat Pasha, or any of his colleagues, and, in an interview with the Marquis of Salisbury on the 26th of December, dwelt much on the indignation which any concession would arouse among his people, adding that his own life was in danger. The English Plenipotentiary took this opportunity of fulfilling certain instructions he had received from Lord Derby, and, alluding to the feeling of abhorrence which had been excited in England by the crimes committed in Bulgaria (so called), represented to his Majesty how great was the sentiment of indignation at the impunity of the chief offenders. The neglect to punish such heinous crimes was characterised by the Marquis as a fatal obstacle to the renewal of those cordial feelings which had once existed between England and Turkey. The Sultan, in reply, contented himself with charging Russia with the responsibility for what had taken place during the suppression of the insurrection; and he hazarded a shrewd guess that the alienation of a large part of the English people was due rather to the partial repudiation of the Turkish debt than to the massacre of the Bulgarians. In the course of this interview, Abdul-Hamid laid much stress on a law to which he had assented, and by which the partial repudiation of the previous year had been repealed, though it had not at that time been possible to make any provision for the payment of the debt. On the same day (December 26th), Safvet Pasha wrote to the Turkish Ambassador in London a despatch indicating the chief features of the new Constitution, and insisting that it was in itself a sufficient guarantee of the reforms which it was intended to carry out.

The relations between the Sultan and the English Government were becoming almost antagonistic, and Lord Salisbury did his utmost to widen the breach. He seemed to consider that the chief part of his business was to threaten and intimidate the Porte, and he was annoyed that the Porte would not be intimidated. On the 25th of December, he telegraphed to the Earl of Derby that Admiral Drummond had found it necessary to leave Besika Bay, and that he had requested him to take the fleet to Athens instead of Salonica, in order to avoid misconstruction, and to support his assertion that no assistance was to be expected from her Majesty's Government. On the following day, Lord Derby signalised his approval of this course; and the year closed in the midst of gloomy anticipations which the ensuing months did not fail to realise. In the final days of December, Odian Effendi, Under-Secretary of State in the Department of Public Works, was sent as a special envoy to England, to give full explanations on the existing posture of affairs. But the autumn meetings had now done their work, and the Government had resolved that, if Russia desired to attack Turkey, she was at liberty to do so.

CHAPTER VIII.

Opening of the Year 1877—Fourth Plenary Meeting of the Conference—Refusal of the Turks to discuss the Chief Proposals of the Ambassadors—Interview of Lord Salisbury with the Grand Vizier—Resort to the Language of Intimidation—Statement by Midhat Pasha of the Reasons why the Sultan could not accede to the Demands of the Powers—Counter-Proposals of the Turkish Minister—Odian Effendi, Special Envoy to London—Sittings of the Conference on the 4th, 8th, and 11th of January—Complaints of the Turkish Plenipotentiaries that the demands of the Powers exceeded the Bases of the English Programme—Ineffectual Attempt to answer their Arguments—Considerable Reduction in the Terms proposed by the Six Powers—Meeting of the 15th of January—Warnings by the Marquis of Salisbury—The New Proposals—Commissions of Control still to be retained—Ineffectual Nature of the Guarantee—Ninth Meeting of the Conference, on the 20th of January—Final Decision of the Porte—Speech of the Russian Minister—Termination of the Conference, and Departure of the Ambassadors—Russian Military Preparations and Financial Embarrassments—Money Troubles in Turkey—Popular Feeling in the Ottoman Empire—Debate in the Grand Council—Hungarian Sympathy with Turkey, and its Causes—Deputation of Hungarian Students to Constantinople—Dilatory Proceedings of the Turkish Government with reference to the Perpetrators of the Bulgarian Massacres—Mr. Gladstone's Pamphlet, "Lessons in Massacre"—Characteristic Exaggerations—Acts of Reparation in the Philippopolis District—Failure of Justice—The Elections under the New Constitution—Fall of Midhat Pasha.

NOTHING could be more gloomy than the prospects of 1877 on the opening day of that year. Russia was committed to a policy of aggression; Turkey was committed to a policy of defiance; England had gone far in a policy of equivocation and menace, which was helping on the designs of the Czar; and the other Powers were awaiting the turn of events, with an air of languor which in some was impotence, and in some was mischief. The fourth plenary meeting of the Conference took place on the 1st of January, when Lord Salisbury expressed his regret that the Turkish Plenipotentiaries had altogether rejected the essential principles of the proposals brought forward by the Powers. He urged them to consider the danger of the position in which Turkey was placed, and stated that the Ambassadors were prepared to discuss the bases which they had recommended for acceptance. All the other foreign representatives adhered to these views; but the Turkish Plenipotentiaries replied that they were not empowered even to discuss the nine following points: viz., the Commission of Supervision; the employment of a foreign gendarmerie; the cantonment of the troops in the fortresses and chief towns; the mode of nominating the Valis; the administrative divisions of the provinces; the encouragement to be given to the Circassians to emigrate to Asia; the judicial arrangements; the financial arrangements; and the rectification of the Montenegrin and Servian frontiers. The Conference thereupon adjourned to the 4th inst., and Lord Salisbury then called on the Grand Vizier, that he might represent to him the extreme danger of the course on which the Turkish Government had entered. The weapon of intimidation was to be employed with great urgency, and the fears of the Porte were to be aroused by the most powerful stimulant that it was within the capacity of the Indian Secretary to apply.

The Marquis pointed out to Midhat Pasha that Turkey stood absolutely alone, and that several other Powers might very probably take part in aggressive operations when the campaign had once begun. "I recalled to his Highness's memory," wrote Lord Salisbury to the Foreign Minister, "the fatal events of 1827–28, and the danger that at least a portion of them might be repeated, and urged upon him that earlier concessions on the part of Sultan Mahmud would probably have preserved Greece as an integral part of the Turkish Empire. I warned him in earnest language against renewing the errors of that period. He stated that he was resigned to the will of God, if it was decreed that the Empire should fall, but that no Turk would yield any one of the nine points which are enumerated in my previous despatch of this date, and which I read over to him. I intimated the possibility of an arrangement being come to in regard to the gendarmerie, if the Porte would undertake to form a corps with foreign officers; but his objection was not so much to the substance of the proposal as to entering into an engagement to carry it out. I gathered that his Highness's strongest objection would be to the nomination of the Valis, with the consent of the Powers, for five years, which he professed to think would lead to the growth of new tributary States." There can be no question that Midhat's objection was well-founded, and that this was the very result contemplated and desired by Russia, if not by the other Powers. Lord Derby, however, conveyed to the Marquis of Salisbury the approval of her Majesty's Government as to the language employed by him on the 1st of January.

Turkey was assuming the high ground of national independence—the only ground on which a nation can either stand with success or fall with dignity. Her attitude was the more courageous because her eyes were fully open to the serious dangers she was incurring. In an interview with Sir Henry Elliot on the 28th of December, 1876, Midhat Pasha admitted that war might be nearly the destruction of the Empire, but added that the country was unanimous in preferring the chance of honourable ruin to the acceptance of conditions which were considered dishonourable, and at the same time fatal. Russia, he said, was aiming at the creation of small autonomous States; and if the Ottoman troops, as regarded Bosnia and Bulgaria, were confined to the fortresses and principal towns, the same result would ensue that had already occurred in Servia: the Turks would be expelled from the province, and a state of quasi-independence would be established. With respect to the introduction of a corps of foreign troops, Midhat Pasha said that the Turkish Minister at Brussels had reported that the Belgian Government would not send such a corps, unless upon the direct invitation of the Porte, and that invitation would never be given at the dictation of foreign Powers. The Sultan, however, was quite ready to engage foreign officers, non-commissioned officers, and men, to organise an efficient gendarmerie; but they must be in the service of the Ottoman Government. The Grand Vizier proposed that a fixed time, such as a year, should be granted to the Porte for carrying out the reforms then being inaugurated, and that the Ambassadors should at the end of that period report whether or not they were being fairly executed. Supposing their decision to be in the negative, the Porte would submit to the appointment of an International Commission, or any other form of control that might be held desirable. The proposal was fair, and involved no inconsiderable concession on the part of an old and haughty Empire; but it was not accepted, because the object of Russia was to break down the independence of the Porte with as little delay as possible, and the other Powers were determined to abet the design.

Odian Effendi, the Special Envoy from Constantinople, reached London at the beginning of 1877, and, in company with Musurus Pasha, the resident Turkish Ambassador, had an interview with Lord Derby on the 4th of January. On this occasion, the envoy repeated the determination of Turkey not to accept the terms suggested by the Six Powers, and the Foreign Secretary again insisted on the necessity of obtaining guarantees, in consequence of the neglect of the Turkish Government to fulfil its former promises. The possibility and even probability of war were clearly contemplated by Musurus Pasha and Odian Effendi; but they said that the Sultan could not submit without a struggle. Turkey had 600,000 men under arms, and was not afraid to risk a campaign with Russia, should that become inevitable. Four days later, Odian Effendi—who is a Christian and an Armenian—called on Lord Beaconsfield, probably hoping that he should obtain from the known Turkish sympathies of the Premier some more comforting assurances than he had derived from the Foreign Secretary. Lord Beaconsfield, however, while professing his strong desire that Turkey should retain her place in the European system, declined to enter into anything like a discussion of the points at issue, because they were then being debated at Constantinople, and could not be negotiated in two places at the same time. He strongly advised the Porte not to reject the proposed terms; but Odian Effendi reiterated his objections, and then proceeded to make a proposal by which he thought the several difficulties might be overcome. Why, he asked, should not the new Constitution be embodied in a protocol, and placed under an European guarantee, thus giving to the Powers the right to interfere on behalf of any portion of the Sultan's subjects who might afterwards suffer from misgovernment? The special constitution granted to the Lebanon was secured by no other guarantee; and, argued Odian Effendi, it had never been alleged that the Porte had failed to fulfil its engagements in that respect. The suggestion was not a wise one, because it conceded the very principle of foreign interference, resistance to which formed the only reasonable ground for the existing Turkish policy.

Meanwhile, the Conference continued its sittings, and on the 4th of January the Turkish Ministers read a long and very elaborate statement of the reasons why the Porte could not accede to the proposals of the Six Powers. In addition to these reasons—which had reference to the independence of the Ottoman Empire, and to the impracticable, injudicious, or unconstitutional character of some of the desired reforms—the two Pashas contended that the proposals now put forth exceeded the bases of the Conference as laid down by the British Government. At the next sitting, on the 8th of January, the Italian Ambassador, Count Corti, replied on behalf of the Powers on the general grounds taken up by the Turkish representatives, while Lord Salisbury undertook to show that the original bases had not been transgressed. The chief point at issue had reference to the question of guarantees; the foreign Plenipotentiaries contending that something more than a mere promise of reform was needed, and the Turkish representatives maintaining that the Constitution was guarantee sufficient. The seventh sitting took place on the 11th of the month, when Lord Salisbury pointed out that the institution of local Commissions, composed of Mussulmans and Christians, charged with superintending the execution of the reforms in Bosnia and the Herzegovina, had been accepted by the Porte in the circular of February 13th, 1876, in reply to the Andrassy Note. The Ottoman Plenipotentiaries had already declared that, in order not to appear to depart from the principle of that circular, they would accept the appointment of the Commissions for Bosnia and Herzegovina, although they did not see the necessity for them under the altered circumstances of the time. But it was now argued by Safvet and Edhem Pashas that between the Commissions thus granted, the members of which were to be appointed by the Porte, and Commissions whose members were to be appointed by foreign Powers, there was an essential and absolute difference. With a perfectly unanswerable appeal to facts, the Turkish Plenipotentiaries pointed out that the English programme did not speak of guarantees to be furnished by the Imperial Government to the Powers, or to the populations through the medium of those Powers: what it demanded was the concession of a system of institutions which should give the populations a control over their local affairs, and furnish some protection against acts of arbitrary authority. The representatives of the Porte, therefore, could not agree to an arrangement which it was impossible to harmonize, either in principle or in form, with the Treaty of Paris, the English programme, or the new situation resulting from the Constitution just conferred upon the Empire.

That there had been a departure from the terms of the English programme was indeed a fact so glaring that the Marquis of Salisbury, at the previous sitting, had been compelled, though with manifest reluctance, to admit it; yet in the same breath he contended, with helpless self-contradiction; that the foreign Commission came properly within the scope of the English programme, although that programme made no mention whatever of any such Commission, but most distinctly stated that the guarantees were to consist of institutions for local self-government, to be granted by the Porte to Bosnia, Herzegovina, and Bulgaria. Such institutions had by this time been conferred on those provinces by the Constitution, together with an Imperial Parliament, which rendered their stability more certain. An attempt was made to show that the question of guarantees was to be interpreted by the terms of the Andrassy Note, which had been accepted by the Porte, and was included in the English bases. But this did not help the matter in the least; for the Commission proposed by the Austrian Chancellor was "a Commission of notables of the country, composed half of Mussulmans, half of Christians, and elected by the inhabitants of the province, according to a system to be settled by the Sublime Porte." Russia very probably hoped to turn this mixed Commission to her own account by influencing the elections through her multifarious agencies, and the proposal may have been nothing better than a concealed attempt at interference; yet in principle it was totally distinct from the later suggestion, which was first clearly expressed in the Berlin Memorandum of May 13th, 1876—a document to which the English Government refused its assent. The proposal of a foreign Commission, by which the authority of the Sultan in his own dominions would be controlled by the representatives of the Six Powers, was therefore a manifest and essential departure from the English programme, and a breach of faith with Turkey.*

The Ottoman Plenipotentiaries had so completely the best of the argument that the foreign Ministers began to see the urgent necessity of bringing the discussion to a close. They therefore determined, at a meeting held on the 12th of January, to make a final communication to the Turkish delegates on the 15th, and to demand a categorical reply. For some time past, they had been considering the

* The records of these transactions are to be found in the "Correspondence respecting the Conference at Constantinople and the Affairs of Turkey: 1876–77" (Blue Book on Turkey, No. 2, 1877). They redound but little to the credit of her Majesty's Government.

advisability of reducing their terms, in the hope that the Porte might thus be persuaded to yield. General Ignatieff had exhibited a very eager desire that the Six Powers should combine in presenting a species of ultimatum, containing a summary statement of the least they would accept; and, to procure unanimity, he had progressively lowered his standard of what was indispensable. The foreign Plenipotentiaries now agreed upon an amended

THE ADMIRALTY PALACE, CONSTANTINOPLE, IN WHICH THE CONFERENCE WAS HELD.

scheme, from which were excluded the four following demands:—1. That a foreign gendarmerie should be appointed. 2. That the Turkish troops should be confined to the fortresses and the chief cities. 3. That the frontiers and geographical divisions of Bulgaria should be re-arranged. 4. That the Governors of provinces should be Christians. When the Plenipotentiaries met for the eighth time on the 15th of January, Lord Salisbury said that he and the other Ambassadors had decided to submit a summary of their modified recommendations for the acceptance of the Sublime Porte; but he added:—"It is my duty to free her Majesty's Government of all responsibility for what may happen, and I am therefore instructed to declare formally that Great Britain is resolved not to give her sanction either to maladministration or to oppression, and that if the Porte, from obstinacy or inactivity, offers resistance to the efforts now being made to place the Ottoman Empire on a more sure basis, the responsibility of the consequences will rest solely on the Sultan and his advisers. In communicating to your Excellencies this modified summary, I am moreover authorised by the Plenipotentiaries to declare that it is the final communication which will be made to you by us, and that if the principles of our proposals are not accepted at the Conference which is to meet on the 18th instant, the representatives of the Six Powers will consider the Conference at an end, and will leave Constantinople according to the instructions that they have received." His Lordship then read the text of the proposals previously adopted by the representatives of the Guaranteeing Powers. It was here suggested that the frontiers of Montenegro should be rectified, with certain additions; that an international Commission of delimitation should be appointed; that

THE "AT-MEIDAN," OR ANCIENT HIPPODROME, CONSTANTINOPLE.

the free navigation of the Boïana should be established, with the neutrality of the forts on that river; that, with respect to Servia, the *status quo ante bellum* should be restored, with a settlement of the boundary difficulties on the side of Bosnia by a Commission of Arbitration; that the Ottoman troops should evacuate the territories of which they held possession in both principalities, should exchange prisoners of war, and should proclaim an amnesty for subjects employed in the enemy's service; that, as regarded Bosnia, Herzegovina, and Bulgaria, the Governors-General (Valis) of the provinces should be named for the first five years by the Porte, with the agreement of the Powers; and that, in various ways which were specifically mentioned, provision should be made within three months for the local self-government of those provinces, for the abolition of tax-farming, for the better administration of justice, for the entire freedom of worship, and for ameliorating the condition of the agricultural classes. The representatives of the Powers had thus receded very considerably from their original proposals; but the conditions to which the Porte principally objected still remained. Besides the provision with respect to the Valis, two Commissions of Control were to be nominated by the Powers to watch over the execution of the new regulations, and to assist the local authorities in the different measures respecting order and public security. These Commissions were to receive special instructions from the Governments of the six countries by which they would be appointed; and it was impossible, by any amount of honeyed phrases, to conceal the fact that they involved a supplanting of the authority of the Sultan in his own Empire. Even had the demand been granted, it could not have led to any good results. To say nothing of the very great probability that the Powers would ere long have quarrelled among themselves as to the degree of interference to be exercised, it is evident that the Commissions could not guarantee the execution of the desired reforms any longer than they themselves continued in force. It was pretended that they were only designed to fill up the interval of time between the promulgation of the new Constitution and its effective organization. But if the bad faith of the Porte was equal to what the Six Powers invariably represented, the Constitution itself might have been swept away as soon as the International Commissions were removed. The more it is examined, the more difficult it is to perceive how such a proposal could have had any other effect than to irritate the Turkish Government and people, without rendering the better government of the country more certain in the future.

The ninth meeting of the Conference, appointed for the 18th of January, did not take place until the 20th, owing to the Turkish Plenipotentiaries requiring more time for the consideration of their final answer. When, on the latter of those days, the representatives of the several Powers reassembled at the Admiralty Palace, Safvet Pasha read a long address, in which he recapitulated the objections entertained by the Porte to the particular guarantees required, but added that, having regard to the gravity of the situation, and in order to avoid exposing themselves to the charge of being guided solely by personal feelings, the Sultan and his Ministers had thought it necessary to appeal, as was usual in such cases, to the judgment and opinions of an Extraordinary General Council. This Council, which was summoned by an Imperial Iradé, met on the 18th of January, and was composed of about two hundred persons, comprising representatives of all classes of Ottoman subjects, and of the various religious bodies. The great questions at issue were discussed with much deliberation; and the result was that the Council pronounced unanimously against the acceptance of the two points having reference to the Commissions of Control, and to the appointment of the Governors-General with the approval of the Guaranteeing Powers. The Sultan nevertheless desired to find some means which would establish an accord between himself and the Western Governments; and he had determined to extend the institution of the Commissions, suggested by Count Andrassy for Bosnia and Herzegovina, to other parts of the Empire. It was consequently proposed that two Commissions, formed equally of Christians and Mussulmans, should be freely elected by the population for a year, and placed under the presidency of a High Commissioner appointed by the Imperial Government. The duties of these bodies would be to superintend the execution of the Constitutional reforms, and to adopt and control the measures necessary for the good government of the provinces, and for the complete security of the inhabitants by means of the gendarmerie to be established by the Porte. Several of the proposed reforms urged by the Marquis of Salisbury were fully accepted by the Turkish Government; some, indeed, were already included in the Constitution, or sanctioned by the laws. "Such," concluded Safvet Pasha, "being in reality the state of the question, the Ottoman Plenipotentiaries are unwilling to believe that the representatives of the Six Powers absolutely insist on retaining in their programme the two points which, without having reference to the whole of the reforms which are to be inaugurated, prevent the discussion of questions of practical utility."

A discussion followed, remarkable chiefly for the haughty tone assumed by General Ignatieff. "The Government of the Sultan," he said, "itself impairs the nature of its relations with the Great Powers, and endangers its right to claim their support, and the benefit of the guarantee acquired by the Treaty [of 1856]. It also assumes the sole responsibility of the serious consequences which may result from this course of action. On this head I think it, therefore, right to declare at once that if, in consequence of the rupture of the negotiations for peace, hostilities against Servia or Montenegro, the recurrence of which the Powers had hoped to prevent, were recommenced, or if the security of the Christians were seriously compromised in the provinces of the interior, or in any of the seaboard towns, the Imperial Government which I have the honour to represent would consider such an eventuality as a defiance of Europe." General Ignatieff then proceeded to add a few words of caution. He said that during the preliminary sittings the people of Thessaly, of Epirus, and of Crete, had brought before the notice of the Plenipotentiaries the several abuses of power from which they suffered. He felt it would not be possible to pass over those claims in silence, and accordingly, on behalf of himself and of the other representatives, called the most serious attention of the Porte to the situation of all the Christian populations of the Empire. Referring to the Constitution, he warned the Turkish Government against possible infringements of the Hatti-Sherif of 1856, and of the ordinances contained in the Firman of the 12th of December, 1875, which would constitute a violation of the engagements entered into with Europe. Particular care should be taken to maintain intact the ancient privileges and immunities conferred upon the Christian communities; and the Porte should make provision for satisfying the holders of Turkish bonds. Throughout his address, General Ignatieff adopted a style as if he were issuing commands to a vassal. Safvet Pasha said but little in reply, and, after a somewhat desultory conversation, the Plenipotentiaries of the Six Powers expressed their opinion that nothing would be gained by prolonging the discussion. The sitting accordingly broke up, and the Conference was virtually at an end.

A final meeting of the representatives of the Six Powers took place at the Austrian Embassy on the evening of Sunday, the 21st of January. Its object was simply that the protocol of the meeting on the previous day should be duly signed. The Ottoman Plenipotentiaries had agreed to be present; but they did not come, nor did they send any excuse for their absence. It was a singular and rather dramatic scene. While the signatures were being attached, a grand ball was going on in another room close by. The time was hardly one for festivity, and the ball may perhaps have been the reason why the Turkish Plenipotentiaries failed to attend. All the Ottoman officials were apparently delighted at the conclusion of the Conference and the approaching departure of the Ambassadors. That departure took place very shortly. Lord Salisbury sailed on the 23rd of January for Athens; but General Ignatieff was compelled to postpone his departure for a while, on account of the tempestuous weather which at that time prevailed in the Black Sea. The Sultan was reported to be indisposed, and therefore unable to receive the Ambassadors previous to their leaving. It is probable that he was glad to avail himself of any excuse for avoiding an interview which must have been embarrassing, and which could have answered no purpose. Most of the foreign representatives applied to his Majesty for a reception; but Lord Salisbury and General Ignatieff were not amongst the number. "May the grace of Allah go with them!" is said to have been the exclamation of a leading Turkish Minister. It is easy to understand that the departure of the Ambassadors was an immense relief to the minds of the Turkish people generally. The questions involved had in effect long passed beyond the stage to which they had been somewhat arbitrarily brought. The discussions in Congress only embittered what they could not cure. By bad management, by false assumptions, by impracticable attempts, and by the gradual kindling of passions which were excited by the very endeavours to allay them, two Empires had been brought to the very verge of war; and if there was still any probability of that issue being averted, such an event was more likely to ensue after the Plenipotentiaries had withdrawn than before. Turkish pride was being perpetually wounded by the dictatorial manner which the foreign Ministers lost no opportunity of making manifest; and it was as well that there should be some means of reconsidering the whole matter in an atmosphere less heated than that of the council-chamber. The discussion now reverted to its more ordinary phases, and the possibility of peace being yet preserved seemed not altogether to have vanished.

The prospect of war breaking out sooner or later was nevertheless so apparent to the Russian authorities that military preparations were pushed forward with as much urgency as if a campaign were on the very eve of commencing. Some difficulty was experienced, owing to want of funds; for the financial resources of Russia are not great, and her credit in the money markets of the world is almost as low as that of Turkey. But when a country is resolved on war, the means of carrying it on are always forthcoming. A reserve of 60,000 men was organized for the army in Bessarabia while the Conference was yet sitting, and mobilisation was gradually extended to districts not included in the original decree. Schools and prisons at Odessa and in the neighbouring towns were diverted from their ordinary purposes, and appropriated to the army and sanitary departments. The usual hardships resulting from a state of war, and even from the preparations for war, began at once to be felt. The prices of nearly all necessaries ran up with alarming rapidity. The municipality of Odessa, one of the richest cities in the Empire, was unable to pay the salaries of its officials. New Customs regulations, making import duties payable in gold instead of currency, raised the price of commodities five-and-twenty per cent., if not more. Trade suffered in consequence; imports dropped to half what they had been in 1875; and several bankruptcies were announced. Other circumstances concurred to hamper the movements of the Russian army in the south. Very speedily it became apparent that the military administration was exceedingly corrupt. Frauds and impositions were discovered from day to day, and it was evident that the troops would not be ready to move for some months. The new organization of the army broke down on the first strain. The weather, moreover, was extremely discouraging. Heavy rain fell in Roumania, through which the invaders from the North would have to make their way to the banks of the Danube. Nothing could surpass the wretched condition of the roads, which the long-continued wet had turned into swamps; and diphtheria, fever, and ague prevailed in the low-lying countries to such an extent that the Russian army, had it made an advance at that season, would have lost a large proportion of its number by disease.

The Turks were equally unfit for active conflict. Unable to meet the necessities of the time in any other way, the Government issued an additional three millions of Turkish pounds in *kaimes* (or in convertible paper currency), which raised the total of paper money afloat to six millions Turkish. This almost produced a panic. The *kaimes* were at once so seriously depreciated that prices were greatly enhanced, and several bakers and other tradesmen, dreading to receive the almost worthless notes of the Government, yet not being allowed by law to refuse them, closed their shops altogether. It was very advisable, if possible, that the Porte should restore its credit abroad; and with this view the decree of the 6th of October, 1875, by which the payment of half the interest on the Turkish debt had been postponed for five years, was definitively withdrawn. The measure, however, did not have the desired effect. Turkish solvency was still considered a doubtful matter, and the Exchequer was compelled to depend chiefly on its paper issues. The war feeling, nevertheless, was very strong. In the early part of January, the inhabitants of Adrianople, both Greek and Turkish, asked the authorisation of the Government to take up arms against the common enemy, as they called the Russians. Upwards of 40,000 Greek inhabitants of Philippopolis telegraphed to their delegates in Constantinople, directing them to submit to the Plenipotentiaries at the Conference a formal protest against assimilation with the Bulgarians; and it was even stated that for some time past Hellenic committees had been making preparations for raising insurrections in Thrace, Macedonia, Thessaly, Epirus, and other places, in case the Porte should grant special rights to the Sclaves. The feeling of the Greeks is not difficult to explain. They were highly indignant at the proposal of the Six Powers, at the instigation of Russia, to include within the administrative boundaries of Bulgaria a large part of Roumelia containing a considerable Greek population. The Hellenes regard the Bulgarians with the utmost contempt, as a dull, unintellectual set of agriculturists; and it mortally offended their pride of race that there should be any idea of merging them in communities to which they believed themselves vastly superior. Among the Turks there was even a passionate eagerness for war. They relied on their ability to conquer, and were impressed with the conviction that, even should they fail, it would be better to die sword in hand than to purchase a disgraceful reprieve by concessions which carried with them the certainty of ruin at no distant date.

This sentiment was very strongly displayed at the Grand Council of Ministers and Dignitaries to which was submitted the grave and difficult question whether or not the Porte should yield to the demands of the Powers with respect to the International Commissions and the appointment of the Governors-General. On the various functionaries assembling, a document, tracing the history of the existing troubles from the outbreak in the Herzegovina downwards, was read by the

Grand Referendary of the Ministry for Foreign Affairs. The reading lasted three hours, and Midhat Pasha then delivered a long speech, in which, after explaining the position of affairs as they stood, he dwelt with great emphasis on the possibility of war, the horrors attending it, the injury to the internal affairs of the country which it would involve, the want of funds necessary to an efficient prosecution of hostilities, and the inability of Turkey to obtain allies. Austria, he admitted, seemed to be neutral; but it was to be feared that she would not long be able to resist the demands of her Sclavonic subjects. Such were the dangers of a policy of resistance: on the other hand, if they accepted the proposals of the European Powers, they must consider their independence sacrificed. One of the most successful harangues of the occasion was that of the Armenian Patriarch. It is said that his earnest and impassioned words drew tears from many of the auditors, and loud expressions of assent rang through the chamber as this venerable ecclesiastic—the head of the Armenian Christians—spoke in favour of resisting the demands of Russia. He said that the question at stake was not one of religion, but of nationality. Christians, he remarked, were free to go to their churches, and Mohammedans to their mosques; but all Ottomans were equally bound to defend the country. This was the general sentiment of the assemblage—of the Christians and Israelites, as well as of the Mussulmans. Only one speaker—the chief of the Protestant community—advised an acceptance of the terms proposed at the Conference. With this single exception, the European demands were unanimously rejected. After the decision, Midhat Pasha asked whether the Sublime Porte might enter into negotiations with the Powers respecting the rejected points. The Grand Council answered in the negative, declaring that the discussion could only be further carried on in regard to the counter-proposals of the Turks.

The Government of the Sultan was indeed finding support in many quarters—in some, even, that were beyond its own jurisdiction. Hungary was enthusiastically in favour of Turkey, and its attitude on the subject had considerable influence on the policy of the Austrian Empire. It is more than probable that the Emperor Francis Joseph was personally well inclined to support the designs of the Czar, and that the three Northern monarchs were in perfect accord as to the programme in agreement with which the map of Europe was to be remodelled for their mutual benefit. Hence the Triple Alliance of which so much has been said, though so little is known as to its exact nature. The Sclavonic element in the Austrian dominions—a very large and important element—was also naturally disposed to sympathise with the Sclaves of Turkey, though perhaps not to the extent of desiring the further aggrandizement of Russia. But Hungary was thoroughly Turkish in her leanings, and this fact seems at times to have swayed the policy of Count Andrassy, while incapable of giving it an entirely different direction. That the Hungarians should feel bitterly towards Russia, and cordially towards Turkey, will surprise no one who is acquainted with the facts. When Hungary rose in arms against the illegal violence of the Kaiser, in 1848–9, she defeated the Imperial troops on so many occasions that the independence of the country was all but established. Austria was clearly overmatched, and would probably have been obliged to recognize the separate existence of Hungary, or at any rate her Legislative and Ministerial autonomy (which was all that was at first demanded, and which rested on the most indisputable historic basis), had not Russia come to the assistance of the Vienna tyranny. By the help of the Czar and his troops, Hungary was crushed, and for nearly eighteen years suffered the unmitigated oppression of a despotism from which she would otherwise have freed herself. The constitutional rights of that interesting land were not restored until the early part of 1867, and the dreary interval was due in no small measure to the dynastic sympathies of that same Emperor Nicholas who a few years later had the audacity to propose to the English Ambassador at St. Petersburg that England and Russia should partition the Turkish Empire. On this account, Hungary has a memory of hatred towards Muscovy: she has also a memory of gratitude towards the Ottomans. The war of independence having reached its disastrous close in the autumn of 1849, several of the military and political leaders escaped into Turkey, the Government of which refused to give them up at the united demand of Austria and Russia. As a species of compromise, and in order to avoid a war which he was in no condition to meet, the Sultan Abdul-Medjid kept Kossuth and his companions confined in fortresses until August, 1851, when, by the intervention of England and the United States, though in defiance of the threats of Austria, they were released. But their captivity was of an honourable character, and it saved them from the vengeance of exasperated autocrats.

In January, 1877, Hungarian feeling in favour of Turkey was made manifest by a deputation of twelve young students from Pesth, who presented a sword of honour to the Turkish Commander-in-Chief, the Sirdar Ekram. The students, who in honour of their Mohammedan hosts had at first adopted the fez, now appeared in their picturesque national costume, with plumed hats and furred mantles. Arranging themselves in a semi-circle opposite the Sirdar, they deputed one of their number to address that functionary. The orator thus selected observed that in 1849 Turkey was the only nation which protected Hungarian refugees after their reverses. The assassin of Poland, he continued, was now about to oppress the nationalities of the Carpathians and the Balkans; and on this account the Hungarians hailed the victors of Djunis (one of the great battles with the Servians in the previous year) as their defenders. The blade of the sabre which was then presented had once belonged to Maria Theresa; the scabbard, which was new, was adorned with figures representing a Turk and a Hungarian trampling down the Russian Hydra. The reply to the deputation was delivered by Safvet Pasha. Alluding to a remark by the leader of the party, to the effect that the Hungarians and the Turks had a common ancestry (which is no doubt ethnologically true to a considerable extent), Safvet said:—"We curse the memory of those who were guilty of the former fratricidal wars between the Turks and Hungarians. If we had been united, perhaps Europe would be differently constituted. It is a pity that Islamism forbids us to send out missionaries. If in old days the Turks had tried to make proselytes, the Hungarians and Turks would now be of one religion." The visit of the Hungarian deputation gave great satisfaction at the Ottoman capital, where it may perhaps have been credited with greater importance than it really possessed. But Hungary was certainly in earnest in her support of Turkey. General Klapka inspected the stores and arsenals, at the request of the Government; and Kossuth, replying to a deputation at Barracone, in Italy, said that the real object of Russia was the formation of small semi-independent States which would in truth be her docile instruments, and enable her to extend her power to the Adriatic.

CLOSING SCENE OF THE CONFERENCE: SAFVET PASHA REJECTING THE ULTIMATUM.

While these matters were going on, the Porte was acquiring fresh discredit among the nations of the West by its neglect to punish the persons chiefly concerned in the Bulgarian massacres. Shefket Pasha, one of those officers to whom Mr. Baring alluded with particular severity, was still at large, and said to be defying the agents of the law to interfere with him, as he had in his pocket evidence that whatever was done by the troops in the revolted districts had been previously ordered by the Government. The Commission under Sadoullah Bey, for inquiring into the outrages, had not pronounced a single sentence up to the beginning of November, 1876; and at the commencement of 1877 the Western Powers were still complaining of shameful dilatoriness, and even of the direct miscarriage of justice. The trial of Achmet Agha, and of others implicated in the horrors of Batak, dragged on for many months, by a resort to interminable quibbles; and Shefket Pasha was ultimately acquitted. Lord Salisbury entered a strong protest against this acquittal, and the Grand Vizier promised a new trial; but not many months elapsed before the Pasha held a command in the armies appointed to resist the Russian invasion. It was these perversions of justice which induced Mr. Gladstone, in March, to issue another pamphlet, to which he gave the title of "Lessons in Massacre." The object was to draw into a focus all the chief crimes committed by the Turkish Government or its agents since the first Bulgarian atrocities. He declared that these acts formed part and parcel of one long scheme of deliberate wickedness, and expressed his belief that the lesson which they were intended to convey was, "Do it again." The pamphleteer proceeded to observe that the lesson was conveyed as plainly to the Mohammedan populations of Turkey as if it had been set forth expressly in a Firman of the Sultan or a Fetwa of the Sheikh-ul-Islam. Assuming the absolute truth of everything said against the Ottomans, and the absolute falsity of everything said in their favour, or in mitigation of their crimes—in other words, begging the whole question in the spirit of an advocate who by some unfortunate mistake has been allowed to arrogate to himself the position

PRESENTATION OF A SWORD OF HONOUR TO ABDUL KERIM PASHA.

of a judge—Mr. Gladstone came to the conclusion that, even were the Turks to alter the character of their proceedings, it was far too late. The Turkish Government was "the great anti-human specimen of humanity." It had said, with Satan, "Evil, be thou my good!" To write this even of a Government is perhaps carrying invective a little too far; but from several passages it is evident that Mr. Gladstone makes no distinction between the Turkish Ministers and the Turkish people. In his eyes they are all alike Satanic. Pursuing his theme with a certain zest of indignation, Mr. Gladstone said:—

"All the acts, and all the non-acts, of the Turkish Government, before the rising, when we knew them scantily, during and since the lamentable scenes, when we know them but too fully, stand forth to view in a dark and fatal consistency. There is a point of development and ripeness in a series of acts, at which tendency becomes proof of purpose; as there is also a point in the accumulation of evidence, at which not to see guilt is in some measure to share it. When deeds admit of no interpretation but one, that one can no longer be honourably avoided. The acts of the Porte through nine long months demonstrate a deliberate intention and a coherent plan. That purpose has been to cover up iniquity; to baffle inquiry; to reward prominence in crime; to punish or discourage humanity among its own agents; to prolong the reign of terror; to impress with a steady coherency upon the minds of its Mohammedan subjects this but too intelligible lesson for the next similar occasion—'Do it again.' I hope that my charge against the Porte is now intelligible and clear. My first duty was to make it so . . . . In what we deem atrocity, the Porte sees only energy. What we think crimes, the Porte holds to be services. To uphold the existing relation of domination on one side, and servitude on the other, by that force in which all along the Osmanli have lived and moved and had their being, is for the Turk the one great commandment 'on which hang all the law and the prophets.' Violence and fury, fraud and falsehood, are sanctified when, in circumstances of adequate magnitude, they are addressed to such an end. The utmost refinements of cruelty, the most bestial devices of lust, become either meritorious or venial when they are the incidental accompaniments of the good and holy work." This, be it observed, is deliberately written of the whole Turkish race, and not simply of the Pashas, Aghas, and office-holders. It is not, then, simply a small coterie that has said, "Evil, be thou my good!" It is a vast nation, counting its many millions.

The opinions of a man of Mr. Gladstone's eminence and intellectual power are always important; but they are not to be received with blind submission. In the present instance they can only be adopted with considerable qualifications. No one will for a moment question that the conduct of the Turkish Government in neglecting to punish the guilty, and in even rewarding some of the greatest criminals, was disgraceful; but it was not more so than that of other Governments under similar conditions. No Power ever punishes or degrades the agents by whom it has been upheld at a period of danger, however detestable may have been their acts. The fact may be in the highest degree discreditable, and no doubt is so; but the discredit falls on human nature generally, and is not peculiar to any section of it. When Russia suppresses a revolt in Poland, Circassia, or Khokand—when France stamps out a rising among the Algerian Arabs—when England crushes insubordination in Ireland or Jamaica, in Hindostan or elsewhere—acts are committed at which humanity stands ashamed; but the perpetrators do not find avengers in the Governments they have saved. If we lived in a state of perfect justice, this of course would not be; but it is the language of passion to charge the fault upon a particular nationality or a particular religion. Let it not be forgotten that the illegalities and cruelties committed in the suppression of the Jamaica insurrection, in 1865, took place under an Administration in which Mr. Gladstone held the most important post after that of the Premier himself; that, beyond the removal of the Governor from office, no kind of punishment was visited on any one of the offenders; and that a large proportion of their fellow-countrymen highly applauded their acts. Yet it would be a little extravagant to call Mr. Gladstone and the British people disciples of Satan, because of this failure to do justice in a flagrant case.*

During the whole progress of the Bulgarian question, Mr. Gladstone could never see more than one aspect of the facts, and was fierce in his denunciations of all whose sight was more inclusive. The great Pashas and military leaders were certainly spared, and in some instances rewarded; but several of the criminals more immediately concerned in acts of outrage were made to suffer for their misdeeds. Acting Consul Calvert wrote to Sir Henry Elliot from Philippopolis, on the 30th of

* The Russell Government, it is true, resigned very shortly after the publication of the Report drawn up by the Commission of Inquiry; but there does not seem to have been any great solicitude for punishment on the part of the members of that Administration, either in or out of office, and certainly Mr. Gladstone did not then issue a pamphlet on "Lessons in Massacre."

November, 1876, that the punishments recently dealt out had tended to suppress the terrorism which since the insurrection of the spring had been exercised by the Mussulmans towards the Christians. This happy result was also due in part to another cause. When the agents for the distribution of English relief arrived in the country, it was thought by the Mohammedans that succour would be extended only to the Christians, and they bitterly complained of the unfairness of such a course, as the Christians had been the first to shed blood. A few acts of charity towards sufferers of their own faith, however, produced a marked change in the feelings of the Moslems, and the threats of massacre, frequent a few weeks before, had entirely ceased by the end of November. Eighty of the burnt houses in Peroushtitza had been wholly or nearly rebuilt; and every family injured in the suppression of the rising had received from the Government from one hundred and fifty to five hundred piastres, for which no bond was required. The village had also received, as a loan, 30,000 piastres for cattle, and a certain proportion of grain; and a doctor, paid by the Government, had been appointed to reside there, in consequence of the sickness that had prevailed. From communications addressed by Mr. Baring to Sir Henry Elliot, it likewise appeared that some of the offenders had been sentenced to various degrees of punishment, and that on the other hand several Bulgarians, implicated in the revolutionary movement, had been released. After a prolonged inquiry, Achmet Agha was condemned to death, and Achmet Chaoush to hard labour for life, by the Philippopolis Commission; but it does not appear that the sentences have been carried out. The Commission was composed of four Mohammedan and four Christian members; and the condemnation of Achmet Agha to death, for his share in the Batak atrocity, was by a majority of five to one. It is evident, however, that the Turkish Government has been very loth to execute these sentences in the case of persons of distinction; and its conduct deserves severe reprobation in that respect, though it is perhaps not altogether so bad as Mr. Gladstone would lead the world to suppose.

A great desire to amend abuses became manifest after the breaking up of the Conference. It was announced that, in accordance with Article 17 of the Constitution, which established the complete equality of all Ottomans, non-Mussulman children were thenceforth to be admitted to military schools. Up to that time, Christians had not been allowed to enter the army; and this had always been regarded as a grievance and an insult, because it put them in the position of an inferior race, which was not to be trusted. A corps of gendarmerie, partly Mussulman and partly Christian, was placed under the direction of Mr. Valentine Baker, formerly a colonel in the English army. The colonisation of large bodies of Circassians in Roumelia was prohibited, together with the employment of irregular troops, excepting when it might appear to be unavoidable. The carrying of arms without special authority was interdicted. An amnesty was issued for persons concerned in the risings of the previous May; liberty of public worship was proclaimed; and provision was made for local self-government. The elections to the newly-created Parliament proceeded with regularity and despatch; but of course many difficulties were encountered, owing to entire want of familiarity with such procedures, and it was said by adverse critics that the choice of members was often dictated by the Pashas. It is very likely that this really occurred in some instances, for the habits of an ancient despotism are not readily set aside. But a Parliamentary system, however imperfectly carried out, is sure to be influenced in some degree by the currents of popular opinion. This was the case with the first Turkish Parliament. Several Christians were elected, and the Legislature, when completely chosen, was fairly representative of the various divisions of the Empire. The method of election was fixed by a special decree, which provided that the electoral lists were to be posted up on the churches, mosques, and other public buildings; that, on a day appointed, the inhabitants of each district were to assemble in a room selected for the purpose, and containing a wooden balloting-urn with two locks; that the Imaums and Mukhtars were first to see that the voters answered to their names in the list; and that each voter was then to throw into the urn a paper inscribed with the names of two of the candidates for the office of electors, one of whom was to be a Christian, and the other a Mussulman. The two candidates with the greater number of votes were then proclaimed the electors of the district, and the selection of members was made by them. Thus, the choice of members was not by the direct vote of the people, but by a body deputed for that purpose, as in the case of the President of the United States.

While the new order was thus being brought into operation, the author of the Constitution suddenly fell from power. On the 5th of February it was announced that Midhat Pasha had that morning been dismissed from the post of Grand Vizier, and had been banished from the Turkish Empire. He had become distasteful to the Sultan, owing partly to his popularity, partly to his too great eagerness in introducing reforms. Latterly he had been disrespectful, and almost defiant, in his demeanour, and it was believed that he had plotted the overthrow of Abdul-Hamid, and his own nomination as dictator. As he had been concerned in the removal of both Abdul-Aziz and Murad, the suspicion seemed not without some warrant; indeed, it was said that letters were discovered which left no doubt as to the fact. Nevertheless, it is far from certain that any such plot existed, and it is perhaps more likely that the Sultan became alarmed at the development of popular power, and inferred from his acts and opinions that Midhat was aiming at a further revolution. Edhem Pasha, the second Turkish Plenipotentiary at the Conference, and formerly Ambassador at Berlin, became Grand Vizier; and Midhat Pasha, the most capable of Turkish administrators, the man most animated by liberal ideas, left for Italy and other western lands, to muse on the fickleness of monarchs and the caprice of fortune.

BANISHMENT OF MIDHAT PASHA.

CHAPTER IX.

Prince Gortschakoff's Circular Despatch on the Failure of the Conference—Circular Despatch of the Turkish Government—Character of the latter Document—The Withdrawal of Sir Henry Elliot from Constantinople—Russian preparations for attacking Turkey—Speeches of Mr. Gladstone in the British Parliament—The Question of Treaty Obligations—Exposition of Government Policy by Mr. Gathorne Hardy—Ambiguous Position of the Cabinet—Publication at Constantinople of a Pamphlet on the Secret Intrigues of Russia—Conclusion of Peace with Servia—Opening of the Ottoman Parliament—Speech from the Throne—Promises of Reform—The Chances of Success—Disturbed Condition of the Ottoman Empire—Spread of Disaffection in Turkey—Agitation in the European Money Markets—Arguments of the Peace Party in Russia—Mission of General Ignatieff to the European Courts—Lord Salisbury and Opinion at St. Petersburg—The Protocol—Preliminary Discussions—Signature of the Document—Accompanying Qualifications—Peace or War?

Now that the Conference had come to an end, and that the Ambassadors had returned to their respective capitals, the two Powers principally interested in the discussion placed their views of the situation before the world in the usual diplomatic form. Prince Gortschakoff's circular despatch bore date the 31st of January, and was addressed to the Russian representatives at London, Paris, Rome, Berlin, and Vienna. It commenced with the remark that the refusal of the Porte to accede to the wishes of Europe had caused the Eastern crisis to enter upon a new phase. Any thought of harbouring exclusive or personal ideas had been repudiated by all the Cabinets, and the question was therefore one of humanity and general interest. After recapitulating the course of events in connection with the Andrassy Note and the Berlin Memorandum, Prince Gortschakoff proceeded :—"At the initiative of the English Government, the Cabinets agreed upon the bases and the guarantees of pacification to be discussed at a Conference to meet at Constantinople. This Conference, in its preliminary deliberations, arrived at a complete understanding, both respecting the conditions of peace and the reforms to be introduced. It communicated the result to the Porte as the firm and unanimous wish of Europe, but met with an obstinate refusal from the Turkish Government. Thus, after more than a year of diplomatic efforts, demonstrating the price which the Great Powers attach to the pacification of the East, and the right which they possess of ensuring it in view of the general interest involved, and their firm desire to obtain it by means of a European understanding, the Cabinets again find themselves in the same position as at the commencement of the crisis, which is, however, still further aggravated by the blood that has been shed, the passions that have been raised, the ruins accumulated, and the prospect of an indefinite prolongation of the deplorable state of things which weighs upon Europe, and justly preoccupies public opinion and the Governments. The Porte pays no regard to its former engagements, to its duties as a member of the European concert, or to the unanimous wishes of the Great Powers. Far from having made a step towards a satisfactory solution, the state of the East has become worse, and remains a permanent menace for the peace of Europe, the sentiments of humanity, and the conscience of the Christian peoples." Under these circumstances, the Emperor wished to know what course would be pursued by the Five Powers, before deciding himself on any further action.

The Turkish despatch (issued January 25th) was a closely reasoned production. It affirmed that the Porte had made every effort to give satisfaction to Europe, consistently with a regard to the national feeling, and with the duty of the Government towards the sovereign and the country. When England suggested that a Conference should be held at Constantinople, Turkey, in accepting that proposal, was careful to state that the basis of the discussion was understood to be the English programme, as communicated by Sir Henry Elliot. At the same time, the Imperial Government formally placed on record, as defining its own views on the subject, the principle of the independence of the internal administration of the Ottoman Empire, as stipulated in the Treaty of Paris of 1856. Such being the case, it was to be regretted that the delegates of the Powers thought fit, before any explanations had been exchanged with the Sublime Porte, to hold preliminary meetings among themselves, with the object of deciding upon the scheme to be presented to the Imperial Government. To this proceeding, "which consisted in deliberating in the absence of the party principally concerned, and in concert with the foreign Power whose position and policy rendered it more particularly interested in the question," the circular attributed, with no little reason, the greater part of the difficulties which followed. "The European delegates," said the Turkish Foreign Minister, "came with a programme decided upon in common, and apparently intended to be imposed upon us by the authority of the agreement previously established between them. It was depriving the Conference in some degree of its proper character, to reduce the discussion which was to have been held among all its members to a simple debate between two parties only—on the one hand, Turkey, completely isolated, and, on the other, Europe, invited with the object of obtaining the acceptance of a programme settled beforehand. However this might be, we had a right to expect that, while deliberating in our absence, the European Plenipotentiaries would not lose sight of the original and essential conditions of the Conference, which, as I have pointed out above, were no other than the terms of the English programme. Unfortunately, the scheme of pacification and agreement adopted by the European delegates was far from confining its scope within the limits traced by the English programme, and from referring to the stipulations of the Treaty of Paris with regard to the non-intervention of the Powers in the internal affairs of the Empire. For Servia and Montenegro, the scheme, contrary to the basis concerning the re-establishment of the *status quo*, demanded cessions of territory, while, for the administration of a considerable portion of European Turkey, it tended to inaugurate a system of institutions which, both as a whole and in its details, practically annulled the sovereign authority. The same scheme further comprised, under the denomination of guarantees, a set of measures which could not have been proposed to any Government wishing to preserve its independence; and while the English programme had only spoken of moral guarantees, resulting from the system of institutions to be conceded to Bosnia and Herzegovina, the scheme in question called upon Turkey to furnish guarantees, material and effective, so to speak, to the European Powers."

The Turkish Minister proceeded to observe that

COUNT ANDRASSY.

they had energetically refused to adhere to any arrangement the effect of which would be to alienate the independence of the State, and that, by the sole force of right and logic, they had succeeded in obtaining the withdrawal of the greater number of those features of the European programme which were incompatible with the moral and material integrity of the Ottoman Empire. Nevertheless, two points remained, to which the Porte was unable to assent. These were, the participation of the Powers in the nomination of the Valis, and the institution of the International Commission appointed to supervise the action of the provincial administrations. The Imperial Government, after consulting the Grand Council, had declined to accede to such requirements. At the same time, however, the Ottoman Plenipotentiaries had announced to the European delegates the intention of the Sultan to substitute for those two measures the institution of two Commissions of Mussulmans and Christians, freely elected by the population, one for Herzegovina and Bosnia, the other for the provinces of the Danube and of Adrianople, which Commissions were to be invested with powers analogous to those which Europe proposed to confer on the International Commission. Such was the Turkish presentation of the case to the judgment of the world. It was necessarily a one-sided statement; but it contained facts which were beyond denial, and those facts carried with them an implied argument of considerable force. An attempt had been made to deprive Turkey of her sovereign

MEETING OF THE OTTOMAN PARLIAMENT.

rights; and it was clear that no independent Power would submit to such terms while it had spirit left to fire a gun. It was also plain, from the barest recapitulation of events, that the Sultan and his Government had been met with a direct breach of faith. The English programme had been violated in letter and in spirit, and the Turks were suddenly confronted with a scheme which fell little short of a project for dismembering the Empire, when they had been led to expect nothing more than a plan for facilitating the execution of their own reforms.

There were some circumstances connected with the withdrawal of Sir Henry Elliot from Constantinople which attracted attention in England. It was true that his return to London was in accordance with general instructions prescribing his line of conduct in the event of the Conference proving a failure. But it was generally thought that he would not resume his functions at Constantinople in any case, and that his conduct of affairs in the Turkish capital was not in accordance with the new policy of the British Government. His views and those of Lord Salisbury were certainly very divergent, and in some of the English papers it was hinted that Sir Henry had done his utmost to thwart the action of the Indian Secretary, and had secretly encouraged the Turkish Ministers to resist the demands of the Six Powers. Charges so derogatory from the honour of the Ambassador should not even have been whispered without something like evidence in their support. But they were suggested, and they found believers. Sir Henry Elliot and General Ignatieff were the very antipodes of one another, and were on terms of so much coldness that the latter was the only one of the Ambassadors who, when the former was departing from Constantinople, did not take leave of him on board the steamer. Shortly after the meeting of Parliament, in February, the Chancellor of the Exchequer was questioned on the subject, and replied that Sir Henry Elliot was still in the service of her Majesty, but that a short time before he had requested permission to quit Constantinople temporarily on sick leave, his health having been affected by the strain of his duties. He was begged to remain some time longer, in consequence of the pressure of business, and in view of the coming Conference. This was done, and the Government professed to have no fault to find with Sir Henry. Yet it was apparent to every one that the Turkish sympathies of that diplomatist were now out of favour at the Foreign Office.

Speaking of the ill-success of the Conference, the Russian paper, the *Golos*, remarked that all that was then wanted was patience, and that waiting would not be difficult, since war was impossible with a State which would perish quicker by the effect of its internal maladies than through the operations of a foreign army. It had become, according to the view of this authority, more to the advantage of Russia, and also of the Eastern Christians, to wait, and see how the course of Turkish decay would shape itself, than to prolong the process of dissolution by interference. Such, however, was not at all the opinion of the Russian Emperor and his advisers; nor was it the desire of the Russian people, except, possibly, in a comparatively few instances. War was not, indeed, to be made at once, for the season was unfavourable to the commencement of hostilities; but it can hardly be doubted that a resort to arms was by that time fully resolved on. In the meanwhile, Europe was to be amused by a pretence of further negotiations which would conveniently fill up the interval between mid-winter and the lengthening days of spring. At the beginning of February, Russia had 220,000 men, duly provided with boats, bridges, steam-launches, and torpedoes, stationed along the line of the Pruth—the river which, towards the south-west, divides the Russian from the Turkish Empire. These regiments were ready at any moment to be let loose on the dominions of the Sultan; but the proper time had not yet arrived, and the matter still remained in the hands of the diplomatists.

The British Parliament met for the first time after the recess on the 8th of February, and the great topic of the day was of course one of the principal subjects of debate. On that occasion, Mr. Gladstone boldly argued that Turkey had placed herself entirely outside the Treaty of March 30th, 1856, by her total disregard of the solemn stipulation into which she then entered. Taken in conjunction with the whole course of Mr. Gladstone's reasonings on the Eastern Question, this was tantamount to affirming that Turkey had no longer any right to require protection of others in the event of her being attacked, but that nevertheless those others had as much right as before to call on her to fulfil her alleged engagements. It has already been shown that the Porte entered into no engagements with the Powers of the nature alluded to, the promises of reform being engagements to the Sultan's own people, and not to other nations. But the answer of Mr. Gladstone's opponents was that, even supposing it to have been as he asserted, it was a defiance of all principles of honour and reason to contend that the Treaty of Peace might be enforced against Turkey, and set aside in so far as it operated in her favour. A further exposition of his views was made by Mr. Gladstone in the course of a debate on Treaty Obligations which took place on the 16th of February, when the right honourable gentleman, after putting a question of which he had given previous notice, went at great length into the whole matter. He then maintained that the Tripartite Treaty of April 15th, 1856, by which England, France, and Austria bound themselves, jointly and severally, to treat any infraction of the independence and integrity of the Ottoman Empire as a *casus belli*, would not apply in the event of Russia attacking Turkey, for the extraordinary reason that Turkey was not a party to that treaty. Nor would he allow that there was any greater efficacy in the seventh article of the Treaty of Peace, by which the contracting Powers (England, France, Austria, Prussia, Russia, and Sardinia) engaged, each on its own part, to respect the independence and territorial integrity of Turkey, to guarantee in common the strict observance of that engagement, and to consider any act tending to its violation as a question of general interest. Reverting to the Tripartite Treaty, he quoted the authority of Lord Palmerston for saying that the nature of the guarantees therein contained was to give a right, but not to impose an obligation, of interference: a contention truly amazing when it is recollected that the language of the treaty is in the highest degree imperative.* Even Mr. Gladstone felt the uncertainty of the ground on which he thus planted himself, and immediately afterwards removed on to the more general assumption that the internal affairs of any State might be subjected to foreign interference, if it were thought that the interest of humanity or the peace of Europe was endangered. Such a principle, if admitted at all, might be applied with as much force against Russia as against Turkey. Humanity is interested in the Poles as well as in the Bulgarians; and if the peace of Europe was endangered in the one case and not in the other, it was because Russia herself endangered it, and other Powers were more conscientious. It is a good maxim in law that no man shall take advantage of his own wrongdoing; and the rule is equally applicable to States.

The credit of the House of Commons was not enhanced by the fact of an eminent statesman, who had once been at the head of affairs, getting up, and attempting to explain away solemn treaty engagements into senseless words. But the honour of the Legislature was amply redeemed by the masterly speech of Mr. Gathorne Hardy, the Minister of War. "When," said Mr. Hardy, "I am asked whether I am bound by a treaty, I must ask what is the view of my co-partners with respect to that treaty, and how far they are bound. I want to know this:—Is Turkey bound by these treaties to Europe, or is she not? If she is, then I say, boldly, peremptorily, and strongly, that Europe is bound by those treaties to her. You cannot escape from that position. Was such a thing ever heard of as that, after having entered into a treaty with a man, you should say to him, 'You have behaved so very ill, I will have nothing to do with you. I have promised you a great deal, and you have promised me something. I hold you to your bargain, but don't look to me to fulfil anything I undertook to you'? I want to know if *that* is the position I have to meet. The right hon. gentleman says he will not say what the obligations of Turkey are. But I am obliged to see to what my co-partners in the treaty are bound, and to what I am bound to them. Why was the Treaty of 1856 renewed in 1871? Because otherwise we should have been released from our obligations under the treaty by the very different form it assumed. Unless we became partners to it under the new form, Turkey and Russia might have agreed between themselves as to the Black Sea. But we had a right to be consulted, and the treaty was re-settled. You say Turkey has forfeited her rights. When did she forfeit them? In 1860, Russia was complaining of the treatment of the Christians by Turkey in exactly the same way as she has complained since. There have been since then the cases of the Lebanon and Crete—instances which called special attention to the conduct of Turkey to her Christian subjects. But when the right hon. gentleman tells us that the catalogue of the crimes of Turkey extends even to her origin, that she is anti-human in herself, and has never been human upon any occasion, it is a lame answer, when he is asked whether in 1871 she had not arrived at such a climax of iniquity as to be out of the pale of civilized society, to refer to a question put in this House to Lord Enfield." In 1872, Lord Enfield, who was at

* Arts. I. and II. of the Tripartite Treaty are thus expressed:—"The High Contracting Parties guarantee, jointly and severally, the independence and the integrity of the Ottoman Empire, recorded in the treaty concluded at Paris on the 30th of March, 1856.—Any infraction of the stipulations of the said treaty *will* [not *may*] be considered by the Powers signing the present treaty as *casus belli*. They will [not may] come to an understanding with the Sublime Porte as to the measures which have become necessary, and will [not may] without delay determine among themselves as to the employment of their military and naval forces." These are the only operative articles of the treaty.

that time Under-Secretary for Foreign Affairs in the Government of Mr. Gladstone, said that the reform edicts of the Sultan were being fairly fulfilled. Mr. Hardy therefore desired to know at what period the violation of those edicts, asserted by Mr. Gladstone, began to take place. He denied that Turkey, by the Treaty of Peace, had entered into any engagement with the Powers as regarded her Christian subjects: the engagement was with the subjects themselves. With respect to the Tripartite Treaty, the War Minister declared that circumstances might happen—though they were certainly remote—in which England might be called upon to fulfil her obligations under that treaty. Therefore he ended as he began, by saying that, without being obliged to go to war for Turkey, we were pledged, not to Turkey alone, but to Europe at large, to maintain the faith of treaties which we have no right to violate.

The debate still left the policy of the Government in some doubt, because it failed to make clear what were the circumstances which would render it imperative for England to go to war in defence of Turkey. But it had at any rate elicited from a Cabinet Minister, holding an important office, the declaration that such a contingency was not absolutely impossible, and that treaties were not things to be sneered out of existence because they did not suit a pet conclusion. It was certainly high time that such an assurance should be given in unequivocal language; for Lord Derby's declaration that, should Turkey prove recalcitrant, no assistance would be rendered by England, even in the event of her being attacked, followed by the tone assumed by Lord Salisbury at the Conference, was operating as a direct incentive to Russia to follow a policy of aggression. The cry on the part of the Opposition in the English Parliament was now that coercion should be brought to bear on Turkey; but no one could be induced to explain exactly what coercion meant. Lord Beaconsfield and other Ministers emphatically declared in Parliament that coercion in any form was out of the question, as far as England was concerned. But the weak point in their position was that, while refraining from action themselves, they were permitting it in another, and that other the very Power most likely to push interference to extremity, and to endanger interests in which Great Britain had a most important share.

During the pause between the Conference and the next diplomatic step, much excitement was caused in Constantinople by the publication of a pamphlet in French, entitled "The Responsibilities," in the production of which Midhat Pasha, in the final days of his power, had some concern. It contained nine confidential letters from General Ignatieff to M. Novikoff, at Vienna; several other documents; and a letter from Ignatieff to the Khedive of Egypt. The papers, according to a correspondent of the *Standard*, ranged from 1871 to 1873. They showed what were the intrigues and plans of the Russian Ambassador, the Russian Consuls, and the Secret Committees, during those years, and furnished important information as to the proceedings of the Russian agents in Servia, Bosnia, Montenegro, Bulgaria, and the Herzegovina. Details were given respecting the introduction of arms into the disaffected provinces, and it was proved (assuming the authenticity of the letters) that large sums of money had been expended in bribing the Bulgarian clergy, and in procuring the dismissal of any persons, whether Greeks or Turks, who opposed obstacles to the schemes of Russia. Among the persons spoken of with great hostility were Mehemet Ruchdi Pasha, Midhat Pasha, the Greek Patriarch, and many of the Greek Bishops. The Greeks, indeed, were attacked in a body with extreme bitterness, for reasons which have already been explained. The alleged letter from General Ignatieff to the Khedive, written in 1871, contained these remarkable sentences:—"For the success of our projects, it is necessary that Egypt should keep herself still tranquil. Arm yourself. Make all the necessary preparations for a long war. Contract treaties of alliance, offensive and defensive, with Greece, Servia, and Roumania, in which we will undoubtedly aid you; and continue to dispute, step by step, the pretensions of the Suzerain Court. If the Egyptian Government shows itself dignified and inflexible in its relations with the Porte, it can be sure of victory. The more they see you firm and intractable, the more the irritation of the Ministers of the Sultan will augment, and ripen to an explosion. It is then that Egypt will know and appreciate Russian friendship, as being entirely different from the French protection, which, after having urged to war the illustrious grandfather of your Highness, is contented to maintain itself platonically, and to abandon the country to Ottoman vengeance." The correspondent of the *Standard* affirmed that there could be no question as to the genuineness of these documents; and a correspondent of the *Daily Telegraph*, in an interview with Midhat Pasha at Brindisi, received the assurances of the fallen Grand Vizier that the papers were all authentic. If so, they leave no doubt as to that conspiracy which Russia had for several years been prosecuting against Turkey.

The armistice with Servia and Montenegro terminated on the 1st of March; but negotiations for peace had been proceeding some time before that date, and, as regarded Servia, peace itself was concluded on the day when, but for such an arrangement, the struggle would have recommenced. The protocol consisted of three points—the maintenance of the *status quo ante bellum*, the granting of an amnesty, and the evacuation of Servian territory in twelve days. The Servian delegates subsequently delivered to the Porte a note, promising that no new fortifications should be erected in Servia; that the Ottoman flag should be hoisted side by side with that of the principality on the existing forts; that the equal rights of Jews and Christians should be recognized; and that armed bands should be prevented from crossing the frontier. On the previous day, a special session of the Skuptschina, or National Parliament, had been opened by an address from the Prince, in which he declared that Servia was unable to continue the war, that Russia desired the conclusion of a separate peace, and that it remained for the Skuptschina to say whether peace should be made, or not. Every article of the proposed treaty was at once voted, and the Assembly was then dissolved. The terms of peace were certainly very favourable to Servia, considering the grave cause of offence which she had given to Turkey; but it would have been extremely injudicious on the part of the Ottoman Government to irritate the European Powers by exacting any reparation for the unprovoked attack of the previous year. With regard to Montenegro, a further extension of the armistice was granted; but it did not lead to peace. The difference resulted from the Montenegrin demand for an increase of territory, including access to the Adriatic, to which Turkey could not be persuaded to assent. That difference was sufficient to destroy all hope of an arrangement.

The time was now approaching when the great experiment of an Ottoman Parliament was to be brought to the test. The initial difficulties had assuredly been great, and that in more ways than one. Certain portions of the Turkish Empire had refused to take any part in the new Constitutional system. Crete, for instance, had altogether declined to elect deputies, alleging that the charter bestowed upon the island had never been respected, and that no faith could be placed in the Constitution of Midhat Pasha. Roumania contended, and not without reason, that, having a Government and Legislature of her own, she could not be merged in the Imperial institutions at Constantinople. The same argument applied to Servia; and the point was conceded by the Turkish Government. The Ottoman Parliament, however, was at last elected, and it contained representatives of the various religions into which the population is divided. On the 19th of March the Chambers were opened by the Sultan, in presence of the Ministers, the dignitaries of the State, the civil, military, and religious authorities, and the foreign *chargés d'affaires*, excepting those of Germany and Russia, who were represented by the dragomans of their Embassies. The speech from the throne was read by the first secretary of the Sultan, and entered at great length into the condition of the Empire. The country, it was remarked, owed its grandeur in former times to the practice of justice, respect for the laws, and good administration. Its gradual weakening was due to the forgetfulness or abandonment of those wise precedents, which were not again brought into force until the reign of Mahmud II., who commenced a series of reforms which had been continued by his son, the Sultan Abdul-Medjid. The benefits of the Tanzimat, however, had been impeded by the Crimean war, which for the first time compelled the Treasury to have recourse to a loan. On the restoration of peace, the country would have entered on a new era of progress and prosperity, had not intrigue and culpable agitation paralysed the efforts of the Government, and added to the national debt by necessitating the maintenance of considerable armies, and the frequent purchase of war-material. The Sultan next alluded to the promulgation of the Constitution—a charter which secured liberty, equality, and justice to all. He then enumerated the principal laws which the two Chambers would be called upon to discuss during the Session. These were—an Electoral Bill; a Provisional Bill; a Bill on Commercial Regulations; a Code of civil procedure; measures for the re-organization of the tribunals, and for the promotion and retirement of public functionaries; a Press Bill; a Bill for the organization of a Court of Account; and the Budget law.

The message abounded in promises as to the determination of the Sultan to offer the creditors of Turkey the most solid guarantees for the execution of the Imperial engagements; and assurances were given that education should be promoted, and that no efforts should be wanting to draw closer the bonds of friendship and sympathy which united Turkey with the great European family. The Royal speech, in fact, had very much the character of other Royal speeches in countries where constitutionalism has been established many years. What gave it special interest was the fact of its novelty in an Oriental land. The East was here, almost for the first time, adopting one of the most distinctive institutions of the West. The ancient Asiatic idea of supreme personal power was by this act set aside in favour of the comparatively modern European idea of a participation by prince and people in the functions of government. The spectacle was imposing in itself; but it was much more so in the possibilities which it opened—in the crowding hopes granted that the chance was only one against many; still it was there, and the world could not afford to disregard the fact. The dumb multitudes of South-eastern Europe, of Asia Minor, of Armenia, and of those other lands which own the immediate authority of the Porte, had at length found a voice; and a nation which can speak for itself has the power of determining its destinies, if there be any

EDHEM PASHA, GRAND VIZIER.

and fears which it excited. In themselves, the promises of the Sultan were worth little or nothing. To promise and to cajole has been the prerogative of despots since the world began. But in that Oriental Parliament—the first Oriental Parliament that the history of the world has known, if we except the Egyptian Legislature established in 1866 (for the Japanese experiment of 1876 seems hardly analogous)—there was at least the chance that a popular power might be established, which would set the country above the need of Imperial favour, or the fear of imperial treachery. Let it be virtue to prompt its utterance, or any courage to maintain its will.

The Turkish Parliament was certainly born in a stormy epoch. Civil war had again broken out in Bosnia. Crete was threatening a renewal of the insurrection of ten years earlier. Greece was watching her opportunity. Servia, though submissive, was not friendly. Montenegro, as usual, was in a mood of fierce antagonism. War with Russia loomed heavily and darkly in a future not remote. The European Powers, without an exception, looked coldly on the fortunes of the Ottoman, and

ST. PETERSBURG: THE NEVSKI PROSPECT.

were indifferent to his fall, if they did not actually desire it. Even amongst the Turks themselves there was much disaffection. Several Softas were arrested in the middle of March for being concerned in the posting up of placards declaring the treatment of Midhat Pasha to be illegal, protesting against the peace with Servia, and calling upon the Porte to reject the demands of Montenegro, and to make war, rather than cede any portion of Ottoman territory. The banishment of Midhat Pasha proved to be an extremely unpopular act. The ability of that statesman was believed to be supreme, and it was considered that he alone had power to defeat the designs of Russia, and save the Empire from ruin. The discontent with Edhem Pasha and his colleagues was deep and general. Night after night, seditious placards were posted up on houses, mosques, and public buildings, with so much secrecy that the police were unable to detect the offenders. The Ministers received anonymous letters, full of invectives against the incapable Government which called out the whole male Mohammedan population, oppressed the country with war-taxes, and yet made a humiliating peace with Servia, and talked about a cession of territory to Montenegrin robbers.* Numerous Ulemas and Softas were transported to St. Jean d'Acre; arrests were effected, and houses searched; but the growing insubordination could not be checked. Worse than all, the new Sultan seemed to be falling into a state of health similar to that of his unhappy brother during the few months of his reign. Like Murad, he was enervated by vicious indulgences; like Murad, he was moody, irresolute, and depressed. Another deposition was openly talked about, and the Sultan himself stood in daily fear of removal from his post, if not of assassination. Such, at any rate, were the accounts circulated in many of the European papers; but Hobart Pasha—an Englishman, though an officer of the Turkish fleet—wrote to the *Times*, stating that the Sultan was in perfect health, and worked day and night for the welfare of his country, and that the Empire, although passing through a fearful crisis, in which the passions and aspirations of five or six different religious communities were roused, was perfectly tranquil.

Europe was hardly less disturbed than Turkey, though in a different way. The fear of war, sometimes varied by spasmodic hopes of peace, agitated every Stock Exchange from the Baltic to the Mediterranean, and from the Atlantic to the Euxine. All kinds of securities fell with alarming rapidity and steadiness, and commerce was deeply affected by the general uneasiness of the time. People still talked of the possibility of peace being preserved; but few really believed it. Nevertheless, there was a peace party even in Russia itself. To some it was doubtful whether the country was prepared for war, and by these it was suggested that Russia was not called upon to constitute herself the sole champion of the oppressed Christians of the East. The cause of those sufferers had been taken up by the Six Powers in concert, and they had arrived at a common agreement. If Turkey refused to submit, it was for the Powers in a body to apply the means of coercion. Five out of the six hesitated as to doing so, or refused point-blank; and it was in no respect incumbent on Russia alone to discharge an obligation which belonged to all. This was the argument of the peace party at St. Petersburg; but it carried little weight, for it was not supported by the national feeling. The Emperor, however, still delayed to commit himself to a position of hostility. The summer was as yet too far off, and it was desirable to temporise a little longer. Besides, General Ignatieff, after a temporary sojourn at St. Petersburg, was on a round of visits to Berlin, Paris, and London; and it was as well to hear precisely what were the last words of Germany, France, and England.

The object of General Ignatieff's mission (which began in the early part of March) was to ask the assent of the Powers to a Protocol which, it was alleged, would dispense with any reply to the Russian circular on the failure of the Conference, and might at the same time enable the Czar to demobilise his armies, the maintenance of which on a war-footing was making very serious demands on the Treasury, without any results to show for the expenditure. The situation was every day becoming more difficult, and, notwithstanding the harmony of the representatives of the Six Powers at the Conference, the intentions of the Cabinets themselves were doubtful. As regarded England, Lord Salisbury had for some time been the chief hope of the Russians and their supporters. Prince Zertelew, the secretary of General Ignatieff, told the Berlin correspondent of the *Standard* that the Indian Minister had at Constantinople become the good friend of the Russians, and that his chief merit consisted in his having destroyed in the minds of Turkish statesmen the last remnant of hope that the Sultan would find allies in case of war. Mr. Gladstone, on the opening night of Parliament, eulogised Lord Salisbury as "an able, honourable English gentleman, with a manly mind," who had done his best under the circumstances, and had brought himself into especial

* Austrian Correspondent of the *Times*.

honour by making Turkey understand her isolation. The St. Petersburg correspondent of the *Daily News*, telegraphing on the 6th of March, remarked that the peaceable attitude of Russia during the preceding few weeks was due to hopes of more decided action on the part of Lord Salisbury. It had been anticipated that he would propose coercion, in alliance with Russia. Such was the opinion which the Special Plenipotentiary of England had earned for himself in the minds of Muscovite statesmen. Russia, it was added, did not wish to act alone. She preferred to act with England; but, if England would not join her, she would be obliged to proceed by herself. Faith in Lord Salisbury, however, was beginning to give way. On returning to London, he had come once more under the influence of his colleagues, and had proved a little less favourable to the interests of the Czar. He had, in fact, gone so far against the Northern Power as to argue in the House of Lords that coercion might lead to serious dangers. Therefore, great disappointment with Lord Salisbury was expressed at St. Petersburg. Prince Gortschakoff had believed that he would take a more decided stand; but, as he seemed gradually reverting to the former position of Lord Beaconsfield, Russia (said a correspondent, with charming ingenuousness) began to perceive that nothing was to be hoped from him.

For several days, great mystery prevailed in London and the Continental capitals, except among the privileged circles, as to the exact nature of the Protocol which General Ignatieff was asking the Powers to sign. It was known that something was going on, and sanguine people hoped it might conduce to peace; but conjecture was baffled as to the way in which such a result would be brought about. The Russian Envoy arrived in England on the 16th of March, and on the evening of the same day the Marquis of Hartington asked the Chancellor of the Exchequer for some information on the subject. Further questions were put on the 19th by Earl Granville in the House of Lords; and from the answers of Sir Stafford Northcote and Lord Derby it appeared that progress was really being made in what it was then believed might prove to be a settlement of the matters in dispute. A draught of a Protocol, intended to embody the views of the Powers as to the situation in the East, had been submitted to Lord Derby by the Russian Envoy, with the expression of a hope that England would join in it. The English Government had proposed certain modifications in its language, and these had been referred to the Cabinet of St. Petersburg, which presently returned the Protocol, with suggestions for further alterations. There, for the present, the information ended; but the air, as usual, was full of rumours, and it was reported that Prince Bismarck had described the Protocol as something which would not commit anybody to anything, and which might be signed with perfect safety by every Power in Europe, from Russia to Monaco. The German Chancellor has a reputation for smart and clever sayings; but, after all, they do not determine the real value of events. In those restless and agitated days, with a million of men preparing for conflict, people wished to know, on some higher authority than a witty speech of Prince Bismarck's, whether, in truth, the Protocol meant peace or war.

It was not until the reassembling of Parliament on the 5th of April, after the brief Easter recess, that the Protocol and the accompanying diplomatic papers were made public. The Government, it appeared, had delayed answering the Russian circular until events should have developed themselves, and until it should be seen what effects would result from the recent change of Government at Constantinople—that was to say, the substitution of Edhem for Midhat Pasha in the post of Grand Vizier. On the 3rd of March, the Russian Ambassador called on Lord Derby, and requested the Government to postpone its reply still further, in expectation of certain statements which the Cabinet of St. Petersburg was about to make. Eight days later—on the 11th of March—Count Schouvaloff placed in Lord Derby's hands a draught Protocol, which the Russian Government proposed should be signed by the Six Powers. The Foreign Secretary replied on the 13th that he had submitted the document to his colleagues, and that the Government was willing in principle to sign such a Protocol, if an agreement could be come to as to its terms. A discussion on the phraseology then took place between Lord Derby and Count Schouvaloff, and on the same day the former wrote a despatch to Lord Augustus Loftus, the English Ambassador at St. Petersburg, in which he reported some remarks made to him by Count Schouvaloff, when handing in the draught Protocol on the 11th. The Count observed that, after the sacrifices which Russia had imposed upon herself, the stagnation of her industry and of her commerce, and the enormous expenditure incurred by the mobilisation of 500,000 men, she could not retire, nor send back her troops, without having obtained some tangible result as regarded the improvement of the condition of the Christian populations of Turkey. The Emperor was desirous of peace, but not of peace at any price. The Governments of the other Powers were at that moment preparing their answers to the Russian circular; and if those replies were not identical, the agreement of the Powers might be broken up, and that might induce Russia to seek for a solution, either by means of a direct understanding with the Porte, or by force of arms. It therefore appeared to the Russian Government that the most practical solution of the difficulty would be the signature by the Powers of a Protocol which should, so to speak, terminate the incident. This Protocol, it was suggested, might be signed in London by the representatives of the Great Powers, under the direct inspiration of the English Cabinet; and the principles embodied might be simply those which would be contained in the replies of the several Governments to the Russian circular. When finally settled, on the 31st of March, the Protocol ran thus:—

"The Powers who have undertaken in common the pacification of the East, and have with that view taken part in the Conference of Constantinople, recognise that the surest means of attaining the object which they have proposed to themselves is before all to maintain the agreement so happily established between them, and jointly to affirm afresh the common interest which they take in the improvement of the condition of the Christian populations of Turkey, and in the reforms to be introduced in Bosnia, Herzegovina, and Bulgaria, which the Porte has accepted on condition of itself carrying them into execution.

"They take cognizance of the conclusion of peace with Servia. As regards Montenegro, the Powers consider the rectification of the frontiers and the free navigation of the Boïana to be desirable in the interests of a solid and durable arrangement. The Powers consider the arrangements concluded, or to be concluded, between the Porte and the two principalities, as a step accomplished towards the pacification which is the object of their common wishes. They invite the Porte to consolidate it by replacing its armies on a peace footing, excepting the number of troops indispensable for the maintenance of order, and by putting in hand with the least possible delay the reforms necessary for the tranquillity and well-being of the provinces, the condition of which was discussed at the Conference. They recognise that the Porte has declared itself ready to realise an important portion of them.

"They take cognizance specially of the Circular of the Porte on the 13th of February, 1876, and of the declarations made by the Ottoman Government during the Conference, and since through its representatives. In view of these good intentions on the part of the Porte, and of its evident interest to carry them immediately into effect, the Powers believe that they have grounds for hoping that the Porte will profit by the present lull to apply energetically such measures as will cause that effective improvement in the condition of the Christian populations which is unanimously called for as indispensable to the tranquillity of Europe, and that, having once entered on this path, it will understand that it concerns its honour as well as its interests to persevere in it loyally and efficaciously.

"The Powers propose to watch carefully, by means of their representatives at Constantinople and their local agents, the manner in which the promises of the Ottoman Government are carried into effect. If their hopes should once more be disappointed, and if the condition of the Christian subjects of the Sultan should not be improved in a manner to prevent the return of the complications which periodically disturb the peace of the East, they think it right to declare that such a state of affairs would be incompatible with their interests and those of Europe in general. In such case, they reserve to themselves to consider in common as to the means which they may deem best fitted to secure the well-being of the Christian populations, and the interests of the general peace.

"Done at London, March 31, 1877.

"(Signed)

"MÜNSTER. DERBY.
BEUST. L. F. MENABREA.
L. D'HARCOURT. SCHOUVALOFF."

The signature of this document was accompanied by certain qualifications which seriously changed its character. Count Schouvaloff made the following declaration, placing, at the same time, a *pro-memoriâ* of it in the hands of her Britannic Majesty's Secretary of State:—"If peace with Montenegro is concluded, and the Porte accepts the advice of Europe, and shows itself ready to replace its forces on a peace footing, and seriously to undertake the reforms mentioned in the Protocol, let it send to St. Petersburg a Special Envoy to treat of disarmament, to which his Majesty the Emperor would also on his part consent. If massacres similar to those which have stained Bulgaria with blood take place, this would necessarily put a stop to the measures of demobilisation." The Earl of Derby read and delivered to each of the other Plenipotentiaries a declaration to the effect that, as it was solely in the interests of European peace that the Government had consented to sign the Protocol, it was to be understood beforehand that, in the event of the object proposed not being attained—viz., reciprocal disarmament on the part of Russia and Turkey, and peace between them—the document in question should be regarded as null and void. The representative of Italy declared that his Government would be bound by the signature of the Protocol only so long as the agreement established by the Protocol itself was maintained; and the signature of the instrument was then proceeded with. When the result was made known to Europe, the general opinion as to its worth was much divided. Some said it meant Peace. Others, with greater penetration, perceived that it meant War.

CHAPTER X.

Remarks on the Protocol, and the Original Designs of Russia in proposing it—Russia's Device to gain Time—Reception of the Protocol by the Turkish Government—Determination to resist its Demands—Rupture of Negotiations with Montenegro—Circular of the Ottoman Government in Reply to the Protocol—Interview of Musurus Pasha with Lord Derby—The Emperor of Russia with the Army in Bessarabia—Departure of the Russian Representatives from Constantinople—Arrival of Mr. Layard as Temporary Ambassador from England, *vice* Sir Henry Elliot—His Views of Turkish Politics—Retirement of Prince Bismarck from the Active Conduct of German Affairs—Warlike Manifesto of the Emperor of Russia (April 24th)—Circular of Prince Gortschakoff to the Five Powers—Turkish Circular in Reply—Appeal to the Eighth Article of the Treaty of Paris (1856)—Address of the Sultan to his Armies—Despatch of Lord Derby to the British Ambassador at St. Petersburg (May 1st)—Vacillation and Insincerity of the English Government.

During the discussion which preceded the signing of the Protocol, some modifications were introduced into the terms to which Russia sought to commit the Powers. The Cabinet of St. Petersburg wished the other Governments to undertake that, if the Porte should again disappoint the hopes of Christian Europe, they would consider in common "the action" they would deem indispensable to secure the well-being of the subject populations of Turkey, and the interests of the general peace. This was ultimately softened down into an undertaking that in the case supposed they would consider "the means" by which the desired ends might be attained. The alteration may appear slight; but the exclusion of the word "action" saved the Five Powers from committing themselves to a policy of warlike interference in the East. It was at first proposed by Russia that the Powers should determine by general agreement, and at whatever time might appear to them fit for such a course, whether or not Turkey was progressing in a satisfactory manner in her work of regeneration; and it can hardly be doubted that, had these stipulations been accepted, England, France, Germany, Austria, and Italy, might at any moment have been required to help Russia in attacking the Ottoman Empire, if a previous agreement had been obtained that the Turkish reforms were not being duly carried out. Such a war, supposing it to have been waged, would probably have had for its object the creation of a number of tributary States; and these, as we have before observed would have been probably the humble but effective agents of Russian ambition. What the Czar really wanted was to gain the assistance of the Five Powers towards the realisation of his own ends. England, however, would not thus be bound, and the language of the Protocol was altered accordingly. Even then, it was considered advisable to obtain from Russia some kind of promise that she would demobilise her troops; and it was said that Lord Beaconsfield had declared that without disarmament he would not consent to the Protocol in any form. Hence the proviso of Lord Derby that the agreement was to be considered null and void unless reciprocal disarmament took place. The Protocol itself made no mention of demobilisation as regarded Russia, though the Porte was "invited" to put its armies on a peace footing; but Count Schouvaloff, in the declaration by which he accompanied the act of signature, promised that the Emperor would consent to disarmament, if the Sultan would first show a willingness to do the same, and would send to St. Petersburg a Special Envoy to discuss the subject. The terms in which this intimation was made were, however, so imperious and exacting that they were not likely to attain their object, if, indeed, their object was what it professed to be.

The Protocol was in truth no better than a piece of waste paper. It left matters where it found them, or perhaps even added to the chances of war by complicating the question with fresh conditions of a vexatious and intermeddling character. The only possible advantage of the document was in its offering to Russia a species of golden bridge, by which she might be enabled to retreat with a semblance of honour from the difficult position into which she had thrust herself. But it is very doubtful whether she had any desire to quit that position, except by way of a further advance. It is much more probable that the Protocol was a clever device for gaining time before a declaration of war. The instrument was signed on the 31st of March; a few more weeks might yet be taken up in further parleyings; and then spring would have arrived. Meanwhile, the army on the Pruth might be strengthened and improved in numbers, material, and organisation; and the commencement of active operations would happily coincide with the season of the year most favourable for warlike undertakings. It is not easy to understand how experienced statesmen could have hoped for a peaceful result from such a lamentable specimen of diplomacy. The Protocol was a worthy child of the Conference. Both resulted from covert intentions, expressed in insincere pretences. They were marked with failure from the first. Perhaps in some quarters they were so designed.

The Protocol was speedily brought before the cognizance of the Sublime Porte by the foreign *chargés d'affaires* whom the Ambassadors, on their departure, had left behind them at Constantinople. On the 3rd of April, the English representative read the document to Safvet Pasha, but without leaving a copy with him. The full text was presented on the following day by the representative of Russia; and the diplomatic agents of France, Austria, Germany, and Italy, supported the declarations of the instrument that had been signed in London. English influence was freely used to induce the Porte to accept the Protocol, and consent to disarm; but, although frequent Cabinet Councils were held, the Turkish Government delayed its answer for several days. Russia became impatient, and demanded an immediate reply. The 13th of the month was mentioned as the date beyond which Russia would not consent to wait any longer. On that day the renewed armistice with Montenegro would expire, and the Cabinet of St. Petersburg demanded that the Porte should send a Special Envoy to the Russian capital before the termination of the period. For a brief time it was thought that the Porte would yield. The *Times* of April 9th published a telegram from Berlin, stating that Turkey consented to disarm, "as she was bid." Peace, therefore, was regarded as certain. This, however, was a totally erroneous announcement. Turkey was not at all disposed to do as she was bid, and even regarded the Protocol as an additional affront. The Porte was inclined to negotiate on the question of demobilization before the signature of the Protocol; but that unfortunate document, taken in connection with the Russian declaration by which it was accompanied, had entirely altered the aspect of affairs by introducing an appearance of coercion. It was rumoured that even then the Porte would not refuse to entertain the proposals that had been made, provided they were based on a

THE GRAND DUKE NICHOLAS (COMMANDER-IN-CHIEF OF THE RUSSIAN FORCES IN EUROPE).

previous cancelling of the Protocol. But this, of course, was entirely out of the question. Whether rightly or wrongly, the Six Powers had committed themselves to a certain policy, and were not likely to draw back in order that the self-love of Turkey might be saved from violation. Every day, indeed, made peace less probable, and war more imminent. In the Russian *pro-memoriâ*, it was stipulated that peace should be concluded with Montenegro, as one of the preliminaries to an amicable arrangement between Turkey and Russia. But the negotiations between the Porte and the Prince of Montenegro came to a conclusion towards the middle of April. The mountaineers would not abandon their claim to an increase of territory. The Turkish Chamber of Deputies decided by a large majority, on the 10th of April, that no such increase should be granted; and the parties separated in anger. Hostilities at once recommenced, and this petty warfare might fairly be regarded as the commencement of the greater struggle which had been threatening Europe in many vague and portentous shapes for more than a year.

UNIFORMS OF RUSSIAN TROOPS.

The Circular in which the Ottoman Government gave expression to its views on the Protocol was telegraphed to the Turkish representatives abroad on the 10th of April. In taking cognizance of the principal document, and of the declarations annexed thereto, the Sublime Porte expressed great regret at observing that the Six Powers had not thought it necessary to associate the Turkish Government with their deliberations, although questions were discussed which concerned the most vital interests of the Empire. The Porte considered itself imperatively bound to protest against such a precedent, and to point out the evil consequences which, in its opinion, might result from it in the future. After alluding to the comprehensive reforms recently established in the administration of the Empire, and to the difficulties in their complete realisation which had been created by revolutionary intrigue and the disturbed condition of the provinces, the Circular proceeded to comment on the gravity of the situation, which every day became more serious. In reply to the declaration made by the Russian Ambassador at London, the Sublime Porte notified to the signatory Powers that, adopting towards Montenegro the same line of conduct which had brought about the pacification of Servia, it had spontaneously informed Prince Nikita, two months previously, that it would spare no effort to arrive at an understanding with him, even at the price of certain sacrifices. Turkey had long considered Montenegro as an integral part of the Ottoman territory, but had proposed a rectification of the line of demarcation, which secured advantages to that principality. With respect to the Empire generally, the Government was prepared to put all the promised reforms in execution, but, in conformity with the fundamental provisions of the Constitution, these could not have a special or exclusive character. The Imperial Government was ready to replace its armies on a peace footing as soon as it should see the Russian Government take measures to the same end. The armaments of Turkey had an exclusively defensive character, and the relations of friendship and esteem which united the two Empires (said the Circular, with a touch of irony) inspired the hope that the St. Petersburg Cabinet would not, alone in Europe, persist in the idea that the Christian populations in Turkey were exposed to such dangers from their own Government that it was necessary to accumulate against a neighbouring and friendly State all the means of invasion and destruction. With regard to the disturbances which might break out in Turkey, and stop the demobilisation of the Russian army, the Imperial Government, while repelling the haughty terms in which this idea had been expressed, believed that Europe was convinced that the disturbances which had troubled the peace of the provinces were due to foreign instigation, that the Imperial Government could not be held responsible for them, and that consequently the Russian Government would not be justified in making the demobilisation of its armies dependent upon such contingencies.

As touching the despatch of a Special Envoy to St. Petersburg, to treat on the question of disarmament, the Turkish Government very pithily remarked that it could perceive no connection between an act of international courtesy, to which, if reciprocal, it would not object, and a disarmament which there was no plausible motive for delaying, and which might be carried into effect by a single telegraphic order. Glancing at that section of the Protocol which alluded to the reforms to be introduced in Bosnia, Herzegovina, and Bulgaria, the Circular denied that Turkey had accepted any special reforms for those localities. The Porte entertained no doubt that its interests and its duty required it to satisfy the legitimate rights of its Christian subjects; but it could not grant that ameliorations should apply exclusively to the Christian element. "It is not admissible," said the Circular, "that ameliorations tending to secure the tranquillity and welfare of Mussulmans should possess no importance in the eyes of just, tolerant, and enlightened Europe. To take measures, or rather to establish institutions, calculated to ensure to all, and everywhere, the free, moral, and material development of the rights of all—such is the end which Turkey now has in view." Against the proposal of the Powers to watch carefully, by means of their representatives at Constantinople and their local agents, the manner in which the promises of the Ottoman Government were carried into effect, Turkey most energetically protested, and with equal spirit repelled the intimation of the Six Powers that, in the event of their hopes being once more disappointed, they reserved to themselves the right to consider in common the means best adapted to secure the ends they had in view. Turkey, in her quality of an independent State, could not acknowledge herself as being placed under any supervision, collective or otherwise.

"Maintaining with other friendly States," said the author of this remarkable document, "relations regulated by international law and treaties, Turkey cannot allow foreign agents, or representatives charged to protect the interests of their compatriots, to have any mission of official supervision. The Imperial Government, in fact, is not aware how it can have deserved so ill of justice and civilization as to see itself placed in a humiliating position without example in the world. The Treaty of Paris gave an explicit sanction to the principle of non-intervention. This treaty, which binds together the Powers who participated in it as well as Turkey, cannot be abolished by a Protocol in which Turkey has had no share. And, if Turkey appeals to the stipulations of the Treaty of Paris, it is not that that treaty has created in her favour any rights which she would not possess without it, but rather for the purpose of calling attention to the grave reasons which, in the interests of the general peace of Europe, induced the Powers, twenty years ago, to place the recognition of the inviolability of this Empire's right of sovereignty under the guarantee of a collective promise. With regard to the clause which, in case of the non-execution of the promised reforms, would seek to confer upon the Powers the right of recurring to ulterior measures, the Imperial Government perceives therein a fresh attack upon its dignity and its rights, a measure of intimidation calculated to deprive its acts of any merit of spontaneity, and a source of grave complication both in the present and in the future. No consideration, therefore, can arrest the Government in its determination to protest against the views enunciated in the Protocol of the 31st of March, and to treat it, as far as Turkey is concerned, as destitute of all equity, and consequently also of all obligatory character. Exposed to hostile suggestions, to unmerited suspicions, and to violations of international law, Turkey feels that she is now contending for her existence. Strong in the justice of her cause, and trusting in God, she determines to ignore what has been decided without her and against her. Resolved to retain in the world the place which Providence has destined for her in this regard, she will not cease to encounter the attacks directed against her with the general principles of public right, and the authority of a great European Act which pledges the honour of the Powers that signed the Protocol of the 31st of March—a document which, in her eyes, has no legal claim to exact compliance. She appeals to the conscience of the Cabinets, which she has a right to consider animated towards her by the same sentiments of elevated equity and friendship as in the past." With an emphatic expression of opinion that immediate and simultaneous disarmament would be the only efficacious means of averting the dangers by which the general peace was threatened, the Turkish Circular came to a close.

The Ottoman Ambassador in England called on Lord Derby on the 12th of April, and left with him a copy of the despatch. Having read this document, the Foreign Secretary expressed to his Excellency his deep regret at the view which the Porte had taken of a proceeding the principal object of which had been to extricate Turkey from a position of extreme embarrassment and danger. It did not, however, seem clear to Lord Derby whether the Porte would or would not consent to send an Ambassador to St. Petersburg, to treat on the question of mutual disarmament. Musurus Pasha replied that his Government was not prepared to adopt any such measure, and he further expressed an opinion that matters could not be settled in a satisfactory manner unless the Powers consented to annul the Protocol. Lord Derby said he did not see what further steps her Majesty's Government could take to avert a war which appeared to have become inevitable. The Turkish Ambassador responded that the attitude of his Government was simply defensive; that Turkey did not desire war, but that she would prefer it to the sacrifice of national independence, which appeared to her to be involved in the acceptance of the Protocol. The final stage in the negotiations had been reached; the last hope of peace had vanished from the darkening horizon of South-eastern Europe.

The Emperor of Russia was now so fully committed to a warlike policy that retreat was impossible, unless at the risk of political revolution, and perhaps even of personal assassination. He left St. Petersburg for Kischeneff—the head-quarters of the army massed in Bessarabia—on the morning of the 20th of April. On the 22nd, he reviewed the Ninth Army Corps at Umerinka and Birsula, and at the latter place addressed the officers of the inspected troops in a brief speech. "Before your departure," he said, "I give you my blessing. If you should encounter the enemy, show yourselves brave, and strive to uphold the ancient glory of your regiments. There are among you young men who have not been under fire. I hope they will not show themselves inferior to their veteran comrades, but will prove themselves their equals. I trust that you may soon return covered with glory. Good-bye, gentlemen!" Either on that or some similar occasion, the Emperor is reported to have said:—"I have done everything in my power to avoid war and bloodshed. Nobody can say we have not been patient, or that the war has been of our seeking. We have practised patience to the last degree; but there comes a time when even patience must end." The Emperor was accompanied by the Grand Duke Nicholas, the Czarewitch, General Ignatieff, General Milutin (Minister of War), and a staff and suite of nearly three hundred persons. It was evident that hostilities had now been fully resolved on; but the positive declaration of war did not follow until a few days later.

Before this declaration had been made, but after formal notification of the suspension of diplomatic relations, the archives and effects of the Russian Embassy and Consulate at Constantinople were handed over to the German Embassy which undertook the protection of Russian subjects during the rupture now about to ensue. This was on the morning of the 23rd of April. In the afternoon, a solemn *Te Deum* was sung in the chapel of the Russian Embassy, and in the evening the entire staff left the city. The arms of the Embassy were taken down in the presence of an immense crowd at half-past five o'clock P.M.; and this was the last act performed at the Russian diplomatic quarters previous to the commencement of hostilities. A few days before the departure of the Russian staff, a new British Ambassador arrived in Constantinople, Mr. (now Sir Henry) Layard, who had been removed from Madrid for that purpose. Mr. Layard did not go to the Eastern capital in any permanent capacity: his mission was simply to fill the place of Sir Henry Elliot until the health of that gentleman was sufficiently restored to enable him to resume his former post. But the fact of even a temporary Ambassador being sent to the Porte seemed to indicate a willingness on the part of the British Government to enter once more into friendly communications with that of Turkey. The inference was all the more probable from the well-known fact that the sympathies of Mr. Layard were strongly Turkish. Probably no Englishman knows the East better than the distinguished author, traveller, and diplomatist who was now charged with the representation of English interests on the shores of the Bosphorus. Nearly thirty years before, he had been *attaché* to the British Embassy at Constantinople; but that formed only one part of his experience. Sir Henry has given the study of a life to the investigation not merely of Oriental antiquity, but of Western Asia as it exists at the present day. His voice has frequently been heard in Parliament on the great questions connected with the internal condition of Turkey, and the relations of that Empire to the European system; and it has been manifest that, however much he may be persuaded, in common with all other men, of the inherent vices of the Turkish Government, he is far from hopeless of the future of Turkey itself, supposing a fair chance to be afforded the Ottoman people for working out their own regeneration. It has always been the opinion of Sir H. Layard that Europe has drifted into a totally false position with reference to the dominion of the Sultans; that interference has been made the excuse for intrigue; that intrigue has resulted in continual revolution or menace; that the anarchy thus fostered has in its turn afforded a pretext for renewed interference; that Russia has for many years carried on an active propaganda for the destruction of Turkish independence; and that reform has been crippled, and in some instances rendered abortive, by a social state, created to a great extent by external agencies, which no Power in the world could have withstood, had it been equally brought within the sway of such disturbing influences. Yet the new Ambassador did not go to Constantinople to flatter Turkish vanity, or to gloss over Turkish crimes. In his first interview with the Grand Vizier and the Minister for Foreign Affairs, which took place on the 21st of April, he alluded to the fact that no one had even then been adequately punished for the Bulgarian massacres. He referred to the injustice of that partial repudiation of the foreign debt which Turkey had in terms rescinded. He condemned both the style adopted in the recent reply to the Protocol (which he characterised as needlessly offensive and ill-considered), and the manner in which that decision had been communicated to the European Powers. He warned the Porte that these and other acts had alienated the sympathy of England, and had rendered her support improbable, if not impossible; and he urged a recourse to peaceful overtures, as a means of avoiding the mischief which might be expected to result from war.* The warning came too late; but words of this nature could not fail to make a deep impression when proceeding from a man of Sir Henry Layard's high repute, and friendly sentiments towards the Ottoman Power.

The same period of excitement was marked by another event of European interest, which, though having no direct bearing on the impending war, may perhaps have been in some degree associated with it. The German Chancellor, Prince Bismarck, was once more suffering in health from the incessant strain of his multifarious duties, and, as on a previous occasion, he retired for awhile from the post he had occupied during many years. His own wish was to abandon his position altogether; but the Emperor requested him to retain the Chancellorship nominally, with a view to a future resumption of active work, while for the present he sought repose at his seat in the country. It was finally arranged that he should have a holiday of some months' duration, and that in the meantime the President of the Imperial Chancellery should represent him in the despatch of business relating to the internal affairs of the Empire, while the Secretary of State, Von Bülow, took charge of foreign affairs. That the health of Bismarck was seriously impaired, seems indisputable; but there were other reasons as well for the course now taken. The great Chancellor was at issue with his colleagues in some important matters of policy. He had not the support of the Emperor to the extent that he formerly enjoyed. The opposition in Parliament was becoming more vexatious and more powerful; and even in the country itself, Bismarck was no longer the popular man that

* Correspondent of the *Daily Telegraph*.

he had been in 1870 and 1871. It seems probable that he and his Imperial master were not quite in harmony on the Eastern Question. The Emperor was apparently inclined to support his nephew of Russia to the utmost extent of a friendly neutrality. Bismarck, to judge from speeches delivered by him about the period when the Reichstag opened, was animated by feelings not altogether favourable to Russia. Nobody, indeed, could quite understand his policy on the subject; whereas the Emperor's was clear and unequivocal. This may have had some share in determining the temporary withdrawal of the former.

The manifesto of the Emperor of Russia, announcing his final resolution to draw the sword, was issued from Kischeneff on the 24th of April. It commenced by asserting the strong interest his Imperial Majesty had always felt in the destinies of the oppressed populations of Turkey. His desire to improve and assure their lot had, he said, been shared by the whole Russian people, who now showed themselves ready to bear fresh sacrifices to alleviate the position of the Christians in the Balkan Peninsula. The desire of Russia, before all others, was to effect such a result by means of pacific negotiations, and in concert with the chief European Powers; but this end had been thwarted. The Emperor recapitulated the course of events during the two previous years, and lamented that the efforts of himself and his allies had failed to attain their object. The Protocol had been as ineffectual as the attempts which preceded it, and the Czar felt compelled, "by the haughty obstinacy of the Porte," to proceed to more decisive acts. "By her refusal," said the Emperor, "Turkey places us under the necessity of having recourse to arms. Profoundly convinced of the justice of our cause, and humbly committing ourselves to the grace and help of the Most High, we make known to our faithful subjects that the moment foreseen, when we pronounced words to which all Russia responded with such complete unanimity, has now arrived. We expressed the intention to act independently when we deemed it necessary, and when Russia's honour should demand it. In now invoking the blessing of God upon our valiant armies, we give the order to cross the Turkish frontier."

On the same day that this manifesto was issued, Prince Gortschakoff gave formal notice of belligerency to the Turkish *chargé d'affaires* at St. Petersburg. The first consequence of the state of war, he remarked, was the rupture of the diplomatic relations of the two countries, and the Ottoman representative was therefore requested to furnish the number and rank of the members of the Embassy, that they might receive their passports. As regarded Ottoman subjects living in Russia, it was intimated that those who were desirous of leaving were at liberty to do so unmolested, while those who should prefer to remain might consider themselves assured of the full protection of the laws. Prince Gortschakoff also addressed, on that eventful 24th of April, a circular note to the Ambassadors of Russia at London, Paris, Berlin, Vienna, and Rome. From the terms of the Protocol, the Russian Chancellor inferred that the Cabinets had foreseen the contingency that the Porte would not fulfil its promises, but not that it would reject the demands of Europe. At the same time it had been established by the declaration of Lord Derby, attached to the Protocol, that, in the event of mutual disarmament and a peaceful arrangement of the difficulties not being obtained, the agreement of the 31st of March was to be regarded as null and void. The rejection of the Protocol by the Porte, and the motives on which that refusal was based, left no hope that Turkey would accede to the wishes and counsels of Europe; excluded every guarantee for the execution of the projected reforms touching the condition of the Eastern Christians; rendered peace with Montenegro impossible; and neutralized the conditions by which alone disarmament and pacification could be brought about. "Under these circumstances," continued Prince Gortschakoff, "the success of any attempt at compromise is excluded, and there remains only the alternative either to allow the state of things to continue which the Powers have declared incompatible with their interests and those of Europe, or to try by coercive measures to obtain that which the unanimous efforts of the Powers did not succeed in obtaining from the Porte by means of an understanding. My exalted master has resolved to undertake that which his Majesty had invited the Great Powers to do in common with him. His Majesty has given his armies the order to cross the frontier of Turkey. You will bring this resolution to the cognizance of the Government to which you are accredited. My exalted master, in taking this step, is fulfilling a duty which is imposed upon him by the interests of Russia, whose peaceable development is impeded by the constant troubles in the East. His Majesty has the conviction that he at the same time responds to the views of Europe."

To the manifesto of the Emperor of Russia, Turkey replied in a despatch to the foreign representatives of the Porte, dated the 25th of April. All occasion for diplomatic reserve being now at an end, Safvet Pasha did not hesitate to accuse Russia

DEPARTURE OF THE RUSSIAN EMBASSY FROM CONSTANTINOPLE.

in the most direct language of having incited those revolutionary movements in the north-western parts of the Empire which were now alleged as the justification of the impending war. "The Imperial Government," said the Foreign Minister of the Sultan, "deems itself bound to declare that the Christian populations of Herzegovina and Bosnia, and of the vilayets inhabited by the Bulgarians, rose in insurrection solely at the instigation of Pan-Sclavist Committees, organised and paid by Russia; that Servia and Montenegro took up arms against the Sovereign Power only through the direct intervention of Russia; that they never could have sustained the struggle without aid from Russia; and that, in fact, all the ills which for the last two years have scourged their portion of the Empire are due to the action, open or hidden, but always present, of Russia. The aggressor of Turkey is as much the enemy of the Christian as of the Mussulman populations; for she has caused them, and is now preparing for them, more ills than ever she could promise benefits when falsely alluring them to civil war." On the previous day (the 24th), Safvet Pasha, in pursuance of a resolution of the Cabinet, arrived at the night before after much debate, addressed a circular to the friendly Powers, proposing mediation. The actual declaration of war had not then been received; but the belligerent party in the Turkish Government was strongly opposed to any such step. In this circular, the Porte asked if Russia was authorized to declare war separately from the other signatories of the Protocol —to make war, that was to say, in the name of the general peace; and it appealed to the Eighth Article of the Treaty of Paris (1856) to show that, in case any disagreement should arise between Turkey and one or more of the other signatory Powers, the Sublime Porte, and each of those Powers, should, before having recourse to the employment of violence, place the other contracting parties in a position to prevent that extremity by their mediatorial action. Relying on this Article, to which Russia was as much a party as the other Powers, Safvet Pasha suggested that the Cabinets of London, Paris, Berlin, Vienna, and Rome should endeavour to arrest the breaking-out of war by arbitrating on the merits of the quarrel. The appeal was perfectly warranted by the terms on which peace had been concluded in 1856; but nothing came of it, and indeed it was not likely, in the excited state of the two Empires, that the attempt would have been successful, had it been made.

GENERAL MILUTIN.

The Sultan shortly afterwards addressed a proclamation to his armies, which said:—"The Russian Government has declared war upon us. Confident in the aid of Providence and of the Prophet, we have been forced in our turn to have recourse to arms. We have always wished for peace and tranquillity, despite the drawn sword which we have held in our hand; and, in our desire for peace, we have listened to the counsels of Europe, and worked with it to attain the desired result. Our enemy having, however, but one object in view—that of completely annihilating our rights and independence—it was impossible to satisfy his desire without sacrificing everything. Thus, without right or real cause, he has marched to attack us. We are convinced that the Judge of Judges, the Protector of right and justice, will grant us the victory by the aid of our own efforts and bravery, and by the union of the material and moral support of our faithful subjects. The enemy will not attain the desired end. I trust in God, who will grant the victory to the just cause. I hope my soldiers will guard the honour and glory of the Osmanli name, and that of our ancestors, and keep our flag without stain. I salute all my generals, officers, and soldiers. They will show at this solemn hour all their ardour, zeal, and courage. Every foot of ground occupied by our soldiers was bought with the blood of our glorious ancestors. Let them defend the rights and independence of the Osmanlis. In so doing they will obtain the victory. The nation takes under its protection the wives and children of the soldiers. The Padishah is with them in his prayers. If needful, he will take in hand the sacred banner, and will join them, ready to sacrifice his life at the head of the army for the rights, the honour, and the independence of Turkey. May God grant us the victory!" The word "Padishah" is one of the titles of the Sultan, and "the sacred banner" is that which is regarded as the flag of the Prophet, and therefore as the symbol of Islamism, the unfurling of which summons the Faithful to a Jihad, or war for religion,—in other

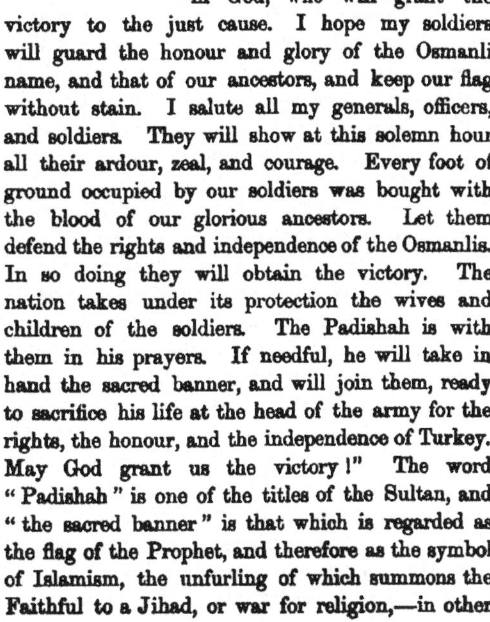

words, to a war of extermination. Resort has seldom been had to this dreadful organization of fanaticism; but it is always a possibility in Mohammedan Empires, and it is a danger especially to be dreaded when accumulated defeats threaten the very existence of a Moslem Power.

The two opponents were now fairly face to face "on the rough edge of battle ere it joined." The question had passed beyond the evasions and insincerities, the mock smiles and muffled hatred, of diplomacy, and had assumed a form which made it necessary for the other European Powers to decide whether or not they would take part in the struggle. The decision of the English Government was conveyed in a despatch from Lord Derby to the British Ambassador at St. Petersburg, dated May 1st. Her Majesty's Ministers, it was here written, had received the announcement made by the Russian Government with deep regret. They could not accept the statements and conclusions with which Prince Gortschakoff had accompanied it, as justifying the resolution taken. The Porte had unfortunately protested against the Protocol; but it had again affirmed its intention of carrying into execution the reforms already promised, and the British Government, therefore, could not admit that the answer of the Porte removed all hope of deference on its part to the wishes and advice of Europe. With patience and moderation on both sides, the objects desired might, in the opinion of the British Government, not improbably have been attained; but Prince Gortschakoff had asserted that all further openings for conciliation were closed, and had expressed the Emperor's conviction that the step about to be taken was in accordance with the sentiments and the interests of Europe. Her Majesty's Government did not agree in that view. The presence of large Russian forces on the frontiers of Turkey constituted a material obstacle to internal pacification and reform; and the entrance of those armies on Turkish soil would not improve the condition of the Christians in the East. But the course on which the Russian Government had entered involved graver and more serious considerations. It was in contravention of that stipulation of the Treaty of Paris by which Russia and the other signatory Powers engaged, each on its own part, to respect the independence and territorial integrity of the Ottoman Empire. In the Conferences of London of 1871, at the close of which this stipulation, with others, was again confirmed, the Russian Plenipotentiary, in common with those of the other Powers, signed a Declaration affirming it to be "an essential principle of the law of nations that no Power can liberate itself from the engagements of a Treaty, nor modify the stipulations thereof, unless with the consent of the contracting parties, by means of an amicable arrangement." In taking isolated action against Turkey, and having recourse to arms without further consultation with his allies, the Emperor of Russia, in the emphatic language of Lord Derby, had separated himself from the European concert, and had at the same time departed from a rule to which he solemnly recorded his assent. It was impossible to foresee the consequences of such an act, and her Majesty's Government felt bound to state that the decision of the Russian Government was not one which could have their concurrence or approval.

The protest, considered by itself, was as admirable in spirit as it was strong and earnest in expression; but unfortunately it was discredited by the source from which it issued. It was simply another turn in the endless vacillations of the Government. Once more, the anti-Russian section of the Cabinet had obtained the ascendancy, and it was Lord Beaconsfield, rather than Lord Derby, who spoke in the despatch of May 1st. Excellent in itself, that despatch was but little in harmony with the policy by which it had been preceded, and the Czar might fairly have complained that he had been deceived and deserted. From the point of view assumed at the Conference by all the Powers, and by none more than England, it is difficult to see how Russia could be blamed for making war on Turkey. It was contended throughout the whole discussion that Turkey had been guilty of abnormal wickedness towards the Christian part of her population; that she was so hardened in guilt that no spontaneous amendment was to be expected from her; that her promises of reform had invariably been broken, and in all probability would be broken again; that her new Constitution offered not the slightest satisfaction to the demands of Christian Europe; and that if she refused the terms presented in common by the Six Powers, she would deserve any fate that might await her, and would receive no assistance, even if invaded and threatened with complete ruin. In spite of these exhortations and menaces, Turkey rejected the requirements of the Powers; and, assuming the correctness of the contention which Lord Salisbury had so earnestly supported at Constantinople, the only alternative was between leaving the Eastern Christians to hopeless, endless, and unutterable misery, and coercing their oppressor. On some grounds there was much to say against Russia; but many persons considered that it was not for Lord Derby and his colleagues to denounce an act which they had almost invited, and, by implication, had certainly condoned.

CHAPTER XI.

Composition of the Russian Army—Its State previous to 1874—Evils and Hardships of the Old System—The Reforms of 1874, and their Chief Provisions—Exceptions to the Rule that every Male is liable to Military Service—Hard Life of the Russian Soldier—System of Punishments—Military Education—Deficiency of good Officers—Virtues and Defects of Russian Troops—Dishonesty among the Officers, owing to insufficient Pay—The Cossacks—Origin and early Services of those Military Tribes—Their present Organization and Position in the Russian Army—Personal Appearance and Disposition—Strengthening of the Russian Forces in all Departments since 1860—Report of General Milutin, Minister of War—Russian Field Artillery—The Army of the Caucasus—General Loris Melikoff and the Grand Duke Nicholas—Mr. Archibald Forbes on the Characteristics of the Russian Soldier—Corruption and Favouritism in the Military Administration—Instances of gross Peculation—The Russian Navy—Monitors, Turret-ships, and Ironclad Vessels—Manning of the Fleet—Errors committed by the Russian Naval Authorities—Unarmoured Ships in the Russian Fleet—Character of the Naval Officers and Crews.

BEFORE entering on the events of the war, it will be advisable to consider the relative military and naval strength of the two Empires. Both wielded immense forces, and were animated by a haughty spirit; but, speaking in the general, it may be stated that Russia had the larger army, and Turkey the larger fleet. The Russian legions—at least, nominally—amount to the enormous total of 3,300,000 men on the war footing, and are divided into the regular army, the reserve, and the militia. Like most other European armies during the last few years, that of Russia has been remodelled with a view to more effective action. The change thus brought about was commenced on the 1st of January, 1874, when a new law came into force, by which military service was made obligatory on the whole nation. The army until then had been recruited from the very dregs of the populace. In the days of serfdom, which lasted until 1863, the rank-and-file had consisted entirely of peasants, and every landed proprietor had to furnish a certain number of soldiers from among his dependents, in conformity with orders issued from time to time by the Emperor. On the Crown estates, the serfs were selected by the magistrates, and, both there and in other localities, the most worthless and dissipated men were chosen to fill the ranks. Even after the abolition of serfdom, the composition of the army continued of a very disreputable character. Idlers, drunkards, and criminals were enlisted under the flag, and it was considered sufficient if a man could perform long marches without exhaustion, obey the commands of his officer with stolid fidelity, and stand against his foe with ordinary courage. These, of course, were good qualities as far as they went; but of intelligence the Russian private had none, and intelligence is every year becoming more and more the ruling force, in armies as in all things else. The extraordinary successes of the Germans in France, during the great days of 1870 and 1871, taught a lesson to Russia as well as to other Powers; and the Czar resolved thenceforth to place his multitudinous battalions on a footing more in harmony with the requirements of modern warfare.

One of the great evils of the old system was the length of service, which operated most cruelly on the masses of the people. In the Guards, men were enlisted for four-and-twenty years; in other regiments, for twenty or twenty-two. The period of liability was from twenty-one to thirty. When these men were sent into distant provinces, it was often equivalent to exile from their relatives for life; it was also equivalent to the loss of their services as labourers on the great estates. Consequently, the best men were kept at home, and the worst were draughted into the army. The term of service was shortened by the Emperor Nicholas; but the character of the men was no better. The poor quality of the Russian soldier was made apparent to the Western nations at the period of the Crimean War. It did not improve between that date and the epoch of the war between France and Germany. The rapidity with which the former country was then over-run, not simply because of the large numbers of the invading hosts, but still more by reason of their trained intelligence and splendid organization, made the Emperor Alexander uneasy as to his own position as the representative of a first-class military Power; and as early as November, 1870, the liability of every Russian male to service in the army was recognized by an Imperial Ukase as a principle for future guidance, though it was not until the beginning of 1874 that any steps were taken for carrying the idea into practice. By the law then promulgated—from the operation of which Finland was excepted—the peace establishment of regular troops was fixed at 760,000 men. The duration of service in the active army was thenceforth to be six years in Europe, and seven in Asia. It is calculated that every year about 700,000 young men attain the proper age for military service, and that from one-fourth to one-fifth of the number is required for the regular army: the remainder pass into the militia, where they must stay for twenty years, during the first four of which they may be called on to augment the ranks of the professional troops. The

COSSACK TYPE.

reserve is formed by those members of the regular army who have served their six or seven years with the colours, but who then become liable to serve another nine years in a modified capacity, during which they may practice any trade or calling, though they are still at the disposal of the

MOUNTED COSSACK OF THE LINE.

State for special requirements. As the new system had not been in operation much more than three years when the war with Turkey broke out, towards the end of April, 1877, the reserve thus provided for had not begun to be created. Even in the active army, the greater number of men had been enlisted under the system recently superseded.

To the rule that every Russian male is liable to military service, there are necessarily several exceptions. The clergy, medical students, chemists, schoolmasters, officers of the mercantile marine, and some others, are either exempted altogether, or allowed a certain postponement of the period of liability; and, by a benevolent provision, the only son of parents who have attained the age of fifty-five is not required to join the army. The Imperial forces, therefore, do not, after all, represent the entire manhood of the nation; but they include a considerable proportion of it. The term of service of recruits possessing even a moderate

COSSACKS ON THE MARCH.

amount of education is shortened by two years, and those who are able to pass an educational test may, by voluntary enlistment, obtain the position of non-commissioned officers after very short periods of training. The system, on the whole, is scarcely so hard as it might at first sight appear; yet it is not a little strict, nevertheless. Those who are well off, or even superficially educated, feel its pressure less onerously; but the poor, ignorant peasant has to endure its full weight. The humble tillers of the soil, who but a few years ago were serfs, are still the chief elements in the army, and their lives are miserable enough. The pay is extremely small—not more than a farthing a day for a full private; and the rations consist of black bread, a small quantity of meat, and a good deal of rice. During the progress of a war, and while manœuvres are being executed in time of peace, the pay is increased to the extent of fifty per cent.; but, under the best of circumstances, the soldier receives so little that he often works as a labourer for such wages as he can get. Yet he is cheerful, willing, and not seldom lively; singing and dancing even on the march, and exhibiting great powers of endurance, though heavily encumbered with weapons, ammunition, and accoutrements. A love of intoxication is among his greatest faults. He will drink as much *vodka* (rye-spirit) as he can get; and, as the liquor is of a coarse and fiery character, its effects are maddening.

The Russian troops are very severely drilled, yet (with the exception of a few picked regiments) do not present the smart appearance of many European armies. Of late years, corporal punishment has been inflicted only on men who, for confirmed bad character, have already been placed on the punishment list; and it may not in any case exceed fifty lashes. Other punishments, of varying intensity, are ordered as occasion may require: of these, the most oppressive is solitary confinement in a dark cell for eight days. As a rule, the Russian soldier is obedient and respectful to his commanding officer; but the officer is frequently not very worthy of respect. An improvement has taken place of late years, for education is spreading even in Russia, and ten elementary military schools have recently been established by the Government, together with others of a more advanced character. But many of the Czar's officers are coarse-living, illiterate men, and we have it on the authority of Colonel Burnaby and other travellers that, in the remote stations of Central Asia, where there is little to do, and consequently a great sense of tedium, the debauchery is excessive, habitual, and shameless. In time, no doubt, Russia will obtain a body of highly-trained military officers, as strenuous efforts are certainly being made towards that end; but for the present the Russian army is not well commanded in the inferior grades. The progress of affairs in the earlier stages of the war of 1877 exhibited great want of readiness, except in a few instances. Officers and men are alike brave, hardy, and constant; but much of the barbarian clings to them, and the inferiority of the Russians to the Germans is as marked in the respective armies as in the respective nations. Regimental schools, however, are now opened during the winter months, and the officers instruct their men—sometimes, it is said, with remarkably successful results—in the rudiments of history, geography, composition, arithmetic, tactics, and fortification. Still, the educated Russian soldier is a rare exception at present, whatever he may become in time. "All in all," says a correspondent of the *Standard*, "the Russian soldier is still the *moushik* [peasant or serf], with all the virtues and vices of the slave; blindly obedient, attached to his officers, but in every respect incapable of governing himself. Widespread drunkenness has unnerved thousands, and other vices have for centuries past been more frequent in the Russian army than in any other: the Russian hospitals are never empty. But otherwise the Russian soldiers are robust, with great powers of endurance, brave, and well drilled. This is especially true of the infantry, which is still frequently reproached, though without reason, with being awkward, and only useful for operations in great masses, but not for skirmishing." The regular cavalry, according to the same writer, is excellent.

The enormous size of the Russian army is one source of its weakness. In proportion to the number of men must be the number of officers, and in Russia there is so small a class of educated gentlemen that the army is under-officered, especially in the scientific corps, and the Emperor is forced to be content with a very inferior set of men for the command of his regiments. The pay of the officers, like that of the privates, is so extremely bad (a full general receiving no more than £300 a year) that men of ability and culture prefer devoting themselves to commerce, or to some of the liberal pursuits, and can with difficulty be persuaded to enter the army. This want of means on the part of Russian officers is one great cause of peculation and dishonesty. Lamentable tales are told of the misapplication of Government stores, and of the ingenious tricks by which money is obtained for articles which the wretched soldier has to do without. In time of war, the pay is increased about fifty per cent., as with the common soldiers, and the officers have certain allowances and privileges which make their lot somewhat more bearable; yet their total remuneration is slight, compared with the services they render, frequently at an immense distance from their homes and kindred. The Russian officer is a stern disciplinarian; but his manner towards his men is often kindly, and the Russian language supplies him with a number of amiable phrases, which are pleasant to hear, though they probably mean but little.

By the new arrangements of 1874, as formerly, military service is performed under special laws by the Cossacks, the non-Russian inhabitants of the Empire, and the population of the Grand Duchy of Finland, which still preserves some of its old Swedish customs, and is permitted to furnish a certain number of soldiers in proportion to the population of each district, and to pay them from the provincial treasury, while the Empire provides for their material wants. The Cossacks are among the most important elements of the Russian army. Generally speaking, the idea of a Cossack at once occurs to the mind whenever the troops of the Czar are mentioned; and Napoleon's celebrated phrase, about Europe in a certain number of years being either Republican or Cossack, was equivalent to saying, "either Republican or Russian." Yet these wild horsemen are to some extent a distinct race, and possess many characteristics very different from those of the pure Muscovite. Their tribes form a species of semi-independent nationality, seated in those parts of the Russian Empire which border on Turkey, Tartary, Mongolia, and China; and their blood is as mixed as their geographical position is extended. Deriving their origin partly from the native Russian stock, they have mingled largely with Tartars and Kalmucks, and their dialect presents a considerable admixture of Polish, owing to their having in former times resided on the frontiers of Poland, and served under the kings of that country. Something of Caucasian blood would seem also to have entered into their composition, for they were long known as Tscherkesses, or Circassians, and the capital of the Don Cossacks is still called Tscherkask. In early ages, the Free Cossacks had their seats in the debateable land lying between Russia and Tartary, where they formed self-governing military republics, professing a certain allegiance to the Czar, but in fact paying very little attention to his edicts, if they clashed with their own ideas or interests. Whenever they came into collision with the subjects of the Turkish Sultan, the Russian monarchs would disavow them, and endeavour to make out that they were brigands, of no nationality whatever; yet it is proved, by documents recently published, that these martial tribes received supplies and ammunition from Moscow.* This was in the first half of the seventeenth century; so early did Russia commence those attacks on Turkey which in our own days

CIRCASSIANS.

have more than once disturbed the peace of Europe. The Czars were in truth very glad to keep on good terms with the Cossacks, for they formed a military barrier along the frontiers on the south and

* Russia, by D. Mackenzie Wallace, M.A., Vol. II., p. 75.

COSSACK OUTPOST.

south-east. The chief communities were those of the Dnieper and the Don,—rivers flowing south towards the Euxine and the Sea of Azof. The former went by the distinctive name of Zaporovians (meaning those who lived beyond the rapids), and dwelt in fortified camps, from which they sallied forth on fishing, hunting, and marauding expeditions. The Cossacks of the Don, of the Volga, and of the Yaïk (now of the Ural), lived in villages, and had more of a Tartar character than those whose homes were to the west; but all were warriors born and bred, and they kept the Tartars in check, as possibly no other organization could have done equally well. Very frequently, however, they conducted forays, marked by every kind of cruelty and excess, into the civilized parts of Russia itself; and more than once—in the seventeenth and eighteenth centuries—they rose in revolt against the sovereignty of the Czars. The chief of each clan is called a Hetman, and his power is considerable; but he is now appointed by the Emperor, and not, as formerly, elected by the communities themselves.

The Zaporovian Cossacks, after an insurrection against the Empress Catherine II. in 1773, were forcibly disbanded, and compelled to emigrate. The majority took refuge in Turkey, where some of their descendants are still to be found; the remainder settled on the Kuban (a river of the Western Caucasus), where for some generations they were engaged in carrying on irregular warfare with the neighbouring tribes of Mohammedans. They are now little more than agriculturists, though still retaining their martial air and appearance.

RUSSIAN MILITARY SCHOOL.

The men belonging to this particular body of Cossacks are a remarkably fine and stalwart race, and the Circassians have on many occasions suffered from their prowess, and doubtless also from their cruelty. Speaking of the Cossacks generally, a well-informed observer has described them as simply a species of mounted militia. In time of peace, the greater number remain at home, with the exception of a short period of drill during the summer; those who are on active service are to be met with in all parts of the Empire, from the Prussian to the Chinese frontier. "In the Asiatic provinces," says Mr. Mackenzie Wallace, "their services are invaluable. Capable of enduring an incredible amount of fatigue, and all manner of privations, they can live and thrive in conditions which would soon disable regular troops. The capacity of self-adaptation, which is characteristic of the Russian people generally, is possessed by them in the highest degree. When placed on some distant Asiatic frontier, they can at once transform themselves into squatters—building their own houses, raising crops of grain, and living as colonists without neglecting their military duties. If they require cattle, they can 'lift' them, either in the territory beyond the frontier, or in the region which they are supposed to protect, precisely as their ancestors did centuries ago. Thus they do their work effectually, at a very small cost to the Imperial exchequer." It has been asserted by several military critics that the Cossack organization is now quite antiquated, and that the soldiers it produces are of little worth in European warfare. The Cossacks themselves, however, consider they are the best troops in the Czar's armies, and boast that they can accomplish the most unheard-of feats of valour. More than one of the Don Cossacks assured Mr. Wallace that if the Emperor had allowed them to fit out a flotilla of small boats during the Crimean War, they would have captured the British fleet, as their ancestors used to capture Turkish galleys on the Black Sea.* It is not unusual with irregular troops to magnify their value, and to imagine that their wild and adventurous spirit is sufficient to effect whatever may be required in the whole range of war. Yet the Cossacks are something more than mere knights-errant. They fill an important page in the military history of Russia, and their usefulness is not yet superseded by any other organization.

It was not until the great war with Napoleon Bonaparte, in the early years of the present century, that the Cossacks first became generally known in Europe as a part of the Russian army. Afterwards, they acquired a sort of melodramatic halo from Byron's poem of "Mazeppa," written in 1818. As a species of irregular cavalry,—daring in spirit, hardy in constitution, rapid of movement, and always self-reliant,—they are undoubtedly valuable troops. Some of them are enrolled in regiments of the Guard and of the Line; but for the most part they maintain their separate and distinctive organization. They form the bulk of the forces employed in Siberia, and are always ready when any hard or difficult service is to be performed. Of infantry they furnish but few: the Cossack is generally a horseman. Unlike other Russians, the Cossacks have at all times enjoyed a remarkable degree of freedom. Serfage has never existed among them: with the haughtiness of a military race, they have combined something of the wild liberty that belongs to pastoral and nomadic tribes, accustomed to the spacious life of the desert. The Cossack commune owns the entire territory on which it is encamped, and all its members have an equal right to the use of the land, together with the pastures, hunting-grounds, and fisheries. The people pay no taxes to the Imperial Government, but are bound to perform military service. The Cossacks of the Ukraine have for a long time lost, to a very great extent, the military organisation for which they were once as famous as their brethren; yet, when France invaded Russia in 1812, they were able to equip at their own expense a force of 18,000 cavalry. The other tribes are still admirable auxiliaries, and in any great war are certain to distinguish themselves. Until recently, every male Cossack from fifteen to sixty years of age was bound to render military service, if called on to do so; and the total number of Cossacks under arms has been lately computed at 129,000. One half of this force is kept in readiness for immediate service; the other forms the reserve; but the whole may at any time be called out at once, and the strength of the regiments may be augmented at the Emperor's pleasure. Each of these warriors is obliged to equip, clothe, and arm himself at his own expense, and to keep his horse; and it is only when on active service beyond the frontiers of his own country that he receives any pay, rations, or provender. In time of war, the period of service is unlimited; during peace, it is confined to three years. The artillery and train are provided at the expense of Government, and the Emperor makes certain yearly payments to the Cossack communities, as a means of securing their services and allegiance. The uniform of these irregular cavalry regiments is not the same in all instances; but for the most part the men wear a short tunic and a long great-coat, blue trousers tucked into high boots, and a black sheep-skin cap. They ride small, wiry ponies, very indifferent to look at, but capable of an extraordinary degree of fatigue; and are armed with a long lance, a carbine, a revolver, a curved sword, and a formidable whip.

In personal appearance, the Cossack is not usually heroic. He is a clumsy man, with coarse and common features of the Tartar type, and his shambling air and manner do not compensate for his want of fine proportions. But his courage, endurance, and fidelity are beyond dispute. On service, these men sleep in the open air, and are extremely useful as scouts; for their predatory habits, quick eyesight, and familiarity with wide tracts of country, enable

* Wallace's Russia, chap. 23.

them to discern with great readiness the features of the ground they are traversing, to fall unexpectedly on small detachments of the enemy, and to disappear with rapidity as soon as the desired mischief has been effected. They elect their own officers, with the exception of those of superior rank, who are named by the Government. Without having the scientific character of more regular troops, the Cossacks will always be useful in the performance of outpost duties, for foraging and scouting, for harassing the adversary's flanks, or for acting as a species of police. Since the commencement of 1875, they have been more strictly organized than before. The active troops are divided into three classes, representing three gradations of age, and consequently three degrees of proficiency; and a reserve is formed out of the veterans, who are liable to be called on for service whenever war occurs. But the Cossack is still a barbarian, and is likely to remain one for many years to come. He is given to plundering, and has not the slightest remorse in taking whatever he wants wherever he can discover it. His cruelty when opposed is extreme, and every country invaded by a Russian army has reason to dread the rapacity and savage caprice of Cossack irregulars. These hordes from the outlying steppes have little idea of civilisation. Badly clothed and equipped, and accustomed to lives of a rough and precarious nature, they are apt to help themselves in any way they find convenient, and resistance to their will is death. In this respect they are no better now than they were a hundred or two hundred years ago. Primitive instincts are not easily subdued, and in Russia there are few influences by which such habits are likely to be mitigated or held in check. The Czar relies on his faithful Cossacks, and any crimes they may commit are matters for their own consciences, which are not likely to be very exacting taskmasters.

RUSSIAN PROVISION-TRAIN ON THE WAY TO KISCHENEFF.

With a view, possibly, to war with Turkey, but at any rate with a steady, persistent purpose of some sort, the Russian army has of late years been augmented and strengthened in many ways. The Minister of War, in a report presented to the Emperor a little before the outbreak of hostilities, stated that whereas, about the year 1860, the reserves of clothing and equipment had been reduced to a minimum, everything had since then been brought into a condition for immediate mobilisation. Still further supplies of clothing could be made with great rapidity, owing to the construction of six large workshops, supplied with the requisite machinery. The doubtful economy of making permanent reserves of provisions, to supply the ordinary requirements of the army, had been abandoned. Since 1870, the War Office had taken steps to secure the maintenance of the army during the first period of an unexpected mobilisation, and to accumulate ample reserves of provisions, especially of flour, groats, &c., for special occasions. The medical service was reported by General Milutin as having undergone a thorough reform, and, both as regarded hospital and surgical material, the supplies in hand were more than sufficient for any emergency. It further appeared that enormous sums had been expended in the manufacture of field-pieces and projectiles. The reserves of lead, which in 1860 had dwindled down to less than six million pounds, had since been increased to a hundred millions. Since 1866, a change had been effected in the entire armament of the infantry and field-artillery, first from smooth-bored muskets and guns to rifles and rifled cannon, then to arms of rapid fire, and lastly to breech-loading weapons. New arsenals had been constructed, additional foundries established, and much money expended in the manufacture of cartridges and ammunition. After the Crimean campaign, the transport-trains, like all other branches of the service, were in a lamentable condition; but in 1866 measures were taken for amending these defects. Waggons were constructed after new models; hospital-carts, divisional and regimental ambulances, and all things belonging to that part of the service, were brought to a state of perfection in accordance with modern requirements; engineering materials were renewed; improved pontoons were built, and an efficient field-telegraph service was organized by the scientific corps.

The Russian field-artillery, at the commencement of the war, was composed mainly of Krupp cannon of the newest construction, purchased during the years 1873, 1874, and 1875. The army has also several mitrailleuses and Gatlings. The artillery officers are stated to have been well educated, and in the ensuing struggle they shewed their ability on many occasions. Extraordinary demands have been made on the War Department to secure the efficiency of the medical corps. It was required that each body of troops should be supplied with an independent staff of surgeons; but the difficulties of this important branch were very considerable. The War Department maintains at its own expense an establishment for the manufacture of surgical instruments and other materials; but, with a few exceptions, medicines are imported from very distant countries, and the cost is necessarily great. When first the probability of war began to appear above the horizon, the Southern Army stationed in Bessarabia consisted of four corps, which had their head-quarters at Kischeneff, Tiraspol, and Orgeieff. It is estimated that these four corps had a strength of about 130,000 infantry and cavalry, with 450 guns and more than 30,000 horses. The whole body was under the command of the Grand Duke Nicholas; and shortly afterwards two additional corps were mobilised—one at Odessa, the other at Sebastopol. The head-quarters of this division were at the former city, and the force was known as the Coast Army.

Such were the legions designed for active service against Turkey in Europe; but the plan of the campaign included operations in Asia as well. The Ottoman dominions have of late been especially vulnerable in Armenia, and the adjacent parts of Asia Minor. Towns and fortresses of great importance lie in those regions, and the nature of the country is such that in the summer military operations can be carried on with facility, though the snows of winter render them equally difficult. In the war of 1853–6, Turkey was particularly unfortunate in the countries which border on the Black Sea, and the Russians, while finding it impossible to penetrate from the Dobrudscha southwards to Constantinople, achieved great successes in that vast table-land which lies to the south-west of Georgia. The Czar therefore, in 1877, determined to strike in this direction as well as in the vicinity of the Balkans; and the troops which he assigned for the purpose are supposed to have amounted, at the least, to 95,000 infantry, 12,000 cavalry, and 300 guns, though on these matters of detail it is sometimes impossible to speak with absolute assurance, since the Russian Government is not unaware of the advantages which accrue from secrecy. The Asiatic force was entitled the Army of the Caucasus, and the chief command was bestowed on General Loris Melikoff, an Armenian well acquainted with the country to be invaded, and experienced in the particular operations he was to conduct, owing to his having served in the same region during the campaign of 1854. The Grand Duke Nicholas, who held the chief command in Europe, was not credited with any great amount of ability. His health was bad, and he had had no practical training in the art of war. The course of events afterwards showed that, when appointing him to so important a post, the Emperor had consulted family feelings, rather than the good of the army, or the successful prosecution of the campaign.

The general character of the Russian soldier has been briefly but strikingly sketched by one of the most acute and instructed observers of the present day. In the pages of a distinguished Review, Mr. Archibald Forbes has shown what are the virtues and what the defects of the Czar's fighting men as they exist in our own times, with such improvements as the slight development of education in Russia has been enabled to effect. "As for the Russian private," writes Mr. Forbes, "I regard him as the finest material for a soldier that the soldier-producing world, so far as I am acquainted with it, affords. He is an extraordinary weight-carrying marcher, tramping on mile after mile with a good heart, with singular freedom from reliance on sustenance, and with a good stomach for immediate fighting at the end of the longest foodless march. He never grumbles; matters must have come to a bad pass indeed when he lets loose his tongue in adverse comment on his superiors. Inured to privation from his childhood, he is a hard man to starve, and will live on rations, or chance instalments of rations, at which the British barrack-room cur would turn up his nose. His sincere piety, according to his narrow lights, his whole-hearted devotion to the Czar—which is ingrained into his mental system, not the result of a process of reasoning—and his constitutional courage, combine to bring it about that he faces the casualties of the battle-field with willing, prompt, and long-sustained bravery. He needs to be led, however; not so much because of the moral encouragement which a gallant leader imparts, but because, his reasoning faculties, for lack of education, being comparatively dormant, he does not know what to do when an unaccustomed or unlooked-for emergency occurs. He is destitute of perception when left to himself. Somebody must do the thinking for him, and impart to him the result of the process in the shape of an order; and then he can be trusted, while physical power lasts, to strive his pithiest to fulfil that order. But if there is nobody in front of him, or within sight of him, to undertake the mental part of the work, the Russian soldier gets dazed. Even in his bewilderment, however, he is proof against panic."*

The main causes of the inferiority of the Russian army to that standard which the excellence of some of its intrinsic qualities would seem to warrant, are three, according to the observation of Mr. Forbes: viz., corruption; favouritism (with its inevitable concomitant and result, intrigue); and the general absence of a sense of responsibility among the officers. Lord Clarendon once observed that nothing was organized in Russia except corruption; and assuredly this organization has been carried to a pitch of great perfection in the Russian army. Mr. Forbes tells us that venality permeates and vitiates the whole military system of the Muscovite. It is not recognized as a crime; it is not even regarded as a thing to be ashamed of. An illustrious personage, high in the army, and near the throne, had mines which produced iron; and, desiring to sell this iron for military purposes, he was compelled to follow the universal usage, and bribe to gain his purpose. Another instance of corruption affected the Roumanian people in a way which must have been anything but pleasant. The Russian Government had an account with the Roumanian Railway, and it would appear that the former was indebted to the latter to the amount of ten million roubles. When the Roumanians pressed for payment, the Russian functionary concerned proposed that the preliminary audit should be a merely formal operation, on condition that he, the Russian functionary, should receive a commission of half-a-rouble on every thousand roubles. The Russian stores, accumulated at various points in Roumania, were hardly in any instance protected by sheds from the influences of the weather. The omission was intentional, because it was to the interest of contractors and others that a large proportion of the stores should be damaged to such an extent as to necessitate the supply of more. "I venture to assert," adds this authority, "that every article of consumption or wear supplied to the Russian army costs, by the time it comes into use, more than double what it ought to do under a well-managed and decently honest system. Of other and yet baser corruption—of the little difficulty with which men, of whom other things might be expected, are to be found willing to be virtual traitors for a consideration, by offering to sell secrets and secret documents—I dare not trust myself to speak. The subject is too grievously melancholy." In many respects, the Russian army suffers from the low tone of morality which pervades the whole official world. Favouritism is found in every rank; the most important commands are given to incompetent men who happen to have influence or money; the really capable officers are kept in the background; and it is only when matters have come to some disastrous extremity that generals like Todleben, Kauffmann, and Bariatinsky are sent for in haste, to repair the errors in which others have involved the army.

Ere quitting this branch of our subject, it is

* The *Nineteenth Century*, November, 1877: article on "Russians, Turks, and Bulgarians at the Theatre of War."

RUSSIAN CIRCULAR MONITOR, "NOVGOROD."

RUSSIAN TORPEDO BOATS.

necessary to give some attention to the Russian navy. Of late years, the Russians have adopted both broadside ships and turret-ships, and each class comprises vessels of very different types. Ships of the American monitor description, and others in accordance with English models, are to be found in the Russian navy; but Admiral Popoff, who occupies the position of extra-constructor to the fleet, has recently inclined rather to English than to trans-Atlantic ideas. Moreover, he is himself an originator of singular designs in the floating armaments of his country; and one of these vessels, called after his own name, and intended for the Black Sea coast-defences, has attracted much attention in all parts of Europe. The Russian navy consists of two great divisions—the fleet of the Baltic, and that of the Black Sea; but each of these includes a number of vessels which belong to other seas, and are only connected with the chief divisions by general orders and unity of command. The number of Russian ironclads at the time of the outbreak of the war was thirteen, and of these the *Admiral Popoff* and the *Peter the Great* carried the most powerful guns to be found in any navy in the world. The *Novgorod* had two 27-ton guns: so also had the *Admiral Chichagoff* and the *Admiral Spiridoff*; the *Admiral Greig* had three guns of the same weight, while the two guns of the *Admiral Popoff*, and the four guns of the *Peter the Great*, were of forty tons each. The armour of the last-named vessel was eighteen inches in thickness; that of the *Admiral Popoff*, fifteen inches; that of the *Novgorod*, eleven inches. The others were also heavily plated, though in a considerably less degree.

Altogether, the Russians had twenty-four iron-clad vessels, the most powerful of which was the *Peter the Great*, constructed in the harbour of Cronstadt, and launched in 1874. This formidable ship is 330 feet in length, and 64 feet in breadth at the battery, with an indicated horse-power as regards her engines, of 10,000. She has two turrets, and the guns are made of Krupp steel. The designer was Admiral Popoff, from whom also proceeded the vessel named after himself, and the *Novgorod*—both of them circular monitors. The *Novgorod* was launched at the dock of Nicholaieff, in the Crimea, in June, 1873. The *Admiral Popoff*, which was built in the same dockyard, was completed in October, 1875. She was even larger than the *Novgorod*, drew less water, and could attain a greater speed. No vessels of this class, however, are very quick in their movements; they cannot steam at a greater rate than eight or nine miles an hour, and are in fact floating fortifications, rather than ships in the old and familiar acceptation of the term. Of the three ironclad frigates owned by Russia, the oldest was the *Sebastopol*, which was the first ironclad constructed for Russia, and was launched at Cronstadt on the 24th of August, 1864. Her prow was provided with a beak or ram of large dimensions; and, as her engines had a force of 1,800 horse-power, she might have proved a dangerous enemy in an encounter. Another of these frigates was built by English engineers at the naval yard of St. Petersburg, and was launched in September, 1866. The armament is placed in a central battery on the gun-deck, and the sides and ends are completely armour-clad. The smaller ironclads are all turret-ships, only partly covered with armour, but of a character to be useful in the minor operations of war. The Russian navy has a very large staff of officers, some of whom are rather military men than sailors. The seamen are obtained, as soldiers are in the army, by recruitment, except where they voluntarily enlist. The crews furnished by Finland are, indeed, obtained entirely by the latter method; but Finland, as we have seen, retains much of its old Scandinavian freedom. The period of service in the navy is nine years, seven of which are spent in active duties, and two in the reserve. The Russian fleet is rendered additionally formidable by being furnished with a large number of torpedoes of terrible efficacy. We shall see as we proceed that one of these frightful instruments of destruction — the fish-torpedo—inflicted damage of the most serious and even irreparable character on some of the Turkish war-vessels.

In the opinion of a very competent authority, Russia committed three grave errors in the construction of her ironclad fleet. According to this view, she expended far too much on Baltic coast-defence monitors and floating batteries—vessels too heavy to be sent conveniently to the south. Secondly, she made a mistake when she adopted the demand for rigged turret-ships of low free-board, and thus saddled herself with four inefficient vessels. Thirdly, she blundered in limiting her navy solely to the ships she can produce in her own country, where the disadvantages of ship-building are enormous, and the cost of ships is equally great.* The sums expended by Russia on her reconstructed navy have been immense; but there is some reason to doubt whether she has even now obtained the most serviceable vessels that might have been had for the money. She has still a large number of unarmoured vessels, including five steam-frigates, twenty-two wooden steam-corvettes and cruisers of various sizes, more than a hundred gunboats and smaller vessels, and fourteen yachts. These structures are of course not without their value; but they cannot be relied on as combatants where the enemy can bring ironclads to bear against them. Armoured ships are the naval combatants of the present, and probably of the future for many years to come; and no naval Power is safe which neglects their construction.

CHAPTER XII.

The Turkish Military System—Reform of the Ottoman Army by Mahmud II.—The Army an Instrument of Mohammedanism—Composition of the Forces—The Regulars, the Reserves, and the Militia—Military Schools—Exemption from Service to be obtained by Purchase—Character of the Turkish Soldiers—Want of Instruction in the Officers—Defects in the Sanitary Arrangements of the Army—Imperfect Drill—Armament of the Several Corps—Strength of the Turkish Army in the Balkans and Armenia at the Outbreak of War—Composition of the Corps of Zaptiehs, or Military Police—The Forces of Egypt—Influence of Religious Fanaticism on Mussulman Soldiers—The Turkish Navy—Size and Armament of the Principal Ironclads—Turkish Sailors and Commanding Officers—Admiral Hobart Pasha and his Antecedents—Defences against Russian Invasion—The Danube—Fortresses on the Southern Bank of that River—Importance of Varna as a Strategical Position—Capabilities of Schumla as a Position of Defence—Tirnova—General Character of the Balkans, with Reference to Defence—Passes through the Mountains—The Frontiers in Asia—Military Position of Armenia.

HAVING in the previous Chapter sketched the general characteristics of the Russian army and navy, it will now be fitting to give a similar account of the land and sea forces of Turkey. It was not until the reign of Sultan Mahmud II. that any successful attempt was made to furnish the Ottoman Empire with an army on the European system. At the commencement of the present century, Selim III. sought to remodel his legions in harmony with Western ideas, and proceeded to some extent with his project; but the Janizaries, fearing the ruin of their privileges and their predominance, deposed the Sultan in 1807, and he was assassinated

* Sir E. J. Reed, late Chief Constructor of her Majesty's Navy, in the *Illustrated London News* War Supplement, May 23rd, 1877.

by Mustapha IV. in 1808. The Turks have always been a military race—indeed, they are more that than anything else; but until recently they managed things according to their own semi-barbarian, Asiatic notions. Every true believer was a fighting man. He was not required to follow menial occupations; that was for the conquered Rayah, or Christian: he was to bear aloft the banner of the Prophet, and to extend by his sword the dominion of the Sultan and of the faith. These ideas and practices, combined with the martial fervour which he inherited with his Tartar blood, made the Turk a soldier to the backbone. The army, however, had somewhat the same character as the levies which in mediæval times were provided by the great territorial lords of Europe at the bidding of the king. The Janizaries revolted in 1826, and were massacred by Mahmud, because that sovereign had resolved to give his army a more scientific and European character. It was a very dangerous time for such experiments. Greece was in rebellion; other parts of the Ottoman Empire were disposed to throw off the yoke; the friendship of the Western Powers had been alienated; and Russia was preparing for invasion. Yet, in that epoch of disaster and peril, the Sultan began to reconstruct his army. His ideas were very far from popular; he was obliged to rely almost entirely on foreigners for drilling and commanding his troops, and the methods of recruitment which he adopted were so despotic that a race less inured to tyranny than the Turks might have resisted in sheer desperation. But an army of some sort was built up with great rapidity, and it was this army which had to encounter the Russians in the unfortunate war of 1828–9. That it was beaten in the end, could have surprised no one; yet it fought sufficiently well to reduce the Russians to very embarrassing straits before peace was concluded at Adrianople.

UNIFORMS OF THE TURKISH ARMY.

The Turkish army has hitherto been composed

almost exclusively of Mussulmans. The Hatti-Sherif of 1856 made an alteration in the law which prohibited arms to Christians; but the army which entered the field against Russia in 1877 was an army of Mohammedan believers. The Christians have until recently paid a personal tax in lieu of military service—a tax not onerous in amount, and only grievous as marking a certain position of social inferiority. A cavalry brigade of Christian volunteers (called Cossacks) was indeed formed in Turkey after the issue of the Hatti-Sherif; but it soon dwindled away to a mere shadow. The Constitution of 1876 has again admitted the Christians to complete equality with the Islamites; but the feeling of exclusiveness is so deeply rooted in the Turkish nature that it will not be readily overcome. The pride of race is fortified by the pride of religion; and the idea of religion is scarcely ever absent from the Turkish mind, either in war or in peace, while in war it is even passionately predominant. The military service of the Empire, in consequence of these exemptions, has hitherto fallen with great weight on the Mussulmans, and especially on the peasant class, for the richer inhabitants of the towns are able to obtain immunity by payment. The Ottoman army is divided into five parts: the Nizam, or standing army; the Ikhtiat, or first reserve; the Redif, or second reserve (which is in itself divided into two classes); the Mustahfiz, or territorial militia; and the Auxiliaries, consisting of volunteers, Bashi-Bazouks, and the contingents from the several tribes and tributaries. Military service extends altogether over twenty years. Four of these are passed in the Nizam; two in the Ikhtiat; three in the first Redif; three in the second Redif; and eight in the Mustahfiz. The Auxiliaries do not come under this arrangement. Of regular troops the Porte has seven army-corps, the head-quarters of which are at Constantinople, Schumla, Monastir, Erzeroum, Damascus, Bagdad, and Yemen. Adding to these the reserves and the militia, the total number of men (excluding the auxiliary troops) should be 700,000; but this number exists only on paper. For some years, owing to the pecuniary embarrassments of the Porte, the lists have not been properly filled up; the Ikhtiat has been almost non-existent; the Redif is badly armed, and in some instances not armed at all; and the Mustahfiz has fallen into a state of complete inefficiency. The Bashi-Bazouks have but little value as soldiers; but the contingents of Arabs, Kurds, and other wild tribes, are excellent as irregular cavalry. They are commanded by their own chiefs, and possess the military virtue of obedience in the highest degree.

The greater number of the Turkish troops are drawn from Asia, as the Mohammedan population of the European dominions has been dwindling for some generations. All men from the age of twenty-one to twenty-four, with certain exceptions, are liable to conscription, which is determined by the drawing of lots. Those who escape the Nizam are draughted into the reserves; but the reserves are composed in part of men who have served their four years in the standing army. The exceptions to military service are the Mollahs, or priests; the Judges; the members of the Ulema, or interpreters of the Sacred Law; those who are physically unfit for duty; and sons who are the only support of aged parents. Constantinople and other large cities manage to evade their liabilities altogether; so that the burden of the conscription, for both army and navy, falls on about 12,000,000 out of the 16,000,000 of Mohammedans to be found in the Empire. It is believed (for there are no exact statistics to be had) that the total population of Turkey, exclusive of the semi-independent States which up to 1877 acknowledged her suzerainty, is 27,000,000. The proportion of the people liable to service is therefore unusually small; and this is one source of the weakness of the Empire, as compared with its great rival and antagonist.

The quality of the army varies considerably in different regiments. In some it is excellent; in others, extremely poor. The population of the Turkish Empire includes many distinct nationalities, and it cannot be said that all are equally good material for the operations of war. Want of education, moreover, is often observable in the officers, some of whom are promoted from the ranks, while others obtain their position in less honourable ways. Yet there are in Turkey several military schools, both preparatory and advanced. The chief of these is the College of Artillery and Engineering, in the neighbourhood of Constantinople. Another is the Imperial Military College at Pancaldi, founded by Mahmud II., where the supply of students is drawn from the preparatory schools, of which there are eight in various parts of the Empire. In these schools, where the course of training extends over four years, ending at the age of sixteen, the instruction consists of the Turkish, Arabic, and French languages, history, geography, mathematics, and astronomy. The preparatory schools now derive their pupils from certain elementary schools, which were established in 1875; but the latter have as yet been so short a time in existence that their effect on the army cannot be determined for some years. To these establishments must be added the Military College of Medicine, at the capital, where a few Christians are admitted, though it is against the rules. Officers of the higher grade in the Turkish army are appointed by favouritism, and are necessarily inefficient in a great many instances.* The Turkish officer is usually brave; but he is often wanting in military science.

The strength of the regular army in time of peace is not more than 99,000 men, and in time of war it does not greatly exceed (even nominally) the sum-total of 170,000. This, for so large an Empire —an Empire military in its origin, and constantly threatened by foes, external and internal—is a very moderate number, and it must be evident that the chief strength of Turkey, if attacked by a foreign Power, lies in her reserves and irregulars. At the best, however, it is not equal to what it should be. By law, the annual contingent of recruits for the regular army, the reserves, and the militia, is fixed at 37,500; but it does not really exceed 25,000. Exemption, and even discharge, can be purchased for sums varying from £36 to £45 sterling. Until 1869 the fine was higher; and when reduced, no fewer than 4,000 men in the Third Army Corps (the head-quarters of which are at Monastir) applied for their discharge, and produced the requisite sums of money. Upon inquiry, it was found that these rather large amounts had been obtained by the sale of landed property—for the most part, to Christians. The fact was curious, as indicating the existence of a widely-spread desire to be freed from military service, even at a cost which to men in humble life must have been serious. The truth is that the old flame of conquest for the sake of religion is extinguished in the breast of the modern Turk. He will still fight splendidly when brought face to face with his enemy; but he has not the same active enthusiasm as formerly. The ideas and manners of the West have chilled his spirit, without much improving his discipline.

The system of army administration existing in Turkey is complicated and embarrassing in itself, and is rendered still worse by corruption and underhand influences. The rations of the troops are good; but here, as in other respects, the Government is cheated by dishonest contractors. The Government itself is often a defaulter to the men for arrears of pay—sometimes even to the extent of two years. Still, the Turkish soldier is rarely mutinous, and may be relied on for doing his duty with the firm and patient heroism which belongs to his race. His courage and persistence are admirable; he handles his weapons well, and (speaking generally) is cool and collected in moments of sudden danger. Mr. Archibald Forbes has recorded that "if the Turk, advancing, finds himself exposed to a flank attack, he needs no officer to order him to change his front: he grasps the situation for himself."† The private is indeed frequently the superior of his officer in relative fitness for the post he holds. Turkish commanders are seldom thoroughly grounded in the principles and practice of the military art as it now exists. They are for the most part ignorant of tactics and of strategy, and have much to learn in some of the most necessary requirements of war. Yet here again there is no lack of valour, nor of a certain native readiness for military life. What is needed is more complete instruction, together with an honest devotion to the interests of the country, apart from corrupt personal ends. One of the best sections of the army is the infantry, which cannot be surpassed for steadiness, quickness, intelligence, and sustained force. The cavalry is not so good, though the Circassians are excellent horsemen, and might do admirable service, if better organized. In the artillery corps many first-rate qualities are apparent; but the want of guns and ammunition is often seriously felt, and the arrangements for military transport are extremely defective. In other matters, the condition of the Sultan's forces is such as to magnify to a grievous extent the unavoidable evils of war. The sanitary arrangements are imperfect and behind the age. There are, it is true, eight military hospitals at Constantinople, into which more than two thousand patients can be received; and in other large towns similar establishments are in existence, and derive their supplies from the School of Medicine at the metropolis. In time of peace, the sick are well cared for; but in war the Turkish wounded and disabled suffer terribly. Ambulances, hospital-corps, and litters, are almost entirely wanting. The injured are sent on the backs of mules, or in carts, to the nearest hospital, and their anguish is incalculably magnified by the absence of alleviating appliances. Care for the wounded is a modern practice, and it has not yet reached Turkey.

A military writer, who has given particular attention to this subject, says that the Turkish troops are drilled mechanically, and that the system in use is only suited to the days of smooth-bore muskets. The duties of outposts and of reconnoitring are left to take care of themselves; and when, no longer ago than 1876, a regiment of the Turkish Guard Corps was reviewed in Crete for the benefit of this writer, the officer in command admitted that his men knew nothing of

* Colonel Baker's "Turkey in Europe," chap. 14.

† *Nineteenth Century*, November, 1877.

skirmishing, which they left to their rifle-battalions.* Skirmishing, or fighting in open order, is a very important part of modern infantry tactics; yet the

TURKISH LANCER.

TURKISH CAVALRY.

Turkish infantry know nothing about it. This branch of the Ottoman service is armed with breech-loading rifles; some of the men with Remingtons, a greater number with Sniders, and several with Martini-Henry weapons. The cavalry are not well mounted, and but indifferently armed; while in the artillery corps the guns are of the most various descriptions. Captain Cooke, of the 22nd Regiment, who has written a work on the Ottoman

TURKISH NIZAMS.

Empire, published by the Intelligence Department of the British Army, relates that in October, 1876, muzzle-loaders and breech-loaders, bronze and steel guns, rifled cannon and smooth-bore cannon, and weapons on the French, the Prussian, and the English systems, were mixed up in the same regiments. Between that date and the breaking out of war, however, nearly the whole of the Turkish artillery was armed with 4-pounder and 6-pounder Krupp guns. The training of the field-artillery is modelled on the Prussian system, and German instructors have been employed with good effect. The greater number of the artillery horses are imported from Hungary; for the efforts that have recently been made to improve the native breed of horses have entirely failed. The transport-train suffers from

* War Supplement to the *Illustrated London News*, May 23rd, 1877.

the want of draught-horses, and in many places the waggons are drawn by oxen.

According to Colonel James Baker, the Turks had probably as many as 600,000 Martini-Henry rifles in store just before the commencement of the struggle, with an equal number of Sniders in the hands of the troops. In 1875, there were 80,000,000 Snider cartridges in store, and orders were shortly afterwards given for very large quantities of Martini-Henry ammunition. The Government was in possession of 50,000 repeating carbines on the Winchester system, and large quantities of Remingtons were also at the disposal of the military authorities. Pontoons for building extemporary bridges were wanting, and there was no provision for field-telegraphs—a device of modern science which in the progress of the war rendered the most important services to the Russians. The keeping up of the supplies was endangered by the financial difficulties of the Empire; yet, on the whole, it was fairly maintained. At the date of the declaration of war, Turkey stood before her gigantic adversary in a position of great inferiority, but yet in one which augured a prolonged and desperate wrestle. North of the Balkans, she had about 128,000 men; viz. (speaking roughly), 55,000 at Widdin, 10,000 at Rustchuk, 15,000 at Silistria, 17,000 in the Dobrudscha, 18,000 at Schumla, and 13,000 at Varna. South of the Balkans, the number of troops seems not to have been more than 30,000; these were chiefly massed at Sophia. Asiatic Turkey was protected by a little over 76,000 men, of whom 22,000 were at Batoum, the same number at Kars, 12,000 at Ardahan, and nearly 20,000 at Erzeroum, with a detachment at Bayazid. A great number of the troops were drawn from the Redif and the Mustahfiz—that is, the reserves and the militia; so that several of the men were but slightly trained. They had the Turk's soldierly instinct, however, and all were animated by a feeling of patriotism and devotion, which made light of hardship and of danger. In addition to these, there were 20,000 Circassian horsemen, who, whatever their faults in some respects, were certainly brave and dashing soldiers. There were also large forces in the Herzegovina, in Albania, at Constantinople,

TURKISH CIRCASSIANS.

EGYPTIAN NIZAMS.

in the islands, and in other localities; so that altogether the army in Europe amounted to 412 battalions, 75 squadrons, and 590 field-guns (with a few batteries of mitrailleuses), 290,000 infantry, and 12,000 horse. Of irregulars, only the 20,000 Circassians of the Danube-Balkan Army, and 12,000 Albanians, could be counted on. The Commander-in-Chief (or Sirdar Ekram) of the Turkish armies in Europe was Abdul Kerim Pasha, who had his head-quarters at Rustchuk. In Asia, Ahmed Mukhtar Pasha acted as Commander-in-Chief, and the force under his orders exhibited a total (as far as could be ascertained) of 104 battalions, 24 squadrons, 96 field-guns and mountain-guns, 73,000 infantry, and 3,600 cavalry.* Many Asiatic irregulars were likewise in the field; but it is impossible to fix their numbers. The other troops in Asia were needed for the protection of the Turkish frontiers in directions far removed from Russia.

The forces of the Ottoman Empire could at any moment be recruited in some slight degree by drawing on the body of men known as Zaptiehs, the police of the towns and country. Their numbers have been variously estimated at from 20,000 to 75,000; they are probably not more than 30,000 at the utmost. Their organization has a military character, and their discipline is said to be good. Many of them were originally in the army, and they could be re-transferred to the ranks with but little trouble. At the commencement of 1877, this force was placed under the orders of Mr. Valentine Baker. It is organised into companies, battalions, and regiments, and each battalion has a company of cavalry. The regiment of Zaptiehs stationed at Constantinople is a very picked body, formed out of the best non-commissioned officers of the army. Here, as in the more regular forces of the country, the pay of the men is greatly in arrear, and the plunder of which the Zaptiehs are often accused is frequently the result of sheer necessity. Apart from this temptation, these military policemen are said to be well-conducted on the whole; but, inasmuch as all are Mohammedans, and a large proportion of the populace north of the Balkans is Christian, the Zaptiehs are in that region looked upon with great disfavour, and doubtless in many instances not without reason.

In addition to the forces of Turkey proper, Egypt is bound to furnish a contingent whenever the Empire is at war. The infantry of the Khedive's forces is recruited entirely from the class of fellahs, or tillers of the soil; and these men coming from a country which is never cold, even in winter, and is generally extremely hot, are unfitted for service in countries such as Bulgaria and Armenia, where the cold is often intense, and all the climatic conditions are such as to afflict an African with the most cruel sufferings. The Egyptian soldier is extremely simple in his habits, and in a warm climate can live, march, and work upon an exceedingly small supply of food. His clothing is light and inexpensive, but for that very reason is ill-adapted to the rigours of more northern lands. The infantry are armed with Remington breech-loading rifles, which they can use with skill; but the cavalry and artillery are said, by those who have had opportunities of observing them, to be exceedingly defective. A few of the generals and colonels in the Egyptian army are natives of the Southern States of America, who quitted their country after the collapse of the great rebellion. The Chief of the Staff to the Khedive is General Stone, who has introduced several reforms into the administration of the army, and has opened educational establishments for the training of officers.† Egypt has recently had some experience of war in her contests with Abyssinia; but the class from which the privates are drawn is not many degrees removed from savagery, and, in these days of elaborate and highly scientific warfare, Egypt's place on any European battle-field is never likely to be distinguished.

The feeling with which Mussulman soldiers enter on any war in which they may consider their religion to be concerned, is very strikingly shown in an address to the army, originally published in a Constantinople journal, and thence transferred to most of the Turkish newspapers. "Oh, brothers!" said this address, "we are warriors, the sons of warriors. God has made us such, and we shall remain what we have ever been. Girt with the sword, and bearing the rifle on our shoulder, we shall always be ready to spring forward at the summons of the Padishah, willing to sacrifice one life or a thousand lives. To us applies the verse, 'Let the chained lion break loose from his fetters, and let the enemy try their worst on him. The coward is disgraced, but the hero bathes his rusty sword in blood. He who loves Allah draws his sabre.' At the cry 'To war, to war!' we forget everything except our country. From the seventh to the seventieth year, all, all, rush to the frontier, and fight like wild animals. Rather than yield an inch of our country to the enemy, we will cover the ground with our corpses. There is not a square foot of ground in this land, but is soaked with the blood of our ancestors. Woe to the insolent enemy

* Correspondent of the *Times*, writing on the 23rd of May from Berlin, but deriving his information from a Turkish source.

† *Illustrated London News* Supplement, May 23rd, 1877.

who dares plant his foot on the inheritance of our fathers! When we were infants in our cradles, our mothers, bending over us, offered up their prayers to Allah. 'Oh, God! we have nothing to give to our country, nothing but these sons of ours. May they live to die martyrs to their country and nation!' Having prayed thus, our mothers lulled us to sleep, singing this song:—'Boy, I have borne thee to become a warrior. Grow up, grow tall and strong, and handle thy sword for thy country. Thy father died a martyr before thee, and, with the bloody shroud around him, is waiting for thee impatiently in the grave. Avenge him!' We are the children whose lullabies were songs like these." Such is the poetry of Moslem fanaticism. Considering how deeply the sentiment of religious faith has penetrated into the Mohammedan mind, it was certain that such appeals would have the most powerful effect in recruiting the army, and raising its spirit to the highest ecstasy of resolve.

Turkey has of late taken high rank as a naval Power. Her fleet of war (1877) consists of twenty-one ironclad ships, including five gunboats, and a hundred wooden vessels. The latter comprise five large steam-frigates, ten steam-corvettes, twenty-six steam-transports, thirty-five small war-steamers, and twenty-four small sailing vessels, brigs, &c. The fleet is manned by 28,462 sailors and 3,600 marines—men well accustomed to the sea, and possessed of many excellent qualities, but badly commanded, and therefore deprived of their full value in the event of a naval war. Of the Turkish ironclads, several were built by Messrs. Samuda Brothers, of Poplar, and others by the Thames Ironwork and Shipbuilding Company, at Blackwall. Some of these were from designs by Ahmed Pasha, chief constructor of the Ottoman navy. One of the largest of the class is the *Mesoudieh* (or *Mesondivé*), which was built by the Thames Company under the superintendence of officers of the British Admiralty, and was launched in 1874. The central battery of this vessel, which is 148 feet long, carries twelve Armstrong guns of eighteen tons each, throwing 400-lb. shot; and there are nine other guns in different parts of the vessel. Another vessel, the *Mendouhizé*, is of similar construction and equal power, and dates from the same year. The armour-plates of the batteries in both these vessels are protected by a shell-proof deck, and are twelve inches thick at the water-line; the ships are further defended throughout by a 12-inch armour-belt; and the bows are fitted with rams of great strength. Among the other ironclads, the largest is the frigate *Osmanieh*, built by Messrs. Napier and Sons, of Glasgow, and launched on the 2nd of September, 1864. This vessel is a ram, armour-plated from stem to stern, 309 feet long and 56 feet broad, with a burden of 4,200 tons. Two smaller ironclads which have attracted attention are the screw-steamers *Avni Illah*, or "Help of God," and the *Muin Zaffer*, or "Aid to Victory," both built on the Thames, and launched in June, 1869. Each of these vessels is 230 feet long and 36 feet broad, with a burden of 1,400 tons, and engines of 600 horse-power. The average thickness of the armour is five inches and a half, and each carries four 12-ton rifled Armstrong guns in a central battery, the construction of which admits of the guns being fired ahead or astern, without the aid of a turret. These two vessels are said to possess the highest degree of speed of any ships of war of the same class and of equal tonnage.

The naval force of Turkey, altogether, has been described as so greatly superior to that of Russia in the Black Sea as to give the Ottoman complete command of that inland water. Supposing all the Turkish vessels to fall into the hands of the Czar, by an unexpected victory, the two navies united would exceed that of England; and the hope of some such stroke of luck had doubtless much to do with the eagerness of Russia to abrogate the neutralisation of the Euxine. The sailors of Turkey are obtained partly by conscription and partly by voluntary enlistment, and the term of service is for eight years. Many Christian Greeks are to be found among the naval forces; for the Greeks have at all times been born sailors, and their religion has not been suffered to stand in the way of their usefulness. The officers have a special school at the island of Khalki, and the Government has also established a three-decker at Constantinople, and another at Ismid, for gunnery instruction on the English system. On the whole, the Turkish navy is undoubtedly a very powerful and efficient force for warlike purposes; but, in the opinion of Sir E. J. Reed, late Chief Constructor of her Majesty's Navy, the Ottoman Porte has fallen into a grave error in making her ironclad fleet too largely and too exclusively a fleet of masted and rigged ships.

The Inspector-General of the Turkish navy is Admiral Hobart Pasha, of whom it may be proper to give some account. He is a son of the Earl of Buckinghamshire, and was born in 1822. Having entered the Royal Navy, he ultimately attained the rank of captain, and, after retiring on half-pay, employed himself, from 1861 to 1865, in commanding a swift blockade-runner on the coast of North Carolina. He managed on several occasions to evade the Federal blockading squadron, and at the close of the war published a narrative of his experiences under the name of "Captain Roberts." There are some men to whom active service is a necessity, and, if they cannot obtain it in their own country, they look for it abroad. The late Lord Dundonald was one of these men, and Captain Hobart is another. He entered the Turkish naval service in 1867, and was placed in command of the squadron sent to watch the coasts of Crete during the insurrection in that island. From a blockade-runner he had now become a blockader, and he shewed as much diligence in the one capacity as in the other. The Greek Government, however, did not admit the legitimacy of this interference in a quarrel where all the sympathies of the Hellenes were necessarily on the side of the Cretans. At the instance of that Government, the English Admiralty, acting in harmony with the views of the Foreign Office, struck Captain Hobart off the British Navy-list. He had certainly committed a breach of naval discipline by accepting service under a foreign Government without leave, and in 1874 he acknowledged his error in a letter to Lord Derby, but at the same time advanced various considerations in excuse for his conduct. He alleged that, while in command of a large Turkish fleet, towards the end of the Cretan revolution, he had prevented much bloodshed, and, in the opinion of many persons, had saved Europe from a general war. He had organised the Turkish navy in a way which had elicited high encomiums from all the Commanders-in-Chief of English fleets which had visited Constantinople during the few previous years. With the assistance of other naval officers, he had established naval schools, training vessels, and gunnery ships. While doing all this towards strengthening the navy of Turkey, which he described as "our ally," he had made many enemies, and it was their habit to say that he had been dismissed the English service, without explaining the cause. He therefore asked that his offence might be overlooked, and that he might be relieved from "the ban of disgrace." Those were days in which the advantages of a friendly association with Turkey had still believers among English statesmen; and Lord Derby supported the application of Captain Hobart "as a matter of Imperial

TURKISH ZAPTIEHS.

policy," since he considered it important that this enterprising English officer should continue to occupy his position in the Turkish navy, without at the same time being exposed to reproach in England. The Lords of the Admiralty accordingly reinstated the petitioner in his former rank as a captain in the Royal Navy; but, after the outbreak of the war between Turkey and Russia, so strong an opinion against his dual position was pronounced in Parliament that he was offered the alternative of remaining in the Turkish service, or retiring from the British. He preferred to continue with his Eastern friends, and was therefore once more removed from the list of English officers.

Turning again towards the land, we may briefly sketch the natural and artificial defences of Turkey against invasion from Russia. As regards Europe, the first natural defence is the Danube—that great river which runs along the southern boundaries of Roumania, and separates the semi-independent State from those dominions which lie under the more immediate sovereignty of the Porte. It was obvious from the first that, as soon as war began, the Roumanian Government would permit the entrance of Russian troops into its territory, and suffer them to form, in the immediate vicinity of the Danube, but on its northern shore, the base of operations necessary to an attack upon the Ottoman Empire. The Roumanians, like their neighbours the Servians, were eagerly desirous of doing every injury to Turkey that they could effect; but, even supposing they had had no such wish, they could not well have acted otherwise, for the Czar would certainly have taken possession of the principality by force, if he had not been allowed to enter after a more peaceful fashion. Thus the invaders were enabled at once to place their forces on the line of the Danube. That stream is a very difficult one to cross, owing to its breadth, the rapidity of its current, and the presence of numerous morasses on the left or northern bank. Yet, when the Treaty of Peace was concluded at Paris in 1856, it was considered advisable to separate Russia from the channel of the Danube, and from its several mouths. The south-western boundary of the Russian Empire was consequently thrown back, and the frontier-line, instead of following the Pruth to the Danube, as it had previously done, was made to quit the former river about thirty miles south of Jassy, and, turning eastward, to strike the Black Sea in the vicinity of the Dniester, so as to leave between the Turkish province of the Dobrudscha and the Russian province of Bessarabia a certain portion of territory, lying partly on the Pruth and partly on the Danube, which by this arrangement was handed over to Roumania. It was evidently thought by the statesmen of those days that Roumania would be faithful to her suzerain, and would thus present a barrier between the opposing forces of Russia and Turkey. Events have shown that the hope was delusive. Russia had very little difficulty in persuading Prince Charles of Roumania (a scion of the Prussian Royal house, and therefore remotely connected with the Romanoffs) that his interest lay in placing his principality at the disposal of the Czar. The Emperor, when at Livadia, told him that he might hope some day to wear an independent crown, and hinted that he might even obtain from Austria the province of the Bukowina, a portion of Hungarian territory inhabited by a people akin to the Wallachians.

It was easily settled, therefore, that the Russian forces were to take up a position on the northern shores of the Danube; but the Danube itself confronted the invader with obstructions of no ordinary kind. Below the Austrian frontier, at Orsova, the channel is, at the least, from six hundred to nine hundred paces wide. The right or strictly Turkish bank everywhere commands the left or Roumanian bank, being considerably higher than its opposite neighbour. The swamps and rush-covered marshes on the northern shore add to the difficulty of approach; and on the southern side there are several fortresses, covering all the available points for crossing These fortresses are —Widdin, Rahova, Nicopolis, Sistova, Rustchuk, Turtukai, Silistria, Hirsova, Matchin, Isaktcha, and Tultcha. As there is no permanent bridge across the Danube below Buda-Pesth, the capital of Hungary, it would be incumbent on the enemy to construct pontoon-bridges—a work of time, labour, and difficulty, which a strong naval force might interrupt, and which in the rough winter season could never afford the invaders absolute assurance of their ability to return whenever they might find it advisable. Of the Danubian fortresses enumerated above, the most formidable is Silistria, situated at the edge of the long and narrow delta (the Dobrudscha) formed by the curve of the river on the one side, and the Black Sea on the other; but even this fortress was not strong in the sense which is required at the present day, when artillery has been brought to so tremendous an acme of power and precision. Other fortresses of importance are those of Varna and Schumla, both situated a considerable distance from the Danube, and therefore of no avail for preventing the passage of that river, though capable of detaining a large body of hostile troops on their march towards the Balkans. Two great authorities in military engineering—Sir

John Burgoyne and Count Moltke—have asserted the importance of Varna as a strategical position. It is planted on the Black Sea, and towards the south-west is bordered by heights which could be defended by powerful outworks. Schumla is also favourably situated for a vigorous defence, and Tirnova, lying about fifty miles from the Danube, at nearly equal distances from Nicopolis, Sistova, and Rustchuk, is at all times capable of being made a strong position, owing to the configuration of the ground. The valleys leading up to the great plateau which nearly surrounds Schumla had been strongly fortified before the outbreak of war, and, in the opinion of Colonel James Baker, a garrison of 40,000

ABDUL KERIM PASHA (GENERALISSIMO OF THE TURKISH ARMY).

men in this position would occupy 70,000 of the enemy's troops to mask the fortress. Its great weakness, however, was that it was dependent on itself for supplies, as it could be turned on the right by the road leading from Rustchuk, and on the left by that from Silistria, so that in this way all communication with the place could be cut off. Schumla may be regarded as an outwork of the Balkans on the right, while Tirnova occupies the same position on the left; but Tirnova was by no means strongly fortified at the commencement of the war.

THE TURKISH FLEET AT BUYUKDERE.

Several of the Turkish fortresses had recently been put in a good state of defence by Colonel Grach, a Prussian officer of distinction; and Silistria, Schumla, and Varna form a triangle which has been compared to the famous Quadrilateral of Northern Italy. The comparison, however, is doubtless too flattering, and the chief protection to Constantinople, the Danube being once passed, lies in the rugged and perplexing character of the Balkan mountains. These might be turned by the coast-line, were it not for the fortress of Varna, which blocks the narrow way between the hills and the sea. Moreover, the ground is in some parts impracticable for guns; so that an invader is compelled to have regard to the passes which here and there penetrate the great wall of barren and precipitous cliffs. Taken in the most extensive sense of the term, the Balkans run from the shores of the Adriatic Gulf to the Euxine, beginning at the peninsula of Sabroncella, opposite the island of Curzola, and terminating at Cape Emineh, south of Varna. But the designation is generally confined to that portion of the range which lies east of Servia, and in which the mountains attain a greater altitude than in the more western parts. This is a truly wild and rugged tract of country, presenting a vast succession of granite peaks and rocky clefts, where the snow lingers far into the summer, and of deep, narrow, and winding chasms, through which the gales often blow with an icy keenness and a tempestuous roar. In the higher parts, a few Alpine plants and lichens struggle into faint and dull existence during the brief season when the snow has disappeared; shrubs and trees shoot up in sheltered nooks a little lower down; and towards the bases of the towering ramparts, which make all the subject lands a shade, lie forests of great density and of primitive gloom. These forests are thickest on the northern face, where the mountains slope down, in vast, subsiding waves of soil, into the valley of the Lower Danube. On the southern face, the climate is so much milder that myrtles bloom upon the lower terraces, and cultivation is carried to a greater height; but the sides of the mountains are here more precipitous then they are to the north. The whole region bristles with difficulties for an invading force, and some of the worst occur in what is properly called Bulgaria.

Near the Black Sea, these mountains are only from two to three thousand feet in height. The highest part of the range, which is believed to be 4,400 feet above the level of the sea, and is perhaps more, lies in the vicinity of Kezanlik. The passes described as practicable for an army are said to be six; but Colonel James Baker considers that the number might be more then doubled, as many of the routes which ordinarily are nothing better than tracks might without much trouble be made available even for artillery. In the western half of the Balkan chain, numerous spurs, with steep sides, run out from the main line;—on the southern side ending abruptly; on the northern, passing with gradations into the rolling plains of the Danube. East of Kasan, the Balkans divide into parallel mountain-chains, stretching to the north-east, and forming a series of valleys, which command several of the routes to the south. The passes best known are those from Tirnova to Kezanlik, by Gabrova; from Tirnova to Slivno, or Slivmia, by Demirkapou; from Tirnova to Kasan, by Osman Bazaar; from Schumla to Karnabad, by Tschalikawak and Dobrol; from Kosludscha to Pravadi, and thence by Koprikoi, or Yenikoi, to Aidos; and from Varna, by Derwisch-Jowann, to Mesembria and Burgas. These roads traverse narrow and rocky defiles, overhung by tremendous precipices, and in many parts are rendered still more difficult by immense forests, by tangled thickets of brushwood, by sinuous rivers and water-courses, and occasionally by morasses. The paths are often strewn with loose stones and boulders, and ascend and descend the rugged slopes with wearisome frequency. Such a country, except during a brief portion of the year, does not offer much for the support of an invader, and the weather is seldom otherwise than violent, while in winter the snow-falls are deep and terrible. The Balkans are therefore far from easy to be forced in presence of a hostile army; but the Russians under Diebitsch managed to penetrate them in 1829, and during the last few years the Turks have for their own purposes made some military roads, which might equally serve the designs of an enemy. During the Crimean War, long before these roads were formed, Colonel Green, with 3,000 Bashi-Bazouks, marched from Gallipoli to Schumla, by the Iron Gate (Demirkapou), in the month of December, without encountering any serious obstacles.

Asiatic Turkey is at all times much more open to Russian attack than Turkey in Europe. At one time, the Caucasus presented a very efficient barrier towards the north-east; but since 1829 Russia has been in possession not only of Circassia, on the one side of that stupendous range, but of Georgia, on the other. Even a portion of Armenia is in the hands of the Muscovite, and a vast tract of Ottoman territory lies open to incursions. Armenia is for the most part an elevated table-land, watered by the rivers Kur, Araxes, Joruk, and Euphrates, and in some small portion by the Tigris. On the eastern side of the plateau rises the volcanic range of Ararat; and the mountains of Taurus and Anti-taurus, of Kurdistan and of the Black Sea, add to the distinctive features of this interesting land. The country was in ancient times very subject to volcanic influences, which, indeed, have not yet exhausted themselves, as was seen in the destruction of Erzeroum by an earthquake in 1859. The climate in the higher regions is hot in summer, but extremely cold in winter; in the valleys, the temperature is more equable. In some portions, Armenia is sterile, owing to a deficiency of water, and there is no great abundance of wood in any part; yet the country is not unfavourable to military operations in the summer and early autumn. In their division of the Trans-Caucasian provinces, the Russians have made good military roads, and their naval power in the Caspian has recently been increased in a very considerable degree. The boundary line between the two Empires in this direction now runs from Fort Nicholas, on the Black Sea, to Mount Ararat, on the frontiers of Persia, south-east of the point from which it started.

A correspondent of the *Daily Telegraph*, writing in February, 1877, described with much detail the wild tract of country in which meet the territories of the Sultan, the Shah, and the Czar. Standing on the summit of Mount Ararat, this writer observes that all around is a tangled mass of mountains, upheaved by some later convulsion than that which built the great Caucasian range. "At our feet as we look northwards," he says, "flows in a south-easterly direction the river Araxes, forming, near its junction with Kura on the great Mogan plain, the Russo-Persian frontier. But the delta of the Kura is all in Russian hands, and their territory thrusts down a long wedge into Persia along the Caspian shore. Along the northern bank of the Araxes, for nearly one hundred miles from Djulfa, runs the main road from Tabriz, in Persia, to Erivan, a Russian fortified town due north of us as we stand on Ararat, and thence again north to Tiflis, the seat of government of the province. Due west-for some fifty miles, the Russo-Turkish frontier follows the crest of the Ararat range, turns northwards, crosses the upper Araxes valley, follows the valley of the Arpa-Tchai, and then, ascending another mountain range, runs north-west along its crest to the Black Sea. This conterminous boundary of Russia and of Turkey is some three hundred and fifty miles in length. On both sides of the Russian frontier lies a strangely tangled web of mountains and of streams, in which at first it seems hard to introduce any idea of order, such as Nature generally shows in all her schemes." Between the interior of Russia and the Trans-Caucasian provinces, there are three means of communication: by the Black Sea and Poti, along the great high-road running nearly parallel with the Caucasus; by the Vladikavkas Railway and the Kasbek Pass to Tiflis; and by the Volga and the Caspian to Baku. The superior naval force of Turkey enabled her to neutralise the first of these routes as soon as war was declared, and the other two are generally made impracticable by winter. The chief artificial defences of Turkish Armenia are to be found in the fortified sea-ports of Trebizond and Batoum (on the south and east coasts of the Euxine), and the inland towns and fortresses of Erzeroum and Kars. These four places form a quadrilateral of considerable strength, covering the greater part of Armenia and Lazistan. Trebizond is the sea-port of Erzeroun, and Batoum of Kars; and the country lying between what may be regarded as the four corners of the quadrilateral should, with good management, be safe from subjection. Yet Turkey has generally been unfortunate in Asia, and the war of 1877 was no exception to the rule.

HOBART PASHA.

CHAPTER XIII.

Crossing of the Turkish Frontiers in Europe and Asia by the Russian Armies—Breach of Rules, and Organized Duplicity—Bad Faith of the Roumanian Government—Conclusion of a Secret Convention with Russia—Position of Hostility towards Turkey assumed by Roumania—Circular of the Ottoman Government with Respect to the Conduct of Prince Charles and his Ministers—Progress of the Russian Troops towards the Danube—Unfavourable State of the Weather—Preparations for active Hostilities—Naval Operations of the Turks against Russian Coast Towns—Gallant Exploit of Admiral Hobart Pasha on the Danube—Early Operations in Asia—The Emperor of Russia at Odessa, Kieff, and Moscow—Speech to the Moscow Estates—Opinion in Russia as to the War—Opinion in Turkey—Loyalty of the Turkish Christians—Feeling of the Greeks—Informal Reply of Russia to the Despatch of Lord Derby—Mr. Gladstone's Resolutions—Meeting in Support of them at St. James's Hall—Division in the Liberal Party as to the Propriety of the Course suggested—Modification of the Resolutions—Progress of the Debate—Government Statement with regard to British Interests—Defeat of Mr. Gladstone by a large Majority—Mysterious Intimations of Mr. Carlyle—Isolation of Turkey—Subserviency of Persia to Russian Interests.

THE Emperor of Russia, when once his resolve was formed, caused his troops to cross the frontiers, both in Europe and Asia, some hours before the actual declaration of hostilities. The Kischeneff manifesto of the Czar, ending with the words, "We give the order to cross the Turkish frontier," was dated, according to the Old Style still observed by Russia, the 12th of April. This was equivalent to the 24th of the month, according to Western computation, on which day the Porte received notice of the state of war; but the crossing of the frontiers had already commenced. In the main, it began late on the evening of the 23rd, and a detachment of Russian troops had reached Bucharest still earlier than that. The Turkish Government, in a circular to its agents abroad, and in the manifesto afterwards published to the world, protested, against the great irregularity of this proceeding, and described it as contrary to the rules which have been universally observed by civilized States. The difference in time was very slight; but it is obvious that if, in such matters, rules are not observed with the utmost rigidity, they may be set aside to any extent that suits the infractor, and a subsequent declaration of war may be made to justify an illegal incursion into a neighbour's territory. Even supporters of Russian policy admitted that the declaration of the Emperor, that at the time of his Moscow speech he foresaw the necessity of acting in a military capacity, and apart from the other Powers, was an evidence of insincerity as regarded the Protocol. The case was not at all helped by the subsequent remark of Prince Gortschakoff, that the Cabinets had anticipated the Porte violating its promises, but not that it would reject the united demands of Europe.

On the 22nd of April, the Grand Vizier sent a telegram to Prince Charles, reminding him of the state of things in Bessarabia, from which an early invasion of the principality by Russian troops was to be apprehended; requesting him to concert with the Sublime Porte as to the proper military measures to ensure the defence of the territory against the eventuality by which it was threatened; and adding that the military authorities could, in any emergency, consult with the Turkish Commander-in-Chief, Abdul Kerim Pasha. The Roumanian Government, replying to this representation on the 23rd, observed that to resist the passage of the Russian army was too serious a step to be determined on by the Executive Power alone, and that the Chambers had been summoned for the 26th of April to consider the question. A small body of Russian troops entered Bucharest on the morning of the day when this reply was despatched, and the Roumanian Government thereupon declared that it yielded to force, and had directed its troops to fall back, in order to avoid a conflict. Had these been all the facts, it would be impossible to blame Roumania. A feeble principality can do nothing against an Empire such as Russia, and a dwarf in the grip of a giant must go wherever the giant chooses to drag him. But Roumania preferred the crooked path to the straight. While begging of the European Powers a guarantee against Turkish invasion, and protesting that if the Russians came it would simply be to pass through the principality on their way south, the Roumanian Government was entering into secret terms with the enemy. A week before summoning the Chambers to deliberate on a state of affairs which had already been foreclosed—a week, also, before the declaration that Roumania yielded to superior force—the Ministers of Prince Charles came to an understanding with Russia to do whatever was required. On the 16th of April, a Convention was signed between Russia and Roumania, the first article of which gave the former the right to use the railways, the rivers, the roads, and the post and telegraph lines, of the latter. Roumanian Commissioners were attached to the Russian army, with powers equal to those of the local authorities; and it was agreed that they were to lend their assistance in the transport of baggage, war-material, and ammunition. In the second additional article of the Convention, the Roumanian Minister of Public Works laid down rules as to the Russian military transport, by which it was provided that, after the Roumanian mail and military trains, the Russian military trains were to have precedence over all others. To further this arrangement, it was determined that the number of passenger-trains should be diminished, and goods-trains altogether stopped, whenever it might appear necessary; while, to prevent unloading, the gauge of the Russian and Roumanian lines was to be assimilated. The Russian military transports were to be in the hands of a Russian superintendent, having power to depose railway officials, with the consent of the Minister of Public Works. The Russians were furthermore to have the right of completing whatever lines they might deem advisable, and the ground necessary for such purposes was to be granted them.

By this Convention, Roumania placed herself in the position of a mere fief of Russia, and it is not surprising to find that many Roumanians considered the independence of their country sacrificed. Yet, on the 30th of April, the Senate, by 41 against 10 votes, approved the Convention with Russia, which had already been adopted by the Chamber of Deputies. M. Cogalniceano, Minister for Foreign Affairs, observed, in communicating this document to the Senate, that the Treaty of Paris had been torn up by the fact of Europe allowing the entry of Russia into Turkey. The laws of honour and good faith, however, are not dependent upon treaties, and were still in force, even supposing the Treaty of Paris to have been reduced to that condition of waste paper which M. Cogalniceano imagined. But Russia had issued her orders, and the principality was bound to obey. Roumania, according to the Minister for Foreign Affairs, would allow the Turks to occupy Kalafat, but would resist any further advance. Even this promise, however, was not carried out. A few days later, the Roumanian artillery at Kalafat, so far from permitting the occupation of that town by the Turks, fired on Widdin, situated on the opposite bank of the Danube, in consequence, it was alleged, of raids committed by Ottoman irregulars. Some acts of hostility had in truth been committed by the Turks against Roumanian ports and open towns; but, after the alliance just established between Prince Charles and the Emperor Alexander, and now revealed to the world, such acts, however regrettable, cannot be considered surprising. Nevertheless, it would have been wiser to abstain from them, as they furnished the Roumanians with the very pretext desired for assuming an attitude of more pronounced antagonism. "I foresee with sorrow," said Prince Charles, in acknowledging the address from the Senate in reply to the speech from the throne, "that all moderation will be of no avail, and that in this case we must meet force by force, as it is our duty to defend our country."

The Turkish Government resented this secret Convention as an act of defiance and disloyalty. The departure from Constantinople of Prince Ghika, the diplomatic agent of Roumania, was insisted on as soon as the Porte became aware of what had been accomplished. The Ottoman Minister for Foreign Affairs addressed a circular on this subject to its representatives abroad, in which the conduct of Prince Charles was very plainly characterized. "While the Sublime Porte," said this circular, "was offering the Roumanian Government the means of defending the country against the invasion of the enemy, the Ministers at Bucharest were secretly treating with Russia, and had concluded, as early as the 16th of April, the Convention which has just been communicated to the Chambers, and by which all the resources of the country were placed beforehand at the disposal of the invader. The publication of this Convention has revealed a state of things which the Sublime Porte was far from suspecting, and which casts the heaviest responsibility upon a Government which, oblivious of all its duties, has not hesitated to contract with a foreigner arrangements which could not be avowed, and which aimed at facilitating the invasion of the Empire, and betraying at the same time the interests of the country, the confidence of the Suzerain Government, and the hopes which all Europe had founded on the institutions of the United Principalities. The judgment which should be passed upon acts stained by such patent disloyalty cannot be too severe." In consequence of this Convention, and of the acts by which it had been accompanied, the Porte regarded the Prince, as well as the legal authorities of the country, as being in the power of the enemy, and it therefore declared null and void whatever decisions might emanate from them under the existing state.

The separation of Roumania from all association with the Porte followed very shortly. On the 11th of May, two orders of the day were brought forward in the Chamber of Deputies, the first of which declared that, as the ties between Turkey and Roumania had been severed, Roumania had become mistress of her own destinies; while the second simply expressed confidence in the measures which the Government might consider it necessary

MAP OF THE SEAT OF WAR IN EUROPE.

THE RUSSIAN ARMY CROSSING THE PRUTH.

to adopt. M. Cogalniceano, the Minister for Foreign Affairs, argued that Turkey had herself created the rupture, and declared war by breaking off diplomatic relations. At a later period of the debate, M. Jonesco addressed the Chamber, maintaining that Roumania had no money, no army in readiness, and no allies, since he could not regard the Russians as such. It was therefore inexpedient to declare war. M. Bratiano, President of the Council of Ministers, replied. He said that Roumania had addressed herself to the Powers, but had received no answer. Being thus abandoned, she must rely upon her own strength. She possessed a good army and good officers, and could now prove her vitality. The country must defend itself, since the Porte had declared war against it. The Deputies then adopted, by 58 to 29 votes, the following order of the day:—"The Chamber,—seeing that Turkey, by her aggressive conduct, has severed the ties uniting Roumania to Turkey, and considering, moreover, that Turkey has commenced hostilities against Roumania, and that Roumanian cannon have already replied to the Turkish declaration of war,—relies upon the sense of justice of the Guaranteeing Powers, which assured Roumania political development in the Treaty of Paris, and empowers the Government to adopt all such measures as will secure the existence of Roumania, and enable her, on the conclusion of peace, to take up a well-defined political position, rendering it possible for her to accomplish her historical mission in the East, unfettered by any dependence." The Senate discussed the question next day, and by 36 against 7 votes adopted an order of the day similar to that voted by the Chamber of Deputies. Shortly afterwards, the Chamber unanimously sanctioned a resolution declaring war against Turkey, breaking off all relations with the Porte, and proclaiming the absolute independence of the principality. The eleventh anniversary of Prince Charles's rule in Roumania was celebrated at Bucharest on the 22nd of May, when he averred that the mission of his reign had had no other significance than the freeing of Roumania from the ties which bound her to Turkey.

On the entry of the Russian troops into Roumanian territory, Prince Charles recorded a formal protest against the proceeding; but the Russian troops knew that they would be received as allies, and, after crossing the Pruth, proceeded towards the line of the Danube as rapidly as circumstances would permit. Only a few could be carried by the railway; the greater number were therefore compelled to march, and, as the roads were deep in mud, owing to an unusually-prolonged rainy season, progress was frequently retarded by mechanical difficulties which could not easily be set aside. The Pruth was crossed at four different points, and 50,000 troops were speedily marching from Tatarbunar, on the Russian frontier, towards Galatz, on the Danube, while five other divisions were advancing in the direction of Ismail, Kilia, and Bilkoff, near the mouths of that stream. With steady though slow persistence, the invaders continued to press forward, and on the evening of the 24th of April occupied the Barbosch railway-bridge over the Sereth—a position of importance which the Turks might have defended by destroying the bridge, had they acted with greater promptitude. Ottoman ships of war were stationed at the junction of the Sereth with the Danube, and it is difficult to understand why they did not open fire on the enemy. On the morning of the 29th, some of the invading troops had reached Ibraila, and the Sereth then lay behind them. The 11th Army Corps occupied Galatz and Ibraila on the 27th, and the 36th Division seized Ismail and Kilia about the same time. The Grand Duke Nicholas, Commander-in-Chief of the European army, now issued an order of the day to the troops, in which he said:—"We do not march to make conquests, but to defend our brethren, oppressed for Christ's sake." Every care was observed to spare the Roumanians as much as possible. No Roumanian towns were occupied; few requisitions were made, and whatever was taken was paid for in hard cash. The postal administration, the telegraphs, and the railway service, remained entirely in the hands of the Roumanian Government; but at each station, on lines traversed by the invading army, a Russian *etappen-commandant* was established. The war had now fairly entered on its initiatory stage; but everything was opposed to a speedy commencement of hostilities on an extensive scale. The rain continued to fall with sullen determination; the Danube was swollen to an unusual degree; the bordering marshes on the northern shore had the character of reedy lakes; and from the flat expanse of stagnant waters went up vapours that carried with them malaria and death. The railways were inundated, and it was necessary to detail five thousand of the Russian troops to repair them. Engineers were set to work to adapt the narrow gauge of Roumania to the wider gauge of the Russian lines; but this of course was an affair of time. The invaders also launched on the Danube some small gunboats, which they had conveyed to Galatz and Ibraila overland; and torpedoes were laid in the bed of the river, to prevent the Turkish vessels getting up the stream.

Turkey was stronger than Russia on the sea, and it therefore seemed not unlikely that the naval power at the disposal of Hobart Pasha would be actively employed. This was a mistaken anticipation; yet, immediately after the declaration of war, the Ottoman ships began operations against various coast-cities of the enemy. The Black Sea was blockaded, and an attack was made on Poti, in Trans-Caucasia, while Odessa, situated on the northern shore of the same inland water, was threatened with a hostile visit. The fleet sent against Poti was composed of two crenelated frigates and three crenelated corvettes. The town was seriously injured by the bombardment, and the sloop *Fetch Bolend* did good service with her central battery of guns. Hobart Pasha was at Rustchuk, on the Danube, when hostilities broke forth, and it was for a time feared that he would experience some difficulty in getting out to sea, by the mouths of the river, in his yacht, the *Rethymo*. In point of fact, the enemy fired at him, but without striking his vessel. The Russians were by that time at Galatz, further down the stream, and were known to be placing torpedoes in the channel. The Turkish Admiral was advised to leave his yacht in the Danube, and return to Constantinople overland; but he declared that he would rather blow up his ship than desert her. He accordingly made arrangements for running the vessel past the Russian batteries in the manner most likely to escape attention. As night approached on the 29th of April, he started on his enterprise. The Danube was running with a very rapid current; and this favoured the hazardous undertaking. All lights were put out; the engine-fires were so managed as to be free from smoke; and in the gathering dusk the *Rethymo* sped down the river. As the batteries were reached, the Russians were seen, by the glimmer of the lanterns they carried, grouped about their heavy guns. A rocket was sent up from the Roumanian shore; others followed in quick succession; bugles sounded and drums beat; and the word of command was heard passing along the ranks. The presence of the yacht had been discovered, and the moment was critical. Hobart Pasha ran his vessel close in-shore, so that the Russian gunners were unable to depress their pieces sufficiently fast to get a good aim. The *Rethymo* went quickly by, and the Admiral, when out of reach of the enemy, ordered his crew to throw a shell into the centre of the Russian camp. Apparently, his greatest danger was from the torpedoes; but either these had not at that time been laid, or the vessel fortunately avoided them.

It was in Asia that the first fighting occurred. The frontier was crossed at three points, and some affairs of outposts took place on the 25th and 26th of April; but the one important fact was that the Russians had made their way into Turkish Armenia, and were advancing in three columns on Batoum, Kars, and Bayazid, from Akhaltsikh, Alexandropol, and Erivan. The Turkish authorities at Erzeroum were at that time actively engaged in collecting provisions. The inhabitants were compelled to contribute whatever they possessed beyond the supplies necessary for six months' sustenance. Prices went up rapidly, and the dearness of all articles of consumption was seriously felt. In Asia, however, as in Europe, the Turks were favoured by the weather. Armenia, like the country on the banks of the Danube, was turned into a swamp by ten days' incessant rain, by the melting of the snows, and by a great overflow of the Tigris—an inundation which was described as more extensive than any previously recorded. The consequence was that the invaders moved with slowness, and the plan of the campaign was damaged by the condition of the country.

During this pause in the operations of the war, the Emperor of Russia appeared most anxious to excite to the utmost of his power the enthusiasm and martial ardour of his subjects. From Kischeneff he proceeded, at the beginning of May, to Odessa, where, accompanied by the Czarewitch and the Grand Duke Vladimir, he arrived on the 2nd of the month. After inspecting the troops and the Russian flotilla, he left for Kieff, and, having visited the monastery in that city, and held a review, departed for Moscow. His Majesty received the Estates on the following morning, and, addressing them, said:—"Six months ago, I here expressed a hope of the peaceful solution of the Eastern Question. I wished to spare to the utmost the precious blood of my subjects; but my efforts have been in vain. God has willed it otherwise. My Kischeneff manifesto has announced to the Empire that the moment I had foreseen has arrived. Fully answering my expectation, the whole of Russia, with Moscow at its head, has responded. To-day it is my happiness, conjointly with the Empress, to be able to thank my people for their patriotism—the patriotism which has been proved by deeds. Their readiness to undergo sacrifices exceeds our expectations. May God assist us to carry out our task, and may He bless our troops who are about to engage in the combat for Faith, Emperor, and Fatherland!" The Czar arrived at St. Petersburg on the 7th of May, but subsequently joined the head-quarters of his European Army. It was very important at such a juncture that the Emperor should ascertain for himself what was the temper of his people with regard to the greatest enterprise of his reign. From what he could observe, he was probably satisfied that on the whole they were well disposed towards the war against Mohammedan Turkey, for which such elaborate preparations had been made. But the national feeling was not universal. At St. Petersburg there was decided coolness on the subject. Moscow, on the contrary, was passionately excited in favour of a warlike policy; but in Moscow the distinctly Russian sentiment is always strongly developed. It was once the capital of the Empire, and is still the traditional home of the race—the so-called Holy City, to which every patriotic Russian turns with a kind of veneration, as the Moslem turns towards Mecca. Kieff shares with Moscow this exaltation of blended feelings, partly national, partly political, and partly religious. In most other divisions of the Empire, the peasantry were disposed to fight, simply because the Emperor told them to do so, and because it was a question of the Cross against the Crescent; but amongst the educated classes doubt and uneasiness were widely spread. The Emperor himself was described as looking thoughtful, and well he might, as upon the issue of the struggle then commencing it was not improbable that both his throne and his life would depend.

BARBOSCHI RAILWAY BRIDGE ACROSS THE SERETH.

In Turkey also there was some diversity of feeling; yet in the main the determination of the country to resist the demands of Russia, even at the risk of a disastrous defeat, was unmistakeably manifest. To this rule the Christians themselves were no exceptions. Several Christian members of the Turkish Parliament protested against the pretext alleged by Russia in her justification—namely, that she had drawn the sword to protect their fellow-believers. They averred that they did not want such protection, and that they were ready to take part in the defence of the Empire. When the Russian declaration of war was read to the Chamber, all the Christian deputies rose one after another, and repudiated the Russian assumption of a right to defend them. The Turkish authorities wisely encouraged this feeling by avoiding everything which could give offence to the members of the Christian churches. Orders were issued by the Imaums to the Turkish journalists to urge moderation towards the Christians, and to divest Mussulmans of the idea that the coming struggle was to be a religious war. In Bosnia, the national militia, which was placed under the orders of Suleiman Pasha, comprised men professing the Greek and Latin forms of Christianity, as well as the faith of Islam. These militia corps elected their own officers, and met twice a week for drill. The force was distinctly a popular one, and it reflected the popular, not the official, mind. In a letter to the Vali or Governor-General of the province, Suleiman Pasha praised the Christian recruits for their willingness to defend the country against all enemies, and strongly recommended the organisation of these mixed forces of Moslems and Christians over the entire Empire.

The feeling in Greece was intensely anti-Russian; yet it cannot on that account be described as pro-Turkish in any important degree. The Greeks, as we have previously explained, had of late years entirely lost their former admiration of the Russians, in whom they saw powerful rivals to themselves for the possession of Constantinople. To thwart such a design, they would probably have joined even with the Turks; but it is not to be supposed that they had any real affection for the latter. Memories of the era when Greece was oppressed and devastated by Ottoman Pashas have not entirely worn out; but they have grown weaker with the lapse of time, and to the Greek imagination at the present day a Turk is no longer the embodiment of every base, cruel, and evil passion in the human breast. Nevertheless, a war-feeling existed in certain sections of the Hellenic population, especially in the army. It was considered that the opportunity of Greece would be found in the dissensions of Turkey and Russia, and that in this way the Greek Kingdom might be enlarged by the acquisition of several provinces which undoubtedly belong to it both geographically and ethnologically. As far as these feelings took any definite form, it was probably that of hoping that some occasion might arise for picking a quarrel with Turkey, and thus obtaining Thessaly, Epirus, and some other territories. But there was never the least thought of entering into an alliance with Russia, or of promoting her designs in any way. On the other hand, Russia looked with jealousy upon Greece. One portion of the Czar's design was to hand over a large Greek population to the semi-independent Bulgarian State which it was proposed to establish. The Bulgarians could readily be made the instruments of Russian ambition; the Greeks had passed beyond that stage. It is easily conceivable that the Turks themselves would have been better pleased than the Russians to see the aggrandizement of the Greek Kingdom. The Turks believed in their ability to hold Constantinople; the Russians desired to obtain it, and did not wish to strengthen the hands of any other claimant.

Political considerations were not entirely set aside by the outbreak of hostilities. The Government of St. Petersburg resolved to make no official reply to Lord Derby's note on the declaration of war; but a document which must be regarded as the informal rejoinder of the Russian Cabinet was issued by the *Agence Russe*. It was here remarked that the Powers which seriously desired to re-establish the former good understanding, and to guarantee the general peace, must seek a basis more in conformity with circumstances, without further dwelling on the mistakes of the past, the results of which were the best refutation of the English despatch. The Turks, in the belief of this writer, had been the first to break the Treaty of 1856. All the documents of that period proved that the Christian Powers did not mean to defend a *régime* oppressive to the Christians. They simply decided against the exclusive protection of Russia, for which they substituted the common protection of Europe. Since that time, there had been interventions in Turkey; but they were of a Platonic kind, and had led to nothing. It therefore remained for Russia to execute alone the duty which the other Cabinets, agreeing with her in principle, hesitated to assume in practice. "The English Cabinet," said the writer, "cannot extricate itself from this dilemma, except by proclaiming that England is the first Mussulman Power in the world, and that she consequently wishes the maintenance of the Turkish dominion over the Christians, even at the cost of their extermination. We hold the English nation in too great esteem to believe that it would sanction such a policy." To this argument it was replied that the Treaty of 1856, renewed and confirmed in 1871, gave no power whatever to the European Governments to interfere in the domestic affairs of Turkey, but on the contrary excluded them from so doing, by the most direct and positive language that could be employed.

The great question again came forward for discussion in the English House of Commons, on the initiative of Mr. Gladstone. At the end of April, that gentleman gave notice that on the 4th of May he would, on the House going into Committee of Supply, move five resolutions, to the effect that the House had just cause for dissatisfaction and complaint in the conduct of the Ottoman Porte with regard to the despatch written by the Earl of Derby on the 21st of September, 1876, relating to the massacres in Bulgaria; that until such conduct had been essentially changed, and satisfactory guarantees on behalf of the subject populations had been provided, the Turkish Government should be deemed by that House to have lost all claim to receive either the material or the moral support of the British Crown; that the House earnestly desired the influence of Great Britain in the councils of Europe to be employed with a view to the early and effectual development of local liberty and practical self-government in the disturbed provinces of Turkey, by putting an end to the oppression that they suffered, without the imposition upon them of any other foreign dominion; that, bearing in mind the wise and honourable policy of England with respect to Greece in 1826 and 1827, the House furthermore desired that the influence of the British Crown might be addressed to promoting the concert of the European Powers, so as to exact from the Ottoman Porte by their united authority such changes in the government of Turkey as they might deem to be necessary for the purposes of humanity and justice, for effectual defence against intrigue, and for the peace of the world; finally, that a humble address, setting forth the prayer of the House, might be prepared, and presented to her Majesty. Mr. Gladstone said he made this motion on his own responsibility, and not as the organ of any party, or section of a party, in the House. It was ultimately arranged that the debate should be opened on Monday, the 7th of May, and advantage was taken of this brief interval to elicit an expression of opinion on the part of the country with respect to the proposed resolutions. The anti-Turkish party was extremely active, and several meetings were held in different parts of England and Scotland in support of Mr. Gladstone's views. One of these, in St. James's Hall, London, was characterised by great excitement. It was held on the very day that the resolutions were to be moved, and the Hall was crowded to excess. Some opponents of the Gladstonian policy were present, but they undoubtedly formed the smaller number. The Duke of Westminster was to have presided, but, being unable to attend, he sent a letter, in which he remarked that since the last meeting, in December, nothing had occurred to shake or weaken their

VIEW OF IBRAILA.

determination to prevent any attempt being made to give either moral or material support to "the most infamous Government in Europe." It was their duty to hold Lord Derby fast to his declaration that England would give no support to that execrable Power. The Duke of Westminster was in favour of active coercion on the part of the Six Powers in carrying out what they had demanded from the Porte. "May God grant," he exclaimed, "that we may shortly see the utter collapse of that great standing curse to Europe, the Turkish Empire." The Duke of Argyle wrote to the same effect, and so also did the Dean of St. Paul's, Dr. Church. The chair was taken by Mr. Thomas Hughes, and the speakers, like their chairman, were men of very secondary reputation.

THE GRAND DUKE MICHAEL, COMMANDER-IN-CHIEF OF THE RUSSIAN FORCES IN ASIA.

Mr. Gladstone had certainly need of as much out-door support as he could obtain, for amongst the Liberal party, as represented in the House of Commons, there was some division of opinion as to whether he had taken a prudent course. The Marquis of Hartington, the official leader of the Opposition, hesitated about supporting the resolutions, and would not give them his sanction until they had been largely modified. Mr. Gladstone was finally induced to accept an alteration in the second resolution, by which all reference to guarantees in the future was omitted, and to refrain from asking the House to pronounce any vote upon the third and fourth resolutions. The effect of these alterations, while still retaining an emphatic expression of opinion that the Porte had by its conduct forfeited all claim to receive any kind of assistance from the British Crown, was to save the House from committing itself to any positive line of action whatever. Mr. Gladstone apparently aimed at coercion, since it would be difficult to put any other interpretation upon his fourth resolution. By the alterations and omissions which he found himself, though unwillingly, compelled to accept, the House was simply asked to rebuke the Ottoman Government for disregarding the reproofs of the Earl of Derby, and to declare that England would do nothing to save Turkey from any ruin which might result from her obstinacy. Sir John Lubbock, one of the Liberal members of the House, had given notice that he would move the previous question. His object was to conceal as far as might be the ominous split which had taken place in the Liberal ranks; and, singularly enough, Sir Henry Wolff, a Conservative member, gave notice of a similar intention, apparently with the desire of shielding the foreign policy of the Government from the possibility of an embarrassing vote. When the question came on for discussion, on the 7th of May, the confusion into which all parties had fallen was painfully, yet almost ludicrously, revealed by two hours of statement, explanation, accusation, and retort, during which no one seemed to understand what anybody else proposed to do. Sir John Lubbock withdrew his notice of amendment, in consideration of Mr. Gladstone having accepted important modifications in his original proposals. But it presently appeared that Mr. Gladstone had only accepted, and not adopted, those modifications, and eventually he made a long and very elaborate speech, and concluded by moving only the first of his resolutions. To this, Sir Henry Wolff moved, as an amendment, a counter-resolution, declaring that the House declined to entertain any resolution which might embarrass the Government in maintaining peace and protecting British interests, without indicating any alternative policy. He objected to Mr. Gladstone's resolutions, as preaching that subserviency to Russia which had been the speaker's object throughout the whole agitation; and he very truly remarked that his speech, if it meant anything, meant war against Turkey.

The views of the Government were on this occasion expressed by Mr. Cross, the Home Secretary, who delivered an able, though not altogether satisfactory, address. The conduct of the Government had been so vacillating that any one undertaking its defence had before him a very difficult task, entailing a corresponding degree of hesitation and contradiction. But Mr. Cross gave the House clearly to understand that, although the policy of the Government was to maintain neutrality, that neutrality had its limits. All the efforts of the Cabinet would be directed towards localizing the war, and reducing its area to a minimum. The Home Secretary pointed out that there were English interests, European interests, and Indian interests—nay, that there were world-wide interests—which might be concerned. In particular, he instanced the Suez Canal, the independence of Egypt, and the possession of Constantinople, involving power over the Dardanelles. Those were matters in which both England and all the rest of the world were concerned; but he did not imagine that Russia would interfere in them. Her Majesty's Government sincerely trusted that no action of Russia would ever require them to protect those interests; but, if they were endangered, it could not be expected that either Europe or England would refrain from action. The debate was resumed on four successive days, and did not terminate until the early morning of May 15th. On these occasions, several members of the Liberal party intimated more or less dissent from the course originally proposed by Mr. Gladstone. Mr. Roebuck, in particular, vindicated the conduct of the Government, declared that Turkey had done no worse than we ourselves had done on several occasions, and warned the country against promoting the designs of an unscrupulous despotism such as Russia. Mr. Jacob Bright, while accepting the first and second resolutions, objected to the third and fourth, as involving a declaration of the doctrine of intervention; and Mr. Forster, though disapproving of a good deal that Lord Derby had done, was not sure that any one else could have done much better. Mr. Goschen thought that Mr. Cross had cleared the air by the statement towards the close of his speech; and some Irish members belonging to the Liberal party evinced dissatisfaction with the Gladstonian views, because they tended to support Russia, the oppressor of Roman Catholic Poland. At the close of the debate, Mr. Gladstone, replying on the whole case, expressed himself once more in favour of a contingent coercion, exercised by the combined European Powers, which might or might not lead to war; and, in case of the continued obstinacy of the Porte, he advocated the application to Turkey of a naval cordon, which he thought would bring the existing war to an end in a fortnight. Finally, Mr. Gladstone's first resolution was put and rejected by 354 to 223 votes—a result which naturally gave great satisfaction to the Government. Sir Henry Wolff's amendment was then adopted without a division, and Mr. Gladstone withdrew the rest of his resolutions. The vote was to a great extent a party vote; yet the discussion had made it perfectly clear that the Liberals were not united in

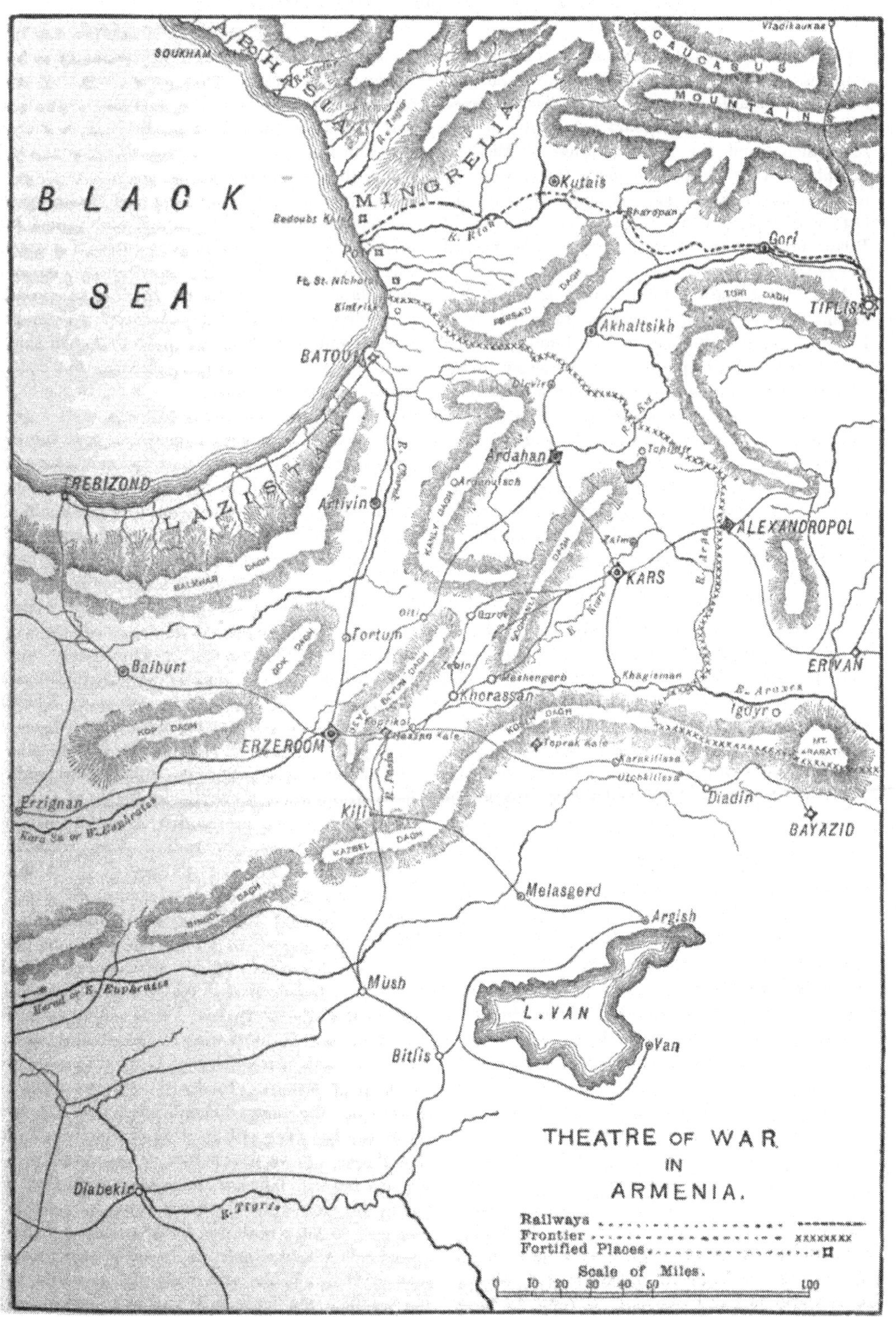

MAP OF THE SEAT OF WAR IN ARMENIA.

supporting Mr. Gladstone's more extravagant opinions. The right honourable gentleman had now fully committed himself to a policy of armed coercion, unless Turkey should be frightened into submission; and the common sense of England saw plainly that we had no more treaty right, or moral right, to adopt such a course towards the Ottoman Empire, than we possessed in the case of Russia itself, or any other country on the face of the globe.

While these matters were being considered, Mr. Thomas Carlyle again came forward with one of his eccentric contributions to an intelligent and candid view of the question. In a letter to the *Times* of May 5th, he mentioned a rumour, everywhere current, that "our miraculous Premier" intended, under cover of a regard for British interests, to send the English fleet to the Baltic, or do something else which should compel Russia to declare war against this country. Latterly, he said, the rumour had shifted from the Baltic, and had become still more sinister on the eastern side of the scene, where a feat was contemplated which would force, not Russia only, but all Europe, to declare war against us. Mr. Carlyle averred that he knew this as an indisputable fact—that he wrote not on hearsay, but on accurate knowledge; and he therefore begged all friends of their country to give immediate attention to the matter while there was yet time, "lest in a few weeks the maddest and most criminal thing that a British Government could do should be done, and all Europe kindle into flames of war." As not the slightest hint was vouchsafed with respect to the nature of the marvellous feat of superhuman wickedness then on the eve of being accomplished, it is not at all surprising that the desired attention was not given to this very cloudy revelation. To have got up a series of meetings, and raged at Lord Beaconsfield, because our miraculous Mr. Carlyle said he had discovered a plot, the features of which he kept studiously in the dark, would have been a height of absurdity too great for the British public to scale, even at the bidding of a philosopher. The "unspeakable Turk" was a very good subject for platform oratory; the half-speaking Mr. Carlyle would scarcely have furnished matter sufficient for discursive addresses. But the admirer of Frederick the Great, having his pen in hand, disburdened himself of some remarks on British interests which must have been productive of very grateful feelings in the breast of the Russian Emperor. There were no such interests visible or conceivable to Mr. Carlyle, except taking strict charge of our route to India by Suez and Egypt, and then steering clear of any copartnery with the Turk. "It should be felt by England," he observed, "as a real ignominy to be connected with such a Turk at all. Nay, if we still had, as in fact all ought to have, a wish to save him from perdition and annihilation in God's world, the one future for him that has any hope in it is even now that of being conquered by the Russians, and gradually schooled and drilled into peaceable attempt at learning to be himself governed. The newspaper outcry against Russia is no more respectable to me than the howling of Bedlam, proceeding, as it does, from the deepest ignorance, egoism, and paltry national jealousy." On this it may perhaps be sufficient to remark that Bedlam howls in many voices, and has more than one object of irrational rage and fury.

In spite of much emphatic language to the contrary, the position of affairs at the commencement of the war was such as to create grave uneasiness lest Russia should acquire undisputed predominance in the East by the entire ruin of Turkey. The alarming fact was that Russia had many allies, if only of a negative character, while Turkey had absolutely none. Russia could count on the friendship of Germany, Austria, Italy, and the Gladstonian party in England. She was very widely regarded as the champion of Christianity, and therefore received the support of many who belonged to Christian communities different from her own. Turkey was without a friend, even among Mohammedan States. The Sultan was said to have an intention of asking the Ameer of Cabul to form a compact Confederation of Semitic peoples; but the idea, if ever entertained, came to nothing. The Bey of Tunis—a tributary of the Porte—was summoned to send a contingent to the Ottoman forces; but he excused himself on the score of financial difficulties, at the same time granting permission to his subjects to join the Turks as volunteers. Those who knew but little of the East imagined that Persia might enter the field as the ally of Turkey. They might as well have expected, in 1870, that Denmark would provoke the wrath of Germany by sending an army to the help of France. Persia has already suffered much from the encroachments of Russia, and depends for her very existence on the good will of that Power. Some day, it is not improbable, this Empire too will fall into the grasp of the Czars: but in the meanwhile the feeble rulers of a feeble race seek to delay their fate by subserviency to the stronger. A bolder and wiser policy would have counselled an alliance with Turkey in opposition to the common foe; but boldness and wisdom are qualities not often to be found in the Persian capital. Another reason operated to restrain the Shah from going to the help of the Sultan. The Turks and the Persians belong to two distinct sections of the Mohammedan religion. The former are Sunnites; the latter, Shiites. Their doctrinal differences are but slight, the quarrel having reference chiefly to the succession of the Caliphate, with respect to which there were two claimants on the death of the Prophet. But the division has been lasting, and has led to feelings as bitter as those which envenom Greeks and Protestants against Romanists, or Romanists against believers whom they regard as heretics—though it can hardly be said that as much blood has been spilt, or as many atrocities perpetrated, in the one case as in the other. The result of these various influences was that the Shah showed very strong Muscovite leanings from the first. He conferred the Order of the Lion and Sun on Prince Milan of Servia, on the Russian General, Von Kauffmann, and on Tchernaieff; and a Special Envoy was despatched to St. Petersburg, to conclude negotiations for the passing of Russian troops and artillery through Persian territory. The Mohammedans of British India, who are mostly Sunnites, warmly sympathised with the Sultan; but these men had of course no power to render help, and Turkey remained, alone and unsupported, face to face with her Titanic adversary, yet determined to risk all upon the hazard of the die.

CHAPTER XIV.

The War in Armenia—Atrocities on both Sides—Rising in Abhasia—Advance of the Russians—Scattered Actions—Capture of Ardahan by the Invaders—Sukhum-Kalé taken by the Turks—Incentives to a Religious War—The Armenian Christians—Pastoral Letter of the Patriarch—Siege of Kars—Operations against the Soghanli Dagh—Retreat of Mukhtar Pasha towards Erzeroum—Dissatisfaction at Constantinople—Advance of General Loris Melikoff through the Passes of the Soghanli Dagh—Further Retreat of the Turks—Erzeroum imperilled—Difficulties of the Russian Position—Concentration of the Turkish Forces—Retreat of the Russian Right—Heavy Fighting before Kars—Further Insurrectionary Movements in Abhasia—Defeat of the Turks at Zeidikan—Victories of Mukhtar Pasha—Attack on the Turkish Centre at the Soghanli Dagh—Retreat of the Russians—Failure of the Campaign—Withdrawal of the Invaders from their advanced Positions—Active pursuit by the Turks—Relief of Kars—Bayazid threatened by the Kurds, but relieved by General Tergukasoff—Naval Operations in the Black Sea—Panic at Odessa—Inactivity of the Turkish and Russian Fleets.

ARMENIA was for the present the chief seat of war; but there also the operations of the invading army were obstructed by the weather. An unusually late winter lingered on the mountain-slopes and in the plains, and by the middle of May the roads were still deep in half-melted snow. Yet the Russians pushed forward, though slowly, and, while waiting for the spring, disgraced themselves by acts of cruelty. On the other hand, the Turks were equally unscrupulous. Parties of irregulars committed their usual atrocities on defenceless women, and Turkish men-of-war, ranging about the Black Sea, bombarded and destroyed coast-towns and settlements which in some instances were devoid of any hostile character. The war-fiend had been loosed, and the usual results ensued with the usual rapidity. In one respect, the Turks acted with remarkable vigour and promptitude. They carried the war into the enemy's territory, and threatened the Russians with a movement in the rear. Numerous Circassians were sent into that region of the Caucasus called Abhasia, in order to rouse the people to a revolt for which the tyranny of the Russians had prepared them. The Abhasians are a wild and fanatical race, whose country lies on the eastern shore of the Black Sea, to the north of Mingrelia. Their religious feelings, as Mohammedans, were powerfully excited by priests of their own faith, and their sympathies as patriots received abundant stimulus from the memory of old oppressions. The movement thus commenced was continued for several months; but, although it excited some alarm amongst the Russians, and obliged them to keep a strong force in the Caucasian provinces, it had but slight effect on the progress of the war, and did not render the Turks as much aid as might reasonably have been expected.

At the commencement of the war, the Russians had some marked successes in Armenia. They were, it is true, repulsed in the neighbourhood of Batoum on the 25th and 26th of April; but the reverse was not important, and the town was shortly afterwards invested. A Russian column, strong in cavalry, and accompanied by a heavy siege-train, marched towards Ardahan, on the road to Kars; and on the 29th a body of troops occupied Artivin, forty miles south of Batoum. Kars was soon besieged by the invaders, and Ahmed Mukhtar

EMBARKING TROOPS AND ARTILLERY AT VARNA FOR THE DEFENCE OF ARMENIA.

Pasha, impatiently sallying forth at the head of a large detachment, gave battle to the enemy on the 29th and 30th of April, but was defeated on both occasions. Bayazid, at the foot of Mount Ararat, was taken on the 1st of May, after very slight resistance; and the Russian army, standing with its back to the Caucasus in three divisions, confronted the Turks in as many different directions. The right flank of the Ottoman forces was now at Erzeroum, the centre was at Batoum, and the left

SUKHUM-KALÉ.

was at Sukhum-Kalé, in Abhasia. The Russians were therefore threatened in their communications; but they did not seem to be much troubled in this respect. They continued to advance in a westerly direction, and to operate against Batoum, a position on the coast of the Euxine. A portion of their right wing, called the Rion detachment, after a river of that name which flows into the sea at Poti, was sent against Batoum, and on the 11th of May encountered a considerable Turkish force, strongly posted on the Khatzubani heights, at the back of the town. The issue of the engagement was not favourable to the Russians, who lost rather heavily, and were compelled to retreat. The Turks fought behind entrenchments, and fought well; the Russians also exhibited great spirit, but appear to have hurled themselves with ill-considered bravery against a line of works which they had not much chance of taking. Meanwhile, Ardahan had been reached, and siege was laid to that place without delay. It was not very strongly defended, and two of the outworks were captured on the 16th. On the following day, General Loris Melikoff proceeded to attack the town itself, which was at length carried by storm, after three desperate assaults, two of which were repulsed with conspicuous gallantry. The Turkish garrison then escaped, and retreated towards the west, while the right wing of the Russians, which had achieved the victory, pushed rapidly forward to Kars (the road being now open), and united with the centre, which was massed before that city. When the last assault on Ardahan took place, the Ottoman commander fled with his staff, and the men followed the example thus set, being unable to do more in the absence of their leaders. The Government not unreasonably directed that the chief officer should be brought before a court-martial; but it would seem that the garrison was really over-matched in point of numbers. Only 10,000 men had been concentrated at this important post, and the Russians, in the final attack, brought up 50,000 troops. The walls of the town had long been in a very ruinous condition, and could not withstand the weight of the Muscovite artillery. Ardahan, therefore, was lost to the Ottomans, and an important position fell into the hands of their enemies.

The Turks had a success at Sukhum-Kalé on the 14th of May. Four ironclad frigates, four large transports, and a despatch-boat, with 10,000 troops, five batteries of artillery, and 50,000 rifles for arming the natives—the whole under the command of Fazli Pasha—appeared on the 13th off the coast of Abhasia, about forty miles above Poti, and began landing troops. The Russian commander at Sukhum-Kalé perceived what was going on, and despatched forces to meet the invaders; but on the night of the same day the Turkish squadron re-embarked the troops, and appeared next morning (the 14th) before the town which it was proposed to attack. The earlier movement had drawn off a portion of the Russian troops, and the Turkish Admiral (Hassan Pasha) bombarded the town without much opposition. He then landed a thousand Circassians, and, aided by the Mussulman part of the populace, took possession of the place. Together with the soldiers, a number of priests were landed at Sukhum-Kalé, for the purpose of preaching a religious war among the revolted Circassian tribes. The capture of the town had considerable effect in spreading the insurrectionary movement amongst the Abhasians, and detached bodies of Russians were defeated in several localities. The people of that country are of a kindred race to the Circassians, and were concerned in the long and heroic struggle which was carried on by Schamyl against the Russians. They are good hands at bush-fighting, but of little value as regular troops. Still, it was embarrassing to the Russians to be thus attacked in their rear, and the religious enthusiasm of the Abhasians made it probable that they would fight their best, whatever that might be worth, against the enemies of their race and faith. For the same reason, the Russians had allies, either secret or avowed, in many of the Christians of Armenia. Not in all, however. On the outbreak of hostilities, Monsignor Narses, Patriarch of the Armenian Church, addressed to his flock a pastoral, calling on them to show, as in previous times, their fidelity to the Ottoman throne. The Armenians, he said, had worked for the good of the Fatherland, to which they had contributed by agriculture, commerce, and manufactures, and even by participation in administrative reforms. He exhorted his followers to remain, as a Christian people, faithful to their traditions; to "render to Cæsar the things that are Cæsar's, and to God the things that are God's." They were to give an example of fraternal love, whether to fellow-believers or otherwise, and above all were to pray that God might deliver them from the implacable enemies who had attacked their country. His Eminence dwelt much on the duty of assisting the Ottoman Government by every possible aid and contribution, and by every moral and material support; and he directed the Armenians to pray for the success of the Sultan's arms, so that their ecclesiastical liberties, their language, and the free administration of their scholastic and religious establishments, might be preserved to them. An address such as this, coming from so high an authority as the Patriarch of the Armenian Church, must necessarily have influenced many who might otherwise have inclined in the opposite direction. The Armenians knew well that Russia had never been tolerant of any form of Christianity differing from her own; and the more sensible must have been aware that their liberties of this nature were more likely to be respected by the Turks than by the soldiers of the Czar. Still, it cannot be doubted that several of the Armenian Christians, whether from a love of political intrigue, or from dislike of the Moslems, sympathised with the invading force, and gave it as much assistance as they could. General Melikoff lost no opportunity of publishing the fact that he was himself an Armenian, both by birth and by religion, or of vaunting that the Czar had several Mohammedan, Circassian, and Tartar generals in his armies; and these arguments he reinforced by a liberal distribution of money among the prisoners, and of seed-corn among the peasantry.

The capture of Ardahan released a large number of Russian troops from the duty of watching the town, and enabled the main body to prosecute its march on Erzeroum with the greater energy. Towards the end of May, Olti was reached—a position lying halfway between Erzeroum and Ardahan. At the same time, the attack on Kars was continued with much vigour. A bombardment was opened, and the Turks were driven from an adjacent village. Frequent assaults were made upon the outworks; but the Ottomans maintained a stubborn defence, and the Russians lost large numbers in their attempts to reduce the place. While these operations were proceeding, the left wing of the Russian army marched from Bayazid, with the object of turning the Turkish position on the Soghanli Dagh from the south. The Soghanli

Dagh is a semi-circular eminence on the river Araxes, to the south-west of Kars; and its reduction would obviously imperil the defence of that city. In the neighbourhood of Lake Van, still further to the south, several enterprises were prosecuted by the Russians, in the hope of holding in check the several bodies of Turkish troops which were moving northwards, and threatening the left flank of the invaders, which was much exposed. Actions of slight importance took place from time to time; but every day the fortunes of the campaign concentrated about the two chief positions of Kars and Erzeroum. The siege of Kars was directed by General Loris Melikoff, whose army consisted of nearly 80,000 men, with 240 cannon. Ahmed Mukhtar Pasha, the Turkish Commander-in-Chief in Asia, made his escape from the city on the 30th of April, after his second defeat, and took up a position on the road to Erzeroum; but on the 29th of May a detachment of his cavalry assailed the Russian encampments near Kars, and, after a gallant engagement, was defeated with much loss. The Turks were now completely separated from Kars by the irregular cavalry of the enemy, and it became doubtful if the Soghanli Dagh could be much longer retained. At Constantinople, great doubts began to be felt as to whether Mukhtar Pasha—whose subsequent career was a singular mixture of good and evil fortune—was fit for the position he occupied. His movements in the first instance appeared somewhat desultory and incomprehensible; but he had then an insufficient force at his command, and events afterwards showed that he was acting for the best.

The weather still continued unfavourable for military operations, and the troops on both sides suffered considerably in health from the rain which had now succeeded to the snows of winter. Yet, on the whole, the Russians continued to press forward, and the Turks to retreat. Leaving a portion of his army before Kars, General Melikoff proceeded towards the Soghanli Dagh, on his road to Erzeroum, and early in June had got through the passes of the mountainous tract of land defending that city to the north-east. By the 6th of the month, the Turkish right wing, numbering about 15,000 men, had been driven along the valley of the Araxes to Deli-Baba, sixty miles east of Erzeroum, while Mukhtar Pasha himself, at the head of not more than 7,000 men, took up a position at Koprikoi, twenty miles nearer the imperilled city. The Russians appeared to be carrying everything before them, and already a large part of Armenia had seemingly fallen into their hands. Those who were favourable to their cause began, with imprudent eagerness, to talk of the Turks suing for peace, and delivering up to their enemies the most important positions in that part of the Empire. But the invaders had embarked on a very onerous enterprise, the difficulties of which were much greater than they had anticipated, or than the forces then at their disposal enabled them to overcome. They were getting perilously far from their base of operations, and were penetrating into the depths of a hostile country, studded with fortified towns which must either be taken or masked. Some of those towns were in their rear, and the safety of their communications was far from assured. Before them rose Erzeroum—a fortified position which had recently been strengthened, and which was not likely to be gained without a serious expenditure of time and life. The Turks, moreover, were now concentrating whatever forces they could command for operations in the field, while the Russians were still divided into three columns, each of which was separated from the others by ranges of mountains. It was time to act with vigour, and some at least of the Russian forces showed no lack of this quality. One of the columns marching on Erzeroum—a body under the command of General Komaroff—is said to have advanced from Ardahan to Olti (a distance of a hundred and fifteen versts), or rather more than seventy-six English miles in two days. The Russians, using their left as a pivot, were swinging round their right, in the hope of securing Erzeroum, and the communications between that city and Trebizond. Komaroff did not, however, stay long at Olti. On the 9th of June he suddenly evacuated that town, and retreated upon Peniak, thus relieving the Turkish left from the danger which menaced it. Before quitting Olti, he threw a quantity of arms and ammunition into the river, and distributed among the peasants all the provisions he could not carry away. An Ottoman corps of six battalions, two batteries, and 1,000 cavalry, subsequently re-occupied the town, and recovered most of the provisions left behind him by Komaroff. At Peniak, only a short stay was made, and Komaroff's column, after a halt of brief duration for the sake of rest, retreated still farther to the east. Mukhtar Pasha had by this time been strongly reinforced, and was now preparing to assume the offensive with greater energy than the means previously at his disposal had permitted him to display.

The middle of June was signalized by heavy fighting before Kars. An attack on the western side was repulsed with loss, and an attempt to establish a battery for Krupp guns of large calibre, to the east, was met by so terrific a cross-fire from two of the forts that the effort was abandoned. Repeated sorties, conducted in great force and with remarkable spirit, took place from time to time, and the Russians had no rest from the incessant activity of their foes. The Turkish field-army now began to advance in an easterly direction, and to recover a portion of the ground it had lost. Some irregulars, commanded by Hassan Bey, even crossed the Russian frontiers in the neighbourhood of Akhaltsikh, put a detachment to flight, and captured many head of cattle. The insurrectionary movement in Abhasia, which had languished for a time, suddenly acquired greater force and animation. The natives of the province flocked to the Turkish standard in great numbers, and a force of 3,000 Abhasians and Circassians was supported by three battalions of regulars. A son of Schamyl arrived to take command of the Caucasian rebels, and the influence of his name alone was calculated to do immense service to the cause. Severe fighting between the Turkish right and the Russian left took place on the 15th and 16th of June among the hills lying in the direction of Zeidikan, ten miles east of Dahar, on the road from Erzeroum to Bayazid. The issue of the first day's combat was indecisive, and the Russians, after bivouacking for the night in their positions, advanced to the attack at an early hour on the following morning, under cover of their guns. A battle, lasting six hours, then ensued, and finally the Turkish army was driven back. The Ottoman troops had been much cut up by the flank fire of a well-posted Russian battery; their supply of ammunition, moreover, had run out. They were therefore compelled to retire behind Deli-Baba, and the Russians took possession of the pass immediately in front of them, where they rapidly threw up fortifications. But a speedy reversal of their good luck was in store. On hearing of the defeat of Mehemet Ali, who had commanded the Ottoman force, Ahmed Mukhtar telegraphed to Raschid Pasha, the commander of the Turkish left (now no longer confronted by an enemy), to hurry up reinforcements with the utmost possible speed; and on the morning of the 17th the Commander-in-Chief proceeded to Deli-Baba with five battalions of infantry, two batteries of artillery, and two regiments of cavalry, thus bringing up the total strength of the Turkish right wing to nineteen battalions, three batteries, and four cavalry regiments. Attacking the Russians under General Tergukasoff with this powerful force, on the 21st of June, Mukhtar Pasha inflicted on his adversary so severe a defeat that the opposing forces were compelled to fall back on Zeidikan. In the course of this action, the ground

LORIS MELIKOFF, COMMANDER OF THE RUSSIAN FORCES IN ASIA.

MUKHTAR PASHA, COMMANDER OF THE TURKISH FORCES IN ASIA.

was taken and retaken twice, and the battle, which commenced at seven o'clock in the morning, did not terminate until eight in the evening. Another great encounter followed on the 25th, when Mukhtar Pasha again fell upon the Russians with sudden and overwhelming violence. Large reinforcements of cavalry enabled him to act with great decision, and at the same time to guard the flanks of his battalions; and ultimately the Russians were compelled to abandon their entrenchments, and take to flight, closely pursued by the Turks.

Mukhtar Pasha, though triumphant, apprehended an attack on his centre at the Soghanli Dagh and Zevin, and that attack came the very next day. To meet it, the Turkish General transferred to the threatened point the battalions he had borrowed from his left wing. In the early hours of the 26th, a force of 16,000 Russians, with four batteries of artillery, advanced to storm the Turkish position. The Ottomans were greatly outnumbered, for their force did not consist of more than 10,000 men, with eight guns. Their position, however, was good, and it had been strongly entrenched. Turks always fight with peculiar doggedness when standing on the defensive behind any cover; and on this occasion their fire told with such excellent effect that the Russians, though bravely renewing the assault again and again, were at length compelled to retire, with ranks disastrously thinned. The victors pursued with great ardour, and the Russians, disorganised and dispirited, suffered from incessant attacks. The defeat was even more serious in its consequences than in itself. It led to a general retreat of the Russian forces in that part of Armenia, and for a time it even appeared doubtful whether the campaign would not be abandoned altogether. The Russians had evidently undertaken a task beyond their strength. Their numbers, though greater than those of the Turks at the commencement of the war, were inadequate for holding so large a tract of country as that which in the first instance they seized. Their supplies were deficient; they committed the common mistake of underrating the enemy; and, scattering their ranks in many quarters, they laid themselves open to multiplied attacks as soon as the Turks had effected their concentration, and had recovered from the dismay into which they were thrown by the early successes of their opponents. The invaders appear also to have reckoned a great deal too much on the degree of succour which they would obtain from the people of the country. Some supporters they did indeed find; but the population generally was not in their favour, and certain bodies of Circassians in their own ranks went over to the enemy. The rising of the Abhasians in their rear was another circumstance which added much to their perplexity. If that rising should spread, their communications might be endangered; and it therefore became absolutely necessary, at the close of June, for the Russians to retire from their more advanced positions, and bring together in a few chosen spots those forces which had been imprudently separated in the prosecution of detached enterprises, now beyond any hope of immediate success.

The Turks pursued their advantage with alacrity. On the 2nd of July, a corps from Alashgerd, which had left Yilanlu in order to cut off the retreat of the enemy's right wing, attacked 10,000 Russians entrenched at Kara-Kilissa. After a sanguinary battle, of several hours' duration, the Russians were defeated and dislodged, but succeeded in rallying their forces on some adjacent heights. The Turks discontinued the pursuit, and encamped for the night in the positions they had won, while the Muscovites retreated in disorder towards Bayazid, which was shortly afterwards surrounded by a body of Kurds from Lake Van, who had for some time past been harassing the Russian left. Fearing the relief of Kars, General Melikoff sent a detached column to occupy a small town fifteen miles north of Zevin, with a view to intercepting any troops whom Mukhtar Pasha might despatch to the beleaguered fortress. Another column, proceeding from Ardahan under command of General Komaroff, attacked a body of 3,000 Turks on the 28th of June, drove them from their positions on the heights of Ardanutsch, and pursued them as far as the village of Batz. On this occasion, the Turkish camp, consisting of two hundred and twenty tents, fell into the hands of the Russians, together with a large quantity of provisions. The column then returned to Ardahan, satisfied with the success it had achieved. The siege of Kars still continued, though the investment had by this time been so much weakened as to be only partial. The situation of the Russians was, on the whole, extremely discouraging, and even in some respects calculated to inspire grave alarm. After the defeat at Kara-Kilissa, the forces under General Tergukasoff (the left wing of the Russian army when advancing) retired to Utch-Kilissa, leaving behind them large stores of ammunition and food, and accompanied by cart-loads of wounded. The Turks followed hotly on their track, giving them not a moment's rest; and Utch-Kilissa was abandoned for Ipek. On the 9th of July, Mukhtar Pasha effected a junction with the Kars garrison, and occupied Djevlikia. The Russian centre then retired to Kurukdara, fifteen miles from Kars, upon the

GENERAL HEIMANN STORMING FORT SINQUAIR AT THE CAPTURE OF ARDAHAN.

Alexandropol road. Here they established an entrenched camp, and the head-quarters, with the greater portion of the infantry, were simultaneously removed to Zaim, ten miles north of Kars. Mukhtar Pasha took up a position at Vera-Kalé, seventeen miles to the south-west of the lately besieged city, and, having relieved and revictualled the fortress, moved his right towards the east, as

BAYAZID AND MOUNT ARARAT.

far as Soubatan. Upon examination, it was found that Kars had suffered but little from the bombardment. It was said that as many as 40,000 shells had fallen within the works; but the outer line of forts had prevented all save a few of these descending into the town itself. The inhabitants had not suffered from lack of food, as the place had been well provisioned for at least a year.

The left wing of the Russians had in the meanwhile undergone a series of varied fortunes. After leaving Ipek, General Tergukasoff followed a bye-road over the hills to the north, and reached Igdyr, where he arrived on the evening of July 8th. Here he replenished his supplies, and, again starting on his way, overtook a column of troops under the command of General Kalbolikhan. Thus reinforced, he marched on Bayazid, and on the 10th defeated the army of irregulars by which the place was surrounded, relieving the garrison from a position of peril which they would probably have been unable to endure much longer. The Russian General was now in command of a force consisting of twelve battalions of infantry, eight regiments of cavalry, and twenty field-pieces. He therefore felt strong enough to attack the column by which he was being pursued. Effecting a retrograde movement towards the Lake of Balykly, he attacked Ismail Pasha, advancing from Ipek, but was signally repulsed, and compelled to retire upon the frontier. For the present, the campaign in Armenia was a failure. The original design had come to nothing; the invaders had been rolled back towards the borders of their own dominion; and, as a large part of the summer had now passed away, it seemed doubtful whether any further action of importance could be taken before the arrival of the early winter common to those regions. Here we must leave the opposing forces for awhile, to follow the course of events in other directions.

Some naval movements occurred during the summer in the Black Sea, but not to the extent that might have been supposed, considering the superiority of the Turkish to the Russian navy. Even the blockade was so feebly enforced that the British and Austrian Governments notified to the Porte that foreign Powers could not be expected to regard it. The active operations of the Turkish men-of-war were few indeed, although at the outbreak of hostilities there had been some talk of bombarding Odessa. A few minor services, however, were performed from time to time. On the 29th of June, some gun-boats were despatched to the Kilia mouth of the Danube to destroy an observatory which the Russians had erected at the village of Zibriami for watching the movements of the Turkish squadron along the coast. The expedition was successful, and the village itself was destroyed, as well as the observatory. The squadron then sailed to Odessa, on the northern coast of the Black Sea, where it excited a great panic, but did not attempt any offensive operations. For some days previously (as a correspondent of the *Times* related), a Turkish man-of-war had been observed out at sea, and, from the evolutions of a number of its boats about the torpedo-lines, it was supposed that the vessel had divers from Lazistan on board, for raising these obstructions. General Semika, commanding the south coast, accordingly gave orders to open fire from all the batteries, and, on that being done, the Turkish man-of-war speedily retired. In consequence of this attempt, the torpedo-lines were closely watched and inspected every day. The appearance of the Turkish squadron created great alarm in Odessa. The population fled to the suburb of Moldavanka, situated on that side of the city which is most remote from the coast; but even here the civilians did not feel safe. On its becoming known that the suburbs of Zibriami and Balabunovka had been bombarded, a general movement farther inland at once set in. The garrison of Odessa was called out, and all the troops stationed in the neighbouring villages were marched into the town; so that, before the day was over, a whole division, consisting of infantry, cavalry, and artillery, was under arms. The batteries were got ready for immediate action, if necessity should arise, and during the night the harbour was illuminated by the electric light. Much anxiety was felt for several hours; but no attack ensued, and on the following morning the lighthouse-keeper signalled the departure of the Turkish squadron in the direction of Sebastopol, in the Crimea. On reaching the vicinity of that town, the commanders of the Turkish vessels felt so nervous with respect to torpedoes that they forbore from taking any active measures, and merely sailed past at a safe distance. At Eupatoria, also in the Crimea, they halted for two or three hours, and bombarded the town until they were driven off by the Russian batteries.

The comparative inactivity of the Turkish fleet is one of the unexplained circumstances of the Russo-Turkish war. It was generally believed that the navy would do much, but in point of fact it did scarcely anything. The Russian fleet likewise was almost totally idle. Its inferiority to the Turks is sufficient to account for its avoiding anything like a general action; yet it might have been supposed that some of the powerful ironclads built by Admiral Popoff would have endeavoured to fight single actions with isolated Turkish vessels. The war of 1877, however, was not a naval war. It was conducted by land forces, and its triumphs and defeats were those of armies in the field, or in fortified positions.

CHAPTER XV.

Affairs on the Danube—Slow Progress of the Invaders—Blowing up of a Turkish Turret-Ship—Taking of a Gunboat—Sinking of a Monitor by a Russian Torpedo—Turkish Apathy—Misconduct of the War—Debate in the Chamber of Deputies at Constantinople—Agitation among the Softas—Address of the Metropolitan of Kischeneff to the Emperor of Russia—Address of the Sultan to the Expeditionary Force sent against Sukhum-Kalé—The Religious Question—Mohammedans and Christians—Decree of the Prophet, granting complete Toleration to Christian Subjects—Disregard of the Rules there laid down—Causes tending to the Development of Fanaticism—The Czar and the Roumanians—Visit of the Servian Prince to the Russian Emperor at Ployesti—Explanations to the Porte—Disaffected State of Bulgaria—Military Operations in Montenegro and the Herzegovina—Despatch of Lord Derby to Count Schouvaloff on English Interests in connection with the War—Reply of Prince Gortschakoff on the Motives and Designs of Russia—The Temptations of Ambition and Success.

WAR often depends as much upon the ways of Nature as upon the designs of princes. The Emperor Alexander was eager to cross the Danube in the early days of May, 1877; but the condition of that river interposed a barrier which the master of many legions was unable to overcome. The stream was more than usually swollen by the spring rains: men had never known it so late in falling. To build pontoon-bridges in the existing state was impossible: they would have been swept away before completion. No other mode of transport for a large army was available; and the Russian commanders had little else to do than to make friends with the Roumanians, and mature their plans for the campaign, against the season when it might be possible to put them in execution. They did indeed manage to throw a small body of troops into the Dobrudscha—a marshy tract of land near the outfalls of the Danube, on the southern side of the river; but the movement was of a very trivial kind, and led to nothing. That the state of war, however, had been fully established, was a fact which every day made sufficiently clear. Towns situated on opposite banks of the Danube assailed one another with shot and shell, and on the 6th of May the Ottomans made an attack on the port of Beket, in Roumania. By the Turks, all passage through the Bosphorus and the Dardanelles was prohibited during the night; and the Russian authorities notified the commanders of vessels at Galatz and other ports near the mouths of the Danube that they would be compelled to leave their anchorages, and proceed to sea, on or before the 7th of May, as the navigation of the Lower Danube would be closed after that date. The right to issue such a notification was very doubtful. The freedom of the Danube was secured by the Treaty of Paris of 1856, and it was questionable whether the declaration of war abolished what had been then established with the sanction of the Great Powers.

Day by day, the Russians continued to advance westward up the northern bank of the river, and by the middle of May about 200,000 men had entered Roumania. The head-quarters of the army were now transferred from Kischeneff, in Bessarabia, to Ployesti, a town forty miles north of Bucharest; and preparations were made for extending the Russian line towards the borders of Servia. These preparations were occasionally interrupted by a Turkish flotilla of gunboats and monitors, which moved up and down the river, throwing shells on to the Roumanian shore. The vessels, however, received more damage than they inflicted. On the 11th of May, a Turkish turret-ship steamed out of Matchin, followed by two gunboats, and placed itself under cover of a wooded island, so that only the three masts were visible above the trees. The Russian gunners in the batteries close to Ibraila opened fire from their light guns, but at first without effect. Two heavier guns were then brought into play, and the second shot, fired at a high elevation with a low charge, dropped on the deck of the turret-ship, and exploded the magazine. "A tremendous flash and glare," said a Special Correspondent of the *Daily News*, who witnessed the catastrophe, "shot up from the interior of the doomed craft, followed by a heavy white smoke, which hung like a pall. Through this white cloud there shot up to a great height a spurt of black fragments, of all shapes and sizes. When the smoke drifted away, all that was visible of the turret-ship was her stern, with the mizen-mast standing, whence still fluttered the Turkish flag. The ship had gone down by the head in shallow water. Two Russian steam-launches put off from Ibraila, boarded the wreck, gained the flag, gathered some of the *débris*, and picked up two men—the fireman and the engineer—both severely injured." One of these afterwards died, and only one man (besides the captain, who was on shore at the time) remained out of a crew of two hundred. In the Russian battery, the enthusiasm was so great that the officers embraced one another; but it has been said that the explosion was really due to an accident in the gunner's storehouse, and not at all to the Russian shot. Another gunboat was lost to the Turks two days later. It had but recently been built at Pesth, and was attempting to steam down to Rustchuk for its armament, when, as it was passing Kalafat a little before midnight on the 12th of May, it was detected by the Russians, and fired at from the Roumanian shore. The Turks at Widdin were mistaken as to its nationality, and fired also; but it contrived to escape this double peril, and to proceed down the river. Early on the morning of the 13th, however, it was compelled to surrender to the Roumanians, after a few rounds of heavy firing.

RUSSIAN BATTERY AT IBRAILA BLOWING UP A TURKISH TURRET-SHIP IN THE MATCHIN CANAL.

The Turks were indeed singularly unlucky in this respect. On the 26th of May, a Turkish monitor was sunk by a torpedo near Ibraila. A detachment of Russian soldiers, under the command of Lieutenant Dubascheff, accompanied by the commander of the Roumanian flotilla, Major Murgescu—all dressed in Turkish uniforms—left the northern shore of the Danube in a number of small boats, and proceeded towards Point Petra Fetei, below Matchin. Aided by the darkness of the night, or rather of the early morning, they managed (according to the relation of the *Times* correspondent at Bucharest) to get near the monitor before being discovered by the Turkish look-outs. When observed by the sentries, they were challenged, and to the question, "Who goes there?" Major Murgescu replied in Turkish, "Friends," and added that his boats had just arrived from Rustchuk. The Turks, evidently not satisfied, commenced firing in the direction of Matchin. The shots flew wide of their mark, and did no damage to the boats. During the firing, several of the Russian soldiers, under the direction of Lieutenant Dubascheff, plunged into the water, swam silently to the hull of the ironclad vessel, and placed the torpedo in close contact with the bottom of the monitor. After the machine had been securely fastened, and the wires of an electric battery accurately adjusted, the men retired to the neighbouring shore of the river, and at half-past three in the morning the monitor was blown into the air, with all the officers and crew.

Before this catastrophe had been reached, "the

other monitors," wrote a correspondent of the *Daily News*, "became alarmed, and, without knowing the cause, fired at random, and a fearful scene of terror and confusion ensued. They not only fired on the Russian launches, which still kept dodging about like mosquitoes, but in their panic and confusion fired into each other. The bullets rattled over the iron awnings of the launches, but did them no harm. They were not once struck, although the bow of one was pierced and sunk by a piece of a shell that exploded near it. The two launches were now on opposite sides of the doomed ship. Dubascheff perceived that the monitor was sinking down before, but very slowly, while the Turks continued to fire away blindly, but incessantly, both with small arms and cannon. Dubascheff cried out to Chestakoff [commanding one of the launches] to try and place another torpedo, in order to make sure of the ship; and the latter slipped in under the stern, and put down another torpedo in the same manner as the previous one. He then shot off until he was at a safe distance, applied the electric battery in the same manner, and a still more terrible explosion followed. Parts of the ship were blown into the air, as they very soon perceived by a large plank which a few seconds later came down endways, driving its way through the iron screen into the boat between two of the sailors, who were back to back close to each other, without injuring either of them. Then the monitor sank rapidly, and after a few moments nothing but her masts was visible above water. The crew had all either been drowned, or had escaped by swimming. Day now began to break, and the position of the two little launches, within the near range of two other Turkish monitors, became very critical. To add to the danger of the situation, the screw of one of them got fouled, and the boat became unmanageable, while they perceived a Turkish launch from one of the other monitors bearing down on them. They opened a fire of small-arms on the Turkish launch, which veered off, and showed no disposition to come any closer. One of the sailors got out into the water, and, after several minutes' exertion, succeeded in clearing the screw; and the two launches, having accomplished their mission of destruction, darted off, passed under the fire of the two other Turkish gunboats, escaped unharmed, and, rejoining their two consorts, returned in triumph to their place of starting." The action of these torpedoes was sometimes baffled by the clever arrangements of Hobart Pasha, who protected the larger vessels by a circle of small boats chained together; but with the destruction of the monitor near Matchin the last of the important ironclads in the Danube disappeared, and the river was left comparatively free for the crossing of the Russian troops.

Both in the army and navy, the Turks exhibited in many respects the apathetic indifference of their race. Near the close of May, Krupp guns, which should long before have been at the Dardanelles and on the Bosphorus, still lay idly on the banks of the Golden Horn. Vessels which might soon be urgently needed for the prosecution of the war remained in an incomplete state, or were put in hand with so much languor that it was impossible to divine when they would be likely to sail. Sir Arnold Kemball, the English Military Commissioner in Armenia, embodied in his reports a deplorable account of the Turkish forces in Asia, which he represented as lacking everything that an army should have, except courage and patience. It was the opinion of this distinguished critic that the Russians would not find any serious military resistance in that part of the Ottoman Empire, and that their only difficulty would proceed from the country and the climate. In this view he proved mistaken; but the Turkish people themselves were dissatisfied with the conduct of the war in its earlier stages. A stormy meeting of the Chamber of Deputies took place on the 19th of May, when the representative of Aidin demanded an explanation of the position and state of the Asiatic forces, and dwelt strongly on what he called the incapacity of Mukhtar Pasha. He contended that Redif Pasha, the Minister of War, was ignorant of the actual situation, and ought himself to go to the front, to ascertain the facts. Referring to the system of keeping secret the movements of the troops, he complained that the Chamber was called on to discuss questions of minor importance while the country was in peril. Other members exhibited a disposition to speak to the same effect; but the President somewhat hastily cut short the debate. The fact of such opinions being openly discussed in a representative Chamber was nevertheless a testimony to the genuine character of the Turkish Parliament. But in many ways the people were resolved to use their newly-acquired liberties without reserve. The Softas, or students of the sacred law, who had so much to do with the deposition of Sultan Abdul-Aziz, began once more to agitate the political world. A number of them gathered clamorously round the Parliament-house on the 24th of May, and raised cries against the War Minister and the unsuccessful commanders in Asia. They required the dismissal of Redif Pasha, and of Mahmud Damat Pasha, the brother-in-law of the Sultan; and several of them either forced their way in, or were admitted as a deputation. Ahmed Vefik, the President of the Chamber, seems to have been in league with the malcontents; for he allowed the deputies to discuss a resolution for the dismissal of Redif Pasha. This resolution was carried by a large majority, and the President then announced to the Softas that they might regard the affair as settled, as the Sultan would never think of resisting the will of the people. But Abdul-Hamid was not disposed to submit to such dictation. Though previously inclined to remove the War Minister, he now determined to keep him at his post, rather than yield to clamour. A Cabinet Council was summoned, and it was decided to establish a state of siege. Redif Pasha became practically the dictator of Constantinople, and the people felt the rigours of martial law, in consequence of the inconsiderate hastiness of a number of law-students who began to think themselves omnipotent in the State. The movement, however, was backed by a good deal of popular feeling, although it is not improbable that the Government exaggerated the danger to which it was exposed. Some of the Softas were arrested, and a military council was established to direct the war.

LIEUTENANTS DUBASCHEFF AND CHESTAKOFF, COMMANDERS OF THE RUSSIAN TORPEDO-LAUNCHES WHICH BLEW UP THE TURKISH MONITOR.

For the present, the Russians were successful, and the war, as a natural consequence, gained in popularity with them. Even at the outset, ambitious designs began to be more openly expressed than before, and the Metropolitan of Kischeneff preached a sermon to the army in presence of the Czar, which took very high ground. "Yours," he said, addressing the Emperor, "is the great destiny to raise the Cross of Christ above the Crescent in the lands beyond the Danube, as upon these shores; to raise above the blasting and annihilating domination of the Mussulman the tree of life, the banner of the victory over death, the blessed Cross, and all the rights of Christian citizenship which are dependent upon it. Before you will go, as in life, the holy

RUSSIAN TORPEDO-LAUNCHES ATTACKING A TURKISH MONITOR BELOW MATCHIN.

images of the ancient Princes of Russia,—Oleg, and Igor, and Sviatoslaf; the majestic and holy forms of the Czars and Czarinas,—Peter the Great, Catherine the Great, the blessed Alexander, the heroic Nicholas; the Romanoffs too, and the Suwaroffs, and the Kutusoffs, with their mighty triumphs. Those, and other mighty men of Russia, made many a time the walls of Constantinople tremble before the weight of their arms. By their glorious achievements they raised up the Russian Empire, and enlarged its bounds by ever wider and richer territories conquered from the Turk. Oh, warriors! how glorious are the memories which will inspire you in your victories and conquests!" Presently the Metropolitan turned to the Czar, and said:—"Orthodox Czar and Master! Leader of the hosts of Russia! Before thy face do I bless the army, beloved of Christ through thee, in the name of our God, the Omnipotent. The Lord Jesus Christ be with thee, who art the champion of the cause of Christ! May he crown thy hero-deeds with glorious victory!" Then turning to the Grand Duke Nicholas, the Commander-in-Chief, the Metropolitan continued:—"Leader, beloved of Christ, of the armies which have assembled on our bounds! By the sacred image of Herbowetz, the sacred image of the chosen one, the celestial Mother of God, the protectress of our city and our land, I bless thee and thy companions in war. I give you all over to the mighty care of the Queen of Heaven, and I pray, and shall continue to pray, that she may continue to lead you from hero-deed to hero-deed, from victory to victory. God guide you back unhurt and uninjured, and crowned with laurels!"

It is curious to note the presence of the religious element on both sides, and the readiness of each combatant to represent that he was acting on behalf of subject races. We have seen what the Metropolitan of Kischeneff said on the Russian behalf. The Sultan was equally emphatic on the part of his own army and people. "Soldiers!" he said, in a proclamation addressed to the forces sent to Sukhum-Kalé, "you go to restore the reign of justice, and to cause the oppressed to recover their rights. Never has a more signal opportunity been given to you of making your names illustrious, of achieving a career in this world, which is perishable, and gaining your salvation in the other, which is eternal. You are now marching, not only under the standard of the Ottomans, but under that of Islamism. You are deputed to fight for your co-religionists. Your Sovereign, therefore, envies you; for, as the verse says, 'Paradise is shadowed by sabres,' which means that you will win Paradise by your victorious blades. God will help you, and the spirit of the Prophet will be satisfied as to one of two things—either that you will sacrifice your lives for the deliverance of your oppressed brethren, and thus fulfil God's orders, or escape death, and remain victorious. In either case, you will receive your rewards, either in this life or the next." In British India, a subscription in aid of the Turks was got up among the Mohammedans, who frequently prayed in the mosques for the welfare of the Sultan, and the security of the faith of Islam. Extreme interest was felt in the war as it progressed, and in some of the Moslem papers it was suggested that Persia and the Central Asiatic States should make war on Russia as a diversion.

With reference to the religious question, it should always be borne in mind that there is nothing in the teaching of Mohammed—nothing, at any rate, in the way of direct injunction or command—which justifies the ill-usage or opprobrious treatment of Christians. On the contrary, Mohammed revered Jesus Christ as one of the great line of Prophets sent by God for the guidance of humanity—indeed, as the greatest of all, short of himself. In the fourth year of the Hejira (626 of our era), he granted to the monks of the Monastery of St. Catherine, near Mount Sinai, and to all Christians, extensive privileges and immunities, at the same time declaring that any Mohammedan who should abuse or violate what was there ordered should be counted as "a violator of God's testament, a transgressor of his commandments, and a slighter of his faith." By this decree, Mohammed undertook himself, and enjoined on his followers, to protect the Christians from every foe, to defend their churches, the residences of their monks, and their places of pilgrimage, and to guard and shelter them from every hurtful action. They were not to be unfairly taxed. No bishop was to be driven out of his bishopric; no Christian was to be forced to reject his religion; no monk was to be expelled from his monastery; no pilgrim was to be detained from his pilgrimage; nor were the Christian churches to be pulled down for the sake of building mosques or houses for the Moslems. The Christians were not expected to sally forth with the Mohammedans to resist the enemies of the latter, on the ground that "tributaries" have nothing to do with war-concerns. Christian women married to Mohammedans were to enjoy their own religion, and not to be subjected to compulsion or annoyance of any kind on that account. "If the Christians," continued Mohammed in this remarkable document, "should become in want of assistance by repairing their churches or hermitages, or for anything concerning their religion, the Mohammedans are to support and favour them. And you are not to consider this as a participation in their religion, but as a mere assistance to their helplessness, and compliance with the ordinances of the Apostle of God, which are made in their favour by the authority of God, and of his Apostle. In time of war, or while the Mussulmans are in a state of hostility with their enemies, no Christian shall be hated or disdained on account of his being resident amongst them (the Mohammedans); and whoever shall thus treat a Christian shall be accounted unjust, obstinate towards the Apostle of God, and disobedient to his will." These privileges were made conditional on the proper conduct of the Christians towards the Mohammedans.

PRINCE CHARLES OF ROUMANIA.

Such were the terms granted by Mohammed to the Christians. They form a splendid charter of liberties—one of the noblest monuments of enlightened tolerance that the history of the world can produce. That Christians, nevertheless, have often been shamefully and cruelly oppressed by Moslems, is a fact beyond dispute. Men are sometimes unfaithful to the better parts of their religion out of the very strength of their devotion to its presumed interests. The highly dogmatic character of the Moslem faith—its imperious tone of self-assertion—its reliance on the sword—its habits of domination and claims to obedience—were all but too likely, despite any commands to the contrary, to encourage an arrogant and persecuting mood; and the passions of a conquering race would do the rest. It must not be forgotten, moreover, that the Crusades had a most unfortunate effect in exasperating the Mohammedans against the Christians. They were not, assuredly, the first causes of persecution; but they intensified and envenomed it. The Moslems felt themselves assailed in their very existence; and countless deeds of ferocity and mad fanaticism, committed by Christian knights in the countries which for a time they conquered or over-ran, left behind them memories of hatred, and longings for revenge, which succeeding times rather magnified than diminished. Unhappily, the decree of Mohammed, granting privileges to the Christians, was not made generally known to the Moslem world. The original was retained by the monks of St. Catherine, who desired to enjoy a monopoly of the benefits it conferred. The only other copy is preserved at Constantinople, where it is kept secret, and regarded with great solemnity as a sacred relic. M. Sálámé (interpreter to Lord Exmouth when he was at Algiers) saw, in 1810, the original of this decree in the monastery where it is preserved, and was the means of giving a translation of it to the nations of Europe. He compared his transcript with the copy in possession of the Sultan, and found that the two corresponded.* This edict shows what is the true position of Mohammedans towards Christianity and its followers, and furnishes an element of hope to a dark and perplexing question.

The Czar, the Czarewitch, the Grand Dukes Vladimir and Sergius, Prince Gortschakoff, Baron Jomini, and other officials, arrived at Ployesti, the head-quarters of the Russian army, on the evening of June 6th. Here the Emperor was met by General Floresco and the municipality of the town, and by a number of Bulgarians, who broke out into a wild song, composed during the insurrection of 1868. "We have suffered long enough," chanted the singers, "and must be true to one another. Oh thou, great Russia, and thou, our sister Servia, why have you forgotten us? Why do you not come and help us?" Further on, more than four thousand of the same nationality sang a new song, thanking the Czar for coming to their aid. Two of the municipal officers then presented bread and salt to the Emperor on a silver plate, on which were engraved the words:—"We are overcome with joy,—we who trust in you; we give praise to you,—we who love your name." Prince Charles, of Roumania, arrived at Ployesti on the 7th, and was received at the railway station by the son of the Grand Duke Nicholas. He visited the Emperor at the Imperial residence, and next day was visited by his Majesty at Bucharest. On the latter occasion, the streets of the Roumanian capital were almost impassable, and the houses along the line of route were crowded to the very roofs. The Czar and the Prince held long conferences on the political situation, and doubtless talked over the terms on which the assistance of Roumania was to be rendered. Bucharest was rapidly becoming Russianised in appearance. Russian soldiers thronged the streets, and a great many of the shops had signs and announcements painted on their fronts in the language of the Muscovites. Contractors from the chief European capitals were gathered about the armies on the banks of the Danube, and three hundred and twenty newspaper correspondents were at hand, to chronicle the approaching war.

Servia was quick in following the example of Roumania, though not to the same extent. Prince Milan requested to know whether the Emperor would receive him at Ployesti, and, on being answered in the affirmative, went there on the 14th of June accompanied by his Minister of Foreign Affairs (General Protic), and Generals Leschjanin and Horvatovich. The Porte was officially informed of the projected visit, but naturally regarded it with great suspicion. After it had taken place, M. Cristics, the Servian diplomatic agent at Constantinople, gave explanations to the Turkish Government respecting the motives of Prince Milan in thus approaching the Czar. He averred that the visit was solely intended as an act of courtesy towards the sovereign of one of the States guaranteeing the Treaty of Paris. M. Cristics admitted the existence of a war-party in Servia, which feared that Roumania might profit by the sacrifices made by the more western State in the previous year. He denied that the Government was following a war-policy, and contradicted the report that works were proceeding at Alexinatz. The object of Servia in the late war, he said, was to gain an extension of territory in the Herzegovina as far as the Marenta, but not to establish Servian independence. The sovereignty of the Porte, he proceeded to remark, was a guarantee for the advancement of Servia and the unity of the race; whereas an independent Servia would soon fall under the domination of Russia or Austria. This, no doubt, was perfectly true; but Prince Milan and his Ministers should have thought of it before. M. Cristics had to make out the best case he could, and no doubt his task was extremely difficult; but his arguments could not have deceived the most trustful of politicians. It is evident, from all that the Prince of Servia said and did in 1876, that his object was to create an independent kingdom, if he could in any way effect it; and it was equally plain that in visiting the Emperor Alexander at Ployesti he was renewing his former intrigues under circumstances that seemed more likely to be attended by success.

* The existence of this little-known document was brought before the attention of the English public by Mr. S. R. Townshend Mayer, in a letter to the *Morning Post* of January 4th, 1878.

At this time, the attitude of the Bulgarians was very hostile, and Sophia was placed in a state of siege. Redif Pasha, the War Minister, issued an order that all Russian subjects, and all Bulgarians supposed to be in league with them, should at once quit the country. An attempt was made to fortify Adrianople, and to erect defences about Constantinople; but, owing to the native listlessness of the people, the work proceeded very slowly. Men were able to obtain exemption from service by a fee of forty piastres, and everybody paid the fee who could afford to do so. A Russian proclamation was now being circulated in Bulgaria. It called upon the Sclaves to rise and join the Russians, and affirmed that the reign of the Turks in that province was virtually at an end. The feeling of disaffection had certainly increased to a very serious extent since the unhappy events of May, 1876. Previously to those events, the mass of the Bulgarians had, in their dull and quiet way, been contented with their lot. The grievances which they suffered were not sufficient to counterbalance the solid comfort of their agricultural lives; and the degree of religious toleration which had existed for some years left nothing to be desired in that respect. A small class of malcontents had formed a league with Russian emissaries; but the great majority of the Bulgarians simply desired to be left alone. Now, however, all was changed. The terrible massacres of a twelvemonth earlier, and the presence of a Russian army on the other side of the Danube, had created a widely-spread desire for putting an end to Turkish domination, once and for ever. Hence the new position of the Bulgarians towards their Ottoman masters. It was a position fraught with peril to the latter.

On the resumption of the war with Montenegro, several actions took place, and at the latter end of April the mountaineers were defeated by the Turks while endeavouring to prevent Suleiman Pasha's advance on Nicsics for the relief of that place. They had taken up a strong position in front of the Dunga Pass, where they were attacked by the Turkish infantry, powerfully supported by artillery. Having driven the Montenegrins back, the Turkish commander entered the pass, and so gained the high-road to Nicsics; but the success, though important, was not conclusive. The Montenegrins were very anxious to obtain possession of Nicsics, a dilapidated fortress in the Herzegovina, commanding a large part of the Montenegrin frontiers towards the north. Since the previous autumn, it had been held by a Turkish garrison, and invested, though somewhat loosely, by the forces of the mountaineers. The garrison stood greatly in need of further supplies, and it was with the object of throwing these in that Suleiman Pasha made his advance. Notwithstanding the discomfiture which he had inflicted on the Montenegrins at the close of April, the Turkish General did not succeed in his design. Further encounters ensued a few weeks later, and the Montenegrins were again forced to retire; but still the object was not gained. To draw off the beleaguering forces from the neighbourhood of Nicsics, simultaneous attacks were made against Kolashin, in the east, and Spitz (or Spizza), in the south. The Montenegrins were in truth very hard-pressed; but, though defeated in the neighbourhood of the Dunga Pass more than once, they still maintained the investment of Nicsics, and two divisions of the Turkish army were severely defeated in the latter part of June, while endeavouring to effect a junction. Much fighting also occurred in the Herzegovina, and both Bosnia and Crete were in a state of revolutionary agitation. In Bosnia, the Turks are said to have committed many excesses against the Christians; but it is tolerably certain that opinion in that province was greatly divided, and that the Turks had many adherents, even among those professing other than the Mohammedan faith.

Thus did matters stand in European Turkey while the Russians were waiting for the Danube to fall, so that they might conduct their forces from the northern to the southern bank, and commence the war in earnest. During the period of suspense, various questions of European policy affected by the condition of hostility were discussed in England with considerable warmth, and with no small admixture of party feeling. A contribution towards this discussion was made in the latter days of June by the official publication of Lord Derby's letter to Count Schouvaloff respecting the interests which the English Government would feel itself bound to defend. The letter was dated May 6th, and commenced by referring to his Excellency's approaching visit to Russia on a short leave of absence. As he would then doubtless have an opportunity of personally conferring with his Government, Lord Derby took that occasion to place before Prince Gortschakoff some considerations of importance to a future good understanding between Great Britain and Russia. Her Majesty's Ministers, it was observed, had lost no time in issuing a proclamation of neutrality. They had warned the Porte that it must not look to them for assistance, and they were determined to carry out the policy thus announced, so long as merely Turkish interests were involved. But, if the war

RECEPTION OF THE CZAR AT PLOYESTI BY GENERAL FLORESCO AND THE MUNICIPALITY OF THE TOWN.

should spread, interests might be imperilled which they were equally bound and determined to defend; and it was desirable that they should make it plain what the most prominent of those interests were. Lord Derby then referred, in the first instance, to the necessity of keeping open, uninjured and uninterrupted, the communication between Europe and the East by the Suez Canal, any attempt to blockade which would be regarded as a menace to India, and an injury to the commerce of the world. An attack on Egypt, or even the temporary occupation of that country, would certainly not be regarded with unconcern by England; nor would her Majesty's Government witness with indifference the passing into other hands than those of its existing possessors of a capital holding so peculiar and commanding a position as Constantinople. Furthermore, serious objections would be felt to any material alteration in the existing arrangements regulating the navigation of the Bosphorus and the Dardanelles. "The course of events," continued Lord Derby, "might show that there were still other interests, as, for instance, on the Persian Gulf, which it would be their duty to protect; but they do not doubt that they will have sufficiently pointed out to your Excellency the limits within which they hope that the war may be confined, or, at all events, those within which they themselves would be prepared, so far as at present circumstances allow of an opinion being formed, to maintain a policy of abstention and neutrality."

Prince Gortschakoff's reply to this communication was dated the 30th of May. Russia, it was here stated, would neither blockade, nor interrupt, nor menace, the navigation of the Suez Canal. As for Egypt, Russia might consider herself at war with that country, seeing that it was a part of the Ottoman Empire, and that its contingents figured in the Turkish army. Nevertheless, she would not bring Egypt within the radius of her military operations. Without being able to prejudge the course or issue of the war, the Imperial Cabinet repeated that the acquisition of Constantinople was excluded from the views of the Emperor. In any case, the future of that capital was a question of common interest, which could not be settled otherwise than by a general understanding, and, if the possession of the city were to be put in question, it could not be allowed to belong to any of the European Powers. So also with the question of the Straits: it was important, in the interests of peace and of the general balance of power, that that question should be settled by a common agreement, on equitable and efficiently guaranteed bases. "The Imperial Cabinet," continued Prince Gortschakoff, "declares that it will not extend the war beyond what is required for the loudly and clearly declared object for which his Majesty the Emperor was obliged to take up arms. It will respect the British interests mentioned by Lord Derby as long as England remains neutral. It has a right to expect that the English Government will, on their side, in like manner take into fair consideration the particular interests Russia has at stake in this war, and in view of which she has imposed such great sacrifices on herself. These consist in the absolute necessity of putting an end to the deplorable condition of the Christians under Turkish rule, and to the chronic state of disturbance provoked by it." This condition had reacted on the internal and external situation of Russia herself; and her international relations, her commerce, her finances, and her credit, were affected by the position of the Christians under the rule of the Sultan. It was to put an end to these evils that his Majesty had decided to impose upon his country the burden of war. The object in view could not be obtained unless the Christian subjects of Turkey were placed in a position in which their existence and security would be guaranteed, and the Emperor was resolved not to lay down his arms without having completely, surely, and effectually, obtained that guarantee.

Such were the explanations which, in the most explicit diplomatic form, were offered by the Russian Chancellor to the English Government at the commencement of the war. In some respects they were as satisfactory as such assurances can be; in other respects they were sufficiently vague to cover a multitude of unavowed designs. But even where the Czar's promises possessed a character the most exact, it was impossible not to feel some uneasiness with regard to the ultimate issue of the struggle then commencing. The temptations of ambition and success are not easily resisted by a despotic power.

CHAPTER XVI.

First Causes of the Rivalry between Turks and Russians—History of Russia—Aboriginal Sarmatian Tribes—Origin of the Russian Nationality—Conquest of Novgorod by Rurik, the Scandinavian—Attacks on Constantinople by the Russians in early Times—Prophecy with respect to the Imperial City—Conversion of Olga to Christianity—Reign of Sviatoslaf—The Grand Duke Vladimir and his Reforms—Anarchy succeeding his Death—Reign of Yaroslaf—Vladimir Monomachos and his Last Testament—Primitive Kingship and its Duties—Martial Character of the Russian Annals—Novgorod an Exception—Establishment of a Free Republican Government in that City—Power and Influence of Novgorod—Decay of its Prosperity—Present Appearance of the Town—Russia invaded by the Mongol Tartars—Ravages of the Golden Horde—Vassalage of the Russian Princes to Tartar Khans—Defeat of the Tartars on the River Don—Dissension among their Communities—Magnificence of their Capital on the Lower Volga—Their Toleration of Christianity—Humiliation of the Russian Princes—Ivan Vasilivitch, First Czar of Muscovy—Inglorious Reign of Vasilii Ivanovitch—Strange Career of Ivan the Terrible—Bad and Good Deeds of that Monarch—Development of Civilisation in Russia in the Sixteenth Century—Intercourse between the Russians and the English at that Period—Admiration of Queen Elizabeth at the Russian Court—Character of the Muscovites early in the Seventeenth Century.

Now that we have brought the two great adversaries face to face on the line of the Danube, it will contribute to an intelligent understanding of the course of events if, while the invaders are yet awaiting their opportunity for crossing the river, we devote some space to a sketch of the origin and development of the Russian and Turkish Empires, their position in Europe, and their relations towards one another. The war of 1877 was not the product merely of dissensions arising within a brief term of years, but resulted from causes dating far off in history, and having their beginnings in rivalries of race, of creed, and of power, such as generally ensure a long course of warfare, until one nation or the other is completely vanquished, or both have learned wisdom from a higher civilisation. Russia and Turkey are old enemies, and the occasion of their enmity cannot be justly estimated by confining our attention to the present time. We must travel back some centuries, and view the two Empires in their cradles. Let us begin with Russia.

The extreme North, whether of Europe or of Asia, was almost entirely unknown to the ancient Greeks and Romans. The name Scythia was used to cover a region of immense extent and indefinite boundaries; everything beyond the fiftieth degree of north latitude was frankly described as "Terra Incognita;" and of the hyperborean countries nothing was related but a few fables touching the existence of some earthly paradise behind the sources of the icy wind. What is now understood by Russia Proper was formerly included in European Sarmatia—a wild and inhospitable desert, into which the cultivated races of the South had little desire to penetrate. The Sarmatians are described by classical writers as a savage people, fierce, warlike, and immoral. In conjunction with other barbarous tribes, they devastated the Roman Empire, and sacked Rome itself, in the declining ages of the Cæsars; but they possessed nothing beyond the military virtues, and those only in the rudest form. The name of one of these tribes was Roxolani, and it has been thought that the word Russian is thence derived, though the point is at the best extremely doubtful. But the Russians, however they may have obtained their name, were not the original possessors of the land. They were Sclavonians, who, advancing northwards from the Danube and the southern parts of the Volga, conquered the Tshudi or Finns of European Sarmatia, and amalgamated with them in the early part of the Christian era. For centuries later, little was heard of them, and the history of Russia cannot be said to commence until about 862, when a Scandinavian freebooter of the Baltic, named Rurik, founded a dynasty which lasted until 1598. A few years before the appearance of Rurik, the Russians, as they had now come to be designated, were made known to the southern and western parts of Europe by some members of that nation who, after visiting Constantinople, formed part of an embassy sent by Theophilus, Emperor of the East, to Louis I., son of Charlemagne, Emperor of the West. These Russians represented the Grand Duke who ruled over their country, and, after discharging their mission, they requested the French monarch to send them back to their own land by sea, as, in journeying to Constantinople, they had been compelled to traverse many hostile nations. This was done, and they returned to the North in 839. It was not long afterwards that Rurik made himself master of the eastern shores of the Baltic.

Before the time of this sea-rover, Russia had been divided into several small independent communities, the principal of which were Kieff and Novgorod. Rurik, who, at the head of his Scandinavians, had been called in by the latter to aid the people against their more powerful neighbours, acquired by his martial deeds a large extent of country, which he consolidated under a despotic government.

His immediate successor, Igor (who during his infancy was represented, after the death of his father, by Oleg, one of the same family), gained possession of Kieff by an act of treachery, and removed the seat of power from Novgorod to that city. The dynasty was thus firmly established on its barbarian throne, and in the tenth century the house of Rurik became masters of the province of Moscow, and of many other regions in the northern parts of Europe, while, towards the south, following the course of the Borysthenes (now the Dnieper), their power was extended almost to the shores of the Black Sea. Even at this early period, the Russians made themselves formidable to the rulers of Constantinople. As their ancestors had attacked the city of the Tiber, so did they make frequent descents on the Eastern metropolis, then swayed by the feeble sceptre of the Byzantine Emperors. Being provided with a large fleet of boats, they descended the Borysthenes on four several occasions in the ninth, tenth, and eleventh centuries, entered the Black Sea to the northwest of the Crimea, and so gained the Bosphorus. It is a remarkable fact that even then it was believed by many that Constantinople was fated to become in time a possession of the Russians. Popular credulity affirmed that in the square of Taurus, in that city, an equestrian statue was inscribed with a prophecy to this effect. Prophecies of such a nature have a tendency to fulfil themselves, by creating ambition on the one side, and apprehension on the other; but this particular foreshadowing still awaits its realisation.

RURIK, FOUNDER OF THE RUSSIAN EMPIRE.

The chief object of the Russians in attacking Constantinople in those days was to load themselves with plunder. Political domination was not at that time a very powerful motive with them. They were little else than a race of pirates, and, having enriched themselves with the gold and silver and the costly stuffs accumulated in the capital of the Eastern Cæsars, they were glad to spread sail once more along the northern shores of the Black Sea, to ascend the winding channel of the Borysthenes, and to escape into the heart of their dim and forest-covered lands. The intercourse between the Russians and the Byzantines, however, was not always unfriendly, and it resulted in the former receiving some elements of civilisation from the latter. It was in this way that the Muscovites were Christianised, and thus it has come to pass that the subjects of the Czar are followers of the Eastern or Greek form of Christianity, instead of the Western or Latin. Olga, the wife of Igor, son of Rurik, reigned over the Russian people after the demise of her husband (whose death at the hands of a hostile tribe she most savagely avenged), and in 945 sailed from Kieff to Constantinople, where she was baptized in the faith she had recently adopted. Her example had less effect than might have been anticipated, and the Russians, for the most part, remained Pagans and idolators for another generation or two. The successor of Olga was her son Sviatoslaf—a rough and courageous warrior, who subdued the nations between the Volga and the Danube, conquered Bulgaria, seized on Adrianople, and menaced the Imperial capital itself. His good fortune, however, came to a termination after a while, and he was at length reduced to such extremities by the military genius of the Emperor John Zimisces that he was glad to accept from that monarch a safe passage to the Borysthenes on his way back to Russia. Before he could reach Kieff, he was slain by some rebellious tribes, near the cataracts of the river, in the year 972.

His dominions were divided among his three sons, two of whom ultimately perished in civil war, so that the third, named Vladimir, became undisputed ruler of the re-united sovereignty in 984. In the early years of his life, he was a devoted follower of the idolatrous religion professed by his countrymen; but he was afterwards converted to Christianity by the zeal of Greek missionaries, powerfully seconded by his own desire to marry Anna, the sister of the Emperors Basil II. and Constantine VIII. (or IX., as he is sometimes reckoned), who reigned simultaneously at Constantinople. Vladimir was very deliberate in his choice of a new religion. In the eastern parts of his realm he came into contact with Mohammedans and Jews; in the western parts, towards Poland, he encountered the missionaries of the Romish Church; in the southern and middle parts, Greek priests had for several years been swaying the minds of his people. The Grand Duke was solicited by all these bodies, and appears in turn to have given some heed to each. His sensual nature was so attracted by the polygamous habits of the Mohammedans, and by the peculiar indulgences promised to the faithful in their Paradise, that he was very near acknowledging the Prophet, and would probably have done so if he could have got his own consent to renounce the use of wine. Had Vladimir become a Moslem, his people would doubtless have become Moslems too, and in that case we should probably have had no Eastern Question at all, or a very different one from that which has since arisen. But the influence of Constantinople prevailed, and Vladimir was baptized as a Greek Christian. He now became as furious an iconoclast as any Puritan of the days of Charles I., and omitted no means of converting his people to the views he had himself accepted. The persuasions of an absolute ruler very speedily take the form of commands, and the subjects of Vladimir soon believed as their master did. Something of Greek art and culture (respectable even in their decadence) entered Russia with the Greek religion; churches and palaces arose in Kieff, then the capital of the State; and a system of education was commenced, where formerly there had been nothing but gross ignorance.

Vladimir was undoubtedly a great monarch, and is deservedly held in high regard by his countrymen to this day. He had the savage and brutal vices of his time; but his powers of organisation and sovereignty were remarkable. He established his sway from the Baltic to the Black Sea, and from Poland and Lithuania (portions of which he subdued) to the Volga. The Crimea submitted to his sceptre, and portions of the neighbouring mainland also acknowledged him as supreme lord. It must not be supposed, however, that he incorporated all these possessions into one homogeneous empire. The more remote parts were rather tributaries than subjects in the most absolute sense; but they yielded to his superior force, and recognized the leadership of Kieff, because Kieff was ruled by a strong man. After his conversion to Christianity, the mildness of Vladimir is said to have been such that he would no longer punish with death even the greatest criminals, but was content to fine them. Considering the character of the age in which he lived, and his own disposition through a large part of his life, this seems improbable. He treacherously murdered his own brother; while a Pagan, he offered up human sacrifices to the idols which he worshipped; and in other respects he was by nature a self-indulgent man. It is not very conceivable, therefore, that so radical a change could have been effected in his heart, especially when we remember that his conversion to Christianity was in a great degree prompted by worldly motives. Towards the end of his life, however, his rule became so weak and inefficient that serious disorders were the result. At length, the city of Novgorod refused to pay its annual tribute to Kieff, and Yaroslaf, one of the sons of Vladimir, is believed to have taken the part of the rebellious citizens. The old monarch assembled an army, with which he marched towards Kieff, but died of grief upon the way, after a reign of forty-five years. This was in 1015, by which time Russia had acquired a position among the States of Europe, though as yet it was but little known to the West. The Russian Church has enrolled Vladimir among her saints, and given him a rank equal to that of the Apostles. He was certainly very far from a saint in the earlier part of his career; but he helped to civilise his country, and his better deeds stand out luminous and distinct against the background of his crimes.

Before his death, Vladimir had divided the dukedom among his twelve sons, thus undoing whatever approach he had made towards consolidating the various portions of his realm. The chief dignity was still attached to the principality of Kieff; but the master-spirit had departed, and a series of civil wars broke out. Poland—then a much more powerful country than Russia—took advantage of this anarchical condition: the Polish King sacked Kieff, and on his return devastated a large tract of country. At length, Yaroslaf became supreme over his brothers, and speedily applied himself to the amelioration of the semi-barbarian state of society which he found. The code of laws which he drew up is still to some extent in force, and, although he can hardly be described as the equal of Justinian, he was in many respects a wise and beneficent prince. Yet he repeated one of the worst errors of his father—indeed, of most of his predecessors—and divided his dominions among his sons. Anarchy again ensued, and the country once more suffered from the incursions of the Poles. In the midst of these commotions, a remarkable man appeared upon the scene. Vladimir Monomachos, Grand Duke of Kieff, and grandson of Yaroslaf, seemed made to be the founder of his country's greatness, though in truth events proved too strong for him. His mother was a daughter of the Greek Emperor, Constantine Monomachos, and he was born in 1052. As a young man, Vladimir fought under his relative, Boleslaf II., King of Poland, whom he joined with an auxiliary force in a war against Bohemia, in 1076. But his martial services were soon required at home, where the division of the Russian nationality into several petty States had led to perpetual warfare among the rival princes. His father was Grand Duke of Kieff, which still claimed a certain authority over the other communities, such as that which was exercised in the Anglo-Saxon Heptarchy, first by Northumbria, afterwards by Mercia, and finally by Wessex. But the supremacy of Kieff was at this time little more than nominal, and was disputed at the edge of the sword by any State which felt itself powerful enough for the task. In the course of these intestine wars, Vladimir Monomachos behaved with the usual ferocity of warrior-princes in those days, and, on taking the town of Minsk, slaughtered the inhabitants without discrimination. Practically, he was the ruler of Kieff during the life of his father, and on the death of that prince lost power rather than gained it. The succession in Russia at that time did not pass from father to son, but from the oldest to the next oldest among the Russian princes. Thus the father of Vladimir was succeeded by his nephew Sviatopolk, Prince of Turov; but Vladimir was already in possession of certain minor principalities, which Sviatopolk permitted him to retain. For some years his life was one of great vicissitudes; but he earned an illustrious name amongst his countrymen by the severe defeats which he inflicted on the Polovtzee, a nomadic tribe from Central Asia, which had entered the southern parts of Russia, and which harassed the people by continual attacks. At sixty years of age, on the death of Sviatopolk, Vladimir Monomachos became Grand Duke of Kieff, and reigned thirteen years, until his death in 1125.

They were years of signal prosperity; for, whatever his faults—and they were the faults rather of his epoch than of himself individually—Vladimir, like his namesake and great-grandfather, was a ruler of high and noble aims, and of large capacity for carrying his purposes into effect. The period of his rule was a time of internal peace. Foreign enemies were repelled; new towns were built; and Russia took higher rank among the nations than she had occupied before. His testament of last instructions to his children exhibits a very remarkable degree of benevolence and wisdom. "O my children!" he there wrote, "love God; love also mankind. It is neither fast, nor seclusion, nor monastic life, which can save you; but good works. Do not forget the poor; feed them, and think that all goods belong to God, and are entrusted to you only for a time. Do not conceal treasures in the bowels of the earth, for this is contrary to the Christian religion. Be fathers to the orphans; judge the widows yourselves, and do not permit the stronger to oppress the weaker. Do not take the life either of the innocent or of the guilty: the life and the soul of a Christian are sacred. . . . In your household, look to everything yourselves, without relying on your stewards and servants; and the guests will not find fault either with your house or with your dinner. In time of war, be active, and be an example to your officers. It is not then the time to think of banquets and enjoyment. Repose after having established the nightly watch. Men may suddenly perish; therefore do not lay aside your armour where danger may happen, and mount your horses early. Above all, respect a stranger, be he a great or a common man, a merchant or an ambassador; and if you cannot give him presents, satisfy him with meat and drink, because strangers spread in foreign countries good and bad report of us. Salute every one whom you meet. Love your wives, but give them no power over yourselves. Remember every good thing which you have learned, and learn what you do not know." Respect for religion, and the practice of a virtuous life, were enjoined by Vladimir in this last testament. It gives one a curious idea of the primitive habits of princes in the east of Europe at that period, to find Vladimir so constantly insisting on the excellence of the monarch doing even menial things with his own hands. "I have myself," he observed, "done all that I could order a servant to do. In hunting and in war, by day and by night, during the heat of summer and the cold of winter, I have not known any repose. I have never relied on magistrates and officers. I never allowed the poor and the widows to be oppressed by the strong. I myself superintended the Church, the Divine service, the household, the stables, the hunt, the hawks, and the falcons." This was unquestionably the original idea of kingship. The king was the man who *knew*; the man who was capable of applying his knowledge; the man of strength and wisdom, of activity and resource. Kingship was chieftainship made permanent and hereditary; and the chief was to approve himself such by showing greater readiness of brain and hand than any of his fellows. Thus, kingship in the early ages of the world was eminently a practical institution, which justified itself by results, and by the plain test of usefulness. In the twelfth century, this conception had not entirely passed away, even in the west of Europe; but it was more completely preserved in the east, where life was simpler, and the patriarchal ideas of the Asiatics had not yet been superseded by the arrangements of a more complex civilization. Vladimir was a perfect specimen of the Russian monarch at a time when Russia possessed its most distinctive characteristics, as a member of the European family dwelling on the very limits of Europe, and within sight of the great eastern deserts. He preached what he practised; it is probable that in the main he had really done as he said, though there may be here and there a touch of boasting or exaggeration. Reviewing the events of his life, he averred that he had undertaken eighty-three important expeditions, not to mention many insignificant ones. He had concluded with the Polovtzee nineteen treaties; he had captured more than a hundred of their best chieftains, whom he had afterwards released; and he had punished, or drowned in rivers, upwards of two hundred. Between the morning and the evening, he had travelled a hundred miles. Amid thick forests, he had with his own hands bound several wild horses at once, and he had had many remarkable escapes from the attacks of savage animals. "When Providence has decreed a man's death," he remarked, with a touch of Oriental fatalism, "neither his father, nor his mother, nor his brethren, may save him." Vladimir was a warrior fit to lead the race of warriors among whom his lot was cast. He has a link of connection with England, from having married a daughter of Harold, the last of the Anglo-Saxon Kings, who, after the death of her father, dwelt at the Court of Swen II., King of Denmark.

NOVGOROD.

For many centuries, the annals of Russia are little else than a record of continual fighting between barbaric chieftains, who considered courage and endurance the chief virtues of man. All is hard and metallic. The clang of armour and the collision of swords echo through great spaces of history

RUSSIAN TYPES.

1. Woman of Novgorod.
2. Girl „
3. Girl of Pskov
4. Woman „
5. Old man of Novgorod.
6. Young „ „
7, 8. Girls of Pskov.
9. Woman of Tver.
10. „ Torjok.
11. „ Kalouga.
12, 13. Citizens of Moscow.
14, 15. Women of Smolensk.
16. Woman of Trogobouge.
17. Girl of Drogobouge.
18. „ Viazma.
19. Woman of Orel.
20. Girl „
21. Boy „
22. Woman of Riasan.
23. Girl „
24. Girl of Saratov.
25. Woman „
26. Man of Kolomnia.
27. Woman „
28. Girl of Koursk.
29. Woman „
30. Girl of Lgov.
31. Man of Koursk.
32, 33, 34. Boy, woman, and girl of Saratov.
35. Girl of Toula.
36, 37. Women of Toula.
38, 39. Workmen „
40. Girl of Dankov en Riazan.
41. Girl of Ranenbourg en Riazan.
42. Girl of Koslov en Tambov.
43, 44. Men of Koursk.
45, 46. Girls of Lgov en Koursk.

extending over many ages, and give interest and character to what would otherwise be a blank. We see but slight evidences of the progress of civilization, of the rise of peaceful communities, or of the creation of a mercantile class, such as, in other countries, counterbalanced the excessive power of the monarch or of the nobles. To this rule, however, there was one remarkable exception. The city of Novgorod (situated on the river Volkhof, a hundred and twenty miles south-east of St. Petersburg) acquired importance as a free community about the middle of the twelfth century. It was at that time a veritable republic, governed by a chief magistrate, whose office was indeed hereditary, but whose power was limited. Novgorod was a commercial city, which ultimately formed a connection with the Hanseatic League, an association of port-towns in Germany, established for mutual protection against the piracies of the Swedes and Danes. War was not the only end and aim of the Novgorodians; but, like the people of other mercantile republics, they knew how to fight upon occasion. In the year 1250, they obtained important victories over the Swedes on the banks of the Neva, and their power became so great that there was a phrase, "Who can resist God and the Great Novgorod?" In the fifteenth century, this Russian city contained 400,000 inhabitants, and was therefore at that time relatively a much more important place than London. Like Venice, and the great commercial cities of the Low Countries, Novgorod held large possessions: its authority extended to the frontiers of Livonia and Finland, covered a part of the province of Archangel, and included lands within the limits of Siberia. Its power aroused the jealousy of the Russian Czars, and in the fifteenth century it submitted to the yoke of Ivan III. In the following age, Ivan IV. desolated the place, and carried away the famous bell, on which the inhabitants had long prided themselves. For about a hundred years, Novgorod was the chief factory of the Hanseatic League, as far as the trade with Russia and Poland was concerned; but in 1553 the arbitrary conduct of Ivan IV., in seizing the effects and imprisoning the persons of the German merchants resident there, induced the association to abandon Novgorod altogether. This was a great blow to the prosperity of the city, which had already lost much of its freedom and its proud pre-eminence, owing to factious divisions among its chief citizens, and to the encroachments of the Grand Dukes; yet for some time longer it continued to be the largest and most commercial city in Russia. It is now little more than a desolate heap of ruins, and its population does not exceed 18,000. At a distance, it strikes the eye, as many other Russian cities do, by the gilded domes of its churches, which even at the present day amount to sixty-three; but the traveller, on entering, finds only scattered groups of small houses, separated by great interspaces of mouldering walls, empty courts, grand buildings ruined and cast down, melancholy wastes of weedy overgrowth, and fields which, by the thinness of the soil, attest that they have formerly been covered by busy streets and squares. The principal church is the cathedral, situated in the Kremlin, or fortress, which stands on a steep hill surrounded with thick walls and towers. It was built in the eleventh century by Greeks from Constantinople, and was dedicated to St. Sophia, in imitation of the great building in that city which is now a mosque. The entrance to the cathedral is through a pair of bronze gates, covered with figures and inscriptions, and doubtless of Byzantine workmanship. The paintings with which the edifice is adorned were executed by Greek craftsmen before the revival of art in Italy, and are distinguished by that stiff, non-natural style of drawing, and that splendour of colour and gilding, which we see in the early Florentine school, and which in recent years have moved the extravagant admiration of our English Pre-Raphaelites.

The anarchy resulting from divided rule, which had long spread over the greater part of Russia, invited the aggression of the Mongol Tartars, vast hordes of whom, led by a son of Genghiz Khan, attacked the Russians, about 1223, in the vicinity of the Sea of Azof, and slaughtered large numbers. They were followed in 1236 by a body of Tartars called the "Golden Horde," led by a grandson of the great conqueror, who laid the whole country waste, and took possession of the government. At that time, fear of the Tartars possessed even the most remote nations, arising not unnaturally from the extraordinary military genius exhibited by several of their princes, and by the people themselves. Issuing from the wide Scythian deserts like a devastating storm, their countless myriads, impelled by the love of conquest and the desire of pillage, poured over the south-eastern parts of Europe, destroying where they could do nothing else, but in some places introducing a new element into the older populations. The countries to the north and west might have appeared safe from these barbarian incursions; but, at any rate, they were not beyond the fear of them. In the year 1238, the people of Sweden and Friesland forbore, from this cause alone, to send their ships to the herring-fisheries on the coast of England, and the absence of exportation reduced the price of these fish to an unparalleled degree. Gibbon, in his celebrated

History, remarks on the whimsicality of the fact that a Mongolian Khan, who reigned on the borders of China, should by his action have lowered the price of herrings in the English market. The English poor were better off because the grandson of Genghiz Khan had made an irruption into Russia and the neighbouring States. But what was a godsend to the Englishman was a severe affliction to the Russian.

During a period of more than two centuries and a half, Russia was held in vassalage by the Tartars who had established themselves at Kaptschak, or Kibzak, in the south-eastern parts of the country. These Mohammedan invaders overspread the plains between the Caspian and the Volga, as well as some of the adjacent lands, and the imperial residence of the Khans was fixed on the banks of that great river which runs through the heart of European Russia, and descends into the sea at Astrakhan. The interior of the country was still left under the government of the native princes; but these were generally nominated by the Khans, who took care to appoint only such as would be favourable to their interests. Kieff had declined from its former importance after the removal of the seat of government to Vladimir in 1157. In 1239, the former city was taken by the Tartars, and the navigation of the Borysthenes, or Dnieper, was then neglected by the Russian princes, who, separated from the sea and from the rest of Christendom, were reduced to abject submission to their Tartar conquerors. Moscow, which had been founded about the middle of the twelfth century, was in 1328 declared by Ivan I. to be the capital of Russia. The principality of Kieff was extinguished in 1321, and Moscow was soon acknowledged as the leading city of Russia. The condition of the country was now undergoing important changes. In 1363, the predominance of Dimitri Ivanovitch, Grand Duke of Moscow, over the other Russian princes, so alarmed the Tartar Khan that he demanded an increase of tribute, and insisted that Dimitri should appear before him as a vassal. The prince refused, and prepared for war. The Tartars were far less strong than they had been a century before, and Dimitri marched with confidence at the head of a large army towards the river Don, on the southern banks of which the Moslem army was drawn up. The Russians demanded to be led at once against their enemy, and the Grand Prince, having crossed the stream, destroyed his boats, that there should be no choice before his soldiers but victory or death. After a sanguinary combat, the Tartars were completely overthrown, and for some years left the Russians in peace. In 1382, however, having by that time recovered their old spirit, they descended in immense numbers on Moscow, when nearly all the inhabitants were put to the sword, the city was given up to plunder, and a large part of it was burned.

Fresh incursions of Tartars, under the great Tamerlane, took place in 1395; but the new-comers did not effect a settlement. Tamerlane retired, and the development of the Russian nationality went on with comparatively little disturbance. The Khans of Kaptschak, however, still maintained themselves in the south-east; but internal dissensions amongst their people had greatly weakened them, and the Christian power was every year recovering its original supremacy. In the days of their greatness, the Tartars reigned with that superb sovereignty which Asiatic nations know so well how to exercise. Besides the city of Kaptschak, they built for themselves a capital called Seraï, on one of the arms of the Lower Volga. Of this place, not the slightest relics are now to be found; but Ibn Batuta, who visited it in the fourteenth century, described it as a great, populous, and beautiful city, possessing stately mosques, fine market-places, and broad streets, in which were to be seen merchants from Babylonia, Egypt, Syria, and other countries. The religion of these Tartars, for more than half a century after their Russian conquests, was a combination of Buddhism and other forms of idolatry, with some admixture of the fire-worship which at one time prevailed in Persia. Christianity was tolerated, and occasionally almost received. One of the Khans allowed a Christian chapel to be erected near his palace, and another was in the habit of publicly taking part in the Easter festivals. Some of them even adopted Christianity in full, and a Tartar Khan is reckoned among the saints of the Russian Church. Even after the conversion of the Golden Horde to Mohammedanism, they continued to favour the Christian clergy, and allowed the followers of the Church a complete enjoyment of their religion. In the middle ages, Moslems were often far more tolerant towards Christians than Christians towards Moslems. It is a lamentable fact that in more recent times so much acrimony and hatred should have been imported into the mutual relations of these religious bodies.

Apart from religion, the conduct of the Tartar Khans towards the unfortunate Russians was insolent in the extreme. When a Mongol ambassador was sent to one of the native princes, the latter was obliged to spread a sable fur under the hoofs of the envoy's horse, to listen on his knees while the Khan's despatch was read, to present the ambassador with a cup of mare's milk, and to lick from the horse's neck any drops that might have fallen on it. The Russian princes must have felt this humiliation bitterly; but for many generations they were not strong enough to resist. On the contrary, they did whatever lay in their power to propitiate their Asiatic despots. By flattery and presents, a prince who desired to enrich himself at the expense of a neighbour would obtain the assistance of the Khan in his military expeditions; and a few married into the Tartar royal family.* For a time, something like a good understanding seemed to exist between the more servile of the Christian princes and the more politic of the Tartar sovereigns; but of course there was no real regard on either side, and when the Tartar power declined, and the Christian power once more rose into ascendancy, it was determined to repay in full measure the accumulated wrongs and insults of many successive years.

CONVENT OF ST. THEODOSIA AT KIEFF.

The Tartar power in Russia was almost completely destroyed by Ivan Vasilivitch (Ivan III.), the first Czar of Muscovy, as the country was then called, who ascended the throne as Grand Duke of Moscow in 1462, and took the title of Czar twenty years later. This sovereign must be regarded as the founder of the present monarchy. His second wife was Sophia, daughter of Thomas Palæologus, a member of the Greek Imperial family, at that time driven out of Constantinople by the Turks; and to the spirit and resolution of this lady, Ivan owed much of his success. It was she who incited him to resist the insolent dictation of the Tartars, and under her influence he raised a large army, with which he attacked the enemy in Kazan, about 1470. Those who had formerly been the exactors of tribute were now compelled to pay tribute themselves. The Tartars were struck with terror and astonishment, and from that time forth

* Mackenzie Wallace's Russia, chap. 22.

there was no more sending of ambassadors to enforce acts of humiliating submission from the native princes of Russia. Towards the conclusion of Ivan's long reign, which lasted forty-three years, and terminated in 1505, the Mohammedans made an effort to regain their ascendancy; but the attempt only involved them in deeper ruin, and their power was annihilated by the operations of the great military leader, Svenigorod. Ivan re-united under his authority most of the minor Russian principalities; but his expeditions against Livonia and Esthonia were unsuccessful. He was surnamed "the Proud," and was not wanting in the faults of despotism: indeed, he and his successors exacted from the nobles a degree of servility till then unknown in Russia. Yet it should not be forgotten that he did more than any of his predecessors towards building up the fabric of a mighty empire. Embassies from Germany, Poland, Venice, the Papal States, and other parts of Europe far more civilised than Russia, were for the first time seen at Moscow during the reign of Ivan Vasilivitch. He encouraged foreigners of distinction to settle in his territories; and by one of these, Aristotle of Bologna, the Russian money was re-coined, and gunpowder, together with the art of casting cannon, introduced into the realm. Silver money had not been coined in that part of Europe until less than a century earlier; so backward was Russia in the ordinary conveniences of social intercourse.

The son of this able prince, Vasilii Ivanovitch, was a very different man from his father. A Tartar horde burst into his dominions, and appeared before the very gates of Moscow; but Vasilii, instead of sallying forth to give battle, induced them to withdraw by the payment of a great ransom, and a promise of renewed allegiance. The Tartars quitted the land, but carried with them a large number of prisoners, whom they sold to the Turks as slaves. Ivan IV., Vasilii's son, inherited the martial genius of his grandfather. The Tartars were repelled by a power greater than their own, and the dominions of Russia were proportionately extended. For the anarchy which existed on his accession to the throne, in 1533, Ivan IV. substituted a condition of order which gave his people some opportunities of developing their prosperity; but this good was not without its attendant evil. Ivan was a despot of the true Russian stamp, and, after the death of his wife Anastasia (whose influence over his character had always been wise and beneficent), he behaved with such systematic ferocity that he lives in history under the designation of "the Terrible." Two of his best and ablest ministers were sacrificed to unreasoning fury, and no man's life was worth an hour's purchase if in any way he had aroused the anger, or even offended the whims, of Ivan. This terrific despotism lasted six-and twenty years, and became intensified with the progress of time and the ravages of ill-health. As in the case of other despots, Ivan was haunted with the fear of conspiracy, and under the influence of this apprehension (which indeed was not without grounds) he retired in 1566 to the fortress of Alexandrovsky, situated in the middle of a gloomy forest Thence he issued a proclamation denouncing the nobles, and ending with a declaration that he resigned the government of the State. The people, dreading a return of the anarchy from which they had so often suffered, begged him to resume his power, and acknowledged that he had over them an imprescriptible right of life and death, which he might exercise in any way he pleased. The Czar returned to Moscow, strengthened in his evil moods by the servility of his subjects. There can be no doubt that by this time he was actually mad, and incapable of restraining his actions. It is recorded by a Russian historian that, although he had been absent not more than a month, his whole appearance had altered so strangely that he could be scarcely recognized. His figure was shrunken and emaciated; his head had become suddenly bald; his ample beard was thin, and wildly scattered over his face; his eyes were dull, and his features marked by a ravenous ferocity. In the sombre depths of the forest, in the solitude of that distant fortress, he had lived on his own distracted thoughts, until the natural man was transformed into the semblance of a fiend. Surrounding himself by a large body-guard, recruited in distant provinces of approved loyalty, he built a great stronghold in the heart of Moscow, and drove out hundreds of people from their houses, that he might apply the land to his own use. He beheaded, he poisoned, he impaled. The nobles were the principal sufferers, on account of their share in an abortive conspiracy; but sometimes the populace were massacred, on the bare suspicion of treason. On one occasion, believing them to have corresponded with the King of Poland, Ivan slaughtered the inhabitants of Novgorod with his own hand, until exhaustion forced him to desist. For more than a month, numbers of unoffending persons were drowned in the rivers, the icy covering of which was broken for the purpose.

The brief prosperity which Russia had enjoyed in the earlier years of Ivan's reign was now succeeded by a series of misfortunes, which threatened to reduce the whole nation to despair. The country was desolated by the plague, and in 1571 the Crim Tartars, instigated by the Poles, made an irruption into the Southern provinces, and, advancing towards Moscow, defeated the Russian army within eighteen leagues of the capital. The miserable tyrant, who had by this time lost the military virtues of his youth, shut himself up in a fortified cloister, together with his two sons and his most valuable effects. The Tartars entered the city, set it on fire, plundered the houses of its nobles and rich men, and destroyed a large number of its inhabitants. Eight years afterwards, Stephen Bathori, King of Poland, declared war against Russia, and in combination with the King of Sweden took Narva, Riga, and the whole of Livonia. The Russian nobles ventured to remonstrate with the Czar against his suffering foreign enemies to ravage the country, and requested that he would permit his eldest son to appear at the head of the army. Ivan, suspecting that the prince had entered into a league against him, turned upon the young man with furious reproaches. The son attempted to justify himself, and the father, in a transport of rage, dealt him a violent blow with an iron-tipped staff. The stroke proved fatal in four days, and Ivan, despite the madness of his savage mood, was consumed with remorse for what he had done. He now endeavoured to rouse himself from the disgraceful lethargy into which he had fallen, and to act with vigour against the Tartars, who had once more poured into Russian territory. He could effect nothing, however, by his sword, and was reduced to the humiliation of entering into terms with those warlike barbarians. On returning to Moscow, he became conscious that his death was near at hand, and the approach of that great change seems to have lifted him out of the murderous insanity of many years, and once more to have directed his thoughts to great and noble ends. He performed several acts of clemency, and enjoined his successor to liberate prisoners, to repeal taxes, and to redress the accumulated injuries which he himself had wrought. He expired in 1584, in the fifty-fourth year of his age, leaving behind him a reputation strangely made up of good and bad, and presenting for ever to the minds of his countrymen one of the most portentous figures that are to be found even in the annals of their dreary land, where despotic passions acquire an intensity beyond that of the south, and are touched with all the gloom and rigour of northern forests and of Arctic seas.

IVAN III. IVAN IV.

It will be pleasant, and indeed salutary, to dwell somewhat on the better acts of Ivan IV. before finally dismissing him. In his vigorous and youthful days, he was not merely a conqueror who added largely to the Russian dominions, but, what was of much greater worth, a reformer of abuses in the lands which he ruled. He introduced discipline into his armies, which until then had been little better than a savage rabble; he established a permanent militia, such as might have proved a defence to the country, had not the Czar himself, in later years, ruined all things by the insanity of his will; forts were built to hold the Tartars in check, and the Don Cossacks were subdued. In the hope of encouraging commerce and the arts, he despatched an embassy to the Emperor Charles V., in 1547, requesting artisans and engineers from Germany for the instruction of his people; and, although this endeavour was not attended by success, the fault does not appear to have been his. A printing-press was by his orders set up at Moscow; a code of laws was digested, which removed many of the abuses under which the people had suffered; and the English were permitted to establish factories in Muscovy. Religious toleration was encouraged, and, by the conquest of Astrakhan, the commerce of the Caspian was opened to Russia, which before then had no ports adapted for the prosecution of a foreign trade. The intercourse between Russia and England at that time was very remarkable. Ivan entered into friendly relations with Queen Elizabeth, and, towards the close of his life, when tortured by the fear of retribution, begged of that potentate an asylum in her dominions. This good understanding between England and Russia resulted in the first instance from an expedition sent out by Edward VI., in 1553, with a view to discovering the north-east passage to China and India—a dream which haunted the minds of all adventurous Englishmen in those days. The commanders of that expedition were Sir Hugh Willoughby and Richard Chancellor. Willoughby and several of his companions were frozen to death; but Chancellor made his way into

KAZAN.

the White Sea, and anchored in the bay of the Dwina, where shortly afterwards arose the city of Archangel. A company of Russian merchants was formed in London, and English factories were established on the borders of the White Sea. Our old geographer, Peter Heylyn, relates that in his time the English had dispersed themselves into all parts of that vast Empire. "And truly," continues this writer, "there is no nation so kindly entertained amongst the Russians, both prince and people, as the English, who have many immunities not granted to other nations. The cause I cannot but attribute to the never-dying fame of our late Queen [Elizabeth], admired and loved of the barbarians, and also to the conformable behaviour of the English in general, which hath been so plausible that when Vasilivitch, or Basiliades,* nailed the hat of another foreign ambassador to his head for his peremptoriness, he at the same time used our Sir Thomas Smith with all courtesy imaginable. Another time, when the Jesuit Possevinus began to exhort him to accept the Romish faith,—upon the information of our ambassador that the Pope was a proud prelate, and would make kings kiss his feet, he grew into such a rage that Possevinus thought he would have beaten out his brains.' Notwithstanding these circumstances, which he reports with a good deal of satisfaction, Peter Heylyn does not seem to have had any great regard for the Muscovites. "The people," he writes, on the authority of Maginus, "are perfidious, swift of foot, strong of body, and unnatural; the father insulting on the son, and he again over his father and mother. So malicious one towards another that you shall have a man hide some of his own goods in his house whom he hateth, and then accuse him for the stealth of them. They are exceedingly given to drink, insomuch that all heady and intoxicating drinks are by statute prohibited, and two or three days only in a year allowed them to be drunk in. The commons live in miserable subjection to the nobles, and they again in as great slavery to the Duke or Emperor. They are altogether unlearned; even the priests are meanly indoctrinated."† Such was Russia early in the seventeenth century. Books and newspaper correspondents in our own days enable us to form some idea how far they have improved, and in what respects they have stood still.

CHAPTER XVII.

Russian History continued—Feodor I. and the Dictator Boris Godunof—Alleged Assassination of the Child Dimitri, Heir to the Throne—Different Versions of the Story—Military Services of Boris—Legalisation of the System of Serfage—Death of Feodor I.—Distracted State of Russia during a Period of Interregnum—Politic Conduct of Boris—His Acceptance of the Throne at the Request of the People—Incidents of his Reign—Liberal and Despotic Measures—Temporary Successes, followed by Famine and Anarchy—Appearance in Poland of "the False Dimitri"—Extraordinary Statement of the Pretender to the Russian Throne—His Claims supported by Poland—His Entry into Russia at the Head of a small Polish Army—Military Successes—Death of Boris—Dimitri enters Moscow in Triumph, and succeeds to the Crown—Unpopularity of his Rule—Outbreak of a Conspiracy, and Murder of Dimitri—Another Period of Anarchy—Appearance of fresh Claimants to the Throne—Election of the First of the Romanoffs—Ceremonies at the Inauguration of the Russian Czars—Oriental Splendour of the Muscovite Court—Invasion of Russia by the Poles and Swedes—Wars with the Cossacks and Turks—Social Reforms of the Emperor Alexis—Early Incidents in the Reign of Peter the Great—Character of that Monarch—Barbarous Condition of Russia in his Days—Ambition of Peter to make his Country a great Naval Power—His Visits to Holland and to England—Building of St. Petersburg—Assumption by Peter of the Title of Emperor—Suspicious Death of his Eldest Son, Alexis—The Extreme Despotism of Peter's Government, and its Effects on Modern Russian History—Reigns of later Sovereigns.

A VERY extraordinary series of events ensued shortly after the death of Ivan the Terrible. It frequently happens that a prince of more than usual strength is followed by one of more than usual weakness. A Charlemagne is succeeded by a Louis; an Edward I. by an Edward II. The throne of Ivan was occupied, on his decease, by Feodor (or Theodore) I.—a person of mild and inoffensive character, totally unfitted to rule such a people as the Russians in the sixteenth century. His father, foreseeing his weakness as a sovereign, had established a Council of Boyars, or noblemen, to assist in the government; but this only led to intrigue and confusion. In time, an ascendancy over the rest was gained by the Czar's brother-in-law, Boris Godunof, a nobleman of Tartar origin, whose disposition was not unlike that of the late monarch, and who soon became, to all practical intents, the ruler of the

* It would seem that the monarch really alluded to was Ivan the Terrible.

† Mikrokosmos: a Little Description of the Great World. By Peter Heylyn. Fourth Edition. Oxford, 1629.

country. He banished or assassinated his rivals, and, seeing that the Czar was not likely to live much longer, conceived the idea of becoming, nominally as well as actually, the supreme head of the State. To accomplish this purpose, it was first necessary to get rid of the Czar's heir, his brother Dimitri (or Demetrius), then a child of nine years old. Having removed the boy, together with his mother, to Uglich, a town far from Moscow, he caused him (as historians generally believe) to be assassinated, on the 15th of May, 1591, as he was playing in the court-yard of the palace. His governess and nurse had left the child for a little while, and on returning found him dead, with a gash in his throat. The mother, furious with grief, denounced some of the adherents of Boris as the authors of the crime; and they were at once massacred by the people. It is but fair to add that Boris always denied any complicity in the death of Dimitri, and even affirmed that he perished by an accident. According to the statements of several witnesses, examined before a body of investigators, the boy, who was subject to epileptic fits, fell down in one of these while holding a knife in his hand, and thus inflicted the wound of which he died. But, as this inquiry was carried on under the immediate influence of Boris himself, the testimony given in fear of his wrath must be received with no little hesitation. The ultimate decision was to the effect that the child had committed suicide, and was accompanied by sentences against his mother and uncles for causing the massacre of the presumed murderers—sentences which Godunof proceeded to execute with terrible severity. He departed for the scene of the tragedy at the head of a large force, compelled the Czarina to take the veil, threw her brothers into prison, and slew or banished to Siberia (then just added to the Russian dominions) so many of the citizens of Uglich that the town was rendered completely desolate. All that we know of Boris raises the presumption that he would not have scrupled to make away with the child, if he could only by those means obtain possession of the throne. But the point is one which can never be satisfactorily cleared up, and he is entitled to the benefit of any doubt arising in the minds of historical students. Subsequent events even rendered it questionable whether Dimitri had been killed at all.

The life and reign of Feodor—if reign it can be called—lasted another seven years; but Boris continued to be the actual dictator. He was at first very unpopular, on account of what had happened at Uglich, and it has been said that he set Moscow on fire, and then treated the inhabitants with great generosity, to obtain their favour. He accomplished this object, however, rather by his courage and genius as a soldier than by any such artifice. The Crim Tartars had invaded Russia, and were advancing on Moscow. Feodor, on being asked to put himself at the head of his armies, replied that the saints who had always protected Russia would protect her then; and Boris immediately took the command. His fitness for the post was soon made apparent. The invading hordes were defeated and driven back with enormous loss, and Russia was again free from foreign domination. This brilliant success increased the power of the conqueror, who, on his return to Moscow, obtained the banishment of the nobles opposed to him, and purchased the devotion of the others by establishing the institution of serfage, until then not actually recognized in Russia. The date of this great change, which had so much to do with shaping the political and social history of the Empire in after times, was 1593; and it was not until two hundred and seventy years later that the vicious system was abolished. In the early ages of Russian history, the peasants were free to change their domicile on St. George's Day, which was the termination of the agricultural year; but some encroachments on this natural right had been made before the time of Boris Godunof. The princes and great nobles had long been much opposed to the migration of their labourers, because, while their estates were of immense size, owing to the vast extent of the country, the population was small, as indeed it still is, relatively to the territorial dimensions of the entire realm. Even in the free communes (of which we shall have to speak further on), labourers were often forbidden to depart until they could produce substitutes. The nobles, less scrupulous than the communes, frequently used violence to hinder the peasants from quitting their estates for others. But all this was exceptional, irregular, and, as far as law can be said to have had any existence in the Russia of that period, illegal. Boris sanctioned, organized, and stamped with the seal of authority, what until then had existed only in an unrecognized form. This procured him the dislike of the peasantry, but, what was much more to the purpose, it rallied the nobles to his cause.

The administration of Boris was in many respects very successful. The Empire was extended and greatly strengthened, and the Swedes were defeated in their attempts to interfere in the internal affairs of Russia. Feodor died at the beginning of 1598, the last direct representative of the house of Rurik, which, under some fifty-six sovereigns, had governed Russia for seven hundred and thirty-six years. Several collateral branches existed, and the present Imperial family is connected in this way with the older stock; but the male line expired with Feodor. The death of that prince has been attributed to poison administered by Boris; but we should be cautious in accepting statements made against a man who had many enemies. When lying on his death-bed, Feodor offered his staff, the emblem of empire, to several of his relatives, all of whom refused it. In a burst of rage, he threw it on the floor, and Boris took it up. By his last will, however, the Czar had bequeathed the throne to his widow Irene, sister of Godunof, who was immediately proclaimed sovereign, but in a few days retired into a convent, where she declared her resolution of remaining for the rest of her life. It was then determined by the nobles to offer the throne to Boris; but, with a politic assumption of reluctance, he refused to accept it. A general assembly of the States, composed of the principal persons among the nobility and clergy, together with deputies from several towns (for Russia was not at that time the absolute despotism it has since become), was convoked at Moscow six weeks after Feodor's death, in order to elect a new monarch, and in the meanwhile public affairs were conducted by a Council of Boyars in the name of the Czarina. Symptoms of anarchy soon appeared, and Godunof was unanimously proclaimed Czar of Moscow, as being the only man capable of saving the country from the ruin which threatened it. For two days, public prayers were offered up that Godunof might be induced to accept the throne; but the object of all this adulation still remained quietly in the convent to which his sister had retired. He had spread a report that it was his intention to take the monastic vows, and had for some time resigned into the hands of the nobility the staff which he picked up from the floor of Feodor's chamber.

On the 20th of February, 1598, a deputation waited on Boris at the convent, and informed him that he had been elected sovereign by the whole Empire; yet he still refused to quit his retirement. Next day, the Patriarch of Moscow, accompanied by the principal clergy and nobility, and by a large body of the people, entered the church of the convent, and, having performed Divine service, again requested Boris to accept the throne. Again he refused; upon which the Patriarch, several of the nobles and bishops, and a multitude of the people, flung themselves on the ground, and declared that they would never rise until Godunof had consented to become their sovereign. The Patriarch, with tears, implored the Czarina to use her influence on behalf of their prayer, and she at length declared that, touched by the distress of the nation, she gave her benediction to Boris as sovereign of Moscow. Even then, however, he refused to accept the crown unless on the condition that they should all assemble in arms, and march with him against the Tartars, who were once more contemplating an invasion of the Empire. This being enthusiastically promised, he exclaimed, with mock humility, "The will of God be done!" and ascended the throne amidst universal acclamations.

Taking the field at the head of an enormous force, he struck such terror into the Tartar Khan that, instead of invading Russia, he begged for a continuance of peace. The brief reign of Boris was in many respects brilliant and striking; but he was not successful in one of his favourite projects—that of contracting a matrimonial alliance between his own family and some one of the reigning Houses of Europe. He failed also in attempts to form, first with Austria, and afterwards with Persia, a league against the Turks. Whatever his crimes may have been, Boris was in many respects an enlightened ruler. He desired to create universities where the young nobles might be instructed in foreign languages, and in scientific knowledge. His projects were defeated by the clergy, who considered instruction in secular matters the natural enemy of religion; but he sent eighteen young men of aristocratical lineage to be educated in Germany, France, and England, and he did his utmost to attract foreigners of repute in the arts into his dominions. His general policy seems to have been a singular mixture of severity and benevolence. He punished drunkenness with death. The institution of serfdom was made continually more stringent: and when the peasants fled in large numbers to the Cossacks, to avoid the tyranny by which they were being ground to the earth, Boris issued an edict establishing an inquisition for the discovery and punishment of the fugitives. On the other hand, it is recorded that when, in 1601 and the two following years, a famine of the most terrible character resulted from a succession of bad harvests, he exerted himself to the utmost to alleviate the calamity, and caused great quantities of provisions, besides money, to be distributed in Moscow. Half a million of people are said to have died in that city alone, owing to the distress, and to the overcrowding of persons who had fled there from the country. A general disorganisation of society accompanied this prolonged famine. Bands of robbers and assassins filled the land, and their chief became so formidable that it was necessary to march an army against him, by which, after a battle in the vicinity of Moscow, he was defeated and taken. In the midst of these disturbances, a strange rumour spread throughout the Russian provinces. It was whispered that Prince Dimitri, who was believed to have died at Uglich, whether by the hand of Boris, by accident, or by suicide, was in reality alive, and was making preparations in Poland to recover the throne. The distracted condition of Russia may have offered an inducement to some impostor to put himself forward under this pretence; but at any rate the pretence was made, and it produced an immense effect amongst the Muscovites.

Various accounts have been given of the way in which the claim first came to be asserted. According to one of these, a stranger fell seriously ill in a Polish town, in 1603, and imparted to his confessor that he was heir to the Russian throne. The confessor communicated this statement to Prince Adam Wisznioviecki, of Brahm in Lithuania, who, on the stranger's recovery, espoused his cause. According to another account, this prince had a page, whom one day he had occasion to correct; whereupon he exclaimed, "If you knew who I am, prince, you would not treat me thus. I am the Czarevitch Dimitri, son of Ivan IV." The account given by the pretender of the circumstances attending his escape from death was to the effect that his physician had feigned to comply with the orders of Boris, but had substituted the son of a serf for the young prince, and that he, the real Dimitri, had for some years been secretly brought up in a convent. His account of the assassination differed in its details from that which had been generally received; but the youth confirmed his story by exhibiting a Russian seal bearing the arms and name of the Czarevitch, and a valuable diamond cross. Assuming him to have been an impostor, he would appear to have been a monk named Otrepief; but many persons believed in his claims, and there are those who still assert them. A Russian, named Petrofski, who saw him when living with Prince Wiszniowiecki, declared that he had known young Dimitri well, and that he recognized the stranger as the same person by two warts—one on his forehead, the other under his right eye—and by one of his arms being a little longer than the other. Obtaining the friendship of the Palatine of Sandomir, the young man was introduced to the King of Poland, Sigismund III., who, at a solemn audience, exclaimed, after listening to his statements, "God preserve thee, Dimitri, Prince of Muscovy! Thy birth is known to us, and attested by satisfactory evidence. We assign thee a pension of forty thousand florins, and, as our friend and guest, we permit thee to accept the counsels and services of our subjects."

The Poles very generally adopted the cause of this claimant to the Russian throne, and were greatly pleased by his abjuring the Greek faith, and entering the Romish Church. He was thus enabled to raise a small army, with which he invaded Russia towards the close of 1604. Previous to his appearance in that country, Boris had attempted to get possession of his person, and had even sent emissaries to assassinate him; but these plots were frustrated, and when Dimitri, as we must call him, entered Muscovy at the head of 4,000 Poles, he was joined by many Russians and Cossacks of the Don, who, in consequence of various oppressions, were disaffected towards Boris. The Czar sent an army against him; but it was defeated, and the adherents of Dimitri became more numerous every day. The Pretender, however, suffered a reverse at Dobruinicki, and was compelled to retreat. His cause began to look grave, when information arrived that Boris, in a fit of despair, after the failure of renewed attempts to assassinate his rival, had put an end to his own existence by taking poison. His death occurred on the 13th of April, 1605, and he was succeeded by his son, Feodor, a youth of eighteen, described as a person of most amiable disposition, but whose reign was short and tragical. He received the oath of fidelity from all parts of the Empire not in the power of Dimitri; but the fortunes of that mysterious person advanced with such rapidity that a rising in his favour took place at Moscow on the 13th of June, and Feodor was dragged with his family from the palace, and imprisoned in a private house, where he was murdered a few days later.

In the meanwhile, the chief commander of the forces opposed to Dimitri had embraced the cause of the Pretender, who was now conducted in triumph to Moscow. Whether Feodor was strangled after his arrival, and by his orders, or whether the event happened a little earlier, seems doubtful; but in either case Dimitri had no longer any rival. Maria, the widow of Ivan the Terrible, was brought from the convent in which she had been confined, and publicly acknowledged Dimitri as her son. He was crowned with great pomp at the Cathedral of Moscow, and received the general homage of the realm. For a little while, Dimitri was popular with the masses; but it was speedily discovered that, whether or not he was a Russian by birth, he was in no respect a Russian in his feelings. Having been brought up in Poland, his ideas were entirely Polish, and therefore in the last degree offensive to the Muscovites. He treated his subjects with studied insolence; the customs of the Russian people were regarded by him with undisguised contempt; surrounded by Poles and foreign guards, he irritated

VIEW OF MOSCOW.

the genuine Russians by his want of reverence for the ceremonies of the Greek religion; and, although his real faith was not actually known, it was suspected. Matters were not improved by his marriage to Marina Mniszek, daughter of the Palatine of Sandomir, to whom he had been betrothed before quitting Poland. The nuptial journey from Cracow to Moscow was marked by extreme magnificence, and extended over three months. On the 12th of May, 1606, the lady made her entrance into the Russian capital, and the discontent of the people deepened from that hour, for Marina was a Romanist. Dimitri, although at times exhibiting considerable generosity, contrived to make himself universally disliked by his patronage of the Poles, whose ideas in religion were detestable to every orthodox Russian. The people began openly to denounce him as a heretic, as a person worse than a Turk, and finally as an impostor. A conspiracy against his rule, headed by Prince Zuiski, was discovered and quelled. Zuiski and his brothers, after being condemned to death, were pardoned by Dimitri, but did not on that account abstain from their plots. The prince told a body of Russians, assembled at his palace on the 28th of May, that their hostility to the reigning Czar was discovered, and that either they or he must perish. It was then determined that the signal of revolt should be given by the great bell at Moscow, and that the other bells of the city should answer to the warning sound.

THE KREMLIN AT MOSCOW.

At the appointed moment, the clamour of 3,000 bells filled the air, and Dimitri, who heard the dreadful announcement, sent to Prince Zuiski's brother to learn the cause. "It is a fire," replied the younger Zuiski, who was on guard at the Kremlin. But Basmanof, one of the Czar's most trusted generals, soon appeared with the information that it was a revolt. The whole populace was in arms. Excited by the fury of national zeal and religious fanaticism, the citizens of Moscow poured down upon the foreigners, with savage exclamations of "Death to the heretics!" In the midst of the terrible reverberations of the bells, and of the raging voices of the people, Dimitri himself was pursued from room to room of his palace, until he leaped from a window thirty feet high, and broke his leg. The mob, inflamed with passion and intoxicated with slaughter, followed with murder in their eyes. They triumphed over the fallen monarch, and denounced him as an impostor. He denied it to the last. "I am the Czar—the son of Ivan!" he exclaimed with failing breath; and the next moment he was slain. A frightful massacre followed, and all opposition was quenched in blood.

A little before the death of Dimitri, his supposed mother was interrogated by the conspirators, and revoked her former acknowledgment, as having been extorted by fear. Dimitri had held the sovereign power scarcely a year, and he left behind him a reputation for nothing but deliberate imposture, alien tyranny, and heretical views of religion. Most of the Russian historians deny his claim to be the son of Ivan; but he has not wanted supporters amongst the literary men of other countries. He was succeeded by Prince Zuiski who found his position one of great difficulty and peril. The imposition of the late Czar, if it was one, did not perish with the man. It was again asserted after a little while that Dimitri was *not* dead. A person, who is generally described as "the second False Dimitri," appeared in arms at Tushino, a village near Moscow, and asserted that he was the Czar. He seems to have been a robber, commanding a horde of brigands, and, having seized Marina, the wife of the late Czar, he induced her—probably under compulsion—to admit that he was her husband. Moscow was besieged for seventeen months by this captain of banditti, who kept Russia in a state of anarchy during four years. He was killed in 1610 by a Tartar chief; but, before that event, Zuiski, having been defeated by the Poles, was compelled to resign the crown. After several years of disturbance, which reduced the whole Empire to the utmost state of misery, the nobles placed upon the throne a boy of sixteen, belonging to the House of Romanoff, who through his mother was connected with the House of Rurik. Two other counterfeit Dimitris appeared at different times; but the prosecution of their claims was not attended by any remarkable circumstances.

Michael Feodorovitch, the founder of the present dynasty, was raised to the throne in 1613, and ruled till his death in 1645. He was the reigning monarch when Peter Heylyn wrote his book of Geography, and is mentioned by that author as "living in a firmer and more constant continuation of peace with Tartar, Turk, Polonian, and Swethlander, than ever any of his predecessors did in times past." Bringing his list of Muscovite rulers to a close, Heylyn gives some account of the manner in which the Czars were invested with the regal office, taking as a specimen the ceremonies that were observed in June, 1584, when Feodor I. succeeded to the throne. That monarch, he relates, "went towards the temple of St. Michael, being the principal church in all Moscow; the streets all covered with flowers; the doors of the citizens crowned with garlands; the air echoing with the noise of flutes and trumpets; and the people so crowding to behold their prince, that, had not the guard with naked swords forced a passage through them, it had been impossible for him to have gone on. Being now come to the church door, the lords of the country went out to meet him, and the Archbishop of Moscow, clad *in pontificalibus*, when he was come into the church, embraced him. The pavement of the church was hidden with tapestry, and the stalls adorned with costly hangings. The Great Duke sat down in his throne, being attired in a garment of silk, buttoned down with golden buttons. On his head he ware a purple cap, spangled with rich jewels, and on his fingers abundance of rings. Being thus seated, the Archbishop prayed unto God to bless him, his people, and his government; which was seconded by the joyful shouts of his subjects, amongst whom no small store of silver money was flung about by the treasurer. And so they returned to the palace." Milton, in his account of Muscovy, gives a still more elaborate description of this observance, from which it would appear that for splendour of costly stuffs, for richness of gold and silver, for affluence of jewellery, and for stately pomp of ceremonial, the Russian Czars were hardly surpassed by the most gorgeous monarchs of Asia.* The early English voyagers to Russia, whose narratives may be read in Hakluyt, are profuse in their details of the great Emperor's magnificence; of his robes made all of goldsmith's work, his crystal sceptre beset with gems, his orient pearls, his royal throne, his arms, his many-coloured velvets and satins, his great lords shining in gold and silver, his waiters who thrice changed their apparel during dinner-time, his wealth of plate, his massy goblets of precious metal, his superfluity of meat and drink. But, with the splendour of the East, these monarchs had all the fitful caprice and furious insolence of Eastern despots.

During the seven years' anarchy intervening between the murder of Dimitri and the accession

* A Brief History of Moscovia, by Milton.

of Michael Romanoff to the throne, the country had been invaded both by the Poles and Swedes, each of whom desired to give a reigning prince to Russia. The Swedes occupied Kexholm and Novgorod, and in 1610 the Polish King, Ladislaus, advanced to Moscow, sent Zuiski prisoner to Warsaw, and for a time ruled in his place. It looked very much as if Russia would have been partitioned by Poland, as Poland was afterwards partitioned by Russia; but the nobles and commonalty rallied to the national cause, and Ladislaus was expelled in 1613. The reign of Michael was an important era in Russian history. Order was restored after a long period of distraction, and the country began to assume a position of importance among the States of Europe. The people recovered some degree of prosperity, and commercial treaties were concluded with England in 1623, and with France in 1629. The Poles were defeated in renewed attempts to subjugate Russia; but on the other hand Finland (which had frequently changed hands) was made over to Sweden. Michael was succeeded by his son Alexis, whose reign was distinguished by two very destructive contests with Poland. The second of these ended, in 1667, in the truce of Andruscof, which in 1686 (ten years after the death of Alexis) was converted into a permanent peace. By the truce, Russia obtained a large increase of territory, and the acknowledgment of her authority over the Dnieper Cossacks, who had revolted, and received the countenance of Poland. An insurrection of the Don Cossacks followed shortly after the conclusion of the Polish war in 1667; but the leader of these rebels, Stenko Razin, was invited to appear at Moscow under a treacherous pretence of being treated with consideration, and was then executed as a rebel. This restored order amongst the malcontent tribes; but Russia was not permitted to be long at peace. The Zaporovian Cossacks had revolted against the Poles, and made a treaty of alliance with Mohammed IV. of Turkey, receiving from him the province of Ukraine in fief. A war ensued between the Poles and the Turks, and Russia took occasion to demand that Azof, which had been taken from the Cossacks by the Ottomans in 1642, should be restored to the Czars. This was the war during which the noble Polish soldier, John Sobieski, distinguished himself by some of the most brilliant military achievements that the history of the world can show. The Czar of Russia assisted in the war, having for once a common object with the Poles; but his arms were signalised by no great success, and he died on the 10th of February, 1676, while the struggle was yet proceeding. Alexis was much more distinguished in peace than in war. He revised and amended the code of laws compiled by Ivan IV.; ordered many works on mathematics, military science, tactics, fortification, and geography, to be translated into Russian; enlarged the city of Moscow, and built two of its suburbs; invited foreign officers into his service; and constructed some ships on the Caspian, under the direction of shipwrights whom he procured from Amsterdam.

MICHAEL I.

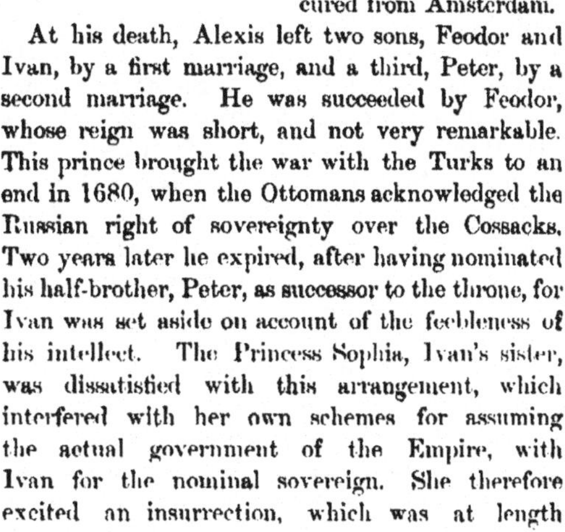

At his death, Alexis left two sons, Feodor and Ivan, by a first marriage, and a third, Peter, by a second marriage. He was succeeded by Feodor, whose reign was short, and not very remarkable. This prince brought the war with the Turks to an end in 1680, when the Ottomans acknowledged the Russian right of sovereignty over the Cossacks. Two years later he expired, after having nominated his half-brother, Peter, as successor to the throne, for Ivan was set aside on account of the feebleness of his intellect. The Princess Sophia, Ivan's sister, was dissatisfied with this arrangement, which interfered with her own schemes for assuming the actual government of the Empire, with Ivan for the nominal sovereign. She therefore excited an insurrection, which was at length appeased by Ivan being proclaimed joint sovereign with Peter, and by the appointment of herself as Regent. The chief agent of the Princess Sophia was the Prime Minister, Prince Galitzin, a person of great energy and talent. When Peter, at the age of seventeen, took the daughter of the Boyar Feodor Abrahamavitch in marriage, during the absence of Prince Galitzin from the seat of government, so much discontent was excited in the party of that nobleman that a new insurrection broke out. It was soon crushed, however; Galitzin was sent to Archangel, and the Princess Sophia was shut up in a convent until her death in 1704. This second insurrection was in 1689, and after its suppression Peter reigned without any rival near the throne. His brother Ivan, who was subject to epileptic fits, died in 1696, and Peter now directed all his energies towards the creation of a new Russia, which should be more in harmony with the Western world than that which had previously existed.

Until then, Muscovy had had very much the character of an Asiatic kingdom; the great ambition of Peter was to give it the character of a European State. It would be superfluous in this place to follow the incidents of his life with any minute attention to detail; but the general effect of his policy on the fortunes of the Empire must not be omitted. Peter was undoubtedly one of the most remarkable men of a coarse and vigorous age. He had the intellect of a genius, and the habits of a savage. Ignorant and debauched, he was nevertheless a true commander of men, possessing quickness of perception, force of will, extraordinary strength of character, and an amount of physical energy which enabled him to be at once the hardest of workers and the most devoted of boon companions. When in England, he used to sit up all night with the Marquis of Carmarthen, drinking brandy mixed with pepper. A public-house near Tower Hill was not too mean a place for this Czar of All the Russias to frequent, that he might smoke his pipe and drink his pot. While living at Sayes Court, near Deptford, the seat of John Evelyn, it was his humour to be driven in a wheelbarrow through bristling holly-hedges. Yet all this fantastic and exuberant vehemence took nothing from the serious power of the man when bent on serious work. His debaucheries had a certain wildness and fury; the graver tasks of his life were conducted with a steady resolution, a quiet intensity of foresight, which generally insured success. The ground had been prepared for him by his father, Alexis, who had invited into his dominions a large number of foreigners, especially Germans and Scotch, and had in this way mitigated in some slight degree the rudeness of his subjects, and opened the door to industrial and social reforms. Yet, when Peter ascended the throne, Russia was still little better than a barbarous country. It was probably less civilized than it had been two or three hundred years before, when contact with the ornate dominion of the Tartars had communicated to Russia a species of fantastic splendour, differing, indeed, from civilization in its highest aspects, yet superior to the dull and brutish condition into which she had sunk in the latter part of the seventeenth century. A long period of alternate anarchy and despotism had by that time impoverished the people and debased the lords. The court might be gorgeous, but it was filthy; the grandees might be rich, but they were ignorant. Decencies of life which had long been familiar to the west of Europe were still unknown to Russia. The mansions of the aristocracy were so wretched, despite their size and a few external emblems of pomp, that they were often over-run by rats, which even threatened the lives of the inmates. The prelacy were so indifferent to learning, or so unable to satisfy any literary tastes they may have possessed, that a few rolls of manuscript formed the sum-total of their libraries. The solitary printing-press set up by Ivan the Terrible had long been destroyed, and neither typography nor book-binding existed in the land. It would not be easy to overstate the downright nastiness of the people, even to the aristocracy. Macaulay describes one of the Ambassadors to England, and the members of his suite, as having gone to the court-balls dropping pearls and vermin.* These men had all the ruggedness of the desert, combined with a low debauchery and foul degeneration which the natural life of the desert will not tolerate, or rather does not know. Peter himself was no better than his subjects, except that in the midst of his coarse and savage humours, his manners which were those of a coal-heaver, and his morals which were those of a sot, he nourished a flame of genius, which kindled the very earthiness of his character into something darkly bright and luridly superb. Perhaps no other great man in the whole course of history exhibits such singular and such dramatic contrasts. His life and character were one series of antitheses. It is impossible to exaggerate the grand grotesqueness of his figure; it is difficult to convey an adequate idea of the greatness, the meanness, the power, the foibles, the vices and the excellencies, of this amazing apparition from the North.

Peter began his reforms by refashioning the army, in which he was assisted by Generals Le

* History of England, chap. 23.

Fort and Patrick Gordon, together with other foreigners of ability. He then determined to create a navy for his Empire. Russia had no ports on the Baltic; her maritime trade was carried on at Archangel; and ships of war were things almost unknown to the ruler of Muscovy. Peter determined that this state should no longer exist; and when he died, he left his country in possession of forty ships of the line and four hundred galleys. The task which he proposed to accomplish might have seemed hopeless to a less earnest man; for Russia had access to none of the great seas and oceans of the world, and was shut out by her geographical position from the pathways of commerce and intercommunication. The White Sea is remote from all the principal seats of trade, and is difficult of navigation through a large part of the year. The Euxine and the Caspian are nothing better than salt-water lakes, land-locked on every side. Yet Peter the Great had no ambition more dear to his heart than that of making Russia a naval Power. He hired Dutch and Venetian shipwrights to help him in his designs. He went to Archangel, where he passed two summers cruising on board English and Dutch ships, and instructing himself in the ways of sea-life, even to the humblest duties of the man before the mast. He sent numbers of young Russians to Venice, to Leghorn, and to Holland, that they might learn the art of shipbuilding; and finally he determined to go personally to the chief countries of the West, and learn for himself whatever they had to teach him that he cared to know.

In the first instance he visited Holland, where he arrived incognito, together with an extraordinary embassy, in 1697. At Saardam he worked as a common ship's-carpenter; living in humble rooms, dressing in humble garb, cooking his own food, and receiving wages for his labour. He was not content unless he knew everything to the minutest detail: rope-making, sail-making, and smith's work, were mastered by his omnivorous mind. Thoroughly true to the character which he had assumed, he associated freely with the other workmen, who little dreamed that their companion was the representative of an old Imperial lineage, the despotic ruler of dominions greater in their superficial extent than those of ancient Rome. To him it was no difficult or irksome matter to live with coarse-handed and coarse-mannered artificers; nor was there anything in his own habits or cast of mind to induce in them the least suspicion that he was other than what he seemed.

From Holland, Peter went to England, where he arrived in January, 1698. His rank was not disguised while he was in this country, and he was a good deal annoyed at the crowds who flocked to see him, and at the festivities given in his honour. Yet, though known to be the Czar, he worked with his own hands at Rotherhithe, where a ship was being built for him. In April he quitted England, taking with him several men of science, together with officers for his army and navy. After a second visit to Holland, which was of short duration, he proceeded to Vienna, to acquaint himself with the discipline and tactics of the Emperor's army, and was about to visit Italy when he received news of a rebellion having broken out among the Strelitzes, or body-guard. He at once hurried back to Moscow, after an absence of seventeen months, and found on his arrival that General Gordon, whom he had left in command, had completely quelled the insurrection. The malcontents were punished with great ferocity, and Peter, conceiving himself to be now secure upon the throne, turned his mind to various matters of social reform which in his judgment were important. The semi-oriental costume which had been common among his people until then, and the beards which all Russians had considered it incumbent on them to wear, were discouraged by the autocrat, as being contrary to the prevalent customs of Europe. In various ways, Peter offended the ancient predilections of his countrymen, and it was only his extraordinary force of will that enabled him to prevail against feelings so inveterate. He touched upon a very sensitive nerve when, in 1703, he determined to transfer the capital of his Empire from Holy Moscow, as it was commonly designated, to a wild and distant spot on the Gulf of Finland, then recently taken from the Swedes—a solitary region of marshes, vexed by northern winds, and bound in icy fetters for nearly half the year. In Peter's character there was nothing of sentiment: Holy Moscow, with its old associations, was a mere phrase to him. It was necessary to his designs that his capital should be seated on the shores of the sea, so that he might have ready access to other parts of Europe, and be able, as it were, to emerge out of the desert which had long hidden the nascent forces of his race. For this purpose, the situation of St. Petersburg, as the new capital was to be called, was sufficiently well adapted. In other respects, a more wretched site for a new city could hardly be conceived. The Neva wandered through great breadths of fen to a sea which was savage in its rigour. Small islands, half engulfed in mud, offered a fragile basis for the stately piles which it was proposed to erect on them. Finland and Lapland lay to the north; and the breath of Arctic oceans touched the weary solitudes as with the touch of death. In less than nine years, the Czar was enabled to transfer his capital from Moscow to the banks of the Neva; but the building of the new city had cost him the lives of 100,000 soldiers and workmen, slain by the cold and by the scarcity of provisions. Even now, after more than a century and a half of existence as a great Imperial metropolis, St. Petersburg betrays the wretchedness of its site through all the splendour of its buildings. Its winter is fierce and long; it is blockaded with ice while happier regions are green with spring, or glowing with the promises of summer; and when the winter has departed, its spacious streets, flanked with structures of granite, of porphyry, and of marble, are so many channels of morass. All this Peter must have foreseen; but he had made his calculations, and he carried them out. At the bidding of his despotic will, troops of workmen were despatched to this dismal waste, and in time palaces and churches, quays and wharfs, the mansions of an aristocracy and the marts of trade, rose over flat and miry lands where until then only the wolf had ravened and the sea-mew cried.

The reign of Peter the Great was characterised by many wars, in which Russia was sometimes defeated and sometimes successful. An attack which the Czar made on Turkey in 1711 was so ill-conducted that the Russian forces were surrounded, and nearly crushed; and the result would have been in the highest degree disastrous, had not Catharine Alexina, Peter's second wife and a woman of humble origin, collected all the plate and jewels she could find in the camp, and sent them to the Grand Vizier as a bribe for concluding a hasty peace. On the whole, however, the Czar was fortunate in his wars, especially in those against Sweden. By the peace of Neustadt, concluded in September, 1721, Sweden ceded to Russia the provinces of Livonia, Esthonia, Ingria, Carelia, Wyburg, and the adjacent islands. Peter had now become one of the most powerful monarchs in the world, and it seemed fitting that he should receive some title greater than that which he had previously borne. The word "Czar" is generally held to be the same as the name Cæsar, though many claim for it a Sclavonic origin. But the Cæsars of Rome were in the first instance rather military dictators than crowned monarchs. When they became the latter, they were dignified by the title of Imperator; and to this highest designation of earthly glory it was considered by the nobles that Peter was now entitled. After some hesitation, which seems to be

PETER THE GREAT. CATHARINE II.

part of the accepted ceremonial in all such cases, the Czar consented to adopt the titles of "Peter the Great, Emperor of All the Russias, and Father of his Country." Fifteen days of rejoicing ensued upon this proclamation; but Peter did not suffer his serious purposes to be forgotten in the blaze of accomplished successes. He saw that the manners of his people were coarse and savage, and, although

STATUE OF PETER THE GREAT AT ST. PETERSBURG.

his own were no better, he desired an improvement for the sake of his land. He united several of the navigable rivers by canals. He encouraged manufactures and science; erected mills; established a manufactory of small arms; opened hospitals; founded colleges and academies, libraries and printing-offices; organised an efficient system of police; and created a uniformity of weights and measures. He paved the streets of Moscow, which until then had been little better than muddy tracks; and, in his desire to arrange all things as by a kind of omnipotence, he attempted to fix the prices of provisions, and to limit the expenses of dress.

His temper was capricious; at times, open and generous,—at others, darkened by the savage passions of an irresponsible despot. One of the most obscure and forbidding incidents of his reign was that which terminated in the death of his eldest son, Alexis. The young man had all his father's faults, without any of his better qualities. He was drunken, selfish, brutal, and immoral; and even his father, though not fastidious in such matters, found it necessary to subject him to reproof. Alexis associated with the disaffected boyars and priests, who detested the innovations which the Czar was bent on introducing. The natural faults of the Prince were perhaps increased by the harshness of his father's conduct; but, however this may have been, he acted in the most outrageous manner. He had married an amiable woman, who, heart-broken by his cruelty, died in 1715, after giving birth to a son. In the following year, Alexis renounced his right of succession in favour of Peter's son by Catharine, and requested permission to retire into a monastery. This was a mere pretence for covering designs of his own. Secretly quitting Russia, he put himself under the protection of the Emperor Charles at Vienna, and was afterwards sent, first to Innspruck, and then to the Castle of St. Elmo in Naples. Being discovered in that retreat, he was induced to return to Moscow, under a solemn promise of forgiveness. Peter, however, had no intention of forgiving him. The Czarewitch had been known to declare that, should he ever come to the crown, he would abolish all that his father had done, and restore the ancient ways of Muscovy. It was therefore determined that his conduct should be made the subject of inquiry by the great officers of State, the Judges, and the Bishops. This investigation seems to have been conducted in the most inquisitorial manner, and was even accompanied by personal severities to the culprit. He was charged with conspiring against his father, and with intending to usurp the throne. Ultimately, a confession was extorted from him, and he was declared by the court to be worthy of death. The sentence was read to him on the 6th of July, 1718, and next day it was reported that his agitation of mind had thrown him into convulsions. On the Czar going to the chamber where he was confined, the Prince implored his forgiveness, which was granted with every appearance of emotion; and Alexis expired the same day. The circumstances of the Prince's death are shrouded in considerable mystery, and it has been supposed that the unfortunate young man was compelled to take poison. His associates were punished with the utmost severity, and the Emperor laid himself open to suspicion by the secrecy of the whole transaction, and the want of feeling which he afterwards exhibited.

Peter died in the metropolis of his creation on the 28th of January, 1725, in the fifty-third year of his age. The state of Russia at that time required a vigorous and even stern ruler; but the system of unmitigated despotism which he confirmed and established did as much evil to Russia as his reforms did good. From his day to the present, Muscovy has been a centre of tyrannical ideas, from which Europe has suffered in many ways, and from which, it may be, she will suffer yet. Government, according to Peter and his successors, is in the main a matter of police and soldiership. The rule of this extraordinary man was the rule of force and cunning, ending, as such systems always do, in enormous corruption, in the debasement of public morals, in a total defect of public honesty, in systematised greed, in cruelty erected into a principle. The work of Peter was in many respects excellent; but his personal influence was bad, with scarcely any qualification. He treated his nobles with a brutal severity which produced—what no doubt he intended—an abject submission on their part to anything he chose to decree. With his own hands he belaboured any of his courtiers who offended him, until their countenances bore unequivocal marks of the resentment they had incurred. It is doubtful whether, in the early ages of Russian history, indignities of this kind were inflicted on noblemen, even by the most ferocious of despots. The Grand Dukes of Moscow were tyrants whose reigns were often disgraced by crimes of the greatest enormity; but the theory of government was not so bad then as it became under Peter and his successors, nor was the practice, as a general rule, so regardless of human rights. The nobles, and even the commonalty, had some degree of influence in the State; but under the new order everything was centred in the will of one man, who might be a murderer or an infuriate drunkard, a madman or an imbecile. Universal servility was the consequence, and this was in turn revenged upon the lower orders in acts of pitiless oppression. Talleyrand was right when he said that Russia was a despotism limited by assassination. For two hundred years it has had no other limitation; it has no other limitation at this hour. In an indirect way, the government may be influenced by modern ideas; the late Emperor, Alexander II. for instance, was an honest and a well-meaning man. His emancipation of the serfs is undoubtedly the most benevolent fact in Russian history. The press is not without some influence, even in those northern latitudes; but the traditions of two centuries of political life exist at this moment with scarcely any modification. Russia is the only country in Europe which has neither a Constitution nor a Parliament. The Emperor may do whatever seems good in his own eyes; but he must accept the penalty of failure in its most evil form, if the last argument of conspiracy should be made to answer the last argument of kings.

Peter was succeeded by his widow, the Empress Catharine I., originally the wife of a Swedish dragoon. She survived the great Czar little more than two years, during which time she carried out to a still further extent the plans to which Peter had devoted his life. Peter II., son of the Prince Alexis, was the next monarch; but his brief reign of three years was characterised by no events of note. He was deposed in 1730, and the crown then passed to Anne, Duchess of Courland, daughter of Ivan V., the elder brother of Peter the Great. The affairs of Poland occupied the attention of this Princess, who also carried on a successful war with the Turks and Tartars, and invaded the Crimea. Previous to her death, in October, 1740, she named as her successor Ivan VI., the infant grand-nephew of Peter the Great. This unfortunate prince was never more than nominally Emperor. A plot having been formed against him, he was imprisoned for life, and Elizabeth, daughter of Peter the Great, ascended the throne in 1741. After languishing many years in a dungeon, Ivan was murdered in 1764. Elizabeth was a woman of strong passions and indolent habits, who suffered her policy to be directed by a succession of favourites. In 1747, during her reign, Russia concluded a treaty of alliance with Maria Theresa in the War of the Austrian Succession, and 36,000 Russian auxiliaries appeared on the Rhine, thus bringing Russia for the first time into direct association with the politics of Western Europe. In the Seven Years' War, a large Russian force, acting in alliance with Austria, invaded Prussia, and on two occasions the soldiers of the Empress defeated Frederick the Great himself. Berlin was taken by the Russians in 1760, and an army of observation was maintained in Poland. Elizabeth died in January, 1762 (New Style), and was succeeded by the Duke of Holstein Gottorp, son of her sister, Anna Petrovna, Duchess of Holstein. Peter III., as the new monarch was called, was a person of weak character, whose reign was limited to a few months. On the deposition of this monarch, his wife, Catharine II., ascended the throne. Her reign conducts us to the portals of modern Russian history, and is filled with so many remarkable events that we must reserve its consideration for another Chapter.

CHAPTER XVIII.

Russian History continued—Conspiracy of the Empress Catharine against her Husband—Peter III. deposed, and shortly afterwards murdered—Reforms instituted by Catharine—Her Policy with Respect to Poland—Previous History of that Country—Noble Career of John Sobieski—His Defeat of the Turks before the Walls of Vienna—Miserable Condition of Poland, owing to the Predominance of the Aristocracy—Ineffectual Attempts of Sobieski to introduce Reforms—Decline of the Polish Power, and Subserviency of the Country to Russia—Reign of Stanislaus Augustus—Religious Oppression by the Roman Catholics, and Interference of the Empress Catharine—League of Russia, Prussia, and Austria, against Poland—Partition of that Country in 1772, 1793, and 1795—Subsequent History of Poland—Despotic Rule of Russia, and Fruitless Attempts at Insurrection—Present State of the Polish Nationality—Domestic Policy of Catharine—Reigns of Paul, Alexander I., and Nicholas—Accession of the Present Sovereign—Emancipation of the Serfs—Enormous Extension of Russian Power—Social Condition of the Empire.

Few more remarkable figures than that of Catharine II. of Russia are to be found in the eighteenth century, fertile as that period was in men and women of note. She was the daughter of the Prince of Anhalt Zerbst, a petty German sovereign; but, by marriage and long residence, she seems to have acquired the Russian character to perfection. Her union with Peter III. took place in 1745, when she was about sixteen years of age, and was productive of little but unhappiness. The Russian court was at that time one of the most profligate in Europe. Intrigues, which in other countries were to some extent hidden under a veil, were there prosecuted with an open and revolting frankness which astonished foreign observers. Peter III. made no secret of his immoralities, and Catharine was well pleased to follow the example of her husband. Dissension had arisen between them before the death of the Empress Elizabeth, who is said to have supported the Princess in opposition to her nephew, the Grand Duke. On coming to the throne, Peter III. talked openly of divorcing Catharine, and marrying his mistress, the Countess Woronzof; and it was not long before a party was formed against him. He had made himself distasteful both to the army and to the Church; himself a foreigner, he preferred to have foreigners about him; and the Russian nobility looked with dislike and suspicion on his designs. Catharine, it is true, was even more foreign than he, having no connection by blood with the Muscovite race; but she flattered, rather than offended, the prejudices of the nation. While living in retirement at the palace of Peterhof, apart from her husband, who had entirely given himself up to the influence of the Countess Woronzof, she gathered about her a number of devoted adherents. On the 8th of July, 1762 (N.S.), she went to St. Petersburg, and induced one of the regiments of the Guards to declare in her favour. Other regiments, including the artillery, immediately followed, and before evening Catharine had been proclaimed Empress, and had received the oath of allegiance from 15,000 men.

For a moment, it seemed as if there might be a

civil war. Peter was staying at his summer palace of Oranienbaum, twenty miles west of St. Petersburg, and the Empress at once marched against him. He was surrounded by his Holstein guards, who were ready to defend his cause to the last; but the Czar himself was so unnerved by the intelligence of the revolt that he could not be induced to give any orders, and, after a few hours of miserable irresolution, he placed himself at the mercy of the Empress. She compelled him, on the 9th of July, to sign an act of abdication, in which he declared his inability to govern, and then sent him as a prisoner to Ropscha, a small palace twenty miles from the capital. It was probably never intended that he should survive very long. Apprehensions of a counter-revolution (for Peter had his friends and supporters) disturbed the successful conspirators, and it was feared that the dethroned monarch might soon be restored. Seven or eight days after the enforced abdication, it was announced that Peter had died of colic. The truth is that on the 14th of July the chief conspirators went to Ropscha, engaged the Czar in a drinking bout, suddenly fell upon him, and strangled him. The principal agent was Alexis Orloff, a man of gigantic stature and enormous strength, one of Catharine's

JOHN SOBIESKI.

numerous admirers; and he is said to have afterwards boasted at Berlin of the crime he had committed. The act may have taken place without any previous knowledge on the part of Catharine; but she was glad to avail herself of its consequences, and subjected the murderers to no sort of punishment. It is probable that she was hardly conscious of a crime. For many generations, murder had been part of the political system of her adopted land.

In the early months of her reign, Catharine had to encounter a large amount of disaffection on the part of her subjects, and to suppress more than one revolt and conspiracy; but, being at length firmly seated on the throne, she did much towards completing the designs of Peter the Great. She encouraged the introduction of those arts and literary masterpieces in which other countries were rich, and Russia was poor; and she gave every inducement to learned and scientific men to settle in her dominions. The sceptical opinions of the French philosophers and encyclopædists were shared by Catharine, as by Frederick the Great. She had little sympathy with anything that did not carry with it a practical value, and the mediæval extravagances of the Greek Church inspired her with nothing but contempt, though as a matter of policy she conformed to its rites. Yet she was not insensible to the advantages, nor perhaps even to the charms, of a stately and pompous ceremonial. In 1766, she dazzled the citizens of St. Petersburg by an elaborate pageant called a carousal, which reproduced the splendid manners of chivalry with great exactness; and at all times her habits were grand and lofty. This, however, was nothing more than so much bullion embroidery on the massive substance of her government. Many of her reforms were really admirable, and prompted by a sentiment of humanity, difficult to reconcile with the crime by which her power had been consolidated. Successive codes of law had been issued by various Russian sovereigns, and Catharine added another to the list in 1768. It abolished the use of torture, and placed the humble Russian on a much better footing than he had occupied before. Education was promoted by this singular woman; and by her encouragement of scientific travellers she acquired a remarkably exact knowledge of the vast and varied dominions which composed her empire.

The foreign policy of the Empress was distinguished by one great iniquity, which Europe suffered to be consummated, and for permitting which she has found her punishment in the supremacy of lawless power. The partition of Poland was to a great extent the work of Catharine, and, while it gave an enormous accession of strength to the purely military conception of government, it lowered the moral tone of Europe, as regarded politics, to an incalculable degree. Poland was originally a part of that immense region, anciently called Sarmatia, out of which Russia itself arose. The people are Sclaves, like the Muscovites; but their civilisation was developed under more favourable conditions, and, when converted to Christianity, they followed the Latin instead of the Greek Church. From a dukedom, Poland grew into a kingdom as early as the year 1000, when the German Emperor, Otho III., recognized its independence of the Empire. Then followed the reigns of five monarchs named Boleslaus, of whom all but the last were successful warriors, conducting expeditions into Germany on the one hand, and Russia on the other. While Muscovy was a struggling principality, scarcely recognized by Europe, and barely guarding her existence against the incessant attacks of Tartar hordes, Poland was one of the leading States in the European system; and even at the close of the seventeenth century she still preserved the splendour of her reputation. Again and again, in many different epochs, the Poles wrested territory from the Russians, and threatened their independence as a nation before the walls of Moscow. Just after the accession of Peter the Great, then a mere child, Poland furnished the bulwark which saved Germany from the stress of Ottoman conquest.

It was the age of John Sobieski—a warrior-prince, it is true, but one with ideas far nobler than any which the sword alone could prompt. Sobieski must be reckoned among those men who save history from the reproach of being nothing better than a record of atrocities—a calendar of successful crimes, committed by monarchs, by soldiers, and by statesmen, to the injury and scandal of the human race. In those days, Turkey was a veritable danger and affliction to Europe. She had absorbed the whole of the south-east; she next proceeded to menace the centre; and Poland, together with Austria, would probably have been subjected to her arms, had not Sobieski repelled the fury of repeated attacks. He vanquished the Ottomans in 1665, in 1667, and in 1673, though they were in alliance with the Tartars and the Cossacks, and presented a most formidable front. On the throne becoming vacant, he was elected King in 1674, but was soon called to arms again by the renewed incursions of the Turks. The Pasha of Damascus, a man of high military fame, was in the field against him at the head of a numerous host. Sobieski could not reckon on more than 10,000 men; but with those he entrenched himself between two villages on the banks of the Dniester, and, after sustaining the Moslem cannonade for twenty days, suddenly broke forth on the 14th of October, 1676, and offered battle to the astonished Turks. The Pasha, fearing a levy of the whole Polish population, proposed honourable terms of peace, which were accepted, and a few years of tranquillity followed this unexpected success.

WARSAW.

But in 1683 a new danger threatened the whole of that part of Europe. The Grand Vizier, Kara Mustapha, had appeared before Vienna, which he closely invested, and it seemed as if Southern Germany would be overwhelmed by the torrent of Mohammedan conquest, as Hungary had already been. All Christendom looked on with apprehension; for the military spirit and power of the Turks in their most successful days were once more active and predominant. It was doubted for a while whether Germany would not share the fate of Greece, of Roumelia, of Bulgaria, of Servia, and of the other nationalities in that remote quarter of Europe, as the Austrians themselves had not sufficient power to resist so immense an inroad of highly-trained and fanatical warriors. In this crisis of affairs, Sobieski advanced to the relief of Vienna at the head of 16,000 Poles, who were speedily joined by several German contingents, so that in September, 1683, he found himself in command of 70,000 fighting men. He took up his position on the mountain ridge of Kalemberg, which overlooks the Imperial city, and from this elevation beheld the plain beneath him covered with the Turkish hosts, glittering in Oriental armour, and provided with a multitude of tents, stretching out in parallel lines, like the streets of a town. Sobieski attacked on the 12th of September, and drove the Turks into their entrenchments. Considering the position too strong for further operations, the Polish King paused, but was suddenly induced to change his resolve by an incident that seemed trifling in itself.

DEFEAT OF THE TURKS BEFORE VIENNA BY JOHN SOBIESKI.

In the early evening, the Grand Vizier was beheld sitting at the entrance to his tent, drinking coffee. It looked to Sobieski like a defiance—as if, from soldiers such as his, nothing was to be feared by soldiers such as the Turks. Stung by this feeling, which was doubtless purely fanciful, Sobieski gave orders for an immediate assault, and the Christians poured down upon their enemies with such amazing impetuosity that the Turks, after a brief resistance, gave way at all points, leaving behind them the camp, the artillery, and the baggage. They were pursued through Hungary, and, though successful in a battle fought at Parang, were finally driven across the Danube.

Sobieski had saved Austria, but he could not save Poland. He could defend it from the inroads of Moslem warriors; he could hurl back the Tartar and the Cossack; but he could not protect his native land from the evils of her own political condition, from the selfishness of her nobles, and the degradation of her serfs. The Constitution of Poland was one of the very worst conceivable. From 1573 it had been an elective monarchy, with a narrow basis of electors. In other words, it was an aristocratical Republic, the leaders of which chose from time to time some prince whom they thought best fitted to promote their own interests, which were certainly not the interests of the nation. Continual intrigue, continual weakness, were the results. The King, in the generality of instances, was the creature of the nobles, and was menaced with the loss of his crown if he sought to be anything else. Even at times when the country was threatened with subjugation, the hands of the monarch were fettered by the jealousies of the great lords. When the King of Sweden invaded Poland, about the middle of the seventeenth century, with an army of not more than 40,000 men, he was enabled to reduce the Government to extremity, because the nobles were wrangling as to what they should do, and the King was powerless to take any steps for the national defence until they had finished their differences. It would have been an easy matter to put 200,000 men in the field, had there been any unanimity; but there was none, and the nation suffered because the nobles were disagreed. To suffer, whether in war or in peace, was indeed the portion of the masses in Poland, and there was little to alleviate their lot, whether in the nature of their country, or in the political forms by which they were bound. Nothing more miserable than the condition of a Polish serf has ever been known in the long annals of human oppression. The aristocracy had power of life and death over their vassals, and neither law nor opinion existed, to check the wantonness of their caprice. The laws favoured a constant accumulation of landed property in the hands of the territorial magnates, and the result was that from age to age the nobles grew more insolently rich, and the peasants more forlornly poor. A nobleman could do most things that he would. If a man had committed any crime, no matter how bad, and could obtain the protection of a noble, there was no power in Poland that could take him from that noble's house. The privileges of the great lords had scarcely any limits but what they themselves imposed. All civil posts, all ecclesiastical dignities, were in their gift, and only noblemen might hold estates, excepting the burghers of Cracow and four other cities. Not that Poland was entirely wanting in the forms of freedom. It had a Parliament in which the chief towns were represented; but the aristocracy was predominant, and the peasants were without voice or influence. The serfs were worked to their utmost capacity of endurance, and suffered to live on the barest necessaries of existence, in cabins constructed of mud and straw. The children herded with the pigs, from which they were not much distinguished in anything that gives comeliness or decency to life; and the wretched parents of these wretched infants are described by an old writer as making use of the hog-trough and cow-rack for table and bed.* The lives of Polish boors were reckoned by their money value; and if a neighbour killed one for his whim, he had only to pay the price to the boor's master, and the laws of Poland had nothing to say to the transaction.

Such was the political and social state which John Sobieski found existing beneath his sceptre, and which he would fain have amended if the nobles would have let him. He brought forward many projects of reform, but they were defeated by the selfishness of those who had an interest in maintaining abuses. They accused him of desiring to perpetuate the sovereignty in his own family; and doubtless he saw the evils of an elective throne. But their real desire was to weaken the monarchy, that the nobles might be strong. The heart of Sobieski was at length worn out by continual opposition. With the penetration of a great mind, he saw what was coming, and told the nobles plainly that retribution would be visited on their sins. At the close of the Diet of 1688, he said to its assembled members:—"What will be one day the surprise of posterity to see that, after being elevated to such a height of glory, we have suffered our country to fall into the gulf of ruin; to fall, alas! for ever. For myself, I may from time to time have gained her battles; but I am

* Jeremy Collier's Dictionary, 1701.

powerless to save her. I can do no more than leave the future of my beloved land, not to destiny—for I am a Christian—but to God, the High and Mighty." The year in which these words were uttered was that in which the Commons and the Lords of England united in the patriotic task of expelling a tyrannical King, and inviting to their shores one whom they had good reason to believe would lead the nation firmly and wisely on the forward path of all reasonable liberty and all healthy progress. Poland had already such a King, without undergoing the disturbance of a revolution; but below that King were insolent lords and embruited serfs, feebly counterbalanced by a few commercial cities. One man cannot save a land. Sobieski stood alone, and the ruin of Poland dates from his brilliant and noble reign.

The monarchs succeeding Sobieski, who died in 1696, felt the weakness of their position, and looked for succour to the Russian Court. Russia had by that time become the greatest Power in the East of Europe. Poland had declined from her former influence and dignity, and she who had once commanded was now compelled to solicit favours from the Czars of Moscovy. The dissensions of the nobility continued, and the majority contended for the maintenance of their privileges. They were supported by the Kings, who, however much their own interests may have been really endangered by the power of a dominant caste, dared not set themselves in a position of defiance against those who at any moment could stir up a turbulent revolution on behalf of their order. The death of Sobieski had been followed by an interregnum, which was terminated by the election of Frederick Augustus of Saxony, who after a while was deposed, and again placed on the throne some years later. He reigned till 1733, when he was succeeded by his son, Frederick Augustus II., after whom came another interregnum, ending in the election of Stanislaus Augustus, son of Count Poniatowski, a Lithuanian, who, after being in the service of

KOSCIUSKO.

Charles XII. of Sweden, married the Princess Czartoryski, a descendent from the family of the Jagellons, who once ruled over Poland. The Czartoryskis belonged to that minority of the nobles who favoured patriotic ideas, and would have made the monarchy hereditary, with a larger degree of popular power for its basis. They were men of ability and culture, who did somewhat to restore the literature of their country, and they had the countenance of their relative, Stanislaus Augustus; but the latter, though an amiable and well-meaning man, was unable to make his will prevail. It is a singular fact that the election of this monarch to the throne was brought about by Catharine II. of Russia, who sent her troops into Poland expressly to effect that result.

One of the great causes of disturbance in Poland at that date proceeded from religious animosities. The greater number of the people were Catholics; but there were also numerous Protestants and members of the Greek Church, who were classed under the general head of Dissidents, and who were equally oppressed by the members of the prevailing faith. They had applied for protection to the Protestant Powers and to the Court of Russia, and their privileges had been affirmed by the Pacta Conventa of 1573, and ratified in 1660 by the Treaty of Oliva, which was guaranteed by the European Governments. Any arrangement by which foreign Powers are placed in a position to guarantee the execution of reforms in another country, is very likely before long to be abused. It is the easiest thing in the world to make a regard for other people's rights the pretexts for acts of violence and wrong, and for the promotion of selfish interests. This is a device well known to Russia, but not exclusively to that country. The provisions of the Treaty of Oliva, however fair-seeming in themselves, and however much, in the first instance, they may have been prompted by a real desire to remove palpable oppressions, were the first causes of the dismemberment of Poland. The Ministers of the guaranteeing Powers met in 1766, and presented memorials in favour of the Dissidents, who had been deprived of all political and civil rights, forbidden to build new churches, exiled, insulted, and treated with the utmost tyranny. Stanislaus was well inclined to support the just claims of these bodies; but the Catholic prelates and nobility violently opposed his fair and reasonable intentions. The Empress Catharine saw her opportunity, and in 1768, under a pretence of favouring religious freedom, marched a body of troops to the very gates of Warsaw. Several members of the Diet, including the Bishop of Cracow, were arrested by the Russians, and sent into Siberia, where they were kept five years. The Diet was intimidated, and granted the full claims of the Dissidents; but this did not bring the troubles to a close. Some Catholic noblemen in the provinces bordering on Turkey rose in revolt, and commenced a civil war, in which the King's troops were more than once defeated. In their despair and apprehension, the King and the Senate petitioned Russia not to withdraw her troops; and the insurgents, conceiving that this interference in the internal affairs of the country justified a similar proceeding on their own part, applied for assistance to the Turks. The Ministers of the Sultan had already represented to the Cabinets of Europe the danger of allowing Russia to acquire predominance in Poland; but their views met with no response, and they now listened to the requests of the Polish malcontents. This led to a war between Turkey and Russia, which broke out in 1769, and caused the devastation of a large part of Poland. The misery of the people was aggravated in 1770 by a dreadful pestilence, which slew many thousands; and it is certain that neither the Dissidents nor their oppressors were any the better for intervention.

The first partition of Poland took place in consequence of this war, and was consummated in 1772. It was concerted between Catharine of Russia, Frederick the Great of Prussia, and Joseph II. of Austria, and the idea is said to have been suggested by the second of those potentates. By this partition, Poland lost more than 83,000 square miles of her best territory, and the provinces thus seized were divided in unequal portions amongst Russia, Prussia, and Austria. There can be no question that Poland had to some extent brought her evil fortune on her own head, by obstinately adhering to a system of manifest injustice; but this does not excuse the partitioning Powers, who committed a crime under hypocritical pretences which must not be suffered to mislead the world. It is entirely beyond conception that nations like Russia and Prussia, as they then were, could have had much regard for liberal principles and the rule of equal toleration. They were not likely, unless as a matter of temporary caprice or fugitive policy, to grant the Roman Catholics of Poland any greater liberty than those believers had themselves permitted to the heretical minority. Desire of territory, and, still more, desire of political predominance, were the real motives which dictated this shameful act. If Poland could be wiped out of Europe, or reduced to the narrowest dimensions, the power of the three partitioning Governments would be proportionately enhanced. A more unscrupulous monarch than Frederick the Great never sat upon a throne. Catharine of Russia had neither a private nor a public conscience; and Joseph of Austria, though in many respects a liberal despot, was well content to support their projects, on the understanding that he should share the booty. It was a simple matter of brigandage, for which a decent excuse was discovered in the real misdoings of Poland. Yet there are those, even at the present day, who would exalt this law of theft into a principle of political morality, and who argue that because a State has done ill in some of the multifarious transactions of its political existence, another State is justified in carrying fire and sword into its territories, and repaying its own loss by acts of unrestrained appropriation.

In the case of Poland, the virtuous pretences of Russia were speedily abandoned, and a few years later the Empress appeared, not as the assertor of reform, however hypocritical the assertion may have been, but as the open and undisguised conservator of evils which had dragged Poland into the abyss of ruin. Roused to exertion by the terrible blow which had fallen on their country, the Poles now set seriously to work to introduce a better system of government into the territory which was left them. Education was encouraged, literature was cultivated, and works of industry received an important stimulus. Count Andrew Zamoyski, Chancellor of the kingdom, prepared a new code, which removed many of the ancient abuses, and to some extent emancipated the peasants. With astounding infatuation, the Diet of 1780 rejected this code; but in 1792 a new constitution was proclaimed, by which, after the death of Poniatowski, the throne was to be made hereditary in the Saxon family, and other reforms were to be effected. This did not at all answer the purposes of Russia, and she determined to overthrow the new political arrangement. Following a line of conduct which she knows so well how to pursue, she fomented disaffection among the nobles, despatched troops into the country, and threatened to support her views by an appeal to force. Stanislaus, whose good qualities were marred by weakness, and who was unquestionably placed in circumstances of the utmost difficulty, joined the coalition against his own country. The King of Prussia (Frederick William II., nephew of Frederick the Great, whom he succeeded) had for a time encouraged the party of reform; but he now added his forces to those of the Russians, thinking probably that if he did otherwise he would have no share in the next act of pillage. A second partition of the unhappy land took place in 1793. The partitioners this time were Russia and Prussia only, and the result was that the former took 83,000 square miles of Polish ground, and the latter 22,500. Poland was allowed to keep 85,000 square miles of her own territory; but the miserable little kindom, while retaining a nominal independence, was a mere vassal of the Russian sovereign. All who dared to love their country, and endeavoured still to serve it by the introduction of liberal reforms, were persecuted with unresting bitterness; and it was then that that great exodus of Poles commenced, which even to the present time has filled every capital of Western Europe with the representatives of their country's wrongs —in many instances, men of noble birth, reduced to the utmost extremities of poverty and want.

Towards the close of the century, one of the greatest of modern Poles, the brave and high-spirited Kosciusko, appeared upon the scene. The success of the French Revolution had plunged all Europe into turmoil, and the moment seemed favourable for a rising in Poland. In 1794, Kosciusko placed himself at the head of a number of peasants, rudely armed with scythes, and by the fury of his onslaught and the passion of his enthusiasm defeated a superior number of Russians. Warsaw was at that time occupied by a strong Russian force, though it was the metropolis of independent Poland; but the soldiers of the Empress were expelled by a popular rising, after a desperate and sanguinary contest. The success of the insurgents, however, was very short-lived. Russia and Prussia poured large bodies of troops into the devoted country. Kosciusko was defeated, wounded, and taken prisoner; and the Russian General, Suwaroff, carried one of the suburbs of Warsaw by storm, and put all the inhabitants to the sword, to the number of 30,000. Warsaw then capitulated, and in 1795 Russia, Prussia, and Austria made a third partition of the land.

It is unnecessary to follow the later fortunes of Poland with much detail. The history of the nation for many years has been one of unrelieved wretchedness, of frantic struggles for renewed independence, and of continual failure, followed by fresh persecutions. The rise of Napoleon's power excited the hopes of Poland, and for awhile those hopes seemed to be on the eve of accomplishment; but Napoleon, after defeating the Russians, concluded an alliance with them by the Peace of Tilsit, in 1807. This was a great blow to the Polish cause; yet the territory which had been taken by Prussia in 1793–5 was erected into a sovereign State, under the title of the Duchy of Warsaw, with the exception of the province of

Bialystok, which was given to Russia. At the peace of 1815, the Congress of Vienna, after handing over certain portions of the Duchy of Warsaw to Prussia, and other parts to Austria, erected the city of Cracow, together with a small surrounding territory, into a Republic, and furthermore established what it was pleased to call the Kingdom of Poland, which, however, was placed under the sovereignty of Russia. In itself, the arrangement seemed fair enough, at any rate in comparison with what Poland had endured for many years; but it was not in the nature of things that it should continue. The new kingdom was endowed with a system of Parliamentary Government, with liberty of the press, with the use of the national language, and with a national army. But this liberal Constitution was placed under the direction of a despotic Power like Russia. No one can have doubted what the end would be. The Poles and the Russians were at issue from the very first as to the meaning of the arrangement. The Poles thought they were granted liberties to the end that they might use them. The Russians regarded those liberties as a convenient means of satisfying the scruples of Western Europe, and it was their determination that they should *not* be used. If the Poles had been content to do exactly as the Russians desired, all might have gone on quietly; but when they evinced a determination to live their national life, which was the very object of the Constitution, the Russian Government undeceived them in the most effectual manner. A national rising in 1830–31 was stamped out with terrible severity, and in 1832 Poland was declared an integral part of the Russian Empire. A little before the close of the insurrection, the Government of Louis Philippe sought the co-operation of England in demanding of the Emperor Nicholas the execution of the stipulations of Vienna. Lord Palmerston was then at the Foreign Office; but, strange to say, although his opposition to Russia was a matter of life-long policy, he declined to interfere, on the ground that Russia had always been our faithful ally. It is probable that he was following the dictates of the Cabinet, rather than his own inclination. Earl Grey was Prime Minister, and, Liberal though he was, he had perhaps not entirely delivered himself from the traditions of the Napoleonic wars. A feeble remnant of Polish nationality still remained in the Republic of Cracow; but this was extinguished, after some revolutionary

THE POLISH INSURRECTION IN 1863: COMBAT IN A FOREST.

movements, in 1846. The three military Powers who have been the evil geniuses of Poland conspired to complete their work, and Cracow was handed over to Austria. The annexation was protested against by England, France, Sweden, and Turkey; but a league of armed sovereigns cares little for protests which are not supported at the point of the bayonet. The three Divine Right monarchs openly tore up the last shred of the Treaty of Vienna, in so far as it affected Poland. They flung their gauntlets in the face of Europe, and Europe took the insult as she generally does.

ALEXANDER I.

The last struggle of Poland to throw off the yoke of her oppressors occurred in 1863 and the following year. It was thought that Napoleon III. might help the rising, as he had helped the cause of Italy in 1859; but the task was too gigantic even for that powerful monarch, unless he could have found an ally in England. Lord Palmerston was then Prime Minister, and he undoubtedly sympathised with the Poles; but neither the Government nor the country was prepared to embark in so perilous an enterprise, and the brief agony of the Poles was terminated by the strong hand of military despotism—terminated with a degree of savage ferocity which moved the indignation and the pity of the world. The administration of Russia in this dependency has been characterised by some good results, as regards internal organization. Serfdom has been abolished, and education promoted, though only in accordance with Russian views. In the early days of the partition, Russia left her Polish provinces in possession of many of their national privileges; but that system has been long superseded. Every kind of separate government was abolished in 1868. and complete union with the Empire was then effected. Poland is now designated "the Vistula Province." The Polish language has been interdicted in courts of law and in public offices, and every possible effort has been made to sink this historic people in the huge mass of Russian nationality. The rising of 1863–4 is said to have resulted in the slaughter of 50,000 men, and the banishment of 100,000 to Siberia. Measures of fierce revenge were taken by the Emperor, and when, in course of the struggle, the European Governments remonstrated on the treatment to which the Poles were being subjected, Alexander replied to the effect that he could not permit foreign Powers to come between him and his rebellious subjects. At that time, he was a believer in the doctrine of non-intervention. His conversion to a different view dates from the rising in the Herzegovina.

The fortunes of Poland have led us far from the reign of Catharine II., to which we must now briefly return. On the whole, that reign was distinguished by many successes, and by a decided advance in the position of Russia as one of the determining forces of the European system. The wars of the Empress with Turkey will be more properly considered when we trace the history of the Ottoman dominion. The domestic rule of Catharine presented some liberal features. Her sceptical views made her tolerant of opinions not generally accepted by the Russians; and although, when the French Revolution broke out, and all the crowned heads of Europe felt anxious for their thrones, she paid particular attention to religion as an instrument of government, there can be little doubt that she had no positive predilections on this subject at any period of her life. In 1782, she erected a Roman Catholic Archbishopric at Mohilow, and made a declaration at Rome that she intended to support the proscribed order of the Jesuits, as the most enlightened and industrious of the religious communities. Yet it must not be supposed that religious liberty existed to any great extent under the sceptre of Catharine. In the midst of much that was genuine and sterling in the character of this remarkable sovereign, there was not a little that was showy and theatrical. When, in 1787, she made a progress through some of her newly-acquired dominions in the south, she lent herself to deceptions which were nothing short of childish. She and her retinue sailed down the Dnieper in fifty magnificent galleys, and the banks of the river were decorated with fictitious villages, peopled for the occasion by peasants who might have been opera-dancers. It cannot be thought that a woman of Catharine's penetration had really any belief in this artificial mirage of the desert. Her chamberlain had got up a magnificent spectacle for her entertainment, and she had the vanity and the folly to be entertained. Towards the end of her life, her thirst for universal empire grew into a disease. She made no concealment of her intention to destroy the Turkish rule in Europe at the first opportunity, and she caused the Grand Duke's second son to be named Constantine, and had him instructed in the Greek language, that he might seem to carry on the traditions of the Byzantine Emperors in the ancient seat of their power. Persia also was to be conquered, and an expedition against that country had been commenced, when a fit of apoplexy put an end to the life of the Empress, on the 17th of November, 1796.

The successor to Catharine was her son, the Emperor Paul, a sovereign who equalled Ivan the Terrible himself in the insane fury of his despotism. Russia was now engaged in a deadly contest with revolutionary France, and anxiety of mind may have contributed to that condition of derangement from which Paul undoubtedly suffered. At first the opponent, he was afterwards the ally of Bonaparte, and he concerted with that successful soldier a plan for the invasion of India. But lunacy was rapidly advancing on him. He interfered in the merest trivialities of individual life, and punished with horrible ferocity any departure from his orders. It was long suspected that his brain was overwrought; and when he published in the St. Petersburg *Court Gazette* a notification that he would propose himself as a champion in single combat against the belligerent monarchs, in order that he might thus terminate the war, the nobles considered that they had proof conclusive of his insanity. A plot was formed among the officers about the person of the Emperor. Entering his bedroom on the night of March 24th, 1801, the conspirators required him to sign an act of abdication. He refused; a struggle ensued; and a scarf being passed round the neck of the Emperor, it was pulled tightly until he was strangled. Next day it was announced that Paul had died of apoplexy, and his son, Alexander I., succeeded to power. It was in the reign of this sovereign that the war with France was brought to a close, and at the peace of 1815 Russia took rank among the greatest of the European Powers. Alexander was a popular monarch, and, though capricious in his ways, as despots are apt to be, was in some respects a wise and beneficent ruler. Nevertheless, it was he who, in September, 1815, originated the Holy Alliance—a league of Russia, Austria, and Prussia, for the suppression of liberal ideas. His brother Nicholas, who followed in December, 1825, was a stronger and sterner man. Poland felt the weight of his hand, and the Russians themselves had little cause for regarding him with affection. Immediately on succeeding to the throne, he was confronted by a dangerous conspiracy on the part of a large body of officers, who were in favour of a Constitutional Government, and this he repressed with a vigour that was absolutely merciless. The political ideas engendered by the French Revolution had found their way even into Russia. The mind of the country had been agitated by the long contest terminating in 1815. In the course of that war, Russia had come into contact with Western Europe and its principles to a greater extent than at any previous date, and the effects began to be visible in a general awakening of intelligence, and in the habit of freely discussing matters which until then had never been discussed at all. The Emperor Nicholas, in his reign of nearly thirty years, extending from the latter part of 1825 to the early part of 1855, set himself with iron will to the repression of those ideas. To some extent he was successful; but he was only so by virtue of a tyranny which has not often been surpassed. Foreign wars were among the means by which he diverted the attention of his subjects from the consideration of domestic affairs; and the old Russian designs on Turkey, which had for some time been in abeyance, were revived on more than one occasion. The first of these was in 1828 and the following year, when General Diebitsch, after gaining several successes over the Turks on the northern side of the Balkans, crossed that mountain range, and advanced to Adrianople, where a treaty of peace was signed on the 14th of September, 1829. The second occasion was the Crimean war, which happened within the memory of the present generation, and in which the ambitious designs of Russia were checked by England, France, and Sardinia, acting in alliance with the Sultan. Nicholas expired while the war was yet proceeding, but with the shadow of probable failure settling like a heavy pall upon his dying hours. The leading features of these two wars will be sketched in a succeeding Chapter.

Alexander II., the next sovereign of Russia, who took up the sceptre left by his father, Nicholas, pursued with a steady purpose, unsurpassed by any of his predecessors, the traditional policy of the Russian Empire, which aims, if not at universal dominion, at a preponderance over other States so enormous and overwhelming as to constitute one of the gravest perils of the future. The one truly magnificent act of his reign was the emancipation of the serfs, which was decreed on the 3rd of March, 1861, and completely carried out two years later. An act of humanity and justice on a grander scale, it would perhaps be impossible to find; for by this decree 23,000,000 Russians were delivered from the thraldom of ages, and elevated to the rank of reasonable beings. But even this noble edict must not make us forget the other characteristics of Alexander's reign. Russia is still an unredeemed despotism; its force is the force of an almost illimitable army, and its designs, as regards foreign policy, are in no respect different from those of Peter the Great or Catharine II. The steady advance of Russian power is indeed a fact of the most prodigious kind. Dr. Lyall, a traveller in Russia during the earlier years of the present century, sketched in a very striking manner the progress that had been made up to his time. "But a few centuries ago," he remarked, "the Russian territory formed a fourth part of the present European Russia, and about a seventeenth part of the present Russian Empire. In the reign of Ivan III., this territory was augmented 10,000 square miles, and, in the reign of Vasilii, 14,000 square miles. Ivan IV. tripled the extent of his dominions, and Feodor I. greatly extended them. In the reign of Alexis, all the provinces that had been taken by the Poles were re-conquered; and, besides, he added 257,000 square miles to the Russian states. Under the sway of Feodor III., the dreary region of Nova Zembla was acquired. Peter the Great extended his dominions 280,000 square miles. The Empress Anne, treading in the same path of augmentation, left behind her a realm of above 324,000 square miles in extent; and while Catharine II. held the sceptre of the North, the territory was increased to 335,000 square miles. In the reign of Paul, and since the present sovereign [Alexander I.] ascended the throne, the Empire has been enlarged to no less than 345,000 geographical square miles, of which 85,000 belong to Europe, and 260,000 to Asia. And we might prophecy, if the same system of aggrandisement be persevered in, he may bequeath to his successor an Empire of 400,000 or even 500,000 square miles."

Alexander II. was assassinated by the Nihilists at St. Petersburg on March 13, 1881. He was succeeded by his son, under the title of Alexander III.

Circassia was acquired by the Emperor Nicholas, who began that series of aggressions in Central Asia which have been continued in so remarkable a degree by the late and present Emperors. A Russian author of the present day, M. Boukharow, has recently boasted that the extension of Russia in the last century was a fact unexampled in history. Her extension in the present century is no less so. She has doubled her territory since 1772. She has advanced three hundred and fifty leagues on the road to Vienna and Paris, has absorbed half Sweden and the larger part of Poland, has conquered from Persia an area equal to that of Great Britain, and has wrested from Turkey, by successive wars and treaties, a dominion as large as Prussia before the war of 1866.* Many of the Central Asiatic States have within the last few years been drawn within the enormous whirlpool of her power, and only a few feeble Governments and a comparatively narrow territory stand between her and the frontiers of British India. There are those who see in this unparalleled growth only a cause for rejoicing. Mr. Carlyle has argued that the mission of Russia is to drill anarchic populations into order; and if we

* *Edinburgh Review*, Oct., 1876.

desire to know what kind of order is the result of this species of drilling, we have only to glance at the recent history of Poland and of Circassia. Others are not so well contented with what has been achieved in the past, nor with what will perhaps be accomplished in the future. Our object in these retrospective Chapters is to furnish the reader with some material for his own judgment on a question of which it is impossible to over-rate the gravity, or to exaggerate the interest.

From the preceding sketch it will have been seen that the political condition of Russia, even at the present day, is that of a highly concentrated autocracy. In the structure of society, however, there are certain elements which seem to offer the hope of a better state in times to come, though it is to be feared that they are equally capable of a bad application. Something of local self-government exists in the village communities of the country, each of which has for its chief administrator an elected official, whose power is limited by the heads of households. In these free communes, a species of village assembly is held, of which the Elder, or elected chief of the little commonwealth, is the president. Regular debates take place on affairs of local interest, and local officials are elected by the votes of all the members. The arable land and pasturage, from which the peasants draw their means of living, belong to the commune, which has to pay an annual sum into the Imperial Treasury. The power of the commune is very considerable, and Mr. Mackenzie Wallace says he has known many instances in which the peasants have defied the police, the Governor of the province, and even the Imperial Government itself, but never any in which they have openly opposed the will of the commune, though that body often orders re-distributions of property which seriously affect individual members. The same writer also observes that, in spite of the systematic and persistent efforts of the centralised bureaucracy to regulate all departments of the national life, the rural communes remain in many respects entirely beyond its influence, and that these communes, containing about five-sixths of the population, are good specimens of representative, constitutional government, of the extreme democratic type. The real authority lies with the assembly, of which all heads of households are members; and even women are included when, owing to the decease of their husbands, they occupy the chief position in the family. The meetings are in the open air, and the discussions are as free as discussions can be. Other local administrations are to be found in Russia, and are permitted by the supreme power. It need scarcely be pointed out that here is a check on the autocratic system of Russia. It is equally certain, however, that these village communes, with their power over the possession of landed property, and their subordination of the individual to the majority, might, under different political conditions, result in a species of communistical despotism, such as the most extreme sections of the French Republicans have repeatedly endeavoured to establish. This, indeed, is the tendency of the popular party in Russia; this is the danger underlying the apparently smooth surface of Russian political life. At the present day, the chief forces in the Muscovite Empire are the military and bureaucratic power wielded by the Czar, and the power of the peasantry, who are unfortunately ignorant and superstitious to a superlative degree. The towns are few, and not very influential; the nobility, for the most part, are not rich; and the emancipation of the serfs has reduced the power of the latter. The two extremities of the social scale are thus brought face to face, and it is not improbable that the next generation or two may witness important changes.

RUSSIAN PEASANTS AT HOME.

CHAPTER XIX.

History of the Turks—Origin of the Race in the Deserts of Tartary—Their Settlement between the Euxine and Caspian Seas—Association of the Turks with the Saracens, leading to their Conversion to Mohammedanism—Establishment of the Turkish Power in Asia Minor—Successful Career of Ertoghrul—Conquests of Othman, or Osman—The Capital of the Turkish Dominions fixed at Broussa—Decline of the Greek Empire—Its distracted Condition in the Fourteenth Century—The Turks invited into Europe, to assist a Claimant to the Throne of Constantinople—Their Conquests under Orchan and his Successors—Crushing Defeat of the Christians at Kossova, in Servia—Death of Amurath I.—Formation of the Corps of Janizaries—Corruption of Turkish Manners—Martial Career of Sultan Bayazid, or Bajazet—His Defeat by Timur, the Tartar Khan—Interregnum in Turkey—Reign of Mohammed I.—Amurath II. and his Achievements—His Contests with the Christians under John Huniades—Bad Faith of the Hungarians and their Allies—Terrific Defeat of the Christians at Varna, in 1444—Extraordinary Career of Scanderbeg—Death of Amurath II.—Political Condition of the Turkish Empire in the Middle of the Fifteenth Century—Recent Reforms—Energy of the Turks under the Rule of Mohammed II.

If we would discover the origin of the Turkish race, we must seek for it in the very same regions whence their great opponents, the Russians, issued forth to people the north-east of Europe. Both nationalities come from out of the immense deserts of Scythia; both are remotely Tartars, either wholly or in part; and both have some characteristics in common. When we speak of Tartars, however, we must bear in mind that the people generally so described, from whom the Russians and the Turks derive much of their ancestry, are totally distinct from the Mongol Tartars (or Moguls) who settled in southern Muscovy, who gave a dynasty to China, and who are identified in name, though in little else, with the splendid Empire of Delhi. The latter were men of the same family as the Chinese—yellow-skinned men, with scanty beards, high cheek-bones, flat noses, and oblique eyes. The Tartars properly so called belong to that Caucasian branch of the human race which has furnished most of the European and many of the Asiatic nations. Numerous were the subdivisions of the Tartar stock; but one of the principal was that of the Turks. Some tribes of these people, after many wanderings in Asia, became known to Europe in the seventh century, when Heraclius, Emperor of the East, took them into his service. They were at that time settled between the Euxine and Caspian Seas, near the region of the Caucasus; and Heraclius thought he saw in them the material for good soldiers. In this he was not deceived. His Turkish auxiliaries so distinguished themselves by fidelity and valour that, in the ninth century, the Saracen Caliphs enlisted large bodies of them in their armies. Their religion up to that date had been partly Zoroastrian, partly a wild farrago of traditions common to the Tartar hordes. But their association with the Arabians and Persians led to their conversion to the Mohammedan faith, and they have ever since been amongst the greatest upholders of that creed. Before the era of their conversion, they were a nation of warrior-shepherds, constantly moving about from place to place in the great plains of Georgia and Armenia, yet keeping a magnificent court, with all the glittering adornments of Oriental monarchy. Afterwards, they assumed a more settled character; and having, before the middle of the tenth century, established an independent dynasty in Egypt, and acquired a preponderating influence in the appointment of the Caliphs, they began to dispute the prize of empire with the Persians and the Byzantine Greeks.

Sultan Solyman, who succeeded to the more western portion of the immense dominions acquired by the Seljukians, a Turcoman tribe, made his power felt in Europe towards the close of the eleventh century. The throne of Constantinople was claimed by two princes, one of whom sought the aid of Solyman, who ruled over part of Asia Minor, or Roum, as these Orientals called it, in recognition of its having formed a portion of the Roman Empire. The result was that the warlike Turk obtained more possessions in that quarter of the world, and speedily excited alarm in the nations of Christendom. The power of this dynasty, however, was for a time overwhelmed by the superior might of Genghiz Khan, whose prodigious empire extended from the frontiers of China to those of Poland and Germany. But the Turks of Asia Minor, whose seat of Government was at Iconium (now Koniah), soon recovered their realm, and in 1241 Solyman Shah, chief of the Oghouz Turks, who dwelt in Khorassan, fled from the attacks of the Mongols, and conducted an army to the assistance of the Western Turks, who were still pressed by foes. He was drowned in crossing the Euphrates, either on his way to the west or on his return; but his son Ertoghrul resolved to remain with his followers under the sceptre of Aladdin, the Sultan of Roum. Proceeding westward, they saw one day, just as they had reached the brow of a hill, two armies drawn up for battle in the valley below. One was evidently weaker than the other, and Ertoghrul, in the spirit of chivalry, immediately took the side which seemed likely to fare the worse. By this unexpected help, the smaller army won the battle, and it then appeared that Ertoghrul had been aiding his kinsmen, the Seljukian Turks, against the Mongols. Aladdin proved his gratitude by bestowing on him and his tribe the fertile pasture-grounds near Angora, and Ertoghrul was permitted to assume the title of Emir, or Prince —a designation implying a certain amount of sovereignty, though not that of a supreme ruler. Ertoghrul assisted the Sultan in other wars with the Mongols, and also against the neighbouring Christians, and was rewarded with further grants of territory, extending to the frontiers of the Byzantine Empire, which possessions he was to hold as a fief, on condition of defending the Turkish dominions from invasion by the Constantinopolitan Greeks. This condition was amply fulfilled, and Ertoghrul died in 1288, after a career of successful bravery, which does not seem to have been sullied by any crimes.

The Emir was succeeded by his son Othman, or Osman, from whom the Turks are to this day called Othmans, Ottomans, or Osmanlis. He was a man of great ability as a ruler, as well as a valorous and brilliant general. Though a conqueror, and an enthusiastic propagator of the religion he professed, his civil administration was wise and just. Triumph after triumph attended his arms, and he gained possession of nearly all Nicomedia and Bithynia. When too old to take the field in person, he deputed the military office to his son Orchan, who, before the death of his father, achieved the conquest of Broussa (or Prusa), which then became the Asiatic capital of the Ottomans. The old man was carried in a dying state into the captured city, and there, shortly afterwards, breathed his last, in the year 1326. To the present day, every Turkish sovereign is girded with the sword of Othman on succeeding to the Imperial throne, and this great conqueror is rightly regarded as the founder of the Ottoman power. He had been completely independent since 1307, when Aladdin was dethroned and killed by the Mongols. That event brought the sovereignty of the Seljukian Turks to a close, except in a few scattered principalities, and the Ottoman now became the dominant power in the north-western part of Asia. Orchan was the second of his father's sons—not the eldest; but he succeeded to the throne, by the desire of Othman, because of his martial qualities. The elder brother, with noble self-abnegation, became Grand Vizier, and proved his fitness for the office by the code of laws he produced for the regulation of society and manners in the realms of Orchan. The reign of that monarch was one uninterrupted series of successes. Advancing westward through Asia Minor, at the head of his highly-trained and invincible warriors, he came in sight of the Propontis and of the shores of Europe. To his army, Orchan added a navy of considerable

BROUSSA, THE ANCIENT CAPITAL OF TURKEY.

size; and his power became so great that the rulers of Constantinople courted his alliance and deprecated his enmity.

The Eastern Empire was by this time in its dotage. It had played an illustrious part in history, and its records, stained as they are with many crimes, will always be regarded as among the most interesting of the early Christian ages. Succeeding to some of the fairest portions of that vast dominion which had accumulated about the seven hills of Rome, the Cæsars of Byzantium had perpetuated their sovereignty to a much later age than that at which the Western Emperors succumbed to barbarism. The successors of Constantine preserved no small part of the ancient civilisation, while the older seat of empire on the Tiber was being ravaged by Goths and Vandals. The depredations of the early Russians, from which Constantinople occasionally suffered, were trifles in comparison with the ruin brought to pass in Italy by the fierce warriors who poured down on it. Beneath the sceptre of the Eastern Emperors, the intellect of Greece had undergone a species of modified revival. The Greek language yet endured. The Greek activity of mind had still a recognised sphere for its operations. Learning, which had almost perished in the West, preserved its cloistral haunts along the shores of the Ægean, and by the waters of the Marmorial Sea. Even Greek art, though in a sadly degenerate form, was preserved within the limits of the Byzantine Empire; and when painting and sculpture were re-born in Florence, it was from Byzantium that the impulse came. Justinian the Great gave laws and protection to a contented people when Rome was lying trampled beneath the feet of savages. The whole East of Europe took its conceptions of Christianity, both in doctrine and in ritual, from the Imperial city on the Bosphorus. Byzantine generals carried on those traditions of a conquering race which had descended from the era of the wolf-suckled twins; and for a time even Rome itself was a dependency of Constantinople. But by the fourteenth century all this had passed. The Byzantines were corrupt, debauched, and enfeebled. Torn by internal factions, and ruined by frivolity and vice, they could no longer hold the outlying portions of their realm; they could scarcely hold the capital itself. The advent of a stronger race was projecting its shadow from the Asiatic shores.

BAYAZID BEFORE TIMUR.

The imbecile rule of the Emperor Andronicus Palæologus invited aggression, and his grandson, Andronicus the Younger, headed a revolt against him in 1328. The insurgent was supported by Joannes Cantacuzenus, who solicited the help of Umur Bey, the Turkish Prince of Aidin; and that chief sent a fleet of 380 vessels, and an army of 28,000 men, to act on behalf of Andronicus the Younger. With these forces he entered Europe, and marched by the Hebrus upon the city of Demotica, which was at that time besieged by the Bulgarians. The siege was raised by Umur, who afterwards, at the head of 2,000 chosen troops, proceeded into Servia, whence, however, the severity of the winter speedily forced him to withdraw. The cause of his friend, Cantacuzenus, was subsequently abandoned by the Prince—it is said, in consequence of a bribe having been paid him; but the power of the rebel was established, and at the conclusion of hostilities the Turks returned to the Asiatic side of the Bosphorus. Andronicus the Younger held possession of the throne until his death in 1341, when it was usurped by Cantacuzenus, who abdicated in 1355.

But the fate of the Eastern Empire had been decided by the fact of requesting Mohammedan assistance. The Turks had seen Europe; they had beheld the magnificent city of Imperial dominion; they had wielded their arms in countries of historic fame, in lands of ancient richness and high cultivation. They had been called in as the arbiters between two claimants to the throne, and, having been taught their power, were not slow to apply the lesson. To any observer of ordinary penetration, it was obvious that the Byzantine monarchy was in a state of rapid decadence. The nobles were corrupt, the masses were servile, the politicians were mere intriguers. In the capital of the Eastern Empire, and in its surrounding dependencies, the Osmanlis saw only an effete people, who could scarcely uphold the sceptre of authority in their trembling hands. The Turks themselves were in their prime. They were vigorous, martial, highly-organized as an aggressive race, unscrupulous, as such races generally are, and little inclined to respect feebleness because it had once been strong. It became a part of Turkish policy to be frequently in alliance with the Emperors, and to lend them the forces which they needed for keeping their subjects in awe; but, when thus called into Europe, the Osmanlis had their own interests in view, much more than the interests of their friends. Thus it happened, about the middle of the fourteenth century, that, having been invited as allies, they remained as conquerors. Orchan wrested from the Emperors numerous valuable possessions in Asia Minor, and even threatened them in Europe; and Solyman, the son of Orchan, seized Gallipoli in 1356.

Amurath, or Murad, who succeeded to the throne in 1359, subdued the greater part of Thrace, and fixed his capital at Adrianople in 1361. Moving with his immense armies still farther north, Amurath crushed the Servians on the plains of Kossova in 1389, and the result of this engagement was that Servia, Bosnia, Bulgaria, and Albania, fell beneath the influence of the Moslem conquerors. The Christian monarchs in that part of Europe had formed an alliance against the threatening power from Asia, and it was not merely Servians, but members of nearly all the south-eastern nationalities, who fought at Kossova. Their army was nearly twice as numerous as that of the Mohammedans; but, although it fought bravely and resolutely, the enthusiasm of the Turks was not to be withstood. The defeat was among the greatest recorded in history, and few have been attended by more important results. It established the power of the Osmanlis in Europe, and handed over to ages of subjection numerous races of Christians who were then beginning to emerge out of the barbarism and chaos of earlier times. The Turks have seldom achieved a more signal triumph; but it was immediately followed by a great misfortune. The principal captives were taken to the tent of Amurath, where Milosch Kobilowitsch, a Servian nobleman, prostrated himself at the feet of the conqueror, and gave every token of submission. Suddenly, however, he leaped up, drew forth a dagger which was concealed under his robe, and stabbed Amurath to the heart. The dying Sultan ordered the Servian King to be instantly beheaded in his presence, and with that fierce satisfaction of his revenge expired as he sat upon the throne.

Not many years after this sanguinary conflict, the Turks penetrated even beyond the Danube, and annexed Wallachia to their rapidly-extending realm. They were not unacquainted with one of the subtlest arts of despotism—that of using the vanquished races as a help towards the achievement of still further conquests. The Ottoman forces at the battle of Kossova had included many Christian tributaries, and wherever the Turks established their power they forced the people into their armies, and employed them without scruple as the weapons of their ambition. In this way arose the celebrated force of Prætorian troops known as the Janizaries. The corps was first established by Aladdin, the brother and Grand Vizier of Orchan, and was afterwards re-modelled by Amurath. By the Mohammedan law, the Sultan is entitled to a fifth part of the spoil and captives taken in battle; and out of the more youthful of the Christian prisoners it was determined to form a body-guard of picked troops, who should have the honour of taking the foremost place in all the greatest enterprises of the Ottoman sovereigns. They were of course educated in the Mohammedan faith, and, whether they really adopted it or not, were compelled to appear as if they did. A celebrated Dervish, being asked to bless the troop shortly after its formation, laid his white sleeve on the head of one of the soldiers, and said, "Let them be called *Jeni-cheri* (the new soldiers). May their countenances be ever bright! May their hands be victorious, their swords keen, and their spears always hanging over the heads of their enemies! Wherever they go, may they return with a white (or shining) face!" Thus did the Sultans of Turkey form a standing army of professional soldiers, long before any such institution was known to the Christian nations of Europe. The Janizaries lasted as an important part of the Turkish military system for about five hundred years, and their power was at times so great that they made and unmade Sultans at their will. The conquests of the Ottoman power in Europe were greatly aided by the forces thus derived from the Christian populations themselves; but it was afterwards determined to make no further demand upon the Christians, and the Rayahs are still exempted from military service on payment of a special tax, though in terms they are now permitted to enter the army if they please.

On the death of Amurath, he was succeeded by his son, Bayazid, more commonly, but less correctly, designated Bajazet, who had already acquired distinction as a successful general, and who, by the rapidity of his movements and the startling suddenness of his blows, had earned for himself the surname of *Ilderim*, or the Lightning. This monarch was characterised by some of the worst features of Oriental despotism. He was ferocious and unrelenting, and immediately after his accession to the throne put his brother Yakoub to death for alleged sedition, though the real motive appears to have been jealousy of the young man's power in the army. His reign, moreover, was marked by a degree of moral corruption from which until that time the Turks had been generally free. When these tribes first issued from the deserts of Tartary, they were a brave, simple-living, hardy, and industrious race, and the luxurious climate and splendid cities of Western Asia made no material difference in their habits. Stern and rigorous they could be; they were not men to let the kinder sentiments of humanity bar the road of their progress. But they were often just; they were neither drunkards nor men of lax morality; and, in a strong, unbending way, they carried out some of the best principles of their religion. The era of their depravity dates from their appearance in South-Eastern Europe. In the Byzantine Empire of the Middle Ages, morals had fallen to the lowest point of degradation. The Greeks of those days were feeble, cowardly, cunning, and dissolute. They retained not a little of that intellectual adaptability which had made their remote ancestors so illustrious; but they retained also some of their worst vices. The Turks might have raised them to a higher level; unfortunately, the Greeks dragged down the Turks. The enormous corruption of the Turkish Empire in later times, the degradation of society in the chief cities of the Sultan, are due, not to anything naturally inherent in the Turkish race, but to the base example of some of the nations which they conquered. It is customary to impute the bad conduct of Greeks, Bulgarians, Bosnians, and Servians, to the influence of the Turk. It would be more correct to reverse the statement, though sweeping condemnations of this kind are generally to be deprecated. There are some special features in the Mohammedan religion which have a tendency to promote much that is objectionable in social life; but it must not be forgotten that the Turks, on their first appearance in Europe, were, in everything except mental culture, a superior race to the degenerate subjects of the Eastern Emperors, and that their own decline is due to a too ready adoption of the manners that they found.

The Ottoman Empire in the reign of Bayazid extended from the Euphrates to beyond the Danube. From point to point of this immense dominion, Bayazid was perpetually moving on warlike expeditions. He conquered the northern region of Anatolia (or Asia Minor), overawed the province of Karamania, and extinguished the independence of several Seljukian principalities. The Byzantine Empire was now reduced to very narrow limits. In Asia, scarcely anything was retained; in Europe, nothing was left excepting a small part of Thrace, the province of Macedonia, Greece, and a few islands of the Ægean Sea. Even these were held only by favour of the predominant Mussulman. The Emperor Manuel Palæologus humbled himself in the most ignominious fashion before Bayazid, that he might be allowed to enjoy in peace the slender remnant of his possessions; but his degradation availed him little. In 1391, the Sultan captured the city of Philadelphia, the last Greek town in Asia Minor which remained faithful to the Empire; and while the Greek commander who held that post was doing his best to defeat the enemy, Manuel was actually assisting the Sultan in the reduction of the place. Five years later, Bayazid defeated at Nicopolis, near the Danube, a confederated army of 100,000 Christians, headed by Sigismund, King of Hungary. The victor was intoxicated by success, and boasted that in a little while he would besiege the Hungarian capital, subdue Germany and Italy, and feed his horse with a bushel of oats on the altar of St. Peter at Rome. In this tremendous fight, the greater number of the Christian forces were slain or driven into the Danube, and the Turks themselves are said to have lost 60,000 men. Furious at the sacrifice of so large a portion of his army, Bayazid gave orders to kill all the prisoners, with the exception of twenty-four nobles, who were ultimately ransomed; then, flushed with success and glutted with revenge, he proceeded to further conquests in the direction of Greece. He now exacted a tribute of the Greek Emperor, and insisted upon his having a Turkish cadi and a Mohammedan mosque at Constantinople. He even threatened, and actually invested, that city, which would probably have been taken some years before its ultimate fate, had not Bayazid been called away to defend his Asiatic provinces from the inroads of a conqueror still greater than himself.

The power of the Mongolian Khans, which had risen to an amazing height under the renowned Genghiz, in the thirteenth century, had considerably declined after the death of that chieftain, whose overgrown dominions were split up amongst his followers. But, in the latter part of the fourteenth century, a warrior as successful as Genghiz once more arose in those Tartarian deserts, and, advancing with rapid strides from victory to victory, seemed as if he were about to establish a universal empire. The realm which obeyed Timur touched that which obeyed Bayazid along the banks of the Euphrates. It was certain that these two Oriental despots would speedily come into collision, and that one would encroach upon the dominions of the other. Timur took possession of Sivas, on the Halys, in 1400, and treated the inhabitants with great atrocity. Four thousand Armenians, who formed the garrison, are said to have been buried alive for defending their charge to the uttermost; and the Mongolian then turned his arms towards Syria and Egypt. Bayazid was unable at the moment to vindicate his authority; but he did not forget the injury he had received. Having strengthened his forces, he took possession of Erzinjan, a town

TURKISH SOLDIERS OF THE FIFTEENTH CENTURY.

situated on the Euphrates, within the dominions of Timur. This led to an open war between the two potentates, and in 1402 a great battle took place between the forces of the Osmanlis and the Tartars, commanded by their respective sovereigns, on the plains of Angora, the capital of the ancient Galatia. Bayazid was defeated with terrific loss, and endeavoured to escape from the field on the fleetest of his horses; but he was pursued and captured, and at sunset was carried to the tent of Timur. The treatment of the vanquished Sultan by his conqueror has been very differently described by different authors, and, according as we believe those accounts, it was either extremely noble or extremely cruel. Bayazid, according to one narrative, was softened by the mild expostulations of Timur; according to another, the Tartar Khan enclosed his captive in a cage of iron, and carried him about in this way from place to place, until he died in his misery and shame, in 1403. The old traveller, Busbequius, who visited Constantinople about a hundred and fifty years later, asserts that Timur treated Bayazid with great ferocity, and that his wife, who was also captured, was grossly insulted before his face. The latter account is certainly much more in harmony with the usual character of Asiatic conquerors than the former. It was for a long time believed in this part of the world, and forms an incident in the play of "Tamburlaine," attributed to the old English dramatist, Marlowe. The cage, however, may possibly have been a species of litter, shut in with bars.

This defeat resulted in a considerable diminution of the Ottoman Empire in Asia, for Timur reinstated several of the Seljukian princes; but the Turkish power in Europe was not affected by the misfortune at Angora. It is very possible that Timur might have pursued the Osmanlis even across the Sea of Marmora, had not his attention been turned in another direction. Having already subdued India, Persia, Khorassan, and some of the more western parts of Asia, he conceived the design of adding China to his territories; but death arrested him on the way, and no one of equal genius arose to carry on his ambitious schemes. Nevertheless, the sovereignty of the Ottomans had been temporarily shattered. The succession to the throne was disputed by four of Bayazid's sons, Solyman, Isa, Musa, and Mohammed, amongst whom the Empire was broken into jarring fragments, and for a period of several years a state of civil war existed, in which sometimes one prince, and sometimes another, acquired a degree of superiority. At length, owing to repeated successes, Mohammed became sole monarch in 1413, and ruled from that year till 1421. He commenced his reign by ordering the murder of his nephew, the son of his late brother Solyman, and in two years expelled the Seljukian princes from the possessions in which they had been reinstated by Timur. The reign of this prince was signalized by some misfortunes; amongst others, by the destruction of a Turkish fleet off Gallipoli, where it was attacked by the Venetians in 1416. Another incident of the period was a revolt of dervishes, who assembled near Ephesus, and propounded certain extreme doctrines of communistical democracy. In 1421, Mohammed paid a visit to the Emperor Manuel at Constantinople, and was received with great splendour. On his return to Gallipoli, he died of apoplexy; but the fact of his decease was kept secret until the succession could be made secure. The soldiers were ordered to cross the Bosphorus to Broussa; but they had heard rumours of the Sultan's death, and refused to go unless they could see him. The body of the monarch was accordingly seated in a dark kiosque, enveloped in a cloak, within the folds of which a page was stationed, who, if we are to believe the story, moved the arm of the dead Sultan sufficiently to give the salute which is usual with the Turkish princes.

Amurath II. succeeded to his father, Mohammed, and was immediately called upon to defend his throne against the pretensions of a person calling himself Mustapha, who alleged that he was the eldest son of Bayazid, supposed to have been killed at Angora. Mustapha had for some time disputed the power of the late Sultan; but, being defeated, he had been held in durance at Constantinople, on payment to the Emperor of a large annual sum. After the accession of Amurath II., Manuel Palæologus thought he could answer his purposes better by releasing the prisoner, and supporting his claim. He accordingly made a bargain with him, to the effect that he would assist in an attack upon the Sultan, on the understanding that Gallipoli, Thessaly, and the shores of the Black Sea, should be restored to the Eastern Empire. The terms were accepted, and for a time everything seemed to go well with the pretender. Gallipoli and Adrianople were subdued by a Greek army under the command of Mustapha, and a Turkish force that was sent against him rallied to his standard. Amurath, however, was in the field at the head of a formidable host. Mustapha, beginning to lose heart, wasted valuable time in considering what he should next attempt, and after a while the Moslems who had joined his army returned to their old allegiance. The pretender was attacked by the Sultan in the neighbourhood of Gallipoli, and, being utterly defeated, was captured, and hanged from one of the towers of Adrianople, whither he had fled after his discomfiture. Amurath revenged himself by desolating a wide tract of country, and by investing Constantinople. On the 24th of August, 1422, he ordered a general assault upon the walls of that city. A terrific struggle ensued, but about sunset the Turks unexpectedly withdrew, owing, as the Greeks averred, to a dazzling appearance of the Virgin, who struck terror into the besiegers, but, as more prosaic historians maintain, to the appearance of a fresh pretender to the Ottoman throne, in the person of Amurath's younger brother, who, like the claimant recently defeated, bore the name of Mustapha. The second candidate fared no better than the first, and the Sultan now entered

JOHN HUNIADES.

on a career of conquest, embracing operations both in Asia and Europe.

At the head of his devoted soldiers, Amurath in 1426 laid waste the island of Zante, belonging to the Venetians, and in the following year subdued the Morea, captured Salonica, and compelled the Venetians to conclude a favourable peace. The Servians and the Wallachians felt the keen edge of his sword, and in 1438 he penetrated into Transylvania, and carried off 70,000 prisoners. He was at length, however, confronted by his match. Transylvania was a dependency of the Hungarian kingdom, and the Voïvode or Governor at that time was the famous John Huniades Corvinus. Being in possession of a valiant and numerous army, Huniades boldly attacked the Moslems, and overthrew them on several occasions, until at length they were compelled to recede across the Danube, with the loss of many of their best troops. They were followed to the southern shores of that stream in 1443, when Huniades, with a magnificent army drawn from several countries in that part of Europe, fell upon the Turks at Nissa, or Nisch, and again put them to flight. Advancing in a south-easterly direction through Roumelia, this brilliant general inflicted still further reverses on the disheartened Ottomans, and then turned back towards his own country, laden with booty, and with a vast number of prisoners. The Turkish sovereign, utterly worn out by his misfortunes, and by the death of his eldest son, Aladdin, now sued for peace, and it was agreed between Turkey on the one part, and Hungary with her allies on the other, that neither should cross the Danube in a hostile manner into the dominions beyond. A little before this event, the Sultan had quelled an insurrection in his Asiatic provinces, fomented by an inveterate enemy named Karaman Ogli, whom he generously forgave. Ogli, however, secretly incited the Hungarians to renew the war, and the Papal legate at Buda absolved the King from his solemn promise, on the ground that oaths to infidels are

THE BATTLE OF VARNA, 1444.

not binding. In ten weeks, the forces of the Christians were again across the Danube, and Bulgaria seemed as if it would fall entirely into their possession. Amurath, immediately on concluding peace, had resigned the Empire to his son Mohammed (then a child), and had retired to Magnesia, where he joined a society of dervishes and hermits, who lived after a very austere and rigorous fashion. But, upon hearing the peril which threatened his dominions, he again placed himself at the head of the army. A great battle took place at Varna, on the Black Sea, in 1444, and Amurath, during the heat of the engagement, caused the late treaty of peace to be borne through his ranks on the point of a lance, while he cried aloud to the troops, "Let the infidels come on against their God and sacrament; and, if their belief of those things be certain, let them, O just God, be their own avengers, and the punishers of their own ignominy!" The combat was fierce and bloody, and, while the issue was yet doubtful, the Hungarian King, Ladislaus, made his way towards the tent of Amurath, and challenged him to single combat. The Sultan pierced the horse of his adversary, who fell, and was at once dispatched by the Janizaries. His head was cut off, and, being displayed on the point of a spear, caused such discomfiture in the Christian ranks that the forces of Huniades, which until then seemed to be driving back their opponents, suddenly gave way in uncontrollable panic. The greater number were either slain or taken prisoners, and Cardinal Julian Cesarini, who had obtained for the King of Hungary the Pope's dispensation from his oath, was among those whose dead bodies were afterwards discovered on the field. Huniades made his escape, and Amurath, considering that all danger to his Empire was at an end, again retired to the privacy of a religious life, to which his meditative temperament seemed naturally to incline him.

But quiet was not to be his portion. Another sedition among the Janizaries, which broke out in 1446, and brought the utmost affliction upon Adrianople, once more drew the Sultan from his hermitage. The insolence of the Prætorian troops was quelled, but another danger had started up in a different direction. At that time, Albania was a principality owing a certain allegiance to the Turks, but governed by its own rulers. The sovereign power, so far as it could be called sovereign, was vested in the family of the Castriots, and George Castriot, son of John, was, when a boy, sent by his father as a hostage to Sultan Amurath, together with three of his brothers. The four youths were carried to Adrianople, where three of them died, not without suspicion of poison. George was brought up under the immediate eye of the Sultan, and, having been educated as a Mohammedan (in contravention of a promise given to his father), was appointed, when only eighteen years of age, to the command of a large body of troops. In this position he so distinguished himself by valour and good conduct that the Turks bestowed on him the title of Iskander-Beg, which in European countries was speedily contracted into Scanderbeg. The designation is an Oriental form of the term "Prince Alexander," for Alexander the Great is a favourite with the Orientals as well as with the Greeks. After the death of his father, in 1432, George Castriot formed a design of returning to his principality. His Mohammedanism had been forced upon him, and was never sincerely professed; he disliked the Turks, and desired to bring about the complete independence of his country, which was now seized by Amurath, and governed in his own name through the agency of a Pasha. Scanderbeg had proposed to himself a very difficult enterprise, and it was necessary that he should cloak his designs till they were ripe for execution. He accompanied the Turkish army to Hungary, but, when there, entered into a secret arrangement with Huniades, and, by a sudden manœuvre of the forces under his command, contributed to the defeat of the Ottomans at Nissa. In the confusion following upon that reverse, he penetrated to the tent of the Sultan's secretary, held a dagger to his throat, and forced him to sign an order to the Governor of Croya, the capital of Epirus (which was often associated with the Albanian principality), to deliver that place into the hands of himself, Castriot. The signature having been obtained, Scanderbeg at once put the secretary to death. Immediately quitting the camp with three hundred Albanians, this daring adventurer appeared before Croya, massacred the Turkish garrison, and, publicly renouncing Mohammedanism, ascended the throne of his fathers. For five successive years, the Sultan led army after army against his rebellious favourite, but, although Scanderbeg was frequently compelled to retire to his mountain fastnesses, he could never be entirely subdued. The personal strength and courage of this remarkable man, his genius as a military leader, and his frequent successes against superior numbers, have spread his fame over the whole east of Europe, so that he is one of the most popular heroes of those border-lands of the Christian and the Moslem. Even the Turks regarded him with admiration, and some time after his death dug up his bones with great respect, mounted them in gold and silver, and wore them as amulets. Amurath was on the point of setting out personally to measure his strength with Scanderbeg, when, in 1448, he heard that Huniades, after ravaging Servia, was threatening to descend into Macedonia, where Scanderbeg was expected to join him. The forces of Huniades were drawn up on the historic plain of Kossova, and here they were attacked by Amurath in October. The Hungarians were greatly overmatched in numbers; Scanderbeg did not arrive to their assistance; and the Christians, in spite of a desperate struggle of three days' duration, were driven in utter ruin from the field. Amurath returned to Adrianople, after an unsuccessful attempt to reduce Albania, and on the 9th of February, 1451, died of apoplexy. The good fortune of Scanderbeg continued during the reign of Amurath's successor, Mohammed II., who in 1461 proposed terms of peace, which were accepted. A few years after, Scanderbeg broke his treaty, and obtained several victories over the Turkish generals; but Epirus, which he ruled in conjunction with Albania, was conquered by the Sultan in 1466. His death took place at Lissa, in the Venetian territories, in 1467, at the age of sixty-three; and it was followed in 1478 by the submission of Albania to the Ottoman rule.

Some account of the Turkish political system, as it existed about the period at which we have now arrived, may fitly close this Chapter. The facts are derived from a recent author, whose knowledge of Turkey is based, not only on books, but on a personal acquaintance with the country and the people.*

When the conquering hosts of the Ottomans acquired a new possession, order was established by creating a feudal system, consisting of what were called Timars, Ziamets, and Beyliks, which were grants of land carrying with them the obligation of providing a military force for the service of the State in case of need. A Timar contained from three to five hundred acres of land, and the owner, who was called a Spahi, or Cavalier, was bound to supply a mounted cavalry-soldier for every three thousand aspers of his revenue. The Ziamets and the Beyliks were still larger grants of land. These fiefs were hereditary in the male line; and when a certain number of grants had been grouped together, the district was placed under an officer who bore the title of Sandjak Bey. A Bey is equivalent to a lieutenant-colonel in the army; but the title is hereditary. Sandjak means a standard or flag, to which was generally attached the command of five thousand horse. To each Sandjak Bey was given a horse's tail, as a distinctive mark of command; for with the Turks, who were originally a nomadic people, the horse was a symbol of power. The whole system of government was based on the idea of feudal tenure—the tenure of land on the condition of giving military service, and helping in the work of protection and government. With respect to political administration, the chief functions were entrusted to the Vizier—a word signifying the bearer of burdens. In the next degree, power was given to the Cadiaskers, who were two in number—one for Europe, and one for Asia. Their duties were legal; and under them were the Khodya, or tutors of the royal princes, the Muftis, or expounders of the sacred law, and, after the capture of Constantinople, the Judge of that city. When these officers assembled in council, they formed the Divan. This deliberative body was attended by a Chief Secretary, the Reis Effendi, who frequently became an officer of great power and importance. The Grand Vizier sat at the head of the Divan, in the absence of the Sultan; but the Sultan himself was often present, and of course on those occasions took the principal place. The term Pasha, which means "the Shah's foot," was originally given to Turkish subjects who had distinguished themselves in any way, though it is now generally associated with military command. A Pasha of three tails was one to whom had been presented three horses' tails as a token of exceptional power.

The territorial possessions of the conquering Ottomans were divided into Church lands, lands set apart for private property, and domain lands. The domain lands contributed to the support of the Sultan, and to the expenses of the State; and it was from these that the great feudal lords received the price of their military service. After a time, the demand for soldiers became so extreme, owing to the continual extension of the Empire, that a system of slavery was introduced, by which a fifth of the conquered races passed into a state of servitude to the victors. Orchan, the son and successor of Othman, began by taking annually a thousand Christian children, ranging from twelve to fourteen years of age, who were educated in the Mohammedan faith, and so trained that in after years they might be fitted for military, civil, or ecclesiastical employment. This, of course, opened to them the highest positions in the State; but it violated the rights of the Christians, because the parents had no choice in the matter, and were compelled to see their children brought up in a religion that was hateful to themselves. It was thus that the corps of Janizaries was formed, and these favoured troops afterwards became the greatest persecutors of the Christians in the whole Ottoman

* Lieut.-Colonel James Baker: Turkey in Europe, chap. 8.

Empire. The treatment of the Christians, however, was not severe in the earlier ages of the Ottoman rule. It was a maxim of the old Turkish law that "the bended head should not be stricken off." But this benevolent rule was forgotten when the Turks became insolent with success, and intoxicated with the grandeur of their extensive Empire. A Mufti was once asked, "If eleven Mussulmans kill, without just cause, a Christian who is the subject of the Padishah, and pays tribute, what is to be done?" The Mufti's reply was—"Though the Mussulmans should be a thousand and one, let them all die." It is lamentable that this noble sentiment should not always have pervaded the conduct of the Turks towards their Christian subjects. But it should in justice be recollected that the fanaticism has not been invariably or entirely on one side; and that if the Mohammedans have frequently abused their power, the Christians have sometimes been excessively difficult to rule in the spirit of moderation and fairness.

The system of government established by the earlier Sultans was in some respects modified by Amurath III., who reigned in the latter part of the sixteenth century, and was again altered by Sultan Mahmud II., in the year 1834. The great object of Mahmud was to reduce the enormous corruption and tyranny which had resulted from the feudal system of administration. The Beys and Pashas formed a species of aristocracy, upon whose power there was very little restraint. As a natural consequence, they acted with extreme selfishness and cruelty. Worse depositaries of power than many of these great landed proprietors, it would be impossible to find. Idle, profligate, and avaricious, they exhausted the resources of the lands they ruled, hindered progress, oppressed the poor, and outraged the Christians. With all his faults, his tendency to violence, and his habits of despotic will, Mahmud appears sincerely to have desired the reform of abuses, and the development of a true prosperity. But he was staggered—as his contemporary, the Russian Emperor Nicholas, was staggered in his own dominions—by the frightful degree of corruption existing in the official world. He found that the only course to pursue was to abolish the Beys, or hereditary feudal chiefs, who until then had been the chief instruments of government in the provinces, and to substitute for them a political system more under the influence of Constantinople. Further changes have taken place in subsequent reigns, and the Empire is now divided into great administrative centres called Vilayets, all of them subject to the general control of the Sultan and his Cabinet. The head of each Vilayet is called a Vali, or Governor-General, and he possesses considerable powers, but can at any moment be deposed by the Sultan. Abdul-Aziz created much discontent during his reign by the frequency with which he changed his Valis, sometimes from corrupt, and sometimes from frivolous, motives.

The state of education in Turkey has undergone a great change in recent times. Until 1846, education was theological. The schools were attached to the mosques, and the whole system of instruction was managed by the priests. But in that year an approach was made towards a system of secular education. In 1869, an Imperial Iradé promulgated an organic law of public instruction, which divided the schools of the Empire into two categories—viz., public schools, which are placed exclusively under the control of the Government; and private schools, which are inspected by Government, but depend on individual enterprise, and are carried on as business speculations.

The power of the Turks was at its height when Mohammed II. succeeded to the throne on the death of Amurath II.; and the Turkish character had at that time attained its most distinctive development. The Ottomans were a conquering race, and they had the faults which are inseparable from military dominion. They were proud and arbitrary, and did not suffer considerations of natural or prescriptive right to stand in the way of their advancing armies. But they had also many of the virtues of a strong and dominant people. As a rule, they were not wantonly cruel, and a nation which submitted to their sway was generally treated with consideration. In many places, they introduced order—though it was, indeed, the order of the drawn sword—amongst communities which had been debased and enfeebled by inherent vice, or by the influence of vexatious and impotent Governments. In the middle of the fifteenth century, the Turks were in the main a virtuous race. Corruption had begun to make its appearance in the higher ranks; but it had not yet spread to any serious degree, and the mass of the people was sound. Even at the present day, the Turkish commonalty are possessed of many admirable qualities; but the profligacy of the official world, and of the upper classes, has eaten deeply into the political and social body. Such was not the case in the days of that great conqueror who wrested Constantinople from the failing grasp of the Greek Emperors. At that time, the fortunes of Turkey were still in the ascendant; its star was literally crescent. Immense energy of will, strong fixity of purpose, religious enthusiasm of the highest order, the masculine virtues in their strongest development, and the accumulated traditions of a race already accustomed to centuries of conquest, all conspired to bear forward with resistless force the vast wave of Ottoman aggression against the bulwarks of the regal city. On the one side was the energy of virile strength; on the other, the languor of approaching dissolution. It was an epoch big with fate for the fortunes of Europe—one of those periods of time to which the mind always looks back with unabated interest, as to a turning-point in the procession of universal history. It seemed to be the beginning of a new era of Ottoman conquest, threatening the very existence of Christendom; it was in fact the beginning of Ottoman decay—a prophecy of loss, coming in the deceitful form of a new and splendid acquisition of imperial power.

CHAPTER XX.

Turkish History continued—Commencement of the Reign of Mohammed II.—His secret Policy with respect to the Eastern Empire—Degraded Condition of Constantinople—Projects of Mohammed for conquering the City—He builds a Fortress on the European Side of the Bosphorus, with a View to closing the Straits—Remonstrances of the Emperor Constantine—Threatening Reply of the Sultan—Warlike Preparations—Enormous Cannon cast at Adrianople—Arbitrary Actions of Mohammed—Fatal Apathy of the Byzantines—Attempt of the Emperor to effect a Union of the Greek and Latin Churches—Ancient Byzantium and Modern Constantinople—Surroundings of the City—Its Defences at the Time of Mohammed II.—Preparations for the Attack—Splendid Appearance of the Sultan's Army—Spirited Defence of the Constantinopolitans—Progress of the Siege—Arrival of Greek Vessels to the Relief of the Citizens, and Defeat of the Turkish Galleys—The Ottoman Fleet carried overland to the Golden Horn—Dissensions in the City—Futile Negotiations between the Emperor and the Sultan. The Grand Assault ordered—Capture of Constantinople on the 29th of May, 1453—Death of the Emperor Constantine—Treatment of the City and of the Inhabitants by the Sultan—The Imperial Family of the Palæologi—Effects on Europe of the Fall of Constantinople.

On ascending the throne of his father, in the twenty-second year of his age, Mohammed II. succeeded to a wide and brilliant Empire, yet one which had of late been somewhat shaken by the military genius of Huniades and of Scanderbeg. Amurath had on the whole been remarkably successful; but he had more than once been foiled, and the reverses which he sustained in his last expedition against the capital of Albania, where the great leader of the rebellion defied his numerous hosts, literally broke his heart and hastened his end. His dying advice to his son was never to despise an enemy, however weak he might appear; and it would have been well for the Ottoman Empire if his descendants had always observed that rule in the conduct of their military affairs. Mohammed was certainly not disposed to underrate possible dangers, and the first act of his reign was one of those atrocious deeds which give such a sanguinary hue to Turkish history. Following an evil example with which the annals of his house had furnished him, he sent the Agha of the Janizaries to strangle his brother, an infant only eight months old, and then despatched the Agha himself, as if to disavow his act. Having in this way secured his power from a possible rival, he made peace with his Christian tributaries, and, marching into Asia, humbled the insolence of Karaman Ogli, who was once more in arms against him. The Sultan now turned his mind to what was to be the great enterprise of his reign—the acquisition of Constantinople. He had but recently renewed, with solemn oaths and assurances, a treaty of friendship with the Greek Emperor; yet it cannot be doubted that from the first he contemplated planting his standard on the walls of the Imperial city. With this view he retrenched the inordinate expenditure of his court, displaced and punished several peculators, improved the discipline of the Janizaries (who were beginning to show a rebellious spirit), and reinforced his army. The new sovereign was stern, even to cruelty. He suffered nothing to dispute the supremacy of his will, and his people obeyed him more from fear than love.

Constantinople had by this time reached its lowest depth of degradation. The frivolity of the people affected their serious studies, no less than their pleasures. While the very existence of Christianity in that part of the world was threatened by a powerful, wily, and unresting foe, they neglected the affairs of State, that they might dispute on barren subtleties of theology, which no one could determine, or was any the better for considering. An ignoble devotion to amusement was visible in every rank of life; and the loss of Imperial dominion seemed a trifling matter, if the passing hour could be fleeted carelessly. The spacious realms of the earlier Byzantine Emperors had dwindled down to the city of Constantine itself, and a small portion of territory beyond. Even that much was held only upon sufferance. On the death of John Palæologus, in 1448, his successor, Constantine XII., dared not take up the sceptre without first obtaining permission of Amurath; and on that account he has sometimes been excluded from the list of Greek Emperors, as not being in truth an independent sovereign at all. John Palæologus had seen what was imminent, and had endeavoured to avert it by a personal appeal to some of the Western Powers for assistance against the encroachments of the Turk. But Byzantium was left to its fate, and Constantine found himself face to face with an inexorable destiny, which no humility could assuage, which no force of his might successfully defy.

Mohammed II. began his reign in 1451, and it was not long before the insincerity of his treaty of friendship with the Emperor began to be obvious. He suppressed the pension which had for some time been paid to the miserable Byzantines, and of which they had imprudently, and with wearisome pertinacity, requested the augmentation; he expelled their officers from the banks of the river Strymon, or Emboli, on the borders of Thrace and Macedonia; and he then proceeded to build a strong fortress on the European side of the Bosphorus, at a distance of five miles from Constantinople, directly opposite the castle which his grandfather, Mohammed I., had erected on the Asiatic side. Cannon had been used by the Turks in the reign of Amurath II., when they had been employed with great success at the taking of Patras and Sicyon, as well as on other occasions; and it appeared to Mohammed that by these powerful engines, planted on both sides of the straits, he could obtain a complete mastery over the passage from the Euxine into the Sea of Marmora. Constantine saw in this act a design to take the city by famine, whenever it suited the Sultan's purposes to do so, as he could easily, by his great guns, prevent the entrance of any vessels into the harbour. Filled with distrust and apprehension, the Emperor sent an embassy to Mohammed in 1452, to complain of what he described as an infraction of the treaty of friendship. The Turk haughtily replied that he would construct what edifice he pleased, without

A COUNCIL OF JANIZARIES.

asking leave of his allies, and that providing for his own safety was not a violation of any engagement. The answer was so unsatisfactory that Constantine sent another embassage, this time insisting that the fort should be abandoned. Mohammed was incensed at what he considered the insolence of a vassal. He told the envoy—with how little truth we may all judge—that he contemplated no enterprise against the city; but he bid him remember that the Empire of Constantinople was measured by her walls. Reverting to what had happened a few years before, he remarked that his father had been reduced to great distress by the league which Byzantium had formed with the Hungarians, when they invaded the Ottoman dominions by land, while the Hellespont was covered by the galleys of the Franks. Amurath had been obliged to force the passage of the Bosphorus, and he had vowed to erect a fortress on the European side. That vow, Mohammed informed the Christian representative, he was himself compelled by a sacred obligation to accomplish; and he added that the ground was his own as far as the shores of the Bosphorus. "Return now in safety," he concluded; "but the next who dares to come with remonstrances shall be flayed alive."

THRONE OF THE BYZANTINE EMPERORS. (*After a Greek MS. in the Imperial Library at Paris.*)

Thus driven to bay, Constantine, whose spirit was equal to the tragic destiny awaiting him, resolved to defy the power which was bent on his annihilation. He was restrained, however, by the pusillanimous advice of his counsellors, who believed it would be better to await the development of events. The winter of 1452–3 passed away without anything being done by the Greeks; but the Ottomans steadily pursued their work. The capture of Constantinople was the one thought that possessed the Sultan's mind. Often his nights were sleepless with the details of this great project; and by day he was perpetually deliberating with his generals on the best methods of prosecuting the contemplated siege. He paid particular attention to his artillery, which he was resolved to make the most formidable in the world. In this design he was greatly assisted by a certain Christian renegade, a founder of cannon, whom Mohammed frequently consulted, and whom he bound to his interests by liberal rewards. One day, he asked this man if he could cast a cannon capable of throwing a ball of stone of sufficient size to batter the walls of Constantinople. The artificer replied that even if the walls were more solid than those of Babylon, he could bring to bear against them an engine which should produce the most tremendous effects. Urban, the person thus consulted, was allowed to establish a foundry at Adrianople, and at the end of three months had completed a piece of brass ordnance surpassing anything previously known. The bore was of immense size, and the stone bullet weighed more than six hundred pounds. The Sultan determined on making an experiment; but, to mitigate the effect of the startling roar on the ears and minds of his people, he announced beforehand that the explosion would take place on a certain day. Nothing could be more satisfactory than the action of this enormous gun. The ball was carried a distance of a mile, and buried itself to the depth of a fathom; and the explosion was heard within a circuit of a hundred furlongs. To remove the work of Urban's skill from Adrianople to the vicinity of the Imperial city, was a task of no small difficulty. It was carried on thirty waggons, linked together, and drawn by sixty oxen; and nearly two months elapsed before the journey of not more than a hundred and fifty miles could be accomplished.

Meanwhile, the construction of the castle on the European side of the Bosphorus was actively pushed forward. A thousand masons were constantly employed on it, and the work proceeded with great rapidity. The form was triangular, and at each angle rose a massive tower. One of these towers stood on the declivity of the hill; the two others guarded the sea-shore. The walls varied in thickness from twenty-two to thirty feet, and the whole building was covered with a platform of lead. When the three towers were completed, Mohammed levied tribute on every vessel that passed the straits. A Venetian ship resisted the exaction, and was immediately sunk by a shot from one of the Sultan's guns. Such of the crew as escaped were beheaded, while the master was impaled; and the power of the Sultan was not again disputed in those waters. Constantine, feeling his utter inability to remedy such evils, sent a humble message to Mohammed, requesting as a favour that the harvest might not be destroyed. He gained nothing, however, by his meekness, and shortly afterwards a disturbance broke out between the garrison of the fortress and some of the neighbouring Christians. The latter were massacred by the troops of the Sultan, and the citizens of Constantinople saw in the immediate vicinity of their own walls the fate which was being prepared for themselves.

That fate, it was but too evident, would not be averted. The citizens were unequal to the stern demands of the occasion, and nothing could rouse them from the apathy into which they had long declined. In the very shadow of approaching death, they played, they jested, they wrangled on their favourite theses of philosophy and religion. Shut up within the walls of their city, they had literally no horizon beyond, save that which was delineated by the gathering legions of their foes. The empire of the first Constantine, embracing some of the finest portions of Europe and Asia, had, under the sceptre of the last Constantine, shrunk to the limits of a beleaguered town. Soon there would be nothing left; yet the people stared at their approaching doom, without lifting a hand against it. Like persons in a trance, they saw the danger drawing nearer day by day, and acted as if its existence were unknown. When the Emperor required of them a contribution for necessary expenses, they refused. Something might yet have been done to defend the existence of the Greek nationality, so far as it could be said to exist at all; but everything depended on the exertion of the citizens, and the spirit of exertion had departed. The military force at the command of the Emperor consisted of about six thousand Greeks, with three thousand Venetians and Genoese; and the navy was confined to a few galleys and ships of war. Attempts were made to strengthen the fortifications, and to lay in a stock of corn; but very little was effected. Out of a population of 100,000, only 4,970 enrolled their names for the defence of the city, and the fortifications could not be properly guarded for lack of men. In his despair, Constantine sought alliances abroad. He even went to the extent of sending an embassy to Rome, with a proposal for the union of the Eastern and Western

Churches. It was hoped that the Pontiff would persuade the Princes of the West to rally to the defence of Constantinople; but Nicholas V. did not take up the cause with much enthusiasm. He promised to send some galleys and troops: all he really sent was Cardinal Isidore, charged with the duty of effecting the promised amalgamation.

If anything had been required to arouse the fanaticism of the people to its full height, a better plan could not have been devised. The Cardinal celebrated divine service in the church of St. Sophia, which Justinian had founded; and of course he followed the liturgy and ceremonial of Rome. The Constantinopolitans were wild with rage and horror. They consulted a famous monk named Gennadius, whose extraordinary sanctity gave peculiar value to his advice. He replied by predicting the most dreadful misfortunes to all who should compromise their orthodoxy by any reconciliation with the Latins. In the service of the mass, the Greeks make use of leavened bread, the Latins of that which is unleavened. Could there be a greater difference, or a more excellent reason for two sects of Christians tearing each other to pieces, while the common foe of both was almost at the gates? Excited to fury by the words of Gennadius, the priests, the soldiers, and the citizens raised a tumult, which convinced Isidore that no accession to the Church of Rome was to be looked for in Constantinople. The people declared that the church of St. Sophia had been defiled. They protested that they would rather see the turbans of the Moslems in their public places than the hats of Roman cardinals. The Papal Legate was equally determined to admit no compromise; and he wrote to the Pontiff every dissuasion from lending any aid to people so determined to resist what in his opinion was the only saving faith.

Next to Rome, Constantinople is the most interesting city of Europe, and the greatest scene of remarkable events, affecting the destinies of mankind. It occupies to a great extent the site of ancient Byzantium, which was founded by a Doric colony from Megara, in the year 667 B.C. In the reign of Darius Hystaspes, Byzantium was taken by the Persians; but, subsequently to the battle of Platæa, it came once more into the hands of the Greeks, by whom it was re-peopled by a mixed colony of Athenians and Lacedæmonians. After passing through many fortunes, it was attacked by Philip of Macedon, whose soldiers were silently approaching the town on a dark night, when suddenly a light shone from the north, and revealed the danger by which the citizens were threatened. It was believed that this was a miracle wrought by the goddess Diana, to whom the inhabitants built an altar as an expression of their gratitude, at the same time assuming the crescent as the emblem of their city. The crescent is now the emblem of the Turks, and it has been thought that they adopted it on taking possession of Constantinople; but there is reason to believe that this figure had long been the symbol of the Moslem faith. Byzantium was compelled to submit to Alexander the Great, and in later ages was ravaged by the Thracians, Scythians, and other barbarous tribes. The Byzantines were a commercial people, and at one time enjoyed a position of great prosperity. They are described by ancient authors as an idle, dissipated set, fond of music, dancing, and gaiety, and little disposed to martial exercises, though, in the second Christian century, they resisted the Roman Emperor, Severus, for three years, and at length capitulated only on account of famine. The town was constantly full of foreign sailors, merchants, and fishermen; and, as good wine was to be found there, the carousing was deep and frequent. The citadel of Byzantium stood on the hill where the seraglio is now built, and the rest of the city lay behind the present gardens of the Sultan.

When the place was taken by Constantine I., after the final defeat of his rival, Licinius, the Emperor was so struck with the situation that he determined to build a new city close by, and to make it the capital of his dominions. This city he at first called Nea Roma, but it afterwards received the title of Constantinople, in honour of himself. Constantine had just adopted Christianity, and in May, 330, the new city, which had been commenced not more than three years earlier, was dedicated to the Virgin Mary, amidst a succession of feasts which lasted forty days. The Roman world being divided into the Empire of the West and the Empire of the East, Constantinople became the capital of the latter. The Eastern Empire commenced, as a settled and permanent political condition, with the reign of Arcadius, in 395 of the Christian era, and it lasted until the period with which we are now concerned. The time of its greatest prosperity was under the rule of Justinian the Great, who reigned from 527 to 565, and who to a great extent rebuilt the city, after it had been almost entirely burned in the sedition of the Nika. For many centuries, the Eastern Emperors maintained a splendid court at Constantinople, and made their power felt over a wide extent of territory. The city, however, had to endure many trials. Numberless revolts, plots, and conspiracies occurred within its walls, and it was menaced at different times by the Persians, the Arabs, the Russians,

STORMING OF CONSTANTINOPLE BY BALDWIN, COUNT OF FLANDERS, 1204.

the Venetians, and others. The Mohammedans of Arabia would probably have captured this great seat of empire, when they attacked it in the seventh and eighth centuries, had they not been repelled by the strength of the walls, and by the surprising effects of the Greek fire which the people poured down on them, and which is said to have been then used for the first time. The city was not so fortunate in 1203–4, when it was besieged by the Venetians, under their blind and aged hero, Dandolo, aided by a body of Crusaders, commanded by Baldwin, Count of Flanders. After a prolonged investment, Constantinople was stormed and pillaged, and became the seat of the Latin Empire, beginning with Baldwin, and lasting till 1261, when the city was recovered by the Greeks, who renewed the Eastern Empire in its old seat of authority. But the majestic days of that dominion had departed; and less than two centuries later, the Imperial capital itself lay at the mercy of a Turkish Sultan.

Constantinople is built on a triangular promontory, projecting into the Sea of Marmora. Two of its sides are washed by that sea and by the Golden Horn, or port; and the third connects the promontory with the mainland of Thrace, at the eastern extremity of which province the city has been reared. In the middle of the fifteenth century, Constantinople was provided with walls on all sides. Towards the port, these walls were of very insufficient strength; but in other directions the defences were everything that could be desired, and from the Egri Kapousi, or Crooked Gate, adjoining the Bosphorus, as far as the Seven Towers, a double wall and a double fosse had been provided for the protection of the town. The base of the fortifications was composed of vast masses of rock, heaped together in the rugged style termed Cyclopean. To an observer from without, the long, high line of wall looked like the perpendicular face of a mountain; but, owing to the hilly ground on which Constantinople is built, there are points from which an external spectator can look over the ramparts into the interior of the city. At the period of Mohammed's attack, the entrance to the port was obstructed by two iron chains, and by the vessels in the harbour; and the suburb of Galata, on the opposite side of the Golden Horn, was strongly fortified towards the land, though accessible from the direction of the sea.

On the whole, the position was a good one to defend, had there only been sufficient men to defend it. It is easy to see with whom lay the moral right; but the material power was with Mohammed, and he cared little for abstract questions, or niceties of conscience, where the extension of his sway was concerned. With sleepless energy, he accelerated his preparations for the grand assault. Every detail in the vast machinery of conquest was superintended by himself. Enormous cannon were day by day planted in the most favourable positions, and high wooden towers, moving upon rollers, were propelled towards the walls, where at the proper moment they were to be filled with troops, who, by means of ladders thrown from the summit of the towers towards the opposing ramparts, would be enabled to cross the ditch, and hurl themselves into the city. Great engines for casting stones, and battering-rams of extraordinary power, were also moved by painful gradations towards the points of attack, and a numerous fleet sailed along the shores of Asia Minor to the Dardanelles. When all was ready for the commencement of active operations, Mohammed advanced at the head of his army. The numbers of that army have been differently stated by various historians. Some speak of 300,000 men, some of 400,000; but Gibbon considers that the total did not exceed 258,000. In any case, however, the greater number consisted of irregular troops, gathered from newly-conquered nations, and inspired with no great enthusiasm for the cause they were compelled to serve. Many of these were without arms, and some were almost without raiment. They were driven forward by the whip or the scimitar, and in all battles were placed in the front ranks, so as to consume a certain amount of the enemy's strength before the flower of the Moslem army rushed on to the assault. The regular troops, by whom the actual work was to be accomplished, were divided into 60,000 horse, and 20,000 infantry.

At the head of his forces, Mohammed set out from Adrianople in the spring of 1453. A Turkish historian, Saad-uddin Effendi, describes in a tone of exultation the magnificence and the formidable aspect of this army as it assembled beneath the eye of the Sultan. Mohammed was delighted with the martial bearing of the men, with the glitter of their arms and armour, and with the splendour of the golden balls surmounting their standards. Having praised the Creator for what had been granted him, he addressed his soldiers, and said, "The Koran declares that to combat for the service of God is a universal commandment, which all must obey." He expounded to them the importance of those precepts in their sacred book which enjoin war against the infidels, and he added that the Prophet had promised, according to the tenor of ancient traditions, that his followers should acquire the spacious city of the Cæsars, and that it should become the residence of his people. The army was followed on its march by the Ulemas, the Sheikhs, and the descendants of the Prophet, by a crowd of holy persons praying for the success of the Sultan's arms, and (to their disgrace be it said) by numerous soldiers of fortune from Hungary, Bohemia, and Germany, who were lured by the hope of plunder. The sun was rising on the 6th of April when this embattled host came within sight of Constantinople. The towers and domes of the Imperial city, seated on its numerous hills, and around them the waters of the Golden Horn, of the Bosphorus, and of the Sea of Marmora, lay disclosed in the fresh light of morning. That sunrise was the sunset of the Eastern Empire.

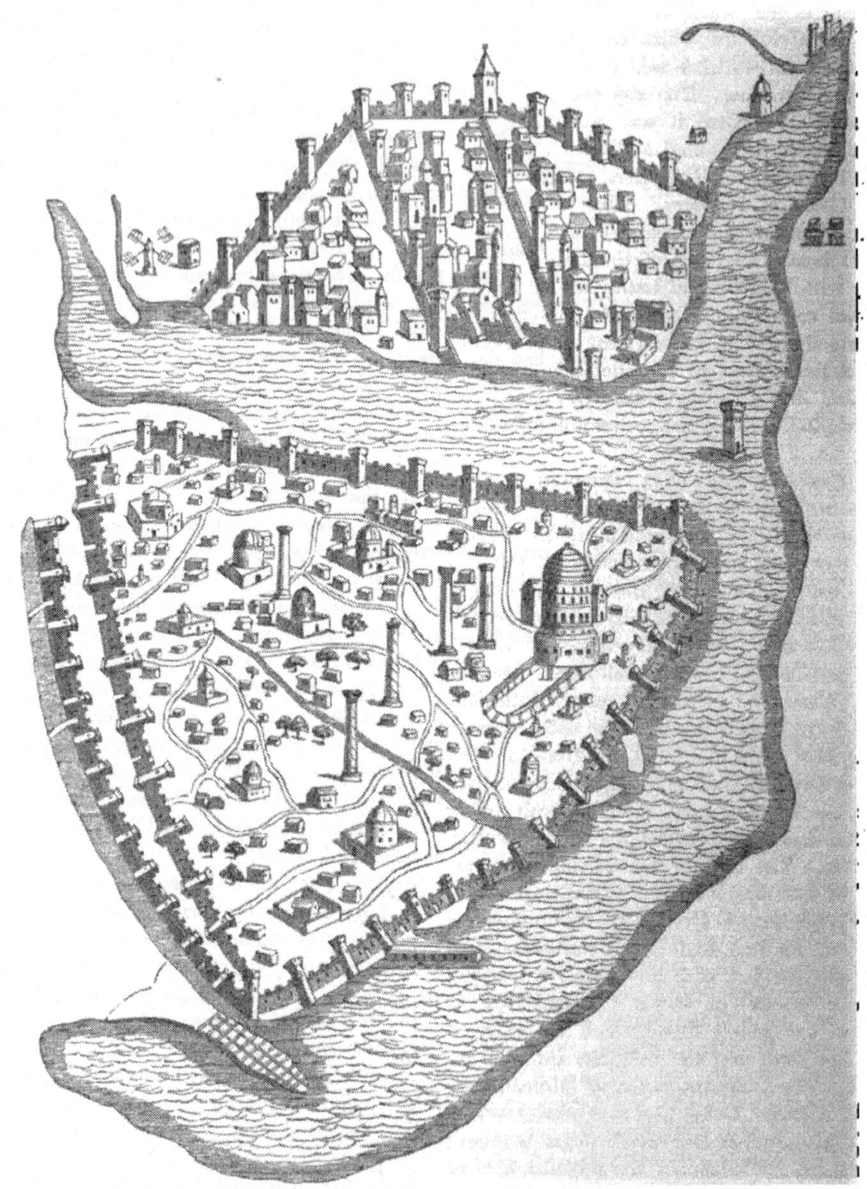

BIRD'S-EYE VIEW OF CHRISTIAN CONSTANTINOPLE.
(From an Engraving in the Imperium Orientale of Anselmo Banduri, Paris, 1711.)

Mohammed halted at a distance of five miles from

SIEGE OF CONSTANTINOPLE BY MOHAMMED II.

the city, and then, advancing in battle-array, planted the standard of the Prophet before the Gate of St. Romanus. The siege began immediately afterwards. The Turkish camp ranged from the Sea of Marmora to the port. Mohammed took his post in the centre of the line, and the Janizaries were stationed in front of his pavilion. To cover his attack, the Sultan cut a ditch parallel to the wall defending the land side of Constantinople. Fourteen batteries were planted opposite the most feeble points in the defences; archers were set to harass the besieged wherever they might show themselves; and subterraneous works were commenced by miners who had been brought from Servia. Within the city, consternation pervaded every rank. To make matters worse, the three thousand Venetians and Genoese who formed part of the defending force were regarded by the Greeks with detestation, because, like other Italians, they were members of the Latin Church. The heart of Constantine, however, did not fail him in this great emergency. He took personal command of the outer wall, and threw some of his own spirit into the crowd of nobles and citizens who formed his subjects. That he had little hope is certain; but he clearly realized from the first that it was his duty to die in the defence of his Imperial city, and to that resolve he continued faithful. The situation, indeed, was not yet desperate. Trenches and mines were opened by the Turks, and some breaches were made in the walls; but these were repaired by the besieged, who were now exhibiting a spirit which, had it been manifested at an earlier date, might have saved them from conquest. They were buoyed up with the fallacious hope of succour arriving from Huniades, who was then acting as the Regent of Hungary; and from time to time they made sorties which staggered the enemy, without driving him from his positions. The stupendous cannon established by Mohammed at various points, with the assistance of his engineer, Urban, proved less effective than had been anticipated. The guns were so unwieldy that with the utmost diligence they could not be discharged more than seven times a day. They were in truth very clumsily worked, until the engineers were better instructed by the Ambassador of Huniades, who was residing in the Turkish camp as a kind of guarantee for the fulfilment by his master of a promise not to assist the Emperor. But if the Turkish artillerymen gained in science with the progress of time, so also did the Christians. Under the direction of Constantine, the besieged after a while kept within the ramparts, and pointed their guns with so much precision that the trenches of the assailants were repeatedly destroyed. Nevertheless, the latter continued to advance, though at an immense cost of life and ammunition. Arriving at the edge of the fosse, the Ottomans attempted to fill up that enormous hollow, and to construct a road to the assault. Fascines, hogsheads, and trunks of trees, were flung into the gap, and the Sultan, directing his men in person, urged them forward with impassioned words and gestures. But Mohammed found the walls and their defences too strong for direct attack, and consequently fell back on the process of mining. This also was a work of extreme difficulty, for the soil was rocky, and the engineers of the Ottomans were sometimes countermined by the Christians. The prospects of the siege began to look so unhopeful that Mohammed considered whether it would not be better to withdraw; but the thought was soon rejected, as unworthy of his martial fame. The struggle grew more desperate on each succeeding day, and every agent of destruction then known to men was used on both sides for determining this tremendous issue. The balistæ of the ancient world stood side by side with the cannon of modern science, and by an elaborate mechanism projected rocks and stones against the ramparts of the city. The besieged, on their side, employed the liquid Greek fire, which appears to have been composed of naphtha, and which in earlier days had saved Constantinople from Mohammedan assaults. Extraordinary spirit and perseverance were displayed by both armies; but the efforts of Mohammed were rewarded by the destruction of the Tower of Romanus, which fell headlong into the fosse, and filled a large portion of the open space. Animated by this success, Mohammed ordered up his men to the assault, which took place under cover of the night, and was splendidly repulsed by the Christians. The commander of the Genoese was John Giustiniani, who seconded the efforts of the Emperor with admirable resolution and skill. The assault having been driven back, he poured forth torrents of burning naphtha and hot oil; and on the following day the Sultan beheld one of his wooden turrets consumed to ashes, the fosse restored, and the chasm caused by the fall of the tower filled up with temporary works.

It was shortly after this sanguinary encounter that succour arrived to the Christians in the shape of five vessels from the island of Chios, or Scio. A strong gale from the south-west carried them through the Hellespont and the Sea of Marmora, and on approaching the Bosphorus they found the multitudinous Turkish ships stretching from shore to shore in the form of a crescent. But the Greek sailors were not daunted. With press of sail and force of oars, they moved forward against a fleet which was to be counted by hundreds. The coasts of Europe and of Asia were crowded by spectators, awaiting the issue of a contest which seemed as if it must necessarily terminate one way. But the Turkish vessels were ill-managed; those of the Christians were handled by sailors to whom the sea is native. Sweeping the waters with their artillery, the Greeks bore down on their adversaries, and, when the latter attempted to board

MOHAMMED ENCOURAGING HIS SEAMEN.

them, vomited forth floods of liquid fire. From the beach, Mohammed, mounted on his horse, watched the varying battle, and encouraged the Ottoman seamen by his voice and actions. He dashed into the sea, as if he could reach his ships, and change the fortune of the battle. His gestures followed the movements of the combatants; when he saw his galleys driven back, he uttered loud reproaches, and urged the sailors to renewed exertions; but all was in vain. The squadron receded after a third attack, scattering in disorder along the opposing shores; and the Christian vessels, which had sustained but little damage, steered along the Bosphorus, and anchored within the chains of the harbour.

This repulse seems to have suggested to the Sultan a device of an extraordinary character, which he proceeded to accomplish. In the course of a single night, he carried eighty galleys overland, by means of machines dragged by multitudes of men over greased planks, extending a distance of some few miles. The vessels were commanded by pilots, and moved with sails set over rugged ground, by the light of torches, and to the sound of trumpets and clarions. The Genoese, who formed the principal inhabitants of Galata, did not dare to offer any opposition to this extraordinary invasion, and the Greeks manning the walls of Constantinople could not understand the meaning of what they saw and heard—the advance of enormous objects through the night, the glare of torches, the gathering of great multitudes, the noise of instruments and of voices. At daybreak, the vessels were launched in the basin of the port, to the utter bewilderment and terror of the besieged, who had no conception that such a thing was possible. The ships had been conveyed from the Bosphorus across the peninsula of Pera, which they traversed by a deep valley joining that of the harbour. It is said that the Genoese sailors at Galata materially assisted the Turks in this transportation, and the device itself has been attributed to a Christian, who is supposed to have learned it from the Venetians. The same thing had been done before at Lake Benacus, and the Christian in the Turkish camp who knew of the fact revealed it to the Sultan. It may, however, have been suggested by a prophecy, frequently repeated in Constantinople, to the effect that the fall of that city was impossible until a sovereign should make his vessels float over the earth with expanded sails. If any hint of this prophecy reached the ears of Mohammed, it is conceivable that it prompted its own fulfilment.

The arrival of the Turkish fleet in the harbour was a new misfortune, which Constantine set himself to encounter with dauntless intrepidity. He sent his vessels to attack the vessels of the foe; but, after losing two ships, which were destroyed by the powerful batteries erected in the port, the Christians were forced to retire. A Venetian proposed to the Emperor to burn the Moslem fleet; but a Genoese betrayed the design to the Sultan, and the attempt, when made, was frustrated. The Genoese came to be generally suspected, though Giustiniani, their commander, was really devoted to the cause of the Empire. Intestine broils broke out from day to day, and were carried to such an extreme that the disputants could scarcely be withheld from shedding each other's blood. The defence was weakened by these unseemly contentions, and Mohammed pressed the siege closer and more sternly every hour. In the narrowest part of the upper harbour, he constructed a mole, fifty cubits in breadth, and one hundred in length. It was formed of casks and hogsheads, strengthened with timber, and braced with iron. Here he mounted his heavy cannon, and combined against the weakest portion of the city the utmost force of his artillery, of his navy, and of his troops. Still the defence went on with heroic resolution, and Giustiniani displayed the greatest readiness in devising new fortifications when the old ones failed. Wild-fire and streams of scalding oil were poured from the ramparts, and the Greeks were supported by the Venetians and the Genoese, notwithstanding that the ranks of the latter were disgraced by some few traitors. For forty days the besieged were scarcely able to rest, either by day or night, owing to the constant necessity of repairing the breaches, and of countermining the advances of the Turks. Khalil Pasha, the Grand Vizier, was bribed to use his influence with the Sultan in the direction of abandoning the siege; and the catastrophe was postponed some few weeks by this method. Yet nothing could avert the end, the imminence of which was apparent even to the most hopeful. Such enormous gaps were torn in the external walls by the action of the Sultan's cannon that the besiegers and the besieged could see each other, and further resistance would soon be impossible. Constantine therefore sent an envoy to the Sultan, proposing to pay whatever tribute he should demand, if he would retire; but the answer of Mohammed was that he must take the city, or the city must bury him. As a counter-proposal, he offered to his adversary a portion of the Morea, if he would give up Constantinople. The Emperor replied that he would rather immolate himself beneath the ruins of his capital than consent to such a humiliation; and in his final message to Mohammed he said:—"Since neither oaths, nor treaty, nor submission, can secure peace, pursue your impious warfare. My trust is in God alone. If it should please Him to soften your heart, I shall rejoice in the happy change. If He deliver the city into your hands, I shall submit without a murmur to His holy will. But, until the Judge of the Earth shall pronounce between us, it is my duty to live and die in the defence of my people." Such was the grand and dignified defiance of one who proved himself worthy to be called the last of the Roman Emperors.

The resolution of Mohammed was now taken. It was the evening of the 28th of May. Rumours were circulating throughout the camp, of assistance to the Greeks being on its way from Italy and Hungary; and it seemed advisable to delay the general assault no longer. The Sultan accordingly issued a proclamation, promising that he would give all the spoil of the capital to his soldiers for three days, if they would win it by their swords. He strictly commanded at the same time that none of the public edifices should be set on fire; but, with this exception, there was no restraint upon the fury of his troops. The proclamation was received with cries of joy. The day had been spent in religious fasting, but the night was given over to festivity and exultation. The countless tents of the besiegers were illuminated; fires were kindled throughout the camp; and, as the night darkened over that imperial scene, innumerable lights shone forth from land and sea, and shouts, as if anticipatory of triumph, rose from the serried ranks of Moslem warriors. It was evident to the beleaguered citizens that the hour of their bitterest agony was at hand. They saw the lights, they heard the shouts, they felt the coil of the great investment drawing closer round the doomed position.

On that terrible evening, the Emperor summoned the leaders of his forces to a consultation at the palace. Gibbon has finely observed that his last speech was the funeral oration of the Roman Empire. The Byzantine historian, Phranza, was himself present at the meeting, and has described what took place. The principal lieutenants of the Emperor were gathered about their master. They wept, they embraced; regardless of their families and fortunes, they devoted their lives to the defence of the city; and each commander, departing to his station, maintained all night a vigilant and anxious watch from the ramparts. The Emperor, accompanied by some of his followers, entered the church of St. Sophia, and devoutly received the Sacrament of the Communion. After briefly reposing in his palace, which echoed with the cries and lamentations of his attendants, he solicited pardon of all whom he might have injured, and, with a firm spirit, though with an entire absence of hope, rode off to the ramparts, and to his death.

The attack began on the following morning, —Sunday, the 29th of May, the feast of All Saints, according to the Eastern Church. Armed with an iron mace, the Sultan proceeded on horseback to the breach. Ten thousand Janizaries surrounded him; more than 100,000 cavalry were on each side, and behind. In various localities, 150,000 infantry were distributed, together with a large number of soldiers in the vessels and on the wooden bridge. The mortal conflict began about daybreak, when the Turks, in the midst of a dead and ominous silence, moved up to the assault by sea and land. The worthless troops were sent first, that they might help to fatigue the defenders, and with the horrible calculation that their heaped-up bodies would fill the ditches, and make a level roadway for the veterans. It was necessary to drive them forward with blows; but on reaching the walls they endeavoured to scale the ramparts with their ladders. These were at once overturned, and for more than two hours the Christians withstood the utmost efforts of their enemy. The Janizaries, and other picked troops, fought with the magnificent courage for which they were always famous. The artillery opened a terrific fire, and Mohammed himself, riding about from point to point of the lines, encouraged his men by every exhortation that his passionate nature could conceive. The first Janizary who mounted the walls of Constantinople, he announced, should be made a Pasha, and be loaded with wealth; others should be rewarded in proportion to their services. There was now no longer any need for the dread silence in which the operations of the day had commenced. The drums and trumpets blared forth with an appalling clamour; and in the midst of endless reverberations, and of the heavy dust of combat, which darkened the heavens and oppressed the air, the resistless troops of the Moslem hurled themselves into the breach. The end had nearly come; the assailants were swarming into the city. Some poured through the gap in the walls in the midst of a ceaseless shower of missiles, consisting of darts, stones, beams of wood, and bars of red-hot iron. Others climbed the ladders and gained the ramparts. But still the defenders would not yield. Women, children, and old men joined in the furious contest, and again the Ottomans were hurled into the ditch. The check, however, was only momentary. Mohammed renewed the assault with fresh animation, and suddenly a cry of victory rose from the Turkish ranks. The seamen in the Golden Horn had gained possession of one of the towers, where they hoisted the standard of the Crescent. Others hewed their way with axes through the city-gates, and Constantinople was now in the grip of her foe. At this moment, a bullet or arrow pierced the hand of Giustiniani. He withdrew to find a surgeon, but was stopped on the way by the Emperor. "Your wound," said Constantine, "is slight; the danger is pressing; your presence is necessary; and whither would you retire?" "I will retire," replied the Genoese, who seems at the last crisis to have lost the courage which he had previously shown, "by the same road which God has opened to the Turks." He passed through one of the breaches in the inner wall, and was seen no more at the front. His example was followed by most of his countrymen, and the defence slackened from that instant. The Emperor, however, still remained at the breach, surrounded by multitudes of dead bodies. He was speedily engulfed in the rushing tide of the Ottomans. "Is there no Christian left alive to strike off my head?" he exclaimed. Then, seeing that he stood in imminent danger of being taken alive, and led in triumph through his own city, he laid aside his gilded armour, and fell amid the tumult as if he had been one of the meanest of his soldiers. The precise manner of his death has been variously reported; but nothing is known with certainty, except that his body was found some time after, beneath a heap of slain, near the breach which he had defended to the last.

The city was pillaged by torch-light, and the Moslem soldiers enriched themselves by an immense amount of gold and precious stones, rich clothes, and costly furniture. More than 40,000 men had been killed in the day's conflict; more than 60,000 were loaded with chains. Every foul and bloodthirsty act which can disgrace a conquering host was committed for three days in the fallen city; then Mohammed restored order, and treated the captives with some leniency. He at once converted the church of St. Sophia into a mosque, from the steps of which a muezzin called the faithful to prayer; but most of the other sacred edifices were left to the Christians. Privileges were conferred on the Greek Patriarch, and liberty of worship was granted to his followers. Cardinal Isidore, the Pope's purchased a number of the Greek captives from his Janizaries, and allotted them the Fanar for their quarter. The Genoese of Galata remained in that suburb, and 5,000 families were chosen out of the Asiatic dominions of the Sultan, and commanded, under pain of death, to settle in the Imperial city by the end of September. The family of the Palæologi survived for some generations. Andrew, son of Thomas, ruler of the Morea, became a Mohammedan at Constantinople after the overthrow of his

WALLS OF CONSTANTINOPLE IN THE SIXTEENTH CENTURY.

Legate, was taken prisoner with the rest; but, having previously changed his clothes, his dignity was unknown, and, being sold for a trifle to a merchant, he found means to escape from captivity, and to return to Rome. Giustiniani soon after died broken-hearted at Chios. Those of the Greeks who were not enslaved escaped into various parts of Europe, but especially into Italy, where their mental accomplishments led to a revival of learning and the arts, which in time spread to remoter regions, and gave birth to that great movement of the modern world which is called the Renaissance. The city of Constantine became almost a solitude, so great was the exodus; but Mohammed afterwards father's principality. Others of the race survived in Italy; and in the parish church of Landulph, in Cornwall, is an inscription on a brass plate, stating that in that spot was interred the body of Theodore Palæologus, of Pesaro, a descendant of the brother of Constantine. This gentleman married an English lady, and died in Cornwall on the 21st of January, 1636. A person calling himself John Anthony Palæologus Lascaris died at Turin in 1874; but his claims were considered doubtful.

Thus fell Constantinople, exactly 1,123 years after its foundation by the Roman Emperor from whom it was named. No event occupies a more important place in history, or is linked in a more remarkable manner with the course of human affairs. The capture of this great city by the Mohammedans marks the final departure of Europe out of ancient into modern annals. As far as Constantinople is concerned, the Middle Ages seem scarcely to exist. The line of the Cæsars continued until the last of the Eastern Emperors fell amongst heaps of slain before the breach that Moslems had effected in the walls of his city. The Greek language, but little corrupted until the dispersion of the Hellenes, still carried on the traditions of the classic ages. But the iron mace of Mohammed shattered the last fragments of a majestic rule, which once had held the world in awe. From that epoch, the Modern Age begins. Something of antiquity, in its vivifying and ever-youthful influences, seems then to have been detached from its stronghold on the Bosphorus, and to have dispersed itself, like winged seeds, over the whole of Europe. Mediævalism shrank before that potent touch; but in the Imperial home of the Greek race a semi-barbaric despotism had planted its stern foot, and the remnants of the old civilization withered beneath the fatal tread.

TREBIZOND.

CHAPTER XXI.

Turkish History continued—Effects of the Fall of Constantinople—Balance between Islamism and Christianity temporarily impaired, but soon restored—Conquest of Greece by Mohammed II.—Suppression of the Empire of Trebizond—Martial Career of the Sultan—His Reverses and his Victories—Character of the Man and of his Reign—Feeble Rule of Bayazid II.—Civil War in Asia—Incidents in the Reign of Bayazid—Mutinous Spirit of the Janizaries—Treacherous Cruelty of the Sultan—Deposition of Bayazid—War with Persia under Selim I.—Persecution of the Shiites—Conquest of Syria and Egypt—Extraordinary Series of Triumphs—Succession of the Sultan to the Spiritual Prerogatives of the Caliphs—Preparations for the Conquest of Persia, and Death of Selim—The Two Barbarossas, and their Conquest of Algiers—Military Achievements of Solyman the Magnificent—Terror inspired by the Ottoman Navy—Political Rule of Solyman—His Merits as a Sovereign—Feeble Character of Selim II.—Depredations of the Barbary Pirates on the Christian Countries of the Mediterranean—The Battle of Lepanto—Great Defeat of the Ottomans—Results of the Christian Victory lost by Want of Energy and Cohesion—Secret Treaty with Venice—The Decline of Turkish Power to be dated from the Reign of Selim II.—Causes of that Decline, as indicated by various Historians.

CONSTANTINOPLE became the capital of the Turkish dominion as soon as Mohammed had won it by his sword; and by this illustrious conquest the Sultans became the heirs of the Eastern Emperors, who were themselves the representatives of the Roman Cæsars. The great city had been lost by the frivolous and disgraceful jealousies of Christendom; for there was strength enough in the chief nations of Europe to have swept back the wave of Ottoman conquest, had there been any principle of union, or any superiority to divisions that concerned only the most paltry issues. The danger to the Western world was of a very serious kind; yet it was permitted to advance undisputed, and it fell at length like a crushing blow, not merely on the regions which it more immediately affected, but on others far removed. It is true that the Turks were seated in Europe before this last achievement of their arms; but the capture of the Imperial city gave them a position of command, both moral and material, such as they had not held before. Christendom awoke to the danger when it was too late. It was now feared that Islamism was about to become the dominant religion of the world, and for a brief period it seemed not improbable that Italy would share the fate of Greece, and that Mohammed would fulfil the threat of Bayazid, and feed his horse on the altar of St. Peter. We must bear in mind that, while the Turks were thus advancing in the south-east of Europe, the Moors were not yet expelled from the south-west. The balance, however, was soon to be readjusted. The union of the crowns of Aragon and Castile, by the marriage, in 1469, of Ferdinand and Isabella, created a strong Spanish monarchy; and in 1492, after the conquest of Granada, the power of the Saracenic princes in the Iberian peninsula was utterly destroyed. By a most remarkable coincidence, it was in that very year—truly an *Annus Mirabilis*—that Columbus discovered America: an event which gave an enormous extension to Christianity, both as regarded the Latin Church, and the several denominations of Protestantism which were shortly to arise.

Never had Christendom stood in so perilous a position since the early conquests of the Saracens, when, in the eighth and ninth centuries of our era, they subdued nearly the whole of Spain and Portugal, invaded France, threatened the Eastern Empire, and established themselves in Sicily. The danger was generally acknowledged, but the remedy was not so obvious, owing to want of cohesion among the Christian princes. Æneas Sylvius, secretary to the German Emperor, and afterwards Pope of Rome under the title of Pius II., bewailed this distracted condition, and described Europe as a body without a head, as a republic without laws or magistrates. Mohammed took advantage of the fact, and proceeded with his conquests. Greece was divided into a number of small and feeble States, quite incapable of resisting a powerful foe. The Sultan turned his arms in that direction, and, in a series of victories extending over several years, added the Morea, and many other parts of Hellas, to his dominions. He had, however, to encounter a formidable opponent in the Venetian Republic, which wrested some of his conquests from him; but on the whole he prevailed, and, in the suppression of the Greek Empire of Trebizond, successfully defied the power of Persia. At that period, Trebizond formed an independent Government, ruled by the Greek family of the Comneni, who, when driven from Constantinople in 1204, took refuge in the ancient Colchis, lying on the southern shores of the Black Sea, where they formed a sovereignty of their own. The Shah of Persia alleged that, on the death of the prince then reigning, the territory would be his by right of descent; but his claims were treated with contempt, and in 1461 Mohammed seized on Trebizond, and put an end to the small State of which it was the capital. This was another blow to the nationality of the Greeks, who now entered on that career of misery and degradation from which they were not rescued until the great uprising which so powerfully moved the sympathy of Lord Byron and his contemporaries.

The long reign of Mohammed, which extended over thirty years, was one unbroken series of martial exploits, which did not always terminate successfully. The Turkish monarch experienced, in particular, a very severe defeat at the hands of John Huniades, whom he besieged at Belgrade. Vast preparations were made for the reduction of that city, and the Sultan himself took the field in person; but, after receiving a dangerous wound in an action fought on the 6th of August, 1456, he was obliged to escape by night with the utmost precipitation. Huniades also was wounded, and died a few days later; but he had the satisfaction of knowing that he had worsted the victor of Constantinople. In Moldavia and Transylvania, the armies of Mohammed suffered discomfiture. Scanderbeg long defied the power of this great sovereign, though, as we have seen, he was finally vanquished. Mischa Palæologus, a Greek renegade, who had been made a Turkish Pasha, was defeated by the Knights of St. John in an attack on Rhodes, in 1480; and Mohammed was so exasperated at this misfortune that he resolved to renew the attack in person, and would probably have done so, had his life been spared. The knights forming the brotherhood had originated in a religious order founded at Palestine about the end of the eleventh century, when the Crusaders seized the Holy Land; and their possession of Rhodes, which they acquired in 1309 or 1310, enabled them to conduct frequent expeditions against Turkish ships, to take rich prizes, and to beard the Ottoman power from the security of their island nest. But against these reverses is to be set the subjugation of Greece, Wallachia, Servia, Bosnia, Albania, Epirus, the Crimea, Karamania, and the principal islands of the Archipelago, or Ægean. With respect to the countries bordering on the Danube and the Adriatic, however, it should be remarked that Mohammed rather restored or confirmed powers of sovereignty which had already been obtained, though never very strongly enforced, than added actually new dominions to the Ottoman Empire. Istria, Carniola, and Dalmatia, on the Adriatic, were ravaged by frequent incursions; Friuli, one of the Venetian States, was invaded; the great maritime Republic was forced to give up Scutari and other places in 1479; Otranto was captured and sacked in 1480; and the Shah of Persia was humbled more than once. The seizure of Otranto spread such alarm throughout Italy that the Pope, Sixtus IV., held himself in readiness to fly beyond the Alps. But the career of Mohammed was nearly at an end. The Persian monarch had entered into a league with some other Eastern princes against the power of the Sultan, whose eldest son, Bayazid, was defeated with great loss. Mohammed fitted out an expedition with remarkable despatch, and departed for the scene of war, but was carried off by a fit of the gout, on the 3rd of May, 1481, at a small town in Bithynia. His remains were buried in Constantinople, and his tomb bore the epitaph,—"I designed to conquer Rhodes, and subdue proud Italy." Grateful for her release, Rome celebrated the death of this persecutor by a three days' festival.

Mohammed was a man of large powers and of superlative wickedness. His cruelty was excessive, even for that age; he was treacherous to a degree scarcely paralleled; no man could depend upon his favour or upon his word. Some acts of fantastic barbarity which have been attributed to him are perhaps apocryphal; but that he never suffered respect for human life to stand in his way, that his displeasure was death, and that he violated his most solemn engagements whenever he found it convenient, are among the best-known facts of history. In morals he was licentious, and his amours seem in no instance to have been qualified by any touch of real affection or nobleness. But his intellect was far above the average. He could speak and write in Arabic, Persian, Greek, and Latin, besides his own language, and possessed an amount of scholarship and taste which is not usual among his countrymen. Poetry was familiar to him, and he was well-read in history, especially in the records of such heroes as Alexander the Great and Julius Cæsar, whom he proposed to himself as models. His own position as a conquerer is undoubtedly one of great distinction. He is said to have subdued twelve kingdoms or principalities, and to have taken more than two hundred towns. In Turkish history he is called Mohammed the Great, or the Victorious; and by Western writers he and his successors were designated Emperors of the Ottomans, in consequence of the acquisition of Constantinople. Though he added so much to the lustre of their arms and the extent of their realm, he was not loved by his own people; partly on account of his cruelty, partly because he was suspected of laxity in religion. He has, indeed, been described as possessing no religion at all. This does not seem to have been the case; but he can hardly have been a very strict Moslem, for he invited to his court the Venetian artist, Gentile Bellini, sat to him for his portrait, and caused him to paint several pictures—things hateful and abominable to every true follower of the Prophet. A singular story is related of this painter's visit to Turkey—a story which is open to some doubt, but which is certainly quite in harmony with the character of Mohammed, and with that of many another despot. The Sultan greatly admired Bellini's picture of the beheading of John the Baptist, but objected that the severed muscles of the neck were not sufficiently retracted. To prove that he was right, he ordered the head of a slave to be smitten off in the presence of the artist; and it is added that Bellini was so horrified at the sight that he never enjoyed another hour's tranquillity until he had returned to Venice.

The conqueror of Constantinople was short, square-set, and remarkable for strength. His complexion was sallow, his aspect melancholy when not ferocious, and his nose large and hooked, dividing eyes that were piercing, hollow, and sunk in his head. So great was his pride that he abolished the custom of allowing the Grand Vizier to dine at the same table as himself; preferring to sit in solitary state, rather than lower his dignity by association even with the chief minister. But the worst thing related of him is that he erected into a law an atrocious custom which had for some time prevailed, and of which he had himself taken advantage—that of murdering the brothers of the reigning Sultan, who might possibly come forward as rivals to the throne. He affirmed that the Ulemas had declared this to be permissible, and that it was necessary for the repose of the world. Yet, notwithstanding all these crimes, Mohammed had some virtues as a ruler. His code of laws, which incorporated portions of what had previously existed at Rome and Constantinople, introduced improvements into the administration of justice. He enforced on all his officers a strict and honest discharge of their duties, and punished with terrible severity any judge who abused his powers. Theft was unknown in

THE GRAND VIZIER DIRECTING THE ASSAULT ON RHODES. *(From Caoursin's MS. in the Imperial Library, Paris.)*

his dominions, and the nation was prosperous, though vexed with continual wars, by which more than 800,000 men are computed to have lost their lives.

The sovereign who filled the throne on the death of Mohammed—Bayazid (or Bajazet) II., son of the great conqueror—was a prince of a poor and irresolute character. It was lucky for the Western world that such was the case; for, had the new monarch pursued with equal vigour the policy of the old, it is impossible to say where the tide of Mohammedan conquest would have stopped. The people of Italy were soon relieved of their fears, for it was evident that the grasp of the Ottomans on that peninsula was getting weaker. Otranto had been seized by Achmet Pasha, the ablest of the late Sultan's lieutenants, and the position was at once fortified by him, as a base of operations for the conquest of the whole country. He then left for Constantinople, hoping to receive final instructions, and to return in the following spring at the head of a great army. The death of Mohammed, however, put an end to the project; and the King of Naples, aided by auxiliaries from Hungary, Spain, and Portugal—for the Christian Powers were now beginning to be seriously alarmed at the progress of Turkish victory—laid siege to the city, and ultimately forced the garrison to capitulate in the course of 1481. The Ottoman Empire was soon threatened by dangers, much more important than the loss of an extraneous conquest. Civil war broke out, owing to the claims of Prince Djem, or Zizimes, a younger son of Mohammed, who had for some time been Governor of Karamania, and who asserted that the will of the late Sultan, by which the sceptre was bequeathed to Bayazid, was a forgery. Djem appeared in arms against his brother, seized on Broussa, the capital of Asiatic Turkey, and advanced towards the Bosphorus. With the assistance of Achmet, Bayazid defeated his forces with great loss; but the Prince renewed his attempt in the following year, and was again worsted. He then fled to Rhodes, where he was hospitably received by d'Aubusson, the military leader who, at the head of the Knights of St. John, had repulsed the Mohammedans in 1480. Fearing, however, to bring upon himself the vengeance of the Turkish Sultan, d'Aubusson sent his captive to France, and he afterwards came into the power of Pope Alexander VI. (the infamous Borgia), who demanded 40,000 ducats a year for his safe custody, or 300,000 ducats for his immediate death. His ultimate fate is not known with absolute certainty; but it is believed that he was poisoned by Alexander, at the desire of his brother Bayazid, in February, 1495.

Numerous wars were waged by Bayazid in the course of his reign, which lasted from 1481 to 1512. Many of these resulted disadvantageously to the Sultan; yet, on the whole, the Ottoman power was increased. The Turkish armies and fleets inflicted great reverses on those of Venice, and at the close of the fifteenth century portions of the north of Italy were invaded by Iskander Pasha. The great object of contention between Turkey and Venice was the possession of various parts of Greece, especially the islands, and, although defeated in some quarters, Bayazid undoubtedly extended his sway over that interesting and valuable region of south-eastern Europe. The reign of this prince was made remarkable by the first treaty ever concluded between an Ottoman Sultan and the Government of Poland, and by the opening of diplomatic relations between the Porte and the Czar of Moscow, Ivan III. The earlier of these events was in 1490; the latter, in 1495. Bayazid was much troubled by the augmentation of the power of Persia which occurred during his time. Shah Ismail, the founder of the Sophi dynasty, seemed as if he would restore that splendour of dominion which has so frequently been seen in Persia; and Bayazid feared him as a rival who might dispute the supremacy in Western Asia. The Shah had in fact encroached on the Sultan's dominions; but the Turkish sovereign was too much occupied in other directions to resent the injury.

An episode in the reign of Bayazid is worth relation, as showing the terms on which these warrior-princes held their power. The Janizaries had with difficulty been restrained by the superior genius of Mohammed, and they now scarcely concealed their want of loyalty towards Bayazid. In 1489, the Sultan conceived a design of reducing their numbers and curtailing their privileges; and in his moments of revelry, when under the influence of wine (to which, despite the prohibition of the Koran, he was addicted), he spoke freely of what he proposed to accomplish. Achmet, whose power with the army, and whose natural independence of character made him singularly bold in opposing the Sultan's humours, reproved his intention, and warned him of the probable consequences. Bayazid accordingly determined on the death of one whose sword had often saved him from ruin, but whose influence was greater than he could endure. He gave a splendid feast, at which Achmet was present, and, after drinking to excess, ordered kaftans of honour to be presented to the guests. That of Achmet was made of black velvet—a sign to its recipient that he was to prepare for death. The other guests retired, and Achmet was left alone in presence of the Sultan and of the executioners. Preserving his self-reliance even under these circumstances, he reproached the Sultan for his vices, and especially for his intemperance. In the midst of his harangue, he was thrown to the ground, and was about to be dispatched, when a eunuch besought the Sultan to respite the Pasha until the ensuing morning, when it would be seen how the Janizaries would act, on the supposition that their leader had been executed. The effect was such as the eunuch probably anticipated. The Janizaries surrounded perfidiously murdered; for, with far less of martial genius, Bayazid had all the tigerish passions which disgraced the character of his father.*

As the reign of Bayazid began with civil war,

DJEM, OR ZIZIMES, DINING WITH D'AUBUSSON, GRAND MASTER OF RHODES.
(From Caoursin's MS. in the Imperial Library, Paris.)

the seraglio, reviled Bayazid in the most insulting language, and threatened him with death; and the revolt assumed so serious a character that it was found necessary to produce Achmet from the dungeon in which he had been confined. At a subsequent period, however, when the Janizaries had been sent away on foreign service, Achmet was so it ended. The Sultan wished to appoint Achmet, one of his sons, as successor to the throne. The eldest son, Kurkud, resisted, and a period of great disturbance ensued, ending in the supreme power being seized, not by either of these princes, but by

* Upham's History of the Ottoman Empire, Vol. I. (Constable's Miscellany, 1829.)

Selim, the youngest son, who was the favourite of the Janizaries. Bayazid quitted the capital, in order to spend the remainder of his life at Demotica, in Roumelia, but died on his journey thither, on the 26th of May, 1512. Selim commenced his reign by the slaughter of his two brothers, and of five of his nephews, the sons of Achmet. The system of government which he established was one of pure terrorism; but it was administered with consummate ability, and it met with the success which is never denied to power. The new Sultan was offended with Persia, because the Shah had espoused the cause of his brother Achmet. He probably found another reason in jealousy of the growing strength of that dominion. He had certainly a third, in religious animosity. The Persians belonged, as they still belong, to a sect of Mohammedans which is regarded by the Turks as heterodox, and the Shah had given great offence to the whole Ottoman people by his treatment of the numerous Sunnites scattered throughout his kingdom. Their mosques had been destroyed, the tombs of their saints had been violated, and they themselves had been subjected to persecution. All these motives conspired to induce in the mind of Selim a spirit of furious hatred against the Persians, and in 1514 he marched into the dominions of his foe. His forces suffered severely in the arid deserts bordering on the Euphrates; but when at length they encountered the Persian army, under the command of Ismail himself, a complete victory was the result, though a victory purchased dearly by enormous losses. Selim commanded his legions to advance in pursuit of the Shah; but they refused, owing to the terrible nature of the desert, and the agonies they had already endured. At the same time, Ismail began to rally his forces, and to march with augmented numbers against the enemy by whom he had recently been repulsed. Selim retreated behind the Euphrates, hotly pursued by the Persians, who slew large numbers of his men; but a second campaign, undertaken in the following year, was attended by greater success. Diarbekr was seized, with the goodwill of its inhabitants; Kurdistan was rapidly overrun; and in a little while the whole mountainous country bordering on the province of Van, and the vast territory comprised within the peninsula of Mesopotamia,

VIEW IN KURDISTAN.

were annexed to the Turkish Empire. The Shiites, or heretics of Persia, were treated with the utmost inhumanity. Forty thousand were put to death, and the Sultan was vindicated in his ferocity by a sentence of the Grand Mufti, who declared that the death of one Shiite was more agreeable to God than that of seventy Christians.

The next enterprise of Selim was directed against Egypt, which he reached by way of Syria, then a dependency of the larger country beyond the Isthmus of Suez. The rulers of Egypt at that period were a race of Mohammedan sovereigns, to whom old English writers gave the title of Soldan—evidently the same word as Sultan. The descendants of the Arabian Caliphs, whose power had now vanished like a dream, dwelt beneath the sceptre of these Egyptian monarchs, who held them in a species of captivity, yet treated them with the reverence supposed to be due to their sacred character as representatives of the Prophet. Although the Caliphs had no longer the slightest tittle of secular power, they were still the Commanders of the Faithful, and were regarded much as the Roman Pontiff is regarded at the present day in the city of the Tiber, whence he issues his spiritual mandates, but where he is no longer a temporal sovereign. The hope of succeeding to the lofty title of Commander of the Faithful may have had something to do with the readiness of Selim to undertake so difficult an enterprise as the conquest of Egypt; but the immediate occasion of that exploit was the alliance that had been concluded between the Soldan and the Shah. The expedition was planned with much skill, and carried out with extraordinary energy. In the neighbourhood of Aleppo, a battle, marked by varying fortune, took place between the invaders and the defenders of the menaced land. Those celebrated horsemen of the Egyptian sovereign, the Mamelukes, inflicted terrible losses on Selim's army, and at one time almost achieved the victory; but in the end success fell to the Sultan, owing partly to the effect of his artillery, and partly to the treachery of some of the Soldan's allies. In this great battle, which was fought on the 17th of August, 1516, the Soldan lost his life, not from wounds, but from the effects of rage and despair, and from the exhaustion caused by his personal efforts to retrieve the fortune of the day. As a consequence of the victory, the cities of Damascus, Tripoli, Beyrout, Sidon, and Antioch, sent deputies to conciliate the goodwill of the conqueror, and to acknowledge his authority; and thus all Syria submitted to the Turkish rule. Damascus, which had long been the residence of the Caliphs, and which has always been one of the most luxurious and entrancing cities of the East, surrounded by gardens of perfect beauty, and in itself majestic with the traditions of successive sovereignties, was an additional ornament of a most noble character to the Empire of the Sultan. Thence, in the intoxication of triumph, Selim proceeded through Palestine, which submitted without a murmur to the rule of this successful soldier. The desert of Cairo, which had been rendered less suffocating by abundant rains, was traversed by the Ottomans in ten days; and in the vicinity of Cairo itself the Turks and the Egyptians again joined battle in 1517. The struggle ended in the renewed success of the former, and the Egyptian commander, Touman Bey, then retreated into Cairo, fortified the gates and avenues, and collected his strength in the chief street. Selim, however, forced his way in, and another desperate encounter took place amongst the houses. The barricades and trenches were valiantly defended by the Mamelukes, and even the women and children took part in the fiery conflict, which lasted two days, and was rendered the more terrific by a portion of the city being set in flames by order of Selim, who for a time despaired of victory. It was not until another division of the Ottoman force had burst in from a different direction that the Mamelukes took to flight. Touman Bey made his escape in disguise, and the city was given up to pillage, and to indiscriminate slaughter.

After achieving this great feat, the Sultan visited Mecca and Jerusalem, and then returned to Constantinople, taking with him Mohammed XII., the last representative of the Abasside Caliphs, from whom he extorted the scimitar, the standard, and the mantle of the Prophet. These were the insignia of the Caliphate, and their possessor is regarded throughout the Sunnite portion of the Mohammedan world as the head of Islam in its spiritual capacity. The desires of this superb conqueror grew more enormous with success. On his way back to Constantinople, he had been met at Aleppo by a Persian ambassador bearing magnificent presents, who saluted him, by the Shah's command, as the Emperor of Emperors. But he was not satisfied with this merely verbal compliment: he desired the reality of power in that great dominion which the Arabian Caliphs had subdued in an earlier age; and he made a public oath at Constantinople that he would never recede a step until he had utterly subverted Persia, and extinguished a race odious to God and man. Vast preparations were commenced for the prosecution of this design; but, before the expedition could set forth, Selim was attacked by a mortal disease, as he was journeying from the capital to Adrianople. He died on the 22nd of September, 1520; and it is said that during the torments of his last illness, which proceeded from an imposthume in the thigh, and lasted forty days, he reproached himself with the blood which he had shed in the course of his reign. There has, indeed, never been a sovereign who in so short a space loaded himself with a greater accumulation of crimes against humanity. As a conqueror, he takes very exalted rank; but in every other respect he has justly earned the execration of posterity.

The extension of the Turkish power over the northern coast of Africa, during the reign of Selim and his successor, is a curious chapter in the records of the sixteenth century. Under the general designation of the Barbary States were included the five kingdoms of Morocco, Fez, Algiers, Tunis, and Tripoli; all of them peopled by a Saracenic race, which had in time mingled with the native African stock. It was from these regions that the warlike Moors issued forth to seize on Spain; and there the descendants of those conquerors are still to be found, mourning over their lost greatness, and dreaming of some distant future which shall restore to them the Paradise of Granada, and the wealth of Andalusian valleys. After the expulsion of the Mohammedans from the Iberian peninsula, the Moors, and their congeners in that part of Africa, were so weakened, impoverished, and cast down, that the Spaniards and Portuguese obtained a footing in several of their cities. But this Christian supremacy was not to continue long without dispute. In the year 1474, a humble potter in the island of Mytilene—a Greek and a Christian—had a son born to him, who was destined, after becoming a Mohammedan, to re-establish the superiority of Moslem power on the southern coasts of the Mediterranean. The youth, when twenty years of age, changed his religion, went on board a Turkish privateer, and took the name of Horush. He then sailed along the coasts of the Mediterranean, capturing rich Spanish and Italian prizes, and in time creating for himself so great a reputation for prowess in this species of warfare that many Turkish and Moorish adventurers applied to serve under him. Thus he became the Admiral of a good-sized fleet, the head-quarters of which were at Goletta, the harbour of Tunis. The reigning Bey of Tunis, Muley Mohammed, was very glad to receive these corsairs hospitably, as, in return for the use of his harbour, they promised to aid him against the Spanish monarch, then threatening hostilities. The name Barbarossa, by which the chief commander was known, is said to have been given him by the sailors of the Christian Powers, on account of his red beard; though some derive it from Baba (Father) Horush, as he was called by his own men. Whatever the meaning of his name, he was the dismay of the European merchant-vessels trading from port to port in those regions; and in an equal degree he was regarded as the hope of the Mohammedan sovereignties in Northern Africa. A petty Moorish prince, who in 1512 had been dispossessed of his territories near Algiers by the Spaniards, solicited the assistance of Horush, who made two unsuccessful attempts to recover the realm, in the first of which he lost his left arm. His failure in this respect, however, did not at all diminish his reputation, and shortly afterwards the Algerines begged his help towards expelling the Spaniards from the little island of Algesiras, in front of Algiers, where they levied a tribute on ships coming there to trade. Horush went to Algiers with a large body of his Turks, and soon changed his manner from that of an ally to that of a master. In 1516 he succeeded in making himself an independent Sultan, whose dominions extended as far west as the frontiers of Fez. But the Spaniards, alarmed at the rise of such a power close to some of their own settlements, sent a large force against Barbarossa in 1518, and the usurper was defeated and killed in an engagement on the banks of the river Maileh.

Nevertheless, the kingdom he had established still remained, and the supreme power was now exercised by the brother of Horush, a leader of equal daring and ability, by the Turks called Khair Eddin, and by the Christians Barbarossa II. As it soon became apparent that he would not be able to resist, unaided, the assaults of Spain, he offered his dominions to Selim, by whom they were accepted, and Khair Eddin became Viceroy of Algeria, with a strong body of Turkish troops to defend the possession. The balance of power was re-established in favour of the Mohammedans, and in 1530 Barbarossa II., after several ineffectual attempts, took the island opposite Algiers which the Spaniards had occupied, and which he then connected with the mainland by a mole which gave security to the harbour. Large numbers of Christian slaves were employed on this work, and also on the extensive fortifications by which the city of Algiers was strengthened. At the same time, the Algerian galleys swept the Mediterranean, striking terror into the crews of Christian vessels, and taking costly argosies, laden with the riches of the old world and the new. Tunis was conquered by Barbarossa about 1532, and some two years later he was appointed by the Sultan Pasha of the Seas, or Great Admiral, to oppose the operations of Andrea

Doria. His career was for the most part one of extraordinary success, both by sea and land; but the Spaniards under Doria took Goletta and Tunis in 1535 (when 10,000 Christian slaves were set at liberty), and these places were not finally recovered by the Turks until 1574, during the reign of Selim II. From that time, the Turkish power on the northern coast of Africa was so strongly consolidated that none of the European nations could compete with it. Algiers and Tunis became names of dread to the whole of Christendom; and after the death of the second Barbarossa, in 1546, the adventurous sea-rover, Dragut, became the most formidable of these banditti. The corsairs who issued from the sea-port towns of Northern Africa enriched themselves by their depredations, and at the same time helped to support the predominance of the Ottoman Empire by the abject fear with which they inspired the coast-towns of Southern Europe through many generations; and the only excuse which could be found for their crimes was in the necessity of keeping some check on the continual depredations of the Knights of Malta committed on Turkish ships. The sufferings of Christian slaves in the

BARBAROSSA II. (*From a Painting by Velasquez.*)

galleys of Algiers are celebrated in numerous legends and ballads, in one of the episodes of "Don Quixote," and in the second chapter of "Robinson Crusoe." To serve in a privateer against the corsairs of Barbary, was long considered the finest manifestation of spirit which a young man could show.

The greatness of the Ottoman Empire was at its height under the sceptre of Solyman the Magnificent, or the Lawgiver, the only son of Selim I. Its military power was unequalled, either in Asia or in Europe, though an attack on Vienna, in 1529, was repulsed. Hungary was reduced to the condition of a vassal State, and the crown of that kingdom was conferred by Solyman on John Zapolya, who received it as a creature of the Sultan. Armenia and Irak, with the cities of Tabriz and Baghdad, were detached, in 1534, from the Persian monarchy. Yemen and other parts of Arabia were subjugated by the Ottoman Pasha of Egypt, and armaments were sent into Guzerat to aid the Indian Moslems against the Portuguese. The Turkish fleet became masters of the Mediterranean, and laid waste the shores of Italy and Spain. Venice, no longer at the height of her august dominion, did not venture to dispute the maritime supremacy of the Ottomans, and Francis I. of France thought it prudent to seek their alliance. The island of Rhodes, which had defied Mohammed the Great, succumbed to Solyman the Magnificent, and the fraternity of religious knights, who were permitted to withdraw, ultimately found a home in Malta. On the death of John Zapolya, in 1541, a large part of Hungary was incorporated with the Ottoman Empire. Transylvania was subdued in 1552, and it was only by continual exertions and immense sacrifices that Austria succeeded in defending her part of Europe from the restless activity of the Turks. Wars were also conducted with Persia, not altogether without success; and a great naval victory, in 1560, over the combined fleets of the Christian Powers, at Djerbeh, on the African coast, confirmed for a time the naval superiority which had been mainly acquired by the two Barbarossas. The Turkish fleet, however, experienced a great reverse in 1565, when, having laid siege to Malta, they were repulsed with extraordinary gallantry by the Grand Master, John de la Valette. Solyman cannot be reproached with the extravagant crimes committed by his father. He was a legislator and reformer, as well as a soldier: the finances of his empire and the administration of justice were established by him on bases so suited to the Turkish character that they remained for many generations the settled constitution of the Ottoman dominions. The excessive power of the Janizaries was balanced by the creation of another body, called the Bostangis, who were nominally gardeners, but in reality soldiers in disguise, appointed to watch over the safety of the monarch. Though not incapable of sternness, the Sultan was a man of generous and noble character. He began his reign by causing it to be proclaimed throughout the Empire that whoever had been unjustly treated, either by his father or his father's ministers, should be indemnified out of the Imperial treasury; and that which he promised, he performed. When, after a most arduous siege, he had taken the island of Rhodes, in 1522, he treated the Grand Master and his followers with leniency; and on other occasions he proved his superiority to those savage and destructive passions which he might well be supposed to have inherited with his blood. As an encourager of the arts, he added greatly to the magnificence of Constantinople, and he facilitated the internal communications of his realm by the construction of roads and bridges. His love of literature, and especially of poetry, softened what might otherwise have been too rigorous in his character; and it is to be regretted, in the interests alike of Christians and of Mohammedans, that Sultans such as he have not been more common. He died in his tent, in September, 1566, while conducting one of his expeditions against Hungary. Mortification at the failure of repeated assaults appears to have brought on one of those apoplectic seizures which ended the lives of so many of the Sultans.

The eight years during which Selim II. occupied the throne were years of changeful fortune. They were not wanting in some splendid triumphs, and the Ottoman Empire, already of vast extent, received further additions under the sceptre of this monarch. But Selim himself was a man of feeble character, and it is from the period of his reign that we must date the decline of Turkish power. The Sultan was an idler, a sensualist, and a drunkard; and, had the conduct of affairs rested entirely with him, his realm would probably have been visited by some great disaster. He was surrounded, however, by able counsellors, and the vigour of the Turkish character, though now beginning to relax, was still capable of performing remarkable feats, when occasions of sufficient importance called it forth. The island of Cyprus was wrested from the Venetians in 1571, after a vigorous resistance; but in that same year the Turkish fleet experienced a reverse which for the first time proved that the Powers of the West, when united and resolved, were more than a match on the ocean for the galleys of the Sultan. The Christian States were so much alarmed by the fall of Cyprus that the Pope of Rome, Philip II. of Spain, and the Venetian Republic, united for their common safety. Selim, becoming acquainted with this powerful combination, ordered his admirals to commit every species of hostility in the dominions of the Confede-

TOMB OF SOLYMAN THE MAGNIFICENT.

rate Powers; and these orders were carried out with so much zeal that the Venetians found it necessary to fortify their capital, and several of their possessions, lest they should fall into the hands of the enemy. Many of the Turkish vessels were little better than pirate ships, commanded by the Barbary corsairs, and manned by sailors whose courage and whose knowledge of the sea were of the highest order, but whose ferocity and love of plunder knew no limits. Ranging about from coast to coast, and from town to town, these men, obeying no law but their own will, and restrained by none of the responsibilities of civilised warfare, were enabled to inflict frightful damage on the places which they visited, and were for many years the terror of the whole Mediterranean sea-board. Their methods of procedure were similar to those afterwards adopted by the buccaneers who ravaged the coasts of South America for the gold, the precious stones, and the rich merchandize, which Spanish and other colonists had accumulated in the ports and harbours. But the Barbary corsairs formed part of a regular navy, and were actuated by religious fanaticism as well as by desire of pillage. Sallying forth in their light, fleet vessels from the Mohammedan towns of Northern Africa, they swarmed over all the neighbouring seas, and fell like a pestilence on the shores of Italy, of Spain,

BATTLE OF LEPANTO.

and of other lands bordering on the Mediterranean. Doubtless, the navy of the Sultans contained honourable warriors as well as pirates; but the rulers of Constantinople did not disdain the assistance of wretches whose trade was robbery and massacre.

Christendom was for a time stunned with dismay at the accumulation of misfortunes thus heaped upon it; but when a more manly spirit once more took possession of its princes, it was resolved to deal boldly with an evil which threatened every maritime State from the Pillars of Hercules to the Ægean. A powerful fleet was fitted out by the Confederated States already mentioned, and in 1571 the several contingents assembled in the Straits of Messina. The principal military commander was the gallant young hero, Don John of Austria, a natural son of the Emperor Charles V. The chief naval commander was Admiral Doria. On board this fleet, besides the seamen, were 20,000 soldiers, amongst whom were several persons of high position, who served as volunteers. The whole enterprise, however, narrowly escaped a disgraceful termination; for the different nationalities began quarrelling amongst themselves before they had seen the enemy, and Don John, in particular, was highly exasperated by the execution of a Spanish captain who had been concerned in some mutinous disturbance. Fortunately, the feud was composed after awhile, and it was then determined to sail directly for Lepanto, where the Turkish fleet was at that time lying. The Gulf of Lepanto is situated near Corinth, and is surrounded by land, excepting towards the west, where it is approached from the Ionian Sea through a narrow channel. The Turkish fleet, which consisted of 335 sail, was lying secure in the harbour, and a question arose among its officers whether it would be advisable to leave that position, and give battle to the enemy. Mohammed Bey, a person of great years and experience, was opposed to taking any active measures; but Ali Pasha, who appears to have been deceived by an erroneous report as to the number of the Christian vessels, strongly recommended that they should engage the Confederates without a moment's delay. His advice prevailed. Twelve thousand Janizaries and Spahis, draughted out of the neighbouring garrisons, and 4,000 other soldiers, were taken on board; and the fleet then stood out of the Gulf, and steered its course for the island of Echinates, halfway between Lepanto and Patras. The Christian vessels at the same time moved up from the west, and the two fleets came in sight on the afternoon of the 7th of October.

The day was far spent before the battle commenced; but this did not hinder either side from fighting with the utmost resolution and fury. The signal being given to the Christian fleet by the hoisting of the Confederate standard, the Turks set up a cry, and fell on six galeasses which lay at anchor nearly a mile in front of the allied forces. The attack was repulsed with much gallantry, and the Turks were now greatly inconvenienced by the clouds of smoke which a brisk wind, just then blowing from the west, carried full in their faces. Nevertheless, they re-formed their line of battle, which had been somewhat broken in the collision with the galeasses, and bore down swiftly on their adversary. Ali Pasha, singling out the galley of Don John, ran upon her with so much violence that the prows of both vessels were broken off, and the encounter now became more close and deadly. The opposing vessels grappled one another; the Turkish ships were boarded again and again; again and again the Christians were driven back with frightful loss; but the issue was not determined for some hours. The combatants fought with spears and swords, with cannon and muskets, with arrows and javelins, with fire-balls, and with every instrument of destruction that they could adopt. Surrounded by four hundred Janizaries, Ali Pasha came into personal combat with Don John, who had with him an equal number of chosen troops, consisting mostly of officers. In other directions, contests of no less fury were proceeding between the Christians and the Moslems. Venieri, the Venetian Admiral, took two of the Turkish galleys; Colonna, the Pope's Admiral, captured one; Ligni, the Genoese commander, had the same success; and Giovanni Contareni seized the vessel of Mohammed Bey, who was slain in the encounter, together with the greater number of his men. Meanwhile, Don John was sustaining the repeated and furious assaults of Ali Pasha, who was at length mortally wounded, and then slain outright. This was the turning-point of the battle. The head of Ali was cut off, and held up on the point of a spear; and at the same moment the banner of the Cross was displayed from the mainmast of the Pasha's galley, the crew of which, enfeebled by their terrible losses, and discouraged by the death of their commander, could offer no further resistance. A shout of "Victory! victory!" ran along the Christian line. The Turkish fleet was struck with dismay; the order of battle was hopelessly broken up; and several vessels fled towards the shore, pursued by the galleys of Candia, which captured large numbers of them. The conflict was prolonged for some time by the left wing of the Turkish fleet, which was opposed to the Spanish contingent at a considerable distance from the other squadrons. In this direction, the fighting was decidedly in favour of the Ottomans; but when their commander understood that his comrades of the centre and right wing were overthrown, he considered it prudent to provide for his own safety in flight.* The general results of this great battle were that the Turks lost 25,000 men killed and 8,000 taken prisoners; that 15,000

VENICE.

Christian slaves were set at liberty; and that 30 Turkish galleys were sunk, 25 burned, and 140 taken: the other vessels escaped. The Confederates lost 15 galleys, and about 10,000 men; and among the wounded was a man who has written his name on the pages of universal literature,—the great creator of one of the greatest characters in fiction,—Michael Cervantes, the author of the immortal "Don Quixote." He has turned his experiences on that occasion to some account in his chief work, where also are several details, evidently historical, of the contests between the Turks and the Spaniards for the possession of Goletta and Tunis.†

At Rome and Venice, the news of the victory was received with transports of joy. It was believed that the naval power of Turkey had been entirely broken, and, although this was a mistake, the Christian success was not without important consequences, since (as Cervantes has remarked) it damaged that reputation for invincibility at sea which the Turks had long enjoyed, and showed that the resources of Europe were in this respect greater than those of the Asiatic Empire. Selim was so astonished and afflicted by the intelligence that for three days he neither ate nor drank, nor suffered

* Universal History, 1781. Vol. X. of the Modern Part.

† See "The History of the Captive," forming the twelfth, thirteenth, and fourteenth chapters, Part IV., of "Don Quixote."

anybody to approach him. On the fourth day he took up the Koran, and, according to the story, accidentally opened it at this passage:—"In the name of God, clement and merciful, I grieve for the victory which the Europeans obtained over the inhabitants of the earth. Gladness shall not be given them any more for victory hereafter." The Sultan accepted these words as a proof that the reverse which he had suffered would speedily be repaired; and to some extent this was the case. The Confederates, still divided by petty jealousies, lost valuable time in debating what they should do next. Finally, they determined to take no further steps of importance till spring, and the months thus wasted were turned to good account by the Ottomans in creating a new fleet. A few scattered successes on the coasts of Greece were obtained by the Venetians; but in the course of the following year the naval superiority of the Turks was again established. Philip of Spain had never been heartily in the enterprise, fearing lest the power of Venice should in this way be aggrandized; and the maritime Republic, apprehensive of being left alone, concluded a secret treaty with the Turks. When the Venetian Minister presented himself before the Grand Vizier at Constantinople, that officer said, in reply to some observations hinting at the recent victory, "Learn that the loss of a fleet to my master the Sultan is as the beard of a man, which grows the thicker for the shaving; but the loss of Cyprus to Venice is as an arm cut off from the body, which no art can replace." By the secret treaty, which was concluded in 1574, Cyprus was confirmed to the Turks, to whom several other places were at the same time ceded. The Venetians, moreover, undertook to pay the Sultan 30,000 crowns in gold, towards defraying the expenses of the war; so that, notwithstanding the brilliant success of the allies at Lepanto, Venice, at the conclusion of peace, was in a worse position than when she entered on the contest.

In other respects, the arms of Selim were attended by good fortune; but this was due, not to any personal qualities on the part of the monarch, but to the signal ability of his Grand Vizier, Mehemet, who in fact exercised the supreme authority in the name of his master. Selim died on September 12th, 1574, after a reign of only eight years, leaving behind him an empire greater in superficial extent than that to which he had succeeded, but weaker in some of the highest essentials of military rule, and already beginning to show signs of that fatal decay which later generations made progressively more manifest. "The line of the great Sultans," says a living historian, "had come to an end. Several of the later Sultans were men of vigour and ability; but the succession of great rulers, which, unless we except Bayazid II., had gone on without a break from Othman to Solyman the Lawgiver, now stopped. The power of the Sultans over their distant dominions was lessened, while the power of the Pashas grew. The discipline of the Ottoman armies was relaxed, and the courts of most Sultans became a scene of corruption of every kind."* Knolles, the author of a History of Turkey published in 1610, has remarked on the same facts,—namely, the culmination of the Turkish power under Solyman I., and the commencement of its decline under his successor. He ascribes the rapid growth of that power to the abilities and long reigns of the first ten Sultans, extending from 1300 to 1566, which gives an average of twenty-six years and a half to each. These Sultans were for the most part men of temperate habits, of great energy, and of marked capacity for the science of government. They were trained to war and business by the command of provinces, before they reached the supreme power, and their counsellors and generals were singularly gifted, both as politicians and as warriors. Other causes of the Turkish success are discovered by Knolles in the admirable discipline and constitution of the professional troops employed by the Ottomans—troops which, being constantly engaged in warlike operations, were far superior to the occasional levies of the Christian States; in their formidable artillery and firearms, which were worked by the most skilful engineers of Europe; in the character of the Turkish despotism, which enabled the Sultans to act with secrecy and despatch against their enemies; and in the extraordinary stimulus to their officers resulting from the fact that, from the highest to the lowest, they depended, even to their lives, upon their master's pleasure. It was an unfortunate feature in the political arrangements of Solyman—unfortunate, that is to say, for the continuance of Turkish supremacy—that he established the system of bringing up the heirs to the throne in the Seraglio, and not, as formerly, in the army, and in the circles of government. In many respects, Solyman was a wise, just, and thoughtful ruler; but in this respect he committed a fatal error. The princes of the House of Othman became thenceforth, except in a few instances, enervated and enfeebled. They succeeded to the throne without any knowledge of affairs, and with little capacity to acquire it; for the society of frivolous and degraded women had contracted their minds and lowered their moral tone to the level of slaves and eunuchs. The consequences were speedily

* The Ottoman Power in Europe, by Edward A. Freeman, D.C.L., LL.D. 1877.

seen in the wide diffusion of luxurious habits, which had in them nothing that was noble, little that was graceful, and everything that was vile. The Pashas soon became as the Sultans, and the huge, overgrown Empire was infected at the heart. The reaction of Christendom against the power of the Osmanlis dates from the battle of Lepanto; but it was many years before any important effect was observable. From the close of the sixteenth century to comparatively recent times, the history of the Turkish Empire is a painful record; and it says much for the inherent excellence of the Turkish character, even under the worst political conditions, that the mass of the Ottoman race should have retained so many virtues, despite the influence of rulers so corrupting and corrupt.

CHAPTER XXII.

Turkish History continued—Decline of Turkey as a conquering Power—Development of Indolence and Sensuality—The Fall of the Turkish Empire anticipated in the First Half of the Seventeenth Century—Speculations of Dr. Heylyn—Predatory Incursions of the Cossacks—War with Persia—Character of Amurath IV.—Recovery of the European Powers from their Depression—Turbulence of the Janizaries—Accumulated Disasters—English Embassy to Constantinople in the Reign of Charles II.—Paul Rycaut's Account of the Turks at that Period—Turkish Fear of the Russians in the Second Half of the Seventeenth Century—Causes of Turkish Decay, according to Rycaut—Treatment of the Christians—Contemptuous Toleration and Harsh Obstruction—Renegades from Christianity—The Austrian Empire as a Rival to the Ottoman Power—War on the Danube—Heroic Efforts of Mustapha II.—The Peace of Carlowitz—Reign of Achmet III.—War between Russia and Turkey (1768-74)—The Treaty of Kainardji—Commencement of the Russian Protectorate over the Eastern Christians—Amelioration in the Condition of the Christians antecedent to Russian Interference—Predominance of Russia in the East—Acquisition of the Crimea—War of 1787-91—Misfortunes of the Turks—The Treaty of Jassy—Russia in the Black Sea—Civil War in the Turkish Empire—Invasion of Egypt by the French under Bonaparte—Turkey at War with England and Russia—The Reforms of Selim III.—Deposition and Murder of Selim—Brief Reign of Mustapha IV.

After the death of Selim II., Turkey lost its distinctive character as a conquering Power, and settled down into a state of comparative repose, which in time became lethargy. Not that the sword was sheathed: military expeditions were still made, and new territories were occasionally acquired. But the immense energy which in previous ages had carried the Turk with the impetuosity of a tidal wave over so large a part of Asia and Europe, and which appeared to gather strength from its own momentum, had now in some degree spent itself. The pretensions of the Ottomans, though by no means abandoned, were not so confidently advanced as before; and it seemed to be considered that, unless under provocation, the Empire should rest content with its achievements. Solyman the Great was wont to say that whatsoever belonged to the Empire of Rome was his by right, as he stood possessed of the Imperial seat and sceptre of the first Constantine, commander of the world. But this assumption, which was not without a certain plausibility, was no longer put forward as the excuse for fresh aggressions. Diplomacy was beginning to take the place of chieftainship. In the reign of Amurath III., extending from 1574 to 1595, Turkey opened friendly relations with most of the European countries, and a commercial treaty was concluded with England. It came to be considered that war is not the only employment of life—that peace has its delights and its duties. Unfortunately, the Turk has always been in the main a soldier, and peace developed some of his worst qualities. The Sultans became mere sensualists; the Pashas grew slothful and corrupt. The traditional vices of Constantinople seem to have entered into the ruling classes, and luxury, pleasure, and idleness, were considered the great ends of life. Whatever their faults, the Turks of earlier ages had certainly not been sluggards; but now they acquired those lounging habits of dreamy reverie which we are apt to associate with the idea of an Oriental. An old English traveller in Turkey relates that one day, when he was taking his ordinary exercise, together with some companions, a Turk demanded of them whether they were out of their way, or out of their wits. If their way lay towards the upper end of the cloister, why did they come downwards? If to the lower end, why did they go back again? To sit on a carpet in the shadow, to shoot languidly at a mark, and to send some of their slaves for the arrows, were the favourite pastimes of the Ottomans in the days of their decline.

The deterioration of the Turkish race, as a dominant force in Europe, proceeded so steadily that, in the first half of the seventeenth century, during the reign of Amurath IV., we find the approaching fall of the Empire a matter of frequent speculation.

The old cosmographer, Peter Heylyn, writing about 1629, puts the case very strongly in his account of Turkey. There were many reasons, he said, for believing that the Ottoman Empire was in the wane. In the first place, the body had grown too monstrous for the head; the Sultans, since the death of Solyman I., never accompanying their armies in person, but rioting in luxury at home. Then the Janizaries had become more factious than ever, and, corrupted by ease and liberty, drowned in prohibited wines, and enfeebled by vicious indulgences, had fallen from their ancient discipline, so as to be far less effective in the camp than formerly. The Ottomans had of late made no increase in their dominions; and it was in those days an article of political faith that Empires built up by violence (as indeed all Empires are) begin to diminish as soon as they cease to augment. Rebellions of a formidable character had recently broken out, and been with difficulty suppressed. The sons of the Grand Signor (as our old English writers delighted in calling the Sultan) were reared up in effeminacy, which they were not able to shake off when they came to the head of affairs. The Turkish power had been successfully defied, not only by the Venetians, the Hungarians, and the Poles, but even by the poor Prince of Transylvania, while the Dukedom of Florence overawed it with six ships. By the avarice and corruption of the court, all peace and war, all counsels and information, all wrongs and favours, were made saleable. Furthermore, the young prince then reigning seemed to the observant eyes of Heylyn but a weak staff for so huge an Empire to lean on; and, supposing the line of Othman to fail, the dominions of the Sultan would be at the mercy of many accidents. The most likely successors to the Imperial power, in the opinion of this writer, were the Janizaries; "unless," he added, "the princes of Christendom, laying aside private malice, join all in arms to strip this proud peacock of her feathers, and (upon so blessed an advantage) to break in pieces with a rod of iron this insolent and burdensome monarchy: a thing rather to be desired than expected." Thus was the future of the Ottoman Empire regarded by an English politician in the early years of the reign of Charles I.

The line of Othman, however, did *not* cease, and Amurath IV., so far from proving a weak prince, did much to re-establish the prosperity of the State. He was only twelve years of age when, in 1623, he succeeded to the throne on the death of his brother, Osman II., and soon after his accession a rebellion occurred in Asia, which resulted in the loss of several provinces. Baghdad fell into the hands of the Persians, and in 1624 the Tartars of the Crimea defeated the forces of the Turkish Pasha who governed that dependency. The Don Cossacks, moreover, were now becoming a source of trouble, if not of actual danger, to the Empire. These tribes were at that time only nominally subject to the rulers of Muscovy, and they pursued their own quarrels for their own ends, though there is every reason to believe that the Czars encouraged and incited them to attack Turkey, in the hope that the strength of the Moslem sovereignty would thus be broken. In the time of Achmet I., who reigned from 1603 to 1617, the Cossacks had descended the Don in a fleet of boats, had crossed the Black Sea, and had surprised the town of Sinope, which they sacked and burned. In 1624, under the sceptre of Amurath IV., these ravages were renewed with still greater audacity. A hundred and fifty long barks, each manned by seventy Cossacks, appeared in sight of Constantinople, and desolated the shores of the Bosphorus. Misfortune followed misfortune for a long term of years, and the Janizaries were at length so wild with rage that in 1633 they assembled in arms, set fire to a part of the capital, and cried out to the Sultan, then twenty-two years of age, that the Empire could be saved only by his sword. Amurath left the Seraglio, and presented himself to the troops, by whom he was received with great enthusiasm; and in 1635 he led a strong army to the rescue of his Asiatic possessions. Erzeroum, Erivan, and Tabriz, were recovered, and frightful tortures were inflicted on the rebels. In December, 1638, Baghdad was taken by storm, when many thousands of Persians were slaughtered, both during and after the attack. Peace was concluded with Persia in the following year, and, although Baghdad and the surrounding country were regained by the Sultan, Erivan was given back to the Shah. Amurath returned to Constantinople, which he entered in triumph, and died in the following year, 1640, of a fever brought on by continual debaucheries. He was undoubtedly an able soldier, and deserved the title of Ghâzi, or the Victorious, which he assumed; but he might with equal truth have been called by the opprobrious nickname applied to Selim II.—viz., the Drunkard. To the vice of intemperance, Amurath IV. was a mere slave, and he took a detestable pleasure in luring his people into the same indulgence. The sale of wine was licensed, to the extreme scandal of all strict Mussulmans; and the Sultan himself drank to so frightful an extent that he often fell into a state of maniacal frenzy, during which he would run half-naked about the streets, killing all whom he met.

The Christian Powers of Europe became stronger as the Ottoman Empire grew weaker. In the closing years of the sixteenth century, Transylvania, Wallachia, and Moldavia refused to pay their annual tribute to the Sultan, and in 1606 Turkey was obliged to conclude a peace with Germany and her allies, by which the Sultan recognised the Emperor as his equal, and abolished the tribute which Austria had paid for her part of Hungary. Poland proved herself equal to the best armaments of the Porte a few years later; and in the reign of Mohammed IV. (1648–87) the Venetians twice defeated the Turkish navy, and destroyed a large number of vessels. Mutinies of the Janizaries were continually occurring during this unhappy period of Turkish history. These insolent soldiers made and unmade sovereigns and ministers at their pleasure, and it was death to oppose their will. In the time of Mohammed IV., they ravaged the environs of Constantinople, and, during the eight years from 1648 to 1656, the administration of affairs was in the hands of fifteen Grand Viziers. At length, however, the Government acquired strength and permanence, and the Turkish arms were brilliantly successful in several quarters. Yet it was in this reign that the Ottomans suffered such severe defeats at the hands of the Austrians, and of the Poles under Sobieski. After subduing a part of Germany, and menacing the very existence of the Empire, the Turkish hosts under Kara Mustapha Pasha, the Grand Vizier, were in 1683 utterly routed before the walls of Vienna, as we have related in a previous Chapter. For a time, it had seemed as if the old conquering spirit of the Ottomans was about to be revived, and Europe trembled for her liberties and her faith, as she had not trembled since the battle of Lepanto. But after the great victory of Sobieski and his allies, the power of the Sultans again recoiled. A large part of Hungary was freed from the Moslem yoke, and the Grand Signor could no longer retain his hold on the lands north of the Danube. The Venetians drove his forces out of Greece, and the Janizaries, once more revolting in 1687, deposed Mohammed, and

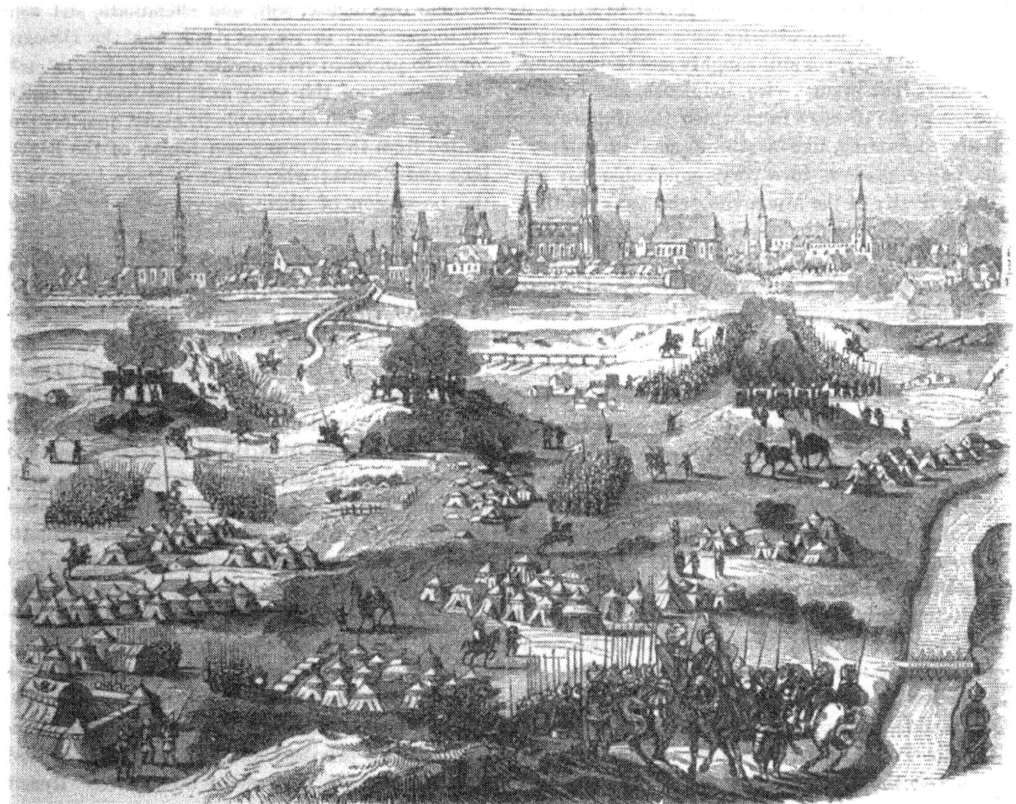

SIEGE OF VIENNA BY KARA MUSTAPHA PASHA, 1683. *(From a Print in Ortelius' "Chronologia.")*

imprisoned him in the Seraglio, where he died in 1691.

During the reign of this Sultan, Charles II. of England sent the Earl of Winchilsea as Ambassador Extraordinary to the Turkish Court. His Lordship had for his secretary a gentleman named Paul Rycaut (afterwards knighted), who made good use of his opportunities for acquiring an intimate knowledge of the Turkish State; and his work on this subject is an admirable account of government and society in Constantinople at the period to which it refers. Rycaut delineates for us a military nation in a state of decay, yet still haughty and threatening. He shows that luxury, vice, indolence, and corruption, were the diseases from which the Empire was slowly consuming, like a strong man in a fever; and he foreshadows in a very remarkable way the coming rivalry of the Muscovite, who was even then thinking of Constantinople as a possible inheritance. "The Turk," says Rycaut, "is well inclined to the Polander, and desires his prosperity beyond others of his neighbour princes; because he looks on him as the only curb upon all occasions of the Moscovite, and whom they may make use of to give some stop and arrest unto the progress of his arms. The Moscovite hath yet a greater fame and renown with the Turks, being reported able to make a hundred and fifty thousand horse; so that he treats with the Turk on equal terms, and fills his letters with high threats and hyperbolical expressions of his power, and with as swelling titles as the Turk. The Greeks have also an inclination to the Moscovite beyond any other Christian prince, as being of their rites and religion, terming him their Emperor and Protector; from whom, according to ancient prophecies and modern predictions, they expect delivery and freedom to their church. But the greatest dread the Turk hath of the Moscovite is from the union with the Sophi, or Persian; which two, uniting together, would be too unequal a match for the Ottoman Empire."*

Although impressed with the splendour, and in some respects with the power, of the Ottoman Empire, Rycaut clearly perceived that the processes of decay had set in, and he gives many details showing that this declension had already proceeded to a not inconsiderable extent. He remarks that he who should take a view of the Ottoman armies as described in history, and should thence infer their existing state, would be very much misled as to the puissance of the Turks, or the rules of their Government. The ancient sublimity of the Emperor was abated; the land forces were reduced, and the maritime power was discredited by ill-success, and by unskilful and slothful seamen. Many of the provinces were dispeopled and desolate, and the royal revenue had greatly fallen off, together with the plentiful stores and provisions of war which in former times had been accumulated. The discipline which had anciently been observed, even in times of peace, was no longer visible; laws and religion had lost their force; the military had become degenerate, soft, and effeminate, and were no longer held in respect; nor was the Ottoman court so prone to remunerate the services or exalt the interests of the army as it had been in earlier times. The ruin observable in many quarters proceeded from the tyranny and rapine of the Beglerbegs and Pashas; who, either in their journeys to the possession of their governments, or on their return from them, exposed the poor inhabitants to the violence and injury of their attendants, as if they had entered the confines of an enemy, or the dominions of a conquered people. In the marches of the troops from one province to another, parties of twenty or thirty were permitted to make excursions into the neighbouring countries, where they not only lived upon free quarters, but extorted money and clothes from the poor vassals, and sold their children into slavery, especially the Bulgarians, Servians, Bosnians, and Albanians; so that, rather than be exposed to so much misery, the unfortunate people often abandoned their dwellings, and wandered into other cities, or sought refuge among the mountains and woods. The military spirit was so much relaxed that soldiers would frequently apply to be placed upon the retired list on account of a mere scratch or flesh-wound. A small sum of money, presented to the commanding officer, would obtain for them this privilege, and they were then entitled to a pension for the rest of their lives. Rycaut assures us that in his time there were great numbers of strong and healthy soldiers receiving what was called "dead men's pay." The Janizaries, having been permitted to marry—a freedom which was formerly denied them—had applied themselves to trade, and in many instances had grown so averse from war that they were almost inclined to mutiny whenever hostilities were spoken of. In short, the Turks were rapidly becoming unfit for their one great vocation of fighting, without having obtained a facility in any other form of human enterprise. Yet they still enjoyed the full extent of their dominions, and, like the sea, if they lost ground in one place, acquired it in another.

With respect to the general treatment of the Christians in the Turkish Empire, the testimony of

* The History of the Present State of the Ottoman Empire, by Paul Rycaut. Fourth Edition, 1675.—The first edition was published a few years earlier.

Rycaut is somewhat contradictory. He admits that Mohammed enjoined toleration when he himself was weak and stood in need of support, but maintains that at a later epoch, when his sword had made him predominant, his edicts were all for blood and ruin, and for the enslavement of those whom he regarded as infidels. The sentences quoted by Rycaut in support of this view seem to refer to the treatment of Christians who took up arms against the Mussulmans, rather than to their ordinary condition; but, however this may be, it is admitted that an open and public profession of the Christian faith was allowed in the Turkish dominions at that time, though under certain disadvantages.* The poverty, ignorance, and stupidity of the Greek and Armenian Churches, on which Rycaut remarks, may possibly have been aggravated by persecution and neglect; but when we find that much the same condition existed at the same period even in Russia, it seems not unfair or unreasonable to charge the greater portion of the blame on the Eastern Churches themselves. The toleration of the Turks has always had in it some element of contempt; and that contempt has been not unnaturally awakened by the puerile absurdities of the Oriental sects. At the time when Rycaut wrote, the Mohammedan religion tolerated Christian churches and houses of devotion in places where they had been anciently founded, but did not admit of any new buildings of the same character. The Christians might repair the old coverings and roofs, but could not lay a stone in a new place consecrated to Divine Service; nor, if fire or any other accident destroyed the superstructure, might they strengthen the foundations for another building. This harsh law was rigorously carried out after the great fires which occurred at Galata and Constantinople in the year 1660. Many of the Christian churches and chapels, which had been burnt to ashes in the conflagration, were rebuilt by the piety and zeal of the Christians, but were afterwards thrown down by public order, as being contrary to the Turkish law. In many ways, the condition of the Christians was made exceedingly irksome, so that there was a perpetual temptation to forsake the proscribed for the dominant religion. To this temptation large numbers yielded, and the Ottoman power was strengthened in a very considerable degree by the genius and energy of renegades. Until about the middle of the seventeenth century, it was usual for the Turks to exact, every five years, a tribute of Christian children, who were educated in the Mohammedan faith. This increased the numbers of the Moslems, and in an equal degree enfeebled the subject races; but, when Rycaut wrote, the custom had in a great measure grown out of use, and it does not appear to have been ever revived. The practical abolition of this oppressive law was a great gain to the unfortunate Christian parents who had suffered from it, and it may possibly have contributed to the decline of Turkish predominance. Nevertheless, the Ottomans did not want for converts. Multitudes of Greeks, Armenians, and Jews, voluntarily adopted the religion of the Prophet, and, having once done so, to recant was death. These renegades were generally amongst the most bitter persecutors of the religion they had forsaken; and when the severity of Mohammedan fanaticism was to some extent moderated—as was the case in the seventeenth and eighteenth centuries—the credit was due, not to the converts, but to the native Turks.

The Ottoman Empire, like that of Rome, had doubtless been too much extended, and it shrank at the extremities from lack of vital force, or from coming into collision with powers strong enough to resist its armies. In the south, Persia gradually advanced on what had been Turkish territory for a greater or less duration of time; in the north, the Austrian Empire, recovering from the dismay into which it had been thrown when Kara Mustapha was besieging Vienna, began to enter into competition with the Ottoman for superiority on the line of the Danube. Since the first quarter of the sixteenth century, Hungary, so far as it was free from Turkish rule, had been united with the Austrian Empire; and this gave an accession of military strength to the sovereigns of that dominion. In other respects, however, it might rather be regarded as a weakness. The Austrians were Roman Catholics; a large proportion of the Hungarians were Protestants; and the former persecuted the latter with such implacable bitterness that the Hungarians sometimes doubted whether they would not be better off under the sway of the Mohammedan. It was thus that the people of Hungary first acquired that sympathy with the Turks which later events have strengthened, and which is now so remarkable a characteristic of the nation. Yet, although the Hungarians disliked their Austrian masters, they were compelled to furnish recruits to the armies of the Empire; so that Austria was in a good condition to defy the strength of the Ottomans, and to push back their frontiers from the advanced positions which had been occupied in

* Rycaut printed in full the decree of toleration granted by Mohammed to the monks of Mount Sinai, of which some account has been given on pp. 176–8 of this volume. He believed in its authenticity, though this was denied by such of the Turks as were inclined to persecute.

earlier ages. The power of the Sultans was attacked even in Servia. Belgrade was taken by the Imperialists in 1688, but retaken by the Turks in 1690. In the following year, the Ottomans were signally defeated at Salenkemen, on the banks of the Danube, near the point where the Theiss empties itself into the larger stream. The Grand Vizier, Kiuprili—the third of that name, and, like his father and grandfather, a man of genius, energy, and liberal principles—commanded the Turkish forces, and was slain at the head of his troops. The consequence of this victory, which cost the Imperialists dear, was that the fortress of Grand-Waradin was surrendered to the Emperor Leopold. Belgrade was invested by the Prince of Baden, but was shortly afterwards relieved by Buyukli Pasha. The successes and failures of the two belligerents were indeed about equally balanced; but it was evident that the Turks were no longer in the position of undisputed conquerors. The Venetians acquired possession of the valuable island of Chios, situated in the Archipelago, in the year 1694, and in 1696 a revolt of Arab tribes gave great disquietude to the Government at Constantinople. Chios was recovered in 1695 by a Tunisian pirate, who offered to destroy the Venetian fleet, if the Government of the Sultan would furnish him with twelve vessels of war. This success, however, was counterbalanced by the failure of the Mohammedan arms in the direction of the Danube. On the side of the Imperialists, Frederick Augustus, Elector of Saxony, afterwards King of Poland, and the celebrated Prince Eugene, in subsequent years the companion of Marlborough, were the generals who chiefly distinguished themselves.

It was at this period that Russia first came upon the scene as the open adversary of Turkey. In 1696, Peter the Great concluded an alliance with Austria, and, by means of the small fleet which he had hastily improvised, and which he made the nucleus of his navy, wrested the town of Azof from the grasp of the Sultans. In the Hungarian campaign, Mustapha II., who succeeded to the throne in 1695, commanded in person, after the manner of the earlier Sultans; but, although his courage and enthusiasm were of the highest order, his military qualifications were hardly equal to those of his Christian opponents. Being at the head of much larger forces than his enemy could command, he was enabled, at an immense sacrifice of men, to gain some successes; but the Austrians were only checked, not defeated. Reorganising their armies, they attacked Temeswar in 1696, and, when the Sultan endeavoured to raise the siege, very nearly inflicted upon him a serious defeat. The Imperialists even penetrated to the Sultan's tent; but Mustapha had left for another quarter of the field, in order to hurry up reinforcements. When these arrived, the Imperialists were driven out of the camp, and found it necessary to abandon their positions, with the loss of all their cannon, and of a considerable number of their men. Mustapha entered upon another campaign in 1697, but on the 11th of September was disastrously overthrown before the castle of Zenta, on the borders of the Theiss. The Sultan and the remnant of his army fled to Temeswar, leaving to the victor, Prince Eugene, the immense riches contained in the Turkish camp, the artillery, and the stores. Utterly crestfallen and humiliated, the Sultan after a while retired to Adrianople, where he perceived the necessity of requesting peace. Negotiations were never very rapidly transacted in those days, and it was not till the 26th of January, 1699, that the arrangements were concluded. This was the celebrated Peace of Carlowitz, by which the condition of the Danubian countries was settled for a time. By the agreement thus sanctioned, the Emperor Leopold acquired the greater part of Hungary, Transylvania, and Sclavonia; Peter the Great retained Azof; Podolia, the Ukraine, and Kaminiek (which the Turks had conquered) were guaranteed to the Poles; and the Venetians were allowed to keep the Morea, together with a strong frontier in Dalmatia. The Turks, on the other hand, retained that part of Hungary called the Banat of Temeswar, together with portions of Transylvania and Sclavonia, and the mainland of Greece. The rule of the Sultans north of the Danube had always been very precarious, and it was now reduced within narrow limits. Wallachia and Moldavia had been rather fiefs of the Porte than actual possessions. At times they were not even that, and they felt an additional security in the triumph of the Christian arms under Prince Eugene. The Peace of Carlowitz was felt throughout the Turkish Empire as a great degradation, and it led to an insurrection in 1703, when Mustapha was deposed.

In the following reign—that of Achmet III.—Peter the Great made war upon Turkey, but with such ill-success that he was obliged to conclude a disgraceful peace by bribing the Grand Vizier. This was in 1711, and the Czar was reluctantly compelled to cede the fortress of Azof to his successful adversary. The Morea was taken from Venice in 1714, and the Emperor Charles VI. then declared war on Turkey, and obtained some important triumphs. The Ottomans were defeated by Prince Eugene at Peterwaradin in 1716, and at Belgrade in 1717. The Peace of Passarowitch followed in 1718, and the Sultan ceded to Austria the Banat of Temeswar, Belgrade, and the western parts of Wallachia and Servia. Like so many of his predecessors, Achmet was deposed by a rising of the Janizaries; but this was not until 1730, and was in consequence of the successes of the Persian Shah, who by a sudden and brilliant movement recovered some territories which had been previously taken by the Ottomans. It was in the reign of Achmet III. that a printing-office was first established in Constantinople; so backward were the Turks in adopting the great invention of Faust.

Another war between Turkey and Austria began in 1737, and came to a close in 1739, when Belgrade, with all that had been won by the Christians in Servia, Bosnia, and Wallachia, was restored to the Sultan. In this war, Austria acted as the ally of Russia, which had come into collision with Turkey a few years before, owing to some Turkish troops, when on the march to attack the Persians, having crossed certain territory, in the neighbourhood of the Caucasus, to which the Muscovites laid claim. Russia was beginning to feel her strength as a European Power, and to form designs pointing to the subjugation of Turkey by slow degrees. The political will of Peter the Great, about which so much has been written, may never have really existed; but it is certain that that monarch regarded Russia as the predestined opponent of Turkey, and that he coveted a position in the South of Europe, such as Constantinople alone could give him. From that time to the present, wars between Russia and Turkey have been of frequent occurrence, and the dominion of the Czars has steadily advanced southwards. Several years elapsed before Russia was sufficiently strong to effect any conquests on a large scale; still, she exercised her arms against the Ottoman chivalry, and occasionally obtained successes which augured well for the future. The first war in which Russia proved her superiority over Turkey was that which commenced in 1768, during the reigns of Catharine II. and Mustapha III. The declaration of war came from the Sultan, and was caused by that interference of Russia in the affairs of Poland which resulted in the first partition. It is worthy of note, however, that, a little while before, Turkey herself had proposed to Austria to share Poland between them. The war lasted until 1774, and was marked by a succession of the most signal disasters to the Turkish arms. The whole of the country between the Danube and the Dnieper fell into the hands of the Russians; the Crimea was conquered; and in 1770 the Turkish fleet in the Bay of Chesmé was defeated by the Russian navy. Abdul-Hamid I. had succeeded to Mustapha III. when peace was concluded at Koutchouk-Kainardji, in Bulgaria, in July, 1774. By this peace, Russia obtained Great and Little Kabarda; the fortresses of Azof, Kimbourn, Kertch, and Yenikalo; the country between the Boug and the Dnieper; the free navigation of the Black Sea, together with a passage through the Bosphorus and the Dardanelles; the co-protectorship of Wallachia and Moldavia; and the protectorship of the Greek Church within the Turkish Empire. This was the commencement of that mischievous interference in the internal affairs of Turkey which Russia was allowed to exercise until the peace of 1856, at the conclusion of the Crimean war; an interference which has hastened the decay of the Ottoman Empire, has led to numerous wars, has involved Europe in the most painful complications, has promoted the boundless ambition of Russia, and has failed in producing any good results, even for those Christian populations whom it was the professed object of the Russian sovereigns to protect.

By the Treaty of Kainardji, the Porte promised protection to the Christian religion and its temples. The court of Russia was empowered to build in the Galata quarter of Constantinople a public Greek church, to be placed under the ægis of the Ambassador; and the subjects of the Russian Empire were to have permission to visit Jerusalem and the Holy Land, without paying any tribute. It is generally held that the ameliorated condition of the Christians in Turkey was due in the first instance to this treaty, and to the active interference of Russia; but the assumption is not warranted by facts. The treaty may have secured to the Christians some privileges which they did not before enjoy; but the stringency of the Turkish despotism had been growing less for some generations. We have seen that more than a hundred years earlier the tribute of Christian children had ceased to be enforced, and the administration of the three Kiuprilis had been characterized by much liberality. Still farther back, during the reign of Selim I., that powerful monarch was several times restrained in his bloodthirsty purposes by the Mufti, who plainly told him that it was against the sacred law of the Koran either to massacre the Christians, or to prohibit the exercise of their religion; and the Sultan submitted. Turkey had in fact shown that she was not entirely beyond the influence of modern ideas. Those ideas, it is true, penetrated the huge mass of Moslem fanaticism with great slowness; but it cannot be said that their influence in any part of Europe was remarkably powerful at the period in question. Even in

England, bigotry and intolerance, though assuming forms more vexatious than cruel, were among the recognized principles of government in the reign of George III. In France, not a hundred years had elapsed since the multitudinous atrocities attending the Revocation of the Edict of Nantes, and a repetition of those atrocities was possible at any moment up to the epoch of the Revolution. In other parts of Europe, Catholics persecuted Protestants, and Protestants persecuted Catholics; while in Russia the Greek Church was the enemy of both. That Turkey should have made any advance, however slight, towards the principles of religious toleration, while in countries far more civilized that advance was not much greater, was a hopeful fact from which a good deal might have been made, if Europe herself had had a clearer perception of the principles of justice and reason. It has often been observed that the continual interference of Russia in the affairs of Turkey has aggravated the oppressions from which the Christians have suffered, and has hindered, instead of promoting, the arrival of a better day. The state of the Christians in the Ottoman Empire has never been so good as it was during the twenty years from 1856 to 1876, when the Treaty of Paris secured the Turkish dominions from the encroachments of unscrupulous ambition.

Russia was not unnaturally elated at the success of her arms and of her diplomacy, as manifested in the war, and in the Treaty of Kainardji which brought the struggle to a close. The Muscovite power now became beyond all question the predominant power in the East of Europe. Not only did Catharine II. acquire a large accession to her realm, but she obtained a position of command which would enable her or her successors to dictate the policy of Turkey whenever a motive for doing so should arise. The reputation of the Ottoman Empire was so seriously damaged that every thinking politician saw the improbability of its ever being restored. The Grand Vizier, Reis Effendi, who signed the treaty, was so overcome with shame and mortification that he died shortly afterwards. The Austrian Ambassador at Constantinople wrote to his Government that the maintenance of the Eastern Empire no longer depended on the good-will of the other Powers, but simply on that of Russia. "In fact," he added, "as soon as Russia is prepared (which cannot be long hence), one may expect any day the capture of Constantinople." The prospect of

BIRD'S-EYE VIEW OF THE ISLAND OF CHIOS IN THE SEVENTEENTH CENTURY.

Russian ascendency in so important a quarter of Europe was not very agreeable to the several Cabinets; but to object to Russian policy, and yet permit it to take its course, has been the usual method of European Governments.

The peace between Russia and Turkey did not last many years, and the occasion of war again breaking out is to be found in the condition of the Crimea. That peninsula of the Black Sea had long been governed by Tartar Khans, vassals of the Sultan, and powerful allies in any war he undertook with the Muscovites. By the Treaty of Kainardji, the Khans were established in a position of nominal independence; but as a matter of fact they were subjected to the influence of Russia, and Catharine II. determined, almost immediately after the conclusion of peace, to obtain a complete mastery over the Crimea, so that she might have the command of the Euxine. It was one of her magnificent designs to drive the Turks out of Europe, and re-establish the Greek Empire in its old seat; but, to do this effectually, it was necessary to seat herself in the fine naval positions presented by the Crimean peninsula. She accordingly issued a manifesto on the 10th of April, 1783, by which the Crimea, the isle of Taman, and Kuban, were taken under the sovereign protection of Russia. The Turkish people were aflame with indignation, and demanded war; but the Sultan, feeling that he was not strong enough to confront the Muscovites, gave his consent to the annexation, which was ratified by a convention signed at Constantinople on the 28th of December, 1783. Very shortly afterwards, the strong fortress of Sebastopol, which the allied armies had so much trouble in capturing in 1854–5, arose on the western side of the Crimea; and over one of the gates of this new city, Catharine, when

SEBASTOPOL.

on a visit there in 1787, inscribed the words, "Road to Constantinople." These words may not have been known to the Sultan and his advisers; but Turkey knew of the enormous fortress which had been reared almost at the threshold of her Imperial city, and she could not have doubted that it was intended as a menace, and as a means of overawing her at some not very distant date. The Ottoman Government became seriously alarmed. Preparations for war were made on a large scale, and the support of foreign Powers was eagerly solicited. England looked with jealousy on the predominance of Russia in the Black Sea, and promised assistance to the Turks in the shape of money for carrying on hostilities. Prussia also was inclined to follow the same course; but Russia found sympathy and support in the direction of Vienna. War was declared by Turkey in August, 1787, and at the commencement of the following year Austria joined her forces to those of Russia. The progress of the war was not favourable to the Turks. The Austrians, it is true, were defeated in many engagements; but the Russians were for the most part successful, and their good fortune continued even after the withdrawal of Austria, in August, 1791. In the previous year, Suwaroff had captured the fortresses of Ismail and Brahilow, and at the former of those places he and his troops disgraced themselves by an atrocious massacre. The fortress had withstood repeated attacks, and Suwaroff, being determined to take it, promised his soldiers the plunder of everything they could find, and ordered them to give no quarter. It was not until three assaults had been made upon the walls that the Russians succeeded in bursting in, when 33,000 Turks were killed or severely wounded. In 1791, the same able general captured Anapa, the key to the Kuban.

Matters now began to look so serious that a coalition against Russia was formed among several of the European Powers. England fitted out a formidable fleet, which was designed for the Baltic; Prussia massed an army of 80,000 men in Silesia; Holland, Spain, and the Two Sicilies signified their willingness to join the league; and the prospect of a general war seemed imminent. At the last moment, however, England began to hesitate, and to propose negotiations. Two Plenipotentiaries in succession were despatched to St. Petersburg; but the Empress could not be induced to recede from any of her requirements, or to give up the positions she had won. Again it appeared as if war were on the point of breaking out; but the progress of the French Revolution, which threatened the stability of all the established Governments in Europe, suggested to those Governments the policy of not quarrelling amongst themselves, but rather of combining against the common enemy. England and Prussia accordingly made proposals to Russia, which conceded to her, as a basis for the opening of negotiations, almost everything for which she was contending. At the same time, the Turks were so disastrously defeated at Matchin that they made proposals for an amicable arrangement, and the preliminaries of peace were signed at Galatz on the 11th of April, 1791. When, however, Field-Marshal Prince Potemkin, the Commander-in-Chief of the Russian army, arrived at Galatz, he accused the Russian Plenipotentiary of exceeding his powers, and declared the convention null and void. A Congress having been opened at Jassy, demands of the most extravagant kind were made by Potemkin on behalf of his sovereign; but the Russian Field-Marshal died shortly after, and the Treaty of Jassy was signed on the 9th of January, 1792 (N.S.). The Russian terms had been in some degree moderated, yet they were sufficiently hard. The stipulations of the Treaty of Kainardji were renewed; the river Dniester was recognized as the frontier of the two Empires; Oczakow was ceded to Russia, with the large space comprised between the Boug and the Dniester, where the Russians soon built the city of Odessa; the Crimea, the island of Taman, and part of the Kuban, were confirmed to the Empress; and it was stipulated that an indemnity of 12,000,000 piastres should be paid to Russia for the expenses of the war. The other conquests of the Russian arms were restored to Turkey, and, as soon as the treaty was signed, the Empress renounced the payment of the indemnity, and declared herself satisfied with the fact of its having been conceded. One of the most important articles of this treaty was that which, following the precedent of the Treaty of Kainardji, permitted Russian ships to enter the Straits of the Bosphorus, and to navigate the Black Sea. Under cover of this provision, foreign vessels of other nations often found an effectual protection by using the Russian flag, and Russia herself acquired a fresh grasp upon the unfortunate Empire which she had resolved, sooner or later, to destroy.

Two wars with Russia within a short space of time had convinced the ruling classes in Turkey that the strength of the Ottoman Empire was gravely overmatched by that of the Northern Power. The Turks are the most conservative people in the world; but the ruling Sultan, Selim III., saw clearly that the old methods, which had been sufficient to give the most brilliant triumphs to Turkey in the Middle Ages, were altogether

ATTACK ON THE SERAGLIO BY THE JANIZARIES.

inadequate to withstand the forces of Europe at the close of the eighteenth century. The nations of Christendom had been advancing for many generations; the Turks had been falling back; and the disproportion of resources was now alarmingly manifest. Selim determined to organize his armies on European models, and to introduce several much-needed reforms into the civil administration of the Empire; but his designs were hindered by the state of anarchy into which his dominions were plunged shortly after the conclusion of peace. Syria and Egypt were in open rebellion; Paswan Oghlu, Pasha of Widdin, defied the authority of his sovereign; and Ali Pasha, at Janina, acquired a degree of power which seriously threatened that of the Sultan. In the midst of these troubles, Selim concluded an alliance with Russia, Naples, and England, in consequence of which a united Turkish and Russian fleet took possession of the Ionian Islands, and in the year 1800 these were constituted into a Republic, the protectorship of which was vested in the Sultan, on condition of his consenting to the incorporation of Georgia with Russia. Egypt had been invaded by the French under Napoleon Bonaparte in 1798; but the intruders were expelled by the English in 1801. Peace was concluded with France in the following year, when that country acquired the free navigation of the Black Sea—a privilege which was soon afterwards extended to England and other European Powers.

Selim now devoted himself to the realization of those reforms which he had long contemplated. He was a man of much more enlightened and cultivated mind than is usual with Oriental monarchs. In the seclusion of the Seraglio, previous to his accession to the throne, he had studied Turkish and European history; had conducted a correspondence with eminent Turkish statesmen, and with the French Ambassador, Count de Choiseul; and, it is believed, had exchanged letters with Louis XVI. himself. As soon as the condition of his Empire permitted him, he reformed the system of taxation, reorganized the Divan, and placed his armies on a footing similar to those of the European Powers. The Sultan was at this time much under the influence of the French Ambassador, Count Sebastiani; and, the jealousy of England and Russia being aroused, war against Turkey was declared by those countries in December, 1806, on a variety of pretexts having reference to the freedom of navigation in Turkish waters. Admiral Duckworth passed through the Dardanelles, and threatened to bombard Constantinople; but, fearing soon after that his retreat would be cut off, he returned to the Mediterranean, with the loss of two ships and 600 men at the repassage of the Straits, where the heavy ordnance did fearful execution. Selim exhibited immense energy in the defence of his Empire; but the Russians made progress on the Danube, and the Janizaries, who attributed the misfortunes of the Turkish arms to the new military organization of the Nizam, assembled to the number of 15,000 men, occupied the suburb of Pera, and planted their ordnance against the Seraglio itself. The result was that, by a decree of the Mufti, Selim was deposed, on the ground that he had no heir, and had introduced several innovations into the State. The deposition took place on the 29th of May, 1807, and the first act of his nephew and successor, Mustapha IV., was to abolish the reforms of his predecessor; but the Turkish arms were none the more successful on that account. The fleet was entirely defeated by the Russians off Lemnos, and Baïraktar, the Pasha of Rustchuk, appeared at the head of an army before the capital, in July, 1808, and demanded the deposition of Mustapha. He next entered Constantinople, attacked the Seraglio, and required that Selim should be given up to him. The grim reply of Mustapha was the production of the dead body of the late Sultan, whom he had just strangled. Baïraktar thereupon deposed Mustapha, and placed his brother Mahmud on the throne. The reforms which the Janizaries had endeavoured to suppress were destined to be resumed by the new monarch; but it was not until after a period of extraordinary convulsion and accumulated misfortunes that Turkey was permitted to enter upon the new era which Selim had conceived, and vainly sought to carry out.

CHAPTER XXIII.

Turkish History continued—Turbulent Commencement of the Reign of Mahmud II.—Rising of the Janizaries—Destruction of the Palace of the Grand Vizier, and Death of Baïraktar—The Sultan besieged in the Seraglio—Desperate Fighting in the Streets of Constantinople—Assassination of Mustapha and his Women—Restoration of Tranquillity—Proposed Conditions of Peace between Russia and Turkey—Serious Reverses of the latter—The Peace of Bucharest (May, 1812)—Distracted condition of the Turkish Empire—Romantic Career of Ali Pasha—Commencement of the Revolt in Greece—Claims of the Greek Race—Ineffectual Rising—The Movement in the Morea—Spread of the Rebellion over other Parts of Greece—Enthusiasm for the Greek Cause in England—Shelley and Byron—Progress of the Struggle—Ferocity of the Combatants on both sides—Intervention by England, France, and Russia—Refusal by Sultan Mahmud to accept Terms from the Powers—The Battle of Navarino, and its Results—Internal Reforms of the Sultan—Destruction of the Janizaries—The Treaty of Akerman—Renewed War with Russia—Disasters of 1828-9—The Peace of Adrianople—Action of England in Opposition to Russia—Troubles with Egypt—The Treaty of Unkiar-Skelessi—Death of Mahmud II.

We enter on the modern era of Turkish history when we come to the reign of Mahmud II., sometimes described as Mohammed VI. From an early age, Mahmud, who was born in 1785, had been of a studious temperament, and, while living in the Seraglio, had employed his time in reading Turkish and Persian literature. During the year previous to his accession, he had derived a good deal of instruction from the society of the deposed Sultan, Selim III., who imbued him with his own principles of reform, and gave him a strong bias against the Janizaries, as the opponents of all improvement, and the constant troublers of the Turkish State. When Baïraktar burst into the Seraglio, after a bloody struggle, Mahmud was discovered, according to some accounts, in the furnace of a bath,—according to others, in a room where he had been concealed under a heap of carpets and books. In any case, he expected instant death, if he should be found; and there is no more dramatic surprise in fiction then the sudden conversion of this menaced fugitive into the despotic chief of a great Empire. He had succeeded, however, to no easy task. The Janizaries were dissatisfied with the new monarch, and with Baïraktar, who was made Grand Vizier. It was believed that both were bent on carrying out those reforms which had cost Selim his throne; and the unpopularity of Baïraktar was so great that, whenever he went abroad on state affairs, he found it necessary to surround himself with an armed guard. The Janizaries were secretly planning his destruction, and in a few months the storm burst. Assembling in force about the middle of November, 1808, these turbulent soldiers surrounded the palace of the Grand Vizier by night, and set it on fire. Baïraktar, aroused from sleep by the roaring of the flames, retreated into a strong, square tower, which he appears to have thought would be proof against the conflagration; but the fire gained upon him, and he was finally blown up by the explosion of a magazine, to which it is believed he had himself applied the torch, on finding that escape was impossible.

In the meanwhile, the Sultan himself was besieged in his Seraglio by the infuriated Janizaries. The gates of the city had been shut by the malcontents, so that no troops might be sent in from other parts of the Empire; and a fearful struggle ensued between the mutinous soldiers and those who supported the ruling sovereign. Fighting continued throughout the 15th of November, and the vessels of the Capitan Pasha, lying in the harbour, played upon the Janizaries' barracks. On the 16th, Cadi Pasha, with a column of four thousand men, and a number of cannon, drove the Janizaries before him, and set fire to a barrack in which five hundred of them had taken refuge. The rebels, recovering themselves after awhile, beat back their opponents at various points, and for some hours a murderous conflict deluged the streets with blood, and the chief positions were taken and retaken several times. Massacre, pillage, and arson, were added to the horrors of that dreadful day; and Mahmud, mounting to a high tower of the Imperial palace, saw his capital ablaze from the walls of the Seraglio to the aqueduct of Valens. The magnificent dwelling of the Vizier was now nothing more than a smoking mass of ruins, covering a vast space; and the Janizaries had by this time so completely gained the upper hand that the other troops refused to fight against them any longer. During the height of the convulsion, Mahmud took a step of a desperate nature, involving a number of atrocious crimes, but crimes for which the annals of his house furnished him with abundant precedents. He ordered his brother Mustapha to be strangled, together with the infant son of that deposed sovereign. Four of his women, who were likely to become mothers, were sewn up in leathern sacks, and drowned in the Bosphorous; and Mahmud thus became the only living representative of the line of Othman. It is a popular tradition among the Turks that their dominion will endure no longer than the family of its great founder. When, therefore, the Sultan was enabled to show that he was the only one of the race remaining, the Janizaries abandoned their defiant attitude, and the Sultan further conciliated them by ordering his ships to cease firing on the town,

GATE AT CONSTANTINOPLE.

and by disbanding a newly-formed body of troops who were excessively disliked by the Prætorian soldiery. The friends of the late Vizier were safely embarked on board a vessel at the Seraglio-point, and sent to distant parts; and Mahmud found himself in a position of command, such as his energetic nature especially required.

The time abounded in dangers for the Turkish Empire. The country was in the midst of a serious struggle with Russia, and the hopes of assistance held out by the French Empire had proved deceptive. Some very considerable successes on the Danube had been achieved by the Turks; but it was doubtful whether they could long resist the immense forces that were being arrayed against them. Napoleon had entered into a friendly understanding with Russia at the Peace of Tilsit, in the summer of 1807; and in the following year the French sovereign was reluctantly persuaded to forego his opposition to the Emperor Alexander's desire of annexing Wallachia and Moldavia. A convention was concluded at Erfurt, in the circle of the Lower Rhine, on the 27th of September, 1808, by which Napoleon undertook neither to assist nor oppose the coveted appropriation of territory. The Czar accordingly submitted to the Porte certain conditions of peace, of which the leading features were that the Danubian Principalities should be ceded to Russia; that Turkey should recognise in that Power a right of protection over Georgia, Imeritia, and Mingrelia, situated south of the Caucasus; and that Servia should be made independent under a Russian guarantee. Such was the state of affairs with which Mahmud found himself called upon to deal when he had restored order at Constantinople. Turkey now relied on the countenance of Austria, and, offended by such humiliating conditions, resolved to risk a continuance of the war. The Russians then crossed the Danube in three places, and, in April, 1809, seized the fortresses of Tultcha and Ismail, lying on opposite sides of the river. At Silistria, however, they experienced a severe reverse in the autumn, and in 1810, though successful at several points, they were checked at Rustchuk, Schumla, and Varna. The Turks were at length driven from the town of Rustchuk, though not from the fortress, and in 1811 the Russians were compelled to set fire to the city, and abandon it. On the whole, however, the campaign of 1811 was disastrous for the Turks. An army which had crossed the Danube into Wallachia, in September, was obliged by General Kutusoff to surrender on December 8th, and the Grand Vizier escaped with difficulty.

RUSTCHUK.

Before events had reached this pass, some irregular negotiations had been conducted between the opposing generals, as to the conditions upon which Turkey would be inclined to treat for peace. Russia was disposed to abandon her demand for the whole of Wallachia and Moldavia, on the understanding that she was to have that portion of the latter principality which is bounded on the west by the river Sereth, and that the Czar should receive a sum of 20,000 piastres as an indemnity for relinquishing Wallachia and the rest of Moldavia. The Turks, however, refused the cession of the territory bounded by the Sereth, and proposed the Pruth as a more suitable frontier-line; and peace was ultimately made on these terms. The superiority of Russia at the close of the war was so great that she would probably have insisted on the line of the Sereth, had she not felt the necessity of making peace with Turkey on almost any conditions, in order that she might repel the threatened invasion of her own dominions by Napoleon.

Peace was therefore concluded at Bucharest on the 28th of May, 1812, when it was agreed that the Pruth, instead of the Dniester, should thenceforth be the boundary between the two Empires; that the navigation of the Danube should be free; that the whole of Wallachia and the greater part of Moldavia should return under the suzerainty of the Porte, with special guarantees for their liberties; that the people of those Principalities should be exempt from taxation for two years; and that the Asiatic frontiers should remain the same. A general amnesty was to be granted to the Servians, and their country was to have local self-government, and to pay a definite tribute to the Sultan. The whole of Bessarabia was thus secured to Russia by the advancing of the boundary-line in Europe from the Dniester to the Pruth.

The terms of peace might certainly have been worse for Turkey; yet they were severe, and it may seem strange that Mahmud, knowing the danger in which his adversary was placed by the aggressive designs of France, should not have resisted further. But the demands of Russia were supported at Constantinople by the English Ambassador; a large English fleet lay near at hand in the Mediterranean; and the Sultan considered it prudent to obtain peace at the sacrifice of a portion of his dominions. The Russians evinced so much joy at the conclusion of the war that a foreign Minister resident in London expressed his surprise to the Russian Ambassador. The treaty, he observed, was no better than a piece of waste paper, and had probably been signed only to deceive the Russians. It was impossible that the Turks should not seize the first opportunity, on the withdrawal of the Russian armies, to re-commence the war, and take back their own: no Christian Power, according to this diplomatist, could resist such a temptation, and it was not to be expected that the Turks should. The Russian Ambassador, Prince Lieven, replied, "Little do you know the Turks. The ink of that bond is worth to us 100,000 men."* So great was the faith which the Russians themselves placed in the pledged word of their Ottoman foes. In an earlier age, it had been declared by the religious authorities of Turkey that the followers of Islam were not bound to keep faith with infidels. The Pope had sanctioned the same immoral doctrine on behalf of Christians as against Moslems, and the Hungarians, as the reader has seen, broke their pact with Amurath almost before the ink was dry. But for the most part the Turks have honourably observed treaties, though no small part of their misfortunes has resulted from the systematic perfidy with which they have been met.

The internal state of Turkey was still desperate. Several of the Pashas were in rebellion, and the Sultan was distracted by many anxieties. Intrigue was being fomented in Servia by the Prince of Wallachia; but Mahmud sent a large army into the former State in the summer of 1813, and the Servians were reduced to submission. Some of the rebellious Pashas were defeated, and punished by the loss of their heads; and a renewed insurrection in Servia was appeased, after some degree of interference on the side of Russia, by concessions which gave partial independence to the people. Equal success attended the efforts of the Sultan in Asia. Rebellion was put down in many places, and the Wahabees, a sect of reforming Mohammedans, who consider themselves the only true followers of the Prophet, and who had seized on Mecca, were completely crushed by Mehemet Ali, the Pasha of Egypt. But fresh troubles were in store for the unhappy Empire, and it can hardly be questioned that they were due in part to the sleepless intrigues of Russia. Greece was that portion of the Ottoman dominions which was next to be revolutionised. Mahmud had long suspected that Ali Pasha, of Janina (whom Byron visited when in that part of the world, and whom he has described in "Childe Harold"), was meditating a rebellion in the Hellenic provinces; and this was rendered the more probable by the excessive court paid to Ali in his Pashalik by England and France. When the Venetian Republic was destroyed by the Treaty of Campo Formio, in 1797, the territories which that State possessed on the coast of Albania were made over to France; but, in the constant changes of those troublous days, they fell into a condition of mere anarchy, and Ali Pasha acquired an ascendency in them. By successive additions to the sphere of his power, he had in time come to be the ruler (in little more than nominal subordination to the Sultan) of Albania, Epirus, Thessaly, and the whole of Continental Greece. He was an Albanian, and in early life had been a robber, like many other of his countrymen, who are not supposed to lose caste by the adventurous life of a brigand. Having made himself useful to the supreme Power in the latter part of the eighteenth century, he obtained a confirmation of the authority which he had usurped at Janina, in Epirus, and for many years continued to improve his dominions, of which, owing to the distracted condition of the Turkish Empire, he was almost the independent sovereign. That he aimed at complete independence is certain. The Govern-

* A Fragment of the History of Servia, by the late David Urquhart. 1843.

ment of the Sultan was well aware of this, but for a long while hesitated to attack him. His power was great; his valour and ability had on several occasions done good service to the Porte; and it was feared that, if provoked, he would be a formidable opponent to the Imperial dominion. But his insolence became greater than could be endured, and it was resolved to take measures of repression. Ali, though in some respects a wise and successful governor, was a man of the most unprincipled and ferocious disposition, and he gained his ends sometimes by deceit, and sometimes by assassination, torture, and terrorism. But he was now growing old, and it seemed unlikely that he would display the same vigour of resistance that might have been expected at an earlier time. Having attempted to procure the murder of one of his confidants, who had abandoned his court, and obtained an appointment in the Seraglio at Constantinople, he was excommunicated at the beginning of 1820, and all the Pashas of Europe were ordered to march against him. The struggle was prolonged and difficult, and the Greeks, who at the commencement had opposed the usurper, afterwards changed sides, and supported his cause. In any form of defiance to Turkish rule, they saw the opportunity of achieving their own independence; and such proved to be the case. The fortunes of Ali, however, were on the wane. His armies being at length worsted by the Turks, he surrendered on the 1st of February, 1822, under a promise that his life and property should be spared. He had often broken faith with others: the lieutenants of the Sultan now broke faith with him. Sentence of death being pronounced, he was killed on the 5th of February, and his head was sent to Constantinople, where it was displayed at the Seraglio-gates.

The revolt of Greece against the Ottoman sovereignty took its rise from these convulsions. The spirit of independence, however, had been fostered for some years by the action of certain societies, professedly of a literary character, but really political in their objects. The most remarkable of these was that entitled Philikó Hetairia, or Association of Friends, which was founded by some Greek merchants in 1814. It is a significant fact that this body originated at Odessa, a Russian city. That its members were really patriotic in their aspirations, cannot be doubted; but it is equally obvious that there was a connection between the popular movement and the covert designs of Russia. From this centre of revolution, agents were sent forth into Greece, to kindle the flame of disaffection, and to prepare for a rising whenever a favourable opportunity should occur. The design had every probability of success. The Greeks had been oppressed and misgoverned for centuries; the resources of their splendid country had been wasted and misapplied; and a state of almost universal anarchy and brigandage had succeeded to the prosperity of former days. Assuredly the Greek had no reason to love the Ottoman. He felt that he was the superior of his tyrant in all but material strength. He recollected that in the ancient world his race had been the greatest race in Europe—the most intellectual, the most artistic, the most capable of influencing universal thought. He still felt that he had mental powers larger than those of the Turk; and he was not unaware that at Constantinople itself some of the ablest ministers had been men belonging to his own nationality. Greece, in fact, though degenerate, had never been entirely extinguished. It was still a country with a distinct character, a distinct history, a distinct language. The modern Hellenes may to some extent have been mixed up with Sclavonic immigrants; yet the qualities of the race have always been maintained in a marked degree, and the idea of a revival seemed within the scope of possibility. The Greeks are one of those nations which may be said to have a right to separate existence, because Nature, and art, and history, have clearly singled them out from surrounding populations. When, therefore, they dreamt of freedom in the earlier years of the present century, they formed to themselves an ideal which had its roots in fact. Geographically speaking, Greece is a well-defined country; ethnologically speaking, the Greeks are a well-defined people. They had lost their independence through division; they might regain it through union. It was not with them as with some other races subjected by the Osmanlis: they had not been conquered because of their inferiority, but because the old Greek spirit of mutual jealousy had so weakened the several governments of the peninsula that the door was opened to the Turk. When the French Revolution had thrown all Europe into a turmoil, and had set men thinking on the first principles of politics, these ideas not unnaturally presented themselves to the quick intelligence of the Hellenes. Hence the success of the Hetairia in creating a spirit of resistance to the Turkish rule.

The contest between Ali Pasha and the Sultan seemed to offer the desired opportunity for rousing the whole of Greece to action. The leading member of the Philikó Hetairia was Prince Alexander Ipsilanti, the eldest son of a previous Hospodar of Wallachia. Here again the connection of Russia with the contemplated Greek movement is very apparent. Ipsilanti had served in the armies of the Czar, and had lost his right arm in battle. The association was unfortunate, but it does not impeach the good faith of the Greek Prince. It was determined that the movement should commence among the Greek population of the Danubian Principalities; that in this way a base of operations should be formed; and that Greece should be revolutionized by forces sent from that direction. The Greeks, however, were a minority in Wallachia, and a minority very much disliked by the mass of the people. The Hospodars, or Viceroys of that province, had for several years been chosen from among the Fanariote Greeks of Constantinople, and they had always been regarded as alien oppressors. Prince Ipsilanti and a few friends crossed the Pruth from Russianised Bessarabia, in March, 1821; but the movement was a disastrous failure. The Hetairists began murdering and plundering, and Ipsilanti was unable to restrain them. He appears to have reckoned on the assistance of Russia; but it did not suit the purposes of that Power to identify itself with an ill-planned expedition, and, as soon as the Turkish Government could send sufficient forces against the insurgents, the rising was put down in blood. In the Morea, however, a much more important outbreak occurred in the spring of the same year. At the beginning of April, the Greeks of several towns rose against the Turks, slaughtered large numbers of them, and reduced the others to submission. The revolt spread with extraordinary rapidity, and the Ottoman Government was not in a position to send reinforcements into the country. A great many acts of atrocity were committed by the Klephts, or robber-chiefs of Greece; but on the whole the movement was that of a people determined to be free, and prepared to fight rather than yield. Continental Greece followed the example of the Morea in a few days. Several of the Greek islands joined the rebellion shortly afterwards, and this placed at the disposal of the insurgents a number of ships, until then used for commercial purposes, but capable of being fitted out as vessels of war, and manned by a race of seamen among the finest in the world. For a time, therefore, the insurrection prospered; but the cold-blooded murders of Turks, by which it was disgraced, led to equally horrible acts of revenge on the part of the Sultan. He executed several of the Greek residents in Constantinople; amongst others, the Patriarch Gregorios, whom he suspended from his own gate on Easter Day. Shortly afterwards, four more Bishops were hanged, and all over European Turkey the fanaticism and fears of the Mohammedans found expression in numerous acts of spoliation and murder. The Emperor Alexander now appealed to his right of interference as established under the Treaty of Kainardji, and remonstrated with the Porte on what was taking place. For the present, he did nothing more than remonstrate; but he kept his attention fixed on the course of events in Turkey. In the meanwhile, the Greek revolution proceeded with uninterrupted success. In December, a National Assembly met at Epidaurus, and on the 13th of January, 1822, a Constitution was announced, by which a Legislative Assembly was created, together with an Executive of five members, under the Presidency of Prince Alexander Mavrocordato, formerly Secretary for Foreign Affairs to the Hospodar of Wallachia. At the same time, however, a Senate which had been formed in the previous June was sitting in the Morea (the Peloponnesus of ancient Greece), and the jealousies of these two bodies proved a source of weakness which no one had sufficient authority to remove.

The uprising of Greece was hailed throughout Europe as the most interesting fact of modern times. It was believed that the glories of the elder world were about to be revived; that the Greeks were degenerate simply because they had been kept down, and that with the return of freedom they would once more illuminate the nations by the grandeur of their genius. This was hoping too much; but the error was excusable, for it proceeded from generous emotions. All the men of intellect were on the side of Greece, and naturally so, when it is considered how much of modern intellect is Greek in its origin. Some of the best feelings of humanity were enlisted on the same behalf, for the Hellenes had undoubtedly been oppressed, and were bravely striving to throw off their oppressors. The enthusiasm for struggling Italy which arose in our own times, when Victor Emmanuel and Garibaldi were fighting the Austrian and the Neapolitan, did not equal that which kindled, not only England, but most of the Continental nations, in the days to which we are now referring. The adventurous flocked into Greece, to aid the cause of the insurgents; men of the noblest genius gave it the service of their pens. Before the close of 1821, Shelley had consecrated to that cause one of the finest of his poems—the Lyrical Drama of "Hellas"—the dedication of which, to Prince Alexander Mavrocordato, is dated from Pisa, November 1st, 1821. It is very curious to find Shelley, in the preface to this work, uttering much the same reproaches against his countrymen that Mr. Gladstone uttered later in connection with the Bulgarian movement. "The English," wrote Shelley, "permit their own oppressors to act according to their natural sympathy with the Turkish tyrant, and to brand upon their name the indelible blot of an alliance with the enemies of domestic happiness, of Christianity and civilization. Russia desires to possess, not to liberate, Greece, and is contented to see the Turks, its natural enemies, and the Greeks, its intended slaves, enfeeble each other until one or both fall into its net. The wise and generous policy of England would have consisted in establishing the independence of Greece, and in maintaining it both against Russia and the Turks." Byron was no less strongly moved in favour of the Hellenic rising; and in 1823 he personally joined the movement, and died of fever, in 1824, in the pestilential air of Missolonghi.

For some years, the War of Independence continued with extraordinary spirit. By land and by sea, the Greeks exhibited much of their old courage and heroic resolution, and Constantine Kanaris, one of the Greek Admirals, distinguished himself in many a gallant encounter. On the other hand, the Turks fought with the utmost fury, and at the taking of Chios, on the 11th of April, 1822, committed an atrocious massacre of unarmed people. The Greeks themselves discredited their cause by many acts of cruelty and bad faith, and the struggle was urged on both sides with all the ferocity of internecine war. The Ottoman armies made but little progress, and in 1824 the Sultan requested the Pasha of Egypt, Mehemet Ali, to send his adopted son, Ibrahim, to conquer the Morea, on the understanding that it should be given to him for his Pashalik. The offer was accepted, and Ibrahim landed in Greece on the 24th of February, 1825. The arrival of these Egyptian troops, under the command of an able and energetic officer, turned the scale against the Greeks, who were divided amongst themselves by opposing counsels and rival leaders. In North-western Greece, Redschid Pasha made considerable progress, though checked for a while by the magnificent defence of Missolonghi. Still greater successes were obtained by the Ottomans in 1826 and 1827; yet the Greeks refused to abandon their hopes. By this time, many foreign volunteers had joined the revolutionary movement, and of these several came from our own country. Lord Cochrane gave the Greeks the benefit of his skill and experience as a seaman; Sir Richard Church was made Generalissimo of the Greek army; General Gordon and Captain Frank Hastings did effectual service on the same side; and Mr. Trelawney, the friend of Byron and Shelley, entered the ranks of the insurgents in the spirit of a modern knight-errant. Nevertheless, the Turks continued to prevail, and it seemed as if within a little while their authority would be entirely re-established over the whole of Greece.

But the sympathy of Europe in the cause of the insurgents was about to take a more practical form. Russia had given expression to some views pointing to intervention as far back as 1823; but they did not satisfy the requirements of the Greeks, and the war went on without assistance. On the 4th of November, 1824, the Greeks appealed to the British Government, and received from the Foreign Secretary, the eloquent George Canning, an assurance that England would be willing to mediate between them and the Sultan, and to guarantee any settlement which might thus be effected. In August, 1825, Greece put herself under the protection of England, and in 1826 authorized the British Ambassador at the Porte to treat for peace, on the understanding that Greece should receive local self-government, but should recognise the Sultan as its suzerain, and should pay him a yearly tribute. Nothing was then settled; but, after Canning had succeeded to the Premiership in 1827, a treaty was signed in London (July 6th), by which England, France, and Russia undertook to enforce by armed intervention an armistice between the Turks and the Greek insurgents, so as to enable them to carry out the proposed settlement. Mahmud, believing himself to be in a position of command, refused to allow any interference, or to entertain the project of erecting Greece into a vassal State. From one point of view, it is difficult to blame the Sultan. The Greeks had defied his power, and, after several years of arduous fighting, had been reduced to the utmost extremity. It was therefore expecting too much of a sovereign prince that, having gained the day, he should concede nearly the whole of what had been originally demanded and refused. We can easily understand how Russia would reply to a similar requisition, if placed under similar circumstances; and the rule is as good for the Ottoman as for the Muscovite. But the three allied Powers had determined to secure the independence of Greece, whether in a greater or less degree; and their naval forces prepared for active operations.

The Turkish and Egyptian fleet was at that time lying in the Bay of Navarino, on the western coast of the Morea; and here, on the 20th of October, 1827, the combined fleets of England, France, and Russia, under the general command of the English Admiral, Sir Edward Codrington, inflicted on the Ottomans a terrific defeat, resulting in the destruction of more than thirty of the Sultan's ships several of which were blown up, or burned, by the Turks themselves. It is a remarkable fact that this great battle had not been preceded by any declaration of war. An informal armistice had shortly before been concluded between the Greeks and the Ottomans. This was perfidiously broken by the former, who despatched their English friend, Captain Hastings, on an expedition to Salona. When Ibrahim Pasha sent a squadron against Hastings, Codrington drove it back. Ibrahim then recommenced his ravages in the Morea, and the allies began to lose patience; but the action of Navarino was precipitated by the Turks firing on an English lieutenant and a Greek pilot, who had been sent to parley with them. The allied fleets, however, had previously drawn up in line of battle, and it seems impossible to deny that the representatives of the three nations had acted after a most irregular and domineering fashion, and had committed a flagrant violation of international right, in attacking a country with which they were at peace. The action, which was fought between the fortress of Navarino, on one side of the Bay, and the batteries of Sphakteria, on the other, was undoubtedly a great triumph of courage and seamanship; but the news was not received in England with unmitigated satisfaction. The Duke of Wellington characterized the destruction of the Turkish fleet as an "untoward event;" and to many others it appeared obvious that the power of Russia would be enhanced, to the extent that Turkish power was diminished. General Jackson, when President of the United States a few years later, told the English Minister at Washington that England and France had helped

THE PIRÆUS, GREECE.

to aggrandise Russia by bad policy, and th[illegible]ey would some day weep tears of blood for [illegible]ing her at Navarino: a prophecy which may [illegible]dly said to have been fulfilled in the Crime[illegible]ar. The words, "untoward event," together [illegible] an expression of regret at a collision "wholly [illegible]expected by his Majesty," occurred in the [illegible]yal Speech at the opening of Parliament in [illegible]28, at which time the Duke of Wellington had [illegible] Premier. England and Russia, almost imm[illegible]ly after the battle of Navarino, withdrew fr[illegible] the war, if war it can be called; but France la[illegible] an army, which compelled Ibrahim Pasha to ev[illegible]ate the Morea, in September, 1828.

While the struggle in Greece was proceeding

THE BATTLE OF NAVARINO.

Mahmud had been busily engaged with his internal reforms, many of which were of a nature to offend the prejudices of his subjects. His great object was to give a European character to the institutions and the manners of his country. He introduced the western style of dress into Turkey; abandoned the use of the turban, which Mohammedans generally regard with much veneration; and gave musical and theatrical entertainments within the sacred enclosure of the Seraglio. He resolved also to re-commence the military reforms of his uncle Selim, and again to establish the Nizam Jedid, or body of troops organized after European models. This last design roused once more the savage fanaticism of the Janizaries. On the 15th of June, 1826, when the Sultan and the Grand Vizier were in the country, the dissatisfied troops rose in insurrection, and committed great excesses. The Grand Vizier, hastily recalled to the metropolis, took measures for vindicating his master's authority, and at once found himself supported, not only by the new troops, but by the Ulemas and Students. Mahmud arrived shortly afterwards at the Seraglio, and by his orders the Mufti unfolded the standard of the Prophet, and summoned all faithful Mohammedans to rally round that holy symbol. The city was soon divided into two hostile factions. The Janizaries concentrated their forces in one of the great squares, and threw up entrenchments. The supporters of the Sultan gathered in their front, and an attack was made by ordnance, before which the Janizaries retired into their fortified barracks, where they continued to fight with the resolution of despair. Heavy guns, however, were brought to bear upon the walls; fusees were thrown upon the roof; and the building was presently on fire from one end to the other. The frightful struggle was continued in the midst of the flames; all who endeavoured to escape were at once shot down; and before the day was over, 6,000 Janizaries had perished at the hands of their fellow-troops. Fifteen thousand who had not taken part in the movement were exiled to different places in Asia Minor, and on the following day a Hatti-Sherif pronounced the abolition of a corps which had contributed so much to the military predominance of Turkey, but which had at length become a source of internal danger too great to be suffered by any monarch who was resolved that *his* will, and not that of his soldiers, should prevail. During many ages, the turbulence of the Janizaries had been the greatest obstacle to any improvement in the Turkish State. Whenever a weak sovereign held the reins of power, the Janizaries were practically at the head of affairs, and ruled by a species of terrorism which had no other object than the promotion of their own interests. The destruction of this body was a terrible and tragic event; but the rebels had provoked their fate, and it was simply a question of whether they or the Sultan should perish in a conflict which they had themselves begun.

In that same year, 1826, Russia pressed the Porte very hard for a more complete settlement of affairs having reference to the position of Servia and the Danubian Principalities, and to the navigation of the Black Sea. After some negotiations, the Treaty of Akerman, in Bessarabia, was signed on the 6th of October, 1826. This document confirmed the provisions of the Treaty of Bucharest, concluded in 1812, and added many others, admirably calculated to break down the independence of Turkey, and place her at the mercy of her great rival. It was stipulated that the Dardanelles and the Black Sea should be open to Russian merchant-vessels, and that Turkey should not attempt to re-capture any fortress on the Eastern coast of that sea. Servia and the Danubian Principalities were secured in their virtual independence, excepting that Russia reserved to herself a certain right of interference; and Turkey undertook to make compensation to all Russian merchants who had suffered losses on account of any restrictions of a commercial character imposed by the Ottoman Government in previous years.

The independence of Greece was now practically accomplished; but it was not yet recognised as a matter of form. Mahmud was exasperated by the attack on his fleets in the Bay of Navarino, and was even less inclined than before to make concessions to the Allies. He was determined not to admit the intervention of the three Powers; he would not allow that Greece was in fact independent. In these resolutions he was supported by a Council of State, and by public feeling generally. It was seen that war was inevitable, and the Sultan called to arms all who had strength to fight. In a proclamation addressed to his people near the end of 1827, he remarked, and with unquestionable truth, that for sixty years the Russians had been incessantly creating opportunities for war with them. They had encouraged and aided, if they did not originally excite, the rebellion in Greece, and they had extorted from the Turks, in the moment of their distress, the injurious Treaty of Akerman, which the Sultan now openly repudiated. "Their final aim," said the proclamation, "is nothing less than to destroy Islam itself. We have to fight, not for a province, nor for a boundary line, but for our faith. Let every true follower of the Prophet obey this call to arms.

Let life and property, body and soul, be devoted to this sacred war for the defence of Islam." The determination of Mahmud had a certain grandeur and greatness in its audacity; but it was assuredly rash. The Allies had destroyed the larger portion of the Turkish fleet a few weeks before. The Sultan himself had destroyed the best part of his army in the previous year. His finances were in disorder; his Empire was in a state of chaos. It is impossible to conceive a Power in a less favourable position for a great war than Turkey then occupied. The number of Turkish soldiers who had received a military training under the new system is said not to have exceeded 80,000. To these were to be added about 100,000 Asiatic horsemen; but the latter were barbarian warriors, not at all well fitted to encounter the disciplined armies of Europe. It was necessary to keep 30,000 regular troops at Constantinople, to repress any disturbances that might occur, and the Government found itself incapable of providing more than 25,000 men for the garrisons on the Danube, or more than 30,000 for operations in the field. The troops were little better than a rabble, armed with weapons of different sizes, and provided with very bad artillery. On the other hand, the Russians, when the war broke out in 1828, could at once set 100,000 men in battle order, and the number was increased in the following year. Russia, moreover, had sixteen ships of the line in the Mediterranean, and eleven in the Black Sea, besides frigates and smaller vessels, while Turkey had only the miserable remnant of a fleet which had escaped from Navarino.

VARNA.

Yet the war was conducted by the Turks with extraordinary valour, and for a time with marked success. They defended Ibraila, on the Danube, for forty-four days. Schumla resisted the Russian assaults successfully to the last. The armies of the Czar were defeated at Silistria in the first campaign, and had the utmost difficulty in taking the city in 1829. Varna was defended with equal stubbornness, and was at last compelled to succumb only by the treachery of Youssouf Pasha, and the neglect of Omar Vrioni. But, notwithstanding all these gallant endeavours, the Turks were too tremendously overmatched to have much chance of success. The second campaign—that of 1829—was on the whole very favourable to the Russians. In Europe, Field-Marshal Diebitsch advanced over the Balkans, and took Adrianople on the 20th of August. In Asia,

Erzeroum was captured by Field-Marshal Paskiewitsch, who in the previous year had conquered Kars, Akhaltsikh, Anapa, and Poti. The Emperor Nicholas had succeeded in his purpose—partly, it is said, by an excessive resort to bribery, with which he had corrupted some of the Turkish generals, and obtained possession of fortresses not otherwise within his power. But his success had been accomplished at an enormous cost. Count Moltke, who as a young man was present with the Russians during the campaign, and who has since published a work on the subject, remarks that in order to reach the gates of Adrianople Russia had expended 100,000,000 roubles, and had sacrificed considerably more than 50,000 men. With a meagre force of 20,000 men Diebitsch entered the second city of European Turkey, and it has often been said that the Turks might yet have prevailed, if they had had spirit enough to prolong the contest. It is well known that the Russian commanders were extremely anxious as to their position. Their numbers were few; their men were exhausted by long marches and continual fighting; and they were in the heart of the enemy's country. But the Turks did not know the full extent of their opponent's weakness. They were themselves discouraged and worn out, and they believed that in a speedy peace was their only hope of saving Constantinople itself from foreign occupation. A little more resolution and activity on their part might, in the opinion of Count Moltke, "have hurled Diebitsch from the summit of victory and success to the lowest depths of ruin and destruction." But the issue seemed too doubtful to be risked, and the Turks gladly availed themselves of the mediation of England and the other Powers, and entered into negotiations for a peace, preceded, on the 29th of August, by an armistice. Diebitsch was a clever diplomatist, as well as an able general, and he managed to extort very favourable terms from the crest-fallen Ottomans. By the peace of Adrianople, concluded on September 14th, 1829, Russia acquired parts of the eyalets of Childir and Kars, towards the Caucasus, with the fortress of Anapa, near the mouth of the Kuban (though at the outset of the war she had disclaimed all intention of territorial aggrandizement); the Sultan acknowledged the independence of Greece; the separate administration of Wallachia and Moldavia was guaranteed by Russia; Servia was recognized as a vassal state; an indemnity of 10,000,000 ducats was exacted from Turkey; and the Russians were permitted to occupy the Danubian Principalities, and the town of Silistria, until the money had been paid. Russia became possessed of the whole eastern coast of the Black Sea, with the free navigation of the Straits, and obtained complete command of the chief mouths of the Danube, which had been only partially acquired by the treaty of 1812. She also secured the protectorship of the Greek Church throughout the whole of Turkey.

Such were some of the results of the War of Independence in Greece. They were far from agreeable to the English people, and the glowing enthusiasm of the days of Byron and Shelley had entirely departed in 1829. England, as well as France and Russia, had withdrawn her Ambassador from Constantinople when the Porte refused to recognise the independence of Greece; but it was now perceived that a less hostile attitude towards Turkey must be adopted, if the designs of Russia were to be checked in any degree whatever. We had in fact been outwitted by the Czar and his Ministers, as we so often are. On the 4th of April, 1826, a protocol had been signed at St. Petersburg by Count Nesselrode and the Duke of Wellington, providing for the autonomy of Greece, but binding the Powers "not to seek for themselves or their subjects any territorial or commercial advantages or influence which should not be equally applicable to all other nations." Six months later, Russia extorted from the Sultan the Treaty of Akerman, which undoubtedly secured to that Power special advantages of a very valuable kind. The Peace of Adrianople was a still further concession to the selfish interests of Russia; and the Duke of Wellington, as Prime Minister, found himself compelled to assume an attitude of cautious antagonism towards the Colossus of the North. Before the conclusion of peace, he ordered the British fleet to be in readiness to enter the Dardanelles in the event of the Russians marching on Constantinople. This policy undoubtedly restrained the Russians in some degree; but it came too late to effect any important results. The mistake was in ever having entered into any agreement with Russia for the promotion of ends which, however good in themselves, were certain to be used by that Power as a means of forwarding her own ambition. Unfortunately, the political state of Greece for many years was not such as to justify the brilliant hopes that had been entertained. Turbulence, lawlessness, brigandage, petty intrigues, political dishonesty, and general feebleness, were the prevailing characteristics of the Greek Kingdom; and the subserviency to Russia was so great that, during the war in 1854, France and England were obliged to occupy the Piræus, to restrain the Government and people from aiding the Czar by attacks on Turkey. The Duke of Argyll—a bitter enemy of the Ottoman—declared in 1867 that the Greek Government was the worst in Europe, after that of Turkey; and it does not stand very high even now. It must be admitted, however, that the position of a small and incomplete kingdom, surrounded by enemies, was a very difficult one; and progress of late years has been genuine and steady.

After the conclusion of peace, Mahmud busied himself for some years in creating a new army and navy, and in recruiting his finances. His Empire was desperately involved, and the demand upon his Exchequer, caused by the indemnity which he had promised to pay the Czar, was so onerous that he was at length compelled to solicit the remittance of about one-third. New troubles, moreover, soon arose. Mehemet Ali, Pasha of Egypt, had made himself almost independent, and his increasing power gave great uneasiness to the Turkish Sultan. The Empire was indeed divided against itself. In 1831, Ibrahim Pasha directed his forces against the Pasha of Damascus, and conquered Syria. From this province he refused to withdraw, and the Sultan declared war against his vassal on the 15th of April, 1832. Ibrahim advanced as far as Broussa, the Asiatic capital of the Ottoman Empire, and Mahmud would probably have been hurled from power, but for the interposition of Russia, to whom it was much more important that a feeble rule should be perpetuated at the Porte than that a vigorous and enterprising man like Ibrahim should obtain the sceptre. A Russian fleet appeared off the Bosphorus in April, 1833, and landed a strong body of troops opposite Constantinople. This put an end to the war; but Mehemet Ali, though still remaining a tributary of the Sultan, obtained the addition of Syria and Adana to his dominions. On the 8th of July in the same year, Mahmud concluded with Russia the famous Treaty of Unkiar-Skelessi, by which the Czar bound himself to assist Turkey with an army whenever she should require it, in consideration of a promise on her part that no armed ship of any foreign nation should be allowed to pass the Dardanelles without the permission of Russia. Here was another evil consequence of the mistaken policy adopted by the Western Powers, which had forced Turkey to become the ally of Russia, and to grant that country privileges of the most injurious kind to the interests of other lands.

The remaining years of Mahmud's reign were occupied with preparations for another war with Mehemet Ali. This was long postponed by the mediation of England, France, and Russia; but it broke out at length in 1839, in consequence of an evident determination on the part of the Viceroy to conquer Arabia. It commenced with a fresh misfortune to the Turkish army, which was utterly defeated on the 24th of June near Nisibis, or Nezib. This crowning calamity of a disastrous reign was never known to the Sultan. The news of the defeat had not arrived at Constantinople when, on the 1st of July, 1839, Mahmud II. reached the termination of his life. He had reigned since 1808, and during that long period of thirty-one years very few successes had attended his arms or his policy. Yet, with all his crimes, all his mistakes, and all his misfortunes, Mahmud was in some respects a great sovereign. He created a new Turkey in the midst of blood and fire, and any hope of regeneration which the Empire may have since enjoyed is to be attributed to his initiative.

CHAPTER XXIV.

Turkish History concluded—Accession of Abdul-Medjid—Progress of Affairs in Syria and Egypt—The Hatti-Sherif of November, 1839, confirming and enlarging the Reforms of the late Sultan—Negotiations with Mehemet Ali—Interposition of England, Russia, Austria, and Prussia—Action of the Four allied Powers in Syria—Submission of Mehemet Ali—Singular Career of that Ruler—Toleration in Turkey under the Sceptre of Abdul-Medjid—Favourable Opinion of Lord Shaftesbury in 1854—Social Reforms and Development of Prosperity—Position of Turkey towards the Rest of Europe—The Sultan and the Hungarian Refugees—Designs of the Emperor Nicholas—His sounding of the British Government in 1844—The Dispute between France and Russia with Respect to the Guardianship of the Holy Places (1850-53)—Extravagant Demands of Russia—Ultimatum of Prince Menschikoff—His Retirement from Constantinople on the Rejection of the Russian Demands by Turkey—Manifesto of the Czar—Crossing of the Pruth by the Russians—United Action of France and England—Position of Napoleon III.—Preliminaries of the War of 1853-6—Turkish Disaster at Sinope—Russian Advances towards England—Sir Hamilton Seymour's Conversations with the Czar about "the Sick Man"—Declaration of War by France and England against Russia—The Crimean War and the Peace of 1856—Subsequent Condition of Turkey.

TURKEY was in a position of the greatest internal danger when Abdul-Medjid ascended the throne, and the general posture of affairs was rendered more serious by the youth and ignorance of the new sovereign. Like other Turkish princes, he had been brought up in the harem, and his education was as defective as priests, women, and eunuchs could make it. Mahmud had desired to give his son a European training; but Mohammedan fanaticism was so strongly opposed to such a course that the Sultan was forced to recede. Abdul-Medjid, therefore, came to the administration of affairs with the ordinary incapacity of a boy, and the special unfitness of one who had seen nothing beyond the walls of a seraglio. He was but sixteen years of age, and, with an utter want of experience in the concerns of life, he was suddenly called upon to guide the fortunes of a great Empire in a state of dissolution. News of the disastrous defeat at Nisibis, which had taken place on the 24th of June, arrived at Constantinople a few days after his accession on July 1st. Ibrahim Pasha was on his road to the capital, and all the adherents of the old ways regarded him as the hope of Islam. In this terrible conjuncture, a new misfortune befel the Empire. By an act of stupendous treachery, the Capitan Pasha, Achmet, deserted to Mehemet Ali with the whole of the Turkish fleet, and arrived at Alexandria on the 14th of July. It was the act of one who desired the success of the Old Turkish party, and who thought that in this way the downfall of the Sultan might be effected, or the progress of reform be checked by fear of the consequences. But Abdul-Medjid was supported by able and courageous Ministers, who were resolved to persevere in those schemes of regeneration which Mahmud had begun, but had very imperfectly carried out. On the 3rd of November, 1839, a Hatti-Sherif, solemnly issued at Gulhané, ratified and confirmed the civil reforms of the late sovereign, and added some others. By this measure, the Sultan guaranteed to all his subjects, without regard to rank or religion, security for person and property, and promised to introduce a regular and impartial system of taxation, public administration of justice, the right of free transmission of property, an amelioration of the system of the conscription (which pressed with great hardship on the poorer classes), and some other improvements. The concessions were of an exceedingly liberal character, and the fears of the priestly party were so much aroused that plots were formed for dethroning the Sultan. But a few timely executions restored tranquillity, and Abdul-Medjid became in time a very popular sovereign in most parts of his Empire.

Immediately on his accession to the throne, the young Sultan forwarded to the Viceroy of Egypt an offer of pardon, together with the hereditary possession of his province, on the understanding that he would conform to his duties of obedience and submission. Mehemet Ali might perhaps have accepted these terms, but for the arrival at Alexandria of the Turkish fleet under the traitor Achmet. This immense accession of strength encouraged him to continue his resistance; but the European Powers stepped in to adjust what threatened to be a very serious complication. Their mediation was welcomed by Abdul-Medjid, but Mehemet Ali objected to the proffered terms, and it was then resolved to take more peremptory measures. On the 15th of July, 1840, a convention was signed at London, by which England, Russia, Austria, and Prussia, agreed to submit to the Egyptian ruler certain proposals in the form of an ultimatum. The Pasha was to have the hereditary sovereignty of Egypt, and possession of the government of St. Jean d'Acre, in Syria, for life. If, within ten days from the notification of these terms, the Pasha should not have accepted them, the Sultan was to offer him Egypt alone; and if he still persisted in refusing, the four Powers were to compel him by force to accede to the proposed settlement. France had joined in the earlier stages of the negotiations, but separated from the other four Powers in the adoption of this agreement. The Viceroy of Egypt, finding himself face to face with a powerful combination, endeavoured to temporise by offering to open negotiations with the Porte, and by despatching an envoy to Constantinople, charged with instructions. The suggestions of Mehemet Ali, however, were not considered satisfactory by the Turkish Ministers, and the Sultan pronounced the formal deposition of the Pasha. On the arrival at Alexandria of a firman to this effect, Mehemet Ali announced his intention of repelling force by force; and the four allied Powers then declared the ports of Syria and Egypt in a state of blockade. On the 9th of September, a combined English, Austrian, and Turkish fleet appeared off Beyrout, which was bombarded and captured in October, when the Egyptian army lost 7,000 men in killed, wounded, and prisoners, together with twenty pieces of cannon. Sidon had been captured on the 27th of September, and Acre followed on the 3rd of November. Even Alexandria was blockaded, and Mehemet Ali, now an old man of more than seventy, found it necessary to come to terms. The principal towns of Syria had been evacuated by their Egyptian garrisons, and some of the Pasha's forces, while endeavouring to make their way through Palestine into Egypt, had been taken prisoners of war. The Syrian tribes began to forsake the failing cause, and the garrison and inhabitants of Jerusalem returned to their allegiance to the Sultan in November. Negotiations having been opened, an arrangement was concluded in January, 1841, by which Mehemet

Ali restored the whole of the Turkish fleet; his son, Ibrahim Pasha, was directed to relinquish Syria; and the Sultan bestowed on Mehemet the hereditary possession of Egypt. This remarkable man—a Macedonian peasant in early life, who by military genius alone had raised himself to the position of a great ruler—was in many ways an enlightened and beneficent sovereign. Despotic and arbitrary he undoubtedly was; but he added much to the prosperity and good government of Egypt, and reorganized on intelligent and liberal principles a state of society which had sunk to the lowest depths of misery and degradation. The arts and sciences, and some of the institutions, of Europe were introduced into this primæval land by one who until his thirty-fifth year was unable to read; the Christians were protected by a wise toleration; and the magnificent resources of the country, which had lain dormant for ages, were developed to an extent, and with a rapidity, which excited the surprise of all political observers. Mehemet Ali died on the 2nd of August, 1849, a few months after the death of Ibrahim, and was succeeded by Ibrahim's son, Abbas Pasha. The present ruler, Ismail, began his Viceroyalty on the 18th of January, 1863, and received from the Sultan the title of "Khedive," meaning King or Lord, on the 14th of May, 1867. It would lead us too far afield to follow in this place the career of the Sultan's Egyptian vassal.

BEYROUT.

For some years after the conclusion of peace in Syria, the rule of Abdul-Medjid was distinguished by no very remarkable events. The Sultan was a man of rather weak character, much given to the forms of indulgence which prevail in Mohammedan countries; but he was mild, just, and well-intentioned. The reforms instituted in 1839, which sometimes go by the general designation of the Tanzimat, were carried out with evident sincerity, though often thwarted by the prejudice and intolerance of the Old Turkish party. In 1849, Christians were admitted to office in Turkey, and it is undeniable that in many respects their condition underwent a great improvement. But the progress of amelioration was necessarily slow, for the obstacles were numerous and difficult. The Hatti-Sherif was in some points violated, yet it was very far from being a dead letter. The personal wishes of the Sultan were liberal and benevolent, and many of the great officers of State were equally well inclined to follow the new policy to its legitimate conclusions. But the bigots were numerous all over the Empire, and they sometimes made their will prevail. The difficulties of the position were increased by the underhand influence of Russia, which was sedulously exercised to embroil the Sultan with his subjects, and to create the very evils which it was afterwards designed to allege as the excuse for open intervention. Intrigues were always proceeding at Constantinople, and the Ambassadors of the leading Powers schemed against one another for predominance, while the unfortunate Empire suffered by the agitation thus artificially maintained. The faults of Turkish rule have no doubt been most serious; but a disposition to inaugurate a better state had been manifest for some years, and that disposition was rendered partially inoperative by the selfish cabals of the European representatives. No country, however well-organised, could have passed without injury through such a series of trials; and the fact of her not being entirely ruined by pretended friends and secret enemies is proof that, with all her errors, Turkey must possess some sterling virtues, which under healthier conditions might have been more fully developed. It must always be recollected to the credit of Abdul-Medjid that he accustomed his people to the idea of toleration. The Earl of Shaftesbury, speaking in the House of Lords on the 10th of March, 1854, bore testimony to the liberality with which Protestants had been uniformly treated by the Sultan then reigning. On that occasion, he denounced the assertion contained in a Russian manifesto, that England and France, which were then just entering into an alliance to repel the ambition of the Czar, were fighting for Mohammedanism, and that Russia was fighting for Christianity. The question, he truly remarked, was not one of religion, but of justice. If he were compelled to choose between the two, he would infinitely prefer the Turkish to the Russian civilization. The wrongs suffered by the Christians in Turkey were mainly attributable to themselves, being caused by intrigues and disputes among the sects, or by the ambition of the Greek priests. The Porte had allowed books, missionaries, printing-presses, and all the agencies of improvement and proselytism, full scope throughout the Turkish dominions; whereas in Russia the frontier was hermetically sealed against any such importations, and for thirty years not a single copy of the Bible printed in the vernacular tongue had been allowed to circulate. The Earl of Shaftesbury traced the secret motives of Russian interference in Turkey to jealousy of the toleration shown by Turks towards Protestants; and he showed in the most irresistible manner that religious liberty had nothing to gain, but everything to lose, by the substitution of Muscovite for Ottoman rule.

It is singular to contrast these utterances with the tone adopted by Lord Shaftesbury at a more recent period. It is true that Abdul-Medjid has long since departed; but the spirit of toleration did not depart with him. The Bulgarian massacre was an isolated instance of fanaticism, bursting out with sudden ferocity on the application of an exciting cause, which had been in all probability deliberately devised with a view to that end; but it does not disprove the general fact that for many years all the religious bodies in Turkey had enjoyed a remarkable degree of freedom, though subject to some disabilities, similar to those of English Dissenters up to a recent period. Under Abdul-Medjid and his successor, the Christians were in fact protected from one another; the extravagant claims of the Greek Church, which had been felt by the Bulgarians as a galling yoke, were effectually checked; Greek and Romanist were withheld from mutual extermination; and the Protestant missionaries pursued their work in peace. The progress of Turkey during the first fifteen years of the reign of Abdul-Medjid was indeed remarkable. For the greater portion of that time, the Empire was tranquil. Old industries were revived; trade and commerce were developed; and there seemed a reasonable probability that Turkey would eventually be assimilated to the ideas and habits of Europe. A Council of Education was established in 1846, and the Sultan soon afterwards founded a University, extended the system of primary schools, and opened military, medical, and agricultural colleges. The days had passed when Turkey was a danger to Europe. She was no longer a conquering Power. She did not threaten the independence of any country or race. She had no ambition beyond the natural desire to retain what she held, and the creditable wish to improve her state by adopting the forms of Western Europe. To some extent, it may be said that the existence of a Mohammedan Empire within the European circle is an anomaly. But this is a world of anomalies, or what appear such to our half-instructed judgments; and it is hard to show in what respect Christianity was the worse for the existence of a Moslem sovereignty between the Danube and the Sea of Marmora. The Turks, it is true, had obtained their position by conquest; but the same may be said of every other dominant Power, and if four or five centuries of possession do not confer a right, as rights are construed in political morality, it would be difficult to say how such a right can be established at all. Only one European

Power had any positive interest in the destruction of Turkish rule; and at the period of the Crimean War it was apparent to the other Governments, not merely that Turkey had a claim to be supported, but that it was to the interest of the Western world generally that that support should be given.

The Crimean War had been preceded, a few years before, by a rupture of diplomatic relations between Russia and the Porte, consequent on the noble conduct of the Sultan towards Kossuth, and the other Hungarian and Polish refugees. Russia, as we have already related, had lent her aid to Austria in murdering the liberties of Hungary, and, when the beaten patriots fled into the Turkish dominions in the autumn of 1849, Austria and Russia demanded their extradition, which the Porte, upheld in its determination by the English Government, persistently refused. Upon this, Russia suspended all intercourse with Turkey, and the British fleet, in view of a possible rupture, cast anchor in Besika Bay on the 13th of November. The quarrel was accommodated by the close of the year; but there is no doubt that it rankled in the mind of the Czar. This, however, was certainly not the principal motive for the course afterwards adopted by the Emperor Nicholas. A desire to obtain Constantinople for the Russian capital was probably the chief operating cause which led to the sanguinary struggle in the Crimea. The scheme had been cherished for some years; indeed, it is very likely that it had been secretly entertained by the Czar throughout the whole of his reign. Nothing could be more agreeable to the inordinate ambition of a sovereign who regarded military success as the greatest form of human excellence, than to give tangible shape to a project which had formed one of the lofty dreams of Catharine II., and doubtless of Peter the Great. When the Emperor Nicholas visited England in 1844, he conversed with Lord Aberdeen—an old friend of his, at that time Foreign Secretary—with the Prime Minister, Sir Robert Peel, and with the Duke of Wellington, respecting what he regarded as the approaching dissolution of Turkey. On his return to Russia, he embodied these views in a memorandum drawn up by Count Nesselrode, which was transmitted to the English Government. Its existence, however, was not made known until March, 1854, when negotiations were proceeding, the failure of which led to the war with Russia. The *Times* had by some means become acquainted with this document, and an intimation of its existence was thus published to the world. By that time, the Earl of Aberdeen, whose views were always friendly towards Russia, had attained to the position of Prime Minister; and, being questioned on the subject in the House of Lords, he was obliged to confess that, when Foreign Minister ten years earlier, he had so far listened to the suggestions of the Czar that that potentate had been induced to put his ideas into

SCHOOL IN BULGARIA.

the definite form of a diplomatic paper, which would probably never have seen the light, but for the discovery of its existence by the *Times*. From this document, and from the previous conversations, it is evident that from the year 1844, if not from an earlier date, the Emperor had formed designs against Turkey. But he approached the execution of those designs after a very distant, cautious, and tentative fashion. He had occupied the Danubian Principalities from 1848 to 1850, under the pretext of suppressing revolutionary movements; but this had led to nothing, and a fresh project was now to be set on foot.

For every war an excuse of some kind is needed, and the excuse found by Russia was the custody of the Holy Places at Palestine. The Greek and Latin Churches had long contended for the guardianship of those sacred monuments. In the reign of Francis I. of France, they were placed under Latin monks, protected by the French Government; but the Greek Church was jealous of so exalted a privilege being conferred upon its rival, and from time to time obtained firmans from the Porte invalidating the rights of the Latins, who were expelled in 1757. The buildings were then committed to the care of the Greeks; but the French seem never to have abandoned their claim in this respect. The subject was revived in the year 1850, and the Porte then proposed that a mixed commission should adjudicate on the respective demands. A great deal of warm discussion ensued between the representatives of Russia and France; but on the 9th of March, 1852, the Sultan issued a firman ratifying and consolidating the rights previously granted to the Greek Christians, and declaring that the Latins had no excuse for claiming exclusive possession of certain holy places specified. Here was a great triumph for Russia; but her demands grew in proportion as they were gratified. While on the whole pronouncing against the Latin Christians, the Sultan allowed them to possess keys of the church at Bethlehem and of other places, as in former times. This was regarded by Russia as a mortal offence, although the French Government had acquiesced, with some reluctance, in the general settlement. The fatal Treaty of Kainardji, which has been at the bottom of so many of Turkey's misfortunes, was now invoked by the Czar, as conferring on him a right to protect the Christians in all parts of the Turkish Empire. The position of the Sultan was peculiarly difficult, since he had pleased neither the Russians nor the French, and was open to attack from both. But he showed considerable fairness, and at the same time maintained the independence of his Empire with much spirit and dignity. On the 28th of February, 1853, Prince Menschikoff arrived at Constantinople as Envoy Extraordinary from the Russian Emperor. His demands, however, were so extreme that all hope of an arrangement speedily disappeared, and in May he departed from the Turkish capital, after the rejection by the Turkish Government of the ultimatum which he had presented. In that ultimatum, his Imperial master had demanded that the protectorate of the Greek Christians should be again conceded to him, and that the Russo-Greek Church should receive specifically, and by solemn treaty, all the rights and privileges, in regard both to the Holy Places and to other matters, that it had ever claimed. He also required that the Greek Patriarch at Constantinople should be irremovable, unless guilty of proved high treason or gross misconduct, and even then only with the consent of Russia. Up to that time, the Patriarch had been removable at the pleasure of the Porte; but, by the condition now demanded, he would become nothing else than a Russian subject, exercising very great and exceptional powers in the midst of the Turkish Empire. By the advice of Lord Stratford de Redcliffe and M. de la Cour, the English and French Ambassadors, the Sultan, on the 13th of May, refused to comply with such demands, and Menschikoff quitted Constantinople on the 21st of the month.

The object of the Emperor Nicholas was patent to all the world. He sought to put Turkey in the position of a vassal State to Russia, and thus to carry to its legitimate conclusions all that had already been done by his predecessors in the same direction. For nearly a century, Russia had been advancing towards the great end of her foreign policy. She had absorbed Ottoman territory; she had obtained something like suzerain rights in the very heart of Turkey; and she was now endeavouring to increase those rights, and to put the Sultan more completely in the position of a satrap. But it was necessary to give these designs some colour of disinterestedness; and the Czar accordingly issued, on the 26th of June, a manifesto to the Russian people, in which his contemplated action was attributed entirely to solicitude for the rights of the Orthodox Church. He affirmed that numerous arbitrary acts of the Ottoman Government had recently endangered those rights, and threatened finally to destroy the whole order of things sanctioned for centuries, and dear to the Orthodox faith. The failure of the Czar to obtain the satisfaction of his demands had induced him to order his troops to enter the Danubian Principalities. Nevertheless, he added, it was not his intention even then to commence war: he merely desired to obtain a necessary pledge. "We do not seek conquests," he concluded; "Russia does not need them. We demand satisfaction for a legitimate right openly infringed. We are ready even now to stop the movement of our troops, if the Ottoman Porte engages to observe religiously the integrity of the privileges of the Orthodox Church. But if obstruction and blindness obstinately desire the contrary, then, invoking God to our aid, we will leave it to His care to decide our differences, and, placing our full hope in His all-powerful hand, we will march to the defence of the Orthodox faith."

Nearly three weeks before the issue of this manifesto—viz., on the 6th of June—the Sultan had published a Hatti-Sherif confirming all the rights and privileges of the Greek Christians, and had at the same time appealed for support to his allies. The English and French fleets had anchored in Besika Bay on the 13th of the month, so that matters had already begun to look very warlike. On the 2nd of July, the Russians, under General Luders, crossed the Pruth, and entered Moldavia; and on the same day the Russian Minister, Count Nesselrode, addressed a circular note to the Russian Envoys at Foreign Courts, in order to justify the step which had been taken. The movement of the English and French fleets towards the waters of Constantinople was here alleged as the reason why Russia had determined upon crossing the Pruth. But, as the French Foreign Minister, M. Drouyn de l'Huys, well observed in reply to the Russian circular, the action of his own Government and that of England had been preceded by preparations for war, which for several months past had been made in Bessarabia, and in the harbour of Sebastopol; and also by the departure from Constantinople of the Russian Envoy, Prince Menschikoff, who had previously conveyed to Redschid Pasha a very clearly expressed threat of an approaching occupation of the Danubian Principalities. Moreover, the English and French naval forces did not, by their presence outside the Dardanelles, infringe existing treaties, while, on the contrary, as M. Drouyn de l'Huys observed, the occupation of Wallachia and Moldavia constituted a manifest violation of those treaties. A reply of a similar nature was despatched by the English Cabinet to St. Petersburg, and the project of an English and French alliance began to excite attention.

The French Empire had but recently been restored in the person of Louis Napoleon, who, elected as President in December, 1848, and as Dictator for ten years in December, 1851, had received from the popular suffrages the Imperial dignity of France in November, 1852. As a democratic sovereign, and the representative of a new line, Napoleon III. was regarded with dislike by the older European Monarchies. As a Bonaparte, he was watched with suspicion and fear, as one who in all probability cherished schemes of European conquest, similar to those which gave a brief and lurid splendour to the reign of his uncle. His position at home was scarcely more favourable than his position abroad. Although supported by the great majority of the French people, he was bitterly opposed by an irreconcileable faction, which, while weak in numbers, was powerful in the literary abilities of many of its supporters, in the extravagance of a licentious press, in the turbulence of a discontented working class, and in the plots of men whose dreams had been shattered by the convulsions of 1848. It was essential to the continued prosperity of Napoleon III. that he should obtain some great success, especially of a military order, which should give him a recognized position among the Powers of Europe, and dazzle the populace by the renovated glory of France. These considerations undoubtedly had their share in determining the action of the French Emperor; but it would be unjust to deny that there were other motives also, and those of a larger and more permanent kind. Napoleon III. was at that time in the zenith of his mental powers. He was not yet broken by sickness and advancing years. He had not acquired that fatal habit of vacillation which towards the end of his reign ruined all his better projects, and betrayed him into his worse. He distinctly perceived and clearly understood that the predominance of Russia in the south-east of Europe was a danger to the world. He knew that if the principles of Russian rule were made stronger in any one direction, the principle of popular rule, which he himself represented, would be menaced by a deadly peril. The Imperialism of a Romanoff and the Imperialism of a Bonaparte are two distinct things, which the identity of the designation should not persuade us to confound. The Emperor of the French comprehended the principles of his own rule, and was not slow to perceive that the older forms of Imperialism must give way to his, or his must give way to them. For all these reasons combined, Napoleon III. was doubtless eager for a war with Russia; but he would hardly have cared to enter on such a war without the assistance of England. The English alliance was a double advantage to him. It added to his material strength, and it immeasurably increased his moral power. The approximation of the two countries on this question was to some extent mutual; but it was much warmer and more emphatic on the part of France than on that of England. The English Government was directed by Lord Aberdeen, a statesman of decidedly Russian sympathies; and the hesitation of the Cabinet, despite the warlike tendency of some of its members, was marked and obvious. It was still hoped that arrangements might be made, and, though Russia was evidently bent on hostilities, ministerial England talked of peace with almost wearisome pertinacity, and Paris was ahead of London in the disposition to bring Russia to a sharp account.

Events dragged on through the whole of 1853 with great slowness, but with an ever-increasing probability of war. Without waiting for any decision, either by diplomacy or by arms, the Emperor of Russia assumed towards the Danubian Principalities the position of a Dictator. In the course of July, he signified to the Hospodar of Moldavia that his relations with the Porte were to cease; that the tribute which Moldavia had been in the habit of transmitting to Constantinople was to be placed at the disposal of the Russian Government; and that the sovereign power of Turkey was temporarily suspended during the military occupation of the provinces. Under these circumstances, Lord Clarendon, the English Foreign Minister, considered it improper for the British Consuls to continue to exercise authority in those provinces; and he lost no time in communicating that opinion to Lord Stratford de Redcliffe. At the same period, a Conference was being held at Vienna, on the initiative of the English and Austrian Governments. At this Conference, England, France, Austria, and Prussia were represented, and a note containing the bases of a settlement was agreed to on the 31st of July. Its object was to bind the Sultan in specific language to a recognition of the rights of his Christian subjects, and to satisfy the demands of Russia with respect to the position of Russian ecclesiastics in the Holy Land. This note was accepted by the Czar on the 10th of August; but the Sultan, on the 19th of the same month, required certain modifications, not affecting the essential conditions of the proposed arrangement, but qualifying the peremptory language in which some of those conditions were expressed. These modifications the Czar rejected on the 7th of September, and Austria thereupon withdrew from further joint action with the Western Powers, and despatched special instructions to its representative at Constantinople to press on the Sultan the acceptance of the Vienna note as it originally stood. Even had he been personally inclined to do this, the Sultan would not have dared so far to oppose the wishes of his subjects. The popular feeling at Constantinople was passionately in favour of hostilities. Inflammatory placards were posted throughout the city, denouncing the too pacific policy of the Ministers, and urging the Sultan to a holy war. The Ulemas were much excited, and began to talk of war or abdication. Troops were rapidly forwarded to Varna; the Russians from day to day strengthened themselves in the Principalities, and marched an army-corps upon Bucharest; and on the 14th of September two English and two French ships entered the Dardanelles.

It was not long before Turkey resolved to defy the power which was evidently bent on her destruction, and to resent the occupation of the Danubian Principalities which had taken place at the beginning of July. On the 5th of October—the opening of the year in Turkey—a manifesto of the Sultan, containing a declaration of war against Russia, was publicly read in all the mosques. Omar Pasha, one of the most able and distinguished of the Turkish generals, was instructed to communicate the resolve of the Sultan to Prince Gortschakoff—not the same Prince Gortschakoff who now holds the highest position in the Russian Government, but an officer of distinction, who had command of the invading forces in the Principalities. In transmitting this communication, Omar Pasha said that the Sublime Porte, as a last expression of its pacific sentiments, proposed the evacuation of the two provinces, and granted a term of fifteen days for the decision of the Prince. The proposal was of course rejected, and the Czar issued a counter-declaration of war on the 1st of November. The Turks had already, on the 23rd of October, fired on a Russian flotilla off the fortress of Isaktcha, and shortly afterwards they crossed the Danube at Widdin, and occupied Kalafat, in Wallachia. The English and French fleets entered the Bosphorus on the 2nd of November, and fighting between the Russians and the Turks soon began in earnest. The Russians were defeated at Oltenitza, on the northern side of the Danube, on the 4th of November; but in the course of the next few weeks the Turks in Asia sustained reverses in three localities. A terrible naval disaster followed on the 30th, when a Turkish fleet of seven frigates, three corvettes, and two smaller vessels, lying in the harbour of Sinope, on the Black Sea, was attacked by a Russian fleet of six sail of the line, two sailing vessels, and three steamers, and totally destroyed, with the exception of one vessel, which conveyed the tidings to Constantinople. The town of Sinope was also bombarded and set on fire. The attack was made under cover of a fog, and was regarded at the time as treacherous. It may be urged that, after a declaration of war, either belligerent may take his enemy at any disadvantage which chance may offer. But what gave exceptional character to the affair

DESTRUCTION OF THE TURKISH FLEET AT SINOPE.

at Sinope was that for a few weeks past there had been a suspension of hostilities (though of an informal nature), and that the Western Powers were still engaged in endeavouring to effect a peaceful solution. Be the morals of the case as they may, however, the misfortune was terrific, and Turkey was dismayed at the crushing blow which had so suddenly fallen upon her. Several of the ships blew up; four thousand lives were lost by fire or drowning; and Osman Pasha, the Turkish Admiral, died at Sebastopol of his wounds. In consequence of this calamity, the allied fleets, listening to an urgent request on the part of the Porte, entered the Black Sea on the 4th of January, 1854. On the 5th of December, 1853, a collective note had been presented at Constantinople by the four Powers, requiring to know upon what terms the Sultan would negotiate for peace. The reply of the Porte, which was dated the 31st of December, proposed, as bases for negotiation, the promptest possible evacuation of the Principalities; a revision of the treaties between Turkey and Russia;. the maintenance of religious privileges among communities of all confessions; and a definite settlement of the convention respecting the Holy Places. All attempts at pacification, however, entirely failed of success; and to the ultimatum of England and France, sent to St. Petersburg on the 27th of February, 1854, the Czar, on the 19th of March, declined to make any response.

The indignation of the English people against the ambition of Russia had been slowly rising, and the publication, in March, 1854, of some reports by Sir Hamilton Seymour, our Ambassador at St. Petersburg, concerning the designs of Nicholas, showed the urgent necessity of checking those designs, even at the cost of war. In despatches to the Foreign Office, written in the early part of 1853, Sir Hamilton Seymour gave details of certain interviews which he had had with the Czar. On the 11th of January, the conversation had been general, and the Emperor was about to close it when Sir Hamilton Seymour respectfully begged that his Majesty would add a few words, which might tend to calm the anxiety of the English Government. In responding to this request, the Emperor, speaking at first with a little hesitation, but, as he proceeded, in an open and unrestrained way, observed:—"The affairs of Turkey are in a very disorganized condition; the country itself seems to be falling to pieces. The fall will be a great misfortune, and it is very important that England and Russia should come to a perfectly good understanding upon these affairs, and that neither should take any decisive step, of which the other is not apprised." After a few words from Sir Hamilton Seymour, expressing his satisfaction that his Imperial Majesty should hold such language, the Emperor proceeded to unfold his views with more particularity. "We have on our hands," he said, "a sick man—a very sick man; it will be, I tell you frankly, a great misfortune if one of these days he should slip away from us, especially before all necessary arrangements are made. However, this is not the time to speak to you on that matter." Sir Hamilton responded:—"Your Majesty is so gracious that you will allow me to make one further observation. Your Majesty says the man is sick: it is very true, but your Majesty will deign to excuse me if I remark that it is the part of the generous and strong man to treat with gentleness the sick and feeble man." The conversation was resumed on the 22nd of January, when the Czar, returning to his illustration of the sick man, said:—"Turkey has fallen into such a state of decrepitude that, as I told you the other night, eager as we all are for the prolonged existence of the man (and that I am as desirous as you can be for the continuance of his life, I beg you to believe), he may suddenly die upon our hands. We cannot resuscitate what is dead. If the Turkish Empire falls, it falls to rise no more; and I put it to you, therefore, whether it is not better to be provided beforehand for a contingency than to incur the chaos, confusion, and the certainty of a European war, all of which must attend the catastrophe if it should occur unexpectedly, and before some ulterior system has been sketched. This is the point to which I am desirous that you should call the attention of your Government." After some more conversation, in which the Emperor made further approaches towards the main point, he continued:—"Now, I desire to speak to you as a friend and as a gentleman. If England and I arrive at an understanding in this matter, it is indifferent to me what others do or think. Frankly, then, I tell you plainly that if England thinks of establishing herself one of these days at Constantinople, I will not allow it. I do not attribute this intention to you, but it is better on these occasions to speak plainly. For my part, I am equally disposed to take the engagement not to establish myself there—as proprietor, that is to say, for as trustee I do not say: it might happen that circumstances, if no previous provision were made—if everything should be left to chance —might place me in the position of occupying Constantinople."

At a subsequent interview, in February, the Emperor pursued the same subject. He professed great suspicion as to the designs of France. Not much more than a month previously, he had apprized the Sultan that, if his assistance were required for resisting the menaces of the French, he was entirely at the service of that sovereign. He then observed that, in the event of the dissolution of the Ottoman Empire, he thought it might be less difficult to arrive at a satisfactory territorial arrangement than was commonly supposed. "The Danubian Principalities," he said, "are in fact an independent State under my protection: this might so continue. Servia might receive the same form of Government. So again with Bulgaria. There seems to be no reason why this province should not form an independent State. As to Egypt, I quite understand the importance to England of that territory. I can, then, only say that if, in the event of a distribution of the Ottoman succession upon the fall of the Empire, you should take possession of Egypt, I shall have no objections to offer. I would say the same thing of Candia [Crete]. That island might suit you, and I do not know why it should not become an English possession." It need hardly be said that Sir Hamilton Seymour gave no encouragement to these proposals, and, in writing to Lord John Russell, who was then for a brief while at the head of the Foreign Office, he remarked that the Emperor's object was apparently to engage her Majesty's Government, in conjunction with his own Cabinet, and probably that of Vienna, in some scheme for the ultimate partition of Turkey, and for the exclusion of France from the arrangement. Lord Clarendon, who had succeeded to the Foreign Office by the 23rd of March, 1853, wrote to Sir Hamilton Seymour on that day some pertinent remarks on the existing state of affairs in the East. Her Majesty's Government, he said, could not admit that the signs of Turkish decay were either more evident, or more rapid, than they had been for some years. "There is still," he continued, "great energy and great wealth in Turkey; a disposition to improve the system of government is not wanting; corruption, though unfortunately great, is still not of a character, nor carried to an extent, that threatens the existence of the State; the treatment of Christians is not harsh, and the toleration exhibited by the Porte towards this portion of its subjects might serve as an example to some Governments who look with contempt upon Turkey as a barbarous Power." The British Government of course entirely repudiated any desire to join in a dishonest plot, and the Czar did not return to the subject with Sir Hamilton Seymour. He made the same attempt, however, with the French Government, notwithstanding the suspicion of France which he had expressed to the English Ambassador; but here also his proposals were met by a refusal. The complication in the East accordingly went on, and before the end of 1853 it became obvious that, if there was to be a European war at all, France and England would be found side by side, opposing the policy of Russia.

Lord Aberdeen was still Prime Minister of England when, undoubtedly with reluctance on his part, a treaty of alliance between England, France, and Turkey was signed on the 12th of March, 1854. The declarations of war by France and England against Russia were issued on the 27th and 28th of March, and the troops of the two Allied Powers were speedily despatched to Gallipoli. A few days before these declarations, the Russians had crossed the Danube into the Dobrudscha, from which, after several defeats by the Turks, they withdrew before the autumn. The summer of 1854 was wasted by the armies of France and England in inactivity at Varna, where large numbers died of cholera, and from the effects of a pestilent climate. It was not until the middle of September that the allies landed in the Crimea, and commenced that series of operations which terminated in the complete defeat of Russia. In the conduct of the war, Sardinia after awhile took part, and, under the political direction of Cavour, attained a position in the European system which materially helped the development of the little Sub-Alpine kingdom into the Italian monarchy which now sways the peninsula from historic Rome. Austria and Prussia stood apart throughout the struggle, excepting that the former, after the evacuation of the Principalities by the Russians in August and September, 1854, occupied those provinces by virtue of a treaty with Turkey. The policy of Prussia excited the utmost contempt in England, and we have since learned how completely the national feeling in this respect was shared by the Queen and the Prince Consort.* Indeed, at that time the English people, with but few exceptions, were united in the determination to repel a danger which threatened, not England only, but the interests of justice and civilisation all over Europe. A small section, headed by Mr. Cobden and Mr. Bright—men of high political genius and noble character, but who in this matter seem to have been the victims of a theory—consistently opposed any resort to war, and were for letting Russia partition Turkey, seize on Constantinople, obtain complete mastery of the Black Sea, and do what she liked with the Bosphorus and the Dardanelles. But the vast

* See Vol. III. of Mr. Theodore Martin's "Life of the Prince Consort," published at the close of 1877.

majority of the nation repudiated such views, and the Prince Consort, in communications to several exalted personages, and in memoranda written at the time, gave clear expression to the great popular instinct of that period. In a letter to King Leopold, of Belgium, the Prince Consort most truly observed:—"All Europe, Belgium and Germany included, have the greatest interest in the integrity and independence of the Porte being secured for the future, but a still greater in Russia being defeated and chastised. For it is to weak States, above all others, of importance as a precedent that, if a strong neighbour seeks to oppress them, all Europe should come to their aid, and repel the oppressor." That is a principle of universal application. It is as true now as it was then; and, so far from its being a contradiction of the great Liberal doctrine of non-intervention, it is the absolute and necessary completion of that safeguard of the weak.

The war was undoubtedly popular in England; but it was terribly mismanaged. A peace of nearly forty years' duration had left us with little capacity for military affairs; and the Peninsular officers, such as Lord Raglan, who were appointed to the chief commands, seemed to have forgotten their old skill. By sea, much was threatened, but little done. Sir Charles Napier was sent to the Baltic; but becoming alarmed at the real or apparent strength of the Russian fortresses, he returned in the autumn of 1854, after destroying the petty town and fort of Bomarsund, and performing some other small services. Sir Edmund Lyons, in the Black Sea, was rather more successful, but had not many opportunties of distinguishing himself. At no time, however, have British courage and endurance been more conspicuously shown than in the operations of the Crimea. It was mainly by the advice of the French Emperor that the troops were sent to that distant peninsula, in order that the power of Russia in the Black Sea might be crippled by the destruction of Sebastopol, which the Empress Catharine had described as the gate of Constantinople. The first battle in which the French and English were concerned was that of the Alma, fought on the 20th of September, 1854; shortly after which, Sebastopol was besieged by the united forces of the Allies. The battles of Balaklava (October 25th) and Inkerman (November 5th) were engagements in which the valour of the British soldier was splendidly exhibited, but which reflected little credit on the science of the generals. Then came the terrific winter of 1854–5, in which, owing to the utter failure of the Commissariat, to mismanagement at home, and to the wicked dishonesty of contractors, thousands of gallant men perished, not from the bullets of the enemy, but from sheer cold and hunger. No one whose memory goes back to that time will ever forget the sense of horror with which England was afflicted in those winter days, when intelligence from the Crimea revealed that our army was dying in the deep snow before Sebastopol for want of the commonest necessaries of life, and that but for the generous assistance of the French the catastrophe would have been even worse. The disclosures of the *Times* and other papers led to the fall of the Aberdeen Ministry. Mr. Roebuck having placed on the paper a resolution for a committee of inquiry into the conduct of the war, Lord John Russell, who was at that time President of the Council and leader of the House of Commons, resigned office on the 23rd of January, 1855, declaring that he did not see how the motion could be resisted. This was followed, a week later, by the resignation of the whole Cabinet, which was announced in the House of Lords by the Earl of Aberdeen on the 1st of February.

Popular opinion had already nominated Lord Palmerston as the fittest man for carrying on the struggle, and he was entrusted by the Queen with the task of forming an Administration. The new Government had not been in office many weeks when the death of the Emperor Nicholas, on the 2nd of March, seemed to offer some prospect of peace. A conference was opened at Vienna on the 15th of the same month, at which Lord John Russell, then Colonial Secretary, attended as the British Plenipotentiary. Russia, however, refused to agree to the proposals for limiting her naval power in the Black Sea, and the attempt came to an end on the 4th of June, long before which time the French and English envoys had withdrawn. Lord John Russell was not supported by the majority of the Cabinet in the approval he had given to the Austrian proposals, which were held to be insufficiently binding upon Russia; but he continued to hold office until the middle of July, when a strong expression of opinion in Parliament, as to what was considered the disingenuousness of his conduct, induced him to resign. In the spring of the same year, the Sebastopol Inquiry Committee, appointed on the motion of Mr. Roebuck, was inquiring into the causes of the national disasters in the Crimea; and in the summer Mr. Gladstone, who had quitted the Government almost immediately after its formation, because he could not agree with his colleagues in accepting the Committee, began to exhibit those Russian leanings which have since been developed in so marked a degree.

All this while, the war proceeded with renewed

energy, and on the 8th of September, 1855, Sebastopol fell beneath the assaults of the Allies. This did not put an end to the contest, but it made the end more probable. The Turks, who had achieved many successes in Europe, were unfortunate in Asia, and the capitulation of Kars, on the 28th of November, after a prolonged and noble defence by General Fenwick Williams, was a serious disaster. Proposals for renewed negotiations were made shortly afterwards, and peace was concluded at Paris on the 30th of March, 1856. The terms of peace have already sufficiently appeared in the earlier pages of this work. It will here be enough to state that they secured the neutrality of the Black Sea, guarded the free navigation of the Danube, provided for the rights of the vassal States, and abolished the Russian protectorate over the Christians of Turkey, first established by the Treaty of Kainardji, in 1774. The history of the Ottoman Empire, from the conclusion of peace to the breaking out of the Herzegovinian insurrection, with which our narrative commences, is a record of struggle, convulsion, intrigue, and accumulated debt. Abdul-Medjid died in June, 1861, and his brother, Abdul-Aziz, was profligate and indolent. The reviving prosperity of the Empire was checked, and Russia took advantage of internal troubles to prepare the war of 1877.

CHAPTER XXV.

Relative Strength of the Turkish and Russian Empires in 1877—Decay of Turkish Prosperity, owing to Misgovernment—Good Qualities of the Osmanlis—Opinions with Regard to Turkey previous to the Crimean War, and before the War of 1877–8—Speeches of Mr. Cobden, Lord Palmerston, Mr. Disraeli, Mr. Bright, and Mr. Layard (1853–4)—Division in the Cabinet of Lord Aberdeen, and in that of Lord Beaconsfield—Position of the Russian Emperor in the Summer of 1877—Preparations for the Invasion of Bulgaria—Crossing of the Danube at Galatz—Fighting on the Southern Shore—The Turks driven back—Evacuation of Matchin—Retirement of the Turks from the Northern Part of the Dobrudscha—Bombardment of Rustchuk—The Hospital and the Consulates cannonaded by the Russians—Protest by the Porte against Russian Outrages—Proclamation of the Czar to the Bulgarians—Plans for a further Crossing of the River—Condition of the Danube and its Banks at Simnitza—Passing of the Stream on June 27th by General Dragomiroff—Heavy Fighting on the Shore—March of Reinforcements under Prince Mirsky—Retreat of the Turks, and Occupation of Sistova by the Russians—Ambulance Arrangements of the Invaders—Operations at Turna Magurelle—Fight between a Turkish Monitor and Four Russian Torpedo-Boats—Pillage of Sistova by the Bulgarians—Further Passage of the Danube—The First Line of Defence abandoned by Turkey.

When the Russians stood on the banks of the Danube, in June, 1877, waiting to cross over into Bulgaria, they had before them an Empire containing a population (exclusive of the vassal States) variously estimated at from 27,000,000 to 28,500,000 people, of whom some sixteen or eighteen millions are Mohammedans, though in European Turkey, considered by itself, the Christians of all creeds reckon nearly 4,788,000 to 3,527,000 of the Moslems. The population of Russia at the same period was about 86,000,000. It will thus be seen how enormously disproportioned was the contest, as far as numbers were concerned; and in other respects also the advantages were greatly on the side of Russia. Both Empires, indeed, were in a bad financial state, and both were threatened by internal dangers of a serious kind; but, on the whole, Russia was certainly more vigorous than her rival. Corruption has long existed, and does still exist, in each sovereignty; but it is more rankly developed throughout the whole Turkish State than in the Russian. An English author, not long removed from us,* has recorded that in Turkey you may see vast districts without an inhabitant, where nevertheless are traces of a large and civilised race, existing there in former times; and that there is a city near the frontier—a city once containing 60,000 inhabitants—which is now absolutely without people. The indolence and profligacy of the official Turk must be charged with these results; while other evils are justly attributable to religious fanaticism. Yet there is good reason to believe that in both respects the sins of Turkey have been exaggerated by partisan writers. The Ottomans, at any rate, understand the virtues of Free Trade, while the Russians are to this day most jealous Protectionists. In the administration of justice, in the machinery of government, in the imposition of taxes, in education, and in religious tolerance, reforms of the most satisfactory kind have been introduced during the last thirty or five-and-thirty years, and to some extent, though not completely, carried out. The Firman of 1856, issued at the close of the Crimean war, added greatly to the privileges of the Christians, and authorized the free exercise of religion. Colonel James Baker has observed that it is not necessary to pass new

* The late Mr. Nassau W. Senior.

RUSSIAN TROOPS MAKING RAFTS ON THE BANKS OF THE DANUBE.

laws, but only to carry out those which already exist. An intelligent Turk told this gentleman that all his country wanted was "Justice within, and justice from without"—a sentence of admirable truth, terseness, and point. What shocks us in Turkey is not the character of the people generally, but the corruption of the office-holders and office-seekers, to which of late years has been added the demoralisation consequent on the recent loans, and the eagerness of capitalists, large and small, to become bondholders, instead of investing their money in land or trade.

"The genuine Osmanli," says Mr. Bosworth Smith, "has many noble social and national characteristics. He is, or was till the example or the precept of the western money-makers influenced him, eminently a man of his word; his word was his bond, and a bond which was a first-rate security. He is still sober, temperate, dignified, and courageous. Terribly cruel as he is when his passions are aroused, he is at other times gentle, hospitable, and humane. Nowhere in Christendom, with the one exception, perhaps, of Norway, are beasts of burden and domestic animals treated with such unvarying kindness and consideration as they are in Turkey; and nowhere, probably, in spite of all the depressing influences of polygamy, and the degradation of women generally, does the mother retain more hold on her children, or do children regard their mother with such constant and indissoluble veneration. It was not a Mussulman, but a Christian missionary, and he a zealous and successful one, who, in rebuking some younger missionaries at Stamboul, who were speaking contemptuously of the Turks, remarked, 'You will see practised here the virtues we talk of in Christendom': an over-statement, no doubt, but still with some truth in it, and truth which we should do well to bear in mind, as a make-weight against the official corruption, and the misgovernment, and the vices, with which the Turks may be justly charged, and which those who most admire what is fine in their national character have the best right to deplore."*

It is curious to observe the way in which the same opinions, both for and against Turkey, were expressed, in almost the same language, before the Crimean War, and before the war of 1877. On the 16th of August, 1853, Mr. Cobden, speaking in the House of Commons, said there was a growing conviction in men's minds that the integrity and independence of the Turkish Empire, as a maxim of policy, had become an empty phrase. It was considered that the Turks in Europe were intruders;

* Quoted by Colonel James Baker in his "Turkey in Europe," chap. 24.

that their home was in Asia; and that the progress of events had demonstrated that a Mohammedan Power could not be maintained in our quarter of the globe. The independence of a country that could not defend itself was not to be extraneously upheld, according to the dictum of Mr. Cobden; who, however, would probably have objected to the absorption of Belgium by France, or of Switzerland by Austria, though neither would have been able to maintain itself unaided. As far as the Christians of Turkey were concerned, Mr. Cobden observed that, if he stood there as the avowed advocate of Russia, he could not have pursued a course more calculated to assist her views. To Lord Palmerston it appeared that the Turkish Empire was not in the state of decay asserted by Mr. Cobden. He held its maintenance to be not only necessary, but worth contending for. Turkey, instead of having gone back during the previous thirty years, had made more improvements in social and moral concerns, and in religious tolerance, than any other country. "So far, therefore," continued Lord Palmerston, "from going with

GENERAL ZIMMERMAN, COMMANDER OF THE RUSSIAN FORCES WHICH CROSSED THE DANUBE AT IBRAILA.

were a Rayah, he should say, "Give me any Christian Government rather than a Mohammedan." He contended that the importance of our trade with Turkey had been over-rated, and affirmed that all our commerce in the Black Sea was owing to Russian encroachments there. What could a country like Turkey, which was destitute of roads, contribute to the commerce of the world? Mr. Cobden protested against its being argued that we were bound, in pursuance of our own interests, to maintain Turkey; and he ridiculed the idea of Russia being in any respect dangerous to England. The converse of these opinions was expressed by Lord Palmerston, who answered Mr. Cobden at considerable length. He observed that, if the honourable gentleman had the honourable gentleman in that sort of political slang which is the fashion among those who want to partition and devour Turkey—so far from talking of Turkey as a dead body, an expiring body, or something that cannot be kept alive—I am satisfied that if you will only keep out of it those who want to get into it, if you will only leave those that are in it to deal with it in the way in which they are now dealing with it, there are countries in Europe, to which the honourable gentleman has referred, that are in much more danger of sudden dissolution from internal causes than Turkey. Turkey, it is certain, has no Poland and no Siberia." On the 31st of March, 1854, Lord Palmerston contended that the rule of the Mussulman was the only one which could combine the scattered provinces and different sects of Turkey into one kingdom—an assertion which may possibly be disproved by experience, but which seems as probable now as when it was uttered. We were arming, he said, to keep Turkey from falling into the grasp of Russia; to prevent the civilised world from lying prostrate at the feet of a single Power; to defend the liberties of Europe, and the independence of nations.

The views of Mr. Cobden and Lord Palmerston in 1853–4 were exactly reproduced in 1877–8 by Mr. Gladstone and Lord Beaconsfield. At the earlier period, Mr. Disraeli, the leader of the Conservative Opposition in the House of Commons, observed a rather cautious policy, and refrained from committing himself or his party to any very definite position. It is remarkable, however, that he brought against the Government of the day—that of Lord Aberdeen—precisely the same charges of vacillation, contradiction, and internal division, that at the later period were brought against his own Cabinet. He alleged—with an evident truthfulness which was afterwards retorted on him—that the manifest want of harmony in the Government had tempted Russia into a policy of aggression, and that a more firm, decided, and consistent tone would have prevented war. "The epithets which Ministers applied to the war," he remarked on the 31st of March, 1854, "the objects they indicated for it, the prospects they drew of its course and results—above all, their appreciation of Turkey, and her possibility of future prosperity—were hopelessly irreconcilable with each other." The familiar names of Mr. Bright and Mr. Layard occur frequently in the debates of 1853–4: the one maintaining that we ought to have helped Russia to impose her will on Turkey; the other arguing that we had supported Russia too much, and that Turkey deserved every aid we could give her. History has repeated itself within a very contracted circle. In 1854, as in 1877, there were Russophiles and Turkophiles, according to the cant ¥ a more recent day: that is to say, there were men who regarded Russia as the champion of Christianity and progress; and others who protested against Turkey being judged by standards different from those which are applied to any Western Power, and who required that, whatever her sins, she should be treated in accordance with the elementary principles of honesty and fair-dealing.

If the division in the Cabinet of Lord Aberdeen—a division which ultimately led to its overthrow—encouraged the aggression of the Emperor Nicholas, it is no less obvious that the division in the Cabinet of Lord Beaconsfield, and still more the immense divergence of opinion in the English nation itself, confirmed the Emperor Alexander in any ambitious schemes he may have formed. As he paused on the northern banks of the Danube, in June, 1877, he must have derived no small comfort from the general aspect of affairs in England. It was not merely that he had his well-wishers in the Government: he had enthusiastic supporters all over the land; he had a party devoted to his cause; he had powerful newspapers, distinguished authors, eloquent orators, a large proportion of the Church, and nearly the whole of the Dissenters, pledged to find the highest reason in every word of his diplomacy, the noblest heroism in every act of his armies. Behind the hesitating Administration of Lord Aberdeen was a united nation, bent on a policy very different from that of the Scotch Earl. Behind the two sections of the Beaconsfield Cabinet were two sections of the English people; and that which supported Russia spoke with a more powerful voice than that which championed Turkey. There had, indeed, been a reaction from the excessive clamour of the previous autumn, when indignation at the Bulgarian atrocities had put all considerations of policy out of court; but there was still a loudly-expressed demand on the part of a large number, including many influential leaders of opinion, that no assistance should be given to Turkey, even if the legions of the Czar should appear at Constantinople. The Emperor Alexander was not ignorant of these facts, and he had little ground for apprehension, so far as England was concerned, as he viewed his regiments gathering in the Wallachian plains, and waited for the falling of the stream.

The stream was unusually late in falling. Its currents were still swollen in the middle of June, and a good portion of the summer was slipping away while the Russian forces lay inactive on the northern bank. An immense amount of rain had descended; the snow on the neighbouring mountains, in melting before the warmth of the advancing season, had added largely to the volume of water; and it was generally observed that the Danube was seldom so long in returning to its ordinary condition. It had been hoped to effect the passage of the river in the latter part of May; but week succeeded week without the desired opportunity occurring. The loss of time, however, had one advantage: it enabled the Russians to complete their preparations, which were certainly in a very unsatisfactory state for some time after the line of the river had been gained. For the Turks, this delay was equally good. They were backward, as they usually are; and weeks of waiting enabled them to repair some of the omissions of the earlier spring. But the Russians worked to the most purpose. Steadily and quietly, they massed their regiments on the banks of the stream; and the proposed points of crossing were kept in such profound secrecy that the Turks had not the slightest chance of discovering where they were to be struck.

The forward movement at length began on the night following the 21st of June, when several boats containing infantry put forth from Galatz, opposite the north-western corner of the Dobrudscha. The number of men forming the first detachment was about 1,800, and they were under done to hinder the Russian design. Nevertheless, the Turks were not unprepared to meet the enemy when he crossed the river at a point about nine miles below Matchin. Nearly 4,000 infantry, with 300 cavalry and two guns, were drawn up on the southern shore, ready to receive the invaders, and their position was a good one for inflicting the greatest amount of damage. The river was still very swollen, and the Bulgarian shore was rendered difficult by a wide tract of marsh, overgrown with reeds and rushes, and covered by shallow water, in

THE FIRST DETACHMENT OF COSSACKS CROSSING THE DANUBE.

the orders of Major-General Inkoff, commanding the first brigade of the Eighteenth Infantry Division. It had been generally supposed that the crossing would be somewhere between Giurgevo and Turna Magurelle, and this was also the belief of the Turks, who had concentrated the greater part of their army between Rustchuk and Nicopolis. Thus the Ottomans were successfully deceived; but they exhibited great apathy even in respect to matters which were within their observation. For some days, the Russians were engaged in the construction of a bridge near Ibraila, a little below the confluence of the old and new channels of the Danube. The work was carried on within sight of the Turkish forces at Matchin; yet nothing was which the boats were unable to float, so that it was necessary for the men to get out, and wade through a tangled swamp, under fire from their antagonists. The first boat-load was at once detected in the act of landing in the early morning of the 22nd, and was hotly attacked. As the distance traversed by the boats was rather more than three miles, the Turks seem to have been remiss in not attempting to sink them in mid-stream. The Russians, however, effected their purpose, and, marching in a southwesterly direction, maintained a desperate fight against superior numbers. While the boats were sent back for reinforcements, the first detachment, taking advantage of every rock, or other inequality in the ground, managed to advance some way into the country, though at a considerable cost in killed and wounded. A second division presently arrived, under General Zimmerman, commander of the Fourteenth Army Corps, and this was accompanied by artillery and cavalry, which were carried over in boats towed by steam-launches. Zimmerman immediately attacked the heights in front of him, and the battle raged along the rising ground for some hours. "Slowly," says a correspondent of the *Daily News*, "the Russians drove back the Turks, following them from rock to rock, from point to point, from summit to summit, from hill to valley, and from valley to hill, over the irregular and uneven ground; and the roll of musketry continued from daylight until two o'clock in the afternoon, until they had reached the heights above the village of Zizila, where the Russians halted, satisfied with their day's work, and the ground already gained." It was admitted by the Russians that the Turks fought with extraordinary courage and vehemence, repeatedly charging with the bayonet, and maintaining a hand-to-hand conflict as long as they could hold their ground. Some of the Ottoman cavalry, who appear to have been Circassians, succeeded in isolating and surrounding an advanced detachment of fifteen or twenty Russians, every one of whom was cut down. The ferocity of these men was such that, although exposed to a heavy fire, by which they lost several of their number, they got down from their horses, in order to cut off the noses and ears of the fallen, and to hack their bodies into little pieces. If these troops were really Circassians, their excesses will hardly excite wonder. They recollected all that had been done by the Russians to themselves and their countrymen, and the passion of revenge was not sufficiently sated by the infliction of death. It sought to heap indignity upon a hated oppressor, and to repay many years of atrocious usage by usage even worse. This took place before the arrival of the reinforcements. When these had been landed, the Turks were steadily pushed back towards Zizila, and Matchin was abandoned on the evening of the same day. During the ensuing night, some Cossacks took possession of the town, and on the following day General Zimmerman and his officers were received by a procession of the inhabitants, who moved forward with banners, holy pictures taken from the churches, and various other religious emblems. Three priests, and some Church dignitaries in full canonical robes, accompanied the deputation, who chanted a hymn as they approached the General. In acknowledgment of this reception, Zimmerman took off his cap, kissed the little wooden cross that was presented to him, and submitted with becoming reverence to a copious sprinkling of holy water, which was dispersed by means of a bunch of green leaves.

The success of the Russians in effecting their purpose struck so much discouragement into the commanders of Isaktcha and Tultcha that they at once abandoned those places, which were indeed too weakly defended to permit of much resistance. The whole of the Turkish forces were withdrawn from the northern part of the Dobrudscha, and concentrated behind hasty defences thrown up in the vicinity of Trajan's Wall. The Russians continued to pass over the Danube in large numbers, and on the 24th of June portions of Zimmerman's command began to cross at Hirsova, about forty miles south of Matchin. Rustchuk, on the Bulgarian side of the river, was heavily bombarded from the opposite bank on the 24th and 25th. The place so called is a fortress of considerable strength, which it was advisable to reduce before the Russians penetrated far into Bulgaria, especially as it commanded the railway to Varna, and several of the roads to the interior. The Russian batteries were at Giurgevo and Slobosio, and they did much damage. They appear, indeed, to have been worked with a reckless disregard of the mischief they might effect. Among the buildings which were struck, was one used as a hospital, where the Red Crescent flag was at that time flying. A correspondent of the *Times*, writing from Schumla on the 29th of June, said it was well known at Giurgevo that the principal building at Rustchuk, distinguished by a flag bearing two red crescents on a white ground, was a hospital; yet on that building the chief fire was directed from the first, and was continued with so much pertinacity that after a while the house was completely destroyed. The sick were brought out, and laid on mattresses spread on the ground; but, as the shells were dropping about the streets at the time, their position must have been in the highest degree perilous. A steady fire was also directed upon the quarter of the town where the foreign consulates were situated. The English consulate received four shells, and was demolished; and the French and other consulates suffered to a serious extent. The Turks replied to this attack, and Giurgevo was a good deal injured; but the mischief there effected did not equal what the Russians had done at Rustchuk. The Porte soon afterwards issued an official despatch on the subject, complaining that the Russians, without any military necessity, had completely destroyed that flourishing town by concentrating their fire on habitations erected outside the fortifications and works of defence. The act was therefore made known "to the justice and humanity of Europe, and to the public conscience." Similar charges with respect to the conduct of the Russians, in Asia as well as in Europe, were brought forward by the Turkish Government, which alleged that the invaders maltreated the relatives of people serving in the Ottoman armies, and dishonoured their wives and daughters. Several outrages at sea, resulting in the explosion of Turkish merchant-vessels, were also alleged by the Porte to have taken place, and it was added that the crews were sacrificed, without affording them time or means for saving their lives. These assertions were afterwards denied or explained away by the Russians; but some of them were indisputably true, though probably not all. That the hospital and consulates at Rustchuk were bombarded as described, is certain, for we have the testimony of the *Times* correspondent, who was there at the period in question. As the Russians are admirable gunners, and were not posted at an excessive distance from the place attacked, it seems impossible that the outrages should have been accidental, and they prove the implacable spirit in which the invaders entered on their campaign.

While these acts were being committed, the Czar was producing a proclamation to the Bulgarians, which was issued in the final days of June. The Emperor commenced by referring to the achievements of his ancestors in securing freedom to the Servians and Roumanians. Time and circumstance, he remarked, had not altered Russia's sympathies with her co-religionists in the East. She still bore the same love and the same solicitude towards all the members of the great Christian family of the Balkan Peninsula. The Emperor had confided to his army the mission of securing the sacred rights of the Bulgarian nationality, which he described as constituting the immutable conditions of civic existence. "Men of the Bulgarian land," continued the Czar, "the aim of Russia is to construct, not to destroy. She is called upon by the decrees of Providence to pacify and conciliate all races and worshippers in every part of Bulgaria where dwell inhabitants of diverse origin and faith. Henceforth, Russian arms will protect all Christians from violence. No injury shall be done them or theirs with impunity. All crimes shall receive punishment. The life, liberty, honour, and property of every Christian shall be equally protected, whatever his faith. Vengeance will not guide us; the sentiment of strict equity will alone prevail, together with the firm determination to introduce progressively order and law in the place of confusion and arbitrary sway. To you, Mussulmans of Bulgaria, I address a salutary warning. It is painful to me to recall the crimes and violence of which several among you have been guilty towards the defenceless Christians. These horrors cannot be forgotten; but the Russian authorities will not hold all responsible for the crimes of some. Regular and impartial justice will deal only with criminals still unpunished, although their names were well known to your Government. Admit the justice of God, which has now reached you; bend to His will; submit to the legitimate requirements of the authorities who will be established wherever my troops appear; become peaceful citizens, and society is ready to accord you the benefits of a regular organization. Your existence and your property, the lives and honour of your families, will be sacred before us Christians." Again turning to the Bulgarians, the Emperor told them that the hour of their deliverance from Mussulman tyranny had at last struck. "Give the world," he said, "an example of Christian love; consign to oblivion your internal dissensions; scrupulously respect the legitimate rights of every nationality; unite, brothers in religion, in the sentiments of concord and brotherly affection, which alone afford the solid bases of a durable edifice; rally closely under the shadow of the Russian banner, whose victories have so often awakened the Danube. Bulgarians, wherever the Russian troops advance into the interior of the country, the Turkish power will be replaced by a regular organization, and the native inhabitants will be at once called upon to participate in it actively, under the high direction of special and new authorities. The Bulgarian legions will serve as the kernel of the local armed force destined to maintain order and security. The anxiety you testify loyally to serve your country, the impartiality with which you perform the great task which duty has imposed on you, will prove to the world that you are worthy of the fate Russia has been for so many years preparing for you, at the cost of such sacrifices. Obey the Russian authorities, and submit faithfully to their directions; for in this lie your strength and your safety."

Cannonading was general along the line of the Danube as June drew towards a close. The Roumanians at Kalafat bombarded Widdin on the 26th, and on the following day Nicopolis was fiercely assailed from Turna Magurelle. The object of all this gunnery practice was to distract the attention of the Turks, and to leave them in doubt as to the point at which the next crossing would be made. Up to that date, the Russians had entered only that part of Bulgaria which goes under the designation of the Dobrudscha—a long and somewhat narrow territory, lying between the Black Sea on the east, and the winding course of the Danube on the west and north. This was not the locality best adapted for a march towards Constantinople. The Dobrudscha is a confined and sandy waste, and the way by the at Alexandria, to the north of Simnitza, a town situated near the banks of the river, facing Sistova. The plan was to cross at Simnitza, and in the first instance to attack the opposite town, which lies in a

PROCESSION OF BULGARIAN PRIESTS, ETC., SETTING OUT FROM MATCHIN TO MEET GENERAL ZIMMERMAN.

sea, which is the only practicable route, is stopped by the powerful fortress of Varna. It was therefore evident that it would be necessary to throw the great body of the Russian army across the Danube somewhere in the middle section of the stream; and the particular point determined on was kept secret from the enemy by this widely-extended bombardment from the shores of Wallachia. The forces designed for the later crossing were massed

plateau overhung by precipices forming the southern shore of the Danube. A small camp of Turkish soldiers had been formed in the immediate vicinity, and above the camp was a battery of heavy guns. Other guns were disposed at different points about the town, and to the right was a small open earthwork. The ground on the Roumanian side also was high; but between Simnitza and the Danube is a broad marshy tract, consisting of

THE CROSSING OF THE DANUBE AT SIMNITZA.

meadow, of river-sand, and of clinging mud, half submerged in water. A narrow arm of the Danube extends between this tract and the town of Simnitza, so that the marshy ground is in reality an island. A raised road and bridge, leading from the town across the flats to the landing-place on the Danube, had recently been destroyed by the floods, and the Russians were obliged to construct a short pontoon-bridge in order to reach the banks of the main stream. Although the river had sunk considerably during the previous fortnight, much of this sandy flat was still under water, or intersected by small winding channels which lost themselves in the swamp. The only cover existing on the intermediate tract consisted of a wood of willows and alders; but these trees were well adapted to concealing an advance. It was determined that the crossing should be effected on the night of the 26th of June, and the troops appointed for the purpose were those forming the fourteenth division of the Eighth Army Corps, commanded by General Radetsky. The officer having the immediate direction of the movement was General Dragomiroff. The Grand Duke Nicholas had announced that the crossing must be made, whatever it might cost; and it was therefore directed that the division commanded by Prince Mirsky should support the main attack by a night march from Lissa, so as to be in position at Simnitza at seven A.M. on the following morning, and assist the other division with all the force at its command.

Preparations for the attack commenced immediately after dark on the 26th of June. Field-guns were planted along the edge of the flats, to sweep the opposite bank of any forces that might be posted there; and while these guns were being placed in position, the infantry were marching across the flats towards the cover of the willow-wood. The night was very dark; the ground to be traversed abounded in difficulties; and the early light of June 27th was coming on before all the preparations of the Russians were complete. On the banks of the river were a number of boats, capable of holding from fifteen to forty men each. Having been dragged through the mud, these were launched from under the boughs of the willow-trees; then, putting off singly, they were rowed across the main channel of the Danube towards a little cove on the Bulgarian side, near to which was the camp of Turkish soldiers guarding Sistova. The Turks had maintained a good watch, and were not caught unawares. They perceived the movements on the opposite shore; they saw the boats putting off, and the dark masses of Russian infantry marching across the flats. Their cannon immediately opened fire, while from the slopes above the cove came a smart fusillade of musketry. The Russian advance was under the command of Major-General Yolchine, whose brigade consisted of the fifty-third and fifty-fourth regiments of the Line. His position was in the leading boat, and, on landing with a small number of men, he bade them lie down in the mud, and then opened a skirmishing fire to cover the landing of the boats that followed. When all had arrived, Yolchine told his men to fix bayonets, and follow their officers. This was done with a ringing cheer, and the Turks, after discharging a volley, gave way. The Turkish guns, however, continued to fire, and one of the shells fell into a boat containing two guns, their gunners, and the commandant of the battery, sinking the frail craft with every one on board. Several of the Russian soldiers were also killed on both sides of the river; yet the work of crossing steadily proceeded, and by seven o'clock in the morning a Russian battery had been established on the southern shore, and Dragomiroff himself had reached the scene of action.

In the hope of silencing the Turkish fire, shells were thrown across the stream almost as far as Sistova; but for a long while the Ottomans continued to reply with undiminished spirit. This artillery duel continued for some hours, and the Russians lost several men, who were rapidly carried off to the ambulances. As the day advanced, Prince Mirsky received final instructions, and ordered his division to move down to the flats, so as to be in readiness to cross, and support Dragomiroff's men, who were now hotly engaged. As these reinforcements were marching towards the swampy ground on the banks of the Danube, it was announced that a Turkish monitor was coming down the stream. This, however, proved to be a mistake. What had been observed turned out to be two large lighters lashed together, which the Russians were sending down to assist in transporting the troops. Untouched by a couple of shells from the Sistova battery, they reached the Roumanian shore, somewhat higher up than the crossing-place, and there waited for their freight. The Turks had by this time rallied on the upper slopes in front of their battery, and soon afterwards they began to recover ground, and to drive the Russian advance some way towards the Danube. But this lasted for only a short time: the Turks were once more hurled back, and the battery then ceased to fire. A little past the middle of the day, the Russians had got full possession of the heights, and had gained a command of Sistova, upon which the Turkish infantry endeavoured to retire. The invaders had thus made good their footing on the southern shores of the Danube in more places than one, and materials for the building of pontoon-bridges began to be accumulated on the northern side. During the whole of the afternoon, evening, and night of the 27th, troops continued to cross, and the number of boats was gradually increased to about three hundred. Being unable to retreat upon Sistova, the road to which was blocked by a Russian skirmishing force, the Turks fell back in the direction of Rustchuk, lying further down the stream to the east. At nightfall, General Dragomiroff brought up a battery of horse-artillery in pursuit of the fugitives, and the Russians encamped themselves on a plateau behind the crest of hills. Sistova was occupied on the afternoon of the 27th by a detachment of Cossacks, who proceeded cautiously through the surrounding fields and gardens. After peering into the shattered earthworks, where only two dismounted field-guns were found, they felt their way into the town, examining street by street, and sending small parties into some of the houses which presented a suspicious appearance. There was no occasion for alarm, however. Sistova had been evacuated, and scarcely any Turks were left. Some infantry followed at a later date, and the Cossacks established their camps in and about the town. An infantry regiment was then stationed mid-way between Sistova and the landing-cove, to guard the Bulgarian end of the bridge which was by that time being constructed further up the stream.

The Special Correspondent of the *Daily News*, from whose report these facts have been derived, gave a very impressive account of the march of the reinforcements under Prince Mirsky, and of the ghastly spectacle which met them as they were passing over the swampy flats. The surgery of the second line had been established on that intermediate ground; and here the more serious cases were being dealt with before they were sent on to the house-hospitals in Simnitza. "As we passed," said the correspondent, "about twenty shattered creatures were lying there on blood-stained stretchers, waiting their turn at the hands of the doctors. More than one I noticed required no further treatment than to be consigned to a soldier's grave. Beyond the first swamp we met a fine young officer of the Guards, carried on a stretcher with a shattered leg. But the youngster raised himself jauntily on his elbow to salute the General, and wrote a telegram in my note-book to acquaint his friends that he was not much hurt. Some distance further on, we passed the second surgery, whither many wounded had been brought. It was within range of the Turkish batteries about Sistova, and the mud around was pitted with shell-holes. But the Turkish fire by this time was nearly crushed by the steady cannonade of the Russians. Here I may speak of the admirably efficient work of the Russian ambulance-service belonging to the army. The ambulance-force is strong, and the casualties were well within its compass, so that the work went like clock-work. The younger surgeons and the ambulance-men were continually up among the fighting men, and the moment a soldier was struck he was attended to. If severely injured, he was put on a stretcher, and carried off after simple bandaging. If lightly wounded, he left the field on foot, assisted by one or two of the ambulance-men. The first destination of all was the surgery of the first line, where the ambulance-waggons were always waiting. The slighter cases went away sitting in the waggons. The severe cases were put on stretchers, and taken to the surgery of the second line. The only hindrance was the deep sand and the deeper mud, which impeded all movement, and sorely distressed the wounded retiring on foot."

The Emperor and the Czarewitch arrived at Simnitza on the morning of June 28th. His Majesty immediately visited the wounded, who numbered about four hundred, and in the afternoon crossed the Danube, and inspected the troops at Sistova, where he was received with great enthusiasm. Having embraced General Dragomiroff, he greeted him as the hero of the previous day, and presented him with the third-class cross of St. George. The soldiers were addressed, and warmly praised for their valour; and the Czar then entered a Bulgarian church in Sistova, the path to which was strewn with flowers by the women and children of the place. Here, after the performance of a *Te Deum*, he took the Sacrament, and at seven in the evening returned to Simnitza. There had been much talk of a simultaneous crossing at Turna Magurelle, further to the west; but no attempt was made at that point, owing to the project having come to the knowledge of the Turks, who concentrated a large number of troops on the opposite shore. The Russians accordingly kept the attention of these forces engaged by apparent preparations for crossing, and thus diverted them from the spot where the operation really took place. The invaders, however, built a bridge at Turna Magurelle, as they had already done at Ibraila and Giurgevo. A large number of boats was also brought together above the town, at the point where the river Aluta falls into the Danube; but these were to be employed only in case it should be found that the Turks on the opposite bank were so few in number as to render the passage safe. Such was not the fact, and the river was therefore not crossed at that particular spot; yet, while the passage was being effected at Simnitza, a demonstration was made at Turna Magurelle, which had the effect of distracting the Turks, and preventing any concentration of their forces at the true seat of action. The city of Nicopolis, opposite Turna Magurelle, was bombarded by the Russians, and several houses were set on fire. On their own side of the river, the Muscovites had set up an electric light, in order that by its intense and far-stretching rays they might discover what was taking place on the Turkish side. Thus aided, they fired from three batteries upon Nicopolis, from which the Turks replied with all the force of their heavy guns. An attempt was made to throw a bridge across from the northern to the southern shore; but the Turks immediately destroyed it. They appeared to consider that they were resisting a real attempt to cross the stream; but the passage, as we have seen, was at that moment being effected in a different locality.

During the passage of the Danube, a singular fight took place near the mouth of the Aluta between a Turkish monitor and four Russian torpedo-boats. The monitor had for some time been shelling the Russian batteries, and destroying the small craft on the river; and it was determined, if possible, to put an end to the annoyance. Four torpedo-boats were hidden behind an island in the Danube, and, as the monitor was steaming past, they suddenly darted out, and rapidly approached their enemy. The Turkish vessel was handled with remarkable skill and courage. Her commander thrust out a number of torpedoes at the end of long spars, and at the same time opened a tremendous fire from a mitrailleuse and numerous small arms. He next endeavoured to run down the Russian boats, and, although this failed, he obliged his antagonists to keep at a considerable distance. It is said that the commander of this vessel was an Englishman; at any rate, he had the appearance of being an European. The contest continued for a long while, and was watched with breathless interest from the shore. Again and again, for more than an hour, the torpedo-boats endeavoured to get at the monitor; but that vessel alternately backed and advanced, turned and re-turned, moving with so much celerity and cleverness that the boats were unable to reach her. At one time, a Russian launch got between the monitor and the shore. The latter vessel, which was turned in the other direction, at once backed towards the launch, with the intention of crushing it against the bank. The current carried the Russian vessel partially aground, and it seemed as if escape were impossible; but one of the crew jumped into the water, and helped to push off. Shortly afterwards, a Russian officer fired three shots from his revolver at the captain of the monitor, who, being quite untouched, took off his hat, and bowed in acknowledgment of the deadly salute. Ultimately, however, he disappeared from the deck, and was thought to have been either killed or wounded; and the monitor then steamed off, evading pursuit.

GENERAL RADETSKY, COMMANDER OF THE RUSSIAN FORCES WHICH CROSSED THE DANUBE AT SIMNITZA.

On the morning of July 1st, the Grand Duke Nicholas, accompanied by General Nepokoitchitsky and a portion of the Staff, crossed the Danube on a visit of inspection. They passed over the newly-made bridge, which was constructed partly of iron, partly of wooden pontoons. Not only was Sistova visited, but a large extent of country south-west from that town. From the furthest point reached, a fine view of the Balkan slopes was obtained; and the Grand Duke then returned to Sistova. The town was entirely deserted by its Turkish inhabitants, whose houses had been sacked and partially destroyed by the Bulgarians. In every direction were the evidences of pillage and wanton violence, and the total destruction of property must have been very large. The eight mosques of Sistova were much damaged, and the Turkish shops and stores were rifled of everything valuable, while the fixtures were broken into fragments. In these disgraceful acts the Russian troops had no share; indeed, they put a stop to them the moment they entered the town. Sistova was a prosperous and picturesquely situated place, and the Turks and Bulgarians forming its population seem to have been equally well off. It is worthy of note that a correspondent of the *Daily News*, who might perhaps have been expected to give different testimony, recorded that the Bulgarians showed few indications of having been materially oppressed, or had perhaps thriven wonderfully on oppression. Many of their houses were large and handsome, and the Bulgarian ladies were not indifferent to the latest Parisian fashions. The more conscientious of the people were ashamed of the injury done to Turkish houses, and on Sunday, July 1st, an edict was read in all the churches, directing that the stolen property should be given into the hands of the police, for restoration to the owners. But it does not appear that restitution was ever made.

The bridge across the Danube was completed by July 1st, and, on the following day, troops, horses, artillery, ammunition, baggage-waggons, ambulances, &c., began to pass over in one unbroken stream. This continued for some days; but in time it appeared that the bridge was not strong enough to answer the immense demands made upon it. Before the close of the first week, it had given way several times, and many hours were lost in effecting necessary repairs. Nevertheless, several divisions had passed over by the 7th of July; but many more still remained upon the northern bank. Meanwhile, the Turks were doing nothing to oppose the advance of their antagonists. Their first line of defence—the great river which separates Bulgaria from Wallachia—had been abandoned with scarcely a struggle, and reliance was now placed upon the second line, namely, the Balkans. Why the first line should have been so quietly relinquished is one of the mysteries of the war, which it is very difficult to explain. It is believed, however, that the Turks were to some extent influenced by the opinion of Count Moltke that the Danube could not be defended. Doubtless it would have been impossible to prevent the crossing of the Russians; yet the passage of the river might have been made to cost them dear. As it was, nothing but a few paltry engagements checked even for a moment the entry of the Russian troops into the territory of the Sultan. In the early days of July, a large invading force stood on Bulgarian soil; and if the Turkish generals had any coherent plan of defence, that plan had still to be unfolded, and events have shown its futility in the most disastrous forms.

CHAPTER XXVI.

Bulgarian Opinion with regard to the Russians at the Commencement of the War—Testimony of Mr. Layard as to the Loyalty of the Bulgarians—The Russians and the Turkish Parliament—Designs of the Czar on Turkish Territory—The Moscow Sclavonic Benevolent Society—Its Affiliation on the Government—Speech of M. Aksakoff, declaring the Real Objects of the Association—Russian Intrigues in Greece—Mr. Archibald Forbes on the Character of the Northern Bulgarians—Self-restraint of the Turks in quitting Sistova and other Towns—Character of the Russian Army—Use of the Lash—Colonel Wellesley and the Grand Duke Nicholas—Opening of the Servian Parliament in July, 1877—Servia and Russia—Agitation in Constantinople—The Egyptian Contingent—Reprehensible Conduct of the Turkish Government—The Russian Advance—Mismanagement in the Invading Army—Sacking of Biela—Occupation of Tirnova by the Russians—Extraordinary Apathy of the Turks—Reception of the Invaders by the Bulgarians—Fear of Disturbances at Constantinople—Destruction of Yeni-Zaghra—Proceedings of the Russians on the River Lom—The Waning Summer, and the Prospects of the Autumn and Winter.

MIDSUMMER had passed ere the main body of the Russian army had crossed the Danube. The season most favourable to active operations had therefore suffered a rather considerable diminution, and the chances of the future were doubtful in many ways. The ostensible object of the war was to liberate the Bulgarians, who were assumed to be labouring under the most cruel oppressions, and to be burning with desire to welcome their Northern champions. But the Russians themselves did not know with any certainty what reception they would find among the great mass of the Bulgarian people. A few deputations of a semi-theatrical character, with girls scattering flowers, priests sprinkling holy water, and peasants waving their caps, gave only a very slight and doubtful intimation of the real feeling spread throughout the land. That feeling might be quite in harmony with the deputations which waited on General Zimmerman and the Emperor; but then it might also be the other way. There were not wanting indications that the popular sentiment might, on the whole, be far from enthusiastic; and these indications, whatever their worth, must have been within the knowledge of the Russian authorities. Mr. Layard, writing to Lord Derby from Therapia on the 12th of May, 1877, reported an interesting conversation he had had with Dr. Washburn, the Principal of the Roberts College, an American institution, at which Christian youths of different races and creeds, subjects of the Porte, are educated together. Dr. Washburn was in constant communication with young men who had been brought up under his superintendence, and who were scattered about in various parts of the Turkish Empire. This gentleman entirely corroborated what had been said to Mr. Layard by the heads of every religious creed in the country—viz., that the Christians of all denominations were convinced they would have a far better chance of preserving and developing their national character and religion under Turkish rule, with all its faults and vices, than under that of Russia. "Their unanimity on this subject," said Mr. Layard, "is very remarkable, and deserves the impartial consideration of those who still believe that Russia has declared war against Turkey for the benefit of the Christians, and at their earnest solicitation. . . . All the Bulgarians brought up at the College, who speak English, and who are capable of forming a fair and accurate judgment as to the condition and wants of their country, were opposed to, and strongly condemned, the proceedings of those who instigated the attempted Bulgarian insurrection, and those who took part in it." The mutual misunderstanding, out of which the dreadful events of a twelvemonth earlier had arisen, had by that time passed away, and a better feeling had supervened. A large number of Bulgarians, according to Dr. Washburn, understood that they had been deceived and misled by Russian and other foreign emissaries; while the more respectable Turks repented of their conduct towards the Christians. Three Turks, belonging to Kezanlik, had died of broken hearts from the remorse they had felt

BRIDGE OF BOATS ACROSS THE DANUBE BETWEEN SIMNITZA AND SISTOVA.

RECEPTION OF RUSSIAN TROOPS AT SISTOVA.

for the murder of innocent Christians, especially children.* Let the fact go in mitigation of a world of wrong and horror.

The evidence tending to show that the Bulgarians were at any rate not wholly in favour of the Russians is in truth very remarkable. On the 19th of April, the Bishop, the chief men, and many other Bulgarian inhabitants of Philippopolis, transmitted to the Porte, through the Governor of that town, an address expressive of grief that Russia, actuated by evil intentions, had assumed the part of ameliorating the lot of the Christians, and especially of the Bulgarians, when in fact her only objects were to sow hate and disorder between two co-resident people, Mussulmans and Bulgarians, and to find a pretext for declaring an unjust war against the Ottoman Empire. Mr. Layard had spoken to the Bulgarian deputies in the Turkish Parliament, and to others, and had reason to believe that the address fairly represented the actual feelings of the majority of Bulgarians.† He reasonably added, however, that the presence of a victorious Russian army in the midst of that population might produce a difference; and Dr. Washburn had previously made the same remark. In a very interesting despatch to Lord Derby, written on the 30th of May, 1877, Mr. Layard observed that the Christian populations of Turkey—or rather those who by their knowledge and intelligence were capable of representing them—believed that the pressure recently brought to bear upon the Porte by the European Powers, and the lesson which the Turkish Government had received, would contribute to the realization of the national aspirations. They were encouraged by the unexpected success of the Turkish Parliament, in which they found that they could freely express their opinions and expose their grievances. They knew that the unchecked success of Russia would at once lead to the destruction of that germ of future liberty and good government; and for this conviction they had considerable warrant. A Russian gentleman said to Mr. Layard:—"Russia looks upon the establishment of a constitution and a Parliament by the Turkish Government as an insult and defiance to her. Their existence would alone furnish us with a sufficient reason to make war upon Turkey. We will never consent to be the only Power left in Europe without constitutional institutions, and, as we are not yet prepared for them, we cannot, it is evident, allow Turkey to have them."‡ For the prosecution of such designs, sympathy with the Bulgarians was as good a cover as could be found.

It is certainly not assuming too much to say that a proportion of the Bulgarians looked with coldness and disfavour on the advance of a Russian army into their land. But the Russians undoubtedly had their partisans, and it would have been singular if they had not, considering the immense amount of pains that had been taken to create a Muscovite sentiment among them. Whether inadvertently or intentionally, the Emperor Alexander revealed this fact in a very striking way, towards the end of that proclamation to the Bulgarians to which we referred in our last Chapter. The unhappy people were exhorted to prove to the world that they were worthy of the destiny which Russia had prepared for them during so many years, at the cost of such great sacrifices. The Sultan could hardly require more authentic proof than is contained in that sentence, of the deliberate and systematic plot against a large part of his dominions which culminated in the invasion of Bulgaria in 1877. But there were other proofs as well. The proceedings of the Moscow Sclavonic Benevolent Committee, originating in a small organization established in the year 1859, had been no secret to those who took note of such matters. Professedly a charitable society, for helping needy persons of the Sclave race, both at home and abroad, and for promoting education, it was in reality an immense agency for bringing all the members of that race under the dominion of Russia. The fact is now admitted, and it is a very significant fact in the history of the war. Just before the commencement of hostilities, this committee was reconstituted as the Moscow Sclavonic Benevolent Society, and as such was recognized and sanctioned by the Government, and placed under statutes issued by the Imperial Minister of the Interior. The *Moscow Gazette* of May 23rd, 1877, contains a speech delivered at the first meeting of the reconstituted association by M. Aksakoff, its chairman, the admissions in which are too remarkable to be passed over. Referring to the previous doings of the Committee, M. Aksakoff said:—"For a length of time, the Committee had to contend against opposition in Russia itself, and even with antagonistic views and inimical influences; for a long time the efforts of the Committee were directed merely towards keeping the spark and smouldering fire alive. We see now that the efforts of the Committee were successful, and that the flame has burst out. The number of members has increased; branches have been established at Petersburg and Kief. Exactly ten years ago, a Sclavonian Congress met at Moscow at

* Blue Book on Turkey, No. 25 (1877).

† Mr. Layard to the Earl of Derby, May 23rd, 1877.—Blue Book on Turkey, No. 26 (1877).

‡ Blue Book on Turkey, No. 26 (1877).

the time of the Ethnographical Exhibition, where representatives of all Sclavonian races met for the first time on Russian soil in the name of their common unity. A few years afterwards, a Russian orthodox temple was raised at Prague, owing to the strenuous efforts of the Committee, and in spite of the protests of *quasi*-sapient and timid partisans of the Sclave cause. There is no necessity for any allusion to recent events; they are too well known. In this manner, slowly and tediously, by narrow paths, dropping many good men on the way, we have at last reached the broad road, and attained the boundary of the promised land. The Russian flag is already waving beyond Russian limits, and this flag has been raised for the recovery of the liberty and human rights of the oppressed, humiliated, and despised by civilized Europe. The slumbering East is awakening; and not only the Sclaves of the Balkan Peninsula, but also the whole Sclave world awaits its resurrection. A new era is approaching; the dawn of the great Sclave day is on the point of breaking."

The British Ambassador at St. Petersburg stated the reasons why this society had been taken under Government control. It had been found to be a danger to the State to allow a political association which was known to be in communication with the Omladina (a revolutionary body in Servia), and through that with the International at Geneva, to levy arms, and equip large bodies of volunteers, for aiding the Servians against Turkey.* To suppress the Committee and its branches would have been a hazardous proceeding: besides, they had been extremely serviceable in preparing the way for the Russian army in Bulgaria. They were accordingly affiliated on the Government, now that all necessity for convenient pretences was at an end. Those who deny that Russia acts after this fashion, deny what the Russians themselves affirm. When the Greek provinces of Turkey rose in revolt at the close of the war of 1877-8, the movement was assisted from St. Petersburg, with scarcely an attempt at concealment. Mr. Bohm, a Russian merchant in London, wrote to a journal enthusiastically devoted to Russian interests:—"An increase of territory to the present Hellenic Kingdom would meet with a cordial approval by the Russian people, and ultimately also by their Government, inasmuch as the majority of the Russians desire the emancipation from Turkish rule of those races who belong to the orthodox faith, and, on the other hand, the Court party at St. Petersburg long to see Queen Olga (the daughter of the Grand Duke Constantine, and niece of the Russian Emperor) installed as Empress at Constantinople. It is an open secret that, in spite of an apparent discouragement on the part of Prince Gortschakoff and General Ignatieff, the adherents of the all-powerful Grand Duke Constantine are supporting by substantial gifts the Greek insurrection." † The policy of Russia may be multiform, but it is controlled by a few general ideas.

From what has been stated, it will be seen that the Russians, in entering Bulgaria, penetrated into a country where it was at least doubtful whether the majority of the people would be very heartily inclined to support the invaders. But they probably reckoned, and with reason, on the strength of their forces, and on the known disposition of the Bulgarians to side with the powerful, not from love, but from pusillanimity. The Russians, from the first, regarded them with a species of quiet contempt, and the Bulgarians had no great reason to like the Russians. Mr. Archibald Forbes, who represented the *Daily News* at the seat of war with all those brilliant qualities as a military correspondent which he has so frequently exhibited, gave a very unattractive account of these peasants, both in his letters from the spot, and in an article on the general subject which he contributed to the *Nineteenth Century* for November, 1877. The latter of those productions presents some curious evidence on the opinions entertained of the Bulgarians by their deliverers. "An outspoken Russian of my acquaintance, after a large campaigning experience of them," wrote Mr. Forbes, "gave it as his belief regarding the North-Balkan Bulgarians that they must either be the result of a temporary lapse in the creative vigilance, or that they must be accepted as a refutation of the Darwinian theory of the survival of the fittest. My Russian friend had doubtless good cause of disgust for the Bulgarians, but I venture to regard his expressions as rather too strong. My experience of the Bulgarians, indeed, is that they have fewer of the attributes calculated to kindle sympathetic regard and beget genial interest than any other race of whose character I have had opportunities of judging. It tells doubtless in favour of the Bulgarian that he is in name a Christian, although his 'evidences of Christianity,' so far as I have cognisance of them, consist chiefly in his piously crossing himself in starting to drive a vehicle for the hire of which he has charged double a liberally reasonable sum, after having profusely invoked the name of the Saviour to corroborate his asseverations that the

* Lord Augustus Loftus to the Earl of Derby, June 4th, 1877.—Blue Book on Turkey, No. 26 (1877).

† *Daily News*, March 27th, 1878.

price he asks is ruinously low. He cannot be denied a certain candour, which sometimes has a cynical flavour in it; as when he coolly tells a Russian, who in the character of his 'deliverer' is remonstrating against his withholding of supplies, or his extortionate charges for them, that 'the Turk was good enough for him,' and that 'he didn't want deliverance.' The Bulgarian is singularly adaptive. He realised his 'deliverance' with extreme promptitude of perception, resulting in arrogance. He drove his ox-cart with nonchalant obstinacy in the only practicable rut, and grinned affably when your carriage springs were broken in scrambling out of it to pass him. In the towns, he held the crown of the causeway; in the country regions, near the forepost lines, he sees it to be expedient to pursue the career of a double spy and a double traitor." The same authority recorded that when Tchernaieff was in England, in the previous winter, he detailed to him the wide-spread ramifications for the organization of revolt spreading over the whole of Bulgaria, north as well as south of the Balkans, of which documentary evidence and full verbal assurances had been furnished by the various committees outside Bulgaria. These assurances of support and co-operation encouraged Tchernaieff to strike across the frontier into Bulgaria as soon as Servia declared war; yet the rising of the Bulgarians in the spring had proved extremely feeble and scattered, and north of the Balkans there was no rising at all. The population had in truth no extreme grievance, such as might lash even a peaceable and mild-spirited people into rebellion. Except under the special excitement of the disastrous outbreak in May, 1876, the Turks had not behaved with cruelty to their Bulgarian subjects, nor, even under the exasperation of war, did they at first act as might reasonably have been anticipated. When the Russians had reached the southern bank of the Danube, the Ottoman troops, according to the testimony of Mr. Forbes, evacuated Sistova without so much as breaking a twig on the front of a Bulgarian house; without filching a Bulgarian goose, or requisitioning a Bulgarian egg. The same thing occurred in other localities; and the Turkish civilians were equally considerate.

PRINCE HASSAN, SON OF THE KHEDIVE, AND COMMANDER OF THE EGYPTIAN CONTINGENT.

It is not proposed to discuss in the present Chapter the many allegations of brutality made against the Russians, as well as the Turks, throughout the course of the war; but some general considerations, with reference to the ordinary character of the invading troops may not be out of place in this connection. A correspondent of the *Standard*, writing from Alexandria, in Wallachia, on the 25th of June, gives some interesting details of military life in the armies of the Czar. What was chiefly noticeable in the Russian forces, as a fact immediately attracting attention, was the prevalence of extreme good-nature. From Archdukes and Field-Marshals down to humble privates, every one seemed kindly, sympathetic, and quick to understand. But the correspondent felt bound to add that, in the opinion of others more experienced than himself, those qualities were only skin-deep, and that Oriental recklessness of human life and suffering was ingrained in the pleasant and courteous gentlemen whose manners so charmed the stranger. In illustration of this belief, he related some particulars which he had derived from apparently authentic sources. Riding out on a Wallachian road, he stayed to rest himself at a wine-shop. Two young soldiers shortly afterwards entered, wearied out and penniless, but still cheerful. The correspondent got into conversation with them, and one of the two stated that they were peasants from the neighbourhood of Moscow. Their rations appeared to be of the barest and most miserable kind, and they confessed that many in their regiment were ill, though few were in hospital. The younger of the two then related a story which, if true, exhibits in a strong light the fantastic cruelty of the Russian military system. "The doctors were fooled yesterday," said he. "One of our company died, and they carried him to the hospital. The doctor came out with his whip, and declared he was not dead; so he cut him over the legs, making great stripes. But the poor fellow was really gone; so everybody laughed at the doctor." The correspondent treated this narrative as a joke, and told the young soldier that he should be careful in talking thus to strangers, as some people might believe him to be serious. "It *is* serious, as God knows," they both answered. "The doctors always flog a man before admitting him into the hospital, and many times he will die under the whip." Such stories must of course be taken subject to possible correction. But the whip is an institution in Russia; brutal manners are common, as the inheritance of ages of slavery; and a story which would be incredible, if related of a more civilised race, seems within the limits of belief when imputed to one which has not yet emerged out of the ferocity of primitive conditions.

Even in the highest quarters, the conduct of Russian military officers was not such as might be expected in an age when courtesy is generally acknowledged as the rule of social intercourse. Lieutenant-Colonel the Hon. Frederick Wellesley, of the Coldstream Guards, who had been sent as Military Attaché to the British Embassy at St. Petersburg, and who in that capacity accompanied the Russian army of invasion, was treated with such marked incivility by the Grand Duke Nicholas, while in Roumania, that the subject was brought before the attention of Parliament on the 25th of June by Lord Dorchester, when the Earl of Derby was obliged to admit that there was truth in the reports. The Foreign Secretary had of course communicated with the Russian Government, and the matter was subsequently arranged. It would seem that Colonel Wellesley had commented rather freely on what he considered the defects of the Russian military system, and that this had roused the ire of the Grand Duke, who placed certain restrictions on his freedom of action, and warned him that he must not testify in an unfriendly spirit. So acutely did the colonel feel the affront that had been put upon him, and through him upon the country he represented, that he doffed his uniform, dressed himself in plain clothes, and retired to Bucharest, whence he wrote home for instructions. Colonel Wellesley was afterwards attached to the head-quarters of the Emperor, by whom he was treated with great courtesy and consideration.

In the war then commencing on Bulgarian soil, of which the professed object was to effect the liberation of the South Sclavonic race, it was highly probable that Servia would sooner or later take some part. Her martial attempt in 1876 had certainly resulted in nothing but disaster; but she had at that time only the indirect assistance of Russia, and she might now reckon on the open and complete co-operation of the great Northern Power. It was therefore important to observe what course would be taken by the Principality when the armies of the Czar had crossed the Danube. A new session of the Servian Parliament began on the 2nd of July; and on that occasion Prince Milan delivered an opening address, which was considered moderate in its tone. The Prince observed that they could look forward with confidence to the results of the recent struggle, in which blood had been shed for the cause of the Eastern Christians, for humanity, and for the future of Servia. He had concluded peace on the advice of the National Assembly; but he had informed the nation that the fate of the Eastern

Christians was in stronger hands than his own, and that they could bring the war to a close without endangering the sacred object they had had in view. The banner of the victorious Czar was at that moment floating not far from the Servian frontier; and, on the occasion of his recent interview with the Russian Emperor, that magnanimous sovereign had graciously given assurance of his future paternal care for Servia and the Servian circumspection, as a false step at so decisive a moment might ruin our fair prospects." Put into more direct language, this simply meant that Servia was not then prepared to join in the war, but that she would certainly do so on the first opportunity.

Constantinople was profoundly agitated and disturbed during the progress of these events. The Government affected to make light of the first cross-

THE EGYPTIAN CONTINGENT ON THE WAY TO CONSTANTINOPLE.

people. Prince Milan of course made no allusion to the speech delivered by the Czar at Moscow on November 10th, 1876, in which he had plainly hinted that the whole Servian people were a race of cowards, because of their ill-success in encountering the troops of the Sultan. The Emperor Alexander had by this time got over his disappointment and ill-humour, and poor little Servia could not afford to quarrel with a patron whose insults of yesterday might be obliterated by his favours of to-morrow. "Although," continued Prince Milan, "Servia is at present in enjoyment of the benefits of peace, events are developing around us of such great importance that the country's welfare imposes ing of the Russians—that which took them into the Dobrudscha; but the people were evidently not at ease. They were nervous, restless, and full of apprehension, and the appearance in the city of semi-barbaric levies from Asia Minor, Arabia, and Egypt, did not add to the general confidence. It was necessary for the police to keep a sharp watch on many of these warriors, whose evil propensities were well known; and as speedily as possible the new-comers were sent off to the seat of war, that Constantinople might be freed from the danger of any outburst of fanaticism against the Christians. The Egyptian contingent, comprising 6,000 infantry and 1,000 artillery, was under the command of Prince Hassan, second son of the Khedive, and Egyptian Minister of War; but, as the Prince was only four-and-twenty years of age, it was hardly to be expected that, either as a commander, or as Minister of War, he should make any great figure. He had in fact been engaged in the recent Abyssinian campaign, and had shown himself very far from successful. But the Egyptian troops were of some value, if only as an adventurous enemy, but to be simply falling back from point to point, and leaving the country open to a hostile advance. In this extremity, the Government did what most Governments do when similarly afflicted; what the French Government did in ample measure during the disastrous days of 1870 and 1871; what the Germans themselves were not above doing when, once in a way,

RUSSIAN OFFICERS CHASTISING THEIR MEN FOR PLUNDERING AT BIELA.

addition to the numerical strength of the Sultan's army. They brought with them a thousand Remington rifles, a million cartridges, one battery of cannon, and three steam-launches, for service on the Danube. These forces arrived shortly before the second crossing of the Danube at Simnitza. Popular opinion was already feeling disturbed, but it became much more so in the early days of July, when it was known that the main body of the Russian army had secured a powerful hold on Northern Bulgaria, while the Turkish commanders seemed to be doing nothing to arrest the progress of their

the fortune of war went against them: they suppressed truths and invented fictions. They also commenced a system of annoyance, directed against the correspondents of English newspapers known to be unfavourable to the Turks. Various difficulties were thrown in the way of these gentlemen when they were dispatching intelligence to their respective journals, either by telegraph or post; and one of the communications of the *Times* correspondent was opened by Tevfik Bey (a political agent of the Turkish Government at Schumla), and subjected to manipulation in several parts, with a view to entirely removing or obliterating whatever was distasteful to the authorities. This was the conduct of a despotic Government, frightened at impending misfortune, and exasperated by the severe criticisms, not always in complete accordance with truth, with which it had been assailed for more than a year. Such acts were of course highly reprehensible; but they are nothing more than what might have occurred under the like provocation at St. Petersburg, Vienna, Berlin, or any other seat of military power.

The Russians had crossed the Danube with little opposition; but their advance towards the Balkans, now that they had reached the southern side of the river, was not very rapid. It was necessary, however, to proceed with prudence, for the invaders were in a country guarded by the four strong fortresses of Rustchuk, Silistria, Varna, and Schumla. These strongholds could not safely be left in the rear, unless they were first taken by the Russians, or invested by sufficient forces to keep a check upon their garrisons. To do this would employ a large number of troops, and the Russians were not then prepared to detach so many regiments from their main body. There seems, moreover, to have been considerable mismanagement in some respects. No attempt was made to keep the retreating enemy in sight, or to learn whither he had retired, or what were his plans. The communications of the invading army were insufficient; the bridge of boats across the Danube was unsafe; and, in the event of a retreat being rendered necessary, nothing could have rescued the army from disasters of the most appalling kind. The commissariat was so defective that the dinner of a general on the southern side of the Danube had to be sent to him from his baggage-waggon on the northern side. This, it is true, was in the very early days after the crossing; but it reveals an absence of provident forethought so great that only an equal amount of blundering on the Turkish side saved the Russians from misfortune. The sanitary arrangements of the camp at Simnitza were as bad as they might have been two hundred years ago. By the end of June, the air was poisonous, and a still hotter season had to come. The wells were almost drained, and the men were drinking semi-fluid mud, for the purification of which there were no scientific appliances in the camp. The Russians, in fact, were slow in all they did and all they determined on doing. After a while, they generally amended their errors; but it was fortunate for them that their adversaries were so lethargic. It was not until the second week of July that they had constructed a second bridge of boats across the Danube; but by that time activity began to be visible in the Russian commands. Traction-engines were set to work on each side of the river, to bring the roads into a better state of repair for the passage of infantry, cavalry, and artillery. The army was preceded by an advanced division, consisting of one brigade of rifles, the Bulgarian Legion, and four cavalry brigades. Of the latter, the first was commanded by Prince Eugene of Leuchtenberg; the second, consisting of two regiments of Cossacks, by General Cherkasoff; the third, a Circassian Cossack brigade, by Colonel Gutoleim; and the fourth by Duke Nicholas of Leuchtenberg. Biela, a small Turco-Bulgarian town on the river Jantra, about twenty miles south of the Danube, and on the main road to Rustchuk, was occupied by a brigade of Russian cavalry on the afternoon of July 5th. The Turks had already retired, without doing any injury to the town or the people; but as soon as their backs were turned, the Bulgarians began to wreak all the mischief possible on the houses of their late masters, and to treat the mosque with indignity. In a little while, however, the people of Biela had some reason to regret the substitution of Russian for Turkish rule. Many of the houses were pillaged by the Muscovite troops, who seemed perfectly indifferent whether the places they were attacking belonged to Bulgarians or Turks. Provision-shops were ransacked, liquor-shops were broken into, and a great deal of drunkenness was the consequence. The utmost licence prevailed for some hours, and it was not until a species of military police was formed that these disgraceful scenes came to an end.

The army of invasion was now divided into three main columns. One, as we have seen, was pushing in a north-easterly direction towards Rustchuk, by way of Biela; another was directed towards Nicopolis and Plevna, west and south-west of Sistova; and the third marched south towards Tirnova and Gabrova. Tirnova was occupied by two brigades of cavalry and artillery on the 8th of July. It had been held by about two thousand Redifs, who withdrew as the Russians advanced. The population of Tirnova was about 16,000, a third of whom were Turks. It was not a place of strategical importance, but offered a convenient base of operations for crossing the Balkans, among the northern spurs of which it is situated. The expedition started from Sistova a little after six o'clock on the morning of July 6th, and was under the command of General Gourko. "Though the morning was bright," wrote a Military Correspondent of the *Times*, "there was no flashing of blades or gleam of bayonets, for the blades, though sharp, are

ENTRY OF RUSSIAN TROOPS INTO TIRNOVA.

dull, and the bayonets which the Dragoons carry in addition to their swords were now sheathed. The way led through a river, and over an undulating country, yellow with standing barley, but broken here and there with patches of green maize. Sometimes for a mile or two—as, for instance, after crossing the river—there was short cropped turf, very much like that on English downs. During the early part of the day, the hills rose steeply on the right, for the ground we were marching over had all the appearance of being the bed of an old lake. The pace was a fast walk, with very few halts, only one of about five minutes before the column reached Kujabunar, where a few Turks were disarmed. All the way, the Guard detachment led, and scouts on either side watched from the top of high hills the country which the column could not see." Twice there was an encounter with the enemy, who on the second occasion held a very advantageous position on a fortified hill, having the river Jantra in front, and a battery of artillery at the top, with a strong force of infantry to defend the works; but the Turks fled with precipitation on being attacked by some squadrons of Cossacks.

The Russians were advancing with apparent recklessness. They had fortified positions in their rear and on their flanks; and if the Turks had shown ordinary capacity and vigour, they might have inflicted on their enemies a severe defeat. The line of the invaders was extended about forty miles, and was necessarily weak in many parts, if not in all; but the Russians seem by this time to have acquired a feeling of perfect confidence, resulting from the extraordinary inaction of their antagonists. Of course it is conceivable that the quiescence of the Turks may have been part of some profound scheme of strategy, which would lead to amazing triumphs; but the game was a dangerous one, and it could only be justified by favourable results. Those results did not ensue, and it seems, therefore, but reasonable to suppose that the carelessness shown by the Ottomans was the apathy of indolence or fatalism, rather than a masterly stroke of policy. The Sultan assuredly had no confidence in this remarkable system of protecting an Empire by abandoning its defences. The Turkish Commander-in-Chief, Abdul Kerim Pasha, exhibited the most astounding indifference to the progress of the Russians; and to the remonstrances of the Sultan he is stated to have replied:—"I beseech your Majesty not to trouble yourself about the passage of the Russians at Sistova; it is of no importance. I have an excellent plan, which will certainly result in the total defeat of the Russians, and will prevent any one of those who have crossed from ever returning alive to his own country." Trochu also had an excellent plan for the defence of Paris in 1870; but, however admirable its character, it did not prevent the Germans from starving out the city, and ultimately occupying it with their victorious legions. The plan of Abdul Kerim may have been equally ingenious; but it has resulted in the dismemberment of the Turkish Empire. Notwithstanding the calm assurances of the Ottoman Generalissimo, the Sultan was far from satisfied. He was disposed to go personally to the head-quarters of the army; but, being dissuaded from that course, he sent his War Minister, Redif Pasha, together with Namyk Pasha, a soldier of experience, and Mehemet Pasha, his aide-de-camp, to investigate the conduct of Abdul Kerim, and report their observations to him. Neither army can be said to have exhibited any remarkable powers of generalship at that time; but the plain fact remained that the Russians continued to advance, and that the Turks were doing nothing to repel a danger which threatened Constantinople itself.

The march from Sistova to Tirnova has been described as more like a military promenade, or a triumphal procession, than a forced march, as it really was. The people were enthusiastic in their welcome of the invaders, or at least appeared to be so. They offered bread and salt to the commanding officers; they pelted every one with flowers. Verdant arches were reared at the entrance to each village; the women presented fruit; the priests advanced singing, with sacred pictures, with standards, and with banners. Everywhere was excitement; everywhere, extravagant demonstrations of delight greeted the new-comers. The soldiers were forbidden by their officers to touch wine or spirits on the march, and Prince Eugene, when encamping near any village, always requested that the people would not bring out strong drinks for the men. By the 12th of July, Tirnova was filled with Russian soldiers, for the greater part of the Eighth Corps had arrived, and at their head was the Grand Duke Nicholas. The people kept open house for the Russian soldiers, and no trouble was experienced in obtaining billets. In one village, however, there was an exception to this apparent uniformity of good will. At Akchair, the people showed great disinclination to sell anything to the Russians; but whether this was owing to real dislike, or to fear that they might be punished by the Turks at some future period, it is impossible to say. Nowhere could any signs of the Turks be detected. They had fled from the villages before the Russians arrived, and in some instances had driven off all the Bulgarian live-stock on which they could lay their hands. Although marching slowly, the Russians had by this time penetrated a considerable distance into Northern Bulgaria; but the Turks still evaded a collision, and hid themselves away among the mountains. In the middle of July, it was confidently reported that there was not a Turkish soldier between Tirnova and Elena, and that no force barred the way across the Balkans. The feeling in Constantinople, which had for some time been that of uneasiness, deepened into that of alarm. The Sultan was haggard and agitated. He was distressed at the mismanagement of the war by those to whom he had entrusted the chief commands, and could not help feeling that his throne, and even his life, were at stake. It was said that he was anxious to see the British fleet moored in the Golden Horn, and that some of his Ministers, including the Grand Vizier, sympathised with him in that view. Another section of the Cabinet, however, objected to the entrance of the fleet, unless it came as the avowed ally of Turkey; and this division in the Government resulted, as might be supposed, in the absence of any definite action. Owing to the restrictions of the state of siege, tranquillity was preserved in the Imperial city; but beneath the treacherous calm were many furious passions, which might some day break loose. The Softas were believed to be conspiring in secret; the more fanatical of the Mohammedans were contemplating revenge; and the Christians were apprehensive of sanguinary disturbances, if any calamity of a serious kind should overtake the Ottoman armies. The householders of Galata, where a large number of Christians reside, established an organization for protecting one another in case of an outbreak. They had their plans ready for the occupation of certain thoroughfares, and even for the destruction of the bridge of boats over the Golden Horn. The danger was certainly one against which it was prudent to make provision; but a correspondent of the *Times* at Therapia, who recorded these facts under date of the 17th of July, believed that the probability of a massacre of Christians by Mohammedans had been greatly overrated, and thought that the peril lay in a different direction. He observed that in and around the suburb of Galata—the Ratcliffe Highway of the East—were gathered a large number of ruffians (nominally Christians) of every race and clime, the very scum and dregs of Levantine humanity. These were for the most part armed, having taken advantage of the opportunity specially provided for them by General Ignatieff when, in the previous winter, he encouraged rumours of an imminent rising of the Moslem against the Giaour. A very slight popular disturbance might, in the opinion of the correspondent, have furnished these men with a pretext for plundering every bank and house within their reach, and cutting the throats of all who resisted them. Obviously, there was a danger from fanaticism on both sides; but in the metropolis the evil was fortunately averted.

Still, the horrors of war are always great, and in this particular struggle few things were more heart-rending than the way in which the populations of villages were turned out of their abodes, either in sheer wantonness, or to answer the strategical necessities of a campaign. A Naval Correspondent of the *Times* beheld an affecting scene of this nature at Yeni-Zaghra, on the evening of July 17th. A piece of ground half a mile in width separated the railway from the town, and here was encamped a small Turkish army, numbering something less than 3,000 men. The whole place was one scene of disorder, with everything littered about, and with a crowd of nearly seven hundred women and children huddled together on the other side of the railway, in close association with the few miserable chattels they had been able to take with them. The town itself was in a state of ruin, the houses burned, and the smoke still curling up from among the stones and rafters. The baths, the mosque, and other public buildings, had been completely destroyed; the shops and private houses had been sacked; and broken furniture was lying confusedly about the ways. A mournful silence hung over the place, and the only living things to be seen were some wretched dogs, a great many ducks and geese, several cocks and hens, and a few stray cats. At the entrance to the village, the correspondent met a Turkish escort, bringing out the last remaining inhabitants (all women and children) who had been found lurking about after the order to depart had been given. They were packed like cattle in trucks and luggage-vans, and sent away to some city a hundred miles off. The observer of these facts went into every kind of house, and all sorts of shops. He saw bedding and clothes, broken looking-glases, pots, pans, plates, musical instruments, letters, account-books, children's toys, dolls, packs of cards, and an immense number of other things, all lying broken and pell-mell. The same kind of mischief was visible in the shops, and the destruction was so complete that it was difficult to imagine how so much could have been done in so short a space of time. The Turkish quarter of the town was not merely ransacked, but reduced by fire to a smouldering mass of ruins. As this quarter was a good deal scattered, and yet every part of it was burned, it was evident that the fire was not the result of accident. It subsequently appeared that the Ottomans had committed a frightful massacre on the people, of which the details will be given in another Chapter. The injury to the town, however, had been partly effected by the Bulgarians, and partly by the Turks. On the 14th of July, the Russians had advanced as far as Hairem Burgas, and the whole Turkish population of Yeni-Zaghra had fled at their approach. The Bulgarians then set fire to the Turkish quarter, but, on the Russians being compelled to retire from Hairem Burgas, the Turks re-occupied the town which they had so hastily quitted. They found the Mohammedan quarter reduced to blackened ruins; and, in revenge, the Bashi-Bazouks sacked the houses of the Bulgarians, and broke everything into shivers. Such, at least, was the account given by the Osmanlis in their own excuse. The Turkish commander afterwards ordered every soul to depart from the town; and thus it happened that the *Times* correspondent, when he arrived at the place, was greeted by the miserable sight of which he reported the details.

Meanwhile, the Russians were creeping on, and the military situation altered from day to day, without as yet leading to any important results. On the 14th of July, a correspondent of the *Daily News* accompanied a patrolling party along the road towards Rustchuk. At Trestenik they found a large abandoned camp, probably belonging to the troops commanded by Ahmed Eyoub Pasha; still nearer Rustchuk, and close to the river Lom, they came across an entrenched position, which seemed to have been occupied by a body of from ten to fourteen thousand soldiers, but which was then quite empty. A little farther on, however, they were stopped by the Turks, with whom a small skirmish ensued; but the collision was an affair of no importance. The Russian camps were frequently visited by the inhabitants of the villages along the Lom, who reported that their effects were despoiled by the Moslems; but no instances of personal violence were at that time alleged, nor was there any sign of burning villages. The Turks were just then conveying supplies from their abandoned positions on the Rustchuk road towards their left flank. In the execution of this manœuvre, they were attacked on the 12th of July by Prince Manueloff, commanding the Eighth Cavalry Division, who, after

TIRNOVA.

considerable resistance, which necessitated the bringing up of his artillery, captured a mass of baggage, provisions, and ammunition, with more than a thousand head of cattle. This was a success as far as it went; but it was a very small affair, and the men got tired of their inactivity. The officers begged for a relaxation of the injunction that the infantry were not to cross the Jantra for a long time. But, although the Czarewitch and his brother Vladimir were among the persons making this request, the Chief Commander of the Rustchuk Army, General Nepokoitchitsky, maintained his prohibition. The troops were to stand strictly on the defensive until orders of a different character should arrive from head-quarters. The position of the Turkish troops was such that a precipitate advance would not have been prudent; yet the advisability of undertaking some active operations as soon as possible was obvious to every one. The invaders had been much delayed by their own want of preparation, and by the swollen condition of the Danube. Even after the crossing of the river, great slowness characterized the movements of all the army-corps; and the middle of July was nearly reached before any action of importance took place. The great mountain-barrier of the Balkans rose sternly in front of the Russians, and it was probable that the efforts of the Turks would be concentrated in those difficult and perilous defiles. It was therefore urgent that, if Adrianople was to be gained that year, the Balkans should be crossed within the next few weeks. In the mountainous regions of Bulgaria, the autumn is as severe as the winter of more favoured lands, while the winter is terrific in its intensity of cold. Had the month been June instead of July, the necessity for rapid movement would not have been so great; but the summer was now waning, and for all practical purposes the campaign had not commenced.

VIEW OF NICOPOLIS.

CHAPTER XXVII.

Russian Attack on Nicopolis—Prolonged and Desperate Fighting—Capture of the Town—Turkish Impassiveness—Hassan Pasha before the Emperor Alexander—Panic in the Imperial Encampment—Establishment of a Russian Government in Bulgaria—M. Aksakoff and Opinion in England—The Turkish Government and the Suez Canal—Despatch of British Vessels to Besika Bay—Explanations of the English Government in the House of Commons—Expedition of General Gourko across the Elena Balkans—His Encounter with the Turks near Osman Bazar—Occupation of three of the Balkan Passes—Explorations of Prince Tserteleff—Actions with the Ottoman Troops—General Gourko at Kezanlik—Fighting in the Shipka Pass—Defeat of the Turks, and Desertion of their Camp—General Skobeleff the Younger—Extraordinary Apathy of the Turks—Mutilation of Wounded Russians—Collateral Expeditions of General Gourko—Rifling of Turkish Houses by the Bulgarians—Changes in the Turkish Commands—Suleiman Pasha—Rumours of Peace and Realities of War—English Troops sent to Malta—Three Days' Fighting before Plevna, and Defeat of the Russians—Affairs in Montenegro and Bosnia—Operations at Sea—Combat between a Russian Merchantman and a Turkish Ironclad—Irritation in Russia against England.

THE first important action between the Russians and the Turks, after the crossing of the Danube by the former, occurred at Nicopolis—one of the fortified positions commanding the great stream. It was towards this city that the right-hand column of the army of invasion was directed at the beginning of the campaign. On the 12th and 15th of July, the town was severely bombarded by the Roumanian batteries at Islaz, and by the Russian field-artillery posted south and west of the fortress itself. Nicopolis was in fact invested on the land side by the Russians, and their shells could be seen from the Roumanian shore bursting in the Turkish fortifications. The heights of Simovitza had been held by the Turks up to the 15th; but on that day a body of Russian troops, strengthened by a detachment of Roumanians from the other side of the river, occupied the line of hills, from which the Turks retreated in great haste, leaving a quantity of ammunition and other war-material to fall into the hands of the invaders. The Roumanians opened fire from their batteries upon the Turkish positions, and the Russians at the same time advanced on Nicopolis under cover of the guns. The fighting on the 15th was very stubborn, and the storming of the southern forts cost the allies a large number of men, owing to the prolonged and desperate resistance of the Turks. After a sanguinary contest of some hours, the Ottomans were overwhelmed by superior numbers, and compelled to retire into the fortress. While the column thus discomfited was effecting its retreat, another battalion of Mussulman troops made a sortie, and attacked the advancing Russians on their flank. The new-comers, however, were speedily obliged to withdraw, owing to the terrific fire from the Roumanian batteries at Islaz; and at nightfall the Russians occupied all the external positions previously held by the Turks. The Russian troops, which were under the command of Baron Krüdener, belonged to the Ninth Corps, and consisted of two divisions of infantry, and one division of cavalry. The losses on both sides were very heavy; but the Russians had succeeded in their object, for, during the night of the 15th, the Ottomans abandoned further resistance, and the town was entered by the conquerors early on the morning of the 16th.

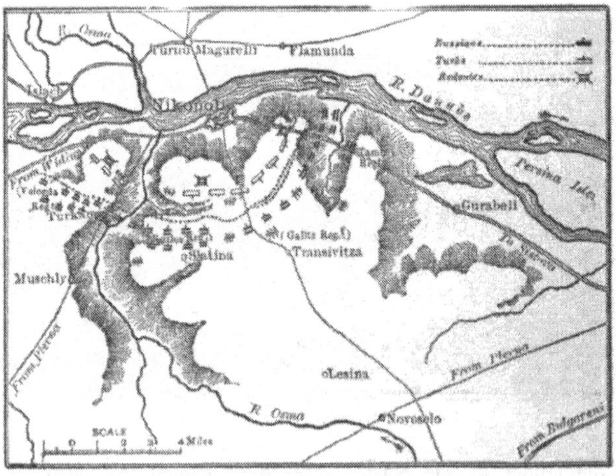

PLAN OF THE ATTACK ON NICOPOLIS.

Previously to surrendering, the Turks burned their stores, and consumed the principal buildings of the town, situated on the wharf. A few stray shots were fired after the entry of the Russians; but the commanders, Hassan Pasha and Ahmed Pasha, had relinquished all hope of success, and 6,000 men, including the garrison, were given up to captivity, together with two monitors and forty cannon. At two in the afternoon of July 16th,

STREET IN NICOPOLIS DURING THE BOMBARDMENT.

the long line of Turkish prisoners began to defile down the road leading from the citadel to the river, and, on reaching the bank, squatted on the sand with true Oriental imperturbability, and awaited their transportation to the Roumanian side of the Danube. A correspondent of the *Times*, who visited the spot, has recorded that a fitting commentary on Turkish energy—by which of course we are to understand want of energy—was visible in the shape of an immense pile of serviceable gabions, intended to protect the gunners, but which had never been filled. No attempt had been made to strengthen the rugged heights by which the city was commanded; and everything was left to the courage and resolution of the individual soldier. "Thousands of rifles, bayonets, and accoutrements," says the same writer, "were piled along the road where the train of three hundred wounded Moslems awaited their removal into the improvised hospitals. The wounded Turks were superior in physique and expression to their more fortunate companions calmly seated upon the bank of the Danube. The whole scene was saddening in the extreme. The air of hopeless resignation upon the faces of the prisoners, the smouldering ruins of the buildings burned by the Turks the night before their surrender, the wretched huts left standing, and the bleak hillsides whitening in the sun, made a picture as unattractive as it is possible to conceive." The Roumanians were delighted with the success obtained, and the Russians immediately set to work to construct a pontoon-bridge across the river from Turna Magurelle to Nicopolis, as an aid to the Simnitza bridges, which were being repeatedly injured by wind and wave, and by the frequent passage of troops.

The conflagration at Nicopolis had been larger than was at first supposed. Four or five acres of ruins were visible to those who visited the town after it had passed into the hands of the Russians, and considerable quantities of grain were destroyed. The battle behind the fortress was the most hotly-contested and the most important which had up to that time taken place in the European seat of war. The high plateau, extending some miles back from the river, was intersected by vineyards, clumps of trees, and fields of grain, and these afforded some degree of protection to the Russians during a portion of their advance; but, when passing from the hollows on to the steep ground where the Turkish guns had been planted, they must have suffered severely. On entering the town, the conquerors found large stores of ammunition and rifles, including stacks of old percussion-guns, and the equipments of artillery horses. The capture of the fortress relieved the Russians from the fear of attack on their right flank, and weakened the Turkish defence in an equal degree. But the garrison had done all they could with the means at their disposal, and it is remarkable that the Ottoman Generalissimo should not have attempted more to save the position, or, supposing that to be impossible, should not have withdrawn the troops to localities where they might have been more useful. Hassan Pasha, of whose prowess the Russians spoke highly, arrived on the 17th of July at the Emperor Alexander's head-quarters, which were temporarily fixed at Pavlo, near the river Jantra. "As he fought when free," says the Special Correspondent of the *Daily News*, "so Hassan Pasha acted when a prisoner, bearing himself before the Great White Czar with true Turkish *nonchalance*. When asked why he capitulated, he said his ammunition was all gone, and he had been obliged to kill with his own hand three or four soldiers who left their duty. He said it was a stupid war, into which the Turks had been mainly led by the English attitude, and the nation would be glad when it was over. He spoke as rank folly of the conduct of a Russian artillery officer who, when one position was barely carried, rode his guns in among the still undefeated Turks, and, unlimbering, came into action against other positions as yet uninjured." Curiously enough, the engagement at Nicopolis was the occasion of a brief panic at the Imperial encampment, which was then at Czarevica, a few miles south of Sistova. On the night of the 15th of July, a Cossack rode in with a hurriedly-written despatch from a telegraph clerk at the bridge across the Danube, to the effect that the Turks were marching from Nicopolis on Sistova, and threatening to sever the Russian communications and destroy the bridge. The Emperor acted with great coolness, and ordered the necessary military dispositions for covering the lines of approach. When this was done, scouts were sent out, who brought back intelligence that the country in the direction of Nicopolis was perfectly quiet. News soon afterwards arrived from Baron Krüdener, respecting his success on the banks of the Danube, and it ultimately appeared that the telegraph clerk had been confused by the sound of firing from the direction of Nicopolis, and, feeling alarmed for the Emperor's safety, had sent off the Cossack with an intimation which proved to be erroneous.

The Russians had now secured a firm grip on Northern Bulgaria, and Turkish rule, except in some few places, was becoming a thing of the past. Immediately after crossing the river, the invaders had proceeded to organize a species of provisional government, at the head of which was placed Prince

Tcherkasski, who was to be assisted in the discharge of his duties by the Bulgarian Legion of the Russian army, acting as a sort of police. He was instructed to seize the landed property of the Mohammedan ecclesiastical establishments, and of the Mohammedan landlords. The latter, who were for the most part Bulgarian renegades, were to be banished from the country, and many influential men, suspected of having oppressed the Christians, were menaced with severe punishment. Some were indeed executed on Bulgarian testimony, and, while the Mohammedans were disarmed, the Christians were provided with weapons. The Czar was bent on Russianizing Bulgaria, and the steps he took were admirably calculated to promote such a design. The institutions established by his commanders were professedly Bulgarian, but actually Muscovite. Orders were issued for the election of a Bulgarian Administrative Council; but, as everything was to be under the supreme direction of Russian soldiers, the character of the Council was obviously determined beforehand. At the time these changes were being effected, opinion in Russia was assuming a very arrogant character. Mr. Lewis Farley, a gentleman connected with the English press, and a friend of Russia, having, during a stay at St. Petersburg, written to M. Aksakoff, requesting his assistance for the establishment in England of a journal intended to mediate between Great Britain and Russia, the President of the Moscow Sclavonic Society replied:—"At a moment when General Kemball is actually in command of the Turkish army in Asia, when England threatens to send her fleet against us, and the English agent at the head-quarters of the Russian army is suspected of acting as a spy on behalf of Turkey—at such a moment, it is highly improper for you to propose to Russia to care for the immediate defence of her policy before English public opinion, and to be out of pocket for the purpose of purchasing English good-will." The allusion to Sir Arnold Kemball, in this passage, as the actual commander of the Turkish Army in Asia, which he simply accompanied in the quality of British Military Attaché, is a curious specimen of the vain imaginings which passion and prejudice may mistake for truths.

The ill-success of the Russians in Asia was to a great extent counterbalanced by the progress they were making in Europe, and it became necessary for England to consider her own position in the East, in view of the not improbable contingency of a Russian advance on Adrianople. The relations of this country to the Ottoman Empire generally were rendered extremely difficult by the existence of a state of war between that Empire and the Government of the Czar; and in the course of June some communications passed between the Cabinets of London and Constantinople with respect to the Suez Canal. From a despatch of Mr. Layard it appeared that the Porte assented to the view of the Queen's Government relating to the free passage of the Canal by all neutral vessels. As regarded hostilities in that great water-way and its approaches, the Ministers of the Sultan stated that, as the Canal was part of the Ottoman Empire, and had never been declared neutral, they could not allow the enemy's ships to have any access to it. They also said that they had taken measures to protect the two entrances from the approach of hostile vessels, but that they reserved the rights of Turkey, and her prerogatives as the territorial Power. Sir Stafford Northcote, speaking in the House of Commons on the 25th of June, observed that, as the Russian Government had declared that they would not bring Egypt within the radius of their military operations, and that they would neither blockade, nor interrupt, nor in any way menace, the navigation of the Suez Canal, her Majesty's Government did not feel it necessary to take any measures for the protection of that route to India, as they relied upon the undertaking of the Russian Government that it would not be endangered. Nevertheless, it was considered advisable to send the fleet to Besika Bay, in order that it might be at a convenient station. The position of that bay, as Sir Stafford Northcote remarked on the 6th of July, enabled the Admiral to communicate at once, if necessary, with the English Ambassador at Constantinople, and with the Government at home. The fleet consisted of eight vessels, of which seven were ironclads, while one was an unarmoured frigate. At the same time, a single ship was stationed in the Suez Canal; but these measures, the Government was eager to explain, were not intended as a hint, warning, or threat, to either of the belligerents. Russia had certainly no cause to complain of the conduct pursued by the British Government since the commencement of the struggle. England kept watch from afar; but the Emperor was still given to understand that, within certain limits, he might treat his adversary as he would.

The operations of the invading force had for the most part been characterized by slowness; but there was one Russian commander whose vigour and enterprise might be described as rash. This was General Gourko, who, at the head of a strong detachment, started southwards from Tirnova on the morning of the 12th of July, with intent to cross the Elena Balkans, to make direct for

Kezanlik, and thus to obtain a command over the Tundja Valley, leading to Adrianople. The enterprise was one of a very adventurous character, for the tracks through the mountain passes were exceedingly difficult, and it was necessary to convey the baggage and provisions upon pack-horses. Such narrow ways are easily defended, and a small force of Turks, supposing any such force to be there, might drive the Russians back with heavy loss. But Gourko had reason to believe that his advance would not be seriously resisted, and that the Ottomans were massed in other localities. He relied also on preparations being made for supporting his column by the main body of the army in the course of a few days. The Russians were now beginning to introduce something like organization into their large invading force. As regarded supplies, Bucharest was turned into a great central depôt, where stores to a vast amount were accumulated. Sistova and Tirnova were the intermediate and advance depôts, and the conveyance of stores was facilitated by the construction of a temporary bridge between Simnitza and Sistova. General Gourko therefore pushed forward with some degree of confidence that he would be able to open the southern slopes of the Balkans to the ulterior operations of his comrades.

GENERAL GOURKO.

His column consisted of eight regiments of cavalry,

and six battalions of the Tirailleur Brigade. The main body marched at once upon Elena; but the General himself, diverging to the left, led a cavalry reconnaissance on the Schumla road, in the direction of Osman Bazar, to ascertain whether the enemy indeed, that he must retire from the neighbourhood of Osman Bazar; but he had obtained the knowledge he required, and, having left a detachment of the Eighth Corps, which had followed him, to watch the Turkish position, he rejoined his main column,

AN AWKWARD CORNER IN THE SHIPKA PASS.

was posted there in force, or not. The result was that he discovered about six thousand Turks, and found that they constituted the left flank of the Turkish line between the Danube and the Balkans —a line extending from the north to the south, and fronting towards the west. With this detachment of six thousand Ottoman troops, General Gourko had an encounter, in which his cavalry suffered some rather considerable losses. It became evident, and pushed forward towards the Balkan passes. Of these, in that particular direction, there are three, nearly parallel with one another, and all leading to the valley of the Tundja. Dividing his troops into three detachments, and guided by the Christian inhabitants of the country, Gourko took possession of all these ravines, and struck southward with as much celerity as the nature of the ground permitted. The central pass, called after the village of Hainkoi, at the southern extremity, he traversed himself, accompanied by the greater number of his troops.

The defile was narrow, winding, and flanked by broken and precipitous cliffs. Indeed, the rugged way was so wanting in breadth that the gun-carriages and mountain-batteries could not be got through until the paths had been widened. As the advance proceeded, the roads were repaired and opened out, and the army made its way through a succession of deep gorges, abrupt glens, and winding defiles, often perplexed with broken rocks, and sometimes darkened by the shadow of dense oak-forests. Occasionally, the close, stony hollows would expand into wider valleys, fair with corn-fields, orchards, and vineyards, and picturesque with primitive little villages; but for the most part the country had the savage grandeur, loneliness, and sterility, which Salvator Rosa loved to represent in his landscapes. Speaking of one of the passes traversed by the army, Mr. MacGahan, in a communication to the *Daily News*, said:—"This pass was discovered by Prince Tserteleff, to whom had been confided the whole business of obtaining information about the roads, the movements of the enemy, their numbers, dispositions, and so on. He soon ascertained that the Turks had fortified the Slivno and Gabrova Passes in such a way as to render the forcing of a passage at either of them a very difficult matter, and he determined to look for another. Count Moltke, in his book, refers to a pass between those of Gabrova and Slivno, but speaks of it as only a path, not practicable for an army. Prince Tserteleff decided to investigate this pass, in the hope that it might lead to something. He soon ascertained that it had a very bad reputation—a place that was generally frequented by brigands, and rarely used either by Bulgarians or Turks. Among the Turks it was a kind of tradition that this pass was in the clouds, that the defiles leading to it were so wild, so savage and barren, as to be unfrequented by either bird or beast—a kind of mountain desert where nothing could live. Pursuing his investigations, the Prince heard of a man who had been through the pass, and, finding him, he learned that he had been through in fact, but that was two years ago, and the road might have become impassable since then. What made the information really important was that he had been through with one of the ox-carts of the country. If an ox-cart could go through, very probably a cannon might be got through somehow, and it was determined to reconnoitre and explore. Three days before the arrival of the Grand Duke at Tirnova, General Rauch went forward with two hundred Cossacks for this purpose, taking with him Bulgarian guides. Without waiting to explore the road to the end, he immediately began preparing it for the passage of artillery. Although these two hundred Cossacks were working three days on this road, with the Bulgarian peasantry coming and going all the time freely, the Turks never got a whisper of their presence there. They even sent three battalions from Kezanlik to Slivno to strengthen the positions before the latter place, and these three battalions passed by Khaini the day before the Russians issued out. And yet, although the whole Bulgarian population of a dozen mountain villages knew the Russians were there, not one man was found among them to inform the Turks. The Turkish staff either did not know of this pass at all, or, knowing it, believed it to be so impracticable that they did not even think it worth while to place a corps of observation there to watch it. The only danger that the Russians had to fear was that some wandering party of Bashi-Bazouks or marauders should pass that way, and discover what they were at, or that the noise made by the Cossacks in repairing the road should excite the curiosity of the small Turkish force which it was known was at Khaini, at the outlet of the defile. They did not dare to use powder for blasting the rocks, by which they might have made the road passable in several places. Prince Tserteleff went forward continually with one or two Bulgarians, reconnoitring the route far in advance of even the advance guard. He even disguised himself in a Bulgarian peasant's clothes, and went forward on foot, anxious to see if the road were really practicable, before the whole column should advance; and he was the first man of the Russian army, and his the first horse, to cross the summit, and the first to open out the defile at Khaini."

The progress of the invaders was most picturesquely described by the Military Correspondent of the *Times*, who, referring to the events of the 13th of July, said:—"The road is good at first, though steep, and there is some light left in the sky to show the way; but soon we arrive in a deep gorge, densely wooded with high trees. Through the valley runs a small stream, and its bed, covered with rocks, is as much the road as that which sometimes winds along the banks. The darkness thickens, and the Staff is completely at the mercy of the Bulgarian guide, for no man who had not often traversed this path could possibly find the way. Sometimes the trees meet overhead, and the riders have to stoop suddenly when a branch appears marked in sombre shade against the bright stars.

Fire-flies flicker among the trees, and lie with blue, lambent light on the rocks. Not a word is spoken, every brain being intent on catching the glimmer of the white cap in front of him; only the horses seem to find their way easily. Sometimes a clatter of hoofs placed violently on rocks, and a splash in a pool, tell that a horse has slipped on a wet rock, for the dew falls like rain, and the rocks are smooth with the ever-wearing passage of water. We halt in profound darkness, and a series of matches is lit to examine the written directions for the route. The little flame gleams on sabre and cap for a few seconds, dances on the flickering water, then dies, and leaves the darkness more profound than before. The sides of the ravine close in overhead; huge rocks hang over the stream, and gaunt, leafless trees stretch out ragged branches like gibbets against the sky. Is the Bulgarian guide true? for at that point there is no longer a road beside the river for a long time. He leads the General up a steep place out of the stream; then, returning himself, quickly disappears down its bed. Are we betrayed? A Cossack dashes after him, but the guide calls to the General to follow. Presently we are aware of something alive on the banks on either side, and a large rock in the middle of the stream is covered with something that, by straining the sight, we discover to be men with rifles and bayonets. Are they friends or foes? The General shouts in Russian, 'Good night, my children!' and, to our relief, from all around comes back in a hoarse growl, rather than a shout, 'Good night, your Excellence!' It is a part of the infantry which passed first, and ought now to be in bivouac further on, where the gorge opens."

A fortified position, held by a body of Turkish Nizams, was suddenly discovered on the 14th in the most difficult part of the ravine; but the Ottoman troops were so struck with astonishment at the appearance of the invaders that, after a brief struggle, in which several were killed and wounded, they fled with the utmost precipitation. In all three passes, battery-emplacements were found in good positions; but they were unarmed, and therefore of no use in repelling the Russian advance. The Nizams, in retiring before their enemy after the collision of the 14th, shaped their course in a westerly direction on Konaro; but, on the 15th, having in the meanwhile received reinforcements, they attacked Gourko's vanguard, and were again repulsed with the loss of two of their camps, and of the little town of Konaro. The telegraphic and railway lines were cut on the same day, and an action of some importance ensued on the 16th. The engagement took place at Uflami, where a body of Turkish artillery, cavalry, and infantry, was found drawn up in a strong position. The Turks fought well, and the Russians lost severely, not only from the enemy's fire, but in the hand-to-hand conflict with sabre and bayonet which followed. Ultimately, however, the Mohammedans gave way, and on the 17th General Gourko approached Kezanlik. The situation of that town is at the mouth of the Shipka Pass, beyond which lies the Tundja Valley. By this time, the Turks had awakened to the necessity of making greater attempts to repel so threatening an invasion. Fighting continued at intervals all through the 17th, and the Russians suffered much from the intense heat, and from the laborious character of the marching. Nevertheless, General Gourko entered Kezanlik on the evening of that day.

The Shipka Pass was held by a considerable Turkish army, which was now in Gourko's rear, and it was part of the original plan of operations that the Russian commander should assail that force from the south, while Prince Mirsky, at the head of the Ninth Division, attacked it from the north. This was on the supposition that the Russian advance would have reached Kezanlik on the 16th, and would be sufficiently rested on the 17th to take part in the operation. But, as we have seen, it was not until the evening of the 17th that Gourko's men arrived at the place of destination, and they were then utterly exhausted by their fatigues. Prince Mirsky was accordingly unassisted in his attack, which was attended by severe fighting. The Turks were strongly entrenched, and Mirsky sent against them only one regiment, divided into three columns. The fortifications of the Ottomans consisted of six tiers of entrenchments, planted with powerful batteries, and defended by picked troops. The right-hand column of the Russians got well into the pass, and then, after an encounter of some hours' duration, effected a lodgment in the hostile lines. The left-hand column missed its way, and was beset by an overwhelming force of Turks. Retreating in the face of superior numbers, this small body of men maintained a sanguinary combat for four hours, and at length got beyond fire, though with such serious losses that only one officer was left standing, and even he was wounded.

The attack in support, which General Gourko was unable to deliver on the 17th, took place on the 18th. As the two battalions of rifles which formed the advance were approaching the rear of the Turkish position, a flag of truce was sent forward, and in a little while negotiations were opened; but while these were proceeding, the

Russians made some alteration in their military dispositions, which seems to have been misunderstood by the Turks, who at once opened a heavy volley from their rifles. The bearer of the flag of truce, who had entered the Turkish fort, was slain, and his body was found next day beheaded and mutilated. A hundred and forty-two men were killed and wounded in a few minutes, and the others, without waiting for orders, rushed upon their enemy with loud cries of wrath. The Turks were speedily driven back, and the Russians occupied their abandoned camp in the rear of the fortifications. Gourko now summoned the Turks to surrender, and after nightfall a letter arrived from their commander, Mehemet Pasha, offering to abandon all further defence. This was speedily followed by an armistice; but early on the following morning it was discovered that the Turks had fled. During the whole of the 18th, Prince Mirsky had remained in his positions, awaiting intelligence from Gourko. On the 19th, a reconnaissance was pushed forward into the pass from the north; but the younger General Skobeleff, who had command of the detachment, passed several lines of fortifications without encountering any opposition. His surprise was naturally great, and became even greater when, on reaching the Turkish camp, he found it entirely deserted. Fires were burning, and rations were in process of being cooked; but the Ottomans had departed. Pressing on, Skobeleff and his men gained the brow of the pass, and in a deep hollow below them, lying to the south, beheld a body of troops in camp. For the moment it was impossible to say whether these troops were friends or foes. A loud Russian hurrah, sent down from the top of the mountain into the depths at its foot, met with no response, and it seemed as if Skobeleff had come unawares upon a detachment of the Turks; but soon afterwards the red-cross flag of the ambulance staff became visible, and there was no longer any doubt that the men were Russians. The two divisions of the invading army speedily effected their junction, and the Shipka Pass was for a time in possession of the invaders.

CAPTURE OF YENI-ZAGHRA.

That the Turks should have made no better defence of this mountainous region at that particular juncture, was of a piece with all their conduct in the early days of the war. The ground in parts was admirably adapted for military operations on the side of those who had to resist an advance. The rugged and beetling rocks which flanked the tortuous way were rendered more difficult by the trees which densely covered them. In addition to these natural obstacles were several lines of fortifications, constructed, it is said, by an English engineer-officer, and extremely well suited to their purpose; yet the Turks had done very little to defend their positions. The prisoners captured by the Russians stated (according to the official reports of the victors) that there were fourteen battalions occupying eight splendid positions, one behind another, throughout the Shipka Pass, all of which were abandoned in the most unaccountable manner by the Turks. The captives stated that the Pasha went away first, and was soon followed by 10,000 men, all of whom were regulars. The positions forsaken by the Turks were so well fortified that the Russians could not help admiring their construction. The victors captured a large quantity of army biscuits, five mountain guns, five Krupp guns, three regimental standards, and a number of tents. Gourko's men were thus masters of a large portion of the Balkans, and could utilize the Turkish fortifications to defend themselves, should they be attacked. The Turks had allowed the Russians to get to the southern side of the chief Balkan range; and although, as it afterwards turned out, this advance was imprudent and premature, it is certain that, had it been properly supported, the whole of Roumelia might have been opened to Russian attack before the end of July. The subsequent progress of the war showed how magnificently the Turks can fight when once they are aroused; but their proceedings at the commencement were imbecility itself. Unfortunately, there was another characteristic—that of ferocity—carried to those appalling lengths which seem natural to Oriental races when they are excited either by rage or fear. According to the reports of General Gourko, all his wounded were despatched, and the dead were either beheaded, or otherwise mutilated. Charges of this nature were often brought against the Turks during the progress of the war, and unquestionably with truth in many instances; but, if we suppose that all the brutality was on one side, and all the humanity on the other, we shall simply make ourselves the fools of a preconception, which neither requires evidence, nor will accept it.

Before arriving at Kezanlik, General Gourko sent a detachment of Cossacks to cut the line of railway from Yeni-Zaghra to Yamboli. He likewise despatched a small body of cavalry to Eski-Zaghra, situated on the higher slopes of the Maritza Valley, south of the Balkans. The business of these cavalry-men was to collect transport materials; but their position was isolated and dangerous. The desired objects having been secured, pioneers were set to work widening the road along the Hainkoi Pass, so that the batteries of field-artillery might be brought through, together with vehicles for the conveyance of stores. For the present, General Gourko had been remarkably successful. He had established himself in Roumelia, and his communications with his base at Tirnova were perfectly open. The Emperor sent him a message of congratulation, and the compliment was assuredly well deserved. Yet, under the circumstances, the enterprise was one of doubtful prudence. Before throwing forward their advance so far, the Russians should have known positively whether or not they were able to support it. If unsupported, it was evident that this detachment from the chief army could not possibly maintain itself against a spirited attack, and would either be overwhelmed or forced to retreat. As matters turned out, the requisite support was not forthcoming, and Gourko's brilliant achievement suffered a discouraging eclipse.

When the Russians entered Kezanlik, they were enthusiastically welcomed by the Bulgarians; but the Turks withdrew into their houses, fearing lest violence should be offered them. From the Russians themselves, speaking generally, they received no molestation; but the native inhabitants were not equally considerate. They obtained the assistance of a few Cossacks, in company with whom they entered several of the Turkish houses, and rifled them of whatever valuables they could find, together with such sums of money as chanced to be at hand. One of the sufferers was a certain Sadoullah Bey, who is said to have plundered the Bulgarians during the troubles of the previous year. In appropriating what they found in this man's house, the Bulgarians maintained that they were simply taking back their own; and so with other houses which were similarly treated, and then reduced to ruins. Doubtless some of the persons thus visited by the popular vengeance deserved the fate that overtook them; but mobs on such occasions are never very discriminating, and there can be little doubt that many unfortunate Turks were robbed for no other reason than that they belonged to the hated race. These disgraceful scenes might have been checked, had General Gourko left a strong guard at Kezanlik; but, as already related, he quitted the town shortly after entering it, in order that he might attack the Shipka Pass, where the Turks were threatening his rear. When, a few days later, some Russian soldiers were sent to Kezanlik to administer the affairs of the place, they did the most they could to stop the work of pillage.

RUSSIAN ATTACK ON THE TURKISH ENTRENCHMENTS AT PLEVNA.

A newspaper correspondent saw Prince Tserteleff lashing many of the offenders with his Cossack whip. On one occasion, the Prince found the interpreter to one of the brigade-commanders dividing spoil with some Cossacks in a Turkish house. Enraged at the sight, he slashed him across the face with his whip, and then ordered him under arrest; but these acts of just severity could not undo the mischief that had already been effected.

Dismay and apprehension fell upon the Turkish Government, and on the people of Constantinople, when intelligence reached the capital that a detachment of the Russian army was actually on the southern side of the Balkans. It was believed on the first alarm that the whole body of invaders would speedily overrun Roumelia; that Adrianople would be occupied, as it had been in 1829; and that Constantinople would stand in peril of capture, if energetic measures were not at once taken for stopping the triumphant advance of the Russians. The Sultan had long been much dissatisfied with his Commander-in-Chief, Abdul Kerim Pasha, and he now determined to dismiss an officer who was evidently incapable of rendering any service to the country. His place was filled by Mehemet Ali, and the command of the Balkan troops was given to Suleiman Pasha, who had recently been operating with success against the Montenegrins. At the same time, Safvet Pasha was dismissed from the Foreign Office, and Aarifi Pasha was appointed his successor. Suleiman Pasha was in the prime of life, barely forty years of age, and presenting every appearance of activity and talent. He has been described as a man of fair complexion, with sandy hair and whiskers and grey eyes; altogether, a northern-looking man, very different from the dark, corpulent, sallow Orientals who form the bulk of Turkish Pashas. On being recalled from Montenegro, he proceeded to an encampment which had been formed on the northern side of Adrianople, near the old palace of the Sultans. The ruins of that palace were broken up, to aid in strengthening the fortifications of the place, and the General immediately set to work incorporating newly-enlisted troops with the veterans whom he had brought with him from Montenegro.

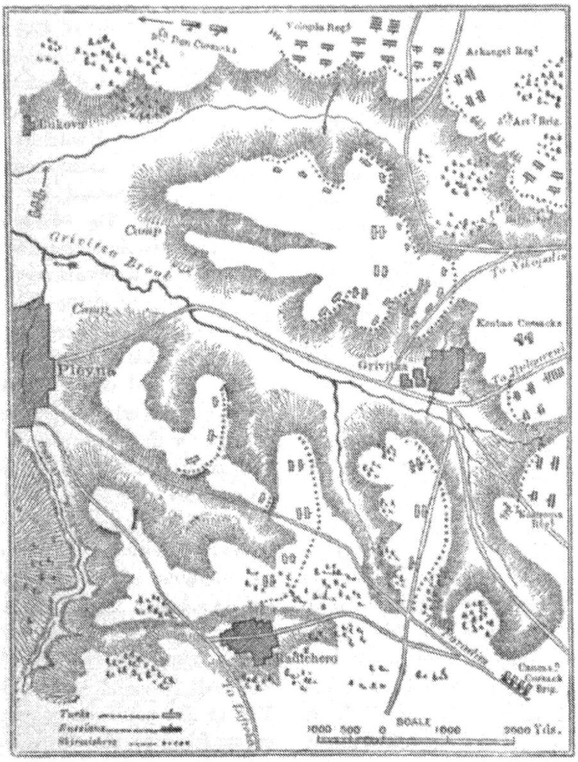

PLAN OF THE BATTLE OF PLEVNA.

The successes of the Russians, and the fact of their now being in force to the south of the Balkans, emboldened the peace-party at Constantinople, and gave rise to some talk of an arrangement. It soon, however, became apparent that Turkey would refuse the only terms which Russia, under the existing circumstances, was likely to grant. The Czar was evidently bent on humbling the pride of Turkey, and on establishing his own power, whether directly or indirectly, in the European dominions of the Sultan. No sovereign of an independent country could accept such a state until reduced to the utmost extremities. Turkey was still a great military Empire, and in Asia the fortune of war had been chiefly on her side. Therefore, although rumours of peace pervaded every capital in Europe, no serious idea of opening negotiations with the enemy was entertained by the Porte at this juncture. Suleiman Pasha infused his own energy into the troops, and his own spirit of hopefulness into the Ministerial circles. When the feeling of panic had passed away, it was seen that the position of General Gourko's force was one of extreme danger, more fitted to inspire alarm in the invaders themselves than in their opponents. So far from the war being on the eve of terminating, it was probably only just beginning; and this appears to have been the impression entertained by the English Government. In the latter part of July, it was resolved to take still further measures for the protection of English interests, if by any extension of the conflagration they should be imperilled. The Cabinet of Lord Beaconsfield determined to augment the garrison of Malta without delay, and to despatch to that island two additional battalions, each numbering about nine hundred men. It was also contemplated to send further drafts at an early date, and orders were at the same time issued to various bodies of troops to hold themselves in readiness for service abroad, if it should be required. Rumour even affirmed that an expedition was about to sail for Gallipoli; that England and Austria were to join in the occupation of Constantinople; and that forty thousand troops were to be sent from India to Egypt. These were fictions, born of the prevalent excitement; but the strengthening of the garrison at Malta was a fact, and it showed that the Government, though still maintaining its position of neutrality, felt uneasy at the progress of the Russian arms in Europe, and as to the probable fate of Constantinople, should the legions of the Czar penetrate still farther south.

While General Gourko was endeavouring to make good his grasp upon the Tundja Valley, some important operations were taking place on the other side of the Balkans, between that mountain range and the Danube. A large portion of the Turkish army of Widdin, commanded by Osman Pasha, was stationed in and about Plevna, a small town to the south-west of Nicopolis. Osman was on his way to relieve the latter place, when news reached him that it had fallen. He therefore turned aside, and occupied Plevna; and here he was attacked, on the 19th of July, by General Schilder-Schuldner, with a portion of the Ninth Corps, consisting of an infantry brigade, with cavalry and artillery. The Ottoman troops numbered about 8,000, and the Russians, after an animated encounter, in which for a brief time they actually occupied the town, were swept back. The attack was repeated more than once, but always with the same ill-success, and a little before dark the Turks took the offensive, and drove the Russians far beyond the positions they had occupied when the battle began. During the ensuing night, General Krüdener, who commanded the Ninth Corps, sent 6,000 troops under General Schilder-Schuldner to reinforce his left. The Turks also were at the same time strengthened, so as to bring their total force up to 20,000 men. This fact was unknown to Krüdener, who, believing that he was in the position of command, ordered a fresh attack on the 20th, though his own forces did not exceed 7,500. Fighting continued all day, with terrible losses to the Russians; yet they gained some important positions and, after nightfall, 3,000 men were sent to their assistance from the garrison at Nicopolis. The battle was once more renewed on the 21st, when, after a sanguinary engagement, which lasted many hours, General Krüdener's troops were driven from their positions, which were then occupied by the Turks. Osman Pasha fixed his headquarters at Plevna, and the Russians established themselves in front of that town, where they were reinforced by two divisions of the Fourth Corps under General Zotoff, and by the greater part of the garrison from Nicopolis, together with troops from the army round Rustchuk. The Turks, who also received further reinforcements, did not follow up the success obtained by them during the three days' fighting. The two armies remained watching one another in their respective positions, occasionally endeavouring to obtain some advantage, but without any immediate results. The delay enabled the Russians to make preparations for a further struggle, and, as at this time troops were pouring through Roumania, and crossing the Danube in large numbers every week, the probability of a sanguinary contest for the possession of Plevna must have been obvious to the Turkish authorities. But it did not occur until after an interval of several days.

At this period, the war in Montenegro appeared to be languishing. The Turks had obtained some considerable advantages over the mountaineers; but the latter were yet in arms, and sufficiently strong to present a threatening front to their enemies. The fortress of Nicsics, in the Herzegovina, was still invested by the Montenegrins, and Fort Vir, at the southern entrance to the Dunga Pass. surrendered to the Christians on the 23rd of July. Other successes were achieved by the same belligerents in the latter part of that month, and the Turkish cause was weakened by the withdrawal of the able and energetic Suleiman Pasha. In Bosnia, the insurrection continued for awhile; and its leader, Despotovich, convoked a meeting of the chiefs during July, at which he put to them the direct question whether, according to a rumour which had recently prevailed, they were going to place themselves under the banner of Austria. They all declared on oath that their faith and loyalty to him, as their general and brother, remained unaltered; and it was then agreed to elect a committee to watch over Bosnian affairs, with power to co-operate with Despotovich, in whose hands was placed the supreme management of the insurrection. It must be recollected, however, that Bosnia was very much divided against itself. The Mohammedans are numerous in that province, and the Turkish Governor, about the same time, issued a proclamation to the Bosnian Mussulmans, in which he declared the Empire to be in danger, and summoned the people to arms against the common enemy, who, he said, affected to represent humanity and civilization, and, after breaking treaties, contemning all international rights, and stirring up the provinces to revolt, was then carrying on a war of extermination among the followers of Islam. On the advice of Ali Bey, commanding in that district, the Governor sent flying corps all over the country, with the object of crushing the insurrection, and great rewards were offered to the Zaptiehs, or rural police, to insure special vigilance in the suppression of discontent. Several of the small towns or villages were attacked by the insurgents, and some were set on fire. But the operations altogether were of a paltry character, not requiring any specific detail; and on the 4th of August Despotovitch was defeated, and compelled to cross into Austrian territory, where he was confined in a fortress. The Bosnian insurrection being then at an end, the insurgents, in parties of several hundreds, took refuge in Dalmatia, and were interned in islands of the Adriatic.

NAVAL COMBAT BETWEEN THE "VESTA" AND "ASSARI TEFVIC."

The attention of the world was so much absorbed by the progress of events in Bulgaria and Armenia that but little regard was paid to the operations of the rival fleets. There was, in truth, but little to observe; yet some movements, occurring from time to time, are not altogether unworthy of record. In July, the Turkish fleet once more appeared within sight of Odessa, but retired without firing, after having produced much agitation among the citizens. On the 14th of the month, Hobart Pasha had two hours' audience of the Sultan, at the close of which he received orders with regard to certain movements of the fleet. About the same period, two frigates and three corvettes made a reconnaissance of Sebastopol. On their approach, five Russian ships, commanded by a Vice-Admiral, retired within the port; but the Turkish squadron, fearing the action of torpedoes, sailed on to Eupatoria, where it destroyed the Russian batteries, together with some portions of the town, and captured a vessel laden with salt. A very exciting collision between a Russian merchantman and a Turkish ironclad took place at this stage of the war. In the early spring, Captain

Baranoff, of the Imperial Russian Navy, published an article in the *Golos* upon the late Mr. Elder's circular vessels, and the general character of ironclads. Russia, in the opinion of this authority, required no ironclads at all, either circular or oblong. It had been proved, he said, by the events of the Crimean War, that ships, however strong their build, will always succumb to the heavier artillery that is brought to bear upon them from the shore. He therefore advised his Government to abandon the construction of ironclads, to avoid naval battles, and to confine operations at sea to the letting loose of a number of cruisers against the enemy's merchantmen. Where an engagement could not be avoided, Captain Baranoff preferred that it should be fought with small, light craft, capable of moving with great speed, and therefore having a good chance of avoiding the attacks of the adversary. The Russian Admiralty appeared to consider that there was some value in these ideas, and it was intimated to the captain that he might put his notions to the proof. The merchant-steamer *Vesta* was placed at his disposal, and was prepared for hostile action by the reception of some six-inch mortars, and by the strengthening of her deck, so as to bear the additional weight.

The *Vesta* was an iron steamer of light build, which until then had been employed in the conveyance of corn and tallow. She now sailed forth from Sebastopol with intent to seek the enemy, and on the morning of the 23rd of July, when thirty-five miles from Kustendji, fell in with the Turkish ironclad *Assari Tefvik*, a vessel protected by a cuirass of twelve inches in thickness, mounted with guns of twelve tons weight, and capable of a speed of thirty knots an hour. This formidable opponent was attacked by Captain Baranoff, who, in his little unarmoured steamer, maintained a combat of five hours' duration. The superior manœuvring of the *Vesta*, consequent on her greater lightness, kept the Turkish vessel in check during the whole of that time, though the distance between the two ships was often very slight. The *Assari Tefvik*, notwithstanding the thickness of her armour, considered it prudent to keep perpetually in motion, so as to avoid, as much as possible, the rapid fire of her antagonist. She was indeed frequently struck by small shot, but during the whole encounter received only three cannon-balls. Of these, one did but little harm; the second went through the deck, setting it for a while on fire; and the third struck the turret, causing great consternation among the Turkish sailors. Considerable injury was of course done to the *Vesta*, which was at one time hit by a grenade close to the powder-magazine. The danger of an explosion seemed imminent; but Captain Baranoff took such speedy and effectual measures to avoid the peril that the safety of the vessel was soon assured. Her rudder was afterwards struck, so that she could not properly obey the helm; yet the Russian captain maintained the contest with extraordinary gallantry, and did not withdraw until the appearance on the scene of two other Turkish vessels, which went to the assistance of their comrade. Battered and injured in many ways, yet not vanquished, the steamer cast anchor at Sebastopol in the early morning of the 24th. Three officers and eleven men had been killed; two officers and four men were seriously wounded; and three officers and eleven men were slightly wounded. Among the last was Captain Baranoff himself; and of the entire crew very few escaped untouched.* All, however, received honours and rewards from the Czar. The value of ironclad ships in naval warfare has yet to be accurately determined; but an incident such as this is worthy of consideration in any estimate of the general question.

As the summer advanced, strong excitement prevailed in Russia with respect to the policy of England. It appears to have been taken for granted that the Government of Lord Beaconsfield had determined on war, and a disposition to accept that issue was apparent in many circles of Muscovite society. The press became extremely violent. Some of the journals laughed at the insignificant force which England could spare for an Eastern war; while others declared that the Egyptian contingent of the Turkish army was being equipped with English money. At the same time it was loftily announced that the Turks were to be entirely expelled from Bulgaria, and that Russia would open the Dardanelles to her war-vessels. In expectation of an attack on the northern provinces of the Empire, supposing war to break out between Russia and England, torpedoes were sunk off all the exposed points on the Finnish and Baltic shores. Helsingfors, Viborg, and Dünamünde, were the chief places thus protected; but Russia was certainly premature in supposing that she was in any danger in those directions. There was undoubtedly a war-party in England; but there was a peace-party too, and it was not unrepresented in the Cabinet itself. Lord Derby had declared that the English Government would do nothing to oppose Russia, as long as British interests were respected; and from that determination there were no signs of any disposition to withdraw.

* Correspondent of the *Times*, writing from Berlin, July 28th, 1877.

CHAPTER XXVIII.

The Tide beginning to turn—Operations of Osman Pasha—Taking of Loftcha by the Turks—March of General Gourko to Yeni-Zaghra, and Capture of the Town—Renewed Fighting with the Turks—Crushing Defeat of the Bulgarian Legion at Eski-Zaghra—Disastrous Retreat of General Gourko to the Northern side of the Balkans—Fortification of the Shipka and Hainkoi Passes—Rise of a Spirit of Mutual Exasperation—A Foolish Prophecy—Accusations by the Turkish Government against the Russian Soldiers—Confirmations from Official Sources of the Truth of those Statements—The Wounded Mussulmans in the Rasgrad Hospital—Massacres of Mohammedans in various Localities—Panic and Flight—Testimony of English Newspaper Correspondents—Outrages on Women—Disingenuous Arguments—Evidence contained in Parliamentary Papers—Ferocity of the Bulgarians—Character of the Russian Soldier—Atrocities committed by the Turks against the Russians—Massacres at Kavarna and Yeni-Zaghra—Horrible Scenes—Mutilation of the Dead and Wounded in the Shipka Pass—Dreadful Incidents in various Parts of European Turkey—Massacre by Kurds at Bayazid, in Asia—Both Belligerents guilty of Murder and Outrage.

WHETHER owing to the removal of Abdul Kerim Pasha, or to the increasing gravity of the situation, the Turks were at length beginning to act with that energy which they are always capable of exhibiting when sufficiently aroused. In the latter part of July, it became apparent that the tide was turning. The defeat of General Krüdener in the three days' struggle before Plevna, on the 19th, 20th, and 21st, made the invaders for the first time aware that their progress through Bulgaria would not be a mere military promenade, varied by a few skirmishes; and Nicopolis was reported to be in danger. The Russians at once called the Fourth Roumanian Division, under General Manu, to their aid, and the Russian head-quarters were removed backwards from Tirnova to Biela. Osman Pasha then marched in a south-easterly direction from Plevna to Loftcha, or Lovatz, which, while occupied by a small body of Turks, had been taken a few days before by an equally small number of Russians. The town was once more seized by the Turks on the 26th of July; but it cost them six hours' hard fighting to get possession of it, and they had to fight again on the following day. Nevertheless, they were now acquiring a position of command in the region of which Plevna may be taken as the centre, so far as these operations were concerned; and the Russians had to consider, not only their laurels, but their safety.

The despatch of Roumanian troops was not popular with the people of the Principalities. A correspondent of the *Times*, writing from Vienna on the 27th of August, said that Prince Charles, on receipt of the first telegram from the Czar after the battles at Plevna, hesitated to comply with it, as there was no convention for regulating the co-operation of the Roumanian army. General Ghika, the Roumanian military *attaché* at the Russian head-quarters, arrived, and urged that the Roumanian troops should be sent over, bringing a promise that everything should be arranged satisfactorily. On this, the Prince transmitted an order to General Manu to cross over and occupy Nicopolis. As the passage was made, not over the bridge, but by boats, it took some time, and another telegram came from the Russian head-quarters to hasten the movement. The Prince then sent his Minister, M. Bratiano, to inquire into the cause of the delay. He found General Manu surrounded by his staff, and, when he told him to hasten the passage, the General replied, "The Division will pass; but you have taken a very ill-advised step in sending it across." This was reported to the Prince, who saw in it a reflection on his policy, and took the first opportunity of recalling the offending officer. General Krüdener sent orders to the Roumanian Division to occupy a position outside Nicopolis, which General Manu refused to do, pleading that his orders from the Prince were merely to occupy the town. He was then recalled, and replaced by General Angelesco.

For the present, we must relate the further operations of General Gourko south of the Balkans. That officer was directed to advance from Kezanlik on Yeni-Zaghra, lying to the south-east; and his forces, which were divided into three columns, were to converge on the point of attack in such a way as to overwhelm opposition. The right column was formed of the Bulgarian Legion, two batteries of artillery, and three regiments of cavalry, and was to march from Eski-Zaghra. The centre column was commanded by Gourko himself, and consisted of the Rifle Brigade, a regiment of Cossacks, and four batteries of artillery, to be directed from Kezanlik; and the left column, starting from Hainkoi, was composed of five battalions of infantry, two batteries, and some Cossacks. On the 29th of July, Gourko set out from Kezanlik, and, after a fatiguing march of forty miles, approached Yeni-Zaghra on the morning of the 30th. He struck the left flank of the Turkish entrenchments in front of the railway station, and attacked the Ottoman troops (a portion of the army of Suleiman Pasha) with sudden and impetuous fury. The resistance was determined, and a succession of bayonet-charges covered the ground with dead and wounded. But by two o'clock in the afternoon the Muscovites had succeeded in driving back the enemy, and taking possession of Yeni-Zaghra. They then blew up the railway station, and destroyed a large quantity of ammunition and stores; but, for want of cavalry, no pursuit was possible until the following day, when the Cossacks fell on the rear of the discomfited Turks. Previously to that, however—namely, on the 30th —General Gourko, having heard that the right column was in great straits, and unable to force its way from Eski-Zaghra, started to its assistance. He reached Karabunar that night, and found the whole valley lit up with blazing villages. Thence, on the morning of the 31st, he proceeded towards Dzuranli; but between that place and Eski-Zaghra no fewer than 30,000 Turks were drawn up. The Russian commander was unaware of this fact until the enemy's batteries suddenly swept the road in his front. He then sent forward his infantry, covered by artillery, and a sanguinary action followed. Gourko's own column came under the fire of guns posted in a wood to the left of the road. "Two Cossack guns," says a writer in the *Times*, "were brought up to a mound to reply to the Turkish fire, and a detachment of the infantry regiments, including the Tirailleur Companies, were thrown into the eastern side of the wood to turn the Turkish flank. This turning movement, as usual, constrained the Turks to retire from their threatening position; but they presently returned, and only yielded place at last under the pressure of shells from the Cossack guns. Within the wood they held their ground well, being so superior in numbers that their fire rained thickly on every point where the Russians tried to gather for a charge, while their battery shelled the high road and a small wood to the right of it, where some of the Czar's troops tried to gain a footing. Much gallantry was shown in this attack on the wood. The colonel of one regiment, finding his men wavering before the tempest of bullets, seized the colours, and dashed forward, crying out, 'Who will dare to lag behind?' With a wild cry, his men sprang after him, and drove back the thickening Osmanlis." The right of the Russian line, however, was very nearly turned, when the cavalry of Prince Eugene of Leuchtenberg, appearing from Eski-Zaghra, whence they had cut their way against heavy odds, saved Gourko from annihilation.

BATTLE OF DZURANLI.

CHARGE OF PRINCE LEUCHTENBERG'S DRAGOONS.

In the meanwhile, the Bulgarians were being badly beaten in the vicinity of Eski-Zaghra, from which they were obliged to retire into a defile leading northwards, and so, by the Shipka Pass, into Bulgaria Proper. The men, though unaccustomed to warfare, seem to have fought very well, and out of the whole body of sixteen hundred, less than five hundred reached Shipka in safety. The whole expedition was a failure. After being reinforced by Leuchtenberg's cavalry, Gourko pushed on until within sight of Eski-Zaghra; but, finding himself threatened by the Turks in flank and rear, he was obliged to leave the Bulgarians to their fate, and to retreat as fast as he could through the Dalboka and Hainkoi Passes, both narrow, tortuous, and difficult. The sufferings of his army were great during those disastrous days. The wounded died in large numbers, and even strong men perished from fatigue and sunstroke. In the fighting of the 30th and 31st of July, General Gourko lost three thousand men, and to this had to be added the losses of the Bulgarians; so that the misfortune to the Russian cause was one of no small proportions. By the 2nd of August, the advanced division of the invading force had gained the northern side of the Balkans; but steps were immediately taken for securing a hold upon the chief defiles. The Shipka Pass was strongly fortified, armed with twenty-eight guns, and garrisoned by a regiment of the Ninth Division. Two regiments occupied the Hainkoi Pass, which was also elaborately defended; and reinforcements were sent southwards, to strengthen the detachments holding the exposed positions.*

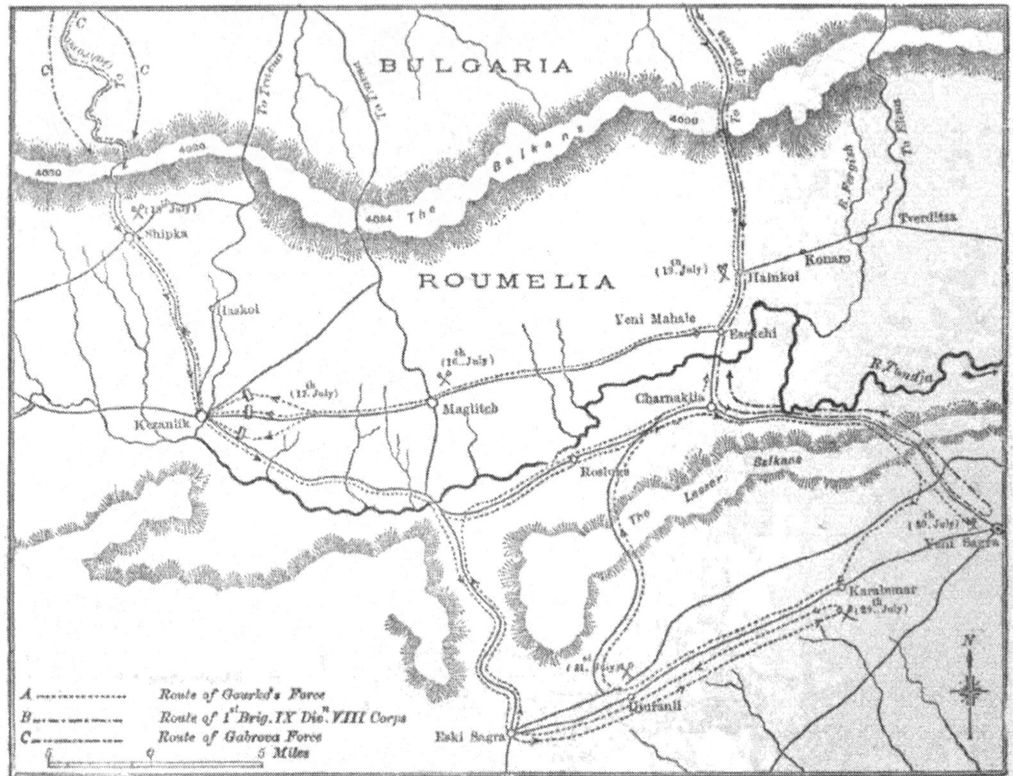

PLAN OF THE TUNDJA VALLEY, SHOWING THE MARCHES OF THE FORCES UNDER GOURKO, WITH THE DATES OF THE SKIRMISHES.

The belligerents had by this time become thoroughly exasperated, and the war was being waged on both sides with merciless ferocity. It was a war in which the utmost fury of religious fanaticism was certain to be enlisted, and in which the pent-up venom of antagonistic races was let loose, with all the frightful results which cool-headed men had foreseen, and lamented beforehand. It has been related, on the authority of one of the

* *Daily News* Correspondent, writing from Sistova on the 8th of August.

most eminent and trustworthy of Special Correspondents, that the Turks, in retiring from the northern parts of Bulgaria, behaved with exemplary self-restraint and consideration, and that their regard for the Christian population was very ill-repaid by the inhabitants of many villages. A few weeks later, the same correspondent reported that all this had changed, and that the Turks were acting with ruthless barbarity. There must have been some reason for so marked a difference, and it appears to be discoverable in the acts of the Bulgarians towards their former masters. In the first instance, the Russian invaders restrained the disorderliness and rapacity of the people; but they were soon infected by the evil spirit of the time. At Kustendji, in the very early days of the war, it was said by the Turks that, if the misconduct of the Bulgarians should lead to reprisals, the Russians would have to remember that it was the Christians, not the Mohammedans, who began the slaughter. Unfortunately, the reprisals came very quickly, and with terrible excesses. These in turn led to acts of revenge on the part of the Muscovites, and, as July advanced, a terrible saturnalia of blood and diabolical license set in throughout the wide extent of country affected by the contending armies. Those who were disinclined to see the grievances of the Bulgarians amended by a Russian invasion had often prophesied that such would be the case. They had pointed out that, although the Turk is far from being "anti-human" under the ordinary circumstances of life, he is a devil if once his religious passions are aroused; and it was therefore suggested that to awaken those passions by foreign interference was the height of mischievous folly. The Russian advocates treated this argument with the utmost contempt. They averred that the Turk was not only a monster of unparalleled cruelty and wickedness; he was also a coward. He would slay or torture any number of women and children as long as he believed himself safe from punishment; but as soon as a Russian army had crossed the Danube, he would crouch in abject terror before his superior, and thenceforth not a hair upon a Christian head would be imperilled. The event showed how lamentably ignorant were such writers of the subject on which they presumed to dogmatize. But it was an unfortunate characteristic of the war between Russia and Turkey that fanaticism and prejudice obscured the judgment even of neutrals.

At a very early period of the war, the Turkish Government began to publish accusations of shocking cruelty committed by the Russians and Bulgarians on defenceless Moslems, especially women and children. Several of these stories may have been inventions; others may have been exaggerated and heightened; and it is not at all improbable that the Porte seized with avidity on such narratives, in the hope that they might turn the tide of English sympathy against the Russians, as the accounts of Turkish atrocities in Bulgaria in 1876 had set popular opinion against the Ottomans. But it cannot be questioned by any reasonable man that great excesses were committed by the Russians and Bulgarians before they were committed by their opponents. It was asserted by a correspondent of the *Pall Mall Gazette*, writing from Therapia on the 27th of July, that before the declaration of war a "Brigade of Vengeance" was formed at Bucharest. It consisted of four battalions of Bulgarian revolutionists, with whom were associated a number of insurgents from other provinces. This brigade was organised with the avowed object of exterminating the Moslems in European Turkey, and of burning the mosques and houses of the Mohammedans; and it was added that these objects were known to the Emperor of Russia. The whole subject is most painful and loathsome—one which the historian would gladly pass over in silence; but it is necessary to any complete record of the war that some exposition should be made of those exceptional crimes which disgraced its course, and in which both sides were implicated. In doing so, the main desire and sole object will be to state the facts fairly and honestly, as far as they can be ascertained, without regard to preconceptions of any kind whatever.

One of the earliest official allegations by the Turks against the Russians was contained in a despatch from the Ottoman Government, received by the Embassy at Paris on the 12th of July, 1877. It was here stated:—"A Russian division, arriving on the 7th at the villages of Kestan and Belovan, disarmed the Mussulman inhabitants, and distributed their arms among the Bulgarians. They then treated the Mussulman population in the same way as previously, massacring men, women, and children, and burning their houses. This tends to show that the Russians have devised a system of exterminating the Mussulmans on the passage of their troops, and that our unfortunate co-religionists must expect the most horrible and barbarous treatment from an enemy who expressly announced himself as the champion of the rights of humanity, and the impartial protector of all our populations. We cannot doubt that Europe will be indignant and deeply moved at the recital of such atrocities." Accusations made by any belligerent against his adversary must of course be received with a certain amount of distrust; but it would be carrying a reasonable caution too far if we refused to accept such testimony altogether. That it was confirmed from independent sources, cannot be denied. It is true that Mr. Archibald Forbes—whose admirable impartiality is no less conspicuous than his brilliant genius—has recorded that, so far as his personal observation went, the Russians committed no acts of atrocity.* But this negative testimony, though valuable in its degree, will not suffice to disprove positive evidence tending to establish the contrary. A Special Correspondent of the *Times*, telegraphing from Schumla on the 17th of July, said that, from cross-examination of six wounded female victims of Cossack barbarity near Sistova, he had learned that women and children were butchered. "I was slow to believe the reports of such senseless barbarism," he added; "but now I find them to be too true." The *Times* correspondent attached to the Turkish Army telegraphed on the same day that, under official authority, he had just seen and talked with seventeen Mussulman fugitives, who had arrived, desperately wounded, at Rasgrad. One of these sufferers, a little girl only two years old, had received a blow on the head, and a shot in the lower part of the body. A woman had three stabs and a blow. Another woman, aged sixty, had received two blows on the head, and a thrust from a lance. A female child of five bore three stabs; a young married woman had been struck three times on the head; and an old woman had been stabbed as well as struck. In addition to these victims, there were five injured women and three old men, who were wounded by long sword-bayonets and fire-arms. A longer account of the cases was afterwards communicated to the *Times* by the same correspondent, who found the victims lying together in a verandah of the Rasgrad hospital. "The wounds of these poor wretches," he said, "were from blows, thrusts, and fire-arms. The first are sabre-strokes, which have been delivered with force; the thrusts are from lances; while the bullet-wounds have evidently been made with pistols. With what degree of thoroughness these deeds of devilry were done, may be gathered from the fact that the seventeen victims showed a total of thirty-six wounds. Of these, for example, a little girl of six years bore four. It would appear, therefore, that the murderers went to work in cold blood, and were not content with killing or wounding at the first stroke." The unfortunate people belonged to a band of fugitives who, on the 30th of June, were hurrying away from Ablanova. Thirty-five of the number are said to have been killed outright by the Russians who fell upon them. That, it is true, is a statement which cannot be brought to the absolute proof which was so eagerly demanded by certain writers whenever Russia was concerned, but which was held to be quite unnecessary when Turkey was the offender. The murdered could not be brought to life to tell their own tale, and the only witnesses were the seventeen sufferers in the Rasgrad hospital, who may possibly be accused of a dishonest prejudice which they did not scruple to support by false testimony. But it is not at all likely that, in order to strengthen this testimony, they inflicted wounds upon themselves, of a character not far short of mortal; and the fact of their bearing those wounds must be accepted as presumptive testimony in favour of the story they related. The wounded people were seen by all the representatives of the European and American press assembled at Rasgrad, and they afterwards attached their signatures to a document testifying to the facts. At Schumla, according to the same authority, forty persons, including women and children, were lying injured; and amongst them was a baby at the breast, whose tiny person bore six wounds.

The Turkish Government renewed its accusations, at a somewhat later period, in another despatch to the Ottoman Embassy at Paris, dated July 23rd. It was here affirmed that a telegram from the Governor of Tirnova to the Grand Vizier established all the barbarities formerly described as committed by the Russians and Bulgarians during the occupation of Tirnova and the neighbouring villages. Fire had been set to a mosque in which the inhabitants of Tiamsi-Keni had taken refuge, and they were burned alive. The Russians, according to this account, forced their prisoners, on pain of death, to fire on the Ottoman troops sent to rescue them; and it was asserted, on the information of Suleiman Pasha, that ten unarmed Mussulmans, inhabiting the village of Eski-Zaghra, were slaughtered by the Russians and Bulgarians. A list was given of the houses burned and Mussulmans massacred (including many hundreds of women) in the villages entered by the enemy; and it was said that in some places scarcely a Mohammedan was left alive. As the names of these villages were stated, the allegations had at least an appearance of accuracy which it is not easy to gainsay. In numerous instances, villages were set on fire, and the people driven back into the flames when they sought to escape. Mr. Layard, writing to the Earl of Derby on the 24th of July, said that the proceedings of the Russians and Bulgarians in Bulgaria

* *Nineteenth Century* for November, 1877.

and Roumelia had convinced the Mohammedans that it was the deliberate intention of Russia either to exterminate the Mussulman population by the sword, or to drive it out of the country. These people were flying in terror from the districts occupied by the Russians, and crowding into Constantinople in a state of extreme misery and destitution. The Sultan gave directions that proper places should be found for their shelter, and that they should be provided with rations, which would be paid for out of the privy purse. He also requested Mr. Layard to entreat the Queen and the British Government to use their influence with the Emperor of Russia for the prevention of such crimes as had been committed. In some places, the Moslem and Christian authorities concerted, and with good effect, for the preservation of order and the repression of panic; and the Turkish Minister for Foreign Affairs ordered the Director of the Press, near the end of July, to cause the editors of the various Ottoman newspapers to be moderate and careful in publishing reports calculated to increase the feeling of exasperation already existing amongst the Mussulmans. But on the whole the prevalent emotions were terror, anger, and revenge.

Further statements to the same effect were made by the Turkish Government from time to time; but the really important fact is that they were confirmed by independent observers. A Naval Correspondent of the *Times*, writing from Adrianople on the 30th of July, said :—"I have seen here, in the house of Achmet Pasha, two Turkish women wounded by Bulgarians, and a child two years old with a wound from a Cossack lance, and its leg shattered by a bullet. Five others were killed in the same onslaught at Tekke." Colonel Borthwick, writing from the camp at Schumla, on July 20th, to friends in England, said that, on the day before, he had visited some of the worst cases of distress among the Mussulman refugees, and had distributed a little help to them. He then visited eighteen wounded women and children in a portion of the military hospital, and gave them assistance. It was bad enough, he remarked, to find helpless women groaning under wounds from lances, bayonets, and swords; but it was still more painful to behold little girls of seven and eight, boys as young, and one infant of nine months, treated in the same way. These things were not done in any sudden access of panic; they were perpetrated by a steadily-advancing army, without provocation, and on unoffending women and children. The *Daily Telegraph* correspondent at Yeni-Zaghra wrote to his journal: —"It is quite impossible to depict the horrible spectacle which the country hereabouts presents after the Muscovite occupation. The whole region is at once a charnel-house and a desert. The cattle roam about untended in what remains not yet burned of the crops and grass, amid the dead bodies of their owners. But there is far worse than this to communicate. The outrages committed all around by the Russian troops upon such as they spared alive have been inconceivably shocking and atrocious. I have seen and talked with hundreds of refugees, and especially with some of the many Jewish families who have escaped from the hands of the invaders. Those who have come in from Eski-Zaghra declare that in that district every woman and girl without exception has been brutally outraged by the Cossacks of Gourko, or by the Bulgarians." The correspondent proceeded to mention one especially horrible case, the details of which he had received, in the presence of the dying girl, from her agonized friends. This particular form of villany—among the very worst of which human nature is capable—was alluded to by Mr. Archibald Forbes in his communication to the *Nineteenth Century*, where mention is made of four Jewish sisters who had been outraged by uncounted Bulgarians in sight of their own father, as he lay dying, murdered in his house at Carlova.

The evidence in support of these terrible allegations was so strong that all but the most extravagant partisans acknowledged its validity. The *Times*, which had taken a decided tone against the Turks, and was on the whole favourable to the Russian invasion, wrote in its leading columns on the 25th of July :—"The testimony of the newspaper correspondents at Schumla makes it clear that women as well as men have been killed or wounded. It is possible, no doubt, that some of those crimes may be explained, and others slightly palliated. . . . But we fear both Russian soldiers and Bulgarian peasants have committed crimes which nothing could excuse; and, indeed, it was but too likely that the war would gain a bad eminence among modern contests for outbursts of savagery." This was the language of a reasonable candour; but it was truly pitiable to see the desperation with which more extreme journals fought to the last to resist any imputation against the objects of their idolatry. On the same day on which the *Times* made the frank admissions just quoted, the *Daily News* observed that the charges came either from the Government at Constantinople itself, or from correspondents who, as one of them had disclosed, obtained their information from official sources, and could only say what pleased the authorities. To put the cruelties imputed to the Russians on the same level as those established against the Turks, was, in the opinion of the writer, to confound accusation with proof. This was said after the publication of statements, made by correspondents of the *Times*, to the effect that they had themselves seen the wounded victims of Russian barbarity, and had received from their lips precise details of many atrocious deeds. But it is curious to observe what a totally different standard of evidence was set up by critics of this stamp, when dealing with Russian misdeeds, to that which had been accepted when the accused were Turks. In the days of inquiry into the Bulgarian massacres, anything was received which advanced the object the writers had in view. That a piece of evidence came at second-hand, or at third-hand,—that it proceeded from declared enemies of the Turks,—that it was extravagant or improbable,—were never admitted to be objections. When, in their turn, the Russians were accused, nothing would suffice but the most rigid demonstration, sometimes even to an extent which the facts themselves had rendered impossible.

THE "TIMES" CORRESPONDENT AT YENI-ZAGHRA.

In spite of these attempts to hide the truth, English opinion in the summer of 1877 was greatly agitated by the doings of Russians and Bulgarians amongst the Turkish population which fell under their power. The subject was mentioned in Parliament, and Lord Derby produced some diplomatic correspondence which had taken place on the subject. The Parliamentary Paper thus given to the world contained the reports of several consuls, the results of whose inquiries confirmed the impression that many horrors had been committed; though it is exceedingly probable that, as in the case of the Bulgarian massacres in 1876, there had been exaggeration, and in some instances entire misrepresentation.* It certainly cannot be said that Mr. Layard was quick to adopt a conclusion adverse to the incriminated parties. In a despatch to Lord Derby, dated July 25th, he expressed a doubt as to the genuineness of some of the stories, observing that they were too like the statements made in the previous year with reference to the conduct of the Turks in Bulgaria. Nevertheless, the truth of some of these assertions was corroborated by several consuls and other agents of the British Government, and by American missionaries. The facts were indeed denied by Count Schouvaloff, the Russian Ambassador at London; and in certain quarters much reliance was placed on a despatch from Colonel Wellesley, dated August 6th, giving his impression, as the result of investigations he had made, that the charges against the Russians were entirely without foundation. But Colonel Wellesley's opinion on the matter was absolutely valueless, since he had not been at the front of the army, nor had visited the hamlets where the alleged acts were accomplished. He could simply base his denial on the negative testimony of certain "trustworthy persons" who had been present at the various engagements, and who said that they had not

* The Parliamentary Paper in question is Blue Book on Turkey No. 28 (1877). Many of the statements made by the consuls are necessarily given at second-hand; but the descriptions of wounded women and children, actually seen by these gentlemen, are not liable to the same qualification. The same Blue Book contains particulars of Turkish as well as Russian iniquities.

witnessed a single case of massacre or cruelty. If the statements to the contrary effect had rested simply on the word of the Turkish Government, those statements, as coming from a party interested in establishing a case against the Russians, would have been inconclusive; but we have seen that this was not the fact. Not merely English consuls—who are sometimes accused of writing to order—but English journalists, German and Austrian journalists, and others who can hardly be suspected of conspiring to misrepresent the truth, testified to the outrages that had been committed by Bulgarians, by Cossacks, and occasionally by regular troops.

The Naval Correspondent of the *Times* was among the most zealous in discovering these iniquities, and in reporting them to his journal. On the 16th of August he wrote :—"The day before yesterday, I went with the Imperial Army to Hain Boghaz. Yesterday, at Laneli, about two hours and a half from the pass, I saw one hundred and twenty persons who had been murdered in a savage manner by Cossacks and Bulgarians. Among the victims were two women, one of whom, very beautiful and young, had been killed, and thrown naked into a pool of water, while the other lay on the ground. I saw with my own eyes families, including children, who had been thrown in a well. The houses of these people, and the handsome embroidered dresses of the women, showed they had been rich. In one house, women and young girls had been shut up, and subjected during ten days to outrages by Cossacks and Bulgarians. According to information given to me by an old woman belonging to this neighbourhood, the house was afterwards set on fire, and fifteen women were burnt to death. The Bulgarians, when they heard of the arrival of the Turkish Army at Hain Boghaz, carried off the Turkish women and children, from three to thirty

BULGARIAN REFUGEES.

years of age, and fled to the Balkans. The victims of whom I spoke above were all collected together, and murdered in succession. Many more were butchered in the same way; but I have not had time to go and see them." It is probable that in the greater number of instances, though certainly not in all, these atrocities were committed by the Bulgarian peasants and the Cossacks; as, on the Turkish side, they were chiefly attributable to the Circassians and the Bashi-Bazouks. A Military Correspondent of the *Times* wrote on the 16th of July:—"This war is not an affair of civilization, but of horror upon horror. The Russian officers do all they can to prevent atrocities of every sort; but the Russian soldier looks on the Turk as an animal whom he has to chase and kill. Discipline prevents the Russians from committing excesses; but the Bulgarians have not the same obedience to orders, and, having felt the Turkish yoke, they will kill if they can. Among the Russian officers it is said, 'We began by making war on the Turks for the sake of the Bulgarians; we shall end by making war on the Bulgarians for the sake of the Turks.'" On several occasions, the Russian officers were obliged to use their whips freely, when they found the Bulgarians pillaging the dead, or slaughtering the wounded. It has sometimes been urged in excuse for these wretches that they had been debauched by centuries of Turkish misrule; but there had been nothing, for many years previous to the war, capable of developing such a hell of evil passions in the Bulgarian population, had there not been something essentially vicious in the very nature of that population, which previous slavery may have helped to develop, but which it could not have entirely created. Yet these were the men whom the Russians systematically armed as they advanced into the country, after first taking all weapons from the unfortunate Mussulmans, who were thus left defenceless. It was hardly possible that the results should have been other than they were.

The truth of these allegations was earnestly and even passionately denied by the Russian Government and the Russian newspapers; but nations never plead guilty to charges of this character. In estimating the value of what was asserted by the many witnesses of Russian misdoings, we have a right to consider the character of the people, as exhibited on former occasions and on different fields. No Englishman who has reached middle age will ever forget the abominations committed by Muscovite troops during the Crimean War. The firing on flags of truce, the cold-blooded slaying of the wounded, the acts of bad faith and inhumanity, may not unfairly be remembered at the present day, and be used as some means of determining the probability of what is alleged to have taken place during the war of 1877. There is nothing in the recent history of Russia to favour the supposition that a single generation has entirely altered the disposition of the race. Moreover, it must in candour be admitted that all armies (though doubtless in different degrees) are at times disgraced by acts of wanton barbarity. We have therefore a general probability to start with, and in the second place we have special evidence to prove several of the particular charges made in so much abundance during those terrible months of 1877. It would be saying too much if we were to allege the truth of everything that was asserted by heated partisans, or by interested persons, to the discredit of the Russian invaders; but, after all fair deductions have been made, a residuum of truth remains; and it is to the interest of justice that that truth should not be denied or obscured, but should take its proper place among the dismal facts of a war prompted by ambition, and prosecuted in the name of violated humanity and outraged right.

The barbarity of the Turks, however, was even worse than that of the Russians or Bulgarians; though it must always be remembered that the atrocities of the former did not commence until after the latter had committed numerous acts of massacre, torture, and incendiarism. Even as late as July 15th, General Zimmerman told Commander Drummond, of her Majesty's ship *Rapid*, that the Turks had committed no personal outrages or murders, as far as his own experience went. And at that time the Bulgarians and Cossacks had been slaying and outraging Turkish women and children for more than a fortnight.* It seems to have been about the middle of July—or perhaps a day or two earlier—that the Turks began to revenge themselves; but the revenge, when it came, was terrible. A correspondent of the *Daily News*, attached to the headquarters of Suleiman Pasha's army, wrote, under date of July 29th, that burning villages belonging to the Christians were to be seen on the line of march, and that the whole population appeared to be flying. The first object which this writer was taken to see, on his arrival at Karabunar, was the severed head of a Bulgarian peasant, which had just been brought in by a Turkish soldier, who had himself performed the operation, in revenge for being fired at. The head was thrown into a ditch close to the station, and there remained in full

* The affair of Ablanova., already mentioned, was on the 30th of June.

view of every one, until some charitable person covered it with earth. Among the worst acts proved against the Turks was the common practice of mutilating the wounded, and outraging the dead, on the several fields of battle. But it was not only the actual belligerents who suffered. A horrible massacre of civilians took place at Kavarna, where fifteen hundred Circassians demanded a contribution of 100,000 piastres (about £900). The population, being very poor, could not pay; whereupon the Circassians commenced an indiscriminate assault. The Christians took up arms, and endeavoured to defend themselves; but they were at length overpowered, when one hundred of them were slain, and the town was given up to pillage. Five hundred fled to Baltchik, whence an Austrian Lloyd steamer took them to Varna, which was at that time crowded with more than 50,000 refugees. At Yeni-Zaghra (the destruction of which town has already been related), a large number of Bulgarians were massacred by the Bashi-Bazouks about the middle of July. A few days later, a correspondent of the *Times* helped to dig up some of the bodies, and ten of these, including two women, were found horribly mutilated. "There was no time to look for more," says the correspondent, "but I imagine there must have been hundreds. The stench of the place was awful, and the destruction complete. No Mussulman corpse was found. The massacre began at mid-day, and lasted until noon next day. It was then stopped by the arrival of Selim Pasha with Turkish regular troops, who collected the Bulgarians under strong military guards, and sent them off to Adrianople." The Bashi-Bazouks, Circassians, and other Turkish irregulars, were treating every village they passed in the same way, burning, ravishing, and pillaging. These men, who seem to have been entirely beyond the control of their superiors, often deserted in small bands, and ranged about on marauding expeditions of their own.

It is a remarkable fact that the Naval Correspondent of the same paper, who visited Yeni-Zaghra on the 17th of July—the day before that on which his coadjutor arrived—could not find the slightest trace of a massacre. He even offered a Napoleon for any corpse that could be produced; but not one was then forthcoming. Together with his interpreter, he took the trouble of looking into every waggon that had been loaded with refugees, and he spent nearly an hour in cross-questioning the people about the alleged affair. Not a single man, woman, or child, he avers, had a scratch to show, and only one man alleged that he had lost a relation. A little boy of ten told him that he knew where sixteen bodies lay, and, conceiving that the grown-up men were afraid of giving evidence, while the child had no such apprehension, he thought he would go to the place. It turned out, however, to be half an hour's drive on the other side of the town; but, as the Russians and the Bashi-Bazouks had had a slight conflict there on the 14th of July, the evidence of the dead bodies did not appear to be worth much. The alleged massacre seemed therefore to be problematical; but unfortunately it turned out to be only too true. The Naval Correspondent made another visit to the town a few days later, and found dead bodies enough—the bodies, in many instances, of women who had first been foully outraged, and then as foully murdered. The tragedy of Yeni-Zaghra was one of the most terrible of the war; but it seems to have been preceded by Bulgarian atrocities.

A perfect manufacture of false reports concerning atrocities committed on both sides was carried on by persons who made it their business to create feelings of animosity with respect to one belligerent or the other. Something of the kind occurs in every war; but it is equally true that acts of the most abominable description were really perpetrated, both by Russians and by Turks. Each nationality professed the highest regard for the humane principles of modern civilization; but trustworthy witnesses have shown too clearly that those principles were outraged alike by Moslem and by Christian. One of the worst accounts was that which was given by a Military Correspondent of the *Times*, who, writing from Kezanlik on the 19th of July, described the state of things which he found in the Shipka Pass after the battle on the 18th. Having described a group of Turkish wounded, whose injuries were being dressed and cared for by their adversaries, the correspondent proceeded:—"A few paces further on is a circle of Russians—officers and men—gazing, fascinated, at a spectacle within. There, at last, are the bodies collected together for examination; all headless, some cut limb from limb, some treated in a manner which is universally regarded as the deepest insult that can be paid to the body of a man, alive or dead. But were these men alive or dead when they were thus treated? With regard to some there may be a doubt, but with regard to others no doubt. Here was to be seen a body with wounded finger dressed, and the rest cut off ruthlessly—perhaps in struggling with the knife. There lay what was a man, in an attitude showing plainly that he had striven to save his throat; near him was another with the red cross on his arm, having, perhaps, dressed the wounded finger of the first-named; one in the terrible exhibition lay with bared belly, slashed across with knives, and showing that blood had run from the wounds; another had been cut limb from limb. A young and well-shaped form, with clearer skin than the rest, had been beheaded and otherwise shamefully mutilated; but there was not a single wound of any description on his body produced by regular warfare. These are only instances. The proof was all too plain. There lay men who had been wounded or unwounded prisoners in the hands of the Turkish 'gentlemen,' who had foully murdered and mutilated them, showing thus that they are savages as cruel as any in Africa or India. And but a few paces distant the Russian medical men were dressing the wounds of these savages, and soldiers standing round guarded them from all evil, even the righteous indignation which filled their own breasts." The Military Correspondent of the *Times* was Lieutenant-Colonel Brackenbury; and this gentleman, together with two French correspondents, and the representative of a Spanish-American illustrated journal, signed a paper in which the frightful and abominable facts were specifically set forth. This was communicated by Colonel Wellesley to the English Government, and is to be found among the documents laid before Parliament in the summer of 1877. It showed the spirit of savage desperation with which the Turks encountered their adversaries, and justly roused the indignation of the English people. But, atrocious as such facts were, they were not so bad as the murder and torturing of non-combatants which occurred during that awful time.

Among the numerous villages sacked by the Turks, with the accompaniment of dreadful outrages on the Christian inhabitants, was one called Kara-atli, situated about sixteen miles from Tirnova, in the direction of Philippopolis. It consisted of more than three hundred houses, but on the 30th of July was completely destroyed by a party of Bashi-Bazouks. A good many of the inhabitants had left before the attack, but some six hundred remained. These were chiefly women and children, who, on the approach of the Turkish irregulars, took refuge in the neighbouring woods and fields. Some were so fortunate as to escape observation; but many others were caught by the merciless savages, and massacred with every circumstance of horror. The place was then pillaged and burned down, and, when the hamlet was visited by an English journalist shortly afterwards, dogs and pigs were devouring the bodies, while donkeys and cattle strayed ownerless about the roads. But a still worse series of atrocities occurred at Geula-Mahalisse, a little off the line of rail between Yeni-Zaghra and Tirnova. The town was visited, on the 27th of July, by a large number of Circassians, who in the first instance carried off a great many young girls, and then returned, full of murderous designs against the remainder of the populace. They found that the women and children had fled for protection into the church. Thither they followed them, and slaughtered all; and a hundred and seventy-five dead bodies were taken out of the building, and buried, by Colonel Lennox and Lieutenant Chermside, R.E., Military Attachés, and Messrs. Leslie and Meyrick, of the Aid to the Sick and Wounded Society. Many other corpses were found in different localities, and the wounds of thirty-six injured persons were dressed by the medical gentlemen. These eye-witnesses described the scene in the church as awful. "The dead and the dying," according to the report of the *Times* Naval Correspondent, "were piled in suffocating heaps; little children crawling about looking for their mothers; wounded mothers trying to move those ghastly heaps to find their children, and when found hardly able to recognise them with the fearful sword-cuts about their little heads. Many women had been subjected to fearful outrages, while others had had their breasts cut off, or their hands chopped off at the wrist. A mother lay stone-dead, and her baby was vainly endeavouring to get the food for which it was starving, while an older child was calling and pushing the dead woman, to try and make her awake. Even while these gentlemen were in the village, the murdering was going on at another part, and so threatening were these ferocious ruffians that their lives stood in very great danger. A Circassian from behind a hedge took a deliberate shot at Mr. Meyrick, but missed him." No regular troops were at that time in the town, so that the Circassians were entirely without check.

A correspondent of the *Daily News* spoke of Bulgarian villages strewn with slaughtered men, women, and children, lying about among the ashes of their burnt houses; of husbandmen found dead in the fields, apparently shot while at their daily labours; and of a Bulgarian having been seen by the side of a well, still living, but desperately wounded, and with the cross scored by transverse cuts on his forehead. At Kaceljevo, some distance up the Lom, occurred a catastrophe similar to that of Geula-Mahalisse. The village was for a time occupied by a regiment of Russian dragoons, commanded by Colonel Bilderling; but these left on a reconnaissance down the river. In their absence, a detachment of Turks, said to have been under the command of a superior officer, entered the little place. The inhabitants shut themselves into the church; but the door was broken open by order of the commanding officer, and all the miserable fugitives were slain. When Colonel Bilderling returned at night, he found the village empty and desolate, and the church reeking with blood. A few persons who had hidden themselves in the neighbouring gardens presently came in, and related all that had passed under their observation. But the wrong-doers had escaped, and were by that time possibly on their way to the commission of fresh crimes.

One of the most dreadful of these events was the butchery committed in and around Eski-Zaghra. After the desperate fighting which occurred between the Russian cavalry and the Turks in the neighbourhood of that town, from the 29th to the 31st of July, the Ottoman troops took possession of the place, and began a frightful massacre. All the Christians, whether men, women, or children, were shot as they left their houses, while those who remained within were burned alive. Many leading Turkish merchants are alleged to have taken part in acts of incendiarism, and one of them collected large numbers of Bashi-Bazouks, and sent them all over the country around Schirpan. The result was that about sixty villages were set in flames; that five hundred schools and colleges, and more than thirty churches, were destroyed; and that many persons were murdered. The total loss of life was stated at from twelve to fifteen thousand; but this was probably an exaggeration. Still, the number must have been large; for the Turks planted soldiers along the road leading to Kezanlik, with directions to shoot down every one passing that way. Similar horrors occurred in Asia. While General Tergukasoff was fighting in the neighbourhood of Deli-Baba, in the middle of June, 22,000 Kurds advanced from Van, and took possession of the town of Bayazid, whereupon the Russian garrison retired into the citadel. After a couple of days' blockade, the latter offered terms, and, these being accepted, half of the garrison (consisting of 1,200 Cossacks) marched unarmed out of their stronghold. Suddenly the Kurds set upon them, and massacred the whole number. The gates of the citadel were then closed; the remainder of the Russians refused to carry out the terms of surrender; and on the 10th of July (as related in Chapter XIV.) the town was relieved by Tergukasoff. It should be added that the massacre was so rapidly effected as to prevent the regular troops from interfering, and that Mukhtar Pasha, the Commander-in-Chief, gave orders that the principal offenders should be shot, together with some wretches who had exhumed and mutilated the Russian dead at Zeidikan.

As regards European Turkey, there can be no doubt that the whole truth was summarised by the Naval Correspondent of the *Times*, when he wrote (under date July 28th):—"I hear on every side the same story—Turks murdered and defiled by Christians, and Christians by Turks. I pass through villages, actually by the hundred, where nothing remains alive but the dogs and poultry, and where every house alike, Turk or Christian, has in its turn been ransacked. The whole Bulgarian population rise like one man on the approach of the Russians, and, as I firmly believe, murder the Moslems, besides destroying telegraphs and railways, and giving every assistance to the enemy. It only depends on the situation of a Russian force whether there is a rebellion of the subjects of the Porte in that particular district, or not. The Russians foster this rebellion in every possible way, and it is needless to say that they draw no small profit from these horrors, whichever way they go. If Moslems are destroyed, it is so many dangerous people out of the way; if Bulgarians or Christians, then so much more is Russia justified in her Holy War."* The writer believed that the Russians themselves were guiltless of atrocities; but, even supposing it to be so (and the assertion is negatived by much independent testimony), the guilt must rest mainly with those who incited the Bulgarians, who provoked the reprisals of the Turks, and who, with deliberate subtlety, prepared the way for a state of anarchy and demoniac rage, such as the worst epochs of the world might be challenged to surpass.

* *Times*, Aug. 16th, 1877.—A great many more instances both of Russian and Turkish ferocity might be added to the present Chapter; but what has been stated will probably suffice, especially as it will be necessary in future pages to refer again, though only incidentally, to this revolting and miserable subject.

MEHEMET ALI PASHA.

CHAPTER XXIX.

Russian Edicts in Bulgaria—Ill Feeling between the Bulgarians and Roumanians—Commission for the Punishment of Offenders—Mehemet Ali Pasha and his Previous Career—Character of Suleiman Pasha—Opinion in Austria with reference to the Developments of the War—Reinforcements of the Russian Army sent to the Vicinity of Plevna—Position of Osman Pasha—General Skobeleff the Younger—Preparations for the great Battle of Plevna—The Order of Advance on the Morning of July 31st—Severe Artillery Fighting—Movement of Schahofskoy's Infantry on the Entrenched Positions of the Turks—A Desperate Enterprise—Magnificent Charge of the Russians—Temporary Success, followed by Failure—Disastrous Defeat—Sufferings of the Wounded—The Russian Army shattered, and forced to retire to New Positions—Urgent Necessity for Reinforcements—Mistakes in the Management of the Campaign—Consternation in Roumania—The Imperial Guard summoned to the Seat of War—Losses by Sickness and Fatigue—Affairs in the Dobrudscha—The Fugitives in Adrianople—Charitable Organizations for the Relief of Distress—Contributions in England towards the Mitigation of Suffering on both Sides—The Triumph of Modern Civilisation.

HAVING gained possession of Bulgaria, the Russians were not slow to exercise the rights of sovereignty. Before the close of July, a law was proclaimed, by which the tax previously paid by the Christians for exemption from military service was abolished; tithes also were to cease from the 1st of January, 1878, and to be replaced by a tax paid in cash. During the current year, tithes were to be collected in the

SKIRMISH BEFORE PLEVNA.

old way wherever the Russian administrators were in want of corn or of other agricultural produce, but in money where there was no such want. Agents to whom the Turkish Government used to farm out the collection of taxes were to receive no indemnity for advances made to that Government. Taxes were to be paid in Russian paper-money, or cash, the value of the assessments to be determined by the Russian authorities; and it was announced that no Turkish paper-money would be accepted. The Czar was in truth taking possession of the conquered land, but the execution of some of the details was left to the Bulgarians themselves. The way in which they used their power was such as might have been expected. In the district of Matchin, situated in the Dobrudscha, many Roumanian families were settled, and they complained bitterly of their treatment by the Bulgarians, alleging that they had to pay all the taxes, and that their new masters frequently extorted these by the whip. A very few weeks of such tyranny made them regret the absence of the Turks, who, they alleged, were more considerate in their depredations. The Bulgarians certainly lacked the power of making themselves loved, and any strong despotism was better than their feeble spite.

Another manifestation of the new authority had reference to criminal matters. A commission was formed under the orders of a Russian general, and consisted of seven Bulgarian members (including the President) and three Turkish. The appointment of any Turks at all on such a body had a look of liberality; but nothing was easier than to outvote them. The three Ottomans, however, seem to have been disposed to do justice in cases where their countrymen were clearly shown to have been guilty of enormities. On the 23rd of July, two Turkish brothers were hanged at Kezanlik for various outrages, and they were unanimously condemned by the Commission. When the prisoners were brought to the place of execution, one of the Turkish members said that they were about to be punished for offences against Mohammedans as well as Christians, and that all men who acted vilely would be similarly condemned, whatever their race or creed. A Bulgarian member proclaimed the same warning on behalf of his fellows, and the men were then executed. As regarded this particular case, there was probably no ground of complaint; but the danger of such a tribunal being turned into an instrument of revenge, whenever the passion of race or religion came into play, must be obvious. The Czar had undertaken to punish the persons concerned in the massacres of 1876; and this he could hardly accomplish without running the greatest risk of sometimes mistaking private animosity for public justice. Such were the fatal difficulties of the time.

But it was not certain whether the Russians would be able to retain their hold upon the province they had seized. The appointment of Mehemet Ali Pasha to the general command of the Turkish forces in Europe, and of Suleiman Pasha to the Army of the Balkans, threw new energy into the Ottoman counsels. The former commander, however, accepted his charge with a heavy heart, and even wrote to the Grand Vizier, expressing the regret with which he assumed the office. His opinion of the army-corps at Schumla was not favourable; and, on the other hand, he was himself far from popular with the soldiers. This was owing to his foreign origin. Mehemet Ali was a German, with the French name of Detroit, and was born at Magdeburg, in Prussia, in 1829. His father was a musician, not very well off; and the boy, after passing through one of the schools in his native town, found he must go forth into the world to seek his fortune. At Hamburg he obtained an engagement as sailor on board a German merchant-ship, and at fifteen years of age left his country, to which he was not destined to return. His life at sea was rendered miserable by the brutality of his shipmates, and he formed plans of escaping on the first opportunity. The vessel being anchored in the Bosphorus, he succeeded in reaching the European coast at Balta Lima, and soon obtained the favourable regards of Ali Pasha, at that time Foreign Minister, who, attracted by the good looks of the boy, offered him a home in his palace. It was not long ere he adopted the religion of Islam, and became a pupil in the Turkish Military Academy, at the same time receiving the name of Mehemet Ali Effendi. The youth made rapid progress in his new studies, and soon became first in his class. In the autumn of 1853, shortly after passing through the last course, he was appointed lieutenant on the staff of Omar Pasha, the chief commander of the Turkish army in the war with Russia then commencing. During the progress of that war, his knowledge of the principal Continental languages proved of great service to his superiors, and procured him the esteem of the foreign officers and other persons of distinction gathered at the Turkish head-quarters, and especially of the eminent Spaniard, General Prim. He followed the whole campaign of the Danube and of the Crimea, and became a Major-General in 1868, when only thirty-nine years of age. A little before the death of his patron, Ali Pasha, Mehemet Ali was appointed Field Marshal. This was in the early part of 1877, and his promotion to the chief command of the European armies followed in the course of a few months. His colleague, Suleiman Pasha, was described by a correspondent of the *Times* as a most unostentatious and reserved man, very self-reliant, prompt, and active, and with a great mastery over all the details of military organization. His tent consisted of a simple piece of canvas stretched across two sticks, under which he crawled at night, and slept on the ground. Guards, sentries, orderlies, and all the pomp of military rank, were dispensed with, and his two or three aides-de-camp bivouacked in like style near him. His two horses were picketed in front of his tent, with their saddles on their backs, to take their chance of forage with the rest of the cavalry, in the same way that their master expected no different fare from the rest of the army.

The campaign was evidently to be no light affair, and both sides mustered all their forces to the grand encounter. A second Roumanian division crossed the Danube to Nicopolis, and Servia began to arm, though it was not until near the end of the struggle that she took the field. The action of Roumania, however, created an uneasy feeling in Austria, and, although that Power refrained from making any objection to the passage of the Danube by the Roumanian troops, she mobilized her own forces as a precautionary measure. It was feared that the war might approach too near her confines, and that the course of events might aggrandize Russia to an extent not favourable to the influence of other Powers. The Cabinet of Vienna was disinclined to see the North Danubian Principalities strengthened in any great degree, lest this should be indirectly a strengthening of Russia. It was equally prepared to object to the incorporation of Bosnia with Servia, which was one of the designs attributed to the Czar. In Hungary, public feeling continued to be greatly in favour of maintaining the Ottoman Empire in its integrity. Meetings in favour of the Turks were held in two hundred Hungarian towns; but in Croatia, where the population is of Sclavonic origin, the sympathies of the people were entirely in favour of the Russian attempt to emancipate the Bulgarians from the yoke of Turkey. A meeting of Sclavonic sympathisers was held at Agram on the 5th of August, and it was attended by about twelve hundred persons. After a long discussion, a resolution was adopted, expressing the conviction of those present that the barbarous and cruel oppression of the Christian peoples in the East would continue so long as Turkey existed, and that the Turkish Empire in Europe must therefore fall, if an existence compatible with the dignity of mankind was to be secured to the oppressed race. The meeting further affirmed its warmest sympathy with those nations which were fighting for freedom, and also with Russia, the ally of Austro-Hungary; and in conclusion it expressed the conviction that Austro-Hungary would not defend Turkey, but would join the frontiers of Dalmatia and Croatia, by occupying Bosnia and the Herzegovina. The difficulty of the Austrian Empire consisted in the diverse nature of its population. The Magyars detested the Russians, while the Sclavonic nationalities not unnaturally desired to see the predominance of their own race. In Austria, there is no one nationality so far superior to the others as to be able to give a decided bias to the policy of the Imperial Government. The German element, now that all association with the rest of Germany is at an end, counts for but little; and the remainder neutralize one another by the equality of their forces. Hence the continual hesitations of Austria throughout the Russo-Turkish War, and the partial effacement of that Power in the counsels of Europe. The Emperor himself was probably well inclined to support his Muscovite brother; but the fear of offending Hungary was a restraining influence which could not be disregarded. Early in August, the Emperors of Austria and Germany had an interview at Ischl, in the Archduchy of Austria, and the result of their discussions appears to have been that the two sovereigns spoke in sympathetic terms of the Czar and his enterprise, but undertook no new engagements.

The Czar was by that time decidedly in need of sympathy, for his fortunes had received a very serious check. After the repeated defeats of Krüdener's corps before Plevna, Prince Schahofskoy, the commander of the Eleventh Corps, was ordered to leave two infantry brigades at Osman Bazar, and march on Plevna with the remainder of his troops. The Thirtieth Division of the Fourth Corps was also transferred to the same place from Simnitza, and was directed to act under the orders of Schahofskoy. That officer marched at the rate of thirteen miles a day, and by the evening of the 28th of July had reached a village twelve miles east of Plevna. At night, his troops encamped in the vicinity of the town, and reconnoitring parties were sent out to ascertain the position and strength of the Turkish commander. From these inquiries it appeared that Osman Pasha was holding Plevna with a force of 35,000 to 40,000 men. He had received reinforcements from Sophia by the valley of the Isker, and was in a good positon for resisting attack. His troops occupied a number of villages about five miles from the point most exposed, and both flanks rested on the river Vid, on the western side of Plevna. The line followed a curve similar to that of a horseshoe, with the convex side towards the enemy. Strong entrenchments had been thrown up, and behind entrenchments the Turks always fight their best. At Grivica, in the direct line of Schahofskoy's march, was an advanced force. Baron Krüdener, the senior commander, was eight miles to the north-west, and it appears to have been thought that, with the reinforcements then hurrying up, the Russians would be enabled to crush their adversary, and drive him from his works.

On the night of July 28th, the younger General Skobeleff joined General Schahofskoy, and was appointed to the command of the Cossack brigade, with orders to march on Loftcha. This officer was described by a correspondent of the *Daily News* as the stormy petrel of the Russian army: wherever there was any hard fighting, there Skobeleff was certain to appear. Another representative of the same journal spoke of him as a tall, handsome man, with a lithe, slender, active figure, and a clear blue eye. He was the youngest general in the Russian army, being only thirty-three years of age, and had greatly distinguished himself during the war in Khokand, the conquest of which province was in a great measure due to his extraordinary energy, abilities, and courage. Even among his countrymen, however, he was looked upon with some distrust as a reckless fighter, who would fling away his own life, and the lives of his troops, in the prosecution of any design on which he had entered. But he had certainly been successful in Central Asia, and there are times in every campaign where dash and resolution are worth more than the profoundest science. He was now ordered to execute a reconnaissance in the direction of Loftcha, and at once rode off into the darkness on his perilous errand. Next morning (the 29th), Prince Schahofskoy and his head-quarters moved from Karajac-Bugarski on the direct road towards Plevna. Grivica was reached without anything being seen of the enemy; but the noise of cannon was heard from the south, in the direction of Loftcha, and Schahofskoy, retracing his steps, bivouacked for the day on a plain near the village of Poradim, with a brigade of infantry in front. The Russian General now made his dispositions with a view to a concentric attack on Plevna, including an attempt to envelop the enemy by cavalry operating on both flanks. Poradim is about seven miles from Plevna, and patrols

RUSSIAN COUNCIL OF WAR.

which were pushed forward touched the adversary at Radisova, Tucenica, Bogot, and Slatina. At night, Skobeleff returned from his expedition towards Loftcha, with the intelligence that it was held by five battalions of Turkish infantry, and that the neighbouring roads were infested by Circassians and Bashi-Bazouks. It seemed also that the Turkish forces were being strengthened; but it was necessary that Plevna should be taken if possible, and preparations for the attack proceeded throughout the 30th. In the afternoon of that day, a council of war was held at Poradim. Baron Krüdener, Prince Schahofskoy, and the leading officers, were present at this council, and it was settled that the action should begin at five o'clock next morning, by a general advance on the Turkish positions in front of Plevna. Prince Schahofskoy and the Staff were to move forward at four o'clock, and several aides-de-camp from the Grand Duke Nicholas were detailed to various points, to make observations, and to carry reports of the battle to the head-quarters at Tirnova.

Owing to a night of heavy rain, and to other causes, the movements of the troops were delayed, and they did not begin their march until six o'clock, instead of four. The number of the infantry was about 32,000, with 160 field-cannon, and three brigades of cavalry. The right was commanded by Baron Krüdener, the left by Schahofskoy; and a brigade of the Thirtieth Division was held in reserve at Pelisat. The plan of battle was that Krüdener should attack the Turkish left flank from Grivica, towards the river Vid, and that Schahofskoy should assail the right from Radisovo. "The main fault of the dispositions," says a military critic of great authority, "was that Krüdener and Schahofskoy were practically independent of each other; that the two attacks were too far apart, and without connecting link. But the gravest evil, which did not rest with the commanders on the spot, was the weakness of the assailing force."* The Turks had had time to entrench themselves, and had now thrown up defensive works of formidable strength. The morning was gloomy, but the Russian soldiers were in good spirits, and in excellent fighting condition. The flanks of the advancing army were protected by the main body of the cavalry; and while Skobeleff, with his Cossacks, guarded the Loftcha road, so as to protect the left of the attack, Lascaroff, with two cavalry regiments, covered Krüdener's right. Schahofskoy's right column marched on Pelisat, four miles from Plevna, whilst the left column made straight for Radisovo, three miles south of the position which was to be attacked. The action began at half-past nine in the morning by Krüdener opening fire from a battery on the Turkish redoubt above the village of Grivica. The Turks were slow in replying, but at length did so with great vigour. The general nature of the country was more favourable to the defence than to the attack. Plevna is situated at the bottom of a valley running north and south, and the ground is broken up into numerous wave-like hills, on most of which the Turks had established several entrenched positions.

Krüdener's operations against Grivica were aided by a simultaneous attack, directed by Schahofskoy against the same point. Subsequently, Schahofskoy's troops attacked the village of Radisovo, situated in a deep valley behind the southernmost ridge of the Turkish position. Under cover of their batteries, the infantry went down into the valley, and Radisovo was captured without much difficulty, being weakly held by only a small number of Bashi-Bazouks, who nevertheless stood their ground until they could stand no longer. In a little while, the Russian batteries compelled the Turkish cannon to quit the opposite height; and the batteries were then enabled to cross the valley, to pass through Radisovo, and to come once more into action in the position vacated by the Ottomans. The assailants had soon planted five batteries on the ridge beyond Radisovo, and from these a converging fire was directed on the Turkish guns crowning the ridge beyond; but the return fire was steady and continuous. Many hundred shells fell into the village, though, by a singular fortune, not one of the inhabitants was injured. The position of the Russian guns was much exposed, and the Turkish practice was good; so that large numbers were killed and wounded about the battery. It was now one o'clock in the afternoon. The action had up to this time been confined to the artillery, and, as Krüdener had made but little advance, Schahofskoy determined to attack with his infantry, without waiting any longer for support. It was a rash decision. The position of the Turks was so strong that, unless the two divisions of the attacking force could have combined, there was no chance of success. It did not appear at all probable that Schahofskoy would receive any assistance from his superior in the very doubtful enterprise which he had resolved to undertake; but this consideration was not suffered to impede the design. At about half-past two, Schahofskoy and his Staff rode on to the ridge from which the batteries were firing, to ascertain whether the artillery had sufficiently prepared the way for the infantry. In this inspection

* Mr. Archibald Forbes in the *Daily News* of August 3rd, 1877.

they nearly lost their lives, owing to the fury of the Turkish fire; but after a while the commanding officer came to the conclusion that the action might enter upon a different stage, and that an attempt might fairly be made to carry the Turkish positions at the point of the bayonet. Schahofskoy had not more than three brigades at his disposal, and one of these was in reserve; the enemy was much superior in numbers, and held strongly-entrenched positions; yet the Russian commander, with a degree of confidence which under the circumstances was almost criminal, resolved to assault the Turkish position, and to risk the safety of his army on an issue where the chances were altogether against him.

His plan having been formed, Schahofskoy ordered the leading battalions of his infantry, who were lying down in the Radisovo valley behind the guns, to rise up, and advance over the ridge. The men started to their feet with cheers, and marched at a rapid pace across the glen, and up the steep slope beyond. They were aided by a heavy artillery fire, under cover of which they passed over the crest of the opposite hill, and descended into the valley where their enemy was posted. While thus proceeding, large numbers dropped under the concentrated fire of the Turkish shells; but the column still pressed on with great steadiness, and for a time in good order. At length, however, owing to frequent losses, and to the natural impatience of the men to get to close quarters, the line broke up into straggling masses, and so dashed onward without any close cohesion. The supports followed quickly; but the precision of military formation was now at an end. "Presently, all along the face of the advancing infantrymen," wrote Mr. Archibald Forbes, "burst forth flaring volleys of musketry-fire. The jagged line springs onward through the maize-fields, gradually assuming a concave shape. The Turkish position is neared. The roll of rifle-fire is incessant, yet dominated by the fiercer and louder turmoil of the artillery above. The ammunition-waggons gallop up to the cannon with fresh fuel for the fire. The

THE BATTLE OF PLEVNA: ADVANCE OF GENERAL SCHAHOFSKOY'S INFANTRY.

THE BATTLE OF PLEVNA

guns redouble the energy of their cannonade. The crackle of the musketry-fire rises into a sharp, continuous peal. The clamour of the hurrahs of the fighting men comes back to us on the breeze, making the blood tingle with the excitement of the fray. A village is blazing on the left. The fell fury of the battle has entered on its maddest paroxysm. The supports that had remained behind, lying just under the crest of the slope, are pushed forward over the brow of the hill. The wounded begin to trickle back over the ridge. We can see the dead and the more severely wounded lying where they fell, on the stubble and amid the maize. The living wave of fighting men is pouring over them, ever on and on. The gallant gunners to the right and to the left of us stand to their work with a will on the shell-swept ridge. The Turkish cannon-fire begins to waver in that earthwork over against us. More supports stream down with a louder cheer into the Russian fighting line. Suddenly the disconnected men are drawing together. We can discern the officers signalling for the concentration by the waving of their swords. The distance is about a hundred yards. There is a wild rush, headed by the colonel of one of the regiments of the Thirty-second Division. The Turks in the shelter-trench hold their ground, and fire steadily, and with terrible effect, into the advancing forces."

He who watched the dreadful scene from one of the neighbouring hills, and who has given us this vivid description of what he saw, heard the tempest-gust of wrath, half howl, half yell, with which the Russian infantry, their bayonets at the charge, rushed on to avenge their colonel, who had been struck down by a Turkish shell. In another moment they were over the parapet and shelter-trench, and in among the Turks like an avalanche. The slaughter was terrific; but the outer edge of the first position was won. The assailants ought now to have turned the shelter thus obtained against the main position of their adversaries; but, inspired probably by their temporary success, they continued to ascend the slope, though in somewhat broken order. The Turkish fire from the next position thinned their ranks to an alarming extent; yet, while hesitating once or twice, they continued on the whole to advance. It took them half an hour to traverse the ground between the trenches they had won and those which rose before them; but, on reaching the latter, the defenders, with one final volley, abandoned the work. The Turks had still a line of batteries in the rear of the second position, and were not inclined to give up fighting. These batteries were planted on a high, isolated hill; but, although the position was one of great strength, Schahofskoy determined to attempt it. Once more he ordered his men forward, and again they advanced, but this time with great slowness and hesitation. The impetus of the first rush had been expended; the men were fatigued, and to some extent disheartened; and in a little while they slackened, hung back, and finally stood still, doggedly firing, but declining to press on. This continued until Schahofskoy threw his reserve brigade into the attack, partly in the rear of his line, partly on the left flank. Re-invigorated by this accession of strength, the attacking force renewed its onward rush; but the Turks themselves had now been reinforced. In time the further position was gained by the Russians, and there was a short though deadly struggle for its possession. For a moment it was carried by the assailants; but the Turks brought up a heavy mass of infantry, and swept the enemy out.

While these events were going on, another portion of Schahofskoy's force moved in the direction of Plevna itself. They were encountered, however, by so determined a resistance that, after charging again and again, they acknowledged the attempt to be impossible. Reinforcements were sent up, but without making any alteration in the state of affairs, and numbers died where they stood, being too much exhausted with their efforts either to advance or retire. Their ammunition had run out, and the waggons which should have supplied them were far behind. Two companies of infantry managed to get round the right flank of the Turkish works, and to enter the streets of Plevna; "but," said Mr. Forbes, "it was like entering the mouth of hell. On the heights all round, the cannon-smoke spurted out, and the vineyard in the rear of the town was alive with Turks." The intruders were compelled to retire as speedily as they could, and, as the sun descended behind the hot and rolling smoke, it was evident to Schahofskoy that his design had utterly failed, and that he was beaten at every point.

As the dusk was falling over that field of mortal conflict, the defeated troops reeled back from the second position, reeled back from the first, and retired to the ground from which they had started in the afternoon, flushed with a hope which there was little to encourage. Schahofskoy had no spare troops to cover the retreat, and the Turks followed, and re-occupied the entrenchments from which they had been expelled. At Loftcha also the Russians had been repulsed, and in no one direction had anything been gained. The village of Radisovo was now filled with Russian wounded, and the

Turkish shells fell amongst the houses, doing still further damage. The injured were being perpetually brought in by their more fortunate comrades; but large numbers were necessarily left where they had fallen. After dark, companies of Bashi-Bazouks moved over the field, killing those who lay there, and whose miserable condition left them no power of self-defence. "Lingering on the ridge till the moon rose," says the account from which we have already derived so much, "the Staff could hear from down below, on the still night air, the cries of pain, the entreaties for mercy, and the yells of bloodthirsty, fanatical triumph. It was indeed an hour to wring the sternest heart." The darkness was illuminated by the flashing of the Turkish artillery, and made dissonant by the scream of shells and the whizzing of rifle-bullets. The retreating wounded and their escorts were frequently struck; and even when the Staff quitted the ridge behind Radisovo, they were still pursued by fears of the Bashi-Bazouks, who were evidently in great force in their rear. Schahofskoy and his officers snatched some brief repose in a stubble-field, but in the course of a few hours were compelled to retreat with rapidity, owing to an alarm of the enemy being close upon them. They had missed their way to Radisovo, and afterwards learned that during the night the Bashi-Bazouks had got into the town, and butchered the wounded without mercy.

RUSSIAN WOUNDED LEAVING PLEVNA.

The defeat had been of the most complete and overwhelming kind. The number of killed and wounded was so great that a company which was told off to guard Radisovo could only be made up out of several regiments. The loss in Schahofskoy's command alone was estimated at not less than 5,000 men; and to these were to be added the losses of General Krüdener, which were in themselves very serious, and had not been counterbalanced by even a temporary success. In the course of the day, Krüdener sent word to Schahofskoy that he could make no headway, and had resolved to fall back on the line of the river Osma, which falls into the Danube near Nicopolis. His plans were in truth completely disarranged, and it was very generally held that he had shown great want of capacity in his management of the whole affair. His own officers loudly condemned him, and alleged that he entirely lost his self-possession during the progress of the attack.

Another Russian general—a divisional commander—was so utterly dismayed, even before the fighting commenced, that he rode off a distance of ten miles, and never appeared on the field at all. He was an old man, who had not seen actual warfare before, and he was now sent back to Russia—"for the benefit of his health." A Special Correspondent of the *Times*, who visited Plevna immediately after the battle, remarked that if ever there was causeless human slaughter, it occurred in front of the Turkish fortifications on that memorable occasion. The Russians themselves were much dissatisfied with the attack, and an officer, who had been badly wounded in the assault on the Turkish entrenchments, told the representative of the *Times* that they could have carried the positions if they had been properly supported. The column, however, was not strong enough, either from want of troops, or from defective generalship; and the Turks, perceiving the fact, drove back their assailants with fearful loss. Not more than half of the attacking column came out of the engagement, and amongst the survivors the wounded were very numerous. Another officer stated that their losses in killed, wounded, sick, and prisoners, including the actions of the 19th, 20th, and 21st of July, as well as the great battle of the 31st, amounted to 10,000 men. General Skobeleff was the only sub-commander who succeeded in bringing away all his wounded, though he had lost nearly half his number; and for this feat he was thanked by the Emperor, when, shortly afterwards, he visited the Imperial head-quarters. On the 2nd of August, the head-quarters of Prince Schahofskoy were on the heights above the village of Poradim, while those of General Krüdener were at Trestenik. By that time everything was in good order; the infantry were drilling, and it was generally believed that with reinforcements Osman Pasha's position could be carried. Some additions to General Krüdener's troops had already arrived, and the Russian line of communication was never for a moment in danger. But large reinforcements were urgently needed, and these could not be had at once. The position held by the troops defeated at Plevna was, however, a very strong one, and any fear of Turkish attack, which may for a moment have been entertained, was now dismissed from the minds of all. If the Ottomans had followed up their success by a vigorous assault while the Russians were still demoralized, fatigued, and cast down, they might have achieved important results; but in the course of a few days any such movement had ceased to be advisable.

Much discredit was thrown on the Russian commanders for this terrible misfortune, and a great deal of mutual recrimination was indulged for several days. General Schilder-Schuldner was despatched to Russia under military escort, that he might be tried by court-martial for his defeat at Plevna when first that place was attacked. Colonel Biskupski, Chief of the Staff to General Krüdener, was also sent home under the same conditions, and Krüdener himself was removed from his command, to which General Zotoff succeeded. The retreat on the line of the Osma was arrested, and the Russians began to entrench themselves before Plevna. But to many it appeared that the Commander-in-Chief of the Russian forces was as much to blame as his subordinates for what had happened. The latter were carrying out the instructions that had been given them, and, although they may not have used a proper discretion in the execution of those orders, the orders themselves appear to have been characterized by great want of prudence. The whole campaign, in short, had been badly managed. The Russians seem to have made up their minds from the first that the Turks would offer but slight opposition, and therefore entered on the war with an insufficient army. The singular apathy of the Ottomans during the early weeks of the war deepened this impression, and tempted the invaders into rash enterprises. They advanced into the country in numerous detached bodies, penetrated beyond the Balkans before they had fully mastered the more northern province, and pushed many miles beyond their base of operations, with fortresses in their rear, a large army on their right flank, and another gathering on their left. Of the strength of this army they appear to have had no definite information; while greatly outnumbered, they attacked a strongly entrenched position; and the calamity of July 31st followed as a natural consequence upon arrangements ill-conceived and feebly carried out.

In Roumania, extreme consternation was created by the news of what had happened at Plevna. After being unduly confident, the people now became unnecessarily gloomy. They feared that the Russians were about to be totally annihilated; that the forces in Bulgaria would be cut off from the Danube; and that the Turks would themselves cross that river, and overrun the principalities. The situation of the Russians was in truth grave, but it was not so bad as alarmists fancied. By concentrating their forces, the invaders would have a considerable army at their disposal, and immediate steps were taken for rendering it still greater. It was now found that the Roumanian contingent was a valuable auxiliary; but it would not do to depend on this alone. Orders were accordingly sent to St. Petersburg for the immediate despatch of troops, and it was determined to summon the Imperial Guard. By the middle of August, the cavalry regiments of that force were quitting St. Petersburg daily for the south. The first to leave was a regiment of Hussars; these were followed on the 15th by a regiment of Lancers, and on the 16th by the Grenadiers. The Landwehr of the first class was also called out, to the number of 188,600 men. Reinforcements were continually arriving at the seat of war, and the Turkish opportunity declined visibly with every hour. Yet for some weeks these reinforcements did nothing more than repair the losses that had already been sustained, if they did even that. Not only had large numbers of men fallen in battle, but many others had died of sickness, or been rendered inoperative by fatigue, exhaustion, and impaired health. Long marches, and exposure to the burning sun by day, and to the soaking dews by night, had produced their inevitable effect upon the soldiers, and to these influences was to be added the depressing consciousness of defeat. It was therefore evident that the Czar would have to make very large demands on the military spirit of his people, and the hopeful anticipations of the spring faded before the searching light of truth.

The worst sickness was experienced by the army of the Dobrudscha, where the climate is always bad in summer. The operations of the Russians in that dreary region had come to a standstill by the commencement of August, and it was not very clear to any one why the troops were retained there. A correspondent of the *Times* remarked that they were doing nothing but occupying a territory which was of no value to the invaders so long as they did not use the Black Sea to bring up supplies. While the passage of the Danube was still problematical, it was wise, in the opinion of this writer, to secure a crossing at Ibraila, which might be utilized if all attempts higher up the river should fail; but as soon as the crossing was effected at Simnitza, the presence of Russian troops in the Dobrudscha ceased to be of importance, as they had not been able either to effect a junction with the Russian army in the other parts of Bulgaria, or to isolate Silistria. General Zimmerman had most of the Fourteenth Corps and a division of another corps in the Dobrudscha, and his main force was encamped about eight miles from Tchernavoda. His operations, up to the period at which we have now arrived, had consisted mainly in sending out detachments of Cossacks in all directions on scouting duty, and these irregular horsemen had frequent encounters with the Circassians. Hirsova was completely abandoned by the Turks, who took with them all their movable property except their dogs, which were so numerous that the Russians were compelled to kill them. While the Osmanlis remained, they were in horrible fear of the Russian torpedo-boats, which they termed devil-fish. They had no less dread of the vessel commanded by Lieutenant Dubascheff, which about this time attacked a Turkish monitor eighteen miles from Silistria, set it on fire, drove the crew ashore, and would have captured it but for the arrival of Turkish reinforcements. Colonel Sankey, the English Consul at Kustendji, assured a newspaper correspondent that since the Russians had entered the Dobrudscha he had heard no complaints against their conduct from any of the inhabitants; but it also appeared that many robberies and much devastation had been effected by the Bulgarians and Roumanians, who, inflamed by a spirit of revenge, worked a great deal of mischief between the departure of the Turkish troops and the arrival of the Russians. The shopkeepers affirmed that the Muscovites paid for everything they had, while the eight thousand Ottoman troops stationed about Kustendji stole whatever they wanted, whenever the opportunity occurred. It is a remarkable fact, that, as the war advanced, Russians and Turks began to entertain a better opinion of one another, while the miserable Bulgarians were looked upon with contempt and hatred by both alike. "Among the Turks," said a St. Petersburg paper, "one meets very sympathetic persons. The prisoners show no hostility to us, and are evidently well content with their position, saying often, 'The Russians, good people!' For the most part they are honest, somewhat proud and vain, conscious of their own dignity, but good-hearted. The prisoners live admirably with each other. I never saw any of them quarrelling, or even disputing; on the contrary, they help each other, and, if one of them has no money, another pays for him."

While the war was progressing with its attendant horrors, charity was doing its utmost to relieve the misery of the sufferers by well-devised organizations, chiefly of English origin. Large numbers of fugitives were collected at Adrianople, where Mr. Blunt, the English Consul, Mr. Black, Director of the Ottoman Bank, and a few other gentlemen, did what they could without funds to relieve the wretched people who poured by thousands into the city from the surrounding country. In every Turkish house there were three or four fugitives, and the Jewish population were sorely tasked to support their fellows. Mr. Blunt obtained permission from the

THE ENGLISH AMBULANCE WITH THE TURKISH ARMY.

Vali to order as much bread as he might require, and was thus enabled to meet the trains with carts containing piled-up loaves. The wounded women and children were taken off in arabas, and provided for as well as might be in the emergency. A small hospital was promptly organised under the direction of a lady who, though of native birth, was the daughter of an Englishman, and who took a house on her own responsibility, and opened it for the reception of fugitive Turkish women, wounded or not wounded. This lady (Mrs. Camara) received rations from the Government, but in all other respects was dependent on her own resources. Some idea of the number of fugitives in Adrianople may be formed from the fact that on the 8th of August no fewer than 13,500 were supplied with rations, of whom it was estimated that 11,000 were Bulgarians. At the same time, there were 3,000 arabas, or country bullock-carts, on the roads leading from Philippopolis and Eski-Zaghra, and these, it was anticipated, would bring the total up to 25,500. So enormous an influx caused a sudden increase in the price of provisions, which in two days ran up ten per cent. A scarcity of flour was feared, and not without reason, as the crops were rotting in the fields. In addition to the civilian fugitives, the city was called upon to provide for more than 2,000 wounded soldiers. Some of the men were nursed in the military hospitals, others in the civil hospital, and others again in buildings specially utilized for the purpose. The Sisters of the Assumption helped in the good work of nursing, and the Red Crescent Society took charge of a hospital which was designed to contain two hundred and sixty patients. The Stafford House Committee, which had rendered great assistance during the Servian War, continued

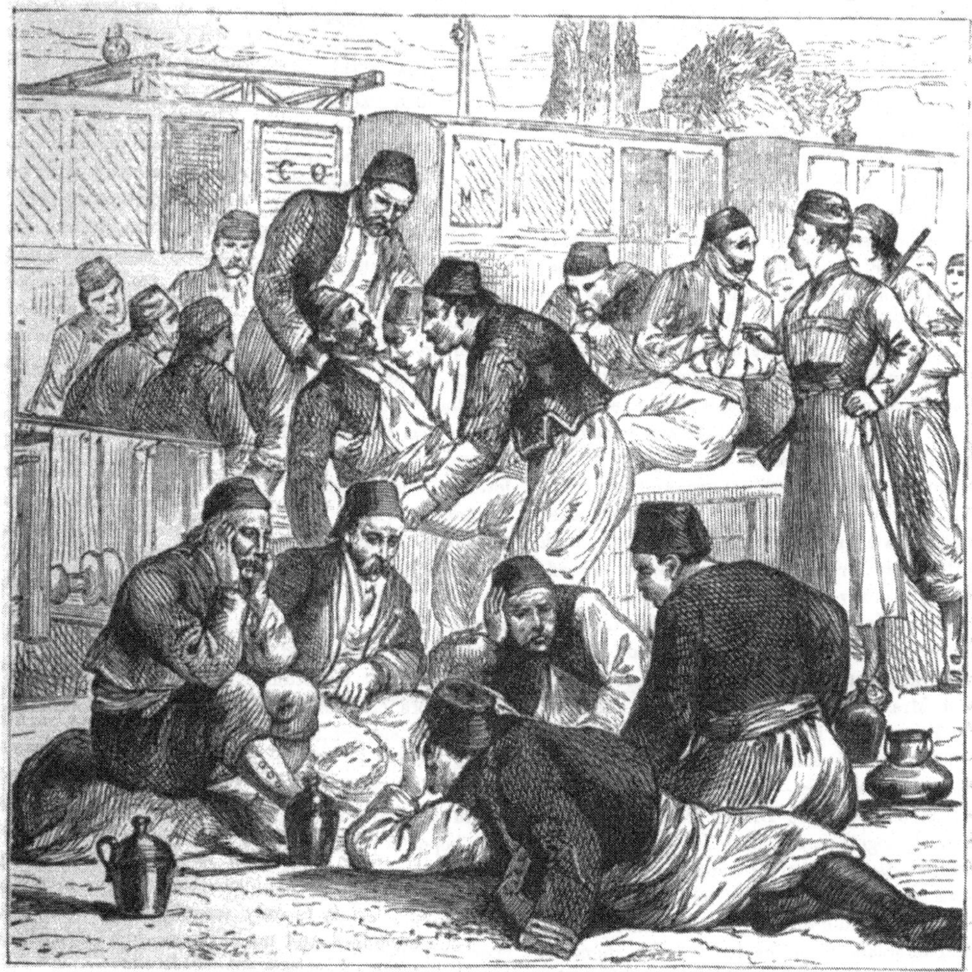

TURKISH WOUNDED SENT TO CONSTANTINOPLE.

its admirable work under the far greater necessities of the time. This body originated with a number of ladies and gentlemen who met at Stafford House, the mansion of the Duke of Sutherland. The director was Mr. Barrington Kennett, assisted in the first instance by seven English surgeons, and afterwards by a larger number, who were distributed in various localities. A waggon-transport, under Colonel Borthwick, did valuable service in the Schumla district, by the transport of large numbers of sick, while other lines of transport operated in other directions. The Stafford House Committee was under the protection, and enjoyed all the privileges, of the Red Crescent, as secured to that body by the Geneva Convention.

The Red Crescent Society was the National Ottoman Society for the Relief of Sick and Wounded, and was established under the patronage of the Sultan, who contributed £2,500 to the subscriptions, and gave the members a committee-room in one of his palaces. The head-quarters were of course at Constantinople; but sub-committees were formed in the principal towns of the provinces. Large contributions towards the support of this Society flowed in from all directions, and especially from the Mussulman population of India. Another association of a charitable character was the British National Society for Aid to the Sick and Wounded. There were also several ladies' committees in Constantinople and along the Bosphorus, the members of which prepared bandages, and made beds, sheets, and other necessaries. Mrs. Layard, Lady Kemball, and Mrs. Hanson, were active at Therapia, and the Princess of Reuss formed a committee at Buyukdéré with the same charitable objects. The three principal societies—the Red Crescent, the Stafford House, and the British National—acted harmoniously together, and each for the most part concentrated its attention on a different section of the work to be performed. The Red Crescent looked after the field-hospitals; the British National took field-ambulances for the front under its care; and the Stafford House Committee worked at the transport-service, and the distribution of stores.* A fund was started by Lady Strangford for the relief both of Turks and Russians, and a purely Russian fund was likewise opened in England. The amount of misery was in truth enormous. It was greater even than is usually the case, because the ferocity with which the struggle was waged had resulted in a destruction of life beyond the ordinary limits of civilized warfare. Large tracts of country were entirely devastated by the fury of the contending armies, and by the uncontrolled excesses of the irregular troops, both Turkish and Russian. The means of life were suddenly snatched from thousands of unoffending persons, and those who until recently had been living in comfort, and who had taken no part in the prosecution of hostilities, were driven, in a state of absolute destitution—in many cases sorely wounded, and in all reduced to the limits of despair—from the outlying districts into the towns and cities. To meet so enormous an accession of misery, funds were needed to no small amount, and they were furnished in a great degree by the exhaustless charity of England. On this exalting ground of pity for human sorrow, political differences were forgotten, except in a few despicable instances, where not even the sight of unexampled wretchedness could shame the bitterness of fanaticism. Although great demands were at that time being made on English charity in respect of the Indian Famine, the sufferers in Turkey, whether they belonged to the one side or the other, were not forgotten. It is some relief from the horrors of unnecessary strife to contemplate this better side of human nature, intent on mitigating, as far as that might be, the ruin caused by ambition, by obstinacy, by ignorance, by want of mutual understanding, and by the complications of a hopeless political question. In some respects, war is worse now than it was in former days, since the means of destruction are so much the greater; but it is only recently that charity has been organized and made thoroughly efficient, and that science has lent its noble aid, to soften in some slight degree the multitudinous wickedness of the sword.

* Correspondents of the *Times*.

CHAPTER XXX.

Serious Position of the Russians—Errors in their Tactics—Incapacity of General Krüdener—Reconnaissance against Loftcha—Bravery of General Skobeleff—The Russian Forces in the Second Week of August—Violent Rains, and Sickness among the Troops—Bad Sanitary Arrangements in the Camps—The Russian Reinforcements—Movements of the Turks, indicating an Intention to assume the Offensive—The Military Position in the Shipka Pass—General Character of the Pass—The Russians attacked on the Morning of the 21st of August—Renewed Fighting on the 22nd—Desperate Struggle on the 23rd—The Russians nearly overwhelmed—Arrival of Reinforcements—The Battle of the 24th—Partial Repulse of the Turks—Devotion of the Russian Medical Staff—Services of Newspaper Correspondents—Mr. Archibald Forbes and the Czar—The Struggle for the Shipka Pass resumed on the 25th of August and two following Days—Splendid Qualities exhibited by both Belligerents—Withdrawal of Suleiman Pasha—Distress in Russia—Roumanian Discontent with Russian Policy—Evils of Paper Currency—Prolonged Fighting with the Army of Mehemet Ali—Defeat of the Russians—General Posture of Affairs at the Close of the Summer.

Grave indeed was the situation of the Russians at the beginning of August. Gourko had been compelled to retreat from his advanced positions south of the Balkans, and General Krüdener had repeatedly failed to drive the Turks from Plevna. The armies of the Sultan were fast repairing the errors which apathy had caused in the earlier days of the campaign. The line of the Danube, indeed, was sacrificed; but Osman Pasha was now strongly entrenched, with a brave and efficient host, at no great distance from the southern shores of the broad river, and the progress of the conquerors was suddenly brought to a deadlock. The Russians had committed the serious blunder of advancing to Tirnova without seizing Plevna, and of pushing through the passes of the mountains while Loftcha, on their right flank, still remained unsecured. It was known that the Turks had considerable forces at Sophia, on the southern slopes of the Balkans; at Nisch, on the borders of Servia; at Widdin, on the Danube; and at Schumla, towards the east. The roads from most of these towns were commanded by Loftcha and Plevna, which the Russians permitted their adversaries to occupy; and thus it happened that the invaders found themselves with the enemy in front, on both sides, and to some extent in their rear. What rendered the mistake more lamentable was the fact that General Krüdener had actually been ordered to occupy Plevna as soon as he crossed the river. This order he disregarded, and even withdrew some cavalry which had been sent thither, that he might employ them in the siege of Nicopolis. That city being taken, he appears to have given himself no trouble to ascertain whether the Turks were approaching Plevna or not; and the consequence was that this important position fell into the hands of Osman Pasha, and that, in the vain attempt to wrest it from him, the Russians lost many thousand men.

To make matters still worse, the invading forces were divided into numerous small bodies, which were scattered far and wide over a large extent of country, and so distributed that, on any sudden emergency, it would have been a very difficult task to re-unite them. The whole necessities of the campaign had been miscalculated. The Turkish powers of resistance, and determination to resist, had been signally under-rated; and the Russians were by this time outnumbered in several places, and out-manœuvred in the general conduct of the campaign. In the management of the last battle before Plevna, General Krüdener seems to have exhibited a strange want of military capacity. He hesitated several days before he could make up his mind whether to attack or not. He was irritable and excited where he should have been calm and thoughtful; and when at length he resolved to act, he gave his orders with such inconsiderate haste that several of the troops were obliged to start without breakfast, and even then were an hour behind the appointed time.* With such an entire failure of skill and forethought, it is not surprising that the Russians were defeated, despite the splendid heroism of the men, or that the Turks should at once have recovered the credit they had lost. It is but fair, however, to add that Krüdener himself asserted that the Grand Duke positively ordered him to attack, against his better judgment.

Nothing was more essential to the well-being of the Russians before Plevna than that the spirit of the troops should be restored by some action in which they might inflict a telling blow on their enemy. General Skobeleff desired to head an attack on the Turks; but his superiors would not permit anything more serious than a reconnaissance. This took place in the early part of August, and was directed against Loftcha. On the 3rd of the month, Skobeleff quitted the head-quarters of the Grand Duke Nicholas, taking with him five battalions of infantry, his own brigade of cavalry, and two batteries of horse-artillery. In time he came out on the road to Selvi, mid-way between that town and Loftcha, and his cavalry then occupied

* Mr. MacGahan in the *Daily News*.

several villages in the direction of Plevna, and in other quarters. The artillery was sent forward on the 6th to some heights beyond Loftcha, which was thus completely encircled. From the elevated ground it was apparent that the Turks were in great force; that they had from fifteen to twenty thousand troops encamped in and about the town; and that the low hills in the vicinity were strongly entrenched. Skobeleff opened fire with his artillery, and the Ottomans replied with animation. But after awhile the Russian commander, not content with firing from a distance, pushed forward his infantry, sending them down a narrow hollow, thickly covered with woods. They reached the foot of the hill in good order, though exposed to a terrific rifle-fire, and advanced in a scattered way against the Turkish lines. To have attacked such a position would have been to court the most crushing defeat, and strict directions had been given that no such attack should be made. But the ardour of the troops carried them too far, and Skobeleff himself was obliged to ride towards the front, in order to turn back his men. Being mounted on a white horse, and dressed in a white coat, he presented a very conspicuous mark to the enemy, and in a few minutes his horse was shot under him, while three out of the six Cossacks who formed his escort were seriously wounded. Mounting another steed, he still dashed forward, shouting and gesticulating, while his trumpeter sounded the retreat. The skirmishers began to withdraw, when suddenly Skobeleff went down, together with his horse. Fortunately, however, he was again untouched, although the Turkish fire was one unbroken fusillade. He now returned up the hill, followed by his too adventurous troops, who were saved from extermination by the daring of this singular officer. The objects of the reconnaissance had been obtained: the Turks had been bearded in one of their strongholds, and it had been discovered that they were so well posted and so numerous as to render any attack hopeless until the invaders had been heavily reinforced. On the following day, the Ottomans made demonstrations of a threatening nature, which warned Skobeleff that it was time to quit a position full of danger for his detachment. This he did under cover of another advance against Loftcha, which was abandoned as soon as the main body of the troops had got fairly on their way.

HOUSE OCCUPIED BY THE CZAR AT GORNY STUDEN.

As the result of the defeat at Plevna, the Russians were now reduced to the necessity of remaining strictly on the defensive. They were waiting for the arrival of further reinforcements, and it was calculated that nearly 100,000 more men would be required before the offensive could be resumed with any probability of success. In the second week of August, the Grand Duke was at Bulgareni, behind the entrenched positions fronting Plevna. Part of Prince Mirsky's division stood between Tirnova and Loftcha, to hinder an advance of the Turks on the former place. This protected the right flank of the Russian communications, while the left flank, running from the Danube to the Balkans, was guarded by the two corps constituting the army of the Czarewitch, and by the First Division of the Eleventh Corps. In the latter instance, 60,000 men were distributed over a long line, so that, had the Turks been then disposed to make a dashing assault, the safety of the Russian forces would have been very questionable. Zimmerman, who was stationed in the vicinity of Trajan's Wall, in the southern part of the Dobrudscha, was afraid of moving his 30,000 men to where they were sorely needed, lest they should be attacked and overwhelmed by Turks from Varna and Schumla. The paucity of troops made it necessary to postpone the investment of Rustchuk, which at an earlier part of the war had been bombarded, though with no great effect. The Rustchuk army, which had crossed the Jantra about the middle of July, after a long delay very trying to the patience of officers and men, was by this time drawn up on the western bank of the river Lom; but the head-quarters of the Twelfth Corps were on the opposite side, between Trestenik and Kadikoi. Rustchuk, therefore, was still threatened, though not subjected to that complete investment which had at one time been designed.

Violent and continued rain fell in the middle of August, turning the roads in Roumania into swamps, and greatly retarding the march of the reinforcements. Large quantities of bread and other necessaries, while being conveyed in the provision-waggons, were spoiled by the drenching and remorseless torrents. This was in many ways a sore trial to the Russian army. The troops were encamped under canvas, which of course offered but little protection to the men. Several, including the Cossacks, were not under cover at all. Great depression of spirits ensued, as the natural consequence of such surroundings, and disease set in with alarming quickness. Diarrhœa and dysentery became frequent; the hospitals filled rapidly; and a keen desire for home—in itself a disease—spread throughout the ranks. The bad health of the troops, however, was due to other causes besides the rain. Previous to the arrival of the wet, the men had suffered much from irregular rations, hard marching, and heat, and still more from the horrible state of the camps, owing to the accumulation of filth and decaying matter. Utterly indifferent to sanitary laws, the Russians never bury dead horses or oxen, or the entrails of slaughtered cattle. The brooding heat of summer turned all this corruption into an aërial poison, which it was impossible to avoid taking into the system. At Biela, the air was filled with a dust compounded of a thousand abominations, animal and vegetable. The plague of flies was also most afflicting, and the foul air produced a perpetual sense of nausea. High and low suffered alike, and many of the officers surrounding the Emperor were struck down with fever. Scarcely any one was thoroughly well, while many were too ill to be capable of duty. The Turkish quarter of Sistova was converted into a succession of hospitals. The abandoned houses were cleared out, furnished with necessary appliances, and filled with wounded men from the region of Plevna. But the sickness was more difficult to deal with than the cases requiring surgical treatment; and a low condition of health was set up, by which the efficiency of the Russian troops was greatly impaired.

The head-quarters of the Emperor were now at Gorny Studen, where his Majesty resided in a good house outside the village, with his suite in tents around. On the 17th of August, he and the Grand Duke Nicholas reviewed the Fourth Rifle Brigade previous to its march for Plevna, where it was designed to assist in forepost work. Reinforcements were now steadily arriving in large numbers; but, to avoid encumbering the more direct thoroughfares, which were left open for supplies, they took a long and circuitous route. It was believed that no fewer than 180,000 men were then actually on the march towards the scene of action, and in the meanwhile the position in front of Plevna was strongly fortified, and armed with artillery. The Fourth Cavalry Division was detached on an independent expedition, with a view to blocking the Orkhanieh Pass through the Balkans, so as to stop the Turkish communications with Sophia. The Turks still continued in the main to act on the defensive; but from time to time they pushed forward cavalry reconnaissances in several directions, and with one of these there was a smart skirmish on the 15th of August, near the village of Tucenica, south-east of Plevna. A general reconnaissance in considerable force followed on the 16th, and was directed along the whole of the Russian left flank. The fighting was but little, yet the fact was important, as seeming to indicate that the Turks were about to assume the offensive. On the same day, a column of Suleiman Pasha's force issued from the Tundja Valley, and made a vigorous attempt to force the Hainkoi Pass. This detachment managed to enter the defile, but was there encountered by the Russian artillery, and by a regiment of the Ninth Division, and ultimately compelled to retire. Demonstrations were also made in other directions about the same period. Skobeleff's position near Loftcha was attacked, and his Cossacks were continually harassed by sudden inroads.

Suleiman Pasha had moved into the Tundja Valley in the early part of August. His lines were described by a correspondent of the *Times* as extending from the village of At-Kieu, about three miles east of the Furdich Pass, to Hain Boghaz, a distance of about seven miles. "The valley of the Tundja at this part," said the same writer, "is about one and a half to two miles wide, lying between the true Balkans and a low range of hills, some 1,500 to 2,000 feet high, running parallel to them. The river winds over shallow shingle-beds, and presents no kind of feature in itself of strategical importance, except that, by the gradual denudation of the valley, and alterations in the bed of the stream, spurs of rock, covered with short scrub and grass, lie diagonally across the plain, and would afford shelter for infantry or commanding positions for artillery. It was a strange sight to watch Suleiman Pasha's great army of 30,000 men, with the vast trains of bullock - waggons and pack - horses, winding through the valley for upwards of seven or eight miles in extent. The head of the columns had already vanished out of sight, and still onward and onward, tramp, tramp, tramp, came the infantry, with the artillery lumbering along in the rear, while as far as the eye could reach streamed the long lines of bullock-waggons, 3,000 or 4,000 in number, with the rear-guard only discernible through the strongest glasses, like ants on the hills in the distance. The entire army is bivouacked in the open, and sleep in the positions they take up. At night, the camp-fires light up the country and hill-sides for miles around, and the far-off specks of light, among the woods and forests on the mountains, point out the position of the videttes and outposts. As night comes on, silence settles down on the great camp, only broken by some far-off bugle-call, or the neighing of the horses tethered in the standing corn."

SULEIMAN PASHA.

The period of inactivity was near its termination, and it was probable that the Shipka Pass would presently be the scene of desperate fighting. At that time, the pass was held by no more than twenty companies, under General Stoletoff, and amongst these were the remains of the Bulgarian Legion which had been so badly beaten at Eski-Zaghra. Suleiman Pasha was believed to be in command of forty battalions, with which he seemed about to attack the defile; and it was therefore imperative for the Russians to strengthen their forces in that direction, if they would guard against the menaced danger. Several brigades were accordingly ordered into the pass, and various military dispositions were made for meeting the probable requirements of the future. Two Roumanian divisions of infantry, and some Roumanian artillery, were now in the camp before Plevna, and they were said to present a good appearance; but at the close of the third week of August the Russians were still awaiting the bulk of their reinforcements, and the fear was, lest they should be attacked before they were sufficiently strong to resist with success. The new regiments marched with extraordinary celerity to strengthen the positions in the Shipka Pass. For two days and nights, they neither slept nor cooked their food, but still kept up with amazing strength and resolution, marching without knapsacks or baggage, that their movements might be the less impeded. The necessity for their presence was indeed urgent, for every day made it more plain that the threatened attack would soon be delivered. On the 19th of August, Suleiman Pasha occupied the village of Shipka, and prepared for active operations. Mr. Archibald Forbes has described the Shipka Pass as being not a pass at all, in the proper sense of the term. It is not a gorge or defile; it is simply a portion of the Balkans where the mountains are of less than the average height, and where the road is more practicable than at other parts. This road traverses the summit of a ridge, the ground on both sides of which is broken up into shallow hollows and deeper gorges. The mountainous spurs, which strike out here and there, afforded the Turks good positions, from which the central ridge might be flanked; and in other respects the region was well adapted to attack, though less suitable than might have been supposed for purposes of defence. The narrow valleys by which it is bordered were in many instances protected from the fire of guns planted on the central ridge; and in some quarters the batteries might be rather closely approached before they could do any mischief to the assailants.

of the assaulting parties came up. Several of the Turks were blown into the air; but this did not prevent their obtaining a moderate degree of success. On the 22nd, the Turks were chiefly engaged in making a wide turning movement on the right and left flanks of the Russian position, and no important results were gained that day. The battle was once more renewed on the 23rd, when the Ottomans assailed their antagonists simultaneously on the front and flanks, and drove in the defenders from

HEAD-QUARTERS OF SULEIMAN PASHA IN THE TUNDJA VALLEY.

their outlying ground. It was to the credit of General Stoletoff and his men that, outnumbered as they were, they were not entirely overwhelmed. They stood their ground with dogged resolution, and on the 23rd reinforcements began to arrive under General Derozinski. The Turks had by this time worked round the Russian flanks, and were climbing the ridge on both sides, so that it seemed not improbable that the Muscovites would be caught between two fires, and entirely crushed. Before the junction of the Turkish divisions had been effected, the Russian commanders sent a telegram to the Czar, telling him what they expected, and conveying the assurance that beneath the

The Ottoman attack commenced on the morning of August 21st, when the Turks made their way up the steep ground leading from the village of Shipka to the head of the so-called pass. The Russians on the heights that morning counted no more than 3,000 men, with forty guns, and their nearest supports were at Tirnova, forty miles away. The Turks had rather the better of the contest, and the outer line of the Russian trenches was carried before the evening closed in. These trenches were on the slopes below Mount St. Nicholas, the highest peak of the Shipka Pass, and were protected by mines which had been constructed in front of them, and which were exploded as the head shelter of their works they could hold out until the arrival of further reinforcements, or that at the worst they would expend the last drop of their blood in defending the position.

Six o'clock in the evening had now arrived, and many of the Russians, being utterly exhausted by the violence of their endeavours, by hunger and by thirst, combined with the terrible heat which scorched the bare sides of the cliff, lay panting on the ridge, under the withering rifle-fire of the Turks. Those who were less fatigued still maintained a savage fight among the rocks a little farther down, and from the moving Turkish line rose shouts of "Allah il Allah!" Stoletoff and Derozinski were standing on an advanced peak, anxiously scanning the road that leads up from the Jantra Valley—a road obscurely traced through masses of rock and heavy overgrowth of trees—when suddenly Stoletoff gave an exclamation of joy, seized his companion by the arm, and pointed down the pass. "Now, God be thanked!" he exclaimed, as a long black column disclosed itself in winding, serpent-like coils, relieved against the brown of the road. The troops sprang to their feet with an inexpressible sense of relief; and at that moment the sunshine smote upon the bayonets of their advancing comrades, and turned the darkness into light. A storm of cheers burst up from the wearied ranks at this reassuring vision, and the triumphant utterances of the Turks were for a moment silenced by the yet louder shouts of their adversaries. The column came slowly on, and in time it appeared that the men were mounted. Cavalry in such a position would have been entirely out of place; but these were not cavalry. The new-comers formed a battalion of the Rifle Brigade, mounted on Cossack ponies, and the rest of the body was not far behind. It was the brigade which had accompanied General Gourko in his expedition a few weeks before, and the men had marched with the utmost swiftness to join their fellows, whom they knew to be overmatched, and to save the Shipka position from the Turks. A mountain-battery was soon brought to bear on the Turkish left; the riflemen scattered themselves among the projecting rocks and crags; and from every available cover the white smoke drifted forth upon the wind. The Rifle Brigade was under the command of General Radetzky, who quickly passed up the sloping road, between the two lines of Turkish fire, and joined his brother officers beside the batteries of the first position. The principal command at once passed into his hands, on account of his being the senior officer present; but he had only praise for General Stoletoff, whose defence had been characterised, not merely by courage, but by all the highest qualities of a soldier.

Early the following morning, an attempt was made to carry the Turkish positions on the right flank. These were on a wooded ridge commanding the Russian lines, and it was necessary for the safety of those lines that the enemy should be dislodged. The Turkish advance had by this time been checked, and the left flank was tolerably safe, but the right was still in considerable danger. About nine o'clock A.M. on the 24th, General Dragomiroff arrived with two regiments of the second brigade belonging to his own division; but large numbers of men were lost in running the gauntlet of the elevated road which marked the summit of the ridge. All through the morning, a terrible struggle went on in the depths of the valley, and in the rocky and wooded hollows into which the ground is broken. The Turks were once more making an attempt to get in the rear of their antagonists' position; but this was no easy matter. The fight swayed to and fro, in vast yet scattered waves, and, although the Russians were often driven back, they generally managed to recover their ground. On the whole, however, they did not improve their position, and towards noon the Turks sent up reinforcements. It was then determined by the Russians to make a counter-attack on the right flank of the Turkish ridge, simultaneously with a renewed assault from below. Two battalions of the Jitomer regiment marched across the level grass-land forming the intervening valley, and were received by a terrible fire from the Turkish mountain-guns, planted on a thickly-wooded peak, and by the rifle-fire of the Turkish infantry. The advance was covered by the Russian artillery; but as soon as the infantry had got into the forest, it was necessary that the guns should cease firing, lest they should strike their own men. An hour's fighting at close quarters then ensued, and the Russians appeared to be gaining ground. The Turks began to withdraw their batteries from both flanks, although on the central peak they yet stood fast. Radetzky perceived that his advanced infantry must be supported: he therefore placed himself at the head of a company belonging to the Jitomer battalions which had been left in reserve; and at the same time the colonel of the regiment led forward another. It may perhaps be doubted whether Radetzky, as the chief commander, should have exposed himself to this extent; but the occasion was grave, and he may have thought that nothing but a personal example would suffice to determine the fortunes of the day. The troops followed him with ringing cheers, and, dashing

ATTACK ON THE SHIPKA PASS.

across the valley, flung themselves against the centre of the hostile line. The breastworks on the peak were carried with a rush, and, after a sharp bayonet-charge, the Turks retreated. They retreated, however, only to advance once more with renewed determination, and a furious attempt was made to retake the position. Another struggle, of nearly an hour's duration, dyed the fierce slopes in blood; but by three o'clock in the afternoon, the Ottomans had abandoned their attempt, and the Russian soldiers, exhausted with their efforts, stood triumphant in the conquered works.

Satisfied with what he had achieved, Radetzky returned to his own position, where, some time before, General Dragomiroff had been seriously wounded in the leg. It was now determined by the chief commander to move a detachment against the outlying positions towards Shipka, which the Turks had seized on the first day. The Podolsk Regiment was accordingly sent forward to the attack, under cover of a heavy artillery-fire, and was partially successful in its allotted task. The Russians had greatly improved their position, as compared with what it had been on the two previous days, and it was by this time known in camp that large reinforcements were hurrying on from the north. But the Turks were being reinforced also, and the sanguinary contest was not yet at an end. The Ottoman troops engaged on those four days were nearly all regulars, and they fought with admirable spirit and constancy. The losses on both sides had been very heavy, but were apparently more serious in the Russian hosts than in the Turkish. Mr. Forbes, who saw the whole of these actions, testifies to the devotion and skill of the Russian surgeons, and to the courage with which they placed themselves in the most dangerous positions, whenever their services were required. It was indeed almost impossible to find a sheltered spot anywhere, and the Turkish bullets came so

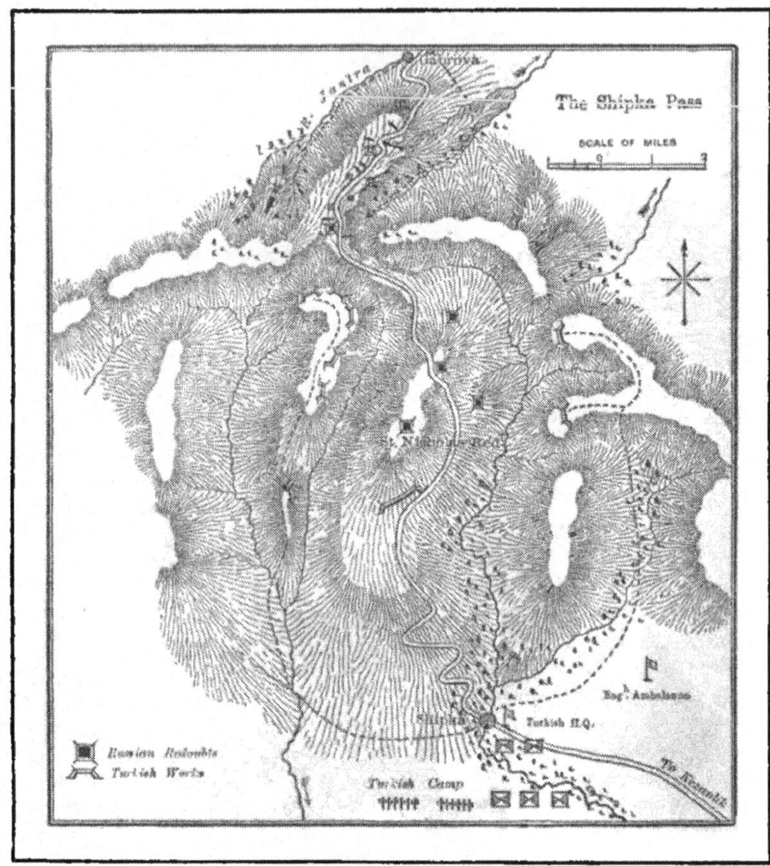

PLAN OF THE SHIPKA OPERATIONS.

thick and fast that one of the patients received a fresh wound while the earlier one was being dressed. The ambulance-men also behaved admirably, picking up the wounded under the hottest fire, and showing so little regard for their own safety that several were themselves injured. Excellent service, moreover, was done by the Bulgarian peasant-boys, who went into the very thick of the battle with jars of water for the soldiers.

Let us turn from the murderous details of battle, that we may recognise with fitting honour the extraordinary services rendered on these occasions by the English press, and especially by the *Daily News*, which has acquired an illustrious reputation for the promptitude, spirit, accuracy, and pictorial power of its war-reports. If the account just given of the four days' fighting in the Shipka Pass has any element of vividness, it is due entirely to the splendid description by Mr. Archibald Forbes. The Special Correspondents of the daily press are becoming almost as important as the commanding officers themselves. It is no longer possible to write history without writing of them; and although Mr. Forbes may have his equals, he has certainly not his superior. After the struggle on the 24th of August, he rode all night long, and through the greater part of the 25th as well, without stopping for either rest or food, in order that he might telegraph his account of the transactions to the journal which he represented.* He reached Gorny Studen, the Imperial head-quarters, in advance of any of the aides-de-camp whom the Grand Duke had sent to the Shipka Pass to report the progress of events. Consequently, the Emperor had received only a few brief telegrams indicating the chief developments of the action in very general terms, and he was glad to hear from the lips of Mr. Forbes the details which that gentleman was so competent to convey. "The concern of the Emperor," writes the correspondent, "was not less strongly evinced than was his thorough conversance with the military art. He expressed an anxious desire that every effort should be made to supply his noble soldiers with the food they so much needed, and expressed great gratification when I was able to tell him I had seen camp-kettles bubbling even amid the whiz of bullets. The simplicity of his Majesty's habit of life is apparent at a glance. He carries no luxury with him, and I have seen a subaltern's tent at Wimbledon far more sumptuously accoutred than the campaigning residence of the Czar of All the Russias." Mr. Forbes next had an interview with the Grand Duke, to whom he gave verbal explanations, accompanied by a roughly-drawn plan of the actions he had witnessed. He then passed on to Bucharest, leaving another correspondent—Mr. MacGahan—to continue the record of what was taking place upon the bloodstained ridge.

Notwithstanding their partial successes, the position of the Russians was critical. The Turks had indeed been compelled to give ground to a certain extent, but they were still on their adversary's flanks. The village of Berdek, on the left of the Russian position, and the mountains on the right, had been seized by the Ottomans, who had constructed a redoubt on the right of the Russian line, and planted batteries which commanded the road leading up to the pass. The redoubt enfiladed the road, and the path was thus rendered impracticable. The battle was renewed with undiminished fury on the 25th of August, and General Petroceni, commander of the First Brigade of the Ninth Division of the Eighth Corps, was killed on the road thus commanded by the Turkish fire. Even on the other side of the ridge, men were sometimes killed and wounded by bullets dropping over. General Radetzky was so doubtful of his ability to retain the position that he recommended the Commandant of Gabrova to hold his people in readiness to fly at a moment's notice. The Russians attempted on the 25th to take the Turkish redoubt, but were driven back with fearful loss. A very insufficient force had been despatched upon this service, and the troops, failing to take the position at a rush, got entangled in the brushwood and trunks of trees with which the Turks had formed their entrenchments. The attack was afterwards renewed with a stronger column, and for a moment it seemed as if it would be successful; nevertheless, the men were once more driven back, and Radetzky himself, followed by a portion of his Staff, then rode on to the ground. A third attack was ordered, and the Russians got into the redoubt, and held it for a few seconds. The struggle was prolonged throughout the day, but, although the redoubt was surrounded, and the rifle-fire of the assailants was terrific, the Turks held their ground to the last, and the Russians had nothing but a long list of killed and wounded to show for their pains.

While this sanguinary contest was proceeding, the Ottomans conducted an attack against the front

* After the great struggle at Plevna, on the 31st of July, Mr. Forbes rode from the scene of battle to Giurgevo, travelled thence by rail to Bucharest, and then, without pausing for repose, crossed the Roumanian frontier to the nearest Transylvanian telegraph-office, whence a message of six columns in length was despatched to England, the whole of which appeared in the later editions of the *Daily News* of August 3rd, 1877. (See an article on "The War Campaign and the War Correspondent," by Major W. F. Butler, in *Macmillan's Magazine* for March, 1878.)

GENERAL VIEW OF THE RUSSIAN POSITION IN THE SHIPKA PASS.

1. Fort St. Nicholas. 2. Redoubts 3. Green Battery. 4. Battery of Mount Bedeck. 5. Turkish Lunette. 6. Redan called Turkish Redoubt. 7. Round Battery. 8. Karanla. 9. Han. 10. Road from Kezanlik to Gabrova. 11. Former Telegraph Lines. 12. Turkish Positions.

BRINGING DOWN THE WOUNDED.

and rear of the Russian position, but were ultimately compelled to retire. The combatants were not yet exhausted by this prodigious series of efforts, and fighting again took place on the 26th and 27th, without any material change in the relative position of the combatants. The Russians still remained unshaken on the ridge where they had first drawn up their forces; the Turks still confronted them with a powerful and menacing host; but neither side can be said to have been victorious. Nothing, however, could surpass the fighting qualities displayed by both belligerents. The firmness of the Russians in resisting a series of terrible assaults was characterized by the finest heroism; while the Turks had incontestably shown that they do not always require to fight behind defences, but can attack again and again an enemy posted upon commanding ground, and provided with every means of effective action. Had the Ottomans succeeded in their design, and driven the Russians over the Shipka Pass, the latter would certainly have been in a very serious position. They would have been hemmed in between the Balkans and the Danube, and, with hostile forces on their flanks, and untaken fortresses in their rear, would probably have been overwhelmed. But this was an achievement beyond the power of Suleiman Pasha and his gallant soldiers. Nevertheless, the Turkish General was still disinclined to give up the attempt, and on the 27th of August telegraphed for reinforcements. A few days later, however, he found it advisable to abandon the position, and by the 31st he had removed most of his troops from the neighbourhood of the pass. A few battalions of Egyptians were left behind; others remained in the village of Shipka, and some cannon were still planted on the heights; but the main body of the army had gone. Suleiman Pasha, with all his energy and all his skill, had in effect confessed himself foiled. The Russians felt so much relieved that a large number of their reinforcements were sent back, and Radetzky stated confidently that he could save the position from any force likely to be brought against him. During the seven days' fighting, the Turks are said to have made upwards of one hundred distinct attacks; but their brief success had been entirely eclipsed. Five thousand of their dead lay between Shipka and the slopes of Mount St. Nicholas. The Russians also had lost heavily, and the air was tainted by the corruption of unburied corpses. The Turkish system of care for the wounded appears to have been extremely bad. In Kezanlik, eight hundred injured soldiers were left in the charge of two Turkish surgeons, and many had to shift for themselves. But the members of the English Society of the Red Crescent did excellent service under the directions of Dr. Leslie Hume and Dr. Sandwith, and the Turkish officers preferred their attendance to that of their own countrymen. As it was, the amount of suffering was fearful; but it would have been still worse without the aid thus generously rendered.

The Russians had defeated the attempt to dispossess them of the Shipka Pass, but the fortunes of the war still looked unpromising. When the highest achievement of invaders consists in their standing successfully on the defensive, it is obvious that the invasion itself has been checked. This was the case with the Russians, and their position in Bulgaria was undoubtedly precarious. In Russia itself, the earlier feeling of enthusiasm had given place to one of despondency, and in many quarters the war was unpopular. The people were beginning to be painfully conscious of the burdens which hostilities impose, and could see no indications that the proposed ends were likely to be attained. The want of money, always considerable, became very serious before the end of August, and it was found necessary to enlarge the issue of rouble notes to the amount of 11,000,000. Since the commencement of the war, Russia had magnified her State debt by two loans, amounting to 300,000,000 roubles, and entailing an annual payment of 17,000,000 roubles for interest. The increase in the issue of paper-money had added 867,000,000 roubles to the floating debt, and, with all this aggravation of the national burdens, the price of provisions was rising, and trade was almost paralysed. The annual fair at Nishni-Novgorod was unusually dull that year, and merchants were requiring delay in the payment of their debts. At the same time, the Czar ordered the State Bank to advance to agriculturists sixty per cent. on the corn and wheat harvested, and appointed a commission to deliberate on the proposition that all passenger-fares and charges for goods-freights on the railways should be collected in gold. Recruiting was vigorously proceeding, and the peasants were in all directions being called off to join the army. The cost of the crusade was ruinous, and for the present the enterprise was a failure. It is not surprising that under these circumstances a large amount of discontent was spread throughout the Empire, and found its expression in secret conspiracies which the police had difficulty in discovering. The revolutionary societies were working beneath the surface, and their influence was not favourable to that spirit of servile devotion on which the Russian Emperors have long reckoned for the effectual prosecution of their designs.

Matters were not mended by the state of opinion in Roumania, where a feeling unfavourable to the Russians was beginning to appear. The Government of the Principality desired to conclude a military convention with Russia, but the Czar was disinclined to any such agreement. The Roumanian Minister, M. Bratiano, and the Chief of the Roumanian Staff, visited the Emperor's head-quarters in the hope of concluding the desired arrangement; but the Grand Duke Nicholas distinctly affirmed that the independent action of the Roumanian army in Bulgaria was not permissible. The Russians, however, were glad to incorporate a Roumanian division with their own troops, and to strengthen their threatened positions in Bulgaria by the soldiers of Prince Charles. The allied nationalities did not get on at all well together, and an incident at Nicopolis almost brought about a collision between the two. The Russian Commandant in that city had a Roumanian soldier flogged for some offence. The countrymen of the sufferer were aflame with indignation at this affront. The officers of the regiment went to their colonel, and declared that, unless satisfaction were made, every one of them would call out the first Russian officer he met. The colonel telegraphed to Bucharest, and Prince Charles communicated with the Russian head-quarters. The answer, however, was not at all favourable to the Roumanian sense of independence. It was replied that the matter was purely one of military discipline; that the Commandant was responsible for order; and that, as the Roumanian Division formed part of the Russian force at Nicopolis, the jurisdiction of that official extended over the men composing it, as much as over the Russians. This was annoying to the Roumanians; but they could only grumble and submit. Shortly afterwards, a special agreement was concluded between the Principality and the Russian head-quarters, by which the Roumanian army, under the personal command of Prince Charles, was to take part in the war. On the night of the 24th of August, a brigade of Roumanian infantry passed over the Simnitza bridge, and three regiments of cavalry crossed the Danube near Turna Magurelle. Six thousand Turks came up to dispute the passage, but arrived too late, and were obliged to retire.

ROUMANIAN CAVALRY CROSSING THE DANUBE.

This concession pacified the Prince, but the Roumanian people were not at all pleased with the turn which events had taken. They had expected much from the war, and it had yielded little that was in accordance with their wishes. A correspondent of the *Times* observed that Roumania had aimed at independence, and would have attained that object by remaining on the defensive, whereas direct participation in the war had endangered her future, and exhausted her financial resources. It was expected that the Russians would disseminate a large quantity of gold; but nothing of the kind had occurred. The Russians spent little money in supplying their wants, for they brought most things by rail from their own country. It was also a source of annoyance that the Russians induced the peasantry to place waggons and horses at their disposal, and that the peasants themselves, attracted by the hope of easy profit, were lured away from the cultivation of their fields. The industrial condition of the country suffered to a very serious degree in this respect, and the anticipated advantages turned out to be purely fictitious. The Russians soon ceased to pay in ready money, and for everything they purchased gave bonds payable at three months' date. It was remembered by the Roumanians that they had once before been paid by the Russians in the same way; that the settlement occupied fifteen years; and that in the end the unfortunate people were forced to be content with three per cent. of what was due to them. No wonder that the inhabitants of Wallachia and Moldavia looked askance upon the presence of their Northern friends.

While the Russians and the Turks were confronting one another on the Shipka heights, Mehemet Ali, the Ottoman Commander-in-Chief, was engaging the enemy in another direction. His centre was for some time near Eski-Juma, about twenty miles to the west of Schumla, on the road between Rasgrad and Osman Bazar. Against this position the army of the Czarewitch conducted frequent reconnaissances, in one of which about 8,000 infantry, with six squadrons of cavalry and fifteen guns, made their way round through the mountainous country midway between Tirnova and Schumla. Starting from Agaslar, on the 20th of August, they entered the valley of Yenikoi, and surprised the Turkish outposts, which they drove in. They then attacked the Turkish right, posted on ground overlooking Haidarkoi. The Turks were considerably overmatched in point of numbers, and the position was for a time in danger; but, about three o'clock in the afternoon, Salih Pasha and Baker Pasha arrived upon the scene, in time to prevent the outposts falling back. The former at once sent three battalions to the support of their comrades, and at the same time four guns and a body of infantry were planted on some heights forming the left shoulder of the valley. Fighting continued until the evening, when the Turks retired, leaving the Russians in a position which seriously exposed their right flank. The following day seems to have passed in quiet; but on the 22nd the Russian guns opened a cannonade at half-past eight in the morning. This was answered by the Turks, and quickly silenced, and the valley on the right flank of the Russians was afterwards occupied by the Osmanlis. The Russian line was then charged with great enthusiasm; the Muscovites fell back, and the positions they had recently held passed into the hands of the Turks. The struggle was prolonged at other points, and at the close of the day the Russians withdrew to strong positions, some way removed from those which they had first occupied. On the evening of the 23rd, they made a sudden attack on the positions wrested from them by the Turks. The adversaries were at that time posted on two hills fronting each other; but, while the ground held by the Russians was covered with brushwood, that of the Turks was open. Under cover of the bushes, the assailants set up masked batteries, which opened a heavy fire upon the Ottomans. In two hours, six hundred shells had been thrown on to the hill occupied by the Moslem troops, and at eight o'clock the Russians moved rapidly across the valley, firing constant volleys. They were met at the point of the bayonet, and a prolonged struggle at close quarters took place during the night. The Russians advanced to the attack again and again, and towards morning occupied the hill which the Turks had so valorously defended. During the 24th, the Turks were reinforced, and after another sanguinary struggle the enemy's line was turned, and finally broken up. In retreating, the Russians left behind them two guns, four artillery caissons, and a large quantity of munitions of war.* Some minor successes of the Turks took place in the same direction at this period; but they were not of much importance as affecting the general issues. Nevertheless, it was now evident that the Russians had to confront an enemy who had at length roused himself from the apathy which had so long paralysed his movements. If the same vigour had been exhibited at the close of June, and in the early days of July, it is not impossible that the invasion would have been entirely repulsed. Even as it was, the Russian arms were exposed to many perils; yet the invaders had planted a strong foot in Bulgaria, and had seized the Balkans with a grip which was not to be shaken off. The mountain passes might have been defended at their northern ends; but when once the Russians had established themselves in those tortuous paths, it was beyond the scope even of Turkish valour to drive them forth.

* Correspondent of the *Daily Telegraph*.

CHAPTER XXXI.

The Campaign in Asia—Relative Positions of the Russians and Turks in the Middle of July—Defences of Erzeroum—Embarrassments of the Russians—The Armenian Fugitives—Abandonment of the Siege of Kars—Proceedings of Mukhtar Pasha—Reconnaissance of Turkish Cavalry on the 17th of July—Encounter on the 18th—Alterations in the Military Positions—Fighting on July 26th—Fresh Positions gained by the Turks—Russian Attack on Great Yahni—Inhuman Conduct of the Turkish Irregulars—Firmness of Mukhtar Pasha in repressing Atrocities—Occupation of the Ruins of Ani by the Russians—Action of the 18th of August—Prolonged Fighting, and Repulse of the Assailants by the Turks—Russian Official Account of the Battle—Desultory Movements—Turkish Attack on the Kizil Tépé—The Hill wrested from the Russians—Severe Fighting for its Recovery—The Turks driven from the Open Ground, but left in possession of the Hill—Patriotism of an Arabian Woman—Improvement in the Turkish Position—Punishment of the Abhasians by a Russian Column—Burning of Villages—Mr. Gladstone and the Greeks—Correspondence with M. Negroponte—Mr. Layard and the Correspondent of the *Daily Telegraph*—Debate in Parliament.

WE must now return to the seat of war in Asia, which we quitted at the close of Chapter XIV. After the relief of Bayazid by Tergukasoff on the 10th of July, General Melikoff concentrated the greater number of his troops in the eastern parts of Turkish Armenia, near his own frontiers, and there awaited reinforcements. But the Turkish commander, no less than his adversary, felt the need of fresh levies, and he recruited large bodies of irregulars, and drilled them as fast as he could. Volunteers from Sivas and the Syrian provinces were passed through a rapid course of instruction at Erzeroum, and numerous guns, intended for field-service and for use in the garrison, arrived in the same city. Between Erzeroum and Kars, four distinct systems of defence blocked the valley of the Araxes, and the mountainous nature of the country was turned to the best account by the skill of the military engineers. Erzeroum itself was protected by the Deve-Boyun range of heights, which by the middle of July had been covered by a triple line of shelter-trenches and redoubts: other lines were thrown out in the direction of Kars. The Russians were at that time quite incapable of attacking such formidable obstacles, and were compelled to stand on the defensive until they had been strengthened by fresh battalions. The insurrection in the Caucasus obliged them to keep a great array of troops in that province, and left all the fewer men for operations in Armenia. General Tergukasoff, moreover, was much embarrassed by the large number of native Christian families who followed his columns with their domestic animals and household goods, and to whom, in the name of the Emperor, he had promised protection. These people alleged that, should they fall into the hands of the Turks, after having identified themselves with the invasion, they would be subjected to the most cruel usage; and it is indeed certain that their treatment would not have been merciful. The Kurds were acting in Asia with the same ferocity as the Circassians and Bashi-Bazouks in Europe, and the rule of the stronger was not likely to be tempered by any scruples of humanity, such as the progress of civilisation has developed among the nations of the West. Tergukasoff therefore conducted the rebellious Armenians beyond the Russian frontier, and then took up a position in the neighbourhood of Igdyr, on the road to Erivan, and about twenty miles from Bayazid, but within the dominions of the Czar.

The siege of Kars had by this time been almost completely abandoned, as the Commander-in-Chief of the Russian forces in Armenia considered his army too weak to conduct siege-operations on a large scale, and at the same time to resist the attacks of Mukhtar Pasha. Melikoff accordingly ordered the heavy guns to be withdrawn, and, removing his divisions to the east of the city, distributed them in two camps—one resting to the south of the main road leading from Kars to Gumri or Alexandropol, the other covering a more southern road to the same fortress, which lies just within the frontiers of the Russian Empire. The Muscovites had in fact virtually admitted their failure, and for a time there was a pause in the campaign. But this did not last long. Mukhtar Pasha followed on the track of his enemy, though with caution, forming entrenched camps east of Kars as he proceeded, and presently began a new series of movements, having for their primary object the collection of intelligence with respect to the enemy's positions, and for their ultimate design an invasion of Russian territory by the soldiers of the Crescent, if such an enterprise should be found possible. With these views, the Turkish Generalissimo directed that a strong cavalry reconnaissance should be pushed up to the Russian outposts. The force was to start from camp by nine o'clock on the morning of July 17th; but it was nearly eleven before the whole body was on the road. Some Circassians, forming part of the First Cavalry Brigade which Mukhtar Pasha despatched on this expedition, carried before them a "holy flag" of green (the colour of the Prophet), bearing in silver letters an inscription from the Koran, together with a smaller rallying standard, on which the crescent and the star were conspicuously blazoned. The force altogether was of a very motley character, including regulars and irregulars, and presenting a great variety of uniforms, some brilliant and picturesque, others ragged, faded, and weather-stained.

The route was over a rocky country, carpeted with lichens and wild flowers, and the destination of the troops was a broad valley between Kars and Mount Alaghez, the latter lying beyond the Russian frontiers. The Arpa-Tchai runs through this valley, and on the farther side were the Russian tents. At the risk of coming into collision with the enemy, the Turkish horsemen advanced close to the hostile camp, and made their observations at leisure. A Mussulman Cossack was seized, and induced to give some information touching the numbers and resources of the enemy; and it was generally believed that the Russians in that locality could not exceed 30,000 at the utmost, and were probably fewer. The Muscovites seem to have considered their position not very secure, for early on the following morning their two camps were drawn nearer to one another, and five or six thousand cavalry, together with a couple of light batteries, were sent out to cover the movement. Mukhtar Pasha then determined on effecting a complete change of front, so as to place his forces parallel with those of the Russians, and at the same time slightly to overlap them on both flanks. The Russian camp was now entrenched behind one of a series of hills dotting the wide plain of Soubatan. The Turks occupied, for the time being, some terraced heights bordering the plain or valley; and the distance between the two armies was but slight.*

On the 18th of July, the Turkish commander sent out a small mounted force from his left, under the direction of Edhem Pasha, of the Second Brigade of Cavalry. This force included three bodies of Circassians (the Cossacks of the Ottoman army), who rapidly moved round by the village of Soubatan, turned the enemy's right, and so got into the rear of three squadrons of heavy dragoons, and one of regular Cossacks. A very animated encounter soon followed, and each body of horsemen charged the other several times. Ultimately the Russians retreated, and, being pursued by the Circassians, were driven within their advanced posts. The cavalry on both sides behaved extremely well; but the superiority rested with the Mohammedans, mainly on account of their being armed with Winchester rifles, whereas the Russians had nothing better than old large-bore rifled carbines, clumsily converted to a more recent pattern. The Russians offered to renew the combat in the evening, but nothing more occurred than the interchange of a few harmless shots at long range. The chief of the Circassians, Mehemet Ghazi, Prince of Lesghie, arrived in camp that same evening. He was the representative of Schamyl, and of course exercised great authority among the mountaineers, whose enthusiasm was kindled by his presence. He at once issued a number of proclamations to the Mussulmans in the Russian army, appealing to their religious feelings to abandon the cause of a Christian oppressor; and these exhortations appear to have borne fruit in numerous desertions of Mohammedan Cossacks from the enemy's ranks. The Turkish army moved to its new lines before nightfall on the 18th, and on the 20th the forces were augmented by five battalions of the Kars corps. The enemy made fresh dispositions to meet these alterations in the Ottoman plans, and the two antagonists remained staring at each other for some days, without attempting any military operations. The weather was rainy and depressing, with much thunder and lightning, and camp-life was wearisome in its monotony. But the Russians hesitated to attack the Turks in their new and stronger positions, and Mukhtar Pasha was under orders from Constantinople not to risk his previous gains by any rash enterprise.

An expedition, however, was sent out by the Turks on the night of July 25th, when Mustapha Safvet Pasha conducted a cavalry raid on to Russian territory. This was answered on the following day by a Russian attack on the Turkish positions. Two battalions of infantry, twenty squadrons of cavalry, and two horse-batteries, moved out of the Muscovite camp in the early morning of the 26th, and shaped their course in the direction of Ara-Oghlu. The Turks at the same time moved forward to Chela, and a heavy cannonade was opened on the Russian column as it advanced. Under cover of this fire, a body of Circassians, commanded by Edhem Pasha, advanced to meet the enemy as his forces debouched into the plain between Ulelltépé and Ara-Oghlu. The Moslem cavalry, however, were repulsed, but at eleven A.M. Mukhtar Pasha sent forward three brigades of infantry to support the Circassians.

* The Armenian Campaign, by Charles Williams, Special Correspondent of the *Standard*.

TURKISH IRREGULAR CAVALRY RECONNAISSANCE.

2 H

This produced the desired effect, for the Russians retired to Ara-Oghlu, and occupied a ridge to the east of the village, from which there was no probability of dislodging them. The artillery practice of the Russians appears to have been extremely bad, and to have made no impression on their opponents. Their movements, indeed, were very slowly and inefficiently conducted, and it was not until two o'clock in the afternoon that Melikoff ordered a division from the Kadikeui camp to support his detachment. The column then sent forward was headed by four regiments of dragoons, in rear of whom were two horse-batteries, followed by two more cavalry corps; then followed a battery, and then two infantry brigades, numbering twelve battalions. Another force advanced simultaneously from a different point, and it seemed for a little while as if an action of a more determined character were about to take place. But nothing ensued beyond a slight cavalry skirmish on the left flank of the Turks, and a reconnaissance which was pushed forward by the Russians to Ani, situated a little within the Turkish territory. This ancient and ruined city was held for a couple of hours by the Muscovites, who then retired, unmolested, in the midst of a heavy shower of rain and hail.

By this time, a strong cavalry camp had been formed by the Russians at Tash-Kalé, about twelve miles to the north-east of the Turkish positions, and it also became apparent that the Kadikeui camp contained one complete division of infantry. The Turks had for a long time maintained that there was nothing but cavalry in that direction; but some English officers who accompanied their forces felt certain that infantry formed the front line of the encampment, and so it ultimately proved. The Russians were therefore stronger than their enemies had supposed; yet they were not strong enough to make any offensive movement of a formidable nature. The general result of the engagement on the 26th was that the Turks were enabled to occupy several positions on the west bank of the Arpa-Tchai which they had not previously held. At a small cost in men, they had proved their superiority to the Russians, and the position of the invaders was each day shown to be more grave than it had appeared the day before. That the commissariat of the army was very deficient, is probable from statements made by deserters. While the officers drank champagne, the men were reduced almost to the level of starving, and these sufferings were not cheered by any immediate hope of an improvement in the fortunes of the war. The spirits of the men would probably have sunk to a dangerous degree, had they not been excited by frequent movements, seeming to promise something effective against the enemy, although in reality they led to nothing. On the 27th of July, the troops of Melikoff again issued from their encampment, and moved across the plain in the direction of the Ottomans. Ten battalions of infantry were accompanied by a strong force of cavalry, and by eighteen guns, including two light cavalry pieces. With this array, an attack was made on Great Yahni, an insulated hill rising out of the level ground about a mile and a half to the north of Mukhtar Pasha's most advanced post on the left. A little before noon, the advancing column reached the foot of this hill, the slopes of which were occupied by three battalions of Turks. The attack was delivered at five points; but at only three of these was the fighting anything more than a feint. Infantry, cavalry, and artillery, were all engaged, and the contest was prolonged for about three hours, when the Russians retired, leaving a small proportion of dead upon the field. Some of the bodies were afterwards stripped, mutilated, and outraged by the Kurds; but such atrocities were firmly punished by Mukhtar Pasha. It is admitted on all hands that the Turkish Commander-in-Chief in Asia evinced an honourable feeling with respect to these abominable acts. To oppose the Kurds and Circassians required no small amount of resolution, for those irregular horsemen were very necessary as auxiliaries, and were not at all well inclined to brook interference with what they regarded as their martial rights. An instance of the difficulty occurred a little before the period to which we are now referring. On the 10th of July, a report was made to Mukhtar Pasha by the head-man of a village near Kars, to the effect that two Circassians had on the previous evening ridden into the place and stolen a lamb, and that, on being remonstrated with by the owner, one of them shot the villager dead. The result of a court-martial which inquired into the case was that the man was found guilty, whereupon it was ordered by the Commander-in-Chief that he should be hanged. The Circassian leaders begged for his life, and one of them threatened that he would retire with his whole tribe if the sentence was executed. Mukhtar refused to alter his resolution on account of this menace; the man was put to death, and on the following day 1,100 Circassians deserted their colours. Not even this incident, however, could shake the firmness of the Mushir. A hundred irregular cavalry having arrived from Diabekir on the 25th of July, and reports having preceded them as to their thievish habits, Mukhtar Pasha gave them to understand that if any man was brought up for the theft of a

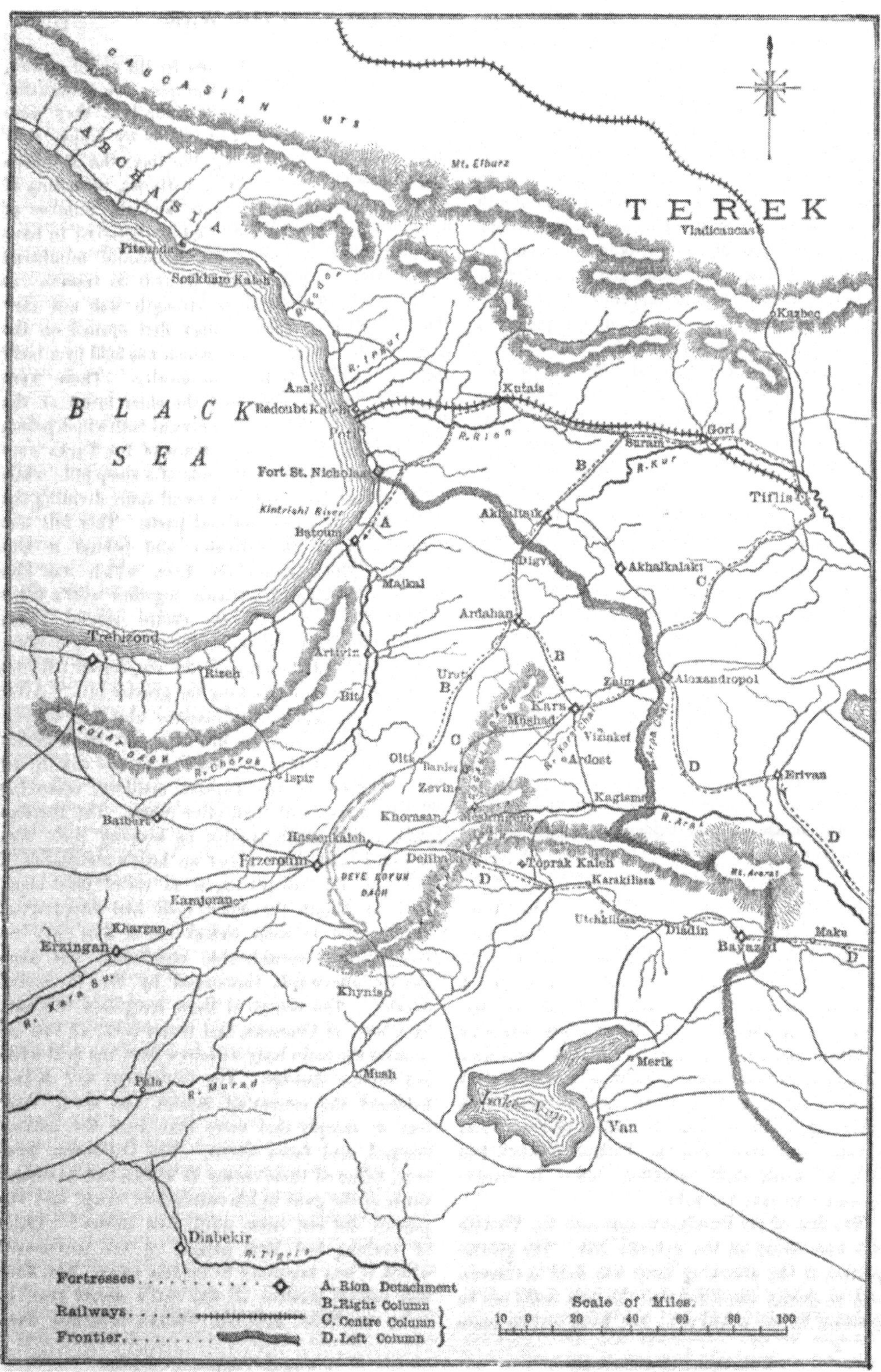

PLAN OF THE INVASION OF ARMENIA, SHOWING THE ADVANCE OF THE RUSSIANS, AND THEIR RETREAT TO THE FRONTIER.

single egg he would hang him, and that if the culprit could not be found he would cause the whole detachment to draw lots in his presence, and execute him on whom the lot should fall.*

The activity of the Russians increased towards the close of July, and on the 30th of that month they carried out a movement of an important character. The plateau of the Kurukdara is varied by a steep and isolated hill, called the Kizil Tépé, or Red Hill, and from behind this eminence General Melikoff threw out his left, and occupied the peninsula upon which Ani stands. The right of the Turkish line nearly touched the ruins of that city, although the ruins themselves were not occupied; and this manœuvre of the Russians was so threatening that it was necessary to oppose it at once. At half-past ten in the morning, a Russian column, the approach of which had been concealed by uplands, appeared within a mile of the old fortifications, and immediately proceeded to pitch tents on the ground thus occupied. The Turks sent out a small force to oppose the movement; but the resistance was extremely feeble, and the Russians were allowed to accomplish their design. From the position then taken up they slightly withdrew six days later, and established themselves a few miles farther to the south—that is to say, still more to the left of their original line; but they returned to the ruins of Ani on the morning of August 8th. For several days, a good deal of elaborate manœuvring went on, and on the 17th of August it was evident that something of importance was being contemplated by the Russians. Before day-break, the camp at Ani was once more broken up, and the troops composing it were moved five or six miles along the Arpa-Tchai to the north-east. Other positions were altered, and large bodies of troops were brought together in the course of the day, as if an attack were contemplated. The attack ensued at day-break on the 18th, when the Turkish outposts were suddenly assaulted by their adversaries, who were advancing in loose order. In time, however, their forces were massed, and brought to bear with effect upon the Ottomans; nevertheless, their advance was slow, and the Turkish soldiers had time to finish their breakfasts before it became necessary to take the field.

The first of the Russians to approach the Turkish line were those on the extreme left. The greater portion of the attacking force was held in reserve, and so closely concealed that the men could not be detected by the naked eye; but from certain parts of the field they could be seen by the aid of glasses, and, as the Turks had telegraphic communication between different sections of their line, they were speedily made aware of the force by which they were threatened. During the day, the Russians brought into action fourteen batteries, consisting of a hundred and twelve guns, and the number of troops employed on their side is believed to have been about 35,000. The Osmanlis numbered 28,000 men in line, with 12,000 in reserve; so that the disproportion of strength was not very great. The Russian artillery first opened on the right of the Ottoman line, which was held by a body of Circassian and Kurdish cavalry. These were speedily driven back; and the chief brunt of the action was on the left and centre, at both which points the fighting was severe. Some of the Turks were posted in rifle-pits, on the side of a steep hill; while others were stationed on a small spur, dividing the mountain into two unequal parts. This hill was called Yahni the Greater, and behind it was another called Yahni the Less, which was also covered with Turkish troops, together with a ridge connecting both with the camps behind. An attack was made on the latter of these eminences, in the hope of drawing off the murderous rifle-fire from the column attacking the greater hill. After a sharp struggle, the Russians obtained a lodgment on the smaller hill by dint of superior numbers; but here the assailants were cut up by the shell-fire of the Turkish artillery, operating from a ravine within effective range. The Russian officers had much trouble in keeping their men together, and, after about an hour's occupation of the hill, the troops began to retire piece-meal, until at length the whole body had disappeared. Having got to some extent out of fire, they re-formed with considerable steadiness, but were shortly afterwards threatened by the Circassian cavalry. The charge of those irregulars was met by a body of Cossacks, and under cover of this encounter the main body withdrew from the field without further damage. The Circassians and Kurds harassed the retreating masses, and stung their rear so sharply that more than once the column stopped, and faced about. The Ottomans, however, followed their enemy to within two thousand yards of the guns in his entrenched camp, and the pursuit did not cease until near sunset.† Little or nothing had been gained by the movement, which it was necessary to explain away. The Russian official account of the battle stated that, in order to divert Mukhtar Pasha's attention from

* Correspondent of the *Times*.

† Williams's Armenian Campaign.

some movements of General Tergukasoff against Ismail Hakki Pasha, General Melikoff caused a demonstration to be made against the position of the Turkish Commander-in-Chief, and that the enemy, deceived by the manœuvre, brought out all his reserves stationed in the rear, thereby exposing his strength. According to this account, it would seem that the only objects of Melikoff were to assist his colleague, and to ascertain the numbers of those opposed to him. The combat, however, appears to have been more prolonged and vehement than is consistent with this explanation, and it is therefore probable that Melikoff really hoped to better his own position by driving the Turks from theirs.

Some desultory movements followed. On the night of the 19th, a column of Russian cavalry was sent out on a scouting expedition to the village of Bulanoch. There they surprised a body of regular Turkish cavalry, who suffered some rather serious losses; but, on fire being opened from a Turkish battery, the Muscovites returned to camp. In the early morning of August 20th, a strong column of cavalry, with a battery of guns, was engaged with the Turkish outposts at Soubatan. This movement looked like the prelude to another serious attack; but the main columns were suddenly countermanded, and the cavalry, finding themselves without support, retired at day-break. It was evident that the Russian commander desired to keep the enemy in a state of anxiety, and at the same time to exercise his own men in the active work of campaigning. Since the 17th of August, the head-quarters of General Loris Melikoff had been established on the Kizil Tépé, or Red Hill. This eminence was occupied by no better force than a single battalion with four field-pieces; but it was considered almost impregnable by reason of its natural strength. The Russians, apparently reckoning too much on the presumed safety of their position, removed the greater number of their troops, on the 24th of August, from the camp at Orta, behind the Kizil Tépé, and the Turks took advantage of their over-confidence. A bright moon was shining in the early morning of the 25th; but the approach of the assailants, who numbered about 7,000, was not observed, owing to the obscurity of a deep ravine, along which they crept stealthily and noiselessly, in a compact, well-concentrated mass. Nothing was known of their presence until they had arrived at the very foot of the hill, from which, with startling suddenness, and with cries of "Allah il Allah!" they rushed towards the summit. The small force holding the position maintained its ground with much firmness, and resisted the enemy at the point of the bayonet. Numerous Turks fell mortally wounded in the fierce struggle; but the Russians were at length compelled to retire, as the ever-thickening numbers of their opponents threatened to over-lap both their flanks. They retreated to their camp, situated at a distance of about two miles from the northern slope of the Kizil Tépé, dragging with them their four guns, and reaching their comrades without being pursued. On the alarm being given, a body of infantry and dragoons promptly turned out, and endeavoured to retake the hill from which the detachment had been driven forth. But this was a task beyond their power, and frequent repulses showed the futility of the attempt.

The noise of the firing, however, had by this time roused the forces at the other Russian camp—that at Kurukdara. A feeling of consternation, almost amounting to panic, spread throughout the divisions, and orders were issued to strike tents, pack luggage, and load everything on the commissariat-waggons, for it was feared that the Turks, if finally successful, might seize both camps, and overwhelm the army. Everything was soon prepared for flight, yet it was resolved meanwhile to make a further effort to drive back the enemy. A large body of troops was sent forward to the Red Hill, the crown of which was now held by a strong force of Ottomans. Across the ravine at its foot, the Tiflis regiment advanced with heroic resolution, but unavailing courage. The Turks were in the position of predominance, and were moreover acting under the influence of fierce religious excitement. An imaum, clad in the flowing robes of his priestly office, moved about among the soldiers, exhorting them, with uplifted hands, to fight and die for the faith. Other priests were to be seen in various directions, animating the less courageous by the proffered rewards of the Moslem Paradise; and such was the devotion of these ministers that one of them was shot. Reinforcements were continually sent up by Mukhtar Pasha in large numbers; and for twelve miles, extending from the neighbourhood of Ani to a point near the road to Kars, the ground was covered with Turkish troops. A movement was made towards the Russian camp at Kurukdara, with the design of out-flanking it; but this project was effectually counteracted by the main body of the Russians. It was some hours before the several divisions could coalesce in one united attack on the Turkish lines. When, however, the necessary combinations had been effected, frequent attempts were made to reconquer the Kizil Tépé by storming; but the endeavour was as frequently defeated by the obstinacy of the Ottoman defenders.

BATTLE OF KIZIL TÉPÉ.

TURKISH WOUNDED TAKEN OUT OF ACTION AT THE BATTLE OF KIZIL TÉPÉ.

The attacks were aided by a fiery rain of shells and shrapnels, and one of these missiles exploded a store of ammunition, and blew numbers of horses and men into the air. "Joy and satisfaction," says an eye-witness, writing to the *Daily News*, "lighted up the faces of the officers around me, and one of them made the sign of the cross." This fortunate stroke inspired the Russian troops with fresh ardour, and the attack was renewed with infinite gallantry and spirit. In the centre of the Russian line, Colonel Komaroff's brigade was engaged in sharp infantry fighting. The Muscovites began to win ground, and the Turks were driven over the plain and the neighbouring undulations, until they were forced into the broad ravine of Soubatan, at the foot of the Aladja mountain. The opposite side of this ravine was covered with entrenchments and batteries, which, in the heat of their success, the Russians would willingly have charged, had they not been expressly forbidden by directions from head-quarters. The Turks accordingly retired, without being pursued, under cover of their defensive works, and in that direction the battle came to an end at one o'clock in the afternoon. In another part of the field, however, the Grenadiers, led by General Cederholm, under the special superintendence of General Heimann, were engaged in active operations. The Grenadiers were opposed by several Arabian battalions—picked troops, who fought with singular determination and vigour. The fighting on both sides was here chiefly with the rifle, and the smoke was so thick that in a little while the men were unable to take good aim. The Moslems, however, were ultimately compelled to fall back on their rifle-pits and entrenchments at the foot of the Yahni Hills. The action terminated with an encounter between the irregular cavalry of both combatants, after which the Turks retired within their lines, and fighting ceased over the whole field at about four o'clock in the afternoon. Nevertheless, although the Ottomans retreated from the open ground, which remained in possession of their adversaries, they had succeeded not merely in taking, but in holding, the Kizil Tépé. For this advantage they paid largely in killed and wounded; but, from a military point of view, the gain was worth the price at which it had been purchased. On the following day (August 26th), Mukhtar Pasha, availing himself of the strong position on the Red Hill, shifted his whole camp down to the plain; and here his men immediately set to work entrenching themselves in lines protected by the Kizil Tépé on the one hand, and the Great Yahni on the other.

The Turkish success of August 25th is said to have been due, in a great degree, to the initiative of a young Arabian woman, named Fatima, acting as chieftain of some Bedouin squadrons. The plan of attacking the Kizil Tépé was communicated by her to Moussa Pasha, who had in former times been a general in the Russian service, but who had since deserted it. Moussa and Fatima rode at the head of the Turkish assaulting columns in the grey moonlight of that eventful morning, and on nearing the menaced position fell in with a patrol of Cossacks, who demanded the pass-word. Owing to his previous military education with the Russians, Moussa was able to answer in the language of that nationality, and in accordance with the arrangements usually existing in the field-service of the Czar. He was likewise acquainted with the pass-word, which had probably been communicated to him by some Mohammedan deserter. The Cossacks were therefore entirely deceived, and in the uncertain light supposed the force before them to be a portion of their own army. The Turks were permitted to advance, and the small force of Cossacks was speedily overwhelmed. The assailants were then close upon the main position, and the garrison, taken at a disadvantage, were unable to defend the post, notwithstanding their courageous efforts to save it from the Turkish inroad. The loss of the Kizil Tépé necessitated a change in the Muscovite positions, and on the 27th of August Melikoff's forces executed a flank march, and took up fresh ground in the vicinity of Utch Tépé (the Triple Hill), situated due east of the eminence recently occupied.

Early in September, indications of the approaching winter began to be visible on the summits of the mountains, though the temperature in the plains was still comparatively warm. The late actions had enabled the Turks to encamp in much more favourable localities. Large fields of uncut corn were at their disposal; water was abundant, and the air was healthy. The spirit of the Ottoman soldiery was greatly improved by their recent gains, and by their discovery of the fact that the Russians were few in numbers, and very far from invincible. In the earlier part of the campaign, Mukhtar Pasha had been under the impression that the Russians were in tremendous force, and that he had no means of opposing such multitudinous legions. This was the reason why the Ottoman Commander-in-Chief had, at the beginning of the summer, retreated from the frontiers, relinquished a large tract of ground to the enemy, and drawn his forces together where he thought they could be most effectually employed. It was now apparent that the Russian army of invasion was but small, and that these deficient numbers were not compensated by any extraordinary ability on the part of the commanders. Thus it happened that the Armenian campaign commenced with seeming triumphs on the part of the aggressors, and was followed by a series of misfortunes, both real and grave.

The insurrection in Abhasia which Turkey had fomented, and which had served its turn in drawing off a large number of Russian troops, was now at an end. Several native chiefs had been concerned in it, and these it was resolved to punish. A column from the Russian army was sent into the interior of the country on the 30th of July, with orders to retaliate sharply the injury that had been done by the Abhasians. The instructions given to the officers were, to force their way along the main road in the direction of the principal villages, to burn everything, and to work as much ruin as possible. The detachment consisted of cavalry, infantry, and artillery, and presented a formidable front to the half savage tribes which it was to attack. Some amount of resistance, however, was experienced, and the expedition was very badly conducted. A correspondent of the *Times*, who rode with the column, was astonished at the confusion which existed among the persons in command. "Every one," he recorded, "spoke at the same time; officers declined to carry out the orders of their superiors; the captain of artillery disputed with the colonel as to the line of action to be taken, and gave orders to a company of infantry; the artillery lieutenant continued to fire shells when he was positively told to stop; the Cossacks, on receiving orders, discussed the matter among themselves; and the only men who showed any discipline were the Russian infantry." Ultimately, some cavalry were sent out as scouts, and returned with the news that the enemy occupied a commanding position on the road below, in the depths of a thick forest, the path traversing which had been strongly barricaded in two places. Nevertheless, when the infantry were sent forward, the resistance was not very prolonged, and the Abhasians fled, after a little desultory fighting. The column then resumed its march, burning the villages on the road; and intelligence afterwards arrived that the Abhasians had occupied a fresh position on the crest of a range of hills, separated from their enemies by a deep valley. From this point they fired on the Russian column with some effect; but in the end the position was taken by the infantry, aided by the four guns which accompanied the expedition. The burning of villages still continued, and an immense amount of damage was effected. All this while, the cavalry had been scouring the country with the same object and the same results. Here and there, the miserable fugitives made a stand, and fired into the ranks of their foe; but the effort never lasted more than a few minutes, and the losses of the Russians were but slight. The country behind the avengers was now a dense mass of smoke, rising from the numerous villages which had been set on fire. At about three in the afternoon the column retreated, having destroyed, according to the estimate of the writer already quoted, about a hundred and fifty houses, in each of which the average number of occupants was five or six. The persons rendered homeless by this raid must therefore have amounted to several hundreds, and the whole expedition had been conducted in a spirit of remorseless cruelty, which may have had its effect in breaking the courage of the Abhasians, but which cannot be recognized as consistent with the rules of modern warfare. Many of the troops employed were Georgians, and therefore to a great extent barbarians; but if Turkey is to be blamed for accepting the services of Bashi-Bazouks and other savage irregulars, Russia must be equally condemned for using a very similar set of marauders as the instruments of her vengeance.

It had been thought that the progress of the war would induce the Kingdom of Greece to take up a position hostile to Turkey, in the hope of increasing its boundaries by the addition of Thessaly, Epirus, and other provinces filled mainly with a population of Hellenic origin; but up to the present time Greece had remained quiet. At the latter end of August, however, the fortunes of the little monarchy were brought prominently before the notice of the English public by a statement in the *Daily Telegraph*, which has since led to so much discussion that some account of the controversy cannot be omitted from these pages. The sympathies of the *Daily Telegraph* were very strongly in favour of the Turks, and on the 28th of August that journal contained a telegram from its correspondent at Pera, to the effect that papers had just been discovered, showing that Mr. Gladstone had been trying to stir up the Greeks against Turkey, in defiance of the neutrality of England, and of his own professions of a desire for peace. About two months previously, according to this telegram, Mr. Gladstone had written a letter to a Greek merchant in Constantinople, urging that his countrymen should unite with the Sclaves in an attack upon the Turks. M. Negroponte, the gentleman addressed, was said to have replied that the interests of the Greeks were different from those of the Sclaves; that the best policy of Greece was rather to fight the Russians than the Turks; and that Greece, if she were wise, would remain tranquil. The statement went on to declare that Mr. Gladstone, in answer to this, wrote a second letter, very curtly worded, saying that he had expressed his views, and was astonished to find the Christians of the East so disinclined to make common cause against the Mussulmans. It was added that he again urged the Greeks to attack the Ottomans, and that M. Negroponte wound up the correspondence by giving it as his conviction that Mr. Gladstone's was not good advice. In answer to these statements, Mr. Gladstone published in the papers a brief notification, saying that his opinions on the subject had been fully expounded in the *Contemporary Review* of the previous December (1876), and that he was "not aware" of having added to them in any letter. On the 15th of September, a communication from M. Negroponte appeared in the English newspapers, emphatically denying that Mr. Gladstone's letter was of the nature attributed to it by the *Daily Telegraph*. "Out of delicacy," said M. Negroponte, "I will not mention the name of the person from whom undoubtedly proceeded the information which gave rise to the despatch to your contemporary, and the perversion of the contents of the letters in question. I leave it, however, to public opinion in England to form a judgment as to how far this may be considered honourable conduct on the part of a person of consequence." Mr. Gladstone afterwards obtained a copy of the first letter to M. Negroponte, published it in the newspapers of September 25th, and at the same time observed that the correspondent of the *Daily Telegraph* had been no more than a dupe in the business. "There is some Polonius behind the curtain," he said; "and I call upon him to come out." Upon this the

ABHASIAN MOUNTAINEERS.

Daily Telegraph remarked that the statement made by its correspondent was based on a description given by several distinguished persons who had seen the letters. It averred that the first letter was one of a series, and that to substantiate the full correspondence it was necessary for its informant to do one of two things—either to obtain complete files from M. Negroponte, or to transfer to the diplomatic authorities all responsibility for naming the original author of the allegation. The correspondent could not answer the first of these conditions, as M. Negroponte withheld the originals; nor could he fulfil the second, because those who had seen the correspondence placed what they had mentioned to him under the seal of confidence. The *Daily Telegraph* therefore, on behalf of its correspondent, withdrew the statement it had made, but at the same time insinuated that this was on purely technical grounds, and because circumstances prevented the substantiation of what, nevertheless, the journal evidently regarded as true.

All who paid any attention to public affairs inferred that the "Polonius" to whom Mr. Gladstone alluded was Mr. Layard, the British Ambassador at Constantinople. Mr. Layard, however, was rather slow in accepting the challenge which had been thrown out. It was not until October 29th that he wrote a despatch to Lord Derby, giving his own version of the facts. He here stated that he had communicated the contents of the letter, through a member of his Embassy, to the correspondent of the *Daily Telegraph;* that the correspondent took time to inquire into the matter; and that, having satisfied himself that a correspondence was going on between Mr. Gladstone and M. Negroponte, and that the Greeks were under the impression that Mr. Gladstone had been stirring them up to unite with the Sclaves, he (the correspondent) telegraphed to that effect on Monday, August 27th, and his telegram was published on the following day. He accused Mr. Gladstone of having suppressed other letters that had passed between him and M. Negroponte, of declining to publish copies of the original correspondence, and of refusing to make known a letter he had received from the *Times* correspondent, which would have disproved the statements of M. Negroponte. Mr. Gladstone, on the 20th of November, required further explanation; but the whole of December, 1877, and the early part of January, 1878, passed without Mr. Layard taking any additional notice of the matter. To a telegram from the Foreign Office, requesting further particulars, the Ambassador replied that he did not think it necessary to prolong the controversy. The discussion, however, was continued in a letter from Mr. Gladstone to Lord Tenterden (secretary to Lord Derby), dated the 28th of January, 1878, and laid before Parliament together with the rest of the Negroponte correspondence. The right honourable gentleman here accused Mr. Layard of having transmitted to the anonymous correspondent of a London journal an injurious accusation against him, which was forwarded by telegraph, and published accordingly. This once more summoned the Ambassador to the field. In a dispatch to the Earl of Derby, written from Constantinople on the 19th of February, 1878, Mr. Layard affirmed that there was no foundation whatever for the charge. He had casually mentioned to a gentleman connected with the Embassy that he might tell the correspondent of the *Daily Telegraph*, as a piece of news, that there was a letter from Mr. Gladstone to M. Negroponte, which was then in the hands of another newspaper correspondent. The statement transmitted to the *Daily Telegraph* was not sent until a week later; it was not suggested by Mr. Layard, and when it appeared was read by him with surprise. It would seem that the letter was in the first instance given by M. Negroponte to the correspondent of the *Times*, who showed it to the Ambassador; and that the representative of the other journal, on hearing from Mr. Layard of its existence, obtained for himself some further particulars, and at once forwarded them to his principals. In his communication to the papers of September 25th, Mr. Gladstone stated that his correspondence with M. Negroponte took place when the Conference was sitting at Constantinople; that is to say, at a time when it was hoped that war would be averted, and when any appeal to the Greek people would certainly have had far less importance than during the crisis of a desperate war, when Turkey was engaged in a life-and-death struggle with an antagonist of overwhelming power. He said nothing of any communication since the outbreak of hostilities; but there was in fact a letter from himself to M. Negroponte, dated July 21st, 1877—a letter which its author published some months after the controversy with the *Daily Telegraph*. In that letter, Mr. Gladstone remarked:—"It was and is far from my intention to pronounce upon the merits of the controversy between Greek and Sclave. I sought only to insist [*i.e.*, in the previous letter or letters] upon the policy and duty of treating the Christian cause as one in the face of the Ottoman power and influence, and of adjourning to a future juncture the settlement of the inter-Christian controversies. It has not been thought right to act upon this principle, but upon the opposite one; thought right, I mean, among the Hellenes of the Empire. *Events seem to me to be rapidly supplying materials for a judgment on the question whether the policy thus pursued has been a wise one.* It certainly has not raised up, at least in this country, one solitary friend to the Hellenic cause. *I hope it is not too late to change.*" On the 21st of July, when Mr. Gladstone wrote that letter, the tide of success, as far as Europe was concerned, was only just beginning to turn in favour of the Turks. The Russians were still on the southern side of the Balkans; Adrianople was still menaced; it was still believed in England that Plevna was in imminent danger. Under these circumstances, Mr. Gladstone was understood to have reproached the Greeks with not going to the assistance of the Russians, and giving the final blow to Turkey. In the opinion of many observers, the cause of Bulgaria was being championed by Russia for her own ends, and those ends would be fatal to the future of the Greeks. This was very well understood in Greece itself; it was understood in all the political circles of Europe; it had been repeatedly pointed out in England. But Mr. Gladstone was angry with the Hellenes for not seeing the question in the same light.

The matter was brought before the attention of Parliament on the 12th of March, 1878, by Mr. Evelyn Ashley, the member for Poole. That gentleman moved that the House, having had laid before it the correspondence between her Majesty's Ambassador at Constantinople and the Foreign Office, relating to certain charges which had been made against the right honourable the member for Greenwich, based on his letters to M. Negroponte, viewed with regret the part taken in the matter by her Majesty's Ambassador. On that occasion, Mr. Layard was ably defended by Mr. Bourke (the Under-Secretary for Foreign Affairs), by the Solicitor-General, and by the Chancellor of the Exchequer; and on a division Mr. Ashley's motion was defeated by 206 votes against 132. But the numerical victory would have been worth little had it not been supported by a preponderance of argument on the side of the Ambassador. In one respect, perhaps, Mr. Layard may have been open to blame. It is not desirable that men of high and responsible position should be in frequent communication with the representatives of the press. The practice has of late years been imported from America, and is growing to an extent which seems to demand some check. Mr. Layard, however, did no more than what a great many public men are doing every day of their lives, and in the particular instance impugned he does not seem to have intentionally wronged Mr. Gladstone. Whether it is consistent with the dignity of an Ambassador to receive information from one newspaper correspondent, and then convey it in a circuitous and imperfect way to another, is a question distinct from the main issue, and one which in this place it would be superfluous to discuss, however interesting it may be as a matter of general policy.

CHAPTER XXXII.

Relative Position of the Russians and Turks after the Struggle for the Shipka Pass—Operations of the Army of the Czarewitch on the Lom—General Leonoff at Karahassankoi—Attack by the Russians on the 30th of August—Prolonged and Sanguinary Struggle—Splendid Resistance of the Russians against Superior Numbers—General Retreat along the whole Line—Fighting renewed on the 31st—Taking of Kadikoi by the Turks—Perils of the Russian Position—Advance of the Turks towards Biela—Seizing of the Bridge at Pyrgos—Sortie from Plevna by the Army of Osman Pasha—The Russians surprised—Hard Fighting, and Defeat of the Turks—Address of Prince Charles of Roumania to his Troops—State of Affairs in the Shipka Pass—Importance of the Position to the Russians—Retaking of Loftcha by Generals Imeretinsky and Skobeleff—Gallant Capture of a Turkish Redoubt—Retreat of the Turks in a Westerly Direction—Preparations for a Renewed Attack on Plevna—The Military Situation before that Town on the 6th of September—Ineffectual Fighting on the 7th—The Struggle resumed on the 8th—Power of the Russian Artillery—Causes of the Failure of the Russian Attack on the Grivica Redoubt—Further Movements on the 8th of September—Desultory Encounters on the 9th—An Eventless Day—Hopeful Anticipations for the Morrow.

August was drawing to a close on the bloodstained fields of Bulgaria, and it was still a very doubtful matter which of the two combatants would finally prevail. The fortunes of Russia had certainly improved in some degree since the closing days of July, when the attacks of Krüdener and Schahofskoy on the entrenched positions at Plevna were defeated with such terrible loss. Reinforcements were beginning to arrive, and the armies of the Czar had shown that they were capable of holding the Shipka Pass against the determined assaults of Suleiman Pasha. Yet the invaders were still able to do little more than stand on the defensive, and the Turks were pushing them hard in several places.

Their position would have been much worse if the three Ottoman armies, under Mehemet Ali, Suleiman Pasha, and Osman Pasha, had been able to unite. Indeed, in that case the Russians must have been overwhelmed. But Osman Pasha was held fast in Plevna, though he could not be dislodged; Suleiman Pasha was unable to get through the Shipka Pass; and Mehemet Ali was fully engaged in the vicinity of the Lom. It was expected that Mehemet would support the movement in the Balkans by attacking the pass from the north, so as to enclose had their influence on the fortunes of the campaign. The Turks did not follow up with energy their success of August 24th, and on both sides a pause ensued for several days. One of the Russian commanders, General Leonoff, was at that time holding with a small cavalry force the little village of Karahassankoi—an advanced position situated on high ground, where the hills separating the Kara or Black Lom from the Ak or White Lom decline into a flat-topped ridge, running southward towards Eski-Juma. The Cossack outposts occupied a por-

RUSSIAN ENCAMPMENT IN A CEMETERY, KARAHASSANKOI.

the Russians between two fires; but this he was unable to do, owing to the repeated and vigorous demonstrations of the army commanded by the Czarewitch. The main body of the Russian left wing had for some time been established in the valley of the Lom, with one extremity stretching towards Rustchuk, and the other towards Osman Bazar; and several unsuccessful attempts to win ground from the Turks had been made by these troops, as already related. The Russians, it is true, failed in improving their position; but they effectually stopped the divisions of Mehemet Ali from going to the assistance of Suleiman Pasha.

The operations of the Czarewitch were continued with much spirit throughout some weeks, and they

tion of this ridge bordering on a small grove of trees, which was full of Circassian videttes; and the Russian line was continued down the valley to the village of Popkoi. Other detachments of the Czarewitch's army were stationed in various hamlets, but were much scattered and exposed. On the 28th of August, General Leonoff was reinforced by a regiment of infantry of the Thirty-fifth Division, commanded by Colonel Nazaroff, who brought with him several field-pieces, which increased the number to ten, though of these only two were of large calibre. A few rifle-pits were dug along the slope; small batteries were erected on each side of Karahassankoi; and it was hoped that the position might be held even against the superior force which was known to be in the vicinity of Rasgrad. This force consisted of 30,000 Turks, with sixty guns; and it was certain that an attack would very shortly be delivered. Operations against the Russian left wing were simultaneously commenced from two points on the 29th of August. One column, under Nedjib Pasha, proceeded from Rasgrad towards Karahassankoi, which stands about three miles to the north of Yenikoi, and six or seven miles south of Agaslar. The other column, commanded by Salih Pasha, left Eski-Juma to join the force already at Agaslar, and both of these co-operated with Nedjib in making a powerful attack on the forces of General Leonoff. Indications of an advance were detected by a Cossack on the morning of the 30th, and immediately afterwards a discharge of musketry burst from out the maize-fields along the ridge, a mile east of the village. General Leonoff's force consisted of about 3,000 infantry, 500 cavalry, and the ten guns already mentioned. The cavalry were at once sent to the flanks; two guns were dragged through the woods on the left into the corn-field; two others (the heavy ones) were posted on the ridge, under cover of some shrubs and bushes; and two more occupied the battery near the village, to the right of the Russian line. A large number of Turkish horsemen soon afterwards moved down the opposite hill-side, galloped across the valley, and burned the village of Sadina. Some shots from the Cossack battery in the corn-field drove them back; but the next moment the whole hill-side swarmed with hostile soldiery, who seemed as if they had suddenly sprung up out of the earth. The Turkish batteries on the opposite slopes opened fire at the same time, and it soon appeared that the Ottomans had brought an extraordinary number of guns into play, and had stationed them in a great many localities bearing with terrible effect on the ridge occupied by the Russians.

Carrying all before them like a torrent, the Turks came trooping on, and the two heavy guns were forced to retire from their position on the ridge. Meanwhile, a desperate struggle was proceeding in the fields covered with the high stalks of the maize, in the depths of which luxuriant growth the opposing cavalry slaughtered each other with sustained and dreadful fury. After a prolonged contest, the Turks forced their way into the village of Karahassankoi, a portion of which was set on fire; but the infantry continued to maintain their positions with obstinate courage. All the guns were sent to the rear, where they again opened fire; but the superiority of the Turks was unmistakable. The situation was the more trying on account of the glaring sun and oppressive heat. Nevertheless, the Russians still presented a defiant front to the enemy, though the whole country for miles around was shadowed by the smoke of Turkish artillery, and by the clouds of dust and earth thrown up by the bursting shells. Large numbers of wounded straggled back towards Gagovo, in the rear of the Russian line, and from that direction reinforcements were anxiously expected. They did not come, however, until about two o'clock in the afternoon, when the action had been going on for nearly six hours; and their number was not more than three hundred—a force quite insufficient to repair the heavy losses which the Russians had endured. The disproportion between the assailants and the assailed was therefore even greater than at first, especially as the Turks were receiving continual accessions of infantry and cavalry. Yet for two hours longer the struggle was maintained with admirable spirit, and the Osmanlis, though still advancing, were confronted by a stubborn foe, who grudged every inch of ground he was compelled to relinquish, and exacted a heavy price for it. Leonoff's infantrymen, however, were at length completely exhausted, and at four o'clock P.M., began to retire. The engagement had extended over some fifteen miles, and, while the chief fighting was being maintained at Karahassankoi, the Turks created a diversion by attacking Haidar-koi, on the opposite side of the Lom, from which the Russians were driven forth. Towards evening, the retreat was general, and the conquerors occupied the positions which their enemies had recently held. The Russians fell back on Papaskoi, with no other consolation for their defeat than the knowledge that they had inflicted on their adversaries a loss nearly equal to their own.

Mehemet Ali, in a despatch to his Government, telegraphed on the day of the battle, stated that the Chief of the Staff, Rifaat Pasha, who had been sent during the day to Karahassankoi, returned in the evening, and reported that a battalion of the Jerusalem Redifs, belonging to the Salih Brigade, had captured a cannon, four ammunition-waggons, and a number of carts, containing two thousand rifles, two thousand coats, and a large amount of military equipments. The English officer, Baker Pasha, greatly distinguished himself in the operations of the 30th, and the horse he rode was struck by a shell. Fighting was renewed on the following day, when the Turkish army concentrated in strong force on the western bank of the Lom, and at the same time eight Ottoman battalions, accompanied by some cavalry, advanced from Rustchuk against Kadikoi, on the road from Rustchuk to Rasgrad,

THE BATTLE OF KARAHASSANKOI.

1. Salina. 2 Karahassankoi. 3. Gagovo destroyed by the Bombardment. 4. Popkoi 5. Haidarkoi. 7. River Lom. 8. Cossack Squadron. 9 Bashi Bazouks 10. Turkish Army coming from Rasgrad. 11, 12, 14, 15. Russian Batteries. 13. Turkish Battery near Rasgrad firing upon 11 and 12. 16, 17, 18, 19. Turkish Batteries. 20. Turkish Riflemen crossing the Lom.

and drove out the Russians. Later in the day, however, the Turks were attacked by the Ukraine infantry regiment of the Twelfth Division, and compelled to retire under the guns of Rustchuk. But the struggle was not over. Kadikoi was again assailed by the Turks on the 4th of September, and once more taken after a sharp action. The Ottoman General on this occasion was Ahmed Eyoub, who on the 5th proceeded ten miles south, and reached Kazelevo, another Russian outpost authorities, or want of sufficient numbers to resist a menacing advance. The Turks were pushing on towards Biela, which until recently had been the head-quarters of the Russian army; and as yet there appeared to be nothing to stand in their way. The garrison of Rustchuk felt themselves so much in the position of superiority that they undertook an enterprise against the boats of the enemy carrying reinforcements over the Danube. Seizing the bridge at Pyrgos, they compelled the divisions

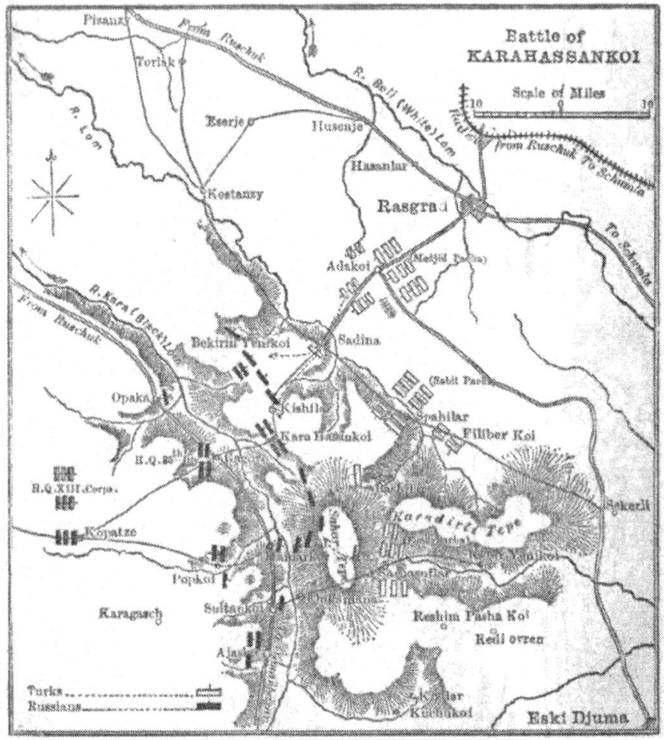

PLAN OF THE BATTLE OF KARAHASSANKOI.

on the Lom, where he defeated the Twelfth Russian Army Corps. As before, the Russians were greatly outnumbered; the position was surrounded, after six hours' fighting, and the town passed into the hands of the Moslems. The whole valley of the Lom had now been recovered by the armies of the Sultan, which had driven their opponents westward, and obtained possession of the road leading from Rustchuk to Osman Bazar. The Russians in that quarter had in truth been overwhelmed. In the battle of August 30th, Leonoff's forces had been overmatched, in the proportion, it is believed, of six to one; but to leave such weak detachments in exposed positions indicated either great carelessness on the part of the Russian military intended for the Czarewitch to go round by the bridge at Sistova, which, being at a considerable distance from Giurgevo—the point opposite Rustchuk where they designed to cross—entailed a serious loss of time, and obliged the Czarewitch to fall back on the line of the Jantra. At the same period, the Grand Duke Nicholas transferred his head-quarters from Gorny Studen to Radenica, a village between Bulgareni and Poradim — thus drawing nearer to the important positions before Plevna.

The chief command of the Russo-Roumanian army in that quarter was conferred, about the end of August, on Prince Charles of Roumania, with General Zotoff as Chief of the Staff, or second in command. On the 31st of the month, these commanders had to sustain a furious sortie by Osman Pasha. At six o'clock in the morning, a large force of Turkish cavalry advanced between Radisovo and Grivica, and drove in the Russian advanced posts on the line between the villages of Pelisat and Sgalince. Two hours later, the Ottomans developed an attack in force on the enemy's positions. The Russians engaged on this occasion consisted of three regiments of the Sixteenth Division, with two battalions of the Thirtieth Division in reserve. These were afterwards joined by the Uhlans and Hussars of the Fourth Cavalry Division, who arrived in time to render assistance to their comrades. The Russians were completely taken by surprise. General Zotoff was paying a visit to Prince Charles, and both were at some distance from the scene of action. No one of sufficient authority to make comprehensive dispositions was on the spot when the attack commenced; so that the several divisions were left to do the best they could by sheer hard fighting until the arrival of Zotoff, who hurried up on hearing what was occurring at the front. From the first it was evident that the conflict would be serious, and the Bulgarian population of the neighbouring villages began to fly with their carts, cattle, and effects. Several of these people were permanently encamped in waggons, or in hastily-constructed straw huts; and whenever the Turks made an advance, they retreated to some fresh position.

The fighting on the 31st was long and bloody. The weak point in the Russian defence was the village of Sgalince and the hollow near it, which formed the centre; and this position changed hands several times during the struggle. The Russian redoubt a mile in front of Pelisat—about eight or nine miles south-east of Plevna—was taken by the Turks early in the fight, and the left wing of the Muscovite force was then driven back on Pelisat, before which trenches had been dug, and lined with troops. This enabled the Turks to operate with effect on the centre, situated at a distance of two miles north of Pelisat; and a desperate engagement, marked by varying fortunes, took place among the hollows of the undulating ground. The entrenchments of the Russians were attacked repeatedly by the Turks, who lost large numbers in the endeavour to carry them. Amazing determination and heroism were exhibited by the assailants in their attempts to drive back the enemy; but to the last the trenches were held by the soldiers of the Czar. Finally, the Turks retreated, carrying off their wounded and many of their slain; yet they still possessed the redoubt in front of Pelisat, and appeared bent on retaining it, even at the cost of another deadly wrestle. The Russians, however, were not disposed to see them in so threatening a position, and accordingly made a spirited attack on the captured work, from which the Moslems were expelled at the point of the bayonet. Nothing could exceed the courage of both combatants during this arduous day, the fighting on which did not cease until four o'clock in the afternoon. The chances of the Turks do not seem to have been very good at any time; for, even in the event of their carrying the trenches, they would have had to encounter large bodies of Russian reserves, which, being fresh, would assuredly have inflicted on them a defeat. Osman Pasha afterwards described the affair as a reconnaissance in force; but it was probably more than that. It seems to have been an attempt to drive the enemy from all his positions; but, if so, the failure of the design was complete.

On being appointed to the command of the Russo-Roumanian army before Plevna, Prince Charles addressed a manifesto to the soldiers of his adopted country, in which he remarked that the war was approaching their frontier, and that, if the Turks were victorious, the united Principalities would be invaded, and made to suffer carnage, pillage, and desolation. Under those circumstances, it was the duty of Roumanians to save their country from the savagery of such foes, and to encounter them on their own soil. The Prince assured his subjects that they possessed "all the old Rouman heart"—by which he no doubt meant the old Roman heart, as the people of the Principalities are said to be descended from Imperial colonists. "Though small in numbers," continued the Prince, "the Roumanian army will, I am sure, earn distinction by its discipline and bravery; it will retain for Roumania the rank which it has hitherto deserved and enjoyed amongst the nations of Europe. This also is the belief of the august Emperor of All the Russias, and, for these reasons, not only will the Roumanians co-operate with the Russians on the same field and for the same end, but the supreme command of the two armies before Plevna has been confided to me." The address, however, did not inspire the Roumanians with any greater liking for the war than they had previously felt. They looked with apprehension on the departure of the army to the southern side of the Danube, arguing that, in case their own forces and those of the Russians should be finally defeated, they would have no means of defending their country successfully against a Turkish invasion.

The position of affairs in the Shipka Pass remained for a long while without alteration after the withdrawal of Suleiman Pasha on the 31st of August. General Radetzky retained the positions he had held with such stubborn determination against the Turkish attacks, and lost no time in strengthening them. His advanced centre was established on Mount St. Nicholas, and his right and left flanks rested upon two crests, which stood a little to the north of that point. To his extreme right and left were ridges extending parallel to the Russian wings, and running northward nearly to answer, he continued, was clear to any one standing upon Mount St. Nicholas. Ravines and mountain-crests lie on all sides of that eminence as far as the eye can reach, even with the aid of a powerful glass. An army holding the chief summit could sweep down upon an enemy defending the southern end of the pass, and, turning his flanks by means of the innumerable ravines which run in every direction, could force him out into the plains of Roumelia. "The Balkans," said this authority, "could be traversed by infantry in every direction; and so

ARRIVAL OF PRINCE CHARLES OF ROUMANIA TO TAKE COMMAND OF THE ARMY BEFORE PLEVNA.

the Gabrova road—the only line of communication for the Russian troops. Since the great struggle, the Russians had held the crest formerly occupied by the Turks on their right wing, and the Ottomans had fallen back to the next ridge, where they still kept up a desultory fire with the Russian pickets. Radetzky had also a species of second centre on a peak lying about half a mile to the rear of Mount St. Nicholas. Strong batteries were constructed on all the Russian heights, and they were considered to be practically impregnable. The Special Correspondent of the *Times* in that locality said it might be asked what object the Russians could have in defending so obstinately the centre of the Shipka Pass, while the Turks held the southern end. The

singular is the conformation of the ground that flanking columns could move nearly everywhere without exposing themselves to fire. It would require an army of gigantic magnitude to take up a position in those mountains which could not be turned by a flank movement of infantry carrying four days' rations in their haversacks; and as it is impossible to put artillery in any position not directly connected with the practicable passes, flanking columns of infantry would only find themselves opposed by infantry." The possession of the Shipka Pass, therefore, gave the Russians a command over Roumelia, and it would have been bad policy to sacrifice such a position, even although its retention demanded a large expenditure of life.

But for the present the interests of the struggle lay in a somewhat different direction, and had the country about Plevna for its centre. A brilliant success was achieved by the Russians on the 3rd of September, when Loftcha, which had been captured by Osman Pasha on the 26th of July, was wrested from the Turks. For some days, a body of troops, numbering about 22,000, had been collected under Prince Imeretinsky to the east and south of that town, which is situated twenty miles south of Plevna. It was important that, before the Russians made their next attack on Plevna, Loftcha should once more pass into their hands, since they would thus be enabled to cut off the communications of Osman Pasha with the south. The preparations for this enterprise were made with great secrecy, and the Turks were surprised in the first instance by the seizure of two peaks, to the north-east of the town, by the younger General Skobeleff, who had marched up from Kakrina, on the Selvi road, to join the attacking force. These positions were taken on the afternoon of Sunday, September 2nd, and Prince Imeretinsky then made his dispositions for attacking Loftcha itself next morning. The town is built on the banks of the Osma, at the junction of roads leading to Plevna and Nicopolis, to Selvi, Gabrova, Tirnova, and the valley of the Isker. The fighting on the 3rd of September was conducted by the entire Russian force in that quarter, composed of the Second Division, the Second Brigade of the Third Division, two regiments of Cossacks, ten batteries of artillery, and a brigade of Tirailleurs. The Turks, according to their own account, had only eight battalions of infantry, and at any rate were numerically inferior to their opponents. The battle began at six o'clock in the morning with heavy firing from the peaks previously secured by Skobeleff. The Turks had already fallen back on a fortified range of heights behind the town, and in this position they awaited the attack. Their batteries were well planted on elevated ridges ; two redoubts defended their position, and there were also rifle-pits and trenches in every direction likely to be

TAKING A TURKISH REDOUBT AT LOFTCHA.

assailed by infantry. The lines of defence were therefore strong, and the troops defended them with the utmost energy; yet the fortunes of the day were unfavourable to the Ottomans. The cannonade from Skobeleff's positions helped to divert attention from the forward movement of General Debloffolski, who, with a brigade of Tirailleurs, advanced in the direction of a ridge on the right bank of the Osma, which overhangs the town.

The two redoubts were situated on this ridge, and it was with a view to their reduction that Debloffolski advanced to the attack at seven o'clock A.M. He was joined before nine by two regiments of infantry, and the assault then commenced.

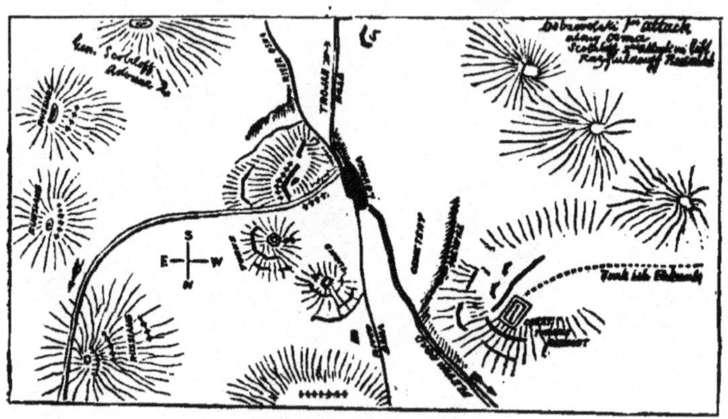

PLAN OF LOFTCHA.

After an hour and a half of desperate fighting, the first redoubt was carried; but the second, called Mount Rous, presented still greater obstacles than the first. The attack on this position was conducted by General Skobeleff at the head of ten battalions. At twenty minutes to eleven in the forenoon, his column was seen moving down the slope of an amphitheatre of hills, and crossing the little valley which intervenes between that declivity and Mount Rous. At the same time the Russian artillery opened a tremendous shell-fire upon the redoubt, but the Turks replied with firmness. A regiment from the reserve was then sent down a defile to the right of the head-quarters, to take Mount Rous in flank, and cut off the Turkish line of retreat. Between twelve and one o'clock, a battery was moved up to support the advance of this regiment, and ten minutes later Skobeleff's column rushed up a causeway leading along the eastern end of the redoubt, and occupied the neighbouring heights with infantry. The garrison of the Turkish batteries then withdrew in a southerly direction towards Trajan, carrying their artillery with them. By one in the afternoon, all the Turkish positions had been taken, with the exception of a redoubt on the Plevna causeway, commanding a little valley at the bottom of the amphitheatre of hills, and strengthened by outlying detached works, designed to flank any attacking force. It now only remained to conquer this position; but the task was one of no small difficulty. An hour was spent in bringing batteries up to the summit of Mount Rous, and placing them in position; but at half-past two the Russian column of attack from the right wing was ordered to advance. A correspondent of the *Times*, who witnessed the action, records that "between the foot of the amphitheatre, and the base of the hill upon which the redoubt was constructed, was a level plain, half a mile wide, forming the bottom of the valley. The attacking force was compelled to cross this little plain under the musketry-fire of the Turkish infantry, securely ensconced behind their parapets. As the Russians emerged from cover, they came upon a level grass-plot from one hundred to four hundred yards wide. Then came the river Osma, about twenty yards in breadth, and a foot in depth, with wide reaches of dry, white pebbles on each bank, where the water runs in time of flood. By the side of the river is the Plevna *chaussée*, and between the *chaussée* and the foot of the hill where the redoubt is situated is an old Turkish cemetery, about four hundred yards in width. The hill of the redoubt was a bluff of some hundred yards opposite the Russian attacking force, and, by a strange oversight, the Turks had no flanking trenches to sweep the face of this bluff. Therefore, when the Russians reached that place, they were safe from fire. Along the *chaussée* and the left bank of the Osma were several low ridges of earth, high enough to cover a man in a creeping posture; and these places of refuge were resting-places in that deadly race for the bluff. The cemetery had a number of tall flagstones standing upright, and they were taken advantage of by the advancing soldiers. The attacking force contained the two regiments named after the German Emperor, and some men of the army-corps which was at Plevna. It was commanded by Major-General Razmindaieff. The men rushed across the valley, amid a perfect hailstorm of bullets. In a few minutes the green sward and the white pebbles were dotted with dead and wounded Russians, and the survivors were resting under the little ridges of the *chaussée* and the Osma. The men advanced in open order at a rush, and the Turks kept up a steady stream of fire. There was not the slightest break in the rain of bullets, and yet it was wonderful to see how small a proportion of the shots took effect. Sometimes a single soldier would run across the whole space between the river and the bluff. There were minutes when no Russian was under fire, and yet the Turks never stopped firing."

It appeared that the defenders were lying down in their trenches, and firing at random over the parapets. The attacking force consequently did not suffer so much as might have been expected, and by three o'clock a considerable body of Russians had collected under the bluff, and were working round to the angle of the redoubt looking up the Plevna causeway. At the same time, another party crept up the face of the bluff, and opened fire on that part of the redoubt which looked towards Loftcha. The latter movement, however, was only a feint to attract the attention of the Turks from the force moving to the right under the bluff. North of the Plevna road, a Russian force soon made its appearance with a battery of artillery to cut off the Turkish retreat. Another attacking column was presently seen advancing up the river from the extreme right of the Russian line, and it soon appeared that its business was to reinforce the troops already stationed under the northern end of the bluff. Two batteries were then advanced along the causeway nearly to the outskirts of the town; but the redoubt still remained untaken. Some of the Turkish trenches within a hundred yards of the ditch were carried at a rush; but four o'clock had arrived without the main work itself being in Muscovite hands. A feigned attack was shortly afterwards made upon the eastern face of the redoubt, and, after a prolonged rifle-fire, the real attack was delivered in another direction. The advance was followed by a steady stream of reinforcements, and the Russian batteries poured a fiery rain of shells upon the redoubt. The attack was conducted in gallant style, and, though several men fell under the rifle-fire of the Turks, the column still pressed on. Then the artillery ceased firing; the men leapt into the ditch, and clambered up the parapet; and another column rushed along the Loftcha face of the redoubt, to clear the advanced trenches. The struggle was soon over, and the Turks had no alternative but to surrender or fly. They chose the latter course, and, firing as they ran, retreated in a westerly direction. Had it been possible, they would naturally have retired upon Plevna; but the dispositions of their antagonists had effectually prevented this. The defeated army was not pursued, and the Russians afterwards acknowledged a loss of 1,000 men in achieving their success. The entire Turkish force in Loftcha is supposed not to have been more than 7,000, and these had for several hours conducted an unequal struggle against 22,000 of the enemy. On the following day (September 4th), Osman Pasha sent twenty-eight battalions to retake Loftcha, but found himself speedily compelled to withdraw his troops, owing to threatening operations in front of Plevna.

It was believed by the Russians that the time had arrived for making a renewed attack on the great fortified position, and thus repairing the numerous disasters which had attended their arms in that direction. They had now in front of Osman Pasha an army consisting of about 80,000 infantry (of whom two-thirds were Russian, and one-third was Roumanian), 10,000 cavalry (half Russian and half Roumanian), and 250 Russian siege-guns. The troops took up their positions on the evening of September 6th. The centre had Poradim for its base, and faced the principal redoubt of the Turks, situated on a saddle-backed ridge above the village of Grivica, or Grivitza, which is about five miles east of Plevna, and eight miles west of Poradim. The right wing, composed chiefly of Roumanians, was to the north and north-east of Plevna, while the left wing stretched down towards Loftcha, and faced Radisovo and the other Turkish posts to the south. The general position of the Turks was undoubtedly of a very formidable character, being aided both by nature and art. On the northern side of a causeway running from Plevna to Biela was a high ridge lying east and west, and terminating at the eastern extremity in a long, smooth slope, while towards the west it ended in a steeper declivity passing into the valley of Plevna The northern side of the ridge formed an extensive natural *glacis;* the southern side was steep, and struck rapidly down towards the causeway. Upon the top and in the centre of this ridge was a strong redoubt, which Baron Krüdener's men had vainly endeavoured to take in the terrible contest of the 31st of July; and the character of the neighbouring land was such as to offer no cover for advancing troops. The western side of the ridge was occupied by a vast entrenched camp, about a mile nearer Plevna than the great redoubt, and immediately in front were several smaller redoubts, constructed so as to protect the approaches to Plevna through the village of Radisovo from the direction of Loftcha.

These redoubts were described as forming in their combination a figure like a broad lance-head, with the point towards the Russians, and were so situated that, supposing one to be taken, the others would command it. To the south-east, and in the rear of Plevna, were various fortifications, and rifle-pits were scattered in all directions commanding the infantry approaches to the Turkish positions. The Russian lines were likewise elaborate. On the farther off were the Russian field-guns, stretching south and south-west as far as the Russian lines extended.* Speaking generally, the Turkish positions took the form of a horse-shoe, of which the convexity pointed towards the east, while the town of Plevna occupied the middle of the base. The Russians had for some time been surrounding the horse-shoe, leaving the base open. Grivica stood in the pointed part of the horse-shoe, and opposite

ROUMANIAN OUTPOST.

northern *glacis*, which stretched for miles without a break, were the Roumanian batteries, commanding the great redoubt, and also extending southwards to the centre line of the ridge. On the southern slope of that ridge, some Russian field-guns were brought to bear upon the redoubt, and the crest of the slope near the village of Grivica was planted with eight six-inch siege-guns, which could concentrate their fire on the same outwork. The head-quarters of Baron Krüdener (who still retained a command, though not the principal) were established two hundred yards in rear of this heavy battery; close by were twelve more guns of large calibre; and the salient angle of the Turkish positions was the Russo-Roumanian centre.

The attack began soon after daybreak on the morning of September 7th—a morning dense with mist, following on the sharp frost of the previous night. This fog afterwards cleared off, and the day became hot and brilliant; but the sun was often obscured by clouds of smoke, which hung over the valleys and the mountains, and revealed only too plainly the grim work which was going on beneath their sulphurous canopy. From the hills all round poured forth the reverberating discharges

* Correspondent of the *Times*.

of the Russo-Roumanian guns, to which the Turks replied with equal energy; and this continued throughout the day. The village of Radisovo was set on fire; but, although an enormous amount of powder had been expended, comparatively little mischief was inflicted by either side upon the other. During the progress of the action, some excitement was caused among the Russian troops by the appearance on the battle-field of the Emperor himself, who seems to have been anxious as to the turn of events. It was the anniversary of his coronation, one and twenty years before. A rude platform was constructed on the field, and from this elevation his Majesty contemplated the scene of conflict. The Grand Duke Nicholas also visited the positions during the day.

The contest was resumed on the following morning, September 8th. During the night, the Turks had repaired the parapet of the Grivica Redoubt, which had been somewhat injured by the Russian guns, and the Ottomans seemed in every way fully prepared to meet their adversaries on equal terms. But the hours of darkness had been turned to account by the Russians likewise, for their working parties were pushed forward in the direction of Grivica, and a battery of siege-guns was erected on an elevation overhanging that village, and at no great distance from the redoubt. This battery came into action as soon as it was light, and was supported by isolated guns of large size. The original battery of siege-guns also lent its aid, and the Turkish redoubt, though replying with spirit, began to suffer visibly. The Russian guns were admirably worked, and occasionally the enemy was silenced by the excellence of their practice; but as soon as the damages were repaired, the Turks renewed their defence with as much spirit as ever. The awful artillery-fire continued on the 8th with scarcely any intermission, and still the Turks replied with the dogged determination which is one of their greatest military characteristics. In the hollows between the Russian batteries—in the valleys now overhung by a curtain of smoke and flame—the Bulgarian villagers went on with their agricultural operations, as if nothing extraordinary were occurring to break the peace of nature. Yet some idea of the tremendous artillery power now being brought to bear on the Grivica Redoubt may be gathered from Mr. Archibald Forbes's description of the Russian battery on the right flank. This battery, consisting of twelve siege-guns, had three faces. The left, armed with six guns, looked down the valley towards Plevna, and concentrated its fire on the redoubt and fortified village known as the Turkish first position. The centre face, with three guns, looked towards a Turkish redoubt behind that of Grivica, and connecting it with the great Plitzitza position on the due north flank of Plevna; while the right face, armed with three guns, fronted the Grivica Redoubt itself. But on the 8th of September the Turks were developing a still wider range of artillery-fire than on the 31st of July, when Krüdener and Schahofskoy vainly endeavoured to take Plevna by assault; so that, in spite of all their preparations, the prospects of the Russians remained far from hopeful.

It was originally proposed that four hundred guns should be brought to bear upon the Turkish lines; but up to September 8th not more than a hundred and twenty at the utmost had been placed in position. The number of shells thrown into the Grivica Redoubt was enormous, yet the effect produced was slight. On the right and centre of the Russian line, the attack had all the character of a siege; on the left, the operations were of a different nature. After the cannonade had continued some hours, a force of Russians, under Prince Imeretinsky and the younger Skobeleff, advanced rapidly along the ridge bordering the road from Loftcha to Plevna. This road, before entering the latter town, passes over a high hill, somewhat thickly covered with trees, the summit of which is about a mile and a half distant from the Turkish redoubts on the bend of the Sophia road. The Turks were posted at the foot of the hill; but the Russians, descending the slope, attacked them with vigour, and drove them back. The greater number retired upon the redoubt, and the Russians then pushed down almost to the bottom of the hill, when they were encountered by a terrible fire from the Ottoman works. The roar of the guns was fearful, and one unbroken flame glared out from the parapets of the opposing fort. The assailants nevertheless continued to advance for about twenty minutes, but were at length compelled to withdraw up the slope. The attack had failed, and the Turks were soon afterwards seen again issuing from the redoubt, and pushing forward as if they would turn the right of the Russian line. This, however, was more than could be accomplished, owing to the Russian infantry lying in large numbers behind the ridge; yet on the whole the Turks had had the best of the encounter when the sun set on the evening of that autumn day.

The failure of the attack was due in a great measure to its having been insufficiently supported from other directions, and to the unaccountable fact that just at the very time when the artillery

THE GIANT BATTERY BEFORE PLEVNA.

of the assailants was most needed, its fire wholly ceased. One small detachment was sent against a strongly entrenched position, without any assistance from other sections of the army. It is not surprising, therefore, that the men were beaten back, and compelled to retire to a position where they were comparatively safe from the Turkish guns. They were not safe, however, from attacks by the Turkish infantry, and one of these was made towards evening. The Ottomans dashed forward with animation up the slope on which the Russians had begun to entrench themselves, but were presently met by so terrific a rifle-fire that they retreated with precipitation, hotly pursued by their antagonists. The Russians had been reinforced, and they advanced with great rapidity and resolution, finding temporary shelter behind trees, banks of earth, or any other object that presented itself. They were now, moreover, supported by the batteries on the right, which had been pushed still nearer Plevna. But by this time the sun was setting. Deepened by the thick volumes of smoke, the evening twilight soon passed into darkness, and, although for some time longer bright jets of flame burst forth from the numerous guns of both combatants, it was evident that no further operations of importance could take place that night. The attempt to seize the redoubt had been unsuccessful, but it had resulted in the Russians obtaining a position much closer to the south of Plevna than they had previously held, and this encouraged them to further efforts in the same direction. A heavy artillery-fire was maintained throughout the night by the attacking force, and during the 9th the centre and right wing got still nearer the fortifications round the town. Some of the batteries were established very close to the Turkish lines; but between them and the points to be attacked was a broad sloping *glacis*, and the fire of the Turkish guns was powerful and threatening. Plevna was now much stronger than it had been on July 31st. Several wholly new redoubts had been erected on the south and south-west; and on the ridge stretching towards the river Vid a row of fortified works had sprung up, connected by a covered way, and affording the Turks excellent protection on their right flank. A perfect maze of fortifications extended in every direction, and the summits and slopes of the northern ridge have been described as a great entrenched camp, studded with redoubts and battery-emplacements. Osman Pasha had certainly made the most of his time since he first occupied Plevna about the middle of July. He had turned a mere village into a fortress of a very elaborate kind. North and south, east and west, and at many intermediate points, the place bristled with redoubts, earthworks, and trenches. Only before Radisovo could a weak point be discovered. The ridge in front of that village had not been occupied by the Turks, and its possession gave an advantage to the Russians.

RED CRESCENT FIELD AMBULANCE AND DOCTOR.

In the early hours of the 9th of September, the infantry commanded by Imeretinsky and Skobeleff withdrew to the summit of the wooded hill from which on the previous day they had conducted their attacks. The artillery-fire was resumed during the 9th, and a Turkish magazine exploded under the Russian shells. Skobeleff was attacked with considerable vehemence; but the Turks were repulsed, and even pursued for some distance at the point of the bayonet. All this while, the Russian guns continued their remorseless fire, and in the afternoon a fresh battery was constructed on the heights above Radisovo. At dusk, General Krüdener moved on to those heights with the Thirty-first Division; the troops took up favourable positions; and preparations were made for a renewed assault the following day. The 10th, however, passed off without any assault being ordered. It was considered advisable to subject the Turks to a further prolongation of the scathing shell-fire, and the 11th was regarded as a more propitious date, because of its being the fête-day of the Emperor. Beyond the continuance of the cannonade, and a few movements of little importance, the 10th of September was an eventless day. The Grand Duke, Prince Charles of Roumania, and General Zotoff, rode about to the several positions; ambulance-waggons were stationed at the most favourable points; and on all hands the morrow was awaited with anxiety, as the day on which a renewed attempt would be made, under more favourable conditions, to seize the fortified lines which the Turks were holding with such grim defiance.

CHAPTER XXXIII.

The Russian Attack on Plevna of the 11th of September—Fighting in a Thick Mist—Temporary Success, and ultimate Failure, of Kriloff's and Krüdener's Divisions—Mr. MacGahan's Account of the Struggle—Successful Attack on the Grivica Redoubt by the Roumanians—The Krishine Redoubt, and Another, taken by Skobeleff—Terrible Slaughter—Subsequent Loss of the Positions by the Russians—Excitement and Despair of Skobeleff—Bad State of the Russian Army—Gloomy Prospects in the Second Half of September—Military Qualities of the Russians—Mismanagement of the Campaign—Inefficiency of the General Staff—Discontent at St. Petersburg—Decline in the Reputation of Russia as a Military Power—The Reaction carried too far—Effect of Turkish Atrocities on the Firmness of the Russian Soldier—Probable Motives of the Turks in waging a War of Extermination—Withdrawal of the Russians from their advanced Positions before Plevna—Preparations for a Winter Campaign—Attempts of General Kriloff to intercept Supplies for the Garrison of Plevna—Failure of his Operations—The Town revictualled—Total Absence of Energy on the Part of the Invaders—Doubts as to the Ultimate Success of Russia.

When morning broke on the 11th of September, everything was veiled in a mist of autumn rain. Distant objects could hardly be detected at all, and even those which were close at hand looked ghostly through the vaporous air. The guns began again at an early hour of the morning, and the thick volumes of smoke added much to the obscurity. Shortly after ten, however, silence fell on the contending ranks, and in that ominous hush—broken only now and again by a solitary gun, which momentarily woke the echoes of the hills—the preparations for the grand assault were made. At exactly eleven o'clock, a rapid fire of musketry broke out on the left of Radisovo, and the Russians pushed on through the gap in the hills along which passes the road from Loftcha to Plevna. Into the dense fog and drizzling mist, made sulphurous and stifling by the gunpowder lavishly consumed, the attacking force descended, as into some under-world of gloom and terror. The Turks replied feebly with their artillery; but it must have been random firing, directed rather by the ear than by the eye. Covered by the general dimness, the Russians continued to advance, and their big guns fired incessantly at the invisible foe. The plan of the attack was that General Skobeleff, who had succeeded to the command of Prince Imeretinsky's force, should attack the Krishine Redoubt, and that other parts of the line should charge the adjacent works, whilst the Roumanians, supported by two Russian regiments, assaulted the Grivica Redoubt.

The mist was in some respects an embarrassment to the Russians; but at eleven, A.M., they moved forward in good order, and Kriloff's divisions got close up to the redoubt on the detached mamelon south-east of Plevna. Their success was only temporary, and the Ottomans, after repelling the attack, advanced against the batteries of their opponents along the whole line. Though fighting with the utmost gallantry, they were in their turn repulsed; but at half-past one in the afternoon the movement was renewed. General Krüdener shortly afterwards arrived on the ground, and his Staff expressed entire confidence in their ability to enter Plevna by nightfall. The Turks were once more driven back, and at half-past three the Russians began a fresh assault. Under cover of a tremendous artillery-fire, a mass of infantry, preceded by a skirmishing line, and followed by supports and reserves, advanced in loose order, drove the Turks out of the shelter-trenches at the foot of the mamelon, and dashed up the southern slope of the mound. They were soon joined by others, and, after a little hesitation, caused by the withering fire of the Turks, the assailants pressed on towards the object of attack. It was a murderous conflict. The inner trenches of the Ottomans extended one above another by the side of the ditch, immediately in front of the fortified position; and from the walls of earth sprang forth an incessant fire of musketry. Nevertheless, the Russians gained ground, though slowly, and with many losses. After awhile, they were threatened on their right flank by some Turkish reinforcements which had been sent to strengthen the garrison. The Muscovites promptly threw back their right, and fired into the advancing Turks, while the remainder of the line continued its advance against the inner trenches. The first of these was at length reached, and for a few minutes it was doubtful whether the fort itself would not be captured. But the slaughter at the foremost of the outworks was so terrific that the Russians were compelled to fall back. Their retreat was slow and orderly at the commencement; but when the Turkish infantry sallied forth in pursuit, sending volley after volley into the ranks of their exhausted opponents, the latter not unnaturally ran with precipitation, to get under the shelter of their own trenches. The dusk of evening shortly afterwards fell over the scene of conflict, and the Turks might fairly have supposed that all fighting was over for the day. Another attempt, however, was presently made to take the position. Fresh regiments were sent forward in the gathering darkness; but they were repulsed in about twenty minutes, and the operations of the day then came to a close. The Emperor and the Grand Duke were on the battle-field till nine o'clock at night, and at a later hour returned to head-quarters.

A SKETCH OF OSMAN PASHA.

Such, stated in outline, were the chief features of the struggle for the possession of Plevna. But a more detailed account, as furnished by an eye-witness, may fitly be appended. Owing to the fog which hung thickly and heavily between foe and foe, the scene was strangely like that described with such wondrous power by Mr. Tennyson in his poem of "The Passing of Arthur":—

"A death-white mist slept over sand and sea;
Whereof the chill, to him who breath'd it, drew
Down with his blood, till all his heart was cold
With formless fear; and ev'n on Arthur fell
Confusion, since he saw not whom he fought,
For friend and foe were shadows in the mist:
And some had visions out of golden youth,
And some beheld the faces of old ghosts
Look in upon the battle; and in the mist
Was many a noble deed, many a base,
And chance, and craft, and strength in single fights,
. . . . . .
Oaths, insult, filth, and monstrous blasphemies,
Sweat, writhings, anguish, labouring of the lungs
In that close mist, and cryings for the light,
Moans of the dying, and voices of the dead."

The semi-fabulous conflict in that western land of Lyonnesse has been interpreted for us by the inspiration of a poet. The actual struggle on the Bulgarian mountains was dimly descried through the mist and smoky fog by one whose duty it was to see whatever he could, and reflect it in vivid language for the information of the world. Mr. MacGahan, one of the Special Correspondents of the *Daily News*, has given us a most striking description of the contest, as it appeared to him with lurid indistinctness through the shadowy pall which cloaked it. "A little to my right," says this observer, "the fire had been raging with fury for nearly two hours—a steady, continuous roll and crash, intermingled with the louder thunder of cannon, which filled the air with the uproar of the bullets and shells. During all this time, there was little to be seen along the crest of the Radisovo ridge, where the Russian guns could be perceived at work, with figures flitting round them, dimly seen through the smoke, strangely magnified by the intervention of the fog, until the gunners appeared like giants, and the guns themselves, enlarged and distorted by the same medium, appeared like huge, uncouth monsters, from whose throats at every instant leaped forth globes of flame. There were moments when these flashes seemed to light up everything around them. Then the guns and gunners appeared for an instant with fearful distinctness, red and lurid, as though tinged with blood. Then they sank back again in shadowy indistinctness. The uproar of the battle rose and swelled until it became fearful to hear—like the continuous roar of an angry sea beating against a rock-bound coast, combined with that of a thunderstorm, and with the strange, unearthly sounds heard on board a ship when labouring in a gale."

For nearly two hours did this fearful storm continue, without any intermission. The redoubt was being battered by the Russian guns; the infantry were firing into the trenches, and the attacking columns were creeping stealthily up to the outworks before making a final rush. At about five o'clock in the afternoon, when a gust of wind had temporarily carried away the fog, a number of Russian soldiers rose up from a field of Indian corn, and dashed forward towards the redoubt in the immediate neighbourhood of Plevna. For a moment the Turkish fire had been almost silenced, but it was only for a moment. The Russians advanced with a shout towards the outer walls of the fort, when from the parapet broke forth a stream of fire, which swayed backwards and forwards under a dense white canopy of smoke. The crash of the discharge was awful; but the Russians plunged into it with a cry as if of joy. Passing over a little hollow, they gained the *glacis* in front of the redoubt; but by this time their numbers were sadly thinned. To take that work they had to break through a circle of fire; yet they got very near the walls. "A rush," writes Mr. MacGahan, "might have done it. Victory was almost within their grasp. But they required a fresh accession of strength; a rush of new men from behind; another wave coming forward with new impetus to carry the first up over the *glacis*; a second wave, and perhaps a third, each bringing new impulsion, new strength. I looked for this wave of reserves. I looked to see if reinforcements were coming up—if the General was doing anything to help the gallant fellows, struggling against that circle of fire. I looked in vain. My heart sank within me, for I saw that all this bravery, all this loss of life, would be useless. While these poor fellows were madly fighting their lives away by hundreds in a desperate struggle, when the victory was trembling in the balance, not a man was sent to help them. They were left to die, overwhelmed, broken, vanquished. It was sublime—it was pitiful. I see a few of them struggling up the *glacis* one by one. They drop. They are not followed; and here they come again, a confused mass of human beings rushing madly back across that corn-field, less than half of those who went forward. When this disorderly remnant was seen flying back, broken, destroyed, two more battalions were sent to pick them up, and carry them back to the assault. Two more battalions! They might as well have sent a corporal and two more men." The two new battalions did all that such a mere handful could do under existing circumstances. They disappeared into the fog, and struggled on towards the walls of the redoubt; but they were repulsed, and soon the whole line was driven back in the direction whence it came.

The attack on the Grivica Redoubt fell mainly to the share of the Roumanians. At half-past two, P.M., the work was assailed by eight battalions of that nationality, aided by three battalions of Russians. The assault was made from different points at the same time, and the men of the first line, who carried scaling ladders, gabions, and fascines, were ordered to reserve their fire, and merely to run forward, fill up the ditch, and plant their ladders. Two other lines followed in due order, and in this way the Roumanians began the attack. By some mistake, the Russians arrived half an hour too late; and, as a consequence, the assault was repulsed, and all, except two companies of infantry, retired. The attempt was renewed at half-past five in the evening, when the redoubt was carried, and the Turks withdrew to another fort, situated a little to the north. Reinforcements were then sent up; but they lost their way in the fog, and the Turks speedily returned, and drove out the allies. Several of the Roumanian guns were disabled, and it was not until after an hour's delay that they could replace them. Towards nightfall, however, a third attack followed, and the redoubt again passed into the hands of the assailants. Four guns and a standard were taken by the Roumanians during this gallant exploit; but their success had been purchased at a terrible cost. On the following day, the village of Grivica was full of ambulance-waggons, and bearers of the wounded were moving to and fro with their melancholy charges. The redoubt was visited by Colonel Wellesley, who described it as heaped full of dead Russians and Roumanians; but what gave additional horror to the sight was the fact that amongst the dead bodies were many persons still living, though desperately wounded. These unhappy beings were left without any care, for the heavy fire of the Turks had hindered the doctors and hospital-men from going to their assistance. The spectacle was so shocking that Colonel Wellesley spoke about it to a Roumanian officer, but was told that the surgeons were obliged to take cases in the order of their occurrence. The Grivica Redoubt was very strong. It was surrounded by a ditch and a covered corridor; the parapets were high and thick, and the only entrance was a narrow opening towards the south. In the covered corridor, the Turks, during their occupancy of the work, seem to have found protection from the enemy's shells; but the redoubt had now changed hands, and was under fire from the Ottomans themselves. At a distance of about two hundred and fifty yards from the captured work was another Turkish fort, which the Roumanians failed to take; and from this a rapid fire was poured upon the principal position.

While the contests just described were being fought out, Skobeleff was operating in another direction. At eleven o'clock in the morning of September 11th, that officer advanced to take possession of a hill fronting the redoubts in the bend of the Sophia road. Immediately he did so, the Turks opened fire, and commenced an attack which spread from the Loftcha road up to the Radisovo ridge, on which the Russians had planted twenty-eight guns, the greater number not more than 1,200 yards from the Turkish redoubts and trenches. A position seriously threatening the Turks was thus created, and the object of the attack was to wrest that position from Muscovite hands. Two attacks were made on the Radisovo ridge, but without success: at the same time, the advancing forces of Skobeleff were thrice assailed; but here also the Ottomans were defeated. The Russian commander ordered his troops to reserve their fire until the Turks came within a hundred yards of them, and then to open a sudden and terrible fusillade. The effect of these tactics was such that not one of the attacks lasted more than ten minutes at the utmost. The attempts upon the Radisovo ridge were of longer duration, but were equally attended by failure and loss. The ill-success of these endeavours had a very depressing influence on the Ottoman troops, and enabled the Russians to conduct their own attack with the greater confidence and spirit. At four o'clock, P.M., Skobeleff brought down twenty pieces of artillery to the spur of the ridge overlooking Plevna, and with these opened fire on the position which he had to attack—a double redoubt, in the bend of the Loftcha road near Plevna. For three hours this fire was maintained, and the Turks replied with equal animation. It was not until after Kriloff's second repulse that Skobeleff, finding the Turkish guns less active than before, determined on commencing the assault. His force consisted of four regiments of the line, and four battalions of sharpshooters. Having formed his attacking column in the little hollow below the redoubt, he caused his artillery to cease firing, and ordered the advance. With music playing and banners flying, but without firing a shot, these devoted men moved on towards the opposing walls. In a little while they wavered and hung back. Skobeleff, who was close at hand, immediately supported them with a fresh regiment, when the advance was resumed with renewed spirit and force, but only for a little while. The fire from the Turkish redoubt was so terrific that flesh and blood could hardly endure it. Another regiment was sent up, to give additional impetus to the assault; and again the line advanced, getting nearer to the fatal position. Every man of Skobeleff's escort was either killed or wounded; but, by some extraordinary fate, the General himself was untouched. Still it was doubtful whether the fort would be taken; for again and again the momentum of the attacking force flagged, or was broken by the deadly fire of the Ottoman soldiery. "Skobeleff," continues Mr. MacGahan, "had now only two battalions of sharpshooters left, the best in his detachments. Putting himself at the head of these, he dashed forward on horseback. He picked up the stragglers; he reached the wavering, fluctuating mass, and gave it the inspiration of his own courage and instruction. He picked the whole mass up, and carried it forward with a rush and a cheer. The redoubt was a mass of flame and smoke, from which screams, shouts, and cries of agony and defiance arose, with the deep-mouthed bellowing of the cannon, and above all the steady, awful crash of that deadly rifle-fire. Skobeleff's sword was cut in two in the middle. Then, a moment later, when just on the point of leaping the ditch, horse and man rolled together to the ground; the horse dead or wounded, the rider untouched. Skobeleff sprang to his feet with a shout; then, with a formidable, savage yell, the whole mass of men streamed over the ditch, over the scarp and counterscarp, over the parapet, and swept into the redoubt like a hurricane. Their bayonets made short work of the Turks still remaining. Then a joyous cheer told that the redoubt was captured, and that at last one of the defences of Plevna was in the hands of the Russians."

His success had cost Skobeleff no fewer than 2,000 men in killed and wounded. A quarter of his entire force had gone; but for the moment his object had been gained. Whether the redoubt could be permanently held, seemed questionable from the very first, and the event showed that the position was untenable. Skobeleff had already demanded reinforcements, and he now requested them again. With additional numbers, he was confident of his ability to hold the works he had taken, and even to carry others which would ensure the fall of Plevna. But reinforcements were not

REPULSE OF THE GRAND ASSAULT ON PLEVNA.

Russian triumph was of a most illusory character. The position was dominated by the redoubt of Krishine on the left, and was moreover exposed, on the side of Plevna, to the fire of various Turkish forces. Nevertheless, Skobeleff kept the fort during the whole of that night; but early on the following morning the Turks opened fire from all sides. Unless the entrenched camp in the vicinity could be taken, together with the Krishine Redoubt, the sent, and with attenuated ranks the Russian commander had to sustain an attack by the Turks, which began immediately after sunrise on the 12th. This was repulsed, together with four others which followed in quick succession. Every moment, however, made it more evident that the redoubt must be given up, unless fresh regiments were thrown into it. Skobeleff had now lost 3,000 men, in addition to the 2,000 of the day before. Some of

CAPTURE OF THE GRIVICA REDOUBT BY THE ROUMANIANS.

his battalions and companies were reduced to the merest shadows. The loss in officers alone was most alarming; of the heads of battalions scarcely one was left alive; yet throughout all this indiscriminate slaughter Skobeleff still remained without a scratch. His extraordinary daring, and amazing freedom from the usual accidents of warfare, inspired his men with the belief that he was almost a miraculous being; and he increased his popularity in the ranks by his cheerful and sympathetic manner. On this occasion he assured the soldiers that help would soon arrive, and that Plevna would soon be taken; but the hours wore away, and no friendly lines were seen approaching the position. It is said that General Levitsky (one of the principal staff officers) formally refused reinforcements—possibly, because he had none to send. About a thousand men were despatched by General Kriloff; but they arrived too late. At five o'clock in the afternoon of that fatal day (September 12th), General Skobeleff, while sitting in his tent on a woody hill opposite the redoubt which he had taken from the enemy, was informed that the Turks were again attacking the right flank of the Russians on the Loftcha road above Plevna. He galloped forward to ascertain the truth of this report, and soon learned that the Turks were also renewing, for the sixth time, their assault on the redoubt. Immediately afterwards, he saw his exhausted regiments pouring out of the fort, and flying back towards their own lines. The Ottomans had brought an overwhelming force to bear against the works from which they were recently expelled, and had swept out the Russians with one supreme effort. A single bastion was held to the last by a young officer in command of a small body of men, all of whom, refusing to fly, were slaughtered where they stood. The heroic efforts of the Russian attacking force had led to nothing but a crushing defeat. The broken remnants of that force were driven back in utter ruin, and General Skobeleff was almost mad with rage and anguish. "He was in a fearful state of excitement and fury," says Mr. MacGahan. "His uniform was covered with mud and filth; his sword broken; his Cross of St. George twisted round on his shoulder; his face black with powder and smoke; his eyes haggard and bloodshot, and his voice quite gone. He spoke in a hoarse whisper. I never before saw such a picture of battle as he presented." At night, the same correspondent saw him again in his tent: he was then calm and collected. He said, "I have done my best; I could do no more. My detachment is half destroyed; my regiments do not exist; I have no officers left; they sent me no reinforcements, and I have lost three guns." "Why did they refuse you reinforcements?" he was asked; "who was to blame?" "I blame nobody," he replied; "it is the will of God."

The renewed attack on Plevna had on the whole disastrously failed. There had been temporary successes, and the Roumanians not only took, but held, the Grivica Redoubt. Yet the Allies were almost as far as ever from driving Osman Pasha out of his stronghold. The Mamelon Redoubt was the key to the position, and that, though three times attacked by the Russians, remained in the hands of its Turkish defenders. Consequently, the former had very little to show for their enormous expenditure of life. In those few days of fighting, they had lost before Plevna some 20,000 men. The medical and sanitary staffs were entirely overwhelmed, and many of the wounded were perforce left to die in their misery, for want of hands to tend them. The surgical arrangements of the Roumanian army, in particular, were disgracefully inefficient, and the doctors acknowledged that a wounded man was seldom looked to until a couple of days after he had been injured. All these facts inevitably tended to lower the spirits of the soldiers, and to create a feeling of despondency and gloom which threatened the most evil results. It was in that month of September that the position of the Russians in Bulgaria appeared to the invaders themselves, and to observers all over the world, in its darkest and most depressing hues. The defeats before Plevna in the second half of July had first opened men's eyes to the fact that the Russians were not invincible, and that the Turks were in some respects more than their match. But it was believed that those defeats would be speedily repaired, and the failure of the Turkish attacks upon the Shipka Pass, a month later, seemed again to incline the balance in favour of the Muscovites. Now, however, the repeated discomfiture of the invaders before the great position created by Osman Pasha, and the frequent errors of judgment committed by the officers of the Czar, induced many persons to believe that the Russians had undertaken much more than they could accomplish. The summer had entirely gone by; the better part of the autumn even had passed; and the armies of the Grand Duke were still held in check on the northern side of the Balkans. A winter campaign seemed inevitable, unless, as some anticipated, the Russians should be compelled to withdraw across the Danube, and to commence the war afresh in the following spring. Those who held this opinion, however, did not take sufficient account of one quality which Russian troops undoubtedly possess in the highest measure. In a certain deadly force of grip, in the power to hold on to a position when once taken up, in the inability to understand when he is beaten, the Muscovite is not surpassed by the Englishman. Some other nations of far higher military genius would probably have given up the task in despair. Not so the Czar and his soldiers. They had fastened with a bull-dog tenacity on the throat of the Turk; and although the Turk stabbed them through again and again, he could not shake them off. The prospects of winter in that mountainous land must have been terrible even to a Russian, accustomed as he is to the extremity of cold; but the resolution had been formed that sooner or later the Ottoman should be beaten, and that resolution seems never to have faltered for a moment. Another element in the case told likewise in favour of the Russians. They had not only a much larger army than the Turks, from which to draw reinforcements; they had a much larger population, from which to recruit their army. It was therefore simply a question of whether or not they would incur the necessary expense to insure an ultimate success. In a war of exhaustion, it was clear that the Russians must prevail over the Turks. They had probably ten men for every one that their adversaries could bring against them; and if they were determined to call up those men, they would assuredly win in the end. There were critics who thought they had not spirit enough to do so; but this belief proceeded from a misconception of the Russian character. The Northern intensity of nature was not to be exhausted by a few months of ill-success.

Apart from the qualities of courage, discipline, and endurance, very little was to be said for the Russian army. "The Turks," wrote Mr. Archibald Forbes, "are better soldiers individually than the Russians. The strategy of both, perhaps, is equally bad; but, as regards both major and minor tactics, the Turks are immeasurably superior. The Turks are better armed than the Russians, both in great and small arms, and have engineers who can design admirable defensive positions; the Russian engineers seem incapable of repairing a hole in a bridge. The Turks seem as well provisioned as the Russians, and are flushed with success; the Russians are depressed by failure after failure." A correspondent of the *Times* was equally severe on the Russian military system. "The chief Russian Generals and their Staff," he observed, "do not keep well enough to the front to be thoroughly informed of what is actually going on at any particular moment. This is not the result of any desire to avoid danger, but proceeds simply from unwieldiness, and not being accustomed to move on horseback. There are too many easy carriages around the different head-quarters. A stranger visiting the armies in Bulgaria would naturally conclude that there was an Emperor with each army-corps. All this prevents that freedom of action which should characterize a general staff, who do all the hard work, while the rest are generally ornamental. The Russian Field and Line are good enough for any purpose desired; but the Staff Departments need a most trenchant reconstruction. I know it is an unpopular task to attack the Staff Departments, to which the correspondent has to look for favours; but justice demands that the brave and efficient Line, which is generally frowned upon by the gorgeous Staffs of an army, should be properly placed before the world, and the blame laid where it justly belongs—upon the gay and unstained uniforms of the chief Staff officers of the Russian army. Individually they are brave fellows; but the system of discipline is lax. Luxury, comparatively speaking, reigns where there should be stern realities; and the result is inefficiency in time of action. The consequence of the unwieldiness of the General Staff is that Staff officers do not accompany the various bodies of troops sent on special missions, to report from actual observation the progress of affairs; and therefore there is a want of that central direction which can only be attained by a numerous, mobile, and experienced Staff, which would act like so many fingers moving the pieces on the chess-board of battle, with the commanding General as the wrists of the organization." The higher officers of the Russian army were for the most part old men, very deficient both in military and general education, inexperienced in war, and addicted mainly to the frivolous enjoyments of the card-table. While the officers of the Line were doing the actual work of fighting, their superiors in station were far away at the rear, drinking champagne, and amusing themselves with the idle recreations of a club.

The military capacity of the Turks was certainly not of the highest; but on the whole it had appeared to greater advantage than that of their enemy. The Russians themselves were beginning to discover their failure. The feeling of discouragement in their camps was very great, and many officers did not scruple to declare that success would be impossible as long as the Head-quarters Staff remained unchanged. So badly was the army appointed that the shovels necessary for siege-operations had been left behind, and the men stood absolutely doing nothing for want of them. The Vienna *Abendpost* of September 13th printed a remarkable letter from its correspondent at St. Petersburg—a letter which must necessarily have been written before the last defeats at Plevna, and which a knowledge of those defeats would probably have made even stronger. In the opinion of the writer of that letter, it appeared which he would doubtless have refrained from publishing in the newspapers of his own country. He alleged that the Turkish troops were better armed than the Russian; that they were more numerous, and that they fought admirably. The difficulties of transport had impeded the movements of the invading troops; there had been a want of proper foresight, and, owing to the absence of storehouses, large quantities of provisions had been left unprotected, and were consequently spoiled by wind

SKOBELEFF AFTER HIS DEFEAT.

more obvious every day that the enemy had been underrated. People who imagined they were conversant with Turkish affairs had deceived themselves, and the leaders of the Russian armies also. This was probably an allusion to General Ignatieff, who had been largely instrumental in bringing the war about, and who had always given his Government to understand that the Turks would succumb at the first blow. The General was now under a cloud, if not in actual disgrace, and the writer from St. Petersburg probably felt himself at liberty to attack the views which Ignatieff had advocated in the days of his power. He wrote, indeed, with remarkable freedom, and asserted a good many things and rain. Peculation and mismanagement were rife in many quarters, and the Bulgarians, for whose delivery such sacrifices were being incurred, did not make a due return for them, but asked enormous prices for everything they had to sell. When these were opinions held by the Russians themselves, it is not surprising that foreign critics were even more outspoken. The reputation of Russia as a military Power fell very low in those dark days; but, as usually happens in periods of reaction, it declined more than a complete consideration of the facts would justify. The Russians commenced the war under a delusion with regard to the strength of their enemy. They were in many respects unprepared for the task they had begun, nor had they sufficiently adapted their military system to the requirements of modern warfare. But when the necessity arose for making more serious efforts, the efforts were made, and that with a success, a rapidity, a concentration, and yet a variety of power, which in the course of a few weeks shattered the Turkish army, and almost the Turkish Empire. They who would persuade the world that Russia, because of a brief period of mismanagement and consequent misfortune, is a feeble Power, which other nations can afford to disregard, are guilty of a gross, and it may be of a dangerous, error. The Colossus of the North is not invincible, but he is a Colossus still; and if at any time he is to be reckoned with, it must be in the spirit which he himself displayed in the latter period of his struggle with Turkey, and not in that which marked his earlier efforts.

One circumstance which contributed to the depression of the Russian troops at this date, was the treatment of the wounded by the Turkish soldiers. There can be no question that the injured, as they lay on the battle-field, were in many instances despatched by the Turks, and often with circumstances of peculiar horror. The Russian soldier had to face this danger, in addition to those which are inseparable from the ordinary events of combat. The knowledge of what might happen to him as he lay mangled and helpless on the ground, had a decided effect in damping his courage, and making him reluctant to meet the enemy. Probably the Turks calculated on their ferocity producing this effect. They may have acted not merely from unreasoning cruelty, but in some instances from a deliberate intention to strike the utmost amount of terror into their opponents. We must recollect that the Asiatic nature is always bloodthirsty when excited beyond a certain point, and that the Turks had undoubtedly had provocation enough to call forth their worst passions with the greatest intensity. For more than a hundred years, the Russians had repeatedly invaded their empire; had taken from them many valuable provinces; had inflicted on the race enormous losses, both in men and money; and had reduced their country from one of the most considerable Powers of the earth to one of the least important. The policy of successive generations had shown their enmity to be implacable, their desire of territory beyond any reasonable satisfaction. After a period of inactivity, secured by the results of the Crimean War, the Russians had once more carried fire and sword across the Turkish frontiers. They had laid waste immense districts, both in Europe and in Asia; they had slain many thousands; they had killed and tortured women and children, the old and the infirm. At that moment, Constantinople, Adrianople, and other Turkish towns, were threatened with a pestilence, because of the over-crowding of famine-stricken fugitives flying from the wrath of Cossack civilizers, with scarcely a rag to cover them, and not a crust to eat, save that which charity afforded. The Turkish soldier knew all this. He knew that the avarice of Russia was insatiable. He knew that her ambition would be appeased by no concessions on the part of the Sultan, short of a complete abnegation of Imperial power. He knew that the entire destruction of his country, and the humiliation of his religion, were the objects which had brought those northern hordes across the Danube. He was not unaware that this last attack was only one in a long series of intolerable wrongs. He found his villages destroyed, his material prosperity ruined, his very existence threatened. It is not surprising under all these circumstances that the barbarism in his blood should have been fiercely kindled, and that, being forced to fight, and feeling the sword at his throat, he fought like a savage, or like a demon. But this is a view of the case which of course it was impossible for the Russians to take; and at best it can only be urged as an explanation of what might otherwise seem beyond the bounds of ordinary human wickedness. The Russian soldier in Turkey, whatever his faults, was brave as the steel he bore; but the nameless horrors of mutilation made him flinch. He could confront the flaming redoubt; he could march coolly up to the mouths of numberless cannon; he could hold his own against the bayonet-charge of Turkish legions; but he feared the crawling wretch who crept over the battle-field when all the flame of combat had burned out, and, with cold-blooded resolution and unfaltering hand, tortured the helpless wounded who looked up for the mercy that they seldom found.

These were considerations which in the main influenced the rank-and-file and the inferior officers, rather than the chief commanders. The latter had to consider their proceedings, not from the point of view of personal danger, but from that of strategical necessity. They perceived that for the present they had no chance of taking Plevna by storm, and they accordingly withdrew their forces to the positions occupied before the opening of the bombardment. Some of the field-artillery still remained on the ground which had been temporarily assumed, and there was talk of a renewal of the attempt in a fortnight or so. But everything indicated the necessity of entering upon a regular siege, and that implied a winter campaign, which would make many serious demands upon the Russian army, not contemplated at the commencement of the war. A railway from Fratesti to Simnitza, for the bringing up of troops and stores, was ordered to be constructed. Steam ice-boats were to be built, so to keep the Danube open in case the winter should be such as to freeze its waters. Contracts for warm clothing, and for the housing of the troops, were authorised. In the meanwhile, very little more was attempted against the Plevna positions, and that little was performed by the Roumanians. Those gallant and spirited troops, who, as we have seen, had taken the main Grivica Redoubt, made repeated efforts to reduce the second fort, by which their conquest was menaced. Having failed to secure the position by direct assault, they opened regular siege operations against it, and advanced by flying sap. The Russians were unable to operate in the same way against other forts, because of that want of shovels to which we have before alluded. Awaiting the arrival of those implements, the Czar's commanders made arrangments for cutting off the Turkish supplies. General Kriloff, who had now succeeded to the command of the cavalry, stationed himself in the rear of Plevna on the road to Sophia; but he was not successful in intercepting the convoys of provisions sent to the relief of Osman Pasha. Two of these convoys were on their way towards the north when Kriloff took the field at the head of his cavalry. The Russian commander did not discover the fact until the waggons, which were some thousands in number, had arrived at Teliche. At that spot, the escort entrenched themselves, and mounted a battery of guns. On the 22nd of September, Kriloff attacked with artillery, and the combat continued all day; but at night the Russians were compelled to seek the position from which they had started. On the following day, the Turks attacked in return, and the artillery duel was renewed. Kriloff was fighting with his back to Plevna, and towards evening two columns of infantry issued out of the town, and assaulted the Russians in their rear. The position was so serious that Kriloff's cavalry was obliged to retire with precipitation towards Trestenik. At the same time, General Lascaroff found it necessary to fall back across the Loftcha road towards Bogot; and the way being thus left open for the passage of the caravan, Plevna was revictualled without any further obstacle. The Turkish escort was under the command of Shefket Pasha, who had been concerned in the Bulgarian massacres. At the same time, reinforcements were thrown into the town; another convoy of provisions got through on the 24th; and Osman Pasha's capacity to resist was largely augmented, at the same time that his rivals were reduced to a state of almost complete inefficiency by their recent defeats and singular want of generalship. The Russian commanders seem not to have known what to do next. The Roumanians were showing much more energy; and in the closing days of September it was a matter of speculation in many European circles whether Turkey would not prove the stronger Power.

BULGARIAN POULTERER AT GORNY STUDEN.

CITADEL OF NICSICS.

CHAPTER XXXIV.

Disturbances in Crete, Thessaly, and Epirus—Address of Kossuth to the Hungarians—Advice of the London Poles to the People of Bulgaria—The Process of dragooning into Freedom—Midhat Pasha and the Paris Positivists—Fruitless Discussions—Speech of Lord Granville at Bradford on the Eastern Question—His Views of Russian and of Turkish Policy—State of Affairs at Constantinople—Remonstrances of European Powers with the Porte on the Treatment of Offenders—Indiscriminate Hangings—"A Turkish Journalist" on the Prospects of Peace, and on the Desertion of Turkey by England—Danger to Europe of an Autonomous Bulgaria—The War in Montenegro and the Herzegovina—Bombardment of Nicsica, and Capitulation of the Place—Renewed Attack by Suleiman Pasha on the Shipka Pass—Fighting at Mount St. Nicholas—Defeat of the Turks—Panic among the Irregulars—Military Situation in the Valley of the Lom—Position of the Czarewitch on the Line of the Jantra—The Battle of Kairkoi—Attack by the Turks, and severe Defeat—Withdrawal of Mehemet Ali—Incidents of the Day—Continued Retreat of the Turkish Army—Relative Position of the Opponents at the Commencement of October.

As the war progressed, its influence was seen in a vague stirring of the revolutionary element in various parts of Europe—sometimes on the side of one combatant, sometimes on that of the other. Greece began to be agitated by warlike aspirations and ambitious views. The people of Crete commenced an insurrection against their Ottoman rulers towards the latter end of the summer, and symptoms of an alarming character were at the same time observable in Thessaly and Epirus. Nineteen districts of the former province were declared in a state of siege, and some fighting with the Turkish troops occurred, though on a very trifling scale. The prospect was sufficiently threatening to induce the Turkish Government to send reinforcements into the disturbed districts, and to station a flotilla of gunboats and cutters on the coasts, to prevent the arrival of volunteers and munitions of war; but as yet the movement did not go for much. On the other hand, those who had suffered from Russian tyranny were inclined to support the Ottoman. Louis Kossuth, the leader of emancipated Hungary in 1849, published an address to his countrymen, in which he appealed to them to associate themselves in arms with the Turks against the common enemy of both. Count Andrassy was exhorted to distrust the promises of the Czar, who, if victorious, would destroy Austro-Hungary, as he had destroyed Turkey. The only way to save the Empire, the Count was told, was to make an alliance with the Sultan against Russia before it was too late, as the conquest of Turkey would inevitably be followed by the ruin of Hungary. But if Andrassy himself was willing to listen to this advice, his Imperial master assuredly was not.

Much the same tone was adopted by the Poles, and the Polish Historical Society of London issued, under date of August 25th, an address to the Bulgarian nation. Speaking to them as "Fellow Christians and Sclavonians," the members of the Society warned the people of the Balkans of the danger attending any reliance on the promises of Russia. The Poles also, they were reminded, were Sclavonians, and Russia had entered Poland, as she was now occupying Bulgaria, with professions of a desire to act as the friend of religious liberty, and with asseverations that she had no selfish object whatever. Many Poles listened to her words, and embraced her assistance. But what had Russian friendship brought to Poland? Before Russia interfered on her behalf, Poland possessed a free constitution. "She has now," continued the address, "no constitution whatever. Before Russia befriended her, the Poles knew nothing of a conscription. Now, her sons are dragged from their homes in order to assist Russia in extending her dominions over the independent races of Asia. Our language —a language possessing a rich literature—is now proscribed, even in courts of justice. Polish children must be instructed in Russian only, and educated (if at all they can be educated) with a much larger number of Russian children, in order that they may be Russianized. No Christian Church is safe in Russia except the Russian Church, which is governed from St. Petersburg." Russia, the writers went on to declare, had made war on Turkey, not for the sake of the Bulgarians, as some of them were weak enough to imagine, but for her own ambitious ends. "She will seek," said the representatives of the London Poles, "to annex Bulgaria, or a large portion of it, as she has taken Bessarabia from Moldavia, and after a few years she will make it a province of Russia. She has, it is said, abolished the tax you paid the Sultan for exemption from military service. In return, Russia will exact from you and your sons fifteen years' military service in Siberia, in the Caucasus, or it may be in Central Asia, and on the confines of China. Instruction will be given to your children in Russian only. The Bulgarian language will not be admitted in courts of justice, because it is unintelligible to the judges whom Russia will furnish to you. Every measure will be adopted to convert you from Bulgarians into Russians. Your ancient Church will be placed under the control, not of a Bulgarian Exarch, but of Russian Bishops, controlled from St. Petersburg. Under the Sultan you might have obtained autonomy and the right of conducting your own affairs; under the Czar you will possess, like the rest of his innumerable provinces, whether Russian, Polish, German, or Finnish, no political privileges whatever, for Russia is a pure and unmitigated despotism, in which the lives and the fortunes of all men lie absolutely at the mercy of the Czar."

The general truth of these statements it was impossible to deny, and the parallel presented by the case of Poland was remarkably exact. When the Empress Catharine sent her troops into that country in 1768, it was under the pretext of securing religious freedom to the Greek Christians and Protestants of the decaying kingdom, who had in truth been very despotically treated by the dominant Church. Yet when, in 1792, the Diet passed a Constitution containing many liberal provisions, Russia again despatched an army into Poland, coerced the Government, and, in association with Austria and Prussia, effected the second partition in the following year. The policy of Russia never changes. What she did at the close of the eighteenth century, she is very likely to do again if it suits her purposes; and even as the members of the Polish Historical Society addressed the Bulgarians, those people were already beginning to feel the strong hand that had been laid upon them. When the Russians entered Gabrovo, a Captain Maslof was appointed Governor, with the assistance of several young Bulgarians who had been educated in Russia; and on certain deputies absenting themselves from a meeting where the affairs of the country were to be discussed, the Governor informed the others that he would severely punish all who sought to avoid their duties in this respect. Bulgaria, in short, was to be dragooned into freedom.

In some intellectual circles the cause of the Moslems was regarded with marked favour. A deputation from the Positivist Society of Paris presented an address of sympathy to Midhat Pasha, who during the month of August was staying in that city. In replying to the deputation, Midhat alluded to the prejudice existing in Europe against the Mussulman religion, which he affirmed to be as consonant as Christianity with modern civilisation. He protested against the policy of those statesmen who allowed religious sentiment to obscure their reason, and who, forgetting all the acts of Russia during the previous two years, could feel indignation only against Turkey. These expressions of opinion found their way into the principal newspapers of Europe; but they had no effect in changing the great current of events, or influencing the policy of rulers. The hereditary antagonists were fairly pitted against one another, and the Powers were content to stand aside, and watch the changing fortunes of the duel. At that particular stage, indeed, it would have been difficult to assign any especial reason for interference. Russia had been told she might work her will on Turkey, provided she did not trench on certain defined interests; and as yet there was no positive evidence that she meant to transgress the stated limits. For the moment, the two belligerents seemed almost equally matched in point of strength and resolution. Winter was not far off, and winter might prove a peace-maker.

Consequently, the eloquence of Hungarians, Poles, and Turks, fell on unheeding ears, and the war pursued its crimson path, while men discussed its moral aspects to little purpose.

Nevertheless, the leading politicians of England continued to debate the Eastern Question from the points of view which party presented. The opening of a new club-house at Bradford, in Yorkshire, on the 28th of August, was made the occasion of a Liberal gathering in St. George's Hall, at which Lord Granville and Mr. W. E. Forster delivered speeches. In the course of his address, Lord Granville complained of the Government for making demonstrations which added nothing to the dignity and strength of the country—demonstrations which inclined more to the ridiculous than to the sublime. He also accused his opponents of inconsistency in objecting to Russia that she was moved by consideration for her own ambitious interests, more than by sympathy for the distresses of her fellow religionists, while at the same time they were proclaiming through a speaking trumpet to the whole world that the only thing which ought to influence a nation is a regard for its interests. In his eagerness to make an epigrammatic point, Lord Granville forgot that what Russia was blamed for doing was an act of aggression against the independence of another, and that all the anti-Russian party in England required was protection against the consequences of that act of aggression, if they should threaten the acknowledged rights of England. Lord Granville was much hurt

ATTACK ON A TURKISH BLOCK-HOUSE.

that unkind things should be said about the Russian army, on the score of atrocities committed against the Turks, and, begging the question in defiance of all evidence, affirmed that the Russian misdeeds had been committed in retaliation for those of the Ottomans; which is very much as if he had said that the persecution of the early Christians by the Roman Emperors was in revenge for the acts of bigotry which discredited the Church in the middle ages. The Russians were the invaders; the Turks were those who had to suffer the invasion; and if anything is clear in history, it is this—that the outrages committed by the Turkish troops did not commence until after numberless provocations by the Bulgarians and Cossacks. But Lord Granville was obliged by the necessities of his case to occupy a very curious position. Partly he argued in favour of Russia, and partly against her. On the ground of humanity, progress, and high moral character, he could see nothing in Russia and her Emperor but occasion for praise; but he thought the statesmanship and the diplomacy of Russia not very able, and he conceived the Empire to be so very weak that nothing could exceed the folly of feeling the slightest apprehension with regard to it. From the severe checks which Russia had encountered, we ought, said Lord Granville, to derive the important lesson not to take upon ourselves alone, and at our own sole risk and peril, responsibilities which rest upon the whole of Europe. "Is this the moment," he asked, "to be alarmed even if Russia succeeds—as probably she will do, in the long run, by the use of all the resources of her Empire—in coping with a semi-barbarous and bankrupt foe, whose subjects are in rebellion, and whose dominion is at her very door? I hope you think I am right in saying that it would not be inconsistent with common-sense and with self-respect if we showed some moderation in our criticism of Russia, and less exaggeration in our indirect compliments to her unbounded power." This rule, however, did not seem to Lord Granville to be applicable in the case of Turkey. He thought the Turkish Government strong, and the Turks themselves extremely wicked. Thus, all the consideration was to be on one side, and all the severity on the other; and if it was an exaggeration to entertain some fear of Russian power, it was very much to the purpose to speak of Turkey as an incarnate fiend, with almost boundless strength for doing evil things. Lord Granville's speech was to some extent called forth by one which had been delivered the day before by the Chancellor of the Exchequer, who, in addressing a meeting of Conservative Associations at Plymouth, vindicated the conduct of the Government in regard to the war. Neutrality, with a watchful eye to British interests, was still the key-note of the Ministerial policy.

The key-note of the Gladstonian policy was, as it always had been, a decided hatred of Turkey. A speech by the ex-Premier was delivered on the 27th of September at a meeting of the Liberal Association of Nottingham, in the course of which he said:—"I will submit to the judgment of any man the speech that I made when the feeling of the nation was at its highest, on the 9th of September, 1876, at Blackheath. I proposed to maintain, if possible—and perhaps you will be surprised to hear it—what is called the integrity of the Turkish Empire; but that we should secure the local liberties of the Christian subjects, and, of course, of all subjects (for we know no distinction between Christian, Jew, and Mohammedan) in the provinces which have been so cruelly oppressed. I did not propose that we should go to war. I will tell you my recommendation, and I abide by it. I proposed that the Powers of Europe should unite, and send their fleets, or a combined portion of their fleets, into the Black Sea, and the Sea of Marmora, and the Archipelago, and say to the Turk, 'Not a man, not a horse, not a gun, not a shilling, shall pass from Asia to Europe, or from Europe to Asia, for the purpose of carrying on your wars.' I said then, and I say now, that if that announcement had been made, as it might have been made, to Turkey, not one drop of human blood would have been shed." In other words, Mr. Gladstone would have committed a most flagrant aggression on the rights of an independent Power, and would have left Russia to reap the advantage, as she always does.

While these matters were being discussed in England, attention was again called in Turkey to the neglect of the Government to punish the persons charged with complicity in the massacres of the previous year. Early in September, the German and French Ambassadors at Constantinople presented to the Porte separate notes, not of identical tenor, concerning the release of certain persons condemned to five years' penal servitude at Widdin for taking part in the assassination of the German and French Consuls at Salonica, in May, 1876. The French Government demanded the re-imprisonment of these convicts, while the German note concluded by declaring that the existing state of things might force the German Government to have recourse to other measures. In consequence of these representations, the men were again arrested. At the same time, great complaint was made, and apparently not without reason, of the severity with which the Bulgarians were being treated. Mr. Layard remonstrated with the Porte on this subject, and received ample promises of amendment, which, however, do not seem to have been carried out. The Grand Vizier assured the English Ambassador that all sentences passed on Bulgarians for murder or outrage since the commencement of the war were referred to Constantinople for confirmation, in order to give time for careful inquiries as to the guilt or innocence of the condemned men. But, on the very day that this assurance was given, an official order was sent to Adrianople, to the effect that the executions were to be continued. The property of the victims was transferred to Mussulmans, and the police were suspected of making accusations simply to extort money. A correspondent of the *Times* alleged that innocent men were sometimes carried, with ropes round their necks, from house to house, in the hope that householders would pay money rather than see an execution carried out before their doors. This particular statement has a quality of grotesqueness, which excites some doubt as to its accuracy; but that many acts of shameful oppression and cruelty were committed is beyond all question. The executions at Adrianople still proceeded, and on the 1st of September thirty-three men were hanged for offences against the Government. In every street, dangling corpses were to be seen, and, as the sufferers were for the most part men of substantial means, it was supposed that they were singled out with a view to the confiscation of their property. Parties of soldiers went about the streets with their prisoners; and every here and there, when they reached a shop with sun-blinds and supporting brackets, the commanding officer cried "Halt!" and a private, carrying a stool and a rope, made the necessary arrangements for executing one of the condemned men. The first thing usually done to a Bulgarian after his arrest on suspicion was to beat him unmercifully; and if he had a long march to make to the scene of his trial, he was often compelled to make it without food or water, and in the heat of the day, so that many arrived in a state of complete exhaustion, too scared and stupefied to defend themselves. On the other side, the Russian Government was expatriating to the interior of Russia all Mohammedans of the Caucasus suspected of disloyalty, and was dividing their worldly riches amongst men who had formerly been in the Russian army. Whether the Bulgarians who were hanged, or the Caucasians who were sent to the interior of Russia, had to endure the worse fate, might form a subject for curious, though not cheerful, inquiry.

In the latter days of the summer, the position of the Turks was much more promising than it had been at the beginning of the campaign. Yet the possibility of ultimate defeat was not excluded from the calculations of public men; and what was considered the desertion of the Turkish cause by the English Government was creating in Constantinople a disposition, in case of the worst, to conclude a separate peace with the victors on the most advantageous terms possible, without any reference to the interests of other European Powers. A Turkish journalist about this time addressed a report to Mr. Layard, in which he set forth, apparently with some official inspiration, the views entertained by his countrymen. The writer began by declaring that, thanks to God, Turkey had displayed a vitality and energy exceeding all anticipations, and the Ottomans were convinced that the country would repel the Russian invasion. Russia had declared war on grounds professedly humane and generous, but which were really dictated by that ambitious policy which for a century and a half had sought to obtain the right of passage through the Dardanelles to the Mediterranean, and thus acquire a position with no parallel in the world, but which, fortunately for the world, belonged to a non-aggressive Power like the Ottoman Empire. England, by refusing her adhesion to the Berlin Memorandum, by sending her fleet to Besika Bay, and by the utterances of several of her public men, had encouraged Turkey to resist Russia, and had consequently assumed a share of responsibility for the existing war. Turkey, nevertheless, had counted on herself. She would even regard as inopportune all foreign assistance, which might impose upon her concessions not less onerous than the triumph of her enemy. The writer proceeded to say:—"After having treacherously tried to ruin us by exciting rebellion, Russia now permits, in the country occupied by her troops, unspeakable atrocities. Yet humanitarian Europe, which professes to be the home of civilization, has done nothing to prevent Russia and her *protégés*, the Bulgarian rebels, from exterminating the Mussulmans. The system of autonomy invented by Russian diplomacy is simply the extension, in disguise, of Muscovite dominion. By it, Russia counts on opening the Dardanelles, which, in the hands of a weakened Turkey, would become a mere passage for Muscovite fleets threatening at every moment the vital interests of Europe. For Turkey, the autonomy of her European provinces would be equivalent to the loss of them. Without them she could no longer successfully resist the assaults of her northern neighbour, who would then have on his side both strength and *prestige*. Treaties will have no hold on a Power which has already shown its contempt for international rights or pledges. There will be no longer any limits to Muscovite ambition, in consequence of the indifference which Europe has displayed for the maintenance of treaties and the balance of power."

To this paper the writer added a postscript, saying that he had just read a recent speech by Lord Beaconsfield in the House of Lords, and that it had produced a painful impression in Turkey. The Turks saw with regret that the considerations which had long constituted the essence of the policy pursued by English statesmen were entirely overlooked,

Lord Beaconsfield no longer talked of resisting the Russian occupation of Turkish provinces, or of going to war for the cause of justice and the maintenance of treaties. He merely declared that England would remain neutral so long as Russia respected the Dardanelles, the Suez Canal, and the Persian Gulf. But was it possible to suppose that the Dardanelles and Constantinople would be safe if Russia succeeded in establishing autonomous Sclave States, receiving their orders from St. Petersburg? Was it not evident that autonomous Bulgaria would be virtually a Russian province, stretching from the right bank of the Danube to the south of the Balkans, and that therefore in the next war the Russian troops would operate from that country as if it were their own, and have the very heart of Turkey laid bare to their attacks? How could the Dardanelles and Constantinople be safe when the Empire had been deprived of its natural lines of defence by the formation of a State which would always be an instrument in the hands of Russia, and when violence and confiscation had driven out its Mussulman population? The writer concluded by saying that, whether Turkey was victorious or defeated, her ancient friends and allies would probably have reason for regret; but the regret would come too late.* This composition is worthy of note, as throwing some light on the general ideas which dictated the Peace of 1878.

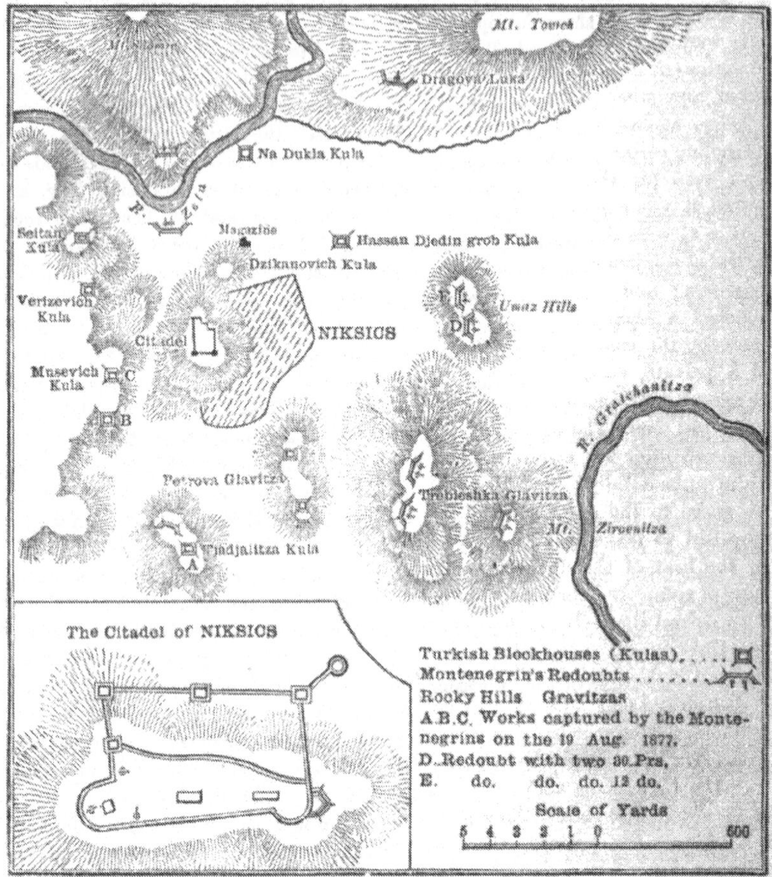

PLAN OF THE LAST INVESTMENT OF NICSICS.

It was not surprising that Turkish politicians should contemplate the worst as a possible contingency in the future. Although the invasion had been checked, the invaders were still in force on the southern shores of the Danube, and it was probable that their strength would be largely augmented every succeeding week. In another direction also, the Ottomans had grounds for apprehension. Their temporary successes in Montenegro and the Herzegovina had come to an end, and the

* *Times*, Sept. 3rd, 1877.

ATTACK ON FORT ST. NICHOLAS.

fortress of Nicsics, which had been invested for several months, was obliged to capitulate on the 8th of September. Further resistance had become impossible, except at an immense sacrifice of life; the people were exhausted with their efforts, and the neighbouring heights had been taken by the Montenegrins. After some negotiations without result, the bombardment was resumed by the besiegers on the 7th. A block-house, and some other positions in the outskirts of the city, were speedily taken, and during the night the Turks abandoned the whole line of hills west of the city, together with the entire defences on that side. Next day, the population refused to fight any more, and forsook the trenches in a body. The regular troops held out somewhat longer, but they fought with little spirit, and presently quitted the redoubts which still remained in their possession. The occupation of these redoubts by the besiegers placed the gunners in the citadel under a cross-fire of artillery from three directions, and of musketry at three hundred yards from another. The place was evidently at the mercy of the attacking force, and the garrison, on receiving assurances of the benevolent disposition of Prince Nikita, surrendered the fortress unconditionally, and were permitted to march out with arms and baggage on their way to Gatschko, where they had elected to proceed. The position was important, and Suleiman Pasha had made great efforts, earlier in the year, to relieve it; but his attempts were unavailing, and after his departure for the Balkans all hope of saving Nicsics was at an end. The officers of the garrison described the artillery-fire of the Montenegrins during the last few days of the siege as very effective, and on the final day the Turkish guns hardly replied at all. The conduct of the Montenegrin troops is said to have been excellent. They mingled freely with the population, and, although both sides retained their arms, no collision occurred between them. The walls were very slightly damaged by the artillery-fire; but, as they had not been repaired for many years, they were now in a ruinous state. Embrasures were filled up with loose stones, and with old cartridge-boxes stuffed with rubbish. Among the war-material surrendered was a complete battery of 12-pounder field-guns, some steel breech-loaders, and a number of heavy bronze rifled guns, mostly disabled, together with a few old smooth-bores—in all, nineteen guns. Large quantities of provisions were found in the magazines; but the people were worn out by prolonged fighting on the ramparts, and were heartily glad that the struggle had come to an end. The garrison had musket-cartridges for only three hours' defence. All the powder for the artillery employed during the previous two days had been taken from the cartridges of old pistols and muskets, which had been in the fortress for years; and when this was exhausted, surrender became inevitable.

Events in Montenegro, however, were of slight importance compared with those which were taking place in Bulgaria. In that principal seat of war, the fortunes of the invaders were being promoted by the bad management of the Turkish Generals. Much had been hoped from Suleiman Pasha; but he had effected nothing, and his obstinate attacks upon the Shipka Pass had had no other result than to diminish his army in a serious degree. Yet, notwithstanding his failure at the close of August, he renewed his desperate enterprise about the middle of September. In the early morning of the 17th, the Turkish troops stealthily approached the right wing of the Russian army. The Ottoman commander thought to take his adversary by surprise; but the advance of the attacking force was discovered by one of the Russian outposts, and the whole of the right wing soon placed itself in a position to withstand the enemy's assault. Captain Ostapoff, commander of the first company of rifles, allowed the Turks to approach to within fifty paces, and then by a volley put them to flight. At a later hour the Turks made two more attacks, but retreated about nine o'clock. The movement against the centre was feeble, and it ceased at a still earlier hour. The chief fighting of the day was that which occurred at Mount St. Nicholas, Radetzky's strongest position in the Shipka Pass. After a bombardment of five hours' duration, the Turks advanced against the eminence in dense masses, hurling hand-grenades among the Russian troops, and driving their opponents out of the front trenches. They then began constructing defences with gabions and fascines which they had brought with them. The assaulting column was nearly three thousand in number, and the men fought with great resolution. Notwithstanding the sustained fire of the Russians, both with guns and small arms, the Osmanlis continued to pour up the ascent, and in a little while had succeeded in securing a foothold on the rock. Some of the works fell into their possession, and, had they been sufficiently supported, it is not improbable that they would have obtained a permanent success. As it was, they held their ground for some hours, though exposed to a galling fire in front and on both flanks. The first counter-attacks were repulsed, but towards noon the Turks were driven from the height, and terribly cut up by three companies of Russians which were sent in pursuit. The retreat became in time disorderly. Rushing down the steep rock in broken masses, the defeated assailants hastily rejoined their comrades, and the only result of the day's action was the loss of a thousand men in killed, wounded, and missing. It is surprising that a panic did not at once set in throughout the whole army, especially as a great perturbation spread through a portion of the ranks at a late hour on the 18th, without any reasonable cause. The night was windy, and the tumultuous movements among the trees, together with the peculiar noises that are commonly produced at such times, seem to have completely destroyed the self-possession of Suleiman Pasha's irregulars. An alarm was given, and the Bashi-Bazouks, who were numerous in the army, caught the sudden infection of fear, and rushed off laden with booty, the result of plundering on the march. The agitation continued for more than an hour; but the regular troops at length restored order by the calmness with which they took possession of the various posts assigned to them. Suleiman Pasha had made so sure of success on the 17th that he telegraphed to the War Office at Constantinople news of his having captured Fort St. Nicholas, when he had only gained possession of some of the outworks; and the intelligence was transmitted by the Government to the Ambassadors at foreign courts. The subsequent failure was rendered all the more mortifying by this act of folly; and confidence in Suleiman Pasha, which had at one time been very high, sank to the lowest point.

WAITING FOR ORDERS TO ADVANCE.

The chief events in the latter part of September were those occurring in the valley of the Lom. For some time past, the forces of Mehemet Ali had been steadily, though somewhat slowly, gaining on those of the Czarewitch. The successes obtained by the Turks in the closing days of August and the early part of September had been followed by a few minor engagements, which enabled the Ottomans to complete their occupation of the country about the Kara or Black Lom. The effect of these operations was to oblige the Czarewitch, as already related, to fall back towards the line of the Jantra. The main body of his forces was now stationed between

Biela and Monastir. His left wing, further to the north, protected the roads to Sistova and the Danube; while his right wing, flanked by the Kara Lom and the Banika Lom, extended towards Osman Bazar. Fuad Pasha's division, which bore the brunt of the fighting at Kazelevo (or Kaceljevo), achieved another success at Sinankoi on the 15th of September. At the same time, Nedjib Pasha's division was established at Voditza, about twelve miles from Sinankoi, and nearly twenty miles south-east of Biela. Skirmishing between the two armies occurred on the 20th of the month, and on the 21st the Czarewitch was attacked by the entire forces of Mehemet Ali. The Russians numbered about 50,000, and their chief position was at Cherkovna, five or six miles to the south-west of their adversaries. The Sultan had for some time been dissatisfied with Mehemet Ali for not gaining greater successes; and he was now peremptorily ordered to engage the enemy, though his forces were considerably less than those opposed to him.

The Turks occupied the territory between the Kara Lom and the Banika Lom—an elevated tract of country, from nine to twelve miles wide. The Russians, commanded by General Tatisheff, were drawn up within a semi-circular range of steep hills surrounding the village of Kairkoi, which lies a little to the south of the Banika Lom. Tatisheff had fortified his line with rifle-pits and small earthworks, and his forces, consisting of infantry, cavalry, and artillery, numbered from 12,000 to 15,000 men. About an hour before noon on the 21st, the attack began with a brisk artillery-fire from the Turkish guns in position on the slope of the hills about Cherkovna. The Moslem infantry soon got possession of a narrow strip of wood, from which they conducted a vigorous attack against the enemy's positions. To reach these, they had to make their way up a steep slope, and the Russians reserved their fire until the assailants were within a hundred yards of the shelter-trenches. The volleys that were then delivered with startling rapidity staggered the advancing Turks, and so completely broke up their line that in a few minutes they retreated into the wood, but only to form once more, and renew the charge. The second attack was gallantly conducted, but as unsuccessful as the first. Hundreds of dead and wounded covered the ground; yet the Ottomans were not inclined to give up the attempt. A shell-fire from the Turkish batteries on the opposite crests was poured without intermission on the rising ground occupied by the Russian batteries, and the gunners fell with alarming rapidity. Even the reserves stationed in the camp behind the ridge were not safe from occasional shells and bullets, and the fire was so terrific that no one dared approach the batteries to remove the wounded. Still the Turkish attack was not attended by success, and at five o'clock in the afternoon the infantry shifted their assault from the right to the left flank. In ten minutes they had cut across the opposing line, and had separated the squadron of Uhlans, stationed on the left, from the infantry posted on the adjoining hill-side. The Uhlans were occupying a vineyard backed by successive terraces, and from one to another of these they slowly retreated, until the arrival of the infantry which had been sent to their support. While falling back, they continued to fight doggedly; but in half an hour their ammunition was exhausted, and the case was becoming hopeless when two companies of infantry marched rapidly through the neighbouring village, partly occupied by Turkish skirmishers, and drove the assailants back into the valley. The firmness of the Uhlans, in resisting an attack made by forces which in that particular direction were superior in point of numbers, prevented a great reverse; for, if the left had been entirely overwhelmed, the line of camps and hospitals in the rear would probably have fallen into the hands of the Turks.

All this while, another attack was being made on the Russian centre. This also was repulsed, and at dark the entire Turkish line was forced to retreat across the little stream in its rear to the point whence it had started. The Ottomans had entirely failed in their object, and their loss in dead and wounded was much greater than that of the Russians. In the first instance, Mehemet Ali boasted of having achieved a victory; but he was afterwards glad to describe his movement as a reconnaissance in force. The Turkish regulars under Nedjib Pasha had fought with admirable bravery; but they were not supported, as had been arranged, by the Egyptian battalions under Hassan Pasha. They were thus outnumbered by the Russians, and the final discomfiture of the whole attack was not surprising. It was evident that Mehemet Ali had been ordered by his Government to undertake a great deal more than he could effect, and he found his position so serious that on the 24th of September he retreated still farther to the east. It was announced from Schumla that this step was taken "out of solicitude to secure supplies, and on account of the massing of very considerable forces of the enemy on the Lom." But the Ottoman General had in truth placed himself in a very dangerous position, and nothing but a timely withdrawal could have saved him from utter ruin. The Czarewitch had recently been strongly reinforced, and the position he had taken up on the Jantra was such as to render an attack extremely hazardous. The first detachment of the Russian Guards had passed through Bucharest to the front on the 18th of September, so that the days of skeleton battalions were at an end, or would shortly be so. Yet for a time the Turks had come very near success in the action of the 21st. Twice on that day, according to a correspondent of the *Daily Telegraph*, the Osmanlis held the keys of the Russian positions; but on both occasions they were compelled to fall back, owing to the want of supports. Three battalions of Salih Pasha's first brigade kept their ground until dark; refused to leave it, even after they had been ordered to retreat; and continued skirmishing for four hours with invincible resolution. The supply of ammunition was well maintained throughout the day, and a continuous stream of ponies, each carrying two boxes of cartridges, was led up to the Ottoman lines, so as to sustain the fire without faltering as long as the action lasted. But, on the whole, the attack was desultory; the Russians were reinforced, and the Turks were not; and defeat followed on the imperfect arrangements of the day.

Mehemet Ali was seriously alarmed for his safety, and continued the retreat he had commenced immediately after the unsuccessful action at Kairkoi. On the 30th of September he began to cross the Kara Lom, and the movement was further prosecuted during the next two or three days. These changes were effected with great suddenness, rapidity, and secrecy, and by the 4th of October the Turkish army was drawn up on the eastern branch of the Lom, around Solenik and Kostanza, and in front of Pizanca, Turlak, and Esirdje. The Russians sent out a detachment to ascertain the whereabouts of the enemy, whose divisions were discovered in seven camps distributed about a wide valley, with droves of cattle feeding on the adjacent hill-sides, and a few isolated rows of large square tents on the distant horizon. After a slight collision between the Russian cavalry and the Turkish outposts—which excited so much trepidation in the nearest Ottoman camp that some preparations for sudden flight were momentarily visible—the little expedition returned to its own lines. The Turks were now in much the same positions as before their advance, a month earlier; and their adversaries also had to a great extent re-occupied the ground they held previously to the retrograde movement. The attempt of Mehemet Ali to break the line of the Czarewitch's forces had completely failed, and the military situation resumed its former characteristics. The opposing armies occupied a long, irregular line from the Danube to Tirnova; but neither was strong enough to break through the ranks of the other, or to do more than march to and fro among the undulating and woody hills which rise along the courses of the Lom.

LAST SHELL BEFORE LEAVING SINANKOI.

THE VALLEY OF THE KARA LOM.

CHAPTER XXXV.

Autumn in Bulgaria—Failure of Supplies—Character of the Country about the Lom—Playing at Hide-and-Seek—Dreary Weather—Mismanagement and its Penalties—Vengefulness of the Bulgarian Peasantry—Mr. Layard on the Extermination of Mussulmans—The Baroness Burdett-Coutts's Fund for the Relief of Turkish Women and Children—Administration of Relief in the Balkans—Ali Suavi Effendi on the Treachery and the Decay of England—Mehemet Ali succeeded in the Chief Command of the European Armies by Suleiman Pasha—Causes of Mehemet's Fall—Depression at Constantinople—Bad Effects of the War—State of Russian Finance—Coming Exhaustion of the Military Resources of Turkey—Expedition of the *Vesta* and the *Vladimir* to rescue wounded Soldiers in Abhasia—Agitation in Hungary—Statement in the Diet by M. Tisza—Plot in Transylvania for aiding the Turks—Feeling in Greece—Position of the Hellenic Kingdom towards Turkey and Russia—Disturbances in Thessaly—Opinions expressed by a Greek Paper published at Constantinople—Declaration of M. Tricoupis—Attempts at Mediation suggested by the English Government—Views of Austria and Germany—Sympathy of the German Emperor with the Russian Cause—Attitude of the Turks and of the Sultan—Dissatisfaction at St. Petersburg—Seizure of a Seditious Pamphlet—Persecution of the Uniate Christians.

AUTUMN had now declared itself unmistakably in the Bulgarian land. The nights, and even the days, were getting cold. Chill winds breathed from the mountains, and frequent rain turned the roads into muddy quagmires. Forage began to run short; fuel also could only with difficulty be obtained; and the men had not yet got their winter clothing. The fences about the houses, and in some instances the timbers of the houses themselves, were being burned by the Russian soldiers; but it was obvious that this resource would be speedily exhausted. The country occupied by the Czarewitch was much desolated by the marching and counter-marching of the opposing armies, so that little remained for the sustenance of man or horse. Neither the Russian nor the Turkish commander seemed very anxious to encounter the other; and the nature of the country was admirably adapted to their mutual evasions. The valley of the Lom is flanked by lofty hills, thickly covered with dwarf-oaks, through the tangled labyrinths of which (otherwise impenetrable) are numerous paths, broad enough for the passage of carts, and therefore of troops with their various accompaniments. The river and its branches wind through the more cultivated part of the valley, and between the principal Lom and the Banika Lom is an irregular, curving plateau, sprinkled with villages, and repeatedly broken up into deep valleys. "The small ridges, with the patches of woodland," said a newspaper correspondent, "formed a succession of screens, behind which it was easy to manœuvre large forces without their being seen by the enemy; and the network of roads, more or less good, made concentration at different points an easy matter. The two armies were facing one another across a valley, perhaps half a mile wide; the foreposts kept up an almost constant guerilla fight; several attacks were made, of more or less importance; and then, suddenly, nothing remained on the hill-tops but empty straw-huts and bush-shelters, and the Cossacks wandered off to find where the Turks were gone." Such was the state of affairs in the days immediately succeeding the retreat of Mehemet Ali.

The weather during the first half of October was extremely bad. Rain poured down incessantly; a dark and gloomy sky hung low over the earth; and it appeared very doubtful whether anything more could be done before the frosts arrived to harden the roads, and set the great military machine again in motion. The rainy season had come several weeks earlier than usual, and the Turks again profited, as they had done at the beginning of the campaign, by atmospheric conditions favourable to themselves, and disadvantageous to their enemies. A dismal prospect spread out before the Russians, and the previous development of the campaign presented little that was calculated to inspire hope for the future. One correspondent was moved to record on the 15th of October that the results of the war so far might be described by saying that the Russians had crossed the Danube, that they had taken the fortress of Nicopolis, and that their loss in killed and wounded amounted to as many as 50,000 men.* It is even probable that the total was greater than that. Not only had the strategy of the invaders been defective, but the general management of their forces betrayed a remarkable want of aptitude. While the Turks were provided with breech-loading rifles, of the newest and best patterns, the Russian soldiers, for the most part, had weapons of a very inferior character, the range of which was a third shorter than that of their enemies' small-arms. The provision for the wounded was in some

BULGARIAN VILLAGE ON THE LOM.

* Mr. MacGahan in the *Daily News*

respects a complete failure, especially as regarded the ambulance-carts, which were so roughly built as to cause, by their jolting, additional anguish to the injured. The engineering service of the army appears to have been singularly inefficient; while the Intelligence Department—an institution which in the war of 1870–71 was of great use to the Germans in providing their commanders with information as to the movements, strength, position, and general resources of the enemy—was either wholly wanting, or negligently managed. When Suleiman Pasha attacked the Shipka Pass, the Russians, though they had then held the ground some weeks, had executed no plan of the position, and were consequently obliged to fight their adversaries in the dark. The result of all these errors was that the Czar made little or no progress with his design, and that he had to face the risks of the coming winter, after having already lost a considerable portion of his army in fruitless endeavours.

What the Russian Emperor had chiefly effected, besides the slaughter of his own troops and the Sultan's, was the production of a vast amount of suffering among the people whom he professed a desire to benefit. The atrocities on both sides continued with little abatement, and even writers unfavourable to the Turks admitted that those of their religion were treated by the Bulgarians with horrible barbarity. "The ill-advised and unfortunate excursion of the Russians south of the Balkans," said one of these writers, "has brought untold misery upon the inhabitants. Unless the Czar and his councillors were prepared to hold as well as to invade the Moslem's territory, it was worse than madness to make the attempt. Experience might have taught them that the Christianity of people like the Bulgarians has no restraining influence against acts of barbarity and inhumanity at which a savage would pause." * The testimony was valuable, coming from such a source; but the writer's reasoning was not very exact. For it was precisely during the occupation of the land by the forces of the Emperor that the chief atrocities south of the Balkans were committed by the Bulgarian peasantry; and the continued occupation of the same places would but have perpetuated the evil. In some quarters, much indignation was expressed against Mr. Layard for having, on the 1st of August, 1877, written, in a despatch to Lord Derby:—"It would be scarcely proper to accuse Russian Generals and the Russian Government of deliberately encouraging or sanctioning the extermination of the Mohammedans of Bulgaria; but I fear that there are influential persons who believe that the only way to Russianise Bulgaria, and to reduce the province to a complete state of dependency on Russia, is to destroy or remove the whole Mussulman population." No one would assert that the Czar's commanders authorized or desired the murder of Mohammedan men, or the outrage of Mohammedan women; but it is beyond question that frightful and abominable deeds were committed on numerous occasions by Cossacks and Bulgarians, and that no effectual measures were taken by the military authorities to prevent them. It is therefore a very fair inference that the Russian Government and its agents were serenely indifferent to the acts of criminality which marked the progress of the Emperor's arms in Bulgaria. Mr. Layard did excellent service in calling attention to these facts, and in bringing before the notice of the English public the admirable work performed by those who had the administration of the Baroness Burdett-Coutts's fund for the relief of Turkish women and children. Never was a work of charity more needed; never was one which reflected greater credit on its promoters. It is a lamentable fact, however, that even charity was not free from the depreciation of partizanship. When the agent of the British National Society offered stores to the Russian hospitals at Bucharest, the chief manager of those institutions, giving way to an almost incredible outburst of petulance, declined to receive them; not because they were not needed, but because of what was described as the ostentatious tardiness of the offer, compared with the prompt and copious assistance afforded to the Turks.

One of the administrators of British relief in the Balkans at this time was Mr. Fawcett, the English Consul-General. When at Carlova, he made a formal protest to the Mudir (or local magistrate) on the subject of the continued outrages of the Bashi-Bazouks and Circassians. The Mudir admitted the truth of the allegations, but, while deploring them, professed his inability to prevent their occurrence, owing to the ruffians being too strong for him. Mr. Fawcett replied, "I came here a good friend to the Turks. I brought money and provisions for Moslems who had suffered by this unrighteous war, subscribed in England by my countrymen, who have admired the courage of your troops in resisting the invader; and, on my own responsibility, at your request, I have diverted part of that money to feeding these starving Bulgarian women and children who are under your protection. But if we have only kept them alive to be further

* *Daily News*, Sept. 13th, 1877: Special Correspondent writing from Adrianople, Aug. 29th.

tortured by blackguards who disgrace the Turkish name, I will, also on my own responsibility, take care to have you punished for it. You are responsible; and as soon as I get back to Constantinople, if my agent here reports that any fresh outrages occur after we have gone, you shall answer for it."* The reign of terror existing at Carlova was inexpressibly dreadful. Acts of assassination were to be counted by the thousand, and the distress among the women and children outran every effort for its relief. Yet still something was done by the brave and humane Englishmen who risked their own lives to succour the trembling, famished, and half-naked survivors.

How those Englishmen who had been largely instrumental in bringing about the war, for the promotion of party ends or the gratification of bigotry, could reconcile to their consciences the unspeakable misery which that war had entailed on Christians and Mohammedans alike, is not easily to be understood. It is much less difficult to comprehend the feeling of indignation, exaggerated though it was, with which many Turks regarded the political conduct of England towards the Ottoman Porte. This feeling found expression, on the 6th of October, in a letter from Ali Suavi Effendi which appeared in the Turkish newspaper called the *Stamboul*. Ali Suavi, of whom we shall hear again further on, was Director of the Imperial Lyceum (the chief Turkish college at Constantinople), and therefore spoke with a certain authority, greater than that of a private individual. This official summed up his ideas of European policy by stating that the source of every political evil, and of every crime, was the English Government. In Europe generally, he averred, there was neither justice nor humanity; but the chief offender was England, acting in combination with Russia. "England," said Ali Suavi, "has attempted the dismemberment of Turkey, and of three other States, in favour of Russia and of herself." But the power of England was decaying. She had undergone great material losses. Her army and navy were nearly powerless. Her mines of coal and iron were used up. Her manufactures were superseded by those of Brussels, and, in order to live, she must in future be content with the position of a porter, and do the work of carrying goods and merchandise for others. These were the utterances of a fanatic; but they suffice to show the current of opinion at the Turkish capital during a very critical time.

* Correspondent of the *Times*.

RAOUF PASHA.

If, however, the Turks were dissatisfied with the English Government, they were not much better pleased with their own commanders. Mehemet Ali had been regarded in July as the hope of the Ottoman armies: by the commencement of October he had sunk so low, in the estimation of the Sultan and of the Turkish people generally, that it was resolved to dismiss him. It was officially announced on the 3rd of October that Suleiman Pasha was to replace Mehemet Ali in the chief command of the Ottoman forces in Europe, as the latter had succeeded Abdul Kerim Pasha; and that Raouf Pasha was to take the command in the Balkans. The officer now removed had always been disliked by his brothers-in-arms, because of his foreign birth, and his having been originally a Christian. He was accused of surrounding himself with foreign officers, especially Germans, and of confiding to them positions of trust, which they betrayed to the Russians. It was also alleged that he neglected to have prayers said previous to action, as other commanders were in the habit of doing. The indifference to religion exhibited by Mehemet Ali would perhaps have been pardoned, had he been fortunate as a commander; but it cannot be denied that he had done little to justify the choice made of him in the summer for the principal

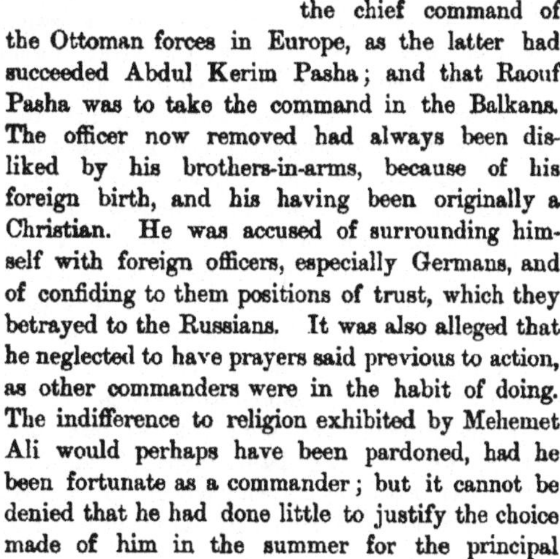

military post. His operations against the Czarewitch, though successful for a time, had failed in the end; and he had in no respect helped either Osman Pasha at Plevna, or Suleiman in the Shipka Pass. For all this, however, it is very possible that he was not personally to blame. The army at his disposal was too small to cope with its adversary after the Czarewitch had been reinforced, and Mehemet Ali attributed his discomfiture on the 21st of September to his having been ordered to make a movement which his own judgment condemned. The interference of the Ministry, indeed, did not end there. It would seem that Mehemet was once more directed to advance against the enemy, and that he declined to take the responsibility of such a step; whereupon his removal followed. He afterwards told a newspaper correspondent at Varna that he had been dismissed because he refused to break his neck against a stone wall. Suleiman's exploits in the Shipka Pass had shown something like a readiness for that species of performance.

The frequent resort to changes in the principal commands indicated the presence of an uneasy feeling at Constantinople, notwithstanding the indisputable fact that the invaders had on the whole been checked and severely punished. It was instinctively perceived that Turkey could obtain no substantial triumph short of driving the Russians back over the Danube; and of this there was only the most doubtful prospect. The prevalent mood, consequently, was one of depression, and it was argued that, as the country was fighting under unfair conditions, the result of the war could hardly be other than disastrous. If she should be beaten, Turkey would be compelled by Russia to give up some of her territory, and Europe would not be likely to make any objection; while, on the other hand, if Turkey were successful, she would not be permitted by the Great Powers to re-possess herself of any of those provinces which had formerly been hers, and thus repay the costs and injuries of the struggle. The Turks had also to fight against the insubordination of a considerable number of their own subjects, and the drain upon the Moslem race was fearful. At the best, they could only hope to preserve the *status quo ante bellum;* at the worst—which was very likely to ensue, owing to the far larger population of the Russian Empire, and the greater size of its army—they would be reduced to the verge of ruin. In some respects they were not far from that already. Commerce had been seriously damaged by the war, as it always is; employment was scarce; the Government could not pay its creditors; and the large issues of paper-money had alarmingly reduced the wages of the labouring class. The financial statement at the close of the summer showed a large deficit, and this necessitated a serious increase of taxation, a fresh resort to loans, and an addition to the ruinous paper-currency. If the enemy had been triumphantly repelled, these evils might have been patiently borne; but the Russians still retained their hold on Turkey, and it was not probable that even the winter would have power to turn them out. The Constantinopolitans, therefore, looked with gloomy eyes upon the war, and hoped but little from its continuance.

The greatest consolation of the Turks was in the knowledge that their own financial condition was hardly if at all worse than that of Russia. The Russian debt at the commencement of 1877 was about £355,000,000 sterling. By the autumn, the internal loans, and the advances obtained abroad, had added £32,800,000 to that already grievous amount. This was for the expenses of the war; and it was calculated that by the close of the year the National Debt of Russia would reach the sum of £387,800,000—that is, more than half the National Debt of England. Of the total thus presented, £375,000,000 had been contracted during the previous forty years; and the debt, while to a great extent nominally incurred for railways and other reproductive works, had been really applied to covering the yearly deficits, and to constructing railways which are not commercial, but simply military, lines. Upon some of these railways there are only two trains a week, while upon the principal line—that between St. Petersburg and Moscow—the locomotive traverses four hundred miles of forest and morass, with scarcely a town, or even a human habitation, in sight.* The cost of maintaining these roads, simply for moving troops and threatening other territories, has been a terrible drain on Russian finance, and one of the causes of that embarrassment by which the Empire has been long perplexed. The people have necessarily suffered in proportion to the Imperial debts; and few nationalities are more severely taxed than the poor Russian peasantry, whose lives are harassed by continual toil, and whose resources are amongst the most meagre in the world. The issue of paper-money is constantly increasing, and its value diminishing; the tariff is higher than that of any other country in Europe; and the Turkish blockade during the war almost put an end to commerce.

The military exhaustion of the Turks was foreshadowed, on the 6th of October, in an announcement that the Government had decided to call out

* Paper issued by the Temple Union, 1877.

all the reserves which had not already been summoned to arms. It was stated that there were still 160,000 men who could be added to the army; but these men were not the best of the Turkish military class. They consisted of the Mustahfiz, or territorial militia, and were in fact the last reserve on which the Government could draw. The losses of the three previous months had been excessive, and those losses, as already observed, fell entirely on the Mohammedan population. Nominally, the Christians had been admitted to military service some years before; but in effect very few Christians had entered the Turkish army, and least of all could they be relied on in a war where the enemy was supposed to represent a Christian cause against its Moslem antagonists. The result was that in numerous Turkish villages nearly the whole of the male population had been swept off to the battle-field, and in several instances to death. In many places the harvest was left unreaped because there were no hands to gather it, and women and children suffered because the heads of families were removed. Some of the best parts of the army had melted away even before the beginning of the war, owing to the protracted and deadly struggles in Bosnia and the Herzegovina, in Montenegro and Servia. The European Turks had been more than decimated before the Russians crossed the Danube, and the ranks were now largely recruited from Asia and from Africa. Many of the new levies were excellent soldiers; but the larger number were very inferior stuff, and it was these men who would shortly have to encounter the Imperial Guards of Russia. Another circumstance which told against the Turks at the period we have now reached, was the fact that they had entered the sacred month of Ramazan, which is kept by Mohammedans as a time of fast. Soldiers are allowed by the law of Islam to disregard the observance while on active service; but the more conscientious do not avail themselves of this permission. During the hours between sunrise and sunset, the strict believer neither eats nor drinks, and it is obvious that under such circumstances effective fighting must be very difficult. It was fortunate for the Turks that during the greater part of that season considerable languor had in most quarters fallen over the operations of the war.

We may take advantage of this pause to relate a naval exploit by the Russians which had occurred in the early days of September. On the 3rd of that month, the *Vesta* and the *Vladimir* left Sebastopol at midnight, with a view to rescuing a large number of wounded men who were lying at Gagri, not far from Sukhum-Kalé, in Abhasia. The expedition was conducted in the most secret and stealthy manner, for fear of detection by the Turks. The *Vesta*, which was under the command of Captain Baranoff, led the way. Every light, in this and in the other vessel, was covered up; the port-holes of the cabins were muffled in felt; and the ships were painted of a bluish grey, so as to be scarcely distinguishable, at a little distance, from the colour of the sea itself. Both started in the darkness of an unusually dark night, and as little noise was made on board as possible. The immediate destination of Captain Baranoff was Kertch, the port of which had not been entered by the Russians since the commencement of the war, owing to the strict watch which the Turkish ironclads were supposed to keep. Kertch is situated at the eastern extremity of a peninsula running out from the south-eastern corner of the Crimea, and separated by the Straits of Kertch from the opposite shores of Asia. Captain Baranoff believed that he would be unable to attain that point without fighting a battle with the Ottoman vessels; but not one was encountered, and the Russian officer landed without opposition to receive his final instructions. Having obtained these, he again embarked, and steered southwards for Gagri Bay. Should he encounter any single ironclad, he was to offer battle, while, if attacked by several, he was to endeavour to escape, and at the worst to take to the boats, and blow the *Vesta* up. After thirty hours' sail, the Russian vessels dropped anchor in Gagri Bay, and a number of armed boats were sent off to the shore. The place appeared to have been burned by the Turks, and presented a general scene of ruin. It was within the district affected by the rising of the Abhasians, and the wounded whom it was desired to succour were Russian soldiers, injured in the encounters of a few weeks earlier. A Russian telegraph-officer was discovered on shore, and it seemed from his statements that the wounded soldiers were then at Gadahout, a coast-village half-way between Gagri and Sukhum-Kalé. To Gadahout, therefore, the *Vesta* at once proceeded, and the village was reached a little before sunset on the 6th of September. At ten o'clock on the same night, lights were seen in front of the *Vesta*, and the men prepared for action. The torpedo-launches were at once got out, and placed under the directions of Prince Galitzin Galovkin, who was second in command on board the *Vesta*. It appeared, from movements that were dimly descried on the surface of the water, that several Turkish ironclads were approaching, and a desperate encounter seemed imminent; but the torpedo-launches had scarcely put off when the sky darkened, and a violent storm came on. Captain Baranoff at once recalled the

A STREET CORNER OF SIMNITZA IN OCTOBER.

expedition, and escaped under cover of the tempest. In this way the ironclads were avoided; and, at one A.M. on the following morning, Captain Baranoff again shaped his course for Gadahout, and at six o'clock once more cast anchor before that village. when they discovered their mistake. The Russian sailors were now informed by the officer in command of the detachment that if they returned to Gagri they would find the wounded ready for embarkation. To Gagri accordingly they went, and the injured

LOADING A RUSSIAN AMBULANCE.

Armed men were seen on shore, and for a time they were evidently under the impression that the *Vesta* was a Turkish vessel. An Ottoman steamer, painted grey, and looking not unlike that which now lay off the coast, had made its appearance the day before; but it left almost immediately. The Russian detachment at Gadahout conceived that the *Vesta* was this Turkish vessel come back, and they were preparing to give it a warm reception soldiers were moved with rapidity on board the Russian vessels, and conveyed to a place of greater safety. During the progress of this expedition, the *Vesta* and the *Vladimir* steamed over 1,807 miles of the Black Sea; thus breaking, along a great extent of territory, the blockade which Turkey had established by the help of a navy much more powerful than that of Russia. A short time before, the Russian Admiral commanding the coast-defences of

Odessa—an officer who was also managing director of the Russian Steam Navigation and Trading Company—eluded the Turkish guard-ships, and passed with a small flotilla through the Kilia mouth of the Danube. He was escorted by two gunboats, the *Novgorod* and the *Vice-Admiral Popoff.* Near the Sulina mouth of the river, a picket of Russian soldiers captured a Turkish rowing boat; and there, as elsewhere, the Sultan's powerful fleet seemed as useless as if it had been sunk beneath the waves.

While the opposing armies were gathering strength for fresh efforts, the political aspects of the question received greater attention than during the crises of combat. Opinion in Hungary was especially agitated, and the Prime Minister, M. Tisza, was questioned in the Diet, on the 27th of September, as to the policy which the Empire might be expected to pursue. In reply to these interpellations, the Minister said that no danger whatever threatened the interests of the Monarchy. The reproach that their neutrality was being exercised in a partisan spirit was not justified. M. Tisza denied that there existed between public opinion in Hungary, and the policy pursued by the Hungarian Government, the sharp contrast which was said to exist, since the aim of both could only be that nothing should happen, in consequence of the war, which could at any time endanger the welfare of the Monarchy. In compliance with a request of the Austrian Minister for Foreign Affairs, the Russian Cabinet had promised at the outbreak of hostilities that Russian troops would not make Servia the seat of warlike operations, and the Porte had consented to take a similar course. It was denied by the speaker that the three Emperors—those of Russia, Germany, and Austria—had entered into any alliance with regard to the Eastern Question, in the sense of having contracted engagements with respect to definite issues. The Emperors and their Governments had only agreed, in the interests of the peace of Europe, to act in harmony, but not in common. This they had done for several years, and their policy had been successful. The fact that the war had not become general was to be ascribed, according to M. Tisza, to the amicable relations existing among the three Governments; and the circumstance that one of those Governments had entered upon a war contrary to the views of the two others, threw no obligation upon either with reference to the great question of the day. In conclusion, the Minister-President asked whether it was a fact that the minds of the people of Hungary were more Turkish than the Turks. He believed it was not; yet the mere asking of the question betrayed a doubt. At that very time, a secret project had just been discovered in Transylvania for sending help to the Turks. Its object was the formation of a Hungarian Legion of 5,000 men, who were to meet at a certain point on the frontiers of Transylvania, with a view to making an irruption into Roumania, where, in conjunction with a Turkish corps, they were to destroy the Roumanian railways, and so prevent the Russian reserves from proceeding to the seat of war. Numerous persons were arrested, and the design was thus nipped in the bud; but, together with other facts, it shewed how strong an agitation in favour of Turkey existed in that part of Europe.

The feeling in Greece was of course very different. In the Hellenic Kingdom, the progress of the war was watched with an interest which implied no sympathy with either combatant. The Greeks were afraid that the Russians, if triumphant, would pay but little regard to the interests of the sovereignty which they had helped to create half a century before. On the other hand, they could not wish success to their hereditary enemies, the Turks. The consciousness of this feeling of antagonism made the Turks exceedingly bitter against all of the Hellenic race, though it would certainly have been wiser policy to conciliate them. Large bands of irregulars were sent into Thessaly, and the usual consequences were seen in acts of plunder, murder, and outrage. Moved by these events, M. Tricoupis, the Greek Foreign Minister, sent a despatch to the *chargé d'affaires* in London in which he remarked that, if the Porte considered the time opportune for intimidating Greece, or aiming a blow at her independence, events would soon prove that such a policy would result in serious dangers. Neither intimidation nor open violence could suppress Hellenism in the East. An unjust attack upon Greece (observed M. Tricoupis) would infallibly rouse the entire Hellenic people to insurrection. There is no proof, however, that Turkey had any idea of subverting the Greek Kingdom. She had quite enough on her hands without undertaking so perilous an enterprise; and even to have made the attempt would probably have drawn down upon her the chastisement of the European Powers. Her action in Thessaly is not at all difficult to understand. The people of that province were agitated by the events of the time, and probably contemplated a re-union with the rest of Greece at the first available opportunity. The Turkish Government feared a general rising, and sought to intimidate the country after the brutal fashion common to Turkish Pashas and Mohammedan irregulars. That there had been some seditious movements in Thessaly appears certain, though it is probable that they were of a very slight and insignificant kind. Whether the Greek Government had any complicity in them is extremely doubtful; but the Thessalians enjoyed the sympathetic good will of their Greek congeners, and bands of armed men crossed the frontiers, to act in any way they could. These men have been described as nothing else than brigands, and it is very probable that plunder was among their principal motives, for robbery and chieftainship have long been common associates in Greece. But it can hardly be doubted that political designs were not entirely absent. Volunteers had for some time past been leaving Constantinople for the Hellenic provinces still subject to Turkish rule, and they did not go with friendly or loyal intentions. Yet the most careful and far-seeing of Greek politicians were opposed to any immediate movement against Turkey, for fear of promoting Russian designs. They saw that the entire success of Russia would injure them in their most vital interests. "The autonomous province into which Russia would form Bulgaria," said a writer in the *Times*, dating from Constantinople, "would not only place at a disadvantage in the race of civilization all provinces still remaining subject to Turkey, but would be little more than a Russianized province, and therefore a hotbed of Pansclavic intrigue, and a sworn foe to the liberal doctrines and aspirations of Hellenism. Greece, in fact, would run the risk of being herself Russianized. She knows, too, that it is the intention of Russia to add to Bulgaria districts which the Greeks believe, with good reason, to be their own. Russian triumph, in a word, means Bulgarian aggrandisement; and to this the Greeks are more opposed than even to Turkish sway, because the former would be a new political force, full of vitality, whereas the latter they look upon as doomed to inevitable decay." In the last resort, however, the policy of the Greeks amounted to an implied declaration that they would not attack Turkey so long as she could hold her own against the enemy who was bent on the dismemberment of her Empire, but that, if she were beaten, and dismemberment seemed likely to begin, they must take their part in the process, lest others should get what the Hellenes considered their own share.

The *Byzantis*, a Greek paper published at Constantinople, admitted that armed bands had entered Thessaly from the Kingdom of Greece, but was sure that the Greek authorities were sincerely desirous of preventing such incursions by all the means in their power. It refused to believe that the affair could be the beginning of a systematic movement of aggression countenanced by the Ministers at Athens, who must know perfectly well that the moment the Sublime Porte was convinced of any such movement being favoured by the Greek Cabinet, it would force on an open rupture, in order to finish the work as soon as possible. No man of sense, observed the writer, could blame Greece for making military preparations which the abnormal condition of the East had rendered prudent, in case the interests of the Hellenic Kingdom should be menaced by an eventual extension of the Sclave movement; but no Greek, or friend of Greece, could approve hazardous and ill-timed acts of aggression, which savoured so much of brigandage. This was probably the view of the Greek Government; but popular passions were inflamed on both sides of the border, and the perils of the future were manifest and grave. The Cabinet of M. Tricoupis, while giving peaceful assurances for the present, refused to undertake for the future not to make war upon Turkey, as suggested officially by the English Government, at the request of the Porte, and declared that such a promise would be tantamount to a termination of the rights of Greece as an independent State, and of her duties to Hellenism. In support of these views, the Greek Premier referred to the protocol of 1832, in which Lord Palmerston, and the Plenipotentiaries of France and Russia, rejected similar pretensions, at that time put forward by the Porte. In answer to a second communication from Lord Derby, early in September, M. Tricoupis declared that Greece would not renounce the privileges resulting from the independence which had been acknowledged by the Powers, and that the dangers to Hellenism resulting from the existing war rendered it more than ever necessary that the Hellenic State should have full liberty of action. The policy of Greece was at any rate sincere and open. She meant to attack Turkey whenever it was convenient to do so, and she would give no engagement to the contrary.

The diplomatists were very busy in those autumn days, and the English Government was among the most active in its endeavours to prevent the war from spreading, and to bring it to a close as soon as possible. Symptoms were observable in Servia of a disposition to join the campaign, and Mr. White, the English Consul-General at Belgrade, was instructed to make the strongest remonstrances to the Servian Government respecting the disloyalty of such a proceeding, and the risks which it would entail. The other Powers were asked to coalesce in the representation, and the British Government seized the opportunity for addressing to those

Powers the question whether they did not think an attempt at mediation would be opportune at that juncture. This was just after the desperate nist to a position of inferiority. So far, therefore, the moment was well chosen for such a proposal as that which was submitted by the British Cabinet

GREEK MOUNTAINEERS.

fighting for the possession of the Shipka Pass. The highest valour and the utmost tenacity of purpose had been exhibited on both sides, and neither could be said to have shewn any marked predominance over the other. It was in fact a species of drawn battle, in which each combatant had vindicated his honour and prowess, without reducing his antago-

to the judgment of the other great Powers. Yet the answers were hardly encouraging. It was generally felt that the time for mediation had not arrived. After the sacrifices she had made, Russia would scarcely have agreed to any peace which did not secure to her very great and decided advantages; while, on the other hand, Turkey, having to a considerable extent repelled the attack that had been made on her independence, was not likely to grant such concessions as would satisfy her enemy. A note on the subject of mediation appeared about this time in several of the German papers, and was clearly traceable to a semi-official source. "It would scarcely be necessary," said this communication, "to point out the groundlessness of the peace-rumours, were it not that the policy of Germany is prominently connected with them. On that point it suffices to repeat the assurance which was given soon after the days of Plevna—namely, that Germany would regard the moment in which the Russian arms have suffered a defeat as the most inopportune and the most hopeless for initiating peace negotiations. Anything that may be conjectured to the contrary shows a complete misapprehension of the position taken up here from the very beginning of the Russo-Turkish question, and rests on entirely erroneous suppositions as to the manner in which the actual state of things is viewed in Berlin."

Whatever the popular feeling in Germany may have been, the official feeling was strongly committed to a desire that the war should not terminate until Russia was in a position of decisive superiority. The German Emperor was heartily on the side of his nephew, the Russian sovereign. He recollected with gratitude the friendly interest which the Czar had taken in his own fortunes during the war of 1870-71, and the positive service which he had rendered by his mere neutrality at a time when the French Government bid high for Russian support. At the conclusion of the war with France, the Emperor William telegraphed to the Emperor Alexander:—"Never will Prussia forget that she owes it to *you* that the war has not assumed the greatest dimensions." The message concluded with the words, "Your grateful friend for life, WILHELM." The author of this effusion was something more than civilly disposed towards the Emperor Alexander: he was warmly and heartily at one with him. The feeling was expressed with perfect unreserve in a telegram sent by the German monarch in reply to one from the colonel of a Russian regiment of Grenadiers bearing his name. The colonel had reported the departure of the regiment for the seat of war, and to this intimation the Emperor William replied:—"Hearty good wishes to the regiment! I hope, with you, that the regiment's colours will be adorned in the present war with fresh laurel-wreaths, and that the regiment will come out of the fight as brilliantly as my soldiers did seven years ago. God preserve you and the regiment!" A similar feeling prevailed in official circles at Vienna. At at court-dinner, given on the 11th of September, in honour of the Emperor Alexander's fête-day, the Russian Military Attaché, Colonel Feldman, was seated on the right hand of the Emperor, who, together with all the guests, appeared at the table covered with Russian decorations. During the banquet, the Emperor rose, and gave the following toast:—"I drink to the health of my dear friend and ally, the Emperor Alexander II. of Russia, whose fête-day we now celebrate." It was afterwards denied that the word "ally" was used; but in any case the tone of cordiality was marked. Such observances may be referred to mere international courtesy; yet they seem on this occasion to have been characterized by a warmth and fervour indicative of a general agreement with Russian policy.

By some of the German papers it was even suggested that the initiative in suing for peace should be taken by Turkey; and they argued that if the Porte asked for the mediation of the Powers, such a request could not well be refused. It seems to have been forgotten by those who gave this advice that any such request on the part of Turkey would be a concession to her adversary of a very important and valuable point, and be tantamount to an admission that she was hopelessly beaten, when in fact the balance of advantages at that time was rather on her side. The Turks, though in the main not sanguine as to the future of the war, were naturally disinclined to put themselves in so humiliating a position before there was a clear necessity. It was hoped by some among them that the struggle might eventuate in a thorough emancipation of the country from that position of dependence upon Europe which had existed for several years, and of which the disadvantages were perceived to be greater than the benefits. The Sultan was said to have been converted to these views, and certainly his confidence in the ability of his Empire to overcome the difficulties by which it was surrounded, and to resist the aggression of a relentless foe, became stronger with the lapse of time, and with the larger development of the war. A writer from Vienna stated in a communication to the *Times* that people in Constantinople were saying to one another,—"There are two things which we have learned: one is our own strength; the other, that we cannot rely on any one but ourselves." The negotiations which preceded the war might, in the opinion of the correspondent, have been attended with greater success, had the Turkish side of the question been taken into consideration as well as the Russian.

The views of the Sultan at this crisis of his

country's affairs were expressed with no little warmth to a correspondent of the *Daily Telegraph*, who had the honour to dine at the Imperial palace at Yildiz. The interview lasted nearly three hours, and in the course of conversation his Majesty said:—"When Lord Salisbury was here, he came to me one day with a paper which he had written, and which his lordship said contained a summary of the evils which must befall Turkey if we did not accept the conclusions of the Conference. I read the paper, and at length remarked,—'But, my Lord Salisbury, you have left no place here for God Almighty; you have not considered the possibility of His powerful intervention on behalf of suffering but faithful Turkey.' And I felt, as I told Lord Salisbury that, that we yet had reason and right to hope in the Great Ruler of the world. How right I am, the progress of events has shown.

THE RUSSIAN IMPERIAL GUARD ON THE WAY TO PLEVNA.

We prayed to be delivered from war. We dreaded the misery which war must inflict. We hoped such terrible bloodshed as war must cause might be averted; and we hoped that the Czar, guided by the religious books in which he professes to believe, would have refrained. But we were forced to fight, and God has helped us. To Him alone we give the glory. When I ascended the throne,

I found myself surrounded by difficulties innumerable. I did not know how to escape them. In my perplexity, I did what a man does who is assailed in his house with a dagger. He grasps the naked blade, though he knows it must cut his hand, in hope of saving himself. I grasped the situation—the result is in the hands of God. Yet do not suppose that, in trusting to Allah, I myself am idle. My first thought on the resumption of peace will be the re-establishment of the finances and the payment of debts, the improvement of agriculture, and the reorganisation of the forces of the Empire; and I will leave no effort untried till I succeed." These utterances must of course be taken for what they are worth; but they show at least that the Sultan had at that time no thought of yielding to his enemy. In a similar spirit he addressed the Civic Guards on the 5th of October, after attending service at the Mosque. To those citizen soldiers he expressed a hope that when they had concluded a glorious peace, the fruit of their common efforts, they would display equal zeal in co-operating for the realization of reforms which alone could afford a basis for the future prosperity of the country.

The sentiment of patriotism was indeed more manifest in Turkey than in Russia at this period of the war. A curious incident, occurring in the latter Empire, may be quoted, as showing the undercurrent of political feeling which not even the despotic power of Russia could entirely conceal. It was discovered one morning that numerous copies of a placard had during the preceding night been affixed to the walls of several private houses and Government buildings in most of the principal cities and towns of Russia. This placard professed to be a reproduction of a telegram in the *Official Gazette*, dated St. Petersburg, September 5th. It was here stated that, by order of his Majesty the Emperor, a commission had been instituted, composed of representatives of all classes, under the Presidency of Prince Gortschakoff, for the purpose of considering two questions: 1, the discovery of means for the further prosecution of the war, in view of the entire disorganization of the finances, and the exhaustion of all the resources of the Empire; 2, the preparation of Constitutional forms of government. It was not until the agents of the police began to tear down these placards that the people, who had assembled in groups to read them, became aware that the whole thing was a hoax.* In the case of each individual city or town, the placard purported to have been printed at the office of the chief local authority; but it is of course clear that all had been prepared at some revolutionary centre, whence they had been disseminated over the land. Russia was indeed seriously agitated by views fatal to the autocratic tyranny which has always been the chief characteristic of her political system. About the same time that the mysterious placard suddenly appeared all over Russia, the Government was much perplexed by a pamphlet written by an ex-Professor, and entitled "Slavery and Liberty," the object of which was to demand a Constitution, federal government, and religious freedom, under a threat of revolution in case of a refusal. The pamphlet was seized by the police, and its circulation strictly forbidden; but even these measures could not stamp out of the popular mind the growing sense that a new era must of necessity be at hand, and that even Russia cannot for ever be ruled by the traditions of the dark ages. In October, M. Aksakoff, the Pan-Sclavist leader of Moscow, was arrested, together with many other persons, at Kief, charged with having been concerned in a conspiracy against the reigning dynasty. Secret printing-presses were also discovered, and the authorities seized several copies of a revolutionary manifesto. The Government, however, continued to persecute with unrelenting energy. The priests of the Greek Uniate faith were subjected to renewed injuries; and when they offered their services gratuitously as volunteer chaplains with the army for the comfort of Roman Catholic and Uniate soldiers, who were left absolutely without spiritual assistance, the Russian Government declined the offer. No one can say that the Czar was disregardful of religious freedom; but his sympathies were reserved for the Bulgarians, or for other communities which unfortunately happened to be beyond the bounds of his own Empire, and within those of the Sultan.

* *Pall Mall Gazette.*

CHAPTER XXXVI.

The Eastern Question from a European Point of View—Opinions of M. Thiers in November, 1876—England and the Road to the East—An Impracticable Programme—The Danger of a General Conflagration—Ferocity of the Sclaves—Bulgarian Cruelties on the Southern Slopes of the Balkans—Details of Murder and Outrage—Persecution of Jews by Bulgarians—A Tragic Narrative—Toleration as exercised by the Turks and by the Eastern Christians—The Principle and Practice of Non-intervention—Prince Gortschakoff's Views on the Subject in 1856—The Title of "Ghazi" conferred on Mukhtar and Osman Pashas—The Campaign in Asia—Reinforcement of the Russian Army in Armenia—Signs of approaching Operations—Cavalry Skirmishes—Plans of the Grand Duke Michael—Neglect of Mukhtar Pasha to guard against a forward Movement—Determination of the Russians to assault the Little Yahni—The Battle of October 2nd—Capture of the Great Yahni by the Russians—Failure of the Attack in other Quarters—Ghastly Scenes on the Summit of the Great Yahni—Ineffectual Operations against the Aladja Dagh—Attack by the Turks on the Karajal Camp—Brilliant Success of the Russians—Engagement in the Direction of Soubatan—Evacuation of the Great Yahni—Russian and Turkish Losses during the Operations early in October—Miserable State of Kars—Defective Arrangements for the Succour of the Sick and Wounded.

THAT the fate of Turkey should engage the thoughts of every statesman and political observer in the old world was inevitable, seeing that the position of the Ottoman Empire has always been peculiar, and that the interests involved in the war were such as to affect, in a greater or less degree, all the chief countries of Europe. Turkey had for ages been mistress of some of the most important regions of the globe. She was seated in Europe, in Asia, and in Africa. Her possession of Constantinople, and of a formidable fleet, constituted her a Mediterranean Power. Her possession of Asia Minor, and of a large part of Armenia, gave her command of the valley of the Euphrates and Tigris, and of the land approaches to India from the west. By her sovereignty over Egypt, she was to some extent the custodian of the Suez Canal—the water-highway to the same Eastern Empire. The position of Turkey, therefore, was very different from that of most other nations, and the prospect of her subjugation by Russia was alarming, because it would imply a transfer of power from an unaggressive to an aggressive State. This is perhaps the chief reason—it is certainly among the chief reasons—why the fate of Turkey has always been one of the gravest questions of European policy. In that question, England and Russia—the two great rivals for the future government of India—have the most vital interest of any of the Powers; but Germany and Austria possess an interest too, though it may be only the interest of a dishonest compact. The views of those Powers have already appeared in the course of these pages. France was less prominent throughout; for France, since 1870, has scarcely had a foreign policy at all. Nevertheless, there were French statesmen who regarded the Eastern Question with keen and observant eyes; and the utterances of one of the most eminent were given to the English public in the autumn of 1877.

On the 3rd of September, a fit of apoplexy put an end to the long life of M. Thiers, and the opinions of that distinguished man acquired additional value from the fact that the author of them had been removed for ever from the sphere of mortal concerns. It appeared that in November, 1876, a little before the meeting of the Constantinople Conference, the Paris Correspondent of the *Times* had a conversation with M. Thiers, of which he afterwards wrote down a report. Circumstances did not permit of its publication at the moment, but it was inserted in the paper of September 10th, 1877. The great statesman said he had been led to ask himself whether Europe could agree to the eventual disappearance of Turkey, and whether she could abandon to indifference the finest corner of the old continent. His reply to this question was that she could not—that there was nobody who could be put in the place of the Turks, nobody whose presence at Constantinople would be equally reassuring to entire Europe. "Russia," said M. Thiers, "is a powerful nation, which possesses great qualities and very great force of expansion; but she is not yet ripe, and Europe would be alarmed when she placed her broad hand on Turkey, lest she should want to place it on the whole continent. Moreover, even if part of Europe, indifferent or timorous, should agree to let Russia do as she liked, Turkey would defend herself to the last gasp before succumbing, and other nations would, involuntarily as it were, be drawn into the struggle. We should then find ourselves confronted by a terrible convulsion, lasting perhaps twenty or thirty years; for the question, being raised in this way, would not be abandoned before being definitively settled." In such a war, oceans of blood would be shed, without leading either to civilisation or to repose. M. Thiers therefore considered that a conflict on the Eastern Question, occurring between two or more great nations, would be an irreparable misfortune. Among all the races which were in conflict in the East, the Turkish race, in the opinion of this illustrious French statesman, was the one which offered the most resources and character, and which was the least hated of all. Europe, consequently, could hardly condemn Turkey with impunity. At an earlier period, M. Thiers had observed that the three Emperors were apparently endeavouring to settle the great problem by themselves, but that they would have to reckon with France and England, and especially with the latter. "England," said M. Thiers, "has incalculable power; she is invulnerable, both at home and abroad. France, after losing a battle, may be disheartened and overcome; but as for England, one ship sunk is another ship launched and going out to sea. Then, too, she is mistress of the road of the universe. Imagine that by some supernatural event that universal road was suddenly intercepted. Imagine the cataclysm *that* would cause, and how humanity would feel the shock! Well, there is one point which England will not at any price allow to be touched, and that is the road leading to the East. Never at any cost will she let that be touched. Here is what the allied Emperors ought not to lose sight of, but what they will seem to lose sight of if they do not consult entire Europe on the work they want to undertake in the East." The programme to be submitted to the Constantinople Conference was described as impracticable. Turkey was asked to disarm those who were fighting for her, to make all her functionaries elective, and to transform by degrees the manner of collecting her taxes; and she was given to understand that the execution of these reforms must be watched over by a foreign occupation. That meant that the occupation would be permanent. M. Thiers hoped that, in the event of war breaking out, Europe would remain for a long time the spectator of the combat. "Russia," he remarked, "has not to fear being threatened; for all that the Turks would aim at would be to repel her attacks. Europe would have little to do or fear as long as the Turks resisted; but from the moment that the Turks appeared to succumb, Europe would have to consider whether she would consent to leave Russia victorious, to dictate laws to vanquished Turkey, or even whether Turkey should be exposed to the necessity of declaring herself conquered. It is then that the general conflagration, of which I have spoken, would have to be dreaded; for one intervention would call in others, and there would not be a country remaining that would be sheltered from the flames."

The judgments of M. Thiers were not infallible; but they seldom made a nearer approach to accuracy than in these remarks. The observation that the Turkish race was the least hated of any in that part of the world, and therefore the best guarantee of union in an Empire of many nationalities, recalls the same speaker's dictum, some years before, that of all possible Governments in France the Republic was the one which divided men least. It was certain that if the tie of Ottoman dominion were removed without some other being supplied—and that other could only be the rule of Russia—the component parts of the Empire would immediately begin to justle, like atoms in a seething chaos. In particular, the Greeks and the Sclaves were only awaiting their opportunity for an internecine struggle. "I would advise you not to encourage the Sclaves," said M. Thiers, "for there is no knowing what it might lead to." The progress of the war soon showed what it led to, and before his death M. Thiers must have seen abundant justification for his warning. It led to numberless acts of atrocity, such as the Sclavic nature seems to take a keen pleasure in committing. Mr. Fawcett, the English Consul-General—a gentleman who, as we have seen, had no indiscriminate affection for the Turks—reported that, among the few miserable fugitives on the southern slopes of the Balkans who had escaped assassination by the Bulgarian Avengers, he had seen hundreds of women and children wounded with lance-thrusts and pistol-shots. These women and children were always Moslems or Jews; and, as Mr. Fawcett spent two months in investigating the circumstances, it may be fairly assumed that he made himself thoroughly acquainted with what had happened in those localities. Captain Burnaby, in a report addressed to the managers of the Stafford House Fund on the 3rd of December, stated that, while pursuing some recent investigations, he had met Captain Fife, her Majesty's Military Attaché in that part of Turkey. Their conversation turned upon the tragedy of Eski-Zaghra, and Captain Fife informed Captain Burnaby that he had asked a missionary in that place for particulars of what had occurred there. The reverend gentleman, replying to a question as to whether the Russians had committed any atrocities in the town, said, "No; but the Bulgarians were let loose, and they did." In the village of Oflande, the commissioner of the Turkish Compassionate Fund relieved two hundred and twelve widows and orphans whose male relations had been massacred by Bulgarians living in the same village. "I was taken," writes the commissioner, "to the spot where the bodies of these poor men were, and I counted seventy-five within the small space of a quarter of an acre. The Bulgarians received their orders from Cossacks who were present the whole time of the massacre. At the village of Muflis, near Hain Boghaz. I relieved a hundred and fifty-eight women and children. Here another horrible slaughter took place, but by Bulgarians only. The victims upon this occasion were all women and children, and over one hundred were murdered, not in the village itself, but at a place some hours distant from it, in the Balkan Mountains. These poor women and children were taken into the mountains; some of them were ravished, and then the slaughter began." The bodies were afterwards mutilated, and the commissioner asserted that he saw things which he could not write about. At the village of Esover, about six miles from Shipka, a hundred and twenty-nine men were murdered in a ravine. The order to murder them came from the Cossacks; but the assassins were Bulgarians, and a priest of the same nationality, who was present, read prayers while the massacre was proceeding, and, when the diabolical work was finished, cried "Long live the Czar!" Such, at least, was the statement afterwards made by two men who escaped from the massacre; and it is so much in accordance with all we know of the Bulgarian nature that it bears the stamp of a reasonable probability. The English commissioner visited the place some time afterwards, and saw the bodies of the victims.

THE SACKING OF SISTOVA.

The relaxation of Turkish rule led immediately to a vast amount of religious intolerance, for which the misdeeds of the Turks could afford no excuse, since the Turks were not always the sufferers. To the orthodox Bulgarians, Jews were as much the objects of murderous hatred as Moslems. A Bucharest correspondent of the *Standard*, writing in the early part of the autumn, stated that some three hundred and fifty Jewish refugees, mostly widows and orphans, were at that time residing in the Roumanian capital. These were the miserable remnant of Hebrew communities lately settled at Kezanlik, Eski-Zaghra, and other places in Roumelia and Bulgaria. Their story was, that just before the Russians entered Kezanlik the

Kaimakan, or sub-govenor of the province, came to those places, and, convoking the Jewish citizens, told them that an invasion was imminent, and suggested that, as they might anticipate ill-treatment from which he would not be able to protect them, they had better leave for a place of safety. Alarmed at this prospect, they followed the Turkish inhabitants into a forest on the Balkans; but two or three very poor families stayed at Kezanlik. A few days after the others had departed, General Gourko's troops arrived. Some conferences then took place between the Russian officials and the representative Bulgarians of the town, and, as the result of these deliberations, the Jews who had remained behind were told to seek out their co-religionists, and give them an assurance that they might return with safety. They returned accordingly, and as long as the Russians remained were not subjected to any injuries. But as soon as the soldiers of the Czar had passed on, the Bulgarians seized every man, woman, and child of the Jewish community, and forced them into the synagogue and its court-yard. The richest men amongst them were singled out, and demand was made for a large sum of money. This was not at once granted, and the Bulgarians fired several volleys into the crowded court-yard, killing many persons on the spot. The unfortunate Jews then gave up all the money they possessed, and the jewellery of the women and girls was next required. Before it could be delivered, the ruffians plunged in amongst the terrified creatures, tearing off necklaces, bracelets, rings, and ear-pendants, and often mutilating the living owners in their eagerness to get at the valuables. This was on a certain Saturday, and, after an interval of drunkenness and church-going on the following day, the Bulgarians were prepared for fresh outrages on the Monday. The violence done to the women, and the murderous cruelties inflicted on the men, will not bear particular description; but the general result was that by the end of the day the number of the Jews was reduced from nine hundred to less than half. Towards evening, the music of an approaching detachment of Russian dragoons and Cossacks was heard; and the Bulgarians ran off, leaving the survivors for a time at rest. Not for long, however. The Bulgarians plied the Cossacks with drink, and another horrible massacre soon took place. Men and women were impaled on the spikes of iron railings, and children pinned to the doors and seats of the synagogue with lances. Another detachment of Russian dragoons endeavoured to escort the survivors (now not more than seventy-two) to Shipka; but they were after a time abandoned by their protectors, and the greater number perished beneath renewed assaults.

Turkish rule had at any rate prevented such tragedies as these, so far as the Jews were concerned; and the atrocities towards the Christians, with which it was justly chargeable, resulted from the interference of revolutionary bodies, acting under Russian guidance. During many years, the Moslem scimitar had kept order between contending factions, and M. Thiers was quite right in saying that there was no other force equally well calculated to do the work. In Roumania, as in Bulgaria, the unoffending Israelites were subjected to much ill-usage, and there was every prospect that this spirit of persecution would be extended wherever the Ottoman power was destroyed. The Eastern Christians have no greater idea of tolerance at the present day than the Western Christians had five hundred years ago. Debased, servile, and ignorant, they recognize few virtues apart from the theories of a priesthood as ignorant, and perhaps nearly as debased, as themselves. The military caste and the priestly caste share the eastern lands of Europe between them, and there are no checks upon the excesses of either, such as are furnished in the West by the multitudinous developments of secular life, by the strength of opinion, by the predominance of literature, by the subtle influence of science in perpetually lowering the force of dogma, and by that long accumulation of humane traditions which has now become part of the habitual life of more civilized countries. The most tolerant Government in the East of Europe is that of Turkey, and even there the principle has been liable to sudden and murderous disruption whenever anything has occurred to rouse the fears of the Mussulmans. That it existed as a rule for several years—allowing for a certain amount of insulting scorn, to which the Ghiaours were frequently subjected, and for some special disabilities—is beyond dispute. The causes of that tolerance, such as it was, are to be found in the indolence of the Turkish nature, and in the weakness resulting from a long process of decay. When the Turk was strong, he persecuted: in the decrepitude and senility of age, he was willing to let Jew and Christian go their ways, provided they did not threaten to cut his throat, or burn his mosques. The effect of recent intervention in the East has been to advance the cause of religious toleration to this extent, and no other—that it has substituted for the influence of a Power which would persecute, but could not, the influence of one which will persecute, and can.

With equal penetration, M. Thiers saw that the proposed foreign supervision of the suggested reforms, to be enforced by a foreign occupation, was a scheme fraught with mischief and danger. It was the abandonment of a principle which had long received the adhesion of some of the wisest politicians—the principle of non-intervention in the internal affairs of other countries. Granting the worst that has ever been said about Turkish tyranny and misrule, it is impossible to define on what ground of right the European Powers could thrust themselves into the place of the Sultan, and supersede his authority in his own house. Nor is it easy to see how any kind of liberal progress could be facilitated by a practice which has always been one of the favourite weapons of despotism. The sovereign right of every State to be respected within its own dominion is among the noblest doctrines of modern political science. The tyrants themselves can assert it when it suits their purposes; but it should be the glory of free communities to uphold the theory and practice at all seasons, as the greatest check on military despotism that can be exercised. It is a curious fact that when, in 1856, England and France put some pressure on the King of Naples, on account of his cruel and oppressive government, Prince Gortschakoff protested against the implied right of one State to interfere in the domestic concerns of another. "We can understand," said the Russian Minister, writing from Moscow on the 2nd of September in that year, "that, in consequence of a friendly predisposition, one Government might offer to another advice inspired by kind interest, and that this advice might even assume the character of exhortation; but we think that this is the extreme limit at which it ought to stop. Less than ever is it now permitted in Europe to forget that sovereigns are equals among themselves, and that it is not the extent of territory, but the sanctity of the rights of each, which regulates the relations existing between them. To wish to obtain from the King of Naples concessions as to the internal *régime* of his States by threatening demonstrations, is to wish to govern in his place, and to proclaim the right of the weak over the strong."* Nothing can be better than this doctrine; and if Russia had only fairly adhered to it in 1849 and 1877, there would have been no interposition of her forces in support of an illegal despotism in Hungary, or of Pansclavic conspiracies in Turkey.

JEWISH REFUGEES AT RASGRAD.

All these questions came up for discussion when, in the early autumn, there seemed some probability of negotiations for peace being opened. But the time was not yet ripe for any pacific settlement, and the war soon entered on new phases, unaffected by abstract considerations of political morality. Attention was now once more attracted towards the campaign in Asia, where active operations were resumed after a brief pause. For some months, the Turkish commander had been in the superior position; and the Sultan, in his gratitude for many brilliant services, conferred on Mukhtar Pasha the title of "Ghazi," or the Victorious—an honour which was

* Attention was called to this interesting despatch by Mr. Algernon Borthwick in an address on the Eastern Question delivered at St. James's Hall, January 10th, 1878.

RECONNOITRING PARTY.

also at the same time bestowed on Osman Pasha, the hero of Plevna. The Turks have an opinion that assumptions such as these, where the issue is yet in suspense, are always revenged by some signal misfortune. Certain it is that, shortly after the two Generals were thus distinguished, the star of their success began to wane. The Russians in Armenia were much stronger towards the latter end of September than they had been a month or so earlier. Two complete divisions had recently arrived, and these included about 16,000 of the Moscow Grenadiers—powerful troops, well-armed, and possessed of a warlike spirit. It was evident that something important would soon be attempted by the Russians, and Mukhtar Pasha himself seemed to anticipate an early attack. He paid particular regard to the Kizil Tépé entrenchments, examined them closely, and ordered the construction of additional earthworks. The Russians had for a long time been preparing for active operations, so that, when the next blow was struck, it might be delivered with a fair chance of success. The numerical inferiority of the Russians had necessitated a cautious policy; but that inferiority was now at an end, and it was resolved to try conclusions once more with an enemy whose power it was not safe to disregard.

On the 30th of September, news reached the Turkish camp that General Komaroff had been reinforced by a division from Akhaltsikh, and that he had detached a brigade of four battalions, one field-battery, and one regiment of cavalry, to strengthen the Russian head-quarters. Hassan Hamet Bey, who commanded at Peniak, endeavoured to prevent the proposed junction, and detached a regiment of Arab cavalry to watch the enemy's course. The Arabs gained the banks of the Kars-Tchai simultaneously with the Russian brigade, but omitted to take proper precautions against an attack. The result was that they were suddenly assailed after nightfall, and put to flight, with the loss of forty or fifty of their number. This was followed by some other cavalry movements of no great importance, except as indicating that operations on a much larger scale were probably about to commence. The design of the Grand Duke Michael, Commander-in-Chief of the Russian forces in Armenia, was to wear out Mukhtar's army by continual attacks and the accumulation of petty losses, and then to get between the Turks and Kars, so as to compel the enemy to abandon the Russian frontier, and fall back on his base of operations at Erzeroum, thus enabling the Russians to capture Kars, and endanger the whole of the Sultan's Asiatic army. Mukhtar Pasha appears not to have divined this intention, and to have calculated on remaining in his advanced position throughout the winter. A site was selected on the eastern slopes of the Soghanli Dagh for a standing camp. Kars was supplied with extra ammunition and provisions, and many of the Christian inhabitants were warned that their houses would be required for quartering the troops. The Turkish commander had reason to believe that the Russians were making similar preparations in the positions they then occupied, and this induced him to suppose that no forward movement was contemplated. He had heard from deserters that his adversary was heavily reinforced; but he disbelieved the information, and therefore took fewer precautions than he would have considered necessary had he credited the improved condition of the Russians. Nevertheless, he strengthened and entrenched the Little Yahni and the Kizil Tépé. The former was a point of great importance, and it was there that the Russians resolved to strike. The position was garrisoned by six battalions of Turks, and mounted with eight guns; and the general command was entrusted to Captain Mehmed Pasha. Although the Little Yahni was to be the chief object of attack, the plan of operations was to embrace other positions as well. General Sholkownikoff, in temporary command of the Fortieth Division, to the left of the Russian line, was ordered to turn the Aladja Dagh, from Ani, with five battalions and a battery, and, having done this, to fall on Mukhtar Pasha's rear. A demonstration, simply to engage the enemy's attention, was at the same time to be made against the Kizil Tépé. General Heimann, with the Circassian division of Grenadiers, was to attack the Turkish centre and main body, so as to prevent the withdrawal of troops from Soubatan to reinforce other positions. It was not intended to make any direct assault on the Great Yahni, but to concentrate the chief strength of the attack on the Little Yahni—an isolated elevation, with a broad, flat top, and steep, craggy sides, which the Russians had ineffectually attacked on the 18th of August. This hill completely blocked the way from Kurukdara to Kars, and was therefore important for the Turks to retain, and for the Russians to seize, if they could effect it. The general object of the Russians in the impending operations was to carry out a complete turning movement on both wings of the opposing force, so as to cut off Mukhtar's communications with Kars. If this could be brought about, the surrender of the Turkish army was anticipated as a probable consequence; but, although the Russians were to some extent fortunate in their attack, they did not succeed to the extent which they had contemplated and desired.

The troops designated for the advance left their

camps at eight o'clock on the evening of October 1st. When they arrived before the Little Yahni, they found its summit crowned with breastworks, ditches, rifle-pits, and masked batteries. The approach of the Russians was discerned by the Turkish garrison

BATTLE OF LITTLE YAHNI.

at dawn on the 2nd of October, when a signal-gun was fired from the Olya Tépé, to give notice to the whole line that the enemy was in motion. Columns were to be seen advancing in heavy masses along the road to Kars, while others threatened the Little Yahni, and others again were making demonstrations against various parts of the Turkish front. By seven o'clock in the morning, thirty-four battalions, sixty-one guns, and six regiments of cavalry, were drawn up in front of the Little Yahni, and preparations were made for an assault. This had been preceded by several hours' cannonading, which, however, had produced very slight effect on the Turkish positions. On the left of the Russian line, General Heimann hurled his divisions in skirmishing order against the Aladja Dagh and the Olya Tépé. It was in the latter of these positions that the main body of the Turkish forces had been concentrated, and from their breech-loading rifles burst out incessant volleys, causing great loss to the attacking troops. The position consisted of a series of rocky terraces, strengthened by entrenchments, and by barricades of stone; and it soon became evident that in this particular direction the Russians had littie chance of succeeding. The attack altogether was ill-managed. The cavalry were kept under fire without doing anything, and large numbers of the infantry simply frittered away their time in idle skirmishes. The men thus engaged formed for themselves extemporary shelters behind heaps of stones, from which every now and then they fired at their opponents, who, being also under cover, received but little damage. After the general action had gone on some hours, it was found, by examining the position through field-glasses, that the garrison of the Great Yahni was exceedingly feeble. The position in itself was strong, for the sides of the hill were steep, and from the base to the top rose a succession of rifle-pits and ditches, constructed in the most elaborate and formidable manner. But the paucity of the numbers guarding the mount seemed to invite attack, and Melikoff accordingly ordered a general assault. The troops advanced from three sides, and at the same time the artillery redoubled its fire. The defenders also fired with persistent resolution; but the Russian Grenadiers scrambled up the steep slopes of the hill, and arrived in front of the fortifications. It took them an hour to get there, but, having arrived, they made short work of the Turkish battalion which they found on the summit. This battalion counted scarcely five hundred men; but all showed the most stubborn heroism in resisting the overwhelming numbers brought against them. Being unsupported, their efforts were in vain; the entrenchments were carried after an obstinate defence, and the hill was completely occupied by the conquerors. Only three junior officers and thirty-seven men escaped to join their comrades, and to tell the story of their loss.

The movement on Little Yahni was less successful. The Russians threw column after column against that difficult position; but these repeated attacks were as constantly flung back, with terrible loss to the assailants. The defence of the hill was in good hands. Mehmed Pasha held his ground with unflinching resolution, though his soldiers were only Redifs, or men of the second reserve, whose acquaintance with the realities of warfare could not have been recent. Notwithstanding that they were exposed for some hours to a galling fire from sixty guns, these men never quailed for a moment; yet it was apparent to Mehmed Pasha that, unless speedily reinforced, he would be driven by sheer weight of numbers from the Little Yahni. He therefore despatched urgent messages to Kars for aid; but before this could be sent, the Russian assaults on his position began to relax, and a division, numbering fifteen or sixteen battalions, with twelve guns, moved off to join in the attack on the Great Yahni. These were not the only movements during the day's operations. From an early hour, General Heimann, as already stated, had been making a series of desperate attempts to take the Aladja Dagh and the Olya Tépé, and he now persuaded General Melikoff to strengthen the attack on those positions. The Olya Tépé was inaccessible from the plain at the foot of the Aladja Dagh; but at other points it was vulnerable, and this fact had been ascertained by the cavalry patrols of the Russians. The southern side of the ridge was wholly unoccupied by the Turks, who, considering the neighbouring position of the Great Yahni to be safe from all assaults, had neglected to concentrate a sufficient number of men on the Olya Tépé, to which the Great Yahni was the key. The conquest of the latter eminence by the Russians brought the neighbouring position within range of their operations, and, as the point was one of much importance, it was determined to order an attack. General Heimann, in an interview with General Melikoff, assured his superior with the utmost confidence that his troops, advancing from the Soubatan Plain, were quite equal to capturing the Olya Tépé, and that therefore the forces under the immediate command of Melikoff might be advantageously employed against the Little Yahni and the garrison of Kars. Melikoff's Staff saw that the advice was not good; but the General himself was persuaded by his subordinate's reasoning. The Olya Tépé was attacked, but not taken; the Russians were repulsed with great slaughter; and at all points, except the Great Yahni, the failure of the operations was complete.

A newspaper correspondent, who visited the summit of Great Yahni after the close of the fighting, has described the ghastly sight which it presented. "All the pits and ditches around," he says, "were filled with the corpses of the Turks. The dead were almost all shot through the head, because the remaining parts of their bodies had been sheltered by the parapets. Here they lay as they fell, on their backs or faces, side by side, or one above the other. A negro with grinning teeth hung right across a white soldier, and his long arms stretched out over the rocky abyss. Some preserved the ferocious expression which they had borne when still alive, and lay with clenched fists and distorted limbs; others, calm and quiet, looked like stone. In a pit opposite each other sat two Softas. Though in the uniform of soldiers, they were easily recognised as religious students by the white muslin band tied around their fezzes. One had his skull laid open by a shell-fragment; the other was shot through the temple. Both had obviously been killed by the same shrapnel. Some hundred dead bodies encumbered the trenches; others lay strewn over the hill-side." Towards the close of the day, General Sholkownikoff's brigade obtained temporary possession of the Aladja Dagh, where they were in a position to threaten the rear of Mukhtar Pasha's camp near Soubatan; but Mukhtar made a counter-demonstration, of such a nature as to compel the Russian officer to retire without delay. A large number of men had been sacrificed by General Melikoff in the execution of his plans, and, when night closed in, he had only the Great Yahni to show for all his expenditure of life. That position, however, was worth having, and the conqueror took measures to secure it. Two battalions were despatched as a garrison to occupy the hill, and they were ordered, in combination with the sappers, to strengthen the entrenchments with additional earthworks. Divisions were posted near at hand, to support these troops in case they should be attacked. But Mukhtar Pasha did not contemplate any movement in that direction, for he knew the position was such that it must of necessity be relinquished by the Russians very soon. Not a drop of water was to be found for ten miles round Great Yahni, excepting a little stream which remained within the Turkish lines. Man and beast were already suffering from the want of this necessary, and they would of course suffer in a still greater degree in proportion to the length of their stay.

The 3rd of October did not pass without some severe fighting in other directions. Early in the afternoon, the Turks began an attack on the Karajal camp, being apparently under the belief that the bulk of the Russian forces had been concentrated in a different quarter. The assailants numbered about 15,000 men; their front extended a distance of three miles, and they were preceded by two batteries, and followed by supports and reserves. Their right wing was covered by the Kizil Tépé, and they advanced with much rapidity, confidence, and spirit. General Lazareff, in command of a large force, lay in ambush to receive the enemy. Only a small number were sent out to meet the advancing line; the rest lay behind heaps of stones, or any other cover which presented itself. The Turks believed they had merely a feeble detachment before them, and rushed forward with renewed ardour. Their batteries opened fire, and at the same time the guns on the Kizil Tépé flung numerous shells on to the field of combat. Suddenly the Ottomans were confronted by the rifle-barrels of the Russians, projecting over the little mounds of stone or earth which protected the infantry-men. The Turks fired with redoubled energy; then the Russian volleys burst out, the whole line disclosed itself, and the Turks perceived that they were in presence of a large force, prepared to dispute the ground with all the solid firmness of their nationality. Alternately firing and advancing, they bore down on their adversaries. Smitten full in the front by this unexpected blow, the Turks faltered and hung back. Their resistance was maintained for a little while by rapid firing; but they were soon in retreat, still keeping their faces to the enemy, and availing themselves of every undulation in the ground to make a fresh stand. The Russians followed like a torrent, and the Turks, losing heart, turned round, and ran towards the shelter of their pits and breastworks. Even from these, however, they were dislodged at the point of the bayonet, and shortly after nightfall were in rapid retreat to their fortified camp at the foot of the Aladja Dagh. General Lazareff followed for some time longer; but, at length losing sight of his opponents in the black darkness, he ordered the cessation of the pursuit, satisfied with having so completely defeated what looked like a formidable attack. It was evident from this affair, as well as from one or two other recent actions, that the Russians were beginning to recover that spirit of self-reliance which they had lost in consequence of the many misfortunes attending their arms at an earlier period of the war. Their commander on this occasion appears to have acted with true soldierlike ability, and the Grand Duke expressed himself highly gratified with what had been effected. General Lazareff had not been caught unawares; his arrangements were excellently adapted to the occasion, and were carried out with entire mastery over the details. His men also had greatly distinguished themselves, and their success was complete and striking. The superiority of the Turks, which for some months had been unquestionable, was now beginning to wane. Mukhtar Pasha ceased to be victorious in the very moment of assuming his boastful designation. He seems to have lost his foresight and his judgment; his plans were wanting in method, and his blows, aimed wildly at the enemy, recoiled upon himself.

Yet he was still successful in resisting attack. On the evening of October 3rd, the Russians made a movement in the direction of Soubatan, which induced Mukhtar Pasha to telegraph instructions to Moussa Pasha, commanding the Kizil Tépé, to send out some battalions for resisting any assault that might be meditated. The Ottoman detachment was much weaker in numbers than that to which it was opposed; but, owing to the configuration of the ground, the Russians were unable to bring all their battalions into action. "It was upon the infantry fire," writes an English observer, who acted as correspondent of a London paper, "that the result depended; and such infantry fire it is not given to one man to see twice in a life-time. It is nothing to say that the roar was continuous; but, as the night drew on, the lines of fire remained as it were ruled upon the face of the terrain. Now dim through the smoke, now golden as liquid iron, anon bright as the electric spark, the fire of the Turkish troops was blasting as forked lightning, and seemed to be absolutely unintermittent."* The Russians replied with vigour; but their rifles were not so good as those of the Turks, and the discharges were consequently much less rapid. The encounter continued far into the evening, and, when the Russians retreated, they left a large number of dead and wounded on the ground. The antagonists had never been nearer to one another than from six hundred to seven hundred yards; yet their rifles told with terrible effect. In this direction the Turks were victorious, and the Russian design, whatever it may have been, was frustrated.

Finding it impossible to maintain their position on the Great Yahni hill, owing to the want of water, the Russians abandoned that eminence on the morning of October 4th, and the head-quarters were transferred to the Kaback Tépé, or Gourd Hill. Mukhtar Pasha and his Staff shortly afterwards re-occupied the Great Yahni, and some shells were then directed against the Kaback Tépé. In moving towards the latter position, the Russians were pressed somewhat closely by Mehmed Pasha from the Little Yahni, and by Hassan Pasha with a brigade from Hadji-veli. Some heavy fighting ensued, and for five hours the artillery of the two combatants was hotly engaged. About four o'clock in the afternoon, Mukhtar Pasha sent orders that the pursuit was to cease, and the Muscovites were glad to get under the shelter of their new position, without attempting any reprisals. When the Ottomans returned to the Great Yahni, they found that the Russians had constructed upon the outer slopes, not merely entrenchments for their infantry, but redoubts for their guns; and it is said that these redoubts, though thrown up in a single night, were perfect in their construction and beautiful in their finish. On the morning of the 5th, the Turkish Commander-in-Chief attempted a diversion by sending some artillery and cavalry towards Utch-Tépé, and an engagement followed, which, though lasting till nearly nightfall, was unattended by any important results. The series of operations commencing on the 1st of October had now come to an end, and it had not been productive of any permanent advantage to the Russians. It had led, however, to heavy losses. Official returns spoke of 3,360 men killed, wounded, or missing; 54 officers had been wounded, and one colonel of artillery was killed. Spies and deserters from the Turkish side alleged that Mukhtar Pasha had lost 8,000 of his troops; but the statement was probably an exaggeration. Two hundred and forty Ottoman prisoners were in the hands of the Russians; but this was poor compensation for the depletion of their own ranks. Reinforcements were again demanded, though only with respect to particular localities. The renewed activity of the Russians had been severely felt by the Turks; yet the former had done little or nothing towards advancing the fortunes of the campaign, or repairing the errors of the summer.

The number of Turkish wounded in Kars led to a very deplorable state of things in that city. Before the engagements just described, four thousand sick and wounded were congregated there; and the number was now largely increased. Only four doctors in the place were fit for duty, and it followed of necessity that they were dreadfully overworked, and that many urgent cases were neglected. The whole of Kars could not provide hospital accommodation for more than 1,200 men, and there were cots for only three hundred patients. Scarcely half the wounded were provided with shelter; yet the barracks and places of rest for travellers were filled to overflowing. Many of the sufferers were crowded into small, ill-ventilated huts; and typhoid fever, dysentery, and scurvy, abounded among the miserable victims of the war. "It was practically impossible," says a representative of the *Times*, "for one fourth of these men to be visited by the doctors; indeed, it was impossible that the medical men could know where all their patients were housed. Fresh cases came daily to notice, and men were hourly found who had been lying for days with undressed wounds, unset limbs."† The Stafford House stores sent out early in September were by this time completely exhausted, and the hospitals were without carbolic acid, lint, charpie, bandages, splints, and other necessaries. At Olti and Bayazid, also, great distress was experienced, and it was computed by the medical authorities that at that time fourteen per cent. of the whole strength of the Armenian army was on the sick list. The Turkish authorities were much

* Williams's Armenian Campaign.

† Armenia, and the Campaign of 1877. By C. B. Norman, Special Correspondent of the *Times* at the Seat of War.

reproached with their cruel indifference to the sufferings of the wounded, and the criticism seems to have been deserved. An English surgeon related that he had seen soldiers whose wounds had been professedly dressed, but which had in truth been simply hidden by bandages, and left to gangrene. By some of the Turks these facts appear to have been regarded without the least regret or shame. An Ottoman official of high standing said one day to an Austrian gentleman, "Do you know the history of my country? Do you know that for centuries we went on from victory to victory till we forced our way up to the very walls of your own capital, Vienna? We had not then in our armies one ambulance or one medical man. Why should we have any now?" The Austrian retorted, "I can see but little difference between your old and your new system. In those days you killed your soldiers without doctors; you now kill them with." Medicine in Turkey is indeed at so low an ebb as to be quite unworthy of the name of science; and had it not been for foreign assistance, the sacrifice of life would have been even more appalling than it was.

KURDISH TYPES.

CHAPTER XXXVII.

Previous Career of Ahmed Mukhtar Pasha—His Services in Montenegro, Arabia, and other Parts—Honourable Features in his Character—Military Virtues of the Turkish Soldier—Testimony of Russian Wounded in the Hospital of Odessa—Withdrawal of Mukhtar Pasha from his advanced Positions—Expedition of General Lazareff towards the Rear of the Turkish Head-quarters—Disproportion of the Turkish and Russian Forces—Advance of the Grand Duke Michael—Heavy Bombardment—Progress of the Flanking Movement—Lazareff in the Rear of the Turkish Army—Description of the Ground—Action of October 14th—Plans for a Simultaneous Attack—Operations against the Olya Tépé on the 15th—The Position carried—Capture of Vezinkeui—Abandonment by the Turks of the Aladja Dagh and Little Yahni—Panic-stricken Flight towards Kars—Prisoners of Distinction—Incidents of the Final Collapse—State of Kars, and its Military Position with Reference to Defence—Retreat of Mukhtar Pasha to the Soghanli Dagh—Movements of Ismail Pasha—Junction of his Forces with those of the Commander-in-Chief—Continued Retreat of the Turkish Army—The New Position on the Deve-Boyun, in Front of Erzeroum—Preparations at Erzeroum for resisting the Russians—Energy of Faizi Pasha—Surprise and Rout of Ismail Pasha's Troops—Despatch of Reinforcements to Erzeroum—The Military Position on the Deve-Boyun—Expulsion of Newspaper Correspondents.

AHMED MUKHTAR PASHA was on the eve of a serious defeat; but as yet he stood in a position of proud pre-eminence, and much interest was excited in his previous career. His life had in some respects been remarkable, as he had risen from a family engaged in trade to a sphere of great importance. His grandfather was Hadji Ibrahim Agha, head of the guild of silk-merchants of Broussa, the ancient capital of Turkey, a city still famous for its silk-looms. Losing his father at an early age, Mukhtar, who was born in 1837, was brought up by his grandfather, and sent in 1849 to the preparatory military school of his native city. Here he showed considerable aptitude, and in five years quitted the establishment first of his class. He then entered the Military Academy at Constantinople, where he remained four years, and acquired the rank of lieutenant while he was yet pursuing his studies. On leaving, in 1858, he was made a captain on the Staff, and in that capacity joined the head-quarters of Omar Pasha, in Montenegro, three years later. It was not long ere his courage and ability were conspicuously shown. Finding himself one day with some cavalry near the defile of Ustruck, then in possession of the enemy, he charged the mountaineers with great spirit, and drove them out of the pass, which he held for some hours until reinforcements arrived. This was shortly before the close of the campaign, in 1862; and after the conclusion of peace Mukhtar was appointed Professor of Astronomy, Military Architecture, and Fortification (a singular combination) in the Constantinopolitan Academy where he had finished his education. He continued to rise in his profession, and in 1865 accompanied Prince Youssouf Izzedin, eldest son of Sultan Abdul-Aziz, in a tour to Austria, Germany, France, and England. During this trip, Mukhtar received from several European sovereigns the Legion of Honour, the Red Eagle, the Crown of Iron, and other honorary decorations, and in 1867 returned to Constantinople, where he was appointed one of the Commissioners for regulating the frontier of Montenegro, and in that capacity preserved to the Ottoman Empire the strategical point of Veli Malou Berdu, between Spitz and Podgoritza. His scientific knowledge of the art of fortification enabled him to construct the *tête du pont* of Vezir Kupri—an advantage over the Montenegrins which the latter sought to revenge by an attempt on the life of the young Turkish officer. On the conclusion of these labours, in 1869, Mukhtar was made a member of the Council of War, and, after a few months, General of Brigade under Redif Pasha, then commanding an expedition against the Arabs of Yemen. Redif falling ill, the actual conduct of affairs fell to Mukhtar, who distinguished himself by some brilliant feats of arms, and by the suppression of the rebellion. He became Mushir (or Field Marshal), and Governor of Yemen, in 1871, and two years later was transferred to Crete. After filling several other important posts, he was appointed to the command of the Turkish forces in Bosnia, Herzegovina, and Montenegro, shortly after the outbreak of the troubles in those regions. It is alleged by his friends that while on this service he gained twenty battles, and lost only one. However this may have been, he certainly exhibited his usual ability and resolution, and on the outbreak of the war with Russia was considered the fittest man for commanding the troops in Asia. He had only three weeks in which to provide for the defence of Armenia, and the early part of the campaign was unfortunate, owing to the want of preparation by which every movement was impaired.*

The word "Ghazi" originally meant "fanatic," but is now understood to signify both Defender of the Faith and Conqueror. Besides this title of

* Williams's Armenian Campaign, Appendix C.

honour, the Sultan conferred on Mukhtar Pasha the First Class of the Medjidié in diamonds, two fine Arab horses, and a sword in brilliants. The Mushir had certainly deserved these recognitions, for, besides being an excellent soldier, he had shown himself an honourable and humane man. As we we have already seen, he did his utmost to restrain the thievish and brutal propensities of the Kurds, Circassians, and other irregular troops; and when, nevertheless, outrages occurred, he was sincerely grieved. The regulars under his command behaved for the most part with exemplary discipline and self-restraint. The peasantry were safe from exactions at their hands. Whatever they required was paid for in coin; and if the soldiers had no money (as was frequently the case), they contented themselves with the small modicum of meal allowed them for their rations, which they mixed with water, and baked on heated iron plates. Mukhtar Pasha is short of stature, but strongly built, his face browned with the sun, and his appearance and bearing those of a thorough soldier. His personal habits throughout the campaign were extremely unostentatious, and the equipment of his tent consisted of nothing more than a camp-bedstead and a couple of camp-stools. In this respect he resembled Suleiman Pasha, but differed from the generality of Turkish commanding officers, who are usually surrounded by great pomp and state. In battle, he exposed himself with almost reckless courage, and his men regarded him with the mingled love and veneration which bravery and frequent success will naturally inspire.

CONVEYING AMMUNITION TO THE FRONT.

The troops were worthy of their commander—always excepting the infamous irregulars. A correspondent of the *Daily News* said it was perfectly wonderful to see these men, wretchedly fed, badly clothed, and many of them without shoes, marching cheerfully along, full of confidence and spirit, to meet the enemy in battle. No one thought of murmuring at his lot; no one deserted his colours; all were willing to die at the word of command. The writer doubted whether these fine soldierly qualities could be referred to either patriotism or fanaticism, as the one feeling does not exist in Turkey, and the other would not operate continuously. He believed that they resulted from the Turk's dogged determination to execute at any hazard the orders he receives, and from that insensibility to fear which seems inherent in the Turkish character. But, whatever the origin of these military virtues, the correspondent entertained no doubt that, if well-commanded, paid, and fed, the Turkish troops would be the very best in the world. In some respects, the two sets of combatants were beginning to entertain feelings of mutual admiration. The Turk acknowledged the firmness, solidity, and vigour of the Russian; the Russian saw that the Turk was very far from worn out and ineffective. The wounded in the hospital at Odessa spoke with generous emulation of the bravery displayed by most of the Turkish regulars. One man said to a correspondent of the *Times*, "When *we* are badly wounded, we cease fighting; whereas *they* go on firing until the breath is out of their bodies, or they are taken prisoners." The Circassians and Bashi-Bazouks, however, were denounced as miscreants and wretches; and certainly the irregular troops on both sides threw discredit on the armies with which they were associated in the prosecution of the war.

The fighting in Armenia during the early days of October had on the whole been unfavourable to the Russians; yet they were not discouraged. Great activity was observable in their army, and Mukhtar Pasha, with his diminished numbers, felt uneasy as to the designs that were being prepared against him. He perceived that he could no longer occupy the advanced position in the plain which he had so carefully fortified; and on the night following the 9th of October he secretly withdrew from that stronghold, as well as from the Kizil Tépé and Great Yahni, and returned to his entrenched encampments half way up the Aladja Dagh. The entrenchments on the Kizil Tépé were afterwards found by the Russians to be of very careful and elaborate construction. The guns, which were taken away with them by the Turks, had all been placed in deep cuttings, and covered with double, crossed rows of timber, surmounted by thick layers of earth. To give up such a position was extremely mortifying, especially as, after the Russian reverses at the beginning of the month, the Turks were for a few days animated by a lively hope of entering Alexandropol, in Russian Armenia, before long. The retreat was therefore at once a surprise and a disappointment. As far as secrecy was concerned, the movement was well conducted; but everything was in hopeless confusion. The commanding officers seemed to have no exact knowledge as to where the new position was situated, and battalion stumbled against battalion on the rugged mountain-sides, all through the dark and starless night.

It was necessary that Mukhtar should concentrate his troops within stricter limits; but the necessity was in itself a sign of coming disaster. At the very time he executed his retrograde movement, General Lazareff, one of the most energetic of the Russian officers, was operating, at the head of twenty-six battalions, forty-eight field-pieces, and six regiments of cavalry, against Mukhtar's line of communication with Kars. Lazareff acted after the most scientific fashion of modern warfare. A field-telegraph was laid from the Russian head-quarters at Karajal to the detachment set apart for this important expedition, and followed it during a circuitous march of forty miles across a mountainous and difficult country. Although some of the posts were at one time thrown down by a storm of wind, the line was repaired and at work again in two hours; and its existence enabled the Russian commanders to conduct a simultaneous movement of two distinct columns, the object of which was to surround Mukhtar Pasha, and starve him out. The success of this design was rendered probable by the large accession of force which had recently come to the Russians, and which continued from day to day. On the 6th and 7th of October—just after the succession of battles which had, on the whole, resulted unfortunately for the Muscovites—several heavy columns of troops reached Karajal, and the fact speedily became known to the Ottoman General. It was this circumstance which determined his withdrawal from the more exposed parts of his line; but the step should have been taken earlier, and perhaps have been carried farther. Mukhtar had, at the very utmost, not more than 30,000 men under his orders when the October battles began; and the number had considerably decreased by the 7th of the month. The Russian force was much larger than that, both in men and guns. It had regained its freedom of movement in regaining its strength, and the period of inactivity ended with the arrival of fresh regiments. On the Turkish side, reinforcements had been refused by the Commander-in-Chief during the month of August, on the ground that the men were more urgently needed in Europe; and the Ottomans were now seriously, and as it proved hopelessly, overmatched by the thickening masses of the enemy.

The retrograde movement of Mukhtar Pasha was followed, on the 9th of October, by a corresponding advance on the part of the Russians, who occupied the Kizil Tépé, Soubatan, Hadji-veli, and the eastern slopes of the Great Yahni. Here they were exposed to the artillery-fire from the whole of the Turkish guns; but their own guns were speedily sent forward, and replied with effect. On the 10th, the Grand Duke Michael bombarded the Turkish camp throughout the day, and at the same time threatened the position with dense masses of infantry. Very little was done on the following day; but on the 12th the Russians poured a destructive fire into the Turkish shelter-trenches, and harassed the enemy by perpetual menaces of an infantry assault which was not in fact delivered. Mukhtar Pasha seems to have been at this time the victim of an undue confidence. He maintained that it was absolutely impossible for an army to move round the rear of the Aladja Dagh—an opinion which probably resulted from his ignorance of the ground, which it is believed he had never examined. The consequence of this error was that he had regard merely to his front, leaving his flanks and rear in the most feeble and exposed condition. Lazareff was much indebted to his adversary's negligence for the ultimate success of his turning movement. The Mushir appears to have known nothing of the impending danger until a day or two after it had commenced, and by that time the Russian General had placed himself in a position of command, from which his adversary was unable to drive him out.

The march of General Lazareff, which began early on the morning of the 10th, was a good deal impeded by his artillery and military train, and he was compelled, by the difficult nature of the ground, to follow a circuitous route. Proceeding southwards along the eastern bank of the Arpa-Tchai as far as Kotchiran, he there crossed the river to Dighur, on the western bank, and, after leaving two battalions in that locality, made his way northwards to the heights of Orlok: altogether, a distance of forty miles. Lazareff had now worked round the right flank of the Ottomans, and Mukhtar, on discovering the fact, took measures to repel the enemy. A detachment, consisting of twelve battalions of infantry, some cavalry, and eighteen guns, was sent against the Russian forces, and the command was entrusted to Mukhtar's brother-in-law, Raschid Pasha—a brave soldier, but an officer of little judgment or experience. He encountered General Lazareff, on the 12th, near Orlok, and at first drove him back by the impetuosity of his onslaught; but the smallness of the force prevented his maintaining this temporary success. The Turkish Generalissimo had furnished his lieutenant with as many troops as he could spare; but they were few in comparison with those brought against him. A feeling of despondency, a dim presentiment of evil, had taken possession of the Turkish soldiers, and, on the night of October 10th, upwards of seven hundred deserted. Mukhtar Pasha was therefore ill-prepared to resist the threatened assault; and Lazareff improved his position on the 13th by getting to the rear of the Turkish left, and occupying the Oghur Hill, after a sharp engagement. On the same day, the Russians made a reconnaissance towards Kars, and some heavy firing occurred in that direction. A little before evening, two big guns, placed in position near Soubatan, threw shells close to the Turkish headquarters, from a distance of seven thousand yards. The correctness of the áim was remarkable, and, as the tents were hidden behind rocks and fortifications, the place seems to have been indicated by spies. Extreme uneasiness was felt by the Turks, and Dr. Casson, who had charge of the ambulance hospital, considered it prudent to remove his wounded from the exposed position in which they were lying to the upper slopes of the Aladja Dagh, where it was thought they would be out of range.

To explain the battles which took place on the 14th and 15th of October, a slight description of the ground was given by a correspondent of the *Daily News* attached to the Turkish camp. The Aladja Dagh, according to this authority, "is a mountain 8,800 feet in height, its base of an elongated oval form, running east and west. The summit, of a conical form, is towards the south-eastern extremity of the oval. At the same point it throws out a large spur to the southward. Both the summit and this spur were strongly entrenched, and occupied by eight or ten battalions, and some batteries of field-artillery. The bulk of the Turkish forces occupied the lower portions of the northern slope, and numbered from thirty-five to forty thousand regular troops. On the extreme right (east) is a flat-topped hill, named Lakiridgi Tépé and on the left a similar one, Evliatepessi (the Olya Tépé) which, as will be seen later on, played an important part in the fighting. To the north of Aladja is an immense plain, the mouth of the Kars valley. To the east of this plain are the isolated hills of Karajal, Kizil Tépé, and Utch Tépé, all three in the possession of the enemy at the commencement of the fighting. Towards Kars, that is westward, the plain is bounded by two hills, the greater and lesser Yahni. The greater Yahni is midway between Evliatepessi (the Olya Tépé) and the lesser Yahni, and was occupied by the Russians after the retrograde movement of the 8th. The other two hills were in our hands and strongly entrenched. Continuing the line formed by these three hills, to the south of the western extremity of Aladja are three similar isolated hills, one exactly opposite the long end of the Aladja oval. Then comes a large plain-like valley, and beyond, at some eight miles' distance, a chain of mountains,

DEFEAT OF THE TURKS. RUSSIANS STORMING THE OLYA TÉPÉ.

gradually lessening in height towards Kars, and slightly oblique to Aladja."

The morning of the 14th passed without any event of importance, though immense bodies of Russians were seen by the Turks moving incessantly to and fro in the vast plain beneath the several eminences. At about half-past two in the afternoon, however, the noise of heavy firing was heard at the Turkish head-quarters from a direction south of the Aladja Dagh. The Ottoman guns in that locality were opening fire on the enemy, who had established a couple of batteries on the Oghur Hill, taken by Lazareff the day before. Some Turkish battalions were at once despatched across the valley, and the combat soon raged with fury. Fighting continued until near sunset, when the Turks, finding themselves defeated, retired towards the extremity of the range of hills next Kars. "The Russians," says the correspondent already quoted, "had advanced half way from the higher hill, whence they had commenced, to the final conical hill which terminated abruptly in the flat valley. Mukhtar Pasha, deeming the day's fighting over, turned rein and rode with his Staff over the long slopes leading to his head-quarters. A quarter of an hour passed, and streaks of fire were seen issuing from the point to which the Russians had advanced. Little by little, these streaks increased in number, and the terminal hill seemed all ablaze with bursting projectiles. But there was no sound of artillery. The enemy was bombarding the position with Congreve rockets. The fire was so rapid that the sky was all ablaze. At least sixty per minute were discharged. Then I saw long lines of flickering fire go up the hill, parallel to the crest of flame that crowned the crest. Half-a-dozen times these fiery lines approached and recoiled. Then they mingled; then came a pause. Rocket and musketry-fire ceased. I retired to my tent with sad misgivings." In the course of the ensuing night, the Turkish left began to retreat in the direction of Vezinkeui—a strongly entrenched position, which secured the Ottoman communications with Kars; and the prospects of the morrow looked extremely dark.

BOMBARDING THE TURKISH POSITION WITH CONGREVE ROCKETS.

Previously to these events, General Lazareff had telegraphed to the Grand Duke's head-quarters, reporting the partial success he had obtained, and requesting that, on the resumption of his operations, a simultaneous attack might be directed against other portions of the Turkish lines. The suggestion was adopted, and it was determined to carry the Olya Tépé at any cost. The possession of the Great Yahni, which the Turks had abandoned and the Russians occupied, enabled the latter to make a fresh attack on the Olya Tépé with every hope of success. General Heimann was charged with the operation, and the Caucasian Grenadiers, with fifty-six cannon, were placed under his command for this purpose. The Moscow Grenadiers formed the reserve, and were ordered to refrain from acting until the hill was taken. Their position was on the left of the Russian attack, in the vicinity of Soubatan; and here they were joined, early on the morning of the 15th, by the Grand Duke and General Loris Melikoff. The right wing of General Heimann's forces was covered by the Ardahan brigade, under General Komaroff, and by some regiments of cavalry, designed to hold in check the garrison of Kars, together with the Turkish troops still occupying the Little Yahni.

A tremendous fire was now directed against the Olya Tépé. Fifty-six Russian guns were planted before that position, at a distance sufficiently near to produce considerable effect. Shells incessantly burst amongst the Turkish lines on the summit; but the defenders were not slow in replying, and clouds of smoke hung over the scene of combat, or slowly drifted away on the still air. Every now and then the Turkish fire was silenced, but broke forth with renewed energy as soon as fresh men had supplied the places of those killed or wounded. With these slight intermissions, the combat continued for three hours, and then came to a more prolonged stand-still. The Russian line made no advance, and the Grenadiers still lay about the northern side of the hill, without the least attempt at movement. Suddenly, cannon were heard from the direction of Soubatan, beyond the left of the Russian line; and some Turkish tirailleurs were observed descending the Aladja Dagh, and advancing to the succour of their comrades on the Olya Tépé. To fulfil this intention, it was necessary for them to cross the ravine separating the one eminence from the other; but they were speedily driven back by a Russian detachment, and at that moment three columns of Grenadiers moved up the side of the Olya Tépé. Firing as they climbed, these men approached the summit in face of a tremendous fire from the Turks. To those who watched them from below, they soon became invisible in the dun smoke which they and their opponents were equally producing; but nothing checked their advance. The Russian batteries at the foot of the mountain poured a tempest of shells upon the crest; the Grenadiers concentrated their lines as they got nearer to the point of attack; and at length, with repeated shouts of triumph, they jumped across the ditches, and scaled the parapets. The Turks resisted to the last, but were finally compelled to fly. General Heimann then rode to the top of the hill with his Staff, and, parading his soldiers, ordered a close pursuit of the enemy. The position was fully in the hands of the Russians, and a most important point had been gained in the scheme of concerted operations by which it was hoped to crush Mukhtar Pasha, and redeem the fortunes of the campaign in Asia.

The four Turkish battalions (numbering about 2,000 men) which had held the crown of the Olya Tépé suffered terribly from the Russian guns, which for the most part fired timed fuses, bursting with deadly accuracy amongst the opposing lines. Every possible effort for the defence of the hill was made by the men holding it; but they were outnumbered, and finally crushed. The five battalions sent to their assistance behaved ill, with the exception of the leading half-battalion, which succeeded in gaining the crest. The others were seized with a panic when they were half-way up the slope, and, staggering under the fiery storm that fell upon them as they were nearing the summit of the interposing ravine, they turned, and retired slowly to the Aladja Dagh. Their officers were unable to rally them, and indeed do not appear to have been very energetic in the attempt. The failure of these battalions to relieve their fellows sealed the fate of the position which General Heimann was assailing, and the capture of that position by the Russians carried other misfortunes in its wake. The defeated Ottomans fled towards the Aladja Dagh, and the Russian commander, pressing up the ravine, interposed his forces between the Turkish troops on the mountain and those at Vezinkeui. The latter position was next attacked; the fortified plateau in front of the village was stormed within an hour of the time when the Olya Tépé succumbed to Heimann's assault; and at the same moment General Lazareff operated on the farther side of the village, and, assailing the Osmanlis in their rear, cut off their retreat to Kars. The Turks were now widely scattered in various localities, and made a desperate endeavour to escape, so that they might re-combine in some position more favourable for defence. But in every direction they found themselves opposed by immense masses of infantry, cavalry, and artillery, and in a little while despair settled upon their ranks, and placed them almost beyond the influence of military command. It was only on the Aladja Dagh and the Little Yahni that the Ottomans continued to make a stand; and even there the resistance did not continue long. After a brief struggle, the troops on the Aladja Dagh lost all hope, and even all self-respect. They were alternately entreated and threatened; but their ranks broke up into ragged, disorderly masses, and a panic-stricken flight towards Kars speedily set in. The garrison of the Little Yahni also escaped in the same direction, but in a more deliberate manner, and at a later hour. Watching their opportunity, when the attention of the Russians was occupied by the combat at Vezinkeui, they got off with their stores, cannon, and ammunition. The Russian cavalry did nothing to prevent their retreat, alleging that it was too dark to carry out such an operation; but in other localities immense numbers of prisoners were taken, and Colonel Kavalinsky, Chief of the Staff of the Cavalry, reported to the Grand Duke, at nine o'clock P.M., that seven Pashas, thirty-six guns, and twenty-six battalions, had surrendered and laid down their arms. Many more were captured on the following day, and the army of Mukhtar Pasha was shattered, and all but annihilated. Amongst the prisoners were Raschid Pasha, Lieutenant-General and President of the Military Council; Hussein Kyazim Pasha, Chief of Mukhtar's Staff; Mustapha Pasha; Shefket Pasha, commanding the Second Division; and three other Generals of distinction. Five thousand men had been killed and wounded, and twelve thousand taken prisoners; while forty-two (according to some accounts, fifty-six) pieces of artillery, together with three thousand pack-animals, had passed over to the enemy. Mukhtar Pasha, who had directed the operations of the day from Sevri Tépé (an eminence south-west of the Olya Tépé), and who exhibited throughout the most admirable courage and firmness, escaped to Kars, together with Sir Arnold Kemball, after the capture of the main positions.*

In their flight towards the nearest place of refuge, the Ottoman troops probably behaved no worse than other armies in moments of extreme disaster; but it is certain that, with few exceptions, they gave way to feelings of uncontrolled terror. Not only the irregular cavalry, chiefly composed of Arabs from Orfa and Aleppo, but even the infantry of the Line, rushed pell-mell from the positions they could no longer defend, and lost all military cohesion in the frantic endeavours of each individual to secure his own life and freedom. The final collapse was described in vivid colours by the *Daily News* correspondent on the Turkish side. "Nearer and nearer," writes this gentleman, "advanced the Russian batteries in front and flank. I left the commanding ridge of plain on which I stood, and made for our last position, the hill of Vezinkeui, not far from Kars. This is an isolated hill in the plain, and takes its name from a ruined Armenian village close under its brow. Here, around a large water-reservoir, were accumulated the waggons, mules, and camels of the commissariat, sent off the night before from Aladja. Some four thousand irregular cavalry and panic-stricken infantry were mixed up with the ox-waggons and camels. It was a scene of utter confusion. A reserve battalion of regular troops, deployed in open order with fixed bayonets, prevented the runaways from flying to Kars. Nearer and nearer thundered the Russian guns, and each detonation thrilled the disorganised mass with terror. The road to Kars was cumbered with ox-waggons, baggage, mules, and what was supposed to be their escort. All were running at full speed. The oxen galloped like horses. The mules careered madly, and often, when their burdens slipped from their backs, the frightened conductors went on, not daring to lose time in picking up their charge. The panic was complete. A mile farther on was a line of infantry with levelled rifles, threatening all runaways, and firing repeatedly on those who sought to get off by a side movement. As I neared Kars, the guns of the lower forts were firing on bands of fugitive cavalry." The correspondent himself was threatened by a Turkish colonel, and forced to ride back in the direction of the field of battle. It was only with great difficulty that he got into Kars, and here everything was in a state of the wildest disorder. Terror-stricken crowds filled the streets, and Mukhtar Pasha dared not show himself in public, for fear of assassinatior

The sanitary condition of Kars was in itself a subject for the gravest alarm. Typhoid fever was raging among the sick and wounded, and, though provisions were abundant, firewood was scarcely to be had, and fodder for the horses was equally wanting. It was certain that the victorious Russians would soon lay siege to the place, and it possessed no military force of sufficient strength to resist a powerful attack. The number of armed citizens was considerable; but these extemporised soldiers are seldom worth very much. Of guns and ammu-

* The foregoing narrative of the Turkish defeat has been derived from an examination of various reports. These are in some respects contradictory, and not one is clear as to the exact order and chronological sequence of events. But it is believed that, by a process of comparison, the truth has been here disentangled from the somewhat chaotic obscurity of the first hastily-written accounts.

nition there was no lack. The batteries had been recently repaired; extra traverses had been erected on the eastern and western hills; and additional bombproof accommodation had been provided for the garrison of the forts. But, on a careful examination into the state of the army after his arrival at Kars, Mukhtar Pasha found that not more than 13,000 men fit to bear arms could be collected in the city, and he knew that, unless he could throw a force between Kars and Erzeroum, the Russians would very speedily advance upon the latter place, and take possession of it. He therefore determined to leave Hussein Hami Pasha at Kars with 10,000 men, while he himself, with the remainder, and ten mountain-guns, fell back on the Soghanli Dagh, a range of mountains to the west of Kars, rising to a height of 9,369 feet, and covered with snow the greater part of the year. A telegram was despatched to Ismail Pasha, who was at that time in Russian territory, near Igdyr, ordering him to retire immediately on Koprikoi. On the 19th of October, Ismail, who was one of the Kurdish chiefs largely employed in the war, destroyed all his spare ammunition and commissariat stores, and detached six battalions, with a battery, to Bayazid, while he himself, with the remaining twenty-two battalions and thirty-three guns, fell back on the Araxes. By this time, Mukhtar had given up all hope of again seeing the bulk of his forces on the Aladja Dagh. Thirteen battalions had indeed cut their way through the masses of the enemy, and the soldiers composing them came dropping in from day to day. But by far the greater number, with the artillery, commissariat, hospital equipments, and baggage, had fallen into the hands of the Russians.*

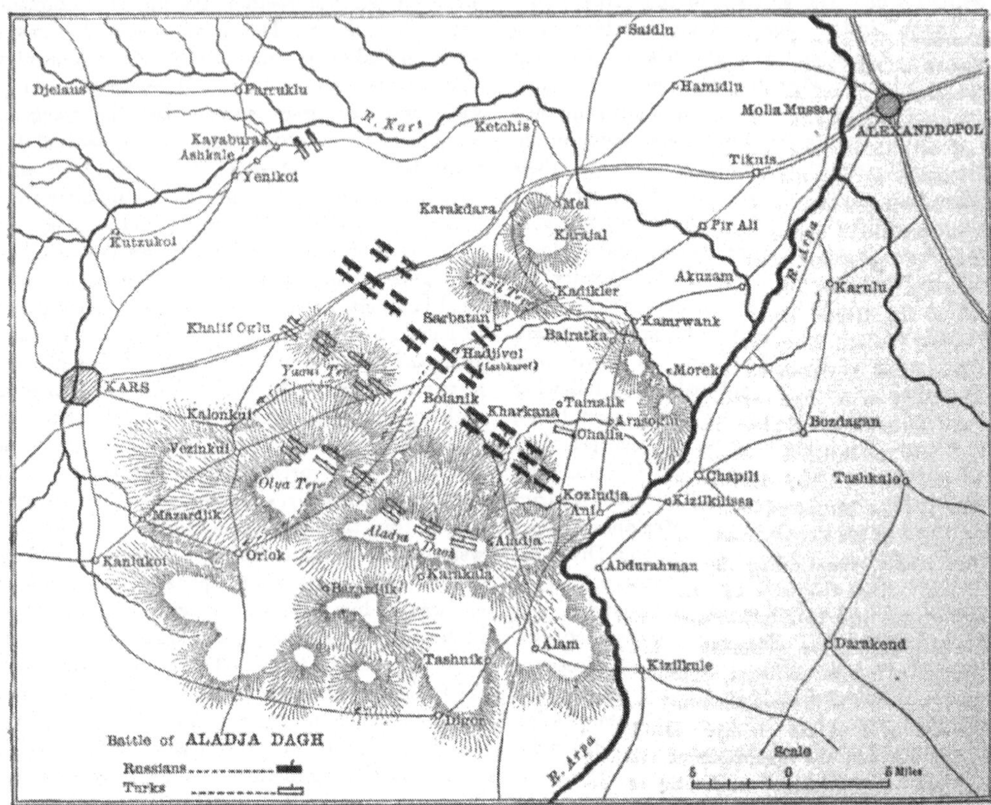

PLAN OF THE BATTLE OF ALADJA DAGH.

Mukhtar Pasha attributed his defeat to the superiority of the Russian guns, and to the desertion of the chief positions by his soldiers, who, as it seemed to him, took to flight without sufficient reason. Unfortunately, the occasions of defeat continued to exist, and the improbability of the Turkish fortunes in Armenia being retrieved, either by Mukhtar Pasha or any other commander, must have been apparent to every one. Ismail Pasha,

* Captain Norman's Armenia, and the Campaign of 1877, chap. 20.

however, succeeded in effecting his junction with the Mushir, though not without considerable trouble. He left Zeidikan on the 24th of October, and was menaced by a Russian army coming from the north. In passing through the defiles of the Kose Dagh range, he divided his force into two columns, of which that to the left was attacked on the 26th by a brigade of Cossacks, but succeeded in repelling the assault. Mukhtar, who in the first instance had retired on Yenikoi, was compelled, owing to the rapid pursuit of General Heimann, to fall back on Koprikoi, which he reached on the 27th. Here he was joined, almost directly afterwards, by Ismail Pasha, from whom he learned that Tergukasoff, as well as Heimann, was in pursuit. The shattered remnants of the army accordingly retreated to the plains of Hassan Kalé on the 28th, and, on the night of the same day, in consequence of the rear-guard being assailed, withdrew still farther to the defile of Deve-Boyun, or the Camel's Neck—the last line covering Erzeroum.

Having made the best arrangements possible under the circumstances, Mukhtar Pasha pushed on towards Erzeroum, leaving directions with Ismail Pasha to retire at once on Hassan Kalé. The movement was carried out on the 28th of October; and three hours after the Turks had left Koprikoi the Russian advance-guard entered the place, where they found large quantities of grain, which Ismail had had no time to destroy. All this while, preparations were being made at Erzeroum for resisting the Russians to the last extremity. The chief commander in that city was Faizi Pasha, an old Hungarian, of great energy and good military abilities. He had long anticipated the misfortune which had now fallen on Mukhtar; and when the news arrived, he hurriedly collected all the able-bodied men in the city, and despatched them to the batteries on the neighbouring range of heights. He also sent forward forty guns, the majority of which were breech-loaders of the Krupp pattern. The entrenchments were improved; redoubts were thrown up on the advanced spurs of the mountains; and the roads by which the city was approached from the east were swept by a cross-fire from the heights above. It would have been well for Ismail Pasha if he had acted with equal promptitude and intelligence; but, instead of taking precautions to guard his position at Hassan Kalé, he bivouacked his men in the open plain to the south, without throwing out a single picket. The advance-guard of General Heimann was not slow in discovering this fact, nor did the General himself lose time in turning it to advantage. He sent a force round by the north, so as to take the Turks in flank after they had retired to rest, and himself advanced, about midnight of the 28th, on Hassan Kalé. The Turks were surprised, terror-stricken, and put to flight. Hardly any resistance was offered, and the Ottomans, throwing down their arms and abandoning their guns, dashed in a confused rout along the road to Kurudjuk. The troops at that place, hearing the noise of firing from the direction of Heimann's attack, turned out with great readiness, to cover the retreat of the fugitives; and on the 29th Ismail Pasha again united his forces with those of Mukhtar.

Telegrams had ere this been sent to Constantinople, urgently requiring all available help, and the Commander-in-Chief was now informed that five battalions had been despatched from Batoum, and that twelve more, together with two batteries, were already on the march from Constantinople. Even without these additions, Mukhtar Pasha had been able to guard the Deve-Boyun ridge with 16,000 troops and sixty guns. With a hopefulness which seems characteristic of his nature, and which is sometimes carried to the extent of an imprudent confidence, he believed that he could withstand the attacks of his enemy; but he had under-estimated the force which General Heimann could bring against him, and supposed his own strength to be greater than that of his adversary, when it was in fact much less. Faizi Pasha was more sensible of the danger which threatened Erzeroum, though he maintained a cheerful bearing, and endeavoured to take the most sanguine view of the case that facts permitted. Had the Turkish Generalissimo possessed a larger and better force, the position was one which might have been easily defended. Its natural capabilities were excellent, and its artificial works were far from contemptible. "The pass of Deve-Boyun," says the *Daily News* correspondent from whom we have already quoted, "is a narrow valley, leading due east from Erzeroum to the wide plain of Hassan Kalé—the latter an old-fashioned Turkish town, near which are the fountains of the Araxes. The pass is skirted by rounded hills, and near its eastern extremity is crossed by a ridge which constitutes the second line of defence. Then comes a deep, precipitous ravine, and immediately beyond another ridge. Opposite the centre of this ridge, slightly to the left, is a long hill crowned by a steeply-bounded plateau, narrow like the hill itself. To the right are two conical hills, somewhat oblique to the front, on which were two redoubts, armed with guns of position, and occupied by several battalions. To the left of the long hill was a rounded mamelon, projecting spur-like from the lofty mountains which fringe the plain. From this mamelon long trenches extended further east, to secure the left flank. In front of all run two rivulets, which, uniting, form one of the tributaries of the Araxes." Here were many elements of strength; but the weak points in the position were two valleys, to the north and south, both debouching into the plain before Erzeroum. Still, the advantages of the situation prevailed over its disadvantages; and Mukhtar Pasha was not without some reasonable ground of hope that, when his reinforcements had arrived, he would be able to save the chief military position of Turkish Armenia from the clutch of Russia.

FLIGHT OF THE TURKS. FUGITIVES IN A TURKISH VILLAGE.

As the difficulties of the war increased, the presence of newspaper correspondents at the respective camps, which had at first been tolerated, became a subject of annoyance to the commanders on both sides. Many of these gentlemen were hampered by vexatious difficulties, while some were actually dismissed. Early in the autumn, the *Agence Russe* announced that, by order of the Commander-in-Chief of the Russian army of the Danube, the correspondent of the London *Standard*, Mr. Frederick Boyle, had been expelled from the Roumanian territory for having, in a letter from Poradim of the 24th of August, described the Russian positions and entrenchments, and spoken in hateful and malevolent terms of the Russian army, despite the hospitality received by him. Captain Norman, the representative of the *Times* in Armenia, was accused of exaggerating the reverses and the misdeeds of Turkish soldiers, and was obliged to quit the scene of operations, in consequence of orders to that effect from Constantinople, though Mukhtar Pasha himself regretted the step. The correspondent of the same journal, accompanying the Russian forces in Asia, complained that he was treated with marked discourtesy, and subjected to so many restrictions that he was unable to perform the duties of his office. Simply because he was an Englishman, he was set down for a Turkish spy; and after a while the feeling of admiration for the Russians, with which he had commenced his work, gave place to sentiments of a very different order. With respect to the Russian armies in Europe, however, a correspondent of the *Daily News* denied that any of his brethren were forbidden to enter Bulgaria, and affirmed that they were only withheld from visiting the positions around Plevna. Even this prohibition, he added, was entirely owing to the indiscretion of some correspondents, who revealed the exact position of each division, brigade, and regiment before Plevna during the September attacks, so that the Turkish Ambassador in London had ample time to telegraph all the dispositions of the Russians and Roumanians to Osman Pasha before the assault began.

CHAPTER XXXVIII.

General Todleben entrusted with the Investment of Plevna—Changes in the Russian Commands—Character of Osman Pasha—Plevna and its Fortifications—Life at Gorny Studen, the Imperial Head-quarters—Daily Routine of the Emperor Alexander—Kindness to the Sick in Hospital—Russian Hostility to England—Opinions of Prince Tcherkasski with respect to the Progress of the War—State of Bulgaria—Desperate Condition of the Roads—Damage to the Bridges of Boats—The Russian Reinforcements—Capture of a Russian Convoy by Mehemet Pasha—Arrangements by the Russians for a Winter's Campaign—Destruction of a Turkish Gunboat by Torpedoes—Taking of Gorny Dubnik by General Gourko—The Investment of Plevna rendered more strict—Concentration of the Russian Fire—Capture of Teliche and Dolny Dubnik—Completion of the Investment of Plevna—Improved Prospects of the Russian Invasion—Serious Position of Osman Pasha—Gallant Achievement of Skobeleff—A Position secured within the Russian Lines—Capture of Vratza by Gourko—Turkish Women and Children driven into Plevna—Death of Prince Sergius of Leuchtenberg—The Point at which Emperors begin to feel.

NOTHING was more evident throughout the progress of affairs in Europe than that the Russian troops had not been efficiently handled, except on a few isolated occasions. The Grand Duke Nicholas had been made Commander-in-Chief on the strength of his being the Emperor's brother, and he furnished convincing proofs that an Emperor's brother is not necessarily a Napoleon. Some of the other officers showed ability on special occasions, but were apparently inadequate to the conduct of a great campaign. The system of making furious attacks on strongly entrenched positions, defended with all the obstinate courage of the Turks, was seen to be a complete failure, and the Czar could not conceal from himself that other measures were necessary, and other counsellors desirable. He therefore summoned to the field of action a soldier who had done excellent service during the Crimean War. The defence of Sebastopol, in those memorable days, was conducted by General Todleben—an engineer officer, admitted throughout Europe to be a master in his particular branch of the military art. When the Allies appeared on the south side of the great Crimean stronghold, Todleben devised, and created with extraordinary rapidity, a series of earthworks, ramparts, and batteries, of the most formidable character, which were not overcome until after a year's siege. The genius he displayed on that occasion raised him to a very high place in the estimation of his Imperial master, and he was considered the most likely man to reduce the similar works which Osman Pasha had multiplied around the village of Plevna. It is true that he had now to attack, instead of to defend; but it was rightly judged that his knowledge and experience were capable of a double application.

Todleben arrived in Bulgaria at the latter end of September, and at once replaced General Zotoff as Chief of the Staff to Prince Charles of Roumania. That is to say, the actual conduct of the operations against Plevna was consigned to him, and he at once perceived that a regular siege would be necessary. Other changes in the commands were made shortly after. General Gourko, who had not been actively employed since his retreat from the southern side of the Balkans, was appointed to the command of the entire cavalry force concentrated about Plevna. The younger Skobeleff was placed at the head of the Sixteenth Division. General Dundukoff Korsakoff received the command of the Thirteenth Army-Corps; Prince Imeretinsky was made Chief of the Staff of the Russian army; and General Zotoff obtained the command of the corps vacated by Prince Imeretinsky. These alterations were carried out at the beginning of October, and it was not long ere their effect was seen in greater vigour and activity. An improvement was undoubtedly much needed. The imbecility in some of the Russian commands was very strikingly manifested in the escape of the Turkish convoys sent to the relief of Osman Pasha, the details of which have been already given. Kriloff, who had command of the intercepting cavalry on that occasion, was an infantry officer, and seems to have been totally unfitted for the ordering of mounted troops. He actually took credit to himself for his skill in "watching" the road whereby the two convoys, which he failed to stop, made their way into Plevna. In this respect, as in others, the Roumanians showed much greater aptitude than the Russians. A third convoy, consisting of eighty waggons, was captured on the 28th of September by the soldiers of the Principality, who at the same time pushed forward, with remarkable energy and perseverance, the approaches they were making towards the second Grivica Redoubt. An attack on this position was delivered on the 19th of October, and the fort was actually taken for about twenty minutes; but the Turks then rallied, and the Roumanians, after suffering terrible losses, were compelled to retire.

The Allies had a formidable opponent in Osman Pasha. A correspondent of the *Daily Telegraph* said he could hardly find words to express the demeanour of this General during the actions early in September. His coolness and self-possession, even in unforeseen circumstances and at moments of sudden peril, were remarkable. He never for an instant spoke or acted hastily, and was ready with a joke now and then, while intently watching the tactics of the enemy. Such was his conduct at all times, and it procured for him the love and admiration of the troops. Yet he was a strict disciplinarian, and the precision and rapidity with which his men carried out their orders proved the excellence of their drill, and the firmness with which they were managed. A good many wild rumours were in circulation with respect to this commander. Some said he was no other than Marshal Bazaine, the capitulator of Metz; others, that he was one of the Confederate Generals of the American Civil War. Neither story had any foundation in fact. Osman Pasha was born in Asia Minor in 1822 or the following year, and was educated in the Military School of Constantinople. He had never been in Europe, except in European Turkey, but spoke a little French. His figure was tall and spare, and at the time in question he was in delicate health, though his attention to his duties never flagged. Every detail of the army passed under the superintendence of the chief commander, who directed the particular manner in which his orders were to be fulfilled. The place he had to defend was described by the correspondent of the *Daily Telegraph* as one of the most labyrinthine towns in the world. "It is situated," he went on to say, "between a huge marsh and an odorous ditch, called by courtesy the river Vid. Its streets are paved on the principle of one huge boulder to three great holes. It boasts a mosque, a huge Christian church, a prison, and a khan. In itself it is not of the slightest importance. Were Plevna, with the whole of its inhabitants, blotted out of existence, the world would run its round, and nobody would say much about Plevna departed. But it chances to lie at the base of three ridges, which describe a triangle intersected at the base and furthermost angle; and so it has been chosen by both Russian and Turk as a battle-ground. It has really but very few advantages to offer a supine defender. If a sleepy man held it, he would gain nothing whatever from the conformation of the ground. But in the hands of the energetic Osman Pasha it has suddenly become one of the strongest positions to be found anywhere. With great skill, and a very great deal of sound common-sense, the Marshal, immediately on arriving at Plevna, picked out the salient points of the position, and ran up redoubts there. Fort after fort was made and manned; if any point commanded a redoubt, it was entrenched, bastioned, and armed, too; and so the work went on with marvellous perseverance, till Plevna is, humanly speaking, impregnable." The worst of these positions of so-called impregnability is that they can always be starved into surrender, unless there is an army in the field strong enough to keep open the communications, and to overmatch the armies of the enemy. Paris was probably invulnerable to direct assault in the war of 1870-71: yet the Germans reduced it by famine, because the relieving armies could never break the iron circle of investment by which it was held as in the grip of fate.

In striking contrast with the wretchedness of Plevna was the comfort of Gorny Studen, which the Russian Emperor had made his head-quarters since the 14th of August. Compared with most

THE CZAR AND HIS STAFF AT GORNY STUDEN.

Bulgarian towns, Gorny Studen is regular and symmetrical. "In the middle of the village," wrote an occasional correspondent of the *Times*, "stands the church, built in the form of a parallelogram, with a semi-circle added on the eastern side, and a portico supported by three arches, with columns in the façade. The northern slope of the valley was occupied chiefly by Turkish houses, which were deserted by their owners when the Russians approached. Standing out prominently from among these was a large building, with extensive outhouses, the whole surrounded by a strong fence. That house belonged to a rich Bulgarian trader, who was not only a friend of the Turks, but had even become secretly a Mohammedan. When the Turkish population fled, this Bulgarian fled with them, and his house became the temporary residence of the Emperor. Round about it tents were put up for the persons attached to the Imperial Head-quarters. Those who did not find accommodation in the tents lived in the neighbouring houses of the Turkish fugitives. A little to the west, and somewhat higher on the slope, were the quarters of the escort, composed of two squadrons of the so-called 'Escort of his Imperial Majesty,' and half a company of Life Guards. On the opposite slope were the head-quarters of the army. The tent of the Commander-in-Chief, situated near the centre, was easily recognized from the distance, in the day-time by the great standard waving over the entrance, and at night by the two lanterns hoisted on the flagstaff. At the entrance stood the carriage of the field-telegraph, in which was arranged a whole telegraph-station." The Emperor led a very active life. He rose early, and devoted the morning to current affairs. Towards noon on each day, the suite, composed of about fifty officers, assembled in a large tent in front of the Imperial residence. Exactly at twelve, his Majesty entered, saluted all present, and sat down to table. The first course consisted of caviare, Swiss cheese, sardines, raw herrings, and three kinds of *vodka* (rye-spirit). Soup and roast meat formed the second course; and *café noir*, or tea, completed the repast. After breakfast, as this meal was called, the Emperor again occupied himself with affairs, or drove out. At six, dinner was served. It consisted of three or four courses, and lasted about an hour. At nine, there was tea, and at ten or half-past his Majesty retired for the night. On fête-days, a little more gaiety marked the general aspect of affairs; but for the most part life at head-quarters was monotony itself.* A correspondent of the *Novaya Vremia*, a paper published at St. Petersburg, spoke of the large amount of work which the Czar got through every day, and stated that telegrams arriving during the night were taken to him at once. When at table, he generally spoke a good deal, unless when anything had occurred to annoy him. On the days when couriers were despatched to St. Petersburg, he was especially busy. The inconveniences of camp-life were borne with great equanimity, and the Emperor showed much solicitude for the sick and wounded in hospital. "Sometimes," said the courtly writer, "the tears came into his eyes, and he endeavoured in vain to conceal them. Never were the relations between the Czar and his people so close and warm as here. This war will certainly create a whole cycle of legends, and the name of Alexander II. will remain for ever graven in the memory of the people. Yesterday he came into the field-hospital with a heap of presents, in commemoration of St. Alexander's Day. There were shirts, and tobacco-pouches, and purses, and knives, and books, and I know not what more. He had discovered beforehand who played on the harmonica, and asked the others whether they smoked, and whether they could read. The gifts were distributed accordingly. 'The Empress has sent you some presents,' he said on entering, and then proceeded to give two or three to each, asking them at the same time about their wounds, and about the affair in which they had been wounded. The men kissed the Emperor's hand as they accepted the presents, and he stroked their faces as if they had been children." It would be ungenerous to doubt that a good deal of real kindness was mixed up with this solicitude; but a military autocrat would be out of his senses if he were indifferent to the soldiers whose bayonets uphold him.

* *Times*, September 21st, 1877.

The Russian sentiment of hostility towards England grew in intensity as the difficulties of the situation increased. A gentleman observed to the St. Petersburg correspondent of the *Times* that they were fighting against England as well as against Turkey. It was England, he said, that supplied the Turks with money, arms, and officers: and there was a general belief—notwithstanding its absurdity—that the British Government was secretly subsidising that of Turkey. Similar statements were made in the Russian newspapers: and when the Czar's troops were repulsed at Zevin, the *Moscow Gazette* expressed its conviction that the reinforcements previously received by Mukhtar Pasha were Anglo-Indian soldiers in disguise. Englishmen were believed to be largely engaged in the Ottoman navy; and it was reported that a British sloop-of-war had entered the harbour of Kustendji, to obtain information regarding torpedoes, for the benefit of the Turkish Admiral. The Bey of Tunis, it was added, was entirely in the hands of Mr. Richard Wood, the English representative, who had persuaded him to send gold, horses, mules, and grain to Constantinople, despite the protest of all the European Powers except England. These stories, whether they were truthful or not, created in Russia a great feeling of irritation against the British people and their Government. In other respects also, the prevalent mood was that of discontent. This, indeed, was the case to so serious a degree that Prince Tcherkasski, who shortly after the invasion of Bulgaria was appointed Russian Governor of that province, rebuked the desponding and over-critical spirit of his countrymen. His remarks were uttered in conversation with the War Correspondent of the *Novaya Vremia*, and are worthy of note as an illustration of Russian opinion in the crisis of the war. The Prince complained that the Russians of these days are always either over-confident, or depressed at a trifle. Formerly it was not so. "In the memorable war of 1812," continued Prince Tcherkasski, "public opinion kept up the spirit of the army and of the Government, and now it ought to do the same. There have been mistakes and incapacity, but such are to be found everywhere. Great aims are attained not by generals, but by the people. We have never had a great general since the time of Suwaroff. We have been spoilt by the recent Prussian campaigns, and do not study our own history. In 1828–9, we fought for two years with the Turks. It took us two years to pacify Poland. And this time we imagined that we should have a triumphal march to Constantinople. I do not know anything of military affairs, but I am certain that Moltke himself, if he were here, would not advance as triumphantly as he did in France, where he found railways, bridges, provisions, and all the instruments of civilisation. . . . . In the Russian people there is one miraculous quality, called patience. They have patiently borne all kinds of things—the Mongol domination, Ivan the Terrible, serfage. They will bear this war too." Those were brave and spirited words, whatever we may think of the cause; and they proved prophetic.

In the meanwhile, the mismanagement of the Russian army tried to the utmost the faith of patriotic believers like Prince Tcherkasski. The condition of the roads in Roumania and Bulgaria was atrociously bad, and the Russians did little to amend it. Their operations in this respect were described by an English observer as being characterised by unutterable stupidity and inefficiency. In Simnitza, the heavy traffic had worn the centre of the streets concave, and in those deep depressions the rain-water collected as in the bed of a canal. With a little expenditure of energy, trenches might have been dug from the road towards the ditches which flanked it; but nothing of the kind was done, and the water, consequently, had no means of escape. The road from Sistova to Plevna was so damaged by rains as to be almost impassable, and in other directions the mischief was nearly as bad. The arrival of General Todleben was followed, though slowly, by some improvement in these matters. Regular roads were formed across the flat, sandy islands between the sections of the pontoon-bridges across the Danube; but the ways on the Bulgarian side long continued in their state of muddy and marshy rottenness. These heavy sloughs wore out the baggage-animals with fearful quickness, and the waggons, with their contents, were often upset in deep holes of mire and stagnant water. At length the work was taken in hand, but not until after an immense deal of valuable time had been lost. As an engineer officer, Todleben knew well that the most skilful military tactics will be unavailing if troops and artillery are scarcely able to move from one point to another, owing to the bad condition of the roads. The first good results of his supervision were seen in the attention given to these matters of plain necessity.

Not only were the roads in a wretched state, but the Russian communications with the northern side of the Danube were gravely imperilled. On the 5th of October, a storm damaged the bridges at Sistova and Nicopolis; on the 12th, the latter bridge was completely carried away by a storm, and the only remaining link with Roumania was the frail and shaken line of boats extending from Sistova to the opposite shore. Before this event occurred, however, the main body of the Russian reinforcements had arrived in Bulgaria. These reinforcements were formidable, both as to number and quality. The three divisions of the Guards counted 10,000 men, without including the cavalry; and the First and Third Divisions of the Line were before Plevna also. This placed Osman Pasha in a much more serious position than before; yet the investment of his stronghold could not even then be completed. Shefket Pasha succeeded in effecting a junction with Osman on the 11th of October. The number of troops under Shefket's orders does not clearly appear; but the addition, whatever it may have been, was of doubtful value, seeing that it implied several more mouths to feed. Plevna was already getting short of provisions; but a happy achievement by Mehemet Pasha gave relief for a time. That commander, while in the neighbourhood of Telik, near Plevna, about the 13th of October, came across a large Russian convoy, very insufficiently guarded. He attacked at once, and, in spite of reinforcements which were hurried up by the Russians, captured the whole. The supplies thus obtained were set down at 20,000 sheep, 500 head of cattle, and 100 horses; and these animals were got into Plevna, to the great advantage of the garrison. The relief was probably needed, for some prisoners, taken a day or two before, reported that the garrison was at that time in want both of food and ammunition, and that the number of sick and wounded was very large. Osman Pasha alone, according to this account, refused to surrender; the others were said to be much disheartened.

TRAIN OF AMMUNITION, ETC.

If any idea of abandoning Bulgaria had ever been entertained by the Russian Emperor and his advisers, it was now entirely given up, and the invaders resolved to remain throughout the winter, if the Turkish opposition could not be broken before then. The Imperial head-quarters were removed, early in October, from Gorny Studen to Sistova, and the latter place was full of contractors (principally Germans) who had undertaken to provide for the troops during the ensuing months of cold weather. Twenty thousand additional waggons were ordered for transport. A contract was made for the building of barracks, and another for furnishing immense supplies of conserves. On the heights overlooking the town, and commanding its approaches, strong fortifications were erected, and large numbers of guns, with corresponding stores of ammunition, were brought together. While these matters were being arranged, a fortunate circumstance for the Russians occurred at the Sulina mouth of the Danube. Some torpedoes had been sunk in the river during the night following the 8th of October, and, on the 9th, a Turkish three-masted gunboat, coming up to the assistance of another which the Russians had fired on, passed over the hidden mischief, and was suddenly blown to fragments. The incident was followed by a bombardment of Sulina, and of the Turkish squadron in the river, which, however, did very little damage. The Turks had been singularly unlucky in the matter of torpedoes. Either there were no means of determining where they had been laid, or the Ottomans were strangely remiss in taking precautions. Several valuable ships, with a large number of sailors, were thus lost to the Empire, and the greatest naval triumphs of Russia during the war were not gained in open fight, but by the skilful adaptation of scientific means to the destruction of the enemy's vessels. The Russian torpedoes used

GORNY DUBNIK.

on the 9th of October are said by a newspaper correspondent to have "combined in their construction both the elements of safety in placing them, and the certainty of explosion when struck by a passing body. Small bichromate of potass batteries are placed all round the case, screwed into small cylinders; and each of these is what is called placed in a circuit, with a fuse inserted amongst the gun-cotton. These electric circuits are not completed until the mine is placed, and every one has retreated to a safe distance, when, the main wires being joined, the affair is ready for action. The solution of bichromate of potass is placed in a glass tube, hermetically sealed, and protected from accidental fracture by a thick lead covering. When a ship or other passing object strikes this arrangement, which projects outside the torpedo-case, the glass tube is broken, and, the solution coming in contact with the zinc and carbon plates, a current of electricity is immediately generated, and the torpedo explodes."

For some time after his arrival at Plevna, Shefket Pasha was enabled to keep open the communications, and thus facilitate the arrival of reinforcements and provisions; but one of the first designs of General Todleben was to terminate this state of things by completing the investment of the town. General Gourko, now at the head of the cavalry, was ordered to take the necessary measures, and he acted with promptitude and success. As the Russian reinforcements arrived, they were placed in line round the left flank of the army already on the spot, so that they extended from the Loftcha road, occupied by the Sixteenth Division, under General Skobeleff, to the road between Sophia and Teliche. The duty of General Gourko was to guard the extreme left of the line, for which purpose he was provided with a force of infantry and cavalry, amounting to about 35,000 men.

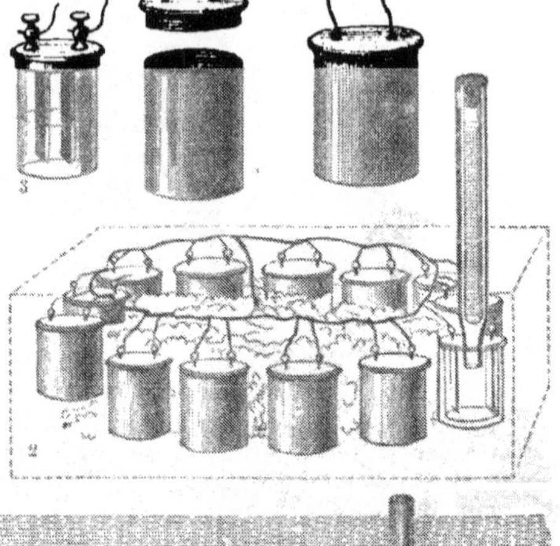

TORPEDO BOX, SHOWING (1) EXTERIOR VIEW, (2) INTERIOR VIEW, (3) SEPARATE CELLS.

Between Gorny Dubnik and Teliche, the Turks had established a fortified position of considerable strength, called after the name of the first place. It was here that General Kriloff had so egregiously failed to stop the convoys under Shefket Pasha on the 22nd, 23rd, and 24th of September; and since then the Turks had erected a number of small forts along the Sophia road. These positions it was the object of General Gourko to seize, so that the Turks should no longer be able to revictual Plevna, or in any way help its garrison. He accordingly crossed the river Vid, at Churikovo, about the 17th of October, and on the 24th vigorously attacked the Gorny Dubnik position. In this operation he was assisted by a heavy bombardment, having the effect of retaining Osman's forces in the outworks, and by a demonstration on the part of the Second Roumanian Division against the north-west of the town. The Turks had recently strengthened the position with formidable entrenchments, and the fort itself consisted of a large redoubt, flanked by two smaller works. It was situated near the road, in the middle of a plain, and on a slight eminence. The Russians attacked with twenty-four battalions, sixty-four guns, and a regiment of cavalry. The garrison is supposed to have comprised between five and six thousand troops, well armed with breach-loaders, and the Russians afterwards acknowledged the loss of two thousand five hundred men in securing the position. The Turks themselves lost two thousand, together with a battery, and at least seventy officers, including the commandant, Hifzi Pasha. Success was with difficulty purchased; for the fighting lasted from six in the morning to the same hour in the evening, when five out of the twelve Turkish battalions escaped to Plevna, and the remainder surrendered.

The Imperial Guards particularly distinguished

themselves in this battle, which was the first of the war in which they had been engaged. It was at one time doubtful if the attack would not end in failure, as the Turkish fire was so terrific that the Russians often wavered, hesitated, and declined to advance. But at length they scaled the parapet with a resistless rush, and Gorny Dubnik was secure in Muscovite hands. The capture of this position nearly completed the investment of Plevna, and the Russian lines were soon connected by a telegraph encircling the town, so that the besiegers could concentrate at a moment's notice upon any point of the circle that might be attacked. The Russians were also aided by the nature of the ground, which enabled them to see every part of the Turkish positions from some point or other of the exterior lines. As long as daylight lasted, any concentration of Turkish troops could be plainly discerned; and if Osman Pasha desired to make a sortie, he could only do so in the night, or at any rate his preparations must be carried out under cover of darkness. The position of the Turkish commander was therefore becoming serious, and people speculated whether he would attempt to break out, or would lie behind his entrenchments and redoubts until he was either relieved by some external force, or compelled by famine to surrender. The chances of getting through, if he determined to make the endeavour, were exceedingly bad, for on every side large armies barred the roads, and, should he escape one, he was likely to fall into the hands of another. In the meanwhile, he remained under the protection of his guns; but he was now beginning to discover that the siege was a reality. General Todleben had all the distances around Plevna divided into small sections, and some four hundred guns were planted about the town. The whole of these guns could be directed on any one point, if it were considered desirable; and this was frequently done when masses of troops could be observed drawn together in an exposed situation. A simultaneous fire was on such occasions ordered by telegraph, and two or three hundred shells would be almost instantaneously hurled within a small space. In this way, sometimes the redoubts, and at other times the buildings in the town itself, were visited by a rain of fire; yet the effect was less than might have been expected.

On the same day that Gourko attacked Gorny Dubnik, a division of the Guards was sent against Teliche, situated to the west of the other position, but was repulsed with heavy loss. Nevertheless, this second position was captured on the 28th of October, when, after a feeble resistance, five battalions surrendered to the assailants. An attempt to recover Teliche, made by Shefket Pasha on the 31st, proved a complete failure, and revealed the growing weakness of the Turks; on the same day, Teteven, near Orkhanieh, was taken by the Russians. On the 1st of November, General Gourko, at the head of a division and a half, accompanied by sixty-four guns, advanced against Dolny Dubnik, east of Gorny Dubnik. The town was held by five thousand Turks; but shortly after Gourko had opened a cannonade, followed by rifle-firing, the Ottomans considered it prudent to abandon the place, and retire upon Plevna, the road to which was still open to them. They had in fact made no resistance at all, and Gourko did not lose a man. The road from Plevna to Sophia, through Orkhanieh, was soon after closed, and the investment of Plevna was then absolutely complete. The country to the south was for many miles at the mercy of the Russian cavalry, which scoured the roads, and captured the supplies intended for Osman Pasha. That enterprising officer counted upon his being delivered by an army of relief; but the event showed that his calculations had no sufficient basis. The respective position of the combatants had entirely changed within a few weeks. The Russians were no longer a miserable handful of men, desperately clinging to points of defence, from which they might at any moment be expelled by an onslaught of the enemy. They were now a powerful host, well-equipped and intelligently commanded; and the whole Turkish scheme of operations, so far as it can be said to have had a definite or consistent character, was rendered futile by the greater resources and better management of the invaders. There had been a time when the failure of the Russian plans seemed highly probable, and when a vigorous and concentrated series of attacks might have been attended by striking results; but that time had passed. Either the three principal Turkish armies had been really unable to co-operate, or there had been mutual jealousy among the commanders, if not dishonest motives, leading to calculated inefficiency. The secret history of the war is not yet known, and no one can presume to speak with certainty on the subject; but the rapid collapse of the Turks, after their prospects had appeared so fair, must necessarily excite surprise, and prompt conjectural explanations. In September, many competent judges doubted whether the Russian failure would not soon be irreparable; before the close of October, the ruin of Turkey was as plainly visible as a mountain peak upon a clear horizon.

The Russian soldiers had by this time built for themselves comfortable huts all along the line of investment before Plevna, and their supplies were not likely to fall short. West of the Vid, the country between the Danube and the Balkans was fully capable of supplying them with all they wanted; east of the same river, food could easily be obtained from Roumania. The spirits of the army became greater with each succeeding week, for it was seen that the worst was over, and that Osman Pasha was held as in a vice, from which there was little probability of his escaping. A very excellent effect, moreover, was produced by the appointment to principal commands of such men as Todleben, Gourko, and Skobeleff, although the Staff commanders still remained as they were. The inherent excellences of the Russian army, which had hitherto been obscured by bad management, were now certain to be brought out in their full vigour; and it was at the same time equally apparent that the Turkish army had done its best, and would become progressively weaker and less efficient. By the beginning of November, all the battalions before Plevna had been brought up to their full strength, and the investment became stricter in proportion to the added numbers of the besieging troops. Only at one part of the line had the Russians lost ground. After the desperate fighting before Plevna in the first part of September, Skobeleff, acting in accordance with orders, fell back upon Tucenica, completely abandoning the Loftcha road, and placing a deep ravine between himself and the Turks. Subsequently, he endeavoured to re-occupy his old positions, but found that the Turks had thrown forward their lines in that direction, and had built four new redoubts. Nevertheless, he succeeded in occupying Brestovec, on the left of the road, and in constructing a redoubt and a line of trenches. The redoubt was in such a position that it projected some way into the Turkish lines; it was therefore of necessity much exposed, and liable to assaults that might have been disastrous. Skobeleff accordingly determined to seize a small wooded hill immediately in front of the right wing of the investing force, as he perceived that its possession would greatly reduce the chances of attack. This hill, which was situated between the Loftcha road and the ravine already mentioned, was defended by trenches, and held by a strong force. Yet Skobeleff believed that he could take it, and he arranged that Gourko should simultaneously open fire all along the line, and occupy the position in front of him towards the bridge over the river Vid. The 9th of November was the date fixed for the attack, and five o'clock in the evening was the hour settled for the commencement of operations.

BATTLE OF CHERKOVNA.

The day was foggy, and the evening very dark. A little before the appointed time, Skobeleff reviewed his troops, and, moving about amongst the men, gave them very particular directions as to what they should do, occasionally cheering them with a joke or a quaint observation. He determined on leading the assault himself, since it was necessary that the soldiers should be restrained from advancing too far, as they had done upon a previous occasion, and that the proposed entrenchments should be properly made. "On the approach of darkness," says Mr. MacGahan, writing in the *Daily News*, "the roar of eighty guns was heard, that vomited splashes of flame upon the murky fog, and then were silent. Then came the scream of eighty shells, seeking their destination in the obscurity. Then there was the crash of the infantry-fire along the whole line, except on the point of the attack; for it was Skobeleff's design to use the fog for cover, and take the Turks by surprise." Another writer in the same journal supplied some further details of the combat. "In the dense fog," he observed, "every noise was magnified, and, as the shells screamed past, and exploded with a sharp, ringing sound behind us in the village, it seemed as if they were ten times the ordinary size. The darkness was impenetrable. An officer, or a couple of stretcher-bearers, loomed up occasionally through the fog, and dodged and jumped into the ditch as the leaden shower came over us. Down below in the hollow we could see no flash; only from that darkness came a hot spitting of lead, that made it almost certain death to face. The fog began to condense and gather on the ground, and the cold increased; and still the battle roared, and rose and fell, ceased and began again. At last it was evident from the firing that the position was taken, and we retired to the village, to the music of the shells and bullets. Here we awaited the next burst of battle, which we knew was sure to come. At a quarter past ten it broke again, and the same fiendish noise and rattle went on as before." The Turks had been as completely surprised as Skobeleff desired. It was not until the Russians were within a hundred yards of their lines that they perceived the approach of the enemy. Instantaneously seizing their arms, they delivered two volleys; but the next moment the Russians charged them at the point of the bayonet, and in a little while the Ottomans were put to flight, leaving several of their number dead upon the ground. Every man in the attacking force was provided with a shovel, and trenches were thrown up with astonishing rapidity, so that in a very few minutes the troops were under cover. The Turks were firing upon them from the next hill; but, although this was near at hand, the practice proved so bad that very little execution was done. At ten o'clock, P.M., Skobeleff quitted the ground, and returned to Brestovec to supper, but had only just arrived when firing again broke out on the right flank. Without a moment's pause, he once more took to his horse, galloped off into the darkness, and did not return until the morning.

His reappearance was opportune, for the Turks were endeavouring to re-capture the position, and the Russian reserves had lost their way in the fog, and were being fired into by their own comrades. The Ottoman attack was repulsed, and so also were two others which followed. On three successive nights, renewed assaults were made by Osman's troops, but without effect. Skobeleff remained every night in the trenches, and succeeded in pushing his lines to within a hundred yards of the Turks. The Guards had at the same time advanced to a position immediately under the Krishine Redoubt, and two days later they and the Roumanians got within rifle-shot of the bridge over the Vid. These successes enabled the besiegers to draw the circle of investment still closer, and the Turks felt the difficulties of their position all the more keenly. The chances of their being starved out were increased by the capture, on November 10th, of Vratza, or Vraca, by General Gourko. The town is situated west of Plevna, and was important as forming a considerable depôt of ammunition and provisions, which of course fell into the hands of the Russians. The families of the Turks taken on this occasion were driven into Plevna, in order that, by increasing the numbers in the town, they might the sooner exhaust its resources. It is said that this hard measure was taken in consequence of the Turks having expelled a number of Bulgarians out of the beleaguered place. But it should be recollected that the Bulgarians thus dispossessed were certain to find support wherever they found refuge, whereas the families of the captured Turks were being forced into a trap, where in all probability they would starve. The *lex talionis* is doubtless an admitted rule, and may in some instances be justifiable in practice; but there are limits which it should never transgress, and the infliction of extreme suffering upon women and children seems inexcusable under any circumstances of provocation whatsoever. Besides the men, the party forced into Plevna consisted of about a dozen women and twice as many children—all in a state of extreme destitution, poorly clothed, and half-wild with hunger. One of the women was accused of having shot a Russian sergeant dead in the streets of Vratza after the town was occupied; but it is affirmed that she was well used by the soldiers of the escort conducting the miserable creatures to the outskirts of Plevna. When, however, we find a writer in the *Daily News* commending with effusive admiration the tender kindness with which the Russian

FUNERAL OF PRINCE SERGIUS.

officers and men treated these poor outcasts, previous to driving them into what was little better than a prison where they would probably die of famine, it is impossible to refrain from characterizing such humanity as a pretence, and such commendation as a form of cant. A similar act was committed by the Prussians during the war of 1870—71; but it was very generally denounced as unjustifiable.

In the vicinity of the Lom, little was being done at this period of the war; but attention was attracted towards the army of the Czarewitch by the death of Prince Sergius Maximilianovitch of Leuchtenberg, who since the beginning of the campaign had acted on the Staff of the Czarewitch, and taken part in several battles, in which he had distinguished himself by an almost reckless courage. On the morning of October 24th, the Grand Duke Vladimir made a reconnaissance directed against three places on the Black Lom. The first person killed was Prince Sergius, who, accompanied by several officers, was watching the movements of the enemy from what was supposed to be a place of safety in rear of the Russian reserves. The little group appeared to be actually out of fire, and indeed the Turks had not been operating in that direction. Nevertheless, a chance shot struck the Prince, and put an end to his existence on the instant. A Russian officer on horseback was standing a few paces to the left front of his Highness, whose field-glass he was carrying. The Prince asked for it; and just as the officer was turning round to fulfil this request, he heard him exclaim "Ah!" at the same time pressing his hand to his forehead. Reeling in the saddle, he would have fallen to the ground, had he not been caught by the officers surrounding him; but before any measures could be taken, it was seen that he was dead. The missile which struck him was a spent ball, and it was believed that, had he stood a few yards further back, he would have escaped with nothing worse than a contusion. "With the present long-range guns," observed the correspondent of the *Times* who recorded the sad event, "there is no such thing as absolute safety anywhere near a field of battle." Prince Sergius was third son of the Duke of Leuchtenberg and the Grand Duchess Maria, eldest daughter of the Emperor Nicholas. Consequently, he was nephew of the Emperor Alexander, and the Czar is stated to have felt his death most keenly—to such an extent, indeed, that his physicians were alarmed as to its effect on his health. The Prince was not quite twenty-eight years of age, tall and fair, with an affectionate disposition, which had gained him a large number of friends. The funeral rites took place at St. Petersburg on the 6th of November, when the remains were laid in the St. Catherine chapel of St. Peter-Paul's Cathedral, near those of the deceased's mother. All the Court dignitaries, Ministers, and generals present in the capital, joined in paying the last honours to the fallen soldier, and the streets through which the procession passed were thronged with a sympathising crowd. The emotion exhibited by the Emperor when he heard the painful intelligence did honour to his nature; but it is much to be desired that great potentates would feel more acutely for the countless multitudes of humble men whom their ambition consigns to death or torture. The fate of Prince Sergius was no worse than that of innumerable Russians and Turks who had already suffered the utmost miseries of war; yet the Emperor Alexander seems to have been incapable of recognizing the evil until his own affections were lacerated. In countless graves over all that reddened Bulgarian soil, lay the victims of a real greed and a hypocritical pretence. In countless homes all over Turkey, all over Russia and Roumania, were broken-hearted women and orphaned little ones, who might have been happy but for the great crime which an Emperor had committed, and which hosts of slavish adulators had applauded him for committing. Yet not until a stray bullet struck down that Emperor's nephew could he understand in any vivid sense the sorrow which is without comfort while life endures.

CHAPTER XXXIX.

Agitation in Constantinople—Position of Mahmud Damat Pasha, the Sultan's Brother-in-Law—Supposed Conspiracy in Favour of Murad—Interview of the Sultan with English Members of Parliament—His Views of Reform—The Consular Courts in Turkey—Opinion in England on the Future of Turkey and the Designs of Russia—Lord Mayor's Day at the Guildhall—Speeches of the Greek Foreign Minister and Lord Beaconsfield—Vacillations of the English Government—Feeling in the East—Mr. Gladstone at Holyhead—Utterances of Lord Hartington and Mr. Bright—British Interests and their Critics—A Turkish Journal on the Betrayal of Turkey by England—The Ottomans and the Roman Catholics—Anti-Russian Feeling at the Vatican—The Undeveloped Riches of Russia—Further Opinions of Mr. Gladstone—The Danger of Muscovite Predominance—Virtues of the Russian Soldiery—Kindness of the Turks—Exaggerations of Partisanship—The Men of the Imperial Guard, and their Equipment—Superiority of the Turkish to the Russian Arms of Precision—Unpopularity of the War in Roumania—Intentions of Russia towards Roumanian Bessarabia—Antagonism between the Roumanians and Bulgarians—The Stern Hand of Military Despotism—Preparations of Servia for entering into the War—Revival of the Insurrection in Bosnia.

CONSTANTINOPLE felt the shock of the recent Turkish disasters, and trembled through all its nerves. Usually, the Turk is impassive, and takes both good and evil fortune with equal placidity. But in the autumn of 1877 the popular heart was deeply stirred, for it was seen that the Infidel was winning serious triumphs over the Faithful. The Old Turkish party gave strong expression to its views, and attributed the misfortunes of the national arms to the favours conferred on Christians, and the spread of religious tolerance. These opinions were shared by the Sultan's brother-in-law, Mahmud Damat Pasha, who was at that time Mayor of the Palace. Yet by some of the patriotic party this very person was regarded as one of the principal causes of the late defeats, and of the impending ruin of the Empire. He was even accused of selling the country to Russia, and fierce demands were made for his dismissal. In the first week of November, placards were posted in the capital, summoning all patriots to rise, and accusing the Government of ordering the military commanders to spare the enemy, and of secretly negotiating with the Russians to conclude a disastrous peace. Such a peace, it was observed, the Turkish people would never sanction; and they were exhorted to fight to the last gasp, and chase the enemy from the soil. "If we cannot conclude an advantageous peace, if the Most High abandons us," continued the address, "let us first kill the miscreant, Mahmud Damat, and then die." The placards were quickly removed, but they had had their effect.

On the 7th of November—the day following that on which this popular appeal was made—a rumour spread over the city that Damat had been poisoned. The statement was at once denied by his medical attendants, who, however, admitted that he had had a fit of apoplexy, though not of a serious character. He was certainly ill in some way, for the physicians paid repeated visits to his residence, and passed the night with him. In a little while he recovered, but his position at court seemed shaken. He was thought to be associated with a band of malcontents who were desirous of restoring Murad. The deposed monarch was living under surveillance, and on the 2nd and 3rd of November the Government considered it prudent to surround the Palace of Cheragan, where he then was, with soldiers. A few days later, forty or fifty persons in the service of the ex-Sultan were arrested, and it was afterwards said they had been strangled, though the Turkish papers spoke only of exile. The circumstances were mysterious, and are not known with exactness. According to the *Political Correspondence* of Vienna, Mahmud Damat Pasha accused the ex-Sultan of conspiring; in consequence of which, the reigning Sultan had his brother removed from the Palace of Cheragan to the Old Seraglio. This was forcibly opposed by Murad's servants, who considered his life in danger; and it was on this account that they were strangled. Murad was then closely confined as a prisoner of State, and in the meanwhile many partisans of Midhat Pasha were arrested. The attempt to poison Mahmud Damat Pasha had, according to the same account, been frustrated by his physician; and the excitement prevailing at Constantinople was increased by a rumour that the Prophet had appeared to the Sultan, commanding him to conclude peace, as the safety of the Mohammedan faith depended on it. The story went on to say that Abdul-Hamid thereupon consulted his chief astrologer, who said that he also had seen the same vision. The Sheikh-ul-Islam, moreover, was alleged to have had the story of the dream narrated in the mosques, as if to prepare the public mind for peace; but there was in truth no disposition to a pacific policy just then at the Turkish court. Russia herself was more desirous of coming to an arrangement than Turkey. Yet the Ottoman Government feared that a change in the popular sentiment might any day set in, and the newspapers were frequently warned that they would be suspended if they published disquieting reports.

The dread of revolution was not unnatural at such a time of trial; but the Sultan had acted so as to offer no excuse for change. He produced a favourable impression on two English members of Parliament—Mr. Henry Edwards and Mr. Goldney —who, together with Admiral Hornby, were paying a visit to Constantinople in October. These gentlemen were presented to his Majesty on the 17th of the month, and a very interesting conversation ensued. The Sultan (according to a report in the *Times*) expressed himself extremely desirous of carrying out the reforms and improvements he had indicated in his recent decree. He regretted that he had prejudices of long standing to deal with, and that it was impossible without danger to proceed otherwise than gradually; but he was fully resolved to form a basis for further reforms. He was specially anxious for such measures as would ensure the equality of all his subjects. The Parliament would, of course, require time to develop itself, and to show real practical results; nevertheless, he felt quite sure that the freedom of discussion permitted to its members, and the publication of their speeches and of the measures they passed, would accustom the people to take a more active interest than before in the affairs of the Empire. It might be impossible for the present to recognize anything like a system of Party Government by the Parliament, as the people, in their want of familiarity with Parliamentary institutions, could not help looking upon opposition to the Ministry as hostility to the lawful Government. He had read in the papers of English Parliamentary proceedings, and quite understood the benefits that might arise from a system of government such as ours in a country where it was of gradual growth. Eventually, as he hoped, the laws would be firmly administered, and the promised reforms resolutely carried out. He declared himself much gratified at the satisfaction expressed by one of the guests at the change he found in Constantinople since his last visit during the Crimean War, and for his approval of the system of freedom extended to religious education, and the acquisition and tenure of property irrespective of race or creed. What was wanted to secure and perfect this was, in his opinion, one uniform code administered by the native Judges, instead of the variety of Consular Courts of every nation accredited to the Porte, which lowered and impaired the powers of the Government, and led to the greatest complications and difficulties. This last remark touched upon a very important matter. By an arrangement long existing in Turkey, and generally referred to as the Capitulations, the consuls of foreign Powers are invested with the right of administering justice in the case of persons belonging to their own nationality. It was felt that this was a serious interference with the independence of Turkey as a sovereign State; and in June, 1869, Sultan Abdul-Aziz addressed a memorial to the European Governments, setting forth the Ottoman objections to so unusual a privilege. Modifications were agreed to in April of the following year, and in 1872 the Sultan decided on the abolition of the system in Egypt. But it still exists in Turkey Proper, and it is difficult to conceive a custom better calculated to undermine the self-reliance of a nation, to degrade it in its own eyes and those of others, and to encourage perpetual intrigues. It is a part of that policy of interference, of treating Turkey differently from European Empires, which has had no other fruit than the destruction of the Ottoman Power, and the triumph of Russian policy in the East. No wonder that Abdul-Hamid expressed his dissatisfaction with a system so prejudicial to his realm.

MAHMUD DAMAT PASHA.

It was in the midst of agitation at Constantinople, and of Turkish defeat in Bulgaria and Armenia that the annual civic festival in London, on the 9th of November, gave Lord Beaconsfield and other persons of note an opportunity of expressing their views on the existing phase of that great question which was then disturbing Europe. In the Court of Exchequer, the Chief Baron, on receiving the new Lord Mayor (Alderman Owden), according to usual custom, made some rather elaborate remarks on the foreign politics of the time. The burden of his argument was that the balance of power had been almost entirely destroyed by the aggrandizement of Prussia, the weakening of France, and the development of Russia. He asked if it were possible that Constantinople, the Bosphorus, and some of the fairest portions of Asia Minor, should fall to the lot of the Czar. Would the dominion of Turkey be parcelled out by the two great military Powers, Russia and Germany, as Poland, in the last century, had been partitioned by Russia, Prussia, and Austria? If so, what was to become of the dearest interests of England—the freedom of her commercial intercourse, and the safety of her possessions in the East? England might indeed be able to meet any number of States banded against her; but it would be at the expense of hundreds of thousands of precious lives, and of many millions sterling of money. The warlike tone expressed in this address was at that time very prevalent throughout the country, and it was not absent from the speeches delivered in the evening at the Guildhall banquet. One of the most curious of those speeches was that of the Turkish Minister, M. Musurus, who, although a Greek by race and a Christian by religion, spoke with pride of his being "a faithful subject and servant of his Ottoman Fatherland." The era of the regeneration of Turkey, he said, dated from the suppression of the military system existing under the Janizaries, which was an obstacle to all progress. Sultan Abdul-Medjid had inaugurated his reign by a proclamation guaranteeing the life, property, and honour of all his subjects, without distinction of race or creed. These principles were afterwards developed in numerous political and administrative reforms, and the great work had recently been crowned by the granting of a complete liberal constitution, based on the free representation of all the populations of the Empire. "Myself a Christian," continued Musurus, "I have the honour, like some of my Christian fellow-countrymen, to be a Senator—a member of the Upper House of the Ottoman Parliament. I do not doubt that this political transformation of the Empire on English principles gives pleasure to Englishmen. I know that there is some incredulity as to the reality of the change—an incredulity, or rather ill-will, arising out of political dissensions and the exciting circumstances of the present war, in which my country is defending its independence and its integrity. But I must remind such sceptics that the ultimate appreciation of the facts is reserved for the verdict of history—that impartial judge, who is not the inebriated, but the sober, Philip."

The most important address of the evening was of course that of Lord Beaconsfield. The policy of the Government had been marked by so many oscillations that men were glad to hear from the chief Minister of the Crown a re-statement of that policy, as affected by the existing posture of affairs. Lord Beaconsfield again affirmed that the neutrality of England was conditional on the interests of England not being assailed or menaced. The Premier spoke scornfully of those "cosmopolitan critics—men who are the friends of every country save their own"—who had denounced that policy as selfish. "My Lord," said the speaker, "it is as selfish as patriotism; but it is the policy of her Majesty's Government, which they adopted from the first, and which they have maintained throughout." He then proceeded to dispute a "dogma of diplomacy" which had been confidently asserted for some years—viz., that Turkey was a phrase, and not a fact; that its Government was a phantom, that its people were effete, and that it was used by statesmen merely as a name to maintain the balance of power, and to secure the peace of Europe. If that were really the case, the sooner it was proved to be so the better. But the experience of the year had shown the very contrary. Turkey had exhibited a vigour and a fertility of resource which made it manifest that she had a right to be recognized among the sovereign Powers of Europe. "The independence of Turkey," continued Lord Beaconsfield, "was a subject of ridicule a year ago. That independence, whatever may be the fortunes of the war—and war changes like the moon—is not doubted now. It has been proved by half a million of warriors, who have devoted their lives to their country, without pay and without reward." With respect to the prospects of peace, his Lordship said that he did not take the desponding view some persons took. "I am encouraged," he observed, "not to take a desponding view, because I remember what has been the conduct on principal occasions of the chief belligerents in the contest. I cannot forget that the Emperor of Russia, with a magnanimity characteristic of his elevated character, announced, on the eve of the commencement of this war, that his only object was to secure the safety and the happiness of the Christian subjects of the Porte, and that he pledged his Imperial word of honour that he sought no increase of territory. I cannot forget that his Highness the Sultan has declared in the most formal manner that he is prepared to secure all those changes which will give to the Christian subjects of the Porte that safety and that welfare which the Emperor of Russia desires; and therefore, when I have these two statements from such high authority, made in a manner so solemn and so earnest by the two sovereigns who are at this moment in collision, I think I have a right to say that peace ought not to be an impossible achievement and conclusion. But then, it is said, there is a difficulty which prevents the Emperor of Russia and the Sultan of Turkey, though they are entirely agreed on every subject, from bringing about the peace which is desired. It is said that the military prestige of Russia demands a continuance of the war. Well, there are different opinions upon the subject of military prestige. In my opinion, military prestige does not depend on a single victory either way. A single victory may depend on chance or fortune; may even, with a bold commander, depend on transient circumstances which may not again occur. But what is the real foundation of military prestige? It is when a great country and a powerful Government can command the military services of a nation great, determined, and disciplined. Now, whatever may be the accidents of the present war either way, no one can say of the Russian soldier that he has not proved himself an enduring, a disciplined, and a most courageous man. There have been feats of valour performed by him, even in defeat, which have rarely been excelled—such, for example, as were exhibited before the fortifications at Plevna. And therefore I cannot conceive, totally irrespective of the news of the hour, which may bring military prestige to either of the contending parties, if it is to be defined by a single victory—I cannot understand that under any circumstances the military prestige of Russia will have been injured."

The confidence in Turkey's powers of resistance, affirmed by Lord Beaconsfield in this memorable speech, would have come with greater force and effect a few weeks earlier than at the time when it was expressed. The tide, as we have seen, was again turning, both in Europe and Asia, and it was a very doubtful matter whether Turkey would be able, unaided, to preserve that independence which the English Premier believed no one would any longer think of questioning. But his remarks gave comfort to the Sultan and his advisers, and revived in their breasts the almost extinguished hope of English assistance. As a matter of fact and of fair inference, there was nothing in Lord Beaconsfield's speech, nor was there anything in the conduct of the Government generally, which could support such a hope. The Ministerial policy, it is true, had in many respects been vacillating. It had altered a good deal since the days preceding the autumn agitation of 1876. Even after that change, it was impossible to say how far the Government would sanction, and how far oppose, the designs of victorious Russia, assuming her to be victorious. The Cabinet was manifestly divided; and according as one section or another prevailed, the tone adopted towards Turkey was either cold or friendly. But nothing had been said which could reasonably encourage the belief that England would forcibly interfere to terminate the struggle, or to save Turkey from a crushing defeat and consequent loss, unless certain things were done by Russia which at that time it did not seem probable she would even attempt. Nevertheless, a vague reliance on England undoubtedly existed at Constantinople, and it derived some degree of countenance, though without any true justification, from the Guildhall speech of Lord Beaconsfield. Probably nothing encouraged this feeling so much as the repeated statements by Opposition speakers in England, and in the Opposition newspapers, to the effect that the Government was resolved, sooner or later, to drag the country into war for the sake of Turkey.

Lord Beaconsfield's manifesto, if it may be so called, provoked a slight degreee of response from Mr. Gladstone, who, speaking at Holyhead on the 12th of November, referred to the recent Ministerial utterance. He maintained that the speech of the Premier was animated by that spirit of sympathy with Turkey which had disastrously marked all his efforts, and had impressed itself on the policy of the country for the previous eighteen months. The Earl, he said, represented "Turkism" in a very developed form; yet in his late address he had dropped the integrity of the Ottoman Empire. That, in the opinion of Mr. Gladstone, was a most significant fact. But at the same time he exhorted his auditors to beware of any indications of a disposition, under whatever pretext—whether that of British interests, or any other—to engage this country in the existing quarrel, "and on the wrong side." From these qualifying words, it would seem that Mr. Gladstone was still not unwilling to see England committed to what he believed to be the right side—the side, that is to say, of Russian aggression and territorial greed. In this very speech he expressed a mild hope that Russia would be moderate if success crowned her arms, but in the same breath gave her an encouragement to be the reverse, by saying "it would be too much to expect that she should exact nothing in requital for her enormous efforts." The speaker's favourite idea of coercing Turkey was once more brought forward in his Holyhead address. "Austria, twelve months ago," he said, "declared in favour of naval coercion. And what did naval coercion mean? It meant everything. Turkey was fighting her battle in Europe with Asiatic soldiers. He had suggested fifteen months ago that a naval barrier of the fleets of Europe should be interposed between Asia and Europe. Then Turkey could not lift an arm; she could not have maintained the contest for a week. Italy was known to be in general concurrence with Germany; and of France we had not the least reason to suppose the reverse. It was England that was the barrier to this settlement." Mr. Gladstone, in fact, would have had us bind Turkey hand and foot, in order that the assassin might more readily despatch her. The bare statement is sufficient. To make any comment on the morality of such a course, would be the merest garrulity of superfluous criticism.

Some other expressions of opinion on the part of public men were reported at the same time, and must not be passed over in this connection. The Marquis of Hartington, the leader of the Liberal Opposition in the House of Commons, made a speech at Glasgow on the 7th of November—two days before the Premier's harangue at the Lord Mayor's banquet. His Lordship's tone was much more moderate than that of Mr. Gladstone, as indeed it was throughout the whole question. He thought the Government entitled to credit for having up to that time preserved a neutral policy; but he hinted a doubt whether the policy would be always maintained. As regarded the future, he hoped that, when peace was made, such arrangements would be enforced, in combination with the other Governments of Europe, as would put an end to a condition which had resulted in continual insurrection, intrigues, and warfare. On the same day, Mr. Bright was addressing the Rochdale Liberal Association, and of course he touched upon the Eastern Question. He said he had observed within the last week or two that the papers which supported the Government had been writing to the

SERAGLIO POINT, CONSTANTINOPLE.

OSMAN PASHA RECONNOITRING THE ENEMY'S POSITIONS BEFORE PLEVNA.

effect that something dreadful was about to happen, and that it was necessary for England to be stirring with a decided policy, and to take some explicit line in connection with the East of Europe. One thing Mr. Bright was quite certain of, and that was that, if the country exerted the most ordinary common-sense—if it looked back to its course twenty years before—if it looked forward to the utter hopelessness of good resulting from any contest it might then enter into,—neither the existing Prime Minister nor any other would venture to go to war for merely visionary questions, or would act upon the idea that England was perpetually to dam up the Dardanelles against one of the greatest Empires of the world, and so prevent its ships having free passage into the Mediterranean. That was an object with which no other nation had any sympathy, and for which we could obtain in no part of the world a single ally. To suppose that the Government would go to war with such a view, was to suppose that its members were in a condition which would justify their being confined in lunatic asylums; and therefore Mr. Bright felt confident that no such absurdity would be committed, especially if the country—by which he meant those who held the same view with himself—were in earnest in its opposition to such a policy.

At this period of the war, the opinions of the Russophiles were curiously divided on one point. According to some, we had no interests at all in the preservation of the Turkish Empire; according to others, the interests might exist, but were not worthy of consideration in comparison with the superlative duty of destroying the Turkish Empire. The former was the opinion of Mr. Bright; the latter was the contention of Mr. Gladstone, or at any rate of his followers. There were those who thought that Mr. Bright's view was the more honest of the two, though perhaps also the more foolish. Certainly, the ostentatious way in which the Gladstonian party trampled on the interests of England, as if they were matters of no account whatever, disgusted many who might possibly have been won by a more decent argument. These were the persons to whom Lord Beaconsfield alluded in his trenchant definition of "cosmopolitan critics" as "men who are the friends of every country save their own." The phrase was conceived in the highest spirit of concentrated wit; but it would not have struck half so hard or deep, had it not been barbed with truth.

How little hope of English assistance existed in Turkey just before the delivery of Lord Beaconsfield's speech, may be judged from an article which appeared in the Constantinopolitan journal, *Bassiret*, about the close of October. It had become evident, according to the Turkish writer, that the inconstant and tortuous policy of England throughout the Eastern Question was preparing great disasters for that country. There were three eventualities to be considered as the final results of the war: the victory of the Russians; the victory of the Turks; and the autonomy of the Turkish provinces of Europe, by the intervention of one or more of the Powers. Supposing Russia to be victorious, England would entirely lose her influence in the East, and her interests would be absolutely compromised. Should Turkey be victorious, the Ottoman Empire would come out of the trial resplendent with glory. "In such a case," continued the Turkish journal, "England, whose policy towards us has been one of unbounded selfishness and inconsistency, will have no cause to rejoice. The Sultan is the supreme head of all the Mussulmans, and in this capacity he exercises over them a sovereign influence. His victories would increase his prestige, and particularly in the eyes of the Mussulmans of India." Some day, Russia would attack the English possessions in that Empire, and the writer hinted that the Mohammedans of India would then turn against their English masters. In the event of other Powers taking into their own hands the work begun by Russia in European Turkey, Roumelia would fall under the rule of Sclaves, and that would imply a double loss to England—the loss of influence, and the loss of commercial advantages. The journalist went on to observe that the only means by which Great Britain could repair her errors, and efface the remembrance of her faults, would be to come to an understanding with Turkey, and declare war on Russia. This, very naturally, was the general opinion throughout Turkey; but it was also an opinion which found many adherents in England itself.

On the whole, however, Turkey enjoyed little official support in any of the European countries; but she would probably have had a friend in the Pope, if the Pope had been in a position to be a friend to any one. As the people of Constantinople, just before its capture by the Turks, were better disposed to admit the turbans of the Moslems than the hats of Roman Cardinals, so the Catholics of the present day would ally themselves with the Sultan rather than with the Czar. And for this there are in truth good reasons. The persecution of Romanists all over the Russian Empire has had no parallel in the Turkish dominions. The followers of the Latin Church have accordingly, for the most part, taken sides with the Ottoman against the Muscovite; and Pio Nono, in the failing months of his life, showed that his sympathies were much more with the Turk than with the great military Power which was attacking him. The Italian Kingdom was decidedly Russian in its leanings; but this was only an additional reason for the Vatican to lean in the opposite direction. The Turkish Ambassador at Rome was treated by the old Pope with marked consideration; and the Catholic organs all over Europe espoused the cause of the Moslem against the schismatic. One of them even went the length of speaking with some tenderness of the Koran. This new-born enthusiasm, however, seems to have given a little offence to more moderate controversialists; and the *Germania*, an organ of the Ultramontane party in Germany, observed that Russia, though an enemy of the Church, and a persecutor whose pride ought to be abased, should not be altogether humiliated, and that joy at the victories of Turkey should not be suffered to degenerate into friendship for the Ottoman Power. Still, the feeling of most Catholics was strongly anti-Russian, and therefore of necessity pro-Turkish in a greater or less degree. The disposition of the Vatican caused some uneasiness in Germany, where it was regarded as a sign that the Ultramontanes were ready to contract any foreign alliance which, by fostering European complications, might promote their own ends. The subject is believed to have been talked over by Prince Bismarck and Count Andrassy at a sort of informal interview which they had, on the 19th and 20th of September, at Salzburg, in Austria. The result of that interview was to establish more clearly than ever the substantial agreement of Austria and Germany on the great question of the day; and Turkey was still left alone to encounter the full strength of Russia, in which tremendous task the goodwill of the Vatican was but a slight support.

The chief difficulty of the Russians at this stage of the war proceeded from the want of money. The scarcity of the precious metals was most embarrassing, and much was thought of the patriotism of a great landed proprietor in one of the central provinces, who sent his silver plate to the Mint to be melted down for coin. The *Moscow Gazette* considered that the example ought to be generally followed; but it does not appear to have been. A project was at one time advanced for seizing the valuables belonging to the Church which were not absolutely essential for the conduct of the services. A Russian paper remarked that in all probability millions could be realised by the sale of jewels, and of gold and silver vessels, then lying idle in the vaults of various churches and monasteries. This assertion, however, was declared by another Russian journal to be greatly exaggerated, as ninety-nine churches out of a hundred were so far from possessing hidden treasures that they were in need of pecuniary support. It was also alleged that a great part of the costly donations bestowed on the Church in the course of time consisted of silver vessels, which, on being melted, would, at the low standard then existing, only reach the value of a few million roubles. The wealth of Russia is in truth much less than is generally supposed, and the resources of the Empire had already been sorely tried by the necessities of the campaign. The State Bank had a reserve of £25,000,000 sterling; but this was not to be touched, unless under a great emergency. The reality of its existence was affirmed by a correspondent of the *Times*, in opposition to the opinion of many, who believed it to be a myth.

In any case, Russia found herself perfectly well able to carry on the war. Her tone grew more confident with the return of success, and her attitude became so arrogant and self-assertive that even her English friends felt a little uneasy. Mr. Gladstone, in a lecture on "Russians, Turks, and Bulgarians," delivered on the 23rd of November at Hawarden, expressed, though with some hesitation, a doubt as to whether the Czar might not be tempted into going further than was right. Some, he observed, were apprehensive lest Russia might be thinking about Russian interests, as we were thinking of British interests. Whether she was or was not, Mr. Gladstone would not pretend to say. He believed in the honour of the Emperor, and in the strong humanity of the people; but he knew that in other countries besides Russia classes working under ground, and watching their opportunity, sometimes got their way against the nation; and in such classes he had no confidence. He lamented the errors which gave to Russia the opportunity of concentrating so much power in her hands; but if she should misuse it, the world, he hoped, was strong enough to prevent the mischief that might follow. To many it seems that Mr. Gladstone's statesmanship in such matters is to let the evil be done, in order that that vague entity called "the world" may have the honour of undoing it. Mr. Gladstone observed that there was a strong feeling in the country, in which he shared to a certain extent, that it would be a misfortune if Russia should acquire an exclusive or dominating influence in the Sclave Provinces. With others, he had laboured to the best of his ability to prevent this mischief; but the so-called friends of the Turk had done all in their power to bring it about. The "certain extent" to which Mr. Gladstone agreed with the strong feeling in the country, appears to have been very uncertain; and when we recollect that, on his own showing, he would have used the naval force of this country to impose a complete paralysis on Turkey, while Russia with her armies effected all that she desired to effect on land, the degree of agreement with an anti-Russian policy which Mr. Gladstone professed to have entertained becomes exceedingly difficult to realize. But there are mysteries in politics into which it may be profane to inquire; and Mr. Gladstone, though generally frank, even to imprudence, has in this respect furnished posterity with a riddle which it may be amusing, though not very satisfactory, to make attempts at guessing.

The composition of the principal armies employed in the struggle was a subject continually engaging the attention of military critics, and it is one which will bear some further examination in these pages. A correspondent of the *Times*, writing from Bucharest on the 4th of October, observed that what was mainly wanting in the Russian army was the habit of spontaneous action, which could result only from the education and modes of thought of a free people. Whether in consequence of serfdom, or whether from too much Imperialism, the power of initiative was wholly absent. When a Russian soldier was told what to do, he did it like an obedient child; but in a whole year it would never occur to him to originate the thing himself. None the less were his virtues very great. Never in his life had this critic seen so quiet, so gentle, so well-conducted an army: in 200,000 men, he had not come across one drunkard. His account is assuredly in direct opposition to what is generally related both of the Russian army and the Russian people; but it is only fair that the Muscovite soldier should have the benefit of this flattering testimony. The writer admitted it to be the popular idea in England that the Russian is a hard-drinking, noisy, violent, brutal boor; but he maintained that there could be no greater fallacy. The principal drink of the army, he averred, is tea, which is substituted four times a week for the authorized daily ration of *vodka;* consequently, the soldier is remarkably sober, not at all given to violent words or blows, and so scrupulous in paying for all he buys that he allowed himself to be fleeced uncomplainingly by the Bulgarians for whom he was fighting. Always patient, always cheery, his principal amusement was singing in chorus. Whenever a company or a battalion was on the move, the singers were called to the front, when they shuffled out of their places, and formed up in a loose group of fours at the head of the column, which marched off to the music of their singing, varied occasionally by a few taps on the drum. Another popular fallacy in England, according to the report of this correspondent, was that the Russian soldier lives under constant subjection to blows—that the knout and the stick are his only ruling motives. The fact was that nowhere is the soldier managed so entirely by moral means as in the armies of the Czar. A word from his officer, or even a look, is sufficient. He seems to feel reproof as much as an Englishman would feel a blow; but then, we are told, reproof is rarely deserved. The bulk of the Russian privates are themselves small landowners, and so get on very well with their officers, who sometimes, however, in their recklessness of human life, seem to forget that their men are no longer serfs. Even in time of war, the Russian soldier, it appears, is not liable to corporal punishment for any offence whatever, unless he has, by previous bad conduct, and by judgment of a court, been placed in a degraded or inferior class, one of the special disadvantages of which is this liability. The favourable testimony of the *Times* correspondent was to some extent confirmed by a statement in a Russian official paper, to the effect that, since the mobilisation of the army in the early part of 1877, there had been only three capital sentences in a host of 200,000 men. One was passed on a soldier who had attacked a correspondent of the Havas Agency; the second was for insulting an officer; and the third was for desertion. No doubt the discipline of the Russian army is good; but the writer in the *Times* represented a state of ideal perfection which is difficult of belief, which has certainly not its parallel in the world, and which much that we know of Russian soldiers, and of the Russian peasantry, very strongly contradicts.

But if the Russian soldier had his admirers, so also had the Turkish. Another correspondent of the *Times*, writing from the camp of Suleiman Pasha, near Kadikoi, on October 16th, gave an enthusiastic account of the virtues of Suleiman's troops. These men, it seems, formed for themselves a species of rude dwellings by burrowing like sand-martens into any steep bank of earth they could find; and out of those caves, which they made somewhat more habitable by spreading the ground with straw or dry foliage, they would greet the passers-by with friendly amiability, sometimes asking for a little tobacco. If the person addressed had any to give, a hearty expression of thanks rewarded the donor; if not, the only answer was, "May your way be blessed!" The same writer testified that among the Turkish soldiery not only had he never experienced an uncivil word, nor heard a jest at his expense, but he had to acknowledge numberless small services, rendered by cheerful, willing hands, and with all the hearty disinterestedness of patriarchal hospitality. "It imports little," said this observer, "that my heart should ache because the great cause of humanity demands the wholesale slaughter of these brave and gentle folk; but it does so ache, and I wish that some of our bitterest anti-Turkish agitators could spend a month in a Turkish camp, that they might see these people for themselves." The truth no doubt is, that there were excellent human beings in both armies, and that where the excellence really existed it was brought out with additional lustre by the rough test of war. Yet unfortunately it is none the less true that in all armies there are numerous men whom the excitement of combat turns into devils, and perhaps a still larger number who, being neither very good nor very bad, are gradually debauched by the iniquities which they are forced to see, and even to assist in committing. We shall do no good by exaggerating either human wickedness or human virtue. Only by a sober and equitable judgment can we redress the balance which passion is continually endeavouring to disturb.

The Imperial Guards, now in front of Plevna, were the choicest troops in the Russian army. By some of the English newspaper correspondents they were described as worn and fatigued, even before their task had begun; but this would seem to have been only the temporary effect of their long journey from the North, and to have speedily passed away. A writer from the spot affirmed that the men were stalwart, ruddy, and well-fed, and marched with great spirit, singing in chorus as they went, and moving in long, loose, flexible files on both sides of the road, so as to avoid the worst places, and leave the middle for the guns. The average height of the infantry was at least equal to that of our own household troops; the ages of the men ranged for the most part from twenty-six to thirty years; and a considerable proportion wore the yellow chevron which marks a six years' period of service. The soldiers of the Guard had the Berdan rifle, which carries well up to 1,100 yards. The Line, with the exception of one division, were still armed with an old-fashioned rifle, converted into a breech-loader by a clumsy imitation of the Snider breech-lock, and effective at not more than six hundred yards. The Turks carried the Peabody-Martini rifle, which is sighted for 1,200 yards, and can do considerable damage at least four hundred yards farther. It was commonly believed by the Russians that these Turkish rifles came from England; but they were in truth imported from America, and were manufactured by the Providence Tool Company, Rhode Island.*

The Christian races on the Danube, for whose liberation the war was ostensibly being waged, were beginning to look on Russia with some feeling of suspicion, as it became increasingly evident that ambition, and not humanity, was the real motive which had determined the action of the great Northern Power. In Roumania, there was a serious agitation against the Government, and a desire amongst considerable numbers that the Chambers should be convoked, with a view to recalling the army. It was even said that the majority of both Chambers were determined to assemble of their own accord, if the Government declined to summon them. The partisans of the Ministry were themselves doubting the wisdom of the course that had been adopted. The people had in the first instance been pleased at the gallantry which their troops exhibited in Bulgaria, especially as the value of those troops had been questioned by the Russians, and by other nations as well. But the arrival of long trains of wounded in Bucharest and the minor Roumanian cities created a different feeling, and led to a sentiment of disgust at a war in which the suffering seemed to be greater than the glory or the substantial advantages. There was another reason why the subjects of Prince Charles regarded the development of affairs with considerable misgiving. It was very generally suspected--and the event has shown the correctness of the suspicion—that Russia intended, on the conclusion of peace, to reclaim that portion of Bessarabia, adjoining the Kilia branch of the Danube, which had been made over to Moldavia by the Treaty of Paris in 1856. It was believed that any such design would be aided by the Bulgarians who had settled in this region, and who formed the great majority of the population. These Bulgarians were not at all friendly to their new rulers, whom they accused of endeavouring to destroy their nationality; and the feeling of mutual dislike had very considerably increased since the commencement of the war. The Bulgarians of Roumania were among the chief instigators and contrivers of the insurrectionary movement which broke out south of the Danube in May, 1876, and which led to such terrible reprisals on the part of the Turks. They were more Russian in their feelings than the Bulgarians still remaining under Turkish rule, and the Roumanians dreaded what might ensue if they and the Muscovites combined for despoiling the Principality. Thus, the first enthusiasm for the war had in Roumania very nearly died out by the autumn; and, although Prince

* *Times*, October 16th, 1877.

RUSSIAN SOLDIERS.

Charles was determined to go on with what he had begun, it was with difficulty that he could make his policy prevail. Among the Bulgarians of the Balkan districts, the feeling of affection towards Russia was not very great. The stern hand of military despotism had been laid upon the people, and the enthusiasm of spring and early summer had been greatly lowered by an experience of the hard and bitter facts of war.

In Servia, on the contrary, there was a marked increase in the disposition to take part in the struggle. Troops were ordered towards the Turkish frontier; ammunition and provisions were sent in the same direction; officers and surgeons on leave were recalled to their respective posts; the Kragujevatz Arsenal was kept working day and night; and at the beginning of October it was announced that the Servian Minister of War had concluded contracts with four native firms for revictualling the army, and that the first provision-train had left for the south-west, where fourteen battalions had for some time been concentrated, as a corps of observation to watch the Turkish troops collected on the other side of the border. Russia was pressing Servia closely to obtain her assistance; but some of the Ministers were opposed to such a step, and the Prince hesitated between a desire to engage once more with Turkey, and the fear of what might ensue if he should again be beaten. It was necessary also to come to some understanding with Russia as to what Servia should get for her adhesion, in the event of a successful termination of the contest; but in principle it had been almost resolved to take the field at the first opportunity which might seem favourable to such a step. The warlike preparations of Servia were not unknown to the Turkish Government, which demanded of the Servian Agent at Constantinople some explanation of what was intended. A rather warm discussion ensued, and the Agent reproached the Foreign Minister of the Sultan with having ordered the concentration of Turkish troops along the western frontier of Servia. Ultimately, the Ottoman Minister promised to withdraw a portion of his troops; but it does not appear that this concession met with any reciprocity on the part of Prince Milan.

Turkey, however, could have had no wish to add to her existing difficulties. Besides the war in Bulgaria and Armenia, she had to encounter a renewal of the insurrection in Bosnia, where it had ceased for a time. The Government issued an appeal to its rebellious subjects in that quarter, exhorting them to confide in the Sultan's clemency and pardon, and arguing that Russian intervention in favour of the Rayahs had never done them any service. "The Ottoman Empire," said this appeal, "is large enough for all the Sultan's subjects, without distinction of race and creed." This, no doubt, was true enough; but Russian conspiracy and Turkish misgovernment had created a condition in which the antagonisms of race and creed had assumed a character of chronic war and internecine hate. In the latter part of November, a further attempt was made to restore a feeling of mutual reliance between the governors and the governed. The Grand Vizier, in the name of the Sultan, addressed a proclamation to the Bulgarians, rebuking them for their rebellion, but at the same time promising a pardon to all who appealed to the magnanimity of their sovereign, and returned to their homes. Very little effect was produced by this address, and it can hardly have been supposed that it would be instrumental in bringing back the Bulgarians to their allegiance. The seed of blood had been sown, and it was producing its deadly harvests. The Bulgarians were committed to the cause of revolt, and, with a successful foreign army to uphold them, they were not likely to recede. So the Sultan made his promises to unheeding ears, and the sanguinary struggle went on, disgraced in its progress by every foul and unutterable crime, as in its origin it had sprung from craft and violence, from ambition and revenge.

CHAPTER XL.

Condition of Plevna—Objects of Osman Pasha in holding the Position—The Russian Line of Investment—Arrival of Reserves at Constantinople—Horrors of the Road between Plevna and Teliche—State of the Wounded in the Beleaguered Town—The English Doctors and Osman Pasha—Treatment of the Injured Turkish Soldiers—Plevna and its Inhabitants during the Siege—Bad Management of the Russian Soldiers in Camp—Gloomy Weather—A Jewish Sorceress—Approaching Exhaustion of Osman's Resources—Mukhtar Pasha on the Deve-Boyun—Advance of the Russians—Flanking Movement of General Heimann—Attack on the Turkish Left and Right—The Assault repulsed—Cavalry Demonstration against the Centre of the Turkish Position—An Unsuspected Ambush—Sudden Appearance of the Russian Infantry—Utter Defeat of the Turks, and Tumultuous Retreat on Erzeroum—Terrible State of the City—Hopefulness of Mukhtar Pasha—Resolution to defend the Fortress to the Last—Siege Works commenced by the Russians—Lieutenant-Colonel Tarnaieff, and his Project for entering Erzeroum—Attack on the Azizi Works—Temporary Success, and ultimate Repulse—Horrible Treatment of the Wounded—Renewed Attack on the Forts—Second Failure, and Change of Tactics—Erzeroum completely invested.

PLEVNA was surrounded, but still defiant. Osman Pasha did not easily lose heart, but, in proportion as the legions of the enemy thickened about him, added to the great network of the defences with which his skill and energy had guarded the position. Even before the end of October, it was calculated that the entrenched line along the Sophia road extended over fifteen miles, and that the whole circumference of bank and ditch, strengthened at short intervals by formidable field-works, embraced five-and-twenty miles of front from right to left. When the Roumanians made their unsuccessful attempt to storm the second Grivica Redoubt, on the 19th of October, they had to face three successive tiers of rifle-fire, one above another, which poured forth shots at the rate of about twenty thousand a minute. It was a marvel that the fort should have been taken at all; but it was impossible to hold it. This, however, was only one of the many difficulties by which Plevna was environed, and the Russians knew that their best ally would be famine within the walls. The Turkish commander foresaw the danger, and endeavoured to keep open his communications by planting a line of forts along the road to Sophia. The futility of such an attempt became apparent as time wore on. The successes of the Russians at the latter end of October, by which they were enabled to occupy various outlying positions, as already related, completely isolated Plevna, and the growing weakness of the Turks diminished the chances of relief. Yet Osman clung with desperate tenacity to the stronghold he had created. One thing was certain: the existence of Plevna as a fortified position, with masses of fighting men behind the walls, detained a large Russian army north of the Balkans, and forbade any advance in force until the place could be reduced. If Osman Pasha could have held out till the ensuing spring, the fortunes of the war might have been different; and it was probably in the hope of doing so that he rejected all idea of surrender at a time when his subordinates appear to have been disheartened.

The Russians, however, understood their game, and were determined to play it out. They strengthened their investing lines, kept a vigilant watch all round, and awaited the event. At the beginning of November, the dispositions of the besieging force were sufficiently formidable to make the escape of the Turks very unlikely. In the vicinity of Grivica, the Thirty-first and Fifth Divisions, constituting the Ninth Corps, the head-quarters of which were at Pelisat, extended as far as Vladina, where the line was taken up by the Thirtieth Division of the Fourth Corps. Next came the troops under Skobeleff, who greatly improved his position by the seizure of the woody hill on the 9th of November. From the ground occupied by that commander, the line turned north-west, passing by Tyrnen to the Vid. The artillery occupied the ridge before Radisovo, and on the other side of the river the line crossed the Sophia road, whence it curved in a north-easterly direction, until just below the village of Opanes, from which point it extended eastward round the Grivica Redoubt. The country west of the Vid was held by the Guards and the Fourth Roumanian Division, while the north-eastern districts were occupied by the other divisions of the Roumanian army, and the Fourth Rifle Brigade. The length of the investing line was stated at thirty miles, and the army consisted of about 120,000 men. This number would have been insufficient for a secure investment, had it not been for the facilities for rapid concentration afforded by the system of field-telegraphy. As it was, Osman Pasha was strictly held, and the autumn deepened towards winter, without much prospect of relief to lighten the surrounding gloom.

What made the general situation more disastrous

for the Turks, was the fact that they had nearly come to the end of their resources. The latest reserves, which were called out near the end of October, arrived at Constantinople in the early days of November, and were at once marched up to the War Office, that they might be drilled and provided with uniforms. Being for the most part middle-aged men, it was evident that the flower of the population had already been taken; but the feeling of patriotic devotion was unquestionable. The Turks had only to look around for evidence of the evils which they were called on to encounter; but unfortunately those evils were largely increased by the ferocity of their own irregulars. A correspondent of the *Times* said that the road from Plevna to Teliche was rendered melancholy by the perpetual recurrence of unburied bodies. "We grew callous at last," he wrote; "so callous that a dead body touched us no more than a mile-stone might have done. Murder with violence awakened a languid interest. I do not know how I can more clearly or more terribly indicate the horrors of the journey than by telling the simple truth about that one matter—that the sight of the body of any poor wretch done to death by famine, or beaten to death by cruel stripes, or stabbed, or shot, or stoned, awakened in the hearts and minds of half-a-dozen Englishmen no more than a momentary sensation of pity or of anger. We had grown accustomed to these things, and emotion had grown tired, and would not be stirred by any one of them." Many of these dead bodies were the bodies of Bulgarians slain by the Turks; but the latter also had suffered in numerous instances, owing to the mortality among the women and children of fugitives. The correspondent

NEWSPAPER CORRESPONDENTS IN THE ADVANCED TRENCHES BEFORE PLEVNA.

scarcely passed a mile without witnessing a funeral, and the mourners, probably desiring to screen their Moslem rites from the eyes of Christians, would suspend some fragment of cloth from the lower branches of trees, or even hold it up at arm's length, between the performers of the ceremony and the public highway.

The state of Plevna itself was equally bad; but this was mainly caused by the neglect of the Turkish wounded. The writer just quoted spent a few days in the beleaguered town, and was conducted over the hospitals by Dr. Ryan, a young Irish surgeon in the Turkish service. Nothing could exceed the horror of what he there witnessed. Sick and wounded were huddled together in the midst of unutterable filth and stench, without help, without the commonest necessaries of their condition, and with every aggravation of their misery that could result from the abominations in which they lay. For these terrible afflictions, Dr. Ryan was in no degree responsible. He was without assistance until the arrival of three English doctors with the correspondent; nor had he any splints, bandages, chloroform, medicines, stimulants, or other appliances. Infectious diseases were of course rampant under such arrangements, and in the chief hospital, taken in conjunction with a smaller one close by, there was an average of forty-three deaths a day. Four thousand five hundred wounded from Plevna passed through the English Ambulance at Orkhanieh about this time, and received their first dressings at that place. Some of them had been lying wounded for weeks, without bandages; yet, when the English Ambulance proposed to enter Plevna with a large supply of hospital stores, Osman Pasha, it is alleged, refused to admit them. The ambulance was on this account established at Orkhanieh, a distance of two days' ride from Plevna. The Turkish commander thought the place quite near enough, or rather, as some of his critics affirm, was indifferent to the whole matter. Dr. Ryan would sometimes join in the actual work of fighting, and Osman is said to have declared that that was the kind of doctor he wanted, and that he did not see the use of any other.

The day following that on which the English surgeons reached Plevna, Dr. Bond Moore, together with his secretary, Captain Morisot, waited on Osman Pasha at the camp, and made a formal tender of the Stafford House Society's volunteers and stores. A similar proffer was at the same time made by Dr. McKellar, on behalf of the Red Crescent Society. The doctors, however, were bluntly told that they were not wanted, and were ordered to return. Dr. Moore informed the Pasha that he had inspected the hospitals, and he handed in to him a description of the patients and their sufferings. But Osman appears to have been in no respect moved by this revelation of misery. He stated that he intended immediately to transfer his sick and wounded to Sophia; and when Dr. Moore observed that a six days' journey for men in so bad a state would result fatally in hundreds of cases, the Pasha showed signs of displeasure at the persistence with which the claims of humanity were urged on him. The services of the English doctors, he said, were not needed at Plevna: if they wished to do anything, they must go to Sophia. Dr. Moore replied that the immediate transport of the wounded would be a barbarity shocking to Europe; and the deputation then retired. Although naturally discouraged by this reception, Dr. Moore made another appeal to the Commander-in-Chief. Before leaving Plevna, he wrote to the Pasha, acknowledging the receipt of a communication from his Excellency, in which he declined to accept the assistance of the English medical staff. Dr. Moore went on to observe that by a personal inspection he had convinced himself of the urgent need of help. He had found fever, small-pox, famine, and gangrene, rife amongst the unhappy patients; but, in accordance with his Excellency's command, he would leave the camp on the following day. "Humanity," he added, "will not allow me to deprive your Excellency's unfortunate men of the comforts sent out for them from England; and I therefore have given over to your Excellency's Chief Turkish Surgeon, Colonel Assib Bey, the whole of the medicines, bandages, stretchers, appliances, soups, &c., which I brought with me, since it is your Excellency's wish that an English surgeon should not administer them. I should not be doing my duty as the only Stafford House surgeon here, were I not urgently to protest in my professional capacity against the unnecessary transport of the wounded to Sophia. The villages of Lukavitza and Avlanitza, and the town of Orkhanieh, are ready to receive them; and to transport to Sophia men in the deplorable condition in which I have found them, will result only in sowing the Orkhanieh Pass with corpses." Osman Pasha hereupon consented to let the men be removed to the places suggested by Dr. Moore, instead of Sophia; but this was the utmost concession he would make, and he insisted that they must go at once. The correspondent of the *Times* saw the first convoy of a thousand leaving the town, and the spectacle was heartrending. The wretched soldiers stretched out their hands for pity and assistance, shrieked and groaned, or writhed in dumb but most expressive agony. Yet Osman persisted in his policy of indifference to the sufferings of his troops. When Dr. Stokes's ambulance reached Plevna, two days after the arrival of Dr. Moore and his companions, Dr. Stokes was informed that he might fill his arabas with wounded if he liked, but that he must take them away, and that he need not trouble himself to return. In other quarters, the efforts of the English surgeons were met with gratitude and co-operation by the Turks; but Osman Pasha was penetrated with the old Turkish idea that a soldier is simply a fighting machine, and that, if disabled, the sooner he dies out, or is removed, the better.

Another correspondent of the *Times*, however, suggested that the Ottoman commander was bound to consider the preservation of his military position above all other things. The wounded consumed food without being able to render service: they were therefore ordered to be sent out of Plevna, and the doctors, of course, were sent with them. It was urged that Osman may have thought it hard that, in order to save a limited amount of life and suffering, he should imperil, not merely the safety of his entire army, but the welfare of the whole Turkish nation. He may have considered it right to make a certain sacrifice, in order to avert one of an infinitely greater character. In the same stern spirit (which, if exhibited by an ancient Roman, we should probably admire), he declared that he would fire on any Turkish families whom the Russians might endeavour to drive into Plevna. Dr. Ryan, in a report to Mr. Barrington Kennett, the Stafford House Commissioner, affirmed that the reception of the English doctors by Osman Pasha was perfectly courteous. "He told them," said Dr. Ryan, "he was very glad to see them, but that if they were sent in the real cause of 'humanity,' and to assist his wounded, he much preferred their leaving for Sophia, and establishing themselves there. He was sending nearly all the wounded to Sophia, and for those who were remaining he had a sufficient staff of surgeons. His reasons for sending away the wounded must appear most obvious to any one knowing the circumstances of the case. I believe that it is always one of the first considerations of a general after a battle to send off as soon as possible all wounded who are in a state to travel, in order to make room for further fighting. In addition to this main consideration, I must state that our accommodation was very insufficient; that many of our hospitals consisted of houses without windows, and we were fearfully overcrowded, often having thirty men in a room only large enough for ten. Then, again, we had no beds, and could not procure them, as there was no wood to make them of. Another great consideration was that we had not sufficient nor proper food, having only the bare necessaries of life, such as biscuits and meat. From a sanitary point of view it was also extremely desirable to remove them as quickly as possible, thereby lessening the chances of an epidemic, which is always liable to break out when such a large population is confined in a small area. Of the 4,500 wounded, I believe that all but 250 were sent off, the wounds of those remaining being of the very gravest character. Most of the wounds of those sent away were very slight, being flesh-wounds caused by bullets, and which would be perfectly healed in from twenty to thirty days." On the whole, therefore, it would seem that Osman's conduct, if inflexible, was not so heartless as might at first appear.

The Ottoman forces in the camps about the town had by this time made themselves huts for their winter quarters, and were in good spirits, notwithstanding the hardships to which they were exposed. The troops in the town itself, though in some respects better off, were not so cheerful, and during the rainy season wandered listlessly about the streets, in a mood of abject despondency. With its closed-up shops, its muddy roads, and its depressed and idle populace, Plevna was dreary in the extreme; and it was almost a relief to the general stagnation and gloom when a shell from the Russian guns dropped in the public ways, and either burst, or buried itself in the soil. The people soon became accustomed to the danger, and disregarded it; but casualties happened every now and then. Unexploded shells lay thickly scattered about the open ground surrounding Plevna, and they were so many mines of peril to the heedless passer-by. A more serious danger, however, was that of the unburied corpses, which filled the air with the elements of deadly disease. Bodies of Russians, stripped absolutely naked, lay in every direction, and the neighbourhood of Grivica, in particular, was a mere pest-house. The Turks refused all offers for the burial of the dead, and the frightful atmosphere generated by their decomposition spread like a subtle poison over the neighbouring lands. After the departure of the English surgeons (including Dr. Ryan) from Plevna, the sufferings of the wounded were even greater than before. There were now only Turkish doctors in the place, and their treatment of the injured was described as almost childish. In the case of a gunshot wound in the thigh, they would simply bandage up the limb as tightly as they could, all the way from the foot to the trunk, when, the circulation being stopped, the patient had very little chance of his

MAKING TRENCHES BEFORE PLEVNA.

life. Some of the Turkish officers even said, "These unfortunates will never handle rifle again. If they die now, they will go to Paradise; if their lives are saved, the Sultan will have to pay them pensions for forty years, and Turkey is not rich enough to afford that." The mortality was, of course, terrific; but Osman Pasha had the fewer mouths to feed, and this was now becoming a consideration of the greatest importance.

The sufferings of the Russians were of a different nature, and resulted principally from the bad management of their camps. The Russian soldier, according to a correspondent of the *Daily News*, has little facility in making himself comfortable. The rainy weather had caused the Bulgarian soil to be soft and miry, and the consequence was that the tents outside Plevna were often flooded with water. Ditches might easily have been dug, to carry off the superfluous moisture; but it never occurred to the Russian troops to perform this very simple piece of engineering. The tents were thin and badly constructed, and nothing was done to make them more habitable, or better fitted to exclude the weather. The troops bore their troubles with extraordinary patience; but patience is at once one of the virtues and one of the defects of the Muscovite soldier. It is his virtue, because it enables him to endure an enormous amount of hardship without actually breaking down: it is his defect, because it induces him to tolerate a number of evils, which, with a little more spleen and energy, he would soon overcome. In conducting the siege of Plevna, and in waiting for the inevitable fall of that stronghold, the investing troops suffered an amount of misery which nations of a higher intelligence and a quicker spirit would have escaped, or rather have brushed aside.

THE DEVE-BOYUN PASS.

The weather around Plevna is said to have been curiously affected by the heavy artillery-fire of the besiegers and the besieged. The immense amount of sulphurous air, poured forth by the guns of both combatants, raised the general temperature, and obscured the heavens with thick mists. This happened with so much regularity that a moist and foggy day was always expected after a bout of heavy firing, and the anticipation seldom proved erroneous. The gloomy and depressing character of the atmosphere seems to have disposed the minds of people within the walls to a kind of tampering with the supernatural world. Inside Plevna there was an old Jewess, who contrived to make a good deal of money by fortune-telling. From morning to night, her house was filled with officers and soldiers, eager to question the planets as to what was in store for them. It is even said that Osman Pasha himself consulted the ancient sorceress, who predicted for him a brilliant future, provided he were not made prisoner before the 12th of December. It is a singular fact that Osman's surrender took place exactly two days earlier than that date, so that the negative side of the Jewess's prophecy may be said to have been fulfilled. A month earlier, however, the Turkish commander must have known, without any supernatural revelation, what would inevitably happen at no great distance of time, unless the line of investment could be broken through, of which there was then little more than the possibility. A Russian *parlêmentaire* was sent into Plevna on the 12th of November, with a suggestion that the Pasha had better capitulate at once. To this he replied that he had not yet exhausted his entire means of defence, nor done all that his duty as a military commander required him to do. The answer itself proved that his resources were getting low, and the Russians must have been abundantly satisfied that with perseverance they would surely win. Yet Plevna was still some weeks from the last extremity. A want of winter clothing was said to be the principal trouble experienced at that time by Osman Pasha; but he was a great economist in such matters, and made the most of his resources. When the weather was fine, he deprived his soldiers of their boots, and stowed them away in magazines until cold or wet made a re-issue advisable. In all other respects he appears to have been equally careful, and his determination to die hard must have been as well known to the Russians as to himself.

Mukhtar Pasha in Asia was in no better position than Osman Pasha in Europe, though he considered himself well able to repel any assault that the Russians might make on the heights he was now occupying. The Deve-Boyun was in truth, as we have already shown, one of the most formidable positions a commander could hold. The narrow defile forming the pass of the Deve-Boyun is the only road from the plain to Erzeroum, and it leads up the face of a mountain, every portion of which is commanded by the batteries on the summit. The roadway is only wide enough to allow of two waggons travelling abreast, and the military works which had been created by the energy of Faizi Pasha (the Hungarian, General Kohlmann) were such as to offer every opportunity for a successful defence. It was about the close of October that Mukhtar Pasha took up his position on this mountain, and he was followed with alacrity by the Russian Generals, Heimann and Tergukasoff, who occupied in succession Olti, Koprikoi, Deli-Baba, and Hassan Kalé. On the 3rd of November, the Russians were within ten miles of Erzeroum, and had even pushed forward a reconnaissance to the foot of the Deve-Boyun. At that time, the extreme left of the Turkish army held Gurgee Boghaz; the centre occupied the Deve-Boyun Pass; and the right extended to the end of the ridge forming the Soghilhar Dagh. By this disposition of the Ottoman forces, Erzeroum was completely covered, and the pass itself was occupied by Mukhtar Pasha's own men, who, as disciplined and veteran troops, might be expected, notwithstanding the disaster they had recently undergone, to encounter the enemy with firmness and resolution. The Turks, however, were considerably outnumbered. It is probable that the Russians were as two to one, and they were inspired by the confidence naturally resulting from a brilliant success, achieved over the very men whom they were now about to attack once more.

The chief anxiety of the Turks was with reference to the valleys on their flanks, which, unless strictly guarded, might be turned. It was believed that the Russians would not dare to assail the heights in front; yet this was the very thing which they had resolved on doing. The attack, which had been carefully prepared, was delivered on the 4th of November, when the entire Muscovite force was sent forward against the position. The Turks had imprudently abandoned an outlying fort on the last spur of the Soghilhar Dagh, to the east of the ravine, and the withdrawal from this work allowed the invaders to advance within a mile and a half of the Deve-Boyun front. Mukhtar Pasha was ill-provided with field-artillery; but he had ten batteries, consisting of sixty guns, and eighteen of these commanded the pass. The Russians possessed a hundred and twenty guns, planted at several points along their line, which extended over about eight miles. Heimann knew the formidable character of the position he had to attack, and he saw that he must either execute a strong flanking movement, or by means of a stratagem entice the Ottomans from their entrenchments. He finally resolved to combine both methods, and on the night of November 3rd sent off a strong column along the mountain road towards Partak, and another towards Navi-Kui, with instructions to conceal themselves in the numerous ravines on both sides of the road leading up to the Turkish centre. In the uncertain light of dawn, on the morning of the 4th, the Russian infantry crept noiselessly over the intervening ground. The path was rugged and difficult, and occasionally some slight murmurs of the impending danger reached the ears of the Turkish sentinels; but no alarm was given. The Turks are generally neglectful in the matter of night-outposts, and they paid the penalty on this occasion, as on many others. The assailants made their way towards the assigned positions, and soon found shelter among the precipitous rocks which thickly cover the ground.

Between eight and nine on the morning of the 4th, the Russians were seen advancing across the plain in the direction of the Turkish left. It was at first supposed that this was a movement of no consequence; but it soon proved to be seriously intended. The left of the Turkish line was commanded by Captain Mehmed Pasha, a Prussian, whose men occupied a flat-topped, conical hill, enfilading the whole Turkish front, and commanding all the ground within its vicinity. This hill was so important as to be the key of the entire position, and the attempt to carry it was made with the most determined gallantry. Again and again the height was assailed by a strong body of troops; but the Turks succeeded in repelling all attacks. They lost very severely, however, and towards midday Mehmed Pasha sent to the Commander-in-Chief for assistance. Three battalions and two batteries were at once despatched to reinforce the Prussian captain, who disposed of them with so much ability that the Russians, finding themselves raked by the guns which Mehmed had promptly thrown forward, abandoned the attempt they had been so obstinately making, and retired out of range, leaving a large proportion of their number on the ground. In this struggle the artillery had played a prominent part, and the Russian guns were worked with so much precision that the Turks believed the gunners to be either English or Prussian. The Turkish right was simultaneously attacked, and the noise of firing on both flanks was incessant for some hours. Two Turkish Pashas fell at their posts; but the Ottomans still held their ground, and it seemed as if the result of the day's fighting would be a victory for the Crescent. The Turks had had time to send several battalions to the threatened positions on the flanks, and the Russians were compelled to recoil from both sides, firing sullenly as they drew back.

A front attack against the centre of the Russian position, commanded by Mukhtar Pasha in person, might well have seemed hopeless, owing to the difficult nature of the ground, and the strength of the artillery by which it was swept. Yet Heimann, on finding himself foiled at the flanks, resolved on making the attempt, under cover of a stratagem. He brought together all his squadrons of cavalry, and manœuvred them in the open plain. Presently they were observed by the Turks stretching out towards the foot of the pass; but it was thought hardly possible that horsemen could be really sent on such an enterprise, especially as they were unsupported by artillery or infantry. The truth was, however, as the reader is aware, that forty-five battalions of foot-soldiers were lying in ambush among the gullies and small lateral glens of the Deve-Boyun. Of their presence there the Turks had not the slightest conception, owing to the movement having been carried out during the night. It was believed, therefore, that the cavalry were acting by themselves, and that there would be no difficulty in repelling so rash an assault. On came the horsemen in gallant style, seeming as if they would ride over the position by sheer force of will; but the Turks allowed them to approach untouched until near enough for effective operations. At length, when they had gained the very foot of the hill, Mukhtar Pasha gave the word to his soldiers to leave their entrenchments, and charge the enemy. The Turks rapidly sprang down the slope, and began to open fire on the audacious Cossacks. The latter slowly retired, and the Ottomans, full of confidence in their presumed superiority, pursued with ardour, and were drawn still farther into the trap. Their shots told with deadly effect, and all seemed going well for the Osmanlis, when in a moment everything was changed.

What ensued was strikingly described by a correspondent of the *Daily Telegraph*, who wrote:—"From many places on the hill-sides, where but a moment before there was nothing to be seen but the bare ground, started up dense files of Russian infantry. The hills were covered with them; their shouts echoed from side to side. In an instant they were pouring fearful volleys, at murderously short distances, on both flanks of the unsuspecting, unprepared Turks. Too confident, too anxious to punish the over-daring of the Russian cavalry, Mukhtar's men had advanced so far down the valley that there was no longer the possibility of recovery. The narrowness of the road, the closeness of the overwhelming fire, the advantageous positions secured by the enemy—above all, the suddenness of the attack—unmanned and paralysed them. Panic-stricken, the Turks ran hither and thither—terrified, bewildered, unable to offer the least resistance. Up the hill-side dashed the victorious Russians. They reached the trenches as soon as the surviving Turks themselves; position after position they assailed and took with amazing celerity. They had it all their own way. Practically, there was no defence of a position that just before was deemed invincible. The Turks, no longer a disciplined force, but only a panic-stricken crowd, were driven over the crest of the hill, abandoning munitions, arms, everything." They were under the impression that the Russian army was even more numerous than it was in fact, and, when they found their retreat cut off by that portion of the attacking force which had clambered over the rocks to the upper part of the slope, despair overwhelmed them, and they were no longer capable of resistance. The terror of the infantry on the open hill-side was shared, with less excuse, by the threats of the inferior officers. Afterwards, Faizi Pasha endeavoured to rally them, but with no greater success. He pointed out that, if they would only cling to the hill on the right, above Topalack, they would be able to enfilade the Russian advance, and so check the pursuit. The discomfited soldiers of the centre had no ear for such advice, but dashed in wild confusion along the road to Erzeroum. Mukhtar Pasha wished to die by the Russian bullets, but he was swept away in the general rush. The only troops who conducted themselves with

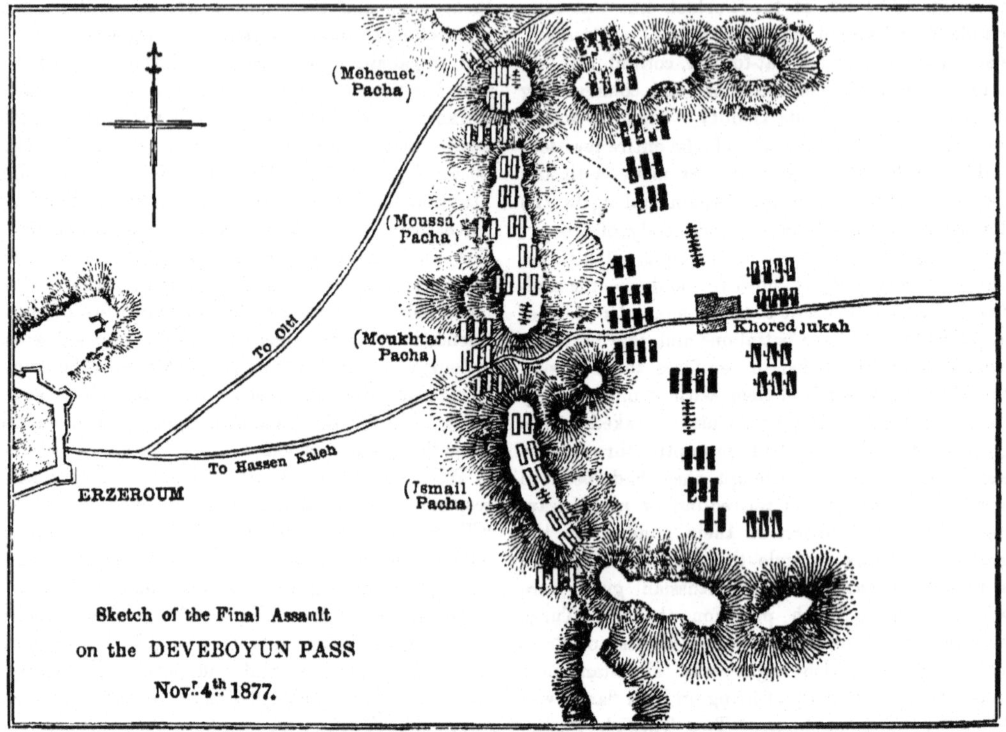

PLAN OF DEFEAT OF THE TURKS IN THE DEVE-BOYUN PASS.

the gunners in the trenches. As soon as they perceived the Russian foot-soldiers starting up as it were from the very earth, they abandoned their artillery without firing a shot, and, cutting the traces, rode off at full speed. The Turkish infantry maintained the struggle for a little longer, but at last joined the flying masses of their comrades, with the exclamation, "Defeat, defeat! It is the will of Allah."

When the true nature of the offensive movement became apparent, Mukhtar Pasha placed himself at the head of two battalions, and endeavoured to stem the torrent of the Russian attack. But it was too late to effect any change. The troops would not listen to the exhortations of their commander, or to resolution were those of the two European officers, Faizi and Mehmed Pashas, who commanded the right and left wings. These men presented so steady a front to the enemy that the pursuit slackened and moderated. But for this interposition, the Russians, in the opinion of Captain Norman, might have crossed the Deve-Boyun at once, and entered Erzeroum that night. The road to the capital presented a spectacle of utter ruin and complete military disorganization. The struggle in front of the entrenchments had been short, but decisive, and early in the afternoon the Turkish army was in full retreat. Infantry and cavalry, gunners and teamsters, officers and men, Circassians and Kurds, Bashi-Bazouks and camp-followers, camels, oxen, and various kinds of vehicles, were all jumbled together in one inextricable tangle. The commissariat animals blocked the way, and the Circassian and Kurdish cavalry cut a path with their swords through the struggling and frightened mass, while the infantry rushed over the low hills on both sides of the road. Outside Erzeroum, the scene was even worse. The Governor, on hearing of the defeat of his countrymen on the Deve-Boyun, had closed the gates of the city, fearing the disorders that might ensue from the sudden inroad of a defeated and demoralised army. The fugitives, on reaching the walls, and finding all ingress barred against them, became frantic with fear and rage, and a bloody struggle ensued between those on the ramparts and those below, in which both sides used their rifles with deadly earnestness. About midnight, when the excitement had in some degree abated, strong guards were placed at the gates, and the fugitives were permitted to enter.* The barracks, however, were so filled with sick and wounded men that the new-comers were unable to find any place of shelter. A bitter fall of sleet had set in, and the weary and famished soldiers sank down into the half-frozen mud, and slept the sleep of exhaustion.† Faizi and Mehmed Pashas reached the city a little beyond midnight; the latter after a most harassing retreat, in which he had to fight continually, to preserve his force from capture. The losses were fearful. Forty-two guns, and nearly all the baggage, had passed over to the enemy; and 4,500 men, at the lowest computation, had been killed, wounded, or taken. Mukhtar Pasha himself afterwards acknowledged a loss of 1,000 men in killed alone, and it was probably more. A magnificent position, seemingly impregnable, had been abandoned in headlong flight, and the retention of Erzeroum itself became thenceforth extremely doubtful.

During the night following that lamentable day, Mukhtar Pasha and his lieutenants held a council of war, at which they expressed a very strong opinion that Erzeroum should be defended to the last. The Governor of the city, and the principal inhabitants, pleaded for a surrender, representing that the army was disorganised and utterly broken; that the Russians, flushed with victory, were in possession of the heights commanding the town; and that, consequently, a successful defence was impossible. The hopeful nature of Mukhtar Pasha would not permit him to take this gloomy view of the facts. He believed that his soldiers might be rallied to a sense of duty, and that Erzeroum was strong enough to resist a siege. Yet there was little in his surroundings to encourage a sanguine mood. At daybreak on the 5th of November, a large number of the populace left the city; the archives, together with vast quantities of baggage, were sent away; and everything indicated a total want of self-reliance on the part of the citizens. It was reported that the enemy's advanced posts were at a distance of two miles, and that a considerable force of cavalry had been seen hovering about during the night. The Russians were said to have threatened an immediate bombardment, unless the place were at once surrendered; and even some of the soldiers quitted Erzeroum, and marched in a north-westerly direction towards Baiburt, whither the English Military Attaché, General Sir Arnold Kemball, had already gone. Under all these disheartening circumstances, Mukhtar Pasha preserved his courage and cheerfulness, and in the course of a day or two succeeded in imparting some of his own spirit to the people about him. On the 6th, a *parlementaire* arrived from General Heimann, with a demand for a surrender; to which the Mushir answered evasively, that he might gain time for communicating with Constantinople. He had 12,000 troops in garrison, provisions in plenty, and abundance of ammunition. The situation, therefore, was not immediately threatening, though it could not be said to offer many elements of hope. A telegram was sent to the capital, requesting instructions; and the reply was that the Field Marshal was to defend the place to the last man and the last cartridge. Finding himself thus supported, he sent a messenger to the Russian General, to the effect that he would hold the fortress while one stone remained upon another. It was indeed obvious to the Sultan and his Ministers that with the loss of Erzeroum the Asiatic campaign would be virtually at an end, and the whole of Turkish Armenia would lie within the power of the Czar. It is therefore not surprising that Mukhtar Pasha was commanded to retain his grasp on the position at every risk and cost.

The Russians were equally bent on seizing this great stronghold. On the 7th of November they threw up a redoubt facing the eastern side of the town. It was situated about 2,500 yards from the Tope Dagh (or Cannon Hill), and entirely commanded the city. The Turkish Generalissimo was in no position to hinder the progress of the work, the construction of which went on, day and night, with great rapidity. He therefore confined himself to preparations for the defence of the city, which he knew would be soon assailed. The fortifications of Erzeroum were in many respects very

* According to some accounts, the gates were forced by Mukhtar's soldiery.

† Captain Norman's Armenia, and the Campaign of 1877.

RUSSIAN ATTACK BEFORE DAYBREAK.

strong, and the walls were mounted with more than a hundred and fifty Krupp siege-guns, many of which were of large calibre. In addition to the garrison were several thousand armed inhabitants, bringing up the total strength to at least 20,000 men. This gave four men per yard for the defence of the walls, and the number was considered by a competent observer sufficient to render any assault extremely hazardous. Heimann, however, was impatient to get the city into his possession, and on the 9th attempted to carry the outworks by storm, but signally failed in his endeavour. The scheme originated with a Staff officer named Tarnaieff—a man of Armenian extraction, who had already distinguished himself during the campaign, and who, having been employed for some years in the Russian consulate at Erzeroum, nominally as a dragoman, had acquired, in his real capacity of a spy, a considerable knowledge of the place. He was killed in the action which followed, and plans of all the works were found upon his body. "The act of employing Staff officers as dragomans in the consulates of fortified towns," observes Captain Norman, "is a novel feature in diplomacy —one that redounds more to the far-sightedness of the Russian Government than to its honour." At a council of war, held in General Heimann's tent on the evening of November 8th, Tarnaieff volunteered to undertake the capture of the outlying Azizi works, if he were entrusted with the command of three battalions, and were supported by a complete brigade. The project at first seemed ridiculous; but the young Lieutenant-Colonel at length carried his point, which was particularly attractive to Heimann, himself a dashing and adventurous soldier. It was finally agreed that Tarnaieff should attack the Azizi outworks, commanding the whole eastern range of fortifications, and that the movement should be supported by a simultaneous attack on the south-western face, near the Kremedli Redoubt.

MUKHTAR PASHA SIGHTING A KRUPP GUN IN THE REDOUBT AT ERZEROUM.

The troops were paraded for action at midnight on the 8th, when Tarnaieff led the right column of attack, at the head of three battalions, with seven others in reserve, two miles to the rear. The Armenian Colonel was accompanied by a single field-battery, and, advancing quietly through the darkness, arrived within three-quarters of a mile of the fort. He then detached two of his battalions, and proceeded with the third towards the walls. The battalions left behind were instructed to push on, directly they heard the firing commence; and in the meanwhile Tarnaieff, with the other, was to plant scaling-ladders against the fort, and endeavour to obtain a passage into the interior. His approach, though executed with great skill and secrecy, had not escaped the attention of one of the Turkish sentries in a lunette forming an outwork of the Azizi Fort. Hearing a noise, which he thought indicated the advance of troops, this man reported the matter to the officer of the guard; but his story found no credence. Daylight, however, proved that he was right, for in the early dawn of the 9th two bodies of Russian troops broke into the lunette, one from the parapet in front, the other from the open gorge in the rear. The place was at once in possession of the enemy; but Captain Mehmed Pasha, who commanded at Azizi, placed himself at the head of half a battalion, and proceeded to the spot, having heard a disturbance which convinced him that all was not right. Before he reached the lunette, the presence of the Russians was visible, and Mehmed ordered an immediate charge. This was executed with so much spirit and impetuosity that in a little while the intruders were driven out of the work, from which, however, they had already removed the garrison, consisting of twenty officers and five hundred men. Tarnaieff's reserve battalions endeavoured to retake the lunette, and the fighting soon became general. The citizens, excited by the religious exhortations of their priests, who shouted to them from the minarets, flocked to the citadel, where they were hurriedly armed; and large crowds of these extemporised soldiers were soon on their way to the Azizi Fort, determined to resist the Russian attack to the utmost extremity of their power. A sanguinary struggle ensued, lasting until past mid-day; but early in the afternoon the Russians were driven back at the point of the bayonet, swept out of the lunette, and pressed up to the walls of the Tope Dagh Redoubt. In the other direction the attack had been equally unsuccessful, and Heimann recalled his column at two P.M. The Turkish casualties on this occasion amounted to about 700 killed, and 1,500 wounded, whilst twenty officers and 500 men were left prisoners in the hands of the enemy. The Russian loss was even heavier, and amongst the killed was the brave young Armenian Colonel who had devised the attack. Being wounded early in the engagement, he had surrendered to a Turkish officer, but seems to have been afterwards slain in cold blood His dead body was found next day in the lunette, and it was evident from its condition that horrible mutilations had been inflicted upon the corpse, if not upon the living man. Unfortunately, Tarnaieff was not the only person on whom this iniquity had been practised. Nearly every Russian found lying on the ground was decapitated, or otherwise mangled; and these dreadful crimes appear to have been perpetrated by women from the city, who, when it was seen that the Russians were defeated, issued forth with knives, hatchets, and other household weapons, to despatch the wounded who lay gasping on the ground. In strong contrast with this diabolical conduct was the heroism of Dr. Featherstonhaugh, Mr. Consul Zohrab, the youthful sons of that gentleman, and the old consular cavasse, Mustapha, who went about the field under a storm of bullets, giving such aid to the wounded as they were capable of rendering.*

In an official report afterwards issued by General Heimann, that commander stated that several columns of the attacking force lost their way in the darkness, and that the principal operation failed on that account. But the assailants had certainly come very near success, and, besides carrying off a considerable number of prisoners, had spiked twenty guns in the Azizi Fort. Had it not been for Mehmed Pasha's prompt and gallant advance, the work would probably have remained in the hands of the Russians; indeed, the partial success of November 9th encouraged Heimann to make another attempt a few days later. On the night of the 12th, large bodies of men were sent against the position, but only to fail more signally than before. The night was pitchy dark, bitterly cold, and rendered the more depressing by torrents of icy rain. Neither side fought with much animation, and Heimann, seeing the futility of these somewhat random attacks, determined to wait for reinforcements, and in the meanwhile to cut off the communications with other parts of Armenia by the help of his cavalry. The Cossacks were already scouring the plains about Erzeroum, and in a little while they advanced along the neighbouring mountain heights, so as to interpose themselves between that city and Trebizond, on the Black Sea, from which place reinforcements had been sent towards the beleaguered fortress. It was not long ere Erzeroum was completely invested, and Mukhtar Pasha was probably the only man who looked towards the future with any confidence.

* Norman's Armenia.

CHAPTER XLI.

Blockade of Kars—Capabilities of Defence—Movements of the Grand Duke Michael—Temporary Seizure of Fort Hafiz Pasha—Bombardment of the City and its Works—Discouragement of the Garrison—Russian Council of War—Determination to assault the Fortress—Dispositions for the Attack on the Evening of November 17th—The Forward March—Inadequate Defence of the City—Desperate Fighting at the Khanli Fort—Scaling of the Karadagh by the Russians—Reduction of Kars on the Morning of the 18th—Triumphal Entry of the Grand Duke Michael—Alleged Treachery on the Part of a Turkish Officer—The Story of Hassan Bey—Effect of the Fall of Kars at Constantinople and in other Places—Russian Rejoicings—Divine Service and a Salvo of Artillery—Proposal to march across Asia Minor to Constantinople—Movement of General Melikoff on Erzeroum—Operations of Heimann before that City—Expedition of Komaroff—Preparations of Mukhtar Pasha for the Defence of Erzeroum—Interview of a Newspaper Correspondent with the Mushir—The Russians in the Snow—Arrival of a Caravan from Persia—Defences of the Beleaguered City—Operations of Suleiman Pasha on the Lom—The Civic Guard of Constantinople—Affairs in Thessaly, Epirus, and the Kingdom of Greece—The Case of the Geshoffs—The Sultan and the Greeks—Ineffectual Attempts to conciliate the Hellenic Nationality.

Kars was effectually blockaded after the great defeat of Mukhtar Pasha on the 15th of October. No one could go in or come out without being stopped, and several Turks and Armenians were captured in the endeavour to escape. From the early part of November, an artillery-fire from a battery of long-range twenty-four-pounders, established in the neighbourhood of the Little Yahni, was kept up day and night, and the inhabitants of the city soon began to despair. It was seen that the place would be left to its resources; that it was not likely the Turkish Government would be able to send a force to its relief; and that in time surrender must inevitably ensue. The commandant was Hussein Hami Pasha, a Lieutenant-General in the Turkish army; and the garrison consisted of not more than 10,000 Nizams and Redifs, with whom were associated a rather inconsiderable number of armed citizens, whose services added but little to the strength of the fortress. The difficulties of the defence were increased by the presence of 3,500 sick and wounded, who crowded the hospitals and the khans, and were even to be found lying about in the covered markets. Of food there was sufficient for six months' consumption, and the stock of ammunition, except as regarded small shells, was plentiful, as a large stock of siege-projectiles had been laid in after the relief of Kars in July. The Russians were well-informed by their spies of the general condition of the city, and it was considered that an assault would be the most likely means of ultimate success. But, as a matter of form, a summons to surrender was first of all sent in. This was despatched on the 25th of October, and Hussein Hami at once submitted the question to a council of war, by whom it was unanimously determined to hold the fortress as long as possible. On the following day, Melikoff occupied the valley of the Kars-Tchai, together with some heights behind the city which the Turks had left unguarded; and the bombardment began in earnest on the 4th of November.

The Grand Duke Michael determined to bring a powerful force to bear on this great stronghold of the Ottoman rule in Armenia, and on the 5th of November moved round from Karajal to Vera-Kalé. His flank was much exposed during the march, and Hussein Hami, rapidly sending out the greater part of his garrison, attacked the Russians with such sudden vehemence that the division was thrown into temporary confusion. The men, however, quickly rallied, and the Turks were pressed back at the point of the bayonet into their defences. The repulse, indeed, was carried to greater lengths than the Russians themselves anticipated, for with the full impetus of their rush they actually entered Fort Hafiz Pasha at the south-east angle of the *enceinte*. Here they dismantled the guns and removed the breech-pieces; but, the column being unsupported, as there had never been any deliberate intention of seizing the work, the assailants were subsequently obliged to withdraw, in the execution of which movement they suffered great losses. On the following day, the Grand Duke again sent a *parlementaire* to the city, to require its surrender; but Hussein Hami declined even to discuss the subject, and threatened to fire on any other messenger who should approach the fortress on a similar errand. There was nothing to be done, therefore, but to carry on the bombardment with vigour. In May and June, the siege had been conducted against the northern face of the city; but this was found to be not the most vulnerable part, as the defensive works in that direction are situated on lofty hills, and therefore beyond effective cannon-range. The guns were now planted against the southern and eastern sides of Kars, and a greater effect was speedily observable. When the siege-batteries were finished, they extended from the Kars-Tchai, near Komadsoi, to the foot of the hills near Vezinkoi. On the 6th of November, the Russians had sixty siege-pieces in position, and a few days later they suspended their fire, that other batteries might be constructed.

As the month wore on towards the middle, the bombardment became terrific. Hussein Hami

Pasha, telegraphing to Mukhtar Pasha at Erzeroum, confessed that his men were so utterly cowed and dispirited that the fortress would probably fall at the first assault. General Loris Melikoff was of the same opinion, and preparations were made for the grand attack. This was in the first instance ordered for the night of November 13th, and the assaulting columns even advanced so far as to attract the notice of the Turkish sentries, when General Lazareff pointed out that the ground was too slippery, and too much involved in water, to allow of the operation being successfully conducted. The troops were therefore withdrawn, after a slight skirmish; and the bombardment was resumed, though with some irregularity. On the 16th, Fort Hafiz Pasha was silenced, and the south-eastern angle of the works was thus left entirely undefended. The probabilities of a triumphant assault were now all the greater, and on the 17th of November the Grand Duke Michael assembled a council of war, at which the question was discussed. To the generals it appeared that there were several reasons why a favourable result was to be anticipated, if the effort were vigorously made. The garrison of Kars was small—so small that at least one-third of the works could not be defended; the troops were disheartened, and little disposed to fight with resolution; typhoid fever was making terrible havoc in the city; and it was reported that dissensions existed amongst the Turkish commanders. Accordingly, the upshot of the conference was that Kars should be immediately assailed.

The attack took place that very night. For some time past the weather had been bad, with a bitterly cold temperature, a good deal of rain, and some snow. But these evils had now abated, and the condition of the ground had improved since the 13th. The moon was near the full; but the sky was so obscured with clouds that not much light reached the earth. The columns of attack formed up about six o'clock on the evening of the 17th, and two hours later were sent forward on their perilous undertaking. In all, the Russian forces amounted to at least 30,000 men; but only 18,000 took part in the actual fighting. These were directed by General Melikoff himself, who planned the whole scheme of operations. The orders of that commander were that the column on the extreme right, advancing from Vezinkoi, was to threaten the Karadagh works, and at the same time to seize Fort Hafiz Pasha; after which it was to climb the southern slopes of the Karadagh, and to take Fort Ziaret in reverse. General Lazareff, who had executed the flank march round the Aladja Dagh in October, commanded the right wing, which consisted of the Fortieth Division. The central column, extending from Magardjik to Komadsoi, on the Kars-Tchai, was commanded by Count Grabbe, and comprised a regiment of the Thirty-ninth Division, together with the Moscow Grenadiers and the Caucasian Rifles. Its special business was to attack the Khanli and Suwarri Forts, to the south of Kars. Generals Roop and Komaroff were stationed on the western bank of the Kars-Tchai; and while the first of these officers was directed to attack the Tahmasp Fort with the remainder of the Moscow Grenadiers, the second was to advance against the Mukhliss Fort at the head of the Ardahan Brigade. A hundred and forty-four field-guns were sent with the assaulting columns, and proved very useful in the struggle which ensued.

The columns advanced under cover of a heavy fire from fifty-two siege-guns, and each of these columns was accompanied by a ladder-party; but, when the moment for action came, the ladders were found to be too short. The commanders to the south and east had been directed to carry the works opposed to them at all costs; while those on the north and west were only to make a serious demonstration, without going to the extent of an actual assault. The attack began in the centre, at the Suwarri or Cavalry Fort, where the Arabs of the second reserve, who held the position, offered a very weak resistance. Kars was one of the strongest fortresses in Turkey, owing to the labours of English and Prussian engineers, and was so constructed that each part supported and commanded the other parts. But the most formidable stronghold is vulnerable if it be unprovided with a sufficient number of men to conduct the defence, and if those who guard the ramparts are depressed and apprehensive as to the result. The Turks, it is said, had not more than six hundred soldiers to each mile of parapet; and the armed citizens, who were reluctantly goaded to the outer walls, and were worse than useless when they got there, did not increase the proportion to more than a thousand men per mile. The difficulties of the moment were made all the greater by the darkness of the night; for the gunners could not distinctly see where to fire, and the assailants were thus enabled to approach the walls pretty closely before anything effective could be done against them.

Although the attack in some quarters was not very vigorously met by the Turks, the assault on the Khanli Fort, in the centre, was attended by the death of Count Grabbe, who, while leading the foremost ranks of his brigade, fell pierced by a rifle-bullet. This work was held by Anatolian Nizams (regular troops from Asia Minor), who fought with the utmost resolution and fury. The officer who succeeded to the command of the Russians was a colonel of engineers, and it appeared to him better to abandon the direct attack, and work round to the gorge. Here his progress was stopped by a blockhouse of heavy masonry, the massive gates of which were speedily blown in. The garrison were then informed that, in the event of further resistance, the walls would be mined, and shattered to fragments by that dreadful explosive, dynamite; and they were offered the alternative of unconditional surrender as the only means of avoiding the catastrophe. They determined on capitulation, and the Russians obtained a most important position, from which it was found impossible to expel them, although attempts were made from adjoining redoubts to bring the heavy guns to bear on the intruders. The assailants were not less successful in other directions. Fort Hafiz Pasha, attacked by General Lazareff, was hastily abandoned by the troops holding it, owing to the want of artillery; and the Russian commander then directed his men up the steep, rocky slopes of the Karadagh. To scale these heights was an arduous task; but it was not attended by much loss of life, as the ascending columns were sheltered from the fire of the guns on the crest, and the other forts were unable, by the development of the attack, to render any aid. Having reached the top, one brigade of Lazareff's division advanced against Fort Ziaret, which was speedily taken, while the other attacked the citadel, an antiquated work, defended only by a few heavy guns, and by two companies of artillery of the second reserve, or Redif. The fighting was not very prolonged at this spot, and in a little while the citadel passed into the hands of the Russians, together with an immense amount of small-arms, ammunition, ordnance-stores, &c.

Thus the greater part of the fortress of Kars was hopelessly lost to the Turks; but the struggle was still desperately maintained at some other points. At one of the redoubts, a furious encounter was kept up for ten hours, and the Russians were hurled back again and again, but always returned to the charge with fresh accessions of strength. The work was not taken until six o'clock on the morning of the 18th of November, when the garrison, being utterly exhausted, had no choice but to submit. Some of the other positions were seized at an earlier hour; but, on the whole, the fighting extended through the greater part of that long winter night. To the west of the Kars-Tchai, General Roop took Fort Tahmasp, and by eight o'clock in the morning the fortress was entirely in possession of the Russians. Several of the garrison made a frantic attempt to cut their way through the serried ranks of their opponents; but the division under Komaroff, aided by a body of dragoons, captured the greater number. The commandant, Hussein Hami Pasha, nevertheless succeeded in escaping, together with some few horsemen; but by noon nearly the whole of the garrison, several Pashas, two hundred and fifty-seven siege-guns, and sixty field-guns, were in the hands of the Russians, who, however, had suffered considerably in achieving their success. A loss of more than 2,500 men in killed and wounded was admitted by the assailants; but on the other hand the Turks lost no fewer than 5,000, to say nothing of the prisoners.*

General Loris Melikoff, who had directed the engagement throughout, entered the town at eleven o'clock, A.M., on the 18th, and on the following day the Grand Duke Michael (who in all the operations of the Armenian campaign seems to have been little better than a puppet) made a solemn entry into Kars, that he might receive the homage of the inhabitants. He afterwards visited the citadel, where he entertained his officers at breakfast in the palace of the civil Governor. Forts Hafiz and Khanli were subsequently inspected by this ornamental but not very useful soldier, and the Grand Duke, having thanked the troops in the name of the Emperor, passed several battalions in review, and caused the artillery to be paraded before the conquered fortifications. Kars, however, was not a very safe place to remain in. The town was full of Turkish sick and wounded—all of them in the filthy and neglected condition which appears to be the miserable fate of Ottoman soldiers when they are once disabled; and the air was so pestilential that, a day or two after, the Grand Duke shifted his quarters to Vera-Kalé, near Ardost, leaving a garrison to occupy Kars, while Melikoff, with the bulk of his troops, was sent forward to aid the siege of Erzeroum. The people of Kars behaved with orderly submission as soon as they perceived that the Russian strength was too great to be any longer resisted. A Governor was named by the Grand Duke; native inhabitants were enrolled as police; and, from that time forth, Kars became a Muscovite possession.

The capture of this stronghold, though not effected without some severe fighting, is believed to have been in part attributable to treachery in the fortress itself. How far the story is true, it is very difficult to determine; but a writer with many opportunities of information has recorded his belief

* Williams's and Norman's works on the Armenian Campaign; *Daily News* Correspondence.

in the alleged facts. Those allegations cannot be here omitted, and are given on the authority of the writer to whom reference is made. According to this gentleman, a certain European doctor in Pera

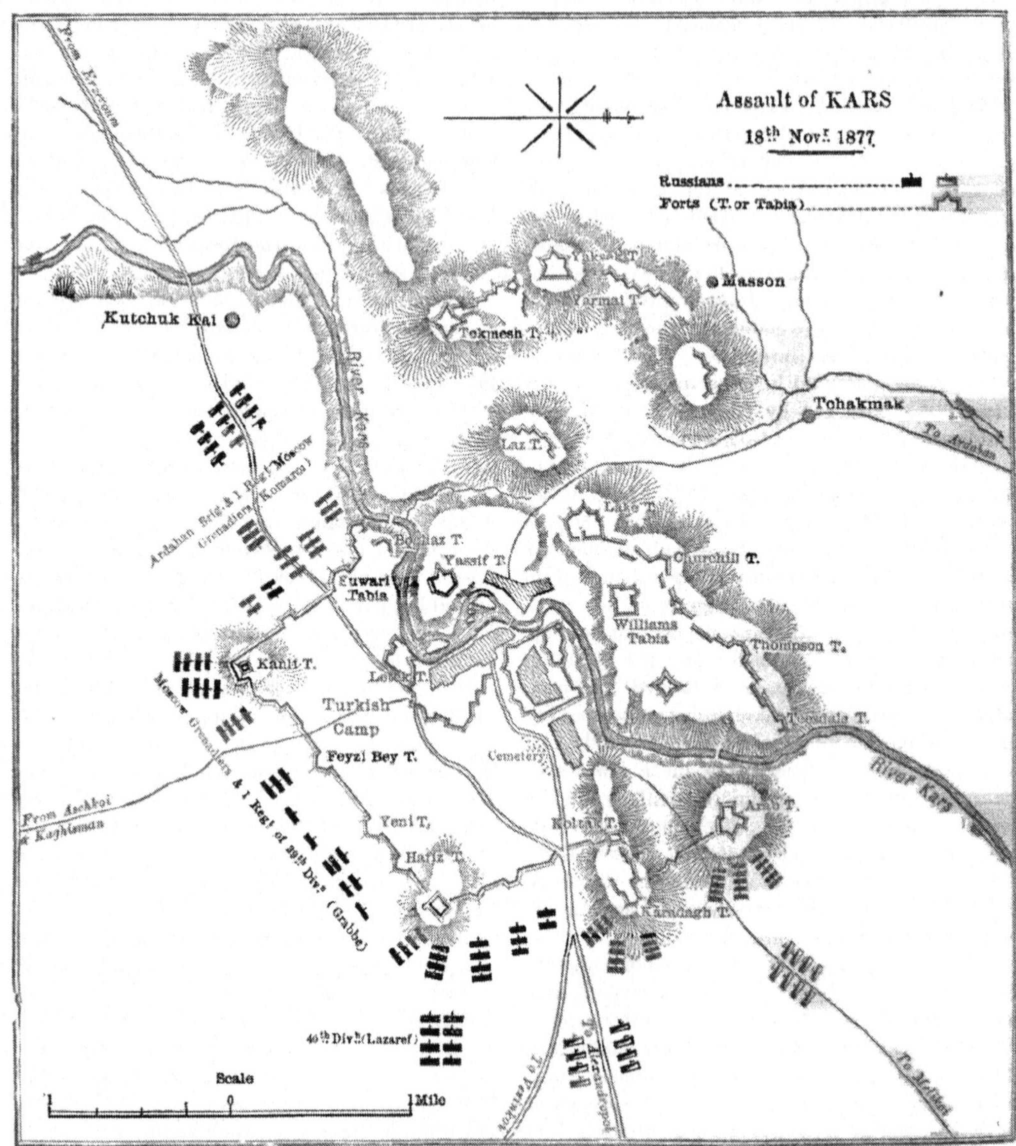

PLAN OF THE SIEGE AND CAPTURE OF KARS.

obtained a divorce from his wife, who presently married one Kibrisli Mohammed Pasha. The lady shortly afterwards had a son, who was brought up as a Mohammedan, and named Osman. The youth was educated at the military school of Constantinople, and, after entering the army, was attached to the Embassy at Paris as a military pupil. He also visited England, and on his return to Constantinople was promoted to the grade of Major on the Staff, and appointed to Van, where he remained some years. Here he quarrelled with the Governor, fell into disgrace, and, at the commencement of the Russo-Turkish campaign, offered his sword to the Czar. His services were at once accepted, and he received a high appointment on the Intelligence Branch of the Staff of the Caucasus. Before his desertion of his country, Osman Bey had formed an acquaintance with one Hassan Bey, a colonel in the Turkish artillery, and at that time commandant of the citadel at Erzeroum. Both these men had

STORMING AND CAPTURE OF KARS.

received a European education, and knew English and French thoroughly; indeed, Hassan had been a military student at Woolwich. Before the outbreak of the war, the higher Ottoman officials in Erzeroum had remarked, not without misgivings, that Osman and Hassan held aloof from other Turkish officers, and were frequent guests at the house of M. Obermüller, the Russian Consul; and at a later period Mukhtar Pasha became aware that Osman Bey was in Melikoff's camp, and that the Russians had obtained through him an accurate knowledge of the organisation of the Ottoman army, and of the construction of the fortresses. The disloyalty of Hassan was not suspected by the Turkish Generalissimo, and it is possible that it did not exist until called forth by a feeling of personal annoyance. Hassan Bey, who was now acting as commandant of artillery at Kars, had expected to be promoted to the rank of general of brigade. Mukhtar Pasha doubted his fitness for so high a post, and accordingly passed him over. The slight appears to have rankled in the mind of the young officer, and to this cause his disaffection has been imputed. At any rate, it would seem that early in November the commandant of artillery volunteered to take a flag of truce to the Russian camp, so as to ascertain the exact strength of the enemy, and the number of troops detached in pursuit of Mukhtar Pasha on his retreat to Erzeroum. During the Russian operations against Kars in the summer, Hassan Bey had behaved with so much zeal and gallantry that his motives on the present occasion were not doubted. He received permission to go forward with the flag of truce, and, under cover of that pretence, visited Lazareff's camp in the vicinity of Magardjik. What passed between him and the Russian General can only be guessed; but he returned to Kars with the story that Osman Bey was disgusted with the treatment he had received at the hands of his existing employers, and ardently desired to rejoin his countrymen. He added that the Russians were not numerous, and were devoid of siege-guns, and that accordingly no fear need be entertained for the safety of Kars. On the 12th of the same month, Hassan Bey was allowed to visit the Russian camp once more, to observe if the enemy were then in a position to bombard or assault the town. He again reported that the Russians were extremely weak, and so incapable of risking an attack that there was not the least necessity to repair or occupy Fort Hafiz Pasha. The very next day, the Russians, as already related, sent forward their assaulting columns against the fortress, but withdrew them on finding that the ground was not in a proper state for the attempt. This must have directed some degree of suspicion against Hassan Bey, and the feeling was confirmed on the 14th by a circumstance which ought to have been conclusive on the subject. A Circassian was seized while endeavouring to pass the sentries at night with a letter to Hassan Bey from the traitor Osman. The letter was expressed in ambiguous phraseology, from which no meaning could be extracted; but this very fact should have cast a stronger light on the intrigues of Hassan. On being sent for, however, the commandant of artillery denied all knowledge of the letter, and suggested that the bearer should be put to death. Strange to say, his excuses were accepted, and the unfortunate Circassian was flung from the citadel cliff. The result was that Fort Hafiz Pasha was left undefended by guns, and captured on the first assault. This enabled the attacking column to scale the southern cliffs of the Karadagh, and to seize the works and the citadel on that eminence with comparative ease. Hassan Bey was successful in his treason, and became an honoured guest in the camp of the Grand Duke, being the only Turkish officer who was permitted to wear his sword. The authority we have been following states that his father sold Varna to the Russians in 1828.* In that case, the traitor of 1877 inherits disloyalty and bad faith in his very blood; but at all events it was extremely fortunate for Hassan Bey that his treason was not discovered until too late. The carelessness and blind trust shown by the Turks are remarkable.

Before Plevna, the news of the fall of Kars was received with the simultaneous firing of a salute from all the batteries around the circle of investment, extending thirty English miles; and on the night of November 19th General Skobeleff constructed a transparency, which he erected on the Green Hill, and which bore an inscription in large letters, setting forth, in the French language, "Kars is ours. Ten thousand Turks taken prisoners. Long live the Emperor!" The Turks riddled the transparency with bullets until the lights were extinguished; but unfortunately they could not extinguish the fact. In Constantinople, the disastrous news was kept secret as long as possible; indeed, the state of feeling at the capital, even before the truth was known, was such as to justify the gravest fears. The aspect of the war had become so discouraging that the Sultan was recommended to unfurl the Standard of the Prophet at once. This would have meant the opening of a religious war, and would have entailed an incalculable multiplication of all those atrocities which had already shocked and angered the civilised

* Captain Norman's Armenia, and the Campaign of 1877.

world. The Sultan, however, opposed the advice thus given him, saying that, until the Russians were in possession of Erzeroum and Adrianople, he would not resort to so extreme a measure. Fortunately, the measure was not resorted to at all; but it is to be feared that if, at any future period, a further attack should be made on Turkey, with a view to her complete extinction, the step will be taken, as any other desperate step might be by men who are fighting for bare existence. For the present, the Russians thought not of any such extremity; and they certainly had occasion enough for rejoicing, and even for a little boastfulness. Their congratulations, nevertheless, sometimes assumed very questionable forms, and they were severely criticised for a circumstance which took place on the 19th of November. On that day, Divine service was performed in one of the redoubts before Plevna, in presence of the Emperor, expressly to celebrate the capture of Kars; and after the conclusion of this religious observance, all the Russian batteries fired salvoes against the beleaguered fortress, as though ostentatiously to connect the thanksgiving with one of the murderous facts of war. The *Times* correspondent with the Russians before Plevna said, when describing this performance:—"Half-way between Brestovec and Tyrnen, where the Russian lines cross the Vid, I was startled by a tremendous roar of artillery, which echoed and re-echoed round the whole Plevna lines of circumvallation. The first salvo was followed in rapid succession by three or four others, so that the air became full of hundreds of hissing shells, speeding simultaneously into Osman Pasha's entrenchments. These salvoes, I found, were fired in celebration of the capture of Kars. The effect of the whistling endured for several minutes in vibrations of the atmosphere, and resembled the distant cheering of many thousands of men so closely that I believed for the moment a general assault was being made on the Krishine Hill, opposite Skobeleff's position. The Turks did not respond." War, of course, cannot be made without terrible and tragic facts; but to associate a religious observance with an act of slaughter was certainly in very doubtful taste, if indeed we are not to apply to it a severer condemnation.

The Russians were so much intoxicated by their success at Kars that to some the event appeared to offer an opportunity of terminating the war by means of an expedition starting from the vicinity of the captured fortress. Among the officers composing the Russian head-quarters in Armenia, the question was discussed whether it might not be possible to approach Constantinople by a westerly march across Asia. A great council of war was held at Kars on the 18th of November, when, according to a correspondent of the *Standard*, one of the ablest of the Russian commanders, General Philippoff, very energetically advocated the idea. General Philippoff, who was said to have an intimate acquaintance with Asia Minor, proposed that Erzeroum should be covered by a corps of observation, instead of being surrounded with a view to siege operations, and that a large army should then be directed towards Scutari. Supposing it to reach that point, it was certain that the Turkish powers of resistance would very speedily collapse; but the colleagues of General Philippoff wisely judged that the perils of the enterprise were too great to be risked. The line of communication with the base of such a movement would have been so long that it would necessarily have been exposed to frequent, and probably fatal, attacks. The intervening country, moreover, presented but little means for the sustentation of so large an army on the march; and the weather, at that winter season, would have tried the men to the utmost. It was therefore determined to proceed by regular methods against the remaining Turkish stronghold in Armenia, and General Loris Melikoff, moving by Tcharpakli and Bardez, endeavoured to push forward a brigade to Olti, so as to enter the Erzeroum valley by Gurgee Boghaz; but deep falls of snow, combined with the rugged character of the road, hindered his progress, and forced him to return. The troops from Kars then entered the Passin plain, where they found the army under General Heimann, who, after the failure of his attempt to carry the Azizi works, had detached a brigade to Madirga, some five miles north-east of Erzeroum, to prevent the garrison of that fortress obtaining supplies from the villages in the Euphrates valley. For the support of this detachment, Heimann had constructed a road to Kiossa Mahomed; but the Turks speedily burned the village and destroyed the road. The Russian army was now being desolated by typhoid fever, and it was necessary to give the men some rest. Little or nothing, therefore, was at that particular time being done against Erzeroum; but, by order of the Grand Duke, General Komaroff was despatched to Ardahan, the civil and military administration of which was to be settled by him, previous to his entering upon further undertakings calculated to reduce Armenia to submission. Ardahan, it will be remembered, had been captured in May, and since then had not passed out of Russian hands. Komaroff, on arriving there, found that the administration required no interference from him, and accordingly pushed on towards Batoum, encountering on the way a band of Lazi irregulars at Ardanutsch, where he had defeated a similar body on the 28th of June. The resistance of the

MINARETS AT ERZEROUM.

irregulars was slight, and Komaroff immediately afterwards occupied Ardanutsch, which he placed under the jurisdiction of the Governor of Ardahan.

The pause in the Russian operations before Erzeroum enabled Mukhtar Pasha to bring up re-inforcements, both of men and guns, from Batoum, Trebizond, and Constantinople. Reserves of food were also procured from the neighbouring villages, and laid up in the city. All inhabitants not volunteering to bear arms were at once expelled, and houses were stripped of their wood-work to increase the stock of fuel. Faizi Pasha had previously collected large stores of wheat, and they were now ground into flour by the numerous mills which existed in the vicinity of Erzeroum. Had the Russians been more vigilant, they would have put a stop to some of these preparations for resisting a lengthened siege; but they seem to have been stupefied by the deep snow and wintry rigour, or perhaps were exhausted for a time by the vehemence of their previous efforts. By the close of November, Mukhtar had about three men for the defence of every yard of front, and could rely on more than four months' full provisions for his army. The spirit of the inhabitants, however, was very bad. They were in a state of continual alarm, and were doubtless well disposed to send in their submission to the Russian commander. Although frequently exhorted to show a more patriotic spirit, they could hardly be persuaded to keep their shops open, and the Civil Governor was obliged to impose a fine of five pounds on those who refused to comply with his orders in this respect. It appears that they were afraid of having their goods pillaged by the Bashi-Bazouks; and even among the regular troops there were cases of insubordination, with which Mukhtar Pasha was obliged to deal severely.

The fall of Kars necessarily produced an evil effect on the people of Erzeroum, who feared that a similar fate would soon be theirs. Rumours got about that the Commander-in-Chief himself was preparing to quit the place, and that he had already sent away his personal effects. A correspondent of the *Daily News*, who was at that time residing in the city, feared that there might be some truth in this report, and determined to visit the Marshal, that he might hear from his own lips what he proposed to do. "It was three o'clock in the afternoon," says the correspondent, "when I called on Mukhtar Pasha at the Yeni-Kishlar, the principal barracks of Erzeroum. It is a wide, desolate square of sad-coloured limestone, looking like a model European prison. A crowd of ragged camels and Rosinante-like pack-horses stray perpetually in its immediate vicinity. I entered by the main gate. Four sentinels on either side guarded it. I flung my horse's bridle to one, and, taking a dirty staircase to the left, arrived at a long, wide corridor, desolate and dirty as the staircase. Awkward-looking soldiers, with yellowish-white baggy overcoats, stood about, and came uneasily to 'attention' as any unknown, tolerably-dressed stranger and possible Pasha came by. A long line of great arched windows fronted an equal extent of blank, dreary wall, along which hung, like so many funeral palls, the sombre-coloured curtains closing the entrances to the different apartments. No. 1 is that of the captain of the guard—where that functionary, clad in brown flannel, sits gloomily staring at the dingy, whitewashed walls, smutted by the smoke of the tottering stove that roars like a small tempest in the corner. Next door are a couple of aides-de-camp, one of whom, after conducting you to the neighbouring chamber of the secretary, lifts the drapery before the Marshal's doorway, and you are in the presence of the redoubted Ghazi Ahmed Mukhtar Pasha, Commanding-in-Chief the Ottoman armies of Armenia. The room, like the others, is bare and whitewashed. A low divan runs round two of its sides. Opposite the door, on the divan, is a wolf-skin and a cushion—the bed of the Marshal. In another corner of the divan is a sheepskin, stained red." On that sheepskin the Marshal was found sitting cross-legged, after the Oriental fashion. Although not more than a couple of weeks had elapsed since the correspondent had seen Mukhtar Pasha, that short interval had wrought considerable changes in him. The fresh colour and bright eye which he had formerly possessed were no longer observable. His cheeks and brow were furrowed with thought and care, and, although the eye was still animated with a feverish fire, it was rather that of desperation and fierce resolve than the buoyant expression of earlier but still recent days. The correspondent told him that sinister rumours were prevalent in the town, and that people believed the evacuation of Erzeroum to be imminent. "Is your Excellency about to leave us?" he asked. With unusual warmth, Mukhtar Pasha turned almost fiercely on his questioner. "Never, never!" he exclaimed. "While I have a man to stand by the guns, I will not abandon Erzeroum."

It was now near the end of November. Winter had set in with savage intensity; snow and sleet lay thickly over that dismal land, and piercing winds blew across the white surface of the earth, chilling the besiegers to the very marrow in their bones. The Russians had by this time encamped in the Deve-Boyun Pass, and were in some degree protected by tents covered with thick felt, in each of which was a stove, supplied with wood. Intelligence of these facts was brought in by a caravan from Persia, the individuals forming which had, for inexplicable reasons, been allowed to pass through the Russian lines, and enter the besieged city. Although unmolested by the enemy, the people of the caravan suffered somewhat from their friends. They had not taken the precaution of sending forward a flag of truce; so that when the Turkish sentinels on the ramparts of Erzeroum dimly perceived the long column of men and camels approaching from the Deve-Boyun Pass, they believed that a storming party from the Russian camp was advancing upon them, and accordingly opened fire. The caravan was broken up in wild disorder as the first shells burst within its line, and it was some hours before the component parts could be again collected. The correspondent who reported these facts thought it advisable, shortly afterwards, to leave Erzeroum for a neighbouring village, that he might be in a more favourable position to retreat, should the worst arrive. As he rode out of Erzeroum, he noticed that Mukhtar Pasha had taken very elaborate precautions against assault. On the ramparts were sentries, at a distance of fifty yards from one another; in the covered ways a similar line was posted; fifty yards from the crest of the *glacis*, a first line of sentinels was stationed in rifle-pits not twenty yards apart; fifty yards farther out was a similar line; and a body of irregular cavalry under Muhir Ali incessantly patrolled the ground over which the enemy must advance, if he advanced at all. A surprise at any one point was therefore improbable; but Mukhtar Pasha admitted that he feared a general assault on the forts, and simultaneously on the lower ramparts in the plain.

In Europe, little had been done by Suleiman Pasha since his appointment, at the beginning of October, to the chief command of the Turkish forces in that part of the Ottoman dominions. His first proceeding was to inquire into the defensive capabilities of the chief fortifications north of the Balkans; his next, to send in a report of what he had observed. He is said to have advised the withdrawal of Osman from Plevna to Orkhanieh; but the War Council at Constantinople rejected the plan. Indeed, Suleiman found himself thwarted in divers ways, and it was only with difficulty that he could enforce any of his views. The particular scene of his operations was the line of the river Lom—a difficult country, complicated with the most elaborate intricacies of hills, and valleys, and perpetually-winding streams. The new commander did not feel at home in this region, of which there were no good maps; and his character as a fighting general gave place to extreme caution. He did little more than stand on the defensive, occasionally ordering reconnaissances, which revealed the weakness of the enemy's line. An ill-judged attack on Kadikoi, made by the Russians on the 24th of October, ended in their signal defeat; and an attempt on Rustchuk, the following day, was equally unsuccessful. Other actions, of no great importance, occurred in the early part of November, and the army of the Czarewitch showed a disposition to fall back in the direction of Plevna. The chief portion of Suleiman's forces then took up a strong defensive position on the Beli Lom, stretching due south towards the former line from Karahassankoi to Osman Bazar. On the 19th of November, the Turkish right attacked the adversary's positions at Pyrgos and the vicinity, drove the Russians out of the town, and, either accidentally or intentionally, burned the place to ashes, and destroyed large stores of provisions and ammunition. The positions, however, were afterwards re-taken by the Russians; but on the 23rd the latter were defeated in an attack on the right rear of Suleiman's army, which was suddenly assailed by a detachment of Zimmerman's corps. Further severe fighting took place on the 26th, and the Turks were again discomfited, as well as on subsequent days. On the whole, Suleiman did not add to his laurels by the conduct of affairs on the Lom.

Despite all causes of discouragement, the Government of the Sultan still determined to persevere in the war. A new levy of 150,000 Civic Guards was ordered in the course of November, and it was announced that the non-Mohammedan subjects of the Porte would be allowed to enrol themselves. An Imperial decree to this effect was issued after consultations with the Greek and Armenian Patriarchs, and with the Chief Rabbi; but the determination was something like that of the Confederate States of America, in the last days of their existence, to put arms into the hands of the negroes. If any good was to result from such a step, it came too late, and that which might have been accepted as a liberal concession, if made a few years earlier, was now regarded as nothing else than a humiliating confession of weakness. Omar Fenzi Pasha was appointed provisional commander of the new force, and the Grand Vizier issued orders that any member of the Guard who proved insubordinate at drill should be incorporated with the regular army. At Kossova, in Old Servia, now reckoned a part of Albania, a fresh Turkish army was being formed, and 4,000 irregulars were sent into Thessaly, to put down the disaffection which had recently shewn itself in that province. These amateur troops behaved with the lawless ferocity common to their order. They levied black mail everywhere, and caused immense terror amongst the Greeks. At Larissa, under the very eyes of the authorities, they pillaged houses and shops. At Fricala, they ill-used the police; and in the village of Vlako Hiva they burst in upon a party of Greeks who were holding a Church festival, killed twelve men, and committed other atrocities. Popular opinion in the Greek Kingdom was greatly agitated by these and similar facts; and on the 26th of November the Chamber held a sitting with closed doors, at which the general condition of Hellenism was discussed. Shortly after this, the Porte consented to withdraw the Bashi-Bazouks and Zeibeks from Thessaly and Epirus, and it was stated that this concession was due to the intervention of England.

On more than one occasion, the good offices of this country were humanely used for mitigating the severities of the Porte. The case of the Geshoffs excited considerable interest in the autumn of 1877. They were Bulgarian merchants of good social standing, and several members of the family were arrested under suspicion of having given information to the London newspapers of the atrocities committed by the Turks in the previous year. After a lengthened imprisonment, they were condemned to death, and it was feared that the sentence would be carried out. The facts, however, were brought before the notice of the English public by statements in the papers, and earnest efforts were made for sparing the lives of the unhappy men. Mr. Layard took up the case energetically, and so also did the American Minister. The result was that the Geshoffs were released from prison in November, and, together with their families, removed from Philippopolis to Constantinople, where Mr. Layard was promised they should be considerately treated. In the capital they were simply detained at the Ministry of Police, and Mr. Layard was informed by the Grand Vizier that they would be exiled to Aleppo; but even that punishment was not inflicted. It was about this time that the Turkish Government instituted a reform for which it should receive due credit. An order was issued, decreeing the abolition of public executions. According to traditional usage, capital punishment had been inflicted by preference in the most frequented thoroughfares, and this often led to revolting and demoralising scenes, probably equalling what may have been witnessed, until the last few years, in the Old Bailey; but the vicious system is now abrogated in Turkey, as in England.

In more ways than one, the Turkish Government considered it necessary, in the days of its gathering disasters, to conciliate those ideas of European civilization which it had often disregarded. It was thought advisable to pay court to the Greeks, and the Sultan even went the length of inviting the Greek Patriarch to dine with him. To that functionary he expressed his desire to see all degrees of his subjects happy and contented; and there is no reason to suppose that the wish was other than sincere. Unfortunately, people find it difficult to believe in promises made under the pressure of inexorable events, and are apt to think that the promises will be forgotten when the pressure is removed. As regarded the Greeks, it was announced that the Sultan intended to appoint two or three of that nationality as Governors-General of some of the chief provinces; that M. Zarifi, a leading banker at Constantinople, was to be honoured with the highest class of the Order of the Medjidié; and that others of the same family were also to be decorated. With a few exceptions, however, the Christians of the Ottoman Empire were not won over by these courtesies, while on the other hand the Turks regarded such concessions as a sign of embarrassment, and as a subjection of the privileged race to those antagonistic races which were only awaiting their opportunity to destroy the whole fabric of dominion. Greeks and Armenians have long been employed by the Porte in high positions; but the former have not in the main been induced to identify their fortunes with those of the Crescent. The Armenians, until excited by Russian intrigues, may have been very well disposed to remain under the rule of the Sultan; but the Greeks cannot forget their distinct nationality and their ancient renown. If the Turks are ever to be expelled from Europe—if Constantinople is once more to be a Christian city—it is certain that the Greeks are the only people entitled to take up the Imperial sceptre which the Osmanlis will in that case have dropped. A profound belief in this future animates the Hellenic heart wherever it beats within the circuit of the Turkish realms; and it was not likely that a few civilities, or a few favours more or less substantial, would induce the patient and quick-witted Greek to forswear that splendid dream, or barter the visions of prospective power for the enjoyment of any present gain.

CHAPTER XLII.

Preparation of an Army of Relief for Plevna—The Turkish Reinforcements—General Strength of the Ottoman Army in November, 1877—Mehemet Ali at Orkhanieh—Expedition of General Gourko into the Etropol Balkans—The Turks entrenched near Pravca—Determination of General Gourko to outflank the Enemy—March of General Rauch—Fatiguing and dangerous Passage over the Mountains—Attack on the Turkish Positions—Defeat of the Ottomans, and Withdrawal to Orkhanieh—Evacuation of Etropol by the Turks—Character of the Town—Acts of Spoliation and Outrage by the Ottomans—Flight of Mohammedans towards the South—Public Opinion in England—Deputation of Turkish Sympathisers to the Foreign Office—Speech of Lord Derby on Russian Policy and British Interests—Rigid Neutrality—The Two Parties in the Cabinet—Russianizing Policy of Lord Derby—Opinion at Berlin, St. Petersburg, and Pesth, on the Observations of the Foreign Secretary—Lecture of Mr. Archibald Forbes on the Character and Prospects of the War—Patriotic Agitation in Greece—Designs of Italy—The Turkish Blockade—Rumoured Garibaldian Expedition into Albania—Views in Constantinople as to the Terms of Peace—The Turkish Empire and Europe.

DESPERATE as was the situation of Osman Pasha at Plevna, as the November gloom deepened with the advancing month, the Porte did not give up all hope of extricating that brave commander from the trap in which he had been caught. It was not likely that he would be able to cut his way out; his stock of provisions was gradually dwindling; the Russians were becoming stronger every day; and it was certain that they would reduce the place by famine, sooner or later, unless they could be forced to raise the siege. To effect this desirable result, the Ministers of the Sultan now bent all their energies. A secret Grand Council of War was held at the Seraskierate, or War Office, on the night of November 14th, and it was resolved to send all available troops for the augmentation of a relieving army which was then being formed under the directions of Mehemet Ali, who, since his removal from the chief command of all the European forces, had been appointed to this service. His head-quarters were now at Sophia, where he was busily engaged organizing, or rather creating, a corps of sufficient strength to march northwards, and assail the legions under Todleben with some prospect of success. The Government informed the Austrian Ambassador at Constantinople, about this time, that Osman Pasha could hold out for another four weeks; and the calculation proved remarkably near the fact. But the period available for operations in the field was confessedly very small; and if Osman Pasha was to do anything, it was obvious that the attempt must be made with as little delay as possible.

Everything depended on the ability of the generals and the unexhausted resources of the country. As regarded the latter, the *Times* correspondent with Suleiman Pasha gave some statistical details in a communication from Varna, dated November 4th. According to this writer, the measures agreed upon by the Seraskierate for the extension of the Army, and the numbers computed to result from them, stood thus:—All the recruits liable by ordinary course of law to serve in the following year were in October summoned to service. By this measure there were raised 28,900 infantry, 4,320 field-artillery, 3,980 cavalry, 4,960 fortress-artillery, and 1,700 engineers: in all, about 44,000 men. At first it was intended to form these recruits into an army-corps consisting of 12 tirailleur battalions, 34 infantry battalions, 2 field-artillery regiments, and 14 batteries. After more mature consideration, however, it was determined to distribute them among the troops of the Line, for the purpose, mainly, of covering any retreats which, out of tactical considerations, might be made in the course of the war. Next followed the calling out of the Redifs. The troops thus summoned were formed into independent corps in the following manner:—The First Corps was at Schumla, with 28 battalions, equal to 22,000 men; the Second Corps comprised 31 battalions, or 25,000 men; the Third Corps, at Monastir, had 40 battalions, or 32,000 men: in all, 99 battalions, equal to 80,000 men. In Asia, 11 battalions, or 8,700 men, were at Karput; 10 battalions, or 8,000 men, at Sivas; 11 battalions, or 8,600 men, at Erzeroum; 7 battalions, or 5,700 men, at Kars; 9 battalions, or 7,000 men, at Bayazid; while at Diarbekir there were 9 battalions, equal to 7,000 men: in all, 57 battalions with 45,000 men. In the district of the Syrian corps, 18 battalions, with 14,000 men, were stationed. Thus, according to the *Times* correspondent, the new levy consisted of 174 battalions with 139,000 men, and, including the recruits who were raised formerly, showed a grand total of 183,000 troops.

In addition to these levies, the Turkish army in the field (said the same writer) was about to receive a strong reinforcement in the Corps of Baghdad and Yemen, then on their march to the seat of war. The first of these corps, which was designed for service in Asia, counted 19,000 men, with 78 guns.

The Yemen Corps did not amount to more than 9,000 men, with 34 guns. Of the Fifth Corps of Damascus, seven Nizam battalions, twenty reserve battalions (of the four different classes), and nine Mustahfiz battalions, were ready for departure to the scenes where they were so much needed. Thus, the regulars, the reserves, and the militia, were all represented in the general body of reinforcements, of which the grand total amounted, according to the regulations, to about 230 battalions, with 20 batteries, or nearly 250,000 men. But it was reasonably pointed out that the actual number would fall considerably short of these figures. "The rapid summoning of so many recruits," said the writer we have been following, "cannot be done without deductions. The march, also, for weeks, and even months, of so many men—poorly clad, poorly fed, and exposed to all the damaging influences of the worst season of the year—from the most distant parts of Turkey to the seat of war, cannot but be attended with heavy losses. All deductions made, the actual number of recruits which the measures of the Seraskierate should obtain will probably fall somewhat short of 200,000 men. That is still, no doubt, a very considerable fighting power; but, when compared with the present strength of the enemy, and the additions they also are continually making to their numbers, the situation of the Turks will not appear too assuring." In addition to these numbers, however, there was a still further reserve, which, if called out, would yield an increase of 183 battalions, or 146,000 men; and the militia system, when fully enforced, would reach a total of 467 battalions, of which only thirty-three had at that time come forward. Altogether, the total military force of Turkey, not summoned to arms in the first half of November, was about 500,000 men.*

ORKHANIEH, FROM THE ROAD TO PLEVNA.

The forces at Sophia under Mehemet Ali seem to have consisted of some sixty battalions, with 150 guns; and shortly after the middle of November they moved forward, and took up a new position at Orkhanieh, under the Etropol Balkans. But the Turkish commander was anticipated in his plans by a southward move on the part of General Gourko, who on the 16th suddenly started from Dolny Dubnik at the head of a considerable force.

* *Times*, November 19th, 1877.

On the 18th he reached Jablonica, and, sending out a large number of scouts, soon acquired some trustworthy information with respect to the Turkish forces in front of him. It appeared that these were far less numerous than had been supposed, and it was accordingly resolved to give a bolder and more important character to Gourko's expedition. The Turks had occupied very strong positions near the village of Pravca, at a spot where, before entering the Orkhanieh valley, the road passes through a narrow, winding defile, flanked by steep and rugged mountains. The ground is such that a direct attack upon the Turks was impossible, and it was therefore necessary to turn the positions by means of a flank movement. These positions were nearly all on the side of the road which was to the right of the Russian advance. The other side was indeed occupied, but in that direction no redoubts had been erected and no trenches dug, for the possession of the right side, if it could be maintained, would be sufficient for all purposes of defence. Two small redoubts commanded the defile, and the trenches in front of them were such as to present very formidable obstacles. After examining the positions, General Gourko determined on attacking, from its two extremities, the ridge held by the Turks.

The execution of the chief part of the design was entrusted to General Rauch, who took with him the Simionowsky Regiment of the Guard, the first and second battalions of sharpshooters, one battery of horse-artillery, and six squadrons of cavalry. Rauch started from Jablonica on the 21st of November, with orders to march all night towards the western extremity of the ridge on which the Turks were posted. General Gourko, judging by what he could infer from maps, thought that his lieutenant would arrive at the point of attack by noon next day; but the difficulties of the mountain road made the distance, in effect, much longer than it seemed to be, and Rauch did not get to the end of his journey until near the evening of the 23rd. It had been a most toilsome and even dangerous passage. In many places the road was so narrow that the broader artillery-carriages hung with one wheel over the precipice, and were withheld from tumbling down by ropes passed round the guns, and held firmly by the soldiers. The heavy munition-waggons also gave an immense amount of trouble, and rapidity of march was quite impossible. A correspondent of the *Daily News*, describing the advance, said that "the way led over great ledges of hard, flinty rock, full of seams and fissures, so difficult for the horses to pass that several of them caught their feet in the crevices, and tore the hoof from the bone. Horses were not too numerous, and it was impossible to proceed without them; so the hoofless feet were bound up in rags, and the poor beasts limped along, dragging the heavy caissons and guns. The whole day of the 22nd they climbed along the mountain paths, step by step, not advancing two *kilomètres* an hour. Three caissons full of ammunition went over, in spite of all efforts to prevent the accident; and two horses were killed, and one Cossack mortally wounded: the other men who were with the caissons scrambled up in time to save themselves." The troops suffered in many ways. Bending under loads of ammunition, they had to drag themselves up from rock to rock; and their food consisted entirely of hard bread, for, as they feared discovery by the enemy, fires by night were forbidden, and nothing could be cooked, nor could even tea be prepared. "Two men," says the account previously cited, "died of fatigue on the spot; the rest were so worn with want of sleep and severe exertions that they were like drunken men. Every man of the outposts was found by the officers who went the rounds to be dead asleep, and no scolding or threats could keep them awake, although they were in the very face of the enemy. The horses trembled all night, not from cold, but from overwork; and they threw themselves flat, the moment they were taken from the traces." The dense fogs which steamed up from the valleys at night rendered it in the highest degree dangerous to proceed after dark; so that Rauch was unavoidably delayed, and Gourko, who had advanced to Osikovo, waited for news of him with great anxiety. On the evening of the 22nd he heard from his subordinate that he had not got farther than Kalugerovo, and all hope of an immediate attack was at an end.

Time had not been wasted by General Gourko on the 22nd, for the day was devoted to several preparations for an assault on the end of the ridge opposite to the one against which Rauch's detachment had been sent. It was likewise considered advisable to make a demonstration in front, and to occupy the hills on the left of the road, facing the Turkish positions. This was done with scarcely any loss, the Ottomans retiring at once from ground which they do not seem to have considered worth a contest. Having thus secured the heights on one side, the Russians proceeded to plant a battery of horse-artillery, and another of mountain-howitzers, in such positions as to command the Turkish guns, while another battery was established on the lower slopes of the ridge, to the right of the Russian advance. All these guns were placed in position on the night of the 22nd, and opened fire on the

Turks next morning. The reply was very feeble, for the Ottomans had only two guns, and those were badly served. During several hours the unequal contest went on; and about four o'clock on the afternoon of the 23rd Rauch's troops were seen at the other end of the ridge, on the crest dominating the Turkish lines. This important point had been seized by the Russians with a loss of not more than twenty-nine men wounded and two killed, and the Turks hastily retreated to a more secure locality. Previous to this encounter, the Russians had been so utterly worn out that it seemed as if they would drop upon the craggy, mountainous ways from mere exhaustion. But the sight of the enemy animated them with fresh spirit; and when their officers, divesting themselves of swords and revolvers, told the men that they were going against the Turks unarmed, in perfect confidence that no harm would come to them in association with such brave and adventurous troops, the enthusiasm of the soldiers knew no bounds. The previous fatigue was forgotten, and the result was speedily apparent in the withdrawal of the Ottomans.

When Rauch's men were perceived to have attained the summits at the farther end of the ridge, to the left of the Turkish positions, the Moscow Regiment, stationed on the side of the road facing the Turkish centre, began to descend into the valley near Pravca, and the enemy on the opposite heights at once opened fire. By following a circuitous route, however, the men avoided all damage, and occupied Pravca under cover of the darkness. General Dondeville advanced on Etropol, to the right of the enemy's line; and the Turks, being now threatened on both flanks and in front, retreated during the night to Orkhanieh, in the direction of Sophia. The success of the Russians had been complete, but it had involved an immense amount of arduous labour. The central column was unable to advance farther than the top of the ridge north of the gorge, owing to the redoubts and batteries by which the road was commanded; yet the Turks were on the whole worsted by the superior dispositions of their opponent. "The horse-artillery," said a writer from the spot, "got pieces mounted hundreds of feet above the road by sheer lifting and hauling. The Turks, who on their side had dug a ziz-zag road all the way up the mountain for their troops and cannon, were surprised, and reasonably, at the Russian energy and rapidity of movement; and they did not lose any time in evacuating their positions the moment they understood they had only one road left open to them." Their camps were found deserted by the advancing Russians, and in many places the camp-fires had not yet died out. In one direction, however, the Turks had been successful. The main Russian attack was assisted by a demonstration from Vratza, consisting principally of cavalry, divided into two columns, the one marching to Novatchin, the other to Ludikovo. Owing to the prevalence of a thick fog, the former of these columns passed the place at which it was intended to stop, and was shortly afterwards surrounded and cut off by a body of Turkish infantry and irregulars. By dint of hard fighting, the men at length got through; but they had lost a large number in killed and wounded, and had suffered a mortifying reverse at the hands of a despised and hated enemy.

Etropol was evacuated by the Turks during the 23rd. The place was captured without loss, as the Ottomans, finding themselves overmatched, made no serious attempt at defence. Their earthworks were constructed on some mountains near the village; but the adjacent summits were unoccupied, and these commanded the whole valley, together with the Turkish redoubts. On the opposite heights the Russians planted several cannon, which they had dragged up with the help of the Bulgarians, who brought their mountain cattle to aid in the work, and to pull the heavy guns up acclivities where no horses could have gone. The Ottomans, considering it impossible that any one should climb the hills in their vicinity, contented themselves with leaving an outpost in the redoubt situated within the first line of their earthworks, while the main body remained in the camp some way farther back on the hill-side. This carelessness gave the Russians the opportunity they wanted. Some of them set off to climb the heights on which the Turks were posted, and were approaching the redoubt when the Turks in camp perceived them. The question now was as to which should gain the redoubt first, and, as both strained every nerve, the issue hung for some time in suspense. It was finally determined in favour of the Russians, who climbed the parapet a little before the arrival of their antagonists. The struggle that ensued was of short duration, and ended in the withdrawal of the Turks, who soon afterwards abandoned the place, and fell back upon their fortifications in the Slatica Balkans, leaving three Krupp guns behind them. Etropol may be described either as a large village or a small town. It is situated on the Mali Isker, a rough mountain stream, over which many of the houses are built. The streets, as in most Oriental towns, are crooked and narrow, and on the entry of the Russians, which took place on the 24th of November, nearly all the shops were found

RUSSIANS CROSSING THE BALKANS: AN AWKWARD CORNER.

to be fast closed with the heavy wooden shutters commonly used in Turkey. The inhabitants were half Turkish and half Bulgarian, and the sacred edifices of both religions stood almost side by side. The peasantry in that part of Bulgaria are said to be better looking and more intelligent than those bordering on the Danube, and their air of indepen-

DEFILE IN THE BALKANS.

dence and self-reliance moved the admiration of a newspaper correspondent. During the occupation of Etropol by the Turks, nothing was burned or destroyed; but some acts of spoliation and violence were committed by the army. The girls were hidden in the mountains on the approach of the Moslem forces; but the soldiers hunted them out, and ten were seized and carried away. Nine came back after a time, and eight of these, unable to bear the dishonour to which they had been subjected, drowned themselves in the Mali Isker, although their priests had given them absolution, and declared them purified.* Such were the episodes of a war in which the principles of civilisation seem to have been utterly forgotten.

The people of Etropol welcomed General Gourko with much joy, and showed themselves willing to do whatever the Russians told them; but, with the exception of the treatment which the young women had suffered, they admitted that the Turkish soldiers had done them but little damage. Reassured by the presence of the Muscovites, the Bulgarians soon returned to their abandoned villages, and in many instances installed themselves in houses that had belonged to Turks. It was now the turn of the Moslems to fly, and large numbers of them quitted the region of the Balkans with the utmost precipitation, and made their way towards the south. The road from Orkhanieh to Sophia was darkened by forlorn outcasts, carrying their goods and chattels,

* *Daily News* Correspondence.

and eagerly looking out for some place where they might rest in safety beneath the Turkish Crescent, undisturbed by any immediate fear of the dreaded invader. The country for miles around was beautiful and fertile in itself, but had been rendered desolate by the remorseless operations of war, and by the general disruption of society consequent on the outbreak of hostilities. The weary fugitives were accompanied by their wives and children, and it is difficult to realize, as it would be impossible to exaggerate, the sufferings of those miserable beings. Cold winds blew from the north; rain fell with wearisome persistence; and when the rain ceased, it was followed by the still greater affliction of snow. Winter was close at hand, and winter in the Balkans is a fierce and deadly season.

The successful advance of the Russians into the Etropol mountains reduced the Turkish chances of defence so considerably that public opinion in England was again excited in the highest measure as to the probabilities of the immediate future. The party in favour of a Russian policy, and that in favour of a Turkish policy, were much agitated towards the end of November, and omitted no opportunity of urging their respective views upon the Government and the nation. The advocates of a Turkish alliance were perhaps the most active at that particular time, for they had every reason to fear their cause was losing, and that even the Ministry of Lord Beaconsfield included those who were not greatly desirous it should succeed. On the 28th of November, the Foreign Secretary, Lord Derby, received a deputation from the Society for the Protection of British Interests against Russian Aggression in the East, the Turkish Defence Association, and the Polish Society of the White Eagle, who waited upon his Lordship for the purpose of presenting a memorial urging upon the Government to depart from their policy of inaction, and to bring about a desirable peace. Sir Henry Hoare, one of the members of the deputation, pointed out that the possession of Constantinople had an important bearing upon British interests. If Russia occupied that city, he argued, the question of the free passage of the Dardanelles would follow, and the position of our Indian Empire might be seriously compromised. The proper route to India was by the Euphrates Valley; and if the Russians made a railway through that valley, they would be able to compete with the Suez Canal. Sir Henry therefore asked Lord Derby to disregard the assertion of Mr. Gladstone that the whole of the Nonconformist body supported the "bag-and-baggage" policy he had advocated. On the contrary, many believed in the policy of defending Turkey, and were persuaded that far greater danger to civil and religious liberty was to be apprehended from Russia than from the Porte. In replying to this speech, and to the addresses of other members, Lord Derby expressed his disagreement with the opinion that our true line of communication with India lay through the Euphrates Valley. So long as the Suez Canal was uninterrupted, we had a communication sufficient for all purposes; nor did he think there was any danger that, if the Afghan people turned against us, they would be joined by the Mohammedan population of India. One of the speakers having expressed his conviction that Austria was ready to act in the sense desired, provided we gave her some encouragement, Lord Derby observed that he might claim for himself a greater opportunity of knowing the feelings and ideas of the Austrian Government than any one outside the Foreign Office was likely to have had; and, without going into details, he contented himself with expressing an entire disagreement with the views to which allusion had been made. The inaction of the Cabinet had not, according to Lord Derby, been forced upon himself and his colleagues by popular opinion. "We have held the same course throughout," he added; "and on that point I may remind you that, as long ago as May, 1876—before there had been any expression of opinion on the part of the country—before there had been any Bulgarian agitation—in fact, before much attention had been called to the subject,—I expressly warned the Turkish Government that, under the circumstances of the case, they were not to look to us for any military assistance." The Foreign Secretary alluded to the anxiety exhibited by a section of the country that we should take part in the American and Franco-German wars, and he begged the deputation to consider what unnecessary calamities we should have brought upon ourselves had we done so. "For my own part," said Lord Derby, "believing that, unless a war is necessary, it is a crime, I think we ought to be most careful to do and to say nothing that may tend unnecessarily to bring it about. It seems to be required that we should strengthen the Mediterranean garrisons, and send our fleet up to Constantinople. I quite admit that, in the unsettled and unquiet state of Europe, it is not desirable that our garrisons should be left below their usual strength, and we did in the course of this year raise them to their proper complement. But if it were proposed to put them upon a war footing, it would be necessary to consider, not merely certain military and administrative difficulties which would undoubtedly occur, but also what the moral effect of that would be, and whether the attitude of menace which might seem to be assumed would be justified by the circumstances of the case. As to sending up a fleet to Constantinople, it could not be done without the consent of the Porte, and the Porte, being free to withhold its consent, might, and very probably would, refuse to give it, except upon certain conditions. How far those conditions might be at variance with the attitude of neutrality which we still maintain, is a matter upon which I think there may be some considerable difference of opinion. I do not think Constantinople is in that immediate danger in which some seem to consider it. I think they have very much underrated the difficulties which the Russian armies have, and which they will continue to have, before them. But upon that point I can only again refer you to the language held by us as to the conditions of our neutrality at the beginning of the war. From the opinions then expressed we do not intend to deviate in the slightest degree, on one side or the other."

This address of Lord Derby was really of very great importance, since it revealed, indirectly, but not the less plainly, that division in the Cabinet which had been long suspected, which had been frequently denied by the organs of the Government, but which subsequent events placed beyond the possibility of any further equivocation. The position of Lord Derby was peculiar. In the earlier phases of the dispute between Russia and Turkey, he was generally supposed to represent a policy very much in accordance with that of Lord Beaconsfield himself, and he shared with the Premier, in almost equal measure, the severest criticisms of the anti-Turkish press. A little later came signs of vacillation, and later still it was evident that the pro-Russian party in the Cabinet (if the phrase be permissible) had no more earnest member than the Foreign Minister. The fact was reflected in the changed tone towards that statesman observable in the same newspapers which a few months before had denounced him as something very like a fool, with the additional qualifications of a knave. If his lordship now figured in the totally different character of a wise, sober, and enlightened politician, it was due to the fact that he had come unequivocally forward as the friend of Russia and the enemy of Turkey. That he should ever have been regarded in any other light, is surprising when we consider that the evacuation of the Servian fortresses by Turkey in 1867 was chiefly brought about by his contrivance, and that the opening of the Servian door of invasion to the armies of Russia is attributable to him more than to any other man in the world. Yet Lord Derby had undoubtedly adopted an ambiguous tone in the summer and autumn of 1876, and it was not until he had the support of the popular agitation on the Bulgarian massacres that he found courage to assume what must be regarded as his true position on the Eastern Question. His speech on the 28th of November simply re-confirmed what had at that time been known for several months. It produced, however, a great effect in political circles abroad. At Berlin, according to a correspondent of the *Daily News*, the address was regarded as a complete departure, if not from the policy which the English Cabinet had intended, at least from that which Europe had expected. "The public belief," says this writer, "was that Lord Beaconsfield's opinions would prevail, and that intervention was imminent; and intense satisfaction prevails at Lord Derby's sensible declarations." Equal satisfaction was very naturally felt at St. Petersburg, where, according to the *Agence Russe*, the speech produced an impression tending to lessen the effect of the Earl of Beaconsfield's harangue at the Lord Mayor's banquet. A conviction prevailed in the Russian capital that, if the whole Cabinet were to use similar language, the Porte would lose all hope of drawing England into the war, and the interests of peace would thus be favoured. At Pesth, the feeling of depression equalled the sentiment of delighted admiration experienced in the cities to which allusion has just been made. The Hungarians had always based their hopes on an alliance between England and Austro-Hungary for the maintenance of the Ottoman Empire, and these hopes were almost entirely destroyed by the reply of Lord Derby to the deputation. That the Foreign Minister's observations were extremely imprudent, inasmuch as they implied a direct encouragement to the aggressive spirit of Russia, can hardly be questioned; but, for some reason which it is yet impossible to divine, Lord Derby was allowed to commit the English Government and the English nation to a policy which his chief undoubtedly disapproved, and which found its warmest supporters in the party opposed to Lord Beaconsfield and to the entire Cabinet.

It was just at this time that Mr. Archibald Forbes, one of the Special Correspondents of the *Daily News*, who had recently returned to England for a little much-needed rest, gave a series of public addresses on the character and prospects of the war, which, coming from so acute an observer, possessed more than temporary interest. In the course of a lecture, delivered on the 30th of November at the Royal United Service Institution, Mr. Forbes observed that no man could say what might not have been the issue if the Turks had boldly taken the offensive in the first week of August. He believed the Russians would have had at least to concentrate round Sistova, if Suleiman Pasha, instead of braining his army on the rocks of the Shipka Pass, had crossed the Balkans by the defile of Kazan and the Iron Gate, and joined his forces with those of Mehemet Ali. But the Turks did not move in earnest, and the Russians held on, adhering with wonderful pertinacity to the key of their position, the Shipka Pass. From the 21st to the 26th of August, their grip on that position, according to Mr. Forbes, was very sorely strained. Russian battalions were hurried to and fro by forced marches; and want of system, combined with a sort of gasping nervousness of direction, aggravated the troubles of a situation which at the best was precarious enough. Mr. Forbes related that on the 24th of August he ventured respectfully to suggest to the Grand Duke Nicholas that he should treat the Shipka positions as a sort of leviathan picket, and keep an army-corps for its defence; three brigades to be always within hail in and about Gabrova, and one brigade, regularly relieved, on duty at the most exposed point. The reply of his Imperial Highness was startling. "My God!" he exclaimed, "where am I to find an army-corps? I have not a spare battalion." Referring to the probabilities of the future, and to the character of the war, Mr. Forbes said:—

"I would, with all caution, refrain from prophecy; but there can scarcely be a doubt that, supposing Plevna to fall by Christmas or the new year, and the winter to be hard and close, of which there is every prospect, there can interpose no very serious obstacle to hinder a large Russian army from crossing the Balkans by the Shipka Pass. In war, the weight generally tells sooner or later. In conclusion, I would point out how little the Turkish method of fighting has changed since the wars which preceded the commencement of the present century. In his remarks on the long series of Ottoman wars closing with 1811, Major Frank Russell, in his valuable work, 'Russian Wars with Turkey,' says:—'What strikes one in reading the history of these wars is the extraordinary manner in which both sides alike made use of entrenchments. The Turks more especially appeared to regard the spade as their most valuable weapon: in place of rapid manœuvring and skilful combination, they had no thought of anything but moving to a position, then fortifying themselves, and making subsequent sorties. The Ottomans, whether regular troops, irregular, or untrained inhabitants, have always fought brilliantly behind entrenchments; in fact, they seem especially to rely on this quality as their strong point and safeguard. The wars not unfrequently were little else than a succession of sieges, in which the Russians often had the worst of it.' Substitute for the word 'sieges' the phrase 'investments of position,' and you have a description of the present war." Mr. Forbes was one of the most skilled and competent critics of the campaign, and the general effect of his strictures was, that considerable want of military aptitude had been exhibited by the chief commanders on both sides.

All this while, the patriotic agitation in Greece continued to gather intensity. A small camp of 5,000 soldiers was formed under the eye of the King, and these men were methodically instructed in the various details of war. The place of gathering was Thebes, and, with the exception of one battalion, the men wore European uniforms, carried European arms, and lived in a camp furnished with all the modern appliances of military life in the field. The various manœuvres in which the troops were instructed are said to have been acquired with great facility and creditable intelligence, and the officers were fine, soldierly-looking men, in no respect distinguished from those of other European forces. The King and Queen were staying at Thebes in a small, unpretending house, of which the ground-floor was occupied by a tobacconist's and a cobbler's shop. His Majesty rose each day at or before sunrise, to inspect the troops at their morning drill, and at a later hour he was accompanied by the Queen. It was soon announced that no fewer than 50,000 reserve troops were to be concentrated in the camp at Thebes. The Government ordered 15,000 more rifles, and entered into negotiations with the house of Krupp for the purchase of artillery. A special envoy was sent from Athens to the Russian head-quarters; and all Greek subjects living in Servia, and liable to military service, were ordered by their consul to return home. Greece, in short, was actively preparing to take part in the war, in the hope of emancipating those Hellenic provinces which were still subject to Turkey; and there can be no doubt that she would have added her armies to the hosts of Russia, but for the subsequent dissuasion of England, who led her to suppose that her best interests would be consulted by the maintenance of peace.

Italy, though with less excuse, was also desirous of joining the struggle on the side of Russia. There are unemancipated Italian provinces, as well as Greek; but the former are not under the rule of the Moslem, and it was only indirectly, if at all, that Italy could have gained by war. To many Italians it appears that their country can never be complete until it has acquired the Southern Tyrol, Trieste, Istria, and other provinces now under the rule of Austria, but possessing a population wholly or partially Italian. It seems to have been considered by the more speculative class of politicians that if Italy joined the war on the side of Russia, Austria might be provoked into a similar course on the side of Turkey, and that in such a case peace would not be concluded without an entire re-adjustment of the South-east of Europe. The hope was that in this re-adjustment Italy would obtain what she wanted, and would issue out of the struggle with a considerable increase both of territory and population. The game was a highly dangerous one, for it would probably have resulted in bringing England into the field as the champion of Turkey and the ally of Austria, and in that case Italy might rather have suffered diminution than have gained extension. Yet the desire for war was very strong in particular circles of the Peninsula during the latter part of 1877, and it was only with difficulty that the prudent and experienced Victor Emmanuel, then at the very termination of his life, and the cool-headed Ministers by whom he was surrounded, could restrain the popular passions from hurrying the country into a policy of rash adventure. An incident, which happened about the close of November, gave considerable impulse to what may be called the patriotic feeling, and made it all the less easy for the Government to act with circumspection. The Turkish blockade in the Black Sea had been very laxly enforced, and two Italian vessels which had passed the line were seized when they entered the Bosphorus. The Italian Minister, Count Corti, threatened that if they were not released he would proclaim the blockade to be ineffectual. He alleged that forty-five ships had been allowed to pass the line of blockade with free passes from the Turkish Minister of Marine, and that there had never been a single Ottoman cruiser in the Black Sea. The difficulty was soon overcome by the concessions of the Turkish Government; but it created a feeling of much irritation for a short time. This, however, was not the only cause of unsatisfactory relations between Italy and the Porte. Notwithstanding the denials of the Italian Government, the Ministers of the Sultan affirmed that they had positive information showing that a Garibaldian expedition was preparing to land in Albania; and the Porte had long suspected the Italian Government of working against Turkey through the Catholic clergy of that province, who were mostly Italians, or Catholic Albanians educated at Rome.

In whatever direction she turned her eyes, Turkey saw nothing but danger and menace. Her enemies were many; her friends were few, if it can be said that she had any friends at all. A letter from Constantinople, dated November 29th, and written by one who held a position of trust connected with one of the highest personages in the Ottoman Empire, was published in the *Times*, and may be taken as expressing the feeling very generally entertained in Ministerial circles at that period of gloom and desolation. The author of this epistle said that his countrymen were beginning to open their eyes to the gravity of their disasters. Their military honour, patriotism, and fidelity to the faith, had been saved; but their cause was lost. They might still have a gratifying moment; they might still make their enemy pay dearly for his ultimate success; but that success they knew well they could no longer prevent. Their means were exhausted; their treasury was empty; their provisions were consumed; and their soldiers felt that they were advancing towards privation and death. Europe had abandoned them, or rather it had condemned and delivered them up, because they preferred death to dishonour. Want had stolen within their walls, and in the innermost recesses of their houses were to be heard only the lamentations of women and the maledictions of old men. Such being the case, the writer asked what they were to do; and he replied that nothing remained but to treat directly with the victors, and to treat with them only. Mr. Layard would vainly tell them that they had no right to do so—that they defended interests which were not theirs alone: they would not listen to him. "Europe," said the writer, "can ask nothing of us. We know it no longer; we only know our enemy and our personal defence. The Russians are now those who least hate us; what they wanted we have always known, for they have never concealed it, and they have not disappointed our hopes. The so-called common interests are those which least affect us. The Dardanelles and the Bosphorus matter little to us. When the Russians reach Adrianople, we shall prefer giving up the Bosphorus to letting them march on Constantinople. We shall save the suzerainty over our European possessions, and place ourselves under Russian protection, rather than rely on pretended protectors who fold their arms during our agony. The protection of Russia will be sincere as soon as she has obtained the conditions she means to impose. We have fought alone, and will discuss our ransom alone. We are told we shall thus lose Egypt. No matter; we are not strong enough to hold Egypt. It is for Europe to see whether this suits her. But we know very well that Europe exists still less than we do. Germany hands us over to Russia. She is repaying her debt of gratitude at our expense. Austria would not mind if her complaisance were requited with slices of the Turkish body; but her insatiable desires will be balked. France played a Russian policy as long as she had a voice in the matter. Now she says nothing, because nobody listens to her any longer. Italy is watching Austria. She, too, would like something, and she is waiting for Austria to furnish her with a pretext. The two nations will some day avenge us on each other. As to England, with her we are at present most angry of all. We hate her more than the Russians, and we should infinitely prefer to see a Russian fleet in the Bosphorus to an English one. We do not know whether those who call themselves Tories have done us the more harm; but both parties have done their best to hasten our destruction. The Russians are well aware that they will never enter Constantinople. We would sooner set fire to it ourselves, and recross the Bosphorus by the light of its flames. It might soon be done: from Stamboul to Pera, and from Pera to Galata, every one would lend a hand in it."

The opinions here expressed were undoubtedly those which influenced the Porte when peace was made. They are such as might fairly have been anticipated from a very early period of the war. When the writer spoke of Europe, he was in the main considering England; and it was against England that such a peace as the one foreshadowed would be chiefly directed. The argument of the Turks was perfectly natural, however impossible it may have been for English statesmen to sanction it. If England abandoned Turkey in the hour of her supremest trial, it was not to be expected that Turkey should consider the interests of England when at length the necessity arose of making terms with her enemy. Such was the practical dilemma to which a subservient policy had reduced the British nation; and when the crisis came, it was the painful task of the Government to encounter the difficulties which passion and party feeling had piled up mountains high.

BULGARIAN WOMAN.

VIEW OF RAHOVA.

CHAPTER XLIII.

Capture of Rahova and Provitz by the Roumanians—The Dobrudscha—Situation and Military Strength of Bazardjik—Raouf Pasha in the Shipka Pass—Elaborate Fortifications—Osman Pasha's Criticisms on the Conduct of the War—Superiority of the Turkish Privates over their Officers—Progress of the Russians in the Balkans—Alleged Cowardice of Mustapha Pasha at Etropol—Stratagem of Russian Hussars—Movements of Generals Dondeville and Ellis—Encounter with the Turks on the 29th of November—A Rough Mountain Road—Assistance rendered by the Bulgarians—Russian Attack on the Turkish Positions, December 3rd—Courage of Mehemet Ali—Fighting in other Directions—Turkish Attack on the Position of Count Schouvaloff—The Russians checked in their Advance—Severe Weather in the Balkans—Sufferings of the Russian Wounded—State of Etropol—Appearance of the People—Mehemet Ali removed from his Command—Attempts to evade Military Service—Story of a Roumanian Soldier—Re-opening of the Roumanian Chambers—Subjection of Roumania to the Designs of Russia—Siege of Antivari and Spitz by the Montenegrins—Alleged Attempt to assassinate the Prince of Montenegro—Changes at Constantinople—Intrigue and Favouritism—The Vienna Cabinet—Statement of Count Andrassy—True Character of the Austrian Policy.

After the fall of Kars, the great interest of the war centred in and around Plevna, and every isolated movement tending to the reduction of that stronghold acquired a value from its possible effects in the future. The main object of the invaders was to seize all positions of importance in the vicinity of Osman Pasha's fortress, so as to embarrass the Turkish commander in every conceivable way. In this respect, the operations of the Roumanians contributed in their degree to the desired result. Those energetic troops directed their attention, shortly after the middle of November, to the town of Rahova, situated on the southern shore of the Danube, to the north-west of Plevna. On the 19th of the month, the First Division of the Roumanians, under Colonel Slaniceanu, coming from Nicopolis, and pursuing the line of the river in a westerly direction, appeared suddenly before Rahova, and made an attack on the outworks defending the town, taking some, and bombarding the place from the points of vantage thus obtained. During the night of the 20th, a force under General Lupu crossed the river in boats from the opposite side of the Danube, and the two columns, after some hard fighting, got possession of Rahova on the morning of the 21st, by means of a combined attack made under cover of a heavy river-fog. The garrison, consisting of about a thousand men, managed to escape; but a detachment was immediately sent in pursuit. In this affair, the Roumanians lost three hundred men killed and wounded but the success they had obtained was sufficient compensation for the expenditure of life it had involved. On the 23rd of November, the Roumanians captured Provitz, a small town situated five or six miles west of Lom Palanka; and in this instance also the garrison got away in the confusion of the moment, and evaded pursuit. It was at one time supposed that the Russians would conduct important operations in or near the Dobrudscha; but General Zimmerman, who had command of the troops stationed there, effected little or nothing. Nevertheless, it was feared by Suleiman Pasha that his rear might be attacked from that direction, and he therefore took measures for meeting the danger, should it come. He in fact suffered from some reconnaissances, but not to any grave extent. It was apparent to the Russian commander that a forward movement on the road to Bazardjik would be an error in strategy which might entail serious consequences. The country between Trajan's Wall and the Turkish positions on the Lom was of such a nature as to render the sending out of supplies extremely difficult. Bazardjik, moreover, was admirably situated for defence, and its capture, besides necessitating a considerable loss in men, would only have been possible after a lengthened siege. "The fortification," said a writer in the *Times*, "is planted on a plateau which rises precipitously on the left bank of a brook, at present quite dried up. Where the brook leaves the plateau, and opens into a widening valley, stands the town of Bazardjik, with its 30,000 promiscuous inhabitants, comprising Turks, Greeks, and Tartars, with a sprinkling of Jews and Bulgarians. The town has little military importance, in consequence of a plateau which rises abruptly on the right bank of the brook. Its immediate neighbourhood is level and without cover, offering free movement to troops of all arms, and was not protected from the view and fire of the Turkish position on the left bank." That position had recently been much strengthened by a large number of earthworks, partly open and partly closed, which were constructed on the front and flanks, and so judiciously disposed that the capture of the lines would have tasked even a superior force to the utmost. The garrison of Bazardjik was now somewhat formidable. It had originally consisted of nothing more than a few Egyptian battalions; but these were increased in the autumn by the addition of several troops from Varna, Schumla, and other places. At the same time, the garrison of Silistria was augmented. The Turkish troops in the Dobrudscha generally were protected from the weather under canvas, and, being provided with an excellent commissariat, were in perfect health and spirits.

The chief command of the Ottoman forces in the Shipka Pass, now that Suleiman Pasha was removed to other duties, rested with Raouf Pasha—a person of affable manners, possessing a familiarity with the French language which newspaper correspondents found convenient. Great pains were taken to render the camp as strong as possible, and to provide for the comforts of the men. The soldiers were sheltered in rude dwellings of straw, with heavily thatched roofs, or in earth-huts dug out of the solid mountain. Raouf Pasha and Chakir Pasha lived in wooden barracks, while the subordinate officers occupied tents. To give additional security to the position, a wall was built round the camp, and beyond this a deep trench was dug, with steep, sloping sides. The inside of the wall was strengthened with wood and shrubs, and the various tumuli scattered about the ground were thus connected with one another, and, being mounted with guns, were converted into points of support for the line of fortifications. On the summits of neighbouring mountains were other Turkish positions, all of which were difficult of access, and held by troops of approved and stubborn valour. But Raouf Pasha, while feeling satisfied as to his ability to hold his entrenchments against the attacks of the Russians, was not inclined to imitate the tactics of his predecessor, and fling his army against the fortified positions of the enemy. Warned by the failure of Suleiman Pasha to carry the Shipka Pass, the present commander determined on the observance of a waiting and watching policy, so that, while checking the advance of the Russians in his front, he might be prepared to act on the offensive, should a fitting occasion arise.

Osman Pasha, who in his fortified retreat at Plevna heard from time to time of what was going on in the outer world, dissented from many of the arrangements of the War Office and of the other Pashas. It appeared to him as if some malevolent spirit were pushing on the Government to commit blunder after blunder. A young aide-de-camp, in the confidence of Osman, assured a correspondent of the *Times* that his chief had only too much reason for what he said, and he told an anecdote in proof of this. They had asked for some armourers to be sent from the arsenal at Constantinople for the repair of arms. A certain number were accordingly directed to proceed to Plevna; but it was found that they were not furnished with a single instrument of their craft. They were consequently useless, and were sent back next day. The root of the evil, according to this young officer, was to be found in the defective system of organisation existing in Turkey, and in the impassiveness of the national character. "I will relate to you," continued the aide-de-camp, addressing the correspondent, "another fact, which will show you how clearly Osman foresaw and anticipated the events which led to the investment of this place. Osman Pasha, after having beaten the Russians, and taken possession of Plevna, fortified it in such a manner as caused the memorable defeat of the enemy on their first attack on the place. At this time he heard that Suleiman Pasha had succeeded in expelling the Russians from Thrace towards Shipka, and received intelligence that an expedition, counselled by some harebrained Poles, was about to start from Constantinople for the Caucasus. Without delay, he wrote to the Minister of War, dissuading him against the expedition, and advising him, on the contrary, to establish a large camp at Sophia, and to concentrate on that spot not only all the available regular troops then at Constantinople, who mustered pretty strong, but also all the Nizams forming the garrisons of the different vilayets in the vicinity of the capital. Had this disposition been carried out, Sophia would not only have become a central depôt for stores, &c., but would have contained an army of from 120,000 to 150,000 men, which, well commanded, would have rendered the investment of Plevna impossible. Osman Pasha was also strongly against any attack on Shipka, maintaining that a force of from 10,000 to 15,000 men, strongly entrenched at the entrance of that pass, was quite sufficient to hold the Russians in check." Plans the very opposite of what Osman desired were in fact adopted, and certainly the result had not been such as to justify the policy of the Seraskierate, or to discredit the advice that came from Plevna. The progress of the war, however, showed more clearly with each succeeding month the great superiority of the Turkish privates over the mass of their officers; and the soldiers themselves knew it. In Plevna, the only person whom they allowed to interfere between them and the Commander-in-Chief was the Imam or priest of each company, who recited prayers for them regularly five times a-day.

The abandonment of Etropol by Mustapha Pasha, the commandant of that town, was fraught with the most serious consequences for the Turks, as it left the Russians free to pursue their advance over the Balkans. Mehemet Ali, it is said, threatened to shoot Mustapha for cowardice, as well as for bad generalship in retreating while it was light, instead of waiting for darkness, when he might have saved all his guns. Had Mustapha telegraphed to his superior, Mehemet could have spared some battalions to assist him; but he seems to have acted in a panic. His men were infected with the same spirit of apprehension. Their retreat soon became a rout, in which a large number of guns, a great many head of cattle, and vast quantities of munitions and supplies, were left upon the road. A few squadrons of Hussars were sent in pursuit, and the advance-guard of this body, consisting of only eight men, rode boldly up a mountain path, and, with a great noise of bugles and cheering, skirmished with the rear-guard of the Turks. The bugle-notes and cries were multiplied by the rocky sides of the mountains, and the fugitives believed that a large force was close upon their rear. After a time, one of the Hussars was sent back for reinforcements, and a squadron and a half speedily arrived on the ground. The buglers, of whom there were several, purposely sent to produce an effect, were scattered all along the line, and sounded their calls from a dozen different points at once. Again the echoes gave an impression of much greater numbers than were really present, and it appeared to the Turks that the woods were swarming with hidden foes. Struck with terror, they crowded within the shelter of their entrenchments, and the Hussars then advanced to within half a rifle-shot of the enemy's posts.

The authorities at Constantinople hoped much from the advancing winter, and from the physical obstruction of the Balkan mountains; but their reliance in both respects proved ill-founded. Undeterred by snow or bitter winds, General Gourko continued to penetrate the great chain of rugged hills and valleys which barred his way to the south, and the harassed Turks were unable to resist his progress. At the close of November they had lost Pravca, Orkhanieh, Osikovo, and Etropol, and it was probable that before many days were over they would be compelled to abandon several other places too. On the 26th of the month, General Dondeville was sent with a column of troops due south from Etropol, with instructions to operate against the heights of Greot. This position he captured on the 28th, and the Turks at Wratchesh, finding their rear menaced by Dondeville's success, abandoned the little town in hot haste, and retreated to Arab Konak—a strong position on the Orkhanieh-Sophia road. Wratchesh was immediately afterwards occupied by a Russian column from Orkhanieh under General Ellis, who captured a considerable quantity of ammunition and stores, together with a small pontoon-train. Following on the heels of the enemy, Ellis, on the 1st of December, connected his left flank with the right of Dondeville, who, having turned westward, threatened Arab Konak from the east.

Dondeville, however, had not been altogether fortunate in his proceedings, as he had suffered a severe repulse in attacking a Turkish fort. In front of the head-quarters of Mehemet, at Kamarli, were six redoubts, which crowned the summit of a high range of the Balkans. They were at right angles with the main road from Orkhanieh, and the most westerly of the series stood across the road, while the others were erected on ascending ridges of the mountains. Towards evening on the 28th of November, the Russians appeared on the heights immediately opposite the Turkish positions. Descending the slope, they reached a ravine clothed with wood, from which the Ottomans were speedily driven out. The assailants bivouacked for the night among the trees, and in the deep snow which at that time covered the ground. Chakir Pasha, who was stationed at the end of the pass nearest Orkhanieh, was attacked during the same day, and, finding his retreat jeopardised, communicated with Mehemet Ali, who ordered him to fall back, so as to effect a junction with the main body at the camp. The movement was carried out during the night, and, by some extraordinary want of enterprise on the part of the Russian commander, was not in the slightest degree interrupted, though the noise of the transit must have been clearly perceptible. The morning of the 29th was so foggy that the Russians had much difficulty in finding their way to the redoubt which it was proposed to attack—the highest of the series. Six Russian battalions were engaged in the assault, which was conducted with so much gallantry and spirit, in face of a tremendous fire from the Turkish batteries, that the advancing columns gained a temporary footing at the base of the work, and one man even leaped upon the parapet, but was shot down immediately after. As many as five attacks were made on the redoubt, all of which were repulsed with considerable loss, and the gaps in the Russian line were not filled up by reinforcements. At length the Turks sallied forth from their defences, drove back the enemy at the point of the bayonet, and brought the action to a close. Mehemet Ali was greatly relieved by the issue of the day's fighting, and declared that, had he lost the battle, his situation would have been most precarious.

The road of the Turkish retreat from Etropol had been hastily cut, a short time before, through a forest of beech and birch, but cut so roughly that no attempt was made at levelling the ground, or clearing it of boulders. Nothing could exceed the roughness of the track, which at several points was almost impassable. The crest of the heights crowned by the Ottoman earthworks was approached from the east and from the north by two distinct lines of mountains, separated by deep ravines, at the bottom of which, far below the upper ranges, foamed and roared the shallow but rapid streams of that land of rocks and forests. The Russian forces had great difficulty in following the Turks up these rugged mountain-sides, and in getting the guns on to the higher ridges, where alone they would be effective against the enemy; but the task was at length accomplished by a great expenditure of labour. As in the previous advance to Etropol, several Bulgarian peasants, with fifteen or twenty yoke of oxen and buffaloes, assisted in the transport of the guns, shrieking, yelling, singing, and gesticulating, like a crowd of demons. Their efforts undoubtedly contributed to the desired end; but the Russians looked with some jealousy on their interference. The natives were not regarded with any favour by their deliverers, and the feeling of soldierly pride was piqued at having to accept aid from civilians. But to get the artillery into position was a matter of paramount importance, and even Bulgarians could not be altogether despised. It took nearly two days to drag the cannon up; but, when at length brought to the designated spot, they were within very short range of the opposing batteries at Kamarli.* A camp was then formed by the Russians, and artillery-fire was interchanged between the antagonistic armies.

When the detachments of Dondeville and Ellis had effected their junction, on the 1st of December, the combined force was sufficiently strong to feel confidence in its position. At the same time, another column, under General Kurnkoff, was despatched towards Slàtitza. Meeting with but little opposition, this column reached the village of Kilisch-koi, within five miles of the point proposed, on the 3rd, and Kurnkoff was soon able to co-operate with the other divisions of the army. The 3rd of December did not pass over without severe fighting. At daybreak, a heavy cannonade was opened by the Russians from some guns which they had, during the previous night, planted on the hills opposite the western redoubt of the Turks. Mehemet Ali had given orders that entrenchments were to be made in advance of this redoubt; but his directions had not been carried out, and the fort was consequently open to attack. The action took place in a piece of wooded ground in front of the redoubt, and it was contested with varying fortune until late in the afternoon, when the Russians withdrew their guns, though still retaining hold of some portion of the ground they had won. The brunt of the fighting on the Turkish side was borne by two battalions from Bosnia, who decapitated the wounded—a savage custom, which so much disgusted Mehemet Ali that he gave orders for its discontinuance, under the heaviest penalty. The action was directed by Mehemet Ali in person, and his escape without injury was remarkable under the circumstances. He was shelled by the Russian batteries on the ridge immediately in front of him, but, with unflinching coolness, remained in his position of danger during the greater part of the day. The head-quarters' camp of the General and his Staff was rendered untenable by the Russian shells, which were continually bursting in every direction; and the officer in charge of the nearest redoubt, by imprudently firing on the Russians, drew from them a response which it would have been judicious to avoid. Towards evening, Mehemet Ali was persuaded to pitch his tent in a more sheltered spot, and it was with a

* *Daily News* Correspondent.

great sense of relief that his personal attendants found themselves at liberty to remove out of the line of fire.

On the same day (December 3rd), General Ellis succeeded in carrying the heights to the west of the Sophia road, which dominated the Turkish position at Arab Konak. The success, however, was not obtained without very hard fighting, and at one time the position of the Russians was critical. When, after the third attack, the Turks were decisively repulsed, the Russians proceeded to fortify the positions they had won, and the Ottoman lines at Arab Konak and the vicinity were bombarded. An additional column, under Colonel Count Komarowski, simultaneously advanced south from the neighbourhood of Teteven, so as to threaten the Turks on the east; and Mehemet Ali was now effectually held in his positions at Kamarli and Arab Konak. Nevertheless, that commander was not inclined to let the Russians remain in quiet, and, about eleven o'clock on the morning of December 4th, commenced a series of demonstrations against the positions of his antagonists. A strong detachment was sent round the mountain lying to the Russian right, and the men, having gained the crest, charged down upon the Russian sharpshooters, who were not protected by entrenchments. Continuing their course, they neared the position held by Count Schouvaloff, who received them with such staggering volleys of shrapnel that their lines began to waver. They speedily recovered their formation, however, and advanced with the cry of "Allah! Allah!" Presently, they were within pistol-shot of the Russians, and, although their ranks were thinned by repeated volleys from the Muscovite guns, the impetus of the charge was but slightly checked. In fact, they got so near the artillery that for a time it seemed doubtful whether the pieces would not be taken; but, after a fierce struggle, the attacking force was driven back, though only for a time. The assault was renewed again and again, and, to save the position from capture, it was necessary for the Russians to work the guns so quickly that many of them became too hot for further use. At length, only one gun could be fired, and resistance was confined to the bayonets. Animated to fresh exertions by their partial success, the Turks flung themselves with fanatical desperation against the bristling steel; but they might as well have flung themselves against a rock. In a little while they were broken to fragments by the fury of their own onslaught, and by the cold and solid resolution with which they were received. The ground was covered with dead and wounded, and the attacking force, losing its cohesion, reeled backwards down the slope it had so triumphantly ascended, and sought the shelter of its own lines. One more attempt was made towards the close of the day; but it failed equally with those which had preceded it. Still, the Turks were not disheartened, and on the following morning another attack was directed against the important position of Count Schouvaloff. By that time, however, the Count had been strongly reinforced, and the assault was relinquished after a rather brief attempt. The Turks had failed in their endeavour to drive the Russians by main force from the ground they had taken up; but they had not failed in every respect. They were themselves in so excellent a position, and made such good use of the opportunities it gave them, that for a while the Russian advance was stopped, and General Gourko, instead of pursuing his triumphant march across the Balkans, was obliged to entrench himself where he stood, and to take every precaution against surprise. The recklessness which this officer had displayed in his earlier movement across the mountains had given place to extreme caution; but it has been said that care was enjoined on him by his superiors, who were fearful lest he should lose too many of his troops, and again find himself in a dilemma similar to that which had cost so much in the days of July.

Both sides had now a relentless enemy in the weather, and the Turks even more so than the Russians—partly because they were less inured to the influences of frost and snow, and partly because they were not so well provided with the comforts of camp life. Many deserters came into the Russian lines, and related, with every appearance of truth, that their comrades were enduring terrible hardships. These desertions were serious, for the number of the Turkish troops was far from large. It was mainly owing to the excellence of their position amongst the mountains and ravines that they were able for the present to oppose the Muscovite advance; but, supposing their ranks to be greatly thinned, it was doubtful whether they would be able to do this much longer. Further south, the feeling of apprehension was extreme. The people of Sophia were leaving the city in large numbers, fearing that the Russians would be there within the next few days. The condition of the town was truly miserable, for it was crowded with sick and wounded, and typhus was raging, as it is certain to do under such conditions. To make matters worse, the weather was more than usually bad. On some days, snow fell heavily; on others torrents of rain rushed from the clouds with scarcely a moment's intermission; and in either case the cold was piercing. Furious storms howled up and down the mountain-passes, and, as the winter was just beginning, there was no prospect before the unhappy soldiers and the shrinking fugitives, except that every week would make matters worse until the arrival of the distant spring.

The Russian wounded, in the several actions fought at this period, suffered in no slight degree. Owing to the abrupt and craggy nature of the ground, it was impossible to take the ambulances anywhere near the scenes of conflict, so that the injured were conveyed on stretchers from rock to rock over four miles of mountainous road to the nearest hospital-station. Thence, generally on the following day, they were carried in carts still further to the rear. Their ultimate destination was Simnitza, a journey of nearly a fortnight; and, the season being inclement, and the carts rough, hard, and springless, the unfortunate men endured a degree of torture which frequently ended in death. A stoppage on the road, such as would occasionally happen, often led to the wounded soldiers remaining without food until the obstacle could be overcome, and the next town be reached. The number of surgeons and nurses was insufficient for the terrible demands made on them; and a good deal of suffering may be fairly set down as preventible. The men, however, bore their afflictions with extraordinary heroism, and uttered no complaint with their lips, however eloquent their wounds may have been. In the virtue of quiet patience, Russians and Turks are certainly worthy rivals.

HEAD-QUARTERS OF MEHEMET ALI AT KAMARLI.

While these events were going on in the Etropol Balkans, the little town itself was quiet enough. "At Etropol," said a writer from the spot, "one has little idea of what is passing in the mountains. All day and night we hear the echoes of the cannonade sounding in the ravines, and now and then the dull roll of a fusillade of brief duration comes down through the still air, audible above the rattle of the carts on the pavement, or the clatter of horses' feet on the bridges. We are almost within rifle-shot of the positions, and are to all intents as far from the battle as at Bucharest. No wounded men are seen in the streets; there is no hurrying of troops, or rapid movement of artillery. Once in a while, a Cossack comes clattering in with a despatch, or a general passes with a small suite;

LEFT REDOUBT IN MEHEMET ALI'S LINES NEAR KAMARLI.

but the occupations here are leisurely and peaceful. The Bulgarians gather in crowds at the corners of the narrow streets, and keep up an animated discussion; the girls—and very pretty ones too—every evening promenade down to the fountain with their water-jugs, so coquettishly dressed for the occasion, and with such a conscious air, that one sees at once they are parading a little before the handsome Hussars in red jackets, all covered with cord and braid." The dress of the women among these Etropol Balkans is highly picturesque. It consists of a robe with long sleeves and open neck, bound to the waist by a broad belt of square links of chased silver. On the arms are heavy silver bracelets; round the neck hang chains of yellow, red, and green glass beads; and the head is enveloped in a dark-coloured handkerchief, falling down the back. The young men also are given to showy and effective costumes. The members of a small volunteer company, formed at Etropol, wore broad red sashes, stuck full of knives and pistols, sheepskin caps, raw-hide boots, and any accidental addition to their dress, of a rich and jaunty character, that they could pick up. Whether they were of any great value as soldiers, remained to be seen; but the Russians were certainly suspicious as to their qualities. They appeared to regard the whole business in a somewhat theatrical light; whereas to the Russians it was real enough—a tragedy of actual life and actual death.

Mehemet Ali, it was now evident, would not be able to conduct an army to the relief of Plevna; but he was nevertheless doing good service in thwarting the southward advance of Gourko. The Porte, though tardily, sent him reinforcements in rather considerable numbers, and he would probably have soon been able to do still more, had he not been unexpectedly removed from his command about the 10th of December. It was considered that he had acted with too much caution, and he had in truth lost many positions of great importance, in which the Russians were by this time installed. But the blame of these reverses was attributable rather to his subordinates than to himself, while some were perhaps inevitable with so weak a force as that which he originally possessed. At the very moment when his ranks were being augmented, he was deprived of power, and directed to hand over his command to Chakir Pasha, who had lately been acting in conjunction with Raouf Pasha in the Shipka Pass, and still more recently at Orkhanieh. As on the occasion of his previous dismissal, Mehemet Ali is said to have been deprived of power because of his refusal to obey what he considered an imprudent order to attack. The truth is that something like despair had taken possession of the Turkish people, from the highest to the lowest. In the army, not only were desertions numerous, but every attempt was made to evade the liabilities of military service. Several of Mehemet Ali's soldiers purposely disabled themselves by shooting away the forefinger of the right hand, in order that they might be dismissed the ranks; and on one occasion the Commander-in-Chief ordered seven men, who had evidently pulled the trigger with their own feet, to be shot in the presence of their battalions, as a warning to the others.

This crime, however, was not confined to the Turks. A correspondent of the *Times*, writing from Biela on the 22nd of October, related a singular incident which had occurred in the Princess of Roumania's hospital at Bucharest, just before he left that city for the front. He was shown a man dying of pyæmia (blood-poisoning), and was told that when the poor fellow was given up by the surgeons, a priest was sent for, to whom he made confession, but nevertheless appeared extremely restless. At length he begged to see the Princess Elizabeth alone, but declined to give any reason for his wish, though frequently pressed to do so. His uneasiness rapidly increasing, a message was communicated to her Highness, who immediately went to the man's bedside, and received from his dying lips the story he desired to reveal. He stated that his company had been in the first assault on the Grivica Redoubt, which took place on September 11th; that when he saw his comrades falling around him he became frightened; and that he then shot off the end of his forefinger, ran to the rear, got into an ambulance, and was carried to the hospital. He was satisfied that his death from so trivial a wound was the result of a providential punishment for unfaithfulness to his sovereign and country; and he could not die without the forgiveness of the Princess for his conduct on the field of battle.* It is to be suspected that, in all armies, cases of this kind are more frequent than is ever publicly known, although it may be seldom that they awaken such conscientious remorse as that which was exhibited by the poor Roumanian soldier.

Turning our eyes at present from the several fields of conflict, we must note the re-opening of the Roumanian Chambers on the 27th of November. The tone adopted in the speech from the throne was of the most sanguine character. "On the fall of Plevna," said the Prince, "we hope to reap on its ruins the peace so dear to us. We are also convinced that out of its ruins we shall see the

* *Times*, Nov. 2nd, 1877.

independence of Roumania recognised by all Europe, thanks to our patriotism, the bravery of our soldiers, and their blood shed in a noble cause. I have the firm belief, and the Senate and Chamber will certainly share it with me, that the guaranteeing Powers have by this time become convinced that Roumania is a country possessing real vitality; that she is a nation able to fulfil the mission reserved for her on the Lower Danube, having the perseverance to accomplish it, and the energy to defend it when necessary. The time of foreign tutelage and vassalage has passed away from us: Roumania is now, and will for ever remain, a free and independent country." Never were congratulations more ill-placed, or destined to a more ignominious falsification. By the secret Convention with Russia in the preceding April, Roumania had completely sacrificed the position of virtual independence which she had long enjoyed, and had made herself practically a fief of the Russian Empire. The best and most respectable Roumanian politicians had seen at the very moment to what disastrous ends that act inevitably tended, and already their prophecies of evil were beginning to assume definite shape. At the close of November, it was strongly suspected, if not absolutely known, that, whenever peace was concluded, Russia meant to extort from Roumania that territory on the banks of the Danube of which she had been deprived in 1856, and which she burned to regain. It was for the promotion of this purpose that Roumania had sold her honour, had betrayed her Suzerain, had entered into a dishonest compact, and had sent her sons to die in desperate enterprises which the Russians themselves were glad to evade. Under the nominal sovereignty of the Porte, Roumania had been actually free; free to make her own laws, to choose her own Prince, to form her own army, and even to persecute those Jews who were tolerated in Turkey Proper, but found little mercy or justice beneath the sceptre of Prince Charles. With nominal independence, she was rapidly passing into a condition of real servitude—of subjection to an autocrat who uses the promises of freedom only to betray, and advocates the cause of nationalities with no other object than to promote the universal empire of the Sclaves.

The Montenegrins were not idle while affairs of greater moment were passing in other quarters. Prince Nikita, having reconquered the positions in the northern parts of his domain which had been lost in the early days of the summer, and being unable to advance further in that direction, owing to the want of a sufficient supply-train, turned towards the south, and achieved some important successes over the small and scattered bodies of Turkish troops still remaining in the Principality. Pursuing his career without check, he bombarded Antivari, in the Turkish province of Albania. Antivari is a seaport town of some importance, situated on the coast of the Adriatic, at the mouth of the river Boïana, which forms the outlet of the Lake of Scutari. It was peopled during the Middle Ages, when under the rule of Venice, by Italian colonists, and is still the see of a Catholic Archbishop, though the inhabitants are for the most part Mohammedans. This town, the people of which are almost entirely seamen, forms the port of Scutari, and is the depôt of the valley of the Drin. It is defended by a fortress, which the Montenegrins attacked in November, 1877. The citadel, however, held out against a prolonged bombardment, during which the greater part of the town was reduced to ashes. At the same time, the mountaineers despatched troops against Spitz, which was subjected to a vigorous attack. These performances were regarded with some jealousy by Russia, and the Czar is said to have conveyed to Prince Nikita an intimation to that effect. The Prince was certainly engaged in a dangerous enterprise, from which he was not likely to obtain sufficient advantages to repay the cost and risk. On the 9th of December, if we may credit a report, which, however, was contradicted, an unsuccessful attempt was made to take his life. During the operations against the citadel of Antivari, he inhabited the house of one Selim Bey; and on the day in question, when his Highness, fortunately for himself, happened to be out, the structure, which had been undermined, is said to have been blown up. Seven of the Prince's body-guard were in the building at the time, and one of these was killed, while the other six were injured by the force of the explosion.

Intrigues continued at Constantinople. Mahmud Damat Pasha, the Sultan's brother-in-law, was still the great object of popular dislike, and a faction at the palace lost no opportunity of undermining his influence. At length, early in December, it was announced that he had been sent from Constantinople to inspect the fortifications of the Balkans; but everybody understood that this was only another way of announcing that he had been removed from court. At about the same period, Mustapha Pasha was dismissed from the Ministry of War, where he was succeeded by Raouf Pasha. Redif Pasha then undertook the command of the army at Sophia; but these repeated vicissitudes, while totally unproductive of any good effect, revealed only too plainly the desperate straits

SACRED BANNER OF THE MONTENEGRINS.

into which the Government was now drifting. The Porte was not devoid of excellent soldiers, and even two or three able generals were at its disposal; but the great majority of the officers were hopelessly incompetent, and palace intrigues fettered the hands of those who might really have struck effective blows for the liberation of the Empire. "Every general," observed a correspondent of the *Daily News*, "has his party, and the real battles of the war appear to be decided in the Seraskierate, as the partizans of each gain the upper hand in the councils of the Sultan. Favouritism takes the place of merit, from the appointment of a Mushir down to the nomination of a cadet." In some degree, the same charge may be brought against the management of the Russian army; but the evil has not proceeded to an equal extent with the advisers of the Czar as with those of the Sultan. The constant changes in the Turkish army at that gloomy and disastrous time augured ill for the future; and as the year 1877 drew towards a close, there were few who had any hopeful anticipations for the period that was to follow.

In this state of things, the intentions of the Austrian Government, which had throughout been veiled and ambiguous, became the subject of eager speculation throughout the whole of South-Eastern Europe. In several foreign newspapers it was said that the Cabinet of Vienna had addressed itself to Russia, Servia, and Montenegro, in order to explain the attitude it had assumed with regard to the Eastern Question, and to define with exactness the nature of those Austro-Hungarian interests which were supposed to be involved in the struggle. The report met with little credence in Austria itself; but its existence showed how widely-spread was the anxiety prevailing on the subject. The reality of this feeling was recognised by the Austrian Government itself, when Count Andrassy made some statements on the policy of the Empire, in answer to a Hungarian delegation. To the members of that body, who had an interview with the Minister on the 10th of December, Count Andrassy expressed his concurrence in the opinion that another factor in Europe, besides the treaties, must be taken into the account—namely, force; and that the validity of treaties could only be assured in so far as it could be energetically maintained. Referring to the alliance of the three Emperors, Count Andrassy declared that the Monarchy was the free arbitor of its own destiny, and that no State in Europe could more securely reckon upon its just and reasonable interests obtaining proper satisfaction. The Minister then glanced at the position of the small frontier States, and confessed himself strongly opposed to the Christian populations of the East being any longer abandoned to the injurious effects of prejudice, as if Austro-Hungary had no heart for their welfare, and as if it were her interest to maintain unchanged the state of things that existed in Turkey previous to the war then raging. He would not consent to employ the power of the Monarchy for an object which no statesman in Europe, nor even in Turkey, believed to be either just or possible. Finally, Count Andrassy repudiated what he described as the erroneous belief that Austro-Hungary was acting under pressure from another Power, and declared that no country could undertake the settlement of the Eastern Question without the Austro-Hungarian Monarchy. In concert with other Powers, Austria would be able materially to serve European interests; and as for her own specific interests, she would stand up for them alone, if necessary.

This statement evoked much comment at the time; but in truth it placed the position of Austria in no clearer light than before. It simply revealed, in very general terms, that which had all along been suspected—namely, that Austria had a distinct understanding of some nature with the two Northern Empires; that she was following a policy of abstention because she hoped to win more by that course than by any other; and that when the time for making peace arrived, she would have a very sharp eye for her own interests. The desire of the Hungarians was to some extent sentimental—to some extent, a mere instinct of self-preservation. They recollected what they had endured in 1849 at the hands of Russia; they dreaded the extension of Russian power, as likely to involve still further injuries to themselves; and on this account they wished to see the Turkish Empire sustained in its plenitude, and the armies of the Czar driven back in ruin over the waters of the Danube. Such was not at all the policy of Austria. The Emperor Francis Joseph would have been very well content to see the Turks expelled from Europe, and the Russian territories augmented, provided he could at the same time extend his own dominions in a south-easterly direction. This is what he was working for; this, in all probability, was what had long ago been settled between himself and his two brother-Emperors; and this is what, by an astute policy of inaction, he finally succeeded in effecting.

CHAPTER XLIV.

The Army of Suleiman Pasha—Capture of Mahren by the Turks—Desperate Action before Elena, and Retreat of the Russians—Details of the Engagements—Elena evacuated—Sacking of the Town by the Ottoman Troops—A Scene of Turmoil and Confusion—Position of Prince Mirsky at Jakowitza—Arrival of Reinforcements—Further Advance of the Turks—Defeat of Suleiman Pasha—Withdrawal of the Turks from Elena, and Re-occupation of the Town by the Russians—Suleiman Pasha and Mehemet Ali—Affairs in Armenia—The Peace Party in Russia—Fluctuations of Opinion with respect to the War—Demands for Territorial Compensation—Development of Political Discontent—Pamphlet of M. Dragomanoff—Is Russia qualified to act as the Champion of Freedom?—Louis Kossuth on the Designs of Russia and the Duty of Austria and Hungary—Popular Feeling in Constantinople in December, 1877—Fatalism of the Turkish Character—Speech of Sir Henry Havelock on the Eastern Question—The Dardanelles and British Interests—Russian and Turkish Cruelty—Treatment of Prisoners—The Turkish Sick and Wounded in Kars—A Deadly March through the Snow—The Principles of the Geneva Convention.

Affairs were hastening towards a great disaster for the Turks; yet they still presented a bold face to the enemy. By the beginning of December, it was evident that Gourko had checkmated Mehemet Ali in his endeavours to relieve Plevna; but it was possible that Suleiman Pasha would effect the same purpose by a series of movements which he was then commencing. On the morning of December 4th, two brigades of Suleiman's army, commanded by Raschid and Renzi Pashas, moved against the Russian positions at Mahren, or Mariani, about four miles east of Elena, and therefore amongst the Balkans. The place was taken at a rush, and the Turkish forces, being then strengthened by a reserve brigade under Hussein Pasha, advanced on Elena, which they vigorously attacked. The possession of the town was strategically important to both belligerents, as it stands on the road from the Balkan Passes to Tirnova. It was consequently worth fighting for, and the engagement was long and bloody. The struggle lasted eight hours, and the Russians disputed every inch of ground, but were at length compelled to retire upon Jakowitza, a few miles to the west, where, under protection of a fortified gorge in the mountains, they awaited reinforcements. Their losses had been extensive. Sixty officers and 1,800 men were killed and wounded, and the discomfited troops, on their retreat, were obliged to leave eleven guns behind, for want of horses to carry them away.

Such were the general results of the fighting, and they were creditable to the Turks, as well as fortunate for their cause; yet in some respects there had been mismanagement on the part of the assailants, and the course of affairs was not exactly what Suleiman Pasha had intended. The taking of Elena was to have been only an incident in a concerted movement, by which it was proposed to advance upon Tirnova from three points. Kerim Pasha, occupying a position at Lailankoi, about twelve miles from Osman Bazar, and to the right of the Turkish positions, was to attack the Russian entrenchments at Kesarova, four miles further on. Fuad Pasha, on the left, was to make his way by Elena to Tirnova; while Asmi Pasha, commanding the centre, was to advance by the Ahmedli road, and to effect a junction with Kerim Pasha at Arnaoutkoi. It was part of the original design to make simultaneous movements from right and left on two lines of heights running towards Elena, with a view to surrounding and capturing that place; and the success of this plan was regarded as so certain that the summons to capitulate was drawn up two days previously in several languages. The attack was precipitated by Raschid Pasha, who was in command of the left division of the forces converging on Elena, and who, for some unexplained reason, opened fire with his artillery at the very commencement of the advance. This put the enemy on the alert, and a small force came out of Mahren, but was speedily driven back. Crossing the river Jantra, the Russians were reinforced by some troops encamped in an oak-wood on the opposite hills; but Mahren was in possession of the Turks. The inhabitants had for the most part made their escape, though a few were lying dead in the streets, and a woman was among the killed. Thus far, the Russian reverse was not very important; but, as we have seen, it presently assumed much more serious dimensions. The Turkish troops followed their enemy across the river under a heavy fire, and advanced towards the neighbouring hills where a sanguinary struggle took place. These heights were approached by the Turks from a gorge on the right, and were carried after a prolonged resistance, which strewed the hollow with the bodies of the Russian slain. Near the river, some forty of the Ottomans dropped seriously wounded, and were conveyed to the Stafford House ambulance in the village at the rear. But the Russian camp on the slope of the main hill was now in the hands of the assailants, and a further advance was made towards the table-land at the summit.

The Muscovites retreated, sullenly firing as they

withdrew, and losing many more men than their opponents. The Turks pursued with unwavering steadiness, and, when the last of the beaten troops had disappeared over the hill, Fuad Pasha brought up his artillery to the brow of the plateau, and opened fire against some Russian batteries which, from a considerable distance, were shelling the victorious line of the Ottomans. One of these batteries was planted on a hill close to Elena, a large part of which it masked. On the opposite side of a small valley was another battery, and a third stood further to the right. All these sent a plunging fire towards the Turks; but the advance continued without check. In a little while, the Russians at Elena were taken in flank, and, although they were strongly posted amongst hills, ravines, and copses, and were aided by entrenchments in the most favourable localities, it was found impossible, as the reader is already aware, to save Elena from capture. From one position to another the Muscovites fell back, savagely resisting the enemy at every point, but resisting in vain. At some places the struggle was maintained with desperate resolution long after it had ceased at others; but the fortune of the day could not be retrieved. Pressed in front and on the flanks, the Russians began to remove their guns into Elena, though only to find that the town itself was untenable. The retreat, which at first was orderly and composed, soon degenerated into a rout. It was evident that the day was hopelessly lost, and the troops gave way to that feeling of consternation which is natural under the circumstances. The final stand was made in a long earthwork before the camp, which stood just outside the town; and here the slaughter was terrible. But the stand was short, and rather an effort of despair than a piece of deliberate generalship. The last trench was speedily abandoned, and the last remnant of the discomfited army was in hurried flight. Before the catastrophe was reached, the Turkish commander had sent round two squadrons of cavalry to intercept the retreat along the Tirnova road, which was already overlapped by the infantry. The formal surrender of Elena took place immediately afterwards, and the success of the Ottomans was complete as far as it went, though it had not, in conformity with the original programme, included the capture of Tirnova.*

SULEIMAN PASHA DICTATING HIS ORDERS.

* *Times*, Dec. 24th, 1877.

Few acts of ferocity were committed by the Turks on this occasion; but Elena was sacked by the elated soldiery, many of whom were still further inflamed by the large stores of *raki* and other spirits which they found in the town. "It must have been a Bulgarian feast-day," said a correspondent of the *Times* who accompanied the army of Suleiman Pasha; "for in all the grocers' and bakers' shops there was holiday cake, upon which the Bashis pounced with childish delight. Now a draper's show was tapped, and the yarns and rougher goods were thrown out to be trampled under foot, while the long yards of calico and cloths were dragged forth, the pillagers chopping off with their yataghans such lengths as they could secure. From the vintners' the casks of wine were rolled into the street, and the heads stove in; bottles were hurled into the air, and came smashing down among the crowd by the score. From time to time a troop of scared pigs would come rushing into the street, hounded out of their styes by the side currents of the looters. Then there was a shout and a chase, and the poor beasts were bayoneted, or shot by rifles or revolvers recklessly fired amid the crowd. Before a silk-store lay an old Bulgar, shot through the chest, lying as he fell; and a little further, laid out stiff and straight under the projecting front of a cook's shop, was the body of a Russian, clad in shirt and drawers, clean and fine of texture, apparently the remains of some civil functionary. Here and there along the street lay bodies of Russian soldiers, and one or two Bulgarians; but they were soon so trampled and crushed that by the time I came back they were but hideous and shapeless heaps of carrion. Stretched across the street in its broadest part, and about midway, was the triumphal arch, raised by the inhabitants to greet the arrival of the Russians, bearing the inscription, 'Welcome to the deliverers of the Bulgarians!' It was but a poor structure of wood and branches, draped with pink and white calico, and very forlorn looked its withered branches and faded hangings stretched over the cruel irony of the scene beneath. Great was the struggling over the furrier's stores; but the greatest struggle was for Bulgarian woollens—the beautiful long-woolled rugs, the 'chools,' the rolls of shyak and felt."

The official bulletin of the Russians admitted, without any attempt at concealment, that serious reverses had been experienced at Mahren and Elena. The force which encountered the Turks at the former place consisted of a brigade of the Ninth Division, belonging to the Eighth Army Corps. At the beginning of the action, the Turks were opposed by not more than eight battalions, which suffered severely; but reinforcements afterwards came up. Prince Mirsky, at Elena, had part of the second brigade of the Ninth Division, which, after the defeat at Mahren, was joined by the remnants of the force flying from that village. It would appear that Suleiman had contrived, by a long series of reconnaissances and feints, to deceive his opponents as to his real designs, and to induce in them a belief that he contemplated striking in another direction. This would account for the Russians being so badly prepared to parry the blow when at length it came; but it does not excuse their keeping so poor a watch on the movements of their enemy. The disaster, however, might have been worse than it was; for the Turks did not make the best of their success, and Mirsky was able to concentrate his shattered battalions at Jakowitza, where he was speedily reinforced by troops from the army of the Czarewitch. On the 5th of December—the day following the battle—Suleiman Pasha was chiefly engaged in strengthening his position at Elena; but a distinct Turkish column, under Salek Pasha, marched from Osman Bazar towards Kesarova, on the direct road to Tirnova, when the Russians, fearing to be surrounded, fell back during the night on Djutin, after breaking down the bridge across the river. A fresh attack on Prince Mirsky was made on the afternoon of the 6th; but the Turks withdrew on receiving information that the column to their right—the force under Salek Pasha—had been driven back on Bebrova from Slataritza, where some of the Russian reinforcements had arrived. On the morning of the 12th, Suleiman Pasha, after having pushed a number of reconnaissances along the whole Russian line, attacked with his right wing the Twelfth Corps under the Grand Duke Vladimir, posted in the vicinity of Matchka. The Turks were in great strength, and the action included six assaults on the Muscovite positions, all of which were repulsed with heavy loss. Nevertheless, the issue of the engagement hung in suspense until the arrival of Russian reinforcements, when a general advance was made, and the Ottomans were driven back to Krasna, on the River Lom, which they re-crossed under a heavy fire. The loss on both sides was severe; but the most serious fact to Suleiman Pasha was that his advance, which for a moment seemed to promise such favourable results, had been changed into a retrograde movement. Elena could no longer be held by the Turks, and it was evacuated by them on the 14th of December, after being first set on fire. The Russians re-entered the place shortly afterwards; and thus ended the attempt of Suleiman Pasha to penetrate westward, and scatter the hosts of the Czarewitch. The discontinuance of the advance upon Tirnova, though immediately attributable to the pressure of the enemy's reinforcements, was due in some measure to the failure of Mehemet Ali to carry out a concerted movement. That commander had been directed by Suleiman Pasha, as Generalissimo of all the European armies, to make an attack in aid of the operations against Elena and the neighbouring positions, so that the enemy might be withheld from strengthening Tirnova with troops drawn from Gabrova and Selvi. From whatever motive, Mehemet Ali did not obey this order, and the Turks under Salek Pasha soon found themselves out-numbered, and devoid of that support which a simultaneous advance from the west would have afforded them. One cause of Turkish failures throughout the war was the absence of co-operation among the several commanders, who often seemed to be acting rather with a view to their personal ends than to the common good.

FUAD PASHA CAPTURING A GUN.

Co-operation itself was unavailing in Asia, where, as the year drew towards its last, the severity of the weather hindered all actions on an important scale. The Turkish forces were hard-pressed, not merely at Erzeroum, but elsewhere; and Dervish Pasha was compelled to withdraw his troops from their positions on the Khatzubani heights, in front of Batoum. In consequence of this movement, a small column of Russians attacked Khatzubani itself on the 28th of November, and captured the Turkish camp. In the early part of December, strong working divisions were engaged in clearing the snow from the roads over the Soghanli Dagh, to facilitate the transport of the Russian heavy ordnance to Erzeroum, so that active operations might be pursued as soon as the weather was favourable to such a purpose. In the meanwhile, typhus fever continued to spread with alarming rapidity among the forces, and the troops attacked by this terrible disease were separated from the main body, and conveyed to distant villages. Erzeroum was now invested on three sides; but it was still open towards the west, and communication with other parts of Armenia was not entirely cut off. Before the middle of December, a portion of the troops from Kars, together with the heavy guns, had reached Deve-Boyun, and the siege of the great fortress speedily commenced. The capture of Ardanutsch by General Komaroff, to which allusion has previously been made, took place on the 17th of December, and the successful occupation of several villages in the vicinity of Erzeroum rendered the isolation of that fortress more complete. Towards the end of the month, the Grand Duke Michael and General Loris Melikoff arrived before the walls with fifteen battalions and twelve siege-guns from Kars; and on the 25th Mukhtar Pasha quitted his stronghold for the position of the Kop Dagh, on the road from Erzeroum to Baiburt, in order that he might harass the enemy's rear. For this purpose he took with him four thousand men, with artillery, leaving Ismail Hakki to conduct the defence of the threatened city. But immediately afterwards Mukhtar was recalled to Constantinople, and started for the capital in the closing days of the year.

The continued success of the Russians had a marked influence on opinion among the subjects of the Czar. Although, on the whole, the war had been popular at home, a section of the people had looked upon the outbreak of hostilities with much ill-will and many serious forebodings. The views of these persons had been strengthened, and apparently justified, by the numerous reverses attendant on the Russian arms in the summer and early autumn. But the pessimists were now completely silenced by the extraordinary run of good luck which seemed to have set in steadily, both in Europe and Asia. For a time, however, the opponents of the war had a good deal to say for themselves, and they said it with much boldness. They were chiefly to be found in St. Petersburg, for the people of Moscow, Kieff, and the other old cities of Russia, were too much imbued with the patriotic Russian spirit to feel the slightest doubt that when their Czar summoned them to the field it was right that they should go there, and certain that they would win. The malcontents of St. Petersburg were more influenced by the critical habit of modern times, and they saw a hundred reasons why it would have been much wiser to let the Turks alone. The well-informed St. Petersburg correspondent of the *Times* interpreted for English readers, in a letter dated November 30th, the general arguments of the pacific party. "Though we condemn the misrule and tyranny of the Turks," said these gentlemen, "we do not think that Russia should embark in the great enterprise of Sclavonic emancipation. So gigantic a work demands material and moral resources which we do not possess. Our Chauvinists and small-beer patriots ought to look at things a little nearer home. They wish to fight for people whom they call brothers, but of whom they know little or nothing. The Sclavonic idea is still a very vague conception, and we have many home questions to which we ought to direct our attention. We have our own Herzegovinians in the person of overtaxed, uneducated peasants. Is it not ridiculous to fight for the liberty of others, when we have not yet obtained liberty for ourselves?" When the Russian armies in Turkey were defeated again and again, and it was a doubtful matter whether they would not be obliged to withdraw across the Danube, the opponents of the war asked very triumphantly what the Chauvinists thought then of the Sick Man whom they wished to bury without his consent. "Oh, you editorial heroes!" they exclaimed, "who lashed yourselves and the public into a fury, and cried out for war when there was no occasion for it, are you satisfied now? Look into the depths of your native Russia, which you do not know; look at the families whom you have made orphans; listen to the weeping which may now be heard throughout the whole country! And all this is for what? To help people who do not desire our assistance, and who are more prosperous than ourselves. The Bulgarians have suffered more from this war than they would have done from twenty years of Turkish oppression, while we have thrown ourselves back, economically and financially, for half a generation." These representations had great effect in the day of thickening disasters; but they were speedily silenced when victory again lighted on the Imperial standards. Nevertheless, the opinions of the war party had themselves undergone some change. The patriots of Moscow, and of the other historic towns, no longer talked of simply emancipating the Sclaves, and doing a work of generosity for the mere pleasure of performing it. Ambition took the place of sentiment, and it was asked what compensation Russia was to receive for the 70,000 precious lives, and the hundreds of millions of roubles, which she had sacrificed. The Russian people, it was said, must of course secure the end for which the war was undertaken; but they must also remember their own interests. They could not content themselves with a rotten peace, which would compel them in a few years to fight the battle over again. Not only must they secure the independence of Bulgaria, Bosnia, and Herzegovina, but they must at the same time obtain guarantees that that independence would be respected. Consequently, the conditions of peace must include the free passage of the Dardanelles, and the annexation of Kars, Ardahan, and Batoum.

The opinion of the anti-war party, that a vast amount of misgovernment existed in Russia, which should be reformed before the Russians undertook to emancipate other nations, revealed the wide diffusion of political discontent which recent years have developed in Russia. Not merely has that feeling found expression in the plots of secret societies, bent on effecting a revolution of the most extreme and sweeping nature, but the press itself has lent its aid, notwithstanding the censorship of the Russian police, to disseminate the same views throughout the whole mass of Muscovite society. When it has been found impossible to advocate such ideas in Russia itself, they have been put forth by Russians in foreign lands, either in the hope of influencing European opinion, or with a view to smuggling the prohibited writings across the frontiers of the Czar's dominions. A pamphlet, published at Geneva during the year 1877, and written by M. Dragomanoff, formerly a professor at the Kieff University, bears singular evidence to the bitterness with which some Russians can regard the institutions and habits of their native land. "What we consider revolting in Turkey," said this writer, "exists equally in Russia. The Russian people are exhausted by unjust imposts—by a system of taxation, superannuated and long since condemned, which lays all the charges of the State on the poor peasant, who has become a Russian Rayah. The agents of the Government possess and exercise a most arbitrary power. There is an utter absence of guarantees for the security and liberty of the subject; and, moreover, Russia is beset with an amount of religious and national intolerance not to be found in Turkey. These ills are so old in Russia, we have got so much accustomed to them, that we regard them with almost perfect indifference, although they are just as bad as the Bulgarian atrocities which shock us." M. Dragomanoff went on to say that there had been agrarian troubles in various parts of Russia, similar to those which had broken out in the Herzegovina, and that they had produced a chronic famine in many rural districts. During the past few years, thousands of persons had been confined in deadly casemates, or transported to distant places, and many barbarous sentences had been pronounced in State prosecutions. A girl of seventeen had been condemned to hard labour in the mines for selling one of the little Socialist pamphlets which circulate by thousands in the west. Five newspapers had been suspended, or entirely put out of existence, although at the time of the Cretan insurrection Prince Gortschakoff affirmed that the press was free in Russia. The Polish language had been excluded from the tribunals of Poland. The prisons were full of persons dissatisfied with the existing laws. The independence of the Universities had been destroyed, and young women of the Mohammedan persuasion were forbidden to exercise the profession of governess. Wherever he turned his eyes, M. Dragomanoff saw nothing but matter for reprehension and discontent. He would not allow that the Russian Empire had any mission to teach the nations how to live; on the contrary, he very fervently denied that his country, in its then condition, was entitled to talk of carrying the principles of civilization and freedom into the dominions of the Sultan. "In a word," said the ex-professor of Kieff, "a State where a frightful administrative despotism dominates under the form of autocracy, where class privileges still exist in the system of taxation, where the policy of forcing everything to become Russian reigns paramount, where the dominant Church is supported by the police, where there exists no trace of individual liberty—such a State cannot support the cause of freedom and self-government among the Sclaves of Turkey. The influence of such a State on the Sclaves delivered from the Turkish *régime* cannot be otherwise than fatal, and can only create among the Servians, Bulgarians, &c., a hatred which will easily extend from the Russian Government to the Russian nation itself. . . . Russian society, brought up by such a Government, is not better than Sclave society, as was proved by the volunteers who went to support the Servians against the Turks. This volunteer movement, thanks to the enthusiasm of the Russian public, who are easily aroused, was welcomed by the press as a proof that Russian society had arrived at maturity, and that it was capable of acting by itself. Well, let us see what principles, what habits, what examples, the 'ripe Russian society' took with it to Servia. The volunteers were forgiven their drunkenness on account of their incontestable bravery; for the same motive, people overlooked the irregularity of their pecuniary dealings; but other manners and customs showed themselves. Most of these volunteers were officers who had been used to unlimited control and violence in Poland and the Caucasus. Consequently, during the few months of the Servian war, there arose on the banks of the Danube, the Save, and the Morava, a system of cuffing and kicking, the like of which was never seen in Russia, even in the most remote districts. Soldiers and peasants, students and professors, Servians and Bulgarians, all were subjected to the same mode of civilization. It was in this way that the Russians sought to teach the Servians and

Bulgarians the art of war; and not only our infantry officers, but also our journalists, did not appear to be aware that the Servians, and even the Bulgarians, had, under the complicated yoke of the Turks, preserved a sentiment of personal liberty and inviolability much deeper than what we feel. They did not understand that, thanks to the primitive state of Ottoman tyranny, there was much more freedom and equality in Turkey than in Russia. The Servians and Bulgarians must have

RUSSIAN PRISONERS ON THE WAY TO CONSTANTINOPLE.

looked on our volunteers as Russian Bashi-Bazouks, and it may now be said that they know what the Russian Turk is like. With these facts before us, what must be thought of our countrymen who still talk of delivering other Sclaves—the Sclaves of Austria, Hungary, Prussia, Roumania, &c.? So long as the Turkish system exists in Russia, it is simply ridiculous to demand the deliverance of 'our Sclave brethren,' who are far less enslaved than we are."*

Views similar to these were expressed in the *Contemporary Review* for December, 1877, by no less illustrious a man than Louis Kossuth, who contributed to that periodical an article on "Russian Aggression, as specially affecting Austria-Hungary and Turkey." After confessing his personal obligations to the Porte, which had saved him from the vengeance of Austria and Russia in 1849, M. Kossuth urged Austria to maintain the independence of Turkey as a barrier against the extension of Russia, and earnestly exhorted the Austro-Hungarians not to accept additional territory for themselves as a bribe for becoming tacit accomplices in the dismemberment of the Turkish Empire. The Viennese Cabinet, he observed, had always considered that, whenever the Russians committed robbery, Austria must rob as well. This had been done in the last century, when Poland was partitioned; and the policy of Vienna was unchanged. "As to Russia," said M. Kossuth, "it is impossible not to feel indignation when we see that the Power which rose by trampling down freedom, from the Vistula to Behring Straits, covers its dangerous schemes with the veil of humanity, and increases continually the giant stature of its power by systematic consistency and pitiless cruelty." Russia, in the view of this distinguished politician, was using the Christian nationalities as the instruments of her own ambition, and that to the injury

* *Standard*, April 26th, 1878.

RUSSIAN CAMP BEFORE PLEVNA.

of the nationalities themselves. As far as the Porte was concerned, he remarked, Servia was a free country, even more independent than Hungary was of Austria; but she was not free with regard to Russia. The Servians were driven into revolt against their Suzerain by the action of Russian agents, and Servia was at that moment a vassal of Russia. The Hungarians had been accused of fearing the advent of freedom to their neighbours, the Sclavonians. M. Kossuth denied that they were afraid of liberty; but they did not want to see the Sclavonian nations fettered to the Russian yoke. Such a result would have a tendency to enslave Hungary as well, and to prepare for her the fate of Poland. The Russian Emperor had written on his banner, "The Sclavonic Cause;" but Pan-Sclavism had substituted race for nationality. The Turkish Empire was attacked first; the Hungarians and the Austrians would come next. The Muscovite papers had proclaimed as much; and thus Pan-Sclavism would develop into Pansclavo-Czarism. The remedy for this evil, in the opinion of Kossuth, was to be found in an alliance between the Austrian and Turkish Empires; but he seems to have had little faith in such an alliance being established.

In Constantinople, the recent misfortunes to the Turkish arms were received with that quietude which can alone result from the spirit of fatalism encouraged by the Mohammedan religion. When the Russians first crossed the Balkans, in the month of July, there had been a momentary exhibition of fear and anxiety; and for a little while it was apprehended that something like a revolutionary outbreak, of a savage and fanatical character, might take place. But the agitation speedily passed, and by December the Turks had long settled down again into their usual mood of apathy. Even the fall of Kars did not greatly stagger them. They comforted themselves with the reflection that, after all, the possession of Kars was not an important matter, so long as Erzeroum remained to the Faithful. They considered that Kars was a stronghold which they were fated to lose. They had lost it in 1829, and again in 1855; and yet, somehow or other, it had come back to them. Moreover, it was pointed out by a writer from Constantinople that, even if the people had been excited by this loss, they had no means of giving vent to their feelings, since they were wanting in all those organizations that are supplied in other countries by clubs and societies. The Softas of Constantinople had during the last few months been almost entirely suppressed: many had been imprisoned, some had been banished, others had become voluntary exiles, while numbers had entered the army, and were by that time either dead, or face to face with the Russian. The few revolutionary spirits left in the capital were kept in subjection by the rigours of the state of siege. Any man suspected of disaffection might be quietly removed, without his most intimate friends knowing what had become of him; so that feelings of discontent which may possibly have existed were stifled by the pressure of authority.* Still, it may be doubted whether there was any wide diffusion of revolutionary sentiment. The Civic Guard which the Porte had recently established was in every sense of the term a popular body; and if the Government had been generally regarded with hatred or contempt, here was the weapon which might have struck it down.

In the hour of her misfortune, Turkey found but little sympathy in England. She had her friends, it is true; but her enemies were more active. In the course of December, several public addresses were made on the Eastern Question; but the advocates of a good understanding with Russia were more frequently heard than those who would have brought that Power to a sharp account. Sir Henry Havelock, the member for Sunderland, and son of the celebrated General Havelock, who so nobly distinguished himself during the Indian Mutiny, addressed his constituents on the 20th of December; and, having recently returned from the East, where he had for a short period acted as one of the correspondents of the *Times*, his observations on the existing condition of affairs acquired a greater importance than they might otherwise have possessed. His opinions had been considerably modified by personal experience of Turkey, and he now confidently declared there was no truth in the allegation that British interests were involved in the contest with Russia. The actual risk to our commerce, he affirmed, would be while it was on its way between Malta and Port Said. He admitted that there would be a certain amount of hazard to our Eastern commerce if Russia, or any other Power, were to seize the whole navigation of the Black Sea, and afterwards to obtain possession of one side of the Dardanelles, so as to be in a position to open and close that passage at will, and to exclude us from it. But in point of fact Russia had never asked for either bank of the Dardanelles; indeed, it was believed that she desired to dismantle the forts, and leave the passage free to every one. If at any time Turkey were compelled by Russia to close the Dardanelles against our ships of war, we should still have our remedy by purchasing the island of Mitylene, so that our fleet could face

* *Times*, Dec. 17th, 1877.

the entrance to the straits. Sir Henry Havelock argued strongly against England going to war in favour of Turkey, or even sending an army to Gallipoli; and he denounced with considerable warmth the atrocities to the Russian wounded of which the Turks were accused. He did not believe it possible to produce one authenticated instance of violence, even in a minor degree, committed by any of the Russian officers or soldiers during their occupation of the Turkish provinces; while, on the other hand, the Turks had never attempted to restrain the barbarism of their irregular troops, nor of their regular forces either. He had seen long lines of Russian ambulance-carts, two thousand at a time, coming from the scene of action, with wounded Russians and Turks lying side by side, the latter being received into the hospitals, and treated with the same care as the former. But the Turks killed and mutilated the wounded Russians as they lay upon the field of battle.

That Sir Henry Havelock greatly exaggerated the humanity of the Russians, and placed entirely out of view many facts to their discredit, the readers of this History do not need to be told; but one or two circumstances, as affecting the conduct of both sides, may here be mentioned in addition to what has appeared in earlier Chapters. It was frequently said that no Russian prisoners were to be found with any of the Turkish armies after a victory; but there is direct evidence to the contrary.* After the battle at Elena, the *Times* correspondent with Suleiman Pasha spoke of two hundred and fifty captives, who do not appear to have been ill-treated. Other war-correspondents of the same journal frequently referred to Russian prisoners in the hands of the Turkish Army of the Lom; and, although it is undoubtedly true that the wounded were often slain and mangled on the ground where they fell, it is going a great deal too far to assume that such was the invariable practice. On the other hand, the Russians themselves are not free from blame on this very score. A correspondent of the *Daily News*, accompanying the Russians in Asia, said, under date of August 31st:—"The internecine character of the fighting is beyond doubt. Two sharp engagements took place on the 18th and 25th instant. I have seen the official records of the dead and wounded; but no mention of prisoners is made, and no wounded hostile soldier has been brought to the hospitals, although our skirmishing lines had passed theirs in the centre. This fact leads me to suppose that short-handed reprisals for so many outrages committed on the Russian wounded and prisoners are now taken by their comrades." Retaliation was made the apology for these as for so many other acts of ferocity; but the records of the Crimean War justify a doubt whether the Russians waited for even this excuse. Although, in the course of the late war, they may not have been stained by the sheer barbarism which so often disgraced the Turks, it is beyond a question that they committed many acts of refined and cold-blooded cruelty, which deprive them of any right to be considered the champions of humane observances. In the closing month of 1877, they were guilty of a most horrible deed in Armenia. Two thousand sick and wounded had been left behind at Kars when Mukhtar Pasha made his retreat from that fortress. In the dead of winter, and while the ground was covered with snow, these unhappy men were expelled from the hospitals, and forced to march, with the thermometer twenty degrees below zero, all the way to Erzeroum. It was urged in justification of General Loris Melikoff that he had sent notice to the Turkish authorities of his intention to perform this act; but the Porte declined to give its approval to the measure, and in a circular despatch, dated the 12th of December, implored the Powers to use their influence with the Russian Government to change its design, and prevent the prisoners from being "doomed to certain death." If the men could have been removed with safety, the military authorities at Erzeroum would doubtless have been delighted to receive them, as they would have added materially to the fighting capacity of the garrison; but it was only too clear that their removal at that inclement season would entail a fearful mortality. The measure was contrary to the provisions of the sixth article of the Convention of Geneva, which stipulates that belligerents shall be bound to give proper care to all wounded or sick prisoners of war; but the captives were removed, and a very large proportion died in the attempt to reach Erzeroum.† On behalf of the Russians it was alleged that the Turkish soldiers left voluntarily, and performed their fatal march across the snow because they desired to do so; but the statement is simply incredible.

Much has been done of late years to soften the rigour of war; but the savage spirit of former ages still bursts forth with uncontrolled fury. The principles of the Geneva Convention have yet to penetrate the minds of men, and to incorporate themselves with the policy of nations. Most countries now take greater care of their

* The facts were acutely pointed out by Mr. A. R. Fairfield in a letter to the *Daily News* of December 29th, 1877.

† *Morning Post*, Dec. 25th, 1877.

own wounded than was usual a generation or two ago; but the wounded of the enemy fare badly in many instances. Perhaps it is too much to hope that this will ever be entirely remedied; for if we arrive at such a height of humane enlightenment, it is difficult to believe that there will be any wars at all. Yet it is to be hoped that, if wars are to continue, the better practice of modern times with respect to the belligerent's own soldiers will be extended in some degree to those of his opponent. That an advance in this direction has already been made, it would be disingenuous to deny; but the Russo-Turkish War proved how numerous and how terrible are the exceptions.

CHAPTER XLV.

Position of Osman Pasha in the First Week of December—Plevna invulnerable to Assault—Inability of the Turkish Garrison to escape—The Last Month of the Investment—Preparations for a Sortie—The Russians on the Alert—Abandonment of Redoubts by the Turks on the Morning of December 10th—Movement of Ottoman Troops towards the Bridge over the Vid—Furious Encounter with the Russo-Roumanian Army—Total Defeat of the Endeavour to break through—Negotiations for a Surrender—Interview of General Skobeleff with Tefvik Bey—Capitulation of Osman Pasha—General Features of the Situation—Osman Pasha and the Grand Duke Nicholas—The Emperor at Plevna—Losses of the Turks and Russians—The Surrender Premature—Motives by which Osman was probably influenced—Sufferings of the People of Plevna—Frightful Condition of the Hospitals—Brutality of the Bulgarians—Ghastly Struggles for Food—Osman Pasha's Life at Plevna during the Siege—Heroic Conduct of the Army and its Commander—Letter of Osman Pasha on the Surrender—Russian Rejoicings—Military Strength of the Two Belligerents—Effects of the Fall of Plevna—Gloomy Prospects of the Turks towards the Close of the Year.

In the first week of December, Osman Pasha was at bay, yet he was not quite reduced to the last extremity. The only question was as to how long his remaining provisions would last; for the strength of the fortress was such that the Russians had small chance of taking it by assault, and were therefore content to wait until famine had done its work. Cold and hunger were beginning to tell upon the garrison; but behind his walls Osman was secure from direct attack. The line of forts was tremendous, and the Russians had made very little approach towards reducing them. Their allies, the Roumanians, had, it is true, taken the first Grivica Redoubt; but the second of the same name was still in the hands of the Turks, and it entirely commanded its neighbour. General Skobeleff had pushed his own positions to within two hundred yards of the Turkish works on the southern side of Plevna; but he had not been permanently successful in seizing any of the adversary's forts. What the Russians had really accomplished was to put such a girdle round Osman's position that the chances of escape were reduced to the very lowest. In every direction were the most formidable obstacles to any attempt to break through the circle of investment. Supposing the Turkish commander to make a dash at the Roumanian line in the direction of the Vid, he would be met by a bristling series of trenches and redoubts, and, if he succeeded in passing those, would soon be compelled by the Danube to turn either to the right or to the left, in both of which cases he would be encountered by the forces of the enemy. The road to Sophia was effectually blocked by the Imperial Guard, who were strongly posted in that direction. On the Loftcha road, Skobeleff was planted in the midst of a great array of trenches and earthworks; and at every other point were large and well-appointed bodies of troops, which there was little probability of Osman being able to evade or overcome. Thus the prospects of the beleaguered Pasha wore an aspect of almost unmitigated gloom. If he remained, he would ere long be reduced to the fiercest extremities of hunger. If he endeavoured to escape, he would in all likelihood be captured by an enemy whose forces were much greater than his own.

The weakest part of the investing line was towards Radisovo, on the south-east of Plevna; but even there, sixty-two guns were ready, in the early days of December, to sweep the intervening ground. The fire of cannon and of rifles was being continually interchanged between the besiegers and the besieged, and in some places the parapets of the Turkish works were injured, but not to any serious extent. From time to time, animated sorties were made by the Ottomans, who were always repulsed with heavy loss; and, on two occasions about the middle of November, General Skobeleff, who always exposed himself in the most reckless manner, and who was popularly said to bear a charmed life, was wounded, though but slightly. The head-quarters of this commander were indeed so much affected by the Turkish fire that it was found necessary to remove them from Brestovec to Uzendol, three-quarters of a mile off. But weeks passed by, and nothing of serious moment occurred either within or without Plevna, except the steady augmentation of the Russian forces, and the gradual diminution of the Turkish stock of provisions. Both sides were waiting, but the one with far greater hopefulness than the other. The Russians were looking forward, with a degree of confidence which could afford to dispense with hurry, to the approaching exhaustion of the enemy. Osman Pasha was still expecting the arrival of an army of relief. He knew little of what was going on in the outer world; but he must have been aware that efforts were being made for his succour, and, though day after day slipped by without any sign of deliverance, the hope had not entirely departed even at the beginning of December. Food, however, was getting short; and if anything was to be done, it must be done rapidly. But at that very time Mehemet Ali was held in check by the forces under Gourko, and Suleiman was vainly endeavouring to reach Plevna by way of Tirnova.

By the 7th of December, Osman Pasha appears to have considered the position desperate, and to have resolved, as a last resource, on endeavouring to break through. The knowledge of this fact reached the enemy's camp on the night of that day, and preparations were immediately made for defeating such an attempt. The trenches were kept full of troops; the outposts were trebled; and the several commanders were ordered to be on the alert. It was expected that something would be done on the following day; but the 8th passed off in perfect quietude, and the 9th was equally uneventful. The Russians, as usual, bombarded the forts with their siege-guns; but the Turks had for some time ceased to reply. About noon on the 9th, snow began to fall heavily, and in a few hours the country all round was one vast expanse of white. In the evening, a spy came into Skobeleff's head-quarters, with the information that Osman had issued three days' rations to his troops, together with a hundred and fifty cartridges, and a new pair of sandals, to each man. It should here be explained that the foot-gear of the Turkish soldier, in numerous instances, consists of nothing more than a fragment of linen, round which is wrapped a piece of untanned leather, roughly fastened by thongs of the same material. The contrivance is a very poor substitute for a boot, and does not withstand any large amount of wear. The issue of new sandals was therefore one of the most convincing proofs that a movement of the troops was about to take place, and the watchfulness of the Russians was redoubled. At ten o'clock, P.M., another spy arrived, with news that the Turkish troops were concentrating near the bridge over the Vid. On the further side of Plevna, a great many lights were observed moving about, and, as this was an unusual circumstance, it seemed to betoken an immediate attempt to break out. Nevertheless, the dreary night wore on without anything further being detected. The snow at length ceased; but dark clouds drifted across the sky, and the keen wind was now and again burdened by showers of sleet. At three o'clock on the morning of Monday, the 10th, a third spy reported that the Krishine redoubts were being abandoned; and on Skobeleff sending forward a body of troops, with directions to feel their way cautiously, this was discovered to be the fact. The positions were then seized by the Russians, and at once put in a state of defence, in case the Turks, being repulsed in their attempt to get away, should endeavour to recapture them.

The dim wintry morning broke slowly over the snow, and Osman Pasha put his troops in motion for the supreme effort. He had during the night abandoned all his positions, from Grivica to the Green Hill taken by Skobeleff on the 9th of November, and had concentrated the greater part of his army on the further side of the Vid, which he had crossed by means of five bridges—the permanent stone bridge, and four temporary structures. The river flows at some little distance west of Plevna, and the design was to gain the shelter of Widdin, lying on the Danube in the north-western part of Bulgaria. The Turkish commander took with him about three batteries of artillery, and a train of five or six hundred carriages drawn by bullocks; and the main attack was directed against the positions held by the Grenadiers north of the Sophia road. Extending as far as the vicinity of Opanes, the line of the Grenadiers was at that point joined by the Roumanians; but Osman seems to have considered that he should encounter less opposition than proved to be the case. Desperate indeed was the attempt which the heroic defender of Plevna was now engaged in making; but it was his last and only chance. His men advanced under cover of the bullock-waggons, which afforded excellent protection until the animals were either killed or scared into flight. In a little while, however, the battle became too wild and furious for either belligerent to avail himself of shelter. The noise of a gigantic contest—a contest of heroes on both sides—tore the heavy December air, and rolled over hill, and valley, and plain, in waves of reverberating thunder. "The country behind Plevna," said the late Mr. MacGahan, writing to the *Daily News*, "is a wide open plain, into which the gorge leading up to Plevna opens out like a tunnel. The plain is bounded on the Plevna side by steep rocky bluffs or cliffs, along whose foot flows the Vid. From these cliffs, for a distance of two miles, burst here and there, in quick, irregular succession, angry spurts of flame, that flashed, and disappeared, and flashed out again. It was the artillery-fire of the Turks and Russians, which appeared intermingled. The smoke, running round in a circle towards the Vid, rose against the heavy clouds that hung right up on the horizon, while low on the ground burst forth continuous balls of flame, that rent the blackness of the clouds like flashes of lightning. Through the covering of smoke could be seen angry spits of fire, thick as fireflies on a tropical night. Now and then, through an irregular curving stream of fire, we had indistinct glimpses of bodies of men hurrying to and fro, horses, cattle, carriages, running across the plain; and, above all, the infernal, crashing roll of the infantry-fire, and the deep booming of more than a hundred guns."

TURKISH SOLDIERS BEGGING BREAD.

Finding the way too strongly barred in the direction of Opanes, Osman turned his attention to another point, and personally headed an attack on the Russian positions near Gorny Etropol. With loud shouts and irresistible impetus, the Ottomans bore down upon the line of trenches held by the Sibrersky or Siberian Regiment, swept over them, entered the battery beyond, and, after bayoneting the gunners and their officers almost to a man, took possession of the conquered works. The Sibrersky Regiment had been almost annihilated; the first circle of investment was broken in, and even the second was partially carried. But a third lay beyond, and this the Turks never reached. For the Russians, seeing that

THE LAST SORTIE FROM PLEVNA.

matters were beginning to look grave, exerted their utmost powers to repel the threatened danger, and defeat the enemy's design. They opened a tremendous artillery-fire upon the captured works, and upon the reserves drawn up in the rear, which were much exposed. The bombardment was maintained for more than an hour, and the first brigade of Grenadiers was then ordered up to retake the positions. These troops were commanded by General Strukoff, of the Emperor's Staff, and advanced in splendid style towards the scene of conflict. A desperate hand-to-hand fight ensued, and the Turks, who clung to the captured guns with deadly resolution, fell in large numbers. The earthworks were speedily retaken, and the head of Osman's column of attack was turned back on its supports. The Roumanians now prepared to move against the Turkish right flank, while the Russians holding the Brestovec line of heights advanced towards Osman's left wing. The valley of the Vid, on the western side of the river, was darkened by the smoke of that fierce contest, which gave an added gloom to the leaden December sky, livid with cloud and mist. A fiery storm of shells poured into the Turkish ranks from the hills on the opposite side of this valley, and the men at length fell back, and crowded towards the river, which they re-crossed, getting as speedily as possible under cover of the banks, where they resumed their fire. The battle continued at long range for between three and four hours longer; but the sortie was virtually at an end when the attack on the first two lines was repulsed. The Russians apprehended another attempt to break through, but the Turks saw the hopelessness of the endeavour. Nevertheless, the artillery continued to blaze forth, and the two belligerents looked keenly at each other, wondering what would next ensue.

About noon, the firing began to diminish on both sides, and in a little while stopped entirely. A strange and almost startling silence crept over the field of battle, and the smoke, no longer augmented by fresh discharges, drifted slowly away upon the sluggish air. A pause of half an hour followed, during which the Russians kept close watch, lest the sortie should break forth again. Suddenly, however, a white flag was seen waving from the road leading around the cliffs beyond the bridge. A great shout went up from the Russian army the moment the flag was recognised; for it was accepted as a token that the defence of Plevna was at an end, that the sortie was finally repulsed, and that Osman Pasha and all his forces were prepared to surrender. The noise of the shouting, says the correspondent who witnessed this great scene, swept over the dreary plain, and was re-echoed by the sullen, rugged cliffs that overhung the road. Immediately afterwards, a Turkish officer came riding over the bridge, with a white flag in his hand. He approached General Ganetsky, who was in command of the Grenadiers; but that officer sent him back, with instructions to require some one of the rank of a Pasha. General Skobeleff, with thirty or forty companions, then galloped down the road towards the bridge, until close to a large number of Turkish soldiers who were massed on the other bank of the river. White handkerchiefs were displayed by way of signal, and this was answered from the Turkish side by the waving of a piece of muslin attached to a flagstaff. Under cover of white flags, two officers crossed the bridge towards the Russians, and stated that Osman himself was coming out to negotiate the terms of surrender. This was an unexpected announcement, and one which created the liveliest interest. The Russian officers agreed that Osman had acquitted himself like a thorough soldier, and had made an heroic defence. Skobeleff pronounced him the greatest general of the age, as he had saved the honour of his country. "I will proffer him my hand, and tell him so," he added. It was settled that the troops must present arms, and that the Turkish commander should be respectfully received. The scene of the expected interview was characterised by all the horrors of war. The ground had been ploughed into ridges by the Russian fire, and the bodies of dead and wounded Turks, and of mangled horses and oxen, lay thickly around, intermingled with shattered carts, spent balls, and exploded shells.

After a rather long pause, two horsemen were seen approaching, under the usual protection of a white flag. The principal of the new-comers proved to be Tefvik Bey, Chief of the Staff to Osman Pasha—a man about thirty-five years of age, presenting no appearance of having suffered from the rigours of captivity in Plevna. The Russians saluted as this officer rode up, and after a moment's silence he began to speak in French, though with some hesitation, as if he felt embarrassed in delivering his painful message. Osman Pasha, he said, was wounded, but he did not know whether seriously or not. "Where is his Excellency?" he was asked. "There," he replied, pointing to a small house overlooking the road beyond the bridge. Then came another pause, during which neither side seemed to know what next to say or do. Tefvik Bey did not intimate that he had come to negotiate a surrender; and had he done so, there was no officer present on the side of the Russians who was competent to treat with him.

General Skobeleff stammered out, "Is there anybody you would like to see? With whom do you wish to speak?" But still Tefvik Bey sat silently on his horse, and Skobeleff, fairly driven to despair, at length said, "General Ganetsky is in command here, and will arrive presently, in case you would like to speak to him." Tefvik Bey simply nodded in reply; but it appears that he is habitually of a taciturn nature, and that on Russians were standing, and many thousands were congregated on the cliffs, not more than fifty yards off. Had treachery been intended, it might easily have been carried out, and there was a degree of mystery about the circumstances which justified some apprehension. But the Turks were acting in good faith, and it was not long before this was made sufficiently apparent. In a little while, General Ganetsky came up, and, together with

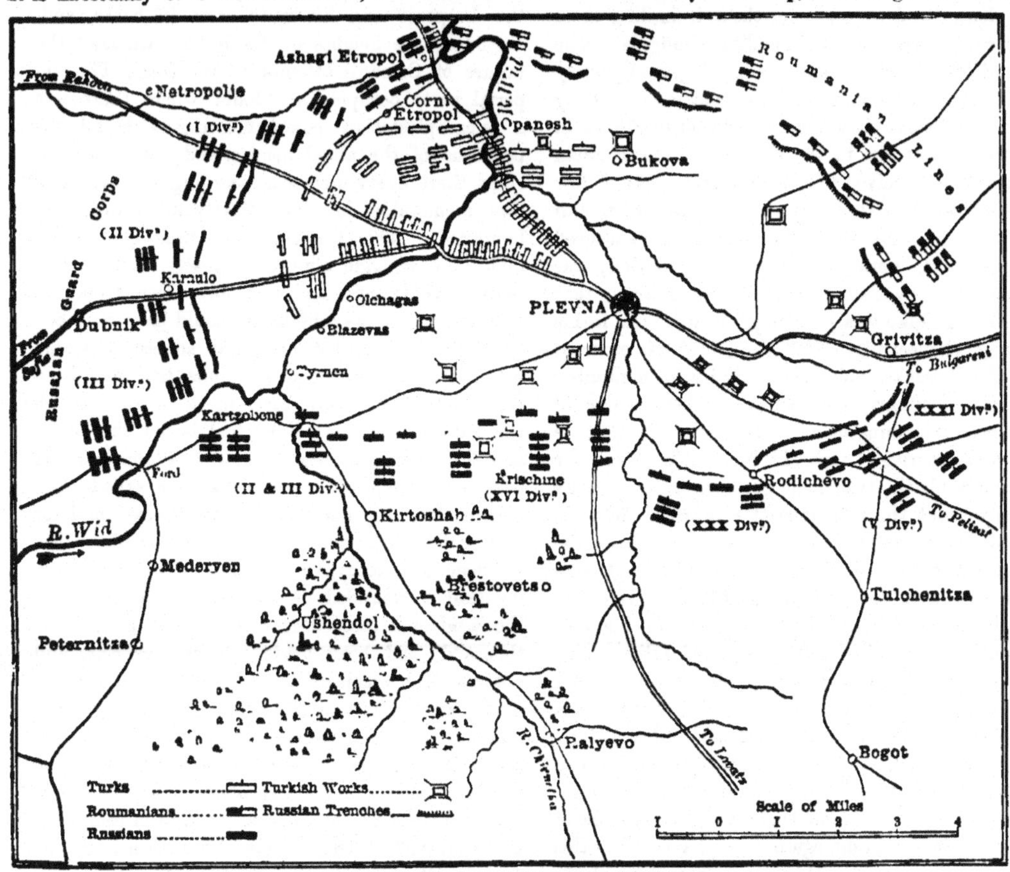

PLAN OF THE LAST SORTIE FROM PLEVNA.

the present occasion he was suffering from great emotion. Some of the Russian officers tried to converse with him by praising his Commander-in-Chief; but not a word was to be extracted from his lips.

The situation was embarrassing, but was presently relieved by the arrival of General Strukoff, who was empowered to enter into negotiations with the Turkish General. Tefvik was then asked if he had authority from Osman Pasha to treat for a surrender. He replied that he had not, and shortly afterwards rode back across the bridge for further instructions. Some of the Turks came up, with arms in their hands, to the spot where the General Strukoff and some other officers, crossed the bridge towards the house where Osman Pasha was lying wounded. The conference between the representatives of the two belligerents did not last more than a few minutes; for the surrender was unconditional, and there was but little to arrange. Osman Pasha was in fact so utterly beaten that he had no choice but to place himself absolutely at the disposal of the victors. To make his sortie, he had been compelled to abandon all his fortified positions about the town of Plevna. These were now occupied by the Russians, and to regain them was impossible. The forces of his enemy were three times as large as his own, and they were closing in upon him with a stricture like that of the rattlesnake.

The interview with Osman Pasha took place about two o'clock in the afternoon, and an hour later all the Turkish soldiers had laid down their arms. They had done this in the most literal sense of the term, each man depositing his rifle in the mud where he was standing. "The ground was littered with arms," says the *Daily News* correspondent, "and we rode over them, trampling them under our horses' feet, and spoiling hundreds." The Grand Duke Nicholas and his Staff arrived shortly after the conclusion of the capitulation; but by that time Osman Pasha had driven off to Plevna in a carriage sent him by the Emperor. The Russian Prince was received with cheers, and spoke a few soldierly words to the troops, who greeted them with acclamation. He then rode towards the captured fortress, and, while pursuing his way thither, was encountered by Osman Pasha, who, hearing that the Grand Duke was following, turned back in his carriage to meet him. The fallen chief was escorted by fifty Cossacks, and close behind were a number of Turkish officers, mounted on ponies—nearly all of them very young men. "The Grand Duke rode up to the carriage," says Mr. MacGahan, "and for some seconds the two chiefs gazed into each other's faces without the utterance of a word. Then the Grand Duke stretched out his hand, and shook the hand of Osman Pasha heartily, and said:—'I compliment you on your defence of Plevna. It is one of the most splendid military feats in history.' Osman Pasha smiled sadly, rose painfully to his feet in spite of his wound, said something which I could not hear, and then re-seated himself. The Russian officers all cried 'Bravo!' 'Bravo!' repeatedly, and all saluted. Prince Charles, who had arrived, rode up, and repeated unwittingly almost every word of the Grand Duke, and likewise shook hands. Osman Pasha again rose and bowed—this time in grim silence. He wore a loose blue cloak, with no apparent mark on it to designate his rank, and a red fez. He is a large, strongly-built man, the lower part of whose face is covered with a short black beard, without a streak of grey. He has a large Roman nose, and black eyes. The face is a strong face, with energy and determination stamped on every feature—yet a tired, wan face also, with lines on it that hardly were graven so deep, I fancy, five months ago; and with a sad, enduring, thoughtful look out of the black eyes. 'It is a grand face,' exclaimed Colonel Gaillard, the French military *attaché*. 'I was almost afraid of seeing him, lest my expectation should be disappointed; but he more than fulfils my ideal.' 'It is the face of a great military chieftain,' said young Skobeleff. 'I am glad to have seen him. Osman Ghazi he is, and Osman the Victorious he will remain, in spite of his surrender.'" Skobeleff has much that is chivalrous in his nature, and his recognition of the Turkish commander's merits was generous and ample.

The noise of the great battle had aroused every one in the Russian head-quarters at Bogot; and telegrams were at once sent to Poradim, whence the Emperor and his suite came in haste, and, ascending the heights of Radisovo, witnessed the failure of Osman's attempt to get free. The Imperial party occupied a redoubt where there was a telegraph-station communicating with all the positions of the allied armies, and despatches arrived there every moment, recording the events of that memorable day immediately after they had happened. The Emperor was thus enabled to follow the struggle almost as closely as if he had been present; and he must have seen from the commencement that the battle could have only one termination, and that his great adversary would inevitably be crushed in the toils that had been cast around him. The attempt to break through the Russo-Roumanian lines had lasted six hours, and the only result was to show how hopeless had been the movement. The Turks had saved their honour, but they had saved nothing else; and for this satisfaction they had paid a terrible price. Between four and five thousand of their number lay dead or wounded on the field. Twenty-seven thousand men (according to some accounts, forty thousand) had been made prisoners of war, and not one had escaped through the Russian lines. Sixty cannon, with all the transport-train and the bullocks attached to the waggons, were in the hands of the allies. Plevna itself was in the grasp of the enemy; the greatest obstacle to the southward advance of the Russians had been removed; and against this tremendous accumulation of success the Ottomans had nothing to set on their own side of the account, beyond the reflection that they had done their duty in the highest spirit of heroism, and had at any rate delayed a triumph which it was not within their power to avert. On the side of the Russians, the killed and wounded numbered 1,500 men, of whom the greater number were in the Grenadier Regiment of the Grand Duke Nicholas, which retook the captured redoubts, and drove back the Turkish column of attack. The Roumanian losses were comparatively slight; and altogether it cannot be said that the allies paid dearly for their success, considering the magnitude of the achievement, and the importance of the results which would probably flow from it.

Osman Pasha had three weeks' provisions still on hand when he evacuated Plevna, and in the transport-train of his army were rations for ten days. Yoked to the waggons that accompanied the sortie were at least a thousand head of cattle, and there were also several horses which might have been killed for food. It seems, therefore, rather strange that Osman should not have postponed his attempt until a later period. Had he held his position for another three weeks, the main body of the Russian army would have been prevented from crossing the Balkans for a similar period, and this would have been a very important gain for the general defence. Mehemet Ali, or his successor, would have had more time for organizing the army which had been formed for the relief of Plevna, and the southward march of the Russians might have been impossible until the ensuing spring, by which time it is not unlikely that the whole aspect of affairs would have been changed. Several reasons have been alleged as those by which the Turkish commander was influenced. According to one of these, the sortie was precipitated by the breaking out of a violent epidemic among the garrison. This malady is said to have had the character of the plague, and it was feared that in a few days it might destroy the whole population of the town, as well as the army. It is also urged that Osman really hoped to cleave his way through the Russian lines, and that the sortie was not merely intended to save his military honour from the disgrace of a tame capitulation. He appears to have supposed that Gourko's departure with the Guard had so weakened the Russian environment to the north-west as to offer a fair chance of success. Gourko had indeed taken with him more than 30,000 of the best troops that Russia possesses; but their places had been supplied by others, and this qualifying fact was unknown to Osman. A third reason for the sortie occurring when it did has been discovered in an order stated to have been received from Constantinople, to the effect that Osman was to cut his way out of Plevna at all hazards.* Whether such an order was actually sent, is far from certain; but it is not impossible, when we consider that the Seraskierate must by that time have been aware that neither Mehemet Ali nor Suleiman Pasha had any immediate chance of relieving Plevna. In any case, the result was unfortunate. Osman Pasha, there can be no doubt, acted for the best, and with every belief that he was serving his country; but the sortie of December 10th was in truth a most happy circumstance for Russia. Todleben had succeeded in creating round Plevna a series of fortified positions as strong as the town itself; but he was not likely to carry Osman's works by storm. The attempt to break through gave him the very opportunity he wanted, and Plevna fell into his hands several days before there was any absolute necessity for its surrender.

* *Daily News*, Dec. 17th, 1877.

The suffering in Plevna had for some weeks past been extreme. Dead bodies lay about the streets, and men were not available to bury them. The mortality accordingly increased with every week, and many hundred sick and wounded were in the hospitals, with scarcely any medical advice or trained attendance. Hunger, cold, and disease were doing their fell work, and mental depression, resulting from the gloomy situation, added to the malefic influences of the time. "Plevna," said a correspondent of the *Daily News*, writing on December 17th, "is full of horrors, and after the turmoil of the last four months the complete silence seems strange and oppressive. As I rode into the town along the Loftcha road, just after sunset, not a sound broke the dead quiet, and the only living thing I met was here and there a stray dog, which slunk away to his horrible meal among the shallow graves in front of the redoubts on the hills." The houses were filled with dead and dying; and miserable creatures, homeless, famine-stricken, and perishing with mortal disease, made the public ways doleful with their cries for help. The Russians did not hurry themselves to relieve the wretchedness they found. When the victorious hosts entered Plevna, on the 11th of December, the day was made one of rejoicing, and the unhappy sufferers in the hospitals received no attention. Hundreds died during that dreadful time, while the Czar and his Staff were visiting the conquered positions, and exchanging congratulations on the great event. It was not until the morning of the 12th that the Russians entered the hospitals, and began to separate the living from the dead.

The mosques, the larger houses, and many of the smaller dwellings, had been converted into temporary receptacles for the sick and wounded, and, owing to want of attendance and the total absence of sanitary precautions, the mortality was appalling. "The first room entered in one of these charnel-houses," says a writer in the *Daily News*, "contained ninety odd Turks. Of these, thirty-seven were dead, and many others on the point of death. Piteous groans came from between rigid lips, and painful cries for water; and some made feeble signs for food. One or two of the strongest raised themselves, and fixed their hideous, sunken eyes with such a beseeching stare on those who had come to

REMOVING THE WOUNDED.

free them from the company of the dead, that it would have softened the hardest heart. The small room, dimly lighted by a high window with one pane of glass, was crowded with the forms of thirty or forty ragged, filthy human beings. Many of these forms were motionless, and scarcely audible groans were heard from one or two, who raised with difficulty their bony hands to their lips, to signify the need of food. There were faint whispers of 'Some water! some water!' piteous to hear. The dim light was concentrated on the half-naked body of an old man stretched across the entrance, whither he had dragged himself in the last hours of his agony, in hope of succour, or at least of a breath of fresh air; for in the unventilated room the air was thick with putrid odours, which burst out when the door was opened, overpowering strong men, and causing them to turn sick and faint. The old man's hands were clutched, in the rigour of painful death, on his nude and meagre breast, and his head lay against the very crack of the door, so that it was opened only by rude force. Living and dead were lying together undistinguishable along the walls behind the door and under the window. This room was one of fifty where a similar spectacle was presented. The pavement of the mosques was covered with crouching forms, some moving at intervals, others motionless and silent. Here and there the faces of the dead came out in ghastly relief, with a fixed expression of great agony."

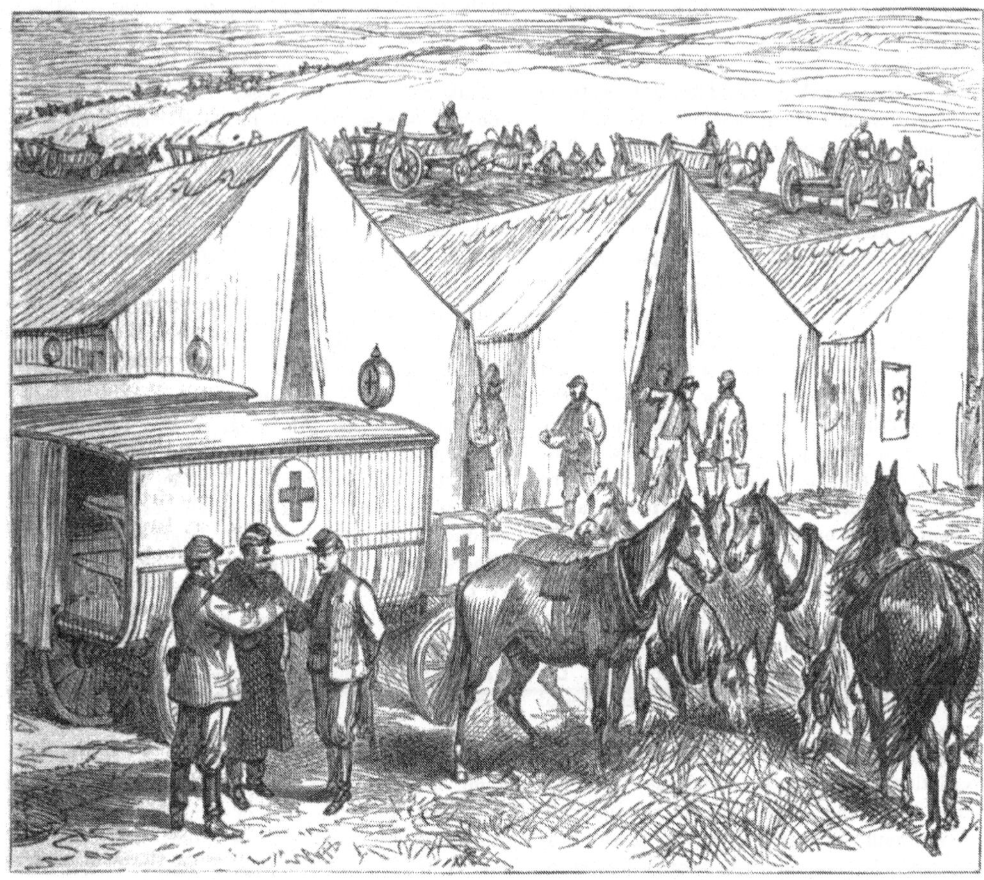

RUSSIAN RED CROSS HOSPITAL BEFORE PLEVNA.

Nothing could be done but to drag the dead from the living, to let in light and air, and to give water and nourishment to the survivors. But only a very small body of men was set aside for this task; and for the removal of the dead not more than three open ox-carts, such as are used by the peasantry, were forthcoming. In these vehicles the dead bodies were slowly removed to the ditches outside. After a day or two, some of the Bulgarians were compelled, or permitted, to serve in place of the Russian soldiers; and they acted, according to our authority, with a brutality terrible to witness. They dragged the bodies down the stairs by the legs, so that the heads knocked heavily from step to step; then, after trailing them through the mud outside, they flung them into the cart so carelessly that portions of the corpses hung dangling over the sides. The conversation which accompanied this work was no less horrible than the work itself. Sometimes a body would be brought forth which bore unmistakable signs of life. One of the Bulgarians, more conscientious than the others, would call attention to the fact, but would be met by some such exclamation as "Devil take him! he will die before to-morrow, any way. In with him!" The *Daily News* correspondent said he had seen this happen, and one of the men who had charge of the hospitals told him he doubted not that such cases occurred several times a day. The dead lay for many hours unattended, and these dreadful sights and sounds went on in the public streets, crowded with men, women, and children. A few Russian Sisters of Charity gave aid and comfort to the sick and wounded, and after several days the care of the miserable creatures was reduced to something like system; but it is much to the discredit of the Russians that organizations for alleviating the wretchedness which was certain to be found in the town were not set on foot before the catastrophe arrived.

Those who were found alive in the hospitals had been reduced to the last stage of weakness from actual want of food. The famine was so extreme that, when bread at length was brought, the sufferers fought with each other in their mortal agony to obtain it. Some, propped up against the wall, ate slowly and feebly until the white rigour of dissolution came over them, and they could stir no more; when the morsel of food remaining in their hands would be snatched away by those whose life was not yet spent, and who wrangled over the spoil until, in some instances, death ended the frightful dispute. The prisoners who were taken in the sortie were also left to suffer, not merely from the severity of the weather, but from insufficiency of food. On the plain near the bridge over the river, from 15,000 to 20,000 captured soldiers were bivouacked in the open air, in the midst of hundreds of unburied dead, the exhalations from whom conveyed subtle poison into the blood with every breath. Even where there had been some attempt at burial, it was only to the extent of a few spadesful of earth thrown over the rotting corpses; and in many instances dogs and birds of prey had routed out these dread remains, for the sake of the horrible food on which they fattened.

During the whole siege of Plevna, Osman Pasha had dwelt in a tent, although there were many comfortable houses at his disposal. The Turkish chief was a true soldier, and, living with his men, shared their hardships as well as their perils. His mode of life was simplicity itself, and his meals were little better than those of the rank-and-file. To defend Plevna was a heavy task. For a long while there were no reserves; the men were either in the entrenchments, or at the redoubts, day and night; and their food consisted for the most part of biscuits and very bad bread. Twice a week, buffalo-beef was served out, but it was so tough and ill-flavoured as to make but a poor addition to the ordinary diet. For drink, the men sometimes had coffee, but, ordinarily, were obliged to be content with water. When not actually on duty, they were protected against shot and shell by the little caves which they had burrowed in the earth, and which served as their temporary houses. Such sleep as they could obtain amidst the noise of the bombardment was taken at intervals upon the bare ground; and this was subject to continual interruptions. Yet, in the midst of numerous trials, the soldiers exhibited a quiet, cheerful, kindly demeanour, such as moved the highest admiration of an English observer.* To these virtues the soldierly conduct of Osman himself very largely contributed. Wherever the danger was greatest, he was always at the head of his men, and the marvel is, not that he should have been wounded at last, but that he should have survived at all. His tent was frequently under shell-fire, and so meagrely furnished as to be but little preferable to the open trenches. He seldom slept more than two or three hours at a time, and at any moment of the day or night might suddenly appear among his troops. Flinching from the post of danger was severely punished; and when officers threw themselves on the ground, to avoid a passing storm of shot and shell, Osman beat them with his own hands, in presence of the soldiers. Most of his aides-de-camp were killed or wounded; indeed, to go from any one part of the main position to another, or to take orders to the various redoubts, was a service of the highest danger. Yet, notwithstanding the severity of his discipline, Osman was decidedly popular with the army he commanded. It was seen that he never spared himself, and every man felt that only by the utmost devotion could the position be saved from capture. In a military sense, the great difficulty of the Pasha proceeded from want of sufficient guns. He was frequently obliged to remove his artillery from point to point of the lines, to repel some unexpected attack; and his earthworks would

* Correspondent of the *Daily Telegraph*.

probably have been multiplied, if he had had cannon to place on them. In two or three places there had been no time to erect batteries: in particular, Osman greatly regretted his inability to do more for the protection of Plevna towards the north-west, where he ultimately endeavoured to break out. The business of the defence was managed by the agency of nine or ten telegraphic wires, connecting the various parts of the position with the head-quarters' camp. Here messages were continually being received by Osman, or transmitted by him to his subordinates; and in this way a large amount of labour was saved, and the galloping to and fro of subordinate officers became unnecessary. A large part of the enemy's lines, however, could be scanned by the eye, and Osman Pasha's tent was in such a position that it was commanded by the Russian batteries.

A week after the capture of Plevna, it was reported that Osman was dead. Some accounts stated that he had poisoned himself; others, that he had died of vexation; and others, again, that his wound had proved mortal. All these accounts were purely fictitious. Osman Pasha was a man of too genuine and strong a nature to take refuge from defeat in the melodramatic absurdity of suicide; nor was he likely to succumb to the natural feeling of mortification at having lost a splendid army and an important position. His wound, which was in the leg, was more painful than serious; and in the hands of his conquerors he was treated with care and consideration. On the 13th of December, he wrote to his brother-in-law, Riza Bey:—"You must know that we were completely blockaded in Plevna for six weeks. During this time we received no outside help, and all our attempts to make a sortie remained without result. Our provisions being totally expended, I determined to make a supreme effort to break the iron line surrounding us on every side. You know the result. I am a prisoner, with the remnant of my brave army. The courage and intrepidity of my soldiers have been highly appreciated by the Russian Emperor, and by his brother, the Grand Duke Nicholas. All our soldiers are prisoners, and are treated with benevolence. Our wounded are cared for with kindness." In this testimony to the good feeling of the Russian commanders, Osman Pasha seems rather to have observed a form of courtesy, usual on such occasions, than to have paid strict regard to the facts. He had not been in the hospitals, where the vindictive Bulgarians were permitted to wreak their dull ferocity on dead and dying Turks. Individual acts of kindness, on the part of Russian and Roumanian soldiers, were indeed not wanting; but the treatment of the prisoners, speaking generally, was a disgrace to civilisation.

The victors in this great contest were inspected by the Czar on the 14th of December, when 58,000 Russian and 12,000 Roumanian troops were drawn up on the battle-field of Plevna. The Emperor was accompanied by the Grand Duke, by Prince Charles, and by a numerous Staff, and was received with enthusiasm by the soldiers. On reaching the ground, he embraced General Witrinsky and General Daniloff, who had commanded the reserve which marched to the rescue on the famous 10th, and the line which had first received the Turkish attack. On this occasion, a few wounded Turks were found lying about the ground, where they had been four days without food or water, exposed to the cold winds of that bleak region. Many of the Turkish dead were still unburied, and there was a great mortality among the prisoners; but this did not prevent the Russians from enjoying their triumph. At St. Petersburg, a Thanksgiving Service was celebrated on the 11th in the church of the Winter Palace; after which the Empress held a Grand Court. All the officers in the capital who had been injured in the war were commanded to attend, if their health permitted. The theatres celebrated the victory by special additions to their programmes; illuminations were general; the National Anthem was sung without stint; and enthusiastic popular demonstrations in honour of the Imperial family and of the army were made in the streets and public places of the metropolis.

Now that Plevna had fallen, the respective strength of the two belligerents became additionally interesting, as bearing on the future course of affairs; and an elaborate statistical paper, published in the *North German Gazette*, threw some light upon this subject. The Russo-Roumanian army in Europe, it was here stated, presented a grand total of 119,000 men, with 558 field-guns. The forces in the Balkans counted 30,000 men, with 162 guns. The Army of the Lom, commanded by the Czarewitch, consisted of 73,000 men, with 432 guns; and the forces in the Dobrudscha and Eastern Roumania comprised 38,000 men, with 440 guns. The Turkish army was composed—first, of the forces in Western Bulgaria, 92,000 men, with 132 guns (including the battalions of Osman, now captured by the Russians), to which were to be added 4,000 irregulars; secondly, of the forces in the Balkans, 26,000 men, with 76 guns and a number of mortars, augmented by 3,000 irregulars; thirdly, of the Army of the

PRISONERS OF WAR.

Quadrilateral and the Dobrudscha, which, including the garrisons, counted 135,000 men, with 386 guns, and about 60,000 irregulars. Here was a very formidable array of troops, whether for attack or defence; and the darkening winter days, the depth of snow that covered a wide extent of territory, and the natural fortress of the Balkan range, offered many opportunities to the Turks, of which it was expected they would, with their usual tenacity, make the most; so that even in the middle of December some military critics were still in doubt whether the Russians would not be compelled to retreat before the combined influences of a rigorous climate, a difficult country, and the embattled hosts of the Crescent.

Yet it was obvious that the fall of Plevna added greatly to the difficulties of the Ottomans. The same event which deprived the Sultan of a large body of hardened troops, familiar with all the varied exigencies of war, added practically to the resources of the Czar, by setting free the regiments that had kept watch upon a fortress now no longer to be dreaded. An advance in force over the Balkans was certain to be made with as little delay as possible. The obstacle to Gourko's movements presented by the army of Mehemet Ali would be swept aside when the Russo-Roumanian legions from Plevna appeared among the mountain-passes. The Turks would then have no alternative but to fall back on Adrianople and the Roumelian valleys; and when such a catastrophe as that is reached, Constantinople is always in danger. Although the Sultan could still reckon upon the services of numerous armed men, it was to be feared that their discipline would be relaxed by that pressure of adverse fate which, in an Oriental mind more than any other, is apt to generate the very evils that it apprehends. The Government at Constantinople knew these things only too well, and the hope of foreign intervention was so slight as to be scarcely worth consideration. England was the only Power whose interests were sufficiently affected by recent events to create even the smallest chance of diplomatic action tending to the employment of force; and in England the peace party was strong enough to impose its will on a Government many of whose members were not unwilling to be so influenced. The Porte, therefore, could see nothing but discouragement, whether at home or abroad; and the old year drew towards its close in the midst of shadows that were deeper than the darkest night.

CHAPTER XLVI.

Meeting of the Ottoman Parliament in December, 1877—Ceremonies at the Opening—Speech from the Throne—Programme of Reforms—Determination of Servia to join the War—Preliminary Action on the Part of that Power—Proclamation of Prince Milan, setting forth his Reasons for declaring War against Turkey—Crossing of the Frontier by the Servian Army—Proposals by Turkey for the Opening of Negotiations with a View to Peace—Circular Note to the Powers—The Turkish Case, and its Weak Point—The Demands of Russia enhanced by her Success—Force the Ultimate Argument of the Conqueror—Cold Reception of the Turkish Circular by the Great Powers—Determination of the Russian Emperor to resist Mediation and Intervention—Return of the Czar to Russia—Enthusiastic Reception at St. Petersburg—Splendid Scene in the Kazan Cathedral—The Emperor and the People—Universal Rejoicings—Religious Ceremonial in the Cathedral of St Peter and St. Paul—The *Te Deum* in the Chapel of the Winter Palace—Russian Feeling of Irritation against England—Parliament summoned for the 17th of January, 1878—Intentions of the Government with Respect to the War.

SELDOM, if ever, has a representative body met under more tragical circumstances than those which environed the second Turkish Parliament when its members assembled on the 13th of December, 1877. Three days earlier, Plevna had passed into Russian hands, and the battalions of Ghazi Osman had been compelled to lay down their arms. Suleiman Pasha was hopelessly defeated in his assault upon the Czarewitch's lines. The forces of Mehemet Ali were held in check among the defiles of the Balkans, which General Gourko had partially crossed for the second time. In Asia, Kars had fallen, and Erzeroum was threatened. Towns had been taken, provinces had been won, subject populations had been revolutionised, and suzerain States had proved unfaithful. Danger and loss were visible in every direction, and it was not easy to see how all this accumulation of misfortune was to be remedied. The Turkish people, however, were quiet, and the Sultan did not fear to call the national councillors together, that the affairs of the Empire might be debated by its representatives. The first Turkish Parliament had been little more than a Constituent Assembly for laying the bases of the new political state, and a general election had taken place during the recess. In the second Parliament, as in the first, the Mohammedans were of course in the majority, because the followers of the Prophet are more numerous in the Empire than the professors of all other creeds put together. But the Christians were represented by numerous members, and among three nominees selected by the Chamber of Deputies for its President, one was a Christian. The choice of the Sultan, however, ultimately fell on a Moslem of known liberality and tolerance.

The place of meeting was the Grand Hall of the Throne, in the Dolmabaghtché Palace. Although the event was one of importance, it seemed to create scarcely any interest among the people of Constantinople, and no crowd was gathered about the entrance to the building. The ceremony, however, was impressive, owing to the magnificence of the hall, and the picturesque intermingling of European and Oriental costumes. The proceedings were managed with admirable order, and the inherent dignity of the Turkish character was apparent throughout. The hall was lined with the Civic Guard of the Palace, forming three sides of a hollow square. Within this, the audience made three sides of a smaller square, of which the fourth side was open, and contained the throne. All stood during the ceremony; indeed, the throne was the only seat in the place. On the right, forming one side of the inner square, were ranged the Ministers according to their rank, all in full uniform, and accompanied by the Under-Secretaries of State. Immediately behind the Grand Vizier were the heads of the non-Mussulman communities, in their ordinary black robes and head-dress, wearing their Turkish decorations, but bearing no mitres, croziers, or other religious emblems. The chief of these was the Greek Patriarch. Opposite the throne stood the Councillors of State, the Senators in uniform, and the Deputies in ordinary dress. The left side was occupied by the Mussulman ecclesiastical dignitaries, headed by the Sheikh-ul-Islam, clad in white woollen robes and a green turban, and attended by the Cadiaskers and Mollahs of the provinces, in gold-laced turbans and robes of various colours. Further back, on the same side of the hall, were the members of the Diplomatic Corps, in full-dress uniforms; and a few journalists and visitors completed the scene.

All having assembled, the folding doors of the side entrance were thrown open, a few minutes past noon, by the chief master of the ceremonies, and the Sultan entered, attended by the palace officials. He was received by a series of modulated cries, taken from the Turkish national hymn, and uttered by a body of retainers placed at the further end of the hall, and specially kept for such purposes. His Majesty was dressed very simply in a plain frock coat, with no other decoration than the order of the Osmanlie; and, slowly advancing up the open space, in the midst of countless salaams and genuflexions, he arrived at the throne, when he faced round, and returned the salutations of the assembly. Without seating himself, he handed a written copy of his speech to the Grand Vizier, who, after putting it reverentially to his forehead, kissed it, and handed it on to Said Pasha, Marshal of the Palace. Repeating the same reverences, Said took up a position to the right of the Sultan, at a respectful distance, and read the speech. This being done, the Pasha made an obeisance to his Majesty, which was repeated by all present. The Sultan then bowed in return, and left the hall in the midst of the same cries which marked his entrance. The whole ceremony had lasted less than ten minutes, and the members shortly afterwards dispersed as quietly as they had met.*

The speech from the Throne had been modified at the last moment, owing to the critical state of affairs; but after all it did not throw any light on the intentions of the Government with reference to the future course of the war. The address commenced by affirming that Russia had begun hostilities, and that Turkey was compelled to defend herself against aggression. It then referred to the disturbances which, two years and a half before, had broken out in the Herzegovina, and spread into other localities. "In spite," said the Sultan, "of the equality in the eyes of the law which all our subjects enjoy, and the immunities which secure their nationality and their language, a part of our population suffered itself to be drawn, without any known motive, into the path of illegality. These misguided men not only injured their fatherland and their fellow-citizens, but brought upon themselves the gravest prejudice. The united Principalities [Wallachia and Moldavia], which had the fortune to possess an independent internal administration, assumed an attitude of hostility towards our Government, without any legitimate reason. These grave events, unprecedented in our history, have considerably increased the difficulties of the war; but the country, in order to make head against them, has put forth all the powers of resistance of which it is capable. All Ottomans, by the abnegation of which they have given proof in this war, have shown that they were prompted by the highest sentiments of patriotism. The courage and valour of our soldiers have been the admiration of the whole world. I continue to appeal to the aid and patriotism of all of you, in order to protect our

* *Times*, Dec. 14th, 1877.

sacred rights. The formation of the Civic Guard, which is daily perfecting and completing itself, and the eagerness with which our non-Mussulman subjects present themselves to take part in this patriotic service, are matters of real satisfaction to our Government. The Constitution, while confirming and corroborating the rights and immunities which our non-Mussulman subjects enjoyed, granted them equality of rights, from which results equality of duties. It was therefore but natural that they should be called to military service, which is the first of duties, and even the foundation of equality. The proof which they have given of their conscientiousness in the way of duty has been duly appreciated, and it has been decided to throw open all ranks of the other branches of our armies to the non-Mussulman population." The salvation of the Empire, it was remarked, depended entirely on the complete and sincere carrying out of the Constitution. The Sultan's dearest wishes were to see all classes of his subjects enjoy the blessings of complete equality, and the country profit by the acceptance of modern ideas, by financial ameliorations, by the fulfilment of all engagements, by the proper distribution, in accordance with the principles of political economy, of the taxes and dues, by the collection of the revenue so as not to injure the interests of the population, and by such reforms as the revision of the judicial system and of the methods by which landed property was acquired, the formation of communes as the basis of an administrative system, and the reorganization of the Gendarmerie. The war, however, had postponed the fulfilment of these wishes, and had, moreover, been productive of frightful calamities to non-combatants, especially to inoffensive women and children, whose life and honour ought to have been respected. Important Bills, elaborated by the Council of State, would be submitted to the Parliament, with a view to settling great Constitutional questions, and deciding certain matters relative to the vilayets, the press, taxation, and the state of siege. "Gentlemen Deputies," concluded the Sultan, "truth can be elicited on questions of

PALACE OF THE SULTAN AT CONSTANTINOPLE.

political and civil rights only by perfect liberty of discussion. That liberty having been conferred by the Constitution, you require from me no further instructions or encouragement. Our relations with the friendly Powers are most cordial. May the Most High bless our common efforts!"

Much surprise was felt that the speech contained no allusion to the fall of Plevna, or to the possibility of peace. A belief in the imminence of a pacific settlement had taken hold of the public mind, and it was generally suspected that the Government, notwithstanding its reticence, was engaged in negotiations with the Powers. This was really the case; but while these diplomatic confidences were being interchanged, the war had entered on a new phase, and the invaders had been strengthened by a fresh ally. Servia had for some months been evincing an eager desire to make another attack on Turkey; or rather the Servian Government had shown this desire, for the people themselves had too painful a recollection of the last war to be enthusiastic about repeating the experiment. Had the Principality been left to itself, it is not unlikely that peace would have been preserved; but Russia lost no opportunity of inciting Prince Milan to a martial policy. The personal ambition of the young Prince seconded these efforts, and, as autumn passed into winter, it became perfectly evident to bystanders that the concentration of troops upon the frontier, and the warlike preparations all over the little State, were not merely defensive measures, but were intended with a view to active operations. Servia, although a small country, was capable of rendering an appreciable service to Russia, and Russia was very willing to avail herself of any assistance that might be forthcoming. The Principality could put several thousand men into the field; and, although these men were not the very best of soldiers, they could at any rate threaten the communications of the Turks, and still further harass an enemy who was already overmatched. Even before any public declaration of a rupture, it was openly announced in the papers that commands would be distributed among forty Russian officers, of whom eight belonged to the Staff, and that twenty officers formerly attached to the Prussian service would enter the Servian army. The Ottomans knew they would shortly be attacked, and the people around Widdin were accordingly withdrawn into the fortress, and armed. There could in truth be no doubt as to the intention of the Servian Prince, though the actual declaration of war was still postponed. On the 10th of December, the regular troops and militia in Belgrade, accompanied by batteries of artillery, began their march for the frontier; and the inhabitants of the districts about the capital, who were liable to military service, received orders to hold themselves prepared for action at any moment. During the few previous weeks, negotiations had been going on with Russia; for Servia could not afford to move without a subsidy, and dared not risk the chances of another war unless she had an assurance from her great patron that in any case she should be held harmless. These conditions were at length satisfied, and all reasons for hesitation were at an end. But in Europe generally Servia found little sanction for the course she was about to take. It was felt that to delay the attack until Turkey was reduced to a state bordering on exhaustion was cowardly, and that to strike at all was ungrateful after the extremely lenient treatment of the Principality at the close of the unprovoked war of 1876—a leniency, by the way, which was mainly due to the eager interposition of Lord Derby, who seems at all times to have been very solicitous that Servia should be in the best possible position for making treacherous attacks on her Suzerain.

The 12th of December was the anniversary of the recognition of Servia's autonomy by the Powers, and on this occasion a *Te Deum* was chanted in the metropolitan church of Belgrade. The Archimandrite Nestor delivered a warlike discourse to the congregation, which included Prince Milan, the Princess, and most of the diplomatic agents; and on the previous night there had been a popular demonstration before the residence of the Russian agent, together with illuminations in honour of the fall of Plevna. It was certain that the declaration of war would not be much further delayed, and it came on the 14th, when a proclamation was issued, announcing that the Servian army had received orders to cross the Turkish frontier. Salvoes of artillery gave additional importance to this notification, and M. Cristics, the Servian diplomatic agent at Constantinople, was instructed to inform the Foreign Minister of the determination that had been reached, and at once to leave the Turkish capital. At the same time, Prince Milan published a series of edicts proclaiming a state of siege and a state of war; instituting military tribunals and military laws for volunteers, as well as courts-martial; requiring the employment of officials and of the clergy in military service; announcing that public functionaries would be dismissed if they infringed the laws, or promoted agitation against the war; suspending the local self-government of the communes; providing State help for the indigent families of soldiers

SERVIAN PRIEST PREACHING THE WAR.

and volunteers who might be killed; ordering a *Moratorium* for the benefit only of men serving at the seat of war; and issuing regulations for the field-post and telegraph systems throughout Servia.

It was necessary to give some reasons for an act of hostility which had not been provoked by any conduct of Turkey towards Servia; and these reasons, such as they were, appeared in the proclamation of Prince Milan, dated the 14th of December. In his manifesto of the 5th of March, the Prince had told his people that the defence of the holy cause for which they had taken up arms in 1876 had passed into stronger hands. But after Servia had concluded peace with the Porte, the Turkish race, according to Prince Milan, had "enriched its history with new and unheard-of horrors, imprisonments, and devastations." Of all nationalities included in the Turkish Empire, the brethren of the Servians had suffered most from Mussulman fanaticism, which had been specially directed against those persons who had found shelter in Servia during the late war, and who on their return to Turkey had been cruelly persecuted, notwithstanding the fact that, by the treaty of peace concluded on the 1st of March, 1877, a complete amnesty was promised them. The Ottoman Government had given solemn promises to that of Servia; but those promises had been broken. "We cannot look on with indifference," continued the proclamation, "nor without humiliation remain further connected with a Government deriving its power from devastation, incendiarism, bloodshed, and fanaticism. Although Servia behaves towards Turkey honourably, the Porte prepares new perils for our country, besides concocting secret conspiracies against our internal security. The Ottoman Foreign Minister threatens us openly with innumerable injuries, without being formally at war with Servia." The Prince then proceeded to argue that it would be a pusillanimous abandonment of duty if they refused at such a moment to aid the brave Russian army, then engaged in championing the cause of the Christians. Their martyred brethren would curse them, if they were found indifferent when, on their very frontiers, rivers of blood were being shed in fighting against the common enemy. "On entering the field," said the Prince, who certainly appreciated the advantage of allying himself with strength, "we find on our side the victorious Russian army, our heroic Montenegrin brethren, and our brave Roumanian neighbours. We take up arms to-day for the holy, national, Christian cause. Following my grandfather's example, I am about to place myself at the head of the armed Servian nation. On the banner which Obrenowitsch IV. unfurls, is written 'National Liberty,' 'Independence.' Under this banner you have already proved your patriotism and readiness to sacrifice all. Let us now fulfil the great national task which the old heroes of Takova so gloriously began, and which we renewed last year. Let us move forward alongside of the victorious banner of the Czar, the Liberator, with Christian faith in God Almighty, the Protector of right; and success is sure. It is God's will."

The Proclamation was well received at the capital though not by the people generally. A deputation of Belgrade citizens waited on the Prince to congratulate him on having taken so decided a step towards liberating the country for ever from Turkish thraldom. At night, the city was illuminated, and the Municipal Council organized a torchlight procession from the Town Hall to the Konak. Bands of music paraded the streets, playing Servian and Sclavonic airs; the Philharmonic Society sang the National Anthem; and an enthusiastic professor delivered a speech, in which he said that Kossova must be avenged. As, however, Servia had been practically free for several years, and had itself been the aggressor in 1876, as it was now once more in 1877, it was ridiculous to talk of avenging a defeat which had happened as long ago as 1389. The Prince started for the frontier on the 16th of December, and it was arranged that his head-quarters were to be at Alexinatz. The Servian troops, under the command of Generals Leschjanin and Benitzki, crossed the frontier on the 15th, and took possession of the heights dominating Maramor, where the Turks had entrenched themselves with a view to opposing the march of the Servian forces upon Nisch. Simultaneously, General Libibratics, who had distinguished himself at the beginning of the Herzegovinian insurrection, left for the Drina frontier, where he was to command the volunteers. On the 23rd of December, the battalions under Horvatovich effected a junction with Skobeleff near Belgradjik, after having defeated a small Turkish force in the St. Nicholas Pass. Other bodies of troops seized various positions on the frontiers, from which they would be able to join in concerted movements against the enemy, and several preliminary skirmishes occurred from day to day, the general effect of which was to show that the Turks were quite unable to oppose with vigour this new invasion of their territory. As a punishment for his disloyalty, Prince Milan was deposed by a decree of the Porte; but the sentence was one which could not be executed, and which therefore it would perhaps have been more dignified not to pronounce.

It was in the midst of these Servian demonstrations that the Turks made their proposals for a pacific solution of the vexed questions between themselves and their antagonists. Even as early as the 11th of December—the day following that on which Plevna had capitulated—Server Pasha, the Foreign Minister of the Porte, had had some conversation with the English and Austrian Ambassadors at Constantinople, to whom he expressed his conviction that the time had come when Turkey might invoke the mediatorial aid of the Powers. He professed to speak only from a personal point of view; but he added that he should bring the proposal before the Cabinet, and strenuously urge its acceptance. A council was held on the 12th, just before the opening of the Turkish Parliament, when Server's project met with general concurrence, and it was determined to address a circular note to each of the Great Powers. Telegraphic intercommunication between Constantinople and the chief European capitals became very active immediately after this resolution had been formed, and the diplomatic world was agitated from day to day by fresh rumours of an approaching termination of the struggle. The Circular, which was despatched in the course of a few days, began by observing that the Turkish Government had not in any way provoked the war which it was carrying on against Russia, and had indeed done everything to avoid it. At the summons of their Sovereign, the people of the Empire had assembled, to fulfil, simply and heroically, the duty of defending their threatened territory; but on their own side they had not threatened, nor did they then threaten, anybody. "It is not easy," said the document, "to discover the reasons by which Russia can justify her aggression. Does she wish to see founded and developed, for the benefit of certain populations which are the objects of her solicitude, institutions and reforms calculated to ameliorate their lot? The Sublime Porte has anticipated this desire by deciding to reorganize its judicial system, and to accomplish in the country useful and practical reforms, intended to meet the wishes of the people, without distinction of race or religion. This work of reorganization has for its base the Constitution granted by his Imperial Majesty, the Sultan. The country has received with delight and gratitude this charter, the application of which, free from every hindrance, is to produce all the effects which have been vainly expected from incomplete measures and unauthorised reforms. A partial reform, to be applied only to certain provinces, to the exclusion of the rest of the Empire, would be attended with grave inconveniences. In matters of administration, the exceptions and favours accorded to certain provinces could not but set against one another the peoples of various races who live under the sceptre of his Imperial Majesty, the Sultan, and would offer a premium to rebellion." The Circular pointed out that nothing was so likely to hinder the due execution of the contemplated reforms as the continuance of a state of war, which was calamitous to the general prosperity of the nation, which killed agriculture and industry by keeping under arms the best of the labouring population, which was attended with heavy charges on the Treasury, and which thus obstructed the economical and financial improvement of the Empire. The subject of reform, therefore, being entirely out of consideration, the question had arisen, What reason could exist for continuing so disastrous a war? The desire of conquest for conquest's sake had, from the commencement of hostilities, been publicly repudiated by the Emperor Alexander. The military honour of the great Empire which he governed remained intact, in spite of the varying fortunes of the campaign; and the armies confronting each other had equally covered themselves with glory on the battle-field. What object, then, asked the Turkish Ministers, could be attained by prolonging the desolation and ruin of their respective countries? It seemed to the Sultan's advisers that the moment had arrived when the two Empires might conclude peace without forfeiting their dignity, and when Europe might usefully interpose its good offices. The Constantinople Cabinet was ready to ask this, though careful at the same time to observe that the country was not yet at the end of its resources. "There are no sacrifices," said the Circular, "which the whole nation would not make, in order to maintain the independence and integrity of the Fatherland. But the duty of the Imperial Government is to avert, if possible, any further effusion of blood. In the name of humanity, therefore, we make this appeal to the sentiments of justice of the Great Powers, and we hope that they will be inclined to regard with favour the step we have taken."

The issue of this circular was unquestionable evidence that the Turkish Government was deeply impressed with the doubtful, if not absolutely hopeless, prospects of the war. It was, indeed, explained in official circles at Constantinople, that Turkey did not approach the Powers as a vanquished State, since she had still two lines of defence—viz., the Balkans, and the fortifications round Constantinople—which the Government believed they would be able to hold. But no Power with a veritable feeling of confidence in the future would have sought to propitiate its enemy by a proposal which, however guarded, betrayed the inherent weakness of the situation. Nevertheless, it may be doubted whether the Turkish Government even then fully understood the terrible conditions of the problem which presented itself for solution.

It was thought that, as the war began owing to the Turkish refusal to accept the requirements of the Conference, it might now be terminated by concessions on the same basis. This was to suppose that nothing had happened between the beginning

RECEPTION OF THE CZAR IN BUCHAREST.

and the close of the year; that there had been no war, or that at any rate there had been such an even balance of success as to leave matters in the same position as before the outbreak of hostilities. Nothing could be more futile than such a supposition; nothing more certain to result in failure, or to entail still heavier disasters in the rapidly-approaching catastrophe. The determination to maintain the struggle to the last—to defend barrier after barrier until nothing remained between the advancing Russians and the very walls of Constantinople—was natural, was heroic. It was simply what had been done against the Turks themselves by the last of the Constantines. It was a course such as every great military Empire which had not entirely lost its spirit would assuredly have taken under the circumstances; for when men are driven to bay by a remorseless oppressor, it is not surprising that they should make him pay dearly for his success, even though it may be evident that that success cannot possibly be averted. But if the Turkish Government really believed itself in a position to secure a diplomatic triumph, the delusion

RETURN OF THE EMPEROR TO ST. PETERSBURG.

is one of the most remarkable in history. There was not the slightest ground of probability for supposing that Russia would quietly go back to the terms that had been refused by Turkey ere yet a single drop of blood had been shed. To say this is no special imputation against Russia; it might be predicated of any other Power as well. The proposals made at Constantinople at the close of 1876, and revised at the beginning of 1877, were in truth a compromise. Whether those proposals were good or bad—whether they were moderate or extreme—it is certain that they were very far from meeting all that Russia really desired in the settlement of the Eastern Question. They were attenuated to the utmost, to satisfy the objections of other Powers, especially of England, and to avoid the necessity of war. But war had come, and Russia had paid enormously, both in life and money, for the fulfilment of her programme. It could not, therefore, be expected that she would now be satisfied with what, perhaps, she might have gladly accepted to avoid the cost of so terrible a struggle. The circumstances had altered, and the conditions had altered with them. This, of course, did not justify Russia in pursuing a policy of ambition, or of territorial aggrandisement; still less could it excuse any violation of pledges actually given; but a more radical settlement of the Eastern Question than had been accepted a year before was certain to be required, and could not successfully be refused. The reforms instituted by the Sultan may have been much more fitted to secure the ostensible ends of Russia than any interposition on the part of the Emperor; but it was quite certain that the Emperor would not think so, and that he was in a position to enforce his views. The question was not whether such a settlement was desirable or undesirable; the only point for consideration was whether matters had not come to such a pass that large concessions to Russia were no longer to be avoided. The right of the conqueror may be nothing more than the right of strength; but that is the very argument which is most effective at the termination of a war.

The semi-official press in the chief Continental capitals was far from taking a favourable view of the Turkish Circular. The *Montags Revue*, of Vienna, observed that public opinion had construed the note as a demand for mediation, but wrongly so, for not only had the Turks not asked for this, but even the basis for such intervention could not be laid down until they had resigned themselves to the consequences of the war. The Berlin *Norddeutsche Allgemeine Zeitung* and the *National Zeitung*—both more or less Ministerial papers—agreed in holding that the Turkish cry for help would not be listened to by the Powers. The former journal told Turkish diplomatists that the Circular would be as little attended to as the solicitations of M. Thiers during his European tour in 1870. Even before the issue of the Note, when Server Pasha was making his first tentative advances, the Austrian Government said plainly that it could not hold out any hope of successful mediation. Germany definitively declined the Turkish request for its good offices, while Mr. Layard informed the Turkish Government that England would continue to observe neutrality. Nevertheless, the British Cabinet thought that the Note might be taken as a starting-point, and that it ought to be communicated confidentially, if not officially, to the Russian Government, when an opportunity might be afforded of ascertaining under what conditions Russia would be disposed to treat. France and Italy avoided any direct expression of opinion, but were willing to act with the other Great Powers when any common ground of interposition could be discovered. The hope of mediation speedily vanished, and the Czar, in reply to a congratulatory deputation from the German Foreign Office, which he received while on his way back to St. Petersburg, made use of some expressions which unmistakably indicated the determination he had formed. "Europe," he said, "follows our actions with confidence. England alone seems desirous to exercise pressure on the freedom of our movements. We shall not agree to mediation, however, and we are armed against intervention." But intervention was not at that time contemplated by the English Government, though it was foreseen that, when negotiations for peace were at length opened, the demands of Russia might be such as to compel England to draw the sword in defence of her own interests. On the 19th of December, the Turkish Ambassador in London called on Lord Derby, and, while dwelling much on the unexhausted resources of Turkey, referred more than once to the possibility of English intervention; whereupon the Foreign Secretary repeated the warnings he had given on many previous occasions, that no such interposition was to be expected.*

For some time past, the return of the Czar to Russia had been very much desired in that country. In many quarters, the presence of the Emperor with the army was looked upon with considerable disfavour, as it was thought he would be there exposed to the uncontrolled influence of one particular set of politicians. His Majesty himself was inclined to remain, and is said to have been

* Blue Book on Turkey, No. II. (1878).

much impressed with the necessity of staying with his troops, as the only means of preserving harmony among rival commanders. After the fall of Plevna, however, he yielded to the solicitations of his Ministers, and, together with Prince Gortschakoff, quitted the scene of hostilities for St. Petersburg, where he arrived on the 22nd of December. He had had a glowing and effusive welcome at Bucharest on the 17th, and, on leaving the frontiers of Roumania, had addressed a telegram to the Princess Elizabeth, thanking her for his reception by the Roumanians, and adding, "God watches over us, and will permit us soon to sign an honourable and glorious peace." His Majesty was enthusiastically received by the citizens of St. Petersburg. The terminus was splendidly decorated; the streets glittered with martial pageantry; balconies and windows were hung with cloths of brilliant colours; and everywhere crowds of sightseers were assembled in holiday attire. The pealing of church bells mingled with the roar of artillery; and the joyful voices of the people added a different and still more welcome note to the universal clamour. After a reception at the station by the Mayor of St. Petersburg, who presented an address of congratulation in the name of the Town Council, the Emperor, accompanied by his son, the Grand Duke Sergius, drove off in a little sledge, followed by a distinguished Staff and an escort of the Horse Guards, to the great Kazan Cathedral.

The scene within the edifice itself was superb. "One passed the massive doors," says a correspondent of the *Daily News*, "to find the semi-darkness of a gloomy morning relieved by the radiance of multitudinous candles, from which the light flashed on the polished, sparkling surface of huge pillars of Finland granite, and on the gold frames of the sacred pictures. The soft light gleamed on the chased surface of the holy door behind which lies the high altar, and on the precious stones with which are so profusely adorned the sacred effigies which break the glistening, silvery surface of the Iconostas. The gorgeousness of a worship which appeals to the soul through the senses was visible everywhere: in the massive candelabra of solid silver; in the name of the Almighty rendered in precious stones in the centre of the screen, with dazzling rays of glory encircling it; in the glitter of innumerable gems; and in the polished beauty of rare marbles." People had spent the night sleeping on the floor, that they might be sure of a place in the morning. All ranks and classes were represented in that motley crowd, in the midst of whom ladies passed to and fro, carrying boxes in which they received contributions for the wounded. As the Emperor approached, the doors of the Cathedral were flung wide open, and, together with the frosty outer air, a great gust of sound, formed by the cheering of the people, the firing of artillery, and the clashing of church bells, swept into the vast enclosure. Headed by the Metropolitan, who was clad in gorgeous robes, and wore a mitre which was one radiant mass of jewels, the clergy advanced in procession towards the door, and at the same moment the choristers raised the chant of thanksgiving. The Metropolitan, having received the Emperor at the outer doors, returned with him into the Cathedral, and the crowd, breaking through the slight restraints which had been placed upon them, pressed forward to greet their sovereign as he returned from the hard-fought campaign. The Emperor slowly passed on towards the altar, and, ascending the steps, touched with his lips the glittering image of the Holy Virgin of Kazan. That done, he moved again towards the door, making his way through throngs of enthusiastic men and women, who strove to kiss the hem of his garment. The pressure, indeed, was so great that the Czar was actually lifted off his feet, and reached the door only by dint of a violent struggle; while his daughter-in-law, the Czarevna, was whirled away by the great human eddy, and at length got out by a side door. Driving off towards the Winter Palace, the Emperor stood for a few moments on the terrace in front of that building, acknowledging the welcome of his subjects; but even this did not satisfy the popular demands, and his Majesty was compelled to show himself again and again at the window of the palace. During the whole day, multitudes of people remained in the wide area of the Alexander Platz, incessantly huzzaing; the soldiers at the barracks cheered far into the night; and after dark the streets of the capital were brilliantly illuminated.

On the morning of the 24th, the Emperor was present at a ceremonial in the Cathedral of St. Peter and St. Paul, where he commemorated the centenary of the birth of his uncle, Alexander I. The Emperor entered the Cathedral followed in single file by the male members of the Imperial family then in St. Petersburg. He wore a splendid Huzzar dress, with fur pelisse hanging from the shoulder, and acknowledged with much dignity the obeisances paid him by the spectators. A solemn funeral service was conducted by the Metropolitan before the tomb of Alexander I., and the scene was very impressive as the strains of the Requiem swelled along the aisles of the spacious Cathedral. The marble monuments of the deceased Emperors were shrouded in the foliage of exotic shrubs; and floral wreaths and crosses, of every rich and tender hue, lay upon the tomb of Alexander. As the anthem was being sung, the Emperor took from one of his Ministers a commemorative medal, struck for the occasion, and laid it reverently on the tomb; whereupon all knelt, each with a lighted taper in his hand, and the Metropolitan was heard pronouncing the benediction in sonorous tones. The Czar afterwards visited in succession the tomb of each member of his race, over which he bent, and kissed the marble. At the conclusion of these pious ceremonies, the Emperor returned the bows of the congregation, and quitted the Cathedral about noon. A magnificent reception was subsequently held in the State apartments of the Winter Palace. All who had been present at the

METROPOLITAN OF ST. PETERSBURG.

funeral service paid their respects to his Majesty, and numerous ladies in superb costumes added to the attraction of the scene. The whole party then went in procession to the chapel of the palace, at the entrance to which their Majesties and the Imperial family were received by the Metropolitan and his clergy. A solemn *Te Deum* was celebrated, accompanied by prayers for the Emperor and Empress, their children, and the entire Russian people.* A salute of a hundred and one guns accompanied the music of the *Te Deum*, and enhanced the grandeur of an effect which appealed as much to national and military pride as to the sentiment of religion.

Prince Gortschakoff is said to have observed about this time that if England wanted war, she would have to declare it; that if she wanted peace, she would have to wait for it. The existence of a very irritable mood on the part of Russia towards England was unmistakably obvious at the period of Turkey's unsuccessful attempt to invite mediation. An uneasy feeling was equally apparent in England itself, and the possibility of war against the great Northern Power assumed greater consistency as the wintry days wore on. It was probably in consequence of this sentiment that the Cabinet determined to summon Parliament at an unusually early date. On the 19th of December it was announced that the two Houses would meet for the despatch of business on the 17th of January, 1878, about three weeks sooner than the usual time. The resolution was come to at a Cabinet Council held on December 18th, and it plainly revealed the sense of grave responsibility which was felt by Lord Beaconsfield's Government in view of recent events at the seat of war. In the estimation of the Ministry, affairs in the East had reached a stage which imperatively demanded some distinct expression of the national will. As yet, there had been no such expression in any full, complete, or authentic form. There had been abundance of opinions; there had been excessive agitation of the popular mind; there had been meetings, speeches, newspaper articles, pamphlets, arguments, passion, prejudice, sentiment—everything, in short, but the clear, calm, determined utterance of a mature resolve, whether on the one side or the other. For this omission the Ministry were more responsible than the people. The vacillation which had marked the policy of Government for the previous year and a half, and which unquestionably proceeded from divided councils, had left every man in a state of entire uncertainty as to what course England would take, if the successes of Russia were pushed so far as to endanger the existence of the Turkish Empire. No one doubted what Lord Beaconsfield thought, or what he would do if he could have his own way; but the question was, how far his will was operative, and up to that point the presumption was rather against its having much influence in the Cabinet than in favour of its potency. The early summoning of Parliament was therefore important, because the national representatives would either uphold the Premier in those anti-Russian views which he was known to entertain, or else support that section of the Cabinet which was willing to sacrifice Turkey for the sake of peace. That the Legislature would probably incline to the views of Lord Beaconsfield, rather than to those of Lord Derby, may be inferred from the fact that the anti-Turkish Press was greatly displeased at what it considered the unnecessary summoning of Parliament. It seems to have been thought that a subservient policy towards Russia was more likely to be carried through when the representatives of the nation were scattered about the country than when they were assembled at Westminster. On the other hand, the journals representing a more distinctly English sentiment approved the step that had been taken, and argued that the popular sanction was needed to give force and efficacy to acts of self-protection which were urgently demanded by the existing posture of affairs. The determination of Russia to reject all offers of mediation, and to drive the war home to the very heart of Turkey, had doubtless much to do with the decision at which the Government had now arrived. By many it was believed that the Queen and her advisers had actually determined upon a declaration of war; but those who were better informed, or more intelligent in their power of construing events, knew that no such issue was necessarily implied. The aid of Parliament was asked, because additional expenses were about to be incurred; but, although the probability of war was to some extent increased by this decision, the possibility of a peaceful solution still remained.

It was indeed out of the question that the Government should go on much longer in the hesitating and feeble manner that had marked its course ever since the autumn agitation of 1876. Living, as it were, from hand to mouth; accepting the policy of the Opposition sufficiently to ruin their own, and yet retaining enough of their own to exasperate the Opposition; cowering before the organization of the platform, and begging the aid of those who spurned them; afraid of Russia, yet more afraid of Russia's friends; shifting their position from day to day, not because the current of

* *Daily News*, Dec. 24th and 25th, 1877.

events shifted, but because they had no fixity of purpose, or cohesion of resolve,—her Majesty's Ministers had, by their fatal imbecility and time-serving, reduced the country to a state of considerable ignominy and of some danger. Lord Beaconsfield unquestionably perceived these facts, and determined to make an attempt to remedy them by the assistance of the national representatives. He had been greatly to blame in yielding to a passing clamour, and in suffering the opinion of subordinates to over-ride his own better judgment; but it was certain that his views had never changed, and that he would hail any opportunity of reasserting them. He could still rely on an immense Parliamentary majority; and he looked to that majority for the support which he found but imperfectly in the composition of his Cabinet. The real objects of the war, which had seemed vague, far-off, and doubtful, as long as the balance of success was fairly maintained, became alarmingly real and threateningly imminent when Plevna had surrendered, and when, both in Europe and Asia, the Turkish power was seen to be tottering to its fall. The Balkans still remained to be crossed; but it was known that the Balkans were not insuperable, even in the depth of winter. If Adrianople should be taken, and Constantinople be menaced, the Turks, as in 1829, would probably make peace on any terms the victors chose to demand; and the question of British interests would then arise with an urgency which even the politicians of St. James's Hall could scarcely disregard. Hence the action of the Government, which was doubtless in the main the action of Lord Beaconsfield.

What may be accepted as the average opinion of the country, setting aside extreme views in either direction, was well expressed by the *Daily Telegraph* when it observed:—"The Queen's Government, in fervently desiring to see an end put to the cruel and ruinous war now raging, represents the heartfelt wish of the country; and the way to this consummation lies primarily through mediation, which the Circular Note of the Porte has just invoked in terms characterised by a dignity and a propriety denied only by a few bitter partizans. But mediation, to be useful, must have behind it fixity of purpose and visible strength; nor would there be much hope of result if we were to undertake the task of recommending peace in the helpless manner suggested by certain bewildered advisers. The House of Commons must supply the Administration with those material resources of which it is the steward; and since it will do this most gladly and liberally, the mere promulgation of the Royal summons constitutes in itself, and by anticipation, a reinforcement of Ministerial action, the value of which cannot be overlooked." The Government had in fact determined that the armaments of England must be increased, in view of the alarming complications which existed in the East of Europe; and for that purpose funds were needed, which Parliament could alone supply.

END OF VOL. I.

PRINTED BY CASSELL & COMPANY, LIMITED, LA BELLE SAUVAGE, LONDON, E.C.

Lightning Source UK Ltd.
Milton Keynes UK
UKOW04f2330221116
288330UK00010B/674/P

9 781248 158555